The
GARDEN CENTRE GROUP

Passionate about plants and gardening

Our 120 centres include some of Britain's best known garden centres; they range from much loved tiny local businesses such as Beaconsfield to the likes of Syon Park and Bridgemere, one of the largest garden centres in Europe.

We have decades of experience in the garden centre world and take enormous pride in our top quality growing stock, some of which is grown in our own nurseries.

All our centres sell a huge variety of plants ranging from old favourites to the new and exotic, as well as almost every gardening product imaginable, giftware, greeting cards, food and much more.

Our staff are enthusiastic and helpful 'horti experts' who like nothing more than dispensing good practical gardening advice and sharing their love of gardening with expert and amateur gardeners alike.

We run a popular Gardening Club that is free to join and offers great benefits including reward points and vouchers, exclusive seasonal offers and invitations to preview events - please ask at your local centre for details.

Throughout the year we also run a wide-ranging programme of gardening events, seasonal demonstrations and entertaining children's activities to inspire the gardeners of the future.

Please visit **www.thegardencentregroup.co.uk** to find out what's on at your local garden centre - we look forward to welcoming you there soon.

BLOOMS   BRIDGEMERE   HEIGHLEY GATE   Jack's Patch   Old Barn   Peter Barratts   Sanders   Woodlands   Wyevale

Yonder Cottage, Somerset

Cerney House Gardens, Gloucestershire

The Grove, Derby

Contents

ngs gardens open for charity

Published by The National Gardens Scheme
A company limited by guarantee. Registered in England & Wales.
Charity No. 1112664. Company No. 5631421

Registered & Head Office: Hatchlands Park, East Clandon,
Guildford, Surrey GU4 7RT

T 01483 211535 **F** 01483 211537 **W** www.ngs.org.uk

© The National Gardens Scheme 2011

The Yellow Book 2011
Production Team: Elna Broe, Linda Ellis, Julia Grant, Rachel Hick,
Kali Masure, Elizabeth Milner, Chris Morley, Wendy Morton,
Azam Parkar, Jane Sennett, Sally Stevens. With thanks to our
NGS County Volunteers · Designed by Level Partnership Ltd ·
Maps designed and produced by Global Mapping · Map Data ©
The People's Map · Data manipulation and image setting by Chat
Noir Design, France · Printing and binding by Pindar pic

Front cover: Brook Farm, Worcestershire by Julia Stanley.

Who's who in the NGS

Every year the National Gardens Scheme provides enormous pleasure to countless people across the country. For those without their own garden, the visits are rejuvenating and often provide an oasis of peace in an increasingly frenetic world. For the gardeners, they are opportunities to exchange tips and find inspiration. And every sort of garden is open for viewing. Some gardens are tiny jewels of colour and show what can be achieved in an urban setting; others are masterpieces of perspective, drawing on the best traditions of Charles Bridgeman, Capability Brown and Thomas Mawson.

The teas and homemade cakes served to visitors are, in some cases, almost as famous as the gardens themselves and are a special part of the remarkable hospitality and generosity shown by the garden owners who throw open their garden gates. To ensure the future sustainability of the Scheme, each year visitors are encouraged to open their own gardens, supported by some of the older hands. This continuity could not be more important, not least because of the significant fundraising for charities involved in nursing, caring and gardening, and I am delighted that two charities of which I am Patron, Macmillan Cancer Support and the Marie Curie Cancer Care, are both very grateful beneficiaries.

I can only wish the volunteers, staff and garden owners of The National Gardens Scheme another happy and rewarding year, bringing a very special pleasure to the thousands of visitors who will walk through those welcoming garden gates.

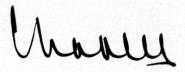

Chairman's Message
Penny Snell

© Ellen Forsström

Welcome to the 2011 Yellow Book which lists an array of gardens from north to south and east to west, over 3700 gardens in all. There are big gardens and small gardens in a diversity of styles to suit all tastes. One thing they have in common is the warm welcome they offer their visitors. By buying this book and visiting the gardens, you will be supporting a host of good causes.

We are always looking for new gardens to open for us. If you have a neighbour with a wonderful garden or an exceptional garden of your own, please contact our County Teams who are listed at the end of each county.

Again this year we are supported by Rensburg Sheppards who generously continue their sponsorship. To them, to all our garden owners and to you, the visiting public, our warmest thanks for helping us raise such wonderful sums to pass on to our benefiting charities. None of this would be possible without the enthusiasm and dedication of our voluntary County Teams and our hard working office staff all of whom contribute to the continuing success of this unique charity.

Our Chief Executive Julia Grant has left us to work for a venture philanthropy charity in London. Julia has taken the NGS forward in many ways, not least by developing the charity so that charitable distributions are now over £2.5m per annum, an increase of over 70%. We wish her every success in her new role.

Enjoy your garden visits and thank you for supporting the NGS.

About the NGS

By visiting an NGS garden you can really make a difference. Gardens which open on behalf of the NGS in England and Wales welcome over three quarters of a million visitors annually, raising much-needed funds for the charities to whom we make donations.

As a consequence of the generosity, support and hard work of garden owners, visitors and our volunteer team in 2010 we donated over £2.6m to charity.

What we do
Many of the 3,700 gardens that open for the NGS are privately owned and open just a few days each year. Others are open to the public on a regular basis and support the NGS in various ways. Some gardens open as part of a group, street or village opening which gets the whole community involved.

Most of the money raised at the garden gate goes straight to our beneficiary charities because we keep overheads low. Donations made by the NGS to beneficiaries are 'unrestricted', which means our money can be invested in projects and work which these charities consider vital to future development, and which might be difficult to fund from other sources.

Our long tradition of opening gardens is supported by our Patron HRH The Prince of Wales, and our President, Joe Swift. The NGS is a registered charity, established in 1927 and in the last 10 years we have raised over £26 million to support nursing and caring charities

Who we support

WE ARE MACMILLAN.
CANCER SUPPORT

As well as funding nursing posts at Macmillan Cancer Support, the annual donation from the NGS supports financial advice, physiotherapy and counselling. In fact, a total of 135 different services are supported and the NGS is proud to be Macmillan's largest ever single donor.

Marie Curie Cancer Care

Over the last decade, the contribution from the NGS has funded Marie Curie Cancer Care. The charity provides high quality nursing, totally free, to give terminally ill people the choice of dying at home, supported by their families. The Marie Curie Nursing Service operates across the UK, from villages and towns to the hearts of our largest cities.

CROSS ROADS CARE

Did you know that 83% of carers suffer from increased stress and anxiety? Crossroads Care are the people carers turn to when they need some time to themselves, and the donation from the NGS supports those vital services.

Help the Hospices

The NGS has supported Help the Hospices since 1997, funding a wide range of training programmes, strategic work and support for quality care. We also give emergency grants to hospices facing urgent financial difficulties.

Qni — The Queen's Nursing Institute

The Queen's Nursing Institute aims to protect and improve the quality of nursing patients receive at home, by funding practical ways to improve care, appointing Queen's Nurses to lead by example, and lobbying for better education for community nurses.

National Trust

Our donation to the National Trust helps to fund the Trust's 'gardening careership' programme, to train and educate heritage gardeners of the future.

PERENNIAL
Gardeners' Royal Benevolent Society
Helping Horticulturists in Need Since 1839

Through Perennial, the NGS helps horticulturists who are facing need or crisis.

THE ROYAL FUND FOR GARDENERS' CHILDREN

The annual donation to The Royal Fund for Gardeners' Children enables ongoing support to orphaned and needy children.

In short, every visitor to an NGS garden is making an essential contribution to someone's life, and especially those who really need care or support through chronic and life-threatening illnesses.

the perfect
transition space

A veranda lets you enjoy the sights and sounds of your garden
but with a sense of freedom you don't get with
a conservatory. Feel the breeze, smell the flowers,
hear the birds, relax in the company
of good friends... your garden
feels more alive than ever.

VERANDA LIVING

Rensburg Sheppards

INVESTMENT MANAGEMENT

An ⊕ **Investec** Group Company

It gives me great pleasure to provide these words of welcome to The Yellow Book 2011. Record numbers at English and Welsh gardens last year provided ample reward for the hard work and dedication of the garden owners.

I would encourage you to pause for a moment whilst looking at the next few pages of this book, in order to appreciate the enormous good work carried out by the charities supported by the National Gardens Scheme. With our financial support, combined with yours as visitors to the gardens, there is a great deal of benefit being provided to some immensely deserving causes. I hope that you will find this book useful when planning your garden visits in 2011.

The summer of 2010 saw the acquisition of all the outstanding shares in Rensburg Sheppards by our longstanding major shareholder, Investec plc. This is a development that we welcome, as it secures our future in partnership with a strong and respected company with shared values. It is also a privilege for me to have recently assumed the role of Chief Executive of Rensburg Sheppards at such an exciting point in the company's development.

Jonathan Wragg
Chief Executive

www.rensburgsheppards.co.uk

Tending to your future

You may never have considered engaging the services of an Investment Manager, but your assets and savings could grow into something even more rewarding. At Rensburg Sheppards we offer insight and expert advice to help you formulate a sound investment strategy. A strategy that will assist you in weathering the storms of the current economic climate and beyond. Our specialist, experienced team shares a philosophy of placing our clients first, above all else, and our reputation for personal service is outstanding. We believe great relationships start with a conversation, so why not give us a call?

For further information, please contact my colleague, Chris Sandford on 020 7597 1038 or email chris.sandford@rsim.co.uk

As you would expect, the value of your investments may go down as well as up and you might not get back the money you've put in.

Jonathan Wragg
Chief Executive

Rensburg Sheppards

How to use your Yellow Book

This book lists all gardens opening for the NGS between January 2011 and early 2012. It is divided up into county sections, each including a calendar of opening dates and details of each garden, listed alphabetically.

There are three simple ways to find gardens to visit:

1 **If you are looking for a specific garden**, you can look it up in the index at the back, or if you know which county it is in, you can go straight to the relevant county section.

2 **If you want to find out more about gardens near you or in a specific location**, go to the relevant county map (at the front of each section) and look for the numbered markers. Use those numbers to look up further information in the county listings.

3 **If you are looking to see what is open near you on a specific date**, go straight to the relevant county. There is a calendar of opening dates after each county map.

County name
Gardens in England are listed first, followed by gardens in Wales.

Directions
A simple set of directions to each garden. Most gardens also list postcodes for use with computer or satellite navigation systems.

Admission price
The admission price applies to all visitors unless exceptions are noted e.g. child free.

Description
A short description of each garden covers the main features. This is written by the garden owner.

Group opening information
Showing gardens that open together on the same day or days.

---

242 HAMPSHIRE

garden and glasshouses. Early stage arboretum. Pond area and formal lawns.
&. 🐕 ❀ 🍵

97 SILVERWOOD
28 Green Lane, Warsash SO31 9JJ.
Nick & Ginny Foy. *4m W of Fareham. From M27 J9 follow A27 towards Southampton. At Parkgate L into Locks Rd. Continue to end, R at r'about into Warsash Rd, 1st L into Fleet End Rd, 300yds past Jolly Farmer PH is Green Lane. Please park in Fleet End Rd, disabled parking only at Silverwood.* Home-made teas.
Adm £3, chd free. Sun 10, Mon 11 July (1-6).
½-acre peaceful, informal garden with many mature trees sloping down to natural woodland and stream. Wealth of herbaceous plants, hardy geraniums, heucheras, phlox. Fernery and fish pond. Many quiet seating areas including the mystical 'Moon Garden' set with crystals.
❀ 🍵

GROUP OPENING

98 SOUTHSEA GARDENS
Southsea PO4 0QE. *Turn into St Ronan's Rd from Albert Rd at junction opp Trinity Methodist Church. Alternatively follow signs from seafront and then follow yellow NGS signs from Canoe Lake and Eastern Parade. Park at Craneswater School in St Ronan's Rd. Entrance to all gardens from St Ronan's Ave.* Home-made teas (Sun). **Combined adm £5, chd free.** Sun 12 June (2-6). Evening Opening £6, wine, Sat 25 June (5-8).

27 ST RONAN'S AVENUE
Mr & Mrs S C Johns

Ronan's Avenue and landsca been used to create a moder concept with exuberant plant 'inside-out' garden at 87 St F Road captures busy urban liv best, with an impressive dinir and sitting room with a perm outside fireplace. 28 St Rona Avenue (see separate entry) showcases a mixture of tend and dry-loving plants along w traditional incl king protea, ba ferns, agave, echeveria and e
🍵

99 NEW SPINDLES
24 Wootton Road, Lee on t Solent PO13 9HB. Peter & Arnold, 02392 550490. *App. of Fareham. Exit A27, turn L Rd A32. At r'about 2nd exit C Rd Newgate Lane B3385. Th r'abouts staying on B3385, t Marine Parade B3333 onto V Rd.* Home-made teas. **Adm chd free.** Sun 29 May; Sun 27 June (2-5). **Visitors also** welcome by appt in June & Plantswoman's delightful sma with all-yr interest. Ferns, gra succulent collection, scented covered pergolas, hostas and clematis. Unusual trees and p bananas, ginger lilies and exi herbaceous borders. Mini bo garden, soft fruit and herbs. I to new and experienced gard
🍵 ☎

Unusual trees a palms, bananas ginger lilies and exuberant

Symbols explained

NEW Gardens opening for the first time this year or re-opening after a long break.

◆ Garden also opens on non-NGS days. (Gardens which carry this symbol contribute to the NGS either by opening on a specific day(s) and/or by giving a guaranteed contribution)

&. Wheelchair access to at least the main features of the garden

🐕 Dogs on short leads welcome

❀ Plants usually for sale

NCCPG Garden that holds a Plant Heritage Collection

🛏 Gardens that offer accommodation. For details see the Accommodation section

🍵 Refreshments are available, normally at a charge

☎ Gardens that welcome visitors by appointment. See the garden entry for details and contact information

Children must be accompanied by an adult

Photography is at the discretion of the garden owner; please check first. Photographs must not be used for sale or reproduction without prior permission of the owner.

Share To indicates that a proportion of the money collected will be given to the nominated charity.

WCs are not usually available at private gardens

Geographical area map

The areas shown on this map are specific to the organisation of The National Gardens Scheme. The Gardens of Wales, listed by area, follow the Gardens of England.

Discover wonderful gardens near you

Over 3,700 gardens across England and Wales open on behalf of the NGS every year. In the last 10 years the NGS has donated £26 million to nursing caring and gardening charities.

How you can support the NGS:

Visit a garden – with so many uniquely different gardens to visit you could be spoilt for choice. All our gardens offer something special. A visit typically offers the chance to meet the garden owner and the opportunity to enjoy a cup of tea in lovely surroundings.

Open your garden – this is a rewarding way to share your passion and hard work whilst raising money for charity. Size is not critical, many NGS gardens are no larger than typical back gardens. Visitors are looking for interesting planning and design, a good range of plants and gardens which have been tended with love and care. A good cup of tea and cake is important too. Why not discuss the possibility with our friendly volunteer team?

Volunteer – join our local teams of volunteers. A range of roles is available, so you don't need to be a gardening expert, but should enjoy being part of a team and working with and meeting new people.

Make a donation – support this wonderful 85 year tradition by making a donation online at www.justgiving/ngs.com

To find out more about any of these opportunities and to sign-up to receive our newsletter please visit www.ngs.org.uk or phone 01483 211535.

Save our garden lawns

Gardeners across the British Isles are being encouraged to sign-up to save our 'at risk' garden lawns and help protect the environment.

Research shows that up to 15% of our 17 to 20 million lawns are at risk of being dug up to provide car or caravan parking, for building extensions or to provide decking or hard landscaping.

John Deere's awareness campaign, National Gardens Park, is dedicated to protecting our lawns, safeguarding the vital environmental and social benefits they bring in our increasingly urbanised society.

The benefits of garden lawns include:

- Reducing the risk of flash flooding by allowing rain to permeate the soil reaching nature's natural reservoirs

- Converting harmful CO2 into oxygen

- Providing an essential natural environment for insects, mammals, birds and invertebrates

- Controlling pollution by absorbing sulphur dioxide and carbon dioxide

- Helping cool down summer temperatures

- Helping control allergies by filtering allergens and trapping pollen and dust

'The vast majority of lawns are inevitably in urban and inner city locations where the natural environment they create is essential for a balanced eco-system. They are an essential part of our green infrastructure,' says John Deere's David Hart.

He points out that 100 square metres of lawn will produce sufficient oxygen each day to support nearly two adults and the total area of domestic lawn supports half of the population.

Explaining the name John Deere's National Garden Park he explains that using a conservative estimate the total number of domestic lawns equates to 772 square miles, an area larger than the recently created South Downs National Park (627 square miles).

Our National Gardens Park is equivalent to our third largest National Park, just smaller than the Lake District – 885 square miles with a lot of water – and Snowdon at 827 square miles but with lots of rock.

'The challenge,' says David, **'is encouraging people to appreciate that their garden lawn, regardless of its size, is a vital piece in a much larger jigsaw and we all know the effect of a missing piece. Every garden lawn in this country is absolutely vital and must be protected and retained, for the benefit of us all.'**

Show your support, sign up and help save our garden lawns at www.johndeere.co.uk/ nationalgardenspark – membership is totally free.

What a great act to follow

National Gardens Park
sign up online
www.JohnDeere.co.uk

All our products, from a large agricultural tractor to the smallest walk behind lawn mower, share the same uncompromising commitment to quality. It's a commitment that began more than 175 years ago and still drives everything we do today.

Whatever John Deere model you choose, you can be confident it's engineered for performance, comfort and reliability. You can also enjoy the support of a world class dealer network with an equally uncompromising commitment to service. What a great act to follow!

 JOHN DEERE

Freephone 0800 085 25 22

JohnDeere.com

Harlow Carr

Dutch Bulbfields

Inca Ruins, Ecuador

Villandry, Loire

Royal Horticultural Society

Quality Garden Holidays

Brightwater Holidays operate a unique range of garden and special interest tours on behalf of the Royal Horticultural Society with tours throughout the gardening world.

Our overseas programme now includes a brand new tour to see **Japan's** amazing **Wisteria Festival** at Ashikaga as an addition to our popular spring and autumn tours there.

Other new tours visit gardens in **Russia, Denver** and **Bhutan,** exciting destinations that complement existing holidays to **South Africa** and **Ecuador.**

In Europe, we'll enjoy the early colour of the **Menton Lemon Festival,** the world famous **Keukenhof Gardens** in Holland on our Dutch Bulbfields river cruise and the traditional Spanish festival, the **Patios of Cordoba.** A timeless combination of gardens and architecture continues to make our **Andalucian** and **Italian** tours popular choices, and with new tours to **Slovenia, Belgium** and **Germany** we have an enviable portfolio of garden tours.

Of course, we never forget that some of the best gardens in the world are here in Britain and we offer a comprehensive choice of garden tours. These range from **Tresco** in the south to a superb new tour of private gardens in **Caithness** and **Sutherland**; classic garden tours to **Kent** and **Sussex, Somerset** and **Devon** and the western seaboard of **Scotland,** and not forgetting the wonderful **RHS Flower Shows** - a must-see for any garden enthusiast.

Join us for a wander through the great gardens of the world.

To obtain a copy of the RHS Worldwide Garden Holidays brochure, please call Brightwater Holidays on:

01334 657155

brightwater
holidays

Brightwater Holidays Ltd, Eden Park House, Cupar, Fife KY15 4HS
rhs@brightwaterholidays.com
www.brightwaterholidays.com
© the RHS Provided under licence granted by the RHS Reg Charity No 222879/SC038262

Travel with your society, friends or hobby group - with 14 years' experience in cultural tours and special interest breaks in the UK and overseas, Travel Editions can tailor-make an interesting itinerary for your group, no matter its size, or you can join one of their pre-arranged escorted tours.

New for 2011, Travel Editions has teamed up with an esteemed French Garden specialist who has sought out some truly hidden garden gems, many of which never usually open to the public. Over the past few years, the French have discovered their passion and talent for gardening just like the English did some 30 years ago; and their creations, both modern and traditional in form, colour and texture, are truly inspiring.

Contact Travel Editions and they will help create a truly beautiful and mesmerising garden tour for your group.

Specialists In • French Gardens • Italian Lakes, Art & Opera • Spanish Art & History • The Baltic Capitals • Imperial Russia • The Dutch Masters • Great British Heritage • Rail & Air Travel

Personal service guaranteed - to discuss your requirements, contact **Jo Blair 020 7251 0045** *or* **jo.blair@traveleditions.co.uk** or for inspiration visit **www.traveleditions.co.uk**

ABTA

ABTA No.V3120

AiTO

Magical Mystery Tour

Whatever your tastes, the NGS has a garden that will appeal. Naomi Slade takes a tour around four very different ones.

Every National Gardens Scheme garden is a surprise. Although tempted by the edited highlights in The Yellow Book, the reality is still an adventure and each garden is as varied and individual as its owner. In a garden the size of a postage stamp you can find 90 varieties of snowdrop. Elsewhere, you can be met by vistas set out by medieval nobility. From roses to rare breeds via sculpture, vegetables and herbaceous perennials every shade of garden passion is catered for.

In Herefordshire, Moors Meadow meanders across a hillside with views over the Kyre Valley.

Recently voted the most romantic garden in the Midlands, it began in 1955 when Tom and Ros Johnson moved to the smallholding. Great plant lovers, they simply planted everything that took their fancy and the garden expanded to its current seven acres, now tended by daughter Ros Bissell.

Made up of a loose patchwork of settings linked by winding paths, it brims with unusual plants. There are herbs and fruit in the kitchen garden, a lake, grasses, a fernery, herbaceous borders and woodland underplanted with countless spring bulbs. It is also home to barn owls, stoats, badgers, pipistrelle bats and great crested newts.

Carved from tranquil countryside, Moors Meadow is a relaxed symphony of greens punctuated by specimen trees including the New Zealand Kowhai, *Sophora tetraptera,* and *Oxydendrum arboreum.* There are also two artist blacksmiths on site. This organic, eclectic garden is full of plantaholic appeal and pretty close to my idea of heaven.

Like Moors Meadow, many NGS gardens have been created from scratch by their owners in a triumph of vision, persistence and hard work.

Opposite Irises and specimen trees mingle with native plants for a relaxed scene at Moors Meadow.

In Sussex, Richard and Ann Montier, owners of the Oast House, transformed a small pond in a cow field into a large s-shaped lake which dominates their 2 acre garden

Around the edge, a boardwalk hovers over the water while a double-helix mound is a neat and artistic solution to all the spoil that was removed. On this exposed site, a conventional garden would be flattened by the prevailing winds, so the Montiers opted for fluid prairie-style planting using tough plants like grasses, *Verbena bonariensis, Echinacea* and *Sanguisorba* in gentle colours. Though textured and vivid, the wildness is tamed by neat wooden edges and contrasts beautifully with the flat expanses of water and the vertical accents provided by young birches and mature oaks.

This is a garden full of movement, from shimmering grasses and foliage, birds, insects and the reflected sky. Swallows and martins swoop over the water and there are many thousands of bees. The core design is strong and the contrasts work superbly, making it an eminently habitable space.

Above At the Oast House Sedums, *Verbena bonariensis* and drifts of grasses sweep around the serpentine pond.

In Northamptonshire, the garden at Foxtail Lilly is a very different prospect, vibrant and intense rather than expansive

Set around a barn shop, it is made up of three interlinking areas and has no lawn. Olive and bay trees mark the entrance, setting the scene for a dry garden, packed with lavender, Californian poppies and alliums all interwoven with shingle paths. A gate then leads to a cutting field where owner Tracey Mathieson grows flowers to sell in posies. In her pretty and practical garden, she has paid attention to colour and scent, and at different times of the year, tulips, dahlias and cornflowers flourish in little raised beds.

The sheltered back garden is naturalistic and densely planted with big drifts and clumps, and subtle, plummy hues. Bold tussocks of purple sage and lots of *Nepeta* 'Six Hills Giant' contrast with textured, structural plants like phormiums, bamboo and *Melianthus major*. But to save one from a surfeit of good taste, there is an edgy sprinkle of humour. Deep in the bamboo, a wild boar skeleton lurks and a gas mask with antlers hangs from a tree, and these touches lend the garden personality and idiosyncrasy above and beyond mere planting.

Above Contrasts of texture and shape characterise the densely planted plot at Foxtail Lilly.

Left Outdoor living country style!

Just a short stroll from the centre of Norwich, Will Giles's city space is awash with luxuriant and often astonishing plants

Not all NGS gardens are in the countryside and urban spaces have been an expanding feature in recent years. They are usually smaller but with walls, fences, buildings and a favourable microclimate, they have a lot to offer in terms of style and design and are a rich source of ideas for visitors. In this garden themes segue from Mexico to India, Italy and California with a vast tree house in the centre and a new xerophytic area for cacti and succulents. It is dramatic and theatrical, like a hyper-real illustration of a hot climate.

Will effortlessly mixes texture, colour and form, spiky palms and serrated leaves contrast with large, smooth *Ensete ventricosum* and assertive dahlias, cannas and brugmansias. Dense undergrowth evokes the palm house at Kew – Will's childhood inspiration – and the garden is packed with ferns, gingers, colocasias and agaves, while wired-on bromeliads emulate tropical epiphytes.

With specimens from across the globe, the result is eclectic. Plants that are continents apart and that would never normally meet thrive together with spectacular effect, the overarching tropical look winning through.

Will's urban plot is about as far from an English country garden as you can get, yet the enthusiasm and inventiveness is a leitmotiv of NGS gardeners. To a person they make the most of their natural advantages while ingeniously battling challenges. They stamp their own imprint and play out their ideas, passions, successes and failures before throwing open their doors for the enjoyment of visitors and the benefit of charity.

Above A miniature jungle of foliage and flowers screens the treehouse.

Right Will's desert garden is overlooked by an Italianate loggia.

For opening and all other details please see the individual garden listing

People find our staff extremely approachable.

If you're thinking of selling at auction, come to Bonhams for a more rewarding experience.

info@bonhams.com
www.bonhams.com

Bonhams
101 New Bond Street
London W1S 1SR
+44 (0) 20 7447 7447

Year Round Conservatory Living

Transform your conservatory into a beautiful and comfortable living space with tailor-made blinds from Thomas Sanderson

Enjoy your conservatory to the full and create a cool, calm interior with tailor-made blinds designed to transform your space into a beautiful and comfortable living area all year round.

Thomas Sanderson has an extensive range of fabrics and finishes to choose from, including more than 1,000 colour and styling combinations. Their advanced solar reflective fabric technology will help you to control the temperature of your conservatory, keeping intense heat and glare at bay and protecting plants and furnishings from fading by reflecting the sun's rays away from the glass in the hot summer months. And in the winter, the insulating properties of the fabric means warmth and heat are retained in the conservatory, ensuring you can enjoy this room whatever the season.

Each conservatory blind from Thomas Sanderson is individually measured and then handcrafted in their UK factory before being installed by a team of experts to ensure a long-lasting, precise fit. And because Thomas Sanderson specialises in blinds for the conservatory, they have developed specialist techniques that mean they can fit blinds to any size or shape window, and are an expert when it comes to blinds for the roof, the area where the majority of heat and glare builds up during summer and escapes in winter.

So if you're looking to get more out of your conservatory, blinds are a practical, stylish and valuable addition that will allow you to enjoy year-round conservatory living – on the hottest of summer days and the crispest of winter evenings.

 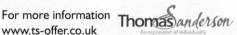

Meet the owner

Central to The National Gardens Scheme are the very people who open their gardens. Each creation is unique and each visit offers an unparalleled opportunity to learn from the gardener themselves.

Unlike public gardens, the owners are almost always there on open days, ready to chat and share their motivations and experiences and to tell visitors about their horticultural journey.

It is an ideal way to get tips and discover new inspiration, hear about their successes and failures and be enthused by their passions. So whether your interest is unusual vegetables or rare snowdrops, hostas, dry gardening, water features, modern roses, wildlife or woodland there is a home-grown expert just around the corner.

NGS gardeners are a generous bunch. As well as justifiable pride in their horticultural achievements, it is this generosity that motivates them to open for charity and they are equally free with gardening advice and information.

From the outset, NGS visitors discovered a new and inspiring way to learn about gardening. United by a love of plants, they are living the joys and challenges of horticulture, whether planting a couple of window boxes or a couple of acres. For visitors, NGS garden owners represent an unparalleled pool of expertise and it is the perfect forum in which to find out more.

Pictures Owners enjoy meeting and chatting to their visitors.

Time for Tea!

While galloping around someone else's plot is enormous fun, it can be hungry work. Fortunately sustenance is usually at hand so grab a cuppa and a cupcake and relax in beautiful surroundings.

Here is a selection of plaudits from our tea connoisseurs:

Berkshire The Priory, Beech Hill. *'The best spread in Berkshire'* Heather Skinner, NGS Trustee

Buckinghamshire Watercroft, Penn, Nr Beaconsfield. Owner Mary Berry is widely regarded as the Queen of Cakes and is a judge on BBC2's *The Great British Bake Off*

Oxfordshire Waterperry Gardens, Wheatley, nr Oxford. Voted *'Best Afternoon Tea'* by *BBC Gardeners' World* Magazine

Essex Court View, Leigh-on-Sea, *'marvellous cakes and a cookery book for sale!'*

Derbyshire 334 Belper Road, Stanley Common, Derbyshire. *'Highly recommended home-made cakes'*

London 5 St Regis Close, Muswell Hill, London. *'Just astonishingly good cake'* Penny Snell, NGS Chairman

Pictures For many visitors, tea and cake in the garden is an essential part of the NGS experience.

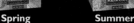

Retail Therapy

With such a variety of gardens, collections and nurseries opening for the NGS it should come as no surprise that there are some fantastic plants to be had. Here are a few to choose from, or check out a plant sale near you!

Northamptonshire
67/69 High St, Finedon

Northamptonshire
Coton Manor, Guilsborough

Devon
Bickham House, Kenn, Nr Exeter

Yorkshire
Dove Cottage Nursery, nr Halifax

Yorkshire
Stillingfleet Lodge, Stillingfleet, nr York

Cumbria
Summerdale House, Nook, nr Lupton

North East
Herterton House, Hartington, Northumberland

Cornwall
Ellis Gardens and Nurseries, Polyphant

Carmarthenshire
Cilgwyn Lodge, Llangadog

Pembrokeshire
Dyffryn Fernant, Fishguard

Pictures Shopping for unusual and home-grown plants is a highlight when visiting many NGS gardens.

Six new flower mugs from Emma Bridgewater

For Spring 2011 the team at Emma Bridgewater has added six new flowers mugs to their growing range. With fifteen favourite flowers now available, this year's new designs for the half-pint mugs are Daisy, Rose, Lily, Cosmos, Crocosmia and Nasturtium. There are also now eleven flowers in the baby mug range including Camellia, Auricula, Daisy, Rose and Lily, all new this year. Perfect for Mother's Day and birthday gifts, the flower mugs continue to be one of Emma Bridgewater's bestselling ranges and the NGS receives a donation for every piece sold. In 2010 the total amount of money donated by Emma to the NGS as a result of this was an amazing £30,000.

Emma Bridgewater®
Some of the nicest things in your kitchen...

New cards from Woodmansterne

Woodmansterne has recently added a new NGS notecard box to their successful range of NGS greeting cards. The unique concertina-folding stationery box unfurls to reveal eight notecards with envelopes. The small square notecards have no message inside so are perfect for any occasion.

Woodmansterne's 40-strong NGS greeting card range continues to share the values of our unique charity with a wider audience. Keep an eye out for new additions - cards not only feature our favourite blooms in season, but also now include plenty of humour from the garden with images featuring gnomes, chickens and even scarecrows!

The cards are available from independent card shops and are also stocked by WH Smith, Waitrose, Ocado and John Lewis.

Woodmansterne

Plants from Crocus available from the NGS

Early in 2011 the NGS joined forces with highly regarded plant supplier Crocus to offer you a fabulous range of plants for your garden. The really fantastic news is that as a result of each order placed Crocus will be making a donation to the NGS.

Since they opened ten years ago, Crocus have gained a reputation for the quality and depth of their plant range, currently in excess of 4,000 varieties. To date they have won 11 gold medals for gardens they have created at the Chelsea Flower Show, and now supply plants to most of gardening's 'A' list.

However, when they started their ambitions were much more modest. Speaking recently Peter Clay, co-founder of Crocus, said: 'When I was trying to create my garden in Herefordshire, I found it very difficult to source the range of plants that I wanted. It seemed that the amateur gardener was denied the same choice as the professional. Crocus was our attempt to redress that bias.'

'Like the NGS we want to open the garden gate as wide as possible. So we are delighted to be selling plants on their behalf and thereby adding to the amazing totals they donate each year to charity.'

So if you are looking to purchase plants to re-stock your garden you can now buy them from the NGS website knowing that they will be of fantastic quality and the team at Crocus will be providing excellent customer service to you. And at the same time you will be helping to raise money for the nursing, caring and gardening charities that the NGS supports.

For full details please visit
www.ngs.org.uk

TRADITIONAL FAMILY VALUES
quality and service assured

Dear Fellow Gardener

As one of the country's favourite gardening companies we have long admired the work of The National Gardens Scheme – **it is a very worthwhile charity and one that we are pleased to support.**

We also admire the generosity of private individuals and public organisations that open their gardens to the public, and the reciprocal generosity of their fellow gardeners who are willing to pay an entrance fee in order to support the beneficiaries of The National Gardens Scheme.

This year, in recognition of your generosity, we would like to offer a **SPECIAL 10% DISCOUNT** to all supporters of The National Gardens Scheme – that's garden owners and their visitors. For every order we receive we will make a further **5% donation to The National Gardens Scheme.** It's for a good cause so please feel free to tell your friends too!

All you have to do to claim this discount is **quote promotional code FD11NGS** when placing your order for seed or plants. This offer will be kept open until 31st December 2011.

You can view our range of seed and plants and place your order on-line at **www.mr-fothergills.co.uk** or you can request **FREE** copies of our latest seed and plant catalogues either online, or by calling our **orderline on 0845 371 0518** (lines are open 8.00a.m. to 8.00p.m. 7 days per week).

Above all, we hope that you will **have an enjoyable summer visiting the many gardens opening in support of The National Gardens Scheme** – and you never know, some of the spectacular flowers and bumper fruit & veg crops you see this summer may even have started their life from a packet of Mr Fothergill's seeds!

Happy gardening!

Jeff & John Fothergill

FREE DELIVERY!
for seed only orders

FREE SEED!
2 packets of FREE seed with every seed order

FREE SOWING GUIDE!
with every order of five packets of seed or more

SAME DAY DESPATCH!
on seed only orders placed on the website before 12.00 noon
(see Page 2 for details)

NEW & EXCLUSIVE

MASSIVE CHOICE
Over 1,300 flower & vegetable varieties

A-Z Flower & Vegetable Seed Catalogue 2011

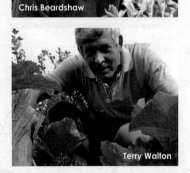

BEDFORDSHIRE

Opening Dates

January

Sunday 30
10 King's Arms Garden

March

Sunday 27
16 The Old Vicarage

April

Sunday 17
19 Swiss Garden
Sunday 24
21 Valley Forge

May

Saturday 7
9 The Hyde Walled Garden
Sunday 15
5 Flaxbourne Farm
6 The Folly
Sunday 22
13 The Manor House, Barton-Le-Clay
20 The Secret Sanctuary
22 Wayside Cottage

June

Sunday 5
18 Southill Park
Thursday 16
14 The Manor House, Stevington (Evening)
Sunday 19
1 31 Broadway
8 How End Cottage
Sunday 26
9 The Hyde Walled Garden

July

Saturday 2
3 22 Elmsdale Road
Sunday 3
3 22 Elmsdale Road
23 16 Wood Lane
Sunday 10
15 Mill End
Saturday 23
7 8 Great North Road
Sunday 24
7 8 Great North Road
12 Luton Hoo Walled Garden

August

Sunday 7
5 Flaxbourne Farm
Saturday 13
3 22 Elmsdale Road
Sunday 14
3 22 Elmsdale Road
11 Luton Hoo Hotel Golf & Spa

October

Sunday 30
10 King's Arms Garden

January 2012

Sunday 29
10 King's Arms Garden

Gardens open to the public

10 King's Arms Garden
11 Luton Hoo Hotel Golf & Spa
14 The Manor House, Stevington

By appointment only

2 Dawnedge Lodge
4 The Firs
17 Park End Thatch

Also open by Appointment ☎

1 31 Broadway
3 22 Elmsdale Road
5 Flaxbourne Farm
7 8 Great North Road
8 How End Cottage
13 The Manor House, Barton-Le-Clay
16 The Old Vicarage
22 Wayside Cottage

Brimming with
glorious blooms
that are perfect
for cutting . . .

The Gardens

ASCOTT
See Buckinghamshire.

1 NEW **31 BROADWAY**
Houghton Conquest MK45 3LT.
Joan Inwood, 01234 742003. *1m N of Ampthill. Turn R off B530 to Houghton Conquest, follow rd through village. 1st turn on L after Royal Oak PH*. Teas at How End Cottage. **Combined with How End Cottage adm £4, chd free. Sun 19 June (2.30-5.30). Visitors also welcome by appt May & June.** Small mature cottage style garden packed with perennials, annuals, bulbs, conifers and trees. Lots of pots and containers, small wildlife pond and water features. Ferns, auricula theatre and many other items of interest. Not an inch of space is wasted in this garden designed for all round interest. Woodturning demonstration. Featured in Bedford in Bloom, Best Small Garden.

❀ ☕ ☎

COWPER & NEWTON MUSEUM GARDENS
See Buckinghamshire.

2 **DAWNEDGE LODGE**
Woburn Lane, Aspley Guise MK17 8JH. Phil & Lynne Wallace, 01908 582233, lynnewallace@hotmail.co.uk. *5m W of Ampthill. 3m from J13 M1. In Aspley Guise, turn L in centre of village at Moore Place Hotel*. Home-made teas. **Adm £3, chd free. Visitors welcome by appt groups & individuals welcome.** Victorian walled 1-acre hill top garden with great views to Woburn, rescued 12yrs ago, with borders described in garden magazine as 'brimming with glorious blooms that are perfect for cutting' Oak pergola, stone patio with many terracotta pots including 20+ acers, agapanthus aeoniums and agaves. Alliums good. Featured in Garden Answers magazine.

☕ ☎

3 NEW **22 ELMSDALE ROAD**
Wootton, Bedford MK43 9JN. Roy & Dianne Richards, 07733 222495, roy.richards60@ntlworld.com. *4m from J13 M1 join A421 towards Bedford, follow signs to Wootton. Turn R at The Cock PH follow rd to Elmsdale Rd on R*. Home-made teas. **Adm £3.50, chd free. Sats, Suns 2, 3 July; 13, 14 Aug, (Sats 2-6),**

(Suns 12-6). Visitors also welcome by appt.
Topiary garden greets visitors before they enter a genuine Japanese Feng Shui garden incl bonsais, every plant is strictly Japanese, large koi pond with bamboo bridge and tea House. The garden was created from scratch by the owner and has many interesting features.

4 ▶ THE FIRS
33 Bedford Road, Sandy SG19 1EP. Mr & Mrs D Sutton, 01767 227589, d.sutton7@ntlworld.com. *7m E of Bedford. On B1042 between Sandy town centre and the A1. On road parking.* Home-made teas. **Adm £3, chd free (share to The Leprosy Mission - Sandy Branch). Visitors welcome by appt group & individual most welcome.**
$^1/_4$ -acre town garden with many garden features reflecting the different conditions from full sun to shade. Designed and created from scratch since 2000 this garden is productive in fruit, flowers, vegetables and wildlife. Run organically, this garden has everything from shrubs, trees, alpines, perennials, to water features and railway memorabilia. Group visits can have an additional talk on the history of this Victorian Gentleman's Residence - from Mr R Humbly-Humbly Esq to the present day.

5 ▶ FLAXBOURNE FARM
Salford Road, Aspley Guise MK17 8HZ. Geoff & Davina Barrett, 01908 585329, carole@boa.uk.com. *5m W of Ampthill. 1m S of J13 of M1.Turn R in village centre, 1m over railway line.* Home-made teas. **Adm £4, chd free, concession £3.50. Suns 15 May; 7 Aug (2-6). Visitors also welcome by appt conducted tours for groups of 10+, coaches permitted.**
Beautiful and entertaining fun garden of 3 acres, lovingly developed with numerous water features, windmill, modern arches and bridges, small moated castle, lily pond, herbaceous borders, Greek temple ruin. Recently established three way bridge, planted up with Japanese acers, tree ferns, echiums, bananas and zinnia creating a tropical full of the Wow Factor! New for 2011 Japanese garden with flyover walkway inspirational woodland setting. Crow's nest, crocodiles, tree house with zip wire for children. Huge Roman stone

arched gateway as recently featured in ITV's This Morning programme and BBC One Show. Music by Woburn Sands Band.

6 ▶ THE FOLLY
69 Leighton Road, Toddington LU5 6AL. Gillian & Edward Ladd. *5m N of Dunstable. J12 M1 follow B5120 to village. Turn R at Bell PH. Garden 0.2m on L.* Home-made teas. **Adm £3, chd free. Sun 15 May (1-5).**
Wheelchair friendly $^1/_3$ acre created over 15yrs. Many mature shrubs and trees with various foliage. Small woodland walk, orchard and vegetable garden. Greenhouse and potting shed with cacti garden. Many interesting features incl numerous old farming implements.

15 GADE VALLEY COTTAGES
See Hertfordshire

7 ▶ 8 GREAT NORTH ROAD
Chawston MK44 3BD. D G Parker, 01480 213284. *2m S of St Neots. Between Wyboston & Blackcat r'about on S-bound lane of A1. Turn off at McDonalds, at end of filling station forecourt turn L.* Light refreshments, home-made teas & wine. **Adm £3.50, chd free. Sat 23, Sun 24 July (2-6). Visitors also welcome by appt all year.**
1 acre garden, $^1/_2$ acre young trees and shrubs. Cottage garden of $^1/_2$ acre crammed with bulbs, herbaceous, water and bog plants, ferns, grasses, shrubs and trees. Rare, exotic and unusual plants abound, large pond, level grass paths. Yr round interest where plants provide structure and form, 2500sq metre glasshouse mainly growing Chinese vegetables.

Topiary garden greets visitors before they enter a genuine Japanese Feng Shui garden . . .

8 ▶ HOW END COTTAGE
Houghton Conquest MK45 3JT. Jeremy & Gill Smith, 01525 404121, smith201@btinternet.com. *1m N of Ampthill. Turn R 1m from Ampthill off B530 towards Houghton Conquest. How End Rd 300yds on RH-side. Garden at end of rd, approx $^1/_2$ m.* Home-made teas. **Adm £3.50, chd free, Combined with 31 The Broadway adm £4, chd free. Sun 19 June (2.30-5.30). Visitors also welcome by appt.**
Approx 1 acre garden with 2 ponds, large vegetable garden, greenhouse and orchard. Large lawn gives an uninterrupted view of Houghton House. The garden contains mature trees and beds with many types of slow growing fir trees. Flower beds contain home grown bedding plants and roses. 3 acres of paddocks, wood and further pond. Many spring bulbs.

9 ▶ THE HYDE WALLED GARDEN
East Hyde, Luton LU2 9PS. D J J Hambro Will Trust. *2m S of Luton. M1 exit J10/10a. A1081 S take 2nd L. At E Hyde turn R then immed L. Junction entrance on R. From A1 exit J4. Follow A3057 N to r'about, 1st L to B653 Wheathamstead/Luton to E Hyde.* Home-made teas. **Adm £3.50, chd free. Sat 7 May; Sun 26 June (2-5).**
Walled garden adjoins the grounds of The Hyde (not open). Extends to approx 1 acre and features rose garden, seasonal beds and herbaceous borders, imaginatively interspersed with hidden areas of formal lawn. An interesting group of Victorian greenhouses, coldframes and cucumber house are serviced from the potting shed in the adjoining vegetable garden. Bluebell walk in season, as featured in the film Brightstar. Gravel paths.

10 ▶ ◆ KING'S ARMS GARDEN
Ampthill MK45 2PP. Ampthill Town Council, 01525 755648, bryden.k@ntlworld.com. *8m S of Bedford. Free parking in town centre. Entrance opp old Market Place, down King's Arms Yard.* **Adm £2, chd free. For NGS: Sun 30 Jan (2-4); Sun 30 Oct (2-4.30). 2012 Sun 29 Jan. For other opening times and information, please phone or email.**
Small woodland garden of about $1^1/_2$ acres created by plantsman the

The Manor House, Stevington

Be tempted by a plant from a plant stall ✿

late William Nourish. Trees, shrubs, bulbs and many interesting collections throughout the yr. Maintained since 1987 by 'The Friends of the Garden' on behalf of Ampthill Town Council.

11 LUTON HOO HOTEL GOLF & SPA

The Mansion House, Luton Hoo, Luton LU1 3TQ. *Approx 1m from J10 M1, take London Rd A1081 signed Harpenden for approx $^1/_2$ m - entrance on L for Luton Hoo.* Light refreshments & home-made teas. **Adm £5, chd free. Sun 14 Aug (11-4).**
The gardens and parkland designed by Capability Brown are of national historic significance and lie in a conservation area. Main features - lakes, woodland and pleasure grounds, Victorian grass tennis court and late C19 sunken rockery. Italianate garden with herbaceous borders and topiary garden.

12 ◆ LUTON HOO WALLED GARDEN

Luton Hoo Estate, Luton LU1 3TQ. Exors of N H Phillips, 01582 721443, www.lutonhooestate.co.uk. *A1081 between Luton & Harpenden. Take New Mill End turning, turn L after 100m. Follow Walled Garden Project signs. NO entrance from Luton Hoo Hotel. Disabled parking next to garden.* **Adm £3, chd free. For NGS: Sun 24 July (11-5).** For other opening times and information, please phone or see garden website.
The 5 acre Luton Hoo Walled Garden was designed by Capability Brown and established by Lord Bute in the late 1760s. Successive owners of the estate adapted the garden to match changing horticultural fashions, only for it to fall into decline in the 1980s. The garden is now being restored. Exhibition of research material on the history of the garden. Guided tours. Illustrated talks. Exhibition of old tools.

13 THE MANOR HOUSE, BARTON-LE-CLAY

87 Manor Road, Bedford MK45 4NR. Mrs Veronica Pilcher. *Off A6 between Bedford & Luton. Take old A6 (Bedford Rd) through Barton-le-Clay Village (not the by-pass) and, Manor Rd is off Bedford Rd. Parking in paddock.* Home-made teas. **Combined with Wayside Cottage adm £4, chd free. Sun 22 May (2-5). Visitors also welcome by appt please apply in writing.**
The garden was beautifully landscaped during the 1930s and much interest is created by picturesque stream which incorporates a series of waterfalls, colourful streamside planting incl an abundance of arum lilies. Sunken garden with lily pond and a magnificent wisteria thrives at the rear of the house. Partial wheelchair access, 2ft wide bridges.

An evening of roses, music and wine with hot refreshments . . .

14 ◆ THE MANOR HOUSE, STEVINGTON

Church Road, nr Bedford MK43 7QB. Kathy Brown, 01234 822064, www.kathybrownsgarden. homestead.com. *5m NW of Bedford. Off A428 through Bromham.* Light Refreshments. **Adm £4.50, chd free. For NGS: Evening Opening wine, Thur 16 June (6-9). For other opening times and information, please phone or see garden website.**
A modern country garden with unusual twists, designed and cared for by owners Simon and Kathy Brown. Roses festoon the cottage garden, the walls, the trees, pergolas and arches. Elsewhere the edible flower border, renewed formal parterres, Wild flower meadow, naturalsitic grass gardens and major container displays offer contrasting areas of interest. An evening of roses, music and wine with hot refreshments, plants and Stevington honey for sale. Featured in Country Homes & Interiors, Homes & Garden, The Flower Arranger and Dream Gardens of England, GGG with a starred entry. Gravel and grass paths.

THE MENAGERIE
See Northamptonshire.

15 MILL END

Potton Road, Wrestlingworth SG19 2EZ. Mr & Mrs R Whitlock. *4m E of Biggleswade. On the B1042 out of Wrestlingworth towards Potton.* Home-made teas. **Adm £4, chd free. Sun 10 July (2-6).**
2 acre ornamental and vegetable garden planted by present owners since building house 21 yrs ago. Extensive mixed borders, large collection euphorbias, rose pergola, arboretum of 100+ unusual and interesting trees. Further into the 13 acre site is an old orchard, woodland of indigenous trees and wild flower walk through coppiced area harvested for the house wood burner. Musical entertainment at 2.30 and 4.30. Games for the children.

16 THE OLD VICARAGE

Church Road, Westoning MK45 5JW. Ann & Colin Davies, 01525 712721, ann@no1colin.plus.com. *2m S of Flitwick. Off A5120, 2m N of M1 J12. $^1/_4$ mile up Church Rd, next to church.* Light refreshments & cream teas in church. **Adm £3.50, chd free. Sun 27 Mar (1.30-5.30). Visitors also welcome by appt April to June.**
A traditional 2 acre vicarage garden on sandy soil with box and laurel hedges, formal lawn, large magnolia grandiflora and numerous other mature shrubs and trees. More recent improvements include many colour co-ordinated herbaceous beds, an eye-catching cornfield meadow, english rose garden, pond, rockery, and small vegetable garden. A striking show of hellebores and daffodils in spring.

17 PARK END THATCH

58 Park Road, Stevington MK43 7QG. Susan Young, 01234 826430, susankyoung@btconnect.com. *5m NW of Bedford. Off A428 through Bromham.* Home-made teas. **Adm £3, chd free. Visitors welcome by appt May, June & July. Advance bookings only, min 8, max 20 visitors.**
$^1/_2$ -acre cottage garden set within old orchard. View of Stevington windmill. Sunny borders of flowering shrubs with herbaceous planting. Fragrant roses and climber covered pergola. Winding grass paths shaded by trees. Trellice border featuring colour and texture groupings. Fruit production and herbs. Garden cultivated to be

drought tolerant. Wildlife friendly. Main path is gravel on a slight slope, grass paths.

SOUTHILL PARK
nr Biggleswade SG18 9LL. Mr & Mrs Charles Whitbread. *3m W of Biggleswade. In the village of Southill. 3m from A1 junction at Biggleswade.* Cream Teas. **Adm £3.50, chd free. Sun 5 June (2-5).**
Large garden, with mature trees and flowering shrubs, herbaceous borders, rose garden and wild garden. Large conservatory with tropical plants. The parkland was designed by Lancelot 'Capability' Brown in 1777.

ST MICHAEL'S CROFT
See Hertfordshire

19 SWISS GARDEN
Old Warden Park, Old Warden, Biggleswade SG18 9EP. Shuttleworth Trust in Partnership with Central Beds Council, www.shuttleworth.org. *2m W of Biggleswade.* Signed from A1 & A600. Light refreshments & teas. **Adm £5, chd free (share to Friends of the Swiss Garden). Sun 17 Apr (10-5).**
Designed in 1820s. 9-acre miniature landscape garden with winding paths, intertwining ponds, wrought iron bridges, fernery grotto and tiny buildings. Peacocks wander around splendid trees and shrubs, with daffodils, rhododendrons and roses in season. Adjacent further acres of native woodland. Plants for sale.

20 THE SECRET SANCTUARY
Whipsnade Road, Dunstable LU6 2NB. Kevin Claridge, www.gardencare-services.co.uk. *1m W of Dunstable Town centre.*

From Dunstable town centre, 1m W, turn L on Whipsnade Rd, past Pipers Croft, & The Secret Sanctuary (formerly known as Craigwen) is 3rd on L approaching the brow of the hill, opp the downs - limited onsite parking. Home-made teas. **Adm £4.50, chd free. Sun 22 May (11-5).**
This exciting garden comprises of individually styled areas, featuring a large lake, waterfalls complemented with a number of focal points and walkways. This inspirational garden is a haven for wildlife and its location offers some stunning views of the local area. Come spend time in the tranquill surroundings and experience this area of outstanding natural beauty. Haven for beautiful birds, butterflies and a comfortable home for unwanted pets. Also visit the snake retreat to see some rare reptiles. Featured in Bloom in Dunstable Portfolio.

THE TOWER HOUSE
See Buckinghamshire

21 VALLEY FORGE
213 Castle Hill Road, Totternhoe LU6 2DA. Pat & Mike Sutcliffe. *2m W of Dunstable. Turn R off B489 Aston Clinton rd, 1/2 m from Dunstable centre, signed Totternhoe. Fronting main rd, corner of Chapel Lane, 1m through village. On rd parking (but not directly outside the house).* Home-made teas. **Adm £3.50, chd free. Sun 24 Apr (2-5).**
A true cottage garden to rear of C17 grade 2 listed thatched cottage (not open). 1/2 -acre sloping site planted from scratch by owners 18yrs ago. Imaginatively landscaped, terraced on 4 levels, long pergola, archways and steps connecting to meandering pathways that lead intriguingly through the foliage. 'Sun trap' garden planted with an orange /yellow theme. Ponds on 2 levels connected by small

cascade. Large range of shrubs, perennials and trees compatible with chalk, including the indiginous Aylesbury Prune. The site also houses The Mike Sutcliffe Collection of early Leyland buses (1908-1934).

22 WAYSIDE COTTAGE
74 Manor Road, Barton-Le-Clay MK45 4NR. Nigel Barrett. *1m off A6. Take old A6 (Bedford Rd) through Barton-Le-Clay Village (not the by-pass), Manor Rd is off Bedford Rd. Parking in paddock at the Manor House.* Teas at The Manor House. **Combined with The Manor House, Barton-Le-Clay adm £4, chd free. Sun 22 May (2-5). Visitors also welcome by appt please apply in writing.**
The garden is sited on a 1/2 -acre plot. Developed over 50yrs it has mature trees, shrubs and flower borders. A well-stocked pond with fountain and waterfalls. A variety of attractive outbuildings nestle within the old walled garden for a tranquil scene with plenty of hidden corners.

23 16 WOOD LANE
Cotton End MK45 3AJ. Lesley Bunker-Nixon & Eddie Wilkins. *2m S of Bedford. A600 signed Shefford from Bedford, 2nd L at The Bell PH, into Wood Lane, past Hall Way on RH-side.* Light refreshments & teas. **Adm £3, chd free. Sun 3 July (12-5).**
150ft garden consisting of cottage style garden, containers and bygones. Formal garden with large koi pond with beautiful fish, borders and lawns. Japanese garden with bonsai trees, wooded area with stream. Vegetable garden based on an allotment. Wildlife area with folly and chickens, also facade of an old water mill.

Bedfordshire County Volunteers

County Organisers
Mike & Pat Sutcliffe, Valley Forge, 213 Castle Hill Road, Totternhoe, Dunstable LU6 2DA, 01525 221676,
sutcliffes@leylandman.co.uk

County Treasurer
Colin Davies, The Old Vicarage, Church Road, Westoning MK45 5JW, 01525 712721, colin.davies@which.net

Publicity
David & Susan Sutton, The Firs, 33 Bedford Road, Sandy SG19 1EP 01767 227589, sutton7@ntlworld.com

Assistant County Organisers
Geoff & Davina Barrett, Flaxbourne Farm, Aspley Guise, Milton Keynes MK17 8HZ, 01908 585329, carole@boa.com
Lesley Bunker-Nixon & Eddie Wilkins, 16 Wood Lane, Cotton End, Bedford MK45 3AJ, 01234 741580

NGS supports nursing and caring charities

BERKSHIRE

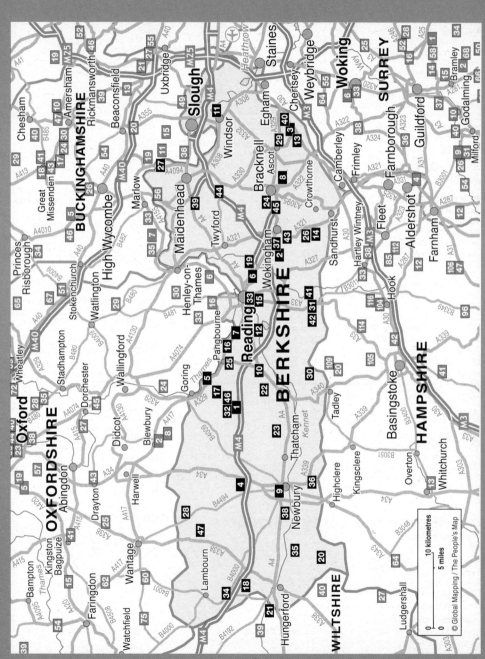

Opening Dates

March
Saturday 26
39 Stubbings House
Sunday 27
39 Stubbings House

April
Sunday 10
15 The Harris Garden
Sunday 17
27 Odney Club
28 The Old Rectory Farnborough
Wednesday 27
18 Inholmes
34 Rooksnest
38 Stockcross House
Saturday 30
42 Thrive's Trunkwell Garden Project

May
Sunday 1
14 Glenmere
26 Oak Cottage
Friday 6
44 Waltham Place Gardens
Saturday 7
39 Stubbings House
Sunday 8
28 The Old Rectory Farnborough
39 Stubbings House
Friday 13
44 Waltham Place Gardens
Sunday 15
30 Padworth Common Gardens
33 The RISC Roof Garden, Reading
Tuesday 17
12 Frogmore House Garden
Friday 20
44 Waltham Place Gardens
Sunday 22
1 Ashampstead Common Gardens
2 Bearwood College
Wednesday 25
38 Stockcross House
Friday 27
44 Waltham Place Gardens
Saturday 28
21 Littlecote House Hotel
Sunday 29
21 Littlecote House Hotel
Monday 30
40 Sunningdale Park

June
Friday 3
44 Waltham Place Gardens

Sunday 5
17 Hook End Farm
24 Moor Close Gardens
35 Rose Cottage
Wednesday 8
17 Hook End Farm
Friday 10
44 Waltham Place Gardens
Saturday 11
11 Eton College Gardens
21 Littlecote House Hotel
45 Whitehouse Farm Cottage (Evening)
Sunday 12
16 Highveldt
17 Hook End Farm
20 Kirby House
21 Littlecote House Hotel
45 Whitehouse Farm Cottage
47 Woolley Park
Wednesday 15
32 Pyt House
38 Stockcross House
46 Willow Tree Cottage
Friday 17
44 Waltham Place Gardens
Sunday 19
4 Chieveley Manor
22 Mariners
24 Moor Close Gardens (Evening)
28 The Old Rectory Farnborough
Wednesday 22
18 Inholmes
34 Rooksnest
Friday 24
44 Waltham Place Gardens
Saturday 25
21 Littlecote House Hotel
Sunday 26
21 Littlecote House Hotel
24 Moor Close Gardens
31 The Priory
41 Swallowfield Horticultural Society

July
Friday 1
44 Waltham Place Gardens
Saturday 2
25 Newlands
Sunday 3
25 Newlands
33 The RISC Roof Garden, Reading
Wednesday 6
38 Stockcross House
Friday 8
44 Waltham Place Gardens
Saturday 9
21 Littlecote House Hotel
Sunday 10
21 Littlecote House Hotel
42 Thrive's Trunkwell Garden Project

Friday 15
9 Donnington Castle House
44 Waltham Place Gardens
Saturday 16
21 Littlecote House Hotel
Sunday 17
6 68 Church Road
19 Ivydene
21 Littlecote House Hotel
42 Thrive's Trunkwell Garden Project
Friday 22
44 Waltham Place Gardens
Friday 29
44 Waltham Place Gardens

August
Friday 5
44 Waltham Place Gardens
Sunday 7
3 Boxwood House
13 The Garden Lodge
33 The RISC Roof Garden, Reading
Friday 12
44 Waltham Place Gardens
Friday 19
44 Waltham Place Gardens
Saturday 20
21 Littlecote House Hotel
Sunday 21
21 Littlecote House Hotel
Friday 26
44 Waltham Place Gardens
Sunday 28
29 Old Waterfield

September
Friday 2
44 Waltham Place Gardens
Friday 9
44 Waltham Place Gardens
Saturday 10
33 The RISC Roof Garden, Reading
Sunday 11
33 The RISC Roof Garden, Reading
Friday 16
44 Waltham Place Gardens
Saturday 17
42 Thrive's Trunkwell Garden Project
Friday 23
44 Waltham Place Gardens
Friday 30
44 Waltham Place Gardens

October
Sunday 2
21 Littlecote House Hotel

You are always welcome at an NGS garden

Gardens open to the public

10 Englefield House
44 Waltham Place Gardens

By appointment only

5 Church Farm House
7 17 Clevedon Road
8 Devonia
23 Miles's Green House
36 Sandleford Place
37 21 Simons Lane
43 Timberlea

Also open by Appointment ☎

2 Bearwood College
3 Boxwood House
4 Chieveley Manor
13 The Garden Lodge
14 Glenmere
17 Hook End Farm
18 Inholmes
19 Ivydene
21 Littlecote House Hotel
22 Mariners
24 Moor Close Gardens
31 The Priory
32 Pyt House
34 Rooksnest

The Gardens

GROUP OPENING

1 **ASHAMPSTEAD COMMON GARDENS**
RG8 8QT. 7m J12 M4. 2m E of Yattendon along Yattendon Lane. L into Sucks Lane, ¹/₂ m, R opp common. Start visit off at Farriers Cottage in lane off Sucks Lane nr Yattendon. Home-made teas. **Combined adm £5, chd free.** Sun 22 May (2-5).

BAGGAGE CHUTE
Colin & Caroline Butler

FARRIERS COTTAGE
Jackie Lomas

2 gardens linked by pretty walk through medieval woodland. Stunning bluebells in May. Start at Farriers Cottage. **Baggage Chute**: lower terraced garden with colourful mix of shrubs and perennials leading to large informal pond. Vegetable and cutting garden. Hillside slopes feature prairie style mix of flowers and grasses with long views over surrounding countryside. Featured in The English Garden. **Farriers Cottage**: small immaculate cottage garden designed and planted by owner. Formal front garden in woodland setting leading to colourful mix of shrubs and herbaceous planting at the back.

❀ ☕

---

2 **BEARWOOD COLLEGE**
Winnersh RG41 5BG. Richard Ryall, 0118 974 8300, secondmaster@bearwoodcollege. co.uk. 5m SE of Reading. Off B3030, 1m S of A329/ B3030 intersection at Winnersh, midway between Reading and Wokingham. Look for Bearwood Rd & College sign. Cream teas. **Adm £4, chd free.** Sun 22 May (2-5). Visitors also welcome by appt, groups welcome in spring and summer.
Late C19 mansion and parkland once owned by the last private owner of The Times newspaper, now an independent school. Azaleas, rhododendrons, walks through mature woodland. Pinetum, lake, natural margins, ice house. Extensive hidden Pulham rock and water garden under restoration. Visits include access to some of the mansion rooms. Nature trail, charcoal making (weather dependent).

🎪 ❀ ☕ ☎

Two gardens linked by pretty walk through medieval woodland. Stunning bluebells in May . . .

3 **BOXWOOD HOUSE**
Heathfield Avenue, Sunninghill SL5 0AL. Mr J P H Morrow & Mr R E G Beard, 07730 201925, paulmorrow@talktalk.net. 6m S of Windsor. From A30 at Sunningdale, take Broomhall Lane, after ¹/₂ m follow signs to car park. From A329 turn into Silwood Rd and R to Larch Ave. Home-made teas. **Adm £3.50, chd free** (share to The Dogs Trust). Sun 7 Aug (2-6). Visitors also welcome by appt in July & Aug for groups of 25+ (can be combined with The Garden Lodge).
Very fine ³/₄ -acre designer's, plantsman's and flower arranger's garden in woodland setting with emphasis on plant and colour association. Large range of herbaceous perennials, large leaved hostas, acers, grasses, topiary, climbers, interesting foliage plants with pergola, woodland garden, natural style pond and many tender plant combinations in pots. Now extended down steps to hot colour themed area and raised pond. On open day shuttle transfer available from car park to visit The Garden Lodge. Featured in The English Garden.

❀ ☕ ☎

4 **CHIEVELEY MANOR**
Chieveley, nr Newbury RG20 8UT. Mr & Mrs C J Spence, 01635 248 208, spence@chieveleymanor. fsworld.co.uk. 5m N of Newbury. Take A34 N, pass under M4, then L to Chieveley. After ¹/₂ m L up Manor Lane. Home-made teas. **Adm £3.50, chd free** (share to Naomi House Hospice). Sun 19 June (2-5). Visitors also welcome by appt June & July only, max group 25.
Large garden surrounding listed house (not open) in the heart of Chieveley village. Attractive setting with fine views over stud farm. Walled garden containing lovely borders, shrubs and rose garden, evolving every year.

♿ ❀ ☕ ☎

5 **CHURCH FARM HOUSE**
Lower Basildon, Pangbourne RG8 9NH. Mr P Olive, 07738 516187, gardenwithsteve@msn.com. 2m NW of Pangbourne on A329. Into Lower Basildon, 200yds past petrol stn turn R down lane to large barn and follow signs to field parking. **Adm £3.50, chd free.** Visitors welcome by appt June 13 to July 15, for groups of 6+.
10 acres of organic garden with formal and natural planting set in Thames Valley with views across Chiltern Hills. Formal lawn and pond, herbaceous borders, vegetable plots, fruit cage, large greenhouse, wild flower meadow, young woodland, paddock with small coppices and layed hedges. Hard rolled chippings and flat grassland.

♿ ☕ ☎

NEW **68 CHURCH ROAD**
Earley, Reading RG6 1HU. Pat
Burton. *E of Reading Town Centre.*
Off A4 at Shepherd's House Hill,
turning into Pitts Lane, into Church
Road, across r'about 3rd on L.
Home-made teas. **Combined adm**
with Ivydene £3.50, chd free. Sun
17 July (11-5).
A fascinating urban garden with
changing elements throughout the
seasons. Different areas showcase a
variety of interesting plants, pergola,
raised fishpond and small
summerhouse. The working
greenhouse is also home to alpines
grown yr-round and seen as
specimen plants in the garden.
Children can seek out the 'Hobbit
Home'.

7 **17 CLEVEDON ROAD**
Tilehurst RG31 6RL. G Emmerick &
G Preston, 01189 427317,
jgpgae@aol.com. *3m W of Reading*
centre. A329 to Tilehurst stn, L into
Carlisle rd, R into Clevedon rd. Home-
made teas. **Adm £5, chd free (incl**
tea & cake). Visitors welcome by
appt 1 to 15 July for groups of 8+.
¼-acre yr-round town garden on 3
levels featuring circular lawn and
octagonal vegetable plot, planted with
a mix of English and Mediterranean
horticultural delights, incl grasses,
climbers, shrubs, fruit and trees. A
tranquil oasis with views to Arthur
Newbery Park.

8 **DEVONIA**
Broad Lane, Bracknell RG12 9BH.
Andrew Radgick,
aradgick@aol.com. *From A329M*
take 3rd r'about, 2nd exit into Broad
Lane and over 2 r'abouts. 3rd house
on L after railway bridge. From A322,
Horse & Groom r'about, take 4th exit
into Broad Lane. **Adm £3 or £5 with**
refreshment. Visitors welcome by
appt in July & Aug for groups of 6+.
⅓-acre plantsman and plantaholic's
garden designed for all seasons and
planted to require minimal watering.
Divided into several areas to provide
appropriate conditions for over 1300
different shrubs, climbers, perennials,
bulbs and alpines, incl many rare and
unusual. Hot and dry front garden,
shady and sheltered corners to the
rear. A new garden of coloured
foliage.

DIPLEY MILL
See Hampshire.

9 **DONNINGTON CASTLE**
HOUSE
Castle Lane, Newbury RG14 2LE.
Mr & Mrs B Stewart-Brown. *1m N*
of Newbury. Follow signs to
Donnington Castle. Entrance on R
towards top of main castle entrance.
Car park through wooden gates. Light
Refreshments & home-made teas.
Adm £4, chd free. Fri 15 July
(10-5).
Large mature garden with additional
planting during last 5yrs. Attractive
herbaceous borders, roses, mixed
borders, fine mature trees, lawns,
woodland and garden walks.

DORNEYWOOD GARDEN
See Buckinghamshire.

10 ◆ **ENGLEFIELD HOUSE**
Englefield, Reading RG7 5EN.
Mr & Mrs Richard Benyon,
01189 302221,
www.englefieldestate.co.uk. *6m W*
of Reading. 1½ m from J12 M4. 1m
from Theale. Entrance on A340 3m S
of Pangbourne. **Adm £3, chd free.**
For opening times and information
please visit website or telephone.
9-acre woodland garden with
interesting variety of trees and shrubs,
stream, water garden descending to
formal terraces with stone
balustrades making background for
deep borders. Small enclosed
gardens of differing character incl
children's garden with joke fountains.
All enclosed by deer park with lake.
Open every Monday throughout yr &
Mons -Thurs, Apr - Oct (10-6). Gravel
paths.

11 **ETON COLLEGE GARDENS**
Windsor SL4 6DB. Eton College.
½ m N of Windsor. Parking off B3022
Slough to Eton rd, signed to R, S of
junction with Datchet Rd (Pocock's
Lane), walk across playing fields to
entry. Cars with disabled badges will
be directed further. Tickets and map
at entrance to Head Master's garden.
Cream Teas. **Adm £4, chd free.**
Sat 11 June (2-5).
A chance to visit a group of central
college gardens surrounded by
historic school buildings, incl
Luxmoore's garden on an island in the
Thames reached across an attractive
bridge. Also opportunity to explore
the fascinating Eton College Natural
History Museum. Limited wheelchair
access to 3 central gardens and over
grass to Luxmoores.

Hook End Farm

Find a garden near you at www.ngs.org.uk

12 FROGMORE HOUSE GARDEN

Windsor SL4 2HT. Her Majesty The Queen, www.royalcollection.org.uk. *1m SE of Windsor. Entrance via Park St gate into Long Walk (follow AA signs). Visitors are requested kindly to keep on the route to the garden & not stray into the Home Park. Stn & bus stop in Windsor (20 mins walk from gardens), Green Line bus no 701, from London. Limited parking for cars only (free). Coaches by appointment only.* Light refreshments & teas. Garden only adm £5. Seperate charge for house entry. Tickets available on the day. Tue 17 May (10-5.15, last admin 4pm). 30 acres of landscaped gardens rich in history and beauty. Large lake, fine trees, lawns, flowers and flowering shrubs. Gravel paths. For advance tickets please go to NGS 'Shop Online' or apply to NGS, Hatchlands Park, East Clandon, Guildford, Surrey GU4 7RT, tel 01483 211535.

13 THE GARDEN LODGE

Bagshot Rd, Sunninghill SL5 9JG. Mr & Mrs J Bolsover, 07730 201925, paulmorrow@talktalk.net. *6m S of Windsor. This garden has no immediate parking. Please follow directions to Boxwood House car park (see separate entry) and use shuttle transfer provided.* Adm £3.50, chd free (share to Tomorrow's People). Sun 7 Aug (2-6). Visitors also welcome by appt in July & Aug, for groups of 25+. Can be combined with Boxwood House. Lovely 1.5-acre plantsman's garden. Attractive gravelled drive leads down steps to hot colour-themed border, lawn, greenhouse and herb garden. Walled garden with box-edged planting in pastel colours and terrace with elevated view of long double mixed borders towards water garden in woodland setting. Photographed by Nicola Stocken Tomkins. Featured in The English Garden.

14 GLENMERE

246 Nine Mile Ride, Finchampstead RG40 3PA. Heather Bradly & John Kenney, 0118 9733274. *2.5m S of Wokingham. 7m J10 M4. A329 towards Reading. On B3430 E of California Crossroads r'about.* Teas & plant sale at Oak Cottage. Open with Oak Cottage. Combined adm £3.50, chd free. Sun 1 May (2-5). Visitors also welcome by appt.

Japanese style garden with waiting arbour, raked gravel area, tea house, Torii gate, dry stream bed with bridge and pond. Vegetable garden, greenhouse and soft fruit area. Attractive in all seasons,with added colour during August. Featured in Amateur Gardening.

GRANGE DRIVE WOOBURN

See Buckinghamshire.

15 THE HARRIS GARDEN

Whiteknights, Pepper Lane, Reading RG6 6AS. The University of Reading, School of Biological Sciences, www.friendsofthe harrisgarden.org.uk. *1½ m S of Reading town centre. Off A327, Shinfield Rd. Turn R just inside Pepper Lane entrance to campus. Use RG6 6UR for satnav.* Home-made teas. Adm £3, chd free. Sun 10 Apr (2-5.30). 12-acre amenity, research and teaching garden. New bulb meadow for 2011, floral meadows, herbaceous borders, stream garden and pond, notable trees and shrubs, some very rare. Plant Heritage Digtalis collection. Some gravel paths.

HEARNS HOUSE

See Oxfordshire.

HIGHER DENHAM GARDENS

See Buckinghamshire.

Small urban gardeners' garden, with mature tree fern walkway and many unusual hostas . . .

16 HIGHVELDT

Beech Road, Purley-on-Thames RG8 8DS. Ben & Dorothy Viljoen. *4m NW Reading, off A329. From Pangbourne Beech Rd is 1st R as you enter Purley. From Reading, cross T-lights at Long Lane, cross r'about, take 1st L.* Home-made teas. Adm £3, chd free. Sun 12 June (2-6). Attractive ⅓ -acre terraced garden retaining much of original 1930s layout. Down steps through trellis

arch to circular lawn with box balls and lavender. Pass through a secret garden that shows a very small space used to maximum effect, then into main terracing incl herbaceous borders, lawns and Chiltern views. Featured in Amateur Gardening, article entitled 'Me and My 1930s Garden'.

17 HOOK END FARM

Upper Basildon RG8 8SD. David & Fiona Ambler, 01491 671255, fiona@hookendfarm.com. *3m W of Pangbourne. From A329 L into Hook End Lane, 1m on R.* Home-made teas. Adm £3.50, chd free. Sun 5, Wed 8, Sun 12 June (2-5). Visitors also welcome by appt in June, for groups of 10+. 2-acre hillside walled garden and orchard in tranquil rural valley with outstanding views. Atmospheric garden with wild natural look. Over 250 varieties of roses, other interesting plants and shrubs filling box parterres, secret corners and arbours. Collection of stationary engines.

18 INHOLMES

Woodlands St Mary RG17 7SY. Lady Williams, Contact Patrick Hoare, paddy@dte.uk.com. *3m SE Lambourn. J14 M4 from A338 take B4000 towards Lambourn, Inholmes signed.* Home-made teas. Adm £4, chd free. Combined adm with Rooksnest £6, chd free. Weds 27 Apr; 22 June (11-4). Visitors also welcome by appt via email or letter. Set in 10 acres with views over parkland. Lots to enjoy with large walled garden, rose beds, cutting and sunken garden. Individual touches incl brightly painted gates and benches and spooky wood. Walks to lake and meadow. Bluebell wood in spring and in summer the inspirational borders burst with colour.

19 IVYDENE

283 Loddon Bridge Road, Woodley, Reading RG5 4BE. Janet & Bill Bonney, 0118 9697591, janetbonney2003@aol.com. *3½ m E of Reading. A4 from Reading towards Maidenhead. Woodley lies midway between Reading & Maidenhead. Loddon Bridge Rd is main rd through the small town. Garden about 100yds S of the 'Just Tiles' r'about. Parking in adjacent rd.* Home-made teas.

Open with **Oak Cottage**. Combined adm £3.50, chd free. Sun 17 July (11-5). Visitors also welcome by appt for groups of 10-20.
Small urban gardeners' garden, with mature tree fern walkway and many unusual hostas, ornamental grasses and plants. Overflowing herbaceous borders and rose bed, using mainly patio roses.The garden also features stained glass and ceramic art to complete the picture.

20 **KIRBY HOUSE**
Inkpen RG17 9ED. Mr & Mrs R Astor. 3¹/₂ m SE of Hungerford. A4 to Kintbury. L at Xrds in Kintbury (by Corner Stores) towards Inkpen. 2m out of Kintbury turn L immed beyond Crown & Garter PH, turn L at junction, house at bottom of hill on R. Adm £3.50, chd free. Sun 12 June (2-5).
7 acres in beautiful setting with views of S Berkshire Downs and historical Combe Gibbet, across lawn with ha-ha and parkland. C18 Queen Anne House (not open). Formal rose borders, double herbaceous border, colour themed border between yew buttress hedges, Lily pond garden by Harold Peto, reflecting pond with fountain, lake, recently-designed walled garden and contemporary sculptures.

21 **LITTLECOTE HOUSE HOTEL**
Hungerford RG17 0SU. Warner Leisure Hotels, 01488 682509, martyn.smith@bourne-leisure.co.uk. 2m W of Hungerford. From A4 turn R onto B4192 signed Swindon. 1¹/₂ m exit L & follow signs. Light refreshments. Adm £4, regret, no children. Sats & Suns 28, 29 May; 11, 12, 25, 26 June; 9, 10, 16, 17 July; 20, 21 Aug; Sun 2 Oct (10-5). Visitors also welcome by appt 1 June - 17 July only.
Beautiful setting around Grade I listed house with views of the Kennet Valley over lawns and parkland. Herbaceous borders, rose and herb garden, clipped yew and box hedging, fruit trees, unique stumpery. Carp pond and large selection of hanging baskets and planters. Plants for sale. Music on the lawn most dates. Raffle. Apple and pear tasting on 2nd Oct plus fruit to take home. Gravel paths, some steep slopes.

22 **MARINERS**
Mariners Lane, Bradfield RG7 6HU. Anthony & Fenja Anderson, 0118 9745226, fenjaanderson@aol.com, www.mariners-garden.com. 10m W of Reading. M4 J12 take A4 direction Newbury 1m. At r'about exit A340 direction Pangbourne. 400yds L direction Bradfield. 1m, L direction Southend Bradfield. 1m opp signpost direction Tutts Clump turn R into Mariners Lane. Home-made teas. Adm £4, chd free. Sun 19 June (2-6). Visitors also welcome by appt May 29 to July 17, groups and individuals welcome (donation to NGS).
1¹/₂ -acre sloping site with creative feature made of slopes. Rich mixture of herbaceous planting incl unusual plants and grasses arranged in colour themes. Old varieties of shrub roses, species and climbing roses. Streamside walk, orchard, sundial garden and 1-acre wild flower meadow. The garden is constantly being developed with new planting and projects. Featured in The Countryside Magazine. Some steep slopes and gravel paths.

MARYFIELD
See Buckinghamshire.

23 **MILES'S GREEN HOUSE**
Briff Lane, Bucklebury RG7 6SH. Mr & Mrs Eric Lloyd, lloydmgh@gmail.com. 6m NE of Newbury, off A4. From Thatcham take Harts Hill Rd N to Bucklebury. Adm £3.50, chd free. Visitors welcome by appt from mid-May to mid-June.
3-acre tranquil valley garden in woodland setting with small lake, bog garden and adjacent pond. Specimen trees and shrubs feature on well-maintained sloping lawns with island beds of choice and unusual plants. Herbaceous beds combine shrubs, roses and perennials. Meadow with grass paths.

24 **MOOR CLOSE GARDENS**
Popeswood Road, Binfield RG42 4AN. Newbold College, 01344 452427, Dr Harry Leonard, avtm96@ntlworld.com. 2m W of Bracknell. From B3408. From Bracknell turn R at Binfield T-lights, from A329(M) take B3408, turn L at Binfield T-lights. Follow signs. Home-made teas at Newbold Church Centre. Adm £2.50, chd free. Suns 5, 26 June (2-5). Evening Opening 19 June (5-8). Visitors also welcome by appt when garden not open. Not Sats.
Small Grade II listed garden designed 1911-13 by Oliver Hill and a rare example of his early work. Lavender garden, water parterre, remains of Italianate garden. Undergoing long-term restoration, it currently offers most interest in its historical architecture rather than planting. Music in the garden on19 June.

25 NEW **NEWLANDS**
Courtlands Hill, Pangbourne RG8 7BE. Mr & Mrs Peter Sketch, www.sketch.cc/newlands. 1/4 m S of village centre off A340. From J12 M4 take A340 to Pangbourne. Home-made teas. Adm £2.50, chd free. Sat & Sun 2, 3 July (11-5). Newly developed 1/3 -acre garden. Contemporary tiered borders, densely planted in a naturalistic/prairie style, wrap around the Edwardian house. Small vegetable and fruit garden contains raised beds and glass house. Newly planted mini orchard with wild flowers. Planting chosen to tolerate chalk and drought and attract beneficial insects.

26 **OAK COTTAGE**
99B Kiln Ride, Finchampstead RG40 3PD. Ms Liz Ince. 2¹/₂ m S of Wokingham. Off B3430 Nine Mile Ride between A321 Sandhurst Rd and B3016 Finchampstead Rd. Home-made teas. Open with Glenmere. Combined adm £3.50, chd free. Sun 1 May (2-5).
Recently developed 1/4 -acre garden with woodland feel. Many mature trees underplanted with spring bulbs and unusual shade-loving plants incl selection of ferns and acers. Herbaceous border and interesting pine pergola with various climbers, island beds and eclectic planting. Small vegetable patch with fruit trees. Potager-style planting in front garden.

27 **ODNEY CLUB**
Odney Lane, Cookham SL6 9SR. John Lewis Partnership. 3m N of Maidenhead. Off A4094 S of Cookham Bridge. Car park in grounds. Home-made teas. Adm £4, chd free (share to Thames Valley Adventure Playground). Sun 17 Apr (2-6).
This 120-acre site beside the Thames is continuously developing and, with lovely riverside walks, can take a full

afternoon to visit. A favourite with Stanley Spencer who featured our magnolia in his work. Magnificent wisteria, specimen trees, herbaceous borders, side gardens, spring bedding and ornamental lake. Some gravel paths.

THE OLD RECTORY
See Wiltshire.

28 THE OLD RECTORY FARNBOROUGH
Wantage OX12 8NX. Mr & Mrs Michael Todhunter. *4m SE of Wantage. Take B4494 Wantage-Newbury Rd, after 4m turn E at sign for Farnborough.* Home-made teas. Adm £4, chd free (share to Farnborough PCC). Suns 17 Apr; 8 May; 19 June (2-5.30).
In a series of immaculately tended garden rooms, incl herbaceous borders, arboretum, boules, rose, pool and vegetable gardens, there is an explosion of rare and interesting plants, beautifully combined for colour and texture. With stunning views across the countryside, it is the perfect setting for the 1749 rectory (not open), once home of John Betjeman, in memory of whom John Piper created a window in the local church. Awarded Finest Parsonage in England by Country Life and the Rectory Society. NGS film for Japan TV. Some steep slopes & gravel paths.

OLD THATCH & THE MILLENNIUM BARN
See Hampshire.

29 OLD WATERFIELD
Winkfield Road, Ascot SL5 7LJ. Hugh & Catherine Stevenson. *6m SW of Windsor. On A330 (Winkfield Rd) midway between A329 and A332 to E of Ascot Racecourse. Parking on Practice Ground (by kind permission of Royal Ascot Golf Club) adjacent to house.* Home-made teas. Adm £3, chd free. Sun 28 Aug (2.30-5).
Nestling in 4 acres adjacent to Ascot Race Course the original cottage garden has attractive herbaceous borders and lovely views. Large productive kitchen garden full of fruit and vegetables, natural pond, specimen trees, a young orchard and mixed hedging.

GROUP OPENING

30 NEW PADWORTH COMMON GARDENS
Padworth Common RG7 4JB.
Between Reading & Newbury. From A4 take Padworth Lane at the Holiday Inn. Keep straight on for 2m. From Tadley, take the Burghfield Rd & turn L into Rectory Rd. From Burghfield turn R into Rectory Rd. Home-made teas. Combined adm £4, chd free. Sun 15 May (2-6).

NEW HATCH FARM HOUSE
Peter & Shoffy Lowndes

NEW HUNTERS LODGE
John & Carol West

Two quite different gardens bordering Padworth Common which is a popular walking and wildlife centre. The tiny, charming church with a Norman arch and wall paintings is a mile away. Considering poor gravel soil, and frequent visits from deer, rabbits and badgers, the gardens are normally a riot of colour. **Hatch Farm House** is a traditional country garden around a 16C farmhouse & barns. Over 1 acre with herbaceous and rose borders, sunken lawn with pretty walls, small orchard and vegetable garden. **Hunter's Lodge** :1½ -acre garden developed over 30 yrs from field, surrounded by mature oaks and visiting wildlife. Wisteria walkway, sunken garden, rockery, rhododendrons and wildflower lawn. Large pond with water feature and busy ducks.

31 THE PRIORY
Beech Hill RG7 2BJ. Mr & Mrs C Carter, 0118 9883146, tita@getcarter.org.uk. *5m S of Reading. M4 J11. Follow signs to A33 Basingstoke, turn L at 1st set T-lights signed Spencers Wood & Swallowfield. After 1½ m turn R by Murco garage signed Beech Hill. In village turn opp church into Wood Lane, then R down Priory Dr. House at end of drive.* Home-made teas. Adm £3.50, chd free. Sun 26 June (2.30-6.30). Visitors also welcome by appt.
Extensive gardens in grounds of former C12 Benedictine Priory (not open), rebuilt 1648. The mature gardens are in an attractive setting beside the R Loddon and are being restored and re-developed. Large formal walled garden with espalier

fruit trees, lawns, mixed and replanted herbaceous borders, vegetables and roses. Woodland, lake and new Italian style water garden in progress. Fine trees. Mostly gravel paths.

32 PYT HOUSE
Ashampstead RG8 8RA.
Hans & Virginia von Celsing, virginiacelsing@gmail.com. *4m W of Pangbourne. From Yattendon head towards Reading. Rd forks L into a beech wood towards Ashampstead. Keep L and join lower rd. ½ m turn L just before houses.* Combined adm with **Willow Tree Cottage £5, chd free. Wed 15 June (2-5). Visitors also welcome by appt 1 Apr to 8 July.
4 acres planted over the last 5yrs. Mature trees, yew, hornbeam and beech hedges, pleached limes, modern perennial borders, orchard and vegetable garden.

33 THE RISC ROOF GARDEN, READING
35-39 London Street. RG1 4PS. Reading International Solidarity Centre, www.risc.org.uk/garden. *5 mins walk from Oracle shopping centre. Limited parking at back of building.* Light refreshments & teas at RISC Global Cafe. Adm £2.50, chd free (share to RISC). Suns 15 May; 3 July; 7 Aug; Sat & Sun 10, 11 Sept (12-4).
Small town centre roof forest garden developed to demonstrate sustainability and our dependance on plants. All plants in the garden have an economic use for food, clothing, medicine etc, and come from all over the world. Demonstration of renewable energy, water harvesting and irrigation systems. Garden accessed by external staircase.

34 ROOKSNEST
Ermine Street, Lambourn Woodlands RG17 7SB.
Mrs T Sackler, 07766 130398, lisa.rooksnest@hotmail.co.uk. *2m S of Lambourn. J14 M4 from A338 Wantage rd, along B4000. Rooksnest signed.* Light refreshments & home-made teas. Adm £4, chd free. Combined adm with Inholmes £6, chd free. Weds 27 Apr; 22 June (11-4). Visitors also welcome by appt 28 Apr to 10 July.
Approx 10-acre exceptionally fine traditional English garden. Rose and

herbaceous garden, pond, herb garden, organic vegetables and glasshouses. Many specimen trees and fine shrubs, orchard and terraces renovated and recently replanted. Garden mostly designed by Arabella Lennox-Boyd from 1980 to today.

35 NEW ROSE COTTAGE
RG17 9TR. Mr & Mrs D Smith. *6m W of Newbury. 4m E of Hungerford.*

From A4 between Hungerford & Newbury take rd signed Kintbury. Cross level crossing, river & canal bridges into village centre at shops. Church St on R. Lunches at Blue Ball from 11.30 & teas at St Mary's Church Hall from 2pm. **Adm £2.50, chd free.** Sun 5 June (12-5). ¼ -acre plantswoman's garden behind a C17 cottage, developed in stages over the past 10yrs by the owners. Emphasis on perennials, beautiful cornus, roses and topiary.

Courtyard, C19 church lych gate, gravel areas, water features and shaded area behind gothic facade. A garden to enjoy and relax in. Domesday Village situated on Kennet & Avon Canal. Popular with visitors, walkers and cyclists. Horse-drawn boat outings, C11 church plus many other attractions. Awarded Kintbury Horticultural Society (RHS) Garden Cup.

The RISC Roof Garden

36 SANDLEFORD PLACE

Newbury RG20 9AY. Mr & Mrs Alan Gatward, 01635 40726, melgatward@bigfoot.com. *1½ m S of Newbury on A399. House is at W side of Swan r'about at Newtown.* Home-made teas. **Adm £4, chd free. Visitors welcome by appt all year.**
A plantswoman's 5 acres, more exuberant than manicured with R. Enborne flowing through. Various areas of shrub and herbaceous borders create a romantic, naturalistic effect. Wonderful old walled garden, potager and herb bed. Yr-round interest from early carpets of snowdrops, crocus-covered lawn and Spring daffodils, to Autumn berries and leaf colour.

  🚶 ☕ ☎

37 21 SIMONS LANE

Wokingham RG41 3HG. Jill Wheatley, 0118 9780500, jill.wheatley@btinternet.com. *1m W of Wokingham. Off A329 between Woosehill r'about and Sainsbury cross roads, on L.* Home-made teas. **Adm £3.50, chd free. Visitors welcome by appt mid April to end June for groups of 12 to 20.**
Peaceful, wildlife haven on outskirts of Wokingham. An organically-run garden, developed since 1996, intensively planted with wide variety of shrubs, herbaceous perennials, climbers,roses, vegetables and fruit. Rear garden designed around natural pond where newts and dragonflies breed. Large hosta collection in courtyard. Display of quilts and ceramics. Information on organic methods of culitvation and pest control. Plants for sale incl those seen in the garden and hostas. Gravel paths.

  🚶 🌿 ⊗ 🛏 ☕ ☎

You may see a model train, an orchid house and probably donkeys and special sheep . . .

38 STOCKCROSS HOUSE

Stockcross RG20 8LP. Susan & Edward Vandyk. *3m W of Newbury. From M4, J13, take A34 S to A4 junction. Exit direction Hungerford, take B4000 to Stockcross.* **Adm £3.50, chd free.** Weds 27 Apr; 25 May; 15 June; 6 July (11-4).
2-acre garden developed over past 15yrs with emphasis on plant partnerships and colour combinations. Specimen trees, herbaceous borders, long wisteria-clad pergola, rich variety of roses, cascade and pond, wild flower lawn, vegetable and cutting gardens; all enhanced by sculptural elements by local artists. Gravel on drive and vegetable garden.

  🚶 ⊗ ☕

STOKE POGES MEMORIAL GARDENS

See Buckinghamshire.

39 NEW STUBBINGS HOUSE

Henley Road, Maidenhead SL6 6QL. Mr & Mrs D Good, 01628 825454, info@stubbingsnursery.co.uk, www.stubbingsnursery.co.uk. *2m W of Maidenhead. Private rd access from Henley Rd opp Stubbings Church. See website for further directions.* Home-made teas & light refreshments. **Adm £3, chd free.** Sats & Suns 26, 27 Mar; 7, 8 May.
Landscaped garden of 10-acres accessed through 1 acre walled garden of retail nursery adjoining C18 house, home to Queen Wilhelmina of the Netherlands in WW2. Long herbaceous border facing 60m wall of wisteria. Notable trees incl historic Cedars and Araucaria, large lawn with ha-ha and parklands vista beyond. Attractive woodland walks providing access to 250 acres of adjacent National Trust woodland (Maidenhead Thicket). Firm, gravel paths. Level site.

  🚶 🌿 ⊗ ☕ ☎

40 SUNNINGDALE PARK

Larch Avenue, Ascot SL5 0QE. National School of Government/Verve Venues. *6m S of Windsor. On A30 at Sunningdale take Broomhall Lane. After ½ m, R into Larch Ave. From A329 turn into Silwood Rd towards Sunningdale.* Home-made teas. **Adm £4, chd free.** Mon 30 May (2-5).
Over 20 acres of beautifully landscaped gardens in Capability Brown style. Terrace garden and Victorian rockery designed by Pulham incl cave and water features. Lake area with paved walks, extensive lawns with specimen trees and flower beds, impressive massed rhododendrons. Lovely 1m woodland walk. Grade II listed building (not open). Free garden history tour at 3.30.

  🚶 🛏 ☕

41 SWALLOWFIELD HORTICULTURAL SOCIETY

RG7 1QX. *5m S of Reading. M4 J11 & A33/B3349, signed Swallowfield. Tickets and maps at Doctor's surgery in The Street.* Home-made teas. **Combined adm £5, chd free (share to Thames Valley Adventure Playground).** Sun 26 June (11-5).
Swallowfield has survived as a real village beside the Blackwater meadows and offers a minimum of 8 gardens to visit, ranging from tiny and perfect to large and shaggy (some immaculate ones too). Some are full of special plants, others developed in a variety of styles. You may see a model train, an orchid house and probably donkeys and special sheep. There are always views to love. Orchid house & treasure hunt.

  ⊗ ☕

42 THRIVE'S TRUNKWELL GARDEN PROJECT

Beech Hill, Reading RG7 2AT, www.thrive.org.uk. *7m S of Reading. M4 J11, follow signs to A33, Basingstoke. L at 1st set of T-lights signed Spencers Wood & Swallowfield. After 1¼ m, R by Murco garage into Back Lane to X'rds. L to Beech Hill. From S keep thorugh Swallowfield on B3349, after Mill House restaurant turn L into Back Lane until X'rds. L to Beech Hill. Signs in village.* Home-made teas. **Adm £3.50, chd £1 (share to THRIVE).** Sat 30 Apr; Suns 10, 17 July; Sat 17 Sept (2-4.30).
3-acre site with Victorian walled garden run by Thrive, a national charity which uses gardening to support and inspire disabled people. Formal and informal interest, pond, butterfly garden, trained fruit and cut flower areas, potager, glasshouse, sensory and cottage gardens. Chelsea Gold medal winning garden and new gardens to be unveiled this yr.

  🚶 ⊗ ☕

43 TIMBERLEA
17 Oaklands Drive, Wokingham
RG41 2SA. Mr & Mrs F Preston,
0118 978 4629,
fred.nina@tiscali.co.uk. *1m SW of
Wokingham. M4 J10 or M3 J3. From
Wokingham take A321 under 2 railway
bridges, Tesco store is between.
Immed turn R at mini r'about, Molly
Millars Lane. 3rd rd on L is Oaklands
Drive. After 100yds, R into cul-de-sac.*
Cream Teas. **Visitors welcome by
appt late May to early Sept,
individuals & group of up to 30.**
Something of interest at every turn!
Triangular $^1/_7$ - acre plot lends itself to
hidden corners with different levels
and vistas. Arches, pergolas and
walls give height to replanted borders.
Water feature with shade loving
plants. Kitchen garden has raised
beds, fruit cage and greenhouses.
Front garden incl small waterfall,
stream, pond and private decking.
Limited wheelchair access.

♿ ✿ ☕ ☎

TYLNEY HALL HOTEL
See Hampshire.

THE VYNE
See Hampshire.

**44 ◆ WALTHAM PLACE
GARDENS**
Church Hill, White Waltham
SL6 3JH. Mr & Mrs N Oppenheimer,
01628 825517,
www.walthamplace.com. *3$^1/_2$ m W
of Maidenhead. From M4 J8/9 take
A404. Follow signs for White
Waltham. Pass airfield on RH-side.
Take L turn signed Windsor/Paley St.
Pass the church, round the bend,
entrance on the left by red post box.
From Bracknell/Wokingham A3095 to
A330 direction Maidenhead. Turn L at
Paley St B3024 to White Waltham.
Turn R into Church Hill, look for brown
Waltham Place signs.* **Adm £4, chd
£1. For NGS: Every Friday 6 May
to 30 Sept incl (10-4). For other**
opening times and information,
please phone or see garden
website.
Influenced by Henk Gerritsen, who
collaborated with Strilli Oppenheimer
to embrace a naturalistic philosophy
which seeks to combine forces with
nature, producing a haven for an
abundance of insect and animal life,
fungi and indigenous flora. The
gardens feature naturalistic plantings
with woodlands and an organic and
bio-dynamic kitchen garden and farm.
Different themed walled gardens,
including a small Japanese garden
and potager. Walled gardens have
paved paths, disabled access to
other areas depends on weather.

♿ ✿ ✿ ☕ ☎

Atmospheric
cottage garden
of 'rooms' with
brick, china and
decorative pebble
areas . . .

WEST SILCHESTER HALL
Silchester. See Hampshire.

WHITE GABLES
See Hampshire.

THE WHITE HOUSE
See Buckinghamshire.

**45 NEW WHITEHOUSE FARM
COTTAGE**
Murrell Hill Lane, Binfield
RG42 4BY. Louise Lusby,
01344 423688,
garden.cottages@ntlworld.com.
*Between Bracknell & Wokingham.
From A329 take B3408. At 2nd set of
T-lights turn L into St Marks Rd, 2nd L
(opp Roebuck PH) into Foxley Lane. L
into Murrell Hill Lane. Car parking in
lanes.* Home-made teas on Sun. **Adm**

£3, chd free (share to Sam Beare
Hospice). **Sat 11 June Evening
Opening £4, wine, (8-10.30); Sun
12 June, £3, chd free (2-6).**
Atmospheric cottage garden of
'rooms' with brick, china and
decorative pebble areas - riotously
planted with roses, herbs, ferns and
other favorites. The courtyard with pot
and lily ponds leads to terrace with
circular domed seating area. Pond
garden contains a pretty summer
house and glasshouse. Candle lit for
the evening opening.

✿ 🛏 ☕ ☎

WHITEWALLS
See Buckinghamshire.

46 WILLOW TREE COTTAGE
Ashampstead RG8 8RA. Katy &
David Weston. *4m W of
Pangbourne. From Yattendon head
towards Reading. L fork in beech
wood to Ashampstead, keep L, join
lower rd, $^1/_2$ m turn L before houses.*
**Combined adm with Pyt House £5,
chd free. Wed 15 June (2-5).**
Small pretty garden of the cottage
that was originally build for gardener
at Pyt House. Substantially
redesigned and replanted over last
5yrs. Perennial borders, vegetable
garden, pond with ducks and
chickens.

♿

WOGSBARNE COTTAGES
See Hampshire.

47 WOOLLEY PARK
Woolley, nr Wantage OX12 8NJ.
Lady Wroughton. *5m S of Wantage.
A338. Turn L at sign to Woolley.* **Adm
£3.50, chd free. Sun 12 June (2-5).**
Two linked walled gardens sensitively
planted with a wide variety of
interesting plants incl climbing roses,
herbaceous borders and vegetables.
Set amongst parkland with fine trees
and views.

Berkshire County Volunteers

County Organiser
Heather Skinner, 5 Liddell Close, Finchampstead, Wokingham RG40 4NS, 01189 737197, heatheraskinner@aol.com

County Treasurer
Hugh Priestley, Jennetts Hill House, Stanford Dingley, Reading RG7 6JP, 01189 744349, hughpriestley1@aol.com

Publicity
Linda Kirkpatrick, April Cottage, The Street, Swallowfield RG7 1QY, 0118 988 2837, wychwoodint@yahoo.co.uk

Assistant County Organisers
Gerald Emmerick, 17 Clevedon Rd, Tilehurst, Reading RG31 6RL, 01189 427317, jgpgae@aol.com
Elspeth Ewen, Blossoms, Clay Lane, Beenham RG7 5PA, 01189 712856, ken.ewen@btinternet.com
Jill Wheatley, 21 Simons Lane, Wokingham RG41 3HG, 01189 780500, jill.wheatley@btinternet.com

BUCKINGHAMSHIRE

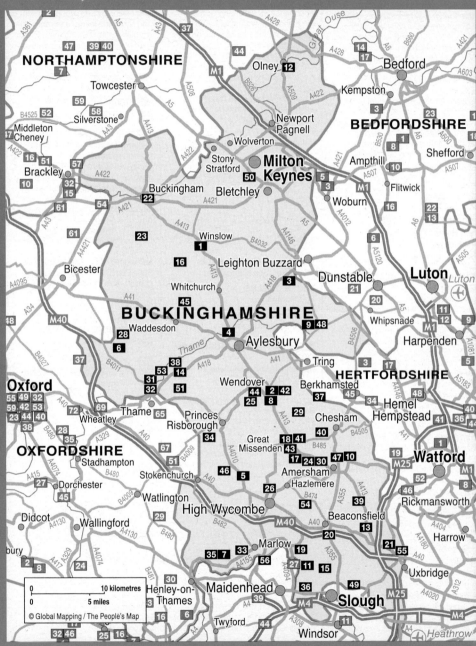

Opening Dates

February

Sunday 13
21 Higher Denham Gardens

Sunday 20
19 Magnolia House, Grange Drive Wooburn

Sunday 27
45 Quainton Gardens

March

Sunday 27
10 Chesham Bois House

April

Saturday 2
49 Stoke Poges Memorial Gardens

Sunday 3
41 Overstroud Cottage

Saturday 9
47 Rivendell

Sunday 10
47 Rivendell

Sunday 17
31 Long Crendon Spring Gardens
56 Whitewalls

Tuesday 19
15 Dorneywood Garden

Wednesday 20
15 Dorneywood Garden

Sunday 24
41 Overstroud Cottage

Monday 25
24 Hollydyke House

Wednesday 27
18 Gipsy House
43 The Plant Specialist

May

Sunday 1
34 The Manor House, Bledlow

Monday 2
3 Ascott
38 Nether Winchendon House
51 Turn End

Sunday 8
41 Overstroud Cottage

Wednesday 11
18 Gipsy House
43 The Plant Specialist

Sunday 15
10 Chesham Bois House
44 The Plough
49 Stoke Poges Memorial Gardens

Sunday 22
29 The Lee Gardens at Swan Bottom

Thursday 26
6 Bunyans Cottage
28 Laplands Farm

Sunday 29
16 East Claydon Gardens
17 Fressingwood

Monday 30
40 The Old Sun House
44 The Plough

June

Sunday 5
35 The Manor House, Hambleden
41 Overstroud Cottage
47 Rivendell

Thursday 9
18 Gipsy House
25 Homelands
33 Lords Wood
43 The Plant Specialist

Saturday 11
12 Cowper & Newton Museum Gardens

Sunday 12
5 Bradenham Manor
7 Burrow Farm
12 Cowper & Newton Museum Gardens
26 Hughenden Manor
32 Long Crendon Summer Gardens
45 Quainton Gardens
55 The White House

Wednesday 15
13 Craiglea House
15 Dorneywood Garden
49 Stoke Poges Memorial Gardens
53 Upper Farmhouse

Saturday 18
2 Acer Corner
42 11 The Paddocks

Sunday 19
2 Acer Corner
9 Cheddington Gardens
13 Craiglea House
34 The Manor House, Bledlow
42 11 The Paddocks
50 The Tower House

Friday 24
42 11 The Paddocks (Evening)

Terraced lawns with specimen and ornamental trees, panoramic views to the Chilterns . . .

Saturday 25
23 Hillesden House
48 Rose Cottage (Evening)

Sunday 26
4 Aylesbury Gardens
19 Grange Drive Wooburn

Wednesday 29
19 Grange Drive Wooburn

July

Saturday 2
36 Maryfield
42 11 The Paddocks

Sunday 3
30 Little Missenden Gardens
36 Maryfield
42 11 The Paddocks
51 Turn End

Sunday 10
56 Whitewalls

Wednesday 13
18 Gipsy House
43 The Plant Specialist

Friday 15
25 Homelands (Evening)

Saturday 16
11 Cliveden

Sunday 17
10 Chesham Bois House

Sunday 24
14 Cuddington Gardens

Saturday 30
2 Acer Corner
15 Dorneywood Garden

Sunday 31
2 Acer Corner
21 Higher Denham Gardens

August

Thursday 11
25 Homelands

Monday 29
3 Ascott

September

Thursday 8
33 Lords Wood

Sunday 11
44 The Plough
56 Whitewalls

Saturday 17
11 Cliveden
36 Maryfield

October

Saturday 15
2 Acer Corner

Sunday 16
2 Acer Corner

February 2012

Sunday 19
- **21** Higher Denham Gardens

Sunday 26
- **19** Grange Drive Wooburn
- **45** Quainton Gardens

Gardens open to the public

- **3** Ascott
- **5** Bradenham Manor
- **11** Cliveden
- **12** Cowper & Newton Museum Gardens
- **26** Hughenden Manor
- **38** Nether Winchendon House
- **43** The Plant Specialist
- **49** Stoke Poges Memorial Gardens

By appointment only

- **1** Abbotts House
- **8** Cedar House
- **20** Hall Barn
- **22** Hill House
- **37** Montana
- **39** North Down
- **46** Red Kites
- **54** Watercroft

Also open by Appointment

- **2** Acer Corner
- **7** Burrow Farm
- **10** Chesham Bois House
- **13** Craiglea House
- **19** Grange Drive Wooburn
- **21** Higher Denham Gardens
- **23** Hillesden House
- **25** Homelands
- **16** Inglenooks, East Claydon Gardens
- **19** Magnolia House, Grange Drive Wooburn
- **34** The Manor House, Bledlow
- **36** Maryfield
- **41** Overstroud Cottage
- **42** 11 The Paddocks
- **50** The Tower House
- **53** Upper Farmhouse
- **45** The Vine, Quainton Gardens
- **9** Westend House, Cheddington Gardens
- **56** Whitewalls
- **21** Wind in the Willows, Higher Denham Gardens

The Gardens

1 **ABBOTTS HOUSE**
10 Church Street, Winslow
MK18 3AN. Mrs Jane Rennie,
01296 712326. *9m N of Aylesbury.
On A413 into Winslow. From town
centre take Horn St & R into Church
St.* Adm £2.50, chd free. **Visitors
welcome by appt.**
Garden on different levels divided into
4. Courtyard near house with arbour
and pots, woodland garden (planted
5yrs ago) with rose arbour, swimming
pool garden with grasses. Walled
Victorian kitchen garden with glass
houses, potager, fruit pergola, wall
trained fruit and many mediterranean
plants. House & garden adm £8.80,
chd £4.40.

2 **ACER CORNER**
10 Manor Rd, Wendover
HP22 6HQ. Jo Naiman,
07958 319234, jo@acercorner.com.
*3m S of Aylesbury. Follow A413 into
Wendover. L at clock tower r'about
into Aylesbury Rd. R at next r'about
into Wharf Rd, continue past schools
on L, garden on R.* Adm £2.50, chd
free. **Sats & Suns 18, 19 June; 30,
31 July; 15, 16 Oct (2-5). Visitors
also welcome by appt May to
October. Individuals & groups.**
Medium-sized garden with Japanese
influence and large collection of
Japanese maples. The enclosed front
garden is oriental in style. Back
garden is divided into 3 areas: patio
area surrounded by shrubs; densely-
planted area with many acers and
roses and area recently developed
which includes a productive
greenhouse and intersting planting.

3 ◆ **ASCOTT**
Wing, Leighton Buzzard LU7 0PS.
Sir Evelyn de Rothschild, National
Trust, 01296 688242,
www.nationaltrust.org.uk. *2m SW of
Leighton Buzzard, 8m NE of Aylesbury.
Via A418. Buses: 150 Aylesbury -
Milton Keynes, 100 Aylesbury & Milton
Keynes.* Adm £4.40, chd £2.20. **For
NGS: Mons 2 May; 29 Aug (2-6).
For other opening times and
information, please phone or see
garden website.**
Combining Victorian formality with
early C20 natural style and recent
plantings to lead it into the C21, with
a recently completed garden
designed by Jacques and Peter Wirtz

who designed the gardens at Alnwick
Castle, and also a Richard Long
Sculpture. Terraced lawns with
specimen and ornamental trees,
panoramic views to the Chilterns.
Naturalised bulbs, mirror-image
herbaceous borders, impressive
topiary incl box and yew sundial.

ASHRIDGE
See Hertfordshire.

GROUP OPENING

4 **AYLESBURY GARDENS**
HP21 7LR. *¾ m SE of Aylesbury
Centre. 4 town gardens S of town
centre, 2 off A413, 2 off A41.* Home-
made teas at 2 Spenser Road. **Adm
£4, chd free. Sun 26 June (2-6).**

> **2 SPENSER ROAD**
> Mr & Mrs G A Brown

> **110 TRING ROAD**
> Julia & Ken Keasley

> **13 WALTON DENE**
> Joe & Marian Benham

> **90 WALTON WAY**
> Mr & Mrs R Lewis-Smith

4 mature town gardens showing a
wide range of ideas and specialities.
Each garden displays the individuality
of its owners and their passions, incl
tender perennials and herbaceous
borders, raised alpine beds and
ponds. Other features incl an
interesting Victorian greenhouse,
vegetable beds and cottage style
gardens. Featured in Aylesbury in
Bloom competition. 110 Tring Road
won Best Formal Garden and 13
Walton Dene won Best Front and
Vegetable garden. Wheelchair access
at 13 Walton Dene & 110 Tring Road.

4 mature town
gardens showing
a wide range of
ideas and
specialities. Each
garden displays the
individuality of its
owners . . .

5 ◆ BRADENHAM MANOR

HP14 4HF. National Trust,
www.nationaltrust.org.uk. *2¹/₂ m
NW of High Wycombe, 5m S of
Princes Risborough. On A4010, turn
by Red Lion Pub, car park signed on
village green.* Adm £3.50, chd free.
For NGS: Sun 12 June (1-4.30).
For other opening times and
information, see garden website.
Unique opportunity to see the ongoing restoration of the C17 gardens,
with views of the village and
countryside. Reinstated victorian
summer border, yew hedges, parterre
and wilderness at various stages of
restoration. Guided tour at 2pm, £1
donation. Gravel & cobbled paths,
steep grass slopes.

  ♿ 🐕 ☕ ☎

6 NEW BUNYANS COTTAGE

5 High street, Brill HP18 9ST. Peter
& Josie Symes. *5m N of Thame.
4m from A41 through Ludgershall.
3m from B4011 Thame/Bicester rd,
signed to Brill. In centre of village.*
Combined adm with **Laplands
Farm** £3.50, chd free. Thur 26
May (2-5).
Pretty, established cottage-style
garden in conservation area of village.
Constantly evolving, mini orchard and
productive areas with lovely view of
parish church.

  ♿

7 BURROW FARM

Hambleden RG9 6LT. David Palmer,
01491 571256. *1m SE of
Hambleden. On A4155 between
Henley and Marlow, turn N at Mill
End. After 300yds, R onto Rotten
Row. After ¹/₂ m, Burrow Farm
entrance on R.* Home-made teas.
Adm £5, chd free (share to
Buckinghamshire Community
Foundation). Sun 12 June (2-6).
Visitors also welcome by appt
June/July. Groups 35 max.
Burrow Farm and the adj Cottages
(not open) are part Tudor and part
Elizabethan, set in the Chilterns above
Hambleden Valley where it meets the
Thames. Views of pasture and
woodlands across the ha-ha greatly
enhance the setting. Special features
are the parterre, arboretum and C15
barn, where teas are served.

  ♿ 🐕 ❀ ☕ ☎

8 CEDAR HOUSE

Bacombe Lane, Wendover
HP22 6EQ. Sarah Nicholson,
01296 622131,
jeremynicholson@btinternet.com.

Chesham Bois House

*5m SE Aylesbury. From Gt Missenden
take A413 into Wendover. Take 1st L
before row of cottages, house at top
of lane.* Adm £3.50, chd free.
Visitors welcome by appt from
May-Sept for groups 10+, no
coaches, parking for 10 cars only.
A chalk garden in the Chiltern Hills
with a steep sloping lawn leading to a
natural swimming pond with aquatic
plants. Wildflowers with native
orchids. Shaped borders hold a great
variety of trees, shrubs and
perennials. A lodge greenhouse and a
good collection of half hardy plants in
pots. Steep slope.

  ♿ ☎

CHARLTON GARDENS

See Northamptonshire.

GROUP OPENING

9 CHEDDINGTON GARDENS

LU7 0RQ. *11m E of Aylesbury, 7m
S of Leighton Buzzard. Turn off B489
at Pitstone. Turn off B488 at
Cheddington stn, turn off
Cheddington/Long Marston rd.*
Home-made teas at Methodist
Chapel on green. **Combined adm**

£5, chd free (share to local
charities). Sun 19 June (2-6).

**CHEDDINGTON
ALLOTMENTS**
Cheddington Parish Council

**CHEDDINGTON COMBINED
SCHOOL**

CHILTERN HOUSE
Rev. Roger & Deborah Hale

NEW **7 HIGH STREET**
Irene & Tony Johnson

6 MANOR POUND ROAD
Mrs Cheryl Sibley

THE OLD POST OFFICE
Alan & Wendy Tipple

ROSE COTTAGE
Mrs Margery Jones
(See separate entry)

WESTEND HOUSE
Mrs Sue Foster
Visitors also welcome by appt.
01296 661332
suefosteruk@hotmail.com

WOODSTOCK COTTAGE
Mr & Mrs D Bradford

Long village with green. Nine very
diverse gardens with 1 new garden
this yr. ¹/₂ -acre cottage garden filled

with small rooms with a balance of evergreens resulting in a garden for all seasons. Courtyard and patio garden with small fountain at base of ancient elder tree with front laid to gravel and assorted shrubs. Small garden designed to blur the boundaries, stained glass and mosaics. Cottage style garden softly planted with lavender, roses, clematis and shaded area with small pond. Converted chapel with pretty cottage style and gravel planting. A garden of mixed planting with connecting paths and seating area. School sensory garden planted by the children with willow tunnel walk leading to outdoor classroom. Large pond and wild plant area. Varied and individual allotments with wide views of Chilterns and over 50 plots. 2-acre garden restored and extended, steel bird sculptures and rare breed hens and pigs. Best Kept Village in Class - Buckinghamshire Association of Local Councils. Wheelchair access at Chiltern House, Cheddington Allotments, Westend House & Rose Cottage only.

& ⊗ ☕

> Gardening was,
> of all
> employments,
> that in which
> I succeeded
> best . . .

10 **CHESHAM BOIS HOUSE**
85 Bois Lane, Chesham Bois HP6 6DF. Julia Plaistowe, julia.plaistowe@yahoo.co.uk, www.cheshamboishouse.co.uk. *1m N of Amersham-on-the-Hill. From Amersham-on-the-Hill follow Sycamore Rd, over double mini r'about, which turns into Bois Lane. Past village shops, house is ¹/₂ m on L. Parking in road or on R at school & at scout hut.* Home-made teas. **Adm £3.50, chd free.** Suns 27 Mar (2-5); 15 May; 17 July (2-5.30). Visitors

also welcome by appt. Please contact by email if possible.
A plantsman's garden with walled garden, small ornamental canal and rill with gazebo, lovely herbaceous borders with some tender and unusual plants, topiaried trees and wide lawns. In spring, fine display of primroses, daffodils and hellebores. Gravel in front of house.

& ⊗ ☕

11 ◆ **CLIVEDEN**
Taplow SL6 0JA. National Trust, 01628 605069, www.nationaltrust.org.uk. *2m N of Taplow. Leave M4 at J7 or M40 at J4 & follow brown tourism signs.* **Adm £8, chd £4. For NGS: Sats 16 July (10-5.30); 17 Sept (2-5.30). For other opening times and information, please phone or see garden website.**
Separate gardens within extensive grounds first laid out in C18. Water garden, secret garden, topiary, herbaceous borders, woodland walks and views of R Thames. Timber steps lead down yew tree walk to river.

& ⊗ ☎

12 ◆ **COWPER & NEWTON MUSEUM GARDENS**
Market Place, Olney MK46 4AJ. Mrs E Knight, 01234 711516, www.cowperandnewtonmuseum. org.uk. *5m N of Newport Pagnell. 12m S of Wellingborough. On A509. Please park in public car park in east street.* Light refreshments. **Adm £2.50, chd free. For NGS: Sat 11, Sun 12 June (10.30-4.30). For other opening times and information, please phone or see garden website.**
Restored walled flower garden with plants pre 1800, many mentioned by C18 poet, William Cowper, who said of himself 'Gardening was, of all employments, that in which I succeeded best'. Also Summer House Garden in Victorian kitchen style with organic, new and old vegetable varieties. Herb and medicinal plant borders in memory of the garden's original use by an apothecary. Lacemaking demonstration.

& ⊗ ☕ ☎

13 ◆ **CRAIGLEA HOUSE**
Austenwood Lane, Chalfont St Peter, Gerrards Cross SL9 9DA. Jeff & Sue Medlock, 01753 884852, jeffmedlock@hotmail.com. *6m SE Amersham. From Gerrards Cross*

take B416 towards Amersham. Take L fork after ¹/₂ m into Austenwood Lane, garden ¹/₃ m. Park at St Joseph's Church or Priory Road. Home-made teas on 19 June only. **Adm £4, chd free. Wed 15, Sun 19 June (2-5). Visitors also welcome by appt. Visits can also be arranged for Spring display.**
1 acre garden. Formal gardens surround Arts and Crafts house (not open) incl white garden with central fountain, pergola, rose garden, and herbacious and mixed borders. The less formal area has wildlife ponds, vegetable garden, fern walk and mixed borders. Many varieties of Hosta. Lots of seats affording lovely views of the garden. Featured in Home Counties magazine.

& ⊗ ☕ ☎

GROUP OPENING

14 **CUDDINGTON GARDENS**
Nr Thame HP18 0AP. *3¹/₂ m NE Thame, 5m SW Aylesbury. Off A418. Parking signed in village. Wheelchair visitor parking phone 01844 291526.* Home-made teas at Tyringham Hall & The Bernard Hall. **Combined adm £5, chd free. Sun 24 July (2-6).**

33 BERNARD CLOSE
Mr & Mrs Tony Orchard

THE OLD PLACE
Dr & Mrs Michael Straiton

NEW **THE OLD RECTORY**
Mr & Mrs R J Frost

NEW **TIBBYS COTTAGE**
Anthony & Evelyn Hatch

TYRINGHAM HALL
Mrs Sherry Scott

Picturesque Midsomer Murders village. 5 gardens open (2 new for this yr), ranging from that of a small cul-de-sac semi-detached in Bernard Close to the 3-acre Old Rectory garden, all accessed within a circular walk, also taking you past 'chocolate box' cottages complementing the pretty village greens, romantic dell with waterfall adjoining Tibby's Cottage in Tibby's Lane and C13 church with attractive churchyard and wild flower reserve. Winners, regional Best Kept Village competition. Wheelchair access at 33 Bernard Close, Tyringham Hall & The Old Place only.

& 🐕 ⊗ ☕

15 DORNEYWOOD GARDEN

Dorneywood Road, Burnham
SL1 8PY. National Trust. *1m E of
Taplow, 5m S of Beaconsfield. From
Burnham village take Dropmore Rd,
at end of 30mph limit take R fork into
Dorneywood Rd. Entrance is 1m on
R. From M40 J2, take A355 to Slough
then 1st R to Burnham, 2m then 2nd
L after Jolly Woodman, signed
Dorneywood Rd. Dorneywood is about
1m on L.* Home-made teas. **Adm
£4.50, chd free. Tue 19, Wed 20 Apr;
Wed 15 June; Sat 30 July (2-5).**
8-acre country house garden on
several levels with herbaceous
borders, greenhouses, roses, cottage
and kitchen gardens, lily pond and
conservatory. Admission only by
written application, or e-mail;
opendaydorneywood@btinternet.com
to the Housekeeper 2 weeks in
advance for all dates.

GROUP OPENING

16 EAST CLAYDON GARDENS

MK18 2ND. *1½ m SW Winslow. In
Winslow turn R off High St, follow NT
signs to Claydon House.* Home-made
teas at the Village Hall. **Combined
adm £4, chd free. Sun 29 May
(2-6).**

9 CHURCH WAY
Margaret Landon

INGLENOOKS
Mr & Mrs David Polhill
Visitors also welcome by appt
June & early July for roses.
Please phone to arranging
bookings. 01296 712059

THE OLD VICARAGE
Nigel & Esther Turnbull

Small village, originally part of the
Claydon Estate (Claydon House, NT
is 1½ m). Typical N Bucks cottages,
C13 church. Inglenooks is an informal
cottage garden with different areas of
interest, many roses, surrounding
C17 timber-framed thatched cottage
(not open). The Old Vicarage, a large
garden on clay. Mixed borders,
scented garden, dell, shrub roses,
vegetables and natural clay pond.
Small meadow area and planting to
encourage wildlife. Access via gravel
drive. 9 Church Way is a small rural
garden with outstanding views over
the N Bucks countryside.

EVENLEY WOOD GARDEN
See Northamptonshire.

FARTHINGHOE GARDENS
See Northamptonshire.

17 FRESSINGWOOD

Hare Lane, Little Kingshill
HP16 0EF. John & Maggie Bateson.
*1m S of Gt Missenden, 4m W of
Amersham. From A413 Amersham to
Aylesbury rd, turn L at Chiltern
Hospital, signed Gt & Little Kingshill.
Take 1st L into Nags Head Lane. Turn
R under railway bridge & 1st L into
New Rd. At top, turn into Hare Lane,
1st house on R.* Home-made teas.
**Adm £3, chd free. Sun 29 May
(2-6).**
Thoughtfully designed garden with
yr-round colour. Shrubbery with ferns,
grasses and hellebores. Small formal
garden, herb garden, pergolas with
wisteria, roses and clematis. Topiary
and landscaped terrace. Newly
developed area incorporating water
with grasses. Herbaceous borders
and bonsai collection. Many
interesting features.

15 GADE VALLEY COTTAGES
See Hertfordshire.

18 GIPSY HOUSE

Whitefield Lane, Gt Missenden
HP16 0AL. Mrs Felicity Dahl. *5m
NW of Amersham. A413 to Gt
Missenden. take Whitefield Lane, opp
Missenden Abbey entrance, under
railway bridge. Small Georgian house
on R, park in field opp.* Home-made
teas. **Adm £4.00, chd free.
Wed 27 Apr; Wed 11 May; Thur
9 June; Wed 13 July (2-5). Also
opening with The Plant Specialist
27 April, 11 May, 9 June, 13 July.**
Late Roald Dahl's garden. York stone
terrace, pleached lime walk, with
hostas, hellebore and allium. Sunken
garden, water feature, sundial garden,
topiary oaks, herbaceous perennials,
assorted roses. Walled vegetable
garden, espalier fruits, herbs,
greenhouse with vine, peaches and
nectarines.Yew garden with roses and
perennials. Wild flower meadow. See
the hut where Roald Dahl wrote his
stories, the Gypsy Caravan featured in
'Danny Champion of the World' and
find your way through the maze.
Wheelchair access available but very
limited.

GROUP OPENING

19 GRANGE DRIVE WOOBURN

Wooburn Green HP10 0QD. *On
A4094, 2m SW of A40, between
Bourne End & Wooburn. From
Wooburn church, direction
Maidenhead, Grange Drive is on L
before roundabout, from Bourne End
left at 2 mini roundabouts,then 1st
right.* Home-made teas & light
refreshments. **Adm £3.50, chd free.
Sun 20 Feb (11-2) Sun 26, Wed
29 June (2-5). Sun 26 Feb 2012.**

MAGNOLIA HOUSE
Alan & Elaine Ford
Visitors also welcome by appt.
Please phone or email for
details.
01628 525818 (07836 224855)
alan@lanford.co.uk
www.lanford.co.uk/events

THE SHADES
Pauline & Maurice Kirkpatrick
Not open Feb dates.

Two diverse gardens in a private tree-
lined drive which formed the entrance
to a country house now demolished.
Display of local paintings/craft.
Magnolia House is a ½ acre garden
with many mature trees incl
magnificent copper beech and
magnolia reaching the rooftop, a small
cactus bed, fernery, stream leading to
pond and greenhouses with 2 small
aviaries. 10,000 snowdrops in spring
and many hellebores. The Shades
drive is approached through mature
trees and beds of herbaceous plants
and 60 various roses. A natural well is
surrounded by shrubs and acers. The
garden was improved in 2010 to
include a natural stone lawn terrace
and changes to existing flower beds. A
green slate water feature with alpine
plants completes the garden. Featured
in Country Life (for snowdrops).

*Thoughtfully
designed garden
with year-round
colour . . .*

20 ► HALL BARN

Windsor End, Beaconsfield HP9 2SG. The Hon Mrs Farncombe, jenefer@farncombe01.demon.co.uk *1/2 m S of Beaconsfield. Lodge gate 300yds S of St Mary & All Saints' Church in Old Town centre.* **Adm £4, chd free. Visitors welcome by appt. Individual or groups. Written appointment/email required.**

Historical landscaped garden laid out between 1680-1730 for the poet Edmund Waller and his descendants. Features 300yr-old 'cloud formation' yew hedges, formal lake and vistas ending with classical buildings and statues. Wooded walks around the grove offer respite from the heat on sunny days. One of the original gardens opening in 1927 for the NGS. Open-air Shakespeare festival in mid-June (covered seating). Gravel paths. Dogs on leads.

   ♿ 🪺

GROUP OPENING

21 ► HIGHER DENHAM GARDENS

Higher Denham UB9 5EA. *6m E of Beaconsfield. From A40 take A412. 1/4 m from the junction turn L at part-time traffic lights into Old Rectory Lane. 1m on turn into Lower Rd signed Higher Denham.* **Home-made & cream teas at Village Hall 31 July only. Combined adm £4 (Feb) £5 (July) chd free (share to Community garden and playing fields). Suns 13 Feb (2-4.30); 31 July (1-5). Sun 19 Feb 2012. Visitors also welcome by appt.**

   11 LOWER ROAD
   Anne Ling

   86c LOWER ROAD
   Jo Mucho

   19 MIDDLE ROAD
   Sonia Harris.
   Not open 13 Feb.

   WIND IN THE WILLOWS
   Ron James
   Visitors also welcome by appt.
   Groups welcome by appointment. One month's notice please.
   07740 177038
   r.james@company-doc.co.uk

Gardens in this small, semi-rural village nestling in the delightful Misbourne Valley with its idyllic chalk stream will be open at a NEW time of year, July, to give our returning visitors a chance to see the gardens in summer. Two gardens will also open in February. A map will guide you firstly to our 3-acre garden then onto the smaller gardens. Wind in the Willows for over 350 shrubs and trees, informal, woodland, and wild gardens including riverside and bog plantings and a collection of 80 hostas. 'Stunning' was the word most often used by visitors last year. 11 Lower Road. A wildlife haven owned by a master composter containing trees, shrubs, colourful borders and vegetables. 19 Middle Road. July 31st only. A garden crowded with as many plants as possible. Some fruit bushes, a few vegetables. Terrace overlooking the garden. 86c Lower Road. July 31st only. A NEW garden in our group where the owner has used her experience of working in a nursery to create a garden on two levels with a Mediterranean feel and a touch of the exotic. Composting demonstration & plant sale 31 July.

   ♿ ✿ ☕

Guinea fowl and ducks wander freely while tumbler pigeons fly above . . .

HILL GROUNDS
See Northamptonshire.

22 ► HILL HOUSE

Castle Street, Buckingham MK18 1BS. Mr & Mrs P Thorogood, 07860 714758, leonie@pjtassociates.com. *Town centre. On L of vehicle entrance to Parish Church (spire very visible) parking in the churchyard. Castle St clearly marked as you face Old Town Hall at central town r'about.* **Adm £3, chd free. Visitors welcome by appt mid May to end Sept.**

*1/3 -acre town garden on old castle walls, aiming at ease of maintenance, yr-round interest and colour.

   ♿ ✿ ☎

23 ► HILLESDEN HOUSE

Church End, Hillesden MK18 4DB. Mr & Mrs R M Faccenda, 01296 730451, suefaccenda@aol.com. *3m S of Buckingham. Next to church in Hillesden.* **Home-made teas. Adm £4, chd free. Sat 25 June (2-5). Visitors also welcome by appt Visits welcome between April and July - 10 persons or more.**

By superb church 'Cathedral in the Fields'. Carp lakes, fountains and waterfalls. Mature trees and large conservatory. Rose, alpine, foliage and herbaceous gardens. 5 acre formal area surrounded by about 100 acres of deer park, wild flower areas and extensive lakes developed by owner. Lovely walks, lots of wildlife and many birds.

   ♿ 🪺 ✿ ☕ ☎

24 ► HOLLYDYKE HOUSE

Little Missenden, Amersham HP7 0RD. Bob and Sandra Wetherall. *2 miles NW Old Amersham. Take A413 north from Amersham. First turning left to Little Missenden. 6th house on right.* **Home-made teas. Adm £3, chd free. Mon 25 Apr (1-5).**

A 3 acre garden with year round interest set in the Misbourne Valley. At the end of April the garden should be full of tulips and other spring flowers. Close to the house is a black and white garden; a newly developed kitchen garden. Gravel paths.

   ♿ 🪺 ✿

25 ► HOMELANDS

Springs Lane, Ellesborough HP17 0XD. Jean & Tony Young, 01296 622306, young@ellesborough.fsnet.co.uk. *6m SE of Aylesbury. 4m NE of Princes Risborough. On B4010 2m W of Wendover. Springs Lane is between the village hall at Butlers Cross & St Peter & St Pauls Chruch. Narrow lane, uneven surface.* **Home-made teas. Thur 9 June; Thur 11 Aug (2-5) Evening Opening wine, Fri 15 July (6-9). Visitors also welcome by appt.**

Secluded *3/4* -acre garden on chalk adjoining open country-side. Evolving design; wide range of features incl secluded seating areas, wildlife pond, mature wild flower meadow, deep borders and gravel beds with exotic late summer and autumn planting. Featured in WI Life National Magazine.

   ♿ 🪺 ☕ ☎

◆ **HUGHENDEN MANOR**
High Wycombe HP14 4LA. National Trust, 01494 755573, www.nationaltrust.org.uk. *1¹/₂ m N of High Wycombe. On W side of Gt Missenden Rd A4128, past church, into NT woodland car-park.* **Adm £2.90, chd £2.10. For NGS: Sun 12 June (11-5).** For other opening times and information, please phone or see garden website.
Mary Anne Disraeli's colour schemes inspire spring and summer bedding in formal parterre. Unusual conifers, planted from photographs taken at time of Disraeli's death. Old English apple orchard with picnic area. Beech woodland walks. Mediterranean border. The walled garden Learning Zone will be open too, with guides available. Meet the Gardener at Hughenden for 1st hand gardening advice. House & Garden adm £7.50, chd £3.50.

&. ✿ ☕

28 **LAPLANDS FARM**
Ludgershall Road, Brill, Aylesbury HP18 9TZ. Roger & Hilary Cope. *Between Brill & Ludgershall. 3m from A41 through Ludgershall towards*

Brill. 3m from B4011 Thame/Bicester rd, via Oakly through Brill. Home-made teas. **Combined adm with Bunyans Cottage £3.50, chd free. Thur 26 May (2-5).**
Self-made country garden of borders dug out of a field incorporating a pond and stream. Majority of plants coming from anywhere but garden centres therefore the garden has evolved rather than planned. Guinea fowl and ducks wander freely while tumbler pigeons fly above. Vegetable area and interesting rare breed fowl.

&. ⊨ ☕

GROUP OPENING

29 **THE LEE GARDENS AT SWAN BOTTOM**
Gt Missenden HP16 9NU. *3m N of Great Missenden, 3m SE of Wendover. From A413, Gt Missenden to Wendover, take 3rd R up Rocky Lane. For Kingswood House after 2m turn L at 1st X-rds. 200yds turn R down drive. For 2 Kingswood Cottages after 2m turn L at 1st X-rds. 200yds turn L down unmade road,*

1st drive on R. Home-made teas at Kingswood House. **Adm £5, chd free. Sun 22 May (2-6).**

2 KINGSWOOD COTTAGES
Jon & Trish Swain

KINGSWOOD HOUSE
Mr & Mrs T Hart

Swan Bottom is a hamlet less than 1m N of the secluded and picturesque village of The Lee, at the centre of which is the green created by Arthur Liberty who founded Libertys of Regent Street. C13 church with fine wall paintings. 2 Kingswood Cottages 2-acre informal garden in the peaceful Chiltern Hills. Children (and adults) love following winding paths, discovering sculptures and artefacts en route, beehives, chickens, specimen trees. Kingswood House 4-acre mature garden in an AONB. Large, colourful, mixed borders with many unusual plants. White garden surrounding a formal pond with fountain, scented sundial garden. Hot colour theme beds adjacent to tennis court. Fruit and vegetable areas. Interesting trees.

&. ✿ ☕

Homelands

Look out for the gardens with the ☎ – enjoy a private visit . . .

46 LINCOLN ROAD
See London.

GROUP OPENING

30 **LITTLE MISSENDEN GARDENS**
Amersham HP7 0RD. *2¹/₂ m NW of Old Amersham. On A413*. Home-made teas. **Combined adm £5, chd free. Sun 3 July (2-6).**

HOLLYDYKE HOUSE
Bob and Sandra Wetherall

KINGS BARN
Mr & Mrs A Playle

THE MANOR HOUSE
Mr & Mrs T A Cuff

1 MILL END COTTAGES
Philip & Eileen Sharman

MILL HOUSE
Terry & Eleanor Payne

MISSENDEN HOUSE
Wilf Stevenson

NEW **TOWN FARM COTTAGE**
Mr & Mrs Tim Garnham

7 gardens set in this attractive Chiltern village in an area of outstanding natural beauty to incl; 3-acre garden with herbaceous borders, shrubs and trees. Old fashioned roses, koi and lily ponds, collection of conifers and kitchen garden. A new garden in an old setting where the owners have tried to reflect the rectangular form of the barn and its plot by picking this theme in its design. Large 9-acre garden consisting of lawns, flower beds, woods and pasture in a glorious setting and a 1-acre semi-formal topiary garden with open views, glasshouse and vegetable area. Rose pergolas, architectural and sculptural features. A garden with mill stream (the R Misbourne) flowing both through the garden and the original Mill House. A garden using a mixture of traditional and modern with herbaceous and lawns together plus Zen garden by Christopher Bradley Hole and a bamboo playground. Traditional English garden of 1-acre where lavender borders and roses are a feature with beech, yew hedging and some topiary. Newly planted herbaceous borders, acers and mature trees incl a willow. Less formal part of the garden has a wild flower area. (Anglo-saxon church built 975). Village used several times as a set for film and TV. Limited wheelchair access due to gravel paths and some steps. Sorry, no dogs at Missenden House.

  ♿ 🐕 ☕

GROUP OPENING

31 **LONG CRENDON SPRING GARDENS**
HP18 9AN. *2m N of Thame. On B4011 Thame-Bicester rd*. Home-made teas at Church House. **Adm £5, chd free (share to Long Crendon Day Centre). Sun 17 Apr (2-6).**

BAKER'S CLOSE
Mr & Mrs Peter Vaines

BARRY'S CLOSE
Mr & Mrs Richard Salmon

48 CHILTON ROAD
Mr & Mrs M Charnock

25 ELM TREES
Carol and Mike Price

MANOR HOUSE
Mr & Mrs West

THE OLD CROWN
Mr & Mrs R H Bradbury

A large variety of gardens to visit during a lovely walk round an attractive village with many old/listed buildings incl St Mary's church which dates from the C13 and the NT Court House which dates from the early C15. The gardens range from a 2-acre sloping garden with an interesting collection of spring flowering trees and shrubs; 1¹/₂ acres on a SW slope with numerous beds, many varieties of clematis and spring bulbs. 4 acres with 2 ornamental lakes and fine views towards the Chilterns with a mix of plantings for sun and shade: two cottage style gardens, with mixed shrub and herbaceous borders, vegetables areas: 2 acres on SW slope, partly walled with courtyard, terraced lawns, rockery with pond, shrubs, bulbs and wild area.

  ♿ 🐕 ❀ ☕

GROUP OPENING

32 **LONG CRENDON SUMMER GARDENS**
HP18 9AN. *2m N of Thame. On Thame/Bicester rd B4011. Maps available for all visitors. Please note parking can be congested at the church end of the High Street*. Home-made teas & Light Refreshments at Croft House, Church House, St Mary's Church, Ketchmore House. **Adm £5, chd free (share to Long Crendon Day Care Centre). Sun 12 June (2-6).**

COP CLOSE
Sandra & Tony Phipkin

CROFT HOUSE
Cdr & Mrs Peter Everett

KETCHMORE HOUSE
Mr & Mrs C Plumb

MULBERRY HOUSE
Mr & Mrs C Weston

THE OLD CROWN
Mr & Mrs R H Bradbury

TOMPSONS FARM
Mr D Tye

A large variety of gardens to visit during a lovely walk round an attractive village with many old/listed buildings incl St Mary's church which dates from the C13 and the NT Court House which dates from the early C15. The gardens range from a walled garden with a variety of plants and shrubs, some unusual and of interest to flower arrangers, an interesting cottage garden, divided into rooms. A restored vicarage garden incl a formal knot garden and notable monkey puzzle and mulberry trees. 1¹/₂ acres with numerous beds, large number of roses and clematis, pots and containers and two sizeable vegetable plots, large woodland garden with mature trees sweeping down to an ornamental lake and a developing garden with large herbaceous borders and a shaded slope to become a wild garden.

  ♿ ❀ ☕

Be tempted by a plant from a plant stall

33 LORDS WOOD
Frieth Road, Marlow Common
SL7 2QS. Mr & Mrs Messum. *1¹/2 m
NW Marlow. From Marlow turn off the
A4155 at Platts Garage into Oxford
Rd, towards Frieth, 1¹/2 m. Garden is
100yds past Marlow Common turn,
on L.* Home-made teas. **Adm £4,
chd free. Thurs 9 June; 8 Sept
(11-4.30).**
Lords Wood was built in 1899 and
has been the Messums family home
since 1974. The 5-acres of garden
feature extensive borders in widely
varying styles. From vegetable, flower
and herb gardens, to large water
gardens and rockery, orchard,
woodland and meadow with fantastic
views over the Chilterns. We are
always bringing new ideas to Lords
Wood, you will find something
different to enjoy with every visit.
Partial wheelchair access, gravel
paths, steep slopes.

Informal garden,
sweeping lawns,
mature trees and
an exceptional rose
garden . . .

**34 THE MANOR HOUSE,
BLEDLOW**
HP27 9PB. The Lord Carrington,
01844 274292,
lordc@carington.co.uk. *9m NW of
High Wycombe, 3m SW of Princes
Risborough. ¹/2 m off B4009 in middle
of Bledlow village.* Home-made teas.
**Adm £5, chd free. Suns 1 May;
19 June (2-6).** Visitors also
welcome by appt.
Paved garden, parterres, shrub
borders, old roses and walled
kitchen garden. Water garden with
paths, bridges and walkways, fed by
14 chalk springs. Also 2 acres with
sculptures and landscaped planting.
Partial wheelchair access.

**35 THE MANOR HOUSE,
HAMBLEDEN**
RG9 6SG. Maria Carmela,
Viscountess Hambleden. *3¹/2 m NE
Henley-on-Thames, 8m SW High
Wycombe. 1m N of A4155.* **Adm £4,
chd free. Sun 5 June (2-6).**

Informal garden, sweeping lawns,
mature trees and an exceptional rose
garden designed by Peter Beales with
a profusion of old fashioned scented
roses. Large terrace on the S side of
the house takes you to a magnificent
conservatory with stunning plants
climbing 30ft.

36 MARYFIELD
High Street, Taplow SL6 0EX.
Jacqueline & Roger Andrews,
01628 667 246,
japrivate@btinternet.com. *1m S
Cliveden, ¹/2 m E Maidenhead. From
M4 J7 or M40 J4 follow signs for
Taplow. Drive past the Church and
drive up High St. Maryfield is on your
left on the bend of the High Street.*
Home-made teas & light
refreshments. **Adm £4, chd free.
Sats & Suns 28, 29 May; 2, 3 July;
Sat 17 Sept (2-5.30).** Visitors also
welcome by appt. Groups
encouraged. £7 per head incl
afternoon tea & cakes.
2-acres wrapped around our Victorian
home in the heart of Taplow Village.
Walled vegetable/potager and herb
garden bordered by fruit trees,
overlooked by a mature lime walk, lily
pond surrounded by generous
borders, extends into herbaceous
planting and rose garden, mature yew
hedging, pond area, orchard and
Japanese-inspired garden. Roger
Andrews is an accomplished
gardener, garden designer and artist,
who also created the planting for the
NGS stand at Chelsea last yr.
Featured in Berkshire Life,
Maidenhead Advertiser, filmed by
BBC & Scottish TV for cookery/
gardening programmes. Also featured
on Berkshire Radio. Limited
wheelchair access. Some narrow
paths.

37 MONTANA
Shire Lane, Cholesbury HP23 6NA.
John & Diana Garner, 01494
758347, montana@cholesbury.net.
*3m NW of Chesham. 3m S of Tring,
3m SW of Berkhamsted. Leave A41
junction signed A4251 North Church.
Follow Wigginton signs turn L after
r'about up The Twist. Out of
Wigginton on Chesham rd turn R after
Champneys into Cholesbury Rd. 2nd
R after 1m Shire Lane. Montana ¹/2 m
on L.* Home-made teas. **Adm £3, chd
free.** Visitors welcome by appt
March to August. Groups welcome
but no coaches.
A 4 acre woodland garden
surrounded by beech and silver birch

trees with year round interest:
daffodils, spring flowers, young
camellias and rhododendrons, sweet
peas and dahlias. Peaceful seating,
meandering paths, an apiary and
chicken runs; vegetable patch and
two greenhouses. Unusual shrubs,
flower beds plus a newly extended
fernery and many young specimen
trees.

**38 ◆ NETHER WINCHENDON
HOUSE**
Nether Winchendon HP18 0DY.
Mr Robert Spencer Bernard,
01844 290101,
www.netherwinchendonhouse.com
6m SW of Aylesbury, 6m from Thame.
**Adm £4, chd free. For NGS: Mon
2 May (2-5.30).** For opening times
and information please visit
website or telephone.
5 acre garden with fine and rare trees.
A variety of hedges and shrubs.
Founder garden (1927) Medieval and
Tudor manor house set in stunning
landscape. Lawn runs down to R
Thame. Picturesque village with
interesting church.

39 NORTH DOWN
Dodds Lane, Chalfont St Giles
HP8 4EL. Merida Saunders, 01494
872928. *4m SE of Amersham, 4m
NE of Beaconsfield. Opp the green in
centre of village. At Crown Inn turn
into UpCorner, on to Silver Hill. At top
of hill fork R into Dodds Lane. N
Down is 6th opening on L. Limited
parking in Dodds Lane.* **Adm £3, chd
free.** Visitors welcome by appt
from May to Sept, incl groups, no
coaches.
³/4 -acre sloping N-facing
compartmentalised site with mature
trees. Difficult stony soil. Designed
with scenic effect in mind and interest
throughout the yr. Large grassed
areas with island beds of mixed
perennials, shrubs and some unusual
plants. Variety of rhododendrons,
azaleas, acers, clematis and a huge
kiftsgate rose up an old apple tree.
Displays of sempervivum varieties,
alpines, grasses and ferns. Small
patio/water feature. Greenhouse.
Italianate front patio to owner's
design.

ODNEY CLUB
See Berkshire.

40 THE OLD SUN HOUSE

Pednor, Chesham HP5 2SZ. Mr & Mrs M Sharpley. *3m E of Gt Missenden, 2m W of Chesham. From Gt Missenden take B485 to Chesham, 1st L & follow signs approx 2m. From Chesham Church St (B485) follow signs approx 1¹/₂ m.* Home-made teas. **Adm £3.50, chd free. Mon 30 May (2-6).**
5-acre garden abundant with wildlife, on a Chiltern ridge giving superb views over farmland. The garden is surrounded by mature trees with inner plantings of unusual trees and shrubs. Features incl large ornamental pond, vegetable and herb garden, woodland walk, chainsaw tree sculpture, pheasantry and chickens. A natural not manicured garden. Music by the Germains Male Voice Choir.

  ♿ 🏵 ⊗ ☕

Small peaceful garden with mixed borders of colourful herbaceous perennials . . .

41 OVERSTROUD COTTAGE

The Dell, Frith Hill, Gt Missenden HP16 9QE. Mr & Mrs Jonathan Brooke, 01494 862701, susie@jandsbrooke.co.uk. *¹/₂ m E Gt Missenden. Turn E off A413 at Gt Missenden onto B485 Frith Hill to Chesham rd. White Gothic cottage set back in lay-by 100yds up hill on L. Parking on R at church.* Cream teas at Parish Church. **Adm £3.50, chd 50p. Suns 3, 24 Apr; 8 May; 5 June (2-6). Visitors also welcome by appt Apr to July, min group 15.**
Artistic chalk garden on 2 levels. Collection of C17/C18 plants. Potager/herb garden, spring bulbs, hellebores, succulents, primulas, pulmonarias, geraniums, species/old fashioned roses and lily pond. Garden studio with painting exhibition. Share of flower painting proceeds to NGS. Cottage was once C17 fever house for Missenden Abbey.

  ⊗ ☕ ☎

42 11 THE PADDOCKS

Wendover HP22 6HE. Mr & Mrs E Rye, 01296 623870. *5m from Aylesbury, on A413. At Wendover after approx ¹/₂ m, turn L at mini-r'about into Wharf Rd. Entrance is 2nd on L. From Gt Missenden, turn L at Clock Tower, then R at next mini-r'about.* **Adm £2.50, chd free. Sats & Suns 18, 19 June; 2, 3 July (2-6) Evening Opening, wine, Fri 24 June (5-8.30). Visitors also welcome by appt during June and July.**
Small peaceful garden with mixed borders of colourful herbaceous perennials and a special show of David Austin roses and a large variety of spectacular named 'Blackmore and Langdon' delphiniums. A tremendous variety of colour in a small area. White garden with peaceful arbour. 'The Magic of Moonlight', created for the BBC. Delphiniums in wonderful colourful profusion, reaching spectacular heights.

  ♿ ⊗ ☎

PATCHWORK

See Hertfordshire.

43 ◆ THE PLANT SPECIALIST

Whitefield Lane, Gt Missenden HP16 0BH. Sean Walter, 01494 866650, www.theplantspecialist.co.uk. *5m NW Amersham. A413 to Gt Missenden. Whitefield Lane opp Missenden Abbey. Under railway bridge on the L.* **For NGS: Wed 27 Apr; Wed 11 May; Thur 9 June; Wed 13 July (2-5). Combined with Gipsy House. For other opening times and information, please phone or see garden website.**
Plant nursery with herbaceous perennials and grasses, container grown bulbs and half hardy perennials in attractive garden setting and display garden. Feaured in Saga magazine, Telegraph & on BBC radio. gravel paths on gentle slope.

  ♿ 🏵 ⊗ ☎

44 NEW THE PLOUGH

Chalkshire Road, Terrick, Aylesbury HP17 0TJ. John & Sue Stewart. *4m S of Aylesbury. Entrance to garden and car park signed off B4009 Nash Lee Rd. 200yrds E of Terrick r'about.* **Adm £3, chd free. Sun 15, Mon 30 May; Sun 11 Sept (1-6).**
Formal garden with open views to the Chiltern countryside, designed as a series of outdoor rooms incl vegetable and fruit gardens, woodland walk and newly planted orchard featuring traditional Buckinghamshire varieties. Access to garden via field car park.

  ♿ 🏵 ⊗ ☕

GROUP OPENING

45 QUAINTON GARDENS

HP22 4AY. *7m W of Aylesbury, 2m N of Waddesdon A41. Nr Waddesdon turn off A41. Maps given to all visitors.* Home-made teas, soup, tea/coffee (27 Feb) at Quainton Parish Church: Teas (12 June) at Church or Brudenell House if fine. **Combined adm £4, (27 Feb), £5 (June) £4 (26 Feb 2012), chd free. Suns 27 Feb (12-4); 12 June (2-6); Sun 26 Feb 2012.**

CAPRICORNER
Mrs Davis

MILL VIEW
Jane & Nigel Jackson
millviewquainton.com

135A STATION ROAD
Mr & Mrs Carter
Not open 27 Feb.

THORNGUMBALD
Jane Lydall

THE VINE
Mr & Mrs D A Campbell
Visitors also welcome by appt.
01296 655243
david@dacampbell.com

4(Feb) and 5(June) gardens of different styles. Village lies at foot of Quainton Hills. Fine views over Vale of Aylesbury to Chiltern Hills. C14 church with outstanding monuments, C19 working windmill milling Quainton flour (open Sundays am), steam railway centre. Heavy clay but well-watered from hills. The Vine - many exotic plants largely from Himalayas and China. Winter flowering shrubs and spring bulbs. Open hill grazing above garden. Stream runs through bog garden into pond. 135a Station Road - mature heavily planted garden with shrubs, herbaceous areas, roses and climbers. Vegetable patch and fruit trees.Capricorner - small garden planted for yr-round interest with scented plants, winter flowering shrubs and bulbs, small woodland glade. Mill View - themed areas,wild flower meadow, insectivorous plants, scented plants, standard wisteria. Greenhouse with orchids and insectivorous plants with automated environment and rain water harvesting. Thorngumbald - well-planted cottage garden with fine display of spring flowering plants.

46 RED KITES

46 Haw Lane, Bledlow Ridge HP14 4JJ. Mag & Les Terry, 01494 481474, les.terry@lineone.net. *4m S of Princes Risborough. Off A4010 halfway between Princes Risborough and West Wycombe. At Hearing Dogs sign in Saunderton turn into Haw Lane, then ³/₄ m on L.* **Adm £3, chd free. Visitors welcome by appt groups of 15+.**
Chiltern hillside garden with terracing and superb views. Planted for yr-round interest, the 1¹/₄ acres encompasses various mixed and herbaceous borders, wild flower orchard, established pond, vegetable garden, managed woodland area and hidden garden. Wide use of climbers and clematis throughout.

47 RIVENDELL

13 The Leys, Amersham HP6 5NP. Janice & Mike Cross. *Off A416. Take A416 N towards Chesham. The Leys is on L ¹/₂ m after Boot & Slipper PH. Park at Beacon School, 100yds L.* Home-made teas. **Adm £3, chd free. Sat & Sun 9, 10 Apr; Sun 5 June (2-5).**
S-facing garden featuring a series of different areas with wide variety of perennials, especially hellebores. Alpine bed, box-edged herbaceous beds, sedum and thyme path leading to rose and clematis arbour. Raised woodland bed under mature trees, bog garden, gravel area with grasses and pond, vegetable plot, auricula theatre, developing topiary.

48 ROSE COTTAGE

68 High St, Cheddington LU7 0RQ. Margery R Jones. *11m S of Aylesbury, 7m S of Leighton Buzzard. Turn off B489 at Pitstone, turn off B488 at Cheddington Stn, turn off Cheddington, Long Marston rd.* Wine. **Adm £2.50, chd free. Evening Opening wine, Sat 25 June (6-9).**
¹/₂ -acre cottage garden filled with small rooms with maximum use of space. A balance of evergreens and deciduous resulting in a garden for all seasons, incl a late border with herbs, vegetable parterre and wildlife pond.

2 Kingswood Cottages

ST MICHAEL'S CROFT
See Hertfordshire.

STEANE PARK
See Northamptonshire.

49 ◆ STOKE POGES MEMORIAL GARDENS

Church Lane. SL2 4NZ. South Bucks District Council, 01753 537619, memorial.gardens@southbucks. gov.uk. *1m N of Slough, 1m S of Stoke Poges. From Stoke Poges, B416 towards Slough, R at Church Lane. From Slough, Stoke Poges Lane, leads into Church Lane. By St Giles Church.* **Adm £3.50, chd free. For NGS: Sat 2 Apr; Sun 15 May; Wed 15 June (1-5). For other opening times and information, please phone or see garden website.**
Unique 20-acre Grade I registered garden constructed 1934-9. Rock and water gardens, sunken colonnade, rose garden incl 500 individual gated gardens. Spring garden, bulbs, wisteria, rhododendrons. Recently completed £1m renovation. Guided walks on the hour.

STRESA
See Hertfordshire.

9 TANNSFIELD DRIVE
See Hertfordshire.

TILE HOUSE FARM
See Northamptonshire.

50 NEW THE TOWER HOUSE

12 Fortescue Drive, Shenley Church End, Milton Keynes MK5 6BJ. Kerry Lintott, 07787 106636, kerry-lee@fsmail.net. *Approx 1m from central MK. Signed off A5.* Home-made teas. **Adm £2.50, chd free. Sun 19 June (2-6). Visitors also welcome by appt.**
An urban cottage garden of 1/4 acre with a hugh collection of perenials. Several varieties of delphiniums, iris, clematis, roses and geraniums with many other beautiful plants.
The garden is divided into 9 compartments of interlinking circles, a large sunken pond area and lots of seating. Definitely one for the plantaholic. Gravel & some narrow paths.

TREETOPS
See London.

51 TURN END

Townside, Haddenham HP17 8BG.
Peter Aldington,
www.turnend.org.uk. *3m NE of
Thame, 5m SW of Aylesbury. Turn off
A418 to Haddenham. Turn at Rising
Sun to Townside. Please park at a
distance with consideration for
neighbours.* Home-made teas.
**Adm £3.50, chd £1. Mon 2 May;
Sun 3 July (2-5.30).**
Architect's own post-war listed house
(not open). Garden less than 1 acre,
space used to create illusion of size.
Series of enclosed gardens, sunken
or raised, sunny or shady, each
different yet harmonious, contrast
with lawns, borders and glades.
Spring bulbs, irises, old roses and
climbers. Courtyard with fish pool.
There is an artist in residence.
Featured in Book 'A Garden & Three
Houses' by Jane Brown now
reprinted. gravel paths and some
steps.

Series of enclosed
gardens, sunken
or raised, sunny
or shady, each
different yet
harmonious . . .

TURWESTON GARDENS
See Northamptonshire.

TURWESTON HOUSE
See Northamptonshire.

TURWESTON MILL
See Northamptonshire.

VERSIONS FARM
See Northamptonshire.

53 NEW UPPER FARMHOUSE

Chilton Road, Chearsley, Aylesbury
HP18 0DN. Mrs Vanessa Doyle,
01844 208317,
vanessa.doyle@dsl.pipes.com.
*6m SW of Aylesbury. Thame - B4011
- Long Crendon. Mini r'about R -
Chearsley Rd. 2m Chearsley; 1st
L - Chilton Rd; 50 yds on L before
de-restriction sign.* Teas in village tea
shop on green. **Adm £3, chd free.
Wed 15 June (2-6).** Visitors also
welcome by appt, max group size
10.
¹/₃ acre plantsman's garden in a very
difficult windy and exposed site.
Garden composed of different areas
incl a gravel garden, woodland area
and traditional perennial borders
featuring many unusual plants.
Stunning panoramic views.

54 WATERCROFT

Church Road, Penn HP10 8NX. Mr
& Mrs Paul Hunnings, 01494
816535. *3m NW of Beaconsfield, 3m
W of Amersham. On B474 from
Beaconsfeld, 600yds on L past Holy
Trinity Church, Penn.* Home-made
teas. **Adm £4.** Visitors welcome
by appt June & July only, groups
20-40.
Mature 3-acre chalk and clay garden.
Large weeping ash. Rose walk with
350 roses. Courtyard with new roses
and summer pots and box topiary.
Large natural old pond with diving
ducks, newly extended pond edge
planting and replanted perennial
border. Italianate garden with 17yr-old
yew hedges and fine view. Wild flower
meadow with wild roses. Formal herb

garden with culinary herbs, small
vegetable garden with hebe hedge.
Glasshouse with unusual
pelargoniums.

WATERDELL HOUSE
See Hertfordshire.

55 THE WHITE HOUSE

Village Road, Denham Village
UB9 5BE. Mr & Mrs P G Courtenay-
Luck. *3m NW of Uxbridge, 7m E of
Beaconsfield. Signed from A40 or
A412. Parking in village rd. The White
House is in centre of village.* Home-
made teas. **Adm £4, chd free.
Sun 12 June (2-5).**
Well established 6-acre formal garden
in picturesque setting. Mature trees
and hedges, with R Misbourne
meandering through lawns.
Shrubberies, flower beds, rockery,
rose garden and orchard. Large
walled garden with Italian garden and
developing laburnum walk. Herb
garden, vegetable plot and Victorian
greenhouses. Gravel entrance drive.

56 WHITEWALLS

Quarry Wood Road, Marlow
SL7 1RE. Mr W H Williams, 01628
482573. *¹/₂ m S Marlow. From
Marlow cross over bridge. 1st L, 3rd
house on L, white garden wall.* **Adm
£2.50, chd free. Suns 17 Apr;
10 July; 11 Sept (2-5).** Visitors also
welcome by appt.
Thames-side garden approx ¹/₂ acre
with spectacular view of weir. Large
lily pond, interesting planting of trees,
shrubs, herbaceous perennials and
bedding, large conservatory.

WOODCHIPPINGS
See Northamptonshire.

Buckinghamshire County Volunteers

County Organiser
Maggie Bateson, Fressingwood, Hare Lane, Little Kingshill HP16 0EF, 01494 866265, jmbateson@btopenworld.com

County Treasurer
Tim Hart, Kingswood House, The Lee, Great Missenden HP16 9NU, tim.hart@virgin.net

Publicity
Sandra Wetherall, Holydyke House, Little Missenden, Amersham HP7 0RD, 01494 862264, sandra@robertjamespartnership.com

Assistant County Organisers
Rosemary Brown, 2 Spenser Road, Aylesbury HP21 7LR, 01296 429605, grahama.brown@virgin.net
Janice Cross, Rivendell, 13 The Leys, Amersham HP6 5NP, 01494 728291, gwendalice@aol.com
Judy Hart, Kingswood House, The Lee, Great Missenden HP16 9NU, 01494 837328, judy.hart@virgin.net
Mhairi Sharpley, The Old Sun House, Pednor, Chesham HP5 2SZ, 01494 782870, mhairisharpley@btinternet.com
Trish Swain, 2 Kingswood Cottages, Swan Lane, The Lee, Great Missenden HP16 9NU, 01494 837752, swaino@talk21.com

Visit the website for latest information

Rivendell

CAMBRIDGESHIRE

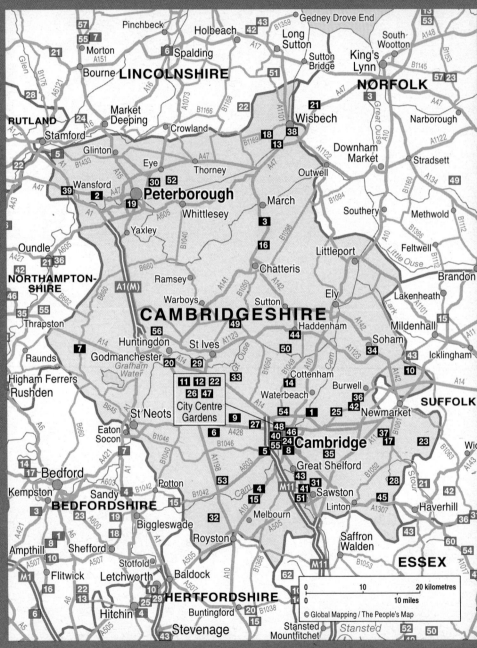

Opening Dates

February

Sunday 27
39 6 Robins Wood

March

Sunday 27
23 Kirtling Tower

April

3 April to 24 April
40 Robinson College

Sunday 3
23 Kirtling Tower
24 Leckhampton
34 Netherhall Manor

Sunday 10
5 Barton Gardens
46 Trinity College, Fellows' Garden
48 Trinity Hall - Wychfield

Sunday 17
11 Churchill College
52 Willow Holt

May

Sunday 1
8 Chaucer Road Gardens
26 Lucy Cavendish College
34 Netherhall Manor

Monday 2
8 Chaucer Road Gardens

Saturday 7
38 Peckover House
54 The Windmill

Sunday 8
15 Docwra's Manor
25 Lode Gardens
54 The Windmill

Saturday 14
50 Ty Gwyn

Sunday 15
36 The Paddock
42 Shadworth House
50 Ty Gwyn
52 Willow Holt

Sunday 22
5 Barton Gardens
16 Doddington Gardens
28 Manna Ash House
37 Pavilion House

Saturday 28
13 Clear View

Sunday 29
2 Ailsworth Gardens
13 Clear View
20 Island Hall
21 Kenilworth Smallholding

Monday 30
21 Kenilworth Smallholding

June

Sunday 5
35 The Old House
45 Streetly End Gardens

Saturday 11
44 53 Station Road
49 Twin Tarns
50 Ty Gwyn

Sunday 12
7 Catworth, Molesworth, Spaldwick & Brington Gardens
9 Childerley Hall
25 Lode Gardens
27 Madingley Hall
42 Shadworth House
43 Shelford & Stapleford Gardens
44 53 Station Road
49 Twin Tarns
50 Ty Gwyn

Sunday 19
1 15 Abbots Way
51 Whittlesford Gardens
52 Willow Holt

Sunday 26
4 Barrington Gardens
16 Doddington Gardens
22 King's College Fellows' Garden
56 Wytchwood

Thursday 30
38 Peckover House

July

2 July to April 2012
40 Robinson College

Sunday 3
10 Chippenham Park
12 Clare College Fellows' Garden
41 Sawston Gardens

Saturday 9
50 Ty Gwyn

Sunday 10
6 Cambourne Gardens
25 Lode Gardens
50 Ty Gwyn

Sunday 17
11 Churchill College
31 Mary Challis Garden
52 Willow Holt

Saturday 23
3 The Barn

Sunday 24
3 The Barn
53 Wimpole Hall

Sunday 31
34 Netherhall Manor

August

Friday 5
55 Wolfson College Garden

Saturday 6
50 Ty Gwyn

Sunday 7
14 Cottenham Gardens
18 Elgood's Brewery Gardens
34 Netherhall Manor
50 Ty Gwyn

Sunday 21
47 Trinity Hall

Sunday 28
52 Willow Holt

September

Saturday 3
50 Ty Gwyn

Sunday 4
50 Ty Gwyn

Sunday 25
52 Willow Holt

Gardens open to the public

15 Docwra's Manor
18 Elgood's Brewery Gardens
29 The Manor
38 Peckover House
53 Wimpole Hall

By appointment only

17 Dullingham House
19 39 Foster Road
30 38 Martinsbridge
32 Mill House
33 5 Moat Way

Look out for the gardens with the ☎ – enjoy a private visit . . .

Also open by Appointment ☎

- **9** Childerley Hall
- **11** Churchill College
- **13** Clear View
- **5** Farm Cottage, Barton Gardens
- **7** 32 High Street, Catworth, Molesworth & Brington Gardens
- **21** Kenilworth Smallholding
- **25** 21 Lode Road, Lode Gardens
- **35** The Old House
- **37** Pavilion House
- **39** 6 Robins Wood
- **7** 7 Thrapston Road, Catworth, Molesworth & Brington Gardens
- **49** Twin Tarns
- **50** Ty Gwyn
- **8** Upwater Lodge, Chaucer Road Gardens
- **52** Willow Holt
- **54** The Windmill
- **56** Wytchwood

The Gardens

1 15 ABBOTS WAY

Horningsea CB25 9JN. Sally & Don Edwards. *4m NE of Cambridge. ½ m off A14. No access from Abbots Way. Follow signs in Horningsea to garden & car park.* Home-made teas. **Adm £4, chd free (share to St Peters Church, Horningsea).** Sun 19 June (2-5.30).
1¼-acre sloping garden, with many herbaceous beds. Views to church and over the R Cam and its water meadows. Interesting plants and use of colour. 180ft double herbaceous borders; 116ft pergola with large collection of roses, clematis and other climbers. Natural pond with fish and bridge.
🐾 ☕

A fusion of ideas influenced by Japanese, Italian and traditional English features . . .

GROUP OPENING

2 NEW AILSWORTH GARDENS

Ailsworth PE5 7AF. *4m W of Peterborough. Easy access from the A47 after the Thorpe Wood r'about or from the A1 at Wansford. Ailsworth/Castor is one large village. From Peterborough take A47 Leicester Rd & follow signs to Castor. Cont through Castor to Ailsworth. Turn R into Main St from A1 exit at Wansford onto A47 to Peterborough, until r'about signed Castor/Ailsworth. Turn L at T-junction into Main St.* Home-made teas. **Combined adm £3, chd free.** Sun 29 May (2-6).

NEW 54 MAIN STREET
Michael & Angela Husdon-Peacock.
Last house on R in Main St

NEW THE MALTING HOUSE
Tony & Jennie Corke.
63b Main Street

NEW THE STEADINGS
Neil & Chris Remnant.
15 Maffit Road

At the heart of the villages is the unique St Kyneburgha Church built on the site of a Roman palace and featured in the Time Team series. The 3 gardens occupy land reclaimed from a farmyard, pig farm and malt house. 54 Main Street a garden of approx ¼ acre, once a farmyard created over the past 10yrs. It consists mainly of shrubs, borders front and rear with unusual perennials, raised corner terrace, circular beds of gravel and slate featuring a variety of grasses, driftwood and metal sculptures. Ornamental trees, hostas and a newly created raised vegetable plot. Several seating areas. The Steadings is a small walled garden, formerly the site of a pig farm. A fusion of ideas influenced by Japanese, Italian and traditional English features. Structural planting with tree ferns, shrubs, clematis and grapevine, incl several water features. The Malting House a C18 red brick cottage with a long narrow garden evolved from a rectangular lawn and vegetable (rubbish!) plot. The garden is now an area of many curves, nooks and seats with ornaments, pond and eclectic mixed planting. Featured in Castot & Ailsworth Open Gardens & Flower Festival. Wheelchair access 54 Main Street only.
🌸 ☕

BANK FARM
See Norfolk.

3 THE BARN
Mill Hill Lane. PE15 9QB. Mark Pocklington. *On A141 March bypass turn into Knights End Rd at the Knights End Xrds. Signed March South travel along Knights End Rd approx 400m turn R into Mill Hill Lane.* Home-made teas. **Adm £2, chd free.** Sat 23, Sun 24 July (10-5).
1 acre garden comprising of open grassed areas and informal island beds of shrubs and perennials. Informal borders and pergola leading to Japanese style garden. Small vegetable patch and orchard area. New pond and bog garden for 2011.
♿ 🌸 ☕

GROUP OPENING

4 NEW BARRINGTON GARDENS
Barrington CB22 7RN. *6m S of Cambridge. M11, J11, take A10 to Harston, turn R before Foxton railway to Barrington. For Ivy Haus 1st house on L entering village. For No's 11 & 8 West Green continue through village, L at church. Parking in car parks or considerately on green.* Home-made teas. **Combined adm £3.50, chd free.** Sun 26 June (1-5).

NEW IVY HAUS
30 Foxton Road. Mr & Mrs P Hollidge

NEW 11 WEST GREEN
Roger & Diana Leech

NEW 8 WEST GREEN
Steven Woolgar & Clare Corcoran

3 contrasting gardens in picturesque village with many thatched cottages set around a large village green. Ivy Haus: contemporary home and garden leading down to a river with beautiful views within a setting of mature trees. Modern courtyard with water feature. 11 West Green: modern fruit and vegetable garden softened with herbs and flowers. 3-acre meadow with walk to river. 8 West Green: designer garden densely planted, set within mature hedges and trees, created with wildlife in mind incl pond. Contrasting rear garden with water feature in a contemporary style. Artists studio will be open with ceramics and painting at Ivy Haus.
🌸 ☕

GROUP OPENING

5 BARTON GARDENS
Barton, Cambridge CB23 7AY.
3¹/₂ m SW of Cambridge. M11 J12.
Take A603 towards Sandy, in village
turn R for Comberton Rd. Home-
made teas at village hall. **Combined
adm £5, chd free. Suns 10 Apr;
22 May (2-5).**

FARM COTTAGE
18 High Street. Dr R M Belbin.
On corner of Ivy Field & High St
Visitors also welcome by appt.
01223 263058
Meredith @belbin.com

GLEBE HOUSE
1 High Street. David & Sue
Rapley.
Top of High St
Not open 10 Apr.

114 HIGH STREET
Meta & Hugh Greenfield

KING'S TITHE
13a Comberton Road. Mr & Mrs
Cornelius Thorne
Not open 22 May.

31 NEW ROAD
Dr & Mrs D Macdonald

THE SIX HOUSES
33-45 Comberton Road.
Perennial (GRBS).
*Last property on LH-side going to
Comberton*

247 WIMPOLE ROAD
Ray & Nikki Scrivens
Not open 10 April.

WINDY CORNER
245 Wimpole Road. Mike &
Jules Webber
Not open 10 April.

Delightful group of large and small
gardens reflecting different
approaches to gardening. Farm
Cottage: A landscaped cottage
garden with herbaceous beds and a
themed woodland walk. Glebe
House: is a 1-acre mature, partly
wooded and walled garden with large
duck pond formal fruit/herb garden,
with an Italiante-style courtyard
garden and a secret garden. 114 High
Street: small cottage garden with an
unusual layout with several areas incl
vegetables, fruit and a secret garden.
King's Tithe: is a spring garden with
many bulbs, shrubs, and fruit trees.
31 New Road: large, wildlife friendly
cottage garden with good show of
spring flowers, mature shrubs, trees
and a kitchen garden. The Six

Houses: recently renovated garden,
and includes winter and dry gardens,
lovely spring bulbs and small wood.
247 Wimpole Road: evolved over
30yrs, and has several 'outdoor
rooms'. A loggia provides cover and a
setting for varied climbing plants.
Windy Corner: an adventurous
bustling array of shrubs and
perennials in a long, narrow country
garden setting. Featured in Farm
Cottage and Cambridgeshire Life.

♿ 🐕 ❀ ☕

**BURGHLEY HOUSE PRIVATE
SOUTH GARDENS**
See Lincolnshire.

GROUP OPENING

**6 NEW CAMBOURNE
GARDENS**
Great Cambourne CB23 6AH. *8m
W of Cambridge. W from Cambridge
on A428 dual carriageway. L at
Cambourne junction into Great
Cambourne. Follow signs to start at
any garden.* Teas available locally.
**Combined adm £4, chd free.
Sun 10 July (11-5).**

NEW 22 JEAVONS LANE
Mr Sheppard.
*Entry through back garden via
Chervil Way*

NEW 43 MONKFIELD LANE
Tony & Penny Miles

NEW 23 ORCHARD WAY
Lower Cambourne. Andrew &
Clare Thacker

NEW 9 ORCHARD WAY
Lower Cambourne. Melissa
Ambery

NEW 5 QUIDDITCH LANE
Mr & Mrs C Mckay

**NEW 7 WATERMEAD
CRESCENT**
Lower Cambourne. Mr & Mrs
Cave

NEW 17 WATTLE CLOSE
Jeremy & Linda Carmichael

Seven small modern gardens in the
new villages of Great and Lower
Cambourne, separated by green
space and a country park with two
lakes. No garden is more than 10yrs
old and many are much younger.
They demonstrate how imagination
and gardening skill can be combined
in a short time to create great effects
from what might have seemed
unpromising or awkward plots. The
grouping incl a garden inspired by the
French Riviera complete with a river of
lavender and perfect miniature
meadow as well as a foliage garden.
Another devoted entirely to raised
beds of vegetables and fruits. Sunny
patios and cool pools abound. Stroll
these villages with your street plan or
take a guided route for disabled
visitors. Featured on regional TV.

♿ ☕

Docwra's Manor

GROUP OPENING

7 **CATWORTH, MOLESWORTH, SPALDWICK & BRINGTON GARDENS**
nr Huntingdon PE28 0PF. *10m W of Huntingdon. For Catworth & Brington turn off A14 onto B660 (Catworth S bound) approx 7m W of A14 junction with A1. Village is on the N side of A14 flyover. Molesworth is on the A14, 8m W of the A1.* Home-made teas. Combined adm £3, chd free. **Sun 12 June (2-6).**

32 HIGH STREET
Catworth. Colin Small
Visitors also welcome by appt & groups, June & July.
01832 710269
sheila.small@btinternet.com

MOLESWORTH HOUSE
Molesworth. John Prentis.
Next to the church in Molesworth

7 THRAPSTON ROAD
Spaldwick. Stewart & Mary Barnard.
Take J18 off A14 to centre of village, garden approx 50 metres from George PH
Visitors also welcome by appt any time June & July.
01480 890060
mnbarnard@tiscali.co.uk

YEW TREE COTTAGE
Brington. Mr & Mrs D G Eggleston.
After village sign past school, up hill, garden is thatched cottage on L
Four varied gardens showing the best of planting, design and creativity representing classic traditions but with a modern twist. 32 High Street is a long narrow garden with many rare plants incl ferns. An informal patio, with containers of unusual foliage plants leads to a lawn with herbaceous borders and a native woodland area. Molesworth House is a Victorian rectory garden with a bit of everything; old-fashioned and proud of it but with a groovy tropical house. 7 Thrapston Road the owners have gardened on site for 29yrs. Mature trees under planted with mixed borders of shrubs, bulbs and herbaceous plants, fish pond, greenhouse. A pleasant outlook to the rear over the village church and mature trees. Yew Tree Cottage comprises flower beds, lawns, vegetable patch, boggy area, copses and orchard. Plants in pots and hanging baskets.
♿ ❉ ☕

GROUP OPENING

8 **CHAUCER ROAD GARDENS**
CB2 7EB. *1m S of Cambridge. Off Trumpington Rd (A1309), nr Brooklands Ave junction. Parking available at MRC Psychology Dept on Chaucer Rd.* Home-made teas. Adm £5, chd free. **Sun 1, Mon 2 May (2-5).**

16 CHAUCER ROAD
Cambridge. Mrs V Albutt

UPWATER LODGE
23 Chaucer Road. Mr & Mrs George Pearson
Visitors also welcome by appt.
07890 080303
jmp@pearson.co.uk

16 Chaucer Road ½ -acre garden, divided by arches and hedges into separate areas, each with its own character. Spring flowering shrubs and trees, bulbs in borders and wildlife area. Waterproof footwear advised. Upwater Lodge- 6 acres with mature trees, fine lawns, old wisterias, and colourful borders.Small potager and newly planted vineyard. A network of paths through bluebell wood leads down to water meadows by the R Cam and small flock of rare breed sheep. Enjoy a walk by the river and watch the punts go by. Home made teas and some stalls.
♿ ❉ ☕

9 **CHILDERLEY HALL**
Dry Drayton CB23 8BB. Mrs Jenkins, 01954 210271, cej443@btinternet.com. *6m W of Cambridge. Between Caldecote r'about and Cambourne on old A428.* Home-made teas. Adm £4, chd free. **Sun 12 June (2-5).** Visitors also welcome by appt 1 May to 10 July. Romantic 4-acre garden (grade II historic garden) surrounds part Tudor house (not open). Winding paths lead through herbaceous borders to secret areas. Large collection shrub roses and good variety of plants and trees.
☕ ☎

10 **CHIPPENHAM PARK**
Chippenham, nr Newmarket CB7 5PT. Mr & Mrs Eustace Crawley, www.chippenhamparkgardens.info. *5m NE of Newmarket. 1m off A11.* Refreshments all day. **Adm £4, chd free. Sun 3 July (11-4).**
The house (not open), gardens, lake, canals and 350-acre park enclosed by wall 3½ m long, built after Admiral Lord Russell petitioned William III in 1696 for permission to make a park. Gardens have been extended and restocked by Anne Crawley, descendant of John Tharp who bought the estate in 1791. Superb display of narcissus and early flowering shrubs followed by extensive summer borders and dramatic autumn colours. Many plant stalls. A great garden which is still improving. Featured in GGG 2 stars.
♿ ♻ ❉ ☕

11 **CHURCHILL COLLEGE**
Storey's Way, Cambridge CB3 0DS. University of Cambridge, 01223 740926, john.moore@chu.cam.ac.uk, www.chu.cam.ac.uk. *1m from M11 J13. 1m NW of Cambridge city centre. Turn into Storeys Way from Madingley Rd (A1303), or from Huntingdon Rd (A1307).* Home-made teas. Adm £3.50, chd free. **Suns 17 Apr; 17 July (2-5).** Visitors also welcome by appt out of university term 18 Apr to 11 June.
42-acre site designed in 1960s for foliage and form, providing a peaceful and relaxing visit with courtyards and large open spaces. Recent additions incl 75m long parterre incorporating 1400 box plants and herbaceous plantings. Beautiful grouping of 20 Prunus Tai Haku (the great white cherry) trees forming striking canopy in spring and naturalised bulbs in grass elsewhere. The planting provides a setting for the impressive collection of modern sculpture.
♿ ❉ ☕ ☎

12 **CLARE COLLEGE FELLOWS' GARDEN**
Trinity Lane, Cambridge CB2 1TL. The Master & Fellows, www.clare.cam.ac.uk. *Central to city. From Queens Rd or city centre via Senate House Passage, Old Court & Clare Bridge.* Adm £3.50, chd free. **Sun 3 July (2-6).**
2 acres. One of the most famous gardens on the Cambridge Backs. Herbaceous borders; sunken pond garden, fine specimen trees and tropical garden.
♿

Winding paths lead through herbaceous borders . . .

Plant sales, preserves, great tea and cakes! . . .

 CLEAR VIEW
Cross Lane, Wisbech St Mary
PE13 4TX. Margaret & Graham
Rickard, 01945 410724,
magsrick@hotmail.com (subject -
NGS). *3m SW of Wisbech, off Barton
Rd. Leave Wisbech on Barton Rd
towards Wisbech St Mary. L at Cox
Garage Xrds into Bevis Lane. 1st L
into Cross Lane. Clear View garden
4th on R with iron gates. Home-made
teas.* Adm £3, chd free. **Sat 28; Sun
29 May (10-5). Visitors also
welcome by appt, between 1 April
& 30 June. The lane is very narrow
so no LARGE coaches.**
Approx 1-acre with lake incorporating
large wildlife area. Secluded cottage
garden with many old fashioned
plants, herbaceous border, gravel
garden with raised bed and pond.
Large rose beds, allotments and small
orchard. Plenty of secluded seating.
Open 28th and 29th May weekend.
Cranwell - clarinet & piano - playing.
Refreshments and homemade cakes,
also homemade jams and honey for
sale.
&♿ ✿ ☕ ☎

GROUP OPENING

 COTTENHAM GARDENS
CB24 8AY. *6m N of Cambridge. Take
B1049 from A14 through Histon to
Cottenham Green. Straight ahead
¹/₂ m, NGS sign. Park on High St.
Teas at 27 High St.* **Combined adm
£4, chd free. Sun 7 Aug (1-6).**

3 CURRINGTONS CLOSE &
MITCHELL HOUSE
Ken & Dawn Marr

NEW 27 HIGH STREET
Ken Elizabeth & Richard Hewitt.
200 metres from parish church

Large village N of the University City
of Cambridge. One of largest in
Cambridgeshire since the C11.
All Saints Church is a prominent
landmark with its 'onion shaped'
pinnacles on the church tower. The
High Street is one of the longest in
the country, with All Saints Church

and the village green a mile apart.
3 Curringtons Close a cottage garden
with herbaceous shrub borders,
climbing roses and clematis over
structures. Gravel garden and formal
box hedge borders. Access to
Mitchell House with mature trees.
Flowers, vegetable garden and lawn.
27 High Street enclosed garden with
unusual plants, mature trees and
informal pond.
&♿ 🎇 ✿ ☕

 ♦ **DOCWRA'S MANOR**
2 Meldreth Road, Shepreth
SG8 6PS. Mrs Faith Raven, 01763
260235,
www.docwrasmanorgarden.co.uk.
*8m S of Cambridge. ¹/₂ m W of A10.
Garden is opp the War Memorial in
Shepreth. King's Cross-Cambridge
train stop 5 min walk.* **Adm £4, chd
free. For NGS: Sun 8 May (2-5). For
other opening times and
information, please phone or see
garden website.**
2¹/₂ acres of choice plants in series of
enclosed gardens. Tulips and Judas
trees. Opened for NGS for more than
40yrs.
&♿ ✿ ☕

GROUP OPENING

 **NEW DODDINGTON
GARDENS**
Doddington, March PE15 0TN.
*Springfield: Doddington clock
tower.Take the B1093 to Benwick for
approx 1m. Manor Estate:Past
school, turn R down Childs Lane.*
Home-made teas. **Combined adm
£3, chd free. Suns 22 May; 26 June
(1-5).**

NEW 36 MANOR ESTATE
Steven Ware

NEW SPRINGFIELD
Benwick Road. Janice &
Jonathan Holdich.
*Look for Springfield signs on L
after layby*

2 contrasting gardens opening for the
first time. 36 Manor Estate is a five
year old,densely planted,sunny
cottage garden situated at the back
of an a typical 1950s council house,
The narrow 30ft x 150ft plot is
adorned with five ponds, colourful
plants, rose arches and a winding
walkway. 1m out of the village is
Springfield. 1¹/₂ acres of rough
Fenland has been transformed slowly

over 18 yrs into a calm, relaxing,
romantic and productive garden.
Large pond, bridges, stream, kitchen
garden, orchard, bee hives,
greenhouses and woodland. Walking
paths and wild areas. Seating and
hammocks. Ample seating available
at both gardens. Plant sales,
preserves, great tea and cakes! Main
path is narrow.
&♿ ✿ ☕

 DULLINGHAM HOUSE
nr Newmarket CB8 9UP. Sir Martin
& Lady Nourse, 01638 508186,
lavinia.nourse@btinternet.com. *4m
S of Newmarket. Off A1304 & B1061.*
Visitors welcome by appt.
The grounds were landscaped by
Humphry Repton in 1799 and the
view remains virtually intact today. To
the rear there is a substantial walled
garden with magnificent long
shrub/herbaceous borders. The
garden encompasses a fine claire voie
and historic bowling green.
&♿ ☎

 ♦ **ELGOOD'S BREWERY
GARDENS**
Wisbech PE13 1LN. Elgood & Sons
Ltd, 01945 583160, www.elgoods-
brewery.co.uk. *1m W of the town
centre. Leave A47 Towards Wisbech
Centre. Cross river To N Brink. Follow
river wall To far end of brewery -
Visitors' Centre Car Park.* Adm £3,
concessions £2.50. **For NGS: Sun 7
Aug (1-4.30). For other opening
times and information, please
phone or see garden website.**
Approx 4 acres of peaceful garden
dating back to Georgian era.
Featuring 250yr old specimen trees
providing a framework to lawns, lake,
rockery, herb garden and a maze.
&♿ ✿ ☕

39 FOSTER ROAD
off Campaign Avenue, Woodston,
Peterborough PE2 9RS. Robert
Marshall & Richard Handscombe,
01733 555978,
robfmarshall@btinternet.com.
*1m SW of Peterborough City Centre.
From Oundle Rd turn N into Sugar
Way at T-lights, L at 2nd r'about onto
Campaign Ave, R at next r'about still
on Campaign Ave, 2nd R at Foster
Rd. Continue to very end of rd.
Entrance via rear gate in green fence.*
Light refreshments & teas. Adm £3,
chd free. **Visitors welcome by appt
individual and small groups most
welcome Feb to Oct.**

Plantsman's garden in small, new estate plot. Informal and formal areas: mixed herbaceous border; woodland/shade; 'vestibule' garden; exotic and ferns; kitchen garden; espaliered fruit; pergola; patio; pond; parterre; numerous pots; octagonal greenhouse; seating and sculpture. Uncommon snowdrops, over 150 hostas, plus daphnes, acers and other choice/unusual plants and cultivars. Year-round plant interest. Three friendly British Shorthair cats. Featured in Cambridgeshire Journal, local press.

20 ISLAND HALL
Godmanchester PE29 2BA. Mr Christopher & Lady Linda Vane Percy. *1m S of Huntingdon (A1). 15m NW of Cambridge (A14). In centre of Godmanchester next to free car park.* Home-made teas. **Adm £4, chd free. Sun 29 May (11-5).**
3-acre grounds. Mid C18 mansion (not open). Tranquil riverside setting with mature trees. Chinese bridge over Saxon mill race to an embowered island with wild flowers. Garden restored in 1983 to mid C18 formal design, with box hedging, clipped hornbeams, parterres, topiary and good vistas over borrowed landscape, punctuated with C18 wrought iron and stone urns. The ornamental island has been replanted with Princeton elms (ulmus americana).

21 KENILWORTH SMALLHOLDING
West Drove North, Walton Highway PE14 7DP. John & Marilyn Clarke, 01945 881332, bookings@kenilworthhouse.co.uk, www.kenilworthhouse.co.uk. *6m E of Wisbech. Off A47 through Walton Highway, at E end of village turn N towards Walpole St Peter, on 2nd sharp bend turn R into Farm Lane.* Home-made teas. **Adm £3.50, chd free. Sun 29, Mon 30 May (11-5). Visitors also welcome by appt.**
Varied country garden set around 100yr-old Bramleys. Beds, large ponds, fern greenhouse and shade garden, herb bed, working smallholding with goats and sheep. Trees lined path past paddocks to secluded mixed desert apple orchard and copse. Teas served in outbuilding housing an exhibition of the development of the smallholding and archaeology. Trail walk to desert apple

orchard. Display of 40yrs history '40 yrs of small holding and Archeology of Area with aerial photographs. Sheep shearing on 30 May.

22 KING'S COLLEGE FELLOWS' GARDEN
Queen's Road, Cambridge CB2 1ST. Provost & Scholars of King's College. *In Cambridge, the Backs. Entry by gate at junction of Queen's Rd & West Rd. Parking at Lion Yard 10mins walk, or some pay & display places in West Rd & Queen's Rd.* Light refreshments & home-made teas. **Adm £3, chd free. Sun 26 June (2-6).**
Fine example of a Victorian garden with rare specimen trees. Woodland walk created in 2009. Gravel paths.

working smallholding with goats . . .

23 KIRTLING TOWER
Newmarket Road, Kirtling, nr Newmarket CB8 9PA. The Lord & Lady Fairhaven. *6m SE of Newmarket. From Newmarket head towards Saxon Street village, through village to Kirtling, turn L at war memorial, entrance is signed on L.* Light refreshments & home-made teas at Church. **Adm £4.50, chd free. Suns 27 Mar; 3 Apr (11-4).**
Kirtling Tower has moat on 3 sides. The garden of 5 acres was created 9yrs ago. Main features are spring garden (planted with 100,000 bulbs of daffodils, narcissus and camassias), secret, walled and cutting gardens. Original Tudor walk. 30,000 bulbs of muscari and chionodoxa planted along 150m church walk. Photographic cards and Kirtling lamb for sale. Refreshments in the church, while you enjoy the organ music.

24 LECKHAMPTON
37 Grange Road, Cambridge CB2 1RH. Corpus Christi College. *Runs N to S between Madingley Rd (A1303) & A603. Drive entrance opp Selwyn College. No parking available on site.* Home-made teas. **Adm £4, chd free. Sun 3 Apr (2-6).**
10 acres comprising formal lawns and extensive wild gardens, featuring

walkways and tree-lined avenues, fine specimen trees under-planted with spring bulbs, cowslips, anemones, fritillaries and a large area of lupins. The Prairie Garden in late summer/early spring is a new feature this year. Gravel and grass paths.

GROUP OPENING

25 LODE GARDENS
CB25 9FW. *10m NE of Cambridge. Take B1102 from Stow-cum-Quy r'about, NE of Cambridge at junction with A14, Lode is 2m from r'about.* Teas & Cake at Carpenter's End. **Combined adm £5, chd free. Suns 8 May; 12 June; 10 July (11-5).**

CARPENTERS END
Mr & Mrs Paul Webb

21 LODE ROAD
Mr Richard P Ayres
Visitors also welcome by appt. 01223 811873

THE OLD VICARAGE
Mr & Mrs Hunter.
not open 10 July

WILD ROSE COTTAGE
Church Walk. Joy Martin

Four varied gardens set in a picturesque village to the E of Anglesey Abbey Garden. Two cottage gardens, Wild Rose Cottage is overflowing with roses and clematis, set against a vegetable garden edged with lavender and sage and a wild flower spiral. 21 Lode Road is planted with bold groups of herbaceous plants creating an element of mystery and delight. These contrast with two recently developed gardens. Carpenters End displays shrubs and trees around a fine lawn. The Old Vicarage is a formal garden with an intricate design formed from box, yew and pleached lime.

26 LUCY CAVENDISH COLLEGE
Lady Margaret Road, Cambridge CB3 0BU. *1m NW of Gt St Mary.* College situated on corner of Lady Margaret Rd & Madingley Rd (A1303). Entrance off Lady Margaret Rd. **Adm £3, chd free. Sun 1 May (2-5).**
The gardens of 4 late Victorian houses have been combined and developed over past 25yrs into an informal 3 acre garden. Fine mature

trees shade densely planted borders. An Anglo Saxon herb garden is situated in one corner. The garden is maintained using organic methods and provides a rich wildlife habitat.

Island Hall

27 MADINGLEY HALL
nr Cambridge CB23 8AQ. University of Cambridge, www.madingleyhall.co.uk. *4m W of Cambridge. 1m from M11 J13.* Home-made teas. **Adm £4, chd free. Sun 12 June (2.30-5.30).** C16 Hall (not open) set in 8 acres of attractive grounds. Features incl landscaped walled garden with hazel walk, alpine bed, medicinal border and rose pergola. Meadow, topiary, mature trees and wide variety of hardy plants. St Mary Magdalene Church open throughout the afternoon (inside garden entrance).

28 MANNA ASH HOUSE
74 Common Road, Weston Colville CB21 5NR. Will & Eugánie Woodhouse. *12m E of Cambridge. 1m E of Weston Colville Village. Between Carlton & West Wickham.* Home-made teas. **Adm £3, chd free. Sun 22 May (10-6).** 1¼-acre long garden with fine views over natural swimming pool and aquatic garden with exotic lilies and irises. Lush planting incl very tall grasses, wild flowers and willow varieties. Open views over undulating Cambridgeshire countryside.

29 ◆ THE MANOR
Hemingford Grey PE28 9BN. Mrs D S Boston, 01480 463134, www.greenknowe.co.uk. *4m E of Huntingdon. Off A14. Entrance to garden by small gate off river towpath. No parking at house except for disabled by arrangement with owner. Park in village.* **For opening times and information, please phone or see garden website.** Garden designed and planted by author Lucy Boston, surrounds C12 manor house on which Green Knowe books based (house open by appt). 4 acres with topiary; over 200 old roses, bearded iris collection and herbaceous borders with mainly scented plants. Meadow with mown paths. Enclosed by river, moat and wilderness. Plants for sale (not in the winter). Gravel paths.

30 38 MARTINSBRIDGE
Parnwell, Peterborough PE1 4YB. Maurice & Lynne Holmes, 01733 766721, maurice53@hotmail.co.uk. *Parnwell Estate, exit Frank Perkins Parkway at Oxney Rd. From Parnwell Way take 1st exit into Saltersgate then into Martinsbridge.* **Visitors welcome by appt** all year round. Plant enthusiasts small town garden, planted on 3 sides for all-yr round interest. Trees, shrubs, wisteria, acers, climbing roses, clematis, bamboos and perennials. Incl water features, walled shady area, gravel and slate beds, mirrors, summerhouse, stepping stones, orfe and gold fish pond with statue.

31 NEW MARY CHALLIS GARDEN
High Street, Sawston CB22 3BG. A M Challis Trust Ltd, 01223 832112. *7m S of Cambridge. Entrance by lane between 60 High St & Billsons Opticians at 66 High St.* **Adm £2, chd free. Sun 17 July (2-5.30).** Given to Sawston in 2006 this 2 acre garden is being restored by volunteers: formal flower garden, vegetable beds with vine house, meadow and woodland, with concern for the flora and fauna - and the village children.

32 MILL HOUSE
22 Fen Road, North End, Bassingbourn SG8 5PQ. Mr & Mrs A Jackson, 01763 243491, millhouseval@btinternet.com. *2m N of Royston. On the NW outskirts of Bassingbourn. 1m from Church, on the rd to Shingay. Take North End at the war memorial in the centre of Bassingbourn which is just W of the A1198 (do not take Mill Lane).* **Adm £4, chd free. Visitors welcome by appt** during snowdrop season and May to early Oct, groups 4+, coaches permitted. Garden created over many years by retired garden designer owners and divided up into interesting enclosures, providing unusual formal and informal settings for many rare trees, shrubs, herbaceous plants, clematis and topiary which provide yr round interest. Wonderful elevated view over countryside and garden. New winter garden with snowdrop collection. Featured in The English Garden & The Mail on Sunday.

33 5 MOAT WAY
Swavesey CB24 4TR. Mr & Mrs N Kyberd, 01954 200568, nicholas.kyberd@fera.gsi.gov.uk. *Off A14, 2m beyond Bar Hill. Look for School Lane/Fen Drayton Rd,at mini roundabout turn into Moat Way, no.5 is about 100 metres on LH-side.*

Visitors welcome by appt. Colourful garden filled with collection of trees, shrubs and perennials. Large patio area displaying many specimen foliage plants in planters, incl pines, hostas and acers.

34 **NETHERHALL MANOR**
Tanners Lane, Soham CB7 5AB. Timothy Clark Esq. *6m Ely, 6m Newmarket. Enter Soham from Newmarket, Tanners Lane is 2nd R 100yds after cemetery. Enter Soham from Ely, Tanners Lane is 2nd L after War Memorial.* Home-made teas. **Adm £2, chd free. Suns 3 Apr; 1 May; 31 July; 7 Aug (2-5).** 'An elegant garden touched with antiquity' Good Gardens Guide. This is an unusual garden which will appeal to those with an historical interest in the individual collections of genera and plant groups: April - Old primroses, daffodils and Victorian double flowered hyacinths. May - Old English tulips. Aug - Victorian pelargonium, heliotrope, calceolaria and dahlias. Author of Margery Fish's Country Gardening & Mary McNurtrie's Country Gardening.

35 **THE OLD HOUSE**
2 Home End, Fulbourn CB21 5BS. Mr & Mrs Charles Comins, 01223 882907, comins@ntufton.co.uk. *4m SE of Cambridge. Opp Townley Village Hall, next to recreation ground, Home End.* Home-made teas. **Adm £3, chd free. Sun 5 June (11-5). Visitors also welcome by appt.** ²/₃ -acre garden surrounded by high flint walls, mature trees, large formal pond with many fish, plants and centre fountain. By the pond a pergola walkway planted with wisteria, clematis and catnip (for our many cats!). Well stocked borders with bulbs, herbaceous plants, roses and shrubs, with central lawn. Rockery with dwarf conifers. Plenty of seating in the garden so come and see us and our plants and rest awhile too! Close to centre of village and Fulbourn Nature Reserve.

36 **NEW** **THE PADDOCK**
43 Lower End, Swaffham Prior CB25 0HT. Judi and Mike Churcher. *10 miles east of Cambridge off B1102. On entering the village from Cambridge, The Paddock can be found at the far end on the left, opposite Rogers Road.* **Combined**

with **Shadworth House adm £4, chd free. Sun 15 May (10-5).** Redesigned 5 years ago. Gravel paths zig zag between shrub and perennial borders. On the way, relax on the deck; on a bench under a birch tree or on a swing seat in the gazebo. Practice golf and explore the playhouse. Round a corner enjoy the colour on the 'flowery mead', where paths snake through herbaceous perennials and ornamental grasses. Artificial putting green, golf practice net, playhouse, gazebo.

37 **NEW** **PAVILION HOUSE**
Station Road, Dullingham CB8 9UT. Mrs Gretta Bredin, 01638 508005, gretta@thereliablesauce.co.uk. *4m S of Newmarket. Take turning off A1304, signed Dullingham, Pavilion House is 1m along this rd, 1st house on R. Parking will be signed.* Home-made teas. **Adm £3, chd free. Sun 22 May (2-6). Visitors also welcome by appt April to July, max 20 visitors. No coaches.** Delightful S-facing 16yr old 1 acre country garden, with traditional colour themed borders. Expansive rural views, wild flower walk, free range bluebelle chickens and stunning raised bed organic vegetable potager. Gravel driveway.

Relax on the deck; on a bench under a tree or on a swing seat in the gazebo . . .

38 **♦ PECKOVER HOUSE**
North Brink, Wisbech PE13 1JR. National Trust, 01945 583463, www.nationaltrust.org.uk. *Centre of Wisbech on N banks of R Nene. Within easy walking distance of town bus stn. Nearest car park in Chapel Rd - no parking on property. Disabled blue badge parking outside property.* **Adm £6, chd £3. For NGS: Sat 7 May (12-5); Thur 30 June (11-5). For other opening times and information, please phone or see garden website.** One of the best Victorian town house gardens, Peckover is a 2-acre site offering many areas of interest. These incl herbaceous borders, bedding, roses, trees, ponds, a propagation

glasshouse, lawns, cut flower border, ferns, summerhouses and an orangery with 3 very old fruiting orange trees and colourful pot plant display. Sat 7 May, Gardeners will be available to answer any questions. Thurs 30 June, Gardeners will be giving tips and advice on rose growing as this opening coincides with the Wisbech Rose Fair. Plant sales money to NGS. Gravel paths.

39 **NEW** **6 ROBINS WOOD**
PE8 6JQ. Carole & Forbes Smith, 01780 783094, caroleannsmith@tiscali.co.uk. *7m W of Peterborough on A1/A47 junction. From A47 turn towards Wansford. At X-rds by church turn W onto Old Leicester Rd. Approx 500yds turn R into Robins Field, follow on to Robins Wood.* Soup & rolls, home-made teas. **Adm £2.50, chd free. Sun 27 Feb (11-4). Visitors also welcome by appt.** Small woodland garden with a collection of 200+ varieties of snowdrops.

40 **♦ ROBINSON COLLEGE**
Grange Road, Cambridge CB3 9AN, 01223 339100, www.robinson.cam.ac.uk. *Grange Rd runs N to S between Madingley Rd (A1303) & Barton Rd (A603). Turn S on Madingley Rd down Grange Rd, on R. N from Barton Rd on L, opp University Library. Park on st, (parking may be limited). Please report to the Porters Lodge on arrival.* **Adm £2.50, chd free. For NGS: Daily Sun 3 Apr to Sun 24 Apr; (2-4). Closed Exam Period May & June 2011. Reopens July 2, 2011 till April 2012. For other opening times and information, please phone or see garden website.** 10 original Edwardian gardens are linked to central wild woodland water garden focusing on Bin Brook with small lake at heart of site. This gives a feeling of park and informal woodland, while at the same time keeping the sense of older more formal gardens beyond. Central area has a wide lawn running down to the lake framed by many mature stately trees with much of the original planting intact. More recent planting incl herbaceous borders and commemorative trees. No picnics. Children must be accompanied at all times.

GROUP OPENING

41 SAWSTON GARDENS
CB22 3HY. *5m SE of Cambridge. 3m from M11 J10. Off junction of A505 & A1301. Sawston village is well signposted.* Light refreshments & cream teas Venue t.b.c. Will be signposted. **Combined adm £4, chd free. Sun 3 July (1-6).**

DRIFT HOUSE
19a Babraham Road. Mr & Mrs A Osborne

54 HIGH STREET
Richard & Marilyn Maunder

35 MILL LANE
Doreen Butler.
Via Mill Lane next to firestation

11 MILL LANE
Tim & Rosie Phillips

30 QUEENSWAY
John & Tessa Capes

VINE COTTAGE
Hammonds Road. Dr & Mrs Tim Wreghitt

Six delightful, peaceful and largely secluded gardens in S Cambs' largest village set off by houses from the C15 to C20. Gardening styles equally varied, incl Vine Cottage Japanese Courtyard, 11 Mill Lane semicircular striped lawn, Drift House classic English with vegetable garden, 35 Mill Lane, waterfall and ponds, 30 Queensway 5yr no-watering policy, 54 High Street kitchen/rose garden and chickens. Many other attractions and features in each incl fountains, paths, decking, mirrors, fruit cage, herb beds, wisteria-clad veranda, 50 varieties of geranium and much more. Most gardens provide some seating. See links to individual gardens for fuller descriptions. Excellent value at less than 60p per garden and time to spend around ½ hour at each. Village shops open until 4pm. WC provided and signposted.Maps to gardens and facilities are provided free to all visitors.
& 🏡 ⊛ ☕

42 SHADWORTH HOUSE
45 High Street, Swaffham Prior CB25 0LD. Mr John Norris, 01638 741465, john.norris@onetel.com.
10m E of Cambridge. off B1102. In the centre of the village. Parking at village hall. **Adm £3, chd free, Combined with The Paddock adm**

£4, chd free, 15 May. Suns 15 May; 12 June (10-5).
The garden is situated between the two Churches and the Red Lion. Many steps (39) lead up to the conservatory and then onto the pond, waterfall and top garden. On a fine day there is the possibilty of a model steam traction engine and thrashing drum running, complete with steam whistle!
🏡 ☕ ☎

GROUP OPENING

43 NEW SHELFORD & STAPLEFORD GARDENS
CB22 5DG. Light refreshments & home-made teas at 59-61 London Road. **Combined adm £4, chd free (share to East Anglia Children's Hospice). Sun 12 June (2-6).**

59 - 61 LONDON ROAD
Stapleford. Dr & Mrs S Jones.
On A1301 next to Church St

NEW CRISPIN COTTAGE
100 London Road, Stapleford.
David & Jean Mann.
Opp The Rose PH

NEW CUIXMALA
39 Gog Magog Way, Stapleford.
Peter & Laura Carr

57 LONDON ROAD
Stapleford. Mrs M Spriggs.
on A1301 next to Church St

NEW MAYLONS
15 High Street, Great Shelford.
Maire & Gilbert Parks

5 PRIAMS WAY
Stapleford. Tony Smith.
Off London Rd, easiest access via 59 - 61 London Rd

NEW 9 STERNES WAY
Stapleford. Mr & Mrs C A Weaver

Contrasting gardens showing a range of size, planting and atmosphere in this village just S of Cambridge. The London Road gardens and Priam's Way form an interlocking series of garden rooms including herbaceous beds, kitchen garden, alpine, pit and summer houses with sculptures set around. Four new gardens incl an established cottage garden with lots of perennials, grasses fishpond and stream a contemporary wheelchair friendly family garden with a studio, an interesting garden with ponds and photographic exhibition and an enclosed garden with a small leaved

lime tree pergola and mirrors.
& ☕

44 NEW 53 STATION ROAD
Haddenham, Ely CB6 3XD. Jo Pooley. *6m SW of Ely. From A142, take A1421. On entering the village from N 200 metres on R.* **Adm £2, chd free. Sat 11, Sun 12 June (10-5). Also open Ty-Gwyn.**
Small organic cottage garden with a traditional mix of planting, vegetable beds and rescue battery hens. Good collection of roses and bearded iris, mini meadow and small orchard.
& 🏡 ⊛

STREET FARM
See Suffolk.

Two C17 cottages (not open), set in a deeply rural hamlet . . .

GROUP OPENING

45 STREETLY END GARDENS
West Wickham CB21 4RP. *3m NW of Haverhill on A1307 between Linton & Haverhill. Turn N at Horseheath to West Wickham, at triangle after R-hand bend turn L.* Home-made teas at Chequer Cottage. **Combined adm £3, chd free. Sun 5 June (12-5).**

NEW CHEQUER COTTAGE 🛏
Mr & Mrs D Sills

CLOVER COTTAGE
Mrs Shirley Shadford

Two C17 cottages (not open), set in a deeply rural hamlet. Thatched Clover Cottage is flanked by a high old red brick wall. The packed front garden has waving swathes of tall aquilegias, with raised fruit and vegetable beds, and borders containing many varieties of hardy geraniums along with several interesting old trees and arches of roses and clematis. Rear garden features a pond and summer house overlooking paddocks and open countryside. Tiled Chequer Cottage has a mixture of cottage and contemporary planting. Monet inspired rose arch entranceway, lawn enclosed by perennial beds featuring iris, delphiniums and roses. Unusual mature trees, pond with bog garden. Elongated vegetable patch flanked by terraced rockery and memento wall, leading into walled garden, featuring evergreen structure plants, damp shade and hot dry beds. Art studio, cakes, honey and preserves all home-made at Chequer Cottage. Plants at Clover Cottage.

46 TRINITY COLLEGE, FELLOWS' GARDEN

Cambridge CB2 1TQ. Trinity College. *Queen's Road.* Adm £3.50, chd free. **Sun 10 Apr (2-5).** Garden of 8 acres, originally laid out in the 1870s by W B Thomas. Lawns with mixed borders, shrubs and specimen trees. Drifts of spring bulbs. Recent extension of landscaped area among new college buildings to W of main garden.

&

47 TRINITY HALL

Trinity Lane. CB2 1TJ. The Master & Fellows, www.trinhall.cam.ac.uk/about/gardens.asp. *City Centre. From Trinity Street in city centre, Trinity Hall is located beween Senate House Passage & Garret Hostel Lane.* Home-made teas. Adm £4, chd free. **Sun 21 Aug (11.30-3.30).** An opportunity to visit the beautiful and tranquil gardens of Trinity Hall. Secluded courtyards offer varied environments in which an array of wall shrubs, herbaceous plants, roses, herbs, fruit and summer flowering bulbs flourish and bloom. The Fellows Garden with its majestic sweeping lawn and attractive mixed borders overlooking the river Cam, provides a peaceful oasis set amongst historic buildings dating back to 1350. Some gravel paths.

48 TRINITY HALL - WYCHFIELD

Storeys Way, Cambridge CB3 0DZ. The Master & Fellows, www.trinhall.cam.ac.uk/about/gardens.asp. *1m NW of city centre. Turn into Storeys Way from Madingley Rd (A1303).* Home-made teas. Adm £4, chd free. **Sun 10 Apr (11.30-3.30).** A beautiful garden that brings together differing garden

environments brimming with a lush range of plants that compliment the interesting architecture. The Edwardian Wychfield House and its associated garden areas contrast the recent contemporary development located off Storeys Way. Majestic trees, shady under storey woodland planting, established lawns, and spring bulbs, working together to provide a picturesque garden. Plant Sale: Some gravel paths.

49 TWIN TARNS

6 Pinfold Lane, Somersham PE28 3EQ. Michael & Frances Robinson, 01487 843376, mkrobinson12@aol.com. *From A14 take St Ives exit. Take A1096 N until B1040. Continue on B1040 which turns into B1086, turn R into Somersham. Turn R on Church St. Park then walk to Pinfold Lane next to church.* Tea & Home-made teas & Light Refreshments. Adm £2.50, chd free. **Sat 11, Sun 12 June (12-5).** Visitors also welcome by appt May to July, Mon to Fri, 10-3. One-acre wildlife garden with formal borders, kitchen garden and ponds, large rockery, mini woodland, wild flower meadow (June/July). Topiary, rose walk, willow sculptures. Hammock. Adjacent to C13 village church. Micro-brewery/cider-house (tasting available). Featured in Cambridgeshire Journal.

50 TY GWYN

6 The Borough, Aldreth CB6 3PJ. Sian & Mark Hugo, 01353 740586, sian@artes-mundi.co.uk, www.artes-mundi.co.uk/garden. *7m SW of Ely. 2m S of Haddenham. The Borough is 2nd on 'L' after entering Aldreth Village. Please park in High St, approx 2 mins walk from garden. Parking for disabled at garden.* Home-made teas. Adm £3, chd free. **Sats, Suns 14, 15 May; 11, 12 June; 9, 10 July; 6, 7 Aug; 3, 4 Sept (10-5).** Also open 53 Station Road Sat 11, Sun 12 June. Visitors also welcome by appt. 1 acre cottage garden in small fenland hamlet. Grass path walks around mature trees, shrubs, perennials and climbers. Wild flower garden, Cactus greenhouse, Vegetable patch, orchard, fishpond. Free range chickens and ducks including rare breeds. Artes Mundi Fair Trade gift shop onsite. Featured in local press.

GROUP OPENING

51 WHITTLESFORD GARDENS

CB22 4NR. *7m S of Cambridge. 1m NE of J10 M11 & A505. Parking nr church, additional parking will be signed.* Light refreshments & home-made teas in Parish Church. Combined adm £3.50, chd free. **Sun 19 June (2-6).**

NEW 11 CHURCH CLOSE
Mrs Val King

19 CHURCH CLOSE
Mr & Mrs V Massey

THE GUILDHALL
Professors P & M Spufford

MARKINGS FARM
32 West End. Mr & Mrs A Jennings.
Parking space

23 NEWTON ROAD
Mr F Winter

NEW 14 NORTH ROAD
Mr & Mrs Adderley

5 PARSONAGE COURT
Mrs L Button.
Please park on rd

RYECROFT
1 Middlemoor Road. Mr & Mrs P A Goodman

11 SCOTTS GARDENS
Mr & Mrs M Walker

There is a sense of going back to older, gentler times with this collection of formal and country gardens. Features include a knot garden, streams ponds and waterfalls and even an allotment consisting of vegetables, fruit, flowers and bird aviary. Informal mixed planting of herbaceous plants and vegetables contrasts with medieval-style herb beds in a C15 walled garden. Planting covers everything from trees and shrubs to herbaceous borders and shade-loving plants.

> There is a sense of going back to older, gentler times with this collection of formal and country gardens . . .

Be tempted by a plant from a plant stall ⊛

52 WILLOW HOLT

Willow Hall Lane, Thorney PE6 0QN. Angie & Jonathan Jones, 01733 222367, janda.salix@virgin.net. *4m E of Peterborough. From A47, between Eye & Thorney turn S into Willow Hall Lane. 2m on R. NOT in Thorney Village.* Adm £3, chd free. Suns 17 Apr; 15 May; 19 June; 17 July; 28 Aug; 25 Sept (11-5). Visitors also welcome by appt.

An intriguing natural garden developed over 18 years from impenetrable undergrowth on a base of rubbish. Hundreds of plants hide strange sculpted creatures alongside meandering paths. 2 acres with ponds, woodland and meadow. A garden to get lost in.

53 ◆ WIMPOLE HALL

Arrington SG8 0BW. National Trust, 01223 206000, www.wimpole.org. *7m N of Royston (A1198). 8m SW of Cambridge (A603). J12 off M11, 30 mins from A1(M).* Adm £4.10, chd £2.20. For NGS: Sun 24 July (10.30-5). For other opening times and information, please phone or see garden website.

New border 2010; a prelude to the walled garden, our showpiece containing fruit, flowers, vegetables. Recreated Sir John Sloane glasshouse, financed with NGS help. Herbaceous borders over 100m long with mixed plantings of perennials, roses and choice shrubs. Dutch Garden and Victorian Parterres. Expanding collection of fine trees and shrubs. Also NCCPG National Collection of Juglans (walnuts).

 NCCPG

54 THE WINDMILL

Cambridge Road, Impington CB24 9NU. Pippa & Steve Temple, 7775446443, mill.impington@ntlworld.com, www.impingtonmill.org. *2¹/₂ m N of Cambridge. Off B1049, turn L into Cambridge Rd.* Home-made teas & wine. Adm £3, chd free. Sat 7, Sun 8 May (2-7). Visitors also welcome by appt March to Sept.

New owners took over this romantic wilderness of 1¹/₂ acres surrounding windmill now stocked with thousands of bulbs, seasonal beds, pergolas, bog gardens, grass bed and herb bank. Secret paths and wild areas maintain the romance. New - hazel avenue completed: composting area vastly extended: green and white planting in Philosopher's Glade now under way. Plant Sale. Mill Tours. Featured on Radio Cambridgeshire. Area round mill gravelled.

55 NEW WOLFSON COLLEGE GARDEN

Barton Road, Cambridge CB3 9BB. Wolfson College. *On SW side of Cambridge. From M11 J12, take A603 into Cambridge. Wolfson College is approx 2m from J12, on L.* Adm £4, chd free. Fri 5 Aug (12-4).

Gardens are a series of lawned courtyards forming a set of garden 'rooms'. The beds and borders contain a wide variety of plants and shrubs which provide structure and interest through the year. Several courts reflect a Chinese influence in the design and planting. The retention of some majestic trees from the original site helps to give an atmosphere of maturity and permanence to a garden which has developed greatly over the last 30yrs.

39 Foster Road

56 WYTCHWOOD

7 Owl End, Great Stukeley PE28 4AQ. Mr David Cox, 01480 454835, robertparker@waitrose.com. *2m N of Huntingdon. On B1043. Parking at village hall, Owl End.* Home-made teas. Adm £3.50, chd free. Sun 26 June (1.30-5.30). Visitors also welcome by appt, May/June only, 12+, coaches permitted.

2-acre garden. Brightly planted borders of perennials, annuals and shrubs, lawns and ponds. 1 acre of wild plants, grasses set among rowan, maple and birch trees leading to spinney. Planted with native trees, ferns, hostas and foxgloves. Plenty of seats and shade. Haven for wildlife. Gravel drive. Featured in GGG.

Cambridgeshire County Volunteers

County Organiser
George Stevenson, 1a The Village, Orton Longueville, Peterborough, Cambridgeshire PE2 7DN, 01733 391506, chrisgeorge1a@aol.com

County Treasurer
Nicholas Kyberd, 5 Moat Way, Swavesey, Cambridge CB24 4TR, 01954 200568, n.kyberd@ntlworld.com

Assistant County Organisers
Pam Bullivant, Rosewell House, 60 Prickwillow Road, Ely CB7 4TX, 01353 667355, pam.bullivant@talk21.com
Dr Lyndon & Alison Davies, 19 Swaynes Lane, Comberton, Cambridge CB23 7EF, 01223 262686, lyndon.alison@tiscali.co.uk
Patsy Glazebrook, 15 Bentley Road, Cambridge CB2 8AW, 01223 301302, glazebrc@doctors.net.uk
Angie Jones Willow Holt, Willow Hall Lane, Thorney, Peterborough PE6 0QN, 01733 222367 janda.salix@virgin.net
Michael Tuplin, 36 Barton Road, Ely CB7 4HZ 01353 612029 miketuplin@yahoo.co.uk
Annette White, 9 Forestry Cottage, West End, Woodditton, Newmarket CB8 9SW, 01638 730876, annette323@btinternet.com

CHESHIRE & WIRRAL

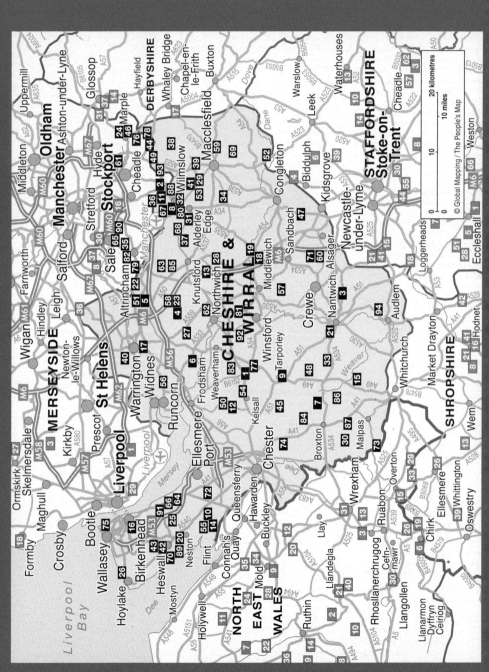

Opening Dates

February
Saturday 12
55 Ness Botanic Gardens
Sunday 13
13 Bucklow Farm
Sunday 20
22 Dunham Massey

April
Sunday 3
62 Parm Place
Sunday 10
74 Saighton Grange
Saturday 16
66 Poulton Hall
Sunday 17
10 Briarfield
22 Dunham Massey
66 Poulton Hall
Sunday 24
48 Long Acre
Monday 25
6 Bluebell Cottage Gardens
Wednesday 27
85 Tatton Park

May
Sunday 1
33 Haughton Hall
89 69 Well Lane
Monday 2
74 69 Well Lane
Saturday 7
42 Inglewood
67 Quarry Bank House Garden
Sunday 8
32 Hare Hill Gardens
35 35 Heyes Lane
42 Inglewood
59 One House Nursery
Saturday 14
8 9 Bourne Street
63 Peover Hall Gardens
Sunday 15
8 9 Bourne Street
34 Henbury Hall
56 Norton Priory Museum & Gardens
60 Orchard Villa
63 Peover Hall Gardens
70 Riverside Lodge
Friday 20
26 29 Forest Road (Evening)
Saturday 21
43 84 Irby Road
46 Leawood
58 The Old Parsonage

76 Sandsend
88 Well House
Sunday 22
1 Abbeywood Estate
21 Dorfold Hall
29 Glynleigh
43 84 Irby Road
46 Leawood
50 Manley Knoll
58 The Old Parsonage
76 Sandsend
88 Well House
91 Willaston Village Gardens
Wednesday 25
15 Cholmondeley Castle Garden
Friday 27
84 Tattenhall Hall (Evening)
Saturday 28
53 The Mount
Sunday 29
12 Brooklands
37 Hillside
53 The Mount
84 Tattenhall Hall
Monday 30
12 Brooklands
37 Hillside

June
Thursday 2
36 73 Hill Top Avenue (Evening)
Sunday 5
2 Adlington Hall
28 Free Green Farm
83 Stonyford Cottage
Wednesday 8
85 Tatton Park
Thursday 9
57 The Old Hough (Evening)
Saturday 11
86 The Valve House
Sunday 12
1 Abbeywood Estate
16 28 Christchurch Road
30 Grafton Lodge
82 199 Stockport Road
86 The Valve House
Thursday 16
57 The Old Hough (Evening)
Friday 17
30 Grafton Lodge (Evening)
Saturday 18
9 Bowmere Cottage
65 17 Poplar Grove
93 Woodsend
Sunday 19
9 Bowmere Cottage
48 Long Acre
64 Plymyard Hall Allotments
65 17 Poplar Grove
69 Ridgehill
93 Woodsend

Thursday 23
57 The Old Hough (Evening)
Saturday 25
52 Millpool
Sunday 26
14 Burton Village Gardens
20 29 Dee Park Road
38 Hillside Cottage
52 Millpool
79 The School House
92 Wood End Cottage
Thursday 30
57 The Old Hough (Evening)

July
Friday 1
4 Arley Hall & Gardens
Saturday 2
5 Beechwood Cottage
17 68 Cranborne Avenue
27 1 Frandley Cottages
94 Yew Tree House Garden & Special Perennials Nursery
Sunday 3
5 Beechwood Cottage
17 68 Cranborne Avenue
23 The East Garden
27 1 Frandley Cottages
94 Yew Tree House Garden & Special Perennials Nursery
Friday 8
3 Alma Villa (Evening)
Saturday 9
41 Hunters Croft
80 68 South Oak Lane
Sunday 10
3 Alma Villa
24 Edith Terrace Gardens
26 29 Forest Road
36 73 Hill Top Avenue
41 Hunters Croft
62 Parm Place
80 68 South Oak Lane
Saturday 16
25 Fieldcrest
31 Greenways
40 10 Hudson Close
47 Little Moreton Hall
73 The Rowans
94 Yew Tree House Garden & Special Perennials Nursery
Sunday 17
25 Fieldcrest
31 Greenways
40 10 Hudson Close
73 The Rowans
77 Sandymere
82 199 Stockport Road
90 West Drive Gardens
94 Yew Tree House Garden & Special Perennials Nursery
Saturday 23
19 Dane Mount
94 Yew Tree House Garden & Special Perennials Nursery

Sunday 24
19 Dane Mount
94 Yew Tree House Garden &
Special Perennials Nursery

Saturday 30
44 4 Keswick Road
78 21 Scafell Close

Sunday 31
44 4 Keswick Road
78 21 Scafell Close

August

Thursday 4
38 Hillside Cottage

Friday 5
38 Hillside Cottage (Evening)

Saturday 6
94 Yew Tree House Garden &
Special Perennials Nursery

Sunday 7
22 Dunham Massey
49 Lyme Park
83 Stonyford Cottage
94 Yew Tree House Garden &
Special Perennials Nursery

Saturday 13
37 Hillside
45 Lane End Farm
81 Springbank
94 Yew Tree House Garden &
Special Perennials Nursery

Sunday 14
36 73 Hill Top Avenue
37 Hillside
39 Hilltop
45 Lane End Farm
81 Springbank
94 Yew Tree House Garden &
Special Perennials Nursery

Monday 29
6 Bluebell Cottage Gardens

September

Saturday 3
61 39 Osborne Street
94 Yew Tree House Garden &
Special Perennials Nursery

Sunday 4
61 39 Osborne Street

Sunday 11
94 Yew Tree House Garden &
Special Perennials Nursery

October

Sunday 9
68 The Quinta Arboretum

Wednesday 12
85 Tatton Park

Sunday 16
22 Dunham Massey

February 2012

Saturday 18
55 Ness Botanic Gardens

Gardens open to the public

1 Abbeywood Estate
2 Adlington Hall
4 Arley Hall & Gardens
6 Bluebell Cottage Gardens
15 Cholmondeley Castle Garden
22 Dunham Massey
32 Hare Hill Gardens
47 Little Moreton Hall
49 Lyme Park
54 Mount Pleasant
55 Ness Botanic Gardens
56 Norton Priory Museum &
Gardens
63 Peover Hall Gardens
67 Quarry Bank House Garden
68 The Quinta Arboretum
71 Rode Hall
83 Stonyford Cottage
85 Tatton Park

By appointment only

7 Bolesworth Castle
11 Brooke Cottage
18 Croco Brook Farm
51 Mayfield
72 Rosewood
75 St Davids House
87 The Well House

Also open by Appointment ☎

3 Alma Villa
9 Bowmere Cottage
14 Briarfield, Burton Village Gardens
12 Brooklands
25 Fieldcrest
26 29 Forest Road
30 Grafton Lodge
31 Greenways
36 73 Hill Top Avenue
38 Hillside Cottage
39 Hilltop
42 Inglewood
48 Long Acre
52 Millpool
53 The Mount
57 The Old Hough
58 The Old Parsonage
60 Orchard Villa
61 39 Osborne Street
62 Parm Place
65 17 Poplar Grove
66 Poulton Hall
73 The Rowans
74 Saighton Grange

76 Sandsend
78 21 Scafell Close
80 68 South Oak Lane
81 Springbank
84 Tattenhall Hall
89 69 Well Lane
92 Wood End Cottage

The Gardens

1 ♦ **ABBEYWOOD ESTATE**
Chester Road, Delamere
CW8 2HW. The Rowlinson Family,
01606 889477,
www.abbeywoodestate.co.uk. *11m
E of Chester. From the west proceed
east from Chester along A51 onto the
A54 following onto A556. Before you
reach the xrds with B5152 turn R into
Abbeywood Estate opp St Peter's
Church. From the east proceed along
A556 towards Chester. Cross over
B5152, rise up the hill & turn L into
Abbeywood Estate.* **Adm £5, chd
free. For NGS: Suns 22 May;
12 June (11-5). For other opening
times and information, please
phone or see garden website.**
Superb setting near Delamere Forest.
Total area 45 acres incl. Mature
woodland, new woodland and new
arboretum all with connecting
pathways. Approx 4½ acres of
garden surrounding large Edwardian
House. Vegetable garden and
greenhouse, walled gardens, chapel
garden, pool garden, woodland
garden, lawned area with beds.
Gravel paths.
&♿ 🐕 ✿ ☕

2 ♦ **ADLINGTON HALL**
Macclesfield SK10 4LF. Mrs
Camilla Legh, 01625 827595,
www.adlingtonhall.com. *4m N of
Macclesfield. Well signed off A523 at
Adlington.* **Adm £5, chd free. For
NGS: Sun 5 June (2-5). For other
opening times and information,
please phone or see garden
website.**
6 acres of formal gardens with
herbaceous borders, rose garden,
rockeries, yew maze, water garden.
Lawns with open views across ha-ha.
32-acre wilderness with mature
plantings, various follies incl a 'Temple
to Diana'; woodland walk. Yew and
ancient lime walks. Flower parterre.
Dogs on leads.
🐕 ✿ ☕

3 ALMA VILLA

73 Main Road, Shavington, Crewe CW2 5DU. Rosemary & Roger Murphy, 01270 567710. *2m E of Nantwich. From J16 M6 take A500 towards Nantwich, at 3rd r'about turn L signed Shavington, L at T-lights into village approx ¹/₂ m take 2nd R into Main Rd, garden approx 300yds on R. From Nantwich follow Shavington signs to Elephant PH turn 1st L into Main Rd, garden approx 400yds on L.* Light refreshments, home-made teas & wine. **Adm £3, chd free. Evening Opening £5, wine, Fri 8 July (6.30-9.30); Sun 10 July (11.30-4.30). Visitors also welcome by appt June & July, coaches welcome.**
Country garden, constantly evolving treasure trove of beautiful mixed herbaceous plants and containers,slate covered front garden with yucca,phormium and grasses. Winding paths lead to rose and clematis covered pergola and arches.Includes alpine bed, water features, bog garden, clipped box,magnificent lavender hedge,mature fruit trees, rill and summer house.Year round interest. Live background music provided by local musician on Friday evening opening. Featured in Cheshire Life.

4 ◆ ARLEY HALL & GARDENS

Northwich CW9 6NA. The Viscount Ashbrook, 01565 777353, www.arleyhallandgardens.com. *4m W of Knutsford. Well signed from M6 J19 & 20, & M56 J9 & 10.* **Adm £7, chd £5. For NGS: Fri 1 July (11-5). For other opening times and information, please phone or see garden website.**
One of Britain's finest gardens, Arley has been lovingly created by the same family over 250yrs and is famous for its yew buttressed herbaceous border, avenue of ilex columns, walled garden, pleached lime avenue and Victorian Rootree. A garden of great atmosphere, interest and vitality throughout the seasons. Specialist nursery adjacent.

5 NEW BEECHWOOD COTTAGE

64 Crouchley Lane, Lymm WA13 0AT. Ian & Amber Webb. *8m S of Altrincham. 4m from J7 or 2m J21 M6 onto A56 turn into Crouchley Lane past Lymm Rugby Club on R, 300yds on R (opp Crouchley Mews).* Home-made teas. **Adm £4, chd free.**

Manley Knoll

Sat 2, Sun 3 July (2-5).
Approx 2 acre garden looking out to fields. Large lawn with herbaceous borders. Formal walkway with rose arches, topiary area and an orchard. Wild flower meadow.

BIDDULPH GRANGE GARDEN

See Staffordshire Birmingham & part of West Midlands.

BLACKWOOD HOUSE FARM

See Staffordshire Birmingham & part of West Midlands.

6 ◆ BLUEBELL COTTAGE GARDENS

Lodge Lane, Dutton WA4 4HP. Sue & David Beesley, 01928 713718, www.lodgelane.co.uk. *5m NW of Northwich. From M56 (J10) take A49 (Whitchurch. After 3 mils turn R at T-lights towards Runcorn/Dutton. Then 1st turning L.* **Adm £4, chd free. For NGS: Mons 25 Apr; 29 Aug (10-5). For other opening times and information, please phone or see garden website.**
The 1¹/₂ -acre south facing garden is on a quiet rural lane in the heart of Cheshire and is packed with thousands of rare and familiar hardy herbaceous perennials, shrubs and trees. Unusual plants available at adjacent nursery. The ancient bluebell woods are usually in full flower for the spring opening.Bluebell Cottage Garden's new Berry Border was represented at RHS Tatton Show in Sue Beesley's back-to-back show garden 'A Banquet for the Birds' which secured a Silver-gilt medal. Partial wheelchair access.

7 BOLESWORTH CASTLE
Tattenhall CH3 9HQ. Mrs Anthony
Barbour, 01829 782 369,
dcb@bolesworth.com. *8m S of
Chester on A41. Enter by Lodge.*
Adm £5, chd free. **Visitors
welcome by appt** April, May & Oct.
One of the finest collections of
rhododendrons, camellias and acers
in any private garden in the NW. Set
on a steep hillside accessed by a
gently rising woodland walk and
overlooking spectacular view of the
Cheshire plain. Formal lawn beside
castle with well stocked herbaceous
borders. Terraces with lawn, rose
gardens and many other plants.
🏵 ☎

Rambling roses, clematis and wide range of plants make this a very traditional English garden . . .

8 9 BOURNE STREET
Wilmslow SK9 5HD. Lucille
Sumner, Melanie & Keith Harris,
www.wilmslowgarden.co.uk. *¼ m
W of central Wilmslow. Take A538
from Wilmslow towards Manchester
Airport. Bourne St 2nd on L after fire
station. From M56 J6 take A538 to
Wilmslow, Bourne St on R.* Home-
made teas. Adm £3.50, chd free.
Sat 14, Sun 15 May (11-5).
Started in 1924 on the site of an
existing orchard, this very unusual
garden has evolved over three
generations of one family. With
winding paths leading into different
and secret areas, featuring
rhododendrons, azaleas and mature
trees. Small glass house with water
features and unusual plants. Hens at
the bottom of the garden.
♿ 🏵 ☕

9 NEW BOWMERE COTTAGE
Bowmere Road, Tarporley
CW6 0BS. Romy & Tom Holmes,
01829 732053, romy@holmes-
email.co.uk. *10m E of Chester. From
Tarporley High St (old A49) take Eaton
Rd signed Eaton. After 100 metres
take R fork into Bowmere Rd, Garden
100 metres on LH-side.* Home-made
teas. Adm £3.50, chd free. **Sat 18,
Sun 19 June (2-5.30).** Visitors also

welcome by appt June/July only.
Mature 1-acre country style garden
around a Grade II listed house (not
open). Mixed shrub and herbaceous
borders, pergolas, two small
courtyard gardens and small kitchen
garden. Rambling roses, clematis and
wide range of plants make this a very
traditional English garden.
☕ ☎

10 BRIARFIELD
Burton, Neston CH64 5TL. Liz
Carter, 0151 336 2304,
carter.burton@virgin.net. *9m NW of
Chester. Turn off A540 at Willaston-
Burton Xrds T-lights & follow rd for 1m
to Burton village centre.* Home-made
teas at Rake Cottage, adjacent to the
main garden. Adm £3.50, chd free.
Sun 17 Apr (2-5). Visitors also
welcome by appt throughout the
year.
Home to many specialist plants, some
available in plant sale. Colourful
shrubs, bulbs, alpines and several
water features compete for attention
as you wander through four distinctly
different gardens. The home garden
has been changed with a wide variety
of unusual trees, shrubs and ground
cover replacing boring area of
bamboo. Increasing emphasis on
Himalayan woodlanders. Plant sale.
🏵 ☕ ☎

11 BROOKE COTTAGE
Church Road, Handforth SK9 3LT.
Barry & Melanie Davy, 01625
536511. *1m N of Wilmslow. Ctr of
Handforth, behind Health Ctr. Turn off
Wilmslow Rd at St Chads, follow
Church Rd round to R. Garden last on
L. Parking in Health Ctr car park.*
Refreshments can be provided on
request. Adm £3, chd free. **Visitors
welcome by appt** June to Aug,
individuals & groups welcome day
& evening.
Garden designer's plant-filled garden
surrounded by trees and shrubs. 3
distinct areas with different. planting
styles. Woodland garden: circ patio,
unusual water feature, tree ferns,
astrantias, hydrangeas, foxgloves,
other shade-loving plants, 20+ types
of fern. Container garden with
banana, cannas, ligularias, bamboo,
daylillies, pond. Colourful naturalistic
style border, island beds, grasses,
late flowering plants.
☕ ☎

BROOKFIELD
See Lancashire Merseyside &
Greater Manchester.

12 BROOKLANDS
Mouldsworth CH3 8AR. Barbara &
Brian Russell-Moore,
ngsmouldsworth@aol.co.uk. *1½ m
N of Tarvin. 5½ m S of Frodsham.
Smithy Lane is off the B5393 via the
A54 Tarvin/Kelsall rd or the A56
Frodsham/Helsby rd.* Home-made
teas. Adm £4, chd free. **Sun 29,
Mon 30 May (2-5).** Visitors also
welcome by appt.
Lovely country style garden in ¾ -acre
with a backdrop of mature trees and
shrubs. The planting is based around
azaleas, rhododendrons, mixed shrub
and herbaceous borders. There is a
small vegetable garden, supported by
a greenhouse. There is also a modest
bonsai collection with some mature
specimens.
♿ 🏵 ☕ ☎

13 BUCKLOW FARM
Pinfold Lane, Plumley WA16 9RP.
Dawn & Peter Freeman. *2m S of
Knutsford. M6 J19, head to Chester
A556. L at 2nd set of T-lights by
Smoker PH. In 1¼ m L at concealed
Xrds, 1st R. From Knutsford A5033, L
at Sudlow Lane. Follow rd, becomes
Pinfold Lane.* Mulled Wine/Mulled
Apple Juice. Adm £2.50, chd free.
Sun 13 Feb (1-4).
Country garden with shrubs, perennial
borders, rambling roses, herb garden,
vegetable patch, wildlife pond/water
feature and alpines. Landscaped and
planted over the last 20yrs with
recorded changes. Free range hens.
Carpet of snowdrops and spring
bulbs. Leaf,stem and berries to show
colour in the autumn and winter.
Cobbles in yard before reaching the
garden. Mainly lawns in garden.
♿ 🏵 ☕

GROUP OPENING

**14 BURTON VILLAGE
GARDENS**
Neston CH64 5SJ. *9m NW of
Chester. Turn off A540 at Willaston-
Burton Xrds T-lights & follow rd for 1m
to Burton.* Maps given to all visitors.
Home-made teas at Burton Manor.
Combined adm £4.50, chd free
(share to Claire House Children's
Hospice). **Sun 26 June (2-6).**

BRIARFIELD
Burton. Liz Carter
(See separate entry)
Visitors also welcome by appt.
0151 336 2304
carter.burton@virgin.net

BURTON MANOR
Burton. College Principal, Keith Chandler

LYNWOOD
Neston Road. Pauline Wright

MAPLE HOUSE
The Village. Ingrid & Neil Sturmey

RAKE COTTAGE
Mrs S Johnson

Burton is a medieval village only 1m from Ness Botanic Gardens. Each garden has a unique character. One has a superb view across the River Dee to the Clwyd hills and an extensive natural stone outcrop; two merge into the Cheshire countryside, while the others nestle under the s-side of Burton Wood (NT). You can compare very different garden styles, from Burton Manor's historic formal garden designed by Thomas Mawson with its terrace, yew hedges, colourful bedding and, opening in 2011, the walled kitchen garden with Edwardian glasshouse; to the delightful wildlife area with pond at Maple House. The owners' interests add diversity; Lynwood has unusual herbaceous plants, Rake Cottage a bubbling water feature amid circled decking and Briarfield an increasing collection of Himalayan woodland plants. Several have productive fruit and vegetable plots. 2 plant sales, Lynwood and Briarfield. At Dovecoat Nursery, Burton, 10% of all sales will be donated to the ngs. Open 10-5.

❀ ☕ ♿

> The planting's lush, the scents are ace with wonderful artefacts to bring smiles to the face! . . .

15 ◆ CHOLMONDELEY CASTLE GARDEN
Malpas SY14 8AH. The Marchioness of Cholmondeley, 01829 720383, www.cholmondeleycastle.com. 4m NE of Malpas. Off A41 Chester-

Whitchurch rd & A49 Whitchurch-Tarporley rd. Adm £5, chd £2. For NGS: Wed 25 May (11-5). For other opening times and information, please phone or see garden website.
Over 20 acres of romantically landscaped gardens with fine views and eye-catching water features, but still manages to retain its intimacy. Beautiful mature trees form a background to spring bulbs, exotic plants in season incl magnolias, rhododendrons, azaleas and camellias and many other, particularly Davidia Involucrata which will be in flower in late May. Partial wheelchair access.

♿ 🐕 ❀

16 28 CHRISTCHURCH ROAD
Oxton CH43 5SF. Tom & Ruth Foster. *1m SW of Birkenhead. From M53 J3 take A552 to Birkenhead. Follow rd passing Sainsbury's cross junction at T-lights (Halfway House PH). Bear L at next T-lights into Woodchurch Rd. Take 2nd L into Bessborough Rd. Christchurch R is 1st L after church. Parking available courtesy of Christchurch Church.* Home-made teas. Adm £3.50, chd free. Sun 12 June (1-5).
Grade II listed Victorian Folly with crenellated towers forms a unique feature in this ¼-acre plot. The garden is on different levels with gravel areas, 3 water features, herbaceous beds and lawns connected by tunnels, pathways and steps. Planting consists of trees (many acers) shrubs and perennials. Christchurch, opp the garden, isopen during the afternoon, when there will be an organ recital. Featured in Amateur Gardening.

🐕 ☕

CLOUD COTTAGE
Simmondley. See Derbyshire.

COURTWOOD HOUSE
See Staffordshire Birmingham & part of West Midlands.

CRAIGSIDE
See Derbyshire.

17 68 CRANBORNE AVENUE
Warrington WA4 6DE. Mr & Mrs J Carter. *1m S of Warrington Centre. From Stockton Heath N on A49 over swing bridge. L at 2nd set of T-lights into Gainsborough Rd, 4th L into Cranborne Ave.* Adm £3, chd free. Sat 2, Sun 3 July (11-6).

Through the gateway you'll embrace an oasis of peace,a secret place. Colour and scent enhance and grace. Water and glass expand the space. The planting's lush, the scent's are ace with wonderful artefacts to bring smiles to the face!

❀

18 CROCO BROOK FARM
Selkirk Drive, Holmes Chapel CW4 7DR. John & Linda Clowes, 01477 532266, gardens@johnclowes.co.uk. *½ m W of Holmes Chapel centre. From M6 J18 take A54 towards Holme Chapel. After Texaco garage turn R A54 Congleton (Chester Rd). After 200yds R into Selkirk Drive, garden entrance 20yds on L. From T-lights in Holmes Chapel village take A54 towards Middlewich, Selkirk Drive 500yds on L. Park along Selkirk Dr.* Adm £3.50, chd free. Visitors welcome by appt parties of 10+.
⅔-acre garden developed since 1980 by the garden designer owner. Containing a wide range of trees, shrubs and herbaceous plants arranged to create interest all yr round. The garden encircles the old farm house (not open) providing the opportunity to create areas with different characteristics. The garden is divided into several areas incl pool, 'hot' garden and inner garden. A wide range of plants for late summer interest. Access may be limited over grass areas in wet periods.

♿ ❀ ☎

19 DANE MOUNT
Middlewich Road, Holmes Chapel CW4 7EB. Mr & Mrs D Monks. *4m E of Middlewich. Approx 1m E of M6 J18.* Cream teas. Adm £3, chd free. Sat 23, Sun 24 July (1.30-5).
¼-acre garden, colourful bedding displays, perennials and show gooseberries, interesting layout, with features incl pottery and garden sculptures.

♿ ❀ ☕

20 29 DEE PARK ROAD
Gayton CH60 3RG. E Lewis. *7m S of Birkenhead. From Devon Doorway/Glegg Arms r'about at Heswall, travel SE in Chester direction on A540 for approx ¼ m. Turn R into Gayton Lane, 5th L into Dee Park Rd. Garden on L after ¼ m.* Adm £3, chd free. Sun 26 June (1-5.30).
The garden has been created over several yrs and has many shrubs, mature trees and borders filled with

Springbank

cottage garden perennials. A mirror in the secret garden reflects shade-loving plants. Gravel areas have a variety of alpines and thymes. Pergolas are framed with roses, clematis and jasmine. The gated entrance by an arbour leads to a garden room with yet more roses and clematis. Water features in a renovated border completes this lovely garden.

DIDSBURY GARDENS
See Lancashire Merseyside & Greater Manchester.

21 ▶ DORFOLD HALL
Nantwich CW5 8LD. Mr & Mrs Richard Roundell. *1m W of Nantwich. On A534 between Nantwich & Acton.* **Adm £5.50, chd £2.50. Sun 22 May (2-5.30).** 18-acre garden surrounding C17 house (not open) with formal approach; lawns and herbaceous borders; spectacular spring woodland garden with rhododendrons, azaleas, magnolias and bulbs.

DOROTHY CLIVE GARDEN
See Staffordshire Birmingham & part of West Midlands.

22 ▶ ♦ DUNHAM MASSEY
Altrincham WA14 4SJ. National Trust, 0161 941 1025, www.nationaltrust.org.uk. *3m SW of Altrincham. 3m SW of Altrincham off A56; M6 exit J19; M56 exit J7. Foot: close to Trans-Pennine Trail & Bridgewater Canal. Bus: No's 38 & 5.* **Adm £7, chd £3.50. For NGS: Suns 20 Feb; 17 Apr; 7 Aug; 16 Oct (11-5.30). For other opening times and information, please phone or see garden website.**
Enjoy the elegance of this vibrant Edwardian garden. Richly planted borders packed with colour and texture, sweeping lawns, majestic trees and shady woodland all await your discovery. See the largest Winter Garden in Britain with over 170,000 bulbs, 50 types of camellia, striking stems, beautiful bark and luscious berries. Many water features. C17 Orangery, Rare Victorian Bark House.

23 ▶ NEW ▶ THE EAST GARDEN
Arley Hall, Northwich CW9 6NA. Charles & Jane Foster. *6m W of Knutsford. Follow signs for Arley Hall & Gardens signed from M6 J19 & J20 & M26 J9 & J10. Parking in Arleys Hall's main car park.* Light refreshments & teas in the Tudor Barn Restaurant, Arley Hall Gardens. **Adm £3, chd free. Sun 3 July (11-5).** Combined with **Arley Hall** adm **£7.50, concession £7, chd £2.**
A beautiful and interesting garden on the E side of Arley Hall developed since 1992 by the owner of Arley Hall Nursery, started in the same year. Old shrub roses, early summer perennials and circular herbaceous borders enclosed by yew hedges. Many varieties of hardy herbaceous perennials - the specialty of the nursery.

GROUP OPENING

24 ▶ EDITH TERRACE GARDENS
Compstall, nr Marple SK6 5JF. *6m E of Stockport. Take Bredbury junction off M60. Follow Romiley-Marple Bridge sign on B6104. Turn into Compstall at Etherow Country Park sign. Take 1st R, situated at end of Montagu St. Parking in village public car parks - short walk to Edith Terrace.* Home-made teas. **Combined adm £4.50, chd free. Sun 10 July (1-5).**

Series of gardens in mixed style from cottage to formal, situated to front and rear of Victorian terrace; described by BBC 'Gardeners' World' magazine as 'a colourful and beautiful living space'. Mixed herbaceous perennials, ornamental backyards and back alleyway. In lakeside setting in the conserved mill village of Compstall, adjacent to Etherow Country Park.

10 FERN DENE
See Staffordshire Birmingham & part of West Midlands.

25 NEW FIELDCREST
Thornton Common Road, Thornton Hough, Wirral CH63 0LT. Paul & Christine Davies, 0151 334 8878, chris@fieldcrest.co.uk, www.fieldcrestgarden.com. *5m S of Birkenhead, 4m SE of Heswall. Exit J 4 M53 Follow B5151 Clatterbridge/ Willaston for 1m Turn L at r'about signed Raby Mere & Wirral RFC. Garden ½ m on R.* Home-made teas. **Adm £3.50, chd free. Sat 16, Sun 17 July (2-5). Visitors also welcome by appt.**
Maturing country garden in 1¼ acres, planted for year round colour and interest. Cottage garden, shrub border, potager with fruit, flowers, herbs and vegetables. Native and rarer trees. Country lane walk, wildflower area with young fruit trees. Wide variety of summer perennials, with phlox. monarda, daylilies and dahlias in July. Cheshire Wildlife Trust Award. Gravel in drive area and some paths.

26 NEW 29 FOREST ROAD
Meols, Wirral CH47 6AS. Graham & Pat Thew, 0151 632 0450, graham@thethews.fsnet.co.uk. *8m NW of Birkenhead. On A553 from Birkenhead towards Hoylake, pass Railway Inn on R. As rd bends L, Forest Rd on R.* Tea & Home-made teas. Glass wine include for evening opening. **Adm £3, chd free. Evening Opening £4, wine, Fri 20 May (5-9); Sun 10 July (2-6). Visitors also welcome by appt between opening dates.**
Suburban seaside garden, a stone's throw from promenade. Curvy and arty with varieties of clematis, picturesque pergola with wisteria. Raised pond in sleepers and slate. Lawned area features revolving sunseeking summerhouse and shady seating areas. Seaside plants, alpines, azaleas, alliums. The bees love it, we hope you will love it too!

27 1 FRANDLEY COTTAGES
Sandiway Lane, Antrobus CW9 6LD. Mr & Mrs N Pemberton. *4m N of Northwich. 2m S of J10, M56. 8m W of J19 M6, ½ m W of Antrobus Village. 200yds W of A559, follow signs to Frandley.* Home-made teas. **Adm £3.50, chd free. Sat 2, Sun 3 July (12-5).**
An organic and wildlife friendly, informal ½ -acre cottage garden with herbaceous, mixed planting, climbers and mature trees. Features incl large wildlife pond with jetty, wildlife meadow, kitchen garden, orchard, hens and butterfly rearing cage. Well stocked and varied planting ensures something for everyone - white border, hot bed, spring border, bog garden, Japanese area and prairie planting.

> Curvy and arty with varieties of clematis, picturesque pergola with wisteria . . . the bees love it, we hope you will love it too! . . .

28 FREE GREEN FARM
Free Green Lane, Lower Peover WA16 9QX. Sir Philip & Lady Haworth. *3m S of Knutsford. Free Green Lane connects A50 with B5081. From Holmes Chapel on A50 turn L after Drovers Arms. From Knutsford on B5081 turn L into Broom Lane, then L into Free Green Lane.* Home-made teas. **Adm £4, chd free. Sun 5 June (2-5.30).**
2-acre garden with pleached limes, herbaceous borders, ponds, parterre; collection of hebes, garden of the senses and British woodland. Collection of ferns. Topiary.

GAMESLEY FOLD COTTAGE
See Derbyshire.

29 GLYNLEIGH
Withinlee Road, Prestbury SK10 4AU. Mr & Mrs C Hamilton. *3m NW of Macclesfield. Take A538 from Wilmslow to Prestbury pass Bulls Head on R, after 1m turn R into Withinlee Rd. From Prestbury follow A538 towards Wilmslow, turn L after top of Castle Hill into Withinlee Rd.* **Adm £5, chd free (share to Friends of Prestbury). Sun 22 May (1-5.30).**
Unique garden designed to create views through the use of a wide variety of unusual planting combinations. Hundreds of mature and recent plantings of rhododendrons and spring-flowering shrubs, trees and groundcovers make this garden strikingly colourful and inspiring. A deep water pond, rockery, rhododendron cone and pergola give added interest.

30 GRAFTON LODGE
Tilston, Malpas SY14 7JE. Simon Carter & Derren Gilhooley, 01829 250670, simoncar@aol.com. *12m S of Chester. A41 S from Chester turning towards Wrexham onto A534 at Broxton r'about. Past Carden Park Hotel & turn L at Cock-a-Barton PH towards Stretton & Tilston. Through Stretton, garden on R before reaching Tilston.* Home-made teas (Sun). wine (Fri). **Adm £4, chd free. Sun 12 June (12-6); Evening Opening wine, Fri 17 June (5-8.30). Visitors also welcome by appt.**
Vibrantly colourful garden of 2 acres crammed with herbaceous plants, shrubs and roses. There are lawns, natural and formal ponds, specimen trees, mixed hedges and garden rooms incl herb garden, standard rose circle, large pergola with sprawling roses and climbers, herbaceous beds, perfumed gazebo, roof terrace with far reaching views.

31 GREENWAYS
82 Knutsford Road, Alderley Edge SK9 7SF. Jenny & Roger Lloyd, 01625 583488. *1m W of Alderley Edge. 1m from Alderley Edge & Wilmslow on B5085 to Knutsford. Close to Chorley Village Hall. Parking at Village Hall. Disabled parking at house.* Home-made teas. **Adm £3.50, chd free. Sat 16, Sun 17 July (2-5). Visitors also welcome by appt May & Aug.**
A garden for plant enthusiasts. A personal collection of unusual and

familiar perennials and shrubs set in 1½ acres, displaying a diversity of planting styles in a range of growing conditions. New plants and beds for 2011. Also, view by appointment for Spring splendour in May and Summer's last hurrah in August. Unfenced pools.

& ❀ ☕ ☎

32 ◆ HARE HILL GARDENS
Over Alderley SK10 4QB. National Trust, www.nationaltrust.org.uk. *2m E of Alderley Edge. Between Alderley Edge & Prestbury. Turn off N at B5087 at Greyhound Rd.* **Adm £3.60, chd £1.80. For NGS: Sun 8 May (10-5). For other opening times and information, see garden website.**
Attractive spring garden featuring a fine display of rhododendrons and azaleas; good collection of hollies and other specimen trees and shrubs. 10-acre garden incl a walled garden which hosts many wall shrubs incl clematis and vines; borders are planted with agapanthus and geraniums. Partially suitable for wheelchairs.

&

Country lane walk, wildflower area with young fruit trees . . .

33 HAUGHTON HALL
Hall Lane, Haughton, Bunbury, Tarporley CW6 9RH. Mr & Mrs Phillip Posnett. *6m SE of Tarporley. Via A49 to Whitchurch & 5m SE of Nantwich off A534 Nantwich to Wrexham rd.* Home-made teas. **Adm £5, chd £2.50. Sun 1 May (2-5).**
Large garden currently being restored. Interesting collection of trees, recently planted borders leading down to lake. Fantastic display of azaleas and rhododendrons. Gravel paths, some steep slopes and cobbles.

& 🐕 ❀ ☕

34 HENBURY HALL
Macclesfield SK11 9PJ. Sebastian de Ferranti Esq. *2m W of Macclesfield. On A537. Turn down School Lane Henbury at Blacksmiths Arms. East Lodge on R.* Home-made teas. **Adm £6, chd free. Sun 15 May (2-5).**
Large garden with lake, beautifully landscaped and full of variety. Azaleas, rhododendrons, flowering shrubs, rare trees and herbaceous borders.

& ❀ ☕

35 35 HEYES LANE
Timperley, Altrincham WA15 6EF. Mr & Mrs David Eastwood. *1½ m NE of Altrincham. Heyes Lane, turning off Park Rd (B5165) 1m from junction with A56 Altrincham-Manchester rd. Or from A560 turn W in Timperley Village for ¼ m. Newsagents shop on corner.* Tea/coffee & biscuits. **Adm £3, chd free. Sun 8 May (2-5).**
Small mature suburban garden 30' x 90' on sandy soil, maintained by a keen plantswoman member of the Organic Movement. Improved accessibility with several changes to this yr-round garden; incl tree haven for birds and new plantings, trees; small pond; greenhouses; many kinds of fruit with a good collection of interesting and unusual plants. A true plantspersons garden with many environmentally friendly features incl wildlife havens, media interest. Dogs on leads. Featured in local press. Partial wheelchair access.

& 🐕 ❀ ☕

HIGH ROOST
See Derbyshire.

36 73 HILL TOP AVENUE
Cheadle Hulme SK8 7HZ. Mr & Mrs Martin Land, 0161 486 0055. *4m S of Stockport. Turn off A34 (new bypass) at r'about signed Cheadle Hulme (B5094). Take 2nd turn L into Gillbent Rd, signed Cheadle Hulme Sports Centre. Go to end, small r'about, turn R into Church Rd. 2nd rd on L is Hill Top Ave. From Stockport or Bramhall turn R or L into Church Rd by The Church Inn. Hill Top Ave is 1st rd on R.* Home-made teas. **Adm £3, chd free (share to Arthritis Research UK). Evening Opening wine, Thur 2 June (5.30-8); Suns 10 July; 14 Aug (2-6). Visitors also welcome by appt, 4+**
⅙ -acre plantswoman's garden. Well stocked with a wide range of sun-

loving herbaceous plants, shrub and climbing roses, many clematis varieties, pond and damp area, shade-loving woodland plants and small unusual trees, in an originally designed, long narrow garden.

🐕 ❀ ☕ ☎

37 HILLSIDE
Mill Lane, Mobberley WA16 7HY. Paul Hales & Mark Rubery. *2m E of Knutsford. Entrance off Mill Lane, next door to Roebuck Inn. Roebuck is sign posted off Mobberley Rd.* Home-made teas. **Adm £5, chd £2 (share to Blackbrook Zoological Park). Sun 29, Mon 30 May; Sat 13, Sun 14 Aug (11-5).**
A magnificent 6 acre garden home to a huge collection of rare birds incl 90 flamingos. The various ponds are adorned with delightful palms trees, tree ferns, bonsais, agaves and citrus trees. On the opposite side is a woodland setting that features a large, delightful waterfall surrounded by many mature plants and trees. Featured in In Cheshire magazine, Knutsford Guardian, Wilmslow Express.

☕

38 HILLSIDE COTTAGE
Shrigley Road, Pott Shrigley SK10 5SG. Anne & Phil Geoghegan, 01625 572214, annegeoghegan@btinternet.com. *6m N of Macclesfield. On A523. At Legh Arms T-lights turn into Brookledge Lane signed Pott Shrigley. After 1½ m signed Shrigley Hall turn L signed Higher Poynton. After 1m turn R at Methodist Chapel. Parking with short walk to garden.* Home-made teas. **Adm £3.50, chd free. Sun 26 June (2-6); Evening Openings wine, Thur 4 Aug (6-8.30); Fri 5 Aug (6-8). Visitors also welcome by appt July/August.**
Set on a hillside, ¼ -acre garden with panoramic vistas, over the treetops of the Cheshire Plain and beyond. Filled with colour, texture and the scent of roses. Landscaped on several levels with a wide variety of shrubs, small trees and 'cottage garden' perennials. Water features and walled patio garden with container planting. Wheelchair access to main areas only.

& ❀ ☕ ☎

39 NEW HILLTOP
Flash Lane, Prestbury SK10 4ED.
Martin & Clare Gardner, 07768
337525,
martin@shutterspeed.demon.co.uk,
www.hilltopcountryhouse.co.uk.
*2m N of Macclesfield. A523 to
Stockport. Turn R at B5090 r'about
signed Bollington, after 1/2 m turn L at
Cock & Pheasant PH into Flash Lane.
At bottom of lane turn R into cul de
sac. Hilltop Country House signed on
R.* Home-made teas. **Adm £4, chd
free. Sun 14 Aug (1.30-5.30).
Visitors also welcome by appt.**
Interesting country garden of approx
4 acres. Woodland walk, parterre,
2 kitchen gardens with herbs,
herbaceous borders, dry stone walled
terracing, lily ponds with waterfall.
Many paths, arches, gateways and
steps to explore. Wisteria clad 1693
house (not open). Mature trees,
orchard, magnificent views to
Pennines and to West. Featured in
Mail on Sunday. Partial wheelchair
access.
 ♿ 🛏 ☕ ☎

40 NEW 10 HUDSON CLOSE
Old Hall, Warrington WA5 9PY. Bill
&Tina Bennell. *3/4 m N of central
Warrington. From Warrington town
centre follow signs for A57 (Sankey
Way) towards Liverpool. At T-lights
turn R onto A574 (Cromwell Ave). At
2nd r'about turn R into Old Hall Road,
then follow signs.* Home-made teas.
**Adm £3, chd free. Sat 16, Sun 17
July (1-5).**
Three year old NW-facing garden
which uses an unusual modern
design to deliver a surprisingly well
stocked garden in 85' x 40' feet of
space. Still evolving, the main features
incl wide herbaceous borders, curved
deck with pergola, raised pond with
water feature, vegetable garden and
small greenhouse. Live piano music
(twice daily) weather permitting.
 ♿ ☕

41 NEW HUNTERS CROFT
Wilmslow Road, Mottram St
Andrew SK10 4QH. Len & Mary
Beth Morris. *3m SE of Wilmslow.
Located on A538, Wilmslow Rd,
between Wilmslow & Prestbury. 1/2 m
from Osteria PH as you drive towards
Prestbury. Parking on L.* Home-made
teas. **Adm £3.50, chd free. Sat 9,
Sun 10 July (1-5).**
1 1/2 acres of undulating lawns and
ever changing borders from traditional
herbaceous, architectural,
rhododendrons and azaleas

surrounding a summerhouse.
Rockery with mature acers and pond
with bog garden. Small woodland,
beech and holly hedges with
pleached lime trees. Topiary.
Greenhouse with vegetable beds and
herb garden. Lovely views.
☕

Dry stone walled terracing, lily ponds with waterfall. Many paths, arches, gateways and steps to explore . . .

42 INGLEWOOD
4 Birchmere, Heswall CH60 6TN.
Colin & Sandra Fairclough,
01513 424645,
www.inglewoodngs.giving.officeliv
e.com. *6m S Birkenhead. From A540
Devon Doorway/Clegg Arms r'about
go through Heswall. 1/4 m after
Tesco's, R into Quarry Rd East, 2nd L
into Tower Rd North & L into
Birchmere.* Home-made teas. **Adm
£3.50, chd free. Sat 7, Sun 8 May
(1-5). Visitors also welcome by
appt.**
First spring opening of 1/2 acre
garden. Stream, large koi pond,
'beach' with succulents and grasses,
wildlife pond and bog area. Brimming
with spring bulbs, acers, conifers,
rhododendrons, azaleas, and
woodland plants. Interesting features
include hand cart, antique mangle,
wood carving & Indian dog gates
leading to secret herbaceous garden.
Featured in Amateur Gardening as the
Reader's Garden.
 ♿ ❀ ☕ ☎

43 84 IRBY ROAD
Heswall CH61 6XG. Gill Edwards.
*1m N of Heswall. Enter Heswall on
A540 travelling N. Turn R at main T-
lights (Lloyd's Bank on L). In 3/4 m
note Harvest Mouse PH on R, turn L
just past this. 84 is 1/4 m up Irby Rd
on R. Large copper beech in garden.*
Home-made teas. **Adm £3.50, chd
free. Sat 21, Sun 22 May (2-5).**
1/3 acre secluded garden, trees,
azaleas, rhododendrons, camellias,

herbaceous, herbs. Two ponds, one
natural, one formal, not quite fully
established. Small patio, secluded
seating, clematis-clad trellis. New
potager (ornamental vegetable plot)
with raised beds, paths. Planting incl
soft fruit, globe and Jerusalem
artichokes, intermingled with flowering
plants. Design of garden invites
exploration, with lovely curving lines.
🐞 ❀ ☕

44 NEW 4 KESWICK ROAD
High Lane, Stockport SK6 8AP.
John & Brenda Waterworth. *4m SE
Stockport. From Stockport, along A6
towards Buxton. At High Lane, turn L
at Horseshoe PH T-lights onto
Windlehurst rd. Take 3rd R into
Keswick Rd.* Home-made teas. **Adm
£3, chd free. Sat 30, Sun 31 July
(1-5).**
A colourful small garden with a
backdrop of tall mature trees. Lawns,
well stocked herbaceous borders incl
shrubs, bamboo and grasses.
Rockery and patio leading to a
descending terraced area, with steps
to a natural stream and specialised
planting for dry and damp, tree-
shaded areas.
❀ ☕

45 NEW LANE END FARM
Leadgate Lane, Huxley, nr Chester
CH3 9BT. Tim & Kate Rayner. *4m
SW of Tarporley. From A51
Tarvin/Tarporley rd, take Corkscrew
Lane, turn adjacent to Bulls Head PH
in Clotton. Continue to T-junction, turn
R then take 1st L into Leadgate Lane
follow signs to garden.* Home-made
teas. **Adm £4, chd free. Sat 13, Sun
14 Aug (2-5.30).**
Approx 1 acre developed over 6yrs.
A garden of 'rooms' designed to
show examples of prairie style
planting, colour-themed borders,
contemporary box garden,
ornamental grasses, 'hot tub' and
vegetable garden. Plentiful seating
with individual views. Maturing yew
hedges divide rooms. Informal
meadow style planting with young
trees surrounds children's area.
 ♿ ☕

46 LEAWOOD
off Longhurst Lane, Marple Bridge
SK6 5AE. John & Mary Hartley. *4m
E Stockport. A626 to Marple - Marple
Bridge, through village, signed Mellor.
100yds on L from car park.* Cream
teas. **Adm £3, chd free. Sat 21, Sun
22 May (11-4).**
*3/4 -acre hidden woodland garden

facing E-W surrounded by trout stream. Large lawns and flower beds of mixed planting giving rise to panoramic view of hillside with rhododendrons, azaleas and camellias. Terraced paths pass small spring fed ponds and wildlife areas of bluebells and unusual shade loving plants. Bird boxes and owl boxes with cameras. Featured in BBC - Owls & Ducklings.

An ever increasing collection of modern ceramics and a most productive vegetable garden in tubs and baskets. Children's discovery trail and craft activity : . . .

47 ◆ **LITTLE MORETON HALL**
Congleton CW12 4SD. National Trust, 01270 272018, www.nationaltrust.org.uk. *4m S of Congleton.* On A34. Adm £7.40, chd £3.70. For NGS: Sat 16 July (11-5). For other opening times and information, please phone or see garden website.
1½-acre garden surrounded by a moat, next to finest example of timber-framed architecture in England. Herb and historic vegetable garden, orchard and borders. Knot garden. Adm incl entry to the Hall with optional free guided tours. Wheelchairs available, ground floor and garden only. Picnic lawn at front of hall.

48 **LONG ACRE**
Wyche Lane, Bunbury CW6 9PS. Margaret & Michael Bourne, 01829 260944, mjbourne249@tiscali.co.uk. *3½ m SE of Tarporley.* On A49. Turn 2nd L after Wild Boar Hotel to Bunbury. L at 1st rd junction then 1st R by Nags Head PH 400yds on L. From A51 turn

to Bunbury until Nags Head. Turn into Wyche Lane before PH car park. 400yds to garden. Disabled parking in lane adjacent to garden. Home-made teas. Adm £4, chd free (share to Guide Dogs for the Blind & St Boniface Church Flower Fund). Sun 24 Apr; Sun 19 June (2-5). Visitors also welcome by appt groups of 10+.
Plantswoman's garden of approx 1 acre with unusual plants and trees. Roses, pool gardens, small vineyard. Exotic conservatory, herbaceous, specialise in proteas, S African bulbs, clivia and streptocarpus. Spring garden with camellias, magnolias, bulbs.

49 ◆ **LYME PARK**
Disley SK12 2NX. National Trust, 01663 762023, www.nationaltrust.org,uk *6m SE of Stockport. Just W of Disley on A6.* Adm £6, chd £3. For NGS: Sun 7 Aug (11-5). For other opening times and information, please phone or see garden website.
17-acre garden retaining many original features from Tudor and Jacobean times. High Victorian style bedding, Dutch garden, Gertrude Jekyll style herbaceous border, Edwardian rose garden, Wyatt orangery and many other features. Also rare trees, lake, ravine garden, lawns, mixed borders and rare Wyatt garden.

50 **MANLEY KNOLL**
Manley Road, Manley WA6 9DX. Mr & Mrs R Fildes. *3m N of Tarvin. On B5393, via Ashton & Mouldsworth. 3m S of Frodsham, via Alvanley.* Home-made teas. Adm £3.50, chd free. Sun 22 May (2-5). Terraced garden with rhododendrons, azaleas etc. Quarry garden with waterfalls and an air of mystery. Far reaching views over Cheshire Plain.

51 **MAYFIELD**
The Peppers, Lymm WA13 0JA. Janet Bashforth, 01925 756107, janetbashforth@talktalk.net. *4m from J7 M56 or 2m J21 M6. In Lymm village turn by Lloyds TSB Bank into Pepper St. Follow NGS signs, take 2nd R leading into The Peppers.* Home-made teas. Adm £3, chd free. Visitors welcome by appt groups welcome.

Constantly evolving plantswoman's garden, approx ⅓ acre. Dry shade area set under mature trees. Colourful mixed borders containing herbaceous perennials and shrubs with a wonderful display of tulips in Apr/May. Front garden has large number of grasses, and vibrant perennial border. Interesting structures and features throughout.

52 **MILLPOOL**
Smithy Lane, Bosley SK11 0NZ. Joe & Barbara Fray, 01260 226581. *5m S of Macclesfield. Just off A523 at Bosley. Turn L 1m S of A54 T-lights. From Leek, turn R, 2½ m N of The Royal Oak PH at Rushton. Please follow direction to parking areas. No parking at garden.* Light refreshments & teas. Adm £3, chd free. Sat 25, Sun 26 June (1-5). Visitors also welcome by appt June to Aug, groups 10-40, coaches permitted.
Garden designed to extend the seasons with colour, texture and scent. Lush herbaceous borders and areas of deep shade. Small stream, pond and bog garden. Gravel plantings, containers and a fine collection of bonsai trees. An ever increasing collection of modern ceramics and a most productive vegetable garden in tubs and baskets. Children's discovery trail and craft activity.

MOSS COTTAGE
See Staffordshire Birmingham & part of West Midlands.

53 **THE MOUNT**
Andertons Lane, Whirley, Henbury, nr Macclesfield SK11 9PB. Nicholas Payne, 01625 422920, ngs@themount1.freeserve.co.uk. *2m due W of Macclesfield. Along A537 opp Blacksmiths Arms. At Henbury go up Pepper St. Turn L into Church Lane then Andertons Lane in 100yds.* Home-made teas. Adm £5, chd free. Sat 28, Sun 29 May (2-5.30). Visitors also welcome by appt.
Approx 2 acres with interesting trees incl *Eucryphia x nymansensis,* fern leaved beech and *Sciadopitys.* Shrubberies, herbaceous border and short vista of Irish yews. Water features and landscaped swimming pool. Far views to Wales.

54 ◆ MOUNT PLEASANT

Yeld Lane, Kelsall CW6 0TB. Dave Darlington & Louise Worthington, 01829 751592, www.mountpleasantgardens.co.uk. *8m E of Chester. Off A54 at T-lights into Kelsall. Turn into Yeld Lane opp Farmers Arms PH, 200yds on L. Do not follow Sat Nav directions.* **For opening times and information please phone or see garden website.**

10 acres of landscaped garden and woodland started in 1994 with impressive views over the Cheshire countryside. Steeply terraced in places. Specimen trees, rhododendrons, azaleas, conifers, mixed and herbaceous borders; 4 ponds, formal and wildlife. Vegetable garden, stumpery with tree ferns, sculptures, wild flower meadow and Japanese garden. Bog garden, tropical garden. September Sculpture Exhibition.

✿

55 ◆ NESS BOTANIC GARDENS

Ness, Neston CH64 4AY. The University of Liverpool, 0151 3530123, www.nessgardens.org.uk. *10 NW of Chester. Off A540. M53 J4, follow signs M56 & A5117 (signed N Wales). Turn onto A540 follow signs for Hoylake..* **For NGS: Sat 12 Feb (10-5); 2012 Sat 18 Feb. For other opening times, admission and information, please phone or see garden website.**

Gardens cover some 64 acres, having a distinctly maritime feel and housing The National Collection of (Sorbus) Mountain Ash. Among some of the significant specimens that still flourish in the gardens are Pieris Forrestii which was collected for Bulley by George Forrest in Yunnan. Mobility scooters avaiable FOC - call for advance booking.

&. ✿ NCCPG ☕

56 ◆ NORTON PRIORY MUSEUM & GARDENS

Tudor Road, Runcorn WA7 1SX. Norton Priory Museum Trust, 01928 569895, www.nortonpriory.org. *2m SE of Runcorn. From M56 J11 turn for Warrington & follow signs. From Warrington take A56 for Runcorn & follow signs, cross Widnes/Runcorn Bridge going S & follow signs.* **Normal adm prices apply. For NGS: Sun 15 May (12-4). For other opening times and information, please phone or see garden website.**

Tatton Park

40 acres of gardens and grounds, 2½-acre Georgian Walled Garden, summerhouses, rock garden and stream glade, rosewalk, colour borders, medieval herb and cottage gardens. Home to the National Collection of Tree Quince, (Cydonia Oblonga). Also including historic Pear orchard and wild flower meadow. John Budworth, our Head Gardener will lead a guided tour of our beautiful quince trees in blossom 2pm - 3pm. Featured in The Telegraph and Kitchen Garden Magazine.

&. ✿ NCCPG

57 ◆ THE OLD HOUGH

Forge Mill Lane, Warmingham CW10 0HQ. Mr & Mrs D S Varey, 01270 526232, jdm@oldhough.co.uk. *3m from Middlewich. 4m from Sandbach. From Middlewich take A530 to Nantwich. At Wimboldsley School turn L to Warmingham L again at* T-junction. Garden ½ m on R. From Sandbach take A533 to Middlewich, ½ m after Fox Inn on L turn into Mill Lane. At T-junction on canal bridge turn R. Stay on this rd. Garden 2m on. Ample parking. **Adm £4, chd free. Evening Openings wine, Thurs 9, 16, 23, 30 June (5.30-9). Visitors also welcome by appt June only, coaches permitted.**

2 acres surrounding rose-covered period house (not open). Double herbaceous borders, wildlife pool with fish and moorhens, sweeping lawns with trees chosen for their bark. Woodland border. Long raised mixed border, clematis, rose garden with rill and pond, ferns and hostas shaded by paulownias. Two black hounds appraise the visitors, naked maidens guard the rill. Some cobbles, small gravelled area, 3 steps at end of route, but can retrace.

&. ✿ ☎

You are always welcome at an NGS garden

58 ▶ THE OLD PARSONAGE

Arley Green, via Arley Hall & Gardens CW9 6LZ. The Viscount & Viscountess Ashbrook, 01565 777277, www.arleyhallandgardens.com. *5m NNE of Northwich. 3m Great Budworth. M6 J19 & 20 & M56 J10. Follow signs to Arley Hall & Gardens. From Arley Hall notices to Old Parsonage which lies across park at Arley Green.* Light refreshments & cream teas. **Adm £4.50, chd free** (share to Save The Children Fund). **Sat 21, Sun 22 May (2-5.30). Visitors also welcome by appt May to July, groups of 6+, coaches permitted.**

2-acre garden in attractive and secretive rural setting in secluded part of Arley Estate, with ancient yew hedges, herbaceous and mixed borders, shrub roses, climbers, leading to woodland garden and unfenced pond with gunnera and water plants. Rhododendrons, azaleas, meconopsis, cardiocrinums, some interesting and unusual trees. Sculpture exhibition at adjoing Arley Hall and Gardens. Wheelchair access over mown grass.

  ♿ 🏠 ✿ ☕ ☎

59 ▶ ONE HOUSE NURSERY

Rainow SK11 0AD. Louise Baylis, www.onehousenursery.co.uk. *2¹/₂ m NE of Macclesfield. On A537 Macclesfield to Buxton rd. 2¹/₂ m from Macclesfield stn.* Home-made teas. **Adm £3, chd free. Sun 8 May (10-5).**

¹/₂ -acre plantswoman's garden featuring hostas, rare and unusual woodland and sun-loving perennials, rockery, gravel garden, sculptures and hornbeam arbour. Stunning views over Cheshire Plain. A short walk away is an atmospheric ¹/₃ -acre historic early C18 walled kitchen garden, hidden for 60yrs and recently restored. Heritage vegetables, gardening and farming bygones, orchard with rare-breed pigs. Sculpture trail and bluebell wood walk.

  ✿ 🏬 ☕

60 ▶ ORCHARD VILLA

72 Audley Road, Alsager ST7 2QN. Mr & Mrs J Trinder, 01270 874833, johntrinder@btinternet.com. *6m S of Congleton. 3m W of Kidsgrove. At T-lights in Alsager town centre turn L towards Audley, house is 300yds on R beyond level Xing. Or M6 J16 to North Stoke on A500, 1st L to*

Alsager, 2m, just beyond Manor House Hotel on L. Home-made teas. **Adm £3, chd free. Sun 15 May (1.30-5.30). Visitors also welcome by appt May to end of Sept.**

The scent of Azara leads past raised beds of phlox,and other alpines. 20ft Clematis montans overlooks a wealth of unfolding ferns, cottage garden plants, camassias, late tulips and early iris. Finally the winding path leads to vegetable and fruit plots. All plants for sale are grown in the garden. Featured in Popular Gardening.

  ♿ ✿ ☕ ☎

61 ▶ 39 OSBORNE STREET

Bredbury, Stockport SK6 2DA. Geoff & Heather Hoyle, geoff.hoyle@btinternet.com. *1¹/₂ m E of Stockport. Osborne St is off Stockport Rd West (B6104), approx 1m from M60. Leave M60 at J27 (from S & W) or J25 (from N & E). Follow signs for Lower Bredbury &/ or Bredbury Hall. Osborne St is adjacent to pelican Xing on B6104. No 39 is across from local shops.* Light refreshments & teas. **Adm £3, chd free. Sat 3, Sun 4 Sept (1-5). Visitors also welcome by appt up to mid-Sept.**

This dahliaholic's garden contains over 300 dahlias in 150+ varieties, mostly of exhibition standard. Shapely lawns are surrounded by deep flower beds that are crammed with dahlias of all shapes, sizes and colours, and complemented by climbers, soft perennials and bedding plants. An absolute riot of early autumn colour. Featured in Amateur Gardening.

  ☕ ☎

62 ▶ PARM PLACE

High Street, Great Budworth CW9 6HF. Peter & Jane Fairclough, 01606 891131, janefair@btinternet.com. *3m N of Northwich. Great Budworth on E side of A559 between Northwich & Warrington, 4m from J10 M56, also 4m from J19 M6. Parm Place is W of village on S side of High Street.* Home-made teas. **Adm £4, chd free** (share to Great Ormond Street Hospital). **Sun 3 Apr; Sun 10 July (1-5). Visitors also welcome by appt.**

Well-stocked ¹/₂ -acre plantswoman's garden with stunning views towards S Cheshire. Immaculate curving lawns, shrubs, colour co-ordinated herbaceous borders, roses, water features, rockery, gravel bed with

grasses. Fruit and vegetable plots. In spring large collection of bulbs and flowers, camellias, hellebores and blossom. A treat in store. Featured in Amateur Gardener.

  ♿ ✿ ☕ ☎

63 ▶ ◆ PEOVER HALL GARDENS

Knutsford WA16 6SW. Randle Brooks Esq. *4m S of Knutsford. Turn off A50 at Whipping Stocks Inn, down Stocks Lane. Follow signs to Peover Hall & Church. Entrance off Goostrey Lane clearly signed.* Light refreshments. **Adm £4, chd free. For NGS: Sat 14, Sun 15 May (2-5). For other opening times and information, please phone or see garden website.**

15 acres. 5 walled gardens; C19 dell, rhododendrons, pleached limes, topiary. Grade II Carolean Stables and C18 park.

  ☕

An atmospheric ¹/₃ -acre historic early C18 walled kitchen garden, hidden for 60 years and recently restored . . .

ALLOTMENTS

64 ▶ PLYMYARD HALL ALLOTMENTS

Bridle Road, Eastham CH62 8BN. Glenn Grant. *6m SE of Birkenhead. From A41 turn into Allport Rd towards Bromborough Station. ¹/₄ m turn L at T-lights into Bridle Rd. L next to Treetops Surgery.* Home-made teas. **Adm £3, chd free. Sun 19 June (2-5).**

Allotments are sited on an area previously used as the gardens of a large house with ha-ha and specimen trees still to be seen. The allotments are well tended, with a variety of vegetables, fruit and flowers on show set against the backdrop of towering trees and pleasant surroundings. A short history of the site, and information on points of interest is available on entry to the site.

  ♿ ✿ ☕

17 POPLAR GROVE
Sale M33 3AX. Mr Gordon Cooke,
0161 969 9816,
gordoncooke.ceramics@virgin.net.
*3m N of Altrincham. From the A6144
at Brooklands stn turn into Hope Rd.
Poplar Grove 3rd on R.* Home-made
teas at The Conservatory. **Adm
£3.50, chd free. Sat 18, Sun 19
June (2-5).** Visitors also welcome
by appt through June.
'A rare synthesis of brilliant planting
and modern sculpture' (The Historic
Gardens of England - Cheshire Vol
2008). Features incl sculpture garden;
pebble mosaic 'cave', scented
garden and living roof. Many tender
and borderline plants thrive in this city
microclimate such as lochroma
australis, Desfontania spinosa and
Vestia foetida'. Garden Ceramics
Exhibition.

66 **POULTON HALL**
Poulton Lancelyn, Bebington
CH63 9LN. The Lancelyn Green
Family, 0151 3342057,
www.poultonhall.co.uk. *2m S of
Bebington. From M53, J4 towards
Bebington; at T-lights R along Poulton
Rd; house 1m on R.* Cream Teas. (Sat
catering by St. John's Hospice). **Adm
£4, chd free. Sat 16, Sun 17 Apr
(2-5.30).** Visitors also welcome by
appt.
3 acres; lawns fronting house, wild
flower meadow. A surprising
approach to the walled garden,with
reminders of Roger Lancelyn Green's
retellings, Excalibur, Robin Hood and
Jabberwocky. Scented sundial
garden for the visually impaired.
Memorial sculpture for Richard
Lancelyn Green by Sue Sharples.
Rose, Nursery rhyme, Witch. Herb,
Oriental gardens. Completely
replanted centre of garden - white
beds, waves of lavender.Art displays
and music recital at 4.p.m. Featured
in local newspaper.

67 ◆ **QUARRY BANK HOUSE
GARDEN**
Quarry Bank Road, Styal SK9 4LA.
National Trust, 0791 755 0425,
www.nationaltrust.org.uk. *2m N of
Wilmslow. Follow NT signs.* **Adm £5,
chd £2.50. For NGS: Sat 7 May
(11-4).** For other opening times and
information, please phone or see
garden website.
A 'picturesque' valley garden created
in the 1790s by cotton mill owner
Samuel Greg. The garden is mainly a
spring garden, with many fine azaleas
and rhododendrons. Some
rhododendrons are unique to the
garden having been commissioned
and introduced by the Greg family
during C19.

68 ◆ **THE QUINTA
ARBORETUM**
Swettenham CW12 2LD. Tatton
Garden Society, 01477 537698
(answerphone),
www.tattongardensociety.co.uk.
*Turn off A54 N 2m W of Congleton or
turn E off A535 at Twemlow Green,
NE of Holmes Chapel. Follow signs to
Swettenham. Park at Swettenham
Arms PH. Entrance at side of PH
through picnic area.* **Adm £4.50, chd
free. For NGS: Sun 9 Oct (12-4).**
For other opening times and
information, please phone or see
garden website.
The 28-acre arboretum has been
established since 1960s and contains
around 10,000 trees and shrubs of
over 2,000 species, some very rare.
Incl National Collections of Pinus and
Fraxinus, large collection of oak, a
collection of hebes and autumn
flowering shrubs. A lake and waymarked walks. A guided tour at 2pm
is incl.
NCCPG

69 **RIDGEHILL**
Ridgehill, Sutton SK11 0LU. Mr &
Mrs Martin McMillan. *2m SE of
Macclesfield. From Macclesfield take
A523 to Leek. After Silk Rd look for
T-lights signed Langley, Wincle &
Sutton. Turn L into Byron's Lane,
under canal bridge, 1st L to Langley
at junction Church House PH.
Ridgehill Rd is opp turn up Ridgehill
Rd, garden on R.* Light refreshments
& home-made teas. **Adm £5, chd
free. Sun 19 June (10-4.30).**
Country garden set in 4 acres
overlooking the Cheshire Plain. Ponds
and water features, shrubbery with
rhododendrons, azaleas, camellias
etc. Herbaceous borders, winter
gardens, topiary areas, walled cottage
garden.

70 **RIVERSIDE LODGE**
19 Oldfield Road, Heswall
CH60 6SN. Tim & Margaret
Ransome. *7m S Birkenhead. From
Devon Doorway/Glegg Arms r'about
go N on Telegraph Rd for 1¹/₂ m. Turn
L at Quarry Rd West. Garden in
Oldfield Rd facing junction with
Quarry Rd West.* Cream Teas.
**Adm £3.50, chd free. Sun 15 May
(1-4.30).**
³/₄ -acre garden set in mature trees
and shrubs. Spectacular stonework
terracing with views to Welsh Hills,
reflecting pool, gazebo, herbaceous
and mixed planting, gravel area and
rose arches. The front garden has
been redesigned by the garden
owners and features a Westmorland
Green Slate water feature.

*A surprising
approach to the
walled garden,with
reminders of Roger
Lancelyn Green's
retellings, Excalibur,
Robin Hood and
Jabberwocky . . .*

71 ◆ **RODE HALL**
Church Lane, Scholar Green
ST7 3QP. Sir Richard & Lady Baker
Wilbraham, 01270 873237,
www.rodehall.co.uk. *5m SW of
Congleton. Between Scholar Green
(A34) & Rode Heath (A50).* **Adm £4,
chd free, concessions £3.** For other
opening times and information,
please phone or see garden
website.
Nesfield's terrace and rose garden
with view over Humphry Repton's
landscape is a feature of Rode
gardens, as is the woodland garden
with terraced rock garden and grotto.
Other attractions incl the walk to the
lake, restored ice house, working
walled kitchen garden and new Italian
garden. Fine display of snowdrops in
February. Open Sat 29 Jan to Sun 13
Mar daily (except Mondays).

72 **ROSEWOOD**
Puddington Village, Neston
CH64 5SS. Mr & Mrs C E J Brabin,
0151 353 1193,
angela.brabin@btinternet.com. *6m
N of Chester. Turn L (W) off Chester
to Hoylake A540 to Puddington. Park
by village green. Walk to Old Hall
Lane, 30yds away then through
archway on L to garden. Owner will
meet you at green by appt.* **Adm £3,**

chd free. **Visitors welcome by appt, groups welcome.**
All yr garden; thousands of snowdrops in Feb, camellias in autumn, winter and spring. Rhododendrons in April/May and unusual flowering trees from March to June. Autumn cyclamen in quantity from Aug to Nov. Perhaps the greatest delight to owner are two large Cornus capitata, flowering in June. Honey from hives in garden available most of year.

73 THE ROWANS
Oldcastle Lane, Threapwood
SY14 7AY. Paul Philpotts & Alan Bourne, 01948 770522. *3m SW of Malpas. Leave Malpas by B5069 for Wrexham, pass church on R, continue for 3m, take 1st L after Threapwood PO into Chapel Lane. L into Oldcastle Lane, garden 1st bungalow on R. Home-made teas.* **Adm £4, chd free (share to Hope House Childrens' Hospice). Sat 16, Sun 17 July (2-5.30). Visitors also welcome by appt June/July for groups 10+.**
This 1-acre award winning garden, has an Italianate theme. Divided into numerous formal and natural areas, in which to sit and enjoy the views and feature statuary. Many mature and unusual trees, several ponds, herbaceous borders, vegetable plots, greenhouse, extensive hosta collection, tranquil secret garden. Something of interest for every visitor.

74 SAIGHTON GRANGE
Saighton CH3 6EN. The Governors of Abbey Gate College, 01244 332077, alan.kift@abbeygatecollege.co.uk, www.abbeygatecollege.co.uk. *4m SE of Chester. Take A41 towards Whitchurch. At far end of Waverton turn R to Saighton. Grange is at the end of village. Home-made teas.* **Adm £3.50, chd free. Sun 10 Apr (1-4). Visitors also welcome by appt.**
The gardens at Abbey Gate College are a little masterpiece of garden design. From the symmetrical vista through the clipped yew hedges, which are undergoing restoration, to the Japanese garden, which is beginning to blossom, all provide a tantalising glimpse of what has been and what is yet to come. This garden is still in a fascinating process of restoration.

75 ST DAVIDS HOUSE
St Davids Lane, Noctorum CH43 9UD. Ian Mitchell, 0151 652 5236. *3¹/₂ m SW of Birkenhead Town Hall. Take A553 then A502 through Claughton Village. After 2 sets of T-lights, 1st L (Noctorum Lane). After Xrds, St Davids Lane is 1st on R.* **Adm £3.50, chd free. Visitors welcome by appt any time of year.**
Victorian garden of 1¹/₂ acres recently restored to original 1864 probable planting. Azaleas, camellias, rhododendrons, herbaceous and mixed borders, rockeries, pond, pine and silver birch copse with winding steep paths. Excellent views of Clwyd Hills, Snowdonia and Irish Sea.

76 SANDSEND
126 Hibbert Lane, Marple SK6 7NU. David & Audrey Bomford. *5m SE of Stockport. Leave M60 at J27. A626 to Marple R at Texaco garage, R at mini r'about into Hibbert Lane ¹/₂ m on R. Or A6 from Stockport via Hazel Grove to High Lane, L at Horseshoe PH into Windlehurst Rd 1³/₄ m towards Marple. Hibbert Lane starts at canal bridge on L 200yds past bridge. Home-made teas.* **Adm £3, chd free. Sat 21, Sun 22 May (1-5). Visitors also welcome by appt, 10 to 24 May only, please apply in writing.**
Long front and back gardens, all-yr round colour, designed for easy maintenance with raised beds, paths journey through shrubs, small trees, lawns and seats to view all aspects. Small pond, hostas, azaleas, rockeries and herbaceous. Sun and shade and abundant birdsong in surrounding mature trees. African craft sale in aid of Christian Relief Uganda.

Sun and shade and abundant birdsong in surrounding mature trees . . .

77 SANDYMERE
Cotebrook CW6 9EH. John & Alex Timpson. *5m N of Tarporley. On A54 about 300yds W of T-lights at Xrds of A49/A54. Light refreshments & teas.* **Adm £4.50, chd free. Sun 17 July (1.30-5).**
16 landscaped acres of beautiful Cheshire countryside with terraces, walled garden and amazing hosta garden. Long views, native wildlife and tranquillity of 3 lakes. Elegant planting schemes, shady seats and sun-splashed borders, mature pine woods and rolling lawns accented by graceful wooden structures. Different every year: witness the evolution of the garden that is now in its 21st yr. Kitchen garden with organically grown vegetables also extensive range of penstemon plants. Limited access for wheelchairs.

78 21 SCAFELL CLOSE
High Lane, Stockport SK6 8JA. Lesley & Dean Stafford, 01663 763015. *On A6 SE of Stockport. 2m past Rising Sun PH. At High Lane turn into Russell Ave opp Dog & Partridge PH, 2nd L to Kirkfell Drive & immed R onto Scafell Close, 21 on the R. Parking on L or to the end in turning circle. Home-made teas.* **Adm £3, chd free. Sat 30, Sun 31 July (2-5). Visitors also welcome by appt, dates around open weekend.**
¹/₃ acre landscaped suburban garden. Colour themed annuals border the lawn featuring the Kinder Ram statue in a heather garden, passing into vegetables, soft fruits and fruit trees. Returning perennial pathway leads to the fishpond and secret terraced garden with modern water feature and patio planting. Finally visit the blue front garden. Plants for sale, tea and cakes available. Partial wheelchair access.

79 THE SCHOOL HOUSE
School Lane, Dunham Massey WA14 4SE. Andrew Bushell & Peter White. *1¹/₂ m SW of Altrincham. From M56 J7 follow signs for Dunham Massey Hall (NT). Turn into Woodhouse Lane becoming School Lane 100yds after Axe Cleaver PH. Car park available from 1pm. Home-made teas.* **Adm £3, chd free. Sun 26 June (1-5).**
Cottage garden divided into rooms. In picturesque setting attached to village hall and beside the Bridgewater canal. Incl herbaceous borders, rose

and bog garden. History of Dunham Massey display in village hall. Walking distance to Dunham Hall (NT). Some gravel paths.

 ❀ ☕

 68 SOUTH OAK LANE
Wilmslow SK9 6AT. Caroline & David Melliar-Smith, 01625 528147, caroline.ms@btinternet.com. ³/₄ m SW of Central Wilmslow. From M56 (J6) take A528 towards Wilmslow, R into Buckingham Rd. From center Wilmslow turn R onto B5086 (Knutsford), 1st R into Gravel Lane, 4th R into South Oak Lane. Park by recreation ground. **Adm £3, chd free. Sat 9, Sun 10 July (11-5). Visitors also welcome by appt July & Aug.** With year round colour, scent and interest, this attractive, hedged cottage garden has evolved over the years into 5 natural 'rooms'. These Hardy Plant Society members passion for plants, reflected in shrubs, trees, flower borders and pond, creates havens for wildlife. Enjoy tranquillity and peace in this plant-packed garden. Fern Garden and Sculpture. Featured in Cheshire Life.

❀ ☎

SOUTHLANDS
See Lancashire Merseyside & Greater Manchester.

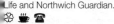 **SPRINGBANK**
670 London Road, Davenham CW9 8LG. Doug & Ann Welch, 01606 43416, doug.and.ann@sky.com. 2¹/₂ m S of Northwich. From Peckmill r'about at S end of Davenham Village on A533 Davenham By-pass take rd signed Davenham & Moulton. Garden on L approx 150yds. Home-made teas. **Adm £3.50, chd free. Sat 13, Sun 14 Aug (2-5). Visitors also welcome by appt.** Lovely interesting garden in ¹/₂ acre sheltered hollow with backdrop of mature trees and shrubs. Large colourful herbaceous border, other mixed borders, roses, pond, bog garden, grasses, hostas and much more. Long pergola with roses, clematis and honeysuckle. High level paths giving views of garden. Chain saw carvings. Featured in Cheshire Life and Northwich Guardian.

❀ ☕ ☎

 199 STOCKPORT ROAD
Timperley WA15 7SF. Eric & Shirley Robinson. 1¹/₂ m NE of Altrincham. Take A560 out of Altrincham, in 1m take B5165 towards Timperley. B5165 is Stockport rd. Home-made teas. **Adm £3, chd free. Sun 12 June; Sun 17 July (1-5).** Overstuffed cottage-style garden full of colourful herbaceous perennials, shrubs and hostas, with a new brick-built pond complete with small koi and goldfish. You will not believe how many plants there are in such a small garden. Small front garden with water feature and new for 2011 shaded plant area.

❀ ☕

♦ STONYFORD COTTAGE
Stonyford Lane, Oakmere CW8 2TF. Janet & Tony Overland, 01606 888128, www.stonyfordcottagegardens.co. uk. 5m SW of Northwich. Fom Northwich take A556 towards Chester. ³/₄ m past A49 junction turn R into Stonyford Lane. Entrance ¹/₂ m on L. Home-made teas on NGS days. **Adm £3.50, chd free. For NGS: Suns 5 June; 7 Aug (1.30-5).** For other opening times and information, please phone or see garden website.
Set around a tranquil pool this Monet style landscape has a wealth of moisture loving plants, incl iris and candelabra primulas. Drier areas feature unusual perennials and rarer trees and shrubs. Woodland paths meander through shade and bog plantings with views across the pool to the cottage gardens. Unusual plants available at the adjacent nursery. Some gravel paths. Open Tues - Sun & BH Mons Apr - Sept 10-5.

♿ ❀ ☕

TATTENHALL HALL
High Street, Tattenhall CH3 9PX. Jen & Nick Benefield, Chris Evered & Jannie Hollins, 01829 770692, jmhollins@hotmail.com - jenbenefield@supanet.com. 8m S of Chester on A41. Turn L to Tattenhall, through village, turn R at Letters PH, past war memorial on L through Sandstone pillared gates. Park on rd or in village car park. Home-made teas. **Adm £4, chd free. Evening Opening wine, Fri 27 May (6-9); Sun 29 May (2-5). Visitors also welcome by appt.**

West Drive Gardens

Plant enthusiasts garden around Jacobean house (not open). 4½ acres, wild flower meadows, interesting trees,large pond, stream, walled garden,colour themed herbaceous borders succession planting,spinney walk with shade plants, yew terrace overlooking meadow,views to hills. Glasshouse, vegetable garden. Wildlife friendly sometimes untidy garden, interest throughout the year. Plant sale of unusual plants. Gravel, grass, and cobble paths, steps and steep slopes.

85 ◆ TATTON PARK
Knutsford WA16 6QN. National Trust, leased to Cheshire East Council, 01625 374400, www.tattonpark.org.uk. *2½ m N of Knutsford. Well signed on M56 J7 & from M6 J19.* **For NGS: Weds 27 Apr; 8 June; 12 Oct (10-6).** For other opening times and information, please phone or see garden website. Features include orangery by Wyatt, fernery by Paxton, restored Japanese garden, Italian and rose gardens. Greek monument and African hut. Hybrid azaleas and rhododendrons; swamp cypresses, tree ferns, tall redwoods, bamboos and pines. Fully restored productive walled gardens.

86 THE VALVE HOUSE
Egerton Green SY14 8AW. Nicola Reynolds. *4m NE of Malpas. From Chester take A41 S, at Broxton r'about turn L onto A534, 1st R after Sandstone PH (to Bickerton). Fork L at Bickerton School. Garden 1st house L. On A49 turn opp Cholmondeley Arms to Cholmondeley Castle. Garden 3m on L.* Home-made teas. **Adm £4.50, chd free. Sat 11, Sun 12 June (2-5).**
½ -acre plantswoman's garden with many interesting features, well stocked herbaceous borders with, apart from many old favourites, an abundance of unusual plants, many of which we will be selling. Lavishly planted wildlife pond with Monet style bridge, productive vegetable and fruit gardens and a well stocked Victorian style conservatory.

WEEPING ASH
See Lancashire Merseyside & Greater Manchester.

88 WELL HOUSE
Dean Row Road, Wilmslow SK9 2BU. Steven & Jill Kimber. *2m N of Wilmslow, via the A34 bypass or Adlington Rd, Well House is on Dean Row Road (B5358), almost at the junction (r'about) with Adlington Rd (A5102). Parking available at the Unicorn PH 300yds, from the house entrance. Next door to the Shell garage. Less able visitors can drop off then park in Chapel Lane but space is limited.* Home-made teas. **Adm £4, chd free. Sat 21, Sun 22 May (1.30-5).**
Landscaped in 2002/3 and hidden from view by mature shelter planting, this 3-acre plot offers woodland with spring bulbs and hellebores, formal and informal gardens, bog area and wild flower meadow.

Lavishly planted wildlife pond with Monet style bridge, vegetable and fruit gardens and Victorian style conservatory . . .

87 THE WELL HOUSE
Wet Lane, Tilston SY14 7DP. Mrs S H French-Greenslade, 01829 250332. *3m NW of Malpas. On A41, 1st turn R after Broxton roundabout, L on Malpas Rd through Tilston. House & antique shop on L.* **Visitors welcome by appt - coach parties welcome, max 50 visitors.**
1-acre cottage garden, bridge over natural stream, spring bulbs, perennials, herbs and shrubs. Triple pond and waterfall feature. Adjoining ¾ -acre field being made into wild flower meadow; first seeding late 2003. Large bog area of kingcups and ragged robin. Antique shop and Victorian parlour.

89 69 WELL LANE
Gayton CH60 8NH. Angus & Sally Clark, 1513423321, aandsclark@aol.com. *7m S of Birkenhead. From Devon Doorway/Glegg Arms r'about travel SE towards Chester for approx ¼ m. Turn R into Gayton Lane for about ½*

m then L into Well Lane. Garden on L. Park on rd or at Maylands. Teas. **Adm £3.50, chd free. Sun 1, Mon 2 May (2-5).** Visitors also welcome by appt.
This undulating established 1-acre garden has a stunning rear setting and is surrounded by a natural woodland backdrop. Many spring flowering shrubs (rhododendron, azalea, magnolia, cornus) with surprises at every corner. Restored old farm buildings with roofless area containing climbers and fronted by cobblestones. Large slate water feature.

GROUP OPENING

90 WEST DRIVE GARDENS
6, 8, 9 West Drive, Gatley SK8 4JJ. Mr & Mrs D J Gane, Mrs B Wingard, Mrs T Bishop & Mr J Needham. *4m N of Wilmslow on B5166. From J5 (M56) drive past airport to B5166 (Styal Rd). L towards Gatley. Pass over T-lights at Heald Green. West Drive is last turn on R before Gatley Village. Cul-de-sac, please do not park beyond the notice.* Home-made teas at No. 6 with extra seating at No. 8. **Combined adm £5, chd free (share to Wythenshawe Hospital, Cardiology Dept). Sun 17 July (10.30-4.30).**
Here are three gardens of distinctly different character, each reflecting their owner's gardening style. Although suburban they are surrounded by mature trees and have a secluded feel. With a rich variety of planting incl grasses, ferns and hostas, as well as herbaceous borders with phlox, echinacea and clematis at their best. Water features, unusual containers and ceramics complete the picture. Please note that no.8 West Drive (not no. 4) is opening this year. Large high-quality plant stall with home-made/grown produce at no.9 as usual.

GROUP OPENING

91 WILLASTON VILLAGE GARDENS
Willaston CH64 1TE. *8m N of Chester. Take A540 Chester to West Kirby rd; turn R on B5151 to Willaston; at village centre turn R into Hooton Rd. Change Lane is ¾ m on R opp garage. All 3 gardens are entered from Change Hey garden.*

Parking available in field at bottom of Change Lane on RH-side. 15 mins walk from Hooton Stn along B5133 in direction of Willaston. Change Lane on LH-side opp garage. Leave M53 J5. Join A41, travel in direction of Queensferry, N Wales. ¼ m at T- lights turn R B5133. Along Hooton Rd, after ¾ m Hooton Stn on L. Then as from Hooton Stn. Home-made teas at Change Hey. **Combined adm £4.50, chd free. Sun 22 May (2-5).**

CHANGE HEY
Change Lane. Keith & Joan Butcher

THE DUTCH HOUSE
Joan & Michael Ring

SILVERBURN
Prof M P & Dr A M Escudier

3 very different gardens in design and planting. Change Hey: 2 acre garden with mature trees, developing woodland area underplanted with rhododendrons and azaleas. The Dutch House: ⅓ -acre cottage-style garden with some formality. The rear garden vista, terminating with a 1920 Boulton and Paul revolving summerhouse, is surrounded on 2 sides by mature beech, oak and pine trees. Some gravel paths. Silverburn: ½ -acre garden designed by present owners. A plantsperson's garden with varied plantings in the herbaceous beds and mixed borders, species and old-fashioned roses, rhododendrons, azaleas, attractive trees, vegetable garden and small orchard. Bridge linking Silverburn and Change Hey not suitable for wheelchairs. Alternative (separate) access possible. Partial wheelchair access.
&. ⊗ ☕

 WOOD END COTTAGE
Grange Lane, Whitegate, Northwich CW8 2BQ. Mr & Mrs M R Everett, 01606 888236, woodendct@supanet.com. *4m SW of Northwich. Turn S off A556 (Northwich bypass) at Sandiway PO T-lights; after 1¾ m, turn L to Whitegate village; opp school follow Grange Lane for 300yds.* Home-made teas. **Adm £4, chd free. Sun 26 June (2-5).** Visitors also welcome by appt.
Plantsman's ½ acre garden in attractive setting, sloping to a natural stream bordered by shade and moisture-loving plants. Background of mature trees. Well stocked herbaceous border, phlox, trellis, roses and clematis, magnificent delphiniums. Choice perennials. Interesting shrubs and flowering trees. Vegetable garden.
⊗ ☕ ☎

Summerhouse, surrounded by deep borders . . .

 NEW WOODSEND
33 Lostock Hall Road, Poynton SK12 1DP. Ruth & Martin Seabrook. *6m N of Macclesfield. From Macclesfield take A523 towards Stockport. At Poynton Centre turn L onto A5149 Chester Rd, turn L immed after railway bridge to Lostock Hall Road.* Home-made teas. **Adm £3.50, chd free. Sat 18, Sun 19 June (2-5).**
Small tranquil garden, owner designed, planted and maintained. Features courtyard patio, rose covered pergola and summerhouse, surrounded by deep borders packed with herbaceous plants, roses and shrubs. An informal shady area planted with ferns, hostas and dicentra, and pond. Front garden with a white planting scheme. Partial wheelchair access.
&. ⊗ ☕

WROXHAM GARDENS
See Lancashire Merseyside & Greater Manchester.

94 YEW TREE HOUSE GARDEN & SPECIAL PERENNIALS NURSERY
Hall Lane, Hankelow, nr Audlem CW3 0JB. Janet & Martin Blow, www.specialperennials.com. *Just off A529, 5m S of Nantwich, 1m N of Audlem. Park at village green, follow Hall Lane left along rear of green. Last house on right before junction with A529. PH, cafes & WC available at nearby Audlem (1m).* **Adm £2.50, chd free. Sats, Suns 2, 3, 16, 17, 23, 24 July; 6, 7, 13, 14 Aug; 3, 11 Sept (1-5).**
Small garden planted in an exuberant cottage style with an abundance of interesting and unusual perennial plants: no lawns just lots of lovely flowers! Specialities include Heleniums, Day Lilies, Phlox, Centaurea, Monarda, Grasses plus lots, lots more. The garden is a haven for bees and butterflies. Attached small nursery selling plants grown in the garden. National Collection of Helenniums (100+ varieties - best Aug) National Collection of Centaurea applied for. Featured in Cheshire Life, Journal of Plant Heritage. Gravel paths, some narrow.
&. ⊗ NCCPG

Cheshire & Wirral County Volunteers
County Organiser
Nicholas Payne, The Mount, Whirley, Macclesfield SK11 9PB, 01625 422920, ngs@themount1.freeserve.co.uk
Deputy County Organiser (& Advertising)
John Hinde, Maylands, Latchford Road, Gayton, Wirral CH60 3RN, 0151 342 8557, john.hinde@maylands.com
Publicity
Graham Beech, 5 Alton Road, Wilmslow SK9 5DY, 01625 529462, gb.ngs@talktalk.net
Peter Johnson, 12 The Stables, Tabley House, Knutsford WA16 0HA, 01565 228213, peterandjane@talktalk.net
Assistant County Organisers
Janet Bashforth, Mayfield, The Peppers, Lymm WA13 0JA, 01925 756107, janetbashforth@talktalk.net
Sue Bryant, Hope Cottage, 39 Stamford Road, Bowdon WA14 2JJ, 0161 928 3819, suewestlakebryant@btinternet.com
Juliet Hill, Salterswell House, Tarporley CW6 0ED, 01829 732804
Romy Holmes, Bowmere Cottage, Bowmere Road, Tarporley CW6 0BS, 01829 732053, romy@holmes-email.co.uk
Ros Mahon, Rectory Cottage, Eaton, Congleton CW12 2ND, 01260 274777
Sally Sutcliffe, Little Somerley, Woodlan Court, Utkinton, Tarporley CW6 0LJ, 01829 730149, sally.sutcliffe1@btinternet.com
Alex Willcocks, Crowley Lodge, Arley, Northwich CW9 6NR, 01565 777381

CORNWALL

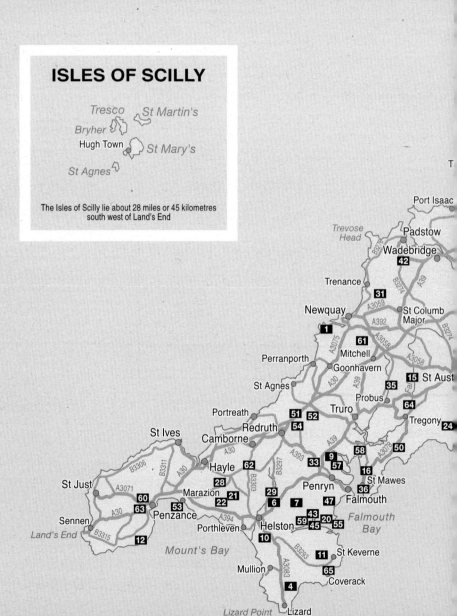

ISLES OF SCILLY

Tresco St Martin's
Bryher
Hugh Town   St Mary's
St Agnes

The Isles of Scilly lie about 28 miles or 45 kilometres
south west of Land's End

Port Isaac
Trevose
Head Padstow
Wadebridge 42
Trenance
31
Newquay St Columb
Major
1
61
Perranporth Mitchell
Goonhavern
St Agnes 15 St Aust
35
Probus
Portreath 51 52 Truro 64
Redruth 54 Tregony 24
St Ives
Camborne 58 50
Hayle 62 9 57 16
St Just 28 33 St Mawes
60 Marazion 21 Penryn 36
63 22 29 47 Falmouth
Sennen 53 Penzance 6 7 43 20 Falmouth
Land's End 12 Porthleven 59 45 55 Bay
Helston 10 11 St Keverne
Mount's Bay 65
Mullion Coverack
4
Lizard Point Lizard

Opening Dates

February

Saturday 5
13 Coombegate Cottage

Sunday 13
13 Coombegate Cottage

Sunday 27
13 Coombegate Cottage

March

Saturday 12
20 Glendurgan

Sunday 13
30 Ince Castle

Sunday 20
27 Higher Truscott

Saturday 26
63 Trewidden Garden

Sunday 27
30 Ince Castle

Wednesday 30
14 Cotehele

April

Saturday 2
58 Trelissick

Sunday 3
2 The Barn House

Wednesday 13
46 Pencarrow

Sunday 17
16 Creek Lodge
47 Penjerrick Garden
54 Scorrier House

Thursday 28
10 Carminowe Valley Garden
23 Headland

May

Sunday 1
3 Boconnoc
12 Chygurno
60 Trengwainton

Monday 2
12 Chygurno
41 Moyclare

Thursday 5
10 Carminowe Valley Garden
23 Headland

Saturday 7
36 Lamorran House

Sunday 8
9 Carclew Gardens
35 Ladock House
56 Trebartha
61 Trerice
67 Woodland Cottage

Tuesday 10
37 Lanhydrock

Thursday 12
10 Carminowe Valley Garden
23 Headland

Sunday 15
30 Ince Castle
38 Long Hay
45 Pedn Billy

Thursday 19
10 Carminowe Valley Garden
23 Headland

Saturday 21
49 Pinsla Garden & Nursery

Sunday 22
43 Navas Hill House
49 Pinsla Garden & Nursery
59 Trenarth (Evening)

Sunday 29
52 Roseland House
62 Trevoole Farm

Monday 30
31 The Japanese Garden & Bonsai Nursery
52 Roseland House

June

Sunday 5
2 The Barn House
17 Cutlinwith
40 The Mill House

Sunday 12
15 Creed House
38 Long Hay

Thursday 16
10 Carminowe Valley Garden

Saturday 18
5 Boscastle Gardens
51 Primrose Farm

Sunday 19
5 Boscastle Gardens
22 Godolphin Hill Gardens
28 Homefield
53 St Michael's Mount
62 Trevoole Farm

Tuesday 21
21 Godolphin (Evening)

Wednesday 22
21 Godolphin (Evening)

Thursday 23
10 Carminowe Valley Garden

Saturday 25
66 Waye Cottage

Sunday 26
1 Arundell
66 Waye Cottage

Thursday 30
10 Carminowe Valley Garden

July

Sunday 3
22 Godolphin Hill Gardens
60 Trengwainton
61 Trerice
62 Trevoole Farm

Sunday 10
6 Bowling Green Cottage

Saturday 16
12 Chygurno
65 Waters Edge

Sunday 17
12 Chygurno
19 Ellis Gardens and Nurseries
30 Ince Castle
65 Waters Edge
67 Woodland Cottage

Tuesday 19
37 Lanhydrock

Wednesday 20
4 Bonython Manor

Saturday 23
1 Arundell

Sunday 24
8 Byeways
50 Poppy Cottage Garden

August

Saturday 6
49 Pinsla Garden & Nursery

Sunday 7
26 Highcroft Gardens
49 Pinsla Garden & Nursery
57 Tregarthen Vean

Saturday 13
25 Hidden Valley Gardens

Sunday 14
25 Hidden Valley Gardens

Monday 15
25 Hidden Valley Gardens

Sunday 21
26 Highcroft Gardens
34 Kingberry

Monday 29
31 The Japanese Garden & Bonsai Nursery
44 Northwood Water Gardens & Gallery

September

Sunday 4
59 Trenarth (Afternoon & Evening)

Saturday 17
58 Trelissick

Sunday 18
7 Bucks Head House Garden
56 Trebartha

Saturday 24
20 Glendurgan

October

Sunday 2
14 Cotehele

February 2012

Saturday 11
13 Coombegate Cottage

Sunday 19
13 Coombegate Cottage

Sunday 26
13 Coombegate Cottage

Gardens open to the public

3 Boconnoc
4 Bonython Manor
11 Carwinion
12 Chygurno
14 Cotehele
15 Creed House
18 Eden Project
19 Ellis Gardens and Nurseries
21 Godolphin
22 Godolphin Hill Gardens
23 Headland
24 The Lost Gardens of Heligan
25 Hidden Valley Gardens
31 The Japanese Garden & Bonsai Nursery
32 Ken Caro
36 Lamorran House
37 Lanhydrock
39 Marsh Villa Gardens
41 Moyclare
44 Northwood Water Gardens & Gallery
46 Pencarrow
47 Penjerrick Garden
48 Pinetum Park & Pine Lodge Gardens
49 Pinsla Garden & Nursery
50 Poppy Cottage Garden
52 Roseland House
53 St Michael's Mount
55 Trebah
58 Trelissick
60 Trengwainton
61 Trerice
63 Trewidden Garden
64 Trewithen

By appointment only

29 The Homestead
33 Kennall House
42 Nanfenten

Also open by Appointment ☎

1 Arundell
2 The Barn House

---

7 Bucks Head House Garden
10 Carminowe Valley Garden
5 Half Acre, Boscastle Gardens
26 Highcroft Gardens
27 Higher Truscott
35 Ladock House
51 Primrose Farm
59 Trenarth
62 Trevoole Farm
66 Waye Cottage

The Gardens

1 ARUNDELL

West Pentire, Crantock TR8 5SE. Brenda & David Eyles, 01637 830071, david@davideyles.com. *1m W of Crantock. From A3075 take signs to Crantock. At junction in village keep straight on to West Pentire hamlet (1m). Park at Crantock Bay Hotel (50yds) or in public car parks at W Pentire. Home-made teas.* **Adm £3.50, chd free.** Sun 26 June; Sat 23 July (1-5). **Visitors also welcome by appt June/July/Aug only, no coaches.**
A garden where no garden should be! - on windswept N coast NT headland between 2 fantastic beaches. 1 acre set around original farm cottage. Front: cottage garden. Side: Mediterranean courtyard. Rear: rockery, shrubbery, more cottage garden leading to pond, stream and bog garden, herbaceous borders, Beth Chatto gravel garden, small pinetum and spectacular exotic garden. Featured in Cornwall Life and Cornwall Today.
☕ ☎

> Garden that shows you can battle with the elements above dramatic cliffs . . .

2 THE BARN HOUSE

Higher Penhalt, Poundstock EX23 0DG. Tim & Sandy Dingle, 01288 361356, rdingle@toucansurf.com. *5m S of Bude. 1m off A39 to Widemouth Bay. Take Millook rd by Widemouth Manor*

Hotel. Follow rd for 1m, signed L at top of hill. Cream teas & light refreshments. **Adm £3.50, chd free.** Suns 3 Apr; 5 June (11-5). **Visitors also welcome by appt Apr to July incl, no coaches.**
Garden that shows you can battle with the elements above dramatic cliffs of N Cornish coast and win. $^1/_2$ -acre garden designed for yr-round interest with many colourful and unusual plants. Divided and enclosed by sheltering hedges. Herbaceous borders, prairie bed, pond, kitchen garden and patio. A walk through fields and wooded valley often gives glimpses of abundant wildlife. Partial wheelchair access.
♿ 🐾 ✿ 🛏 ☕ ☎

3 ◆ BOCONNOC

Lostwithiel PL22 0RG. Mr Anthony Fortescue, 01208 872507, www.boconnocenterprises.co.uk. *4m E of Lostwithiel. 2m E of A390. Turn off A390 at Middle Taphouse.* **Adm £5, chd under 12 free.** For NGS: **Sun 1 May (2-5).** For other opening times and information please phone or see garden website.
Gardens covering some 20 acres, surrounded by parkland and woods. Magnificent trees, flowering shrubs and views. Set in C18 picturesque landscape which surrounds the church and Boconnoc House (both open). Teas in the stable yard designed by Sir John Soane. Newly-planted magnolias.
♿ 🐾 ✿ 🛏 ☕

4 ◆ BONYTHON MANOR

Cury Cross Lanes TR12 7BA. Mr & Mrs Richard Nathan, 01326 240550, www.bonythonmanor.co.uk. *5m S of Helston. On main A3083 Helston to Lizard Rd. Turn L at Cury Cross Lanes (Wheel Inn). Entrance 300yds on R.* **Adm £6, chd £2.** For NGS: **Wed 20 July (2-4.30).** For other opening times and information, please phone or see garden website.
Magnificent 20-acre colour garden incl sweeping hydrangea drive to Georgian manor (not open). Herbaceous walled garden, potager with vegetables and picking flowers; 3 lakes in valley planted with ornamental grasses, perennials and South African flowers. A 'must see' for all seasons colour. Featured in numerous publications.
♿ ✿ 🛏 ☕

Visit a garden in your own time – look out for the ☎

GROUP OPENING

5 BOSCASTLE GARDENS
PL35 0BJ. *5m N of Camelford. Park in doctor's surgery car park at top of village (clearly signed). Limited parking for disabled at both gardens. Maps provided.* Home-made teas. **Combined adm £3.50, chd free. Sat 18, Sun 19 June (1.30-5.30).**

HALF ACRE
Carole Vincent
Visitors also welcome by appt all yr, max 20.
01840 250263

WILDWOOD
Alex Stewart

Boscastle Harbour is well-known to visitors. Both gardens are in older part of village, overlooking cliff, land and sea. Garden paintings exhibition. Half Acre: sculpture in an acre of 3 gardens: Cottage, small wood, the Blue Circle garden, constructed in colour concrete with coastal planting. Studio open. Wildwood: garden of magic deception. Front traditional, rear - lawns leading to wood with pond, tree ferns and shade-loving shrubs. Paintings exhibition.

❀ ☕

6 BOWLING GREEN COTTAGE
Wendron TR13 0NB. Stephen & Carol Lay. *2m from Helston. Signed from Helston - Redruth rd (B3297) and Helston - Falmouth rd (A394).* Home-made teas. **Adm £3.50, chd free. Sun 10 July (1-5).**
2-acre garden compromises informal cottage-style planting, rose beds, perennials and shrubs. Woodlands to explore with wetlands and resident timid moorhens. Mining heritage enhances this tranquil haven which is both exciting and serene in parts. Colour, contrast and creativity abound on this once windswept spot. Featured on BBC2 Open Gardens. If wet, wheelchair access may be difficult in woodland.

♿ 🐖 ❀ ☕

7 BUCKS HEAD HOUSE GARDEN
Trengove Cross, Constantine TR11 5QR. Deborah Baker, 01326 340844, deborah.baker@falmouth.ac.uk. *5m SW of Falmouth. From A394 towards Helston, L at Edgcumbe towards Gweek and Constantine. Proceed for 0.8m then L towards Constantine. Further 0.8m, garden on L at Trengove Cross.* **Adm £3.50, chd free. Sun 18 Sept (2-5). Visitors also welcome by appt July to Sept, max 12.**
Exposed S-facing 1¼-acre garden with panoramic views. Started in 2004 and divided into 3 distinct areas, it contains an evocative collection of trees, shrubs and herbaceous plants. Gale force winds continually threaten but also help create this garden's unique character amidst a rural Cornish landscape.

❀ ☕ ☎

8 BYEWAYS
Dunheved Road, Launceston PL15 9JE. Tony & Margaret Reddicliffe. *Launceston town centre. 100yds from multistorey car park past offices of Cornish & Devon Post into Dunheved Rd, 3rd bungalow on R.* Home-made teas. **Adm £3, chd free. Sun 24 July (12-5).**
Small town garden developed over 4yrs by 2 enthusiastic amateur gardeners, many interesting design features, herbaceous borders, pond, stream and vegetable plot. Areas of interest incl Japanese garden with many young bonsai, shingle grass area, mature cactus, giant rockery. Tropicals incl bananas, gingers and senecio.

❀ ☕

GROUP OPENING

9 NEW CARCLEW GARDENS
Perranarworthal TR3 7PB. *5m SW of Truro. 1m W of Norway Inn, A390 Mylor Rd.* Home-made teas. **Combined adm £3.50, chd free. Sun 8 May (12-5).**

NEW CARCLEW HOUSE
Mr John & Sally Williams

NEW TREVORICK
Mrs Daphne Neale

Carclew House: Part of formal Grade II listed garden undergoing restoration after yrs of neglect. C18 and C19 garden walls and terraces. Plants of note incl rhododendron Sir Charles Lemon and camellia Captain Rawes, one of the finest in the country. Views incl Lucombe Oak, gingko biloba, swamp cypress. New developments incl very beautiful acer glade (30 varieties). Fern dell and woodland walk. Trevorick: Woodland garden

developed around romantic ruin of the old Carclew Mansion over past 40 yrs. Several 1st class specimens of Michelia doltsopa, rhododendron Cornish red and liquid amber Chilean firebush. A garden dominated by trees and shrubs. Partial wheelchair access to both gardens.

♿ ☕

Abundant garden with babbling brook and large natural pond . . .

10 NEW CARMINOWE VALLEY GARDEN
Tangies, Gunwalloe TR12 7PU. Mr & Mrs Peter Stanley, 01326 565868, stanley.m2@sky.com. *3m SW of Helston. A3083 Helston-Lizard. R opp main gate to Culdrose. 1m downhill, garden on R.* Home-made teas. **Adm £4, chd free. Thurs 28 Apr; 5, 12, 19 May; 16, 23, 30 June (10-4.30). Visitors also welcome by appt.**
Overlooking the beautiful Carminowe Valley towards Loepool this abundant garden combines native oak woodland, babbling brook and large natural pond with more formal areas. Wildflower meadow, mown pathways, shrubberies, orchard, nectar beds, cutting garden, kitchen garden, summerhouse. Enclosed cottage garden, tulips in spring and roses early summer provide huge contrast. Gravel paths. Steep valley side in places.

♿ 🐖 ❀ 🛏 ☕ ☎

11 ◆ CARWINION
Mawnan Smith TR11 5JA. Anthony & Jane Rogers, 01326 250258, www.carwinion.co.uk. *3m W of Falmouth. 500yds from centre of Mawnan Smith, turn L at Red Lion PH & follow signs.* **For opening times and information, please phone or see garden website.**
Stunning 14-acre S-facing Cornish

valley garden running down to R Helford. Home of UK's premier bamboo collection. Mixed borders and extensive camellia collection. Wild flowers and ferns abound. A garden of yr-round interest open every day except Christmas Day. Gravel paths & steep slopes in lower garden. Top garden accessible.

12 ◆ CHYGURNO
Lamorna TR19 6XH. Dr & Mrs Robert Moule, 01736 732153, www.gardensofcornwall.com. *4m S of Penzance. Off B3315. Follow signs for The Cove Restaurant. Garden is at top of hill, past Hotel on LH side.* **Adm £4, chd free.** For NGS: Sun 1, Mon 2 May; Sat 16, Sun 17 July (2-5). **For other opening times and information, please phone or see garden website.**
Beautiful, unique, 3-acre cliffside garden overlooking Lamorna Cove. Planting started in 1998, mainly S-hemisphere shrubs and exotics with hydrangeas, camellias and rhododendrons. Woodland area with tree ferns set against large granite outcrops. Garden terraced with steep steps and paths. Plenty of benches so you can take a rest and enjoy the wonderful views. Well worth the effort. Featured in GGG.

COOMBE SCULPTURE GARDEN
See Devon.

13 COOMBEGATE COTTAGE
St Ive PL14 3LZ. Michael Stephens, 01579 383520. *4m E of Liskeard. From A390 at St Ive take turning signed Blunts. Use village car park immed on L, then take 2nd L for 400metres. Parking at house for less mobile.* Home-made teas in Village Hall. **Adm £3, chd free.** Sat 5 Feb (11-4), Suns 13, 27 Feb (1-4). For 2012, Sat 11 Feb (11-4), Suns 19, 26 Feb (1-4).
1-acre garden full of winter colour and scent. Witch hazels, daphnes, hellebores, early rhododendrons, interesting collection of more unusual seasonal plants. Drifts of snowdrops. Sloping site with steps. Open weather permitting - phone to check if in doubt. Art Exhibition in Village Hall 5 Feb 2011. Featured in Country Life and Cornwall Today.

Eden Project

14 ◆ COTEHELE
Saltash PL12 6TA. National Trust, 01579 351346, www.nationaltrust.org.uk. *2m E of St Dominick. 4m from Gunnislake. (Turn at St Ann's Chapel); 8m SW of Tavistock; 14m from Plymouth via Tamar Bridge.* **Adm £6, chd £3, family £15.** For NGS: Wed 30 Mar; Sun 2 Oct (11-4). **For other opening times and information, please phone or see garden website.**
Formal garden, orchards and meadow. Terrace garden falling to sheltered valley with ponds, stream and unusual shrubs. Fine Tudor house (one of the least altered in the country); armour, tapestries, furniture. Gravel paths, some steep slopes in Valley Garden.

15 ◆ CREED HOUSE
Creed TR2 4SL. Jonathon & Annie Croggon, 01872 530372, www.creedhouse.co.uk. *9m W of Truro. From the centre of Grampound on A390, take rd signed to Creed. After 1m turn L opp Creed Church & garden is on L.* Teas. **Adm £3.50, chd free.** For NGS: Sun 12 June (11-5).
5-acre landscaped Georgian rectory garden; tranquil rural setting; spacious lawns. Tree collection; rhododendrons; sunken cobbled yard and formal walled herbaceous garden. Trickle stream to ponds and bog. Natural woodland walk. Restoration began 1974 - continues and incl recent planting. Open all yr.

Be tempted by a plant from a plant stall

16 NEW CREEK LODGE
St Just in Roseland TR2 5JD.
Julian & Alison Davy. *9m S of
Tregony. A3078 from Trogony
towards St Mawes. In St Just in
Roseland village, 2nd R to St Just
Church, garden at bottom of hill on R.*
Home-made teas. **Adm £3.50, chd
free. Sun 17 Apr (2-5.30).**
Small garden situated above St Just
Creek with wonderful views across
water. Garden incl variety of shrubs
with many camellias and flowering
bulbs. Beautiful St Just in Roseland
Church gardens 5min walk, offering
array of colourful shrubs and
subtropical plants.

17 NEW CUTLINWITH
Tideford, Saltash PL12 5HX. Peter
& Mary Hamilton. *1¹/₂ m N of
Tideford, 5m W of Saltash. A38 to
Tideford (10m from Plymouth Bridge)
then rd N opp butcher's shop to
Tideford Cross (1m). R just after sign.
Cutlinwith lane entrance ¹/₂ m further
on R.* Home-made teas. **Adm £3.50,
chd free. Sun 5 June (2-5).**
Cutlinwith is a 3-acre garden in a
small valley. Begun 10yrs ago and
now beginning to mature. The design
aim is to have all yr round interest.
Features trees, borders, water garden
incl stream and ponds. There is also a
developing acer, magnolia and bluebell
walk leading to woodland paths.

18 ◆ EDEN PROJECT
Bodelva PL24 2SG. The Eden
Trust, 01726 811911,
www.edenproject.com. *4m E of St
Austell. Brown signs from A30 &
A390.* **For opening times and
information, please phone or see
garden website.**
The world's largest greenhouses
nestle in a giant 50-metre deep crater
the size of 30 football pitches, the
centrepiece of a spectacular global
garden. Eden is a gateway into the
fascinating world of plants and people
and a vibrant reminder of how we
need each other for our mutual
survival. Free wheelchairs available,
please book in advance. See website
for access details.
♿ ❀ ☕

**19 ◆ ELLIS GARDENS AND
NURSERIES**
Polyphant PL15 7PS. Tim & Sue
Ellis, 01566 86641,
www.ellisnurseries.co.uk. *6m W of
Launceston. From A30 take turning to*

*Blackhill Quarry. Proceed up hill to
village green. L at bottom of green
and keep to L round bend. Garden
4th on R.* **Adm £3, chd free.**
For NGS: Sun 17 July (10-5). **For
other opening times and
information, please phone or see
garden website.**
A developing 1-acre perennial flower
garden with deep herbaceous
borders, willow tunnel, wildlife pond,
white garden, bog garden and new
Mediterranean area. Large collection
of euphorbias planted through the
gardens, many for sale in the nursery.
Full of colour from May to Sept. A
delight to behold. Featured on BBC2
Open Gardens. If wet, wheelchair
access is difficult. Deep, unfenced
pond.
♿ 🐿 ❀

20 ◆ GLENDURGAN
Mawnan Smith TR11 5JZ. National
Trust, 01326 252020,
www.nationaltrust.org.uk. *5m SW of
Falmouth. Take rd to Helford
Passage. Follow NT signs.* **Adm
£6.30, chd £3.20.** For NGS: Sats 12
Mar; 24 Sept (10.30-5.30). **For
other opening times and
information, please phone or see
garden website.**
Valley garden running down to
Durgan village on R Helford. In spring
large displays of rhododendrons,
camellias and magnolias with drifts of
primroses, bluebells and aquilegia
below. Many specimen trees, laurel
maze dating from 1833 and giant's
stride.
❀ ☕

Surrounded by
hedgerows which
are positively
spilling over with
rambling roses . . .

21 ◆ GODOLPHIN
Godolphin Cross, Helston
TR13 9RE. National Trust, 01736
761002, www.nationaltrust.org.uk.
*5m NW of Helston. From Helston
follow A394 towards Penzance, then
B3302 to Hayle, turning L signed
Godolphin Cross.* **Adm by donation.**
For NGS: Evening Openings
Tue 21, Wed 22 June (6.30-8.30).
**For other opening times and
information, please phone or see
garden website.**
A near-miraculous survival from C14
and C16, unchanged by fashions
through the centuries. The garden is
not about flowers and plants but
about the surviving remains of a
medieval pattern. Acquired by the
National Trust in 2007. Summers
evening guided tour of the garden
NGS days only. Enjoy the peace and
tranquility of this atmospheric garden
on a mid-summer's evening. Not
suitable for wheelchairs.

**22 NEW ◆ GODOLPHIN HILL
GARDENS**
Trewithen Terrace, Godolphin,
Helston TR13 9TQ. John & Vicki
Marshall, 01736 762124,
www.thegardenlady.co.uk. *1m S of
Godolphin Cross. From Godolphin
Cross follow sign for Ashton. R at top
of hill, signed Millpool & Trescowe.
300yds down Trewithen Terrace,
garden on R opp phone box.* **Adm
£3.50, chd free.** For NGS: Sun 19
June; Sun 3 July (2-5).
Set high on the southern slope of
Godolphin Hill, this natural, informal
and bio-diverse 3 acre garden has
evolved over 20 years, working with
nature rather than against it. Long
borders containing large variety of
species, shrubs and rambling roses
along with herbs and herbaceous
perennials. Wildlife pond, wildflower
meadow, cut flower garden all
surrounded by hedgerows which are
positively spilling over with rambling
roses. Introduction to moths found in
area by county recorder for Cornwall
Moth Group. Also open Weds/Thurs
25 May - 21 July (2-5). Featured in
Cornwall Today.
♿ ❀ ☕

HARTLAND ABBEY
See Devon.

23 ◆ HEADLAND

Battery Lane, Polruan-by-Fowey PL23 1PW. Jean Hill, 01726 870243, www.headlandgarden.co.uk. ½ m SE of Fowey across estuary. Passenger ferry from Fowey, 10 min walk along West St & up Battery Lane. Or follow signs to Polruan (on E of Fowey Estuary). Ignore first car park, turn L for second car park (overlooking harbour), turn L (on foot) down St Saviour's Hill. **Adm £3, chd £1. For NGS: Thurs 28 Apr; 5, 12, 19 May (2-6). For other opening times and information, please phone or see garden website.** 1¼ -acre cliff garden with magnificent sea, coastal and estuary views on 3 sides. Planted to withstand salty gales yet includes subtropical plants with intimate places to sit and savour the views. Paths wind through the garden past rocky outcrops down to a secluded swimming cove. Featured on Gardeners' World and in Cornwall Today & Here & Now. Partial wheelchair access, wheelchair users please phone beforehand.

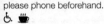

24 ◆ THE LOST GARDENS OF HELIGAN

Pentewan, St Austell PL26 6EN. Heligan Gardens Ltd, 01726 845100, www.heligan.com. 5m S of St Austell. From St Austell take B3273 signed Mevagissey, follow signs. **For opening times and information, please phone or see garden website.** Lose yourself in The Nation's Favourite Garden (BBC poll) and discover the mysterious world of The Lost Gardens. With the finest productive gardens in Britain, a pioneering wildlife project and exotic subtropical jungle just some of the attractions waiting to be explored, you are sure to have a magical day out.

25 ◆ HIDDEN VALLEY GARDENS

Treesmill, Par PL24 2TU. Tricia Howard, 01208 873225, www.hiddenvalleygardens.co.uk. 2m SW of Lostwithiel. From St Austell, take A390 towards Lostwithiel. After 6m turn R on to B3269 signed Fowey, after 200yds turn R signed Treesmill. After 1m turn L, signed to the gardens (½ m). At end of lane after Colwith Farm. **Adm**

£3, chd free. For NGS: Sat 13, Sun 14, Mon 15 Aug (10-6). **For other opening times and information, please phone or see garden website.** 4-acre colourful garden in 'hidden' valley with nursery. Cottage-style planting with herbaceous borders, grasses, ferns and fruit. Gazebo with country views. Iris fairy well. Fishpond, Japanese garden and vegetable potager. Aug opening this yr for special displays of agapanthus, dahlias, asters and crocosmia collections. Many young birds, bees and butterflies and hundreds of tiny frogs and toads. Children's quiz. Featured in The Guardian.

26 HIGHCROFT GARDENS

Cargreen PL12 6PA. Mr & Mrs B J Richards, 01752 848048, highcroftnursery@btinternet.com, www.bjrichardsflowers.co.uk. 5m NW of Saltash. 5m from Callington on A388 take Landulph Cargreen turning. 2m on, turn L at Landulph Xrds. Parking by Methodist Church. Cream teas in Methodist Church. **Adm £4, chd free.** Suns 7, 21 Aug (1.30-5.30). Visitors also welcome by appt. 3-acre garden in beautiful Tamar Valley. Japanese-style garden, hot border, pastel border, grasses, arboretum with hemerocallis and new blue borders. Prairie planting containing 2,500 plants of herbaceous and grasses. Buddleia and shrub rose bank. Pond. All at their best in July, Aug and Sept. Featured on BBC Gardeners' World.

27 HIGHER TRUSCOTT

St Stephens, Launceston PL15 8LA. Mr & Mrs J C Mann, 01566 772755. 3m NW of Launceston. From Launceston B3254 turn W at St Stephens toward Egloskerry. Signed. Home-made teas and soup. **Adm £3.50, chd free (share to RNLI).** Sun 20 Mar (11-5). Visitors also welcome by appt. 1-acre plantsman's garden. Elevated position with fine views. Mainly woodland garden underplanted with masses of hellebores. Freshly-restored rock garden. Alpines in moraine and troughs.

28 HOMEFIELD

20 Pilgrims Way, Fraddam, Hayle TR27 6EJ. Laona & Andy Latham. 2½ m S of Hayle. From Hayle towards Helston on B3302. R at Fraddam Xrds, 350yds on R. Cream teas & light refreshments. **Adm £3.50, chd free.** Sun 19 June (2-5). Small enchanting garden divided into rooms filled with colour and interest. Herbaceous borders, hostas, roses, grasses. A plantaholics' garden. Small lawns, seating areas, water features and Pompeiian oven.

> S-facing border inspired by the planting pioneered by Piet Oudolf . . .

29 NEW THE HOMESTEAD

Crelly, Trenear, Wendron TR13 0EU. Shirley Williams & Chris Tredinnick, 01326 562808, homesteadholidays@btconnect.com. 3m N of Helston. From Helston B3297 towards Redruth. Past signpost Crelly/Bodilly past bus shelter. 1st lane on R then 1st lane L. Light refreshments & teas. **Adm £3.50, chd free.** Visitors welcome by appt Mon-Thur, Apr-Sept, max 20. 3 acres. Mature trees and shrubs. Pond, water features, paths, archways, seating, pergolas, sculptures. S-facing border inspired by the planting pioneered by Piet Oudolf. Poultry, orchard, deciduous woodland, vegetable garden. Apr-May: rhododendrons, camellias, cherries, primroses, daffodils. June: roses, clematis. July-Sept: mixed beds, perennials, grasses, hot and shady areas. Unfenced pond. Uneven paths which can be slippery.

Follow us on Facebook and Twitter

30 INCE CASTLE
Saltash PL12 4RA. Lord and Lady Boyd, www.incecastle.co.uk. *3m SW of Saltash. From A38 at Stoketon Cross take turn signed Trematon, then Elmgate. No large coaches.* Home-made teas. **Adm £3.50, chd free. Suns 13, 27 Mar; 15 May; 17 July (2-5).**
5-acre garden with camellias and magnolias, woodlands, borders, orchard, bulbs, shell house and lovely views of R Lynher. Partial wheelchair access.

31 ◆ THE JAPANESE GARDEN & BONSAI NURSERY
St Mawgan TR8 4ET. Mr & Mrs Hore, 01637 860116, www.thebonsainursery.com. *6m E of Newquay. 1½ m from N coast. Signs from A3059 & B3276.* **Adm £4.50, chd £2, groups 10+ £3.50pp. For NGS: Mons 30 May; 29 Aug (10-6).** For other opening times and information, please phone or see garden website.
East meets West in unique Garden for All Seasons. Spectacular Japanese maples and azaleas, symbolic teahouse, koi pond, bamboo grove, stroll, woodland, zen and moss gardens. An oasis of tranquillity. Entrance free to adjacent specialist Bonsai and Japanese garden nurseries. Gravel paths.

32 ◆ KEN CARO
Bicton, nr Liskeard PL14 5RF. Mr K R Willcock & Mrs Willcock, 01579 362446. *5m NE of Liskeard. From A390 to Callington turn off N at St Ive. Take Pensilva Rd, follow brown tourist signs, approx 1m off main rd. Plenty of parking.*
5-acre connoisseur's garden full of interest all yr round, with lily ponds and panoramic views. Dogs welcome in meadow and woodland walk, plenty of seats in all 10 acres, picnic area. Watch the bird life in the tranquillity of a plantsman's garden. Adm £4.50, chd £2. Daily 27 Feb to 30 Sept (10-5.30). Award winner (Cut Plants) Royal Cornwall Show. Partial wheelchair access.

33 KENNALL HOUSE
Ponsanooth TR3 7HJ. Mr & Mrs N Wilson-Holt, 01872 870557, kennallvale@hotmail.com. *4m NW of Falmouth. A393 Falmouth to Redruth, L at Ponsanooth PO for 0.3m. Garden at end of drive marked Kennall House.* **Visitors welcome by appt all yr.**
12-acre garden/arboretum, beautifully situated in Kennall Valley. Includes typical British species and exotics. Wide variety of trees incl new plantings of rare specimens. Fast-flowing stream with ponds and walled garden. All yr interest.

34 KINGBERRY
Rhind Street, Bodmin PL31 2EL. Dr & Mrs M S Stead. *N side of town, 100yds uphill from Westbury Hotel. Limited parking on hill, otherwise car parks in town centre.* Home-made teas. **Adm £3, chd free. Sun 21 Aug (2-6).**
Surprising haven in centre of this county town. ⅔ -acre formal town garden with abundantly planted herbaceous borders, original stone walls covered in climbers, ornamental pond, gravel terrace, orchard and wild flower garden. Sculptures and unusual plants, many for sale. Bee keeping.

35 LADOCK HOUSE
Ladock TR2 4PL. Holborow family, 01726 882274. *7m E of Truro. Just off B3275. Car park & entrance by church.* Home-made teas in church. **Adm £3.50, chd free. Sun 8 May (2-5). Visitors also welcome by appt March to June, coaches possible if parked by church.**
Georgian Old Rectory with 4 acres of lawns, rhododendrons, camellias and azaleas with many woodland glades, all planted during last 35 yrs. Bluebell walk.

Cornish coastal garden in beautiful but harsh environment . . .

36 ◆ LAMORRAN HOUSE
Upper Castle Road, St Mawes, Truro TR2 5BZ. Robert Dudley-Cooke, 01326 270800, www.lamorrangardens.co.uk. *A3078, R past garage at entrance to St Mawes. ¾ m on L. ¼ m from castle if using passenger ferry service.* **Adm £6.50, chd free. For NGS: Sat 7 May (10-5).** For other opening times and information, please phone or see garden website.
4-acre subtropical garden overlooking Falmouth bay. Designed by the owner in an Italianate/Cote d'Azur style. Extensive collection of Mediterranean and subtropical plants incl large collection of palms and tree ferns. Reflects both design and remarkable micro-climate. Beautiful collection of Japanese azaleas and tender rhododendrons. Large collection of S-hemisphere plants. Featured in Gardeners' World and local press.

37 ◆ LANHYDROCK
Bodmin PL30 5AD. National Trust, 01208 265950, www.nationaltrust.org.uk. *2½ m SE of Bodmin. 2½ m on B3268. Stn: Bodmin Parkway 1¾ m walk.* **Adm £6.75, chd £3.65. For NGS: Tues 10 May; 19 July (10-6).** For other opening times and information, please phone or see garden website.
Large formal garden laid out 1857. Good summer colour with herbaceous borders, shrub garden with fine specimens of rhododendrons and magnolias and lovely views. Wheelchair access route around formal garden. Gravel paths and slopes to higher woodland garden.

38 LONG HAY
Treligga, Delabole PL33 9EE. Bett & Mick Hartley. *10m N of Wadebridge. Take B3314 Pendoggett to Delabole Rd. Turn L at Westdowns from Pendoggett, R from Delabole. Signed Treligga (N). After entering hamlet, follow parking signs.* Cream teas. **Adm £3, chd free. Suns 15 May; 12 June (2-5).**
⅔ -acre abundant cottage garden with beautiful vistas of the N coast and sea. Herbaceous beds, shrubs, pond, greenhouse and lawns. Natural meadow of 1 acre overlooking sea with paths leading to copse, vegetable plots, orchard and greenhouse. Cornish coastal garden in beautiful but harsh environment.

39 ◆ MARSH VILLA GARDENS
St Andrew's Road, Par PL24 2LU.
Judith Stephens, 01726 815920,
www.marshvillagardens.com. *5m E
of St Austell. Leave A390 at St Blazey
T-lights, by church, into Station Rd,
then 1st L, garden 600yds on L.* **For
opening times and information
please phone or see garden website.**
Approx 3-acre garden featuring large
pond, streams, bog garden. Extensive
herbaceous beds, mixed borders,
woodland and marshland walks in
former estuary. New features incl
alpine bed and substantial rose and
clematis pergola. Large fernery/bog
garden, much clearing and re-planting
carried out in 2010.
   ⟨symbols⟩

40 THE MILL HOUSE
Pendoggett, St Kew PL30 3HN.
Trish & Jeremy Gibson,
www.themillhouse.weebly.com.
*2½ m SE of Port Isaac. Take St Teath
rd off B3314 at Pendoggett. Parking
in adjoining field (disabled drop off nr
house).* Home-made teas. **Adm £3,
chd free.** Sun 5 June (2-5.30).
1½ -acre country garden on site of
old mill with ponds, stream and
bridges and extensive views across
farmland. Enclosed formal areas
contrast with open spaces and the
planting throughout is relaxed and
varied. Mature trees and shrubs,
roses, colourful summer and
courtyard gardens, vegetables, fruits,
chickens. Partial disabled access,
drop off nr house.
   ⟨symbols⟩

41 ◆ MOYCLARE
Lodge Hill, Liskeard PL14 4EH.
Elizabeth & Philip Henslowe, 01579
343114, www.moyclare.co.uk. *½ m
S of Liskeard centre. Approx 300yds
S of Liskeard railway stn on St Keyne-
Duloe rd (B3254).* **Adm £3, chd free.
For NGS:** Mon 2 May (2-5). **For
other opening times and
information, please phone or see
garden website.**
Gardened by one family for over 80
yrs; mature trees, shrubs and plants
(many unusual, many variegated).
Once most televised Cornish garden.
Now revived and rejuvenated and still
a plantsman's delight, still full of
character. Camellia, Brachyglottis and
Astrantia (all 'Moira Reid') and Cytisus
'Moyclare Pink' originated here.
Featured in Sunday Times, Western
Morning News and The Cornish
Gardener.
   ⟨symbol⟩

Chygurno

42 NANFENTEN
Little Petherick PL27 7QT. Jackie &
Trevor Bould, 01841 540480,
nanfentengarden@hotmail.com. *3m
W of Wadebridge. A389 to Little
Petherick. Turn into lane next to white
cottage almost opp church, garden
200yds on L.* Home-made teas. **Adm
£3, chd free.** Visitors welcome by
appt **May to Aug. Garden clubs
and large parties welcome.**
²/₃ -acre plantsman's garden on side
of valley. Views of valley and Petherick
Creek to Padstow. Cottage-style
planting, rose walk, small pond. Steep
sloping aspect to rear garden with
many shrubs. Unusual sloping water
feature. Pergola and summerhouse.

Views of mill and water wheel. Many
seating areas. Steep steps.
   ⟨symbols⟩

43 NAVAS HILL HOUSE
Bosanath Valley, Mawnan Smith,
Falmouth TR11 5LL. Aline &
Richard Turner. *1½ m from Trebah
and Glendurgan Gdns. Follow signs
to Trebah Gardens. Pass Trebah on L,
follow rd, past Budock Vean Hotel,
continue for just under 1m, take rd to
R just before sharp L turn at end of
creek, gdn 30yds on R.* Home-made
teas. **Adm £3.50, chd free.** Sun 22
May (1.30-5.30). **Also open
Trenarth** (5.30-8).

Visit the website for latest information

8¹/₂ -acre garden divided into various zones; kitchen garden with greenhouses, potting shed, fruit cages, orchard; 2 plantsman areas with specialist trees and shrubs; walled rose garden; ornamental garden with water features and rockery. Seating areas with views across wooded valley, not a car in sight! There is a lovely bluebell wood walk between the garden and Trenarth (approx 15 mins). Gravel paths.

44 ◆ NORTHWOOD WATER GARDENS & GALLERY
Northwood, St Neot PL14 6QN. Mackenzie Bell, 01579 320030, www.northwoodgardens.com. *2m NE of St Neot. From St Neot Church proceed up steep hill signed Bolventor Colliford & Northwood Water Gardens then follow signs.* **Adm £4, chd free.** For NGS: Mon 29 Aug (11-5). **For other opening times and information, please phone or see garden website.**
Overlooking lovely river valley on S slopes of Bodmin Moor. AONB. 4-acre water garden. 8 delightfully landscaped ponds featuring wildlife, streams, waterfalls and fountains. Idyllic lake and romantic island, giant gunnera, tree ferns, phormiums, acers, water lilies, rhododendrons, pieris, secret walled herbaceous borders. Year round colour. Spectacular hydrangeas in August. Art Gallery.

45 ◆ PEDN BILLY
Bar Rd, Helford Passage TR11 5LF. Dr & Mrs T Bligh. *4¹/₂ m SW Falmouth. Through Mawnan Smith, past Glendurgan and Trebah gardens, L towards Helford Passage, 1st R Bar Rd, last house in rd.* Home-made teas. **Adm £4, chd free.** Sun 15 May (2-5.30).
Half of the 12 acres is ancient woodland with paths winding down to Port Navas Creek and R Helford to private beach. Wild flower areas, beautiful specimen trees, terraced borders. The garden is ablaze with azaleas, magnolias, rhododendrons, camellias and flowering bulbs. Gravel path through woodland, uneven and very steep in parts.

46 ◆ PENCARROW
Washaway, Bodmin PL30 3AG. Molesworth-St Aubyn family, 01208 841369, www.pencarrow.co.uk. *4m NW of Bodmin. Signed off A389 & B3266.* **Adm £4, chd £1.** For NGS: Wed 13 Apr (10-5.30). **For other opening times and information, please phone or see garden website.**
50 acres of tranquil, family-owned grade II* listed gardens. Superb specimen conifers, azaleas, magnolias and camellias galore. 700 varieties of rhododendron give a blaze of spring colour; blue hydrangeas line the mile long carriage drive throughout the summer. Discover the Iron Age hill fort, lake, Italian gardens and granite rockery. Gravel paths, some steep slopes.

47 ◆ PENJERRICK GARDEN
Budock, nr Falmouth TR11 5ED. Mrs Rachel Morin, 01872 870105, www.penjerrickgarden.co.uk. *3m SW of Falmouth. Between Budock-Mawnan Smith, opp. Penmorvah Manor Hotel. Coach parking by arrangement.* **Adm £3, chd £1.50.** For NGS: Sun 17 Apr (1.30-4.30). **For other opening times and information, please phone or see garden website.**
15-acre subtropical garden, home to important rhododendron hybrids and the C19 Quaker Fox family. The upper garden contains rhododendrons, camellias, magnolias, bamboos, tree ferns and magnificent trees. Across a bridge a luxuriant valley features ponds in a wild primeval setting. Suitable for adventurous fit people wearing gumboots. A jungley experience. Featured on BBC1.

Seating areas with views across wooded valley, not a car in sight! . . .

48 ◆ PINETUM PARK & PINE LODGE GARDENS
Holmbush, St Austell PL25 3RQ. Mr Chang Li, 01726 73500, www.pinetumpark.com. *1m E of St Austell. On A390 between Holmbush & St Blazey at junction of A391.* **Adm £6.50, chd £3, concessions £6.** For opening times and information, please phone or see garden website.
30-acre estate comprises gardens within a garden. Some 6,000 plants, all labelled, have been thoughtfully laid out using original designs and colour combinations to provide maximum interest. Rhododendrons, magnolias, camellias, herbaceous borders with many rare and tender plants, marsh gardens, tranquil lily ponds, lake with black swans within the park, pinetum. Japanese garden and arboretum. 3-acre winter garden.

49 ◆ PINSLA GARDEN & NURSERY
Cardinham PL30 4AY. Mark & Claire Woodbine, 01208 821339, www.pinslagarden.net. *3¹/₂ m E of Bodmin. From A30 Bodmin take A38 towards Plymouth, 1st L to Cardinham & Fletchers Bridge, 2m on R.* **Adm £3, chd free.** For NGS: Sat 21, Sun 22 May; Sat 6, Sun 7 Aug (9-6). **For other opening times and information, please phone or see garden website.**
Romantic 1¹/₂ acre artist's garden. Naturalistic cottage garden planting and imaginative sculpture and paths surround C18 fairytale cottage set in tranquil woodland. Acers, bamboos, shade plants, herbaceous succulents and bedding overflow in garden and nursery. Garden sculpture and benches for sale. Some gravel.

50 ◆ POPPY COTTAGE GARDEN
Ruan High Lanes TR2 5JR. Tina & David Primmer, 01872 501411, www.poppycottagegarden.co.uk. *1m NW of Veryan. On the Roseland Peninsula, 4m from Tregony on A3078 rd to St Mawes.* **Adm £3, chd free.** For NGS: Sun 24 July (2-5.30). **For other opening times and information, please phone or see garden website.**
Inspirational plantsman's garden combining colour, form and texture, approx 1 acre, divided into many rooms. From established cottage garden, extra land acquired in 2003

enabled the creation of different gardens filled with many beautiful and unusual shrubs, trees, bulbs, herbaceous and exotics, all colour-themed. Wildlife pond with stream and bridge. Featured in The Most Amazing Gardens in Britain & Ireland, GGG, Sunday Times, Cornwall Today & Amateur Gardening. Gravel car park at entrance.

PORTINGTON
See Devon.

51 PRIMROSE FARM
Skinners Bottom, Redruth TR16 5EA. Barbara & Peter Simmons, 01209 890350, babs.simmons@btinternet.com, www.primrosefarmgarden.blogspot.com. *6m N of Truro. At Chiverton Cross r'about on A30 take Blackwater turn. Down hill, R by Red Lion PH up North Hill, 1st L (mini Xrd), garden approx ½ m on L.* Home-made teas. **Adm £3.50, chd free. Sat 18 June (1-5).** Visitors also welcome by appt.
Rambling informal cottage-style garden with woodland glade. Mature trees and shrubs, herbaceous and mixed borders. Pond with cascades and trickling fountain. Patio area with exotic plants. Gravel path to pergola with scented climbers and summerhouse. Vegetable patch and wildlife pond. New secret garden. A plantsman's garden. Featured on BBC TV Open Gardens.

52 ◆ ROSELAND HOUSE
Chacewater TR4 8QB. Mr & Mrs Pridham, 01872 560451, www.roselandhouse.co.uk. *4m W of Truro. At Truro end of main st. Parking in village car park (100yds) or surrounding rds.* **Adm £3, chd free. For NGS: Sun 29, Mon 30 May (2-5). For other opening times and information, please phone or see garden website.**
1-acre garden subdivided by walls and trellises hosting a wide range of climbers. Mixed borders of unusual plants, Victorian conservatory and greenhouse extend the gardening yr. Holders of National Collection of Clematis *viticella cvs* and Lapageria Rosea cultivars. Featured in The Garden and Cornwall Life magazines. Garden on slope.

 NCCPG

53 ◆ ST MICHAEL'S MOUNT
Marazion TR17 0HT. James & Mary St Aubyn, 01736 710507, www.stmichaelsmount.co.uk. *2½ m E of Penzance. ½ m from shore at Marazion by Causeway; otherwise by motor boat.* **Adm £3.50, chd £1.50. For NGS: Sun 19 June (10.30-5). For other opening times and information, please phone or see garden website.**
Walled and terraced gardens are set against a dramatic backdrop of some 200ft from base of castle. The recently replanted wall gardens were built in C18 while many exotic succulents and other semi-tropicals flourish in the terraces.

54 SCORRIER HOUSE
Scorrier, Redruth TR16 5AU. Richard & Caroline Williams. *2½ m E of Redruth. From Truro A390, at 4th r'about slip road A30 to Redruth for 2½ m, A3047 under railway bridge, L at mini r'about to B3287 for ½ m, R on B3207 for 200yds, R by Lodge House. From Falmouth take A393 to Redruth for 7m then B3258, turn at 2nd lodge.* Home-made teas. **Adm £4, chd free. Sun 17 Apr (2-5).**
Scorrier House and gardens have been in the Williams family for 7 generations. Gardens set in parkland with conservatory, knot garden, formal garden with herbaceous borders and walled garden with camellias, magnolias and rare trees, some collected by the famous plant collector William Lobb. Unfenced swimming pool.

A plantsman's garden and wildlife haven . . .

55 ◆ TREBAH
Mawnan Smith TR11 5JZ. Trebah Garden Trust, 01326 252200, www.trebah-garden.co.uk. *4m SW of Falmouth. Follow tourist signs from Hillhead r'about on A39 approach to Falmouth or Treliever Cross r'about on junction of A39-A394. Parking for coaches.* **For opening times and information, please phone or see garden website.**
26-acre S-facing ravine garden, planted in 1830s. Extensive collection rare/mature trees/shrubs incl glades; huge tree ferns 100yrs old, subtropical exotics. Hydrangea collection covers 2½ acres. Water garden, waterfalls, rock pool stocked with mature koi carp. Enchanted garden for plantsman/artist/family. Play area/trails for children. Use of private beach. Steep paths in places. 2 motorised vehicles available, please book in advance.

56 TREBARTHA
nr Launceston PL15 7PE. The Latham Family. *6m SW of Launceston. North Hill, SW of Launceston nr junction of B3254 & B3257. No coaches.* Home-made teas. **Adm £3.50, chd free. Suns 8 May; 18 Sept (2-5).**
Wooded area with lake surrounded by walks of flowering shrubs; woodland trail through fine woods with cascades and waterfalls; American glade with fine trees. Major but exciting renovations will have started on these fine landscape/woodland gardens.

57 NEW TREGARTHEN VEAN
Mylor Downs, Falmouth TR11 5UL. Mr & Mrs J Williams. *Between Truro and Falmouth 2m off A39. From Truro 1st L after Norway Inn. At rd junction turn L. Over Xrds, 200yds on R.* Light refreshments & cream teas. **Adm £3.50, chd free. Sun 7 Aug (11-5).**
Wide selection of trees & shrubs planted over last 20 yrs. Concentrating on yr-round colour, perennials being added for extended season. Water features and rockeries. Situated in beautiful rural setting. A plantsman's garden and wildlife haven. Limited paths, access over slight grass slopes.

Trewidden Garden

58 ◆ TRELISSICK
Feock TR3 6QL. National Trust,
01872 862090,
www.nationaltrust.org.uk. *4m S of
Truro. Nr King Harry Ferry. On B3289.*
Adm £7.70, chd £3.90. **For NGS:
Sats 2 Apr; 17 Sept (10.30-5.30).**
For other opening times and
information, please phone or visit
garden website.
Planted with tender shrubs;
magnolias, camellias and
rhododendrons with many named
species characteristic of Cornish
gardens. Fine woodlands encircle the
gardens through which a varied
circular walk can be enjoyed. Superb
view over Falmouth harbour. Georgian
house, not open. Now accessible by
foot ferry from Truro, Falmouth and St
Mawes, Apr-Sept. Gravel paths,
some steps, suggested route.

59 TRENARTH
High Cross, Constantine TR11 5JN.
Lucie Nottingham, 01326 340444,
lmnottingham@tiscali.co.uk. *6m
SW of Falmouth. Nearest main rds
A39-A394 Truro to Helston-Falmouth:
follow signs for Constantine. At High
Cross garage, 1¹/₂ m before
Constantine, turn L signed Mawnan,*

*then R after 30yds down dead end
lane. Garden at end of lane.* Light
refreshments & teas. **Adm £3.50, chd
free.** Evening Openings wine, Sun
22 May (5.30-8); Sun 4 Sept (3-
8.30). **Also open Navas Hill House
22 May (1.30-5.30). Visitors also
welcome by appt.**
4-acre garden surrounding C17
farmhouse in lovely pastoral setting -
not a road in sight or sound. Yr-round
interest. Emphasis on unusual plants,
structure and form, with a hint of
quirkiness - not all is what it seems!
Courtyard, C18 garden walls, yew
rooms, prize-winning vegetable
garden, traditional potting shed,
orchard, green lane walk down to R
Helford, new water feature and gravel
garden. Wildlife interest. Sept opening
incl watching bats at dusk leaving
roost for night feeding. Featured in
Cornwall Today & Cornwall Country
Gardener.

60 ◆ TRENGWAINTON
Madron TR20 8RZ. National Trust,
01736 363148,
www.nationaltrust.org.uk. *2m NW
of Penzance. ¹/₂ m W of Heamoor. On
Penzance-Morvah rd (B3312), ¹/₂ m
off St Just rd (A3071).* **Adm £6.50,**

chd £3.20. For NGS: Suns 1 May;
3 July (10.30-5). **For other opening
times and information, please
phone or see garden website.**
Sheltered garden with an abundance
of exotic trees and shrubs.
Picturesque stream running through
valley and stunning views of Mounts
Bay from terrace. Ongoing restoration
of walled kitchen garden showcasing
contemporary varieties of fruit and
vegetables. Large collection of
camellias and rhododendrons. Free
guided tour 2pm on NGS days.
Tarmac main drive, other paths
gravel.

61 ◆ TRERICE
Kestle Mill, Newquay TR8 4PG.
National Trust, 01637 875404,
www.nationaltrust.org.uk. *3m SE of
Newquay. From Newquay via A392 &
A3058; turn R at Kestle Mill (NT signs)
or signed from A30 at Summercourt
via A3058.* **For NGS: Suns 8 May;
3 July (10.30-5). For other opening
times and information please
phone or see garden website.**
Summer/autumn-flowering garden
unusual in content and layout and for
neutral alkaline soil varieties. Orchard
planted with old varieties of fruit trees.
Experimental Tudor garden developed
in partnership with local primary
school. Gravel path around house.

62 TREVOOLE FARM
Trevoole, Praze-an-Beeble,
Camborne TR14 0RN. Mr & Mrs
Stevens, 01209 831243,
beth@trevoolefarm.co.uk,
www.trevoolefarm.co.uk. *3m SSW
of Camborne. From Camborne on
B3303 towards Helston. Past
Pendarves Nature Reserve, L into
lane just after 2 mine chimneys.*
Cream teas. **Adm £3, chd free.** Suns
29 May; 19 June; 3 July (2-5).
**Visitors also welcome by appt May
to Sept.**
The gardens are nestled around C18
smallholding. Old farmhouse and
shade garden, charming courtyard of
restored granite buildings. Old
orchard and herb garden. Patchwork
potager. New bog garden, Victorian
greenhouse, shepherd's hut cottage
garden and rose walk. Shop open
throughout summer selling plants,
produce from garden, homemade
preserves, gardening antiques and
crafts. Gravel paths.

Never immaculate but abundantly-planted . . .

63 ◆ TREWIDDEN GARDEN
Buryas Bridge, Penzance
TR20 8TT. Mr A R Bolitho,
01736 363021/351979,
www.trewiddengarden.co.uk. *2m W
of Penzance. Entry on A30 just before
Buryas Bridge.* **Adm £5.50, chd free.**
For NGS: Sat 26 Mar (10.30-5.30).
For other opening times and
information, please phone or see
garden website.
Historic Victorian garden with
magnolias, camellias and magnificent
tree ferns planted within ancient tin
workings. Tender, rare and unusual
exotic plantings create a riot of colour
thoughout the season. Water
features, specimen trees and
artefacts from Cornwall's tin industry
provide a wide range of interest for all.
Partial wheelchair access, gravel
paths, some steep slopes.

64 ◆ TREWITHEN
Truro TR2 4DD. Mr & Mrs Michael
Galsworthy, 01726 883647,
www.trewithengardens.co.uk. *½ m
E of Probus. Entrance on A390 Truro-
St Austell rd. Signed.* **For opening**

times and information, please
phone or see garden website.
Internationally renowned and historic
garden of 30 acres laid out between
1912 and 1960 with much of original
seed and plant material collected by
Ward Forrest. Towering magnolias
and rhododendrons and very large
collection of camellias. Flattish ground
amidst original woodland park and
magnificent landscaped lawn vistas.
Rose garden currently in
development. Many new plantings
throughout the garden which is now
responding to the challenge of climate
change with many new introductions.
Gravel paths.

65 WATERS EDGE
North Corner, Coverack TR12 6TG.
Lizzie Cartwright. *10m from Helston.
From Helston take B3293. Park in
Coverack car parks, follow yellow
signs, garden next to Porthgwarra
Nursing Home.* Cream teas. **Adm
£3.50, chd free. Sat 16, Sun 17 July**
(2-5).
Coverack, on the unique Lizard
Peninsula, is a Conservation Area and
SSSI. Small, narrow, sheltered
garden, lush and blue in July with
swathes of agapanthus. Hidden
seating, stream, pond and artist's
studio to enjoy. Homemade cakes on
terrace with stunning views of
harbour, beach and sea.

66 WAYE COTTAGE
Lerryn, nr Lostwithiel PL22 0QQ.
Malcolm & Jennifer Bell, 01208
872119. *4m S of Lostwithiel. Village
parking, garden 10min, level stroll
along riverbank/stepping stones.*

Home-made teas. **Adm £3.50, chd
free. Sat 25, Sun 26 June (2-5).**
**Visitors also welcome by appt
most weekends and BHs, please
phone.**
Never immaculate but abundantly-
planted, this 1-acre cottage garden
has large and interesting collection of
plants, some rare and unusual.
Wander along the meandering paths,
sit on the many benches and enjoy
stunning river views. Steep and sadly
only for those sound in wind and limb.
Pretty village, good riverside walks.
No dogs but shady dog crèche
provided.

WICK FARM GARDENS
See Devon.

WILDSIDE
See Devon.

67 WOODLAND COTTAGE
Tregrehan Mills, St Austell
PL25 3TL. Terry & Cassie Corby,
www.woodlandcottage.weebly.
com. *2m E of St Austell. From St
Austell take A390, 1st L after St
Austell Garden Centre, continue
through village for 1m.* Light
refreshments & teas. **Adm £3.50, chd
free. Suns 8 May; 17 July (1-6).**
Enchanting ¾ -acre cottage garden
and 6½ -acre woodland which hides
an old ruined tin mine. Sloping lawns
with island beds. Spring and summer
colour from rhododendrons, azaleas,
large range of perennials and over
200 hemerocallis. Grotto with mature
tree ferns. Many seating areas incl
pretty summerhouse. Not suitable for
wheelchairs.

Support the NGS – eat more cake!

CUMBRIA

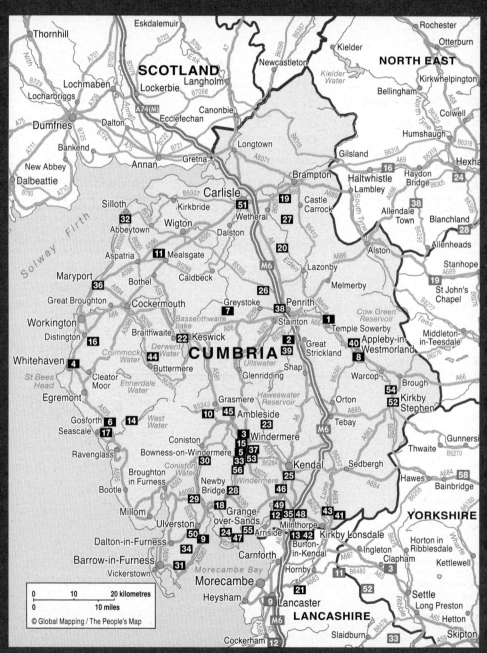

Opening Dates

January

5 Jan to 31 Jan
50 Swarthmoor Hall

February

1 Feb to 28 Feb
50 Swarthmoor Hall
Sunday 27
48 Summerdale House

March

1 Mar to 31 Mar
50 Swarthmoor Hall
Friday 25
10 Copt Howe
Wednesday 30
10 Copt Howe

April

1 Apr to 15 Apr
50 Swarthmoor Hall
Friday 1
10 Copt Howe
48 Summerdale House
Wednesday 6
10 Copt Howe
Friday 8
48 Summerdale House
Saturday 9
10 Copt Howe
Wednesday 13
10 Copt Howe
Friday 15
10 Copt Howe
48 Summerdale House
Wednesday 20
10 Copt Howe
Friday 22
10 Copt Howe
48 Summerdale House
Saturday 23
10 Copt Howe
Sunday 24
10 Copt Howe
48 Summerdale House
Monday 25
10 Copt Howe
Wednesday 27
10 Copt Howe
Friday 29
7 Chapelside
48 Summerdale House
Saturday 30
7 Chapelside
9 Conishead Priory & Buddhist Temple

May

Sunday 1
5 Brackenrigg Lodge
9 Conishead Priory & Buddhist Temple
53 Windy Hall
Friday 6
10 Copt Howe
48 Summerdale House
Saturday 7
10 Copt Howe
15 Gatesbield
Sunday 8
1 Acorn Bank
12 Dallam Tower
Wednesday 11
10 Copt Howe
Friday 13
7 Chapelside
10 Copt Howe
48 Summerdale House
Saturday 14
7 Chapelside
Sunday 15
20 Hazel Cottage
37 Matson Ground
48 Summerdale House
Wednesday 18
10 Copt Howe
Thursday 19
10 Copt Howe
Friday 20
10 Copt Howe
48 Summerdale House
Saturday 21
33 Lindeth Fell Country House Hotel
35 Lower Rowell Farm
Sunday 22
35 Lower Rowell Farm
Wednesday 25
10 Copt Howe
Friday 27
7 Chapelside
10 Copt Howe
48 Summerdale House
Saturday 28
7 Chapelside
10 Copt Howe
Sunday 29
3 Beck Lodge
6 Buckbarrow House
14 Galesyke
21 Heywood House
39 The Nook
Monday 30
6 Buckbarrow House
10 Copt Howe
14 Galesyke
22 High Moss
39 The Nook

June

Wednesday 1
10 Copt Howe
Friday 3
10 Copt Howe
Sunday 5
2 Askham Hall
5 Brackenrigg Lodge
26 Hutton-in-the-Forest
53 Windy Hall
55 Yewbarrow House
Wednesday 8
10 Copt Howe
Friday 10
7 Chapelside
10 Copt Howe
Saturday 11
7 Chapelside
10 Copt Howe
Sunday 12
1 Acorn Bank
11 Crookdake Farm
16 Gilgarran Gardens
Wednesday 15
10 Copt Howe
Friday 17
10 Copt Howe
Saturday 18
44 Rannerdale Cottage
51 Tullie House
Sunday 19
8 Church View
21 Heywood House
30 Lawson Park
31 Leece Village Gardens
32 Lilac Cottage Garden
44 Rannerdale Cottage
48 Summerdale House
51 Tullie House
56 Yews
Wednesday 22
10 Copt Howe
38 Newton Rigg Campus Gardens (Afternoon & Evening)
Friday 24
7 Chapelside
10 Copt Howe
Saturday 25
7 Chapelside
10 Copt Howe
41 Park House
Sunday 26
27 Ivy House
36 Maryport Gardens
41 Park House
Wednesday 29
10 Copt Howe
18 Haverthwaite Lodge
28 Lakeside Hotel

July

Friday 1
34 Little Urswick Village Gardens (Evening)

Support the NGS – eat more cake! ☕

Sunday 3
- **1** Acorn Bank
- **13** Dalton Hamlet Gardens
- **34** Little Urswick Village Gardens
- **55** Yewbarrow House

Friday 8
- **7** Chapelside

Saturday 9
- **7** Chapelside

Sunday 10
- **19** Hayton Village Gardens
- **24** Holker Hall Gardens
- **26** Hutton-in-the-Forest

Thursday 14
- **23** Holehird Gardens
- **45** Rydal Hall

Sunday 17
- **20** Hazel Cottage

Saturday 23
- **46** Sizergh Castle

Sunday 24
- **52** Westview
- **54** Winton Park

Thursday 28
- **45** Rydal Hall

Sunday 31
- **17** Hall Senna
- **25** Horticare

August

Sunday 7
- **55** Yewbarrow House

Thursday 11
- **45** Rydal Hall

Sunday 14
- **34** Little Urswick Village Gardens

Saturday 20
- **49** Sunnyside

Sunday 21
- **49** Sunnyside

Sunday 28
- **4** Berridale
- **48** Summerdale House

Wednesday 31
- **18** Haverthwaite Lodge
- **28** Lakeside Hotel

September

3 Sept to 30 Sept
- **50** Swarthmoor Hall

Saturday 3
- **30** Lawson Park

Sunday 4
- **55** Yewbarrow House

Sunday 11
- **8** Church View

October

1 Oct to 8 Oct
- **50** Swarthmoor Hall

February 2012

Sunday 19
- **48** Summerdale House

Gardens open to the public
- **1** Acorn Bank
- **9** Conishead Priory & Buddhist Temple
- **10** Copt Howe
- **23** Holehird Gardens
- **24** Holker Hall Gardens
- **26** Hutton-in-the-Forest
- **45** Rydal Hall
- **46** Sizergh Castle
- **50** Swarthmoor Hall
- **51** Tullie House

By appointment only
- **29** Langholme Mill
- **40** Olde Oaks
- **43** Pudding Poke Barn
- **47** Stone Edge

Also open by Appointment ☎
- **16** 12 The Avenue, Gilgarran Gardens
- **16** 6 The Avenue, Gilgarran Gardens
- **4** Berridale
- **6** Buckbarrow House
- **7** Chapelside
- **8** Church View
- **11** Crookdake Farm
- **14** Galesyke
- **16** Gilgarran Gardens
- **17** Hall Senna
- **18** Haverthwaite Lodge
- **20** Hazel Cottage
- **22** High Moss
- **28** Lakeside Hotel
- **29** Langholme Mill
- **30** Lawson Park
- **32** Lilac Cottage Garden
- **35** Lower Rowell Farm
- **37** Matson Ground
- **39** The Nook
- **40** Olde Oaks
- **41** Park House
- **13** Pear Tree Cottage
- **43** Pudding Poke Barn
- **31** Raising House, Leece Village Gardens
- **47** Stone Edge
- **48** Summerdale House
- **53** Windy Hall
- **55** Yewbarrow House

The Gardens

1 ◆ **ACORN BANK**
Temple Sowerby CA10 1SP.
National Trust, 017683 61893,
www.nationaltrust.org.uk. *6m E of
Penrith. Off A66; ¹/₂ m N of Temple
Sowerby. Bus: Penrith-Appleby or
Carlisle-Darlington; alight Culgaith Rd
end.* **Adm £4.50, chd £2.50. For
NGS: Suns 8 May; 12 June; 3 July
(10-5). For other opening times and
information, please phone or see
garden website.**
Medium-sized walled garden; herb
garden with collection of more than
250 medicinal and culinary plants;
orchard and mixed borders; wild
garden with woodland/riverside walk
leading to a partly restored watermill
open to the public. Dogs on leads
only in woodland walk. Access map
and information available.
♿ ❃ ☕ ⛏

2 **ASKHAM HALL**
Penrith CA10 2PF. Countess of
Lonsdale. *5m S of Penrith. Turn off
A6 for Lowther & Askham.* Home-
made teas. **Adm £3.50, chd free
(share to Askham & Lowther
Churches). Sun 5 June (2-5).**
Askham Hall is a pele tower (not
open), incorporating C14, C16 and
early C18 elements in courtyard plan.
Splendid formal outlines of garden
with terraces of herbaceous borders
and original topiary, probably from late
C17. Herb garden and recently
created meadow area with trees and
pond. Increasing kitchen garden,
basically organic.
❃ ☕

3 **NEW** ▶ **BECK LODGE**
Bridge Lane, Troutbeck,
Windermere LA23 1LA. Mrs Rachel
Crowfoot. *2¹/₂ m N of Windermere.
From Windermere after Lakes School,
turn R into Bridge Lane, off A591.
Garden on R in ¹/₂ m.* **Adm £3, chd
free. Sun 29 May (11-4).**
Set in the beautiful Troutbeck Valley
this enchanting 1¹/₄ -acre garden is
overflowing with colourful
rhododendrons, azaleas, magnolias
and spring bulbs. A charming pergola
is clothed in a mantle of blue wisteria
complementing well kept lawns and
mixed borders. There is a small but
very productive fruit and vegetable
garden and stunning views of Lake
Windermere.
♿

4 ▶ BERRIDALE
15 Loop Road South, Whitehaven
CA28 7TN. Enid & John
Stanborough, 01946 695467. *From
S, A595 through T-lights onto Loop
Rd approx 150yds on R. From N,
A595 onto Loop Rd at Pelican
Garage, garden approx 1½ m on L.*
Light refreshments & home-made
teas. **Adm £3, chd free. Sun 28 Aug
(2-5). Visitors also welcome by
appt with 2 weeks notice for group
visits June to Sept. Coach parties
welcome any number.**
Large cottage style garden divided
into several areas including Japanese
style, wildlife, patio, large vegetable
garden with fruit trees, show class
vegetables and flowers. Large front
garden, 2 lawns surrounded by flower
borders and small pond. Large pond
with seating area leading to
greenhouse of fuchsias and plants for
sale. Oil paintings by Enid on display.
RHS Banksian Medal for most points
for fuchsia's, also for flower and
vegetables at 2 shows. Limited
wheelchair access.

&♿ ⊗ ☕ ☎

5 ▶ BRACKENRIGG LODGE
Windy Hall Road, Bowness-on-
Windermere LA23 3HY. Lynne
Bush, www.brackenriggs.co.uk.
*½ m S of Bowness. Just off B5284
on Windy Hall Rd, opp Linthwaite
House Hotel entrance.* Home-made
teas at Windy Hall. **Adm £4, chd
free. Combined with Windy Hall
adm £6, chd free. Suns 1 May;
5 June (10-5).**
3 acres of wildlife garden run on
organic lines with a combination of
native and cultivated plants, shrubs
and trees. Water features created
from a diverted culvert giving streams,
waterfall and pond. Woodland area,
bog garden, wild flower meadows.
The new deer fence works a treat.
Stout footwear needed.

🛏 ☕

6 ▶ BUCKBARROW HOUSE
Denton Park Court, Gosforth
CA20 1BN. John Maddison,
01946 725431,
jhnmaddison@googlemail.com.
*13m S of Whitehaven. Turn off A595.
Through centre of Gosforth Village. At
'Y' junction take L fork towards
Wasdale. After 150yds turn L (before
church) into Denton Park. Keep
bearing R. House is last on R in
Denton Park Court.* Tea/coffee &
cakes at no. 7. **Adm £3, chd free.
Sun 29, Mon 30 May (11-5).**

Summerdale House

Visitors also welcome by appt.
Small densely-planted garden approx
23yds x 49yds. Number of
compartments incl wildlife pond,
Japanese style border and gravel
garden, shrub area, cottage garden
borders, natural stream. Decking
area. Decorative stone front garden.
Favourite plant acers. A visitor said 'A
small garden which appears to be
much larger than it is!'.

⊗ ☕ ☎

7 ▶ CHAPELSIDE
Mungrisdale, Penrith CA11 0XR.
Tricia & Robin Acland, 017687
79672. *12m W of Penrith. On A66
take unclassified rd N, signed
Mungrisdale Village. House is far end
of scattered village on L immed after
tiny church on R.* Use parish church
room parking at foot of our short
drive. **Adm £3, chd free (share to
Mungrisdale Parish Church). Fris,
Sats 29, 30 Apr; 13, 14, 27, 28 May;
10, 11, 24, 25 June; 8, 9 July (11-5).
Visitors also welcome by appt.
Teas for groups by arrangement.**
1-acre organic garden below fell,
around C18 farmhouse and
outbuildings, latter mainly open. Tiny
stream, large pond. Alpine,
herbaceous, raised, gravel, damp and
shade beds, bulbs in grass. Extensive
range of plants, many unusual. Art
constructions in and out, local stone
used creatively. Fine views, so unkind
winds. Featured in Garden News.

🐾 ⊗ ☎

8 ▶ CHURCH VIEW
Bongate, Appleby-in-Westmorland
CA16 6UN. Mrs H Holmes,
017683 51397,
engcougars@btinternet.com,
http://www.engcougars.co.uk/
church-view. *Northbound on A66
take B6542 to Appleby. After 2m St
Michael's Church on L garden opp.
Southbound on A66 take Appleby slip
rd, B6542 under railway bridge, pass
R Eden on R and continue up hill to
Royal Oak Inn. Garden next door opp
church.* **Adm £3, chd free. Suns 19
June; 11 Sept (2-5). Visitors also
welcome by appt.**
Developed (2007 - 2008) on a sloping
site. Roses and some shrubs for
structure, but relying heavily on
grasses and herbaceous plants to
create textures, colour combinations
and contrasts in a modern way. Mixed
beds at front with 'woodland corner'.
A small self-contained cottage garden
to get lost in. Featured in The
Cumberland & Westmorland Herald.
The main garden is on a sloping site,
gravel paths.

&♿ ⊗ ☕ ☎

9 ▶ ◆ CONISHEAD PRIORY &
BUDDHIST TEMPLE
A5087 Coast Road, Ulverston
LA12 9QQ. Manjushri Kadampa
Meditation Centre, 01229 584029,
visits@manjushri.org.
www@manjushri.org *2m S of
Ulverston on A5087 Coast Road.
30 mins from M6 J36, follow A590 to*

Ulverston then L onto A5087 Coast Road signed. **Adm £3, chd free. For NGS: Sat 30 Apr; Sun 1 May (10-5). For other opening times and information, please phone or see garden website.**
40 acres of gardens and woodland surrounding Gothic mansion. Temple garden an oasis of peace, wildlife garden, arboretum, cottage gardens. Free map with 3 woodland walks. 6 minute woodland walk to Morecambe Bay. 'It is an amazing house, one of the most spectacular in Cumbria', Hunter Davies in 'Best of Lakeland'. Free guided tours of Temple and house. Cafe and gift shop.

Wide range of home-grown plants available . . .

10 ◆ COPT HOWE
Chapel Stile, Great Langdale LA22 9JR. Professor R N Haszeldine, Please tel 015394 37685 for weekly recorded message. *5m W of Ambleside. On B5343, ¹/₄ m past Chapel Stile.* **Adm £4, chd free. For NGS: Fri 25, Wed 30 Mar; Fri 1, Wed 6, Sat 9, Wed 13, Fri 15, Wed 20, Fri 22 to Mon 25, Wed 27 Apr; Fri 6, Sat 7, Wed 11, Fri 13, Wed 18, Thur 19, Fri 20, Wed 25, Fri 27, Sat 28, Mon 30 May; 11, 25 Ju Weds 1 June to 29 June; Fris 3 June to 24 June (12.30-4.30). For other opening times and information, please phone.**
2-acre plantsman's mountain paradise garden. Superb views Langdale Pikes. Extensive collections of acers, camellias, azaleas, rhododendrons, oaks, beeches, rare shrubs, trees, unusual perennials; herbaceous and bulbous species; alpines, trough gardens; rare conifers; expedition plants from worldwide mountainous regions. Outstanding spring and autumn colour. Wildlife sanctuary, red squirrels, badgers, slow-worms, lizards, hotel for wild birds. Major new garden extensions and features. Featured in many papers, magazines, radio and TV programmes.

11 ▶ CROOKDAKE FARM
Aspatria CA7 3SH. Kirk & Alannah Rylands, 016973 20413, rylands@crookdake.com. *3m NE of Aspatria. Between A595 & A596. From A595 take B5299 at Mealsgate signed Aspatria. After 2m turn sharp R in Watch Hill signed Crookdake. House 1m on L.* Home-made teas. **Adm £3.50, chd free. Sun 12 June (1-5). Visitors also welcome by appt June & July only. No coaches.**
Windswept informal farmhouse (not open) garden with a careful colour combination of planting sympathetic to the landscape incl various different areas with densely planted herbaceous borders, vegetable patch, wild meadow and large pond area home to moisture-loving plants, tame hens and wild moorhens. Featured in Cumbria Life.

12 ▶ DALLAM TOWER
Milnthorpe LA7 7AG. Mr & Mrs R T Villiers-Smith. *7m S of Kendal. 7m N of Carnforth. Nr junction of A6 & B5282. Stn: Arnside, 4m; Lancaster, 15m.* Cream teas. **Adm £3, chd free. Sun 8 May (2-5).**
Large garden; natural rock garden, water garden; wood walks, lawns, shrubs. C19 cast iron orangery.

GROUP OPENING

13 ▶ DALTON HAMLET GARDENS
Burton-in-Kendal LA6 1NN. *4m W of Kirkby Lonsdale. 10m S of Kendal. From village of Burton-in-Kendal (A6070) follow Vicarage Lane for 1m. Parking at Russell Farm (signed).* Light refreshments & home-made teas 2 Bell House Barn. **Combined adm £4, chd free. Sun 3 July (11-5).**

1 BELL HOUSE BARN
Harold & Mary Newell

2 BELL HOUSE BARN
Richard Davey & Jane Hopwood

NEW CROW TREES BARN
Carole Bentham

2 FORESTRY HOUSES
David & Carol Haigh

PEAR TREE COTTAGE
Linda & Alec Greening
Visitors also welcome by appt (see seperate entry).

RUSSELL FARM
Michael & Anne Taylor

6 gardens set in a peaceful rural hamlet near Burton-in-Kendal in SE Cumbria, overlooking the remains of a probable Bronze Age settlement and with lovely country views. Each garden has its own distinctive character, ranging from a farmhouse garden with colour-packed borders and tubs, to a plantsperson's garden with a wildlife friendly approach; one garden making innovative use of its steeply sloping site; another where chickens are free to roam and help with pest control. Well stocked herbaceous borders, mature shrubs and trees, gravel beds, ponds, rare and unusual plants, and a collection of more than 200 different ferns, all within a short stroll of each other. Wide range of home-grown plants available. Limited disabled access due to steps and slopes in several gardens. Featured in Lancaster Guardian.

14 ▶ GALESYKE
Wasdale CA20 1ET. Christine & Mike McKinley, 019467 26267, mckinley2112@sky.com. *From N follow signs to Nether Wasdale, through village take rd to The Lake & Wasdale Head. After approx ³/₄ m Galesyke on R on sharp R-hand bend with wooden fence. From S turn R at Santon Bridge, follow signs to Wasdale Head, Galesyke 2¹/₂ m on R.* Cream teas. **Adm £3, chd free. Sun 29, Mon 30 May (11-5). Visitors also welcome by appt.**
Partially landscaped garden of several acres on banks of R Irt with views of Wasdale Fells, noted for its display of rhododendrons and azaleas. ' During the November 2009 floods the garden suffered some damage; the beds immediately adjacent to the river were completely washed away; and further downstream, several trees were lost. It is possible that this damage may not have been made good in time for the garden opening'.

15 ▶ GATESBIELD
New Road, Windermere LA23 2LA. Gatesbield Quaker Housing Assoc, www.gatesbield.org.uk. *¹/₂ m from Windermere Rail/Bus stn. A5074 300 metres S of Windermere town centre.* Home-made teas. **Adm £3.50, chd free. Sat 7 May (2-5).**
Historic garden surrounding Arts and

Crafts House. Garden adds peace and beauty to lives of the community of residents, who help manage the garden together with volunteers. Rocky outcrops and dells. Several Rothschild rhododendrons, large established King George rhododendron. Unusual trees and ferns. Allotment and composting areas. Refreshments served in Arts and Crafts House, where you can view the Stanley Davies exhibition. Some gravel paths and steep slopes.

GROUP OPENING

16 GILGARRAN GARDENS

Gilgarran CA14 4RD, 01946 830158, pspeakman@sky.com. *5m N of Whitehaven, 5m E of Workington. Turn off A595 towards Distington crematorium. After 1m turn L for Gilgarran. The Avenue 1st rd on R, Pinewoods 2nd rd on R.* Light refreshments & home-made teas at 12 The Avenue. **Combined adm £4, chd free. Sun 12 June (12-5).** Visitors also welcome by appt. Private visits at 12 The Avenue only. Group visits by appt available at all 3 gardens.

STILEFIELD
13 Pinewoods. Brian & Alice Middleton

12 THE AVENUE
Paul & Carol Speakman
Visitors also welcome by appt, 7 days in advance.
01946 830158
pspeakman@sky.com

6 THE AVENUE
Brian & Avril Dixon
Visitors also welcome by appt, group visits. 01946 834434
dixon731@btinternet.com

Small hamlet overlooking the Cumbria coast and fells. Scenic views of the Solway. Three contrasting gardens which vary from a formal landscaped garden, to woodland and wildlife gardens. 6 The Avenue mature garden with seating areas, small woodland garden with summerhouse, leading to ancient woodland. This has been developed into a woodland walk, with a stream and a sandstone bridge dated 1890. Dry river beds, ponds, bridges, leading to views over Irish Sea. 12 The Avenue quiet setting with landscaped lawned terraces, patios, cottage garden, and vegetable garden. Panoramic views of the

Solway Coast. Established trees and shrubs at side contrast with the 'still evolving' rear garden. Array of pots and containers. Stilefield mature house garden with newly developing woodland wildlife garden with pond, shrubs and perennials. Vegetable plot. Refreshments at 12 The Avenue. Plant Sale at Stilefield. Featured in local press and on CFM radio.

17 HALL SENNA

Hallsenna, Gosforth, Holmrook CA19 1YB. Chris & Helen Steele, 01946 725436, helen.steele5@btinternet. *2m SW of Gosforth. Follow main A595 either N or S. 1m S of Gosforth turn down lane opp Seven Acres Caravan Park, proceed for approx 1m.* Home-made teas. **Adm £3, chd free. Sun 31 July (10.30-5).** Visitors also welcome by appt, small parties welcome, no coaches due to limited access.

Tucked away within the hamlet of Hallsenna close to the West Cumbrian coast this garden provides the visitor with many different aspects of gardening. The 1 acre site includes borders fully planted for year round colour and many delightful structures built to provide interest, and punctuate your journey through the garden. Garden tombola, plant sales, homemade teas. Featured in Cumbria Life magazine, Amateur Gardening weekly.

18 HAVERTHWAITE LODGE

Haverthwaite LA12 8AJ. David Snowdon, 015395 39841, sheena.taylforth@lakesidehotel.co. uk. *100yds off A590 at Haverthwaite. Turn E off A590 opp Haverthwaite railway stn.* Teas at Lakeside Hotel. **Adm £3, chd free, combined with Lakeside Hotel £5, chd free. Weds 29 June; 31 Aug (11-4).** Visitors also welcome by appt.

Traditional Lake District garden that has been redesigned and replanted. Gardens on a series of terraces leading down to the R Leven and incl: rose garden, cutting garden, dell area, rock terrace, herbaceous borders and many interesting mature shrubs. In a stunning setting the garden is surrounded by oak woodland and was once a place of C18 and C19 industry.

GROUP OPENING

19 HAYTON VILLAGE GARDENS

Brampton CA8 9HR. *7m E of Carlisle. 3m W of Brampton. From W./J43 M6, A69 E. towards Hexham/Newcastle. 5m turn R signed Hayton. From E./Brampton, A69 W towards Carlisle. 1m turn L at Lane End PH signed Hayton. Maps of garden locations available to visitors. Parking along road on one side only please.* Home-made teas. **Combined adm £3, chd free (share to Hayton Church). Sun 10 July (1-5).**

BRACKENHOW
Mrs Susan Tranter

THE CEDARS
Mrs Lynda Hayward

NEW HAYTON C OF E PRIMARY SCHOOL

KINRARA
Tim & Alison Brown

NEW MILLBROOK
Emily Headon & Angus Dawson

Easily accessible small village of many characterful old sandstone properties, green, church and Stone Inn (Sunday lunches available 12 - 2.30). Not far from Hadrian's Wall, Talkin Tarn, North Pennine fells, Eden Valley and small market town of Brampton with particular attractions such as a Philip Webb church with Burne Jones stained glass. Gardens of varied size and styles all within ½ m. Two new gardens for 2011: Traditional sandstone cottage surrounded by varied planting and featuring large north facing, steeply sloping rear garden with pool and poultry! Secondly, the annual miniature garden competition of Hayton C of E Primary School. Returning gardens: two complementary adjacent front gardens, one with detailed cottage style colour, harmony and containers. The second using slope to create terraces with spring, frog pond and all year texture/colour. A large traditional country garden of sweeping lawns with mixed borders and pergola around patio with outdoor fireplace.

Crookdake Farm

phone or see garden website.
The garden is run by volunteers with the aim of promoting knowledge of the cultivation of alpine and herbaceous plants, shrubs and trees, especially those suited to Lakeland conditions. One of the best labelled gardens in the UK. National Collections of *Astilbe, Hydrangea* and *Polystichum* (ferns). Set on the fellside with stunning views over Windermere the walled garden gives protection to mixed borders whilst alpine houses protect an always colourful array of tiny gems. Consistently voted among the top gardens in Britain and Europe. Partial wheelchair access.

&. ❀ **NCCPG**

24 ◆ **HOLKER HALL GARDENS**
Cark-in-Cartmel, Grange-over-Sands LA11 7PL. Lord & Lady Cavendish, 015395 58328, info@holker.co.uk. *4m W of Grange-over-Sands. 12m W of M6 (J36) Follow brown tourist signs.* **Adm £6.50, chd £3.50. For NGS: Sun 10 July (10.30-5.30).** For other opening times and information please email or telephone.
25 acres of romantic gardens, with peaceful arboretum, inspriational formal gardens, flowering meadow and Labyrinth. Spring sees thousands of bulbs and flowers. Summer brings voluptuous mixed borders and bedding with old-fashioned roses, topiary and box hedging. Discover unusually large Rhododendrons, Magnolisa and Azaleas, and the National Collection of Stryracaceae. Hourly guided tours 11-3. Donations to NGS. Garden map provided indicating position of wheelchair ramps, steps and slopes.

&. ❀ **NCCPG**

25 ◆ **HORTICARE**
54 Wattsfield Road, Kendal LA9 5JN. Mr John Taylor. *From Milnthorpe Rd (A6) turn onto Wattsfield Rd. Take 2nd L onto Wattsfield Avenue. Horticare is across the rd at the end.* Home-made teas. **Adm £3, chd free. Sun 31 July (12-4).**
Horticare is the second 'atypical' garden to join the NGS this year. Horticare is a Horticultural Day Service providing a therapeutic and supportive environment for people with learning disabilities. It is a working nursery growing shrubs, perennials and ornamental bedding as well as providing a garden maintenance service. It is run with a

20 ◆ **HAZEL COTTAGE**
Armathwaite CA4 9PG. Mr D Ryland & Mr J Thexton, 016974 72473, david@dryland73.orangehome.co. uk. *8m SE of Carlisle. Turn off A6 just S of High Hesket signed Armathwaite, after 2m house facing you at T-junction.* Home-made teas. **Adm £3.50, chd free. Suns 15 May; 17 July (1-5).** Visitors also welcome by appt.
Developing flower arrangers and plantsmans garden. Extending to approx 5 acres. Incls herbaceous borders, pergola, ponds and planting of disused railway siding providing home to wildlife. Many variegated and unusual plants. Varied areas, planted for all seasons, S-facing, some gentle slopes.

❀ ☕ ☎

21 ◆ **HEYWOOD HOUSE**
Littledale Road, Brookhouse LA2 9PW. Mike & Lorraine Cave. *4m E of Lancaster. From J34 M6, follow A683 to Caton/Kirkby Lonsdale. At mini island turn R to Brookhouse. At Black Bull PH turn R, garden ³⁄₄ m on LH-side.* Home-made teas. **Adm £3.50, chd free. Sun 29 May; Sun 19 June (11-5).**
Secluded 2-acre garden with many unusual trees and shrubs, sweeping lawns with beautiful herbaceous borders leading to large natural wildlife pond, gravel garden, pergolas with an abundance of roses and

climbers, rockery, folly, woodland garden with natural stream, under development. Garden railway train rides for adults and children.

❀ ☕

22 NEW **HIGH MOSS**
Portinscale, Keswick CA12 5TX. Christine & Peter Hughes, christine_hug25@hotmail.com. *1m W of Keswick. Enter village off A66, take 1st turning R through white gates, on R of rd after ¹⁄₃ m.* Home-made teas. **Adm £3, chd free (share to Keswick Mountain Rescue). Mon 30 May (2-5.30).** Visitors also welcome by appt.
Lakeland Arts and Craft house (not open) and garden currently being restored under supervision of Tom Attwood, returning to the Scheme after many years' absence. 4¹⁄₂ acres of formal and informal S-facing terraced gardens, lawns and paddocks with magnificent views of the fells. Many fine trees, rhododendrons and azaleas.

❀ ☕ ☎

23 ◆ **HOLEHIRD GARDENS**
Windermere LA23 1NP. Lakeland Horticultural Society, 015394 32005, www.holehirdgardens.org.uk. *2m N of Windermere. Off A592 Patterdale Rd. Garden signed on R.* **Adm £3, by donation, chd free. For NGS: Thur 14 July (10-4).** For other opening times and information, please

strong emphasis on recycling and sustainability; much of the potting compost is made from waste sawdust provided by a local business mixed with grass mowings from the garden maintenance service. A small therapy garden, made mainly with reclaimed and recycled materials, offers both tranquillity and a feast for the senses. Information on horticulture as therapy.

26 ◆ **HUTTON-IN-THE-FOREST**
Penrith CA11 9TH. Lord Inglewood, 017684 84449, www.hutton-in-the-forest.co.uk. *6m NW of Penrith. On B5305, 3m from exit 41 of M6 towards Wigton.* **Adm £5, chd free. For NGS: Sun 5 June; Sun 10 July (11-5). For other opening times and information, please phone or see garden website.**
Hutton-in-the-Forest is surrounded on two sides by distinctive yew topiary and grass terraces -, which to the S lead to C18 lake and cascade. 1730s walled garden is full of old fruit trees, tulips in spring, roses and an extensive collection of herbaceous plants in summer.

27 **IVY HOUSE**
Cumwhitton, Brampton CA8 9EX. Martin Johns & Ian Forrest. *6m E of Carlisle. At the bridge at Warwick Bridge on A69 take turning to Great Corby & Cumwhitton. Through Great Corby & woodland until you reach a T-junction. Turn R to Cumwhitton (approx 4m from A69).* Home-made teas in Cumwhitton Village Hall. **Adm £3, chd free. Sun 26 June (11-5).**
Approx 2 acres of sloping fell-side garden with meandering paths leading to a series of 'rooms': pond, fern garden, gravel garden with assorted grasses, vegetable and herb garden, small terrace gardens. Copse with meadow leading down to beck. Trees, shrubs, bamboos and herbaceous perennials planted with emphasis on variety of texture and colour. Partial wheelchair access.

28 **LAKESIDE HOTEL**
Lake Windermere, Newby Bridge LA12 8AT. Mr N Talbot, 015359 30001, sales@lakesidehotel.co.uk. *1m N of Newby Bridge. On S shore of Lake Windermere. From A590 at Newby Bridge, cross the bridge which leads onto the Hawkshead rd. Follow this rd for 1m, hotel on the R.*

Complimentary parking available. Light refreshments & home-made teas. **Adm £3, chd free, Combined with Haverthwaite Lodge £5, chd free. Weds 29 June; 31 Aug (11-4). Visitors also welcome by appt.**
Created for year round interest, packed with choice plants, including some unusual varieties. Main garden areas with shrub roses, herbaceous, foliage shrubs, scented and winter interest plants and seasonal bedding. Roof garden with lawn, herb filled box parterres and espaliered, local, heritage apple varieties. A full menu is available all day.

Organic kitchen garden with bees, pigs and hens . . .

29 **LANGHOLME MILL**
Woodgate, Lowick Green LA12 8ES. Judith & Graham Sanderson, 01229 885215, info@langholmemill.co.uk. *7m NW of Ulverston. Take A5092 at Greenodd towards Broughton for 3³⁄₄ m on L ¹⁄₂ m after school. Parking in front of property.* **Adm £3, chd free (share to NSPCC). Visitors welcome by appt.**
Approx 1 acre of mature woodland garden with meandering lakeland stone paths surrounding the mill race stream which can be crossed by a variety of bridges. The garden hosts well established bamboo, rhododendrons, hostas, acers and astilbes and a large variety of country flowers. Featured in Cumbria Life.

30 **LAWSON PARK**
East of Lake Coniston, Coniston LA21 8AD. Karen Guthrie & Grizedale Arts, 015394 41050, info@grizedale.org, www.lawsonpark.org. *5m E of Coniston. Follow signs to East of Lake/Brantwood. If travelling by car please use Machell's Coppice car park 200m from Brantwood. On foot 15 mins brisk walk up footpath from car park or from Brantwood garden. Minibus shuttle offered throughout open day from Machell's Coppice. Route not suitable for those with*

limited mobility. Garden is steep, uneven and wet in places. Light refreshments & home-made teas. **Adm £4, chd free. Sun 19 June; Sat 3 Sept (12-5). Visitors also welcome by appt. Guided tours & teas offered for groups of between 10-20.**
Smallholding and garden created over the last decade from a reclaimed fellside in spectacular setting overlooking Old Man of Coniston. Sinuous terraces of herbaceous, woodland and water gardens, incl wild flower meadow, organic kitchen garden with bees, pigs and hens. Many seed-grown and unusual perennials, vegetables and shrubs.'This garden is a triumph' (Eric Robson, broadcaster). NGS entry incl access to Lawson Park farmhouse, a recently restored largely C17 building now an artists' residency base. Contemporary art commissions and British design and crafts collection on show throughout house and gardens. Produce for sale. Wheelchair access inside building and in some garden areas.

GROUP OPENING

31 **LEECE VILLAGE GARDENS**
LA12 0QP. *2m E of Barrow-in-Furness. 6m SW of Ulverston. J36 M6 onto A590 to Ulverston. A5087 coast rd to Barrow. Approx 8m turn R for Leece Village (signed, look for concrete sea wall on L). Village parking for gardens. Maps supplied to visitors.* Light refreshments. **Combined adm £3.50, chd free. Sun 19 June (11-5).**

BRADLEY HOUSE
Mrs Ann Waters

BRIAR HOUSE
Jeff & Gill Lowden

NEW **LANE END HOUSE**
Lisa & Alan Sharp

3 PEAR TREE COTTAGE
Jane & Rob Phizacklea

RAISING HOUSE
Vivien & Neil Hudson
Visitors also welcome by appt. 01229 431539

WINANDER
Mrs Enid Cockshott

A small village on the Furness Peninsula 1¹⁄₂ m from Morecombe Bay, rural but not remote, with working farms centred around a small tarn. Gardens of varying size and individual styles, all of which enjoy wonderful views. Features incl a willow yurt, green roof, a white garden, hay meadow with maze, mature trees, wildlife pond, bees, cottage garden, alpines, perennials, shrubs, climbers. and much much more! Raising House, featured in 'Lancashire' magazine.

32 LILAC COTTAGE GARDEN
Blitterlees, Silloth CA7 4JJ. Jeff and Lynn Downham, 01697 332171, lilaccottage@tiscali.co.uk. *1m S of Silloth. On B5300 the Maryport to Silloth rd.* Home-made teas. **Adm £3, chd free. Sun 19 June (11-4).** Visitors also welcome by appt April to Aug.
Approx 1-acre garden set in compartments in a coastal setting. Featuring raised and woodland gardens, herbaceous borders, large lawned areas and sandstone gazebo. Each garden has an individual theme, well stocked with plants and shrubs. In the springtime the magnolias, azaleas, rhododendrons and tulip beds give a fine display of colour, which continues throughout summer and into autumn. Featured in Amateur Gardening and Cumbria Life.

33 LINDETH FELL COUNTRY HOUSE HOTEL
Lyth Valley Road, Bowness-on-Windermere LA23 3JP. Mrs P A Kennedy, www.lindethfell.co.uk. *1m S of Bowness. On A5074. From centre of Bowness opp St Martins church turn L, signed Kendal A5074. 200yds on L after Xrds at Ferry View.* Cream teas. **Adm £3.50, chd free. Sat 21 May (2-5).**
6 acres of lawns and landscaped grounds on the hills above Lake Windermere, designed by Mawson around 1909; conifers and specimen trees best in spring and early summer with a colourful display of rhododendrons, azaleas and Japanese maples; grounds offer splendid views to Coniston mountains. Partial wheelchair access: To terrace in front of house looking over garden and view.

GROUP OPENING

34 LITTLE URSWICK VILLAGE GARDENS
LA12 0PL. *4m W of Ulverston. A590 from Ulverston approx 2m to Little Urswick.* Home-made teas. **Combined adm £3.50, chd free. Evening Opening £5, wine, Fri 1 July (6-9); Suns 3 July; 14 Aug (11-5).**

BECKSIDE FARM
Anna Thomason

REDMAYNE HALL
Jennie Werry

Quiet village setting with houses set around small village green. Two very diverse gardens: Beckside is an organic cottage garden with vegetable plot and raised beds with some unusual herbaceous perennials, mainly grown from seed and cuttings. Redmayne Hall is a very private private garden. Herbaceous borders, more formal area to the rear of the house, paved areas and formal lily ponds.

35 LOWER ROWELL FARM
Milnthorpe LA7 7LU. John & Mavis Robinson, 015395 62270. *2m NE of Milnthorpe. Signed to Rowell off B6385. Garden 1/2 m up lane on L.* Home-made teas. **Adm £3, chd free. Sat 21, Sun 22 May (1-5).** Visitors also welcome by appt.
Approx 3/4 -acre garden. Borders and beds with shrubs and interesting herbaceous perennials. Retro greenhouse and vegetable plots. Very peaceful with open views to Farleton Knott, Pennines and Lakeland hills.

GROUP OPENING

36 MARYPORT GARDENS
Maryport CA15 6ES. *7m W of Cockermouth. At main T-lights on A596, turn uphill beside the church into Wood St, 1st R into Church St & 3rd L into Fleming St, which leads into Fleming Square. Parking available in the Square itself & in streets around it. For The Mount, leave the top of Fleming Sq by Camp St, which turns into Camp Rd. The Mount is on R, almost at the top of Camp Rd.* Home-

made teas at The Priory. **Combined adm £4, chd free. Sun 26 June (2-5).**

THE BROWN HOUSE
Fleming Place. Tim Longville & Celia Eddy

23 FLEMING SQUARE
John & Elizabeth Shea

NEW ▶ THE MOUNT
Camp Road. Dr Brian Money

THE PRIORY
Eaglesfield Street. The Catholic Diocese of Lancaster & Father Bryan Irving

Four gardens behind listed houses in a historic small town by the Solway Firth, three of which are small walled gardens around cobbled Georgian and Victorian Fleming Sq at the heart of the town's Conservation Area, while the fourth is the garden of a large Victorian house (not open) approx 200 metres away and close to the Roman Museum. Beach, harbour, marina, aquarium, cafés and pubs are within easy walking distance. The garden of The Brown House has been described as 'an exotic cottage garden' mixing traditional English favourites with unusual half-hardy plants. The 'quart in a pint pot' garden of 23 Fleming Square combines cottage-garden-style vegetables, soft and hard fruit with a wide range of interesting trees and shrubs. The garden of The Priory, which is still being restored, is more traditional, with mixed borders surrounding two small lawns, while the garden of The Mount is very much a family garden, with colourful borders of perennials and beds of roses. Plants for sale. Wheelchair access at The Mount and The Priory.

37 ▶ MATSON GROUND
Windermere LA23 2NH. Matson Ground Estate Co Ltd, 015394 47892, info@matsonground.co.uk. *2/3 m E of Bowness. From Kendal turn R off B5284 signed Heathwaite, 100yds after Windermere Golf Club. Garden on L after 1/3 m. From Bowness turn L onto B5284 from A5074. After 1/2 m turn L at Xrds. Garden on L 1/2 m along lane.* **Adm £3, chd free. Sun 15 May (1-5).** Visitors also welcome by appt.
2 acre formal garden with a mix of established borders, wildflower areas and a stream leading to a large pond. White garden. Newly planted rose

borders and terrace beds. Walled kitchen garden with raised beds, fruit trees and greenhouse.

38 **NEWTON RIGG CAMPUS GARDENS**
Newton Rigg, Penrith CA11 0AH. University of Cumbria, www.cumbria.ac.uk. *1m W of Penrith. 3m W from J40 & J41 off M6. ¹/₂ m off the B5288 W of Penrith.* Light refreshments & teas. **Adm £4, chd £50p. Afternoon & Evening Opening Wed 22 June (3-8.30).**
The gardens and campus grounds have much of horticultural interest incl herbaceous borders, ponds, organic garden with fruit cage and display of composting techniques, woodland walk, summer scented garden, 2 arboretums, annual meadows, pleached hornbeam walkway and extensive range of ornamental trees and shrubs. Guided tour of gardens by expert gardeners from Newton Rigg, tours incl the organic garden, ornamental garden, the aboretum.

Features including a willow yurt, green roof, a white garden, hay meadow with maze . . .

39 **THE NOOK**
Helton CA10 2QA. Brenda & Philip Freedman, 0797 985 4714, pffreedman@hotmail.co.uk. *6m S of Penrith. A6 S from Penrith. After Eamont Bridge turn R to Pooley Bridge. Fork L to Askham. Through Askham 1m to Helton. Follow signs.* Home-made teas. **Adm £3, chd free. Sun 29, Mon 30 May (11-5). Visitors also welcome by appt, best April to June.**
Plantsman's hillside garden with long views down Lowther Valley. Mainly alpine plants many rare and unusual. Front, cottage garden, side garden has cordon, espalier and fan trained fruit trees, soft fruit and vegetables. Main garden with species rhododendrons, scree garden, troughs, conifers, herb garden and water feature.

40 **OLDE OAKS**
Croft Ends, Appleby CA16 6JW. Chantal Knight, 017683 51304, chantalknight@midwife.plus.com. *1¹/₂ m N of Appleby. Heading N out of Appleby take rd to Long Marton for 1m. 1st L, continue on ¹/₂ m, garden last on R.* Home-made teas. **Adm £3, chd free. Visitors welcome by appt from mid May to end of Aug, incl groups. Coaches permitted.**
A secret ¹/₂ -acre cottage garden.Big sweeping borders filled with interesting and colourful herbaceous perrenial planting.Fabulous views of the Pennines and Lakeland fells.Lovely relaxing garden to sit and relax.2-acre woodland walk with free range hens.Koi carp pond and wildlife pond. Large plant stall-all home propagated. Featured in Cumberland and Westmorland Herald.

41 **PARK HOUSE**
Barbon, Kirkby Lonsdale LA6 2LG. Mr & Mrs P Pattison, 015242 41494 Gardener, matthew@belt7.orangehone.co.uk. *2¹/₂ m N of Kirkby Lonsdale. A65 to Kirkby Lonsdale. Turn at Devil's Bridge onto A683 towards Sedburgh, 3m turn R Barbon village, R at memorial, pass church up hill, follow signs. N.B please note at busy periods parking will be at the village hall, therefore creating a short walk to the event.* Light refreshments & home-made teas. **Adm £4, chd free. Sat 25 (10-4.30), Sun 26 June (11-4). Visitors also welcome by appt, incl cheese and wine evenings for groups.**
Romantic Manor house. Extensive vistas. Formal tranquil pond encased in yew hedging. Meadow with meandering pathways, water garden filled with bulbs and ferns. Formal lawn gravel pathways, cottage borders with hues of soft pinks and purples. shady border, kitchen garden. An evolving garden to follow. Music, wine and cream teas. Featured in Cumbria Life.

42 **PEAR TREE COTTAGE**
Dalton, Burton-in-Kendal LA6 1NN. Linda & Alec Greening, 01524 781624, linda.greening@virgin.net, www.peartreecottagecumbria.co. uk. *4m W of Kirkby Lonsdale. 10m S of Kendal. From village of Burton-in-Kendal (A6070), follow Vicarage Lane for 1m. Parking at farm, 50yds before garden (signed).* Home-made teas.

Adm £3.50, chd free. Also open as part of Dalton Hamlet Gardens 3 July. Visitors welcome by appt June and July, groups of 10+. Coaches permitted.
¹/₃ -acre cottage garden in a delightful rural setting. A peaceful and relaxing garden, harmonising with its environment and incorporating many different planting areas, from packed herbaceous borders and rambling roses, to wildlife pond, bog garden and gravel garden. A plantsperson's delight, including over 200 different ferns, and many other rare and unusual plants. Featured in 'Gardens of the Lake District' by Tim Longville.

43 **PUDDING POKE BARN**
Moorthwaite Lane, Barbon, nr Kirkby Lonsdale LA6 2LW. Gilly Newbery, 015242 76284, gandn.newb@tiscali.co.uk. *2¹/₂ m N of Kirkby Lonsdale. Take Kirkby Lonsdale rd towards Sedburgh (A683). At small bridge with green rails, turn up to village of Barbon. Take R turn at top of hill before Barn, R again, garden is 2nd house (Barn) on R. Park before you get there, one wheel up on the pavementone wheel up on the pavement.* Home-made teas & ploughman's lunches. **Adm £4, chd free. Visitors welcome by appt June to Aug, groups welcome, max 20 visitors.**
1 acre of informal plant lover's garden created over 14yrs from a field mostly with a pickaxe. Organic wildlife friendly with wild flowers in long grass, alongside raised beds, trees and shrubs, herbaceous, vegetables and fruit. Gravel garden, bog and pond. Gothic potting shed and gypsy caravan for children. Featured in Westmorland Gazette and Cumbria Magazine.

44 **RANNERDALE COTTAGE**
Buttermere CA13 9UY. The McElney Family. *8m S of Cockermouth. 10m W of Keswick. B5289 on Crummock Water, in the Buttermere Valley.* Light refreshments & teas. **Adm £2.50, chd free. Sat 18, Sun 19 June (12-5).**
¹/₂ -acre garden with beck and woodland walk overlooking Crummock Water with splendid mountain views. Herbaceous, shrubs, roses, perennial geraniums, tree peonies, pond with fish.

45 ◆ RYDAL HALL
Ambleside LA22 9LX. Diocese of
Carlisle, 01539 432050,
www.rydalhall.org. *2m N of
Ambleside. E from A591 at Rydal
signed Rydal Hall.* **Adm £3.50. For
NGS: Thurs 14, 28 July; 11 Aug
(11-4.30). For other opening times
and information, please phone or
see garden website.**
Formal Italianate gardens designed by
Thomas Mawson in 1911 set in 34
acres. The gardens have recently
been restored over a 2yr period
returning to their former glory. Informal
woodland garden, leading to C17
viewing station/summerhouse, fine
herbaceous planting, community
vegetable garden, orchard and apiary.
Garden and estate tour 1.30pm with
Head Gardener. Partial wheelchair
access.
& 🌿 ❀ 🛏 ☕

Sit and watch birds, butterflies and free range hens . . .

46 ◆ SIZERGH CASTLE
nr Kendal LA8 8AE. National Trust,
015395 69810,
www.nationaltrust.org.uk. *3m S of
Kendal. Approach rd leaves A590
close to & S of A590/A591
interchange.* **Adm £5, chd £2.50. For
NGS: Sat 23 July (11-5). For other
opening times and information,
please phone or see garden
website.**
²/₃ -acre limestone rock garden,
largest owned by National Trust;
collection of Japanese maples, dwarf
conifers, hardy ferns; hot wall border
with fruiting trees. Wild flower areas,
herbaceous borders, 'Dutch' garden.
Terraced garden and lake; kitchen
garden; fruit orchard with spring
bulbs. National Collection of
Asplenium scolopendrium,
Cystopteris,Dryopteris, Osmunda.
& NCCPG ☕

47 STONE EDGE
Jack Hill, Allithwaite LA11 7QB. Ian
& Julie Chambers. *2m W of Grange-
over-Sands. On B5277. Jack Hill is on
L just before Allithwaite Village.
Parking available 10-4.30 in The
Pheasent Inn car park at bottom of
Jack Hill approx 100m. Limited
parking for the not so fit nr house.*
Home-made teas. **Visitors welcome**
by appt by written application.
Gardening on the edge, in harmony
with nature; incl formal box, new
agave garden, pergola with border,
climbers, shrubs and perennials,
herbs grown for use in the kitchen.
Spectacular specimens form a
Mediterranean garden; tree top
balcony's; woodland garden
meanders down to fern garden and
pond. Steep slope in woodland
garden. Pots abound. Fantastic views
over Morecambe Bay. New garden
room with covered walkway,
conservatory, garden room, potting
garden room.
🌿 ☕ ☎

48 SUMMERDALE HOUSE
Nook, nr Lupton LA6 1PE. David &
Gail Sheals, 015395 67210,
sheals@btinternet.com,
www.summerdalegardenplants.co.
uk. *7m S of Kendal, 5m W of Kirkby
Lonsdale. From J36 M6 take A65
towards Kirkby Lonsdale, at Nook
take R turn Farleton.* Home-made
teas (Suns only). Soup and teas
Feb/Apr.Teas May to Aug. **Adm
£3.50, chd free. Suns, Fris, 27 Feb;
1, 8, 15, 22, 24, 29 Apr; 6, 13, 15,
20, 27 May; 19 June; 28 Aug (11-5);
2012 Sun 19 Feb. Visitors also
welcome by appt, groups of 10+.**
1½ -acre part-walled country garden
set around 18c former vicarage.
Several defined areas have been
created by hedges, each with its own
theme and linked by intricate cobbled
pathways. Beautiful setting with fine
views across to Farleton Fell.
Traditional herbaceous borders,
ponds, woodland and meadow
planting provide year round interest.
Large collections of auricula, primulas
and snowdrops. Adjoining nursery
features in RHS 'Britain's Favourite
Plants'. Home made jams and
chutneys for sale. Featured in The
Garden, The Independent - snowdrop
gardens, Best Flower Arrangement-
Japan.
🌿 ❀ ☕ ☎

49 NEW SUNNYSIDE
Woodhouse Lane, Heversham,
Milnthorpe LA7 7EW. Bill & Anita
Gott. *1¹/₂ m N of Milnthorpe. From A6
turn into Heversham, then R at
church signed Crooklands in ¹/₂ m
turn L down lane.* Home-made teas.
**Adm £3.50, chd free. Sat 20, Sun
21 Aug (1-5).**
¹/₂ -acre country cottage garden with
his and hers areas, incl pond and
mixed borders and a stunning display
of prize winning dahlias. Large
immaculate vegetable garden. Sit on
one of our many seats and watch
birds, butterflies and free range hens.
Voted Best Garden in Milnthorpe and
District Show.
❀ ☕

50 ◆ SWARTHMOOR HALL
Ulverston LA12 0JQ. Bill Shaw,
01229 583204,
www.swarthmoorhall.co.uk. *nr
Croftlands suburb of Ulverston town.
A590 to Ulverston. Turn off to
Ulverston railway station. Brown
tourist signs to hall, R into Urswick
Rd, then R into Swarthmoor Hall
Lane.* **Adm £4.50, chd free. For
NGS: Daily Wed 5 Jan to Fri 15
Apr; Sat 3 Sept to Sat 8 Oct;
(10-4.30). For other opening times
and information, please phone or
see garden website.**
Wild flower meadow, snowdrops
January. Wild purple crocus February
- April depending on weather, earlier if
mild winter later if cold and frosty.
Quiet Garden September. Opportunity
to tour the 6 historic rooms of the old
Hall, built around the end of the
sixteenth century. Plants for sale. Tea
and coffee available in the Friendship
room, free if taking the tour, donations
otherwise.
& ❀ 🛏 ☕

51 ◆ TULLIE HOUSE
Castle Street, Carlisle CA3 8TP.
Carlisle City Council, 01228
618737, www.tulliehouse.co.uk.
*City Centre. Signed as Museum on
brown signs, see website for map.*
**Adm by donation. For NGS: Sat 18
(10-5), Sun 19 June (12-5). For
other opening times and
information, please phone or see
garden website.**
Tranquil garden in city centre setting
incl new area for 2011 laid out to
reflect a Roman peristyle garden with
Roman influenced planting incl figs,
vines, myrtle, acanthus, herbs.
Delightful garden to front of Jacobean
house with mature Arbutus unedo
and Cornus kousa growing alongside
Fatsia japonica variegata and
Eucryphia glutinosa. Plant stall,
children's activities, special teas,
garden advice by garden designer.
& 🌿 ❀ ☕

52 WESTVIEW
Fletcher Hill, Kirkby Stephen
CA17 4QQ. Reg & Irene Metcalfe.
*Kirkby Stephen town centre, T-lights
opp Pine Design.* Teas at Winton

Park. Combined with **Winton Park** joint adm £4.50, chd free. **Sun 24 July (11-5).**
Tucked away behind the town centre, this secret walled cottage garden is a little haven. The main garden is filled with perennials, shrubs and large collection of hostas, with small wildlife pond. The adjacent prairie-style nursery beds are at their best in July. Featured in Cumbria Life and Amateur Gardening.

53 WINDY HALL
Crook Road, Windermere LA23 3JA. **Diane & David Kinsman,** 015394 46238, dhewitt.kinsman@gmail.com. *1m S of Bowness-on-Windermere. On western end of B5284 up Linthwaite House Hotel driveway.* Home-made teas. **Adm £4, chd free, Combined with Brackenrigg Lodge £6, chd free. Suns 1 May; 5 June (10-5). Visitors also welcome by appt.**
4-acre fellside garden. Woodland with species rhododendrons, camellias, magnolias and hydrangeas; Japanese influenced quarry garden; alpine gunneras; wildflower meadow; kitchen, 'privy' and 'Best' gardens. Waterfowl garden with gunneras and stewartias. Pond garden, moss path, bluebells and foxgloves in abundance. Wide variety of native birds, many nesting in the gardens. NCCPG Collections *Aruncus* & *Filipendula.* Black, multi-horned Hebridean sheep, rare pheasants from China & Nepal, exotic ducks and geese.

54 WINTON PARK
Appleby Road, Kirkby Stephen CA17 4PG. **Mr Anthony Kilvington.** *2m N of Kirkby Stephen. On A685 turn L signed Gt Musgrove/Warcop (B6259). After approx 1m turn L as signed.* Home-made teas. **Combined**

Beckside Farm

with **Westview** joint adm £4.50, chd free. **Sun 24 July (11-5).**
3-acre country garden bordered by the Banks of the R Eden with stunning views. Many fine conifers, acers and rhododendrons, herbaceous borders, hostas, ferns, grasses and several hundred roses. Three formal ponds plus rock pool.

55 YEWBARROW HOUSE
Hampsfell Road, Grange-over-Sands LA11 6BE. **Jonathan & Margaret Denby,** 015395 32469, jonathan@bestlakesbreaks.co.uk, www.yewbarrowhouse.co.uk. *¼ m from town centre. Follow signs in centre of Grange. Turn R at HSBC Bank into Pig Lane, 1st L into Hampsfell Rd. Garden 200yds on left-follow sign to Yewbarrow Wood at brow of hill.* Cream Teas. **Adm £4, chd free. Suns 5 June; 3 July; 7 Aug; 4 Sept (11-4). Visitors also welcome by appt.**
Mediterranean style garden on 4½ -acre elevated site with

magnificent views over Morecambe Bay. The garden features a restored walled Victorian kitchen garden; Italianate terrace garden; exotic gravel garden; fern garden, Japanese Hot Spring pool. Dahlia trial beds, Orangery, Sculpture and Sensory gardens. Featured in starred garden in GGG & Gardener's World Special feature on Coastal Gardens.

56 YEWS
Middle Entrance Drive, Storrs Park, Bowness-on-Windermere LA23 3JR. **Sir Oliver & Lady Scott.** *1m S of Bowness-on-Windermere. A5074. Middle Entrance Drive, 50yds.* Home-made teas. **Adm £3, chd free. Sun 19 June (2-5.30).**
Medium-sized formal Edwardian garden; fine trees, ha-ha, herbaceous borders; greenhouse. Bog area being developed, bamboo, primula, hosta. Young yew maze and vegetable garden.

Cumbria County Volunteers

County Organiser
Diane Hewitt, Windy Hall, Crook Road, Windermere LA23 3JA, 015394 46238, dhewitt.kinsman@googlemail.com

County Treasurer
Derek Farman, Mill House, Winster, Windermere, Cumbria LA23 3NW, 015394 44893, derek@derejam.myzen.co.uk

Publicity
Paul Burrill, Meadow House, Garnett Bridge Road, Burnside, Kendal LA8 9AY, 01539 724156, p.burrill@btinternet.com

Assistant County Organisers
East Alec & Linda Greening, Pear Tree Cottage, Dalton, Burton-in-Kendal, Carnforth LA6 1NN, 01524 781624, linda@peartreecottagecumbria.co.uk
West John Maddison, Buckbarrow House, Denton Park Court, Gosforth, Seascale CA20 1BN, 019467 25431, jhnmaddison@googlemail.com
North Alannah Rylands, Crookdake Farm, Aspatria, Wigton CA7 3SH, 016973 20413, rylands@crookdake.com

DERBYSHIRE

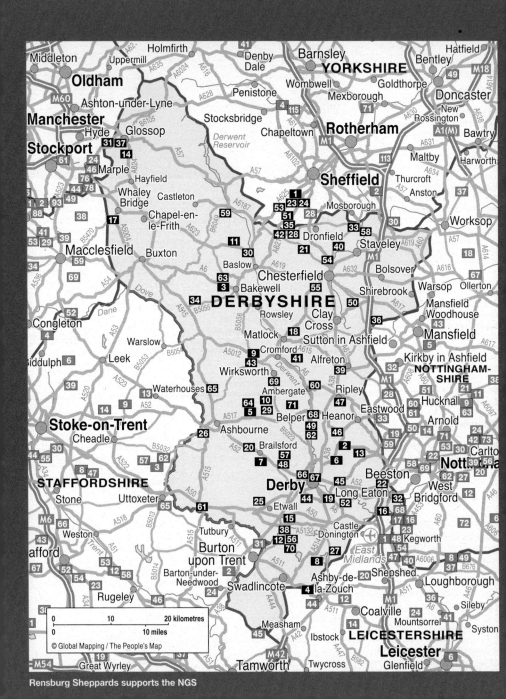

Opening Dates

February

Wednesday 16
4 Bluebell Arboretum and Nursery

March

Wednesday 9
4 Bluebell Arboretum and Nursery

Saturday 19
69 Windward

Sunday 20
69 Windward

Sunday 27
4 Bluebell Arboretum and Nursery

April

Wednesday 13
4 Bluebell Arboretum and Nursery
58 Renishaw Hall Gardens

Saturday 16
52 Old English Walled Garden, Elvaston Castle Country Park

Sunday 17
12 10 Chestnut Way
38 37 High Street
48 Meynell Langley Trials Garden
69 Windward

Sunday 24
4 Bluebell Arboretum and Nursery

Monday 25
7 The Burrows Gardens

May

Sunday 1
31 Gamesley Fold Cottage
54 The Paddock

Monday 2
1 12 Ansell Road
7 The Burrows Gardens

Saturday 7
27 The Dower House

Sunday 8
14 Cloud Cottage
27 The Dower House
30 Fir Croft
71 35 Wyver Lane

Wednesday 11
4 Bluebell Arboretum and Nursery

Saturday 14
64 Tilford House

Sunday 15
6 Broomfield Hall
14 Cloud Cottage
48 Meynell Langley Trials Garden
60 Southfield
64 Tilford House

Sunday 22
14 Cloud Cottage

30 Fir Croft
45 Locko Park
62 2 The Woodridge
69 Windward

Saturday 28
26 Dove Cottage

Sunday 29
4 Bluebell Arboretum and Nursery
13 13 Chiltern Drive
26 Dove Cottage
31 Gamesley Fold Cottage
39 Highfield House
70 Woodend Cottage

Monday 30
7 The Burrows Gardens
42 The Leylands

June

Saturday 4
2 334 Belper Road

Sunday 5
1 12 Ansell Road
2 334 Belper Road
10 Cashel
38 37 High Street
42 The Leylands

Friday 10
57 Rectory House

Sunday 12
23 124 Dobcroft Road
24 122 Dobcroft Road
30 Fir Croft
31 Gamesley Fold Cottage
48 Meynell Langley Trials Garden
66 24 Wheeldon Avenue
67 26 Wheeldon Avenue

Wednesday 15
4 Bluebell Arboretum and Nursery

Friday 17
57 Rectory House

Saturday 18
5 Brick Kiln Farm
34 Green Meadows
53 Owl End
61 Sudbury Hall

Sunday 19
5 Brick Kiln Farm
15 Clovermead
17 Craigside
22 40 Derby Road
25 Dolly Barn
28 Fanshawe Gate Hall
49 Milford Gardens
53 Owl End
71 35 Wyver Lane

Monday 20
7 The Burrows Gardens

Saturday 25
51 9 Newfield Crescent
55 Park Hall

Sunday 26
4 Bluebell Arboretum and Nursery
9 Cascades Gardens

11 Cherry Hill
22 40 Derby Road
26 Dove Cottage
28 Fanshawe Gate Hall
37 High Roost
51 9 Newfield Crescent
55 Park Hall
68 26 Windmill Rise

July

Saturday 2
35 16 The Grove

Sunday 3
1 12 Ansell Road
28 Fanshawe Gate Hall
35 16 The Grove
50 Moorfields
54 The Paddock

Saturday 9
26 Dove Cottage
47 2 Manvers Street

Sunday 10
19 8 Curzon Lane
26 Dove Cottage
28 Fanshawe Gate Hall
43 The Lilies
47 2 Manvers Street
69 Windward

Monday 11
7 The Burrows Gardens

Tuesday 12
36 Hardwick Estate (Evening)

Wednesday 13
4 Bluebell Arboretum and Nursery

Saturday 16
8 Calke Abbey
32 Grange Primary School

Sunday 17
12 10 Chestnut Way
19 8 Curzon Lane
23 124 Dobcroft Road
24 122 Dobcroft Road
32 Grange Primary School
33 The Green
36 Hardwick Estate
70 Woodend Cottage
71 35 Wyver Lane

Sunday 24
15 Clovermead
25 Dolly Barn
48 Meynell Langley Trials Garden
60 Southfield

Saturday 30
16 The Cottage

Sunday 31
4 Bluebell Arboretum and Nursery
16 The Cottage
59 Shatton Hall Farm

August

Saturday 6
34 Green Meadows

You are always welcome at an NGS garden

Sunday 7
46 9 Main Street
68 26 Windmill Rise
Tuesday 9
8 Calke Abbey
Wednesday 10
4 Bluebell Arboretum and Nursery
Sunday 14
12 10 Chestnut Way
48 Meynell Langley Trials Garden
56 22 Pinfold Close
69 Windward
70 Woodend Cottage
Sunday 21
63 Thornbridge Hall
Sunday 28
4 Bluebell Arboretum and Nursery
Monday 29
7 The Burrows Gardens
65 Tissington Hall

September

Saturday 3
61 Sudbury Hall
Sunday 4
43 The Lilies
Wednesday 7
58 Renishaw Hall Gardens
Sunday 11
23 124 Dobcroft Road
24 122 Dobcroft Road
44 Littleover Lane Allotments
48 Meynell Langley Trials Garden
Wednesday 14
4 Bluebell Arboretum and Nursery
Monday 19
7 The Burrows Gardens
Sunday 25
4 Bluebell Arboretum and Nursery

October

Sunday 9
48 Meynell Langley Trials Garden
Wednesday 12
4 Bluebell Arboretum and Nursery
Sunday 30
4 Bluebell Arboretum and Nursery

November

Wednesday 9
4 Bluebell Arboretum and Nursery
Saturday 26
4 Bluebell Arboretum and Nursery

Gardens open to the public

4 Bluebell Arboretum and Nursery
7 The Burrows Gardens
8 Calke Abbey

9 Cascades Gardens
20 Dam Farm House
36 Hardwick Estate
41 Lea Gardens
48 Meynell Langley Trials Garden
52 Old English Walled Garden, Elvaston Castle Country Park
58 Renishaw Hall Gardens
61 Sudbury Hall
65 Tissington Hall

By appointment only

3 Birchfield
18 Cuckoostone Cottage
21 Dam Stead
29 Field Farm
40 Hillside

Also open by Appointment

1 12 Ansell Road
2 334 Belper Road
5 Brick Kiln Farm
6 Broomfield Hall
10 Cashel
11 Cherry Hill
12 10 Chestnut Way
14 Cloud Cottage
15 Clovermead
16 The Cottage
17 Craigside
19 8 Curzon Lane
23 124 Dobcroft Road
25 Dolly Barn
26 Dove Cottage
27 The Dower House
28 Fanshawe Gate Hall
31 Gamesley Fold Cottage
33 The Green
35 16 The Grove
37 High Roost
39 Highfield House
42 The Leylands
46 9 Main Street
47 2 Manvers Street
50 Moorfields
53 Owl End
54 The Paddock
55 Park Hall
56 22 Pinfold Close
59 Shatton Hall Farm
60 Southfield
62 2 The Woodridge
66 24 Wheeldon Avenue
67 26 Wheeldon Avenue
69 Windward
70 Woodend Cottage
71 35 Wyver Lane

The Gardens

1 NEW **12 ANSELL ROAD**
Ecclesall, Sheffield S11 7PE. Dave
Darwent, 01142 665881,
dave.darwent@mypostoffice.co.uk.
*Approx 3m SW of City Centre. Travel
to Ringinglow Rd (88 or 83 bus), then
Edale Rd (opp Ecclesall C of E
Primary School). 3rd R - Ansell. 12 on
L ³/₄ way down, solar panel on roof.*
Home-made teas & light
refreshments. **Adm £2, chd free.**
**Mon 2 May; Suns 5 June; 3 July
(12-4). Visitors also welcome by
appt. Groups 5 to 15. 1 May to
14 August.**
Established 1930s, the garden
contains many original plants
maintained in the original style.
Traditional rustic pergola and dwarf-
wall greenhouse. Owner (grandson of
first owner) aims to keep the garden
as a living example of how inter-war
gardens were cultivated to provide
decoration and produce. More detail
on NGS website. Water features,
ponds, wisteria tunnel, wildlife area,
visiting birds, rainwater harvesting,
information leaflets, feature trail.

25 ASHBY ROAD
See Nottinghamshire.

ASTON GARDENS
See Yorkshire.

BANKCROFT FARM
See Staffordshire Birmingham &
part of West Midlands.

THE BEECHES
See Staffordshire Birmingham &
part of West Midlands.

2 **334 BELPER ROAD**
Stanley Common DE7 6FY. Gill &
Colin Hancock, 0115 930 1061.
*7m N of Derby. 3m W of Ilkeston. On
A609, ³/₄ m from Rose & Crown Xrds
(A608). Please park in field up farm
drive or Working Men's Club rear car
park if wet.* **Adm £2.50, chd free.**
**Sat 4 June (2-5), Sun 5 June (1-5).
Visitors also welcome by appt.**
Relax in our constantly evolving
country garden with informal planting
and features with plenty of seating to
enjoy our highly recommended home
made cakes. Take a stroll across the
field into the young 10-acre wood
with wild flower glades to a ¹/₂ -acre
lake. Recently planted laburnum
tunnel and rose arch.

2 Manvers Street

3 ▶ BIRCHFIELD

Dukes Drive, Ashford in the Water, Bakewell DE45 1QQ. Brian Parker, 01629 813800. *2m NW of Bakewell. On A6 to Buxton between New Bridge and Sheepwash Bridge.* **Adm £3, chd free (share to Thornhill Memorial Trust). Visitors welcome by appt all yr, groups or individuals.** Beautifully situated ³/₄ -acre part terraced garden with pond and a 1¹/₄ -acre arboretum and wild flower meadow. An extremely varied selection of trees, shrubs, climbers, perennials, bulbs, grasses and bamboos, all designed to give yr-round colour.

4 ▶ ◆ BLUEBELL ARBORETUM AND NURSERY

Annwell Lane, Smiṣby, Ashby de la Zouch LE65 2TA. Robert & Suzette Vernon, 01530 413700, www.bluebellnursery.com. *1m NW of Ashby-de-la-Zouch. Arboretum is clearly signed in Annwell Lane, ¹/₄ m S, through village of Smisby off B5006, between Ticknall & Ashby-de-la-Zouch.* **Adm £2.50, chd free. For NGS: Weds 10 Aug; 14 Sept; 12 Oct; 9 Nov; Suns 25 Sept; 30 Oct; Sat 26 Nov (9-4). For other opening times and information, please phone or see garden website.** Beautiful 9-acre woodland garden planted in last 19yrs incl many specimens of rare trees and shrubs. Information posters describing the more obscure plants. Bring wellingtons in wet weather. Please be aware this is not a wood full of bluebells, despite the name. Adjacent specialist tree and shrub nursery. Trees and shrubs for sale in the adjoining nursery. Some grass paths can be difficult for wheelchairs after heavy rain.

5 ▶ BRICK KILN FARM

Hulland Ward, Ashbourne DE6 3EJ. Mrs Jan Hutchinson, 01335 370440. *4m E of Ashbourne (A517). 1m S of Carsington Water. From Hulland Ward, take Dog Lane, past church, take 2nd L 100yds on R. From Ashbourne A517, Bradley Corner, turn L, follow sign for Carsington Water. Approx 1m up on L.* **Light refreshments & teas. Adm £3, chd free (share to Great Dane Adoption Society). Sat 18, Sun 19 June (11-5). Visitors also welcome by appt.**

Garden created 20yrs ago from part of a field. Small courtyard area with pond. Original well complements the reclaimed architectural stone work, leading to lawned area. Well filled herbaceous and shrub borders. Duck pond, pets' memorial garden. Featured on Radio Derby & in Daily Telegraph garden supplement as one of the 50 best small gardens to visit. Partial wheelchair access - garden all on one level, some uneven flag stones and gravel drive.

6 ▶ BROOMFIELD HALL

Morley DE7 6DN. Derby College, 01332 836602, eileen.swan@derby-college.ac.uk. *4m N of Derby. 6m S of Heanor on A608.* **Home-made teas & light refreshments. Adm £2.50, chd free. Sun 15 May (12-4). Visitors also welcome by appt.** Landscaped garden of 25 acres. Shrubs, trees, rose collection, herbaceous borders; glasshouses; walled garden; garden tour guides. Themed gardens, plant centre. National Collection of old roses. New Food Hub cafe & shop with a range of local, fresh, healthy & affordable food. 3 Gold Medals - Harrogate Spring Show, Derbyshire County Show & Bakewell Show. Some gravel paths & slopes but main features accessible by wheelchair.

&. NCCPG

7 ▶ ◆ THE BURROWS GARDENS

Burrows Lane, Brailsford, Ashbourne DE6 3BU. Mr B C Dalton, 01335 360745, www.burrowsgardens.com. *5m SE of Ashbourne; 5m NW of Derby. Follow yellow AA signs from both directions. From Ashbourne: A52 towards Derby 5m to Brailsford. Turn R after Rose & Crown PH, then 1st L. Continue ¹/₂ m, garden on R. From Derby: A52 towards Ashbourne, until 1¹/₂ m after Kirk Langley.Turn L at Xrds Burrows Lane. After ¹/₂ m R at grass triangle, garden in front.* **Light refreshments & home-made cakes. Adm £4, chd free. For NGS: Mons 25 Apr; 2, 30 May; 20 June; 11 July; 29 Aug; 19 Sept (10.30-4.30). For other opening times and information, please phone or see garden website.** 5 acres of stunning garden set in beautiful countryside where immaculate lawns show off exotic rare plants and trees, mixing with old favourites in this fabulous garden. A vast variety of styles from temple to Cornish, Italian and English, gloriously designed and displayed. Plants for sale. Charity events. Featured in Derbyshire Life and Countryside. Regularly featured in Local Press. Most of garden accessible unless wet.

8 ◆ CALKE ABBEY
Ticknall DE73 7LE. National Trust, 01332 863822, www.nationaltrust.org.uk. *10m S of Derby. On A514 at Ticknall between Swadlincote & Melbourne.* **Adm £4.50, chd £2.50. For NGS: Sat 16 July; Tue 9 Aug (11-5). For other opening times and information, please phone or see garden website.**
Late C18 walled gardens gradually repaired over the last twenty three years. Flower garden with summer bedding, herbaceous borders and the unique auricula theatre. Georgian orangery, impressive collection of glasshouses and garden buildings. Icehouse and grotto. Vegetable garden growing heirloom varieties of fruit and vegetables, often on sale to visitors. Garden tours and produce sale on 9 August.

&♿ ❀ ☕ ☎

Wander to the bottom of the garden past the large herbaceous border under the shade of the mature cherry trees . . .

9 ◆ CASCADES GARDENS
Clatterway, Bonsall DE4 2AH. Alan & Elizabeth Clements, 01629 822813, www.derbyshiregarden.com. *5m SW of Matlock. From Cromford A6 T-lights turn towards Wirksworth. Turn R along Via Gellia, signed Buxton & Bonsall. After 1m turn R up hill towards Bonsall village. Cascades on R at top of hill.* Light Refreshments. **Adm £3.50, chd free. For NGS: Sun 26 June (10-5). For opening times and information please visit website or telephone.**
Fascinating 4-acre garden in spectacular natural surroundings with woodland, high cliffs, stream, ponds, a ruined corn mill and old lead mine. Secluded garden rooms provide peaceful views of the extensive collection of unusual plants, shrubs and trees. Gravel paths.

&♿ ❀ 🛏 ☕ ☎

10 ◆ CASHEL
Kirk Ireton DE6 3JX. Anita & Jeremy Butt, 01335 370495. *2m S of Wirksworth, Turn off B5023 (Duffield-Wirksworth rd). Follow rd to Kirk Ireton, take sharp R turn at church corner. Follow lane for 200yds. Garden on R. Parking on L, 80yds beyond house.* Home-made teas. **Adm £3, chd free. Sun 5 June (1-5). Visitors also welcome by appt.**
3-acre garden situated on sloping site, featuring terraced ravine and several wood sculptures by local artists. Open views of surrounding countryside. Many interesting trees, shrubs and plants. Stone circle.

🐕 ❀ ☕ ☎

11 NEW ▶ CHERRY HILL
The Edge, off The Nook, Eyam, Hope Valley S32 5QP. June Elizabeth Skinner, 01433 631036, juneliza.s@btinternet.com, www.peakdistrictart.com. *4m NW of Chatsworth. In the Peak National Park. off the A623. In Eyam past the church on right take 1st R up Hawkhill Rd. Car Park opp. museum. 200yds up hill walk on to The Nook, entrance drive on R.* Home-made teas. **Adm £3, chd free. Sun 26 June (2-5). Visitors also welcome by appt.**
One-acre naturally planted artists' garden. The S-facing aspect is a delightful blend of herbaceous borders, secret areas, and a geranium carpeted orchard. Sculptures hidden amongst the foliage reflect the quirky and different style, which the present owner has brought to this garden. Follow the gravelled paths, under hazel archways where the scarecrows Jack and Jill welcome you into the vegetable plot. Wander to the bottom of the garden past the large herbaceous border under the shade of the mature cherry trees, where hostas and ferns line the pathway. The artist's studio will be open with large oil paintings to small ceramic pieces.

🐕 ❀ ☕ ☎

12 ▶ 10 CHESTNUT WAY
Repton DE65 6FQ. Robert & Pauline Little, 01283 702267, rlittleq@gmail.com, www.littlegarden.org.uk. *6m S of Derby. From A38, S of Derby, follow signs to Willington, then Repton. In Repton turn R at r'about. Chestnut Way is ¹/₄ m up hill, on L.* Home-made teas. **Adm £2.50, chd free. Suns 17 Apr; 17 July; 14 Aug (1-6). Also**

opening with **Woodend Cottage & 22 Pinfold Close (£5 entry)** August 14th. **Visitors also welcome by appt, Groups 10+. Coaches welcome.**
Meander through an acre of sweeping mixed borders, spring bulbs, mature trees to a stunning butterfly bed, young arboretum and new prairie style garden. Meet a pair of passionate, practical, organic gardeners who gently manage this plantsman's garden. Designed and maintained by the owners. Expect a colourful display throughout the yr. Plenty of seats, conservatory if wet. Special interest in viticella clematis and organic vegetables. Featured in The Derbyshire magazine. Some grass and bark paths.

&♿ 🐕 ❀ ☕ ☎

13 ▶ 13 CHILTERN DRIVE
West Hallam, Ilkeston DE7 6PA. Jacqueline & Keith Holness. *Approx 6m NE of Derby. 2m W of Ilkeston on A609. Take St Wilfred's Rd to West Hallam, 1st R Derbyshire Ave, 3rd L is Chiltern Drive.* Home-made teas. **Adm £2.50, chd free (share to Teenage Cancer Trust). Sun 29 May (11-5).**
Small, secret walled suburban garden packed with a myriad of plants, some rare and unusual. Summerhouse, two small ponds and fernery, together with 75 acers and some well-hidden lizards! Garden on two levels separated by steps. A warm welcome awaits all visitors.

❀ ☕

54 CHURCH LANE
See Nottinghamshire.

59 CHURCH LANE
See Nottinghamshire.

14 ▶ CLOUD COTTAGE
Simmondley SK13 6JN. Mr R G Lomas, 01457 862033. *1m SW of Glossop. On High Lane between Simmondley & Charlesworth. From M67 take A57, turn R at Mottram (1st T-lights) through Broadbottom & Charlesworth. In Charlesworth up Town Lane by Grey Mare. Cloud Cottage ¹/₂ m on R. From Glossop, A57 towards Manchester, turn L at 2nd of two mini r'abouts up Simmondley Lane, Cloud Cottage on L after Hare & Hounds.* Home-made teas. **Adm £3, chd free. Suns 8, 15, 22 May (2-5). Visitors also welcome by appt.**
1¹/₄ -acre arboretum and rhododendron garden. Altitude 750ft

on side of hill in Peak District National Park. Collections of conifers, most over 40yrs old. Species and hybrid rhododendrons and a wide variety of shrubs. We have extended the Japanese inspired garden by diverting a stream to make 6 ponds.

15 ◆ CLOVERMEAD
Commonpiece Lane, Findern, Derby DE65 6AF. David & Rosemary Noblet, 01283 702237. *4m S of Derby. From Findern village green, turn R at church into Lower Green, R turn into Commonpiece Lane, approx 500yds on R.* Home-made teas. **Adm £2.50, chd free. Suns 19 June; 24 July (1.30-5). Visitors also welcome by appt.**
Cottage garden set in approx 1 acre. Garden rooms full of perennial flowers. Honeysuckle, roses, jasmine and sweet peas scent the air. Pergolas and archways with clematis, fishponds and bandstand with seating. Greenhouses, large vegetable plot, wildlife orchard. Next to village nature walk & canal walk.

COLLYGATE
See Nottinghamshire.

16 THE COTTAGE
25 Plant Lane, Old Sawley, Long Eaton NG10 3BJ. Ernie & Averil Carver, 0115 8491960. *2m SW of Long Eaton. From Long Eaton green take sign for town centre. Onto B6540 through to Old Sawley, take R at Nags Head PH into Wiln Rd. 400yds take R turn into Plant Lane at the Railway Inn. Garden 200yds on R.* Home-made teas. **Adm £2.50, chd free (share to Canaan Trust). Sat 30, Sun 31 July (2-5). Visitors also welcome by appt late July.**
Cottage garden full of colour, steeped in herbaceous borders. Annual plants raised from the greenhouse. Number of surprising features. Summerhouse in a walled sheltered garden, providing a charming environment. Winners Erewash in Bloom, Best Rear Garden, Hanging Baskets & Planters and Best of the Best Award.

17 CRAIGSIDE
Reservoir Road, Whaley Bridge SK23 7BW. Jane & Gerard Lennox, 01663 732381. *11m SE of Stockport. 11m NNW of Buxton. Turn off A6 on to A5004 to Whaley Bridge. Turn at*

Jodrell Arms/train stn, under railway bridge, immed bear L along Reservoir Rd 1/2 m. Rd narrows to single track with passing places. Park on roadside or 1/2 m walk from village. Cream & Home-made teas. **Adm £3.50, chd free. Sun 19 June (12-5). Visitors also welcome by appt.**
1 acre rising steeply for magnificent views across Todbrook reservoir into Peak District. Gravel paths, stone steps with stopping places. Many mature trees incl 400yr old oak. Spring bulbs, summer fuchsias, herbaceous borders, alpine bed, steep mature rockery, wild flower meadow (we hope). Herbs, vegetables and fruit trees. Featured in Amateur Gardener.

18 CUCKOOSTONE COTTAGE
Chesterfield Road, Matlock Moor, Matlock DE4 5LZ. Barrie & Pauline Wild, 07960 708415, paulinewild@sky.com. *21/2 m N of Matlock on A632. Past Matlock Golf Course look for Cuckoostone Lane on L. Turn here & follow for 1/4 m. 1st cottage on bend.* Light Refreshments on request only. **Adm £3, chd free. Visitors welcome by appt Groups of 10+.**
Situated on a SW-facing, sloping, rural hillside at 850ft, this 1/2 -acre is a plantsman's garden. Developed in under 8yrs it incorporates colour-themed borders, pond, bog garden and conservatory. Large collection of unusual trees, shrubs and perennials make this a yr-round garden but best in late spring and late summer. Large pond. In total over 1200 different species of plants, shrubs, trees.

19 8 CURZON LANE
Alvaston, Derby DE24 8QS. Mrs Marian Gray, 01332 601596, maz@cvnation.com. *2m SE of Derby city centre. From city centre take A6 (London Rd) towards Alvaston. Curzon Lane on L, approx 1/2 m before Alvaston shops.* **Adm £2.50, chd free. Suns 10, 17 July (2-5). Visitors also welcome by appt July only, Groups 10+, no coaches.**
Mature garden with lawns, borders packed full with perennials, shrubs and small trees, tropical planting. Ornamental and wildlife ponds, greenhouse, gravel area, large patio with container planting. Also recently added extra mixed borders and potager garden.

THE DAIRY
See Leicestershire & Rutland.

20 ◆ DAM FARM HOUSE
Yeldersley Lane, Ednaston DE6 3BA. Mrs J M Player, 01335 360291. *5m SE of Ashbourne. On A52, opp Ednaston village turn, gate on R 500yds.* **Adm £4, chd free. For opening times and information, please phone.**
Two acre garden has been developed over more than 30yrs. Among its pleasures and surprises, it boasts an arboretum of rare trees, a collection of cornus and hollies, a colourful scree garden, plus a profusion of roses and diverse herbaceous borders. All of this in an outstandingly beautiful setting which is full of birds and gives striking views from its many well-placed garden benches.

Garden rooms full of perennial flowers. Honeysuckle, roses, jasmine and sweet peas scent the air . . .

21 DAM STEAD
3 Crowhole, Barlow, Dronfield S18 7TJ. Derek & Barbara Saveall, 0114 2890802, Barbarasaveall@hotmail.co.uk. *31/2 m NW of Chesterfield. From A61 Sheffield/Derby take B6051 Barlow at Chesterfield North. Through Barlow, pass Tickled Trout PH on L. Pass Springfield Rd on L then R (unamed rd). Last house on R.* Home-made teas. **Adm £2.50, chd free. Visitors welcome by appt. Groups welcome.**
3/4 acre with stream, weir, fragrant garden, rose tunnel (new), orchard and dam with an island. Long woodland path, alpine troughs/rockeries and mixed planting. A natural wildlife garden-large summerhouse with seating inside and out. 3 village well-dressings and carnival over one week mid- August.

DAVRYL
See Nottinghamshire.

16 The Grove

setting. Walled garden (formerly cow yard) with 17m rill containing different planting styles from tropical, to cottage, to formal box hedging Large well stocked fish pond. Prairie and grass gardens. Large vegetable garden and Mediterranean area around greenhouse. Featured in Derbyshire Life, The Derbyshire and Amateur Gardening.

 ♿ 🏡 ✿ ☕ ☎

DONINGTON LE HEATH MANOR HOUSE
See Leicestershire & Rutland.

26 DOVE COTTAGE
off Watery Lane, Clifton, Ashbourne DE6 2JQ. Stephen & Anne Liverman, 01335 343545, astrantiamajor@hotmail.co.uk. *1¹⁄₂ m SW of Ashbourne. Enter Clifton village. Turn R at Xrds by church. After 100yds turn L, Dove Cottage 1st house on L. Always well signed on open days.* Light refreshments. **Adm £3.50, chd free (share to British Heart Foundation). Sats & Suns 8, 29 May; 26 June; 9, 10 July (1-5). Visitors also welcome by appt.** Celebrating 25 years opening for National Gardens Scheme. Much admired ³⁄₄ -acre cottage garden by the River Dove, with fine collections of, new and traditional hardy plants and shrubs: notably astrantias, alchemillas, alliums, berberis, geraniums, euphorbias, hostas, variegated and silver foliage plants. This plantsman's garden is noted for the number of separate areas, incl a ribbon border of purple flowering plants and foliage, woodland glade planted with daffodils and shade loving plants. Featured on BBC Gardeners' Question Time as an NGS garden.

✿ ☕ ☎

27 THE DOWER HOUSE
Church Square, Melbourne DE73 8JH. William & Griselda Kerr, 01332 864756, griseldakerr@btinternet.com. *6m S of Derby. 5m W of exit 21A M1. 4m N of exit 13 M42. Church Sq is off Church St. On entering square turn R before church immed after war memorial. Dower House is at west end of Norman church. Parking on streets and in Church Square.* Home-made teas. **Adm £3, chd free. Sat & Sun 7, 8 May (10-5). Visitors also welcome by appt.** Beautiful view of Melbourne Pool from balustraded terrace running length of 1838 house. Garden drops steeply by

22 NEW 40 DERBY ROAD
Risley DE72 3SU. Ms Anne Verity. *Leave M1 Jct 25 at Sandiacre/Risley exit onto Bostocks lane. At T-lights turn left to Risley on B5010 (Derby Rd). Park on Derby Rd or Second Ave.* Home-made teas. **Adm £2.50, chd free. Suns 19, 26 June (1-5).** Plant lover's garden. Patio area with scree bed, troughs and pots surrounded by salvias, lavenders and cistus. Gravel paths and mixed borders, especially delphiniums, geraniums and peonies. Many famous old roses incl magnificent ramblers. Around 50 clematis incl herbaceous, many on obelisks, wisteria-covered arbour. Some special trees.

☕

24 NEW 122 DOBCROFT ROAD
Millhouses, Sheffield S7 2LU. Hedley & Margaret Harper. *3m SW of city centre. From city centre take A625 signed Bakewell (Ecclesall Rd S) pass Prince of Wales PH on L. Dobcroft Rd is 5th on L after PH. Follow rd for ²⁄₃m, garden on L.* Home-made teas (incl gluten free) at 124 Dobcroft Rd. **Combined adm with 124 Dobcroft Road £4, chd free. Suns 12 June; 17 July; 11 Sept (11-5).** Attractive long (250ft) garden, with colourful herbaceous borders, 2 wildlife ponds, productive vegetable garden with raised beds and greenhouse. Fine old oak tree. Summerhouse and various secluded sitting areas.

🏡 ☕

23 124 DOBCROFT ROAD
Millhouses, Sheffield. S7 2LU. Dr Simon & Julie Olpin, 01142 960554, simon.olpin@sch.nhs.uk. *3m SW City Centre. From city centre head out on A625 signpost Bakewell. A625 (Ecclesall Rd South) pass Prince of Wales PH on L. Dobcroft Rd 5th L turn after PH. Follow rd down the hill for 1.5km, 124 is on L. Palms in front garden.* Home-made teas, incl gluten free. **Combined adm with 122 Dobcroft Road £4, chd free (share to Sheffield Children's Hospital). Suns 12 June; 17 July; 11 Sept (12-5). Visitors also welcome by appt June to September.** Informal garden using mainly hardy exotics to create a jungle effect. A long (250ft), narrow site densely planted with mature trees, eucalypts, acacias, many large bamboos, palms, tree ferns and bananas. However, flowers are in short supply. Some fine specimen & rare bamboos & many mature trachycarpus & European Fan palms. A good selection of home made cakes available.

☕ ☎

25 DOLLY BARN
Ash Lane, Ash, nr Etwall, Derby DE65 6HT. Glynis & Michael Smith, 01283 734002, dollybarn@ic24.net. *6m W of Derby. From A516 Etwall bypass turn into Ash Lane signed Sutton-on-the-Hill. After 1m take R turn at postbox. Dolly Barn 200yds on R.* Home-made teas. **Adm £3, chd free. Sun 19 June; Sun 24 July (1-5). Visitors also welcome by appt.** Eclectic mix of contemporary, cottage and prairie styles in 2¹⁄₂ acre rural

way of paths, steps and shrubbery to lawn with 70' herbaceous border. Rose tunnel, glade, young orchard, small area of woodland, hellebore bed, rockery, herb garden, cottage garden with roses and vegetables. Wheelchair access is limited to the Terrace, rockery, top shrubbery, woodland and Cottage Garden.

EDITH TERRACE GARDENS
See Cheshire & Wirral.

28 FANSHAWE GATE HALL
Holmesfield S18 7WA. Mr & Mrs John Ramsden, 01142 890391, www.fanshawegate.com. *2m W of Dronfield. Situated on the edge of the Peak National Park. Follow B6054 towards Owler Bar. 1st R turn after church signed Fanshawe Gate Lane. From Owler Bar 2nd L turn. Light refreshments.* **Adm £3, chd free (share to Oesophageal Patients Assoc). Suns 19, 26 June; 3, 10 July (11-5). Visitors also welcome by appt in June & July only. Small coaches, mini buses allowed.**
C13 seat of the Fanshawe family. Old-fashioned cottage-style garden. Many stone features, fine C16 dovecote. Upper walled garden with herbaceous, variegated and fern plantings, water features, topiary, terracing and lawns. Lower courtyard with knot garden and herb border. Restored terraced orchard representing a medieval tilt yard. Newly planted pleached hornbeam hedge. Wildlife pond. Featured in Amateur Gardening, Derbyshire Life, Country Living, GGG & Hortus Gardening Journal.

FELLEY PRIORY
See Nottinghamshire.

29 FIELD FARM
Field Lane, Kirk Ireton, Ashbourne DE6 3JU. Graham & Irene Dougan, 01335 370958, www.fieldfarmgarden.info. *2m S of Wirksworth. At top of Main St, Kirk Ireton turn L signed Blackwall, on sharp RH-bend find Field Lane (unmade rd), Field Farm 400yds. Parking in adjacent field. Home-made teas.* **Adm £3.50, chd free. Visitors welcome by appt Groups 10+ April to September. Coaches must park in village.**
Glorious 2-acre garden for all seasons, set in superb countryside. Gravelled courtyard with specimen

plants. Herbaceous borders, roses and many rare trees and shrubs. Camellias, Rhododendrons and autumn colour. Sculptures and ceramics in the garden. Featured in Open Gardens BBC TV & Japanese TV. Gravel paths and undulating lawns.

> Over the past three years, our children have transformed their sparse grounds into a vibrant growing space . . .

30 FIR CROFT
Froggatt Road, Calver S32 3ZD. Dr S B Furness, www.alpineplantcentre.co.uk. *4m N of Bakewell. At junction of B6001 with A625 (formerly B6054), adjacent to Power Garage.* **Adm by donation. Suns 8, 22 May; 12 June (2-5).**
Massive scree with many rarities. Plantsman's garden; rockeries; water garden and nursery; extensive collection (over 3000 varieties) of alpines; conifers; over 800 sempervivums, 500 saxifrages and 350 primulas. Tufa and scree beds.

FIRVALE ALLOTMENT GARDEN
See Yorkshire.

31 GAMESLEY FOLD COTTAGE
Gamesley Fold, Glossop SK13 6JJ. Mrs G Carr, 01457 867856, www.gamesleyfold.co.uk. *2m W of Glossop. Off A626 Glossop to Marple rd, nr Charlesworth. Turn down lane directly opp St Margaret's School. White cottage at bottom. Car parking in adjacent field. Home-made teas.* **Adm £2, chd free. Suns 1, 29 May; 12 June (1-4). Visitors also welcome by appt in May & June only for any number, coaches permitted.**
Old-fashioned cottage garden. Spring garden with herbaceous borders, shrubs and rhododendrons, wild flowers and herbs in profusion to attract butterflies and wildlife. Good selection of herbs and cottage garden plants for sale.

GARDENERS COTTAGE
See Nottinghamshire.

GORENE
See Nottinghamshire.

GRAFTON COTTAGE
See Staffordshire Birmingham & part of West Midlands.

32 NEW GRANGE PRIMARY SCHOOL
Station Road, Long Eaton NG10 2DU. Grange Primary School. *2m S of J25 of M1. 1m from Attenborough Nature Reserve. Turn off A6005 (Nottingham Rd) onto Grange Rd, then first R onto Grange Drive. Entrance on L. Or turn off Station Rd onto Grange Rd. L onto Grange Drive. Entrance on L.* **Adm £2.50, chd free. Sat 16, Sun 17 July (1-4).**
Over the past 3yrs, our children have transformed their sparse grounds into a vibrant growing space, used for learning and pleasure. They experiment with growing flowers with vegetables, growing new and unusual plants, as well as developing new habitats such as a bog and a tranquil space in the middle of a car park. Plant sale, face painting, cake sale, stringed music, craft demonstration.

33 NEW THE GREEN
Southgate, Eckington S21 4FT. Mr and Mrs North, 07970 650359, alexstyan@designanddig.co.uk, www.designanddig.co.uk. *4m SE of Sheffield. From M1 J30 take A6135 (Sheffield South). After about 3m turn L onto Station Road, after 1/3m turn L onto Southgate. The garden is corner house at end. Pls park on Southgate and walk round to entrance. Home-made teas.* **Adm £3.50, chd free. Sun 17 July (10.30-3.30). Visitors also welcome by appt. Groups welcome June, July and August only (tour included).**
A unique, historic Italian water garden designed by Sir Edwin Lutyens in 1916 for Sir George Sitwell. Now privately owned and 3 yrs into an ongoing restoration to the original plan. Original stonework, rills and water feature. Restored tennis lawn, yew walk and pergola beams with new planting. A copy of the original Lutyens plan and the restoration diary (including photos) will be displayed on NGS day & for private visits.

34 NEW GREEN MEADOWS

Cross Lane, Moneyash, Bakewell DE45 1JN. Mr & Mrs Mike Cullen. *5m West of Bakewell. From centre Bakewell take B5055 to Monyash. At Xrds by village green go straight onto Tagg Lane. At the second bend turn right into Cross Lane.* Home-made teas. **Adm £2.50, chd free. Sat 18 June; 6 Aug (12-5).**
Compact Cottage garden surrounded by enclosures, in superb countryside with far reaching views of the Dales. Herbaceous borders, shrubs, wild flowers, lavender hedges and kit parterre in daily use filled with a profusion of herbs to attract butterflies and wildlife. Water features and limestone garden. Large greenhouse and raised beds.

&. ☕

Our Aga-baked cakes and light lunches are delicious too . . .

35 16 THE GROVE

Totley, Sheffield S17 4AS. Jennie Street, 01142 362302, jennie@hadish.f9.co.uk, www.jenniestreetgarden.co.uk. *6m S of Sheffield.10m NW of Chesterfield. From Bakewell, A621 N to Totley. 1st L after dual carriageway begins, into The Crescent, opp Co-op. 1st L into The Grove. From Chesterfield, A61, L at Meadowhead r'bout onto B6054. after 2 miles, R at T junction down hill. At T junction. R onto Mickley Lane to top. L onto Baslow Road, them immed R into Crescent. L onto The Grove. From Sheffield A621 S to Totley. R opposite Co-op into Crescent, 1st L into The Grove. Maps on garden website. Please park considerately. Parking in Catholic church on The Crescent.* Cream & Home-made teas. **Adm £2.50, chd free. Sat & Sun 2, 3 July (12-5). Visitors also welcome by appt Groups 8-16 only. No coaches.**
Quirky garden on edge of moors, featuring unusual topiary, junk sculptures, national collection watering cans and extensive rainwater collection systems. Organic vegetable garden, 2 greenhouses, 10 compost heaps and comfrey fertiliser production. Chickens, parterre, pond,

herbaceous borders, black border plus other surprises. Plants for sale. . Featured in Sheffield Telegraph, South Side, Radio Sheffield, Derbyshire Times, Amateur Gardening.

❀ ☕ ☎

36 ◆ HARDWICK ESTATE

Hardwick Estate, Doe Lea, Chesterfield S44 5QJ. National Trust, 01246 850430, www.nationaltrust.org.uk. *8m SE of Chesterfield. S of A617. Signed from J29 M1.* **Adm 12 July £10, 17 July £5.55, chd £2.80. For NGS: Evening Opening Tue 12 July (6-8); Sun 17 July (11-5). For other opening times and information, please phone or see garden website.**
The gardens are beautifully presented in a series of courtyards, where you can move from one garden 'room' to the next to explore the herb garden, orchards and colourful borders. Tim Turner, NGS Careership Gardener won Visit Peak District Excell Award for Most Promising Trainee.

&. ❀ ☕ ☎

37 HIGH ROOST

27 Storthmeadow Road, Simmondley, Glossop SK13 6UZ. Peter & Christina Harris, 01457 863888, peter-harris9@sky.com. *³/₄ m SW of Glossop. From M67 take A57, turn R at Mottram (1st T-lights), through Broadbottom & Charlesworth. In Charlesworth turn R up Town Lane by side of Grey Mare PH, continue up High Lane, past Hare & Hounds PH, Storthmeadow Rd is 2nd turn on L. From Glossop, A57 towards Manchester, L at 2nd mini r'about, up Simmondley Lane, turn R into Storthmeadow Rd, nr top, no 27 last house on L. On road parking nearby, please take care not to block drives.* **Adm £2, chd free (share to Manchester Dogs Home). Sun 26 June (12-5). Visitors also welcome by appt.**
Garden on terraced slopes, views over fields and hills. Winding paths, archways and steps explore different garden rooms packed with plants, designed to attract wildlife. Alpine bed, vegetable garden, water features, statuary, troughs and planters. A garden which needs exploring to discover its secrets tucked away in hidden corners. Craft stalls Childrens Curious Creatures TrailChildrens Lucky Dip. Finalist, Daily Mail Garden of the Year.

🐾 ❀ ☕ ☎

38 37 HIGH STREET

Repton DE65 6GD. David & Jan Roberts. *6m S of Derby. From A38, A50 junction S of Derby follow signs to Willington, then Repton. In Repton continue past island and shops. Garden on L.* Home-made teas. **Adm £2.50, chd free. Suns 17 Apr; 5 June (2-5.30).**
Over 1 acre of gardens with bridge over Repton Brook which meanders through. Formal and wildlife ponds, mixed borders of herbaceous, shrubs and trees. Rhododendrons and woodland, grasses, ferns and bamboos. Vegetable garden and greenhouses, container planting for spring and summer colour and alpine troughs. A surprising garden for all seasons with interest for everyone. Open again after a yr off with some changes. Come and see what we have done.

&. ❀ ☕

39 HIGHFIELD HOUSE

Wingfield Road, Oakerthorpe, Alfreton DE55 7AP. Paul & Ruth Peat and Janet & Brian Costall, 01773 521342, peat.ruth@gmail.com. *Approx 1m from Alfreton town centre on A615 Alfreton-Matlock Rd. From Matlock: A615 to Alfreton. Turn R into Alfreton Golf Club. From Derby: A38 to Alfreton. A615 to Matlock. After houses on L of Wingfield Rd, turn L into Alfreton Golf Club.* Light refreshments & home-made teas. **Adm £2.50, chd free. Sun 29 May (11-5). Visitors also welcome by appt late May to mid July for groups of 15+.**
Delightful family garden of ³/₄ acre. Individual areas include a shady garden, small areas of woodland, tree house, laburnum arch, orchard, lawns, herbaceous borders and recently developed productive vegetable garden. Pleasant level walk to Derbyshire Wildlife Trust Nature reserve, where there is a pond and boardwalk and beautiful spotted orchids. A lovely afternoon out. Our Aga-baked cakes and light lunches are delicious too. Some gravel paths and slopes.

&. ❀ ☕ ☎

HILL PARK FARM
See Leicestershire & Rutland.

133 HILLFIELD LANE
See Staffordshire Birmingham & part of West Midlands.

40 HILLSIDE
286 Handley Road, New Whittington, Chesterfield S43 2ET. Mr E J Lee, 01246 454960. *3m N of Chesterfield. From A6135, take B6052 through Eckington & Marsh Lane 3m. Turn L at Xrds signed Whittington, then 1m. From Coal Aston (Sheffield), take B6056 towards Chesterfield to give way sign, then 1m. From Chesterfield, take B6052.* **Adm £3, chd free. Visitors welcome by appt for groups of any size.**
$^1/_3$ -acre sloping site. Herbaceous borders, rock garden, alpines, streams, pools, bog gardens, asiatic primula bed, and alpine house. Acers, bamboos, collection of approx 150 varieties of ferns, eucalypts, euphorbias, grasses, conifers, Himalayan bed. 1000+ plants permanently labelled. Yr-round interest.

HILLTOP
See Cheshire & Wirral.

41 ◆ LEA GARDENS
Lea, nr Matlock DE4 5GH. Mr & Mrs J Tye, 01629 534260. *5m SE of Matlock. Off A6. Also off A615.* **Adm £4, chd 50p. Donation to NGS. For opening times and information, please phone.**
Rare collection of rhododendrons, azaleas, kalmias, alpines and conifers in delightful woodland setting. Gardens are sited on remains of medieval quarry and cover about 4 acres. Specialised plant nursery of rhododendrons and azaleas on site. Featured in Reflections magazine. Free access for wheelchair users.

42 THE LEYLANDS
Moorwood Lane, Owler Bar (Holmesfield) S17 3BS. Richard & Chris Hibberd. *2m W of Dronfield. Situated on the edge of the Peak District National Park, adjacent to the B6054. Moorwood Lane is 1m from the Owler Bar junction with the A621 (Sheffield-Bakewell) or 2nd turn on R after leaving Holmesfield village if travelling W towards Owler Bar.* Home-made teas. **Adm £2.50, chd free (share to Water Aid). Mon 30 May; Sun 5 June (12-5). Visitors also welcome by appt.**
2-acre country garden in which the owners, over the last 30 years, have indulged their individual passions for water and plants. The result is a

garden with a variety of water systems and different types of planting, breeding koi and yr-round interest. New areas have recently been developed. Part of the garden was a working nursery in the 1950s and has been re-developed for plant propagation.

43 THE LILIES
Grangemill, Griffe Grange Valley, Matlock DE4 4BW. Chris & Bridget Sheppard, www.the-lilies.com. *4m N Cromford. On A5012 Via Gellia Rd 4m N Cromford. 1st house on R after junction with B5023 to Middleton. From S Grangemill 1st house on L after Stancliffe Quarry.* Home-made teas. **Adm £2.50, chd free. Suns 10 July; 4 Sept (1.30-5.30).**
1-acre garden being restored after some neglect. Area adjacent to house with seasonal planting and containers, mixed shrubs and perennial borders many raised from seed. 3 ponds, vegetable plot, barn conversion with separate cottage style garden. Natural garden with stream under development from old mill pond. Walks in large wild flower meadow and ash woodland both SSSI's. Early C18 2 storey stone mill. Restricted access. Featured on BBC Radio Derby. Steep slope from car park, limestone chippings at entrance, some boggy areas if wet.

ALLOTMENTS

44 LITTLEOVER LANE ALLOTMENTS
19 Littleover Lane, Derby DE23 6JH. Littleover Lane Allotments Assoc, www.littleoverlaneallotments. org.uk. *3m SW of Derby. Off Derby ring rd A5111 into Stenson Rd. R into Littleover Lane. Garden on L. On street parking opp Foremark Ave.* Tea & Light Refreshments. Barbecue. **Adm £3, chd free. Sun 11 Sept (11-5).**
Allotment site with over 180 plots cultivated in a variety of styles including an apiary garden. A museum collection of heritage gardening equipment. A range of heritage and unusual vegetable varieties grown. Plant and produce sales.

45 LOCKO PARK
Spondon DE21 7BW. Mrs Lucy Palmer. *6m NE of Derby. From A52 Borrowash bypass, 2m N via B6001, turn to Spondon (additional directions on www.lockopark.co.uk).* Home-made teas & light refreshments. **Adm £3, chd free. Sun 22 May (2-5).**
Large garden; pleasure gardens; rose gardens designed by William Eames. House (not open) by Smith of Warwick with Victorian additions. Chapel (open) Charles II, with original ceiling.

46 9 MAIN STREET
Horsley Woodhouse DE7 6AU. Ms Alison Napier, 01332 881629, ibhillib@btinternet.com. *3m SW of Heanor. 6m N of Derby. Turn off A608 Derby to Heanor rd at Smalley, towards Belper, (A609). Garden on A609, 1m from Smalley turning.* Cream teas. **Adm £2.50, chd free. Sun 7 Aug (2-5). Visitors also welcome by appt.**
$^1/_3$ -acre hilltop garden overlooking lovely farmland view. Terracing, borders, lawns and pergola create space for an informal layout with planting for colour effect. Features incl large wildlife pond with water lilies, bog garden and small formal pool. Emphasis on carefully selected herbaceous perennials mixed with shrubs and old-fashioned roses. Additions incl gravel garden for sun-loving plants and scree garden, both developed form former drive.

47 2 MANVERS STREET
Ripley DE5 3EQ. Mrs D Wood & Mr D Hawkins, 01773 743962. *Ripley Town centre to Derby rd turn L opp Leisure Centre onto Heath Rd. 1st turn R onto Meadow Rd, 1st L onto Manvers St.* Home-made teas. **Adm £2.50, chd free. Sat 9, Sun 10 July (2-6). Visitors also welcome by appt in July & Aug.**
Summer garden with backdrop of neighbouring trees, 10 borders bursting with colour surrounded by immaculate shaped lawn. Perennials incl 26 clematis, annuals, baskets, tubs and pots. Ornamental fish pond. Water features, arbour and summerhouse. Plenty of seating areas to take in this awe-inspiring oasis. First prize Ripley Town Council.

MAXSTOKE CASTLE
See Warwickshire.

48 ◆ **MEYNELL LANGLEY TRIALS GARDEN**
Lodge Lane (off Flagshaw Lane), Near Kirk Langley, Derby DE6 4NT. Robert & Karen Walker, 01332 824358, www.meynell-langley-gardens.co.uk. *4m W of Derby, nr Kedleston Hall. Head W out of Derby on A52. At Kirk Langley turn R onto Flagshaw Lane (signed to Kedleston Hall) then R onto Lodge Lane. Follow Meynell Langley Gdns sign for 1½ m. From A38 follow signs for Kedleston Hall (past first entrance).* Light Refreshments. **Adm £2.50, chd free. For NGS: Suns 17 Apr; 15 May; 12 June; 24 July; 14 Aug; 11 Sept; 9 Oct (10-5). For opening times and information please visit website or telephone.**
Formal ¾ -acre Victorian-style garden established 18yrs, displaying and trialling new and existing varieties of bedding plants, herbaceous perennials and vegetable plants grown at the adjacent nursery. Over 180 hanging baskets and floral displays. 85 varieties of apple, pear and other fruit. Summer fruit pruning demonstrations late summer and apple tasting in October. Summer fruit tree pruning demonstrations 24 July. Apple tasting 11 Sept & 9 Oct. Featured in live broadcasts from the garden on Radio Derby.
⌖ ❀ ☕ ☎

GROUP OPENING

49 NEW **MILFORD GARDENS**
DE56 0QA. *7m N of Derby. On A6 running through Milford. Parking next to Strutt Arms PH.* Home-made teas at 2 The Woodridge & Chevin Brae. **Combined adm £4, chd free. Sun 19 June (2-6).**

NEW **CHEVIN BRAE**
David Moreton

NEW **3 HOPPING HILL**
Ceri Booen

NEW **7 HOPPING HILL**
Miss Kelly Adams

NEW **PEAR TREE COTTAGE**
Mrs Ann Whitlock

NEW **1 THE WOODRIDGE**
Aileen & John Hammerton

2 THE WOODRIDGE
Sally & Robert Garner

Nestling on the hillside of this World Heritage Valley are an intriguing collection of generally very steep gardens, all of which make the most of their beautiful views and difficult terrains. A wide variety of approaches have been used by the garden owners and the group incl the garden of a garden designer whose cottage garden has a strongly design-led interest; a druid's naturalistic contemplative garden which has a feeling of real theatre; an organic wildlife garden containing numerous plants and features to provide a wide range of habitats; a rare (for Milford) large flat garden which has over 40 large mature trees; and 2 beautiful cottage gardens one of which also incl a very productive fruit and vegetable plot. In addition to the garden the history of the village is to be seen all around and local information boards explain more about Milford's important industrial past.
❀ ☕

MILLPOOL
See Cheshire & Wirral.

A druid's naturalistic contemplative garden which has a feeling of real theatre . . .

50 **MOORFIELDS**
257/261 Chesterfield Road, Temple Normanton, Chesterfield S42 5DE. Peter, Janet & Stephen Wright, 01246 852306. *4m SE of Chesterfield. From Chesterfield take A617 for 2m, turn on to B6039 through Temple Normanton, taking R fork signed Tibshelf. Garden ¼ m on R. Limited parking on site.* Home-made teas. **Adm £2.50, chd free. Sun 3 July (1-5). Visitors also welcome by appt early May, groups 10+.**
Two adjacent gardens, the larger developed from a field over last few years and has gravel garden, herbaceous island beds, small wild flower area, large wildlife pond, fruit trees and bushes, vegetable patch. Aiming for show of late flowering tulips. Smaller back and front gardens of No.257 feature herbaceous borders. Short walk down field to pet cemetery. Views across to mid-Derbyshire. Free-range eggs for sale.
❀ ☕ ☎

51 **9 NEWFIELD CRESCENT**
Dore, Sheffield S17 3DE. Mike & Norma Jackson. *Dore - SW Sheffield. Turn off Causeway Head Rd on Heather Lea Avenue. 2nd L into Newfield Crescent.* Home-made teas & Light Refreshments. **Adm £2.50, chd free. Sat 25, Sun 26 June (2-6).**
Mature, wildlife friendly garden planted to provide all-yr interest. Upper terrace with alpines in troughs and bowls. Lower terrace featuring one of two ponds with connecting stream and cascade. Bog garden, rock gardens, lawn alpine bed, wilder areas, mixed borders with trees, shrubs and perennials. Featuring azaleas, rhododendrons, primulas. Parking on roadside. No blocked driveways please.
🏡 ❀ ☕

52 ◆ **OLD ENGLISH WALLED GARDEN, ELVASTON CASTLE COUNTRY PARK**
Borrowash Road, Elvaston, Derby DE72 3EP. Derbyshire County Council, 01332 571342. *4m E of Derby. Signed from A52 & A50. Car parking charge applies.* Teas. **Adm £2.50, chd free. For NGS: Sat 16 Apr (12-4). For other opening times and information, please phone or see garden website.**
Visit Elvaston Castle and discover the beauty of the Old English walled garden. Take in the peaceful atmosphere and enjoy the scents and colours of all the varieties of trees, shrubs and plants. Spring bulbs, summer bedding scheme, large herbaceous borders and herb garden. Plant sales. Estate gardeners on hand during the day.
⌖ 🏡 ❀ ☕ ☎

THE OLD RECTORY, CLIFTON CAMPVILLE
See Staffordshire Birmingham & part of West Midlands.

ONE HOUSE NURSERY
See Cheshire & Wirral.

53 **OWL END**
Newfield Lane, Dore, Sheffield S17 3DB. Sue & Roger Thompson, 01142 350830, owlend@googlemail.com. *5m SW Sheffield City Centre. On A625 to Hathersage, turn L at Dore Moor Inn,*

Be tempted by a plant from a plant stall ❀

Park Hall

1st R into Newfield Lane. 200yds on R. Please park considerately on Newfield Lane and surrounding roads. Blue Badges only down drive. Home-made teas. **Adm £3, chd free. Sat 18, Sun 19 June (2-6). Visitors also welcome by appt.** Large garden of 1.5-acres with woodlands and meadow. Herbaceous and mixed borders. Vegetables, soft fruit with polytunnel. Views towards Blackamoor. much of the garden is on slopes and care is needed.

PACKINGTON HALL
See Warwickshire.

54 THE PADDOCK
12 Mankell Road, Whittington Moor, Chesterfield S41 8LZ. Mel & Wendy Taylor, 01246 451001. *2m N of Chesterfield. Whittington Moor just off A61 between Sheffield & Chesterfield. Parking available at Lidl supermarket, garden signed from here.* Cream teas. **Adm £2.50, chd free. Suns 1 May; 3 July (11-5). Visitors also welcome by appt.** ¹/₂ -acre garden incorporating small formal garden, stream and koi filled pond. Stone path over bridge, up some steps, past small copse, across the stream at the top and back down again. Past herbaceous border towards a pergola where cream teas can be enjoyed. Gravel paths & steps.

THE PADDOCKS
See Nottinghamshire.

55 PARK HALL
Walton Back Lane, Walton, Chesterfield S42 7LT. Kim & Margaret Staniforth, 01246 567412, kim.staniforth@virgin.net. *2m SW of Chesterfield. From Chesterfield take A632 for Matlock. After start of 40mph section take 1st R into Acorn Ridge & then L into Walton Back Lane. 300yds on R, at end of high stone wall. Park on field side of Walton Back Lane only.* Home-made teas. **Adm £3.50, chd free (share to Bluebell Wood Children's Hospice). Sat 25, Sun 26 June (12-5.30). Visitors also welcome by appt Apr to Aug for groups of 10+.** 2-acre plantsman's garden in a beautiful setting surrounding C17 house, not open. Four main 'rooms' - terraced garden, park area with forest trees, croquet lawn and new millennium garden now fully mature. Within these are a woodland walk, fernery, yew hedges and topiary, water features, pergolas, arbours, herbaceous borders, rhododendrons, camellias, azaleas, hydrangeas, 150 roses, circular pleached hedge.

56 22 PINFOLD CLOSE
Repton DE65 6FR. Mr O Jowett, 01283 701964. *6m S of Derby. From A38, A50 J, S of Derby follow signs to Willington then Repton. Off Repton High Street find Pinfold Lane, Pinfold Close 1st L.* **Combined adm £5, with Woodend Cottage & 10 Chestnut Way, chd free. Sun 14 Aug (1-6). Visitors also welcome by appt in Aug, for groups of 20-30.** Small garden with an interest in tropical plants. Palms, gingers, tree ferns, cannas, bananas. Mainly foliage plants.

57 RECTORY HOUSE
Kedleston, Derby DE22 5JJ. Helene Viscountess Scarsdale. *5m NW Derby. A52 from Derby turn R Kedleston sign. Drive to village turn R. Brick house standing back from rd on sharp corner.* Home-made teas. **Adm £4, chd free. Fris 10, 17 June (2-5).** Garden re-established 6yrs ago. The 3 acres now has shrub border with rare varieties, grasses, rhododendrons, azaleas and shrub roses. Large pond with candelabra primulas, gunneras, good collection of willows. Part of garden wild but atmospheric with winding paths. Small potager and orchard. Summerhouse to sit in and plenty of seats. Featured in Derbyshire Magazine & Derby Telegraph. Limited wheelchair access.

58 ◆ RENISHAW HALL GARDENS
Renishaw, nr Sheffield S21 3WB. Mrs A Haywood, 01246 432310, www.renishaw-hall.co.uk. *4m W of Sheffield. From J30 M1 take A6135 towards Sheffield. Renishaw Hall is 3m from motorway.* **Adm £3, chd free. For NGS: Weds 13 Apr; 7 Sept (10.30-4.30). For other opening times and information, please phone or see garden website.** Ancestral home of Sitwell family. Romantic, formal 2 Italianate gardens divided into rooms by yew hedges. Bluebell woods, magnolias and rhododendrons in spring woodland gardens. Over a thousand roses in June with peonies and clematis. Deep herbaceous borders with collections of unusual plants. National Collection of Yuccas. Separate children's garden with willow tunnel, maze and trails. Monthly themed garden talks with gardener. Open throughout the season with exhibition on the development & history of the garden. Mercian Vineyard Association - highly commended sparkling wine. Wheelchair route around garden.

RIDGEHILL
See Cheshire & Wirral.

SANDSEND
See Cheshire & Wirral.

59 SHATTON HALL FARM
Bamford S33 0BG. Mr & Mrs J Kellie, 01433 620635, jk@shatton.co.uk. *3m W of Hathersage. Take A6187 from Hathersage, turn L to Shatton, after 2m (opp High Peak Garden Centre).*

After ¹/₂ m turn R through ford, drive ¹/₂ m & house is on L over cattle grids. Home-made teas. **Adm £3, chd free. Sun 31 July (1.30-5). Visitors also welcome by appt Groups 30 max. Coach size max 20 persons.**
Original walled garden of C16 farmhouse now spills out to water gardens and sheltered slopes, planted informally and merging into the picturesque landscape. Among the great variety of unusual plants and shrubs, sculpture and willow features add interest to this maturing and still expanding garden. Planting in front of the house and under the old yew tree has now matured into a substantial feature.

🏡 ❀ 🛏 ☕ ☎

60▶ SOUTHFIELD
Bullbridge Hill, Fritchley, Belper DE56 2FL. Pete & Lot Clark, 01773 852426,
peter@southfield22.fsnet.co.uk. *4m N of Belper. From A610 between Ripley & Ambergate follow signs Bullbridge, Frichley, Crich. In 600yds garden is on junction of Allen Lane (signed Fritchley) and Bullbridge Hill. Turn R into Allen Lane & park in village.* Home-made teas. **Adm £2.50, chd free. Sun 15 May; Sun 24 July (1-5). Visitors also welcome by appt, groups 8+.**
1¹/₂ acre all-year round garden surrounded by mature trees. Lawned areas are interspersed with beds and borders of rhododendrons, flowering and foliage shrubs and herbaceous plants. Rockery with pond and an area of colour themed planting around pavilion. Tea terrace with bedding plants and a court yard garden. Try your hand at Croquet - free trial and tuition. Newly planted in 2010 a David Austin Rose Garden comprising 150 rose plants. Featured in Notts and Derbyshire Country Images Magazine.

🏡 ❀ ☕ ☎

STONEHILL QUARRY GARDEN
See Staffordshire Birmingham & part of West Midlands.

61▶ ◆ SUDBURY HALL
Ashbourne DE6 5HT. National Trust, 01283 585305,
www.nationaltrust.org.uk. *6m E of Uttoxeter. At junction of A50 Derby-Stoke & A515 Ashbourne.*
or NGS: Sats 18 June; 3 Sept (11-5). For other opening times and information, please phone or see garden website.

Original garden design dates from 1700s. Landscaped in 1800s in a naturalistic style popularised by Capability Brown. Wander through the meadow and small woodland, walk by the lake and stroll through our unusual quincunx. Admire the hall from the garden terraces. Virtual tour of Hall available in tea room.

🛆 ❀ ☕ ☎

Wander through this magical setting, admire the unusual trees and listen to the sounds of the countryside . . .

TEBUTTS FARM
See Leicestershire & Rutland.

62▶ 2 THE WOODRIDGE
Milford, Belper DE56 0QA. Sally & Robert Garner, 01332 843129. *7m N Derby. On A6 running through Milford. Parking in large private car park approx 100m diagonally opposite garden.* Home-made teas. **Adm £2.50, chd free. Sun 22 May (2-5). Visitors also welcome by appt.**
Very steep organic wildlife garden situated on 1/4 acre woodlands edge. Developed over past 11 years by keen gardener and wildlife enthusiast. Dense planting contains rare and unusual specimens as well as numerous plants and features to encourage an abundance of insect, bird and animal life. Featured in Garden News.

❀ ☕ ☎

63▶ THORNBRIDGE HALL
Ashford in the Water DE45 1NZ. Jim & Emma Harrison. *2m NW of Bakewell. From Bakewell take A6, signed Buxton. After 2m, R onto A6020. ¹/₂ m turn L, signed Thornbridge Hall.* Light refreshments & teas. **Adm £4.50, chd free. Sun 21 Aug (10-4).**
New this yr, a scented flower terrace set in a stunning 10-acre garden overlooking rolling Derbyshire countryside. This C19, rarely opened garden has many distinct areas incl Italian garden with statuary, knot garden, water garden, 100ft herbaceous border, working potager, koi lake, thatched summer house and

glasshouses. Gravel paths, some steep slopes and steps, stepping stones over water garden.

🛆 🏡 ❀ ☕

64▶ TILFORD HOUSE
Hognaston, Ashbourne DE6 1PW. Mr & Mrs P R Gardner. *5m NE of Ashbourne. A517 Belper to Ashbourne. At Hulland Ward follow signs to Hognaston. Down hill (2m) to bridge. Roadside parking 100m.* Home-made teas. **Adm £3, chd free. Sat 14, Sun 15 May (2-5).**
A 11/2 acre streamside plantlovers country garden. Mixed borders containing some unusual plants lie sympathetically beside untamed areas Raised vegetable beds, fruit trees, collections of hostas, irises and primulas. Wander through this magical setting, admire the unusual trees or just sit and listen to the sounds of the countryside.

❀ ☕

65▶ ◆ TISSINGTON HALL
nr Ashbourne DE6 1RA. Sir Richard FitzHerbert, 01335 352200,
www.tissingtonhall.co.uk. *4m N of Ashbourne. E of A515 on Ashbourne to Buxton rd.* **Adm £4, chd free. For NGS: Mon 29 Aug (12-3). For other opening times and information, please phone or see garden website.**
Large garden celebrating over 70 years in the NGS, with roses, herbaceous borders and 5 acres of grounds.

🛆 🏡 ❀ NCCPG 🛏 ☕ ☎

WARWICK GLEN
See Leicestershire & Rutland.

66▶ 24 WHEELDON AVENUE
Derby DE22 1HN. Laura Burnett, 01332 384893. *1m N Derby city centre. Approached directly from Kedleston Rd or from A6, Duffield Rd via West Bank Ave. Limited on street parking. Good bus services on Kedleston Rd or Duffield Rd.* Light refreshments & teas at 28 Wheeldon Avenue. **Combined adm £3.50 with 26 Wheeldon Avenue, chd free. Sun 12 June (2-5.30). Visitors also welcome by appt May, June, & July.**
Small Victorian garden, with original walling supporting many shrubs and climbers with contrasting colour and texture. Circular lawn surrounded by herbaceous border with main colour scheme of blue, purple, black, yellow and orange tones. This leads to a

small area at rear of garden given to more natural planting to suit shade and natural habitat. This is a garden produced on a low income budget, with varied tones and textures throughout the planting. Hand made cards & Teddy bears for sale (proceeds not for NGS).

67 **26 WHEELDON AVENUE**
Derby DE22 1HN. Ian Griffiths, 01332 342204. *1m N of Derby. 1m from city centre & approached directly off the Kedleston Rd or from A6 Duffield Rd via West Bank Ave. Limited on-street parking.* Light refreshments & teas at 28 Wheeldon Avenue. **Combined adm £3.50 with 24 Wheeldon Avenue, chd free. Sun 12 June (2-5). Visitors also welcome by appt in June & July.**
Tiny Victorian walled garden near to city centre. Lawn and herbaceous borders with newly expanded old rose collection, lupins, delphiniums and foxgloves. Small terrace with topiary, herb garden and lion fountain. House available for filming & photo shoots throughout the year. Featured on BBC & ITV.

68 **26 WINDMILL RISE**
Belper DE56 1GQ. Kathy Fairweather. *1/2 m from Belper market place. Take Chesterfield Road towards Heage. Top of hill 1st R, Marsh Lane. 1st R Windmill Lane, 1st R Windmill Rise. Please do not park on Windmill Rise.* Home-made teas. **Adm £3, chd free. Sun 26 June; Sun 7 Aug (11.30-4.30).**
An original and unusual plant lovers' organic garden with all-yr interest. Large variety of plants, some unusual and rare. Garden divided into sections: woodland, Japanese, secret garden' cottage, edible, patio

gardens. Fish and wildlife ponds, running stream. Specimen fir tree. Lush, restful atmosphere, with paths meandering to many seating areas.

69 **WINDWARD**
62 Summer Lane, Wirksworth DE4 4EB. Audrey & Andrew Winkler, 01629 822681, audrey.winkler@w3z.co.uk, www.grandmafrogsgarden.co.uk. *5m S of Matlock. From Wirksworth Market Place take the B5023 towards Duffield. After 300 yds turn R onto Summer Lane at mini roundabout. Windward is approx 500yds on R.* Home-made teas. **Adm £3, chd free (share to Ruddington Framework Knitters Museum). Sat & Sun 19, 20 Mar; Suns 17 Apr; 22 May; 10 July; 14 Aug (1.30-4.30). Visitors also welcome by appt min 15+.**
Lush, green garden,1-acre, with mature trees and shrubs. Woodland clearings with wild flowers. New butterfly walk, spring bulbs, fernery, grasses, gravel garden, wildlife pond, hostas, roses, rhododendrons and poppies and an impressive Leylandii crinkle-crankle hedge. Small vegetable area. Explore the hidden paths. Find a sheltered seat. Relax and enjoy. Art Gallery. Ruddington Framework Knitters' Museum occasionally demonstrates circular knitting of socks on a Griswold machine. Featured in Derbyshire Magazine.

70 **WOODEND COTTAGE**
134 Main Street, Repton DE65 6FB. Wendy & Stephen Longden, 01283 703259, wendylongden@btinternet.com. *6m S of Derby. From A38, S of Derby, follow signs to Willington, then Repton. In Repton, straight on at*

r'bout through village. Woodend Cottage is 1m on R before Woodend Children's Nursery. Home-made teas. **Adm £2.50, combined adm with 10 Chestnut Way & 22 Pinfold Close £5, chd free. Suns 29 May (1.30-5.30); 17 July; 14 Aug (1.30-6). Visitors also welcome by appt.**
Plant lover's garden with glorious views on a sloping 2½ -acre site developed organically for yr-round interest. On lower levels herbaceous borders are arranged informally and connected via lawns, thyme bed, pond and pergolas. Mixed woodland and grassed labyrinth lead naturally into fruit, vegetable and herb potager with meadows beyond. Especially colourful in July and Aug. Small specialist nursery selling perennials and grasses. Featured in East Midlands Today.

WOODLEIGHTON GROVE GARDENS
See Staffordshire Birmingham & part of West Midlands.

71 **35 WYVER LANE**
Belper DE56 2UB. Jim & Brenda Stannering, 01773 824280. *8m N of Derby. Take A6 from Derby through Belper to T-lights at triangle. Turn L for A517 to Ashbourne, over river bridge, 1st R onto Wyver Lane. Parking in River Gardens, entrance on A6. No parking in Wyver Lane.* Home-made teas. **Adm £2, chd free. Suns 8 May; 19 June; 17 July (1-5). Visitors also welcome by appt April to Aug.**
Cottage garden of approx 500sq yds on side of R Derwent opp Belper River Gardens. Full of hardy perennial plants with pergola, troughs, greenhouse, small pond.

DEVON

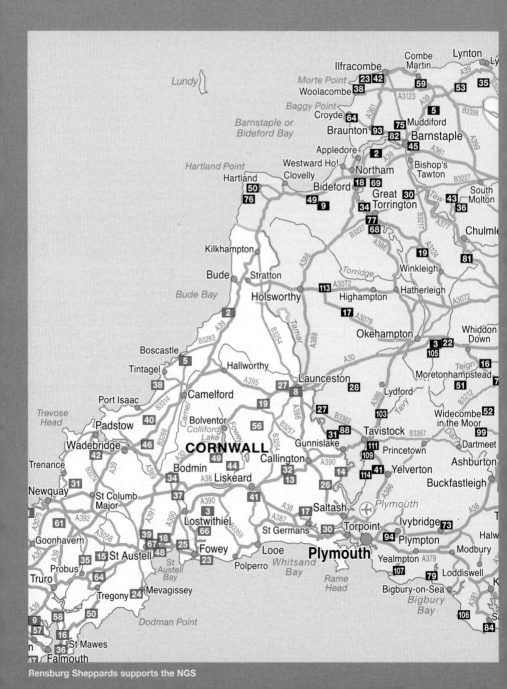

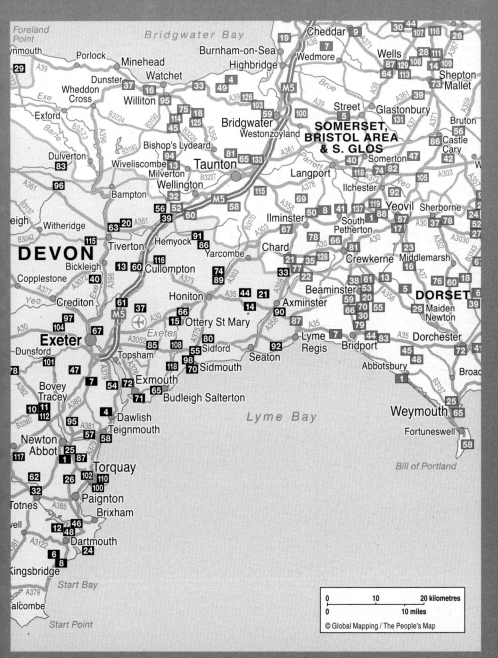

Opening Dates

January

Sunday 2
97 Sherwood

Sunday 9
97 Sherwood

Sunday 16
97 Sherwood

Sunday 23
97 Sherwood

Sunday 30
19 Cherubeer Gardens
67 Little Cumbre
97 Sherwood

February

Sunday 6
19 Cherubeer Gardens
67 Little Cumbre
97 Sherwood

Sunday 13
67 Little Cumbre
97 Sherwood

Saturday 19
86 Pikes Cottage

Sunday 20
67 Little Cumbre
86 Pikes Cottage
97 Sherwood

Saturday 26
86 Pikes Cottage

Sunday 27
86 Pikes Cottage
97 Sherwood

March

Sunday 6
97 Sherwood

Sunday 13
62 Kingston House
97 Sherwood

Monday 14
34 The Downes

Tuesday 15
34 The Downes

Wednesday 16
34 The Downes

Thursday 17
34 The Downes

Friday 18
34 The Downes

Saturday 19
34 The Downes

Sunday 20
34 The Downes
97 Sherwood

Monday 21
34 The Downes

Tuesday 22
34 The Downes

Wednesday 23
34 The Downes

Thursday 24
34 The Downes

Friday 25
34 The Downes

Saturday 26
17 Chapel Farm House
34 The Downes

Sunday 27
34 The Downes
97 Sherwood
104 Summers Place
118 Yonder Hill

Monday 28
34 The Downes

Tuesday 29
34 The Downes

Wednesday 30
34 The Downes

Thursday 31
34 The Downes

April

Friday 1
23 Cliffe
34 The Downes

Saturday 2
23 Cliffe
34 The Downes

Sunday 3
23 Cliffe
34 The Downes
52 Heathercombe
97 Sherwood
113 Wick Farm Gardens
116 Wood Barton
118 Yonder Hill

Monday 4
23 Cliffe
34 The Downes

Tuesday 5
23 Cliffe
34 The Downes

Wednesday 6
23 Cliffe
34 The Downes

Thursday 7
23 Cliffe
34 The Downes
94 Saltram House (Evening)

Friday 8
23 Cliffe
34 The Downes

Saturday 9
23 Cliffe
34 The Downes

Sunday 10
6 Ash Tree Farm

7 Bickham Gardens
23 Cliffe
34 The Downes
45 Gorwell House
59 Jevington Hall
92 Rousdon Cottage Gardens
97 Sherwood
107 Thorn House
116 Wood Barton
118 Yonder Hill

Monday 11
23 Cliffe
34 The Downes

Tuesday 12
7 Bickham Gardens
23 Cliffe
34 The Downes

Wednesday 13
7 Bickham Gardens
23 Cliffe
34 The Downes

Thursday 14
23 Cliffe
34 The Downes

Friday 15
23 Cliffe
34 The Downes

Saturday 16
23 Cliffe
34 The Downes
55 Hillrise

Sunday 17
20 Chevithorne Barton
23 Cliffe
34 The Downes
55 Hillrise
97 Sherwood
101 Sowton Mill
105 Taikoo
118 Yonder Hill

Monday 18
23 Cliffe
34 The Downes

Tuesday 19
23 Cliffe
34 The Downes

Wednesday 20
23 Cliffe
34 The Downes

Thursday 21
23 Cliffe
34 The Downes

Friday 22
23 Cliffe
34 The Downes
118 Yonder Hill

Saturday 23
23 Cliffe
34 The Downes
47 Haldon Grange

Sunday 24
23 Cliffe
34 The Downes

47 Haldon Grange
60 Kia-Ora Farm & Gardens
71 Littleham House Cottage
93 St Merryn
97 Sherwood
113 Wick Farm Gardens
118 Yonder Hill

Monday 25
23 Cliffe
34 The Downes
47 Haldon Grange
60 Kia-Ora Farm & Gardens
113 Wick Farm Gardens
118 Yonder Hill

Tuesday 26
23 Cliffe
34 The Downes

Wednesday 27
23 Cliffe
34 The Downes

Thursday 28
23 Cliffe
34 The Downes

Friday 29
23 Cliffe
34 The Downes

Saturday 30
17 Chapel Farm House
23 Cliffe
33 Dicot
34 The Downes
47 Haldon Grange
79 Mothecombe House
86 Pikes Cottage
89 Pound Cottage

May

Sunday 1
3 Andrew's Corner
6 Ash Tree Farm
23 Cliffe
33 Dicot
34 The Downes
38 Foamlea
47 Haldon Grange
60 Kia-Ora Farm & Gardens
63 Knightshayes Court Garden
71 Littleham House Cottage
79 Mothecombe House
86 Pikes Cottage
89 Pound Cottage
97 Sherwood
116 Wood Barton
117 Yolland Gardens
118 Yonder Hill

Monday 2
3 Andrew's Corner
23 Cliffe
33 Dicot
34 The Downes
40 Fursdon
47 Haldon Grange
60 Kia-Ora Farm & Gardens
86 Pikes Cottage

116 Wood Barton
117 Yolland Gardens
118 Yonder Hill

Tuesday 3
23 Cliffe
34 The Downes

Wednesday 4
23 Cliffe
34 The Downes
47 Haldon Grange

Thursday 5
5 Arlington Court
5 Arlington Court (Evening)
23 Cliffe
34 The Downes

Friday 6
23 Cliffe
34 The Downes

Saturday 7
10 Bovey Country Gardens
23 Cliffe
34 The Downes
47 Haldon Grange
81 The Old Glebe
95 Sedgewell Coach House Gardens
115 Withleigh Farm

Sunday 8
3 Andrew's Corner
7 Bickham Gardens
10 Bovey Country Gardens
23 Cliffe
34 The Downes
38 Foamlea
45 Gorwell House
47 Haldon Grange
81 The Old Glebe
82 The Old Rectory
92 Rousdon Cottage Gardens
95 Sedgewell Coach House Gardens
97 Sherwood
104 Summers Place
112 Whitstone Farm
115 Withleigh Farm
118 Yonder Hill

Monday 9
23 Cliffe
34 The Downes

Tuesday 10
7 Bickham Gardens
23 Cliffe
34 The Downes

Wednesday 11
7 Bickham Gardens
23 Cliffe
34 The Downes
47 Haldon Grange

Thursday 12
23 Cliffe
34 The Downes
61 Killerton Garden

Friday 13
23 Cliffe

116 Wood Barton
117 Yolland Gardens
118 Yonder Hill

34 The Downes
53 Heddon Hall

Saturday 14
17 Chapel Farm House
23 Cliffe
24 Coleton Fishacre
34 The Downes
47 Haldon Grange
75 Marwood Hill
80 The Old Dairy
81 The Old Glebe
83 The Old Vicarage
86 Pikes Cottage
98 Sidmouth Gardens

Sunday 15
16 Castle Drogo
23 Cliffe
34 The Downes
47 Haldon Grange
52 Heathercombe
59 Jevington Hall
60 Kia-Ora Farm & Gardens
62 Kingston House
64 Langtrees
77 Mill Street Gardens
80 The Old Dairy
81 The Old Glebe
83 The Old Vicarage.
86 Pikes Cottage
93 St Merryn
97 Sherwood
98 Sidmouth Gardens
99 Southcombe Gardens
118 Yonder Hill

Monday 16
23 Cliffe

Tuesday 17
23 Cliffe

Wednesday 18
23 Cliffe
47 Haldon Grange
71 Littleham House Cottage

Thursday 19
23 Cliffe
94 Saltram House (Evening)

Friday 20
23 Cliffe

Saturday 21
23 Cliffe
47 Haldon Grange
51 Heather Cottage
55 Hillrise
86 Pikes Cottage

Sunday 22
3 Andrew's Corner
23 Cliffe
38 Foamlea
47 Haldon Grange
51 Heather Cottage
52 Heathercombe
54 High Garden
55 Hillrise
70 Littlecourt Cottages
86 Pikes Cottage
97 Sherwood

99 Southcombe Gardens
103 The Stannary
118 Yonder Hill

Monday 23
23 Cliffe

Tuesday 24
23 Cliffe

Wednesday 25
23 Cliffe

Thursday 26
23 Cliffe

Friday 27
15 Cadhay
23 Cliffe

Saturday 28
9 Bocombe Mill Cottage
21 Cleave Hill
23 Cliffe
47 Haldon Grange
52 Heathercombe
74 Luppitt Gardens
78 Moretonhampstead Gardens

Sunday 29
3 Andrew's Corner
6 Ash Tree Farm
9 Bocombe Mill Cottage
19 Cherubeer Gardens
21 Cleave Hill
23 Cliffe
35 Durcombe Water
38 Foamlea
47 Haldon Grange
52 Heathercombe
60 Kia-Ora Farm & Gardens
74 Luppitt Gardens
78 Moretonhampstead Gardens
97 Sherwood
99 Southcombe Gardens
118 Yonder Hill

Monday 30
3 Andrew's Corner
9 Bocombe Mill Cottage
18 Cherry Trees Wildlife Garden
23 Cliffe
35 Durcombe Water
60 Kia-Ora Farm & Gardens
78 Moretonhampstead Gardens
99 Southcombe Gardens
118 Yonder Hill

Tuesday 31
23 Cliffe

June

Wednesday 1
23 Cliffe

Thursday 2
23 Cliffe

Friday 3
23 Cliffe

Saturday 4
1 Abbotskerswell Gardens
11 Bovey Tracey Gardens
23 Cliffe

44 Goren Farm (Evening)

Sunday 5
1 Abbotskerswell Gardens
3 Andrew's Corner
11 Bovey Tracey Gardens
13 Burn Valley Gardens
20 Chevithorne Barton
23 Cliffe
31 Damerel House
32 Dartington Hall Gardens
44 Goren Farm (Evening)
44 Goren Farm
52 Heathercombe
66 Little Ash Bungalow
97 Sherwood
99 Southcombe Gardens
118 Yonder Hill

Monday 6
23 Cliffe
44 Goren Farm (Evening)

Tuesday 7
23 Cliffe
44 Goren Farm (Evening)

Wednesday 8
23 Cliffe
44 Goren Farm (Evening)

Thursday 9
23 Cliffe
44 Goren Farm (Evening)

Friday 10
23 Cliffe
44 Goren Farm (Evening)

Saturday 11
12 Bramble Torre
17 Chapel Farm House
23 Cliffe
33 Dicot
44 Goren Farm (Evening)
44 Goren Farm
55 Hillrise
85 Owls Barn
86 Pikes Cottage

Sunday 12
7 Bickham Gardens
12 Bramble Torre
23 Cliffe
27 Coombe Sculpture Garden
33 Dicot
40 Fursdon
44 Goren Farm (Evening)
44 Goren Farm
45 Gorwell House
55 Hillrise
57 Hollycombe House
59 Jevington Hall
68 Little Torrington Gardens
76 Docton Mill & Milford Mill Gardens
77 Mill Street Gardens
82 The Old Rectory
85 Owls Barn
86 Pikes Cottage
88 Portington
92 Rousdon Cottage Gardens
93 St Merryn

97 Sherwood
99 Southcombe Gardens
118 Yonder Hill

Monday 13
4 Appletree Cottage
23 Cliffe
44 Goren Farm (Evening)

Tuesday 14
4 Appletree Cottage
7 Bickham Gardens
23 Cliffe
44 Goren Farm (Evening)

Wednesday 15
4 Appletree Cottage
7 Bickham Gardens
23 Cliffe
44 Goren Farm (Evening)

Thursday 16
4 Appletree Cottage
23 Cliffe
26 Compton Castle
44 Goren Farm (Evening)
53 Heddon Hall

Friday 17
15 Cadhay
23 Cliffe
44 Goren Farm (Evening)
72 The Lookout

Saturday 18
9 Bocombe Mill Cottage
22 Cleave House
23 Cliffe
25 Collepardo
36 East Hele
44 Goren Farm (Evening)
91 Regency House
98 Sidmouth Gardens

Sunday 19
6 Ash Tree Farm
9 Bocombe Mill Cottage
13 Burn Valley Gardens
22 Cleave House
23 Cliffe
25 Collepardo
27 Coombe Sculpture Garden
30 The Croft
36 East Hele
37 Feebers Gardens
44 Goren Farm (Evening)
62 Kingston House
64 Langtrees
70 Littlecourt Cottages
72 The Lookout
88 Portington
97 Sherwood
98 Sidmouth Gardens
99 Southcombe Gardens
103 The Stannary
118 Yonder Hill

Monday 20
23 Cliffe
25 Collepardo
44 Goren Farm (Evening)
91 Regency House

Tuesday 21
23 Cliffe
25 Collepardo
44 Goren Farm (Evening)
91 Regency House

Wednesday 22
23 Cliffe
25 Collepardo
44 Goren Farm (Evening)
91 Regency House

Thursday 23
23 Cliffe
25 Collepardo
44 Goren Farm (Evening)

Friday 24
23 Cliffe
25 Collepardo
44 Goren Farm (Evening)
104 Summers Place (Evening)

Saturday 25
22 Cleave House
23 Cliffe
25 Collepardo
44 Goren Farm (Evening)
49 Harbour Lights
56 Holcombe Court
69 Little Webbery
108 1 Tipton Lodge
109 Walreddon Manor Gardens

Sunday 26
22 Cleave House
23 Cliffe
25 Collepardo
31 Damerel House
44 Goren Farm (Evening)
49 Harbour Lights
52 Heathercombe
56 Holcombe Court
60 Kia-Ora Farm & Gardens
69 Little Webbery
97 Sherwood
108 1 Tipton Lodge
109 Walreddon Manor Gardens
118 Yonder Hill

Monday 27
23 Cliffe
44 Goren Farm (Evening)

Tuesday 28
23 Cliffe
44 Goren Farm (Evening)

Wednesday 29
23 Cliffe
44 Goren Farm (Evening)

Thursday 30
23 Cliffe
44 Goren Farm (Evening)

July

Friday 1
23 Cliffe
44 Goren Farm (Evening)

Saturday 2
18 Cherry Trees Wildlife Garden

23 Cliffe
44 Goren Farm (Evening)
44 Goren Farm
90 Prospect House

Sunday 3
18 Cherry Trees Wildlife Garden
23 Cliffe
44 Goren Farm (Evening)
44 Goren Farm
52 Heathercombe
84 Overbeck's
90 Prospect House
114 Wildside
118 Yonder Hill

Monday 4
4 Appletree Cottage
23 Cliffe
44 Goren Farm (Evening)

Tuesday 5
4 Appletree Cottage
23 Cliffe
44 Goren Farm (Evening)

Wednesday 6
4 Appletree Cottage
23 Cliffe
44 Goren Farm (Evening)

Thursday 7
4 Appletree Cottage
23 Cliffe
44 Goren Farm (Evening)
106 Tamarisks

Friday 8
15 Cadhay
23 Cliffe
44 Goren Farm (Evening)
106 Tamarisks

Saturday 9
23 Cliffe

44 Goren Farm (Evening)
44 Goren Farm
54 High Garden
55 Hillrise
83 The Old Vicarage
86 Pikes Cottage

Sunday 10
6 Ash Tree Farm
7 Bickham Gardens
23 Cliffe
29 Cranscombe and Higher Tippacott
40 Fursdon
44 Goren Farm (Evening)
44 Goren Farm
45 Gorwell House
54 High Garden
55 Hillrise
60 Kia-Ora Farm & Gardens
61 Killerton Garden
83 The Old Vicarage
86 Pikes Cottage
92 Rousdon Cottage Gardens
93 St Merryn
96 Shapcott Barton Estate
101 Sowton Mill
118 Yonder Hill

Monday 11
23 Cliffe
44 Goren Farm (Evening)

Tuesday 12
7 Bickham Gardens
23 Cliffe
44 Goren Farm (Evening)

Wednesday 13
7 Bickham Gardens
23 Cliffe
44 Goren Farm (Evening)
96 Shapcott Barton Estate

Knightshayes Court Garden

Support the NGS – eat more cake! ☕

Thursday 14
- 23 Cliffe
- 44 Goren Farm (Evening)

Friday 15
- 23 Cliffe
- 44 Goren Farm (Evening)

Saturday 16
- 17 Chapel Farm House
- 23 Cliffe
- 44 Goren Farm (Evening)

Sunday 17
- 23 Cliffe
- 30 The Croft
- 37 Feebers Gardens
- 44 Goren Farm (Evening)
- 57 Hollycombe House
- 62 Kingston House (Evening)
- 118 Yonder Hill

Monday 18
- 23 Cliffe
- 44 Goren Farm (Evening)

Tuesday 19
- 23 Cliffe
- 44 Goren Farm (Evening)

Wednesday 20
- 23 Cliffe
- 44 Goren Farm (Evening)

Thursday 21
- 23 Cliffe
- 44 Goren Farm (Evening)

Friday 22
- 23 Cliffe
- 44 Goren Farm (Evening)

Saturday 23
- 23 Cliffe
- 39 Fossleigh
- 44 Goren Farm (Evening)

Sunday 24
- 23 Cliffe
- 39 Fossleigh
- 44 Goren Farm (Evening)
- 58 Jason's Garden (Afternoon & Evening)
- 60 Kia-Ora Farm & Gardens
- 96 Shapcott Barton Estate
- 118 Yonder Hill

Monday 25
- 23 Cliffe
- 44 Goren Farm (Evening)

Tuesday 26
- 23 Cliffe
- 44 Goren Farm (Evening)

Wednesday 27
- 23 Cliffe
- 44 Goren Farm (Evening)

Thursday 28
- 23 Cliffe
- 44 Goren Farm (Evening)

Friday 29
- 23 Cliffe
- 44 Goren Farm (Evening)
- 96 Shapcott Barton Estate

Saturday 30
- 23 Cliffe
- 33 Dicot

Sunday 31
- 23 Cliffe
- 33 Dicot
- 100 Southern Comfort
- 102 Squirrels
- 110 4 Wellswood Heights
- 111 Whitchurch Gardens
- 113 Wick Farm Gardens
- 118 Yonder Hill

August

Monday 1
- 23 Cliffe

Tuesday 2
- 23 Cliffe

Wednesday 3
- 23 Cliffe
- 96 Shapcott Barton Estate

Thursday 4
- 23 Cliffe

Friday 5
- 3 Andrew's Corner (Evening)
- 23 Cliffe

Saturday 6
- 3 Andrew's Corner
- 17 Chapel Farm House
- 23 Cliffe
- 102 Squirrels

Sunday 7
- 23 Cliffe
- 68 Little Torrington Gardens
- 102 Squirrels
- 111 Whitchurch Gardens
- 118 Yonder Hill

Monday 8
- 23 Cliffe

Tuesday 9
- 23 Cliffe

Wednesday 10
- 23 Cliffe

Thursday 11
- 23 Cliffe

Friday 12
- 23 Cliffe

Saturday 13
- 23 Cliffe
- 75 Marwood Hill
- 78 Moretonhampstead Gardens

Sunday 14
- 7 Bickham Gardens
- 23 Cliffe
- 40 Fursdon
- 60 Kia-Ora Farm & Gardens
- 78 Moretonhampstead Gardens
- 92 Rousdon Cottage Gardens
- 96 Shapcott Barton Estate
- 103 The Stannary
- 112 Whitstone Farm
- 118 Yonder Hill

Monday 15
- 23 Cliffe

Tuesday 16
- 7 Bickham Gardens
- 23 Cliffe

Wednesday 17
- 7 Bickham Gardens
- 23 Cliffe

Thursday 18
- 23 Cliffe

Friday 19
- 23 Cliffe

Saturday 20
- 6 Ash Tree Farm
- 23 Cliffe
- 39 Fossleigh

Sunday 21
- 23 Cliffe
- 30 The Croft
- 39 Fossleigh
- 66 Little Ash Bungalow
- 105 Taikoo
- 118 Yonder Hill

Monday 22
- 23 Cliffe

Tuesday 23
- 23 Cliffe

Wednesday 24
- 23 Cliffe

Thursday 25
- 23 Cliffe

Friday 26
- 23 Cliffe

Saturday 27
- 23 Cliffe
- 86 Pikes Cottage
- 95 Sedgewell Coach House Gardens

Sunday 28
- 2 32 Allenstyle Drive
- 15 Cadhay
- 19 Cherubeer Gardens
- 23 Cliffe
- 35 Durcombe Water
- 60 Kia-Ora Farm & Gardens
- 86 Pikes Cottage
- 95 Sedgewell Coach House Gardens
- 113 Wick Farm Gardens
- 118 Yonder Hill

Monday 29
- 2 32 Allenstyle Drive
- 23 Cliffe
- 35 Durcombe Water
- 60 Kia-Ora Farm & Gardens
- 86 Pikes Cottage
- 113 Wick Farm Gardens
- 118 Yonder Hill

Tuesday 30
- 23 Cliffe

Wednesday 31
- 23 Cliffe

September

Thursday 1
23 Cliffe

Friday 2
23 Cliffe

Saturday 3
23 Cliffe
90 Prospect House
98 Sidmouth Gardens

Sunday 4
2 32 Allenstyle Drive
7 Bickham Gardens
23 Cliffe
29 Cranscombe and Higher Tippacott
90 Prospect House
97 Sherwood
98 Sidmouth Gardens
118 Yonder Hill

Monday 5
23 Cliffe

Tuesday 6
7 Bickham Gardens
23 Cliffe

Wednesday 7
7 Bickham Gardens
23 Cliffe
43 Glebe Cottage

Thursday 8
23 Cliffe

Friday 9
23 Cliffe

Saturday 10
17 Chapel Farm House
23 Cliffe
55 Hillrise

Sunday 11
2 32 Allenstyle Drive
23 Cliffe
45 Gorwell House
55 Hillrise
57 Hollycombe House
60 Kia-Ora Farm & Gardens
82 The Old Rectory
97 Sherwood
118 Yonder Hill

Monday 12
23 Cliffe

Tuesday 13
23 Cliffe

Wednesday 14
23 Cliffe

Thursday 15
23 Cliffe

Friday 16
23 Cliffe

Saturday 17
23 Cliffe

Sunday 18
2 32 Allenstyle Drive
16 Castle Drogo
23 Cliffe

63 Knightshayes Court Garden
97 Sherwood
118 Yonder Hill

Monday 19
23 Cliffe

Tuesday 20
23 Cliffe

Wednesday 21
23 Cliffe

Thursday 22
23 Cliffe

Friday 23
23 Cliffe

Saturday 24
23 Cliffe
28 Coombe Trenchard
84 Overbeck's
86 Pikes Cottage

Sunday 25
23 Cliffe
28 Coombe Trenchard
86 Pikes Cottage
97 Sherwood
107 Thorn House
118 Yonder Hill

Monday 26
23 Cliffe

Tuesday 27
23 Cliffe

Wednesday 28
23 Cliffe

Thursday 29
23 Cliffe

Friday 30
23 Cliffe

October

Sunday 2
91 Regency House
97 Sherwood
104 Summers Place
118 Yonder Hill

Saturday 8
17 Chapel Farm House

Sunday 9
7 Bickham Gardens
97 Sherwood
118 Yonder Hill

Sunday 16
3 Andrew's Corner
97 Sherwood
118 Yonder Hill

Saturday 22
86 Pikes Cottage

Sunday 23
86 Pikes Cottage
97 Sherwood
118 Yonder Hill

Sunday 30
97 Sherwood
118 Yonder Hill

November

Sunday 6
97 Sherwood

Sunday 13
97 Sherwood

Sunday 20
97 Sherwood

Sunday 27
97 Sherwood

December

Sunday 4
97 Sherwood

Sunday 11
97 Sherwood
113 Wick Farm Gardens

Sunday 18
97 Sherwood

Sunday 25
97 Sherwood

January 2012

Sunday 1
97 Sherwood

Sunday 8
97 Sherwood

Sunday 15
97 Sherwood

Sunday 22
97 Sherwood

Sunday 29
97 Sherwood

February 2012

Sunday 5
19 Cherubeer Gardens
67 Little Cumbre
97 Sherwood

Sunday 12
67 Little Cumbre
97 Sherwood

Thursday 16
19 Cherubeer Gardens

Saturday 18
86 Pikes Cottage

Sunday 19
67 Little Cumbre
86 Pikes Cottage
97 Sherwood

Saturday 25
86 Pikes Cottage

Sunday 26
86 Pikes Cottage
97 Sherwood

Gardens open to the public

- **5** Arlington Court
- **8** Blackpool Gardens
- **14** Burrow Farm Gardens
- **15** Cadhay
- **16** Castle Drogo
- **24** Coleton Fishacre
- **26** Compton Castle
- **27** Coombe Sculpture Garden
- **32** Dartington Hall Gardens
- **40** Fursdon
- **41** The Garden House
- **43** Glebe Cottage
- **46** Greenway Garden
- **50** Hartland Abbey
- **53** Heddon Hall
- **61** Killerton Garden
- **63** Knightshayes Court Garden
- **73** Lukesland
- **75** Marwood Hill
- **84** Overbeck's
- **94** Saltram House
- **96** Shapcott Barton Estate
- **113** Wick Farm Gardens
- **114** Wildside

By appointment only

- **42** The Gate House
- **48** Hamblyn's Coombe
- **65** Lee Ford

Also open by Appointment ☎

- **2** 32 Allenstyle Drive
- **3** Andrew's Corner
- **4** Appletree Cottage
- **7** Bickham Cottage, Bickham Gardens
- **7** Bickham House, Bickham Gardens
- **9** Bocombe Mill Cottage
- **17** Chapel Farm House
- **21** Cleave Hill
- **22** Cleave House
- **30** The Croft
- **31** Damerel House
- **34** The Downes
- **38** Foamlea
- **39** Fossleigh
- **44** Goren Farm
- **47** Haldon Grange
- **52** Heathercombe
- **19** Higher Cherubeer, Cherubeer Gardens
- **54** High Garden
- **55** Hillrise
- **57** Hollycombe House
- **59** Jevington Hall
- **60** Kia-Ora Farm & Gardens
- **62** Kingston House
- **64** Langtrees

- **66** Little Ash Bungalow
- **67** Little Cumbre
- **68** Little Torrington Gardens
- **69** Little Webbery
- **71** Littleham House Cottage
- **76** Milford Mill, Docton Mill & Milford Mill Gardens
- **78** Moretonhampstead Gardens
- **82** The Old Rectory
- **83** The Old Vicarage
- **86** Pikes Cottage
- **88** Portington
- **89** Pound Cottage
- **90** Prospect House
- **91** Regency House
- **92** Rousdon Cottage Gardens
- **98** Runnymede, Sidmouth Gardens
- **93** St Merryn
- **97** Sherwood
- **99** Southcombe House, Southcombe Gardens
- **100** Southern Comfort
- **101** Sowton Mill
- **102** Squirrels
- **103** The Stannary
- **104** Summers Place
- **78** Sutton Mead, Moretonhampstead Gardens
- **105** Taikoo
- **106** Tamarisks
- **108** 1 Tipton Lodge
- **110** 4 Wellswood Heights
- **112** Whitstone Farm
- **115** Withleigh Farm
- **116** Wood Barton
- **74** Woodhayes, Luppitt Gardens
- **118** Yonder Hill

The Gardens

ABBOTSBURY GARDENS
See Dorset.

GROUP OPENING

1 ► **ABBOTSKERSWELL GARDENS**
TQ12 5PN. *2m SW of Newton Abbot town centre. Take A381 Newton Abbot/Totnes, sharp L turn into village or R turn if coming from Totnes. Field car parking at Fairfield or in village. Maps available at all gardens, in Model Stores & Church House.* Home-made teas at Church House. **Combined adm £4.50, chd free (share to Friends of St Mary's).** Sat 4, Sun 5 June (1-5).

BRIAR COTTAGE
1 Monk's Orchard. Peggy & David Munden

COURT COTTAGE
Mr & Mrs A R W Rooth.
50yds from PO, opp Vicarage Rd

---

2 & 8 COURT FARM BARNS
Wilton Way. Mike & Beryl Veale, Pat Mackness

FAIRFIELD
Vicarage Rd. Christine & Brian Mackness

KARIBU
35 Wilton Way. Jenny & Dave Brook

1 LAKELAND
Mary & Alan Wheeler

31 ODLEHILL GROVE
Christine Lewis

NEW ► **TOWN FARM**
Mik & Bryan Wordsworth

18 WILTON WAY
Ced & Viv Bell

10 gardens representing a variety of sizes and styles, in attractive village clustered around C13 church. Have fun finding your way around through hidden pathways beside pretty thatched cottages. Wide ranging views of the lovely valley. Sizes range from the tiny to over 2 acres, incl arboretum and orchard. Varied styles - a plantsman's delight - incl cottage and walled gardens, gardens coping with frequent drought challenges, imaginative ways with pots, arches, terracing, pergolas, rose ropes. Bog garden, ponds and streams to encourage wildlife. Vegetable plots and potagers of different sizes, some with raised beds. Secret jungle garden with bamboos, tree ferns and bananas. Town Farm is a new large garden entry this yr: thatched cottage with courtyard entrance, sweeping lawns, and many mature trees incl liriodendron - hopefully in bloom. Lakeland is a popular garden returning this yr: cottage garden currently undergoing makeover to incl mixed borders, raised vegetable beds and soft fruit area, raised fish pond and wildlife pond. Gardens incl winners of Village Best Gardens competitions - large and small. Botanical art sale. Disabled access to 5 gardens.

Modern kitchen garden with raised beds . . .

2 32 ALLENSTYLE DRIVE

Yelland, Barnstaple EX31 3DZ.
Steve & Dawn Morgan, 01271
861433,
www.devonsubtropicalgarden.
co.uk. *5m W of Barnstaple. Take
B3233 towards Instow. Through
Bickington & Fremington. L at Yelland
sign into Allenstyle Rd. 1st R into
Allenstyle Dr. Light blue bungalow.*
Teas & light refreshments. **Adm £3,
chd free. Sun 28, Mon 29 Aug;
Suns 4, 11, 18 Sept (10.30-6).**
Visitors also welcome by appt Aug
only.
Subtropical planting in small
(50x100ft) garden in mild estuary
location. Bananas, hedychiums
(gingers), palms, colocasia, aroids,
brugmansias, exotic large collection
of passionflowers, prairie planting and
much more. Lots of seating so you
can take your time and enjoy our late
summer burst of scent, colour and
high impact planting.

3 ANDREW'S CORNER

Belstone EX20 1RD. Robin &
Edwina Hill, 01837 840332,
edwinarobinhill@btinternet.com,
www.belstonevillage.net. *3m E of
Okehampton. Signed to Belstone. In
village signed Skaigh. Parking
restricted but cars may be left on
nearby common.* Home-made teas.
**Adm £3, chd free. Sun 1, Mon 2,
Suns 8, 22, 29, Mon 30 May; Suns
5 June; 16 Oct (2.30-5.30). Evening
Openings Adm £5, chd free, wine
& cheese, Fri 5 Aug, Sat 6 Aug
(7-10).** Visitors also welcome by
appt. Guided tour possible for
groups 5+.
Well-established, wildlife-friendly, well-
labelled plantsman's garden in
stunning high moorland setting.
Variety of garden habitats incl
woodland areas, bog garden, pond;
wide range of unusual trees, shrubs,
herbaceous plants for yr-round effect
incl alpines, rhododendrons, bulbs
and maples; spectacular autumn
colour. Organic kitchen garden,
greenhouse and chickens. Wheelchair
access difficult when wet.

4 APPLETREE COTTAGE

Higher Dawlish Water, Ashcombe
Rd, Dawlish EX7 0QW. David & Sue
Stephenson, 01626 895024,
david@stephend.f9.co.uk. *2m NW
of Dawlish. In Dawlish take High St
and follow along onto Old Town St.
Turn R at Swan Inn onto Weech Rd.*

Sherwood

At T-junction R onto Ashcombe Rd
(single track) garden on L after
1¹/₂m. Limited parking. **Adm £3, chd
free. Daily Mon 13 June to Thur 16
June; Mon 4 July to Thur 7 July
(10-4).** Visitors also welcome by
appt.
SW-facing ³/₄ -acre sloping site,
abundantly planted with wide variety
of plants, shrubs and trees.Two pond
areas, bog area plus gazebo with
board walk to larger pond. Decorative
vegetable and fruit garden with
greenhouse. Bordering Dawlish Water
and encouraging and supporting
wildlife.

5 ◆ ARLINGTON COURT

Arlington, Barnstaple EX31 4LP.
National Trust, 01271 850296,
www.nationaltrust.org.uk. *7m NE of
Barnstaple. On A39. From E use
A399.* Adm £6.50, chd £3.25. For
NGS: Thur 5 May (10.30-5) 2pm -
meet the Head Gardener (free with
admission, donations welcome).
Also Evening Opening 6.30pm,
£13 - discover picturesque
Arlington: A garden with a past
(must be pre-booked, evening tour
with Head Gardener, plus 2 course
meal). For other opening times and
information, please phone or see
garden website.
Rolling parkland and woods with lake.

Rhododendrons and azaleas; fine
specimen trees; small terraced
Victorian garden with herbaceous
borders and conservatory. Walled
garden nearly restored, produce for
sale. Regency house containing
fascinating collections. Carriage
Museum in the stables, carriage rides.

6 NEW ASH TREE FARM

Ash Cross, Dartmouth TQ6 0LR.
Ms Stevie Rogers. *2m SW of
Dartmouth. Leave A3122 (Halwell to
Dartmouth rd) at R turn beside white
house just before Sportsman's Arms.
Follow signs to Ash. Ash Tree Farm
1¹/₂ m at 2nd X-rds.* Home-made
teas. **Adm £3, chd free. Suns 10
Apr; 1, 29 May; 19 June; 10 July
(11-5); Evening Opening £5, chd
free, wine, Sat 20 Aug (7-10).**
Interesting, newly-created, colour-
themed garden. Unique, single colour,
cottage-garden style plantings. Large
pond surrounded by wild flowers.
Modern kitchen garden with raised
beds. Whole garden is designed to
attract wildlife; hedgehog houses,
insect homes and bee hives. Full of
original ideas. Wild flower nursery.
Access to walk the farm and bluebell
woods by request. Plenty of seating
areas for the less mobile.

GROUP OPENING

7 NEW **BICKHAM GARDENS**
Kenn EX6 7XL. *6m S of Exeter. 1m off A38. Leave A38 at Kennford Services, follow signs to Kenn. 1st R in village, follow lane for ³/₄ m to end of no through rd.* Cream teas. **Adm £4, chd free, season tickets £10.**
Suns, Tues, Weds
10, 12, 13 Apr;
8, 10, 11 May;
12, 14, 15 June;
10, 12, 13 July;
14, 16, 17 Aug;
4, 6, 7 Sept;
Sun 9 Oct (2-5).
Visitors also welcome by appt.

NEW **BICKHAM COTTAGE**
Steve Eyre
Visitors also welcome by appt.
01392 833964
bickham@hotmail.co.uk

BICKHAM HOUSE
John & Julia Tremlett
Visitors also welcome by appt.
01392 832671
jandjtremlett@hotmail.com

Adj gardens in private valley under Haldon Hills. Bickham House: 7-acre garden with much recent replanting. Colour co-ordinated borders, mature trees, croquet lawn. Fern garden and water garden. Formal parterre with lily pond. 1-acre walled garden with profusion of vegetables and flowers. Palm tree avenue leading to summerhouse. Spring garden with cowslips, bluebells etc. Alpine house with over 100 immaculately displayed plants. Wide selection of well-grown plants for sale. Bickham Cottage: small cottage garden divided into separate areas by old stone walls and hedge banks. Front garden with mainly South African bulbs and plants. Lawn surrounded by borders with agapanthus, eucomis, crocosmia, diorama etc. Stream garden with primulas and glasshouses with colections of nerines and tulbaghias. Pond with large koi carp. Featured in Country Gardener and local press.
♿ ☞ ☕ ☎

Adjacent gardens
. . . season tickets
available . . .

8 ♦ **BLACKPOOL GARDENS**
Dartmouth TQ6 0RG. Sir Geoffrey Newman, 01803 770606, www.blackpoolsands.co.uk. *3m SW of Dartmouth. From Dartmouth follow brown signs to Blackpool Sands on A379. Entrance to gardens via Blackpool Sands car park.* **Adm £3, chd free.**
Tenderly restored C19 subtropical plantsman's garden with collection of mature and newly-planted tender and unusual trees, shrubs and carpet of spring flowers. Paths and steps lead gradually uphill and above the Captain's seat offering spectacular coastal views. Recent plantings follow the S hemisphere theme with callistemons, pittosporums, acacias and buddlejas. Open 1 Apr - Sept (10-4).

9 ♦ **BOCOMBE MILL COTTAGE**
Bocombe, Parkham EX39 5PH. Mr Chris Butler & Mr David Burrows, 01237 451293, www.bocombe.co.uk. *6m E of Clovelly, 9m SW of Bideford. From A39 just outside Horns Cross village, turn to Foxdown. At Xrds take lane signed Bocombe.* Home-made teas. **Adm £3.50, chd £1.** Sat 28, Sun 29, Mon 30 May; Sat 18, Sun 19 June (10-4). **Visitors also welcome by appt Mar to Sept groups of 10+.**
8 new water features, plus new Japanese Pavilion, all set in 5 acres of gardens & wild meadow in small wooded valley, a wildlife haven. Themed flower gardens. Streams, bog gardens & pools. Kitchen garden, orchard, soft fruit garden, shrubbery. All organic. Goats on hillside. Plan & tree guide. Short flower garden walk or circular walk of just under 1m (boots or wellies suggested). Steps & steep slopes. Featured in Western Morning News.
☘ ☕ ☎

BOSCASTLE GARDENS
See Cornwall.

GROUP OPENING

10 **BOVEY COUNTRY GARDENS**
Bovey Tracey TQ13 9LQ. *6m N of Newton Abbot. Gateway to Dartmoor. Gardens between Shewte Cross and cattle grid to moor (2m) on Manaton Rd from fire station r'about. Limited parking at Down Park, parking at Three Corners; extra parking for Holne Brake over cattle grid.*

Combined adm £4, chd free. Sat 7, Sun 8 May (2-6).

DOWN PARK
Shewte Cross. Susan Macready.
1m from Fire Station r'about on Manaton Rd. Parking available

HOLNE BRAKE
Michael & Jennifer Pery.
R after cattle grid on rd to Manaton Rd, 2m from fire stn r'about

THREE CORNERS
Manaton Rd. Jonathan & Sue Clarke.
Up Manaton Rd from Bovey Fire Stn, 1st R after turning into Haytor before Shewte Cross

3 very different gardens on Western edge of Bovey Tracey towards Dartmoor. On the moorland rd towards Manaton is Three Corners, a classic style country garden laid out in 1930s style with croquet lawn, grass tennis court, vegetable garden and vine-clad pergola. Close by is Down Park, a colourful mature garden with a great variety of rhododendrons, azaleas, camellias and unusual shrubs. A mile beyond at cattle grid is Holne Brake, an artist's moorland garden with woodland walks and spectacular views of Lustleigh Cleave. A blaze of colour in spring. Recent clearing of rhododendron ponticum has opened ground for planting of specimen trees. Open studio at Holne Brake. Featured in Country Gardener. Wheelchair access to 2 gardens.
♿ ☘

GROUP OPENING

11 **BOVEY TRACEY GARDENS**
TQ13 9NA. *6m N of Newton Abbot. Gateway to Dartmoor. Take A382 to Bovey Tracey. Car parking available at Mary St, Station Rd, library, Le Molay Littry Way car parks and at Whitstone and Parke. Teas at Gleam Tor & Ashwell.* **Combined adm £4, chd free. Sat 4, Sun 5 June (2-6).**

ASHWELL
East Street. Bill & Diane Riddell

BOVEY COMMUNITY GARDEN
NT and Bovey Tracey Climate Action.
Follow signs to Parke, parking in visitors' car park
www.boveyclimateaction.org.uk

NEW ▶ GLEAM TOR
Brimley Road. Gillian & Colin
Liddy.
*Last house on L at end of Brimley
Rd before rd narrows*

PARKE VIEW
Fore Street. Peter & Judy Hall.
Next to The Old Cottage tea shop

OLD WHITSTONE
Jinny & Richard Aldridge.
Park in Whitstone Quarry

11 ST PETERS CLOSE
Mr & Mrs Gregory.
*Parking available in surrounding
roads*

▾ **WHITSTONE HOUSE**
Laura Barclay.
*Park in Whitstone Quarry at top of
Whitstone Lane*

YONDER
Whitstone Lane,
Moretonhampstead Rd. Mr &
Mrs John Awcock

Pretty cob and Dartmoor granite built
town situated on R Bovey. 8 very
varied gardens. Ashwell: walled
garden with vineyard, orchard, mature
tree and glorious views. Bovey
Community Garden incl restored fruit
garden demonstrating pruning and
cultivation techniques. Gleam Tor:
large recently-redesigned garden,
individually themed areas and
colourful herbaceous perennials.
Parke View: large garden with
meandering stone walls well-stocked
with unusual plants. Restored
Victorian walled garden, now a
flourishing community project
producing traditional and new
vegetables and cut flowers. Old
Whitstone: old farmhouse garden with
herbaceous borders, small steep
wooded orchard, meadow and pond.
11 St Peter's Close: small town
garden packed with interesting plants
and model railway. Whitstone House's
mature garden with undulating
heather feature, woodland walk and
panoramic views of Dartmoor and
Bovey valley. Yonder: exquisite mature
cottage garden with interesting
planting.
🎍 ☕

12▶ BRAMBLE TORRE
Dittisham, nr Dartmouth TQ6 0HZ.
Paul & Sally Vincent.
www.rainingsideways.com. *³/₄ m
from Dittisham. Leave A3122 Halwell
to Dartmouth rd at Sportsmans Arms
and head towards Dittisham. In village*

*turn hard L towards Cornworthy.
Garden ³/₄ m straight ahead - L turn
by gates to park.* Cream teas. **Adm
£3.50, chd free** (share to Trinity
Sailing Trust). **Sat 11, Sun 12 June
(2-5).**
Set in 20 acres of farmland, the
3-acre garden follows rambling
stream through steep valley. Lily
pond, herbaceous borders, camellias,
shrubs and roses are dominated by
huge Embothrium, scarlet in late
Spring against a sometimes blue sky!
Formal herb and vegetable garden
runs along one side of stream while
chickens scratch in an orchard of
Ditsum plums and cider apples on
other side. Well behaved dogs on
leads welcome. Limited wheelchair
access, parts of garden very steep.
♿ ☕

The 3-acre garden
follows rambling
stream through
steep valley . . .

GROUP OPENING

13▶ BURN VALLEY GARDENS
Butterleigh EX15 1PG. *3m W
Cullompton, 3m S Tiverton. From
Butterleigh, take rd to Silverton at T-
junction. After ¹/₄ m, take unmarked L
fork, continue to hamlet. Very narrow
lanes.* Home-made teas at both
gardens. **Combined adm £5, chd
free. Suns 5, 19 June (2-6).**

HIGHER BURNHAIES
Richard & Virginia Holmes

SHUTELAKE
Jill & Nigel Hall

2 different but complementary
gardens separated by stream in the
beautiful Burn Valley, surrounded by
woods and farmland and teeming
with wildlife. Higher Burnhaies:
plantsman's garden within 2¹/₂ -acre
site started in 1997. The planting is a

relaxed tapestry of herbaceous
perennials, trees and shrubs with
ponds and wild edges. Vegetable
garden, old Devon lane and
wilderness walk lead you over the
bridge to Shutelake, where you can
discover a S-facing, terraced garden
surrounding C17 farmhouse. The
varied planting of herbaceous
borders, natural ponds and lakes,
romantic arbours and sculpture
collection invite you to rest and
reflect or you can wander the
woodland escape beside the stream.
Live accoustic music at Higher
Burnhaies.
✽ ☕

**14▶ ♦ BURROW FARM
GARDENS**
Dalwood, Axminster EX13 7ET.
Mary & John Benger, 01404
831285,
enquiries@burrowfarmgardens.
co.uk, www.burrowfarmgardens.
co.uk. *3¹/₂ m W of Axminster. From
A35 turn N at Taunton Xrds then
follow brown signs.*
Secluded 10-acre garden of informal
design with many unusual shrubs
and herbaceous plants. Woodland
with rhododendrons and azaleas,
ponds and large bog garden.
Terraced courtyard featuring later
flowering plants. Rill garden with
water feature; traditional stone
summerhouse with wonderful views.
New area in 2010 featuring late
summer perennials and grasses.
Open 1 Apr - 31 Oct 10-7.
♿ 🎍 ✽ ☕

15▶ ♦ CADHAY
Ottery St Mary EX11 1QT. Rupert
Thistlethwayte,
www.cadhay.org.uk. *1m NW of
Ottery St Mary. On B3176.* **Adm
£3, chd £1. For NGS: Fris 27 May;
17 June; 8 July; Sun 28 Aug
(2-5.30).**
Tranquil 2-acre setting for Elizabethan
manor house. 2 medieval fish ponds
surrounded by rhododendrons,
gunnera, hostas and flag iris. Roses,
clematis, lilies and hellebores
surround walled water garden. 120ft
herbaceous border walk informally
planted with cottage garden
perennials and annuals. Walled
kitchen gardens have been turned
into allotments and old garden store
is now tearoom. Open Fris May to
Sept 2-5.30.
♿ ✽ ☕

16 ◆ CASTLE DROGO
Drewsteignton EX6 6PB. National Trust, 01647 433306, www.nationaltrust.org.uk. *12m W of Exeter. 5m S of A30. Follow brown signs. Limited parking until Aug.* **Adm £5.75, chd £3.15. For NGS: Suns 15 May; 18 Sept (9.30-5.30).**
For other opening times and information, please phone or see garden website.
Medium-sized Grade II* listed garden with formal structures designed by George Dillistone during the late 1920s. These consist of formal rose beds, herbaceous borders and circular croquet lawn surrounded by mature yew hedges. Rhododendron garden overlooks spectacular views of Teign valley gorge and Dartmoor. Visit Devon Attraction of the Year Gold Award. Gravel and some woodland paths.
&. ⊛

17 CHAPEL FARM HOUSE
Halwill Junction, Beaworthy EX21 5UF. Robin & Toshie Hull, 01409 221594. *12m NW of Okehampton. On A3079. At W end of village.* **Adm £3.50, chd free.**

Sats 26 Mar; 30 Apr; 14 May; 11 June; 16 July; 6 Aug; 10 Sept; 8 Oct (11-5). **Visitors also welcome by appt all yr.**
Approx ¹/₂-acre garden started in 1992 by present owners, landscaped with shrub borders, heathers, rhododendrons and azaleas. Alpine bed. Kitchen garden. 2 small greenhouses for mixed use. Small bonsai collection. 3 acres of mixed young woodland with wildlife and flowers. New Japanese garden and stone lantern. Gravel paths, large lawns.
&. ⊛ ☎

18 CHERRY TREES WILDLIFE GARDEN
5 Sentry Corner, Bideford EX39 4BW. Henry and Evelyn Butterfield, cherrytrees.weebly.com. *East The Water. From Bideford Old Bridge, follow up hill past The Royal Hotel. Follow signs to Sentry Corner (approx ³/₄ m), parking at Pollyfield Centre.* Teas & light refreshments. **Adm £2.50, chd free. Mon 30 May; Sat 2, Sun 3 July (2-5).**
Small demonstration garden showing

what can be done to bring wildlife into the town. Incl courtyard garden, summer cornfield, summer wildflower meadow, cottage garden border, woodland edge, and 2 small ponds. Newly-constructed folly and stumpery. Enjoy a friendly chat about wildlife gardening over tea and biscuits with the owners. Small Natural History Collection incl photo wall of garden's wildlife visitors. Featured in BBC 2 Open Gardens.
🐿 ⊛ ☕

GROUP OPENING

19 CHERUBEER GARDENS
Dolton EX19 8PP, 01805 804265, hynesjo@gmail.com. *8m SE of Great Torrington. 2m E of Dolton. From A3124 turn S towards Stafford Moor Fisheries, take 1st R, gardens 500m on L.* Home-made teas at Higher Cherubeer. **Combined adm £4 (Jan/Feb); £3.50, (May & Aug) chd free.** Suns 30 Jan; 6 Feb (2-5); Suns 29 May; 28 Aug (2-6); Sun 5, Thur 16 Feb 2012.

CHERUBEER
Janet Brown

HIGHER CHERUBEER
Jo & Tom Hynes
Visitors also welcome by appt in May & June for groups of 10+.
01805 804265
hynesjo@gmail.com

MIDDLE CHERUBEER
Heather Hynes

The 3 Cherubeers, a family affair, form a small hamlet in rolling farmland at 500 ft at the top of a SW facing valley. Despite the exposed location and stony acid clay soil, the gardens provide a wealth of colour right through the season. Cherubeer: cottage garden set around a C15 thatched house (not open). Ponds, paths, and steps filled with colourful perennials and herbs set off by mature shrubs and trees. Higher Cherubeer: 1-acre country garden with gravelled courtyard, raised beds and alpine house, large herbaceous border, shady woodland beds with over 150 varieties of snowdrops, colourful collection of basketry willows, vegetable garden and National Collection of hardy cyclamen. Middle Cherubeer: colourful small garden. 3 separate areas with bog garden, pond and massed herbaceous perennials

Arlington Court

Follow us on Facebook and Twitter

interlinked with paths. Many cyclamen and snowdrop bank. Featured on BBC2 Open Gardens and Gardeners' World (Higher Cherubeer). Partial wheelchair access due to slopes and gravel. Very little access at Cherubeer.

& ✿ NCCPG ☕

---

20 CHEVITHORNE BARTON
Tiverton EX16 7QB. Michael & Arabella Heathcoat Amory. *3m NE of Tiverton. M5, J27, leave A361 by 1st exit after 300 yds, through Sampford Peverell and Halberton towards Tiverton. Immed past golf course, R then R at next T-junction. Over bridge, L through Craze Lowman, carry on through lanes to T-junction, R then 1st L.* Home-made teas. Adm £3.50, chd free. Suns 17 Apr; 5 June (2-5.30).
Terraced walled garden, summer borders and romantic woodland of rare trees and shrubs. In spring, garden features large collection of magnolias, camellias, rhododendrons and azaleas. Also incl one of only two NCCPG oak collections situated in 12 hectares of parkland and comprising over 200 different species.

🌿 NCCPG ☕

CHIDEOCK MANOR
See Dorset.

21 CLEAVE HILL
Membury, Axminster EX13 7AJ. Andy & Penny Pritchard, 01404 881437, penny@tonybengerlandscaping. co.uk. *4m NW of Axminster. From Membury Village, follow rd down valley. 1st R after Lea Hill B&B, last house on drive, approx 1m.* Cream teas, light refreshments & light lunches. Adm £3.50, chd free. Sat 28, Sun 29 May (11-5). Visitors also welcome by appt.
Artistic garden in pretty village situated on edge of Blackdown Hills. Cottage-style garden, planted to provide all-season structure, texture and colour. Designed around pretty thatched house and old stone barns. Wonderful views, attractive vegetable garden and orchard, wild flower meadow.

& 🌿 ☕ ☎

22 CLEAVE HOUSE
Sticklepath EX20 2NL. Ann & Roger Bowden, 01837 840481, bowdens2@eclipse.co.uk. *3½ m E of Okehampton. On old A30 towards Exeter. Cleave House on L in village,*

on main rd just past R turn for Skaigh. Adm £2.50, chd free (share to NCCPG). Sats, Suns 18, 19, 25, 26 June (10.30-5). Visitors also welcome by appt May to Aug.
½ -acre garden with mixed planting for all season interest. National Collection of Hostas with 1000 varieties. 6 consecutive Chelsea Flower Show gold medals.

& ✿ NCCPG ☎

23 CLIFFE
Lee, Ilfracombe EX34 8LR. Dr & Mrs Humphreys. *3m W of Ilfracombe. Garden is past sea front at Lee, towards top of steep hill on coast rd. Entrance through wrought iron gates on L. Lee Bay car park at bottom of hill (no parking on approach rd).* Adm £3, chd free. Fri 1 Apr to Fri 30 Sept incl (9-4).
Cliff-side terraced garden with spectacular coastal views. Diverse range of habitats from Mediterranean to woodland. Always something to see. In spring, camellias and azaleas, colourful herbaceous borders throughout summer and exotic hedychiums, canna and salvias flowering into autumn. New borders planned for 2011. Featured in The Journal of the Hardy Plant Society.

🌿

Artistic garden in pretty village . . .

24 ◆ COLETON FISHACRE
nr Kingswear TQ6 0EQ. National Trust, 01803 752466, www.nationaltrust.org.uk. *3m E of Dartmouth. Lower Ferry Rd. Follow brown signs. Lane leading to Coleton Fishacre is narrow and can be busy on fine days. Use of passing places and reversing may be necessary. Coach parties must book.* Adm £7.40, child £3.70. For NGS: Sat 14 May (10.30-5). For other opening times and information, please phone or see garden website.
30-acre garden created by Rupert and Lady Dorothy D'Oyly Carte

between 1925 and 1948. Re-established and developed by NT since 1983. Wide range of tender and uncommon trees and shrubs in spectacular coastal setting. Guided tour 2pm focusing on exotic planting of garden and beautiful views.

& 🌿 ✿ ☕ 🐾

25 COLLEPARDO
3 Keyberry Park, Newton Abbot TQ12 1BZ. Betty & Don Frampton. *Take A380 Newton Abbot. From Newton Abbot (Penn Inn) r'about follow sign for town centre. 1st L slip rd before T-lights, then 1st R, 2nd L.* Home-made teas. Adm £3, chd free. Sat 18 to Sun 26 June incl (10.30-5).
⅓ -acre garden laid out in series of interlinked colour-themed garden rooms, explored via 400 metres of meandering paths. Circular rockery of 30 metres enclosing new lawn. Herbaceous and shrub borders, pond, raised walkway, and gazebo allow the visitor every opportunity to view 1,500 varieties of hardy plants, shrubs and trees. Featured in local press. Prizewinner in Supreme Class of the Newton Abbot Britain in Bloom.

✿ ☕

26 ◆ COMPTON CASTLE
Marldon, Paignton TQ3 1TA. National Trust, 01803 843235, www.nationaltrust.org.uk. *3m W of Torquay. 1½ m N of Marldon. From Newton Abbot - Totnes rd A381 turn L at Ipplepen Xrds & W off Torbay Ring Rd via Marldon.* Adm £4.40, chd £2.20. For NGS: Thur 16 June (10.30-4.30). For other opening times and information, please phone or see garden website.
Small formal courtyard gardens, rose garden, herb garden. Access to the usually private fruit and vegetable garden. Incl access to fortified Manor House with restored medieval great hall. Tour of the garden with one of our experienced gardeners, focusing on rose garden, 2pm.

✿

27 ◆ COOMBE SCULPTURE GARDEN
Bradstone Coombe, Bradstone, Tavistock PL19 0QS. Gary & Kay Vanstone, 01822 870208, gv@stoneventures.co.uk. *9m W of Tavistock. On B3362 Tavistock to Launceston rd, garden signed.* Light Refreshments. Lunches and afternoon teas. Adm £4, chd free. For NGS: Sun 12, 19 June (11-5).

For other opening times and information please visit NGS website or telephone.
2-acre S-sloping garden around C17 farmhouse in secluded wooded valley. Variety of garden habitats preserving ancient features with an emphasis on providing for wildlife. Planted with hellebores and bulbs. Unusual trees incl magnolia campbellii, shrubs and herbaceous plants for all-yr colour. Tamar valley fruit orchard, organic vegetable garden. Spring-fed streams, pools and mill pond. Sculptures of Paul Vanstone on display and for sale.

28 COOMBE TRENCHARD
Lewtrenchard EX20 4PW. Philip & Sarah Marsh,
www.coombetrenchard.co.uk. *14m N of Tavistock and W of Okehampton. In Lewdown take turning for Lewtrenchard, at bottom of hill turn R opposite Lewtrenchard Manor Hotel. Garden 100yds on R up unmarked lane.* Home-made teas. **Adm £4, chd free. Sat 24, Sun 25 Sept (2-5).**
Coombe Trenchard's 8-acre Arts & Crafts garden was designed in 1906 by architect Walter Sarel, with terraces, garden buildings, paths and bridges. Still a work in progress, 2 yrs into restoration project, forgotten paths, woodland garden, water gardens and the pattern of long forgotten Edwardian planting schemes have been discovered.

Two contrasting gardens created around old farm buildings . . .

COOMBEGATE COTTAGE
See Cornwall.

COTEHELE
See Cornwall.

COTHAY MANOR GARDENS
See Somerset & Bristol.

GROUP OPENING

29 NEW CRANSCOMBE AND HIGHER TIPPACOTT
Brendon, Lynton EX35 6PU. *1.5m S of Brendon. Both gardens off narrow hillside lane. From Xrds at Brendon village green follow sign to Tippacott. 1m to T-junction fronting moor. Turn R, parking on R for Tippacott, proceed 1m further for Cranscombe on L, parking at top of drive.* Cream teas. **Combined adm £3.50, chd free. Suns 10 July; 4 Sept (1.30-5.30).**

NEW CRANSCOMBE FARM
Gratton Lane. Nicky & David Ramsay

NEW HIGHER TIPPACOTT FARM
Tippacott Lane. Angela & Malcolm Percival

Situated in stunning open countryside, close to Lorna Doone valley and deep within Exmoor National Park, these 2 contrasting gardens, with fine views to moorland, have been created around old farm buildings. Cranscombe, set on the thousand foot contour has interesting levels separated by stone banking around lovely old barn, and an emphasis on indigenous plants viable for moorland conditions. Vast skies and often quickly changing weather patterns enhance the vital nature of this garden. Higher Tippacott has a series of sunny levels with interesting herbaceous planting and stone walls, overlooking its own pretty valley pasture with stream. Vegetable patch and young vines with a distant glimpse of the sea. All organic. The beautiful East Lyn valley with riverside woodland footpaths, riverside pubs serving meals at Brendon and Rockford and NT's Watersmeet are all in immediate vicinity. Sale of recently published local and history series Unforgotten Exmoor, compiled by owner of Cranscombe Farm (all profits to Air Ambulance).

30 THE CROFT
Yarnscombe EX31 3LW. Sam & Margaret Jewell, 01769 560535. *4m NE of Torrington, 8m S of Barnstaple. From A377, turn W opp Chapelton*

railway stn. After 3m drive on L at village sign. From B3232, ¹/₄ m N of Hunshaw TV mast Xrds, turn E for 2m. Parking in village hall car park nearby. **Adm £3.50, chd free (share to N Devon Animal Ambulance). Suns 19 June; 17 July; 21 Aug (2-6). Visitors also welcome by appt.**
1-acre plantswoman's garden featuring exotic Japanese garden with tea house, koi carp pond and cascading stream, tropical garden with exotic shrubs and perennials. Herbaceous borders with unusual plants and shrubs. Bog garden with collection of irises, astilbes and moisture-loving plants, duck pond. New exotic border for 2011 and extension to Japanese garden.

31 NEW DAMEREL HOUSE
Sydenham Damerel PL19 8PU. Mr & Mrs Justin Roberts,
jude@damerelhouse.co.uk. *6m NW of Tavistock. On Tavistock/Launceston rd. 4m from Tavistock turn W following signs to Sydenham Damerel. Through village, follow signs.* Home-made teas. **Adm £4, chd free. Suns 5, 26 June (11-6). Visitors also welcome by appt.**
7 acres of grounds surrounding listed Georgian house on edge of village. Magnificent trees and sweeping lawns with lovely views. Enclosed herbaceous garden abundantly planted with perennials and large formal vegetable garden with box hedging.

32 ♦ DARTINGTON HALL GARDENS
Dartington TQ9 6EL. Dartington Hall Trust, 01803 862367,
gardens@dartington.org. *1¹/₂ m NW of Totnes. From Totnes take A384, turn R at Dartington Parish Church. Proceed up hill for 1m. Hall & gardens on R. Car parking on L.* **Adm £3, chd free. For NGS: Sun 5 June (10-6).**
28-acre modern garden, created since 1925 around C14 medieval hall (not open). Courtyard and tournament ground. Dry landscape Japanese garden. Extensive wild flower meadows and mixed shrub and herbaceous border. Peter Randall-Page sculpture. Guided tour at 2pm. Open dawn to dusk all yr.

33 ▶ **DICOT**

Chardstock EX13 7DF. Mr & Mrs F Clarkson, www.dicot.co.uk. *5m N of Axminster. Axminster to Chard A358 at Tytherleigh to Chardstock. R at George Inn, L fork to Hook, R to Burridge, 2nd house on L.* Home-made teas. **Adm £3, chd £1.** Sat 30 Apr; Sun 1, Mon 2 May; Sat 11, Sun 12 June; Sat 30, Sun 31 July (2-5.30).
Secret garden hidden in East Devon valley. 3 acres of unusual and exotic plants - some rare. Rhododendrons, azaleas and camellias in profusion. Meandering stream, fish pool, Japanese-style garden and interesting vegetable garden with fruit cage, tunnel and greenhouses. Featured on BBC Radio.

34 ▶ **THE DOWNES**

Bideford EX39 5LB. Richard Stanley-Baker, 07782 145337/01237 47551, rsb@usa.net/ glenturret@gmail.com. *3m NW of Great Torrington. On A386 between Bideford & Torrington. Drive leads off A386 4¹/₂ m from Bideford, 2¹/₂ m from Torrington. Do not go to Monkleigh.* **Adm £3.50, chd free.** Daily Mon 14 Mar to Sun 15 May (10-4.30). Visitors also welcome by appt, no coaches.
15 acres with landscaped lawns; fine views overlooking fields and woodlands in Torridge Valley; many unusual trees and shrubs; small arboretum; woodland walks, bluebells.

35 ▶ **DURCOMBE WATER**

Furzehill, Barbrook, Lynton EX35 6LN. Pam & David Sydenham. *3m S of Lynton. From Barnstaple take A39 towards Lynton. On entering Barbrook go past Total garage (do not turn to Lynton) take the next turn R (about 100yds). Follow this single track rd for 2m, gates on L.* Cream teas. **Adm £3, chd free.** Suns, Mons 29, 30 May; 28, 29 Aug (11-5).
Stunning views across Exmoor National Park on the garden approach sets the scene. Silent relaxing garden, enlivened with streams and waterfalls falling 40ft through 8 tiered ponds. Walk from one type of garden into another - the cottage garden, landscaped terraces, the oriental and art gallery gardens, each with colour, scents and beauty.

36 ▶ **NEW** ▶ **EAST HELE**

Kings Nympton, Umberleigh EX37 9TB. Mrs Joan Bradshaw. *3m SW of South Molton, 1m NW of Kings Nympton. Leave S Molton on B3226. Turn off Left to George Nympton. Follow 'Tudor Rose' signs to Hele Farm Shop. Next thatched house down hill.* **Adm £3, chd free.** Sat 18, Sun 19 June (10-5).
The gardens at East Hele cover three acres at the head of a valley. Divided up by low walls of cob and local stone, their higher reaches are rich with beds of varied flowering perennials; lower down, lawns border ponds, rills and areas of young trees. Waterfowl nest in reedbeds. Easy ¹/₂ m circular walk from the garden between woods and fenced pasture giving fine views over the valley and surrounding country. 15m gravel path, then lawn. Help available for wheelchairs.

Rich with beds of varied flowering perennials . . .

GROUP OPENING

37 ▶ **FEEBERS GARDENS**

Broadclyst, Westwood, nr Broadclyst EX5 3DQ. *8m NE of Exeter. From B3181 Exeter to Taunton bear E at Dog Village towards Whimple. After 1¹/₂ m fork L for Westwood.* Cream Teas. **Adm £3, chd free.** Suns 19 June; 17 July (2-6).

1 FEEBERS COTTAGE
Mr & Mrs M J Squires

2 FEEBERS COTTAGE
Bob & Georgina Williams

3 FEEBERS COTTAGE
Richard & Karen Burrell

3 pretty gardens in a Devon hamlet. 1 Feebers Cottage: evolving cottage garden of 1 acre - a maze of pathways, herbaceous, shrubs and trees. In spring, 60 different snowdrops; in autumn, colchicums and cyclamen. 2 Feebers Cottage: colourful, formal garden contrasting the 2 cottage gardens. Delightful flower beds, small alpine house and gravel area with variety of potted shrubs and plants. 3 Feebers Cottage: contemporary cottage garden with formal vegetable area, established fruit trees, flower beds and rose arbour. Some quirky features incl BBQ house and a mini petanque area within a secret garden. Numerous places to sit and enjoy a cream tea. Seasonal produce and plants available for sale.

FERNHILL
See Somerset & Bristol.

38 ▶ **FOAMLEA**

Chapel Hill, Mortehoe EX34 7DZ. Beth Smith, 01271 871182, bethmortepoint@fmail.co.uk. *¹/₄ m S of Mortehoe village. A361 N from Barnstaple. L at Mullacott Cross onto B3343 to Mortehoe. No parking near or at house. Use village car park, L past church, down steep hill, garden further 200yds.* Home-made teas. **Adm £3, chd free.** Suns 1, 8, 22, 29 May (2-5). Visitors also welcome by appt, groups welcome - no coach access.
³/₄ -acre plantswoman's 7 yr-old garden, full clifftop exposure, almost frost-free. Handsome drystone walls throughout. Uneven slate paths lead through many colourful areas filled by exotics, succulents and wide range of shrubs and perennials. Alpine House. Small produce garden. Adjoins SW coastal footpath. Stunning Atlantic view.

FORDE ABBEY GARDENS
See Dorset.

39 ▶ **FOSSLEIGH**

Burlescombe EX16 7JH. David & Glenis Beard, 01823 672907. *3m from M5, J27. From J27 take A38 to Wellington, over M5, 1st L to Burlescombe. 1m, L just before canal bridge. Limited parking, public car park 150m from garden, over bridge then immed L.* Home-made teas. **Adm £2.50, chd free.** Sats, Suns 23, 24 July; 20, 21 Aug (2-5). Visitors also welcome by appt.
The garden borders the Grand

Western Canal. Imaginative use of space, many surprises: Water garden, bog garden, herbaceous borders, Japanese garden, miniature bowling green, sundial vegetable plot, fruit cage, sunken walkways surrounded by flowers and foliage. New this year: fernery, viewing deck. Enjoy a stroll on canal tow-path after your visit.

❀ 🍵 ☎

40 ◆ FURSDON
Cadbury, Thorverton, Exeter EX5 5JS. David & Catriona Fursdon, 01392 860860, www.fursdon.co.uk. *2m N of Thorverton. L (after Xrds by Blue Cross rescue centre) on A3072 travelling from Bickleigh towards Crediton. Fursdon approx 1m from turning. Or go to Thorverton signed on A396 and follow Fursdon signs for approx 2m from village.* Light Refreshments at Coach Hall. **Adm £4, chd free. For NGS: Mon 2 May; Suns 12 June; 10 July; 14 Aug (2-5).** For other opening times and information, please phone or see garden website.
To south are mature trees and lawns with far reaching views. Grass paths lead through shrub and perennial borders to walled garden with roses and herbs. Vine pavilion, thatched roundhouse and hot bed area provide seats near scented and colourful plants. Meadow garden introduces woodland planting and pond. Fursdon House is also open for guided tours on NGS days. See website for details. Featured in Exeter Express and Echo.

& 🎋 🛏 🍵

41 ◆ THE GARDEN HOUSE
Buckland Monachorum, Yelverton PL20 7LQ. The Fortescue Garden Trust, 01822 854769, www.thegardenhouse.org.uk. *10m N of Plymouth. Signed off A386 at Yelverton.* **Adm £6.95, chd £2.75.**
8 acres, incl romantic walled garden surrounding ruins of medieval vicarage. Other areas pioneering 'new naturalism' style, inspired by great natural landscapes. South African garden, quarry garden, cottage garden, acer glade. Stunning views and more than 6000 plant varieties. Famous for spring bulb meadow, rhododendrons, camellias, innovative planting and yr-round colour and interest. Open Mar to Sept 10.30-5.

& ❀ 🍵

42 THE GATE HOUSE
Lee EX34 8LR. Mr & Mrs D Booker, 01271 862409, booker@loveleebay.co.uk. *3m W of Ilfracombe. Park in village car park. Take lane alongside The Grampus PH. Garden approx 30 metres past inn buildings.* **Adm by donation.**
Visitors welcome by appt, open most days throughout the yr but wise to check by phone.
2¼ acres, where no chemicals are used, only few minutes walk from the sea and dramatic coastal scenery. Peaceful streamside garden with range of habitats; bog garden, collection of over 100 Rodgersia, at their best June/July, woodland, herbaceous borders, patio gardens with semi-hardy 'exotics' and large vegetable garden. The Grampus Inn is well recommended for wide variety of home made cakes & cream teas!

& 🎋 ❀ ☎

Orchids early June, butterflies July . . .

43 ◆ GLEBE COTTAGE
Warkleigh EX37 9DH. Carol Klein, 01769 540554, www.glebecottageplants.co.uk. *5m SW of South Molton. Satnav not good. On the road between Chittlehamholt and Chittlehampton - 1m from Chittlehamholt. From A377, in Umberleigh, turn over river onto B3227 towards Southmolton. After 3m, R towards Chittlehamholt at Home Down Cross. After 2m go over Swing Gate Cross, next L lane over field.* **Adm £3.50, chd free. For NGS:** **Wed 7 Sept (2-5).**
Peaceful S-facing cottage garden in rural location. Plantswoman's paradise. Terraced beds and 'brick' garden brimming with rich colour and scent. Artistic containers full of unusual plants adorn the terraces. Small woodland with shade-loving plants. Home of BBC Gardeners' World and Open Gardens presenter. Open Weds, Thurs, Fris Easter til end Oct (10-1) & (2-5). Featured on BBC

Open Gardens, Gardeners' World and new series Carol Klein's Cottage Garden Year.
❀

GOOSEHILL
See Somerset & Bristol.

44 GOREN FARM
Broadhayes, Stockland, Honiton EX14 9EN. Julian Pady, 01404 881335 /07770 694646, gorenfarm@hotmail.com, www.goren.co.uk/gallery. *6m E of Honiton, 6m E of Axminster. From A35 or A30 along Stockland Hill (between Axminster and Honiton) to TV mast. Follow signs from Ridge Cross, (100 metres N of TV mast). Do not go into Stockland itself.* Home-made teas & light refreshments. Lunches at weekends. **Adm £2.50, chd free.** For other opening times and information, please phone or see garden website. **Sun 5, Sat 11, Sun 12 June; Sat 2, Sun 3, Sat 9, Sun 10 July (10.30-6) Evening Openings Sat 4 June to Fri 29 July incl (6-9).** Visitors also welcome by appt.
Wander through 50 acres of natural species rich wild flower meadows. Dozens of varieties of wild flowers and grasses. Orchids early June, butterflies July. Stunning views of Blackdown Hills. Georgian house and gardens. Guided walks at 10.30 and 2:30. Wild flower seed and produce for sale. Featured in East Devon Coast and Country Magazine, Express and Echo. Commended for 2009/2010 Beautiful Farm award.

🎋 ❀ 🍵 ☎

45 GORWELL HOUSE
Goodleigh Rd, Barnstaple EX32 7JP. Dr J A Marston, 01271-323202, artavianjohn@gmail.com. *1m E of Barnstaple centre on Bratton Fleming rd. Drive entrance between two lodges on L.* Cream teas (regret no teas Apr). **Adm £3.50, chd free. Suns 10 Apr; 8 May; 12 June; 10 July; 11 Sept (2-6).** Visitors also welcome by appt.
Created mostly since 1979, this 4-acre garden overlooking the Taw estuary has a benign microclimate which allows many rare and tender plants to grow and thrive, both in the open and in the walled garden. Several strategically-placed follies complement the enclosures and vistas within the garden. Some gravel paths and some slopes.

& 🎋 ❀ 🍵 ☎

46 ◆ **GREENWAY GARDEN**
Galmpton nr Brixham TQ5 0ES.
National Trust, 01803 842382
www.nationaltrust.org.uk. *1½ m SE
of Galmpton. A3022 towards
Brixham. R turn signed Galmpton,
follow brown signs for Greenway
Quay. Entrance 1½ m on L. For ferry
service from Dartmouth or Dittisham
ring 01803 844010.* **For opening
times and information please
phone or see garden website.**
Renowned for rare half-hardy plants
underplanted with native wild flowers.
Greenway has an atmosphere of
wildness and timelessness, a true
secret garden of peace and tranquillity
with wonderful views of R Dart,
associated with many fascinating
characters. One of our experienced
gardeners will be on hand to give a
guided tour, focusing on extensive
camellia garden and wonderful
magnolias.

47 **HALDON GRANGE**
Dunchideock EX6 7YE. Ted
Phythian, 01392 832349. *5m SW of
Exeter. From A30 at Exeter pass
through Ide village to Dunchideock
5m. In centre of village turn L to Lord
Haldon Hotel, Haldon Grange just
past hotel drive. From A38 (S) turn L
on top of Haldon Hill follow
Dunchideock signs, R at village centre
(at thatched house) to Lord Haldon
Hotel.* Light refreshments. **Adm
£3.50, chd free.** Sat 23, Sun 24,
Mon 25, Sat 30 Apr; all Sats &
Suns in May, Mon 2 May, Weds 4,
11, 18 May (1-5). **Visitors also
welcome by appt late Apr to end
May (5 - 40 people).**
12-acre well-established garden with
camellias, magnolias, azaleas and
rhododendrons; rare and mature
trees; small lake and ponds with river
and water cascades. Wheelchair
access to main features.

48 **HAMBLYN'S COOMBE**
Dittisham, Dartmouth TQ6 0HE.
Bridget McCrum, 01803 722228,
www.bridgetmccrum.com. *3m N of
Dartmouth. From Red Lion Inn follow
The Level until it forks & go straight up
steep private rd and through 'River
Farm' gate. Continue straight on to
end of farm track as signed.* **Adm £5,
chd free.** Visitors welcome by
appt, max 25 people. Max 5 cars or
walk from village. No coaches.
7-acre garden with stunning views
across the river to Greenway House

and sloping steeply to R Dart at
bottom of garden. Extensive planting
of trees and shrubs with unusual
design features accompanying
Bridget McCrum's stone carvings and
bronzes. Wild flower meadow and
woods. Good rhododendrons and
camellias, ferns and bamboos, acers
and hydrangeas. Exceptional autumn
colour.

HANGERIDGE FARMHOUSE
See Somerset & Bristol.

49 **HARBOUR LIGHTS**
Horns Cross, Bideford EX39 5DW.
Brian & Faith Butler,
brianbutler@ukonline.co.uk. *7m W
of Bideford, 3m E of Clovelly. On the
main A39 between Bideford and
Clovelly, half way between Hoops Inn
and Bucks Cross.* Home-made teas &
light refreshments. **Adm £3, chd free.**
Sat 25, Sun 26 June (11-7).
½-acre colourful garden with views of
Lundy and countryside. A garden full
of wit, humour, unusual ideas and
surprises. Water features and
polytunnel. You will never have seen a
garden like this! Superb conservatory
for cream teas. Free leaflet. Plants for
sale. Hoops Inn & Clovelly nearby.

50 ◆ **HARTLAND ABBEY**
Hartland, nr Bideford EX39 6DT. Sir
Hugh & Lady Stucley,
01237441264/234 or 01884860225,
ha_admin@btconnect.com,
www.hartlandabbey.com. *15m W of
Bideford, 15m N of Bude. Turn off
A39 W of Clovelly Cross on B3248 to
Hartland. Abbey between Hartland &
Hartland Quay.*
Fascinating family home with
woodland walks through stunning
wild flowers to C18 walled gardens,
beach, gazebo and newly-restored
summerhouse. Bulbs,
rhododendrons, azaleas, camellias,
hydrangeas, herbaceous, climbers,
tender plants and vegetables. Fernery
& Bog Garden by Jekyll. Historic
daffodils. Peacocks, black sheep and
donkeys. Sense and Sensibility filmed
here. Open 1 Apr - 2 Oct except Sats
11.30-5.

51 **HEATHER COTTAGE**
Yeo Cross, Chagford TQ13 8EX.
Nicola Chatterjee. *7m S of
Okehampton. Leave Chagford on
Fenworthy Reservoir rd. At Waye
Cross, R signed Kestor. Yeo Cross
2nd Xrd after 1m.* Cream teas & light
refreshments. **Adm £3.50, chd free.**
Sat 21, Sun 22 May (2-5).
Nestled deep in the heart of Dartmoor
National Park nr Kestor. The natural
granite bolder-strewn garden is
centred around small lake with free
flowing stream which meanders
through the garden attracting many
species of wildlife. Glorious colours in
late spring. Featured in Western
Morning News.

Heddon Hall

52 HEATHERCOMBE

Manaton, Newton Abbot
TQ13 9XE. Claude & Margaret Pike,
Woodlands Trust, 01626 354404,
gardens@pike.me.uk,
www.heathercombe.com. *7m NW
of Bovey Tracey. From Bovey Tracey
take rd to Becky Falls and Manaton.
Continue on same rd for 2m beyond
village to Heatree Cross then follow
signs to Heathercombe. (From
Widecombe take rd past Natsworthy).*
Cream teas & light refreshments.
Adm £4, (£3 April), chd free (share
to Rowcroft Hospice). Suns 3 Apr;
15, 22 May, Sat 28, Sun 29 May;
Suns 5, 26 June; 3 July (1.30-5.30).
Visitors also welcome by appt.
30-acres of varied garden areas in
tranquil wooded valley 1,000 ft up on
Dartmoor. Woodland walks beside
streams, ponds and lake; hundreds of
specimen trees; wild daffodils;
extensive bluebells complementing
fine rhododendrons; wild flower
meadow in orchard; two lovely
summer cottage gardens, bog/stream
garden, woodland garden and
fernery; Seats & sandy paths.
& 🏠 ☕ ☎

53 ◆ HEDDON HALL

Parracombe EX31 4QL. Mr & Mrs
de Falbe, 01598 763541,
info@heddonhall.co.uk. *10m NE of
Barnstaple. Follow A39 towards
Lynton around Parracombe (avoiding
village centre), then L towards village;
entrance 200 yds on L.* Light
refreshments & cream teas. Adm £4,
chd free. For NGS: Fri 13 May;
Thur 16 June (11-4.30). For other
opening times and information,
please phone or email.
Stunning walled garden laid out by
Penelope Hobhouse with clipped box
and cordoned apple trees,
herbaceous secret garden and natural
rockery leading to a bog garden and
3 stew ponds. Very much a
gardeners' garden, beautifully
maintained, with many rare species,
ferns, mature shrubs and trees all
thriving in 4 acres of this sheltered
Exmoor valley. Featured in Country
Life and English Garden.
& 🏠 ❀ ☕

HIDDEN VALLEY GARDENS

See Cornwall.

54 HIGH GARDEN

Chiverstone Lane, Kenton
EX6 8NJ. Chris & Sharon Britton,
01626 899106. *5m S of Exeter on
A379 Dawlish Rd. Leaving Kenton
towards Exeter, L into Chiverstone
Lane, 50yds along lane. Entrance
clearly marked.* Home-made teas.
Adm £3, chd free. Sun 22 May; Sat
9, Sun 10 July (2-5.30). Visitors
also welcome by appt for groups
all yr, Tues to Fris only.
Recently-developed garden for all-yr
interest. 70m double traditional
herbaceous border for high summer
colour. Unusual and choice shrubs
and perennial beds. Large fruit and
vegetable garden. Adjoining
plantsman's nursery open on NGS
days and Tues to Fri all yr. Total area
nearly 5 acres, all planted last 6 yrs.
Featured in Devon Life.
& 🏠 ❀ ☕ ☎

Nearly 5 acres of stunning garden . . .

HIGHCROFT GARDENS

See Cornwall.

HIGHER TRUSCOTT

See Cornwall.

55 HILLRISE

24 Windsor Mead, Sidford
EX10 9SJ. Mr & Mrs D Robertshaw,
01395 514991. *1m N of Sidmouth.
Off A3052 approx ¹/₄ m W of Sidford
T-lights (towards Exeter) signed R to
Windsor Mead. R at top of hill, last on
R.* Home-made teas. Adm £3.50,
chd £1.50. Sats, Suns 16, 17 Apr;
21, 22 May; 11, 12 June; 9, 10 July;
10, 11 Sept (1.30-5.30). Visitors
also welcome by appt Apr to July &
Sept for groups of 10+, minibuses
welcome, no large coaches.
Plant enthusiasts' garden on S-facing
slope. Fine countryside and sea
views. Yr-round colour and interest
from wide variety of plants. Borders
for New Zealand plants, penstemons,
cannas, dahlias, grasses with
kniphofias and hemerocalis,
kaleidoscope border. Fern garden,
shaded area for woodland plants.
Greenhouse with pelargoniums,
streptocarpus, cacti and succulents.
Troughs, hostas, colourful shrubs and
trees. Gold Award large garden
category Sidmouth in Bloom (4th yr).
Featured on BBC radio.
❀ ☕ ☎

56 HOLCOMBE COURT

Holcombe Rogus TA21 0PA. Mr
Nigel Wiggins. *5m W of Wellington.
From J26 or J27 on M5, Holcombe
Rogus is signed from A38.* Light
refreshments. Adm £5, chd free
(share to Holcombe Rogus
Church). Sat 25, Sun 26 June
(10-4).
7 acres of very varied gardens around
Grade I Tudor manor house (not
open). Herbaceous borders, trout
ponds and Victorian rockery.
Recently-restored and recreated
woodland garden and newly-created
vegetable parterre within C18 walled
garden. Espaliers and apple orchard.
& ☕

57 HOLLYCOMBE HOUSE

Manor Rd, Bishopsteignton
TQ14 9SU. Jenny Charlton &
Graham Jelley, 01626 870838,
hollycombealpacas@live.co.uk.
*From Newton Abbot A381, L after
Jack's Patch GC, or from Teignmouth
R at sign Old Walls Vineyard - Church
Rd - R at PH, Radway Hill, L Manor
Rd, R at Rock.* Cream teas. Adm
£3.50, chd free. Sun 12 June;
17 July; 11 Sept (2-5). Visitors also
welcome by appt.
Nearly 5 acres of stunning garden
with magnificent views of the Teign
Estuary. Stylish borders, shrubs for
every day of the yr. Organic
vegetables in raised beds. Attractive
large pond, full of water lilies and fish.
Alpacas, chickens and ducks. All
create an area of individuality.
🏠 ☕ ☎

INCE CASTLE

See Cornwall.

58 ◆ JASON'S GARDEN

Eastcliff Walk, Teignmouth
TQ14 8SZ. The Pope family, 01626
776070, www.jasonsgarden.org.uk.
*Park at East Cliff car park (or
anywhere else in town), follow NGS
signs, walk up tarmac cliff rd with sea
on R.* Home-made teas. Adm £3,
chd free. Afternoon & Evening
Opening Sun 24 July (2-8). Visitors
also welcome by appt.
Magical clifftop garden with high
quality landscaping with modern,
stylish design. Amazing panoramic
view over Lyme Bay and railway
below is complemented by growing
collection of sculptures. Rain water
collection and compost loo add to the
environmental credentials of this
innovative family gathering place.
Garden's underlying ethos leaves a

lasting impression. Highly recommended. Free children's animal trail and adult garden quiz. Sensory design suitable for Blind visitors. Mobility scooter available (book in advance). Talks given to local groups. Short steepish climb to garden (no steps).

59 NEW JEVINGTON HALL
Rectory Road, Combe Martin EX34 0NS. Mrs S A Stevens, 07769 653477, shane@fremingtonhomes.co.uk. *Just outside Combe Martin. 12m from Barnstaple - A39, B3229, A3123, A399.* Home-made teas. **Adm £4, chd free. Suns 10 Apr; 15 May; 12 June (2-5).** Visitors also welcome by appt.
Victorian rectory with Medieval tithe barn with 2 acres of formal gardens extensively restored during last 10yrs. All-yr interest with mixed borders, woodland, ponds and fountains, orchard, meadow, bog gardens, courtyard parterre and walled ornamental kitchen garden. Farmland acquired in 2010, incorporated as ponds and arboretum.

KEN CARO
See Cornwall.

60 KIA-ORA FARM & GARDENS
Knowle Lane, Cullompton EX15 1PZ. Mrs M B Disney, 01884 32347, rosie@kia-orafarm.co.uk. *6m SE of Tiverton. J28 of M5. Straight through Cullompton town centre to r'about, take 3rd exit into Swallow Way, follow rd through houses up to sharp R-hand bend. On bend turn L into Knowle Lane, garden beside Rugby Club.* Home-made teas. **Adm £2.50, chd free. Suns, Mons 24, 25 Apr; 1, 2, 15, 29, 30 May; 26 June; 10, 24 July; 14, 28, 29 Aug; 11 Sept (2-5.30).** Visitors also welcome by appt for groups of 20+, coaches permitted.
Charming, peaceful 10-acre garden with lawns, lakes, ponds and bog garden. Water feature with ducks and wildlife. Mature trees, shrubs, rhododendrons, azaleas, heathers, roses, herbaceous borders and rockeries. Wisteria walk, novelty crazy golf. Surprises everywhere! Traditional homemade Devonshire cream teas and vast array of homemade cakes. Truly scrumptious!

61 ◆ KILLERTON GARDEN
Broadclyst EX5 3LE. National Trust, 01392 881345, www.nationaltrust.org.uk. *8m N of Exeter. Take B3181 Exeter to Cullompton rd, after 7m fork left & follow NT signs.* **Adm £6.60. For NGS: Thur 12 May (11-7); Sun 10 July (11-5).** 10 July (2-5) - meet the gardeners, garden walks (donations welcome), NGS plants for sale, information on NGS. For other opening times and information, please phone or see garden website.
20 acres of spectacular hillside gardens with naturalised bulbs, sweeping down to large open lawns. Delightful walks through fine collection of rare trees, shrubs and herbaceous borders.

Vast array of homemade cakes. Truly scrumptious . . . !

62 KINGSTON HOUSE
Staverton TQ9 6AR. Mr & Mrs M R Corfield, 01803 762235, info@kingston-estate.co.uk. *4m NE of Totnes. A384 Totnes to Buckfastleigh, from Staverton, 1m due N of Sea Trout Inn, follow signs to Kingston.* Light refreshments. **Adm £4, chd 50p. Suns 13 Mar; 15 May; 19 June (2-6); Evening opening 17 July (5-8).** Visitors also welcome by appt, coaches by prior appointment.
George II 1735 house Grade II (not open). Gardens restored in keeping with the period. Walled garden, rose garden, pleached limes and hornbeams, vegetable garden. Unusual formal garden with santolinas, lavender and camomile. Large formal parterre. 6000 tulips in bloom mid-May, maybe!

63 ◆ KNIGHTSHAYES COURT GARDEN
Tiverton EX16 7RQ. National Trust, 01884 254665, www.nationaltrust.org.uk. *2m N of Tiverton. Via A396 Tiverton to Bampton rd; turn E in Bolham, signed*

Knightshayes; entrance ½ m on L. **Adm £7.15, chd £3.65. For NGS: Suns 1 May; 18 Sept (11-5).** For other opening times and information, please phone or see garden website.
Large 'Garden in the Wood', 50 acres of landscaped gardens with pleasant walks and views over Exe valley. Choice collections of unusual plants, incl acers, birches, rhododendrons, azaleas, camellias, magnolias, roses, spring bulbs, alpines and herbaceous borders; formal gardens; walled kitchen garden.

KNOWLE FARM
See Dorset.

64 LANGTREES
10 Cott Lane, Croyde, Braunton EX33 1ND. Paul & Helena Petrides, 01271 890202, angelrest@lineone.net, www.langtrees.info. *10m W of Barnstaple. From Barnstaple A361 to Braunton, L on B3231 to Croyde, past Croyde Bay Holidays on L. Cott Lane on R as rd narrows towards village centre. No parking in lane, park in village car park 200yds L by village hall.* Home-made teas. **Adm £3.50, chd free. Suns 15 May; 19 June (2-6).** Visitors also welcome by appt.
1-acre plantsman's garden with eclectic selection of plants. Many S hemisphere shrubs and other tender species. Yr-round interest with landscaping and design features. Flowers all seasons from rhododendrons and magnolias in spring to salvias, cannas and ginger lilies in autumn. Interesting selection of trees.

65 LEE FORD
Knowle, Budleigh Salterton EX9 7AJ. Mr & Mrs N Lindsay-Fynn, 01395 445894, crescent@leeford.co.uk. *3½ m E of Exmouth.* Light catering & cream teas for groups of 20+ by arrangement. **Adm £5.50, £5 per head for groups of 20+. Visitors welcome by appt for pre-booked groups Mon to Thur (10-4), April to Sept and other times by special arrangement.**
Extensive, formal and woodland garden, largely developed in the 1950s, but recently much extended with mass displays of camellias, rhododendrons and azaleas, incl many rare varieties. Traditional walled garden filled with fruit and vegetables,

Marwood Hill

herb garden, bog garden, rose garden, hydrangea collection, greenhouses. Ornamental conservatory with collection of pot plants and Adam pavilion. Moderately steep slopes to woodland garden.

  ♿ 🐕 ☎

LIFT THE LATCH
See Somerset & Bristol.

66▶ LITTLE ASH BUNGALOW
Fenny Bridges, Honiton EX14 3BL.
Helen & Brian Brown, 01404
850941,
helenlittleash@hotmail.com. *3m W of Honiton. Leave A30 at Iron Bridge from Honiton 1m, Patteson's Cross from Exeter ¹/₂ m and follow NGS signs.* Adm £3.50, chd free. Suns 5 June; 21 Aug (1.30-5.30). Visitors also welcome by appt for groups of 10+ incl coach parties between 25 May and 30 September.
Plantswoman's 1¹/₂ acre garden packed with different and unusual perennials, shrubs, bamboos. Designed for yr-round interest and owners' pleasure. Inspirational colour co-ordinated mixed long borders provide interest in late spring, summer and autumn. Natural stream and damp woodland area with wildlife meadows and gravel/alpine garden. New bridge and shade border for 2011. Featured in local press. Grass paths.

  ♿ 🐕 🌼 🍵 ☎

67▶ LITTLE CUMBRE
145 Pennsylvania Road, Exeter
EX4 6DZ. Dr Margaret Lloyd, 01392
258315. *1m due N of city centre.
From town centre take Longbrook St, continue N up hill approx 1m. Near top of hill.* Suns 30 Jan; 6, 13, 20 Feb 2011; Suns 5, 12, 19 Feb 2012 (12-3.30). Visitors also welcome by appt.
1-acre garden and woodland on S-facing slope with extensive views. Interesting areas of garden on different levels linked by grassy paths. Wonderful display of snowdrops, many varieties, and colourful hellebores. Scented winter shrubs and camellias, spring bulbs. Top garden managed to encourage wildlife. Limited wheelchair access.

  ♿ 🌼 ☎

GROUP OPENING

68▶ LITTLE TORRINGTON GARDENS
Little Torrington EX38 8PS, 01805
623445,
mjsampsonlt@btopenworld.com.
2m S of Torrington on A386. Village signed on A386. Park by village hall. Church Close adjacent to village green, School House 50yds along bridle path. Cream teas & home-made teas at Village Hall. Adm £3.50, chd free. Suns 12 June; 7 Aug (2-5). Visitors also welcome by appt.

CHURCH CLOSE
Karen & John Pollard

SCHOOL HOUSE
Little Torrington, Torrington.
Michael & Jo Sampson

Little Torrington is a small, peaceful rural village. Cluster of houses around village church and the village green. Close to the Tarka Trail, 1m from RHS Rosemoor gardens. The two gardens have differing aspects, one overlooking village green and the other more enclosed. Church Close: ¹/₄-acre S-facing front garden. Beech hedge boundary on Devon bank, mature trees incl superb Cornus contraversa variegata and ginkgo biloba. Herbaceous beds amid acers lead to rear garden of fruit trees, wildlife pond, small vegetable and fruit area, greenhouse and further flower beds. School House: ²/₃ acre informally planted, enclosed by native hedging, rambling roses and honeysuckle. Winding paths through mixed planting areas, some shady, some colour-themed. Mature wildlife pond, 2 other water features. Mature trees, arbour and pergola with variety of climbers. Small raised alpine bed. Village church open.

  🌼 🍵 ☎

69▶ LITTLE WEBBERY
Webbery, Bideford EX39 4PS. Mr & Mrs J A Yewdall, 01271 858206, jayewdall@onebillinternet.co.uk.
2m E of Bideford. Either from Bideford (East the Water) along Alverdiscott Rd, or from Barnstaple to Torrington on B3232, take rd to Bideford at Alverdiscott and pass through Stoney Cross. Cream Teas. Adm £3.50, chd free. Sat 25, Sun 26 June (2-6). Visitors also welcome by appt April-September.
Approx 3 acres in valley setting with pond, lake, mature trees, 2 ha-has and large mature raised border. Large walled kitchen garden with yew and box hedging incl rose garden, lawns with shrubs and rose and clematis trellises. Vegetables and greenhouse.

  ♿ 🌼 🍵 ☎

LITTLEBREDY WALLED GARDENS
See Dorset.

70▶ LITTLECOURT COTTAGES
Seafield Road, Sidmouth
EX10 8HF. Geoffrey Ward & Selwyn Kussman. *500yds N of Sidmouth seafront. From N take B3176 to*

Sidmouth seafront/Bedford Car Park. Take Station Rd, past Manor Rd and immed up Seafield Rd. Garden 100yds on R. Regret no parking at garden, car parks nearby. Home-made teas. **Adm £3, chd free. Suns 22 May; 19 June (2-5).**
Oasis of calm in middle of Sidmouth. A series of rooms for the plantaholic. Courtyard gardens behind house; in front, main lawn and water feature. Rare and tender plants everywhere. Exceptional basket colour.

71 ◆ LITTLEHAM HOUSE COTTAGE
11 Douglas Avenue, Exmouth EX8 2EY. Pat & Phil Attard, 01395 266750. *1/4 m from Exmouth seafront. E along seafront, L into Maer Rd by Fortes Kiosk, L again. Public car park on R. Short 250yd walk to garden. A little unrestricted parking in Douglas Ave.* Home-made teas. **Adm £3, chd free.** **Suns 24 Apr; 1 May (2-5), Wed 18 May (2-5.30). Visitors also welcome by appt.**
This secret garden is full of colour, foliage and flair. Winding paths lead you to horticultural surprises round every corner; spring bulbs, flowering shrubs and other treasures abound in this cottage garden. Organically-grown vegetables, herbs and a variety of fruit trees - something for everyone. Featured on BBC2 Open Gardens. Wheelchair access to main features.

72 ◆ THE LOOKOUT
Sowden Lane, Lympstone EX8 5HE. Will & Jackie Michelmore. *9m SE of Exeter, 2m N of Exmouth. A376 to Exmouth. 1st R after Marine Camp signed Lower Lympstone, 1st R in village into The Strand, past Londis shop, village car park next L. Follow NGS signs, 8min walk. No on-site parking, parking in adj field if dry. Near new Exe Cycle Path.* Cream Teas. **Adm £3.50, chd free. Fri 17 (2-5), Sun 19 June (2-6).**
2 wildlife friendly acres on edge of Exe Estuary. Lovingly created from derelict site over last 7yrs to harmonise with coast and countryside location and maximise on views. Flotsam and jetsam finds amongst naturalistic seaside planting. Circular walk through wild flower meadow to pond, through copse and along riverbank. Walled mediterranean courtyard, small jungley area. Giant sandpit with buckets and spades for children.

Featured in Country Gardener. Limited wheelchair access, some gravel paths, steps, steep slopes.

73 ◆ LUKESLAND
Harford, Ivybridge PL21 0JF. Mrs R Howell & Mr & Mrs J Howell, 01752 691749, www.lukesland.co.uk. *10m E of Plymouth. Turn off A38 at Ivybridge. 1 1/2 m N on Harford rd, E side of Erme valley.* **Adm £4.50, chd free.**
24 acres of flowering shrubs, wild flowers and rare trees with pinetum in Dartmoor National Park. Beautiful setting of small valley around Addicombe Brook with lakes, numerous waterfalls and pools. Extensive and unusual collection of rhododendrons, a champion *Magnolia campbellii* and a huge *Davidia involucrata*. Superb spring and autumn colour. Children's trail. Open Suns, Weds & BH 3 Apr - 12 June (2-6); Autumn Suns & Weds 16 Oct - 13 Nov (11-4). Featured in The English Garden and Daily Telegraph. Partial wheelchair access.

GROUP OPENING

74 ◆ LUPPITT GARDENS
EX14 4TT. *4m E of Honiton.* Home-made teas. **Combined adm £3.50, chd free (share to Luppitt parish church, Woodhayes only). Sat 28, Sun 29 May (1.30-5).**

POUND COTTAGE
John & Naomi Lott
(See separate entry)

WOODHAYES ⬚
Mr & Mrs N Page-Turner.
Take Dunkeswell Rd out of Honiton. Cross R Otter, 150yds R, 1st drive on L
Visitors also welcome by appt.
01404 42011

Both gardens have Dumpdon Hillfort (NT) as backdrop and are 2m apart. Pound Cottage (see separate entry). Woodhayes: 1 1/2 acres of formal garden. Trees, shrubs, herbaceous borders and tree paeonies. 3 levels divided by small stone walls and clipped beech hedges. Rose garden and rockery surrounded by clipped box. Stunning views of R Otter.

75 ◆ MARWOOD HILL
Marwood EX31 4EB. Dr J A Snowdon, 01271 342528, www.marwoodhillgarden.co.uk. *4m N of Barnstaple. Signed from A361 & B3230. Outside Guineaford village, opp Marwood church. See website for map.* **Adm £5.50, chd free. For NGS: Sats 14 May; 13 Aug (10-5).**
20 acres with 3 small lakes. Extensive collection of camellias under glass and in open; daffodils, rhododendrons, rare flowering shrubs, rock and alpine scree; waterside planting; bog garden; many clematis; Australian native plants and many eucalyptus. National Collections of Astilbe, *Iris ensata*, Tulbaghia. Open 1 Mar - 31 Oct 10-5.

♿ 🐕 ✿ NCCPG ☕

> ## Oasis of calm in middle of Sidmouth . . .

GROUP OPENING

76 NEW DOCTON MILL & MILFORD MILL GARDENS
Spekes Valley, Hartland, Bideford EX39 6EA. *13m SW of Bideford. From Bideford at Clovelly Cross on A39, 2nd R turn after r'about. Follow brown tourist signs. From Bude on A39 pass West Country Inn, at top of hill take L turn signed Elmscott. Crossing the moor 1st L turn again to Elmscott. Follow brown tourist signs, approx 3 m from A39.* Light refreshments, home-made & cream teas at Docton Mill. **Adm £4.50, chd free. Sun 12 June (10-6).**

NEW DOCTON MILL
Lymebridge,. Mr John & Lana Borrett
www.doctonmill.co.uk

NEW MILFORD MILL
Mr Paul Case & Mr Simon Forman
Visitors also welcome by appt

1st April to 31st Aug only.
01237 440129
CPookyone@aol.com

Docton Mill: Stunning gardens of 9 acres situated in beautiful valley 1000m from coast. Large herbaceous border over 140m with extensive planting incl unusual and old fashion favourites. Magnolia garden with over 25 varieties. Bog and woodland garden plus river walk. Truly a garden to give variety throughout the seasons. Voted Best Tea Room in 2009. Millford Mill: Wonderfully located riverside garden. Typical 1-acre formal cottage garden backed by woodland including herbaceous borders packed with poppies, roses, lavender and peonies. Bog and woodland planting featuring ferns, primulas and hostas plus woodland walk for you to meanader along. You will enter over an old stone humped bridge, take a breath and enjoy all that is nature's beauty. Toilet facilities at both gardens!

GROUP OPENING

77 NEW MILL STREET GARDENS
Great Torrington EX38 8AW. *7m SE of Bideford, 11m SW of Barnstaple. Take B3227 Langtree/Tadiport rd. Signed just after old dairy buildings, L by Torridge Inn, on street parking 200yds on R up hill.* Light refreshments & teas at Southerlea. Adm £3.50, chd free. Suns 15 May; 12 June (2-6).

NEW HERONS REACH
Mr & Mrs J D Gibbs

NEW SOUTHERLEA
John & Nora Slocombe

NEW WISTERIA COTTAGE
Jill & Philip Dixon

3 delightful and very different S-facing neighbours' gardens sharing wonderful views of Torridge Valley. Southerlea and Herons Reach are sloping gardens, although very different from each other, and created 20 yrs ago when bungalows were built. Southerlea: 1/4 -acre garden with many steps, fishpond, rockeries, climbers, trees, shrubs, small vegetable garden and topiary teddy bear. Herons Reach: terracing, trees, flowers, ponds, lawns and delightful walled cottage garden. Wisteria Cottage: eclectic 50ft x 50ft S-facing

cottage garden with wonderful wisteria, pond, chickens, flowers, raised beds and lots of vegetables. RHS Rosemoor 2m away.

GROUP OPENING

78 MORETONHAMPSTEAD GARDENS
TQ13 8PW. *12m W of Exeter & N of Newton Abbot. On E slopes of Dartmoor National Park. Parking at both gardens.* Home-made & cream teas. Adm £4.50, chd free. Sat, Sun, Mon 28, 29, 30 May; Sat, Sun 13, 14 Aug (2-6). Visitors also welcome by appt.

MARDON
Graham & Mary Wilson.
From centre of village, head towards church, turn L into Lime St. Bottom of hill on R

SUTTON MEAD
Edward & Miranda Allhusen.
1/2 m N of village on A382. R at de-restriction sign Visitors also welcome by appt. 01647 440296 Miranda@allhusen.co.uk

Two substantial gardens offering complementary styles, close to the edge of Dartmoor. Superb walking country, dogs on leads welcome. Mardon: spacious and well-maintained 4-acre garden surrounding Edwardian house (not open) in small Dartmoor coombe. Formal terraces, rose garden, long herbaceous border and wild flowers. Extensive rhododendron and hydrangea planting. Woodland walk along stream leading to fernery and pond with thatched boathouse. Productive vegetable garden. Wild meadow orchard. New agapanthus border. Sutton Mead: 3 1/2 -acre garden of contrasts on gently-sloping hillside. Woodland of mature and recent plantings and rill fed round pond. Potager vegetable garden with unusual concrete greenhouse. Granite walls mingling with imaginative planting of trees and shrubs. Croquet lawn, rhododendrons, azaleas and many varieties of hydrangea. Spring-fed ponds with granite seat at water's edge. Colourful bog garden and orchard. Fine views of Dartmoor from all corners of garden. Featured in Devon Life, Dartmoor Magazine.

79 MOTHECOMBE HOUSE
Holbeton, nr Plymouth PL8 1LB. Mr & Mrs A Mildmay-White. *From A379 between Yealmpton & Modbury turn S for Holbeton. Continue 2m to Mothecombe.* Cream teas. Adm £4, chd free. Sat 30 Apr; Sun 1 May (2-5).
Queen Anne house (not open) with Lutyens additions and terraces set in private estate hamlet. Walled pleasure gardens, borders and Lutyens courtyard. Orchard with spring bulbs, unusual shrubs and trees, camellia walk. Autumn garden, streams, bog garden and pond. Bluebell woods leading to private beach. Yr-round interest.

MOYCLARE
See Cornwall.

Take a breath and enjoy all that is nature's beauty . . .

80 NEW THE OLD DAIRY
Sidbury, Sidmouth EX10 0QR. Alison Carnwath & Peter Thomson. *1/2 m from Sidbury. Off A3052, follow signs to Sidbury. In village, R at church into Church St, over humpback bridge to T-junction then 1st R up Hatway Hill (no rd signs). Proceed 1/2 m, Old Dairy on L down small lane. Park in field.* Home-made teas. Adm £4, chd free. Sat, Sun 14, 15 May (2-6).
Extensive woodland and semi-formal areas providing short or longer walks. Rhododendrons, bluebells, wisteria and early herbaceous plants. Care needed in boggy areas. Panoramic views over Sid and Roncombe valleys.

81 THE OLD GLEBE
Eggesford EX18 7QU. Mr & Mrs Nigel Wright. *20m NW of Exeter. Turn S off A377 at Eggesford Stn (halfway between Exeter & Barnstaple), cross railway & R Taw,*

*drive straight uphill (signed Brushford)
for ³/₄ m; turn R into bridleway.* Home-
made teas. **Adm £3, chd £1 (share
to Friends of Eggesford All Saints
Trust). Sats, Suns 7, 8, 14, 15 May
(2-5).**
7-acre garden of former Georgian
rectory (not open) with mature trees
and several lawns, courtyard, walled
herbaceous borders, bog garden and
small lake; emphasis on species and
hybrid rhododendrons and azaleas,
750 varieties. Adjacent rhododendron
nursery open by appt.

82 THE OLD RECTORY
Ashford, Barnstaple EX31 4BY. Mrs
Ann Burnham, 01271 377408,
annburnham@btinternet.com. *3m
W of Barnstaple. A361 to Braunton.
At end of dual carriageway, R to
Ashford. Approx 1m, follow rd round
to L, 1st house on L.* Home-made &
cream teas. **Adm £3.50, chd free.
Suns 8 May; 12 June; 11 Sept
(11-5).** Visitors also welcome by
appt.
Wide, open aspect, S-facing garden,
with superb views of Taw estuary. Top
garden: large pond with lilies, borders
show interesting planting. Lower
garden: wide variety of unusual plants
and shrubs. Plenty of seating, tea is
served on the terrace.

**THE OLD RECTORY,
NETHERBURY**
See Dorset.

83 THE OLD VICARAGE
West Anstey EX36 3PE. Tuck &
Juliet Moss, 1398341604. *9m E of
South Molton. From South Molton 9m
E on B3227 to Jubilee Inn. Sign to
West Anstey. Turn L for ¹/₄ m then
dog-leg L then R following signs.
Through Yeomill to T-junction. R
following sign. Garden 1st house on
L.* Home-made teas. **Adm £3, chd
free. Sats, Suns, 14, 15 May; 9, 10
July (2-5).** Visitors also welcome by
appt.
Croquet lawn leads to multi-level
garden overlooking three large ponds
with winding paths, climbing roses
and overviews. Brook with waterfall
flows through garden past fascinating
summerhouse built by owner.
Benched deck overhangs first pond.
Features rhododendrons, azaleas and
primulas in spring and large collection
of Japanese iris in summer.

84 ◆ OVERBECK'S
Sharpitor, Salcombe TQ8 8LW.
National Trust, 01548 842893,
www.nationaltrust.org.uk. *1¹/₂ m
SW of Salcombe. Follow NT signs.*
Adm £6.70, chd £3.40. For NGS:
Sun 3 July; Sat 24 Sept (11-5). For
other opening times and
information, please phone or see
garden website.
7-acre exotic coastal garden, Grade
II* listed, with rare plants and shrubs;
spectacular views over Salcombe
estuary.

85 OWLS BARN
The Chestnuts, Aylesbeare
EX5 2BY. Pauline & Ray Mulligan.
*3m E of Exeter airport. A3052 Exeter
to Sidmouth, L at Halfway Inn - after
50yds L fork to Aylesbeare. Straight
on at Xrds until you come to village,
park in Village Way. Garden on R next
to school but approach from The
Chestnuts. 1st rd on R. From Ottery
St Mary through West Hill, L onto
B3180, R at Tipton X. At Aylesbeare,
L through village, garden signed on L.
Disabled parking only at The
Chestnuts.* Home-made teas. **Adm
£3, chd free. Sat, Sun, 11, 12 June
(2-5).**
Peaceful ³/₄ -acre village garden, a
haven for wildlife. Small woodland,
natural bog with pond and gravel
areas. All on N-facing slope of heavy
clay. Contrasting foliage with plenty of
unusual perennials, grasses, billowing
roses, clematis, fruit and vegetables.
Imaginatively-designed with surprises
round every corner.

86 PIKES COTTAGE
Madford, Hemyock EX15 3QZ.
Christine & Bridget Carver, 01823
680345. *7m N of Honiton. Off A30 to
Wolford Chapel, through Dunkeswell
towards Hemyock, then follow signs
from Gypsy Cross. Or 7m S of
Wellington off M5 J26 to Hemyock,
then follow signs. Turn in at gates
signed Pikes Cottage downhill from
Madford Farm & up rough farm track.*
Home-made teas. **Adm £3.50, chd
free. Sats, Suns 19, 20, 26, 27 Feb
(1-5); 30 Apr; Sun 1, Mon 2 May,
Sats, Suns 14, 15, 21, 22 May; 11,
12 June; 9, 10 July; 27, 28 Aug,
Mon 29 Aug; Sats, Suns 24, 25
Sept (2-6); 22, 23 Oct (1-5); 18, 19,
25, 26 Feb 2012 (1-5).** Visitors also
welcome by appt.
Set in 19 acres of bluebell woods (hilly
access). 6 acres of cultivated garden

incl herb garden, scree, prairie
planting, sensory garden,
rhododendrons and other shrubs.
1¹/₂ -acre lawn slopes to large pond
and bog garden. Wisteria tunnel,
steps to snowdrops (Feb) and
arboretum. Children's quiz,
playground, model village. Ample
seating.

*Fascinating
summerhouse
built by owner . . .*

87 ◆ PLANT WORLD
St Marychurch Road, Newton
Abbot TQ12 4SE. Ray Brown,
01803 872939, www.plant-world-
seeds.com. *2m SE of Newton Abbot.
1¹/₂ m from Penn Inn r'about. Follow
brown tourist signs at the end of the
A380 dual carriageway from Exeter.*
The 4 acres of landscape gardens
with fabulous views have been called
Devon's 'Little Outdoor Eden'.
Representing each of the five
continents, they offer an extensive
collection of rare and exotic plants
from around the world. Superb
mature cottage garden and
Mediterranean garden will delight
the visitor. Attractive new viewpoint
café and shop. Open Apr - mid Sept
9.30-5.

88 PORTINGTON
nr Lamerton PL19 8QY. Mr & Mrs I
A Dingle, 01822 870364. *3m NW of
Tavistock. From Tavistock B3362 to
Launceston. ¹/₄ m beyond
Blacksmiths Arms, Lamerton, fork L
(signed Chipshop). Over Xrds (signed
Horsebridge) first L then L again
(signed Portington). From Launceston
turn R at Carrs Garage and R again
(signed Horsebridge), then as above.*
Home-made teas. **Adm £2.50, chd
free (share to Plymouth
Samaritans). Suns 12, 19 June
(2-5.30).** Visitors also welcome by
appt June/July.
Garden in peaceful rural setting with
fine views over surrounding

Bickham House

countryside. Mixed planting with shrubs and borders. Walk to small lake through woodland and fields, which have recently been designated a county wildlife site.

👤 🏠 ✿ ☕ ☎

89 ▶ POUND COTTAGE
Beacon, Honiton EX14 4TT. John & Naomi Lott, 07790 961310, naomilott@yahoo.co.uk. *4m E of Honiton. A30 from Honiton, pass Little Chef, 1st L signed Luppitt. Over bridge, 1.8m up hill, 1st R. Straight on at Pound Farm (no through rd), garden on L. Parking in field on R (limited parking if wet).* Home-made teas. **Adm £3, chd free. Sat 30 Apr; Sun 1 May (1.30-5).** Visitors also welcome by appt April only for rhododendrons. No coaches.
1-acre hillside garden with magnificent views, designed and developed by owners over 28yrs. Collection of over 150 species rhododendrons plus camellias, azaleas, pieris and many unusual shrubs and trees, most of which labelled. Bluebells, vegetable garden and 1 acre across lane with orchard and pond.

🏠 ✿ ☕ ☎

90 ▶ PROSPECT HOUSE
Lyme Road, Axminster EX13 5BH. Peter Wadeley, 01297 631210. *From Axminster town centre (Trinity Square) proceed uphill past George Hotel into Lyme St & Lyme Rd. Garden approx ¹/₂ m up rd on R, just before petrol*

stn. Home-made teas. **Adm £3.50, chd free. Sats, Suns, 2, 3 July; 3, 4 Sept (1.30-5).** Visitors also welcome by appt.
1-acre plantsman's garden hidden behind high stone walls with Axe Valley views. Well-stocked borders with rare shrubs, many reckoned to be borderline tender. 200 varieties of salvia, and other late summer perennials including rudbeckia, crocosmia and grasses. A gem, not to be missed.

✿ ☕ ☎

91 ▶ REGENCY HOUSE
Hemyock EX15 3RQ. Mrs Jenny Parsons, jenny.parsons@btinternet.com. *8m N of Honiton. M5 J26. From Hemyock take Dunkeswell-Honiton rd. Entrance ¹/₂ m on R from Catherine Wheel PH and church. Disabled parking (only) at house.* Home-made teas. **Adm £3.50, chd free. Sat 18, Mon 20, Tue 21, Wed 22 June; (2-6); Sun 2 Oct (11-6).** Visitors also welcome by appt no coaches.
5-acre plantsman's garden approached across private ford. Many interesting and unusual trees and shrubs. Visitors can try their hand at identifying plants with the plant list. Plenty of space to eat your own picnic. Walled vegetable and fruit garden, lake, ponds, bog plantings and sweeping lawns. Horses, Dexter cattle and Jacob sheep.

👤 🏠 🛏 ☕ ☎

GROUP OPENING

92 ▶ ROUSDON COTTAGE GARDENS
Rousdon DT7 3XW, 01297 443712, helena@himalayanlearning.org. *3m E of Seaton, 1¹/₂ m W of Lyme Regis. On A3052 midway between Seaton and Lyme Regis. Look for roadside signs.* Home-made & cream teas. **Adm £3.50, chd free (share to Himalayan Learning). Suns 10 Apr; 8 May; 12 June; 10 July; 14 Aug (11-5).** Visitors also welcome by appt.

CHARTON TREE COTTAGE
Charton. Jane & Sid Gibson

GREEN LANE COTTAGE
Green Lane. Toni & Helena Williams-Pugh

Delightful cottage gardens buried in Devon countryside, each gardening organically and encouraging over 50 species of wild birds and animals from the tiny goldcrest to badgers, hedgehogs and the occasional deer. Charton Tree Cottage: S-facing garden at 500ft, just under 1 acre. 7 rooms, 2 herbaceous borders, water feature. Spring area planted with erythroniums, snowdrops, bluebells, hellebores, pulmonaria plus unusual plants. Kitchen garden with raised beds. Hot border, summerhouse, greenhouse. Green Lane Cottage: double pond water feature, curving lawns and flowerbeds crammed with succession of colour-themed flowers. Circular stone patio with hot tub. Small church window set in tiny folly, sunken walled patio. Wooden staircase to pergola of antique carved pillars from Turkistan and dovecots for over 100 aviaried doves. Photographic exhibition 'The Garden In All Seasons'. Featured in Women's Weekly.

✿ ☕ ☎

93 ▶ ST MERRYN
Higher Park Road, Braunton EX33 2LG. Dr W & Mrs Ros Bradford, 01271 813805, ros@st-merryn.co.uk. *5m W of Barnstaple. In centre of Braunton turn R at T-lights round Nat West Bank. At top of Heanton St L and immed R into Lower Park Rd. Continue to Tyspane Nursing Home on L then L into unmarked lane, R at top. Pink house 200yds on R. Parking where available.* Home-made teas. **Adm £3, chd free.**

Suns 24 Apr; 15 May; 12 June; 10 July (2-6). **Visitors also welcome by appt.**
Very sheltered, peaceful, gently sloping, artist's garden, with emphasis on shape, colour, scent and all-yr round interest. A garden for pleasure with thatched summerhouse leading down to herbaceous borders. Winding crazy paving paths, many seating areas. Shrubs, mature trees, fish ponds, grassy knoll, gravel areas, hens. Many environmental features. Open gallery.

Many environmental features . . .

94 ◆ **SALTRAM HOUSE**
Merafield Rd, Plympton PL7 1UH. National Trust, 01752 333503, www.nationaltrust.org.uk. *3m E of Plymouth. S of A38, 2m W of Plympton.* **Adm £10. For NGS: Evening Openings wine, Thurs 7 Apr; 19 May (6-8). For other opening times and information, please phone or see garden website.**
20 acres with fine specimen trees; spring garden; rhododendrons and azaleas. C18 orangery and octagonal garden house. (George II mansion with magnificent plasterwork and decorations, incl 2 rooms designed by Robert Adam). Good variety of evergreens, incl many tender and unusual shrubs, esp from the S hemisphere. Long grass areas with bulbs and wild flowers. Twilight in the Garden: Join a member of staff for an evening tour of Saltram's garden. Glass of wine and light refreshments in the Orangery.

95 **SEDGEWELL COACH HOUSE GARDENS**
Olchard TQ12 3GU. Heather Jansch, www.heatherjansch.com. *4m N of Newton Abbot. 12m S of Exeter on A380, L for Olchard, straight ahead on private drive.* **Adm £3, chd free. Sats, Suns 7, 8 May; 27, 28 Aug (10-5).**
Heather Jansch, world-famous sculptor, brings innovative use of recycled materials to gardening. 14 acres incl stunning driftwood sculpture, fabulous views from thrilling

woodland bluebell trail down to timeless stream-bordered water meadow walk, pools, herbaceous border, medicinal herb garden. Plentiful seating, come and picnic.

96 ◆ **SHAPCOTT BARTON ESTATE**
(East Knowstone Manor), East Knowstone, South Molton EX36 4EE. Anita Allen, 01398 341664. *13m NW of Tiverton. J27 M5 take Tiverton exit. 6½ m to r'about, take exit South Molton 10m, on A361. Turn R signed Knowstone (picnic area). Leave A361 at this point, travel 1¼ m to Roachhill, through hamlet, turn L at Wiston Cross, entrance on L ¼ m.* **Adm £3.50, chd £1. For NGS: Sun 10, Wed 13, Sun 24, Fri 29 July; Wed 3, Sun 14 Aug (10.30-4.30). For other opening times and information, please phone.**
Large, ever developing garden of 200-acre estate around ancient historic manor house. Wildlife garden. Restored old fish ponds, stream and woodland rich in birdlife. Exotic breeds of poultry. Unusual fruit orchard. Flowering burst July/Aug of National Plant Collections *Leucanthemum superbum* (shasta daisies) and Buddleja davidii. Many butterfly plants incl over 40 varieties of phlox. Kitchen garden and standard orchard. Featured in Exmoor Life.

 NCCPG

97 **SHERWOOD**
Newton St Cyres, Exeter EX5 5BT. Prue Quicke, 01392 851216, prue@sherwoodgarden.eclipse.co.uk. *2m SE of Crediton. Off A377 Exeter to Barnstaple rd, ¾ m Crediton side of Newton St Cyres, signed Sherwood, entrance to drive in 1¾ m. No large coaches.* **Adm £4, chd free (share to Newton St. Cyres Parish Church). Suns 2 Jan to 26 Jun; Suns 4 Sept 2011 to 26 Feb 2012 (2-5). Visitors also welcome by appt.**
15 acres, 2 steep wooded valleys. Wild flowers, especially daffodils; extensive collections of magnolias, camellias, rhododendrons, azaleas, berberis, heathers, maples, cotoneasters, buddleias, hydrangeas and late summer flowering perennials. Woodland garden with shade-loving perennials and epimediums. National Collections of Magnolias, Knaphill azaleas and berberis.

GROUP OPENING

98 **NEW** **SIDMOUTH GARDENS**
Sidmouth EX10 9DX. *10m E of Exeter. On A3052, R at Bowd Inn (B3176) for Runnymede or continue to bottom of hill and R for Woolbrook Park.* Home-made teas. **Combined adm £4, chd free. Sats, Suns 14, 15 May; 18, 19 June; 3, 4 Sept (11-5).**

NEW **RUNNYMEDE**
Orchard Close, Manor Rd. Veronica & Bill Wood
Visitors also welcome by appt. 01395 579638
v.wood@virgin.net

NEW **44 WOOLBROOK PARK**
Barbara & Alan Mence

Sidmouth is situated on the Jurassic Coast World Heritage Site. It has fine beaches, beautiful gardens and magnificent coastal views. 2 contrasting gardens about 2m apart. 44 Woolbrook Park: approx ¼ acre on NW-facing slope, generously planted with trees, shrubs, perennials and bulbs for yr-round interest. Steps lead to wide zigzag path rising gently to woodland edge of birch and rowan, with shady seat under Mexican pine. Benches at every corner and summerhouse looking towards wooded hills. Regret no wheelchairs. Runnymede: beautiful tranquil garden about ¼ acre. All-yr interest. Magnolias, acers, hydrangeas, grasses. Abundance of plants. Artistically landscaped around series of circles, pools and rills. Microclimate, tender plants, woodland areas, gravel garden, rockery. Wheelchair-friendly. Seats, vistas, planting combinations, vegetables, fruit cages, greenhouse, vine. Cup winner large garden category Sidmouth in Bloom.

GROUP OPENING

99 **SOUTHCOMBE GARDENS**
Dartmoor, Widecombe-in-the-Moor TQ13 7TU. *6m W of Bovey Tracey. Take B3387 from Bovey Tracey. After village church take rd SW for 400yds then sharp R, signed Southcombe, up steep hill. After 200yds, pass C17 farmhouse & park on L. Alternatively*

park in public car park in village and walk. Home-made teas. **Combined adm £4, chd free.** Suns 15, 22, 29, Mon 30 May; 5, 12, 19 June (2-5).

SOUTHCOMBE BARN
Amanda Sabin & Stephen Hobson

SOUTHCOMBE HOUSE
Dr & Mrs J R Seale
Visitors also welcome by appt May & June only.
01364 621365

Village famous for its Fair, Uncle Tom Cobley and its C14 church - the 'Cathedral of the Moor'. Featured in RHS 'The Garden'. Southcombe Barn: 3-acre woodland garden with exotic and native trees between long lawn and rocky stream. Clearings blaze with wild flowers and survivor garden flowers. Meadow in recently-cleared area. Southcombe House: 5 acres, SE-facing garden, arboretum and orchid-rich restored wild flower meadow with bulbs in spring and four orchid species (early purple, southern marsh, common spotted and greater butterfly) and over 2,000 specimens in 2010. On steep slope at 900ft above sea level with fine views to nearby tors.

100 SOUTHERN COMFORT
Meadfoot Sea Road, Torquay TQ1 2LQ. Dr Maciej Pomian-Srzednicki & Mrs Ewa Pomian-Srzednicka, 01803 201813, maciej@pomian.co.uk, www.pomian.co.uk/garden. *½ m from Torquay Harbour. From harbourside clock tower take rd uphill towards Babbacombe. 1st R at T-lights, follow main rd up hill. Garden 200yds on L after brow of hill.* Teas at 4 Wellswood Heights. **Adm £2.50, chd free.** Sun 31 July (1-4). **Combined with 4 Wellswood Heights, combined adm £4, chd free.** Visitors also welcome by appt March to June & Sept/Oct, min 5, max 20.
¼ -acre S-facing town plot, part-naturalistic planting of trees, shrubs and herbaceous perennials, many exotic/tender species. Exceptional microclimate, shelter and variety of microhabitats in Meadfoot Valley allows palms, tree ferns, agaves, aloes, bromeliads, aroids, bananas and other individualistic plants to thrive. Emphasis on foliage. Spring-fed pond and rill. Recommended for exotica enthusiasts. Featured in Devon Life.
🕿

101 SOWTON MILL
Dunsford EX6 7JN. A Cooke & S Newton, 01647 252263, sonianewton@sowtonmill.eclipse. co.uk. *7m W of Exeter. From Dunsford take B3193 S for ½ m. Entrance straight ahead off sharp R bend by bridge. From A38 N along Teign valley for 8m. Sharp R after humpback bridge.* Home-made teas. **Adm £3, chd free** (share to Cygnet Training Theatre). Suns 17 Apr (2-5.30); 10 July (2-6). Visitors also welcome by appt.
4 acres laid out around former mill (not open), leat and river. Part woodland with multitudes of wild flowers in spring, ornamental trees and shrubs, mixed borders. Yr-round interest. Mill stream (leat) now used for electricity generation via a crossflow turbine. Partial wheelchair access.
♿ 🏡 ⚘ ☕ 🕿

102 SQUIRRELS
98 Barton Road, Torquay TQ2 7NS. Graham & Carol Starkie, 01803 329241, calgra@talktalk.net. *From Newton Abbot take A380 to Torquay. After Focus DIY on L, turn L at T-lights up Old Woods Hill. 1st L into Barton Rd, bungalow 200yds on L.* **Adm £3, chd free.** Sun 31 July; Sat 6, Sun 7 Aug (2-5). Visitors also welcome by appt Aug only.
Plantsman's small town garden with small ponds and 7ft waterfall. Interlinked areas incl Japanese, Italianate, Tropical. Specialising in fruit incl peaches, figs, kiwi. Tender plants incl bananas, tree fern, brugmansia, lantanas, oleanders, collections of fuchsia, abutilons, bougainvilleas. Colourful pergolas, perennial borders. Environmentally-friendly garden with self-sufficient rain water storage, large disguised compost heaps, home-made solar hot-water panel, many nesting boxes, ducks on slug patrol. Torbay in Bloom Superclass & Environmentally Friendly Garden.
⚘ 🕿

103 THE STANNARY
Mary Tavy, Tavistock PL19 9QB. Michael & Ali, 01822 810897, garden@alifife.co.uk, www.alifife.co.uk/garden. *4m N of Tavistock. On A386 Tavistock-Okehampton rd, towards the north of the village.* Light refreshments and selection of vegetarian lunches. **Adm £3.50, chd free.** Sun 22 May; Sun 19 June; Sun 14 Aug (12-6). Visitors also welcome by appt.

Informal 2-acre garden with magnificent views of Dartmoor. 900ft above sea level, with deer and rabbits, gardening here is a challenge. Originally a field, the planting is naturalistic and abundant, with areas for wildlife, ponds and meadow. New for 2011 vegetable and fruit growing areas. In addition to the openings listed, there will be special events, possibly a musical evening and a wine & cheese tasting. Visit the garden website or phone for details. Featured on Westcountry Television 'Growing Places'. Wheelchair access to almost all of the garden, with some gravel paths.
♿ ⚘ 🛏 ☕ 🕿

Ducks on slug patrol . . .

104 SUMMERS PLACE
Little Bowlish, Whitestone EX4 2HS. Mr & Mrs Stafford Charles, 01647 61786. *6m NW of Exeter. From M5, A30 Okehampton. After 7m, R to Tedburn St Mary, immed R at r'about past golf course. 1st L after ½ m signed Whitestone, straight ahead at Xrd, follow signs. From Exeter on Whitestone rd 1m beyond Whitestone, follow signs from Heath Cross. From Crediton, follow Whitestone rd through Fordton.* Home-made teas. **Adm £3, chd free.** Suns 27 Mar; 8 May; 2 Oct (2-5) Evening Opening £4, chd free, wine, light refreshments Fri 24 June (6-9). Visitors also welcome by appt all yr, 24 hrs notice please.
Original shady sloping garden of trees/shrubs over native/cultivated ground cover. Criss-crossed by rustic paths, walkways and bridges leading to secluded seats, sculptures, follies etc. Divided house area (climbers). Now extended with streamside stroll, grass steps to dewpond, sunnier white orchard (shrub roses etc). Larger, more colour, views and adventure. Arab mares and foals on view.
🏡 ⚘ ☕ 🕿

TAIKOO
Belstone EX20 1QZ. Richard &
Rosamund Bernays, 01837 840217,
richard@bernays.net. *3m SE of
Okehampton. Fork L at stocks in
middle of village. Keep left. Entrance
to Car Park 300yds on R.* Home-
made & cream teas. **Adm £3.50, chd
free. Sun 17 Apr; Sun 21 Aug (2-5).
Visitors also welcome by appt.**
3-acre hillside moorland garden,
recently extended to incl heathers,
grasses and moorland plants.
Interesting collections of
rhododendrons, acers, fuchsias,
hydrangeas, magnolias, camellias,
Chinese and Himalayan roses and
other shrubs and trees. Herb garden.
Sculptures and water features.
Magnificent views over Dartmoor from
terraces of Taipan's house (not open).

 TAMARISKS
Inner Hope Cove, Kingsbridge
TQ7 3HH. Barbara Anderson,
01548 561745, bba@talktalk.net.
*6m SW of Kingsbridge. On entering
Hope Cove, turn L at sign to Inner
Hope. After ¹/₄ m, turn R into lane
beneath Sun Bay Hotel. Tamarisks is
next house. Park opp hotel or in lane
(larger car park in Outer Hope, follow
path leading to Inner Hope in lane).*
Home-made teas. **Adm £3, chd free
(share to Butterfly Conservation &
BTO Birdwatch). Thur 7, Fri 8 July
(11-6). Visitors also welcome by
appt.**
Sloping ¹/₃ acre directly above sea
with magnificent view. Garden is
exciting with rustic steps, extensive
stonework, ponds, rockeries, feature
corners, patios, 'wild' terrace
overlooking sea. Very colourful.
Demonstrates what can flourish at
seaside - notably hydrangeas,
mallows, crocosmia, achillea, sea
holly, convolvulus, lavender, sedum,
roses, grasses, ferns, fruit trees. Bird
and butterfly haven. Information on
Butterfly Conservation and BTO
Birdwatch. Craft exhibition, glass
blowing and enamel work - vases,
jewellery, photos of local area.
Featured in Devon Country Gardener
& Time Off. Garden viewing organised
by AONB.

 NEW **THORN HOUSE**
Wembury, Plymouth PL9 0EQ. John
& Eva Gibson. *5m SE of Plymouth.
A379 Elburton rd to Wembury then
follow signs. Limited parking at house.
Scenic walk from car park.* Home-

made & cream teas. **Adm £5, chd
free. Suns 10 Apr; 25 Sept (2-5).**
Early C19 9-acre terraced garden
beside the Yealm. Arkwright's unique
replica of his garden at Sutton
Scarsdale. Wide variety of tender
trees and plants; many outstanding
specimens of size, maturity or
rareness. Springtime gives the
impression of the foothills of the
Himalayas or Australia's Blue
Mountains. Spectacular autumn
colour. Some steep slopes.

1 TIPTON LODGE
Tipton St John, Sidmouth
EX10 0AW. Angela Avis & Robin
Pickering, 01404 813371,
robin_pickering@hotmail.com. *3m
N of Sidmouth. From Exeter take
A3052 towards Sidmouth. L on
B3176 at Bowd Inn toward Ottery St
Mary. After 1¹/₂ m turn into Tipton St
John. After village sign, 1 Tipton
Lodge is 2nd driveway on R about
100yds before Golden Lion PH.
Parking for disabled only, other
parking in village.* Home-made teas.
**Adm £3, chd free. Sat, Sun, 25,
26 June (11-5). Visitors also
welcome by appt.**
³/₄ acre designed to reflect mid-
Victorian house. Formal grass walks
between double herbaceous borders
and avenue of white weeping roses.
Old shrub roses, small woodland area
incl tree ferns, potager-style vegetable
garden. All organic. Exuberant
romantic planting.

TREBARTHA
See Cornwall.

**WALREDDON MANOR
GARDENS**
Whitchurch, Tavistock PL19 9EQ.
Walreddon Manor Farm. *1¹/₂ m from
Tavistock. From Tavistock take A386
Plymouth rd, at cemetery R on mini
r'about towards Walreddon onto
Brook Lane. Continue for 1¹/₂ m to
manor on R.* Home-made teas. **Adm
£4, chd free. Sat 25, Sun 26 June
(1-5).**
Fully working organic estate gardens
surrounding C15 manor house (not
open). Productive and extensive
terraced vegetable garden with cut
flower bed. Wildflower meadow with
roses. Brand new rose garden full of
climbers, floribundas, T and shrub
with old scented varieties. Orchard
with wild flowers, apple store. At front,
herbaceous borders, shrubs,

climbers, mature magnolias, lawns,
ha-ha, with beautiful views over
parkland, Tavy Valley and beyond.
Wildlife area with deep, dangerous
ponds, wildflowers, fruit trees, mown
paths and gentle woodland walk.
Sloping areas, steep vegetable
garden.

WAYFORD MANOR
See Somerset & Bristol.

Demonstrates
what can flourish
at seaside . . .

4 WELLSWOOD HEIGHTS
Higher Erith Rd, Wellswood,
Torquay TQ1 2NH. Mr & Mrs S W
Tiller, 01803 296387,
sue.tiller@tiscali.co.uk. *1m from
Torquay town centre. From Torquay
harbourside towards Babbacombe,
Burlington Hotel on R. R after red
post box on R into Lincombe Hill Rd
then R at top, garden immed on L.*
**Adm £2.50, chd free. Sun 31 July
(1-4). Combined with Southern
Comfort, combined adm £4, chd
free. Visitors also welcome by appt
July to Sept only, max 15.**
Small exotic garden. Large variety of
exotics incl palms, tree ferns, aloes
and other unusual trees, shrubs and
succulents mainly from S hemisphere.
Side jungle border, succulent bank at
bottom of garden. Unusual plants for
shady areas. Rear courtyard area with
mature bamboos, palm trees and lots
of plants in pots. Featured in local
press.

GROUP OPENING

NEW **WHITCHURCH
GARDENS**
PL19 9RB. *On the SW outskirts of
Tavistock. 1 mile from Tavistock town
centre along the Whitchurch Road.
No parking at the properties but it
should be possible to park on
Whitchurch Road or in Marshall
Close. Some walking will be involved.*

Home-made teas at The Chantry.
Adm £3.50, chd free. Sun 31 July;
Sun 7 Aug (2-6).

> **NEW** **THE CHANTRY**
> Marshall Close. Jan & Ian
> Gasper

> **NEW** **LITTLE MEADOW**
> Chollacott Lane. Janet & Sid
> Ford

> **NEW** **THE SHEILING**
> Chollacott Lane. Sadie & Stuart
> Glynn

Three town gardens, all on steep
slopes as the Tavy valley rises up
towards the Moor. The Chantry is a
very new garden, carefully and
thoughtfully planted taking into
account the scale of the plants against
the high banks towards the top of the
garden which is a little retreat with a rill
and seating area. The Sheiling is
mature and abundantly planted with
some splendid herbaceous plants
planted in drifts leading to a number of
small 'rooms'. Little Meadow is the
largest of the three gardens and
includes open lawn areas and a very
productive vegetable garden.

⊛ ☕

---

112 **WHITSTONE FARM**
Whitstone Lane, Bovey Tracey
TQ13 9NA. Katie & Alan Bunn,
01626 832258,
katie@whitstonefarm.co.uk.

¹/₂ m N of Bovey Tracey. From A382
turn toward hospital (signed opp golf
range) after ¹/₃ m turn L at swinging
sign 'Private road leading to
Whitstone'. Follow lane uphill & bend
to L. Whitstone Farm on R at end of
long barn. Limited parking. Home-
made teas. **Adm £3.50, chd free.**
Suns 8 May; 14 Aug (2-5). Visitors
also welcome by appt, individuals
and groups plus 13th August
specifically for the Eucryphias.
Over 3 acres of steep hillside garden
with stunning views of Haytor and
Dartmoor. Arboretum planted 39yrs
ago of over 200 trees from all over the
world, incl magnolias, camellias,
acers, alders, betula and sorbus.
Major plantings of rhododendron and
cornus. Aug opening for flowering
eucryphias. National Collection of
Eucryphias. Featured in local press.

⊛ **NCCPG** ⌂ ☕ ☎

113 ◆ **WICK FARM GARDENS**
Cookbury, Holsworthy EX22 6NU.
Martin & Jenny Sexton, 01409
253760. 3m E of Holsworthy. From
Holsworthy take Hatherleigh Rd for
2m, L at Anvil Corner, ¹/₄ m then R to
Cookbury, garden 1¹/₂ m on L. **Adm
£3.50, chd free. For NGS: Suns 3,
24, Mon 25 Apr (2-5); Sun 31 July;
Sun 28, Mon 29 Aug (11.30-6); Sun
11 Dec (3.30-8).**
3-acre garden, part arranged into
rooms with fernery, small ornamental
pond, borders, garden sculptures and

park surrounding small lake with
island. Long border developed in
2006 with large variety of plants. All-yr
interest. Plants have been selected to
attract bees and butterflies. 5-acre
arboretum started 2009. Dec opening
with mince pies and mulled wine and
Christmas garden lights. Open Mons,
Tues, Weds 30 May to 15 Sept 2-5.
Featured on Radio Devon.

&. 🐾 ⊛ ☕

114 ◆ **WILDSIDE**
Green Lane, Buckland
Monachorum PL20 7NP. Keith &
Ros Wiley, 01822 855755,
www.wileyatwildside.com. ¹/₄ m W
of Buckland Monachorum. Follow
brown signs to Garden House from
A386. Past Garden House, continue
straight on for 0.7m. Garden 300yds
past village on L. **Adm £4.50, chd £1.**
For NGS: Sun 3 July (10-5). For
other opening times and
information please phone or see
garden website.
Created from field since 2004 by ex
Head Gardener of The Garden
House. Wide range of habitats and
different plant varieties are grown in a
naturalistic style, giving displays of
colour throughout the season. Garden
paintings by Ros Wiley. Featured on
Channel 4 The Landscape Man
showing a year in the development of
the garden.

⊛

115 **WITHLEIGH FARM**
Withleigh, Tiverton EX16 8JG. T
Matheson, 01884 253853. 3m W of
Tiverton. On B3137, 10yds W of 1st
small 30mph sign on L, entrance to
drive by white gate. Home-made
teas. **Adm £4, chd free** (share to
Arthritis Research & Cancer
Research). Sat 7, Sun 8 May (2-5).
Visitors also welcome by appt, no
access for large coaches, drop off
at top of drive then 2 min walk.
Peaceful undisturbed rural setting
with valley garden, 27yrs in making;
stream, pond and waterside
plantings; bluebell walk under canopy
of mature oak and beech; wild flower
meadow, primroses and daffodils in
spring; wild orchids in June. Dogs on
leads please.

🐾 ⊛ ☕ ☎

WOLVERHOLLOW
See Dorset.

Cleave Hill

Be tempted by a plant from a plant stall ⊛

116 WOOD BARTON
Kentisbeare EX15 2AT. **Mr & Mrs
Richard Horton, 01884 266285.** *8m
SE of Tiverton, 3m E of Cullompton.
3m from M5 J28. Take A373
Cullompton to Honiton rd. After 2m
turn L signed Bradfield & Willand on
Horn Rd for 1m, turn R at Xrds. Farm
drive ½ m on L. Bull on sign.* Home-
made teas. **Adm £4, chd free (share
to Action Medical Research).** Suns
3, 10 Apr; Sun, Mon 1, 2 May (2-5).
Visitors also welcome by appt.
Established 2-acre arboretum with
species trees on S-facing slope.
Magnolias, two davidia, azaleas,
camellias, rhododendrons, acers;
several ponds and water feature.
Autumn colour. New planting of
woodland trees and bluebells opp
house (this part not suitable for
wheelchairs).

GROUP OPENING

117 NEW YOLLAND GARDENS
TQ13 7JP. *A38 South ignore 1st slip
rd to Ashburton. Next L in front of
large sign Motel Services Not 24hrs.
100m from main rd R marked Yolland
Hill. Steep hill 1-4 Yolland
House/parking on R.* Cream teas.
Combined adm £5, chd free. Sun 1,
Mon 2 May (2-5.30).

NEW SOUTH BARTON
Angie & Tim Guy

NEW YOLLAND BARTON
Richard Nock

NEW YOLLAND HOUSE
Peter & Sue Munday

3 gardens in secluded wooded valley
that was a dairy farm 30 yrs ago.
Extensive tree planting at that time
now gives shelter with wide variety of
fine evergreen and deciduous
specimens. Yolland Barton: large
garden designed around many
exciting granite features for which 300
tons of stone was brought in mostly
from redundant Georgian and
Victorian buildings. The garden has
been extensively planted with shrubs,
herbaceous and alpine plants to
complement these features. South
Barton has an old-fashioned country
garden air and is planted to provide a
haven for butterflies and bees. Granite
walls and meandering paths. Yolland
House: 4-acre landscaped, terraced
garden with park-like grounds and
interesting trees. Small lake, home to
ducks, geese and moorhens.
Substantial granite rockery with paths
and steps leads back to car park.

118 YONDER HILL
Shepherds Lane, Colaton Raleigh
EX10 0LP. Judy McKay & Eddie
Stevenson, 07864 055532,
judy@yonderhill.me.uk,
www.yonderhill.me.uk. *3m N of
Budleigh Salterton. On B3178
between Newton Poppleford and
Colaton Raleigh, take turning signed
to Dotton, then immed R into small
lane. ¼ m, 1st house on R. Large car
park.* **Adm £3, chd £1.** Sun 27 Mar;
Suns 3, 10, 17, Fri 22, Sun 24, Mon

25 Apr; Sun 1, Mon 2, Suns 8, 15,
22, 29, Mon 30 May; Suns 5, 12,
19, 26 June; Suns 3, 10, 17, 24, 31
July; Suns 7, 14, 21, 28, Mon 29
Aug; Suns 4, 11, 18, 25 Sept; Suns
2, 9, 16, 23, 30 Oct (1-4.30). **Visitors
also welcome by appt.**
3½ -acre paradise with
unconventional planting. Shady
walks, sunny glades, woodland,
ponds, herbaceous and mixed
borders, orchard, vegetables, wildlife
areas incl large pond. Several
collections, many surprises. A garden
with 'soul', must experience to
appreciate. Seating throughout.
Garden attracts great variety of birds,
butterflies, moths and other insects.
Large population of dormice, nightly
visits from badgers and foxes.
Featured in Express and Echo.
Wheelchair and Scooter access on
grass and concrete paths -
wheelchair available, phone to book.

*3½ -acre paradise
with unconventional
planting . . .*

Devon County Volunteers

County Organisers and Central Devon area
Edward & Miranda Allhusen, Sutton Mead, Moretonhampstead TQ13 8PW, 01647 440296, miranda@allhusen.co.uk

County Treasurer
Julia Tremlett, Bickham House, Kenn, Nr Exeter EX6 7XL, 01392 832671, jandjtremlett@hotmail.com

Publicity
Alan Davis, Paddocks, Stafford Lane, Colyford EX24 6HQ, 01297 552472, alandavis27@btinternet.com
Cath Pettyfer, Mill Cottage, Bondleigh, North Tawton EX20 2AH, 01837 89024, cathpettyfer@tiscali.co.uk
Sandra Wallace, Pebbleford Cottage, 2 Church Green, Newton Poppleford, Sidmouth EX10 0DX, 01395 567494
    sandrawallace3@btinternet.com

Assistant County Organisers
North East Devon Dorothy Anderson, Ashley Coombe, Ashley, Tiverton EX16 5PA, 01884 259971, dorothyanderson@uku.co.uk
North Devon Jo Hynes, Higher Cherubeer, Dolton, Winkleigh EX19 8PP, 01805 804265, hynesjo@gmail.com
Exeter Margaret Lloyd, Little Cumbre, 145 Pennsylvania Road, Exeter EX4 6DZ, 01392 258315, margaretlloydhugs@gmail.com
South Devon Sally Vincent, Bramble Torre, Dittisham, Dartmouth TQ6 0HZ, 01803 722227,
    sallyvincent@brambletorre.eclipse.co.uk
South West Devon Ali Fife & Michael Cook, The Stannary, Mary Tavy, Tavistock PL19 9QB, 01822 810897, fifecook@keme.co.uk
East Devon Peter Wadeley, Prospect House, Lyme Road, Axminster EX13 5BH, 01297 631210, wadeley@btinternet.com
Torbay Jan Bond, Clover Rise, 59 Cockhaven Road, Bishopsteignton TQ14 9RQ, 01626 776406, jan@livingtapes.co.uk

DORSET

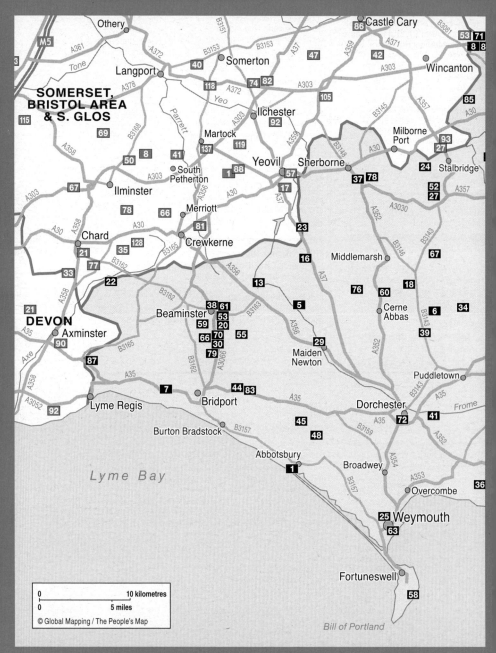

Othery

Castle Cary

86

53 71

8 8

M5

A361

A372

A371

A37

A339

A303

Wincanton

Tone

A378

47

42

A303

Langport

40

Somerton

B3153

B3153

A357

A30

118

A372

85

SOMERSET, BRISTOL AREA & S. GLOS

Yeo

74 82

A303

105

B3145

Milborne Port

115

69

B3168

Martock

Ilchester

92

A303

B3148

A30

93

27

A358

50

8

41

137

119

A353

Stalbridge

South Petherton

1 88

Yeovil

Sherborne

24

67

Ilminster

A303

A356

A30

57

37 78

52

27

78

66

Merriott

17

A3030

A362

81

23

Chard

A30

B3165

Crewkerne

Middlemarsh

B3146

B3143

67

35 128

16

21

77

B3162

13

A37

76

60

18

33

22

B3162

5

Cerne Abbas

6

34

DEVON

A358

Beaminster

38 61

53

59 20

B3163

A356

29

B3143

39

21

Axminster

66 70

55

Maiden Newton

Puddletown

90

30

A35

87

B3165

79

A3066

44 83

A35

Dorchester

72

41

Frome

A352

92

A3052

Axe

7

Bridport

A35

45

B3159

A35

Lyme Regis

Burton Bradstock

B3157

48

Abbotsbury

1

Broadwey

A354

36

Lyme Bay

B3157

Overcombe

25

Weymouth

63

0   10 kilometres

0   5 miles

© Global Mapping / The People's Map

Fortuneswell

58

Bill of Portland

Rensburg Sheppards supports the NGS

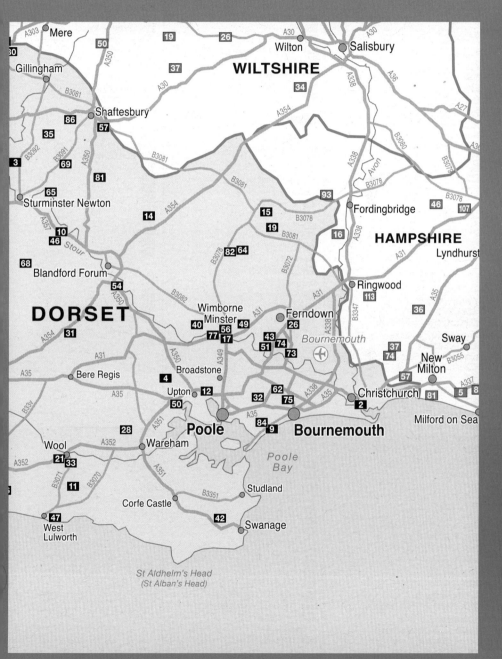

Opening Dates

February

Sunday 27
45 Langebride House
46 Lawsbrook

March

Sunday 13
45 Langebride House
69 The Old Vicarage
72 Q

Saturday 26
80 Snape Cottage Plantsman's Garden

Sunday 27
23 Frankham Farm
24 Frith House
33 Herons Mead
80 Snape Cottage Plantsman's Garden

April

Saturday 2
27 Grange Cottage
52 Manor Farm, Stourton Caundle

Sunday 3
27 Grange Cottage
52 Manor Farm, Stourton Caundle

Wednesday 6
15 Cranborne Manor Garden
19 Edmondsham House

Sunday 10
18 Domineys
39 Ivy House Garden
72 Q
73 Resting Laurels

Wednesday 13
19 Edmondsham House

Friday 15
42 Knitson Old Farmhouse

Saturday 16
42 Knitson Old Farmhouse
44 Knowle Farm

Sunday 17
4 Bexington
5 Broomhill
8 Chiffchaffs
26 The Glade
42 Knitson Old Farmhouse
59 The Mill House
75 46 Roslin Road South
83 Uploders Place

Monday 18
44 Knowle Farm

Wednesday 20
19 Edmondsham House

Saturday 23
80 Snape Cottage Plantsman's Garden

Sunday 24
7 Chideock Manor
12 Corfe Barn
33 Herons Mead
66 The Old Rectory, Netherbury
80 Snape Cottage Plantsman's Garden

Monday 25
7 Chideock Manor
19 Edmondsham House
39 Ivy House Garden
54 Manor House, Blandford

Wednesday 27
19 Edmondsham House
38 Horn Park

May

Sunday 1
9 Chine View
17 Deans Court
26 The Glade
87 Wolverhollow

Monday 2
9 Chine View
17 Deans Court
33 Herons Mead
61 Mount Pleasant
87 Wolverhollow

Friday 6
2 Annalal's Gallery

Saturday 7
9 Chine View

Sunday 8
2 Annalal's Gallery
9 Chine View
18 Domineys
21 The Ferns
23 Frankham Farm
39 Ivy House Garden
72 Q

Wednesday 11
56 Mayfield
69 The Old Vicarage

Friday 13
42 Knitson Old Farmhouse

Saturday 14
42 Knitson Old Farmhouse
75 46 Roslin Road South
76 The Secret Garden

Sunday 15
4 Bexington
16 The Dairy House
26 The Glade
30 Hatchlands
42 Knitson Old Farmhouse
56 Mayfield
59 The Mill House
67 The Old Rectory, Pulham
75 46 Roslin Road South
76 The Secret Garden
86 Wincombe Park

Monday 16
16 The Dairy House

Friday 20
86 Wincombe Park (Evening)

Sunday 22
3 Beech House
21 The Ferns
32 205 Herbert Avenue
51 Manor Farm, Hampreston
66 The Old Rectory, Netherbury
83 Uploders Place
87 Wolverhollow

Tuesday 24
63 'OLA'
87 Wolverhollow

Wednesday 25
56 Mayfield

Saturday 28
80 Snape Cottage Plantsman's Garden

Sunday 29
6 Butts Cottage
10 Coombe Cottage
12 Corfe Barn
17 Deans Court
26 The Glade
33 Herons Mead
46 Lawsbrook
53 The Manor House, Beaminster
57 Mayo Farm
80 Snape Cottage Plantsman's Garden

Monday 30
12 Corfe Barn
17 Deans Court
53 The Manor House, Beaminster
79 Slape Manor

Tuesday 31
63 'OLA'

June

Wednesday 1
57 Mayo Farm
64 Old Down House

Thursday 2
70 Parnham House

Friday 3
2 Annalal's Gallery
11 Coombe Keynes Gardens

Saturday 4
11 Coombe Keynes Gardens
40 Kingston Lacy
58 Mews Cottage

Pleasant place to sit or wander . . .

Sunday 5
2 Annalal's Gallery
27 Grange Cottage
36 Holworth Farmhouse
40 Kingston Lacy
52 Manor Farm, Stourton Caundle
56 Mayfield
58 Mews Cottage
70 Parnham House
72 Q

Wednesday 8
82 Stanbridge Mill

Friday 10
14 Cottage Row (Evening)

Saturday 11
14 Cottage Row (Evening)
75 46 Roslin Road South

Sunday 12
6 Butts Cottage
23 Frankham Farm
51 Manor Farm, Hampreston
64 Old Down House
65 The Old Rectory, Manston
75 46 Roslin Road South

Tuesday 14
63 'OLA'

Wednesday 15
5 Broomhill
64 Old Down House
65 The Old Rectory, Manston

Friday 17
42 Knitson Old Farmhouse

Saturday 18
42 Knitson Old Farmhouse
50 Lytchett Minster Gardens

Sunday 19
3 Beech House
7 Chideock Manor
32 205 Herbert Avenue
42 Knitson Old Farmhouse
50 Lytchett Minster Gardens
53 The Manor House, Beaminster
54 Manor House, Blandford
58 Mews Cottage
68 Old Smithy

Monday 20
53 The Manor House, Beaminster

Tuesday 21
48 Littlebredy Walled Gardens

Wednesday 22
7 Chideock Manor
37 Honeycombe
56 Mayfield
68 Old Smithy

Friday 24
33 Herons Mead (Evening)

Saturday 25
80 Snape Cottage Plantsman's
Garden

Sunday 26
12 Corfe Barn
20 Farrs
33 Herons Mead

37 Honeycombe
80 Snape Cottage Plantsman's
Garden

Tuesday 28
48 Littlebredy Walled Gardens

Wednesday 29
25 3 Gardens at Westham
38 Horn Park

July

Friday 1
2 Annalal's Gallery
31 Hazel Lodge

Saturday 2
49 55 Lonnen Road

Sunday 3
5 Broomhill
25 3 Gardens at Westham
36 Holworth Farmhouse
37 Honeycombe
49 55 Lonnen Road

Sunday 10
4 Bexington
13 Corscombe House
21 The Ferns
25 3 Gardens at Westham
29 Grovestall Farm
34 Higher Melcombe Manor
62 4 Noel Road
74 357 Ringwood Road
75 46 Roslin Road South

Saturday 16
15 Cranborne Manor Garden
47 Little Bindon
58 Mews Cottage

Sunday 17
3 Beech House
23 Frankham Farm
28 Greenacres
34 Higher Melcombe Manor
35 Hilltop
47 Little Bindon
58 Mews Cottage
62 4 Noel Road

Saturday 23
77 The Secret Garden and Serles
House (Evening)

Sunday 24
20 Farrs
32 205 Herbert Avenue
35 Hilltop
77 The Secret Garden and Serles
House

Wednesday 27
59 The Mill House (Evening)
74 357 Ringwood Road

Saturday 30
80 Snape Cottage Plantsman's
Garden

Sunday 31
35 Hilltop
51 Manor Farm, Hampreston
67 The Old Rectory, Pulham

80 Snape Cottage Plantsman's
Garden
84 24a Western Avenue

August

Wednesday 3
67 The Old Rectory, Pulham

Saturday 6
49 55 Lonnen Road
58 Mews Cottage

Sunday 7
18 Domineys
35 Hilltop
36 Holworth Farmhouse
49 55 Lonnen Road
58 Mews Cottage

Thursday 11
77 The Secret Garden and Serles
House

Saturday 13
77 The Secret Garden and Serles
House

Sunday 14
3 Beech House
4 Bexington
35 Hilltop
74 357 Ringwood Road

Sunday 21
5 Broomhill
28 Greenacres
35 Hilltop
58 Mews Cottage

Friday 26
2 Annalal's Gallery

Saturday 27
80 Snape Cottage Plantsman's
Garden

Sunday 28
2 Annalal's Gallery
8 Chiffchaffs
10 Coombe Cottage
17 Deans Court
77 The Secret Garden and Serles
House
80 Snape Cottage Plantsman's
Garden

Monday 29
17 Deans Court
61 Mount Pleasant
77 The Secret Garden and Serles
House

Tuesday 30
81 Springhead

September

Sunday 4
20 Farrs
36 Holworth Farmhouse
54 Manor House, Blandford
73 Resting Laurels

Wednesday 7
71 Pen Mill Farm

Follow us on Facebook and Twitter

Sunday 11
71 Pen Mill Farm
Sunday 18
33 Herons Mead

October

Wednesday 5
19 Edmondsham House
81 Springhead
Wednesday 12
19 Edmondsham House
Sunday 16
18 Domineys
23 Frankham Farm
Wednesday 19
19 Edmondsham House
Wednesday 26
19 Edmondsham House

December

Saturday 10
77 The Secret Garden and
Serles House (Afternoon &
Evening)
Sunday 11
2 Annalal's Gallery

February 2012

Saturday 25
80 Snape Cottage Plantsman's
Garden
Sunday 26
80 Snape Cottage Plantsman's
Garden

Gardens open to the public

1 Abbotsbury Gardens
3 Beech House
8 Chiffchaffs
15 Cranborne Manor Garden
19 Edmondsham House
22 Forde Abbey Gardens
35 Hilltop
36 Holworth Farmhouse
41 Kingston Maurward Gardens
43 Knoll Gardens
48 Littlebredy Walled Gardens
55 Mapperton Gardens
60 Minterne
78 Sherborne Castle
80 Snape Cottage Plantsman's
Garden
81 Springhead

By appointment only

85 Weston House

Also open by Appointment

2 Annalal's Gallery
4 Bexington
5 Broomhill
9 Chine View
10 Coombe Cottage
12 Corfe Barn
14 Cottage Row
18 Domineys
24 Frith House
25 3 Gardens at Westham
26 The Glade
33 Herons Mead
38 Horn Park
39 Ivy House Garden
42 Knitson Old Farmhouse
44 Knowle Farm
45 Langebride House
46 Lawsbrook
49 55 Lonnen Road
56 Mayfield
58 Mews Cottage
59 The Mill House
66 The Old Rectory, Netherbury
67 The Old Rectory, Pulham
68 Old Smithy
71 Pen Mill Farm
72 Q
74 357 Ringwood Road
75 46 Roslin Road South
76 The Secret Garden
82 Stanbridge Mill
87 Wolverhollow

Three neighbours'
gardens - each one
packs a very
different punch . . .

The Gardens

1 ♦ **ABBOTSBURY GARDENS**
nr Weymouth DT3 4LA. Ilchester
Estates, 01305 871130,
www.abbotsburygardens.co.uk. *8m
W of Weymouth. From B3157
Weymouth-Bridport, 200yds W of
Abbotsbury village.* **For opening
times and information, please
phone or see garden website.**
30 acres, started in 1760 and
considerably extended in C19. Much
recent replanting. The maritime micro-

climate enables Mediterranean and
southern hemisphere garden to grow
rare and tender plants. National
collection of Hoherias (flowering Aug
in NZ garden). Woodland valley with
ponds, stream and hillside walk to
view the Jurassic Coast. Limited
wheelchair access, route marked to
avoid steep climbs and gravel.
    NCCPG

2 ♦ **ANNALAL'S GALLERY**
25 Millhams Street, Christchurch
BH23 1DN. Anna & Lal Sims, 01202
567585, anna.sims@ntlworld.com,
www.annasims.co.uk. *Town centre.
Park in Saxon Square PCP - exit to
Millham St via alley at side of church.*
Adm £2.50, chd free. **Fri 6, Sun 8
May; Fri 3, Sun 5 June; Fris 1 July;
26 Aug; Suns 28 Aug; 11 Dec (2-4).**
Visitors also welcome by appt.
Enchanting 100 yr-old cottage, home
of two Royal Academy artists. 32ft x
12½ ft garden on 3 patio levels.
Pencil gate leads to colourful scented
Victorian walled garden. Sculptures
and paintings hide among the flowers
and shrubs. Featured in Garden
News.
☎

APPLE COURT
See Hampshire.

3 ♦ **BEECH HOUSE**
New Street, Marnhull, Sturminster
Newton DT10 1QA. Linda & Peter
Antell. *2m NE of Sturminster Newton.
From A30 take B3092 signed
Sturminster Newton. In Marnhull, just
past The Crown PH, 2nd R beside
church. Garden ¼ m on R, just before
Xrds.* Adm £3, chd free. **For NGS:
Suns 22 May; 19 June; 17 July;
14 Aug (10-5).**
Enjoy being led up the garden path to
discover the intriguing features and
delectable array of flowers in the
series of garden rooms hidden in the
acre behind the house. Arbours,
arches, areas of calm. Pergola, patios
and parterre. Wild, wanton and wacky
aspects. Other open times Tues only
19 Apr to 16 Aug (10-5). Featured in
Dorset Life. Gravel entrance path.
  ☺ ☕

4 **BEXINGTON**
Lime Kiln Road, Lytchett Matravers
BH16 6EL. Mr & Mrs Robin
Crumpler, 01202 622068. *5m SW of
Wimborne Minster. Opp old school at
W end of village.* Cream teas. **Adm
£2.50, chd free. Suns 17 Apr;
15 May; 10 July; 14 Aug (2-5.30).**

Visitors also welcome by appt. ½-acre colourful garden of interest maintained by owners, with spring bulbs to autumn colour. Mixed borders of many interesting and unusual plants, shrubs and trees. Bog garden of primulas, hostas etc, collection of grasses and ferns, with walkways over bog area connecting two lawns.

BRAEMOOR
See Hampshire.

5 BROOMHILL
Rampisham DT2 0PU. Mr & Mrs D Parry, 01935 83266, carol.parry2@btopenworld.com. *11m NW of Dorchester. From Yeovil take A37 towards Dorchester, 7m turn R signed Evershot. From Dorchester take A37 to Yeovil, 4m turn L A356 signed Crewkerne; at start of wireless masts R to Rampisham. From Crewkerne A356, at end of wireless masts L to Rampisham - follow signs.* Home-made teas. **Adm £3, chd free. Sun 17 Apr; Wed 15 June; Suns 3 July; 21 Aug (2-5). Visitors also welcome by appt May to Aug incl.** Delightful 1½ -acre garden in lovely peaceful setting. Pretty trellised entrance leads to island beds and borders planted with shrubs, roses and many unusual perennials giving yr-round colour. Lawns slope to less formal area, late summer border, large wildlife pond, bog garden and small wild flower meadow. Featured in Gardens of Dorset.

6 NEW BUTTS COTTAGE
Plush DT2 7RJ. John & Jane Preston. *9m N Dorchester. At Piddletrenthide (on B3143) take turning E to Plush; after 1½ m follow 'no through rd' sign then 1st R.* Home-made teas. **Adm £3, chd free. Suns 29 May; 12 June (2-5).** Tranquil village garden of ¾ acre sheltered by mature beech trees around C18 cottage in fold of N Dorset Downs. Stream, pond, wild flowers and marsh orchids. Pleasant place to sit or wander amongst wide variety of flowers, vegetables, shrubs and trees. Partial wheelchair access.

CHERRY BOLBERRY FARM
See Somerset & Bristol.

Chideock Manor

7 CHIDEOCK MANOR
Chideock, nr Bridport DT6 6LF. Mr & Mrs Howard Coates. *2m W of Bridport on A35. In centre of village turn N at church. The Manor is ¼ m along this rd on R.* Home-made teas. **Adm £5, chd free. Sun 24, Mon 25 Apr; Sun 19, Wed 22 June (2-5).** Large formal and informal gardens, some in process of development. Bog garden beside stream. Woodland and lakeside walks. Walled vegetable garden and orchard. Yew hedges and mature trees. Lime walk, herbaceous borders, rose and clematis arches. Fine views.

8 ♦ CHIFFCHAFFS
Chaffeymoor, Bourton, Gillingham SP8 5BY. Mr & Mrs K R Potts, 01747 840841. *3m E of Wincanton. W end of Bourton. N of A303.* **Adm £3.50, chd free. For NGS: Suns 17 Apr; 28 Aug (2-5). For other opening times and information, please phone.** A well known mature garden for all seasons planted round thatched cottage with many interesting plants, bulbs, shrubs, herbaceous border and shrub roses. Attractive walk to woodland garden with far-reaching views across Blackmore Vale.

9 CHINE VIEW
15a Cassel Avenue, Poole BH13 6JD. John & Jeannie Blay, 01202 760751, jblay2@tiscali.co.uk. *2m W of Bournemouth. From centre of Westbourne turn S into Alumhurst Rd, take 8th turning on R into Mountbatten Rd then 1st L into Cassel Ave.* **Adm £2.50, chd free. Sun 1, Mon 2, Sat 7, Sun 8 May (2-5). Visitors also welcome by appt in May & June for groups of 10+.** Unique Chine garden with a profusion of azaleas, rhododendrons and sub tropical species. Features incl extensive terraced rockery incorporating 330 tons of Purbeck stone, Palladian rotunda, water features and sculptural pieces. Featured in Gardens of Dorset by Roger Lane. Unsuitable for the less mobile, steep steps and uneven paths.

10 COOMBE COTTAGE
Shillingstone DT11 0SF. Mike & Jennie Adams, 01258 860220, mikeadams611@gmail.com. *5m NW of Blandford. On main rd (A357) in middle of village between Gunn Lane and Old Ox PH. Parking advised in Gunn Lane.* **Adm £2.50, chd free. Suns 29 May; 28 Aug (2-6). Also**

Visit the website for latest information

open **Lawsbrook** 29 May. Visitors also welcome by appt. 0.4-acre plantsman's mixed garden with densely-packed broad borders edged by walls, hedges, fences and arbours. Cottage favourites and more unusual trees, shrubs, herbaceous perennials, climbers, bulbs and self-seeders rub shoulders with late-flowering and bold-leaved subtropicals. Large glasshouse and some non-botanical surprises.

🏡 ⊕ ☎

11 ▶ COOMBE KEYNES GARDENS
BH20 5PS. *B3071 Wool to Lulworth. After 2m fingerpost to L leading directly into village, proceed through village and follow signs for parking in field adjacent to church.* Cream teas. **Combined adm £5, chd free. Fri 3, Sat 4 June (1-5).**
Situated in delightful and secluded hamlet of stone and thatched cottages, former farmyard houses and buildings, C13/C19 church, all renovated and adapted over last 30yrs around small green, conservation area, AONB, adjacent to Jurassic Coast World Heritage Site. Series of village gardens, some classic, some courtyard, some long established, others recently created incl 2 outstanding vegetable gardens, orchards and ponds, vicarage garden adjoining and incl churchyard. Combined with annual village event: produce/book/bric-a-brac stalls within each garden. Partial wheelchair access.

♿ 🏡 ⊕ ☕

12 ▶ CORFE BARN
Corfe Lodge Road, Broadstone BH18 9NQ. Mr & Mrs John McDavid, 01202 694179. *1m W of Broadstone centre. From main r'about in Broadstone, W along Clarendon Rd ³/₄ m, N into Roman Rd, after 50yds W into Corfe Lodge Rd.* Home-made teas. **Adm £2.50, chd free. Sun 24 Apr; Sun 29, Mon 30 May; Sun 26 June (2-5). Visitors also welcome by appt until end of June.**
²/₃ acre on three levels on site of C19 lavender farm. Informal country garden with much to interest both gardeners and flower arrangers. Parts of the original farm buildings and walls have been incorporated into the design. Flower paintings by local artist.

⊕ ☕ ☎

13 ▶ CORSCOMBE HOUSE
Corscombe DT2 0NU. Jim Bartos. *3¹/₂ m N of Beaminster. From Dorchester A356 to Crewkerne, take 1st turn to Corscombe then R signed Church. Or A37 Yeovil to Dorchester, turn W signed Sutton Bingham/ Halstock/ Corscombe. Straight past Fox Inn, up hill then L signed Church.* Cream teas at vicarage or village hall if wet. **Adm £4, chd free. Sun 10 July (2-6). Also open Grovestall Farm.**
Garden in grounds of former rectory with view of Church. Garden rooms with colour-themed cool and hot borders, sunny and shady beds, parterre, reflecting pool, part-walled vegetable garden, orchard and meadow. Secret garden with Mediterranean planting. Featured in GGG and in The Gardens of Dorset.

🏡 ⊕ ☕

> In delightful and secluded hamlet of stone and thatched cottages . . . series of village gardens . . .

14 ▶ COTTAGE ROW
School Lane, Tarrant Gunville, nr Blandford Forum DT11 8JJ. Carolyn & Michael Pawson, 01258 830212, mike.pawson@virgin.net. *6m NE of Blandford Forum. From Blandford take A354 towards Salisbury, L at Tarrant Hinton. After 1¹/₂ m R in Tarrant Gunville into School Lane.* **Evening Openings £4, chd free, wine, Fri 10, Sat 11 June (5-8). Visitors also welcome by appt.**
Young (2005), ¹/₂ -acre, hidden, partly-walled garden. Pergola, arbour, brick paths, Yorkstone terrace, tree house, well, kitchen garden. White wisteria, clematis, shrub and climbing roses, tulips, alliums. This sophisticated cottage garden reflects the owners' passion for unusual plants, structure and an artist's eye for sympathetic colour.

⊕ ☎

15 ▶ ◆ CRANBORNE MANOR GARDEN
Cranborne BH21 5PP. Viscount Cranborne, 01725 517248, www.cranborne.co.uk. *10m N of Wimborne on B3078.* **Adm £5, chd £1, concessions £4.50. For NGS: Wed 6 Apr; Sat 16 July (9-4). For other opening times and information, please phone or see garden website.**
Beautiful and historic garden laid out in C17 by John Tradescant and enlarged in C20, featuring several gardens surrounded by walls and yew hedges: white garden, cottage-style and mount gardens, water and wild garden. Many interesting plants, with fine trees and avenues.

♿ ⊕ ☕

16 ▶ THE DAIRY HOUSE
Behind Manor Farmhouse, Melbury Osmond, Dorchester DT2 0LS. John & Elizabeth Forrest. *6m S of Yeovil. A37, turn W signed Melbury Osmond. 1m into village, L at Xrds, park at village hall. Follow signs to garden, 5 min walk.* Home-made teas in Village Hall. **Adm £3, chd free. Sun 15, Mon 16 May (2-5).**
Previously a farmyard, now 1-acre S-facing mature garden with good examples of garden trees, clematis, climbers and herbaceous borders, shrubs and productive vegetable patch. Lovely views of surrounding countryside. Featured in Dorset Life.

☕

17 ▶ DEANS COURT
Deans Court Lane, Wimborne Minster BH21 1EE. Sir William Hanham, www.deanscourt.org. *¹/₄ m SE of Minster. Just off B3073 in centre of Wimborne. Entry from Deans Court Lane - continuation of High St at 1st T-junction, over pavement by Holmans.* Free parking. **Adm £4, chd free, senior citizens £3 (share to Friends of Victoria Hospital). Suns, Mons 1, 2, 29, 30 May; 28, 29 Aug (11-6). Also open The Secret Garden & Serles House 28/29 Aug (2.30-5.30).**
13 acres of peaceful, partly wild gardens in ancient setting with mature specimen trees, Saxon fish pond, herb garden and apiary beside R Allen close to town centre of Wimborne Minster. The 1st Soil Association accredited kitchen garden within C18 serpentine walls. Lunches and teas served in the garden and tea room, using estate produce (also for sale).

♿ 🏡 ⊕ ☕

DICOT
See Devon.

18 **DOMINEYS**
Buckland Newton, nr Dorchester
DT2 7BS. Mr & Mrs W Gueterbock,
01300 345295,
cottages@domineys.com,
www.domineys.com. *11m N of
Dorchester, 11m S of Sherborne. 2m
E A352 or take B3143. Take 'no
through rd' between Church &
Gaggle of Geese. Entrance
100metres on L. Park & picnic in
arboretum on R, 10metres before
garden entrance.* Home-made teas;
soup lunch as well 16 Oct only. **Adm
£4, chd free. Suns 10 Apr; 8 May;
7 Aug (2-6); 16 Oct (12-5). Visitors
also welcome by appt.**
Our garden around C17 cottage
dates from 1961 and small arboretum
from 1996. Rarities, old favourites,
trees, shrubs, herbaceous, annuals,
bulbs, fruit and vegetables. The aim
has been to paint a picture for all the
seasons with plants in sympathetic
settings reflecting continuing change.
50th yr gardening at Domineys and
25th yr NGS opening. Exhibition by
acclaimed Dorset artist May and Oct.
Featured in Gardens of Dorset by
Roger Lane. Wheelchair access
excludes arboretum.

DURMAST HOUSE
See Hampshire.

EDGEWOOD
See Hampshire.

19 **◆ EDMONDSHAM HOUSE**
Wimborne BH21 5RE. Mrs Julia
Smith, 01725 517207. *9m NE of
Wimborne. 9m W of Ringwood.
Between Cranborne & Verwood.
Edmondsham off B3081.* Tea & cake
NGS days, Weds only. **Adm £2.50,
chd 50p, under 5 free. For NGS:
Mon 25 Apr, Weds, 6 Apr to 27
Apr; Weds, 5 Oct to 26 Oct (2-5).
For other opening times and
information, please phone.**
An historic 6-acre garden of C16
house. Interesting mature specimen
trees and shrubs. Spring bulbs and
blossom, autumn cyclamen. Early
church, Victorian dairy and stable
block, medieval grass cock pit.
Walled garden with vegetables, fruit
and traditional herbaceous borders
planted to sustain long period of
interest. Managed organically. House
tours suitable for wheelchair users.
Gravel paths.

20 **FARRS**
Whitcombe Rd, Beaminster
DT8 3NB. Mr & Mrs John
Makepeace. *Southern edge of
Beaminster. On B3163. Enter through
gate in wall adjacent to museum.*
Home-made teas. **Adm £5, chd free.
Suns 26 June; 24 July; 4 Sept
(11-5).**
Large walled garden behind historic
yew topiary. 4 distinct areas incl
inspirational contemporary grass
gardens designed by John
Makepeace. Jenny's colourful potager
with cleft oak fruitcage, glasshouse
and strawbale retreat. Clipped
Phillyrea define drive alongside border
of cool colours and contrasting
textures. Pools, gravel path with
alternative access through orchard.
Gallery showing John Makepeace
furniture and works by other artists
will be open. Featured on BBC
Regional News and in numerous
publications.

21 **THE FERNS**
East Burton, Wool BH20 6HE. John
& Jill Redfern. *Approaching Wool
from Wareham, turn R just before
level crossing into East Burton Rd.
Garden on R, just under a mile down
this rd.* Home-made teas. **Adm
£2.50, chd free. Suns 8, 22 May;
10 July (2-5).**
Profusely planted with varied
herbaceous borders and shrubs.
Interesting use of hard landscaping.
Fruit and vegetable garden leads to
small woodland garden and stream
and a scene from Dorset clay-mining
history. 'A lovely, secret garden'
(Dorset Life & Country Gardener)
New planted areas. Featured in
Gardens of Dorset.

Dorset Wildlife
Trust Award for
wildlife-friendly
planting . . .

22 **◆ FORDE ABBEY GARDENS**
Chard TA20 4LU. Mr & Mrs Julian
Kennard, 01460 221290,
www.fordeabbey.co.uk. *4m SE of
Chard. Signed off A30 Chard-
Crewkerne & A358 Chard-Axminster.
Also from Broadwindsor B3164.* **For
opening times and information,
please phone or see garden
website.**
30 acres, fine shrubs, magnificent
specimen trees, ponds, herbaceous
borders, rockery, bog garden
containing superb collection of Asiatic
primulas, Ionic temple, working
kitchen garden supplying the
restaurant. Centenary fountain,
England's highest powered fountain.
Gardens open daily. Gravel paths.

FOREST LODGE
See Somerset & Bristol.

23 **FRANKHAM FARM**
Ryme Intrinseca DT9 6JT. Richard
Earle & Susan Ross. *3m S of Yeovil.
A37 Yeovil-Dorchester; turn E; drive
¼ m on L.* Home-made teas. **Adm
£3, chd free. Suns 27 Mar; 8 May;
12 June; 17 July; 16 Oct (2-5).**
3½ -acre garden, created since 1960
by the late Jo Earle for yr-round
interest. Unusual shrubs and trees
from round the world. Spring bulbs
through to autumn colour, particularly
oaks. Dorset Wildlife Trust Award for
wildlife-friendly planting. Avoid slopes.

24 **FRITH HOUSE**
Stalbridge DT10 2SD. Mr & Mrs
Patrick Sclater, 01963 250809. *5m
E of Sherborne. Between Milborne
Port and Stalbridge. 1m S A30. Turn
W nr PO in Stalbridge then follow
signs.* Home-made teas. **Adm £4,
chd free. Sun 27 Mar (2-5). Visitors
also welcome by appt Mon - Fri
only, May - July incl.**
Approached down long drive with fine
views. 4 acres of garden around
Edwardian house and self-contained
hamlet. Range of mature trees, lakes
and flower borders. House terrace
edged by rose border and featuring
Lutyensesque wall fountain and game
larder. Well-stocked kitchen gardens.

GANTS MILL & GARDEN
See Somerset & Bristol.

Cranborne Manor Garden

GROUP OPENING

25 NEW **3 GARDENS AT WESTHAM**
Westham DT4 0LH, *1¹/₂ m town centre. From Jubilee Clock Esplanade, follow sign for Chickerell/Westham/Abbotsbury. Abbotsbury Rd, R opp Sue Ryder. From Abbotsbury B3157 through 5ways junction, 2nd L opp Admiral Hardy PH, 2nd L, look for signs.* Combined adm £3, chd free. **Wed 29 June; Suns 3, 10 July (2-5).** Visitors also welcome by appt May/June, min 20. 07909 282423/01305 771628/01305 778207, gdnswest@live.co.uk

> NEW **HOLLY HOUSE**
> 68 Corporation Rd.
> Mrs Lynne Chalker

> NEW **NONESUCH**
> 70 Corporation Road.
> Mr T Butler

> NEW **A WORK OF HEART**
> 72 Corporation Road.
> The Jones-Barrys

No garden makeovers here. 3 neighbours with gardens next to each other. Small they may be but, contending with sloping ground (steps and narrow paths), each one packs a very different punch. No 68: Rather wild and intriguing, with shaded courtyard, stone statues, roses and scrambling creepers. No 70: A leafy sanctuary. Simple, uncluttered, almost flowerless, with shrubs and trees of contrasting foliage. No 72: An exuberant pot garden. An explosion of colour and energy. Containers of many shapes and sizes which go hand-in-hand with the variety of plants they contain. Within these 3 gardens, not far from the vibrant centre of Weymouth and Old Harbour, there is something for everyone to enjoy. Why not plan a day out and be sure to visit us?

26 **THE GLADE**
Woodland Walk, Ferndown BH22 9LP. Mary & Roger Angus, 01202 872789, mary@gladestock.co.uk. *³/₄ m NE of Ferndown centre. N off Wimborne Rd East, nr Tricketts Cross r'about, Woodland Walk is a metalled but single carriageway lane with no parking bays; please park on main rd and access on foot (5 mins/330yds). Drop-off/pick-up for those with restricted mobility by arrangement only, please phone.* Home-made teas. Adm £3, chd free. **Suns 17 Apr; 1, 15, 29 May (2-5.30).** Visitors also

welcome by appt for groups of 20+ from mid April to mid June.
The name captures the setting. Award-winning 1³/₄ -acre spring garden. Terraced lawns for lingering over tea. Woodland walks through blossom trees, wild anemones, primroses and bluebells. Extensive shrubbery, stream and large wildlife pond with primulas, marginals, waterlilies. Bog garden, wet meadow, spring bulbs and herbaceous and mixed borders. Featured in Gardens of Dorset.
🏵 ❀ ☕ ☎

190 GOLDCROFT
See Somerset & Bristol.

27 **GRANGE COTTAGE**
Golden Hill, Stourton Caundle DT10 2JP. Fleur Miles. *6m SE of Sherborne. Park at Manor Farm or The Trooper PH, walk up hill to thatched cottage on R.* Home-made teas at Manor Farm. Adm £3.50, chd free. **Sat 2, Sun 3 Apr; Sun 5 June (2-5).** Also open **Manor Farm**, combined adm £7.
Come and discover the peace and tranquillity of a real cottage garden. Follow the meandering paths and find many flower borders, box and yew hedging, two ponds, topiary creatures and much more to delight you. Hellebores and spring bulbs a particular feature.

28 **GREENACRES**
Bere Road, Coldharbour, Wareham BH20 7PA. John & Pat Jacobs. *2¹/₂ m NW of Wareham. From r'about adjacent to stn take Wareham-Bere Regis rd. House ¹/₂ m past Silent Woman Inn.* Cream teas. Adm £3, chd free. **Suns 17 July; 21 Aug (2-5.30).**
Approx 1-acre plantswoman's garden situated in Wareham Forest. Lawns punctuated by colourful island beds designed mainly for summer interest. Unusual perennials, shrubs and specimen trees. Themed areas and stone water feature with 2 ponds. Stumpery with collection of ferns and grasses. Various breeds of poultry. Live music and bonsai exhibition.
♿ ❀ ☕

29 **GROVESTALL FARM**
Chilfrome DT2 0HA. Mr & Mrs David Orr. *10m NW of Dorchester. From Yeovil take A37 to Dorchester. 10¹/₂ m turn R into Maiden Newton, R at T-junction and 1st R to Chilfrome. From Dorchester take A37 to Yeovil.*

7m turn L into Maiden Newton, then as above. Follow signs. Caution on narrow final lane. Home-made teas. **Adm £4, chd free.** Sun 10 July (2-6). Also open **Corscombe House.**

2-acre garden created around old farm buildings. Densely planted former yard, walled kitchen garden and 2 small, formal gardens linked by iris and lavender walk. The very rural setting includes a 6-acre 11 yr-old broadleaf wood with mown rides. Featured in Period Living magazine.

30 HATCHLANDS
Netherbury DT6 5NA. Dr & Mrs John Freeman. 2m SW of Beaminster. Turn R off A3066 Beaminster to Bridport Rd, signed Netherbury. Car park at Xrds at bottom of hill. 200yds up bridle path. Home-made teas. **Adm £4, chd free.** Sun 15 May (2-6). Also open **The Mill House, combined adm £6.**

Country hillside garden within 3 acres. Tall yew and box hedges, rose gardens, herbaceous and fuchsia beds and many hardy geraniums beneath a long Georgian brick wall. Open sloping lawns and croquet court, spring-fed pond and mature broadleaf trees in woodland area.

31 HAZEL LODGE
24 Old Oak Way, Winterborne Whitechurch, Blandford Forum DT11 0TN. Brian & Pauline Roberts. 6m SW of Blandford Forum. From A354 turn into Whatcombe Lane signed Winterborne Stickland, Old Oak Way 2nd L, garden 100yds on R. Limited parking, please park sensitively in village. Teas. **Adm £2.50, chd free.** Fri 1 July (2-5). Relaxing, medium-sized garden maintained by owners. Informal colourful mixed borders of shrubs, roses, perennials, acers, vegetable plot. Seating areas give a variety of aspects of garden.

HEDDON HALL
See Devon.

32 NEW 205 HERBERT AVENUE
Parkstone, Poole BH12 4HR. Mr & Mrs Steve Hemsley. 2½ m E of Poole. Herbert Ave lies between A348 Ringwood Rd and A3040 Alder Rd. Home-made teas. **Adm £2.50, chd**

free. **Suns 22 May; 19 June; 24 July (2-5).**
2 bikers garden here: The plants love growing and the wildlife is very much at home. The cleverly divided up and laid out back garden is filled with original features. The use of mirrors, lots of seating in secluded areas, funky paths and wacky colours make this a good fun garden that will not fail to stir your imagination.

33 HERONS MEAD
East Burton Road, East Burton, Wool BH20 6HF. Ron & Angela Millington, 01929 463872, ronamillington@btinternet.com. 6m W of Wareham on A352. Approaching Wool from Wareham, turn R just before level crossing into East Burton Rd. Herons Mead ¾ m on L. Home-made teas. **Adm £3, chd free.** Suns 27 Mar; 24 Apr; Mon 2 May, Sun 29 May; Sun 26 June; 18 Sept (2-5); Evening Opening £4, wine, Fri 24 June (6-8). **Visitors also welcome by appt for groups of 10+.**
½ -acre plantlover's garden full of interest from spring (bulbs, 150+ hellebores, pulmonaria, fritillaries) through an abundance of summer perennials, old roses scrambling through trees and late-seasonal exuberant plants amongst swathes of tall grasses. Wildlife attractive, especially bees and butterflies. Tiny woodland. Cacti. 'Out of the ordinary' (WI Life).

34 HIGHER MELCOMBE MANOR
Melcombe Bingham DT2 7PB. Mr M C Woodhouse & Mrs L Morton. 11m NE of Dorchester. Puddletown exit on A35. Follow signs for Cheselbourne then Melcombe Bingham. Home-made teas. **Adm £3.50, chd free.** Suns 10, 17 July (12-5).
Approached through a lime avenue up private rd, the 2-acre garden is set in quiet valley surrounded by downland. Traditional English garden around C16 manor house and chapel with herbaceous beds, roses and magnificent copper beech and wonderful woodland views.

35 ♦ HILLTOP
Woodville, Stour Provost SP8 5LY. Josse & Brian Emerson, 01747 838512, www.hilltopgarden.co.uk.

7m N of Sturminster Newton, 5m W of Shaftesbury. On B3092 turn E at Stour Provost Xrds, signed Woodville. After 1¼ m thatched cottage on R. **Adm £2, chd free. For NGS: Suns, 17 July to 21 Aug incl (2-6). For other opening times and information, please phone or see garden website.**
The summer garden at Hilltop is a gorgeous riot of colour and scent, the 250 yr-old thatched cottage barely visible amongst the greenery and flowers. Unusual and interesting annuals and perennials grow alongside the traditional and familiar, boldly combining to make a spectacular display. Nursery plants for sale.

> Funky paths and wacky colours make this a good fun garden that will not fail to stir your imagination . . .

HINTON ADMIRAL
See Hampshire.

36 ♦ HOLWORTH FARMHOUSE
Holworth, nr Dorchester DT2 8NH. Anthony & Philippa Bush, 01305 852242, www.inarcadia-gardendesign.co.uk. 7m E of Dorchester. 1m S of A352. Follow signs to Holworth. Through farmyard with duckpond on R. 1st L after 200yds. Ignore 'no access' signs. Home-made teas on NGS days. **Adm £3.50, chd free. For NGS: Suns 5 June; 3 July; 7 Aug; 4 Sept (2-6). For other opening times and information, please phone or see garden website.**
During 32yrs this peaceful garden has been transformed using different styles and a variety of features. Formal and informal, light and shade, running and still water and places to explore. Planted with a wide range of mature and unusual trees, shrubs and perennials. Fine views of Dorset to N and E. Featured in Gardens of Dorset by Roger Lane. Limited wheelchair access.

37 HONEYCOMBE
13 Springfield Crescent, Sherborne DT9 6DN. Jean & Ted Gillingham. *From A352 (Horsecastle Lane), past Skippers PH, turn into Wynnes Rise then 1st L.* Home-made teas. **Adm £2.50, chd free. Wed 22, Sun 26 June; Sun 3 July (2-5).**
Many varieties of clematis scramble through trees, over arches and amongst a sumptuous display of roses, underplanted with a wide variety of herbaceous perennials in colour-themed borders.

38 HORN PARK
Tunnel Rd, Beaminster DT8 3HB. Mr & Mrs David Ashcroft, 01308 862212, angieashcroft@hornpark.fsnet.co. uk. *1¹/₂ m N of Beaminster. On A3066 from Beaminster, L before tunnel (see signs).* Home-made teas. **Adm £4, chd, (under 16) free. Weds 27 Apr; 29 June (2-5).** Visitors also welcome by appt incl groups Tues to Thurs only, Apr to Oct, teas by arrangement, coaches permitted.
Large, plantsman's garden with magnificent view to sea. Many rare and mature plants and shrubs in terraced, herbaceous, rock and water gardens. Woodland garden and walks in bluebell woods. Good autumn colouring. Wild flower meadow with 164 varieties incl orchids. Partial wheelchair access.

39 IVY HOUSE GARDEN
Piddletrenthide DT2 7QF. Bridget Bowen, 01300 348255, bridgetpbowen@hotmail.com. *9m N of Dorchester. On B3143. In middle of Piddletrenthide village, opp PO/village stores near Piddle Inn.* Home-made teas. **Adm £3, chd free. Sun 10, Mon 25 Apr; Sun 8 May (2-5).** Visitors also welcome by appt, groups of 10+ up to early June.
Unusual and challenging ¹/₂ -acre plantsman's garden set on steep hillside, with fine views. Themed areas and mixed borders, wildlife ponds, propagating garden, Mediterranean garden, greenhouses and polytunnel, chickens and bees, nearby allotment. Daffodils, tulips, violets and hellebores in quantity for spring openings. Come prepared for steep terrain and a warm welcome.

40 ◆ KINGSTON LACY
Wimborne Minster BH21 4EA. National Trust, 01202 883402, www.nationaltrust.org.uk. *1¹/₂ m W of Wimborne Minster. On the Wimborne-Blandford rd B3082.* **Adm £6, chd £3. For NGS: Sat 4, Sun 5 June (10.30-6). For other opening times and information, please phone or see garden website.**
43 acres of garden, approached through lime avenue. Parterre and Sunk Gardens planted with Edwardian schemes, spring and summer. Victorian fernery contains 35 varieties. Rotunda. Japanese garden restored to Henrietta Bankes' creation of 1910. 2 National Collections: Convallarias and Anemone nemorosa. Deep gravel on some paths but lawns suitable for wheelchairs. Slope to Visitor Reception & S lawns.

Rachel is delighted to welcome visitors and discuss gardening . . .

41 ◆ KINGSTON MAURWARD GARDENS
Dorchester DT2 8PY. Kingston Maurward College, 01305 215003, www.kmc.ac.uk/gardens. *1m E of Dorchester. Off A35. Follow brown Tourist Information signs.* **For opening times and information, please phone or see garden website.**
35 acres of gardens laid out in C18 and C20 with 5-acre lake. Generous terraces and gardens divided by hedges and stone balustrades. Stone features and interesting plants. Elizabethan walled garden laid out as demonstration. National Collections of penstemons and salvias. Partial wheelchair access.

42 ◆ KNITSON OLD FARMHOUSE
Corfe Castle, Wareham BH20 5JB. Rachel & Mark Helfer, 01929 421681, rachel@knitson.co.uk. *1m NW of Swanage. 3m E of Corfe Castle. Signed L off A351 Knitson, very narrow roads. Ample parking in yard or in adjacent field.* Cream teas. **Adm £3, chd free. Fris, Sats, Suns 15, 16, 17 Apr; 13, 14, 15 May; 17, 18, 19 June (1-5).** Visitors also welcome by appt, max 20.
Mature cottage garden nestled at base of chalk downland in dry coastal conditions. Herbaceous borders, rockeries, climbers and shrubs. Evolved and designed over 50yrs for yr-round colour and interest. Large organic kitchen garden for self-sufficiency. Rachel is delighted to welcome visitors and discuss gardening. Uneven, sloping paths.

43 ◆ KNOLL GARDENS
Hampreston BH21 7ND. Mr Neil Lucas, 01202 873931, www.knollgardens.co.uk. *2¹/₂ m W of Ferndown. ETB brown signs from A31. Large car park.* **For opening times and information, please phone or see garden website.**
Exciting collection of grasses and perennials thrive within an informal setting of shrubs, mature and unusual trees. Mediterranean-style gravel garden, Dragon Garden and Decennium border planted in the naturalistic style. National Collections of pennisetum, deciduous ceanothus and phygelius. Featured on BBC TV, local radio, and in numerous publications. Some slopes. Gravel paths.

44 KNOWLE FARM
Uploders, nr Bridport DT6 4NS. Alison & John Halliday, 01308 485492, info@knowlefarmbandb.com. *1¹/₂ m E of Bridport. Leave A35 signed to Uploders about 2m E of Bridport. Turn back under A35 to reach Uploders. Turn L at T-junction (Crown Inn on L). Knowle Farm is 200yds on R, opp chapel. Careful roadside parking unless using Crown Inn (lunches served).* Home-made teas. **Adm £3.50, chd free. Sat 16, Mon 18 Apr (1-6).** Visitors also welcome by appt.
1-acre informal valley garden on 3 levels bordered by R Asker in conservation area. Tranquil setting with many restful seating areas. Wide variety of interesting and unusual plants in different habitats. Kitchen garden and hens. Large, flower-filled greenhouse. Steep slope on grass to river.

45 LANGEBRIDE HOUSE
Long Bredy DT2 9HU. Mrs J
Greener, 01308 482257. *8m W of
Dorchester. S off A35, well signed.
1st gateway on L in village.* Light
refreshments & home-made teas in
village hall. **Adm £4, chd free. Suns
27 Feb; 13 Mar** (12-4.30). **Visitors
also welcome by appt Feb to July
incl.**
Substantial old rectory garden with
many designs for easier
management. 200-yr-old beech trees,
pleached limes, yew hedges,
extensive collections of spring bulbs,
herbaceous plants, flowering trees,
shrubs and alpines. Some steep
slopes.
♿ ☕ ☎

46 LAWSBROOK
Brodham Way, Shillingstone
DT11 0TE. Clive, Faith & Gina
Nelson, 01258 860148,
cne70bl@aol.com. *5m NW of
Blandford. Follow signs to
Shillingstone on A357. Turn off A357
at PO, continue up Gunn Lane, 2nd
junction on R, 1st house on R
(200yds).* Home-made teas both
dates, ploughmans lunches May only.
Adm £3, chd free. Sun 27 Feb
(10-4); **Sun 29 May** (10-6). **Also
open Coombe Cottage 29 May**
(2-6). **Visitors also welcome by appt.**
6 acres. Over 200 trees incl the
mature and unusual. Borders,
wildflower and wildlife areas,
vegetable garden. February: extensive
snowdrops, hellebores and bulbs.
Relaxed and friendly, lovely
opportunity for family walks in all
areas including wildlife, stream,
meadow. Children and dogs
welcome. Snowdrop walk Feb.
Children's activities. Short gravel path
at entrance.
♿ 🏠 ❂ ☕ ☎

LIFT THE LATCH
See Somerset & Bristol.

47 LITTLE BINDON
West Lulworth. The Weld Estate/Mr
Richard Wilkin. *Park in W Lulworth
BH20 5RJ. Walk to Cove, around it
(shingle) to far side. Ascend steps
(steep, no hand rail, signed), follow
path signed Little Bindon, Range
Walks and Mupes Bay. Wooded area,
wicket gate to garden on R just
before Range flag. 20mins from car
park.* Light refreshments. **Adm £2.50,
chd free** (share to Weldmar
Hospice). **Sat 16, Sun 17 July** (12-
4.30).

Remote and romantic C11 monastic
chapel. Wild, secret garden. Bluebells
and spring bulbs. Exuberant rose
growth, sculptured vegetation,
winding paths and vistas to adjacent
cliffs and hills. Complete tranquillity.
Slightly challenging access as on far
side of Lulworth Cove, repaid by this
special and unusual place, dramatic
coastal scenery en route and beyond.
🏠 ☕

Perfectionist's garden on three levels . . .

THE LITTLE COTTAGE
See Hampshire.

**48 ♦ LITTLEBREDY WALLED
GARDENS**
Littlebredy DT2 9HL. The Walled
Garden Workshop, 01305 898055,
www.littlebredy.com. *8m W of
Dorchester. 10m E of Bridport. 1¹/₂ m
S of A35. Park on Littlebredy village
green by round bus shelter. 400yd
walk to garden, closer parking in
garden car park for less mobile.* **Adm
£4, chd free. For NGS: Tues 21,
28 June** (2-7.30). **For other opening
times and information, please
phone or see garden website.**
1-acre walled garden on S-facing
slopes of Bride River Valley.
Herbaceous borders, riverside rose
walk, lavender parterre and vegetable
and cut flower gardens. Original
Victorian glasshouses, one under
renovation. Walk through old damson
orchard to newly-planted vineyard.
Partial wheelchair access, steep grass
slopes.
♿ 🏠 ❂ ☕

49 NEW 55 LONNEN ROAD
Colehill, Wimborne BH21 7AT.
Malcolm Case & Jenny Parr, 01202
883549. *1¹/₂ m N of Wimborne. From
Canford Bottom r'about where A31
meets B3073, exit N marked Colehill
for 1¹/₄ m, R into Lonnen Rd.* Home-
made teas. **Adm £3, chd free. Sats,
Suns 2, 3 July; 6, 7 Aug** (2-5).
**Visitors also welcome by appt
July/Aug only.**

Perfectionist's garden on 3 levels, with
colour co-ordinated planting using
wide range of plants, with borrowed
view over adjacent fields. Circular box
parterre infilled with vegetables.
Watering cans hang in a row behind
toolshed, by bridge over little stream.
Lots for the eye and senses to enjoy.
❂ ☕ ☎

GROUP OPENING

**50 NEW LYTCHETT MINSTER
GARDENS**
Lytchett Minster BH16 6JF. *3m W of
Wimborne. From A35 Bakers Arms
PH r'about (junction with A351),
follow signs to Lytchett MInster
B3067. L opp St Peters Finger PH,
follow parking signs. Garden
guide/adm at car park.* Home-made
teas at The Old Bakehouse, 55
Dorchester Rd. **Combined adm £5,
chd free. Sat 18, Sun 19 June** (2-6).

NEW 15 ASHBROOK WALK
Sue Allison

**NEW 54 DORCHESTER
ROAD**
Ayla Hill

NEW HERON HOUSE
17 Ashbrook Walk. Geraldine
Stevens

**NEW OLD BUTTON
COTTAGE**
58 Dorchester Road.
Thelma Johns.

NEW 4 OLD FORGE CLOSE
Liz Allen

NEW 10 ORCHARD CLOSE
Daphne Turner

Lytchett Minster, 'The Gateway to the
Purbecks', is W of Poole on the old
Dorchester rd. Mixture of old and new
houses, 2 churches, 2 PHs and an
ancient pound. The 6 small to
medium-sized gardens offer variation
in cottage-style planting with many
varieties of herbaceous perennials
and hardy geraniums, some lush
waterside planting, magnificent
displays of climbing roses, small fruit
and vegetable plots and many other
interesting features. Dogs on leads in
3 gardens. Wheelchair access to 5
gardens, some gravel.
❂ ☕ ♿

**MACPENNYS WOODLAND
GARDEN & NURSERIES**
See Hampshire.

51 MANOR FARM, HAMPRESTON

Wimborne BH21 7LX. Guy & Anne Trehane. *2¹/₂ m E of Wimborne, 2¹/₂ m W of Ferndown. From Canford Bottom r'about on A31, take exit B3073 Ham Lane. ¹/₂ m turn R at Hampreston Xrds. House at bottom of village.* Home-made teas. **Adm £3, chd free. Suns 22 May; 12 June; 31 July (1-5).**
Traditional farmhouse garden designed and cared for by 3 generations of the Trehane family who have farmed here for over 90yrs. Garden now being restored and thoughtfully replanted with herbaceous borders and rose beds within box and yew hedges. Mature shrubbery, water and bog garden. Hardy plant society plant sale.

52 MANOR FARM, STOURTON CAUNDLE

Stourton Caundle DT10 2JW. Mr & Mrs O S L Simon. *6m E of Sherborne, 4 m W of Sturminster Newton. From Sherborne take A3030. At Bishops Caundle, L signed Stourton Caundle. After 1¹/₂ m, L opp Trooper Inn in middle of village.* Home-made teas. **Adm £4, chd free. Sat 2, Sun 3 Apr; Sun 5 June (2-5).**
Also open **Grange Cottage, combined adm £7.**
C17 farmhouse and barns with walled garden in middle of village. Mature trees, shrubberies, herbaceous borders, lakes and vegetable garden. Lovingly created over last 40 yrs by current owners.

53 THE MANOR HOUSE, BEAMINSTER

North St, Beaminster DT8 3DZ. Christine Wood. *200yds N of town square. From Square - up North St (by Red Lion). Entrance signed on L. Parking in Square or central car park. Disabled parking available on site for limited number of cars.* Home-made teas. **Adm £4.50, chd free. Suns, Mons 29, 30 May; 19, 20 June (11-5).**
Set in heart of Beaminster, 16¹/₂ acres of stunning parkland with mature specimen trees, lake & waterfalls. Unusual collection of water fowl incl black-necked swans. Recently restored walled garden with traditional formal planting. New for this yr - renovated woodland walk and wildflower meadow.

54 MANOR HOUSE, BLANDFORD

Church Lane, Lower Blandford St Mary, Blandford DT11 9ND. Mr & Mrs Jeremy Mains. *¹/₄ m E of Blandford. Signed off A350 to Poole from Blandford Forum Ring Road (Tesco r'about).* Home-made teas. **Adm £4 Apr/June; £3 Sept, chd free. Mon 25 Apr; Sun 19 June; Sun 4 Sept (2-5).**
Traditional 4-acre walled garden surrounding Jacobean House (not open). Formal rose beds with mixed herbaceous borders. Stunning spring bulbs. Working fruit and vegetable garden. Large shrub borders with varied collections, climbing roses along walls. Present owners continue to develop and make changes to garden. Gravel entrance.

55 ◆ MAPPERTON GARDENS

nr Beaminster DT8 3NR. The Earl & Countess of Sandwich, 01308 862645, www.mapperton.com. *6m N of Bridport. Off A356/A3066. 2m SE of Beaminster off B3163.* **Adm £5, chd £2.50, under 5 free. For opening times and information please visit website or telephone.**
Terraced valley gardens surrounding Tudor/Jacobean manor house. On upper levels, walled croquet lawn, orangery and Italianate formal garden with fountains, topiary and grottos. Below, C17 summerhouse and fishponds. Lower garden with shrubs and rare trees, leading to woodland and spring gardens. Featured in Mail on Sunday, Ten of the Greatest British Gardens. Partial wheelchair access, upper levels only.

Lovingly created over last 40 years by current owners . . .

56 MAYFIELD

4 Walford Close, Wimborne BH21 1PH. Mr & Mrs Terry Wheeler, 01202 849838, terry.wheeler@tesco.net. *¹/₂ m N of Wimborne. B3078 out of Wimborne, R into Burts Hill, 1st L into Walford Close.* Home-made teas. **Adm £2, chd free (share to The Friends of Victoria Hospital). Weds, Suns 11, 15, 25 May; 5, 22 June (2-5). Visitors also welcome by appt May/June only.**
Town garden of approx ¹/₄ acre. Front: formal hard landscaping planted with drought-resistant shrubs and perennials. Shady area has wide variety of hostas. Back: winding beds separated by grass paths and arches. Pond and greenhouses containing succulents.

57 MAYO FARM

Higher Blandford Road, Shaftesbury SP7 0EF. Robin & Trish Porteous. *¹/₂ m E of Shaftesbury. On B3081 Shaftesbury to Blandford rd on outskirts of Shaftesbury.* Home-made teas. **Adm £3, chd free. Sun 29 May; Wed 1 June (2-5).**
Lovely 2-acre early summer garden, with walled areas, ponds and herbaceous borders, which has spectacular views of Melbury Hill and the edge of the Blackmore Vale. Some uneven surfaces and small steps.

58 MEWS COTTAGE

34 Easton Street, Portland DT5 1BT. Peter & Jill Pitman, 01305 820377, penstemon@waitrose.com. *3m S of Weymouth. Situated on top of the Island, 50yds past Punchbowl Inn, small lane on L. Park in main street & follow signs.* Home-made teas, also light lunches 4 June, 16 July, 6 Aug. **Adm £2, chd free. Sat 4 June (11-4), Suns 5, 19 June (2-5); Sat 16 July (11-4), Sun 17 July (2-5); Sat 6 Aug (11-4), Suns 7, 21 Aug (2-5). Visitors also welcome by appt.**
The 2010 reorganisation is complete, more planned before 2011 openings. National Collection of cultivar penstemon, also raised crevice bed for species penstemon grown from APS seed. New agapanthus are well established. We are delighted with the result so far, but further changes are waiting to be made to bring more colour. Several new dieramas. Ceramics by Tiffany. 2 steps to WC.

59 THE MILL HOUSE
Crook Hill, Netherbury DT6 5LX.
Michael & Giustina Ryan, 01308
488267,
themillhouse@dsl.pipex.com. *1m S
of Beaminster. Turn R off A3066
Beaminster to Bridport rd at signpost
to Netherbury. Car park at Xrds at
bottom of hill.* Cream teas. **Adm £4,
chd free. Suns 17 Apr; 15 May
(2-6); Evening Opening £4, chd
free, wine & refreshments, Wed
27 July (5.30-8). Also open 15 May
Hatchlands, joint adm £6. Visitors
also welcome by appt.**
Gardens arranged round mill, stream
and pond. Formal walled, terraced
and vegetable gardens. Emphasis on
scented flowers, hardy geraniums,
lilies, clematis and water irises. Wild
garden planted with magnolias, fruit
trees and oaks underplanted with
bulbs. Featured in The English
Garden and Gardens of Dorset.
Partial wheelchair access.

The Secret Garden and Serles House

60 ◆ MINTERNE
Minterne Magna DT2 7AU. The Hon
Henry & Mrs Digby, 01300 341370,
www.minterne.co.uk. *2m N of Cerne
Abbas. On A352 Dorchester-
Sherborne rd.* **Adm £5, chd under
12 free. For opening times and
information, please phone or see
garden website.**
20 acres wild woodland gardens
landscaped in C18, laid out in a
horseshoe over 1m round. Home to
the Churchill and Digby families for
350yrs. From spring to autumn the
magnificent mature and newly-
planted specimen shrubs and trees
create surprises and superb vistas
around the lake, ending with
sensational autumn colouring. Regret
unsuitable for wheelchairs.

61 MOUNT PLEASANT
29 Chantry Lane, Newtown,
Beaminster DT8 3ER. Douglas
Gibbs. *½ m N from Beaminster
Square. Up Fleet St, L in 'Newtown',
L again into Chantry Lane. Car
parking in Beaminster School Car
Park just before Chantry Lane, very
short walk.* Teas in Beaminster. **Adm
£2.50, chd free. Mons 2 May;
29 Aug (2-5).**
¼ -acre plantsman's garden created
and looked after entirely by owner.
Divided by hedges and walkways into
smaller spaces. Water garden,
subtropical garden, orchid house.
Camellias, azaleas, hydrangeas all in

pots. Conservatory and rain forest
leading back out into Chantry Lane
with colourful frontage. Expect the
unexpected!. Exhibition of paintings.
Partial wheelchair access, narrow
paths and a few shallow steps.

MULBERRY HOUSE
See Hampshire.

62 4 NOEL ROAD
Wallisdown BH10 4DP. Lesley &
Ivor Pond. *4m NE of Poole. From
Wallisdown Xrds enter Kinson Rd.
Take 5th rd on R, Kingsbere Ave.
Noel Rd is first on R.* Home-made
teas. **Adm £2.50, chd free. Suns 10,
17 July (2-5).**
Exciting small garden, 100ft x 30ft,
with big ideas. On sloping ground
many Roman features incl water and
impressive temple. Most planting is in
containers. Several new features.
Camera is a must. Come and give us
your opinion 'Is this garden over the
top?'. Featured in Gardens of Dorset.

63 'OLA'
47 Old Castle Road, Rodwell,
Weymouth DT4 8QE. Jane Uff &
Elaine Smith. *1m from Weymouth
centre. Follow signs to Portland. Off
Buxton Rd, proceed to lower end of
Old Castle Rd. Bungalow just past
Sandsfoot Castle ruins/gardens. Easy
access by foot off Rodwell Trail at
Sandsfoot Castle.* Home-made teas.

**Adm £3, chd free. Tues 24, 31 May;
14 June (2-5).**
Seaside garden with stunning views
overlooking Portland Harbour. 1930s-
designed garden, once part of
Sandsfoot Castle estate. Mixed
herbaceous borders, shrubs and
roses. Rockeries, fish pond,
vegetables, orchard and '7 dwarfs'
bank. Circular sunken stone walled
area with box bushes and statuary.
Lovingly restored from neglected
overgrown 'jungle'.

64 NEW OLD DOWN HOUSE
Horton, Wimborne BH21 7HL. Dr &
Mrs Colin Davidson. *7½ m N of
Wimborne. From Wimborne take
B3078 Wimborne to Cranborne rd. At
Horton Inn, R to Horton Village. 1st L
to North Farm. and follow track. 5 min
walk to garden down farm track. Drop
off/pick-up for those with restricted
mobility by prior arrangement, please
phone.* Home-made teas. **Adm £3,
chd free. Wed 1, Sun 12, Wed 15
June (2-5).**
Nestled down a farm track, this
³/₄ -acre garden on chalk surrounds
C18 farmhouse. Stunning views over
Horton Tower and farmland. Cottage
garden planting with formal elements,
climbing roses clothe pergola and
house walls along with stunning
wisteria sinensis and banksia rose.
Part-walled potager.

65 `NEW` **THE OLD RECTORY, MANSTON**
Sturminster Newton DT10 1EX.
Andrew & Judith Hussey. *6m S of Shaftesbury, 2¹/₂ m N of Sturminster Newton. From Shaftesbury, take B3091. On reaching Manston, past Plough Inn, L for Child Okeford on R-hand bend. Old Rectory last house on L.* Home-made teas. **Adm £3.50, chd under 12 free. Sun 12, Wed 15 June (2-5).**
Beautifully restored 5-acre garden. S-facing wall with 120ft herbaceous border edged by old brick path. Enclosed yew hedge flower garden. Wildflower meadow marked with mown paths and young plantation of mixed hardwoods. Well-maintained walled Victorian kitchen garden. Access via gravel drive.

66 **THE OLD RECTORY, NETHERBURY**
nr Beaminster DT6 5NB. Simon & Amanda Mehigan, simon@netherbury.demon.co.uk. *2m SW of Beaminster. Turn off A3066 Beaminster/Bridport rd & go over R Brit, into centre of village & up hill. The Old Rectory is on L opp church. Please park considerately in village.* Home-made teas. **Adm £4, chd free. Suns 24 Apr; 22 May (2-5.30). Visitors also welcome by appt 12 May & 8 June only by prior arrangement in writing/email.**
5-acre garden. Formal areas near house, natural planting elsewhere. Extensive bog garden with drifts of irises and primulas. Naturalised fritillaries and orchids. Woodland areas with magnolias and cornus underplanted with bulbs, wood anemones and species peonies. Thornery, beech house and topiary dragon. Steep paths and uneven steps throughout. Featured in The English Garden, Dream Gardens of England and GGG.

67 **THE OLD RECTORY, PULHAM**
DT2 7EA. Mr & Mrs N Elliott, 01258 817595. *13m N of Dorchester. 8m SE of Sherborne. On B3143 turn E at Xrds in Pulham. Signed Cannings Court.* Home-made teas May, July; teas only Aug. **Adm £4, chd free. Suns 15 May; 31 July; Wed 3 Aug (2-6). Visitors also welcome by appt Mon-Fri only incl groups.**
Four acres formal and informal gardens surround C18 rectory with superb views. Yew hedges enclose circular herbaceous borders with late summer colour. Exuberantly planted terrace with purple and white beds. Box parterres, mature trees, pond, waterfall, fernery, ha-ha, pleached hornbeams. Ten acres woodland walks. Flourishing bog garden, stream, island, awash with primulas and irises in May.

68 `NEW` **OLD SMITHY**
Ibberton DT11 0EN. Carol & Clive Carsley, 01258 817361. *9m NW of Blandford Forum. From Blandford A357 to Sturminster Newton. After 6.5m L to Okeford Fitzpaine. Follow signs to Ibberton, park in village hall, 5min walk to garden.* Cream teas in Village Hall. **Adm £3, chd free. Sun 19, Wed 22 June (2-5.30). Visitors also welcome by appt max 20.**
Worth driving twisty narrow lanes to reach rural 2¹/₂ -acre streamside garden framing thatched cottage. Back of beyond setting which inspired international best seller Mr Rosenblum's List. Succession of ponds. Mown paths. Sit beneath rustling trees. Views of Bulbarrow and church. Blackmoor panorama from church. Pub lunches.

Worth driving twisty narrow lanes to reach . . .

35 OLD STATION GARDENS
See Somerset & Bristol.

69 **THE OLD VICARAGE**
East Orchard, Shaftesbury SP7 0BA. Miss Tina Wright. *4¹/₂ m S of Shaftesbury, 3¹/₂ m N of Sturminster Newton. On B3091, Shaftesbury side of 90° bend. Drop passengers at lay-by with telephone box and park in narrow rd to East Orchard nr church.* Home-made teas.
Adm £3.50, chd free. Sun 13 Mar (1-5); Wed 11 May (2-6).
Pretty 1.7-acre country garden, recognised as a Wildlife Wonder Garden by DWT. Meandering grass paths are surrounded by naturalised early spring bulbs, shrubs and mature trees. Wild areas with wild flowers, bulbs and bug hotels. Stunning water features and natural swimming pool. Divine home-made teas, children and dogs welcome. Pond dipping available. Not suitable for wheelchairs when wet.

70 `NEW` **PARNHAM HOUSE**
Beaminster DT8 3LZ. Mr & Mrs M B Treichl. *1m S of Beaminster. Turn R off A3066 1m S Beaminster. Follow signs.* Refreshments available in Beaminster. **Adm £5, chd free. Thur 2, Sun 5 June (2-6).**
Beautifully presented spacious gardens surrounding Elizabethan Manor House. Terraced formal gardens on South side of house with topiary features leading to lake within deer park setting. Walled gardens with themed borders and vegetable area. Ancient wisterias in flower, both blue and white. Partial wheelchair access, gravel paths and steep grass slopes.

71 **PEN MILL FARM**
Penselwood, Wincanton BA9 8NF. Mr & Mrs Peter FitzGerald, 01747 840895, fitzgeraldatpen@aol.com. *1m from Stourhead, off A303 between Mere and Wincanton. Turn off A303 at B3081 junction (Gillingham/Bruton). Take turning to Penselwood from old A303. Continue along lane, 2nd L fork up narrow unsignposted hill. At grass triangle with bench, R to Zeals out of village down steep hill. Garden on R, metal railings and white gate.* Home-made teas. **Adm £3, chd free. Wed 7, Sun 11 Sept (2-5). Visitors also welcome by appt.**
2-acre mature garden planted with unusual acid-loving trees and shrubs where Dorset, Somerset and Wiltshire meet. An attractive natural landscape incl lake, stream and bog garden where shell house is under construction. Over 30 salvias and late summer border. Wheelchair access in dry weather.

PROSPECT HOUSE
See Devon.

72 ▶ Q
113 Bridport Road, Dorchester
DT1 2NH. Heather & Chris
Robinson, 01305 263088,
chriskingpin2@talktalk.net. ½ m W
of Dorchester. From A35 take B3150
into Dorchester. Approx 300m W of
Dorset County Hospital. Home-made
teas. **Adm £3, chd free. Suns 13
Mar (2-4.30); 10 Apr; 8 May; 5 June
(2-5). Visitors also welcome by
appt max 50, teas available on
request.**
A town garden for all seasons where
every inch counts. Themed rooms
transport you from hustle and bustle
of town life. Garden reflects the
owners many interests, featuring
spring bulbs, 80 clematis, water,
gravel and quiet reflective sitting
areas. New features for 2011 incl
Gothic-style folly. Featured on local
radio and in Dorset Evening Echo &
Blackmore Vale magazine.

73 ▶ NEW RESTING LAURELS
14 Chine Walk, Ferndown
BH22 8PU. Paul & Wendy Jefferies.
2m SE of Bournemouth International
Airport. From Parley Cross T-lights, off
Christchurch Rd B3073, 1st R turn.
Home-made teas. **Adm £3, chd free.
Suns 10 Apr; 4 Sept (2-5).**
The immaculate lawns set off the
planting in this ¾ -acre green oasis.
The difficult sandy soil supports many
mature trees and shrubs with good
focal points and an exciting pond
area. Organic kitchen garden. Spring
and autumn colour.

74 ▶ 357 RINGWOOD ROAD
Ferndown BH22 9AE. Lyn &
Malcolm Ovens, 01202 896071,
malcolm@mgovens.freeserve.co.uk
www.lynandmalc.co.uk. ¾ m S of
Ferndown. On A348 towards
Longham. Parking in Glenmoor Rd or
other side rds. Avoid parking on main
rd. Home-made teas. **Adm £2.50,
chd free. Sun 10 July (11-5), Wed
27 July (2-5); Sun 14 Aug (11-5).
Visitors also welcome by appt late
June to end Aug.**
Award-winning His and Hers garden,
much loved. Hers in cottage style with
clematis, phlox, lilies, roses, monarda,
encouraging butterflies and bees,
providing a riot of colour and perfume
into late summer. Through a Moorish
keyhole doorway into His exotic
garden with brugmansias, canna,
oleander, banana, dahlia and
bougainvillea. Ferndown Common

nearby. Featured in Gardens of Dorset
and Garden News and prizewinner
Ferndown in Bloom.

75 ▶ 46 ROSLIN ROAD SOUTH
Talbot Woods, Bournemouth
BH3 7EG. Mrs Penny Slade, 01202
510243. 1m NW of Bournemouth. W
of N end of Glenferness Ave in Talbot
Woods area of Bournemouth. Home-
made teas. **Adm £3, chd free. Sun
17 Apr; Sat 14, Sun 15 May; Sat
11, Sun 12 June; Sun 10 July (2-5).
Visitors also welcome by appt Apr-
July, coaches permitted.**
Plantswoman's ⅓ -acre walled town
garden showing off unusual and rare
plants. Featuring sunken gravel
garden with collection of grasses,
colourful mixed borders, raised
octagonal alpine bed, well-planted
containers, greenhouses and frames.
S-facing wall especially colourful for
April and May openings. Featured in
Garden News. Some narrow paths.

ROUSDON COTTAGE GARDENS
See Devon.

SANDLE COTTAGE
See Hampshire.

76 ▶ THE SECRET GARDEN
The Friary, Hilfield DT2 7BE. The
Society of St Francis, 01300
341345. 10m N of Dorchester, on
A352 between Sherbourne &
Dorchester. 1st L after village, 1st
turning on R signed The Friary. From
Yeovil turn off A37 signed Batcombe,
3rd turning on L. Home-made teas.
**Adm £3.50, chd free. Sat 14, Sun
15 May (2-5). Visitors also welcome
by appt.**
Small woodland garden begun in
1950s then neglected. Reclamation
began in 1984. New plantings from
modern day plant hunters. Mature
trees, bamboo, rhododendrons,
azaleas, magnolias, camellias (some
camellias grown from seed collected
in China), other choice shrubs with a
stream on all sides crossed by
bridges. Stout shoes recommended.

**77 ▶ THE SECRET GARDEN AND
SERLES HOUSE**
47 Victoria Road, Wimborne
BH21 1EN. Ian Willis, 01202
880430. Centre of Wimborne. On
B3082 W of town, very near hospital,
Westfield car park 300yds. Off-road
parking close by. Home-made teas.

Adm £3, chd free (share to
Wimborne Civic Society and for
Sept opening NADFAST). **Sun 24
July; Thur 11, Sat 13, Sun 28,
Mon 29 Aug (2.30-5.30) Evening
Opening £4, chd free Sat 23 July
(7-10) wine & nibbles; Special
Christmas Opening £4, chd free
Sat 10 Dec (2-5) Christmas cake
and tea and (6-9) mince pie &
wine. Also open Deans Court
28/29 Aug.**
Alan Titchmarsh described this
amusingly creative garden as 'one of
the best 10 private gardens in Britain'.
The ingenious use of unusual plants
complements the imaginative treasure
trove of garden objects d'art. The
enchanting house is also open.
Gentle live music accompanies your
tour as you step into a world of
whimsical fantasy that is theatrical
and unique. Santa Claus will be
visiting on 10 December. Featured in
Dorset Country Gardener. Town in
Bloom Best Garden Open to Public,
and Best Back Garden. Some shallow
steps and gravel. No wheelchair
access to house.

³⁄₄ -acre green
oasis on difficult
sandy soil . . .

78 ▶ ◆ SHERBORNE CASTLE
New Rd, Sherborne DT9 5NR. Mr J
K Wingfield Digby, 01935 813182,
www.sherbornecastle.com. ½ m E
of Sherborne. On New Road B3145.
Follow brown signs to 'Sherborne
Castles' from A30 & A352. **For
opening times and information,
please phone or see garden
website.**
40+ acres. A Capability Brown garden
with magnificent vistas across the
surrounding landscape, incl lake and
views to ruined castle. Herbaceous
planting, notable trees, mixed
ornamental planting and managed
wilderness are linked together with
lawn and pathways. 'Dry Grounds
Walk'. Partial wheelchair access,
some gravel and steep slopes.

Be tempted by a plant from a plant stall ⊛

The Mill House

79 SLAPE MANOR
Netherbury DT6 5LH. Mr & Mrs
Antony Hichens. *1m S of
Beaminster. Turn W off A3066 to
village of Netherbury. House ¹/₃ m S of
Netherbury on back rd to Bridport.*
Home-made teas. **Adm £4, chd free.
Mon 30 May (2-6).**
River valley garden with spacious
lawns and primula fringed streams
down to lake. Magnificent hostas and
gunneras, horizontal cryptomeria
Japonica 'Elegans'. Wellingtonias,
ancient wisterias and rhododendrons.
Slightly sloping lawns/grass paths,
some stone and gravel paths,
unfenced water features.
🚻 🏵 🐾 ☕

**80 ◆ SNAPE COTTAGE
PLANTSMAN'S GARDEN**
Chaffeymoor, Bourton, nr
Gillingham SP8 5BZ. Ian & Angela
Whinfield, 01747 840330
(evenings),
www.snapecottagegarden.co.uk.
*5m NW of Gillingham. At W end of
Bourton, N of A303. Opp Chiffchaffs.*
Delicious teas. **Adm £3, chd free.
For NGS: Sats, Suns 26, 27 Mar;
23, 24 Apr; 28, 29 May; 25, 26**

June; 30, 31 July; 27, 28 Aug (2-5);
25, 26 Feb (2-5) 2012. **For other
opening times and information,
please phone or see garden
website.**
Mature country garden containing
exceptional collection of hardy plants
and bulbs, artistically arranged in
informal cottage garden style,
organically managed and clearly
labelled. Specialities incl snowdrops,
hellebores, 'old' daffodils,
pulmonarias, auriculas, herbs, irises
and geraniums. Wildlife pond,
beautiful views, tranquil atmosphere.
The home of Snape Stakes plant
supports. New hay meadow.
🏵 🏵 ☕

81 ◆ SPRINGHEAD
Mill St, Fontmell Magna SP7 0NU.
The Springhead Trust Ltd (Charity
Number: 1112083), 01747 811853,
www.springheadtrust.org.uk. *4m S
of Shaftesbury. From Shaftesbury or
Blandford take A350 to Fontmell
Magna. In centre of village, turn E up
Mill St, opp PH. Follow stream up
twisty, narrow lane to Springhead on
sharp bend. Large, white thatched
house attached to mill.* **Adm £3.50,**

chd under 12 free. **For NGS: Tue
30 Aug (2-6); Wed 5 Oct (10-4). For
other opening times and
information, please phone or see
garden website.**
Large, atmospheric garden created
around lake on ancient site. Spring
water bubbling from beneath chalk
banks; walks, resting places, vistas
and great trees. Bird life on the water,
millrace, unusual planting of
herbaceous and shrub borders, bog
garden, rich autumn colour after hot
summers. New outdoor theatre,
sculpture. Children's entertainment
3pm 30 Aug. Featured in Country
Living magazine. Some gravel paths,
steep slope, wooden bridge with rails.
🚻 🏵 🏵 ☕

82 STANBRIDGE MILL
nr Gussage All Saints BH21 5EP.
Mr James Fairfax, 01258 841067,
emma@stanbridgemill.com. *7m N
of Wimborne. On B3078 to
Cranborne 150yds from Horton Inn
on Shaftesbury rd.* Home-made teas
and a selection of venison burgers
and sausages will be available. **Adm
£4.50, chd free. Wed 8 June
(10.30-5.30).** Visitors also welcome
by appt for groups min 10, max 50,
coaches permitted.
Hidden garden created in 1990s
around C18 water mill (not open) on
R Allen. Series of linked formal
gardens featuring herbaceous and iris
borders, pleached limes, white walk
and wisteria-clad pergola. 20-acre
nature reserve with reed beds and
established shelter belts. Grazing
meadows with wild flowers and flock
of rare breed Dorset Horn sheep.
Plants, local crafts and home-made
produce available. Some areas
around river not suitable for
wheelchairs.
🚻 🏵 ☕ ☎

83 UPLODERS PLACE
Uploders, Bridport DT6 4PF. Mrs
Venetia Ross Skinner. *3m E of
Bridport. From A35 to Bridport or
Dorchester take turning for Uploders
on S side of main rd. R and R again
under A35. At Crown Inn PH
(excellent food) R, 2 bends and
Private Parking notice.* Home-made
teas. **Adm £3.50, chd free. Suns
17 Apr; 22 May (2-5).**
Old yews, cedar of Lebanon and a
tulip tree form the bones of this
newish garden created from
wilderness in 1993. Trees and shrubs
with unusual barks and flowers with
rhododendrons and camellias. A quiet

Sign up to our eNewsletter for news and updates

contemplative meander with the R Asker flowing through. Spring bulbs. Wheelchair access only to terrace by request.

WATERDALE HOUSE
See Wiltshire.

WAYFORD MANOR
See Somerset & Bristol.

84▶ 24A WESTERN AVENUE
Branksome Park, Poole BH13 7AN. Mr Peter Jackson. *3m W of Bournemouth. ¹/₂ m inland from Branksome Chine beach. From S end Wessex Way (A338) take The Avenue. At T-lights turn R into Western Rd. At church turn R into Western Ave.* Home-made teas. **Adm £3.50, chd free. Sun 31 July (2-6).**
'This secluded and magical 1-acre garden captures the spirit of warmer climes and begs for repeated visits' (Gardening Which?) July sees the second flush of roses, lush tropical planting and herbaceous borders at their peak. The feature garden in the review of Gardens of Dorset, April 2010.

85▶ WESTON HOUSE
Weston St, Buckhorn Weston SP8 5HG. Mr & Mrs E A W Bullock, 01963 371005. *4m W of Gillingham, 3m SE of Wincanton. From A30 turn N to Kington Magna, continue towards Buckhorn Weston & after*

railway bridge take L turn towards Wincanton. 2nd on L is Weston House. Home-made teas by arrangement. **Adm £4, chd free. Visitors welcome by appt 16 Mar to 16 Sept, individuals and groups max 25.**
1¹/₂ -acre garden for all seasons; continuing to develop selected areas whilst keeping within the garden's character. Woodland for spring colour, walled borders, mature trees. Interesting formal and naturalistic plantings. New varieties and colour contrasts. Reworked lily bed and new bed of old roses, both gloriously scented. Mainly level lawn and paving, short slope from car park.

WHITE BARN
See Hampshire.

WILLOWS
See Hampshire.

86▶ WINCOMBE PARK
Shaftesbury SP7 9AB. John & Phoebe Fortescue. *2m N of Shaftesbury. A350 Shaftesbury to Warminster, past Wincombe Business Park, 1st R signed Wincombe & Donhead St Mary. ³/₄ m on R.* Home-made teas Sun. **Adm £3.50, chd free. Sun 15 May (2-5) Evening Opening £4.50, wine, Fri 20 May (6-8).**
Extensive mature garden with sweeping panoramic views over lake and woods. Regeneration in progress. Azaleas, rhododendrons

and camellias in flower amongst shrubs and unusual trees. Beautiful walled kitchen garden. Steep slopes and some gravel paths.

87▶ WOLVERHOLLOW
Elsdons Lane, Monkton Wyld DT6 6DA. Mr & Mrs D Wiscombe, 01297 560610. *4m N of Lyme Regis. 4m NW of Charmouth. Monkton Wyld is signed from A35 approx 4m NW of Charmouth off dual carriageway. Wolverhollow is next to the church.* Home-made teas. **Adm £3, chd free. Sun 1, Mon 2, Sun 22, Tue 24 May (11-5).** Visitors also welcome by appt.
Over 1 acre of informal garden. Lawns, with unusual summerhouse, lead past borders and rockeries to shady valley with babbling brook. Numerous paths pass wide variety of colourful and uncommon plants. An area, once field, sympathetically extends the garden with meadow and streamside planting with abundance of primulas! Must be seen.

> ### For Durham please see North East page 398

Dorset County Volunteers

County Organiser
Harriet Boileau, Witcham Farm, Rampisham, Dorchester DT2 0PX, 01935 83612, h.boileau@btinternet.com

County Treasurer
Michael Gallagher, 6 West Street, Chickerell, Weymouth DT3 4DY, 01305 772557, michael.gallagher1@virgin.net

Publicity Officer
Tom Warboys, Pineapple Group, Pineapple Business Park, Broadway Ash, Bridport DT6 5DB, 07748 456367, tom@pineapplegroup.co.uk

Booklet Editor
Judith Hussey, The Old Rectory, Manston, Sturminster Newton DT10 1EX, 01258 474673, judithhussey@hotmail.com

Assistant County Organisers
North Central Caroline Renner, Croft Farm, Fontmell Magna, Shaftesbury SP7 0NR, 01747 811140, jamesrenner@talktalk.net
North East/Ferndown Mary Angus, The Glade, Woodland Walk, Ferndown BH22 9LP, 01202 872789, mary@gladestock.co.uk
North West Victoria Baxter, Longburton House, Longburton, Sherborne DT9 5NU, 01935 815992, victoria@lborchard.co.uk
Central East Trish Neale, Hainsbury House, Hains Lane, Marnhull, Sturminster Newton DT10 1JU, 01258 820152, trishneale1@yahoo.co.uk
Central Wendy Jackson, Vine Cottage, Melcombe Bingham, Dorchester DT2 7PE, 01258 880720, wendyjacks@fsmail.net
West Central Jenie Corbett, Hollytree House, West Chelborough, Evershot, Dorchester DT2 0PY, 01935 83846, jeniecorbett@gmail.com
South Cate Hawkins, 2 Rose Cottages, Warmwell, Dorchester DT2 8HG, 01305 852141, catedereklastridge@btinternet.com
South West Christine Corson, Stoke Knapp Cottage, Norway Lane, Stoke Abbott, Beaminster DT8 3JZ, 01308 868203, christinecorson612@btinternet.com
Bournemouth, Poole and Christchurch Penny Slade, 46 Roslin Road South, Bournemouth BH3 7EG, 01202 510243

Follow us on Facebook and Twitter

ESSEX

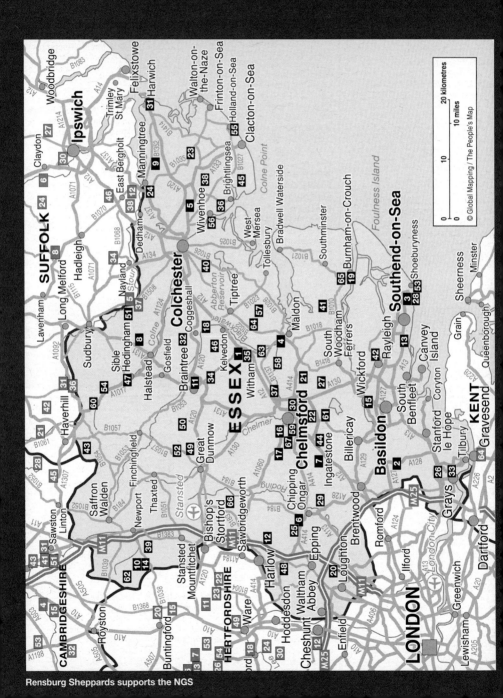

Opening Dates

February

Saturday 19
37 The Old Rectory

Sunday 20
37 The Old Rectory

March

Sunday 27
64 Wood View

April

Thursday 7
44 Peacocks

Sunday 10
3 102 Barnstaple Road
53 South Shoebury Hall

Friday 15
4 Beeleigh Abbey Gardens

Sunday 17
6 Blake Hall

Tuesday 19
41 One Brook Hall Cottages
65 Woodpeckers

Thursday 21
2 Barnards Farm
17 Dragons

Saturday 23
57 Tudor Rose Cottage

Sunday 24
57 Tudor Rose Cottage
64 Wood View

Monday 25
56 Tudor Roost

Tuesday 26
56 Tudor Roost

Thursday 28
2 Barnards Farm
67 Writtle College

Friday 29
63 Wickham Place Farm

May

Sunday 1
25 Hobbans Farm
43 Parsonage House
58 Ulting Wick
60 West End Cottage

Monday 2
18 Feeringbury Manor
21 Furzelea
49 St Helens
60 West End Cottage

Tuesday 3
41 One Brook Hall Cottages
65 Woodpeckers

Wednesday 4
50 Saling Hall

Thursday 5
2 Barnards Farm

Friday 6
63 Wickham Place Farm

Sunday 8
52 Snares Hill Cottage

Wednesday 11
50 Saling Hall

Thursday 12
2 Barnards Farm

Friday 13
63 Wickham Place Farm

Sunday 15
25 Hobbans Farm
33 McPherlynns Dream

Wednesday 18
50 Saling Hall

Thursday 19
2 Barnards Farm

Friday 20
1 Barnardiston House
35 4 Millbridge Road
63 Wickham Place Farm

Saturday 21
9 Chippins
23 Hannams Hall

Sunday 22
23 Hannams Hall
24 Hidden Oasis
46 Porters Farm

Tuesday 24
16 8 Dene Court
17 Dragons

Wednesday 25
50 Saling Hall

Thursday 26
2 Barnards Farm
16 8 Dene Court
17 Dragons

Friday 27
63 Wickham Place Farm

Saturday 28
56 Tudor Roost
62 Wickets

Sunday 29
24 Hidden Oasis
25 Hobbans Farm
36 Moverons
47 Rookwoods
56 Tudor Roost
61 West Hanningfield Hall

Monday 30
36 Moverons

June

Wednesday 1
50 Saling Hall

Thursday 2
2 Barnards Farm

Friday 3
27 The Limes (Evening)
63 Wickham Place Farm

Saturday 4
21 Furzelea
38 The Old School House

Sunday 5
21 Furzelea
27 The Limes
37 The Old Rectory
38 The Old School House
39 The Old Vicarage

Tuesday 7
16 8 Dene Court
17 Dragons
56 Tudor Roost
65 Woodpeckers

Wednesday 8
6 Blake Hall
50 Saling Hall
56 Tudor Roost

Thursday 9
2 Barnards Farm

Friday 10
63 Wickham Place Farm

Saturday 11
38 The Old School House
49 St Helens
64 Wood View

Sunday 12
1 Barnardiston House
10 Clavering Gardens
12 1 The Cottage
25 Hobbans Farm
26 Julie's Garden
35 4 Millbridge Road
38 The Old School House
64 Wood View

Tuesday 14
34 60 Mill Lane

Wednesday 15
19 4 Fernlea Road
50 Saling Hall
62 Wickets

Thursday 16
2 Barnards Farm
67 Writtle College

Friday 17
19 4 Fernlea Road
63 Wickham Place Farm

Saturday 18
38 The Old School House
54 Spencers

Sunday 19
3 102 Barnstaple Road
9 Chippins
13 Court View
30 10 Longmead Avenue
38 The Old School House
52 Snares Hill Cottage

Tuesday 21
44 Peacocks (Evening)
56 Tudor Roost
Wednesday 22
19 4 Fernlea Road
50 Saling Hall
56 Tudor Roost
Thursday 23
2 Barnards Farm
62 Wickets
Friday 24
1 Barnardiston House
35 4 Millbridge Road
63 Wickham Place Farm
Saturday 25
26 Julie's Garden
38 The Old School House
Sunday 26
2 Barnards Farm
22 Galleywood
25 Hobbans Farm
38 The Old School House
43 Parsonage House
Tuesday 28
62 Wickets
Wednesday 29
50 Saling Hall
Thursday 30
2 Barnards Farm
16 8 Dene Court

July

Friday 1
36 Moverons
63 Wickham Place Farm
Saturday 2
11 352 Coggeshall Road
62 Wickets (Evening)
Sunday 3
11 352 Coggeshall Road
29 Little Myles
Wednesday 6
50 Saling Hall
Thursday 7
2 Barnards Farm
Friday 8
1 Barnardiston House
35 4 Millbridge Road
36 Moverons
63 Wickham Place Farm
Saturday 9
56 Tudor Roost
Sunday 10
25 Hobbans Farm
30 10 Longmead Avenue
56 Tudor Roost
Wednesday 13
50 Saling Hall
Thursday 14
2 Barnards Farm
16 8 Dene Court
17 Dragons

Friday 15
15 13 Deirdre Avenue (Evening)
36 Moverons
63 Wickham Place Farm
Saturday 16
48 69 Rundells
Sunday 17
9 Chippins
13 Court View
15 13 Deirdre Avenue
53 South Shoebury Hall
60 West End Cottage
Tuesday 19
56 Tudor Roost
Wednesday 20
50 Saling Hall
56 Tudor Roost
Thursday 21
2 Barnards Farm
Friday 22
36 Moverons
63 Wickham Place Farm
Saturday 23
34 60 Mill Lane
Sunday 24
25 Hobbans Farm
34 60 Mill Lane
55 Trevanne
Tuesday 26
16 8 Dene Court
17 Dragons
Wednesday 27
50 Saling Hall
Thursday 28
2 Barnards Farm
Friday 29
20 56 Forest Drive (Evening)
36 Moverons
63 Wickham Place Farm
Saturday 30
28 Little Foxes
57 Tudor Rose Cottage
64 Wood View
Sunday 31
28 Little Foxes
57 Tudor Rose Cottage
59 45 Waterhouse Lane
64 Wood View

A veritable paradise
with woodland,
herbaceous mixed
borders, dry stream
and gravel beds,
formal topiary and
lawns . . .

August

Thursday 4
2 Barnards Farm
Saturday 6
31 447 Main Road
56 Tudor Roost
Sunday 7
31 447 Main Road
56 Tudor Roost
59 45 Waterhouse Lane
Tuesday 9
16 8 Dene Court
17 Dragons
41 One Brook Hall Cottages
Thursday 11
2 Barnards Farm
Sunday 14
13 Court View
34 60 Mill Lane
Thursday 18
2 Barnards Farm
17 Dragons
Saturday 20
56 Tudor Roost
Sunday 21
56 Tudor Roost
Thursday 25
2 Barnards Farm
Friday 26
13 Court View (Evening)
Sunday 28
14 Deers
59 45 Waterhouse Lane (Evening)

September

Thursday 1
2 Barnards Farm
20 56 Forest Drive
Friday 2
63 Wickham Place Farm
Saturday 3
57 Tudor Rose Cottage
Sunday 4
2 Barnards Farm
25 Hobbans Farm
36 Moverons
59 45 Waterhouse Lane (Evening)
Tuesday 6
20 56 Forest Drive
Friday 9
63 Wickham Place Farm
Saturday 10
49 St Helens
Sunday 11
13 Court View
46 Porters Farm
52 Snares Hill Cottage
Thursday 15
17 Dragons
44 Peacocks

Friday 16
63 Wickham Place Farm
Saturday 17
54 Spencers
Sunday 18
25 Hobbans Farm
58 Ulting Wick
60 West End Cottage
Friday 23
63 Wickham Place Farm
Tuesday 27
41 One Brook Hall Cottages
65 Woodpeckers
Friday 30
63 Wickham Place Farm

October
Sunday 2
18 Feeringbury Manor
Tuesday 11
65 Woodpeckers

Gardens open to the public
4 Beeleigh Abbey Gardens
5 Beth Chatto Gardens
32 Marks Hall Gardens & Arboretum
54 Spencers

By appointment only
7 Brookfield Cottage
8 Byndes Cottage
40 Olivers
42 Orchard Cottage
45 164 Point Clear Road
51 Shrubs Farm
66 Woolards Ash

Also open by Appointment ☎
1 Barnardiston House
2 Barnards Farm
3 102 Barnstaple Road
9 Chippins
11 352 Coggeshall Road
13 Court View
17 Dragons
18 Feeringbury Manor
20 56 Forest Drive
23 Hannams Hall
25 Hobbans Farm
26 Julie's Garden
33 McPherlynns Dream
34 60 Mill Lane
35 4 Millbridge Road
36 Moverons
38 The Old School House
41 One Brook Hall Cottages
44 Peacocks
46 Porters Farm

47 Rookwoods
48 69 Rundells
49 St Helens
50 Saling Hall
52 Snares Hill Cottage
53 South Shoebury Hall
56 Tudor Roost
57 Tudor Rose Cottage
58 Ulting Wick
60 West End Cottage
62 Wickets
63 Wickham Place Farm
64 Wood View
65 Woodpeckers

The Gardens

1 ▶ NEW ▶ **BARNARDISTON HOUSE**
35 Chipping Hill, Witham CM8 2DE. Ruth & Eric Teverson, 01376 502266, ruthteverson@yahoo.co.uk. *A12 S-bound J22 to town centre. At George PH turn R then L at 2 mini r'abouts. Garden opp White Horse PH. A12 N-bound J21, L at r'about to town centre, L at T-lights beyond White Hart Hotel. L at 2 mini r'abouts as above.* Home-made teas. **Adm £3, chd free. Combined with 4 Millbridge Road adm £5, chd free. Fri 20 May; Sun 12, Fris 24 June; 8 July (11-5). Visitors also welcome by appt.**
Medium sized town garden created over last 14yrs. It boasts a magnificent magnolia, lawns, deep borders, raised beds and seating areas. The wide range of unusual plants incl heritage vegetables, fruit and plants that enjoy hot and dry conditions. Partial wheelchair access.
&♿ ✿ ☕ ☎

2 ▶ **BARNARDS FARM**
Brentwood Road, West Horndon, Brentwood CM13 3LX. Bernard & Sylvia Holmes & The Christabella Charitable Trust, 01277 811262, sylvia@barnardsfarm.eu, www.barnardsfarm.eu. *5m S of Brentwood. On A128 1¹/₂ m S of A127 Halfway House flyover. From the junction continue on A128 under the railway bridge. Garden on R just past bridge.* Home-made teas. Light Lunches on Thursdays. **Adm £6, chd free (Thurs), adm £7.50, chd free (Suns) (share to St Francis Church, West Horndon). Thurs, 21 Apr to 1 Sept; (11-4.30); Suns 26 June; 4 Sept (2-5.30). Visitors also welcome by appt weekdays; group visits of 25+ with catering.**
17 hectare, year round interest garden and woodland. Unfenced ponds.Japanese and vegetable gardens, sculpture and woodland walks. Railway. National Malus collection, (blossom April-May) On Sundays: Bernard's 3pm sculpture tour; veteran and vintage vehicle collection; 1920s cycle shop.Our website has a full description, up to date images and news. Picnic areas, ice cream; Sundays: Model T Ford driving and archery lessons.Car park for disabled drivers/passengers. Featured in Yellow Advertiser; Thurrock Gazette; BBC Look East.
& ✿ NCCPG ☕ ☎

3 ▶ NEW ▶ **102 BARNSTAPLE ROAD**
Thorpe Bay SS1 3PW. Ann Safwat, 01702 586615, annstripe@hotmail.com. *2m E of Southend. From A127 follow signs to Shoebury (A1159). At end of Royal Artillery Way take RH lane, straight over r'about into Thorpe Hall Ave. Barnstaple Rd 3rd rd on L. From A13 follow signs to seafront, past Kursall towards Shoebury. At mini r'about L into Thorpe Hall Ave, then R into Barnstaple Rd. Nr Thorpe Bay Stn.* Home-made teas. **Adm £3, chd free. Suns 10 Apr; 19 June (2-5). Also open South Shoebury Hall (Apr), Court View (June). Visitors also welcome by appt May to Aug, refreshments available.**
An ordinary façade belies a plantaholic's secret garden with appeal for everyone. A veritable paradise with woodland, herbaceous mixed borders, dry stream and gravel beds, formal topiary and lawns. A productive area of fruit and vegetables plus greenhouses with stunning cacti. Massed floral display in April, roses in June.
✿ ☕ ☎

Unusual plants including heritage vegetables, fruit and plants that enjoy hot and dry conditions . . .

4 NEW ♦ BEELEIGH ABBEY GARDENS
Abbey Turning, Beeleigh, Maldon CM9 6LL. Christopher & Catherine Foyle, 07779 223321, www.visitmaldon.co.uk/beeleigh-abbey. *1m NW of Maldon. From central Maldon take London Rd. Up past cemetery (on L). 1st R into Abbey Turning. Continue straight down hill 700yds - 1st R into private rd. Access too narrow for coaches.* **Adm £4, chd free. For NGS: Fri 15 Apr (10.30-3.30). For other opening times and information, please phone or see garden website.**
Three secluded acres of spacious gardens in rural historic setting. Mature trees surround variety of planting and water features, woodland walks underplanted with bulbs leading to tidal river, cottage garden, orchard, wild flower meadow, formal rose garden, wisteria walk, magnolia trees, lawn with 85yd long mixed herbaceous border. Scenic backdrop of remains of C12 abbey incorporated into private house (not open). Resident peacocks and specimen trees incl tulip and indian bean.
&. ⊛ ☕

Scenic backdrop of remains of C12 abbey incorporated into private house (not open). Resident peacocks and specimen trees including tulip and indian bean . . .

5 ♦ BETH CHATTO GARDENS
Elmstead Market, Near Colchester CO7 7DB. Mrs Beth Chatto, 01206 822007, www.bethchatto.co.uk. *¼ m E of Elmstead Market. On A133 Colchester to Clacton Rd in village of Elmstead Market.* Light Refreshments. **For opening times and information please phone or visit garden website.**
Internationally famous gardens, including dry, damp and woodland areas. The result of fifty years of hard work and the application of the huge body of plant knowledge possessed by Beth Chatto and her late husband Andrew. Visitors cannot fail to be affected by the peace and beauty of the garden. Large plant nursery and modern Tea Room. Disabled WC and parking. Featured in Daily Telegraph, RHS The Garden, Gardens Illustrated & on Channel 4 The Landscape Man with Matthew Wilson.
&. ⊛ ☕

BEVILLS
See Suffolk.

6 NEW BLAKE HALL
Bobbingworth CM5 0DG. Mr & Mrs H Capel Cure. *10m W of Chelmsford. Just off A414 between Four Wantz r'about in Ongar & Talbot r'about in North Weald. Signed on A414.* Home-made teas served in C17 barn. **Adm £4, chd free. Sun 17 Apr (11-4); Wed 8 June (11-5).**
25 acres of mature gardens, arboretum with broad variety of specimen trees, spectacular rambling roses. Traditional formal rose garden and herbaceous border. Tremendous display of spring flowering bulbs - particularly daffodils. Some gravel paths.
&. ☕

BROMLEY HALL
See Hertfordshire.

7 BROOKFIELD COTTAGE
Hardings Lane, Mill Green CM4 0HZ. Mr Stephen & Carol Poulton, 07719 329369, carolpoulton@btinternet.com. *1m N of Ingatestone. From Ingatestone High St B1002 turn into Fryerning Lane. Turn R at end of lane into Mill Green Rd. The Cricketers PH approx ¼ m on RH-side. Park in lay-by opp PH or in nearby Mill Green Common car park. The garden is approx 5mins walk away down Hardings Lane L of the PH. Please do not drive or park in Hardings Lane as private rd and there is no room to park:* Light refreshments & teas, available by arrangement. **Adm £3.50, chd free. Visitors welcome by appt individual or groups.**
From a formal white topiary garden to a woodland retreat this ⅓ acre garden has been developed by present owners over 20yrs into a series of 'gardens'. Landscaping and mixed planting has been used to create a gardener's garden with all-yr round interest in both colour and form. The garden is set in the conservation area of Mill Green, close to St Peter's Way which is part of a circular country walk popular with ramblers. Nr by are 3 local PHs which offer meals and snacks to suit all tastes and pockets.
☕ ☎

8 BYNDES COTTAGE
Pebmarsh, nr Halstead CO9 2LZ. David & Margaret MacLennan, 01787 269500, byndes2@btinternet.com. *2m N of Halstead. On A131 from Halstead to Sudbury, take R turning signed Pebmarsh & Bures. 3rd house on L before Pebmarsh village round sharp bend.* **Adm £5, chd free. Visitors welcome by appt. Guided tour by owners for groups of 10 minimum. Refreshments included.**
Impressive and still developing garden of 7 acres in rural setting. Planted and maintained by owners with emphasis on labour saving maintenance, conservation and adaptation to evolving climatic conditions. Diverse planting styles, choice plants and habitats. Recent 5-acre arboretum with large population of bee orchids. National Collection of Galanthus.
&. ⊛ NCCPG ☕ ☎

9 CHIPPINS
Heath Road, Bradfield CO11 2UZ. Kit & Ceri Leese, 01255 870730, ceri.leese@sky.com. *3m E of Manningtree. On B1352, take main rd through village. Bungalow is directly opp primary school.* Home-made teas. **Adm £3, chd free. Sat 21 May; Suns 19 June; 17 July (11-5). Also open Hannams Hall 21 May. Visitors also welcome by appt May to July only.**
Artist's garden and plantaholic's paradise packed with interest. Beginning with irises, herbaceous geraniums, hostas and alliums. Featuring meandering stream. Explosion of colour and scent, abundance of tubs, hanging baskets. Wide borders with hemerocallis, swathes of lilies, dahlias, salvias, including Streptocarpus, aeonium, agaves. Exhibition of paintings and photographs by Kit Leese, featuring the garden and local scenes. Featured in Garden News.
&. ⊛ ☕ ☎

GROUP OPENING

CLAVERING GARDENS

CB11 4PX. *7m N of Bishop's Stortford. On B1038. Turn W off B1383 at Newport.* Home-made teas at Piercewebbs. **Combined adm £5, chd free. Sun 12 June (2-5).**

DEERS
Mr & Mrs S H Cooke
(See separate entry)
Also open Sun 28 Aug.

PIERCEWEBBS
Mr & Mrs B R William-Powlett

Popular village with many C16 and C17 timber-framed dwellings. Beautiful C14 church, village green with thatched cricket pavilion and pitch. Deers (see separate entry) for 9 acres, judged by visitors to be a very romantic garden. Piercewebbs is a formal old walled garden with shrubs, lawns, ha-ha, yew with topiary and stilt hedges, pond and trellised rose garden. Extensive views over the countryside. Jamie Oliver was brought up in Clavering where his parents still run The Cricketers PH. Wheelchair access to Deers.

♿ 🐕 ✿ ☕

352 COGGESHALL ROAD

Braintree CM7 9EH. Sau Lin Goss, 01376 329753, Richard.goss@talktalk.net. *15m W of Colchester. 10m N of Chelmsford. From M11 J8 take A120 Colchester. Follow A120 to Braintree r'about (McDonalds). 1st exit into Cressing Rd follow to T-lights. R into Coggeshall Rd. 500yds on R opp bus company.* **Adm £2.50, chd free. Sat 2, Sun 3 July (1.30-5). Visitors also welcome by appt, min group 8.** Sau Lin arrived from Hong Kong to become enthralled with English gardening. 'This is my little heaven', she says of her garden which has various themed areas, perennials, roses and many other plants. Japanese style mixed border garden, fruit trees and shrubs. Various seating and relaxing areas, fish pond with many plants and wildlife. Mediterranean style patio area, with water feature, and numerous patio plants of varying sizes. Many relaxing seating areas. Mature natural fish pond, mature trees, shrubs & roses. Delicious home made cakes & refreshments.

♿ 🐕 ✿ ☕ 📞

45 Waterhouse Lane

🔟 1 THE COTTAGE

Housham Tye, Harlow CM17 0NY. Maria Miola & Cyril Cleary. *3m outside Old Harlow. Leave J7 M11, travel N on A414. At 4th r'about with B183 turn R, then R at 2nd r'about. At T-junction turn L signed The Matchings. After 1m turn R signed Housham Tye, High Laver & Carters Green.* Home-made teas. **Adm £2.50, chd free. Sun 12 June (2-6).** Charming cottage garden of approx ¼ acre with unusual and interesting perennials and shrubs. Natural pond and woodland area contrasts with the gravel garden and lawn. A selection of tree ferns, acers and palms are also displayed.

✿ ☕ 📞

🔟 COURT VIEW

276 Manchester Drive, Leigh-on-Sea SS9 3ES. Ray Spencer & Richard Steers, 01702 713221, arjeyeski@courtview.demon.co.uk. *4m W of Southend, off Kingswood Chase. From A127 London: Under A129 to T-lights. R to Leigh-on-Sea. Right at T-lights. At r'about straight* on. 3rd road on R into Kingswood Ch. Over Bonchurch Ave, L to Manchester Dr.From A13: 3rd rd W from Waitrose turn N into Kingswood Ch, R into Manchester Dr. Home-made teas. Wine for evening opening. **Adm £3.50, chd free. Suns 19 June; 17 July; 14 Aug (1-5); Evening Opening Fri 26 Aug (7.30-10); Sun 11 Sept (2-5). Also open South Shoebury Hall & 102 Barnstaple Road 19 June. Visitors also welcome by appt June to September (incl). Talk and cream tea for groups up to 20. Larger groups with refreshments.** Front garden provides seasonal colour with mixed planting. Clematis and fern walk leads to rear garden. Bold leaved and exotic species. Towering bamboos, palms and bananas. Unusual flowers add to tropical feel. Spiritual sculpture and water add interest. This urban oasis shows how a small suburban garden can appear much larger. Illuminated evening opening with refreshments.

✿ ☕ 📞

14 ▶ DEERS

Clavering CB11 4PX. Mr & Mrs S H Cooke. *7m N of Bishop's Stortford. On B1038. Turn W off B1383 (old A11) at Newport.* Home-made teas. **Adm £5, chd free (share to Clavering Jubilee Field). Sun 28 Aug (2-5). Open with Clavering Gardens Sun 12 June.**
9 acres. Judged by visitors to be a very romantic garden. Shrub and herbaceous borders; 3 ponds with water lilies; old roses in formal garden; pool garden; walled vegetable garden; moon gate; field and woodland walks. Plenty of seats to enjoy the tranquillity of the garden. Dogs on leads.
& 🏡 ☕

Shaded seating areas in this garden allow visitors to watch dovecote and bird boxes . . . admire 'Gladys' in her reflective pool . . .

15 ▶ 13 DEIRDRE AVENUE

Wickford SS12 0AX. Roy & Anne Kebbell. *9m S of Chelmsford. ¹/₃ m from Wickford town centre off the Wickford - Billericay rd (A129 London Rd). From High St (Halls CNR) Deirdre Ave is 4th turning on L.* Home-made teas (Sun). Wine (Fri). **Adm £2.50, chd free. Evening Opening wine, Fri 15 July (6-9), Sun 17 July (11-4).**
Attractive ¹/₄ acre town garden with a wide range of plants incl dahlias, hostas, ferns and climbers. Features pond, stream, bog garden, ivy tunnel and secret corners. Extensive organic vegetable garden featuring a broad range of crops grown together with colourful flowers.
✿ ☕

16 ▶ NEW 8 DENE COURT

Chignall Road, Chelmsford CM1 2JQ. Mrs Sheila Chapman. *W of Chelmsford (Parkway). Take A1060 Roxwell Rd. For 1m. Turn R at T-lights*

into Chignall Rd. Dene Court 3rd exit on R. Parking in Chignall Rd. **Adm £3, chd free. Tues, Thurs 24, 26 May; 7, 30 June; 14, 26 July; 9 Aug (2-5). Also open Dragons (not 30 June).**
Beautifully maintained and designed compact garden (250sq yards). Circular lawn, long pergola and walls festooned with roses and climbers. Owner is well known RHS gold medal-winning exhibitor (now retired), with large selection of unusual clematis. Densely-planted colour co-ordinated perennials add interest from May to Sept.
✿

17 ▶ DRAGONS

Boyton Cross, Chelmsford CM1 4LS. Mrs Margot Grice, 01245 248651, mandmdragons@tiscali.co.uk. *5m W of Chelmsford. On A1060. ¹/₂ m W of The Hare PH or ¹/₂ m E of India Lounge.* Teas. **Adm £3.50, chd free. Thur, Tues 21 Apr; 24, 26 May; 7 June; 14, 26 July; 9, 18 Aug; 15 Sept (10-5). Also open 8 Dene Court 24, 26 May, 7 June,14, 26 July, 9 Aug. Visitors also welcome by appt.**
A plantswoman's ²/₃ -acre garden, planted to encourage wildlife. Sumptuous colour-themed borders with striking plant combinations, featuring specimen plants, fernery, clematis, mature dwarf conifers and grasses. Meandering paths lead to ponds, patio, scree garden and small vegetable garden. 2 summerhouses, one overlooking stream and farmland.
✿ ☕ ☎

18 ▶ FEERINGBURY MANOR

Coggeshall Road, Feering CO5 9RB. Mr & Mrs Giles Coode-Adams, 01376 561946, sonia@coode-adams.demon.co.uk. *12m SW of Colchester. Between Coggeshall & Feering on Coggeshall Rd, 1m from Feering.* **Adm £5, chd free. Mon 2 May; Sun 2 Oct (2-5). Visitors also welcome by appt.**
In April and May, rivers of pink and white tulips under blossom. In June old roses, peonies and wild flowers lead to July, with colourful day lilies, tall daisies and crocosmias taking over. October, a burst of different purples and pinks with michaelmas daises at their peak. Arbours, trellis, gates and sculpture all made by artist Ben Coode-Adams. Featured in Gardeners World, Country Living. Some steep slopes.
& ☎

19 ▶ 4 FERNLEA ROAD

Burnham-on-Crouch CM0 8EJ. Frances & Andrew Franklin, www.franklins.f2s.com. *Take B1010 to Burnham-on-Crouch. Cross the railway bridge then take 4th turn on R, Hillside Rd. Fernlea Rd 2nd L, no.4 nr end of cul de sac on L.* Home-made teas. **Adm £3, chd free. Wed 15, Fri 17, Wed 22 June (2-5).**
Mediterranean cum Moroccan oasis on edge of riverside park. Small (50ft x 50ft) back garden with vine-covered pergola, tranquil water features, mosaics, sculptures, dense planting featuring some unusual varieties. Drought tolerant, low maintenance and with various seating areas (incl a Moroccan style tent!), this garden is for relaxing in. Featured in Good Housekeeping, The Mail on Sunday and Dream Gardens of England: 100 Inspirational Gardens.
& 🏡 ☕

20 ▶ NEW 56 FOREST DRIVE

Theydon Bois CM16 7EZ. John & Barbara, 01992 814459. *2m S of Epping. J26 M25 onto A121 to Wake Arms r'about. 2nd exit B172 to Theydon Bois. Turn L at Bull PH, 1st L into Forest Drive.* Self service teas available in Summerhouse. **Adm £3, chd free. Evening Opening Fri 29 July (2-9); Thur 1, Tue 6 Sept (12-5). Visitors also welcome by appt July to Sept, max 20.**
Elegant, tranquil garden [60ft x 80ft] set on sloping site developed by owners since 1996. Immaculately maintained borders feature specimen trees and plants. Shaded seating areas in this surprisingly secluded garden allow visitors to sit and watch dovecote and bird boxes. Sit on patio and admire 'Gladys' in her reflective pool.
✿ ☕ ☎

21 ▶ FURZELEA

Bicknacre Road, Danbury CM3 4JR. Avril & Roger Cole-Jones. *4m E of Chelmsford, 4m W of Maldon. A414 to Danbury. In village centre (Eves Corner) turn S into Mayes Lane. Take R past Cricketers PH, then L onto Bicknacre Rd. Parking in NT car park. Garden on R.* Home-made teas. **Adm £3, chd free. Mon 2 May (2-5); Sat 4, Sun 5 June (1-5). Also open The Limes 5 June.**
Country garden with a hint of romance in the air. Planted for scent and colour,in ²/₃ acre. Sumptuous mixed borders overflowing with tulips (spring opening), geraniums, peonies,

Be tempted by a plant from a plant stall ✿

poppies, clematis. Roses and yet more roses, clipped box, chamomile steps, lily pond, thatched summerhouse, 'white'garden, topiary, tropical themed courtyard, terrace overflowing with pots, its all here. Delicious homemade cakes for tea. Opp Danbury Common (NT), nr Danbury Lakes and a short drive from RHS Hyde Hall.

GROUP OPENING

22 GALLEYWOOD
Chelmsford CM2 8PD. *3m S of Chelmsford. Exit J16 A12. B1007 go to Eagle PH t-lights, turn L for Martingales in Birches Walk. Turn R at T-lights then 2nd R Well Lane, 1st L Attwoods Close. For Cannon Leys carry on down Watchouse Rd, 5th turn on R Arnold Way.* **Combined adm £5, chd free. Sun 26 June (2-6).**

> **NEW 24 ATTWOODS CLOSE**
> Wendy & John Cummin
>
> **2 CANNON LEYS**
> Penny & George Jennings
>
> **MARTINGALES**
> John & Jenny Perks.
> *Birches Walk off Margaretting Rd*

3 totally different small gardens. 24 Attwoods Close is a small 'Jungle' garden, full of colour and mixed foliage. See the rare 'Man tree' and walk under the Indian Bean tree. A photographers dream. Bring your camera. 2 Cannon Leys is 50ft x 40ft S-facing plantaholics garden packed with unusual perennials and shrubs. Pond with large fish, water feature, slate scree and masses of pots of large hostas, acers, unusual trees etc. Large blue spruce in middle of small lawn, clematis and old fashioned roses. Martingales is an artist's garden paved courtyard garden 60ft x 25ft, N-facing. Separated into 3 small areas densely planted with acers, small hostas and ferns. Water feature, arbour with lead glass panels. On show is a Victorian Style Dolls House.

20 GOLDHAZE CLOSE
See London.

GREAT THURLOW HALL
See Suffolk.

17 GREENSTONE MEWS, E11
See London.

23 HANNAMS HALL
Thorpe Road, Tendring CO16 9AR. Mr & Mrs W Gibbon, 01255 830292, w.gibbon331@btinternet.com. *10m E of Colchester. From A120 take B1035 at Horsley Cross, through Tendring Village (approx 3m) pass Cherry Tree PH on R, after 1/3 m over small bridge 1st house L.* **Adm £3.50, chd free. Sat 21, Sun 22 May (2-6).** Also open **Chippins** 21 May & **Hidden Oasis** 22 May. Visitors also welcome by appt no coaches.
C17 house (not open) set in 6 acres of formal and informal gardens and grounds with extensive views over open countryside. Herbaceous borders and shrubberies, many interesting trees incl flowering paulownias. Lawns and mown walks through wild grass and flower meadows, woodland walks, lovely autumn colour for visitors by appt, ponds and stream. Walled vegetable potager and orchard.

24 NEW HIDDEN OASIS
19 Parrington Way, Lawford, Manningtree CO11 2LZ. P Byford. *8m NE of Colchester. Opp Venture Centre on Wignall St A137, turn into Parrington Way and follow signs to end. Parking at Venture Centre.* Teas. **Adm £3, chd free. Suns 22, 29 May (11-5).** Also open **Hannams Hall** 22 May.
Set in 1½ acres with an historic ¾-acre carp lake with period features. Beautiful mature trees with many shrubs and plants. Fantastic Wisteria and magnolia as well as a biodiversity area. Not suitable for young children (some steep slopes and deep water).

25 HOBBANS FARM
Stoney Lane, Bobbingworth, Ongar CM5 0LZ. John & Ann Webster, 01277 890245. *10m W of Chelmsford. N of A414 between Ongar Four Wantz r'about & N Weald 'Talbot' r'about, turn R past Blake Hall. 1st farm entrance on R after St Germain's Church.* Cream teas. **Adm £3, chd free. Suns 1, 15, 29 May; 12, 26 June; 10, 24 July; 4, 18 Sept (2-5).** Visitors also welcome by appt.
Romantic, tranquil gardens. Herbaceous treasures, honeysuckle, roses, clematis clamber over trees, walls and arches. Crab apples underplanted with narcissi, unusual trees. Walk through meadows to wild garden, wood, pond with bridge to

ancient oak. May - blossom, bulbs. June - riot of roses, peonies, aquilegia, geraniums. July - clambering clematis. Sept - mellow fruitfulness, rich colours. House currenty under renovation. Some narrow paths.

> Quirky, unusual small garden . . . a surprise around every corner, including African, Australian, Indian and beach artefacts and themes . . .

26 NEW JULIE'S GARDEN
163 Whitmore Avenue, Stifford Clays, Grays RM16 2HT. Julie Sadgrove & Harry Edwards, 01375 377780, juliesadgrove@blueyonder.co.uk. *2m E of Lakeside shopping centre. Exit A13 at Grays, take Orsett turn off r'about, follow Stifford Clays Rd for a few hundred metres, turn R into Kingsman Drive, then L into Prince Phillip Ave. At T-junction L into Whitmore Ave. 100 metres on L.* Light refreshments & home-made teas. **Adm £2.50, chd free. Sun 12, Sat 25 June (12-4).** Visitors also welcome by appt in July.
Now for something different. Quirky, unusual small garden (100' x 30') where art and plants combine to bring colour, life and interest. A personal constantly-evolving space which reflects the owners' numerous, varied interests and talents, made using recycled resources. A surprise around every corner, incl African, Australian, Indian and beach artefacts and themes.

42 LATIMER ROAD, E7
See London.

27 THE LIMES
The Tye, East Hanningfield CM3 8AA. Stan & Gil Gordon. *6m SE of Chelmsford. In centre of East Hanningfield across village green from The Windmill PH.* Home-made teas.

Martingales

 Church). Home-made teas. **Adm £3.50, chd £1. Sun 3 July (11-4).** Romantic garden surrounded by wild flowers and grasses, set in 3 acres. Full borders, hidden features, meandering paths, pond, hornbeam pergola and stream. Herb garden, full of nectar-rich and scented herbs, used for handmade herbal cosmetics. Asian garden with pots, statues and bamboo, ornamental vegetable plot, woven willow Gothic window feature and wire elephant.

30 NEW 10 LONGMEAD AVENUE

Great Baddow, Chelmsford CM2 7EF. Jan & Alan Parsons. *1m E of Chelmsford town centre. At Army & Navy r'about exit Great Baddow. 1st L turn into Meadgate Ave follow ¹/₂ m.* Home-made teas. **Adm £3, chd free. Suns 19 June; 10 July (11-4).**
90ft S-facing family garden. Raised beds and pretty mixed borders surround 3 levels and 2 pergolas, with many varied and unusual plants. A water feature tops off the relaxed atmosphere of this beautiful garden. Come and enjoy homemade cakes and a cup of tea in this lovely space.

31 NEW 447 MAIN ROAD

Dovercourt, Harwich CO12 4HB. J Shrive & S McGarry. *1m out of Dovercourt town centre. Follow A120 from Colchester to Harwich. Straight over Churchill r'about at Ramsey onto bypass. Turn R at next r'about up Parkeston Hill, turn R at mini r'about. 300yds on LH-side.* Light refreshments & home-made teas. **Adm £3, chd free. Sat 6 Aug (11-5), Sun 7 Aug (11-4).**
Family town garden with interest for young and old alike, colourful perennial borders with immaculate lawn leading to a tropical oasis complete with Treasure Island. Cannas, bamboo and specimen palms abound lending dramatic height and structure. The decked dining area encompasses a huge stand of banana amidst which nestles a water feature.

32 ◆ MARKS HALL GARDENS & ARBORETUM

Coggeshall CO6 1TG. Thomas Phillips Price Trust, 01376 563796, www.markshall.org.uk. *1¹/₂ m N of Coggeshall. Follow brown & white*

Adm £3.50, chd free. Evening Opening wine, Fri 3 June (6-9); Sun 5 June (2-6). Also open Furzelea 5 June.
Plant lovers' 1-acre well-established 'garden of many rooms' surrounding Victorian house (not open). Owner-designed to lure you round this tranquil garden with its mature trees, interesting planting of shrubs, perennials, grasses, roses and clematis. Also orchard, soft fruit and vegetable area, formal garden and courtyard pots. Grass paths except for gravel drive and formal garden.

28 LITTLE FOXES

Marcus Gardens, Thorpe Bay SS1 3LF. Mrs Dorothy Goode. *2¹/₂ m E of Southend. From Thorpe Bay stn (S-side) proceed E, take 4th on R into Marcus Ave then 2nd L into Marcus Gdns.* Home-made teas. **Adm £3, chd free. Sat 30, Sun 31 July (2-5).**
Award winning ¹/₃ -acre garden offering relaxing afternoon in beautiful surroundings. 7 large island beds packed with flowers and foliage. 400ft of herbaceous and shrubs borders. Ornamental trees and conifers provide seclusion. July features lilies, agapanthus, dahlias, alstromerias and rarely seen burgundy eucomis. Pretty water feature. Many colourful containers incl 25 hostas. A stroll by the sea is only minutes away. Featured on BBC Radio Essex.

29 LITTLE MYLES

Ongar Road, Stondon Massey, nr Brentwood CM15 0LD. Judy & Adrian Cowan. *1¹/₂ m SE of Chipping Ongar. Turn off A128 at Stag PH, Marden Ash, (Ongar) towards Stondon Massey. Over bridge, 1st house on R after S bend. (400yds the Ongar side of Stondon Massey*

tourism signs from A120 Coggeshall by pass. **Adm £4, chd £1, concessions £3.50. For opening times and information, please phone or see garden website.** The walled garden is a unique blend of traditional long borders within C17 walls and 5 contemporary gardens. Inventive landscaping, grass sculpture and stunningly colourful mass plantings. On opp lake bank is millennium walk designed for winter shape, scent and colour surrounded by over 100 acres of arboretum, incl species from all continents. New bridge across the brook making central area usable whatever the weather, from snowdrops to autumn colour.

33 MCPHERLYNNS DREAM
39 Palmers Avenue, Grays RM17 5TX. Martin & Linda McPherson, 01375 411353. ¹/₂ m E of Grays town centre. From Grays follow Orsett Rd E to Palmers Ave (A1013), or from A13 at Brentwood Rd junction follow A1013 W to Grays, this becomes Palmers Ave, just E of town centre. **Adm £3, chd free. Sun 15 May (12-5). Visitors also welcome by appt.**
A side walkway leads to the courtyard, with split levels featuring a sunken pond, mixed border and over 100 pots of hostas, ferns and topiary. An arch leads to a semi-formal garden with deep herbaceous borders, summerhouse and wildlife pond. Walk under Rambling Rector into the vegetable garden.

34 60 MILL LANE
Tye Green, Cressing CM77 8HW. Pauline & Arthur Childs, 01376 325904. 2m S of Braintree. 15m W of Colchester, 5m N of Witham. From M11 J8 take A120 Colchester, follow A120 to Braintree r'about, then take B1018 to Witham approx ³/₄ m (Tye Green), turn R into Mill Lane 400yds on L. House facing you on green. Home-made teas. **Adm £2.50, chd free. Tue 14 June; Sat 23, Suns 24 July; 14 Aug (2-5). Visitors also welcome by appt June to Aug.**
A hidden little gem. Plantaholic's paradise packed with interesting flowers and ferns. Very colourful garden with hostas, penstemons, fuchsias and clematis in profusion, some rather unusual. Three water features add a sense of calm. Relax on patio with delicious home-made

cakes while admiring our beautiful containers, topiary and hanging baskets. Cressing Temple Barns nearby.

35 4 MILLBRIDGE ROAD
Witham CM8 1HB. Sebastian & Andrew, 01376 503112. Exit A12 Witham into Witham Town Centre. Opp HSBC & Barclays Bank is Guithavon St take this rd at the end go straight over Mini r'abouts into Guithavon Road. Millbridge Rd is first on the R. Home-made teas at Barnardiston House. **Adm £3, chd free. Combined with Barnardiston House adm £5, chd free. Fri 20 May (12.30-5); Sun 12 (11-5), Fris 24 June; 8 July (12.30-5). Visitors also welcome by appt.**
Inspirational town garden 129ft x 29ft. Designed into themed areas, to maximise space. Wander through Mediterranean style, British theme, then an Oasis of tranquillity. Mixed borders, perennials, architectural foliage, bamboos & bananas all jostle for position. Large fish pond and hidden features. Several seating areas for contemplation.

36 MOVERONS
Brightlingsea CO7 0SB. Lesley Orrock & Payne Gunfield, 01206 305498, lesleyorrock@me.com, www.moverons.co.uk. 7m SE of Colchester. B1027. Turn R in Thorrington onto B1029 signed Brightlingsea. At old church turn R signed Moverons Farm, follow lane & garden signs for approx 1m. Home-made teas. **Adm £4, chd free. Sun 29, Mon 30 May; Fris 1, 8, 15, 22, 29 July; Sun 4 Sept (11-5). Visitors also welcome by appt groups of 10+.**
Beautiful, peaceful country garden with stunning estuary views. Redeveloped tennis court with raised beds and reflection pool. Courtyard garden, dry stream, natural ponds and a wide variety of planting for varied conditions. A growing collection of decorative and practical metalwork. Magnificent mature native trees give this garden real presence.

37 THE OLD RECTORY
Church Road, Boreham CM3 3EP. Sir Jeffery & Lady Bowman. 4m NE of Chelmsford. Take B1137 Boreham Village, turn into Church Rd at the Lion PH. ¹/₂ m along on R opp

church. Home-made teas. Basic refreshments in garage in February. Tea on terrace and lawn in summer. **Adm £3 (Feb), £3.50 (June), chd free. Sat 19, Sun 20 Feb; (12-3); Sun 5 June (2-5).**
2¹/₂ -acre garden surrounding C15 house (not open). Ponds, stream, with bridges and primulas, small meadow and wood with interesting trees and shrubs, herbaceous borders with emphasis on complimentary colours also vegetable garden. February opening for crocus, snowdrops and cyclamen. First time February opening for species crocus naturalised in grass also snowdrops for sale 'in the green'. Thick gravel drive but wheelchairs can go on lawn to see large part of garden including crocus.

Beautiful, peaceful country garden with stunning estuary views. Redeveloped tennis court with raised beds and reflection pool . . .

38 THE OLD SCHOOL HOUSE
Plough Road, Great Bentley CO7 8LD. Georgie Roberts, 01206 251865, groberts@essex.ac.uk. 6m E of Colchester. In Great Bentley at staggered junction in village, turn across the village green signed Angers Green & the station. House, red brick Victorian on R after shops, next to primary school. Home-made teas. **Adm £3, chd free. Sats, Suns 4, 5, 11, 12, 18, 19, 25, 26 June (2-5). Visitors also welcome by appt.**
Enclosed, formally planned garden around a long box-edged axis running from a paved and gravelled seating area at the back of the house. Within the formal structure planting is relaxed incl pots around the seating area, mixed borders (emphasis on roses). A ruin is surrounded by ferns, other features incl ponds, fountains, small birch grove and French greenhouse.

39 THE OLD VICARAGE
Church End, Rickling CB11 3YL. Mr & Mrs C Firmin. *5m N of Stansted Mountfitchet. B1383 towards Newport. Turn L to Rickling Green through village towards church (1¹/₂ m). Garden on rd to Wicken & Newport.* Home-made & cream teas. **Adm £4, chd free (share to Rickling Church). Sun 5 June (2-5).**
Early Victorian vicarage (not open) surrounded by 1¹/₂ acres of mature gardens. Old walls and well-established hedges provide shelter and excellent backdrop to large closely planted borders, filled with a mixture of shrubs, herbaceous plants and old roses. Lily pond, formal rose garden and walled vegetable garden. Footpath from garden through field to beautiful Norman Church (open). Garden close to Cricketers PH, owned by Jamie Oliver's parents. Gravel paths.

&. ❀ ☕

40 OLIVERS
Olivers Lane, Colchester CO2 0HJ. Mr & Mrs D Edwards, 01206 330575, gay.edwards@virgin.net. *3m SW of Colchester. Between B1022 & B1026. From zoo continue 1m towards Colchester. Turn R at r'about (Cunobelin Way) & R into Olivers Lane. From Colchester via Maldon Rd turn L at r'about, R into Olivers Lane.* **Adm £4, chd free. Visitors welcome by appt, at any time of year. Tour and refreshments for larger groups.**
Peaceful wooded garden overlooking Roman river valley. Dramatic bedding, yew backed borders closely planted with wide variety of plants. Refreshments on terrace of C18 redbrick house (not open) overlooking lakes, lawns and meadow. Woodland with fine trees, underplanted with shrubs and carpeted with a mass of spring bulbs and bluebells.

&. ❀ ☕ ☎

41 ONE BROOK HALL COTTAGES
Steeple Road, Latchingdon CM3 6LB. John & Corinne Layton, 01621 741680, corinne@arrow250.fsnet.co.uk. *1m from Latchingdon Church. From Maldon drive through Latchingdon to mini r'about at church taking exit towards Steeple & Bradwell. Approx 1m turn R at bungalow onto gravel drive.* Home-made teas. **Adm £3. Tues 19 Apr; 3 May; 9 Aug; 27 Sept (11-5). Also open**
Woodpeckers (not Aug). Visitors also welcome by appt, coaches permitted.
¹/₃ - acre organic garden on three levels. Foliage tapestry planted in naturalistic style, subtle colour combinations with unusual herbaceous perennials. Decked area with boardwalk leading to natural pond and bog garden. Formal lawn, pleached limes, box hedges and topiary. Vegetable and cutting garden. Narrow paths, steep steps not suitable for children and people with walking difficulties. Dengie Peninsula is a wild and beautiful part of Essex, a haven for wildlife. Footpath walk to R Blackwater. Collections of auriculas and bonsai trees.

❀ ☕ ☎

42 ORCHARD COTTAGE
219 Hockley Road, Rayleigh SS6 8BH. Heather & Harry Brickwood, 01268-743838, henry.brickwood@homecall.co.uk. *1m NE from Rayleigh town centre. Leave A127 at Rayleigh Weir and take B1013 towards Rayleigh. Pass through Rayleigh and proceed towards Hockley. Please park opp on grass verge.* Home-made & cream teas. **Adm £3.50, or £5 with unlimited tea & cake, chd free. Visitors welcome by appt May, June & July. Groups welcome.**
Award-winning garden of ³/₄ acre. Lawns shrinking as borders expand! Central bed in the front is a mass of colour. May's feature will 100s of aquilegias, plus roses, lilies and numerous herbaceous perennials; July will see exuberant lilies, hermerocallis, agapanthus. Pond, stream with waterfalls, and many flowering shrubs. Featured in BBC Essex.

&. ✿ ❀ ☕ ☎

Dengie Peninsula is a wild and beautiful part of Essex, a haven for wildlife . . .

---

43 PARSONAGE HOUSE
Helions Bumpstead CB9 7AD. The Hon & Mrs Nigel Turner. *3m S of Haverhill. 8m NE of Saffron Walden. From Xrds in village centre turn up Church Hill, follow rd for 1m. Park in field opp. 3m from Haverhill follow signs 'To Village Only' from by-pass. After approx 2¹/₂ m garden is on R. Parking on L 200yds on.* Home-made teas. **Adm £3.50, chd free. Suns 1 May; 26 June (2-5). Also open West End Cottage 1 May.**
C15 house (not open) surrounded by 3 acres of formal gardens with mixed borders, topiary, pond, potager and greenhouse. Further 3-acre wild flower meadow with rare trees and further 3 acres of newly-planted orchard of old East Anglian apple varieties. Featured in Country Life.

&. ❀ ☕

44 PEACOCKS
Roman Road, Margaretting CM4 9HY. Phil Torr, 07802 472382, phil.torr@btinternet.com. *Situated on the B1002 near Margaretting Xroads (towards Ingatestone). From A12 N bound take Margaretting exit and turn R at top of slip rd. From S bound A12 follow signs for Margaretting/Ingatestone.* Light refreshments & teas. **Adm £4, chd free (share to St.Francis Hospice). Thurs 7 Apr; 15 Sept (2-6) Evening Opening Tue 21 June (2-8). Visitors also welcome by appt. Payment required in advance.**
5-acre natural garden with many mature native and specimen trees. Period greenhouse, melon house and potting shed. Formal walled gardens (one under construction), long herbaceous/mixed border. Newly restored temple and 'wildlife lake'. Woodland walk and new orchard/flower meadow. All surrounding Regency House (not open). Small sale of art. See the rose garden on mid summers day/evening.

&. ☕ ☎

45 164 POINT CLEAR ROAD
St Osyth CO16 8JB. Brian & Wendy Wickenden, 01255 821744, briwick@aol.com. *4m W of Clacton. At St Osyth Xrds follow sign for Point Clear, across lake, approx ¹/₂ m on R.* Home-made teas. **Adm £3, chd free. Visitors welcome by appt, any time mid March to Nov, 5 days notice please, coaches welcome.**
³/₄ -acre plantsman's garden that incorporates mixed borders of some 1500 different perennials, shrubs and

trees, many of which are unusual. National Collection of Corydalis. Other features incl a stream of approx 100ft leading to a wildlife lily pond, bridges, scree beds and grasses in a dry garden gravel area. The garden holds colour and interest throughout the year. Plenty of seating areas. Partial wheelchair access, bark paths may be difficult.

 NCCPG

46 NEW PORTERS FARM
Hollow Road, Kelvedon CO5 9DD. David & Judy Starling, 01376 584810, dhsta@tiscali.co.uk. *1 ½ m NW of St Mary's Church Kelvedon on Silver End Rd. Kelvedon is ½ -way between Colchester & Chelmsford.* Home-made teas. **Adm £4, chd free (share to Woodland Trust). Suns 22 May; 11 Sept (2-5). Visitors also welcome by appt min 15+. Coaches welcome.**
C16 house (not open) and barns surrounded by 3-acre garden developed since 1995 using 300yr old pond, old orchard and some existing walls, now festooned with roses and clematis. Round garden densely planted in shades of pink, white and blue. The wilderness, a profusion of white honesty, bluebells and cow parsley. Garden is surrounded by Ruffian Wood (open), 30 acres planted 2005 as part of Woodland Trust's Trafalgar Project (a wood for each ship in Nelson's fleet). The wood is named for HMS Bellerophon (known affectionately as Billy Ruffian).

THE PRIORY
See Suffolk.

47 ROOKWOODS
Yeldham Road, Sible Hedingham CO9 3QG. Peter & Sandra Robinson, 0777 095 7111, sandy1989@btinternet.com. *8m NW of Halstead. Sible Hedingham on A1017 between Braintree & Haverhill. From Haverhill take 1st R almost immed after 30mph sign, turn L by gate lodge through white gates.* Home-made teas. **Adm £3.50, chd free. Sun 29 May (11-5). Visitors also welcome by appt May, June, July & Sept. Large or small groups, coaches welcome.**
Tranquil garden with mature and young trees and shrubs. Simple herbaceous borders with columns of tumbling roses. Pleached hornbeam leading to wild flower bed all being warmed by Victorian red brick wall enhanced with clematis and vitis

coignetiae. Wander through meadow of buttercups to ancient oak wood. Enjoy tea relaxing under dreamy wisteria.

ROSEDALE
See Suffolk.

48 69 RUNDELLS
Harlow CM18 7HD. Mr & Mrs K Naunton, 01279 303471, K_naunton@hotmail.com. *1m from J7 M11 & A414. From M11 J7 take A414 Harlow at r'about 1st exit Southern Way, at 2nd mini r'about L Trotters Rd over 2 speed humps, follow road round bend 2nd L into Rundells. past R turn to Latton Green School/Hillyfield. Garden is situated at top of path ahead as the rd bears to the L.* Home-made teas. **Adm £2.50, chd free. Sat 16 July (2-5). Visitors also welcome by appt.**
Colourful, vibrant, small town garden packed with a variety of shrubs, perennials, herbaceous and bedding plants in over 140 containers. Hard landscaping on different levels incls summer house, seating and various water features. Direct access to an adjacent allotment planted with a variety of vegetables and perennial flower beds.

49 ST HELENS
High Street, Stebbing CM6 3SE. Stephen & Joan Bazlinton, 01371 856495, revbaz@care4free.net. *3m E of Great Dunmow. Leave Gt Dunmow on B1256. Take 1st L to Stebbing, at T-junction turn L into High St, garden 2nd house on R.* Home-made teas. **Adm £3.50, chd free (share to Dentaid). Mon 2 May; Sats 11 June; 10 Sept (11-5). Visitors also welcome by appt for groups.**
A garden of contrasts due to moist and dry conditions, laid out on a gentle Essex slope from a former willow plantation. These contours give rise to changing vistas and unanticipated areas of seclusion framed with hedging and generous planting. Walkways and paths lead alongside natural springs and still waters. Featured in '100 inspirational dream gardens of England' by Barbara Baker, Jerry and Marcus Harpur. (Published Merrell 2010).

87 ST JOHNS ROAD, E17
See London.

50 SALING HALL
Great Saling, Braintree CM7 5DT. Mr & Mrs Hugh Johnson, info@salinghall.com, www.salinghall.com. *6m NW of Braintree. Turn N off B1256 (old A120) between Gt Dunmow & Braintree signed Great Saling & the Bardfields. Saling Hall is at end of village on L.* **Adm £4, chd free (share to St James Church, Gt Saling). Weds 4 May to 27 July (2-5). Visitors also welcome by appt groups, weekdays only, by written application or email, see above.**
Plantsman's country garden of 12 acres, internationally famous for its collections of rare trees and shrubs in a sylvan landscape, chronicled over the past 35yrs by Hugh Johnson in his monthly Tradescant's Diary. 6 ponds, Temple of Pisces, menhir and many vistas make a garden of moods and surprises, beauty and strong botanical interest. House (not open) and walled flower garden dated 1699.

The wilderness, a profusion of white honesty, bluebells and cow parsley . .

51 SHRUBS FARM
Lamarsh, Bures CO8 5EA. Mr & Mrs Robert Erith, 01787 227520, bob@shrubsfarm.co.uk, www.shrubsfarm.co.uk. *1¼ m from Bures. On rd to Lamarsh, the drive is signed to Shrubs Farm.* Light refreshments & teas by agreement with visiting groups. **Adm £5, chd free (share to Holy Innocents Church, Lamarsh). Visitors welcome by appt. May to Sept recommended.**
2 acres with shrub borders, lawns, roses and trees. 50 acres parkland and meadow with wild flower paths and woodland trails. Over 60 species of oak. Superb 10m views over Stour valley. Ancient coppice and pollards incl largest goat (pussy) willow (*Salix caprea*) in England. Wollemi & Norfolk pines, and banana trees. Full size black rhinoceros. Display of Bronze age burial urns discovered by owner's father, Felix Erith FSA on his farm at Ardleigh, Essex. Featured in Braintree District Council Chairman's Summer Reception venue, July 2010.

 You are always welcome at an NGS garden

Snares Hill Cottage

Adm £3.50, chd free (share to St Andrews Church). **Suns 10 Apr; 17 July (1-5). Also open 102 Barnstaple Rd (Apr), Court View (July).** Visitors also welcome by appt.
Delightful, 1-acre established walled garden surrounding Grade 2 listed house (not open) and bee house. Ongoing extension of borders. April is ablaze with 3000 tulips and fritillaria. July shows 90 varieties of agapanthus. Unusual trees, shrubs, rose borders, with 30yr plus old geraniums, Mediterranean and Southern Hemisphere planting in dry garden. Agapanthus for sale. St Andrews Church open to visitors. Garden close to sea. Featured on BBC Essex.
& 🌿 ❀ ☕ ☎

SOUTHLEIGH
See Suffolk.

54 ♦ **SPENCERS**
Great Yeldham CO9 4JG. Caroline Courtauld, 01787 238175, **www.spencersgarden.net.** *Just N of Gt Yeldham on Clare rd. Turn off A1017 in Gt Yeldham at Domesday Oak. Keep L (signed Clare, Belchamp St Paul). Pass 1st entrance at Spencers and ¼ m later turn L at Spencers Lodge.* **Adm £4.50, chd free. For NGS: Sats 18 June; 17 Sept (2-5). For other opening times and information, please phone or see garden website.**
Romantic C18 walled garden laid out by Lady Anne Spencer, grand daughter of the 1st Duke of Marlborough Now overflowing with blooms following Tom Stuart-Smith's renovation. Huge tumbling wisteria, armies of Lord Butler delphiniums ('Rab' lived at Spencers 1970s-80s), vibrant green clover garden. Set in mature grounds with many ancient trees. Victorian woodland garden. Supposedly oldest greenhouse in Essex.
& ❀ ☕

4 STRADBROKE GROVE
See London.

64 THORNHILL ROAD, E10
See London.

55 **TREVANNE**
26 Canterbury Road, Holland-on-Sea CO15 5QJ. Anne & Trevor Legg. *2m E of Clacton. From Clacton follow signs to seafront. Turn L along seafront, approx 2m on L turn into*

52 **SNARES HILL COTTAGE**
Duck End, Stebbing CM6 3RY. Pete & Liz Stabler, 01371 856565, lizstabler@hotmail.com. *Between Dunmow & Bardfield. 1½ m past Stebbing turning past B&T auto salvage yard on B1057.* Home-made teas. **Adm £4, chd free. Suns 8 May; 19 June; 11 Sept (11-4). Visitors also welcome by appt.**
Our peaceful 1½ acre garden is divided into several small areas which include a natural bog garden, orchard, beach garden, fern and fountain gardens, and informal style flower beds. The garden has many water features including a stunning natural swimming pool, bordered by romantic cottage beds, and a herb garden. Featured in Essex Life magazine and Gardeners' World BBC 2.
☕ ☎

53 **SOUTH SHOEBURY HALL**
Church Road, Shoeburyness SS3 9DN. Mr & Mrs M Dedman, 01702 299022. *4m E of Southend-on-Sea. Enter Southend on A127 to Eastern Ave A1159 signed Shoebury. R at r'about to join A13. Proceed S to Ness Rd. R into Church Rd. Garden on L 50 metres.* Home-made teas.

York Rd signed Baptist Church. Take 2nd R into Canterbury Rd, garden approx 200m on R. **Adm £3, chd free. Sun 24 July (2-5).**
Delightful seaside garden beautifully designed by the owners for year round interest. Described as inspirational. Superb pergola with tranquil octagonal seating area around modern water feature. Crescent shaped lawn. Mixed border includes Birch, Catalpa, Mimosa, Koelreuteria, Ginkgo, Cercis. Summerhouse and secret garden provide ideal seating areas to relax and enjoy views of the garden. Exhibition and sale of photographs and crafts by the owners and friends. Seafront walks close by. Featured in Essex Life.

56 TUDOR ROOST
18 Frere Way, Fingringhoe CO5 7BP. Chris & Linda Pegden, 01206 729831. *5m S of Colchester. In centre of village by Whalebone PH. Follow sign to Ballast Quay, after 1/2 m turn R into Brook Hall Rd, then 1st L into Frere Way.* Home-made teas. **Adm £3, chd free. Please confirm opening dates on NGS website or tel. Mon 25, Tue 26 Apr; Sat 28, Sun 29 May; Tues, Weds 7, 8, 21, 22 June; Sat 9, Sun 10, Tue 19, Wed 20 July; Sats, Suns 6, 7, 20, 21 Aug (2-5.30).** Visitors also welcome by appt, groups & coaches anytime.
An unexpected hidden colourful 1/4 - acre garden. Well manicured grassy paths wind round island beds and ponds. Densely planted subtropical area with architectural and exotic plants - cannas, bananas, palms, agapanthus, agaves and tree ferns surround a colourful gazebo. Garden planted to provide yr-round colour and encourage wildlife. Many peaceful seating areas. Within 1m of Fingringhoe Wick Nature Reserve. Featured in Garden Answers.

57 NEW TUDOR ROSE COTTAGE
11 Sawyers Road, Little Totham, Maldon CM9 8JW. Bella D'Arcy Reed, 01621 892737, belladarcy@gardensandpeople.co. uk, www.gardensandpeople.co.uk. *6m NE of Maldon. 2m from A12. From A12 Eastbound turn off at Rivenhall, Silver End turning. A12 westbound, Rivenhall Hotel. Follow Braxted Hall Rd to T-junction B1022.*

Turn R, immed L signed Little Totham. Sawyers Rd on L after entering village. Teas at church hall opp Wood View 24 Apr, 30, 31 July. **Adm £2.50, chd free. Combined with Wood View adm £5, 24 Apr, 30, 31 July. Sats, Suns 23, 24 Apr; 30, 31 July; 3 Sept (1-5).** Visitors also welcome by appt May to Sept, max 6 visitors. Tea or wine if ordered in advance.
Magical garden showing how much can be done in small spaces. Edwardian parterre front garden with wisteria, half-pergola leads into Italian/Greek exotic oasis of perennials, Mediterranean and tropical plants surrounding Koi pool, plus art pieces and bits of former show gardens by its garden designer owner. Seats for visitors. Sale of work by local artists, display of Bella's garden design work. Metal sculptures in garden orginally designed for Chelsea and Hampton Court. Wheelchairs welcome.

58 ULTING WICK
Maldon CM9 6QX. Mr & Mrs B Burrough, 01245 380216, philippa.burrough@btinternet.com. *3m NW of Maldon. Take turning to Ulting (Ulting Lane) off B1019 at Langford, after 2.2m at T-junction, garden is opp.* Home-made teas. **Adm £3.50, chd free (share to All Saints Ulting Church). Suns 1 May; 18 Sept (2-5).** Visitors also welcome by appt min 15.
Colourful 4 acres around C16 farmhouse and listed black Essex barns plus 3 acre woodland planted 2004. Herbaceous borders incl striking pink,dramatic, dahlia filled, cutting garden. Tulips a passion bordering on an obsession! Pond and stream bordered by mature willows, moisture and shade loving plants. Vegetable garden with Victorian style glasshouse. Walk to All Saints Ulting Church by R Chelmer, signed from garden. Church will be open for talk on its history.

WALTHAM FOREST REGISTER OFFICE, E17
See London.

59 45 WATERHOUSE LANE
Chelmsford CM1 2TE. Peter & Julie Richmond. *W side of Chelmsford between Widford & central Chelmsford. Waterhouse Lane is the A1016 between Rainsford Lane &*

Westway. Parking in Bilton Rd opp & between 2 car showrooms. No restriction in Bilton Rd on Sundays. Home-made teas served in neighbours garden, through the garden gate. **Adm £3, chd free. Suns 31 July; 7 Aug (2-5); Evening Openings £10, canapes & wine served in garden, Suns 28 Aug; 4 Sept (7-9).**
A big surprise behind a busy road! Plantsman's town garden with artistic and creative ideas. Subtropical seating area with architectural and exotic plants - dry and shade areas. Display of old garden tools, spring-fed crystal clear pond and stream with ornamental fish. Evening opening will be an illuminated garden visit with wine and canapés. Numbers will be strictly limited to 30 and tickets £10 per head must be booked in advance with the garden owners. No wheelchair access due to gravel in all areas.

Linger in our gravel garden or sit on 'Teletubby Hill' and enjoy long views over rolling countryside . . .

60 NEW WEST END COTTAGE
Drury Lane, Ridgewell, nr Halstead CO9 4SL. Joy & Harry Crane, 01440 788336. *On A1017 Ridgewell is 3m S of Haverhill or 2m N of Great Yeldham. In village follow sign for village hall. Cottage on L a little way past hall.* Light refreshments & home-made teas, wine. **Adm £3, chd free. Sun 1, Mon 2 May; Sun 17 July (11-5); Sun 18 Sept (11-4). Also open Parsonage House 1 May.** Visitors also welcome by appt June to Aug, min 6, max 20 visitors. Refreshments can be requested.
Pretty 150yr old thatched cottage (not open) set in beautiful 1/3 - acre country garden with a formal twist. Quintessential English front garden with shrubs, roses and lavender. Roses and wisteria covered pergola. Herbaceous beds, shrub borders and

gravel garden. Newly planted knot garden. Plenty of seating areas to sit and enjoy refreshments. Well kept village with large green. Gravel drive to garden.

 ♿ ✿ ☕ ☎

61 ► WEST HANNINGFIELD HALL
Hall Lane, West Hanningfield CM2 8FN. Michael & Diana Iles. *5m S of Chelmsford. Leave A12 J16 onto B1007 (S), at Ship PH turn L into Ship Rd, after ³/₄ m turn L into Hall Lane. Or leave A130 onto A132, 1st L at r'about, 1st exit signed Rettendon & the Hanningfields. After 3¹/₂ m turn L signed West Hanningfield. At Compasses PH bear R, L at bottom of hill, 2nd R into Hall Lane.* Wine, soft drinks & crisps only. **Adm £3, chd free. Sun 29 May (11.30-5).** Stunning large country garden surrounded by farmland originally developed over 30yrs ago on a sloping site and considerably extended, altered and restocked during last 10yrs. Lawns with large borders containing shrubs, shrub roses and wide variety of perennials. Features incl formal rose garden, 2 ponds, pergola, vegetable area and collection of young trees. Plant sale by Long House Plants, nr Hyde Hall (RHS) and Hanningfield Reservoir Visitor Centre. Gravel areas, 2 steep slopes.

 ♿ ✿

12 WESTERN ROAD, E13
See London.

62 NEW WICKETS
Langley Upper Green CB11 4RY. Susan & Doug Copeland, 01799 550553, susan.copeland2@btinternet.com. *10m N of Bishops Stortford. Turn W off B1383 (old A11) at Newport. After 5m turn R off B1038 at Clavering, signed Langley. Drive over ford, Upper Green 3m further on. Last house on R of cricket green.* Home-made teas. **Adm £3, chd free. Sat 28 May; Wed 15, Thur 23, Tue 28 June (2-5). Evening Opening £5, music and wine evening, Sat 2 July (5.30-9). Music by duo 'Cambridge Cafe Musicians'. Visitors also welcome by appt May to July, min 10, coaches welcome. Refreshments by arrangement.**
Peaceful country garden and landscaped meadow in 1¹/₂ acres. Wide, informal mixed borders feature

camassia, shrub roses, alliums. Restored lily pond with 'Monet' bridge sheltered by groups of silver birch. Many seating areas. Linger in our gravel garden or sit on 'Teletubby Hill' and enjoy long views over rolling countryside. Best kept Essex small village with large cricket green.

 ♿ ✿ ☕ ☎

63 ► WICKHAM PLACE FARM
Station Road, Wickham Bishops CM8 3JB. Mrs J Wilson, 01621 891282, judith@wickhamplacefarm.co.uk, www.wickhamplacefarm.co.uk. *2¹/₂ m SE of Witham. Take B1018 from Witham to Maldon. After going under A12 take 3rd L (Station Rd). 1st house on L.* Home-made teas. **Adm £3.50, chd free (share to Farleigh Hospice). Every Fris 29 Apr to 29 July; 2 Sept to 30 Sept; (11-4). Visitors also welcome by appt, groups/coaches any day/time.**
14 acres for all seasons. Includes ponds, intricate knot garden and lovely woodland walks with rabbit resistant plants. The ancient walled garden is home to climbers, shrubs, perennials, bulbs and box hedges.Renowned for enormous wisterias (one over 250ft) in May with further flowering in July. In September cyclamen carpets the woodland, replacing earlier bluebells and is a haven for birds. Adjacent to the garden is the last remaining wooden trestle railway viaduct in the country. Nursery offers unusual plants as seen in the garden.

 ♿ ✿ ☕ ☎

64 ► WOOD VIEW
24 Chapel Road, Great Totham, Near Maldon CM9 8DA. Edwin Parsons & Ian Roxburgh, 07540 798135. *5m NE of Maldon. Situated in Great Totham North. Chapel Rd is off the B1022 Maldon/Colchester Road.* Home-made teas at URC Hall (opp). **Adm £3, chd free. Combined with Tudor Rose Cottage adm £5, chd free, 24 April, 30 July, 31 July. Suns 27 Mar; 24 Apr; Sats, Suns 11, 12 June; 30, 31 July (1-5). Visitors also welcome by appt, between March & July.**
Contemporary plantsmans garden containing unusual species. Pergolas and terraces create seating areas in this haven for wildlife. In spring, bulbs and primroses. Summer has herbaceous perennials and shrubs. Display of dahlias and grape covered walkway for autumn. 2 allotments

nearby where refreshments car parking and WC are available. Second-hand garden books (book stall) for sale. Gravel Paths.

 ✿ ☕ ☎

> September's stronger colours and nectar-rich varieties encourage foraging bees and clouds of butterflies . . .

65 NEW WOODPECKERS
Mangapp Chase, Burnham-on-Crouch CM0 8QQ. Neil & Linda Holdaway, & Lilian Burton, 01621 782137, lindaholdaway@btinternet.com. *20m E of Chelmsford. B1010 to Burnham-on-Crouch. Just beyond town sign turn L into Green Lane. Turn L after ¹/₂ m. Garden 200yds on R.* Light refreshments & home-made teas. **Adm £3, chd free. Tues 19 Apr; 3 May; 7 June; 27 Sept; 11 Oct (11-5). Also open One Brook Hall Cottages19 Apr, 3 May, 27 Sept. Visitors also welcome by appt groups 10+, refreshments by arrangement.**
Hedges divide and add structure to exuberant planting in this 1¹/₂-acre country garden. Spring brings blossom in the orchard, wild flowers and drifts of bulbs, later there's summer abundance in the kitchen garden and wide densely-planted borders. September's stronger colours and nectar-rich varieties encourage foraging bees and clouds of butterflies. Garden flowers, produce and preserves for sale.

 ✿ ☕ ☎

66 ► WOOLARDS ASH
Hatfield Broad Oak CM22 7JY. Mr & Mrs Michael Herbert, 01279 718284, mleqh@woolardsash.fsnet.co.uk. *5m SE of Bishop's Stortford. From Hatfield Broad Oak follow B183 N (towards Takeley). After ³/₄ m take 1st*

R (signed to Taverners Green &
Broomshawbury), then 2nd R to
Woolards Ash. From Takeley, B183 S
(towards Hatfield Broad Oak). After
³/₄ m 1st L (signed Canfield & High
Roding), then 2nd L to Woolards Ash.
Home-made teas. **Adm £5, chd free.**
Visitors welcome by appt, April to
July, groups of 10+. Coaches
permitted.
Peacocks, guinea fowl and bantams
roam this beautiful 3-acre garden,
divided into 5 areas by beech and
yew hedges, all set in a pastoral
landscape. The main area has 2 large
subtly planted borders of old roses,
shrubs, herbaceous plants and ha-ha
with distant views. The walled pool
garden provides a tranquil setting for
mature borders with further shrub
borders, mature trees and wild areas
planted with bulbs and old roses,
small vegetable garden.

67 WRITTLE COLLEGE
Writtle CM1 3RR. Writtle College,
www.writtle.ac.uk. 4m W of
Chelmsford. On A414, nr Writtle
village, clearly signed. Teas. **Adm £4,**
chd free. Thurs 28 Apr; 16 June
(10-4).
15 acres; informal lawns with
naturalised bulbs and wild
flowers.Large tree collection, mixed
shrubs, herbaceous borders.
Landscaped gardens designed and
built by students inc. 'Centenary'
garden and subtropical garden.
Development of 13-acre parkland.
Orchard meadow started.
Landscaped glasshouses,wide range
of seasonal bedding. NDH students
will organise and give guided
tours.Horticultural information from
Writtle College tutors.

Chippins

Essex County Volunteers

County Organiser
Susan Copeland, Wickets, Langley Upper Green, Saffron Walden CB11 4RY, 01799 550553,
    susan.copeland2@btinternet.com

County Treasurer
Neil Holdaway, Woodpeckers, Mangapp Chase, Burnham-on-Crouch CM0 8QQ, 01621 782137,
    lindaholdaway@btinternet.com

Publicity & Assistant County Organisers
Doug Copeland, Wickets, Langley Upper Green, Saffron Walden, Essex CB11 4RY, 01799 550553,
    susan.copeland2@btinternet.com
Linda Holdaway, Woodpeckers, Mangapp Chase, Burnham-on-Crouch CM0 8QQ, 01621 782137,
    lindaholdaway@btinternet.com

Assistant County Organisers
Ray Spencer & Richard Steers, Court View, 276 Manchester Drive, Leigh-on-Sea SS9 3ES, 01702 713221,
    arjeyeski@courtview.demon.co.uk

204

GLOUCESTERSHIRE
(for South Gloucestershire see Somerset, Bristol Area & S Glos)

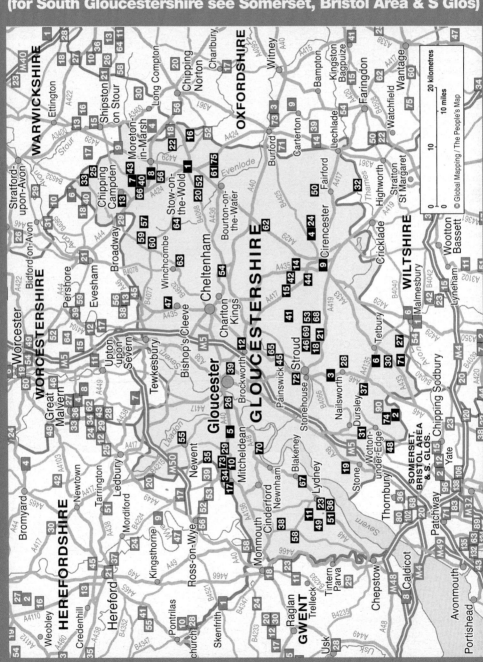

Opening Dates

January

Sunday 30
29 Home Farm

February

Sunday 6
32 Kempsford Manor

Sunday 13
29 Home Farm
32 Kempsford Manor
65 Trench Hill

Monday 14
44 The Old Rectory, Duntisbourne Rous

Saturday 19
32 Kempsford Manor

Sunday 20
32 Kempsford Manor
65 Trench Hill

Sunday 27
19 Edward Jenner Museum
32 Kempsford Manor

March

Sunday 6
32 Kempsford Manor

Sunday 13
23 Green Cottage
29 Home Farm

Sunday 20
23 Green Cottage
47 Pear Tree Cottage
65 Trench Hill

Monday 21
44 The Old Rectory, Duntisbourne Rous

Sunday 27
23 Green Cottage
32 Kempsford Manor

April

Sunday 3
26 Highnam Court

Sunday 10
1 Abbotswood
29 Home Farm
40 Mill Dene Garden
43 The Old Chequer
58 South Lodge
60 Stanway Fountain & Water Garden

Thursday 14
32 Kempsford Manor

Sunday 17
4 Barnsley House
32 Kempsford Manor
38 Meadow Cottage

41 Misarden Park
61 Stone House
66 Upton Wold

Monday 18
33 Kiftsgate Court

Saturday 23
32 Kempsford Manor

Sunday 24
6 Beverston Castle
29 Home Farm
65 Trench Hill

Monday 25
6 Beverston Castle
32 Kempsford Manor
65 Trench Hill

Wednesday 27
36 Lydney Park Spring Garden

May

Sunday 1
18 Eastcombe, Bussage and Brownshill Gardens
22 Grange Farm
26 Highnam Court
51 Ramblers
58 South Lodge
73 Willow Lodge

Monday 2
18 Eastcombe, Bussage and Brownshill Gardens
73 Willow Lodge

Sunday 8
7 Blockley Gardens
14 Cerney House Gardens
27 Hodges Barn
32 Kempsford Manor
43 The Old Chequer
49 Priors Mesne

Monday 9
27 Hodges Barn
44 The Old Rectory, Duntisbourne Rous

Sunday 15
23 Green Cottage
49 Priors Mesne
62 Stowell Park

Saturday 21
11 Brockaran Barn

Sunday 22
11 Brockaran Barn
12 Brockworth Court
23 Green Cottage
58 South Lodge
72 Whiteshill and Ruscombe Gardens

Wednesday 25
35 Lower Farm House

Saturday 28
30 Hookshouse Pottery
34 Longhope Gardens
68 Waterlane House

Sunday 29
23 Green Cottage
30 Hookshouse Pottery
34 Longhope Gardens
39 9 Merevale Road
54 Sandywell Barn House

Monday 30
30 Hookshouse Pottery
35 Lower Farm House
54 Sandywell Barn House

Tuesday 31
30 Hookshouse Pottery

June

Wednesday 1
30 Hookshouse Pottery
65 Trench Hill

Thursday 2
30 Hookshouse Pottery

Friday 3
30 Hookshouse Pottery

Saturday 4
30 Hookshouse Pottery
74 Wortley Farmhouse

Sunday 5
23 Green Cottage
26 Highnam Court
28 Holcombe Glen Cottage
30 Hookshouse Pottery
60 Stanway Fountain & Water Garden
74 Wortley Farmhouse

Wednesday 8
13 Campden House
65 Trench Hill

Saturday 11
3 Atcombe Court
21 France Lynch Gardens
34 Longhope Gardens

Sunday 12
7 Blockley Gardens
23 Green Cottage
27 Hodges Barn
31 Hunts Court
34 Longhope Gardens
54 Sandywell Barn House

Monday 13
27 Hodges Barn

Wednesday 15
13 Campden House
15 Cotswold Farm
65 Trench Hill

Saturday 18
5 Berrys Place Farm
67 Valley View

Sunday 19
5 Berrys Place Farm
15 Cotswold Farm
17 Delves Cottage
23 Green Cottage
31 Hunts Court
37 The Matara Meditative Gardens
46 Paulmead

Visit the website for latest information

58 South Lodge
59 Stanton Gardens
62 Stowell Park
67 Valley View
69 Wells Cottage

Monday 20
5 Berrys Place Farm
44 The Old Rectory, Duntisbourne Rous

Tuesday 21
5 Berrys Place Farm

Wednesday 22
16 Daylesford House
57 Snowshill Manor & Garden
65 Trench Hill

Saturday 25
38 Meadow Cottage (Evening)

Sunday 26
17 Delves Cottage
32 Kempsford Manor
41 Misarden Park
42 Moor Wood
50 Quenington Gardens
53 Rookwoods

Wednesday 29
20 Eyford House
52 Rockcliffe
65 Trench Hill

July

Sunday 3
9 25 Bowling Green Road
24 Herbs for Healing
26 Highnam Court
56 Sezincote
64 Temple Guiting Manor

Monday 4
9 25 Bowling Green Road

Sunday 10
9 25 Bowling Green Road

Monday 11
9 25 Bowling Green Road

Saturday 16
25 Hidcote Manor Garden

Sunday 17
9 25 Bowling Green Road
65 Trench Hill

Monday 18
9 25 Bowling Green Road

Wednesday 27
38 Meadow Cottage

Saturday 30
10 Breenes

Sunday 31
10 Breenes
71 Westonbirt School Gardens

August

Sunday 7
26 Highnam Court
32 Kempsford Manor

Saturday 13
10 Breenes

Sunday 14
8 Bourton House Garden
10 Breenes
32 Kempsford Manor

Monday 15
33 Kiftsgate Court

Sunday 21
4 Barnsley House
24 Herbs for Healing
32 Kempsford Manor
68 Waterlane House

Saturday 27
10 Breenes

Sunday 28
10 Breenes
65 Trench Hill

Monday 29
10 Breenes

September

Sunday 4
26 Highnam Court
31 Hunts Court

Saturday 10
10 Breenes

Sunday 11
10 Breenes
31 Hunts Court
32 Kempsford Manor
65 Trench Hill
70 Westbury Court Garden
75 Wyck Rissington Gardens

Sunday 18
12 Brockworth Court

Saturday 24
10 Breenes

Sunday 25
10 Breenes
37 The Matara Meditative Gardens

October

Friday 14
63 Sudeley Castle Gardens & Exhibitions

February 2012

Sunday 12
32 Kempsford Manor
65 Trench Hill

Saturday 18
32 Kempsford Manor

Sunday 19
32 Kempsford Manor
65 Trench Hill

Sunday 26
32 Kempsford Manor

Gardens open to the public

8 Bourton House Garden
14 Cerney House Gardens
19 Edward Jenner Museum
24 Herbs for Healing
25 Hidcote Manor Garden
31 Hunts Court
32 Kempsford Manor
33 Kiftsgate Court
36 Lydney Park Spring Garden
37 The Matara Meditative Gardens
40 Mill Dene Garden
41 Misarden Park
45 Painswick Rococo Garden
56 Sezincote
57 Snowshill Manor & Garden
60 Stanway Fountain & Water Garden
61 Stone House
63 Sudeley Castle Gardens & Exhibitions
70 Westbury Court Garden
71 Westonbirt School Gardens

By appointment only

2 Alderley Grange
48 Pemberley Lodge
55 Schofields

Also open by Appointment ☎

6 Beverston Castle
9 25 Bowling Green Road
10 Breenes
12 Brockworth Court
34 3 Church Road, Longhope Gardens
15 Cotswold Farm
17 Delves Cottage
29 Home Farm
38 Meadow Cottage
42 Moor Wood
43 The Old Chequer
44 The Old Rectory, Duntisbourne Rous
47 Pear Tree Cottage
51 Ramblers
54 Sandywell Barn House
58 South Lodge
65 Trench Hill
67 Valley View
69 Wells Cottage
73 Willow Lodge

Massed plantings of spring bulbs, heathers, flowering shrubs and rhododendrons . . .

See more garden images at www.ngs.org.uk

The Gardens

Cerney House Gardens

1 ▶ ABBOTSWOOD
Stow-on-the-Wold GL54 1EN. Mr R
Scully. *1m W of Stow-on-the-Wold.
On B4068 nr Lower Swell or B4077
nr Upper Swell.* Home-made teas.
Adm £4, chd free. Sun 10 Apr
(1.30-6).
Massed plantings of spring bulbs,
heathers, flowering shrubs and
rhododendrons in dramatic,
landscaped hillside stream gardens;
fine herbaceous planting in elegant
formal gardens with lily pond,
terraced lawn and fountain created by
Sir Edwin Lutyens.
& 🌿 ☕

2 ▶ ALDERLEY GRANGE
Alderley GL12 7QT. The Hon Mrs
Acloque, 01453 842161. *2m S of
Wotton-under-Edge. Turn NW off A46
Bath to Stroud rd, at Dunkirk. L
signed Hawkesbury Upton & Hillesley.
In Hillesley follow sign to Alderley.*
Adm £3.50, chd free. Visitors
welcome by appt last week May &
all June.
Walled garden with fine trees, old
fashioned roses; herb gardens and
aromatic plants.
& ☎

ASTHALL MANOR
See Oxfordshire.

3 ▶ ATCOMBE COURT
South Woodchester GL5 5ER. John
& Josephine Peach. *2m S of Stroud.
take turning off A46 signed South
Woodchester, Frogmarsh Mill (NOT
turning signed South Woodchester,
The Ram).* Home-made teas. Adm
£3.50, chd free. Sat 11 June (2-6).
12-acre grounds around C17 house
(not open) with later Regency front.
Delightful views over valley with lakes,
mature trees and paddocks. Terraced
herbaceous borders, lawns, extensive
shrubberies, cutting garden mostly
annuals. Long peony border.
Woodland walk through beechwood.
☕ 🌿

4 ▶ BARNSLEY HOUSE
Barnsley, Cirencester GL7 5EE.
Calcot Health & Leisure Ltd,
www.barnsleyhouse.com. *4m NE of
Cirencester. From Cirencester, take
B4425 to Barnsley. House entrance
on Right as you enter village.* Home-
made teas. Light refreshments also
available at The Village PH. Adm £5,
chd free. Suns 17 Apr; 21 Aug

(12.30-4.30).
The beautiful garden at Barnsley
House created by Rosemary Verey is
one of England's finest and most
famous gardens incl knot garden,
potager garden, mixed borders in
Rosemary Verey's successional
planting style. The house also has an
extensive kitchen garden which will be
open with plants and vegetables
available for purchase.
& ⊗ 🛏 ☕

BARTON HOUSE
See Warwickshire.

5 ▶ BERRYS PLACE FARM
Churcham GL2 8AS. Anne Thomas.
*6m W of Gloucester. A40 towards
Ross. Turning R into Bulley Lane at
Birdwood.* Home-made & cream teas.
Adm £3, chd free. Daily Sat 18
June to Tue 21 June; (11-6).
Country garden, approx 1 acre,
surrounded by farmland and old
orcharding. Lawns and mixed
herbaceous borders with some old
roses. Formal kitchen garden and
rose arbour leading to lake and

summerhouse with a variety of water
lilies and carp. All shared with
peacocks and ducks.
& ⊗ 🛏 ☕ ☎

6 ▶ BEVERSTON CASTLE
nr Tetbury GL8 8TU. Mrs A L Rook,
01666 502219,
jarook1@btinternet.com. *2m W of
Tetbury. On A4135 to Dursley
between Tetbury & Calcot Xrds.*
Home-made teas. Adm £3.50, chd
£2.50. Sun & Mon 24, 25 Apr
(2.30-5). Visitors also welcome by
appt.
Overlooked by romantic C12-C17
castle ruin (not open), overflowingly
planted paved terrace leads from C18
house (not open) across moat to
sloping lawn with spring bulbs in
abundance, and full herbaceous and
shrub borders. Large walled kitchen
garden and greenhouses. Access to
some areas of garden but also some
areas of gravel paths, steps & slopes.
& 🌿 ☕ ☎

BLICKS HILL HOUSE
See Wiltshire.

GROUP OPENING

7️⃣ BLOCKLEY GARDENS
Blockley GL56 9DB. *3m NW of Moreton-in-Marsh. Take A44 either from Moreton or Broadway and follow signs to Blockley. Parking and combined entry tickets available at St George's Hall. Home-made teas 8th May at The Old Silk Mill and 12th June at The Manor House.* **Adm £6, chd free.** Suns 8 May; 12 June (2-6).

4 THE CLEMENTINES
Kathy Illingworth.
Open May date only

3 THE DELL
Ms E Powell.
Open June date only

4 THE DELL
Viola & Bernard Stubbs.
Open June date only

GRANGE COTTAGE
Eve & Craig Barnard.
Open June date only.

NEW MALVERN HOUSE
Alistair & Lesley Winrow-Campbell.
Open May date only

MALVERN MILL
Mr & Mrs J Bourne.
Open both dates

THE MANOR HOUSE
George & Zoe Thompson.
Open both dates

MILL DENE
Mr & Mrs B S Dare.
Open both dates
(See separate entry)
www.milldenegarden.co.uk

THE OLD CHEQUER
Mr & Mrs Linley.
Open May date only
(See separate entry)

THE OLD SILK MILL
Mr & Mrs A Goodrick-Clarke.
Open May date only

PORCH HOUSE
Mr & Mrs C Johnson.
Open June date only.

RODNEYS
Duncan & Amelia Stewart.
Open June date only

NEW 2 ST GEORGES TERRACE
Jamie Ball & Brad Hooker.
Open June date only

NEW SPRING HOUSE
Chris & Janet Watts.
Open May date only

WATERSIDE
Patricia Milligan-Baldwin.
Open June date only

This popular hillside village has a great variety of high quality, well-stocked gardens - large and small,old and new. Blockley Brook, an attractive stream which flows right through the village, graces some of the gardens; these incl gardens of former water mills, with millponds attached. From some gardens there are wonderful rural views. Some are on several levels. Small children welcome but close supervision required. Some walking necessary in this fairly large village. Free bus service expected to be available.

Dew pond with Monet bridge leading to island summerhouse, carp and water lilies . . .

8️⃣ ♦ BOURTON HOUSE GARDEN
Bourton-on-the-Hill GL56 9AE. Mr & Mrs R Quintus, www.bourtonhouse.com. *2m W of Moreton-in-Marsh. On A44.* Home-made teas at 16th Century Grade I Listed Tithe Barn. **Adm £6, chd free. For NGS: Sun 14 Aug (10-5).** For other opening times and information, please phone or see garden website.
Award-winning three acre garden featuring wide herbaceous borders with stunning plant and colour combinations; imaginative topiary including knot garden and parterre; water features; unique shadehouse; creatively planted pots. Magnificent late summer garden. The unusual, rare and exotic make this garden a plantsman's delight. Cards and Gifts available. Featured in The English Garden magazine. 70% access for wheelchairs.

9️⃣ 25 BOWLING GREEN ROAD
Cirencester GL7 2HD. Fr John & Susan Beck, 01285 653778, sjb@beck-hems.org.uk. *On NW edge of Cirencester. Take A435 to Spitalgate/Whiteway T-lights, turn into The Whiteway (Chedworth turn) then 1st L into Bowling Green Rd. Please respect neighbours' driveways, no pavement parking.* **Adm £2.50, chd free.** Suns 3, 10, 17 July (2-5); Mons 4, 11, 18 July (11-4). Visitors also welcome by appt June to mid July. Groups very welcome.
Take time out to meander and muse amidst pergolas, paths, pools and pots, and glimpse cool cormorants, friendly frogs and graceful giraffe sharing their space with droves of delightfully different daylilies, romantic roses, curvaceous clematis, glorious grasses, hopeful hostas and priceless perennials in what visitors have described as a floral tardis. Featured in many local publications & local radio. Recieved 30yr NGS award.

🔟 BREENES
Napping Lane, Longhope GL17 0QH. Ann & James Steed, 01452 831286, info@outdoorlivingspace.co.uk. *1/2 way between Gloucester & Ross-on-Wye. 1st turning L after school. Napping Lane up rd 200yds. House at bottom of Napping Lane.* Home-made teas. **Adm £3.50, chd free.** Sats & Suns 30, 31 July; 13, 14, 27, 28 Aug; 10, 11, 24, 25 Sept; Mon 29 Aug (2-6). Also open Longhope Gardens. Please see entry for details. Visitors also welcome by appt June - Oct only.
RHS Gold Medal winners' own private garden set in 1/3 acre with valley views, dramatic planting, interesting level changes throughout, parterre garden, vegetable garden and many places to sit, relax and enjoy a cup of tea and slice of cake. Plenty of yr-round interest. Photography & plants for sale. Featured on BBC Radio Worcester.

11️⃣ NEW BROCKARAN BARN
Blistors Farm, Bream, Lydney GL15 6EW. Louise and Frank McGuinness. *Off main Coleford to Lydney Road at edge of village of Bream. Take Blistors Farm drive and follow signs to Brockaran Barn.* Home-made & cream teas. **Adm £3, chd free.** Sat & Sun 21, 22 May (10-4).

A newly-created (less than 20 yrs) flower arranger's natural woodland garden set in approx 8 acres. Wildflower meadow and sculpture trail. Pond, bog garden, gravel yard, pots, vegetable patch and orchard. Some steep wooded slopes, with lots of seats for visitors to rest and survey the scene. Plants for sale. Some areas of garden not suitable for disabled access.

12 BROCKWORTH COURT

Brockworth GL3 4QU. Mr & Mrs Tim Wiltshire, 01452 862938. *6m E of Gloucester; 6m W of Cheltenham. From A46 Stroud/ Cheltenham off A417 turn into Mill Lane. At T-junction turn R, L, R. Garden next to St George's Church - Court Rd. From Ermin Rd, follow signs to Churchdown and church.* Home-made teas. **Adm £4, chd free. Suns 22 May; 18 Sept (2-5). Visitors also welcome by appt April to Sept. Groups 12+.** Historic manor house (not open) once belonged to Llanthony Priory. CPRE award-winning restored C13 tithe barn. Dew pond with Monet bridge leading to island summerhouse, carp and water lilies. Mostly farmhouse style planting, some new borders and organic kitchen garden. Views of Coopers and Crickley Hills. Arts & crafts workshop/gallery. Jet Age Museum. Featured on Radio Gloucestershire. Gravel paths.

13 CAMPDEN HOUSE

Chipping Campden GL55 6UP. The Hon Philip & Mrs Smith. *¹/₂ m SW of Chipping Campden. Entrance on Chipping Campden to Weston Subedge rd, approx ¹/₄ m SW of Campden, 1¹/₄ m drive.* **Adm £4, chd free. Weds 8, 15 June (2-6).** 2 acres featuring mixed borders of plant and colour interest around house and C17 tithe barn (neither open). Set in fine parkland in hidden valley with lakes and ponds. Woodland walk, vegetable garden. Gravel paths, some steep slopes.

14 ◆ CERNEY HOUSE GARDENS

North Cerney GL7 7BX. Lady Angus, 01285 831300, www.cerneygardens.com. *4m NW of Cirencester. On A435 Cheltenham rd. Turn L opp Bathurst Arms, past church up hill, pillared gates on R.*

Temple Guiting Manor

Adm £4, chd £1. For NGS: Sun 8 May (12-5). For other opening times and information, please phone or see garden website. Romantic walled garden filled with old-fashioned roses and herbaceous borders. Working kitchen garden, scented garden, well-labelled herb garden, Who's Who beds and genera borders. Spring bulbs in abundance all around the wooded grounds. Bothy pottery. Now open from Jan for snowdrops and hellebores.

9 CHURCH ROAD
See Somerset & Bristol.

CONDERTON MANOR
See Worcestershire.

15 COTSWOLD FARM
nr Duntisbourne Abbots, Cirencester GL7 7JS. Mrs Mark Birchall, 01285 821857, ionacotswoldfarm@uwclub.net, www.cotswoldfarmgardens.org.uk. *5m NW of Cirencester. Off the old A417. From Cirencester turn L signed Duntisbourne Abbots Services, then immed R & R again into underpass.*

Private drive straight ahead. From Gloucester turn L signed Duntisbourne Abbots Services. Pass services; private drive on L. Cream teas. **Adm £5, chd free. Wed 15, Sun 19 June (2-6). Visitors also welcome by appt. Groups welcome. Coaches permitted.** Cotswold garden in lovely position overlooking quiet valley on desending levels with terrace designed by Norman Jewson in 1930s; White border overflowing with flowers, texture, scent; Shrubs, trees, shrub roses; Bog Garden; Snowdrops named and naturalised; Allotments in Old Walled graden; 8 native orchids, 100's of wild flowers and Roman Snails;. Family day out. Croquet and toys on lawn; Picnics welcome.

16 DAYLESFORD HOUSE
Daylesford GL56 0YG. Sir Anthony & Lady Bamford. *5m W of Chipping Norton. Off A436. Between Stow-on-the-Wold & Chipping Norton.* Light refreshments & teas. **Adm £5, chd free (share to NSPCC). Wed 22 June (2-5).** Magnificent C18 landscape grounds

Be tempted by a plant from a plant stall ⊛

created 1790 for Warren Hastings, greatly restored and enhanced by present owners. Lakeside and woodland walks within natural wild flower meadows. Large walled garden planted formally, centred around orchid, peach and working glasshouses. Trellised rose garden. Collection of citrus within period orangery. Secret Garden with pavilion and formal pools. Very large garden with substantial distances to be walked.

Snowdrops and wild garlic guide you around, past the herb garden and archaeological dig, to the Grade II listed Temple of Vaccinia . . .

17 DELVES COTTAGE
Wigpool, Mitcheldean GL17 0JN. David & Hazel Ballard, 01594 543288, dballard51@btinternet.com. *1¹/₂ m NW of Mitcheldean. From Mitcheldean turn L by church into Mill End. ¹/₂ m up hill turn R signed Wigpool. After ¹/₂ m take 1st L. Follow NGS signs.* Cream Teas. **Adm £3, chd free. Suns 19, 26 June (2-5). Visitors also welcome by appt.** 1 acre of woodland tranquillity. Mature trees and shrubs give a backdrop of colour and texture to mixed borders of smaller shrubs and perennials incl many hardy geraniums. Cream teas served from garden room overlooking large ponds, with bog areas and marginal planting. Plenty of seats inc carved owl bench. Featured on Radio Gloucestershire.

DORSINGTON GARDENS
See Warwickshire.

DYRHAM PARK
See Somerset & Bristol.

GROUP OPENING

18 EASTCOMBE, BUSSAGE AND BROWNSHILL GARDENS
Eastcombe GL6 7DS. *3m E of Stroud. 2m N of A419 Stroud to Cirencester rd on turning signed to Bisley & Eastcombe.* Home-made teas & refreshments at Eastcombe Village Hall. **Combined adm £5, chd free (share to local charities). Sun & Mon 1, 2 May (2-6).**

> **BEECHCROFT**
> Mr & Mrs R H Salt
>
> **NEW CADSONBURY**
> Natalie & Glen Beswetherick
>
> **HAMPTON VIEW**
> Geraldine & Mike Carter
>
> **12 HIDCOTE CLOSE**
> Mr & Mrs K Walker
>
> **HIGHLANDS**
> Helen & Bob Watkinson
>
> **HOLT END**
> Maurice & Jackie Rutter
>
> **1 THE LAURELS**
> Andrew & Ruth Fraser
>
> **NEW LYNCROFT**
> Rob & Meg Powell
>
> **MIDDLEGARTH**
> Helen & Peter Walker
>
> **ROSE COTTAGE**
> Mrs Juliet Shipman
>
> **23 SIBREE CLOSE**
> Mr & Mrs A Dendy
>
> **WOODVIEW**
> Julian & Eileen Horn-Smith
>
> **YEW TREE COTTAGE**
> Andy & Sue Green

A group of gardens, medium and small, set in a picturesque hilltop location. Some approachable only by foot. (Exhibitions may be on view in village hall). Please park considerately in villages. There will hopefully be an exhibition in Eastcombe Village Hall. Sale of plants by NCCPG. Featured on Radio Gloucestershire. Wheelchair access at 12 Hidcote Close, Holt End, 23 Sibree Close & Lyncroft only.

19 ◆ EDWARD JENNER MUSEUM
Church Lane, Berkeley GL13 9BN. Sarah Parker, 01453 810631, www.jennermuseum.com. *Midway between Bristol and Gloucester just off A38. Follow signs to Berkeley, then brown tourist signs to Jenner Museum.* Light Refreshments at Old Cyder House Shop. **Adm £2.50, chd free. For NGS: Sun 27 Feb (11-4). For other opening times and information please visit website or telephone.** Informal woodland garden at the former home of Dr Edward Jenner. Snowdrops and wild garlic guide you around, past the herb garden and archaeological dig, to the Grade II listed Temple of Vaccinia, the 200yr old plane tree and into the vinery where Jenner's Hampton Court Palace vine grows. Information on the history of the garden and its contents will be provided. Family activities available. Featured in BBC 2 Digging for Britain Channel 4 Genius of Britain & BBC SW documentary, Jenner's Marvellous Medicine. Limited wheelchair access with gravel paths around garden.

20 EYFORD HOUSE
Upper Slaughter, nr. Cheltenham GL54 2JN. Mrs C A Heber-Percy. *Stone Lodge on R, with white iron gates & cattle grid B4068 2¹/₂ m from Stow on the Wold.* **Adm £4, combined adm with Rockliffe House £8, chd free. Wed 29 June (10-6).** 1¹/₂ -acre sloping N facing garden, ornamental shrubs and trees. Laid out originally by Graham Stuart Thomas, 1976. West garden and terrace, red border, walled kitchen garden, two lakes with pleasant walks and views (boots needed). Holy well.

GROUP OPENING

21 FRANCE LYNCH GARDENS
France Lynch, Nr Stroud GL6 8LP. *5m E of Stroud. Turn off A419 at Chalford signed Chalford Hill. Follow signs to France Lynch.* Home-made teas at Orchard Cottage. **Combined adm £4, chd free. Sat 11 June (2-6).**

> **CROSSWAYS**
> Tessa & Trevor Wood
>
> **NEW THE ORCHARD**
> John & Susie Salter
>
> **ORCHARD COTTAGE**
> Pat Willey
>
> **NEW WESSEX COTTAGE**
> Jackie & Nick Topman

THE ANCHORAGE
Carol & Simon Smith

LITTLE OAKS
Jane & David Calvert

Beautiful hillside village of old cottages and pretty lanes. Wonderful views across the valley. Small, medium and large selection of gardens, offering just about everything a garden lover could desire from vegetable and herb gardens to old roses and herbaceous borders. Wheelchair access available at all gardens except Little Oaks.

FROGS NEST
See Worcestershire.

22 GRANGE FARM
Evenlode, nr Moreton-in-Marsh GL56 0NT. Sir John Aird. *3m N of Stow-on-the-Wold. E of A429 Fosseway & 1¹/₂ m from Broadwell.* Tea & Home-made teas. **Adm £3.50, chd free.** Sun 1 May (10-5).
Roses, clematis and wisteria cover the C17 house. Herbaceous borders brim with colourful planting and glorious tulips flower in May. The heart of the garden is the orchard where the ancient apple trees spread over tulips, fritillary and narcissi. The water garden, bordered with primula, hostas and iris adds to the tranquillity. Interesting topiary, sunken garden, yew circle and vegetable garden.

23 GREEN COTTAGE
Watery Lane, Lydney GL15 6BS. Mrs F Baber, www.peony-ukgardeners.co.uk. *¹/₄ m SW of Lydney. Approaching Lydney from Gloucester, keep to A48 through Lydney town. Leaving Lydney turn R into Watery Lane at de-limit sign. From Chepstow take A48 approx 8m. Through Aylburton village, forward at traffic island, Watery Lane 2nd L.* Home-made teas. **Adm £3, chd free.** Suns 13, 20, 27 Mar (1-4); 15, 22, 29 May; 5, 12, 19 June (2-5).
1¹/₂ -acre country garden planted for seasonal interest and wildlife. Mature trees, stream, duckpond and bog garden. Developing woodland area planted with ferns, hellebores, daphnes and other shade lovers. Cottage garden. Wide range of herbaceous peonies, incl National Collection of rare Victorian and Edwardian lactiflora cultivars (June), early peonies May. Featured in

Cotswold Life magazine. Unsuitable for wheelchairs in March due to location of hellebores.
&. ❀ NCCPG ☕

HELLENS
See Herefordshire.

Small, medium and large selection of gardens, offering just about everything a garden lover could desire . . .

24 ◆ HERBS FOR HEALING
Claptons Lane (behind Barnsley House Hotel), Barnsley GL7 5EE. Davina Wynne-Jones, 01285 851457, www.herbsforhealing.net. *4m NE of Cirencester. Turn R after Barnsley House Hotel and R again at the dairy barn. Follow sign.* **Adm £4, chd free. For NGS: Suns 3 July; 21 Aug (12-5).** For other opening times and information, please phone or see garden website.
Not a typical NGS garden, rural and naturalistic. Davina, the daughter of Rosemary Verey, has created a unique nursery, specialising in medicinal herbs and a tranquil organic garden in a secluded field where visitors can enjoy the beauty of the plants and learn more about the properties and uses of medicinal herbs. Teas & cakes made from our herbs plus creams, ointments & remedies from the garden. Featured in The English Garden.
&. ❀ ☕ ☎

25 ◆ HIDCOTE MANOR GARDEN
Hidcote Bartrim, Chipping Campden, nr Mickleton GL55 6LR. National Trust, 01386 438333, www.nationaltrust.org.uk. *4m NE of Chipping Campden. Off B4081, close to the village of Mickleton.* **Adm £10, chd £5.** For NGS: Sat 16 July (10-6). For other opening times and

information, please phone or see garden website.
One of England's great gardens, 10¹/₂ -acre Arts and Crafts masterpiece created by Major Lawrence Johnston. Series of outdoor rooms, each with a different character and separated by walls and hedges of many different species. Many rare trees and shrubs, outstanding herbaceous borders and unusual plant species from all over the world. Approx ¹/₃ of garden accessible to wheelchair users. Map of route can be provided.
&. ❀ ☕

HIGH GLANAU MANOR
See Gwent.

26 HIGHNAM COURT
Highnam GL2 8DP. Roger Head, www.highnamcourt.co.uk. *2m W of Gloucester. Leave Gloucester on A40 towards Ross-on-Wye. DO NOT take Newent turning, but proceed to next big Highnam roundabout. Take R exit for Highnam Court, entrance directly off roundabout.* Light refreshments & teas. **Adm £4, chd free. Suns 3 Apr; 1 May; 5 June; 3 July; 7 Aug; 4 Sept (11-5).**
40 acres of Victorian landscaped gardens surrounding magnificent Grade I house (not open), set out by the artist Thomas Gambier Parry. Lakes, shrubberies and listed Pulhamite water gardens with grottos and fernery. Exciting ornamental lakes, and woodland areas. Extensive 1-acre rose garden and many features incl wood carvings. Large collection of wood carvings scattered around gardens. Steps to refreshment area. Some gravel paths.
&. 🥾 ☕

27 HODGES BARN
Shipton Moyne GL8 8PR. Mr & Mrs N Hornby. *3m S of Tetbury. On Malmesbury side of village.* **Adm £5, chd free. Suns & Mons 8, 9 May; 12, 13 June (2-6).**
Very unusual C15 dovecote converted into family home undergoing restoration (not open). Cotswold stone walls act as host to climbing and rambling roses, clematis, vines, hydrangeas, and together with yew, rose and tapestry hedges create formality around house. Mixed shrub and herbaceous borders, shrub roses; water garden; woodland garden planted with cherries, magnolias and spring bulbs.
&. 🥾

28 HOLCOMBE GLEN COTTAGE

Minchinhampton GL6 9AJ. Christine & Terry Sharpe. *1m E of Nailsworth. From Nailsworth take Avening Rd B4014. Turn L at Weighbridge Inn. Turn L 100yds into Holcombe Glen. 1st house on L. From Minchinhampton 1¹/₄ m via Well Hill or New Rd.* Home-made teas. **Adm £3, chd free (share to Parkinson's).** Sun 5 June (11-7).
3 acres incl springs and ponds. Small waterfalls feed river and stream, giving bog and meadow areas full of wildlife and wild flowers. Above these, terraced walled garden for vegetables and herbaceous plants. Featured on local radio.
🐾 🌼 ☕

29 HOME FARM

Newent Lane, Huntley GL19 3HQ. Mrs T Freeman, 01452 830210, torill@ukgateway.net. *4m S of Newent. On B4216 ¹/₂ m off A40 in Huntley travelling towards Newent.* **Adm £3, chd free.** Suns 30 Jan; 13 Feb; 13 Mar; 10, 24 Apr (2-5). **Visitors also welcome by appt. Groups also welcome on non NGS days (proceeds to NGS).**
Set in elevated position with exceptional views. 1m walk through woods and fields to show carpets of spring flowers. Enclosed garden with fern border, sundial and heather bed. White and mixed shrub borders. Stout footwear advisable in winter.
🐾 ☎

30 HOOKSHOUSE POTTERY

Hookshouse Lane, Tetbury GL8 8TZ. Lise & Christopher White. *2¹/₂ m SW of Tetbury. From Tetbury take A4135 towards Dursley, then take 2nd L, should be signed Leighterton. Pottery 1¹/₂ m on R.* Tea & Home-made teas. **Adm £2.50, chd free.** Sat 28, Sun 29, Mon 30, Tue 31 May; Wed 1, Thur 2, Fri 3, Sat 4, Sun 5 June (11-6).
A combination of dramatic open perspectives and intimate corners. Borders, shrubs, woodland glade, water garden containing treatment ponds (unfenced) and flowform cascades. Kitchen garden with raised beds, orchard. Sculptural features. Run on organic principles. Pottery showroom with hand-thrown wood-fired pots incl frostproof garden pots. Art & craft exhibition incl garden sculptures (May 28 to June 5 only).
♿ 🐾 🌼 ☕

30 HOOKSHOUSE POTTERY

Hookshouse Lane, Tetbury GL8 8TZ. Lise & Christopher White. *2¹/₂ m SW of Tetbury. From Tetbury take A4135 towards Dursley, then take 2nd L, should be signed Leighterton. Pottery 1¹/₂ m on R.* Tea & Home-made teas. **Adm £2.50, chd free.** Sat 28, Sun 29, Mon 30, Tue 31 May; Wed 1, Thur 2, Fri 3, Sat 4, Sun 5 June (11-6).
A combination of dramatic open perspectives and intimate corners. Borders, shrubs, woodland glade, water garden containing treatment ponds (unfenced) and flowform cascades. Kitchen garden with raised beds, orchard. Sculptural features. Run on organic principles. Pottery showroom with hand-thrown wood-fired pots incl frostproof garden pots. Art & craft exhibition incl garden sculptures (May 28 to June 5 only).
♿ 🐾 🌼 ☕

31 ♦ HUNTS COURT

North Nibley GL11 6DZ. Mr & Mrs T K Marshall, 01453 547440, huntscourt@tiscali.co.uk. *2m NW of Wotton-under-Edge. From Wotton B4060 Dursley rd turn R in North Nibley at Black Horse; fork L after ¹/₄ m.* **Adm £4, chd free.** For NGS: Suns 12, 19 June; 4, 11 Sept (2-6). **For opening times and information please visit website or telephone.**
A plant lover's garden with unusual shrubs, 450 varieties old roses, large collection of penstemons and hardy geraniums in peaceful 2¹/₂-acre garden set against tree-clad hills and Tyndale monument. Mini-arboretum. House (not open) possible birthplace of William Tyndale. Picnic area.
♿ 🌼 ☕ ☎

ILMINGTON GARDENS

See Warwickshire.

32 ♦ KEMPSFORD MANOR

High Street, Kempsford GL7 4EQ. Mrs Z I Williamson, 01285 810131, www.kempsfordmanor.com. *3m S of Fairford. Take A419 from Cirencester or Swindon. Kempsford is signed 10m (approx) from each. The Manor is in the centre of village.* For NGS: Suns, 6 Feb to 27 Feb; Sat 19 Feb; Sun 6, 27 Mar; Thur 14, Sun 17, Sat 23, Mon 25 Apr; Suns 8 May 26 June ; Suns 7 Aug to 21 Aug; 11 Sept (2-5); Suns 12 Feb to 26 Feb; Sat 18 Feb 2012 (2-5). **For opening times and information please visit website or telephone.**

Early spring garden with variety of bulbs incl snowdrop walk along old canal. Peaceful, expansive summer garden for relaxation, adjacent to cricket field, croquet and outdoor games and quizzes for children. Occasional plant sales; frequent musical events., New feature - improved vegetable garden, vegetable sales and advice by gardener. Featured on local radio.
♿ 🌼 🛏 ☕ ☎

KENCOT GARDENS

See Oxfordshire.

A combination of
dramatic open
perspectives and
intimate corners . . .

33 ♦ KIFTSGATE COURT

nr Chipping Campden GL55 6LN. Mr & Mrs J G Chambers, 01386 438777, www.kiftsgate.co.uk. *4m NE of Chipping Campden. Adjacent to Hidcote NT Garden. 3m N.E of Chipping Campden.* Light Refreshments. **Adm £7, chd £2.50.** For NGS: Mon 18 Apr; Mon 15 Aug (2-6). **For other opening times and information, please phone or see garden website.**
Magnificent situation and views; many unusual plants and shrubs; tree peonies, hydrangeas, abutilons, species and old-fashioned roses, incl largest rose in England, *Rosa filipes* 'Kiftsgate'. 30% accessible by wheelchair.
♿ 🌼 ☕ ☎

GROUP OPENING

34 LONGHOPE GARDENS

Longhope GL17 0LL. *10m W of Gloucester. 6m E of Ross on Wye. Take Longhope turn off A40 into Church Road. Parking on Church Rd for Court Leet, 3 Church Rd, 6 The Orchards & West View, park on The Wend for Breenes. Limited parking at Springfield House.* Home-made teas.

Support the NGS – eat more cake! ☕

Combined adm £5, chd free. Sats & Suns 28, 29 May; 11, 12 June June (2-6).

BREENES
Ann & James Steed.
(See separate entry)

3 CHURCH ROAD
Rev Clive & Mrs Linda Edmonds
Visitors also welcome by appt May & June only.
01452 831545

COURT LEET
Annie & Gary Frost

SPRINGFIELD HOUSE
Sally & Martin Gibson

NEW **6 THE ORCHARDS**
Ian & Francis Martin

WEST VIEW
Don Vallance

Small village in a valley with wonderful views and C12 church offering six well-planted gardens open to view. Breenes is owned by garden designers and is planted and designed for impact. 3 Church Road is a long garden divided into 'rooms' with a large collection of hardy geraniums, many of them unusual varieties. Court Leet is a densely planted cottage garden around a C17 house (not open) with wonderful blooms and perfume. 6 The Orchards is a small, well planted garden bordered by a stream, with a mix of traditional and contemporary features. Springfield House is a large enclosed garden abundantly planted with shrubs, herbaceous borders and vegetables. West View is a large garden with a wide variety of plants and shrubs, a pond and lovely planting leading to a stream. A good variety of gardens for all tastes.

⊗ ☕

35 LOWER FARM HOUSE
Cliffords Mesne GL18 1JT. Gareth & Sarah Williams. *2m S of Newent. From Newent follow signs to Cliffords Mesne & Birds of Prey Centre (1¹/₂ m). Approx ¹/₂ m beyond 'Centre', turn L at Xrds, signed Kents Green. Garden 150yds down hill on bend. Car park (limited if wet).* Home-made teas.
Adm £3.50, chd free. Wed 25 (2-6), Mon 30 May (1-6).
2-acre garden, incl woodland, stream and large natural lily pond with rockery and bog garden. Herbaceous borders, pergola walk, terrace with ornamental fishpond, kitchen and herb garden; many interesting and unusual trees and shrubs. gravel paths; slight gradients.
♿ 🐕 ⊗ ☕

LYDIARD PARK WALLED GARDEN
See Wiltshire.

Painswick Rococo Garden

36 ◆ LYDNEY PARK SPRING GARDEN

Lydney GL15 6BU. The Viscount Bledisloc, 01594 842844, www.lydneyparkestate.co.uk. ¹/₂ m SW of Lydney. On A48 Gloucester to Chepstow rd between Lydney & Aylburton. Drive is directly off A48. Adm £4, chd 50p. For NGS: Wed 27 Apr (10-5). For other opening times and information, please phone or see garden website.
Spring garden in 8-acre woodland valley with lakes, profusion of rhododendrons, azaleas and other flowering shrubs. Formal garden; magnolias and daffodils (April). Picnics in deer park which has fine trees. Important Roman Temple site and museum .

MARSHFIELD GARDENS

See Somerset & Bristol.

If you hunt, you will find a tiny cricket lawn and pavilion, a rose walk and a 'scratch n' sniff' herb garden . . .

37 ◆ THE MATARA MEDITATIVE GARDENS

Kingscote, Nr Tetbury GL8 8YA. Herons Mead Ltd, 01453 861050, www.matara.co.uk. 5¹/₂ m NW of Tetbury. On A4135 towards Dursley. At the Hunters Hall Inn turn R into Kingscote village. Enter Park at 1st gate on R. Adm £6, chd £3. For NGS: Suns 19 June; 25 Sept (from 1pm). For other opening times and information, please phone or see garden website.
Trees of life - enjoy the tranquil beauty of Matara's meditative gardens and its dedication to the symbolic, spiritual and cultural role of trees. What makes us special are our Chinese Scholar Garden, Japanese Tea Garden, Shinto Woodland, a Celtic wishing tree, labyrinth, healing spiral and ornamental herb and flower gardens.

38 MEADOW COTTAGE

59 Coalway Road, Coalway, nr Coleford GL16 7HL. Mrs Pamela Buckland, 01594 833444. 1m SE of Coleford. From Coleford take Lydney & Chepstow Rd at T-lights in town. Turn L after police stn, signed Coalway & Parkend. Garden on L ¹/₂ m up hill opp layby. Home-made teas. Adm £3, chd free. Suns 17 Apr; Wed 27 July (2-6) Evening Opening Sat 25 June (6-9). Visitors also welcome by appt.
¹/₃ -acre cottage garden, a plantaholic craftworker's creation with shrubs, perennials, spring bulbs in colourful borders and interlinking garden rooms. Lawned area. Gravel paths leading to small pond with waterfall and bog garden. Vegetable garden in raised beds. Gravel garden with grasses, bamboos and pots and containers in abundance.

39 9 MEREVALE ROAD

GL2 0QX. P & J Wilcox. Off Gloucester Ring Rd (A38) 2m E of City Centre. From Gloucester, follow Ring Rd to Cheltenham Rd r'about (University of Gloucester on L). Straight ahead, signed Gloucester Royal Hospital, take 1st L into Kenilworth Ave. At small Xr, continue into Merevale Rd. Adm £3, chd free. Sun 29 May (2-6).
Medium-sized suburban garden consisting of small front garden with gravel area and borders. Collection of acers, patio area with ornamental pots, clematis arch leading to lawn and well stocked herbaceous borders incl many hardy geraniums. Wildlife pond within gravel area planted with grasses. Exhibition of work by Churchdown Photographic. Featured in Gloucester Citizen, BBC Radio Gloucestershire, visited by Heart of England in Bloom committee as part of Gloucester in Bloom's gold award.

40 ◆ MILL DENE GARDEN

School Lane, Blockley GL56 9HU. Mr & Mrs B S Dare, 01386 700457, www.milldenegarden.co.uk. 3m NW of Moreton-in-Marsh. From A44, follow brown signs from Bourton-on-the-Hill, to Blockley. 1.3 miles down hill turn L behind village gates. Parking for 8 cars. Please ring ahead to reserve 'disabled' space. Coaches by appointment. Lunches & cream teas. Adm £5.50, chd free. For NGS: Sun 10 Apr (2-5). For other opening times and information, please

phone or see garden website.
RHS recommended garden, Mill Dene is hidden in the Cotswolds. It surrounds a water-mill and stream. If you hunt, you will find a tiny cricket lawn and pavilion, a rose walk and a 'scratch n' sniff' herb garden with rills.Masses of tulips & bulbs in the Spring. Plant sales, Lunches and Cream teas. Free children's trail. Featured in Korean TV. Gravel paths, some steep but all have grab rails and step alternatives 50% accessible.

41 ◆ MISARDEN PARK

Misarden. GL6 7JA. Major M T N H Wills, 01285 821303, www.misardenpark.co.uk. 6m NW of Cirencester. Follow signs off A417 or B4070 from Stroud. Adm £4, chd free (share to St Andrews church). For NGS: Suns 17 Apr; 26 June (2.30-6). For other opening times and information, please phone or see garden website.
Essentially formal, dating from C17, magnificent position overlooking the Golden Valley. Walled garden with long mixed borders, yew walk leading to a lower lawn with rill and summer-house. Arboretum with spring bulbs en masse. Climbing roses and rose walk linking parterre. Silver and grey border, blue border and scented border. Blue/gold walkway below house.

42 MOOR WOOD

Woodmancote GL7 7EB. Mr & Mrs Henry Robinson, 01285 831397. 3¹/₂ m NW of Cirencester. Turn L off A435 to Cheltenham at North Cerney, signed Woodmancote 1¹/₄ m; entrance in village on L beside lodge with white gates. Adm £3.50, chd free. Sun 26 June (2-6). Visitors also welcome by appt. Please phone.
2 acres of shrub, orchard and wild flower gardens in isolated valley setting. Holder of the National Collection of rambler roses.

43 THE OLD CHEQUER

Draycott, nr Blockley GL56 9LB. Mr & Mrs H Linley, 01386 700647. 2m NE of Moreton-in-Marsh. Nr Blockley. Home-made teas. Adm £3, combined adm with Blockley Gardens 8 May £6, chd free. Suns 10 Apr (1-4); 8 May (2-6). Visitors also welcome by appt April, May, June & July.

A cottage garden, created by owner, set in 2 acres of old orchard with original ridge and furrow. Emphasis on spring planting but still maintaining yr-round interest. Kitchen garden/soft fruit, herbaceous and shrubs in island beds. Croquet lawn, unusual plants, alpines and dry gravel borders.

&. ✿ ☕ ☎

THE OLD CORN MILL
See Herefordshire.

44 THE OLD RECTORY, DUNTISBOURNE ROUS
GL7 7AP. Charles & Mary Keen, mary@keengardener.com. *4m NW of Cirencester. From Daglingworth take rd to the Duntisbournes; or from A417 from Gloucester take Duntisbourne Leer turning and follow signs for Daglingworth.* Adm £5, chd free. Mons 14 Feb (11-4); 21 Mar; 9 May; 20 June (11-5). Visitors also welcome by appt for groups 10+.
Garden in an exceptional setting made by designer and writer Mary Keen. Subject of many articles and Telegraph column. Designed for atmosphere, but collections of galanthus, hellebores, auriculas and half hardies - especially dahlias - are all features in their season. Sheffield meadow now a regular feature. Saxon church. Wheelchair access possible to most of garden. Some gravel paths.

&. ☕

Unique C18 garden from the brief Rococo period . . .

38 OVERBURY COURT
See Worcestershire.

45 ◆ PAINSWICK ROCOCO GARDEN
Painswick GL6 6TH. Painswick Rococo Garden Trust, 01452 813204, www.rococogarden.org.uk. *¼ m N of Painswick. ½ m outside village on B4073.* Adm £6, chd £3. For opening times and information, please phone or see garden website.
Unique C18 garden from the brief Rococo period, combining contemporary buildings, vistas, ponds, kitchen garden and winding woodland walks. Anniversary maze, plant nursery.

🏠 ✿ ☕ ☎

46 PAULMEAD
Bisley GL6 7AG. Judy & Philip Howard. *5m E of Stroud. On S edge of Bisley at head of Toadsmoor Valley on top of Cotswolds. Garden & car park well signed in Bisley village. Disabled can be dropped off at garden prior to parking car.* Adm £4, chd free. Combined with **Wells Cottage** £5. Sun 19 June (2-6).
Approx 1-acre landscaped garden constructed in stages over last 25yrs. Terraced in three main levels: natural stream garden; formal herbaceous and shrub borders; yew and beech hedges; formal vegetable garden; lawns; summerhouse with exterior wooden decking by pond and thatched roof over well head. Unusual tree house.

&. ✿

47 PEAR TREE COTTAGE
58 Malleson Road, Gotherington GL52 9EX. Mr & Mrs E Manders-Trett, 01242 674592, edandmary@talktalk.net. *4m N of Cheltenham. From A435, travelling N, turn R into Gotherington 1m after end of Bishop's Cleeve bypass at garage. Garden on L approx 100yds past Shutter Inn.* Adm £3.50, chd free. Sun 20 Mar (2-5). Visitors also welcome by appt max 1 coach for private visits. March - June inc.
Mainly informal country garden of approx ½ acre with pond and gravel garden, grasses and herbaceous borders, trees and shrubs surrounding lawns. Wild garden and orchard lead to greenhouses, herb and vegetable gardens. Spring bulbs and early summer perennials and shrubs particularly colourful.

🏠 ✿ ☕ ☎

48 PEMBERLEY LODGE
Churchend Lane, Old Charfield GL12 8LJ. Rob & Yvette Andrewartha, 01454 260885. *3½ m SW of Wotton-under-Edge. Off B4058 from Wotton-under Edge through Charfield Village. At top of Charfield Hill, turn L. 2m from M5 J14, at Xrds on B4509 go straight across.* Tea & Light Refreshments. Adm £4.50, chd free. Visitors welcome by appt. Groups of 10+ welcome with advance notice.
Small private garden designed and planted in 2002 by Lesley Rosser. Densely planted for all-year interest and low maintenance. Incorporates trees, shrubs, perennials, grasses, water, gravel and hard landscaping to give an informal and peaceful feel.

Roof garden added in 2006. New garden area recently added.

&. ☕ ☎

49 PRIORS MESNE
Aylburton, Lydney GL15 6DX. Mr & Mrs Brian Thornton. *3m NW of Lydney. At the George PH in Aylburton take St Briavels rd off A48. Go up hill for 2m to T-junction. Turn sharp L, go down hill for approx 200 metres. Turn R into entrance marked Priors Mesne private rd. Go to end of drive 300 metres through auto gate.* Home-made teas. Adm £4, chd free. Sun 8, 15 May (2-5).
Approached down an avenue of mature lime trees, this large terraced garden enjoys distant views over deer park to Severn Estuary and Cotswolds beyond. Collection of rhododendrons, azaleas, magnolias and cornus set amongst three magnificent copper beeches, water feature and woodland walk through bluebells. Featured in The Forester & The Review.

☕

GROUP OPENING

50 QUENINGTON GARDENS
nr Fairford GL7 5BW. *8m NE of Cirencester.* Home-made teas at The Old Rectory. Combined adm £5, chd free. Sun 26 June (2-5.30).

> **BANK VIEW**
> Mrs J A Moulden

> **THE OLD POST HOUSE**
> Mrs D Blackwood

> **THE OLD RECTORY, QUENINGTON**
> Mr & Mrs D Abel Smith

> **POOL HAY**
> Mrs E A Morris

> **YEW TREE COTTAGES**
> Mr J Lindon

A rarely visited Coln Valley village delighting its infrequent visitors with C12 Norman church and C17 stone cottages (not open). An opportunity to discover the horticultural treasures behind those Cotswold stone walls and visit 5 very different but charming gardens incorporating everything from the exotic and the organic to the simple cottage garden; a range of vistas from riverside to seclusion. Fresh Air 2011 Sculpture Show.

🏠 ✿ ☕

Stone House

51 RAMBLERS

Lower Common, Aylburton, nr Lydney GL15 6DS. Jane & Leslie Hale, 01594 843917, jane.hale@virgin.net. *1¹/₂ m W of Lydney. Off A48 Gloucester to Chepstow Rd. From Lydney through Aylburton, out of de-limit turn R signed Aylburton Common, ³/₄ m along lane.* Home-made teas. **Adm £3, chd free. Sun 1 May (2-6).** Visitors also welcome by appt May and June only.

Peaceful medium-sized country garden with informal cottage planting, herbaceous borders and small pond looking through hedge 'windows' onto wild flower meadow. Front woodland garden with shade-loving plants and topiary. Large productive vegetable garden. Apple orchard.

✿ ☕ ☎

52 ROCKCLIFFE

nr Lower Swell GL54 2JW. Mr & Mrs Simon Keswick. *2m SW of Stow-on-the-Wold. 1¹/₂ m from Lower Swell. On B4068. From Stow-on-the-Wold to Cheltenham go through Lower Swell. Climb hill staying on B4068. Converted barn on L. Round corner & start dropping down hill. Rockcliffe halfway down on R.* Home-made teas. **Adm £4.50, combined**

adm with **Eyford House £8, chd free. Wed 29 June (10-6).** Large traditional English garden of 8 acres incl pink, white and blue gardens, herbaceous border, rose terrace; walled kitchen garden and orchard; greenhouses and original stone dovecot with pathway of topiary birds leading up through orchard to it.

53 ROOKWOODS

Waterlane, nr Bisley GL6 7PN. Mr & Mrs Des Althorp. *5m E of Stroud. Between Sapperton & Bisley. Turn down No Through Rd in Waterlane then follow signs.* Home-made teas. **Adm £3.50, chd free. Sun 26 June (2-6).**

3-acre, well structured garden with herbaceous borders to colour themes. Pleached whitebeam around pool area. Wide variety of old-fashioned and modern climbing and shrub roses (mostly labelled), water gardens and outstanding views.

🐕 ✿ ☕

ROSE VILLA
See Worcestershire.

SALFORD GARDENS
See Oxfordshire.

54 SANDYWELL BARN HOUSE

Sandywell Park, Whittington, Cheltenham GL54 4HF. Shirley & Gordon Sills, 01242 820606, shlrleysills@btinternet.com. *4m E of Cheltenham. On A40 between Whittington & Andoversford.* Home-made teas. **Adm £4, chd free. Sun & Mon 29, 30 May; Sun 12 June (11.30-5).** Visitors also welcome by appt June only. Groups of 10+. Coaches welcome.

Plantaholic designer's own 2¹/₂ -acre walled garden. Maintained by owners. Exuberantly planted for form, scent and colour, featuring areas both traditional and contemporary. Herbaceous, roses, climbers, shrubs, trees, lawns, hedges, structures. Formal water features, spring fed stream and small pond.

✿ ☕ ☎

55 NEW SCHOFIELDS

30 Ford House Road, Newent GL18 1LQ. John & Linda Schofield, 01531 820370, linda@hazelschofield.co.uk. *1.5m NE of Newent. At traffic lights on Newent by-pass, take B4215 N signed Dymock. Pass fire station & turn R into Tewkesbury Rd. Continue for 0.9m. Ford House Rd is signed to the L. Take this, then turn L onto concrete road between 2 caravan fields. Continue to 4th house on LH side.* . Refreshments by arrangement. **Adm £3.50, chd free. Visitors welcome by appt Groups of 10+ adults. April-Sept, daytime/ evening. Sun-Fri. Parking for cars & 20 seat coach.**

Tranquil 5 acres developed from 1970s providing: 2¹/₂ -acre spring woodland garden; plantsman's ³/₄ -acres mature trees and shrubs, bulb, herbaceous and hot borders, autumn colour, berries, lavender walk, knot garden, lily ponds; adjacent 1000sq.m exotic glasshouse garden planted with palms, tender and fruiting trees, shrubs, bulbs, climbers and succulents. Enquiries from artist/photography groups welcome. Gravel and bark paths, moderate slopes in woodland.

♿ ☎

56 ◆ SEZINCOTE

nr Moreton-in-Marsh GL56 9AW. Mr & Mrs D Peake, www.sezincote.co.uk. *3m SW of Moreton-in-Marsh. From Moreton-in-Marsh turn W along A44 towards Evesham; after 1¹/₂ m (just before Bourton-on-the-Hill) take turn L, by*

stone lodge with white gate. Light Refreshments. **Adm £5, chd free. For NGS: Sun 3 July (2-6). For opening times and information please visit website or telephone.**
Exotic oriental water garden by Repton and Daniell with lake, pools and meandering stream, banked with massed perennials. Large semi-circular orangery, formal Indian garden, fountain, temple and unusual trees of vast size in lawn and wooded park setting. House in Indian manner designed by Samuel Pepys Cockerell.
 ⚬ ☕

57 ♦ SNOWSHILL MANOR & GARDEN
Snowshill, nr Broadway WR12 7JU. National Trust, 01386 852410, www.nationaltrust.org.uk. *2¹/₂ m SW of Broadway. Off A44 bypass into Broadway village.* **Adm £5, chd £2.50. For NGS: Wed 22 June (11-5.30). For other opening times and information, please phone or see garden website.**
Delightful hillside garden surrounding beautiful Cotswold manor. Designed in the Arts and Crafts style, the garden consists of a series of contrasting outdoor rooms. Simple colourful plantings tumble and scramble down the terraces and around byres and ponds. Garden produce and plants for sale (when available).
⊛ ☕ ☎

58 SOUTH LODGE
Church Road, Clearwell, Coleford GL16 8LG. Andrew & Jane MacBean, 01594 837769, southlodgegarden@btinternet.com, www.southlodgegarden.co.uk. *2m S of Coleford. Off B4228. Follow signs to Clearwell. Garden on L of castle driveway. Please park on the road in front of the church or in the village.* Home-made teas. **Adm £3, chd free. Suns 10 Apr; 1, 22 May (1-5); 19 June (11-5).** Visitors also welcome by appt evenings in May and June only for parties of 12+.
Peaceful country garden with stunning views of surrounding countryside. High walls provide a backdrop for rambling roses, clematis, and honeysuckles. An organic garden with a large variety of perennials, annuals, grasses, shrubs and specimen trees with year round colour. Fernery, vegetable garden, wildlife and formal ponds. New rustic pergola planted with English climbing roses and willow arbour amongst

wildflowers. Featured in BBC Radio Featured on Radio Gloucestershire & on ITV West Country Tonight. Gravel paths & steep slopes.
 ⚬ ⊛ ☕ ☎

SPECIAL PLANTS
See Somerset & Bristol.

59 STANTON GARDENS
Stanton, nr Broadway WR12 7NE. Mr K J Ryland. *3m SW of Broadway. Off B4632, between Broadway (3m) & Winchcombe (6m).* Home-made teas. **Adm £5, chd free. Sun 19 June (2-6).**
An extensive group of over 20 gardens, set in the picturesque C17 Cotswold village of Stanton situated on the edge of the Cotswold escarpment. Gardens range from the formal manor house to charming cottage, which should appeal to all visitors. Plants are for sale in the high street, which have been nurtured by the gardeners of Stanton.
 ⚬ 🏰 ⊛ ☕

> Peaceful country garden in 2 acres with stunning views of surrounding countryside . . .

60 ♦ STANWAY FOUNTAIN & WATER GARDEN
nr Winchcombe GL54 5PQ. The Earl of Wemyss & March, 01386 584469, www.stanwayfountain.co.uk. *9m NE of Cheltenham. 1m E of B4632 Cheltenham to Broadway rd or B4077 Toddington to Stow-on-the-Wold rd.* **Garden only adm £4.50, chd £1.50. For NGS: Suns 10 Apr; 5 June (2-5). For other opening times and information, please phone or see garden website.**
20 acres of planted landscape in early C18 formal setting. The restored canal, upper pond and 165ft high fountain have re-created one of the most interesting Baroque water gardens in Britain. Striking C16 manor with gatehouse, tithe barn and church. Britain's highest fountain at

300ft, the world's highest gravity fountain. Open June, July & Aug, Tues & Thurs (2-5) House & Garden adm £7, chd free, concessions £3.50.
🏰 ☕ ☎

61 ♦ STONE HOUSE
Wyck Rissington GL54 2PN. Mr & Mrs Andrew Lukas, 01451 810337, katielukas@globalnet.co.uk. *3m S of Stow-on-the-Wold. Off A429 between Bourton-on-the-Water & Stow-on-the-Wold. Last house in village behind high bank on R.* **Adm £5, chd £3. For NGS: Sun 17 Apr (2-5.30). For other opening times and information, please phone or email.**
2 acres full of unusual bulbs, shrubs and herbaceous plants. Crab apple walk, rose borders, herb and water garden, meadow walk. Plantswoman's garden with yr-round interest. Private visits welcome March to Sept by prior arrangement.
 ⚬ ⊛ ☕ ☎

62 STOWELL PARK
Northleach GL54 3LE. The Lord & Lady Vestey. *8m NE of Cirencester. Off Fosseway A429 2m SW of Northleach.* Home-made teas. **Adm £5, chd free. Suns 15 May; 19 June (2-5).**
Magnificent lawned terraces with stunning views over Coln Valley. Fine collection of old-fashioned roses and herbaceous plants, with pleached lime approach to C14 house (not open). Two large walled gardens containing vegetables, fruit, cut flowers and range of greenhouses. Long rose pergola and wide, plant-filled borders divided into colour sections. Open continuously for 46 years. Plant Sale 15 May only. Featured in Country Life.
⊛ ☕

63 ♦ SUDELEY CASTLE GARDENS & EXHIBITIONS
Winchcombe GL54 5JD. Aurora Hicks-Beach, 01242 602308, www.sudeleycastle.co.uk. *8m NE of Cheltenham. On B4632 (A46) or 10m from J9 M5. Bus service operates between Winchcombe & Cheltenham or Broadway.* Light Refreshments. **Adm £7.50, chd free. For NGS: Fri 14 Oct (10.30-5). For other opening times and information, please phone or see garden website.**
Award-winning gardens surrounding 15th Century Castle in the Cotswolds incl access to exhibitions, St.Mary's Church and Pheasantry. Plants for

sale incl the David Austin Roses. Rare breed pheasantry, Katherine Parr's tomb. Adventure playground. Wheelchair access to grounds, gardens and coffee shop only.

 NCCPG

SUNNYSIDE
See Gwent.

Small woodland with panoramic views, wild flower areas and thousands of snowdrops and hellebores . . .

64 TEMPLE GUITING MANOR
Temple Guiting, nr Stow on the Wold GL54 5RP. Mr & Mrs S Collins, www.templeguitingmanor.co.uk. *7m from Stow-on-the-Wold. From Stow-on-the-Wold take B4077 towards Tewkesbury. On descending hill bear L to village (signed) 1/2 m. Garden in centre of village on R.* Home-made teas at Tennis Court to side of Gardens. **Adm £4, chd free. Sun 3 July (2-6).** Recently designed formal contemporary gardens to Grade I listed historic manor house (not open) in Windrush Valley. Designed by Jinny Blom, gold medal winner Chelsea Flower Show 2007. New small courtyard garden to newly converted manor barns.

TORMARTON COURT
See Somerset & Bristol.

65 TRENCH HILL
Sheepscombe GL6 6TZ. Celia & Dave Hargrave, 01452 814306, celia.hargrave@btconnect.com. *11/2 m E of Painswick. On A46 to Cheltenham after Painswick, turn R to Sheepscombe. Approx 11/2 m (before reaching village) turn L by telegraph poles, Trench Hill at top of lane.* Home-made teas. **Adm £3, chd free. Suns 13, 20 Feb (11-5); Suns 20 Mar; 24 Apr, Mon 25 Apr; (11-6); Weds 1, 8, 15, 22, 29 June (2-6); Suns 17 July; 28 Aug; 11 Sept (11-6). Suns 12, 19 Feb 2012.**

Visitors also welcome by appt. Approx 3 acres set in small woodland with panoramic views. Variety of herbaceous and mixed borders, rose garden, extensive vegetable plots, wild flower areas, plantings of spring bulbs with thousands of snowdrops and hellebores, woodland walk, 2 small ponds, waterfall and larger conservation pond. Interesting wooden sculptures. Run on organic principles.

66 UPTON WOLD
Moreton-in-Marsh GL56 9TR. Mr & Mrs I R S Bond, www.uptonwoldgarden.co.uk. *31/2 m W of Moreton-in-Marsh. On A44 1m past A424 junction at Troopers Lodge Garage.* Home-made teas & light refreshments. **Adm £7, chd free. Sun 17 Apr (11-5).** Ever-developing and changing garden, architecturally and imaginatively laid out around C17 house (not open) with commanding views. Yew hedges; herbaceous walk; some unusual plants and trees; vegetables; pond and woodland gardens. National Collection of Juglans and Pterocarya. 2 Star award from Good Gardens Guide.

 NCCPG

67 VALLEY VIEW
Chapel Road, Viney Hill, Lydney GL15 4NU. Julia & Adrian Goss, 01594 517117, julia_goss@yahoo.co.uk. *1m S of Blakeney. On A48 take R turn signed Viney Hill. Drive 3/4 m to New Inn on R. Park on road. Garden is 100m walk to end of Chapel Rd (opp New Inn).* Light refreshments & teas. **Adm £2.50, chd free. Sat & Sun 18, 19 June (11-5). Visitors also welcome by appt June & July only.** Hillside garden (steep in places) of approx 1/2 -acre with panoramic views over the Severn Valley towards Gloucester. Comprising densely planted mixed shrub and herbaceous borders, fruit trees, fernery, wildlife pond with waterfall, vegetable and soft fruit plot with raised beds, terraced area with alpines and small wild patch.

68 NEW WATERLANE HOUSE
Waterlane, nr Stroud, Oakridge GL6 7PN. Mr & Mrs Hall. *11/2 m SE Bisley, 11/2 m N W Sapperton. 4m E Stroud 8m W Cirencester on A419 signposted Bisley. At Bisley turn R*

signposted Waterlane 11/2 m. Home-made & cream teas. **Adm £5, chd free. Sat 28 May; Sun 21 Aug (12-6).** Large gardens surrounding house (not open). Front lawn with mixed borders and mulberry tree. Formal garden with round lawn and pergola. Walled kitchen garden with fountain. Impressive pleached hedge surrounding croquet lawn. Avenues of evergreen oak and lime. Woodland, orchard, rose garden and topiary all set amongst sweeping lawns. Most pathways are gravel. Access via lawns to large section of garden.

69 WELLS COTTAGE
Wells Road, Bisley GL6 7AG. Mr & Mrs Michael Flint, 01452 770289, flint_bisley@talktalk.net. *5m E of Stroud. Garden & car park well signed in Bisley village. Garden lies on S edge of village at head of Toadsmoor Valley, N of A419.* **Adm £4, chd free. Combined with Paulmead £5. Sun 19 June (2-6). Visitors also welcome by appt.** Just under an acre. Terraced on several levels with beautiful views over valley. Much informal planting of trees and shrubs to give colour and texture. Lawns and herbaceous borders. Collection of grasses. Formal pond area. Rambling roses on rope pergola. Vegetable garden with raised beds. Main lawn wheelchair accessible, most features visible. Upper garden too steep for wheelchairs.

70 ◆ WESTBURY COURT GARDEN
Westbury-on-Severn GL14 1PD. National Trust, 01452 760461, www.nationaltrust.org.uk. *9m SW of Gloucester. on A48.* **Adm £4.70, chd £2.30. For NGS: Sun 11 Sept (10-5). For opening times and information please visit website or telephone.** Formal Dutch-style water garden, earliest remaining in England; canals, summerhouse, over 100 species of plants grown in England, and recreated vegetable plots, growing crops all from before 1700. Featured in The Guardian. Monty Don's top 10 gardens.

WESTON MEWS
See Herefordshire.

71 ◆ **WESTONBIRT SCHOOL GARDENS**
Tetbury GL8 8QG. Westonbirt School, 01666 881333, www.holfordtrust.com. *3m SW of Tetbury. Opp Westonbirt Arboretum, on A433 (follow brown tourist information signs).* **Adm £5, chd free. For NGS: Sun 31 July (11-5). For other opening times and information, please phone or see garden website.**
22 acres. Former private garden of Robert Holford, founder of Westonbirt Arboretum. Formal Victorian gardens incl walled Italian garden now restored with early herbaceous borders and exotic border. Rustic walks, lake, statuary and grotto. Rare, exotic trees and shrubs. Beautiful views of Westonbirt House open with guided tours. featured in Daily Telegraph article on restoration of the Italian Garden.

WHATLEY MANOR
See Wiltshire.

WHICHFORD & ASCOTT GARDENS
See Warwickshire.

WHITCOMBE HOUSE
See Worcestershire.

WHITEHILL FARM
See Oxfordshire.

72 **NEW** **WHITESHILL AND RUSCOMBE GARDENS**
Whiteshill, Stroud GL6 6BQ. *1m from Stroud. 8m from Gloucester. 3m from M5 J13.* Home-made teas. **Adm £4, chd free. Sun 22 May (2-6).**
Whiteshill and Ruscombe villages will be open together giving visitors a wonderful opportunity to visit at least 10 gardens, large and small, whilst strolling the lanes and footpaths of this beautiful hillside setting. Many gardens enjoy splendid views across the valleys and beyond. Some gardens unsuitable for those with walking difficulties.

73 **WILLOW LODGE**
nr Longhope GL17 0RA. John & Sheila Wood, 01452 831211, wood@willowgardens.fsnet.co.uk, www.willowgardens.fsnet.co.uk. *10m W of Gloucester, 6m E of Ross-on-Wye. On A40 between Huntley & Lea.* Home-made teas. **Adm £3, chd free. Sun 1, Mon 2 May (1-5). Visitors also welcome by appt.**
Plantsman's garden with unusual and rare plants, herbaceous borders, shrubs and alpine garden. Many woodland plants incl trilliums, erythroniums, hellebores etc. Large bog garden with marginals and Asiatic primulas. Fish pond and stream. Exceptional arboretum containing approx 400 different trees and shrubs, from all over the temperate world. Areas of wild flowers in 4-acre grounds. Plants labelled.

WOODPECKERS
See Warwickshire.

74 **NEW** **WORTLEY FARMHOUSE**
Hillmill Lane, Wortley, Wotton under Edge GL12 7QP. Sean and Annabel Mills, www.seanmills.co.uk. *From A46 to Stroud take left turn to Hawkebury Upton, thru Alderley. 1/4 mile cross small bridge. Take turn to Ozleworth on right, see parking.* Cream Teas & Home-made teas. **Adm £3, chd free. Sat 4 (2-6), Sun 5 June (10-6).**
One and a half acres on different levels with wild area, pond, herbaceous borders, textural planting, veg garden and disabled garden.

Sean is a garden designer who also makes garden pots; examples of work to see and buy. Also plant sales and teas. Garden pots for sale and to order both planted and unplanted. Garden designs to see and review. Plant lists available. Plants for sale. Gravel drive. Some steep slopes.

GROUP OPENING

75 **WYCK RISSINGTON GARDENS**
Cheltenham GL54 2PN. *Nr Stow-on-the-Wold & Bourton-on-the-Water. 1m from Fosse Way A429.* Home-made teas in village hall. **Combined adm £6, chd free (share to Friends of St Laurence). Sun 11 Sept (1-5).**

> **NEW** **CHESTNUT COURT**
> Mr & Mrs N Hampton
>
> **COLLEGE FARM**
> Andrea & Hilary Ponti
>
> **NEW** **HOPE LODGE**
> Mr & Mrs R Pye
>
> **STONE HOUSE**
> Mr & Mrs A Lukas
> (See separate entry)

Wyck Rissington is an unspoilt Cotswold village and is unusual because of its wide village green planted with fine horse chestnuts. The gardens open are within easy reach of the convenient parking and of contrasting styles. If you need inspiration for autumn planting or just delight in the mellow hues of September, this is for you. There are 2 new gardens in this popular group opening this yr. Access available to most gardens with limited access at Hope Lodge.

Gloucestershire County Volunteers

County Organiser
Norman Jeffery, 28 Shrivenham Road, Highworth, Swindon SN6 7BZ, 01793 762805, normjeffery28@aol.com

County Treasurer
Graham Baber, 11 Corinium Gate, Cirencester GL7 2PX, 01285 650961, grayanjen@onetel.com *

Booklet Coordinator
Nick Kane, Church Farm, Goosey, Faringdon SN7 8PA, nick@kanes.org, 07768 478668.

Assistant County Organisers
Barbara Adams, Warners Court, Charfield, Wotton under Edge GL12 8TG, 01454 261078, adams@waitrose.com
Pamela Buckland, Meadow Cottage, 59 Coalway Road, Coalway, Coleford GL16 7HL, 01594 833444
Trish Jeffery, 28 Shrivenham Road, Highworth, Swindon SN6 7BZ, 01793 762805, trishjeffery@aol.com
Valerie Kent, 9 Acer Close, Bradwell Grove, Nr Burford, Oxon OX18 4XE, 01993 823294
Shirley & Gordon Sills, Barn House, Sandywell Park, Whittington, Cheltenham GL54 4HF, 01242 820606, shirley.sills@tesco.net
Pat Willey, Orchard Cottage, Lynch Road, France Lynch, Stroud, GL6 8LP, 01453 883736, willey800@talktalk.net

You are always welcome at an NGS garden

HAMPSHIRE

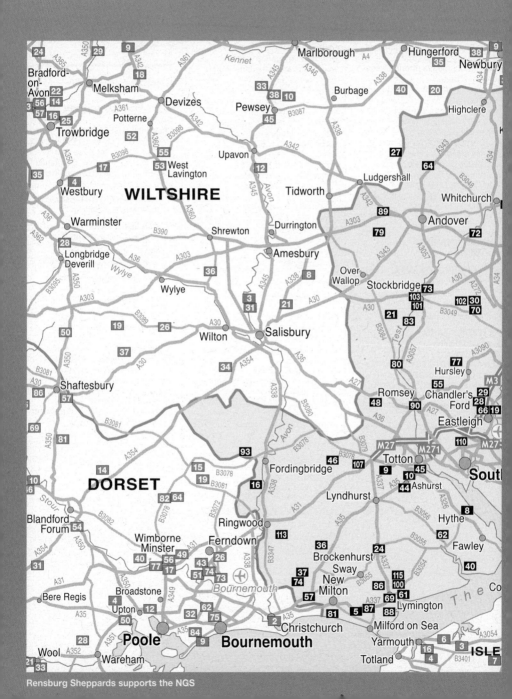

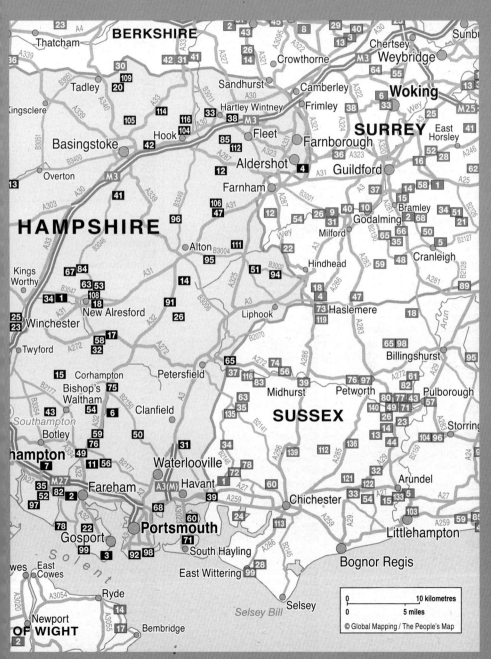

Opening Dates

February

Saturday 12
`18` Brandy Mount House
Sunday 13
`75` Manor House
Sunday 20
`17` Bramdean House
`34` The Down House
`70` Little Court
Monday 21
`70` Little Court
Tuesday 22
`70` Little Court

March

Saturday 19
`8` Atheling Villas
Sunday 20
`8` Atheling Villas
`17` Bramdean House
Sunday 27
`13` Bere Mill
`70` Little Court

April

Sunday 3
`36` Durmast House
`43` Flintstones
Friday 8
`80` Mottisfont Abbey & Garden
Sunday 10
`30` Crawley Gardens
Tuesday 12
`30` Crawley Gardens
Saturday 16
`58` Hinton Ampner
`95` 'Selborne'
Sunday 17
`17` Bramdean House
`68` 60 Lealand Road
`85` Old Thatch & The Millennium Barn
`89` Ramridge Cottage
`95` 'Selborne'
`104` Tylney Hall Hotel
Wednesday 20
`12` Beechenwood Farm
Friday 22
`70` Little Court
Saturday 23
`106` Walbury
Sunday 24
`8` Atheling Villas
`106` Walbury
Monday 25
`1` Abbey Cottage
`8` Atheling Villas
`28` The Cottage

Tuesday 26
`70` Little Court
Wednesday 27
`4` 23 Anglesey Road
`12` Beechenwood Farm
Saturday 30
`71` Littlewood

May

Sunday 1
`15` Blackdown House
`71` Littlewood
`114` White Gables
Monday 2
`28` The Cottage
`43` Flintstones
`94` Sandy Slopes
`114` White Gables
Wednesday 4
`12` Beechenwood Farm
Saturday 7
`8` Atheling Villas
Sunday 8
`2` 80 Abbey Road
`8` Atheling Villas
`61` Hordle Walhampton School
`62` The House in the Wood
`91` Rotherfield Park
Wednesday 11
`12` Beechenwood Farm
Saturday 14
`87` Pennington House
`95` 'Selborne'
Sunday 15
`28` The Cottage
`30` Crawley Gardens
`43` Flintstones
`87` Pennington House
`89` Ramridge Cottage
`95` 'Selborne'
`100` Spinners Garden
Monday 16
`28` The Cottage
`43` Flintstones
`95` 'Selborne'
Tuesday 17
`30` Crawley Gardens
Wednesday 18
`12` Beechenwood Farm
`113` White Barn
Saturday 21
`7` Appletrees
`24` 21 Chestnut Road
Sunday 22
`7` Appletrees
`20` Brooklyn Cottage
`24` 21 Chestnut Road
`49` Great Pecks
`57` Hinton Admiral
`59` Holywell
`68` 60 Lealand Road
`76` Meon Orchard
`108` Weir House

Wednesday 25
`12` Beechenwood Farm
`32` Dean House
`113` White Barn
Sunday 29
`13` Bere Mill
`14` Berry Cottage
`19` 6 Breamore Close
`35` 7 Downland Close
`79` Monxton & Amport Gardens
`88` Pylewell Park
`90` Romsey Gardens
`92` 28 St Ronan's Avenue
`99` Spindles
`107` Waldrons
`109` West Silchester Hall
Monday 30
`13` Bere Mill
`19` 6 Breamore Close
`35` 7 Downland Close
`79` Monxton & Amport Gardens
`90` Romsey Gardens
`94` Sandy Slopes
`107` Waldrons
`109` West Silchester Hall

June

Wednesday 1
`12` Beechenwood Farm
`86` Passford House Hotel Gardens & Wilderness
`113` White Barn
Thursday 2
`86` Passford House Hotel Gardens & Wilderness
Friday 3
`86` Passford House Hotel Gardens & Wilderness
Saturday 4
`8` Atheling Villas
`10` Barhi
`27` Conholt Park
`47` Froyle Gardens
Sunday 5
`8` Atheling Villas
`10` Barhi
`11` 19 Barnwood Road
`15` Blackdown House
`27` Conholt Park
`47` Froyle Gardens
`72` Longparish Gardens
Monday 6
`72` Longparish Gardens
Tuesday 7
`105` The Vyne - **Pre-booking essential**
Wednesday 8
`6` Appletree House
`12` Beechenwood Farm
`27` Conholt Park
`86` Passford House Hotel Gardens & Wilderness
`113` White Barn

You are always welcome at an NGS garden

Thursday 9
- **67** Lake House
- **86** Passford House Hotel Gardens & Wilderness

Friday 10
- **86** Passford House Hotel Gardens & Wilderness

Saturday 11
- **24** 21 Chestnut Road
- **37** Edgewood
- **44** Forest Cottage
- **67** Lake House

Sunday 12
- **17** Bramdean House
- **24** 21 Chestnut Road
- **29** Cranbury Park
- **35** 7 Downland Close
- **37** Edgewood
- **44** Forest Cottage
- **66** 53 Ladywood
- **69** The Little Cottage
- **83** The Old Rectory, Houghton
- **98** Southsea Gardens
- **104** Tylney Hall Hotel

Monday 13
- **35** 7 Downland Close
- **66** 53 Ladywood
- **83** The Old Rectory, Houghton

Tuesday 14
- **43** Flintstones (Evening)

Wednesday 15
- **32** Dean House
- **86** Passford House Hotel Gardens & Wilderness
- **113** White Barn

Thursday 16
- **30** Crawley Gardens
- **86** Passford House Hotel Gardens & Wilderness
- **101** Stockbridge Gardens
- **103** Terstan

Friday 17
- **16** Braemoor
- **37** Edgewood
- **86** Passford House Hotel Gardens & Wilderness

Saturday 18
- **37** Edgewood
- **45** The Fountains
- **58** Hinton Ampner
- **95** 'Selborne'

Sunday 19
- **14** Berry Cottage
- **16** Braemoor
- **30** Crawley Gardens
- **33** Dipley Mill
- **37** Edgewood
- **41** Farleigh House
- **54** Hill Top
- **59** Holywell
- **73** Longstock Park Water Garden
- **81** Mulberry House
- **88** Pylewell Park
- **95** 'Selborne'

101 Stockbridge Gardens
103 Terstan
108 Weir House

Monday 20
- **95** 'Selborne'

Wednesday 22
- **1** Abbey Cottage
- **4** 23 Anglesey Road
- **6** Appletree House
- **34** The Down House
- **86** Passford House Hotel Gardens & Wilderness
- **113** White Barn

Thursday 23
- **27** Conholt Park
- **86** Passford House Hotel Gardens & Wilderness

Friday 24
- **86** Passford House Hotel Gardens & Wilderness

Saturday 25
- **22** 2 Carisbrooke Road
- **26** Colemore House Gardens
- **37** Edgewood
- **98** Southsea Gardens (Evening)

Sunday 26
- **22** 2 Carisbrooke Road
- **34** The Down House
- **37** Edgewood
- **42** Fir Trees
- **46** Fritham Lodge
- **81** Mulberry House
- **96** Shalden Park House
- **99** Spindles

Monday 27
- **26** Colemore House Gardens
- **99** Spindles

Tuesday 28
- **42** Fir Trees

Wednesday 29
- **86** Passford House Hotel Gardens & Wilderness
- **113** White Barn

Thursday 30
- **86** Passford House Hotel Gardens & Wilderness

July

Friday 1
- **16** Braemoor
- **86** Passford House Hotel Gardens & Wilderness

Saturday 2
- **23** Central Winchester Gardens
- **60** The Homestead

Sunday 3
- **16** Braemoor
- **23** Central Winchester Gardens
- **36** Durmast House
- **38** The Elvetham Hotel
- **70** Little Court
- **114** White Gables

Monday 4
- **38** The Elvetham Hotel
- **70** Little Court

Wednesday 6
- **32** Dean House
- **86** Passford House Hotel Gardens & Wilderness
- **113** White Barn

Thursday 7
- **86** Passford House Hotel Gardens & Wilderness

Friday 8
- **86** Passford House Hotel Gardens & Wilderness

Saturday 9
- **21** The Buildings
- **65** Kimpton House
- **82** Oakfields

Sunday 10
- **21** The Buildings
- **39** Emsworth Gardens
- **65** Kimpton House
- **69** The Little Cottage
- **77** Merdon Manor
- **78** Michaelmas
- **82** Oakfields
- **93** Sandle Cottage
- **97** Silverwood
- **109** West Silchester Hall
- **112** Whispers
- **116** 1 Wogsbarne Cottages

Monday 11
- **78** Michaelmas
- **97** Silverwood
- **116** 1 Wogsbarne Cottages

Wednesday 13
- **86** Passford House Hotel Gardens & Wilderness
- **113** White Barn

Thursday 14
- **86** Passford House Hotel Gardens & Wilderness
- **103** Terstan

Friday 15
- **86** Passford House Hotel Gardens & Wilderness

Saturday 16
- **25** 12 Christchurch Road
- **58** Hinton Ampner
- **85** Old Thatch & The Millennium Barn (Evening)
- **105** The Vyne

Sunday 17
- **11** 19 Barnwood Road
- **14** Berry Cottage
- **17** Bramdean House
- **25** 12 Christchurch Road
- **32** Dean House
- **66** 53 Ladywood
- **103** Terstan
- **110** Westward

Monday 18
- **66** 53 Ladywood

Wednesday 20
6 Appletree House
86 Passford House Hotel Gardens & Wilderness
110 Westward
113 White Barn

Thursday 21
30 Crawley Gardens
86 Passford House Hotel Gardens & Wilderness

Friday 22
16 Braemoor
86 Passford House Hotel Gardens & Wilderness

Saturday 23
9 Aviemore
19 6 Breamore Close

Sunday 24
9 Aviemore
16 Braemoor
19 6 Breamore Close
30 Crawley Gardens
93 Sandle Cottage
110 Westward

Wednesday 27
86 Passford House Hotel Gardens & Wilderness
113 White Barn

Thursday 28
86 Passford House Hotel Gardens & Wilderness

Friday 29
86 Passford House Hotel Gardens & Wilderness

Saturday 30
69 The Little Cottage
115 Willows

Sunday 31
24 21 Chestnut Road
69 The Little Cottage
76 Meon Orchard
93 Sandle Cottage
115 Willows

August

Thursday 4
84 The Old Rectory, Swarraton

Friday 5
16 Braemoor

Saturday 6
16 Braemoor
21 The Buildings
69 The Little Cottage
95 'Selborne'
115 Willows

Sunday 7
16 Braemoor
21 The Buildings
32 Dean House
53 Hill House
69 The Little Cottage
95 'Selborne'
109 West Silchester Hall
115 Willows

Monday 8
95 'Selborne'

Tuesday 9
53 Hill House

Thursday 11
84 The Old Rectory, Swarraton

Sunday 14
64 Ibthorpe Tower

Wednesday 17
32 Dean House
64 Ibthorpe Tower

Saturday 20
48 Gilberts Nursery
69 The Little Cottage
111 Wheatley House
115 Willows

Sunday 21
14 Berry Cottage
63 The Hyde
69 The Little Cottage
111 Wheatley House
115 Willows

Tuesday 23
63 The Hyde

Saturday 27
48 Gilberts Nursery

Sunday 28
1 Abbey Cottage
48 Gilberts Nursery
69 The Little Cottage
115 Willows

Monday 29
1 Abbey Cottage
50 Hambledon House
69 The Little Cottage
115 Willows

September

Saturday 3
21 The Buildings

Sunday 4
14 Berry Cottage
21 The Buildings
33 Dipley Mill
63 The Hyde
76 Meon Orchard
85 Old Thatch & The Millennium Barn

Tuesday 6
63 The Hyde

Sunday 11
54 Hill Top

Saturday 17
58 Hinton Ampner

Sunday 18
13 Bere Mill
17 Bramdean House
41 Farleigh House
49 Great Pecks
50 Hambledon House
108 Weir House

Wednesday 21
4 23 Anglesey Road

October

Sunday 9
104 Tylney Hall Hotel

February 2012

Sunday 19
17 Bramdean House

Thursday 23
70 Little Court

Friday 24
70 Little Court

Sunday 26
70 Little Court

Gardens open to the public

3 Alverstoke Crescent Garden
5 Apple Court
17 Bramdean House
40 Exbury Gardens & Steam Railway
55 Hillier Gardens
58 Hinton Ampner
74 Macpennys Woodland Garden & Nurseries
80 Mottisfont Abbey & Garden
100 Spinners Garden
105 The Vyne

By appointment only

31 Crookley Pool
51 Hanging Hosta Garden
52 Heathlands
56 2 Hillside Cottages

The garden is opening for the first time in early May to show off the wonderful bulbs, hundreds of which are planted every year . . .

Also open by Appointment ☎

Aviemore

The Gardens

1 **ABBEY COTTAGE**
Itchen Abbas SO21 1BN. Patrick Daniell, www.abbeycottage.org.uk. 2½ m W of Alresford. On B3047 between Kingworthy and Alresford, ½ m E of the Trout Inn at Itchen Abbas. Home-made teas. **Adm £3, chd free. Easter Mon 25 Apr (12-5); Wed 22 June (11-5, with teas at The Down House, also open); Sun 28, Mon 29 Aug (12-5).**
This 1½ -acre organic garden, on alkaline soil, is a fine garden by any standards. Inside the C18 walls of an old kitchen garden there are enclosures, on different levels, which together make an inspirational garden, designed, created and now maintained by the owner. The adjoining meadow contains specimen trees, an orchard, spring bulbs, summer wild flowers and a plantation of native trees. Hampshire Wildlife Trust Wildlife Garden Award. Big Wildlife Garden (Natural England) Green Garden Award.
&♿ ✿ ☕

2 **80 ABBEY ROAD**
Fareham PO15 5HW. Brian & Vivienne Garford, 01329 843939, vgarford@aol.com. 1m W of Fareham. From M27 J9 take A27 E to Fareham for approx 2 m. At top of hill, turn L at lights into Highlands Rd. Turn 4th R into Blackbrook Rd. Abbey Rd is 4th L. Home-made teas. **Adm £3, chd free. Sun 8 May (11-5). Visitors also welcome by appt incl groups.**
Small garden with extensive collection of herbs and plants of botanical and historical interest, many for sale. Box edging provides structure for more relaxed planting. Interesting use of containers, and ideas for small gardens. 2 ponds and tiny meadow area attract wildlife. Trails for children. Living willow seat, trained grapevine. Art exhibition by local artist.
✿ ☕ ☎

ALDSWORTH HOUSE
See Sussex.

3 ◆ **ALVERSTOKE CRESCENT GARDEN**
Crescent Road, Gosport PO12 2DH. Gosport Borough Council, 023 9242 2467, www.angleseyville.co.uk. *1m S of Gosport. From A32 & Gosport follow signs for Stokes Bay. Continue alongside bay to small r'about, turn L into Anglesey Rd. Crescent Garden signed 50yds on R.* **Adm by donation, open daily all year. For opening times and information please visit website or telephone.** Restored Regency ornamental garden, designed to enhance fine Crescent (Owen 1828). Trees, walks and flowers lovingly maintained by community/Council partnership. Garden's considerable local historic interest highlighted by impressive restoration and creative planting of adjacent St Mark's churchyard. Worth seeing together. Heritage, history and horticulture: a fascinating package. Plant Sale & refreshments Sat, Sun 21, 22 May (10-12). S & SE Britain in Bloom, overall winner Small Park, Green Flag Winner.
  🚻 🐕 ❀

A garden to explore, down narrow winding paths edged with subtle and original plant associations . . .

4 **23 ANGLESEY ROAD**
Aldershot GU12 4RF. Adrian & Elizabeth Whiteley, 01252 677623, adrian.whitely@virginmedia.com. *On E edge of Aldershot. From A331 take A323 towards Aldershot. Keep in R-hand lane, turn R at T-lights into North Lane, then immed L into Lower Newport Rd. Round bend turn immed R into Newport Rd, 1st R into Wilson Rd. Round L-hand bend turn immed R into Roberts Rd, Anglesey Rd 1st on L. Please park considerately in local rds.* Home-made teas. **Adm £2.50, chd free.** Weds 27 Apr; 22 June; 21 Sept (2-6). Visitors also welcome by appt all year, max 12 people.
Larger-than-life garden with a presence that belies its very small size. Designed with generous

asymmetrical borders accommodating an eclectic mix of plants from the everyday to the rare and exotic. Trees and bamboos give a feeling of peace and seclusion while dense planting provides an evolving tapestry of texture and colour.
❀ ☕ ☎

5 ◆ **APPLE COURT**
Hordle Lane, Hordle, Lymington SO41 0HU. Charles & Angela Meads, 01590 642130, www.applecourt.com. *4m W of Lymington. From A337 between Lymington & New Milton, turn into Hordle Lane at Royal Oak at Downton Xrds.* **Adm £4, chd free. For opening times and information, please phone or see garden website.** 1½-acre formally designed and exuberantly planted sheltered walled garden. Theatrical white garden, extensive ornamental grass plantings, subtropical borders. 70 metre hosta walk. International display gardens of day lilies, fern walk, Japanese-style garden with koi pond.
  ❀ 🛏 ☕

6 ◆ **APPLETREE HOUSE**
Station Road, Soberton, nr Southampton SO32 3QU. Mrs J Dover, 01489 877333, jennie.dover@yahoo.co.uk. *10m N of Fareham. A32 N to Droxford, at Xrds turn R B2150. Turn R under bridge into Station Rd, garden 1m. Parking in lay-by 300yds or in rd.* Light refreshments, lunches & home-made teas. **Adm £2.50, chd free.** Weds 8, 22 June; Wed 20 July (12-4). Visitors also welcome by appt.
Very popular, small romantic woodland garden with many varieties of clematis climbing through richly planted beds as well as over obelisks and arches. Meandering paths lead to views of the meadow beyond, and sitting areas afford vistas across the garden. The design belies the actual size: 40ft x 100ft. Featured in Portsmouth Evening News.
❀ ☕ ☎

7 **APPLETREES**
267 Botley Rd, Burridge SO31 1BS. Kath & Ray Butcher, 01489 579429. *From A27 take A3051 Park Gate to Botley, on L after 1½ m. From Botley take A3051, Appletrees is 2m on R.* Home-made teas. **Adm £3, chd free.** Sat, Sun 21, 22 May (11-5). Visitors also welcome by appt.

A garden to explore, down narrow winding paths edged with subtle and original plant associations, leading to secluded seats. Created by flower-arranger owner, with good use of contrasting foliage and flowers. No lawn, just a crown of clipped box contrasting with the relaxed and exuberant planting elsewhere. Sinks and container planting, small pond and waterfall. Featured in RHS The Garden.
❀ ☕ ☎

8 **ATHELING VILLAS**
16 Atheling Road, Hythe, Southampton SO45 6BR. Mary & Peter York, 023 8084 9349, athelingvillas@gmail.com. *7m E of Lyndhurst. At M27 J2, take A326 for Hythe/Fawley. Cross all r'abouts until Dibden r'about. L to Hythe. After Shell garage, Atheling Road is 2nd L.* Home-made teas. **Adm £3, chd free (share to The Children's Society).** Sat 19, Sun 20 Mar; Sun 24, Mon 25 Apr; Sats, Suns 7, 8 May; 4, 5 June (2-5). Visitors also welcome by appt.
Delightful and inspirational all-season ⅓-acre gardens of Victorian villa which appeal to all garden lovers and specialists alike. Shady nooks, sunny flower beds and shrubberies. Winding paths lead through thousands of spring bulbs, hellebores and pulmonarias. Early summer brings wonderful flowering trees, shrubs, bulbs and herbaceous plants, many rare. Teas in gardener's cottage. Self-guide leaflet and children's quiz. Featured in Hampshire Life, Garden News.
❀ ☕ ☎

9 **AVIEMORE**
Chinham Road, Bartley, Southampton SO40 2LF. Sandy & Alex Robinson, 023 8081 3651. *3m N of Lyndhurst, 7m W of Southampton. 5mins from M27 J1. Exit onto A31, ¼ m to Cadnam r'about. 3rd exit A337, signed Lyndhurst, for ¾ m then L into Beechwood Rd for ¾ m to Bartley Xrds. Continue straight & follow signs into Chinham Rd. Also signed on A337, 3m N of Lyndhurst.* Home-made teas. **Adm £3, chd free.** Sat 23, Sun 24 July (2-5).
An 'all-yr-round' small country garden with curving lawns, patios, gravel areas, planted stream banks, raised vegetable beds and an alpine area. Extensive collections of shrubs, small trees, climbers, grasses and

herbaceous plants to interest plants people and hopefully inspire other enthusiasts with ideas for colour combinations and structure.

10 BARHI
27 Reynolds Dale, Ashurst, Southampton SO40 7PS. Ms F Barnes, 02380 860046, fbarnes@barhi.net, www.barhi.net/garden. *6m W of Southampton. From M27, J2 take A326 to Fawley. At 4th roundabout L into Cocklydown Lane. At mini roundabout L into Ibbotson Way. 1st L into Reynolds Dale and follow signs.* Home-made teas. **Adm £2.50, chd free. Sat 4, Sun 5 June (2-5). Visitors also welcome by appt.**
Compact 'modern cottage' garden shared with lively Springer Spaniels, designed around a chambered nautilus spiral. No lawn, so lots of space for plants. The dense planting, meandering paths, secluded pergola, raised formal pond and feature patio have led visitors to describe the garden as 'Tardis-like'.

11 19 BARNWOOD ROAD
Fareham PO15 5LA. Jill & Michael Hill, 01329 842156, thegarden19@btinternet.com. *1m W of Fareham. From M27 J9 take A27 towards Fareham. At top of hill past Titchfield Mill PH turn L at T-lights into Highlands Rd. Take 4th R into Blackbrook Rd, Meadow Bank 4th turn on R. Barnwood Rd is off Meadow Bank. Please consider the neighbours when parking.* Home-made teas. **Adm £3, chd free. Suns 5 June; 17 July (11-5). Visitors also welcome by appt for groups of 10+.**
Step through the gate to an enchanting garden designed for peace with an abundance of floral colour and delightful features. Greek-style courtyard leads to natural pond with bridge and bog garden, complemented by a thatched summerhouse and jetty, designed and built by owners. Secret pathways and hexagonal greenhouse.

12 BEECHENWOOD FARM
Hillside, Odiham RG29 1JA. Mr & Mrs M Heber-Percy, 01256 702300, beechenwood@totalise.co.uk. *5m SE of Hook. Turn S into King St from Odiham High St. Turn L after cricket ground for Hillside. Take 2nd turn R*

after 1½ m, modern house ½ m. Home-made teas. **Adm £3.50, chd free. Every Wed 20 Apr to 8 June incl (2-5). Visitors also welcome by appt mid Apr to mid June, for individuals & small groups. No coaches.**
2-acre garden in many parts. Lawn meandering through woodland with drifts of crocus, daffodils, hyacinths, tulips and bluebells. Rose pergola with steps, pots with spring bulbs and later aeoniums. Fritillary and cowslip meadow. Walled herb garden with pool and exuberant planting incl alliums and angelica. Orchard incl white garden and hot border. Large greenhouse and vegetable garden. Rock garden extending to grasses, ferns and bamboos. Shady walk to belvedere with views over farmland. 8-acre copse of native species with grassed rides. Featured on Alan Titchmarsh's The Seasons: Spring. Gravel drive and some shallow steps which can be avoided.

Riverside walks, species tulips (some growing in grass), peonies, wisteria collection . . .

---

13 BERE MILL
London Road, Whitchurch RG28 7NH. Rupert & Elizabeth Nabarro, 01256 892210, rnabarro@aol.com. *9m E of Andover, 12m N of Winchester. In centre of Whitchurch, take London Rd at r'about. Up hill 1m, turn R 50yds beyond The Gables on R. Drop-off point for disabled at garden.* Home-made teas. **Adm £5, chd free (share to Smile Train). Sun 27 Mar; Sun 29, Mon 30 May; Sun 18 Sept (1.30-5). Visitors also welcome by appt, Fris preferably, min £100 per visit.**
The garden is in a beautiful setting beside the R Test, with carriers and a large lake next to a restored SSSI water meadow. It is grazed by Welsh Mountain sheep, lambs and Belted Galloway cattle. Riverside walks,

species tulips (some growing in grass), peonies, wisteria collection, bog garden. Double perennial beds and swamp cypress avenue. Eastern influence includes Japanese Tea House, many different riverside irises and unique bridges. Unfenced and unguarded rivers and streams. Special drop-off point for disabled at house.

14 BERRY COTTAGE
Church Road, Upper Farringdon, nr Alton GU34 3EG. Mrs P Watts, 01420 588318. *3m S of Alton off A32. Turn L at Xrds, 1st L into Church Rd. Follow rd past Masseys Folley, 2nd house on R opp church.* Home-made teas. **Adm £2.50, chd free. Suns 29 May; 19 June; 17 July; 21 Aug; 4 Sept (2.30-5.30). Visitors also welcome by appt, groups and clubs welcome.**
Small organic cottage garden with all-yr interest. Spring bulbs, roses, clematis and herbaceous borders. Pond and bog garden. Shrubbery and small kitchen garden. The owner designed and maintained garden surrounds C16 house. The borders are colour-themed and contain many unusual plants. Close to Massey's Folly built by the Victorian Rector incl 80ft tower with unique handmade floral bricks, C11 church and some of the oldest yew trees in the county.

15 BLACKDOWN HOUSE
Blackdown Lane, Upham SO32 1HS. Mr & Mrs Tom Sweet-Escott, 01962 777375, rosamond@sweet-escott.co.uk. *5m SE of Winchester. 1m N of Upham, best accessed off Morestead Rd Xrds with Longwood Dean Lane from Winchester or through the village of Upham from Bishops Waltham.* Home-made teas. **Adm £3.50, chd free. Sun 1 May; Sun 5 June (2-6). Visitors also welcome by appt, weekdays only.**
A 5-acre family garden. The 4th year of the 100m long, colourful herbaceous border set against a flint wall. The garden is opening for the first time in early May to show off the wonderful bulbs, hundreds of which are planted every year. There is a 14yr-old wild flower meadow with orchids and cowslips in the spring, a part-walled kitchen garden, orchard and terrace. Jacob sheep and alpacas in the parkland.

7 Beacon Square

16 BRAEMOOR
Bleak Hill, Harbridge, Ringwood
BH24 3PX. Tracy & John
Netherway & Judy Spratt,
01425 652983,
jnetherway@btinternet.com. *2¹/₂ m
S of Fordingbridge. Turn off A338 at
Ibsley. Go through Harbridge village
to T-junction at top of hill, turn R for
¹/₄ m.* Home-made teas. **Adm £3,
chd free. Fri, Suns 17, 19 June; 1,
3, 22, 24 July; Fri 5, Sat 6, Sun 7
Aug (2-5.30).** Visitors also welcome
by appt 17 June to 7 Aug.
In the pretty hamlet of Harbridge, this
³/₄ -acre garden is brimming with bold,
colourful planting and interesting
areas. Step through one of our two
moongates into a seaside haven of
painted beach huts and driftwood
gems. In contrast, walk through to a
cottage garden of overflowing
herbaceous borders with a trickling
little stream running by the lawn to a
pond. Two greenhouses contain
collections of cacti and carnivorous
plants. Enjoy tea on the grass
overlooking the vegetable patch with
our bantam chickens. Small adjacent
nursery.
&. ❀ ☕ ☎

17 ◆ BRAMDEAN HOUSE
Bramdean SO24 0JU. Mr & Mrs H
Wakefield, 01962 771214,
victoria@bramdeanhouse.com. *4m
S of Alresford. In centre of village on
A272.* Home-made teas. **Adm £4,
chd free. For NGS: Suns 20 Feb
(2-4); Suns 20 Mar; 17 Apr;
12 June; 17 July (2-5); Sun 18 Sept
(2-4). Sun 19 Feb 2012. For other
opening times and information,
please phone or email.**
Beautiful 5-acre garden famous for its
mirror-image herbaceous borders.
Carpets of spring bulbs especially
snowdrops. A large and unusual
collection of plants and shrubs giving
yr-round interest incl over 40 varieties
of sweet pea. 1-acre walled garden
featuring prize-winning vegetables,
fruit and flowers. Included in Alan
Titchmarsh's The Seasons.
&. ❀ ☕

18 BRANDY MOUNT HOUSE
Alresford SO24 9EG. Caryl &
Michael Baron, 01962 732189,
www.brandymount.co.uk. *nr
Alresford centre. From centre, 1st R
in East St before Sun Lane. Please
leave cars in Broad St, stn car park,
at Perins School or Longbarn*

Lavender Farm. Home-made teas.
**Adm £3, chd free. Sat 12 Feb
(11-4).**
1-acre, informal plantsman's garden.
Spring bulbs, hellebores, species
geraniums. National Collections of
snowdrops and daphnes. European
primulas, expanding collection of
dwarf narcissi, herbaceous and
woodland plants. 2 raised beds to
display early spring bulbs. Grassing
down of part of long herbaceous
border for bulbs and meadow plants.
Wheelchairs must be supervised.
&. ❀ ❀ **NCCPG** ☕

19 6 BREAMORE CLOSE
Eastleigh SO50 4QB. Mr & Mrs R
Trenchard, 02380 611230,
dawndavina@tiscali.co.uk. *1m N of
Eastleigh. M3 J12, follow signs to
Eastleigh. Turn R at r'about into
Woodside Ave, then 1st L into
Broadlands Ave (park here).
Breamore Close 3rd on L.* Home-
made teas. **Adm £3, chd free. Sun
29, Mon 30 May; Sat 23, Sun 24
July (1-5.30).** Visitors also welcome
by appt in May June & July, for
groups of 10+.
Delightful plant lover's garden with
coloured foliage and unusual plants,
giving a tapestry effect of texture and
colour. Many hostas displayed in
pots. The garden is laid out in
distinctive planting themes with
seating areas to sit and contemplate.
Many clematis scramble through
roses and over a pergola displaying a
magnificent wisteria (flowers 3ft-4ft
long) in May, followed by phlox in July.
Featured in Hampshire Life Magazine.
Small gravel area wheelchairs may
find hard to negotiate.
&. ❀ ☕ ☎

20 BROOKLYN COTTAGE
Little London Road, Silchester,
Reading RG7 2PP. Mrs Althea
Innes. *6¹/₂ m N of Basingstoke, 7m S
of Reading. Off A340, 1m S of
Silchester signed from the Calleva
Arms in centre of village. Parking opp
in Byes Lane.* Home-made teas. **Adm
£3, chd free. Sun 22 May (2-5).**
Small, continually changing cottage
garden in the Roman garrison town of
Silchester. Several seating areas in
which to take afternoon cream teas
whilst contemplating collections of
hostas, acers, ferns and a selection of
interesting mature shrubs. Clematis
and rose-clad gazebo and pergola
with a mature wisteria scrambling up
the C19 cottage walls. Gravel paths.
&. ❀ ☕

21 ▶ THE BUILDINGS

Broughton, Stockbridge SO20 8BH.
Dick & Gillian Pugh. *3m W of
Stockbridge. NGS yellow signs 2m W
of Stockbridge off A30, or 6m N of
Romsey off B3084.* Home-made teas.
Adm £3.50, chd free (share to
Friends of St Mary's Broughton and
St James's Bossington). *Sats,
Suns 9, 10 July; 6, 7 Aug; 3, 4 Sept
(2-5).*
A renovated farmyard, high on the
Hampshire Downs offers gravel
gardens, borders, an exuberant
pergola, all on our thin chalk soil.
Look inwards to the intimate planting
of grasses and perennials, outwards
to spectacular views in all directions.
Featured in The English Garden,
Good Housekeeping & Hampshire
magazine.

Walled city garden
framed by an
ancient Atlantic
cedar and
perfumed by
roses, lavender,
jasmine . . .

22 ▶ 2 CARISBROOKE ROAD

Gosport PO13 0HQ. Chris & Norma
Matthews, 01329 282932,
norma_matthews@hotmail.com.
*3m S of Fareham. Exit M27 J11
signed Fareham Central. Follow A32,
Gosport. Take fork at Newgate Lane
signed Lee-on-Solent. At 3rd
roundabout 1st exit B3334 signed
Rowner. L at T-lights, 1st house on R.*
Home-made teas. Adm £3, chd free.
Sat 25, Sun 26 June (10-4). Visitors
also welcome by appt.
¹/₃ -acre cottage-style garden
developed by owners over 25yrs.
Shrubs, herbaceous perennials,
gravel and alpine gardens give yr-
round interest. Raised organic kitchen
garden. Interesting colourful baskets
and containers with plants
propagated by owners. Wildlife area
and garden, birds enthusiastically
encouraged. Fishpond and miniature
wildlife pond.

GROUP OPENING

23 ▶ NEW CENTRAL WINCHESTER GARDENS

St Cross, Winchester SO23 9SL.
*Central Winchester, parallel to St
James Lane and off Christchurch Rd.*
Home-made teas at No. 10.
Combined adm £5, chd free. *Sat 2,
Sun 3 July (2-5.30).*

4 COMPTON ROAD
Mrs Anthea Fortescue

NEW ▶ 10 COMPTON ROAD
Robin and Allison Jowitt

Enjoy two complementary gardens in
central Winchester. Re-formed over
6yrs, the garden at No.4 Compton
Road (featured in The English Garden)
is a peaceful city haven, intensively
planted with rare trees, unusual
climbers and shrubs. Emphasis is on
colour and shape of foliage and
sculptured form with subtle colour
blending. The concept was to 'paint'
an all-yr plant picture which is in
constant view from large landscape
windows in the contemporary
extension to the house. A plant list of
less familiar plants will be available.
The walled city garden at No.10
features a manicured lawn framed by
an ancient Atlantic cedar and is
perfumed by roses, lavender, jasmine
and nemesia. A series of raised beds
lead to a Mediterranean courtyard
decorated with ornamental iron work
and planted with mature olive and fig
trees with original contemporary
underplanting.

24 ▶ 21 CHESTNUT ROAD

Brockenhurst SO42 7RF. Iain &
Mary Hayter, 01590 622009. *4m S of
Lyndhurst. S on A337 to Brockenhurst,
take R fork B3055, Grigg Lane, opp
Careys Manor Hotel. Garden 500yds
from junction via 2nd L Chestnut Rd
and 2nd L again for no 21. Parking
limited; please use village car park
nearby.* Home-made teas & cakes.
Adm £3, chd free. *Sats, Suns 21,
22 May (2-6); 11, 12 June; Sun 31
July (Sats 11-5, Suns 2-6).* Visitors
also welcome by appt May to Sept,
Weds 2-5, groups of 10+.
Created with passion, cottage garden
favourites and packed showy borders
feature planting for colour, form and
scent. Invaluable ideas for shade/sun
and wet/dry. Flowers, fruit and
vegetables blend in a mix of the

natural and formal. Summerhouse
exhibition of paintings and photos of
American irises, visiting birds and
insects. Home-made jam for sale. No
access to summerhouse for
wheelchairs or to the garden if wet.

25 ▶ 12 CHRISTCHURCH ROAD

Winchester SO23 9SR. Iain &
Penny Patton, 01962 854272,
pjspatton@yahoo.co.uk. *S side of
city. Leave centre of Winchester by
Southgate St, 1st R into St James
Lane, 3rd L into Christchurch Rd.*
Home-made teas. Adm £2.50, chd
free. *Sat 16, Sun 17 July (2-6).*
Visitors also welcome by appt by
prior arrangement.
Small town garden with strong design
enhanced by exuberant and vertical
planting. All-yr interest incl. winter-
flowering shrubs, bulbs and
hellebores followed by more bulbs,
roses, perennials, shrubs and
grasses. 2 water features, including
slate-edged rill, and pergolas provide
structure to offset planting. Small front
garden designed to be viewed from
the house. Featured on front cover
and article in The English Garden.

26 ▶ COLEMORE HOUSE GARDENS

Colemore, Alton GU34 3RX. Mr &
Mrs Simon de Zoete. *5m S of Alton.
Take turning to Colemore (Shell Lane)
off A32, just S of E Tisted.* Home-
made teas. Adm £3.50, chd free.
Sat 25, Mon 27 June (2-6).
Situated in unspoilt country, a 4-acre
garden with unusual plants and trees.
Yew and box hedges, herbaceous
and mixed borders, yellow and blue
garden surrounded by excellent
lawns. Constant development incl a
spectacular water rill, a new formal
reflection pond surrounded with
grasses and ferns and a group of 16
amelanchier trees with interesting
under-planting. Extensive new
planting of trees and landscaping.

27 ▶ CONHOLT PARK

Hungerford Lane, nr Chute
SP11 9HA. Conholt Park Estate,
07917 796826,
conholt.courtyard@tiscali.co.uk.
*7m N of Andover. Turn N off A342
Andover to Devizes rd at Weyhill
Church. Go 5m N through Clanville.
Turn L at T-junction, Conholt ¹/₂ m on
R, just off Chute causeway. A343 to
Hurstbourne Tarrant, turn to and go*

through Vernham Dean, next turn L signed Conholt. Home-made teas. **Adm £4, chd free. Sat 4, Sun 5, Wed 8, Thur 23 June (11-4).** Visitors also welcome by appt. 10 acres surrounding Regency house (not open), with mature cedars. Rose, sensory, winter and secret gardens and fern dell. Restored 1½-acre walled garden with vegetable and flower cartwheels, berry wall, orchard, Ladies' Walk and large (3,000sq m) foot-shaped maze with viewing platform. Visitors are welcome to bring picnic. Dogs on leads.

28 THE COTTAGE
16 Lakewood Road, Chandler's Ford SO53 1ES. Hugh & Barbara Sykes, 2380254521, barandhugh@aol.com. *2m NW of Eastleigh. Leave M3 at J12, follow signs to Chandler's Ford. At King Rufus on Winchester Rd, turn R into Merdon Ave, then 3rd rd on L.* Home-made teas. **Adm £3, chd free. Easter Mon 25 Apr; Mon 2, Sun 15, Mon 16 May (2-6).** Visitors also welcome by appt in Apr & May. ¾ acre. Azaleas, bog garden, camellias, dogwoods, erythroniums, free-range bantams, greenhouse grapes, honey, irises, jasmines, kitchen garden, landscaping began in 1950, maintained by owners, new planting, osmunda, ponds, quiz for children, rhododendrons, smilacina, trilliums, unusual plants, viscum, wildlife areas, eXuberant foliage, yr-round interest, zantedeschia. Watch honey bees in an observation hive. 'A lovely tranquil garden' Anne Swithinbank.

COTTAGE ROW
See Dorset.

29 CRANBURY PARK
Otterbourne, nr Winchester SO21 2HL. Mr & Mrs Chamberlayne-Macdonald. *3m NW of Eastleigh. Main entrance on old A33 between Winchester and Southampton, by bus stop at top of Otterbourne Hill. Entrances also in Hocombe Rd, Chandler's Ford and next to church in Otterbourne.* Home-made teas. **Adm £4, chd free (share to St Mark's Church, Ampfield). Sun 12 June (2-6).** Extensive pleasure grounds laid out in late C18 and early C19 by Papworth; fountains, rose garden, specimen trees and pinetum, lakeside walk and

fern walk. Family carriages and collection of prams will be on view, also photos of King George VI, Eisenhower and Montgomery reviewing Canadian troops at Cranbury before D-Day. Disabled WC.

GROUP OPENING

30 CRAWLEY GARDENS
nr Winchester SO21 2PU. *5m NW of Winchester. Off A272 or B3049 Winchester to Stockbridge rd. Parking throughout village.* Home-made teas in the Village Hall. **Combined adm £5 (April & May) £6 (June & July), chd free. Sun 10 Apr, Tue 12 Apr; Sun 15 May, Tue 17 May (2-5.30); Thur 16 June, Sun 19 June; Thur 21 July, Sun 24 July (2-6).**

BARN COTTAGE
Jane & Kenneth Wren.
Open May & June dates

BAY TREE HOUSE
Julia & Charles Whiteaway.
Open June & July dates

GABLE COTTAGE
Patrick Hendra & Ken Jones.
Open April dates only

LITTLE COURT
Prof & Mrs A R Elkington.
Open April, May, June & July dates
(See separate entry)

PAIGE COTTAGE
Mr & Mrs T W Parker.
Open April & July dates

TANGLEFOOT
Mr & Mrs F J Fratter.
Open May, June & July dates
(See separate entry)

Exceptionally pretty village with thatched houses, C14 church and village pond. A different combination of gardens opens each month from April to July providing seasonal interest from gardens with varied character and style; most gardens benefit from fine country views. Enjoy the spring gardens at Paige Cottage and Gable Cottage, and the 3-acre traditional English country garden at Little Court with carpets of spring bulbs. In late spring and summer, other gardens join in, with traditional and contemporary approaches to landscape and planting, from the rill, pleached limes and prairie style borders at Bay Tree House, the colour-themed borders, herb wheel,

and productive kitchen garden at Tanglefoot, with its traditional Victorian boundary wall, to the exuberant scramble of clematis, roses, jasmine and bee-loving plants at Barn Cottage. There are waterfalls at Gable Cottage and a grass labyrinth and tree house at Little Court which appeals to all ages.

Different combination of gardens opens each month from April to July providing seasonal interest . . .

31 CROOKLEY POOL
Blendworth Lane, Horndean PO8 0AB. Mr & Mrs Simon Privett, 02392 592662, simonprivett@talktalk.net. *5m S of Petersfield. 2m E of Waterlooville, off A3. From Horndean village go up Blendworth Lane between bakery and hairdresser. Entrance 200yds before church on L with white railings.* **Adm £3.50, chd free.** Visitors welcome by appt.
Here the plants decide where to grow. Californian tree poppies elbow valerian aside to crowd round the pool. Evening primroses obstruct the way to the door and the steps to wisteria-shaded terraces. Hellebores bloom under the trees. Salvias, Pandoria jasminoides, Justicia, Pachystachys lutea and passion flowers riot quietly with the tomatoes in the greenhouse. Not a garden for the neat or tidy minded.

32 DEAN HOUSE
Kilmeston SO24 0NL. Mr P H R Gwyn, 07748 094209, julianblackwell@hotmail.co.uk, www.deanhousegardens.co.uk. *5m S of Alresford. Via village of Cheriton or off A272 signed at Cheriton Xrds. Follow signs for Kilmeston, through village and turn L at Dean House sign.* Home-made & cream teas.

Adm £4.50, chd free. Weds 25 May; 15 June; 6 July (10-4), Suns 17 July; 7 Aug (12-5), Wed 17 Aug (10-4). Visitors also welcome by appt, groups welcome.
The 9 acres have been described as 'A well-kept secret hidden behind the elegant facade of its Georgian centrepiece'. Sweeping lawns, York stone paths, gravel pathways, many young and mature trees and hedges, mixed and herbaceous borders, symmetrical rose garden, pond garden, working walled garden and glasshouses all help to create a diverse and compact sliver of Eden. Walled Garden with 135 different varieties of vegetables. On our data base for 2011 we have over 1600 individually documented plant species and cultivars in our collection. Featured in The English Garden.

33 DIPLEY MILL
Dipley Road, Dipley RG27 8JP. Miss Rose & Mr J P McMonigall. *2m NE of Hook. Turn E off B3349 at Mattingley (1½ m N of Hook) signed Hartley Wintney, West Green and Dipley. Dipley Mill ½ m on L just over bridge.* Home-made teas. **Adm £4, chd free.** Suns 19 June (2-6); 4 Sept (2-5). Also open 4 Sept Old Thatch.
An adventure awaits as you wander by the meandering streams surrounding this Domesday Book listed mill! Explore a grotto, scented, fuchsia and Indian gardens, a hothouse, ornamental courtyard and theatrical rose collection. Or just escape into wild meadows. Miniature donkeys.

DORMERS
See Sussex.

34 THE DOWN HOUSE
Itchen Abbas SO21 1AX. Jackie & Mark Porter, 01962 791054, markstephenporter@gmail.com. *6m E of Winchester. On B3047, coming from Winchester, 5th house on right after Itchen Abbas village sign.* Home-made teas. **Adm £3, chd free (share to PCaSo, prostate cancer).** Sun 20 Feb (12-4); Wed 22 June (12-6); Sun 26 June (2-6). Also open 22 June Abbey Cottage. Visitors also welcome by appt, groups of 10+.
2-acre garden developed by owners since 2001, laid out in rooms overlooking Itchen Valley, adjoining the Pilgrim's Way, with walks through

a large meadow to the river. Carpet of snowdrops and crocus, plus borders of coloured stems in winter. Roped rose garden, hot borders, wildlife pond and shady places in summer. Pleached hornbeams, yew-lined avenues, woodland nut and orchard walk. Working vineyard. Live jazz at 26 June event.

DOWN PLACE
See Sussex.

35 7 DOWNLAND CLOSE
Locks Heath, nr Fareham SO31 6WB. Roy Dorland, 01489 571788 / 07768 107779, roydorland@hotmail.co.uk. *3m W of Fareham. Leave M27 J9 (Whitely). Follow A27 on Southampton Rd to Park Gate. Past Kams Palace restaurant, L into Locks Rd, 3rd R into Meadow Ave, 2nd L into Downland Close.* Home-made teas. **Adm £2.50, chd free.** Sun 29, Mon 30 May; Sun 12, Mon 13 June (1-6). Visitors also welcome by appt 15 May to 18 July.
Visit this prizewinning, beautiful, restful and inspirational 50ft x 45ft plantsman's garden, packed with ideas for the 'modest-sized' plot. Many varieties of hardy geraniums, hostas, heucheras, shrubs, ferns and other unusual perennials, weaving a tapestry of harmonious colour. Attractive water feature, plenty of seating areas and charming summerhouse. A garden to fall in love with!

DURFORD MILL HOUSE
See Sussex.

Working walled garden and glasshouses all help to create a diverse and compact sliver of Eden . . .

36 DURMAST HOUSE
Burley BH24 4AT. Mr & Mrs P E G Daubeney, 01425 402132, philip@daubeney.co.uk, www.durmasthouse.co.uk. *5m SE of Ringwood. Off Burley to Lyndhurst rd, nr White Buck Hotel.* Cream Teas. **Adm £3.50, chd free (share to Delhi Commonwealth Women's Assn Clinic).** Suns 3 Apr; 3 July (2-5). Visitors also welcome by appt.
Designed in 1907 by Gertrude Jekyll, Durmast has contrasting hot and cool colour borders, formal rose garden shaped like two halves of a diamond edged with lavender and a long herbaceous border. Many old trees, Victorian rockery and orchard, in spring full of daffodils, crocus, erythroniums and fritillaria. New planting of rare Ghent azaleas: Fama, Princeps and Gloria Mundi. Listed in Hampshire Register of Historic Gardens.

37 EDGEWOOD
175 Burley Road, Bransgore, Christchurch BH23 8DE. Teresa Knight, 01425 672754, teresaknight1@hotmail.co.uk. *3m S of Burley. From Bransgore village take Burley Rd towards Burley for 1m, Edgewood approx ¼ m past Macpennys Garden Centre.* Cream teas. **Adm £2.50, chd free (share to Southampton Hospital Charity).** Sat 11, Sun 18, Fri 17, Sat 18, Sun 19, Sat 25, Sun 26 June (2-5). Visitors also welcome by appt in June & July for groups of 10+.
Our 1½-acre garden is part woodland and part cottage garden with many colourful borders, rose and clematis covered arches, vegetable plots, greenhouse, polytunnel, chickens and bee hives. Come and enjoy our garden for a while, take a peaceful stroll around the wood, relax in one of the many garden seating areas and then why not sample a delicious home-made cream tea?.

38 THE ELVETHAM HOTEL
Hartley Wintney, Hook RG27 8AS, www.elvethamhotel.co.uk. *3m NW of Fleet. On A323, between Hartley Wintney & Fleet.* Light refreshments, wine & teas. **Adm £4, chd free (share to Phyllis Tuckwell & Naomi House Hospices).** Sun, Mon 3, 4 July (11-5).
35 acres surrounding Gothic Victorian mansion circa 1860. Majestic catalogued trees, expansive graceful

lawns, R Hart, fastigate yew avenue leads to Flora's summerhouse, sunken garden, ornamental fish pond. Victorian lean-to greenhouses (working). Oak planted by Queen Elizabeth I contrasts with contemporary bedding and formal pathways. Finalists of Hotel's first photographic competition will be displayed on both NGS days. Gravel paths.

   🕭 🏠 🍵

GROUP OPENING

39 **EMSWORTH GARDENS**
PO10 7PR. *7m W of Chichester, 2m E of Havant. Take A259 W of Chichester, follow signs to Emsworth roundabout N of town centre.* Home-made teas. **Combined adm £5, chd free.** Sun 10 July (1-5).

7 BEACON SQUARE
Emsworth. Annette & Michael Wood.
From Emsworth village, take A259 towards Havant. Take 3rd L (Warblington Rd). After about 200yds, turn L into Seafields, R at end of rd, garden around corner on L
Visitors also welcome by appt for group visits 11 to 15 July. 01243 378482 annettewood06@yahoo.co.uk

23 NEW BRIGHTON ROAD
Lucy Doherty.
From main Emsworth roundabout go N for 1m (signed Rowlands Castle) under railway bridge and flyover, immediately on L up slope

Two complementary gardens close to the centre of Emsworth, an historic fishing and sailing village on Chichester Harbour with numerous pubs, small local museums and walks along foreshore and around mill pond. 7 Beacon Square is an award winning, medium sized garden close to the sea. Exuberant, densely planted, herbaceous beds and borders. Tree ferns, fruit trees, herbs, pond and sculptures. Small, raised beds with vegetables, herbs and salad leaves. Potting shed packed with produce, including melons and aubergines, growing in bags and tubs. Meanwhile, with its eclectic mix of plants and ornaments, the narrow 200ft long garden at 23 New Brighton Road, ranges from full sun to full shade and informal planting maximises the available space. A large number of containers, a wildlife pond, greenhouse, shady reading area and mixed borders. Unusual plants and unusual garden for the plantsperson.

🕭 🏵 🍵

Potting shed
packed with
produce, including
melons and
aubergines,
growing in bags
and tubs . . .

40 ♦ **EXBURY GARDENS & STEAM RAILWAY**
New Forest, Southampton SO45 1AZ. The Rothschild Family, 023 8089 1203, www.exbury.co.uk. *16m S of Southampton. 4m Beaulieu. Exbury 20mins M27 J2.* **Adm £9, chd £2, concessions £8.50, family tickets available. For opening times and information, please phone or see garden website.**
Created by Lionel de Rothschild in the 1920s, the gardens are a stunning vision of his inspiration offering 200 acres of natural beauty and horticultural variety. Woodland garden with world-famous displays of rhododendrons, azaleas, camellias and magnolias. Rock garden, exotic garden, herbaceous gardens, ponds, cascades, river walk and seasonal trails. Superb autumn colour, incl National Collection of Nyssa and Oxydendrum. Steam railway (wheelchair accessible). Buggy tours available. Voted Best Garden to Visit with Children in SE by readers of BBC Gardeners' World magazine.

   ♿ 🕭 🏵 **NCCPG** 🍵

41 **FARLEIGH HOUSE**
Farleigh Wallop, nr Basingstoke RG25 2HT. The Earl & Countess of Portsmouth. *3m SE of Basingstoke. Off B3046 Basingstoke to Preston Candover rd.* Cream teas. **Adm £5, chd free.** Sun 19 June; Sun 18 Sept (2-5).
Contemporary garden of great tranquillity designed by Georgia Langton, surrounded by wonderful views. 3-acre walled garden in three sections: ornamental potager, formal rose garden and wild rose garden. Greenhouse full of exotics, serpentine yew walk, contemplative pond garden and lake with planting for wildlife. Approx 10 acres and 1 hour to walk around. New in 2010 was a shell grotto by Jocelyn Hayden.

   ♿ 🕭 🏵 🍵

42 **FIR TREES**
Bexmoor, Old Basing RG24 7BT. Jan & John Mabbott. *1¹/₂ m E of Basingstoke. M3, J6, follow A339 towards Basingstoke, turn R at 1st r'about signed A30 Hook, L after 40mph sign into Park Lane, 1st L at T-lights, R at T junction. Garden 150yds on L, opp church. Park in The Street.* Home-made teas. **Adm £3, chd free.** Sun 26, Tue 28 June (2-5.30).
Just under ¹/₂ -acre inspiring garden transformed by the owners from an overgrown orchard (photographs on show). Stone terrace leads onto lawn with various themed herbaceous borders. Perennials, shrubs, rose-covered pergolas, acers, old apple trees. Large organic vegetable garden and solar powered rainwater harvesting system. Lots of seating.

   🍵

43 **FLINTSTONES**
Sciviers Lane, Durley SO32 2AG. June & Bill Butler, 01489 860880. *5m E of Eastleigh. From M3 J11 follow signs for Marwell Zoo. From B2177 turn R opp Woodman PH. From M27 J7 follow signs for Fair Oak then Durley, turn L at Robin Hood PH.* Light refreshments & teas in Apr, home-made teas May (n.b. **no teas 2 May**), wine at evening opening. **Adm £3, chd free** (share to Durley Church & Camphill Village Trust). Sun 3 Apr (2-5); Mon 2, Sun 15, Mon 16 May (2-6). **Evening Opening £4.50, wine, Tue 14 June** (6.30-8.30). **Visitors also welcome by appt, Apr to Sept only.**
Garden of great tranquillity. All yr pleasing tapestry effect of contrasting and blending foliage and flowers. Plantswoman's garden developed from a field on fertile acid clay. Large perennial plant collections, especially hardy geraniums. Interesting island beds to wander round and explore. Plant sale (not April). Wheelchair access only when dry, recommend checking by telephone prior to visit.

   ♿ 🏵 🍵 ☎

44 FOREST COTTAGE

135 Lyndhurst Road, Ashurst, Southampton SO40 7AW. Annie & Dennis Hart. *3m NE of Lyndhurst, 5¹/₂ m W of Southampton. From M271 J3, SW on A35 for 3m via Totton bypass to r'about. Continue straight on via 2nd r'about to Lyndhurst Rd. After approx 2³/₄ m, pass The Forest Inn PH on L. Soon see signs for garden on L. Park in side roads opp or further on L by shops. Also signed on A35 from Lyndhurst (3m).* Home-made teas. **Adm £2.50, chd free. Sat 11, Sun 12 June (2-5).**

A beautiful old Bramley apple tree and raised alpine bed is the focal point of this enchanting cottage garden with an abundance of colourful flowers, shrubs and masses of fragrant new roses and clematis, incl 4 new arches. Generously planted perennials benefit bees and butterflies. Appreciate the small container allotment. Enjoy your tea with views from the established pond and patio.

45 THE FOUNTAINS

34 Frampton Way, Totton SO40 9AE. Mrs J Abel, 023 8086 5939. *5m W of Southampton. M271 J3 onto A35 Totton bypass for lm to r'about. Circle r'about and return up A35. Immed L into Rushington Ave, then follow signs.* Home-made teas. **Adm £2.50, chd free. Sat 18 June (2-5). Visitors also welcome by appt.**

Unusually shaped ¹/₄ -acre garden bordered by hedges and filled with a variety of fruit trees, soft fruit cordons and espaliers. Trellis covered in rambling roses, enjoyed with flowers for every season. Plantswoman's garden designed for all yr interest with vegetable plot, wildlife ponds and chickens. 'Cottage garden meets the Good Life' - a garden to relax in and enjoy.

46 FRITHAM LODGE

Fritham SO43 7HH. Sir Chris and Lady Rosie Powell, 02380 812650, chris.powell@ddblondon.com. *6m N of Lyndhurst. 3m NW of M27 J1 Cadnam. Follow signs to Fritham.* Home-made teas. **Adm £3, chd free. Sun 26 June (2-5). Visitors also welcome by appt.**

Set in heart of New Forest in 18 acres; with 1-acre old walled garden round Grade II listed C17 house (not open) originally one of Charles II hunting lodges. Parterre of old roses, potager with wide variety of vegetables, herbs and fruit trees, pergola, herbaceous and blue and white mixed borders, ponds, walk across hay meadows to woodland and stream, with ponies, donkeys, sheep and rare breed hens. Featured in Country Life.

GROUP OPENING

47 FROYLE GARDENS

Froyle GU34 4LJ. *5m NE of Alton. Access to Lower Froyle from A31 between Alton & Farnham, at Bentley. Follow signs from Lower Froyle to Upper Froyle. Maps given to all visitors.* Home-made teas at Lower Froyle Village Hall. **Combined adm £5, chd free. Sat 4, Sun 5 June (2-6).**

BRAMLINS
Lower Froyle. Mrs Anne Blunt

2 COLTHOUSE LANE
West End Farm, Upper Froyle. Susan & Tony Goodsell

THE COTTAGE
Lower Froyle. Mr & Mrs M Carr

DAY COTTAGE
Lower Froyle. Mr Nick Whines & Ms Corinna Furse

THE OLD SCHOOL
Upper Froyle. Nigel & Linda Bulpitt

WALBURY
Lower Froyle. Ernie & Brenda Milam
(See separate entry)

WARREN COTTAGE
Lower Froyle. Mrs A A Robertson

Visitors have been returning to Froyle ('The Village of Saints') for 13 years to enjoy the wonderful variety of gardens on offer, the warm welcome and the excellent home-made teas in the village hall. The gardens harmonise gently with their surroundings, many

Longstock Park Water Garden

Follow us on Facebook and Twitter

with lovely views of beautiful countryside. Seven gardens will open their gates this year, not only providing plant interest, colour and scent, but animals frequently associated with a true cottage garden - as well as vegetables, orchards, greenhouses and wild flower meadows. Look out for the vintage tractors too! Large display of richly decorated C18 church vestments in St Mary's Church Upper Froyle, separate donation.

  🔥 ⊗ ☕

---

48 **GILBERTS NURSERY**
Dandysford Lane, Sherfield English, nr Romsey SO51 6DT. Nick & Helen Gilbert. *Midway between Romsey and Whiteparish on A27, in Sherfield English village. From Romsey 4th turn on L, just before small petrol stn on R, visible from main rd.* Light refreshments & home-made teas. **Adm £2.50, chd free.** Sats 20, 27 Aug, Sun 28 Aug (11-5).
This may not be a garden but do come and be amazed by the sight of over 300 varieties of dahlias in our dedicated 1½ -acre field. The blooms are in all colours, shapes and sizes and can be closely inspected from wheelchair-friendly hard grass paths. An inspiration for all gardeners.

  🔥 ⊗ ☕

The collection of over 1200 hosta cultivars is one of the largest in England, displayed at eye level to give a wonderful tapestry of foliage and colour . . .

---

49 NEW **GREAT PECKS**
Blind Lane, Wickham, Fareham PO17 5HD. Mrs Marie du Boulay. *Leaving Wickham follow A334 Winchester Rd N to top of hill, turn R at T-lights into Blind Lane.* Home-made teas. **Adm £3.50, chd free.** Suns 22 May; 18 Sept (2-6).
1½ -acre garden, beautifully redesigned by current owner. Exuberant borders spilling over with grasses and tall perennials. Formal areas with box edging, topiary, pleached and espalier trees. Vegetable plot, dry garden and lovely view. Wooded area with bee hives, hens, geese, sheep and pigs. Something for everyone.

  ☕

---

50 **HAMBLEDON HOUSE**
Hambledon PO7 4RU. Capt & Mrs David Hart Dyke, dhartdyke@tiscali.co.uk. *8m SW of Petersfield, 5m NW of Waterlooville. In village centre.* Home-made teas. **Adm £3.50, chd free.** Mon 29 Aug; Sun 18 Sept (2-5). Visitors also welcome by appt incl groups, May to Sept.
2-acre partly walled plantsman's garden for all seasons. Large borders filled with wide variety of unusual shrubs and perennials with imaginative plant combinations. Large collection of salvias, hardy geraniums and ornamental grasses. Hidden, secluded areas reveal surprise views of garden and village rooftops. Interesting new projects and planting for 2011. Exhibition of watercolours on 29 Aug.

  ⊗ ☕ ☎

---

51 NEW **HANGING HOSTA GARDEN**
Narra, Frensham Lane, Lindford, Bordon GU35 0QJ. June & John Colley, 01420 489186, hanginghostas@tesco.net. *Approx 1m E of Bordon. From the A325 at Bordon take the B3002, then B3004 to Lindford. Turn L into Frensham Lane at X-rds, 3rd house on L.* **Adm £3.** Visitors welcome by appt 11-16 July & 18-23 July, max 30.
This garden is packed with almost 2000 plants. The collection of over 1200 hosta cultivars is one of the largest in England. Hostas are displayed at eye level to give a wonderful tapestry of foliage and colour. Islamic garden, waterfall and stream garden, cottage garden. Talks given to garden clubs.

  ⊗ ☎

---

52 **HEATHLANDS**
47 Locks Road, Locks Heath, nr Fareham SO31 6NS. John & Josephine Burwell, 01489 573598, johnburwell@dsl.pipex.com. *5m W of Fareham. From M27 J9, go W on A27 towards Southampton. After 1m in Parkgate (just after pelican crossing) turn L into Locks Rd. No. 47 is 1m down on R.* **Adm £3, chd free.** Visitors welcome by appt.
This peaceful 1-acre garden has 7 very different areas. It is a green garden but with many seasonal flowers. Children are welcome and enjoy the wandering paths and the quizzes.

  🔥 ☎

---

53 **HILL HOUSE**
Old Alresford SO24 9DY. Mrs W F Richardson, 01962 732720, hillhouseolda@yahoo.co.uk. *1m W of Alresford. From Alresford 1m along B3046 towards Basingstoke, then R by church.* Home-made teas. **Adm £3, chd free.** Sun 7, Tue 9 Aug (1.30-5). Visitors also welcome by appt, July & Aug only.
Traditional English 2-acre garden, established 1938, divided by yew hedge. Large croquet lawn framing the star of the garden, the huge multi-coloured herbaceous border. Impressive dahlia bed and butterfly-attracting sunken garden in lavender shades. Prolific old-fashioned kitchen garden with hens and bantams both fluffy and large. Small Dexter cows, possibly with calves.

  🔥 ⊗ ☕ ☎

---

54 NEW **HILL TOP**
Damson Hill, Upper Swanmore, Southampton SO32 2QQ. David Green. *1m NE of Swanmore. Junction of Swanmore Rd and Church Rd, turn N up Hampton Hill into Park Lane. Sharp L-hand bend. After 300yds, junction with Damson Hill, house on L.* Home-made teas. **Adm £3.50, chd free.** Suns 19 June; 11 Sept (2-6).
2 acres with extensive colourful borders and wide lawns, this garden has stunning views to the Isle of Wight. The glass houses produce unusual fruit and vegetables from around the world. The outdoor vegetable plots bulge with well-grown produce. Many potted specimen plants. Colour and interest are maintained throughout the season.

  🔥 ⊗ ☕

55 NEW ♦ **HILLIER GARDENS**
Jermyns Lane, Ampfield, Romsey
SO51 0QA. Hampshire County
Council, 01794 369318,
www.hilliergardens.org.uk. *2m NE
of Romsey. Follow brown tourist signs
from A3090 Romsey to Winchester,
or A3057 Romsey to Andover.* Adm
**£8.70, chd free, concessions £7.50.
For opening times and information,
please phone or see garden
website.**
Established by the plantsman Sir
Harold Hillier, this is a 180-acre
garden and landscape with a unique
collection of 11,000 different hardy
plants from across the world. It
includes the famous Winter Garden,
Himalayan Valley, Gurkha Memorial
Garden, Magnolia Avenue, spring
woodlands, fabulous autumn colour,
12 National Collections and 350
Champion Trees. Featured on Radio
Solent.
&. ✿ NCCPG ☕

56 **2 HILLSIDE COTTAGES**
Trampers Lane, North Boarhunt
PO17 6DA. John & Lynsey Pink,
01329 832786,
landjpink@tiscali.co.uk. *5m N of
Fareham. 3m E of Wickham. From
A32 at Wickham take B2177 E.
Trampers Lane 2nd on L (approx 2m).
Hillside Cottages approx ¹/₂ m on L.*
Adm **£2.50, chd free.** Visitors
welcome by appt.
This 1-acre garden, on gently rising
ground, contains so much of interest
for plantspeople. Many rare and
unusual specimens are shown off in
sweeping borders in a tranquil setting.
The National Collection of salvias is
well displayed, all colours, sizes and
growing habits. Something for
everyone and an ideal venue for a
group visit from spring through to
autumn.
&. 🏠 ✿ NCCPG ☎

57 **HINTON ADMIRAL**
Christchurch BH23 7DY. MEM Ltd,
www.hintonadmiral.myzen.co.uk.
*4m NE of Christchurch. On N side of
A35, ³/₄ m E of Cat & Fiddle PH.* Adm
£5, chd free. Sun 22 May (1-4.30).
Magnificent 20-acre garden (within a
much larger estate) now being
restored and developed. Mature
plantings of deciduous azaleas and
rhododendrons amidst a sea of
bluebells. Wandering paths lead
through rockeries and beside ponds
and a stream with many cascades.
Orchids appear in the large lawns.
The 2 walled gardens are devoted to

herbs and wild flowers and a very
large greenhouse. The terrace and
rock garden were designed by Harold
Peto. No refreshments, but picnics
may be taken in the orchard. Gravel
paths.
&. 🏠

58 ♦ **HINTON AMPNER**
Alresford SO24 0LA. National Trust,
01962 771305,
www.nationaltrust.org.uk. *3¹/₂ m S
of Alresford. S on A272 Petersfield to
Winchester rd.* Garden adm **£7.50,
chd £3.45. For NGS: Sats 16 Apr;
18 June; 16 July; 17 Sept (11-5).
For other opening times and
information, please phone or see
garden website.**
12 acres; C20 shrub garden designed
by Ralph Dutton. Strong architectural
elements using yew and box topiary;
spectacular views. Bold effects using
simple plants, restrained and dramatic
bedding. Orchard with spring wild
flowers and bulbs within formal box
hedges; magnolia and philadelphus
walks. Dell garden made from chalk
pit. Shrub rose border dating from
1950s. Restored walled garden.
&. ✿ ☕

59 **HOLYWELL**
Swanmore SO32 2QE. Countess of
Clarendon. *12m SE of Winchester.
On A32 S of Droxford between
Droxford and Wickham.* Light
refreshments & home-made teas.
Adm **£4, chd free.** Suns 22 May;
19 June (2-5).
Large garden in rural woodland and
lakeside setting. Colourful organic
kitchen garden, greenhouse, borders,
roses, trees and shrubs. Pergola
walk. Mature woodland garden with
many acid-loving specimens.
Gardened with great sensitivity for
wildlife. Compost and green manure
sustain the fertility of the organic
vegetable garden.
&. ✿ ☕

Something for
everyone and an
ideal venue for a
group visit from
spring through to
autumn . . .

60 **THE HOMESTEAD**
Northney Road, Hayling Island
PO11 0NF. Stan & Mary Pike, 02392
464888, jhomestead@aol.com,
www.homesteadhayling.co.uk. *3m
S of Havant. From A27
Havant/Hayling Island r'about, travel
S over Langstone Bridge & turn
immed L into Northney Rd. 1st house
on R after Langstone Hotel.* Home-
made teas. Adm **£3, chd free.** Sat 2
July (1.30-5). Visitors also welcome
by appt June to Sept, individuals &
groups welcome.
1-acre garden developed and
maintained by owners. Features
incl pleached lime walk, pergola,
arbour and ponds. Lawn surrounded
by herbaceous beds and shrub
borders with additional alpine beds
and interesting trees. Small walled
garden contains trained fruit trees,
formal herb garden and vegetables.
New beds and folly under
construction.
&. 🏠 ✿ ☕ ☎

61 **HORDLE WALHAMPTON
SCHOOL**
Beaulieu Road, Walhampton,
Lymington SO41 5ZG. Hordle
Walhampton School Trust Ltd. *1m
E of Lymington. From Lymington
follow signs to Beaulieu (B3054) for
1m & turn R into main entrance at 1st
school sign 200yds after top of hill.*
Home-made & cream teas. Adm **£4,
chd free (share to St John's
Church).** Sun 8 May (2-5).
Glorious walks through large C18
landscape garden surrounding
magnificent mansion (not open).
Visitors discover 3 lakes, serpentine
canal, climbable prospect mount,
period former banana house/
orangery, shell grotto, glade and
terrace by Peto (c1907) and terrace,
drives and colonnade by Mawson
(c1914). Seating; guided tours with
garden history. Gravel paths, can be
muddy when wet, some slopes.
&. 🏠 ☕

62 **THE HOUSE IN THE WOOD**
Beaulieu SO42 7YN. Victoria
Roberts. *8m NE of Lymington.
Leaving the entrance to Beaulieu
motor museum on R (B3056) take the
next R turn signed Ipley Cross. Take
2nd gravel drive on RH-bend, approx
¹/₂ m.* Cream Teas. Adm **£4, chd free.**
Sun 8 May (2-6).
Peaceful 12-acre woodland garden
with continuing progress and
improvement. New areas and streams
have been developed and good acers

Visit the website for latest information

Fritham Lodge

made teas. **Adm £4, chd free.** Sun 14, Wed 17 Aug (2-5.30). Visitors also welcome by appt on Weds, groups only.
3½ acres of garden planted in contemporary style, focusing on colour and texture, in tranquil spot, elevated and with glorious views. Large wildlife pond, woodland garden, potager and long banks and large borders planted with hardy perennials in imaginative drifts.

KENT HOUSE
See Sussex.

65 KIMPTON HOUSE
Lower Durford Wood, nr Petersfield GU31 5AS. Mr & Mrs Christopher Napier. *1½ m NE of Petersfield. B2070 N of Petersfield towards Rake. Pass A272 junction to Midhurst. ½ m further on turn R into white gates marked 'Durford Wood, Lower Wood only'. Kimpton House ½ m on R.* **Adm £3.50, chd free.** Sat 9, Sun 10 July (2-5).
10 acres of gardens with panoramic views of S Downs. Large traditional herbaceous and shrub borders with topiary in a formal setting. Contemporary tropical garden where temperatures regularly reach 110°F. Formal French garden of pleaching and topiary. Herb garden. Woodland areas. Water features and wild flower butterfly meadow.
&

66 53 LADYWOOD
Eastleigh SO50 4RW. Mr & Mrs D Ward, 023 8061 5389, sueatladywood@btinternet.com. *1m N of Eastleigh. Leave M3 J12. Follow signs to Eastleigh. Turn R at r'about into Woodside Ave, then 2nd R into Bosville. Ladywood 5th on R. Park in Bosville.* **Adm £3.50, chd free.** Sun 12 (11-5), Mon 13 June; (2-5); Sun 17 (11-5), Mon 18 July (2-5). Visitors also welcome by appt May, June & July, groups of 10+ preferred.
This lovely garden, only 45ft x 45ft, is full of ideas and creative ways of using every available space to grow over 2000 different plants. Clever uses of unusual unusual foliage plants enhance the flower borders throughout the seasons. Pond garden and tiny shade garden are created using trellis onto which many climbers are grown.

planted among mature azaleas and rhododendrons. Used in the war to train the Special Operations Executive. 'A magical garden to get lost in' and popular with bird-watchers.

63 THE HYDE
Old Alresford SO24 9DH. Sue Alexander. *1m W of Alresford. From Alresford 1m along B3046 towards Basingstoke. House in centre of village, opp village green.* Home-made teas. **Adm £3.50, chd free.** Suns, Tues 21, 23 Aug; 4, 6 Sept (1.30-5).
Tucked behind an old field hedge, a delightful ¾ -acre garden created by the owner to attract wildlife and reflect her flower arranging passion for colour and texture. Flowing borders contain an abundant mixture of perennials, half-hardies, annuals, grasses and shrubs. Wonderful ideas for late summer colour. National collection of Patrinia. Short gravel drive at entrance.
& ⊛ NCCPG ☕ ☎

64 IBTHORPE TOWER
Windmill Hill, Hurtsbourne Tarrant, Andover SP11 0DQ. Mr & Mrs P Gregory, kate_ibthorpe@yahoo.co.uk. *5m N of Andover. Off A343 at top of Hurstbourne Hill, signed The Chutes and Tangley. 1st turning on R.* Home-

67 LAKE HOUSE

Northington SO24 9TG. Lord Ashburton, 01962 734293, lukeroeder@hotmail.com. *4m N of Alresford. Off B3046. Follow English Heritage signs to The Grange, then directions.* Home-made & cream teas. **Adm £4, chd free. Thur 9, Sat 11 June (12.30-5).** Visitors also welcome by appt.
2 large lakes in Candover Valley set off by mature woodland with waterfalls, abundant bird life, long landscaped vistas and folly. 1½ -acre walled garden, with rose parterre, mixed borders, long herbaceous border, rose pergola leading to moon gate. Formal kitchen garden, flowering pots, conservatory and greenhouses. Picnicking by lakes.

68 60 LEALAND ROAD

Drayton, Portsmouth PO6 1LZ. Mr F°G Jacob. *2m E of Cosham. Old A27 (Havant Rd) between Cosham & Bedhampton.* Home-made teas. **Adm £2, chd free. Suns 17 Apr; 22 May (1-5).**
Small, unique garden with a difference, created by the owner since 1969. Plants from around the world incl palms, yuccas, echiums and cannas. Designed for maximum effect with lily ponds and rockery. Incl collection of bamboos and grasses, also cacti and other exotics in greenhouse.

69 THE LITTLE COTTAGE

Southampton Road (A337), Lymington SO41 9GZ. Peter & Lyn Prior, 01590 679395. *1m N of Lymington town centre. On A337 opp Toll House Inn.* **Adm £2.50, chd free. Suns 12 June; 10 July, Sats, Suns 30, 31 July; 6, 7, 20, 21, 28 Aug, Mon 29 Aug (all dates 2-5).** Also open nearby Willows: 30, 31 July; 6, 7, 20, 21, 28, 29 Aug. Visitors also welcome by appt 12 June to 30 Sept.
Garden of unique and artistic design using unusual and interesting plants arranged to form pictures with arches, arbours and urns in secret rooms. Each room is hidden from the next and contrasts sharply in style and colour to stimulate, calm, excite or amaze, incl an outrageous black and white garden.

70 LITTLE COURT

Crawley, nr Winchester SO21 2PU. Prof & Mrs A R Elkington, 01962 776365, elkslc@tiscali.co.uk. *5m NW of Winchester. Off A272 or B3049, in Crawley village; 300yds from either village pond or church.* Home-made teas at Village hall. **Adm £3 (Feb) £3.50 (Mar, April & July), chd free. Sun 20, Mon 21, Tue 22 Feb; Sun 27 Mar; Fri 22, Tue 26 Apr; Sun 3 July (2-5), Mon 4 July (2-5.30). Thur, Fri, Sun 23, 24, 26 Feb 2012.** Also opening with Crawley Gardens 10, 12 Apr; 15, 17 May; 16, 19 June. Visitors also welcome by appt all summer, groups welcome.
3-acre traditional C19 country garden in contrasting walled sections. Carpets of crocus, prolific summer flowers, giving harmonious colour throughout the year, with fine lawns. Walled kitchen garden, a house in an ash tree suitable for all ages, and extensive farmland views. A garden of great tranquillity loved by artists and photographers. Featured in Country Living & Japanese TV documentary.

> Bluebell wood and spring flowering garden surrounded by fields and near sea . . .

71 LITTLEWOOD

West Lane, Hayling Island PO11 0JW. Mr & Mrs Steven Schrier. *3m S of Havant. From A27 Havant/Hayling Island junction, travel S for 2m, turn R into West Lane and continue 1m. House set back from rd in wood. Disabled come to very top of drive.* Home-made teas. **Adm £3, chd free. Sat 30 Apr; Sun 1 May (11-5).**
2½ -acre bluebell wood and spring flowering garden surrounded by fields and near sea, protected from sea winds by multi-barrier hedge. Rhododendrons, azaleas, camellias and many other shrubs. Woodland walk to full-size tree house. Features incl pond, bog garden, house plants, summerhouse and many places to sit outside and under cover. Dogs on leads and picnickers welcome.

GROUP OPENING

72 LONGPARISH GARDENS

nr Andover SP11 6PS. *7m E of Andover. Off A303. To village centre on B3048. Parking at Lower Mill only, except for disabled.* Home-made teas at Longmead House. **Combined adm £6, chd free. Sun 5, Mon 6 June (2-6).**

LONGMEAD HOUSE
John & Wendy Ellicock
Visitors also welcome by appt, May to July for groups of 10+.
01264 720386
jhe777@googlemail.com

LOWER MILL
Mill Lane. Mrs K-M Dinesen

Longparish is a small beautiful village on R Test with many thatched cottages. Two gardens offer a wide variety of interest. The 2½ -acre organic and wildlife garden at Longmead House is full of interest with a large, hedged vegetable garden, polytunnel, greenhouse, fruit cage and composting area. There are also fish and wildlife ponds and a wild flower meadow, as well as herbaceous and shrub borders and a woodland walk. At Lower Mill there are approx 15 acres to explore, with tranquil natural walks beside the R Test. The spacious garden shows an enormous variety of design and planting incl a formal bed, courtyard and water garden. Exciting lake created 2010 on the site of previous crayfish beds. Limited wheelchair access at Lower Mill.

73 LONGSTOCK PARK WATER GARDEN

Leckford, Stockbridge SO20 6JF. Leckford Estate Ltd, part of John Lewis Partnership, www.longstockpark.co.uk. *4m S of Andover. From A30 turn N on to A3057; follow signs to Longstock.* Home-made teas at Longstock Park Nursery. **Adm £5, chd £1. Sun 19 June (2-5).**
Famous water garden with extensive collection of aquatic and bog plants set in 7 acres of woodland with rhododendrons and azaleas. A walk through park leads to National Collections of *Buddleja* and *Clematis viticella*; arboretum, herbaceous border.

LOWDER MILL
See Sussex.

74 ◆ MACPENNYS WOODLAND GARDEN & NURSERIES
Burley Road, Bransgore, Christchurch BH23 8DB. Mr & Mrs T M Lowndes, 01425 672348, www.macpennys.co.uk. *6m S of Ringwood, 5m NE of Christchurch. Midway between Christchurch & Burley. From A35, at Xrds by The Crown Bransgore turn R & proceed $^1/_4$ m. From A31 (towards Bournemouth) L at Picket Post, signed Burley, then R at Burley Cross. Garden on L after 2m.* **Adm by donation. For opening times and information, please phone or see garden website.**
12 acres; 4-acre gravel pit converted into woodland garden with many unusual plants. Offering interest all yr but particularly in spring and autumn. Gold Medal & Best in Class, Trees and Shrubs, at New Forest Show. Partial wheelchair access.
  ♿ ✿

MALT HOUSE
See Sussex.

75 MANOR HOUSE
Church Lane, Exton SO32 3NU. Tina Blackmore, 07977 223368, tinablackmore@dsl.pipex.com. *Off A32 just N of Corhampton. Next to Church.* Home-made & cream teas. **Adm £3.50, chd free. Sun 13 Feb (12-3). Visitors also welcome by appt.**
Step into enchanting mature walled garden with views to Beacon Hill fort. Woodland walk, masses of spring bulbs and plants.
♿ ✿ ☕ ☎

MANOR HOUSE
See Wiltshire.

76 MEON ORCHARD
Kingsmead, N of Wickham PO17 5AU. Doug & Linda Smith, 01329 833253, doug.smith@btinternet.com. *5m N of Fareham. From Wickham take A32 N for 1$^1/_2$ m. Turn L at Roebuck Inn. Continue $^1/_2$ m.* Home-made teas. **Adm £3.50, chd free. Suns 22 May; 31 July; 4 Sept (2-6). Visitors also welcome by appt, groups of 20+ only. Easy coach parking.**
1$^1/_2$ -acre garden designed and constructed by current owners. An exceptional range of rare, unusual and architectural plants incl National Collections of Eucalyptus, Podocarpaceae and Araliaceae. Much use made of dramatic foliage plants from around the world, both hardy and tender, big bananas, huge taros, tree ferns, cannas, hedychiums and palms. Streams and ponds, combined with an extensive range of planters, complete the display. Colour themed borders from hot oranges and yellows to gentle pinks and blues. From spring azaleas to autumn brugmansias. Owners available to answer questions. Plant sale of the exotic and rare Sun 4 Sept. Featured in RHS Garden Magazine & on BBC TV Gardeners' World. Garden fully accessible by wheelchair, reserved parking.
♿ ☎ ✿ NCCPG ☕ ☎

77 MERDON MANOR
Hursley SO21 2JJ. Mr & Mrs J C Smith, 01962 775215/775281, vronk@bluebottle.com. *5m SW of Winchester. From A3090 Winchester to Romsey rd, turn R at Standon to Slackstead; proceed 1$^1/_2$ m.* Home-made teas. **Adm £3.50, chd free. Sun 10 July (2-6). Visitors also welcome by appt.**
5 acres with panoramic views; herbaceous border, water lilies, large wisteria; selection of roses; fruit-bearing lemon trees and small secret walled water garden. Ha-ha and black Hebridean (St Kilda) sheep.
♿ ☎ ✿ ☕ ☎

78 MICHAELMAS
2 Old Street, Hill Head, Fareham PO14 3HU. Ros & Jack Wilson. *4$^1/_2$ m S of Fareham. From M27, J9 take A 27 signed Fareham. After approx 3m at gyratory follow B3334 to Gosport. After 2$^1/_4$ m at 2nd r'about in Stubbington go straight over, signed Hill Head. Approx 500yds turn R into Bells Lane. 1m pass Osborne View PH, next R is Old Street.* Home-made teas. **Adm £2.50, chd free. Sun, Mon, 10, 11 July (2-5).**
Very cheerful, colourful small garden with the 'wow' factor. A variety of tall plants for a tall lady! Many are grown from seed or cuttings. Small vegetable garden, greenhouse, garden room, pot-grown vegetables and flowers. Styled in the fashion of a country garden with a wide range of plants with the emphasis on perennials. 1 min walk from beach, 5 min walk from Titchfield Haven Nature Reserve.
✿ ☕

> 11 borders arranged around a communal space surrounded by converted stable blocks in historic mews . . .

GROUP OPENING

79 MONXTON & AMPORT GARDENS
SP11 8AY. *3m W of Andover. Between A303 & A343; parking in field next to Amport Village Green.* Cream teas at Village Hall. **Combined adm £5, chd free. Sun 29, Mon 30 May (2-5.30).**

NEW AMPORT PARK MEWS
Amport Park Mews Ltd

BRIDGE COTTAGE
Jenny Burroughs

WHITE GABLES
Mr & Mrs D Eaglesham

With many thatched cottages, Monxton and Amport are two pretty villages linked by Pill Hill Brook. Visitors have three gardens to enjoy. Bridge Cottage is a 2-acre haven for wildlife, with the banks of the trout stream and lake planted informally with drifts of colour, a large vegetable garden (not suitable for wheelchairs), fruit cage, small mixed orchard and arboretum with specimen trees. White Gables also has a collection of interesting trees, incl a young giant redwood - an unexpected feature in a cottage-style garden - along with old roses and herbaceous plants. The $^1/_3$ -acre garden leads down to Pill Hill Brook. New this year, Amport Park Mews has 11 borders arranged around a communal space surrounded by converted stable/carriage blocks in historic mews, once attached to Amport House, now 9 private dwellings. An unusual arrangement which charms the eye with interesting architectural features (e.g. clock tower) in a village setting. No wheelchair access to White Gables.
♿ ✿ ☕

80 ◆ MOTTISFONT ABBEY & GARDEN
Romsey SO51 0LP. National Trust, 01794 340757, www.nationaltrust.org.uk. *4¹/₂ m NW of Romsey. From A3057 Romsey to Stockbridge turn W at sign to Mottisfont. 6 wheelchairs & battery car service available at garden.* Adm £8.50, chd £4.50. **For NGS: Fri 8 Apr (10-5).** For other opening times and information, please phone or see garden website.
Built C12 as Augustinian priory, now house of some note. 30-acre landscaped garden incl spring or 'font', from which house derives its name, magnificent ancient trees and walled gardens with National Collection of over 300 varieties of old roses. Tranquil walks in grounds, along the R Test and in the glorious countryside of the estate. Large new developing Winter Garden, and thousands more spring bulbs. Talks with the garden team.

81 MULBERRY HOUSE
7 Moorland Avenue, Barton-on-Sea, New Milton BH25 7DB. Rosemary & John Owen, 01425 612066, rojowen@btinternet.com. *6m W of Lymington. From the A337 (S of New Milton), going W, take L turn into Barton Court Ave and 4th R into Moorland Ave.* Home-made teas. Adm £2.50, chd free (share to Oakhaven Hospice). **Suns 19, 26 June (2-5).** Visitors also welcome by appt.
Pretty family garden of ¹/₄ acre with old-fashioned and modern roses; a scramble of clematis; traditional fruit trees incl medlar and mulberry; good selection of hardy geraniums, and fruit and vegetable areas. Relaxed, organic garden with much native planting to attract insect and bird life. Productive hens in an Eglu. Limited wheelchair access, some narrow paths.

82 OAKFIELDS
45 Segensworth Road East, Titchfield, Fareham PO15 5EA. Denise & Dudley McGowan. *2m W of Fareham. From M27 J9 take A27 towards Fareham. At Titchfield Mill PH turn L into Mill Lane. 1st L after Titchfield Abbey into Segensworth Rd East. Garden 200yds on L.* Cream teas. Adm £3.50, chd free. **Sat 9, Sun 10 July (1-6).**
Discover the many aspects of this large, organic wildlife-friendly garden.

The pathways meander alongside naturalistic cottage planting. Fruit garden, vegetables, orchard, meadow and jungle follow. Wildlife ponds and Mediterranean area complement the herbaceous beds and the scent of jasmine permeates the air. Resident bees and hens share the garden. Fareham in Bloom, Gold and overall winner Plantsman's Back Garden & Wildlife Back Garden categories. Outstanding Horticultural Excellence Award.

Gold and overall winner Plantsman's Back Garden & Wildlife Back Garden . . .

83 THE OLD RECTORY, HOUGHTON
Church Lane, Houghton, Stockbridge SO20 6LJ. Mr & Mrs Richard Priestley, 01794 388015. *2m S of Stockbridge. From Stockbridge take minor rd S signed to Houghton (2m). Turn R by war memorial (opp Boot Inn) into Church Lane. Garden 200yds on R before church, parking in field on L.* Home-made teas. Adm £3, chd free. **Sun 12, Mon 13 June (2-5).** Visitors also welcome by appt in June.
Fine views of the church and Test Valley from this 4-acre village garden. Traditional flint and cob walled garden with prolific old-fashioned roses. Mixed herbaceous borders, rockery, herb potager with pond, yew and thuja hedges, rolling lawns. Teas in the attractive yellow and blue pool garden.

84 THE OLD RECTORY, SWARRATON
Swarraton, Alresford SO24 9TQ. Pam & Peter Davidson, 01962 732897. *4m N of Alresford. Follow B3046 N from Alresford to Swarraton, or from A33 turn at dual carriageway to Northington, then R at T-junction.*

Parking in field. Home-made teas. Adm £3, chd free. **Thurs 4, 11 Aug (2-5).** Visitors also welcome by appt, groups of 10+ July & Aug only.
Interesting, well designed 2-acre garden enveloped by 13 acres of Glebe land. Courtyard garden with topiary alongside thatched barn. Subtle combinations of perennials and unusual annuals, raised in Victorian-style greenhouse, cascade down terraced beds with flint walls. Mature trees, long traditional border, young orchard, vegetable corner. Woodland walk through Parsons Belt with old beeches and countryside views. Alpacas. Unfenced ponds, some gravel paths and slopes.

GROUP OPENING

85 OLD THATCH & THE MILLENNIUM BARN
Sprats Hatch Lane, Winchfield, Hook RG27 8DD. Jill Ede and Mr & Mrs S White, www.old-thatch.co.uk. *3m W of Fleet. From A287 Odiham to Farnham rd turn N to Dogmersfield. L by Queens Head PH and L opp Barley Mow PH. From Winchfield stn car park turn R towards Dogmersfield and after 1.3m R opp Barley Mow. Follow signs for parking in adjacent field. Limited disabled access on site.* Home-made teas (Apr & Sept). Combined adm £3, chd free. **Suns 17 Apr; 4 Sept (2-5.30) Evening Opening with wine, music & candlelight, £5, Sat 16 July (7-10pm).** Also open 4 Sept Dipley Mill. Visitors also welcome by appt. It may be possible to charter Canal Society's narrow boat for an NGS private visit. Please visit garden website for details.

THE MILLENNIUM BARN
Mr & Mrs S White

OLD THATCH
Jill Ede

Two gardens in one! A small secluded haven sits under the old oak tree next to the pond, surrounded by year-round colour and seasonal fragrance from roses and honeysuckle. You can listen to birdsong, wind-chimes and the trickling of a small waterfall whilst enjoying views of Old Thatch and the cottage garden beyond. Who could resist visiting Old Thatch, a 'chocolate box' thatched cottage, featured on film and TV, and evolving smallholding alongside the Basingstoke Canal (unfenced). A succession of spring bulbs, a profusion of wild flowers, perennials and home-grown annuals pollinated by our own bees and fertilised by the donkeys, who await your visit. Over 30 named clematis and rose cultivars. Lambs in April, donkey foals in summer. Children enjoy our I-spy quiz on Sunday openings. Dads love the cakes. Mums enjoy the music and candlelight in the evening. Why not arrive by boat? Surrey & Hants Canal Society may have boat trips to coincide with opening dates. Please contact Marian Gough on 01962 713564 **only for boat enquiries**. Featured in Hampshire Life & Daily Mail.

---

86 ▶ PASSFORD HOUSE HOTEL GARDENS & WILDERNESS
Mount Pleasant Lane, Lymington SO41 8LS. Ian & Carolyn Hudleston, 01590 682398, ian@passfordhousehotel.co.uk, www.passfordhousehotel.co.uk. *From Brockenhurst 4m on A337. After 'Welcome' sign for Lymington, over 2 mini r'abouts, 1st R into Sway Rd. Approx 1m, bear R onto Mount Pleasant Lane, hotel ¹/₂ m on R.* **Adm £3, chd free.** Every Wed, Thur & Fri 1 June to 29 July (11-4). **Visitors also welcome by appt.**
Originally the 'Wilderness' was a field. Ian and Carolyn admired Claude Monet and decided to emulate Giverny. This was achieved by removing trees, creating a pond and installing arches and flower beds. We have also created a winter garden to give colour and interest through the seasons. Please come and enjoy.

---

87 ▶ PENNINGTON HOUSE
Ridgeway Lane, Lower Woodside, Lymington SO41 8AA. Sue Stowell & John Leach. *1¹/₂ m S of Lymington. S on A337 from Lymington approx ¹/₃ m to Pennington r'about. Turn L into Ridgeway Lane. At L bend, fork R to continue along Ridgeway Lane for ¹/₃ m until Chequers PH. Turn R immed by post box into private drive.* Home-made teas (weather permitting). **Adm £3.50, chd free.** Sat 14, Sun 15 May (2-4.30).
7 acre garden created around 1910 and entirely organic for the last 16yrs. Substantial rockery of mature acers.

Stream and pond. Italian sunken garden, rose garden, organic ¹/₂ -acre walled Victorian kitchen garden in full use. Magnificent wisteria on the house. Some gravel paths.

---

88 ▶ PYLEWELL PARK
Lymington SO41 5SJ. Lord Teynham. *2m E of Lymington. Beyond IOW car ferry.* **Adm £3.50, chd free.** Suns 29 May; 19 June (2.30-5.30).
Very large garden of botanical interest, dating from 1900. Fine trees, flowering shrubs, rhododendrons, with walk beside the lakes and seashore.

---

89 ▶ NEW ▶ RAMRIDGE COTTAGE
Weyhill, Andover SP11 0QG. Mr & Mrs Raymond Henley. *2m W of Andover on A342 towards Ludgershall. Through Weyhill, turning on R.* **Adm £4, chd free.** Suns 17 Apr; Sun 15 May (2-5).
5-acre garden incl formal garden, pergola, 2 walled gardens, white garden and woodland walk. Extensively planted with spring bulbs, tulips and daffodil maze.

GROUP OPENING

90 ▶ ROMSEY GARDENS
Romsey SO51 8EU. *Town centre, all gardens within walking distance of Romsey Abbey, clearly signed. Car parking by King John's Garden.* Home-made teas at King John's House. **Combined adm £4.50, chd free.** Sun 29, Mon 30 May (11-5.30).

NEW ▶ DOCTOR'S CORNER
S Dale

KING JOHN'S GARDEN
Friends of King John's Garden & Test Valley Borough

4 MILL LANE
Miss J Flindall
Visitors also welcome by appt, suitable for painting groups of 12 to 20.
01794 513926

NEW ▶ 1 SPRING PLACE
A Burn

Small attractive market town with notable Norman C12 Abbey which forms a backdrop to 4 Mill Lane. There are no hills and all shops are

within walking distance. Belonging to the listed C13 house (not open), King John's Garden is a historic garden, planted with material available up to 1700. It also offers an award-winning Victorian garden and North Courtyard with water features. This contrasts with the small, long floriferous town garden at 4 Mill Lane with its original sculpture and attractive hard landscaping, the small Spring Place garden and colourful Doctor's Corner. All have splendid views of the Abbey.

Extensively planted with spring bulbs, tulips and daffodil maze . . .

---

91 ▶ ROTHERFIELD PARK
East Tisted, Alton GU34 3QE. Sir James & Lady Scott. *4m S of Alton on A32.* Home-made teas. **Adm £3, chd free.** Sun 8 May (2-5).
Take some ancient ingredients: ice house, ha-ha, lime avenue; add a walled garden, fruit and vegetables, trees and hedges; set this 12-acre plot in an early C19 park (picnic here from noon) with views to coin clichés about. Mix in a bluebell wood and new grass amphitheatre. Good disabled access to walled garden.

---

92 ▶ 28 ST RONAN'S AVENUE
Southsea PO4 0QE. Ian Craig and Liz Jones, 02392 787331, ian.craig93@ntlworld.com, www.28stronansavenue.co.uk. *Turn into St Ronan's Rd from Albert Rd at junction opp Trinity Methodist Church. St Ronan's Ave is a cul-de-sac off St Ronan's Rd. Park at Craneswater School in St Ronan's Rd.* Home-made teas. **Adm £2.50, chd free.** Sun 29 May (2-6). Also opening 12 & 25 June with Southsea Gardens. Visitors also welcome by appt.
Town garden 145ft x 25ft, 700m from the sea. A mixture of tender, exotic and dry-loving plants along with more traditional incl king protea, bananas,

ferns, agaves, echeverias, echium and puya. Wildflower area, wildlife pond. Two different dry gardens showing what can be grown in sandy soil. Recycled items have been used to create sculptures. Featured in Portsmouth Evening News.

SANDHILL FARM HOUSE
See Sussex.

Edgewood

93 ▶ SANDLE COTTAGE
Sandleheath, Fordingbridge SP6 1PY. Peter & Yo Beech, 01425 654638, peter@sandlecottage.com, www.sandlecottage.com. *2m W of Fordingbridge. Turn R at Sandleheath Xrds. Entrance 50yds on L. Ample field parking*. Home-made teas. **Adm £3.50, chd free.** Sun 10 July with music from Sandleheath Band. Suns 24, 31 July (all dates 1.30-5.30). **Visitors also welcome by appt in July only for groups of 25+, coaches welcome.**
We invite you to visit our 3 acres to stroll through the walled garden, well-stocked with vegetables, relax to the sound of the fountain in the sunken garden, tiptoe across the manicured lawn with its sharp edges, relax in the summerhouse within its own cottage garden. Explore the woodland walk, visit the productive greenhouses and discover the waterfall. Find fabulous fuchsias, admire the sweet peas (best 10 July) and enjoy the formal beds of annuals and dahlias (best 31 July).

SANDLEFORD PLACE
See Berkshire.

94 ▶ SANDY SLOPES
Honeysuckle Lane, Headley Down GU35 8EH. Mr & Mrs R Thornton. *6m S of Farnham. From A3 take B3002 through Grayshot, on to Headley Down. Turn L at mini r'about by garage, down hill to 2nd turning L, bungalow 3rd drive on R. From Headley village take B3002 towards Grayshot, after S bend on to sharp L bend up hill to Honeysuckle Lane on R. Parking very limited*. Home-made teas. **Adm £3, chd free.** Mons 2, 30 May (2-5).
Sloping and partly terraced plantsman's and garden lecturer's garden with many special features incl woodland with rhododendrons, camellias, meconopsis, primulas and other seasonal plants. Stream and pool, herbaceous mixed shrub borders. Rock gardens. Many trees

and unusual plants within about ¼ acre incl davidia, cornus and paulownia.

95 ▶ 'SELBORNE'
Caker Lane, East Worldham, Alton GU34 3AE. Brian & Mary Trigwell-Jones, 01420 83389, mary.trigwell-jones@virgin.net. *2m SE of Alton. On B3004 at Alton end of East Worldham opp The Three Horseshoes PH (please note, NOT in the village of Selborne). Parking signed*. Home-made teas. **Adm £3, chd free** (share to St Mary's Church in May & June, Tafara Mission Zimbabwe in Aug). Sat, Sun 16, 17 Apr; Sats, Suns, Mons 14, 15, 16 May; 18, 19, 20 June; (2-5); 6, 7, 8 Aug (2-6). **Visitors also welcome by appt, individuals and groups very welcome, mid Apr to mid Aug.**
A garden of surprises. ½-acre mature garden with old established orchard of named varieties. Meandering paths provide changing vistas across

farmland. Mixed borders feature a large collection of hardy geraniums and other herbaceous plants and shrubs. Soft fruit garden, containers, metal and stone sculpture and summerhouses. Relax and take tea in the dappled shade of the orchard, or in the conservatory. Book stall, garden quizzes for children, sandpit. Featured in Herald Group of Newspapers. Some gravel paths.

96 ▶ SHALDEN PARK HOUSE
The Avenue, Shalden GU34 4DS. Michael D C C Campbell. *4½ m NW of Alton. B3349 from Alton or J5 M3 onto B3349. Turn W at Golden Pot PH marked Herriard, Lasham, Shalden. Entrance ¼ m on L*. Light refreshments & home-made teas. **Adm £3, chd free.** Sun 26 June (2-5).
4-acre garden surrounded by woodland, redesigned in 2005/6 by Georgia Langton. Extensive views. Herbaceous borders. Walled kitchen

garden and glasshouses. Early stage arboretum. Pond area and formal lawns.

97 SILVERWOOD
28 Green Lane, Warsash SO31 9JJ. Nick & Ginny Foy. *4m W of Fareham. From M27 J9 follow A27 towards Southampton. At Parkgate L into Locks Rd. Continue to end, R at r'about into Warsash Rd, 1st L into Fleet End Rd, 300yds past Jolly Farmer PH is Green Lane. Please park in Fleet End Rd, disabled parking only at Silverwood*. Home-made teas. **Adm £3, chd free. Sun 10, Mon 11 July (1-6).**
¹/₂ -acre peaceful, informal garden with many mature trees sloping down to natural woodland and stream. Wealth of herbaceous plants, hardy geraniums, heucheras, phlox. Fernery and fish pond. Many quiet seating areas including the mystical 'Moon Garden' set with crystals.

GROUP OPENING

98 SOUTHSEA GARDENS
Southsea PO4 0QE. *Turn into St Ronan's Rd from Albert Rd at junction opp Trinity Methodist Church. Alternatively follow signs from seafront and then follow yellow NGS signs from Canoe Lake and Eastern Parade. Park at Craneswater School in St Ronan's Rd. Entrance to all gardens from St Ronan's Ave.* Home-made teas (Sun). **Combined adm £5, chd free. Sun 12 June (2-6). Evening Opening £6, wine, Sat 25 June (5-8).**

27 ST RONAN'S AVENUE
Mr & Mrs S C Johns

28 ST RONAN'S AVENUE
Ian Craig and Liz Jones
(See separate entry)

87 ST RONAN'S ROAD
Miss Judy Walker

85 ST RONAN'S ROAD
Mr Mike Hodges

Four town gardens conveniently within 100m of each other. Each has a distinctive style, with different designs showing what can be achieved in an urban setting. 85 St Ronan's Road is a city garden with a classical twist, featuring a Neptune water feature in a pool of smoke. There is exceptional design at 27 St

Ronan's Avenue and landscaping has been used to create a modern family concept with exuberant planting. The 'inside-out' garden at 87 St Ronan's Road captures busy urban living at its best, with an impressive dining area and sitting room with a permanent outside fireplace. 28 St Ronan's Avenue (see separate entry) showcases a mixture of tender, exotic and dry-loving plants along with more traditional incl king protea, bananas, ferns, agave, echeveria and echiums.

99 NEW SPINDLES
24 Wootton Road, Lee on the Solent PO13 9HB. Peter & Angela Arnold, 02392 550490. *Approx 6m S of Fareham. Exit A27, turn L Gosport Rd A32. At r'about 2nd exit Gosport Rd Newgate Lane B3385. Through 3 r'abouts staying on B3385, turn L Marine Parade B3333 onto Wootton Rd.* Home-made teas. **Adm £2.50, chd free. Sun 29 May; Sun 26, Mon 27 June (2-5).** Visitors also welcome by appt in June & July. Plantswoman's delightful small garden with all-yr interest. Ferns, grasses, succulent collection, scented rose-covered pergolas, hostas and clematis. Unusual trees and palms, bananas, ginger lilies and exuberant herbaceous borders. Mini bog garden, soft fruit and herbs. Interest to new and experienced gardeners.

Unusual trees and palms, bananas, ginger lilies and exuberant herbaceous borders . . .

100 ◆ SPINNERS GARDEN
School Lane, Boldre SO41 5QE. Andrew & Victoria Roberts, 01590 612089, www.spinnersgarden.co.uk. *1¹/₂ m N of Lymington. Follow the brown signs off the A337 between Lymington and Brockenhurst. Also signed off the B3054 Beaulieu to Lymington Road. Map on website.* Cream Teas on 15 May. **Adm £4, chd**

free. For NGS: Sun 15 May (2-6). For other opening times and information, please phone or see garden website.
Peaceful woodland garden on a slope overlooking the Lymington river valley. Azaleas, rhododendrons, magnolias, camellias and other rare shrubs interplanted with a wide variety of choice woodland and groundcover plants. Particularly good in spring are the erythroniums and trilliums. The garden is under development and new areas are now open.

GROUP OPENING

101 STOCKBRIDGE GARDENS
Stockbridge SO20 6EX. *9m W of Winchester. On A30, at junction of A3057 & B3049. Parking on High St. All gardens on High St/Winton Hill.* Home-made teas. **Combined adm £5, chd free** (share to St Peter's Church). **Thur 16, Sun 19 June (2-5.30).**

LITTLE WYKE
High Street. Mrs Mary Matthews

SHEPHERDS HOUSE
Winton Hill. Kim & Frances Candler

TROUT COTTAGE
High Street. Mrs Sally Milligan

WATERLOW
High Street. Mrs Pamela Marples

Stockbridge with its many listed houses, excellent shops and pubs is on the famous River Test. Four gardens are open this year offering a variety of styles and character. Trout Cottage has a small walled garden tucked in behind the High Street. Waterlow is a densely planted garden bounded by a carrier of the River Test. Little Wyke, also on the High Street next to the Town Hall, has a long mature town garden with views over the water meadows. Shepherds House, 50yds east of the White Hart roundabout, is south-facing on 3/4acre of rising ground around a Georgian House. Ongoing renovation includes lawns and terraces around the house, new mixed borders and vegetable/fruit areas, and a belvedere enjoying views overlooking the village.

Clever hard landscaping with theme of ovals and circles, changes of level and vistas . . .

SWALLOWFIELD HORTICULTURAL SOCIETY
See Berkshire.

102 TANGLEFOOT
Crawley, nr Winchester SO21 2QB. Mr & Mrs F J Fratter, 01962 776243, fred@tanglefoot-house.demon.co.uk. *5m NW of Winchester. Private lane beside entrance to Crawley Court (Arqiva). Drop-off & disabled parking only at house, parking in field 50m.* **Adm £3, chd free. Also opening with Crawley Gardens 15, 17 May; 16, 19 June; 21, 24 July.** Visitors welcome by appt, summer only. Approx ¹/₂ acre on chalk, designed and developed by owners since 1976. Features incl colour-themed herbaceous and mixed borders, raised lily pond, herb wheel, wild flower area, traditional Victorian boundary wall with trained fruit and greenhouse. Visitors remark upon the productive kitchen garden and number of unusual flowering plants. Images by Marianne Majerus. Featured in German magazine, Garden Style.

103 NEW TERSTAN
Longstock, Stockbridge SO20 6DW. Alexander and Penny Burnfield, terstan@waitrose.com, http://terstangarden.blogspot.com. *¹/₂ m N of Stockbridge. From Stockbridge (A30) turn N to Longstock at bridge. Garden ¹/₂ m on R.* Home-made teas. **Adm £3, chd free. Thurs, Suns 16, 19 June; 14, 17 July (2-6). Visitors also welcome** by appt in June and July only. Farm cottage surrounded by contrasting garden spaces: an element of surprise and views to the R Test meadows and Stockbridge Down. Clever hard landscaping with theme of ovals and circles, changes of level and vistas, imaginative, unusual and colourful planting, a Showman's caravan, and a maze-like kitchen garden. Featured in Japanese TV documentary. Some gravel paths.

THRIVE'S TRUNKWELL GARDEN PROJECT
See Berkshire.

104 TYLNEY HALL HOTEL
Ridge Lane, Rotherwick RG27 9AZ. The Manager, 01256 764881, sales@tylneyhall.com, www.tylneyhall.com. *3m NW of Hook. From M3 J5 via A287 & Newnham, M4 J11 via B3349 & Rotherwick.* Light refreshments & teas. **Adm £3.50, chd free. Suns 17 Apr; 12 June; 9 Oct (10-5). Visitors** also welcome by appt, groups only. Large garden of 66 acres with extensive woodlands and fine vistas being restored with new planting. Fine avenues of wellingtonias; rhododendrons and azaleas; Italian garden; lakes, large water and rock garden, dry stone walls originally designed with assistance of Gertrude Jekyll. In 2011 Tylney Hall celebrates its 25th anniversary of opening as a hotel. Head Gardener, Paul Tattersdill, awarded 2nd place in Gardener of the Year, Hampshire County Magazine.

105 ◆ THE VYNE
Sherborne St John RG24 9HL. National Trust, 01256 883858, www.nationaltrust.org.uk. *4m N of Basingstoke. Between Sherborne St John & Bramley. From A340 turn E at NT signs.* **Adm £6.10, chd £3.05. For NGS: Tue 7 June (3.15-5) NGS Special Event: Exclusive garden tour and cream tea, £8.50** bookable in advance only, limited numbers. Sat 16 July (11-5). For other opening times and information, please phone or see garden website. A good mix of garden areas including C18 landscape, Edwardian-style summerhouse garden, and a walled garden which incl new glasshouse and vegetable plots. Vegetables grown by gardeners from the charity Thrive. Some gravel paths, mostly level access.

106 WALBURY
Lower Froyle, Alton GU34 4LJ. Ernie & Brenda Milam, 01420 22216, walbury@uwclub.net. *5m NE of Alton. Access to Lower Froyle from A31 between Alton and Farnham at Bentley. Walbury nr village hall where parking available.* Home-made teas. **Adm £2.50, chd free.** Sat, Sun 23, 24 Apr (2-5). **Also open with Froyle Gardens Sat, Sun 4, 5 June. Visitors also welcome by appt May to July, coaches permitted.** Three gardens in one. All gardens have a cottage garden atmosphere in different styles. Each one is packed with plants in colour-themed borders incl many unusual plants. There are water features, an alpine house and fern walk.

107 WALDRONS
Brook, Bramshaw SO43 7HE. Major & Mrs J Robinson. *4m N of Lyndhurst. On B3079 1m W from J1 M27. 1st house L past Green Dragon PH & directly opp Bell PH.* Home-made teas. **Adm £3, chd free. Sun 29, Mon 30 May (2-5).** Visitors have always been pleasantly surprised when they visit our well cared for 1-acre garden hidden behind a high hedge. We have interesting mixed herbaceous beds for yr-round interest, raised gravel and kitchen garden and brick-based greenhouse. Unique display of textiles made by local artists on display in garden room converted from an old stable block.

108 WEIR HOUSE
Abbotstone Road, Old Alresford SO24 9DG. Mr & Mrs G Hollingbery. *¹/₂ m N of Alresford. From Alresford down Broad St (B3046) past Globe PH. Take 1st L, signed Abbotstone. Park in signed field.* **Adm £5, chd free. Suns 22 May; 19 June; 18 Sept (2-5).** Spectacular riverside garden. Contemporary vegetable and cut flower garden incorporating many different crops, surprising uses for scaffolding and painters' ladders and sculpture by Mark Merer. Children can use the playground at their own risk. Newly designed pool garden.

109 **WEST SILCHESTER HALL**
Silchester RG7 2LX. Mrs Jenny
Jowett, 0118 970 0278,
www.jennyjowett.com. *7m N of
Basingstoke. 7m S of Reading, off
A340 (signed from centre of village).*
Home-made teas. **Adm £3, chd free.
Sun, Mon 29, 30 May; Suns 10
July; 7 Aug (2-5.30).** Visitors also
welcome by appt groups of 12+
May to Sept, coaches permitted.
This much loved 2-acre garden has
fascinating colour combinations,
inspired by the artist owners.
Herbaceous borders crammed with
rare and unusual plants, very good
clematis, pots full of half hardies, wild
pond garden and self-supporting
kitchen garden with lovely view across
to field of grazing cattle. Exhibition of
botanical and landscape paintings by
owners. Large plant sale. Nr Roman
site Calleva Atrebatum. Featured in
GGG. Gravel drive.

110 **WESTWARD**
11 Ridgemount Avenue, Bassett,
Southampton SO16 7FP. Jan &
Russ Smith, 023 8076 7112,
janetdsmith@btinternet.com. *3m N
of Southampton city centre. From end
of M3 J14 continue down A33 to 2nd
r'about and head back to M3.
Ridgemount Ave 2nd on L.* **Adm £3,
chd free. Sun 17, Wed 20, Sun 24
July (1.30-4.30).** Visitors also
welcome by appt.

Very colourful ¼-acre garden with
diverse selection of planting incl, in
summer, lilies, heucheras, acers,
clematis and hydrangeas. Many
baskets and containers full of summer
colour. Hosta border, vegetable
garden, summerhouse, koi pond,
waterfall and wildlife pond. Large
collection of aeoniums, echeverias
and cacti. New raised water feature in
front garden.

111 **WHEATLEY HOUSE**
between Binsted and Kingsley
GU35 9PA. Mr & Mrs Michael
Adlington, 01420 23113,
mikeadlington36@tiscali.co.uk. *4m
E of Alton, 5m SW of Farnham. From
Alton follow signs to Holybourne &
Binsted. At end of Binsted turn R
signed Wheatley. ¾ m down lane on
L. From Farnham/Bordon on A325
take turn signed Binsted at
Buckshorn Oak. 1½ m turn L signed
Wheatley.* Home-made teas. **Adm
£3.50, chd free. Sat, Sun 20, 21
Aug (1.30-5).** Visitors also welcome
by appt for groups of 15+, coaches
permitted.
Magnificent setting with panoramic
views over fields and forests.
Sweeping mixed borders, shrubberies
and grasses. 1½ acres, designed by
artist-owner. The colours are
spectacular. 'White & black' border.
Craft stalls in Old Barn.

112 **WHISPERS**
Chatter Alley, Dogmersfield
RG27 8SS. Mr & Mrs John Selfe.
*3m W of Fleet. Turn N to
Dogmersfield off A287 Odiham to
Farnham rd. Turn L by Queen's Head
PH.* Home-made teas. **Adm £3.50,
chd free (share to Samantha
Dickson Brain Tumour Trust).
Sun 10 July (12-5).**
Visitors say you could spend all
day discovering new plants in these
2 acres of manicured lawns
surrounded by large borders of
colourful shrubs, trees and long
flowering perennials. Alstromerias
and salvias a speciality. Wild flower
area, water storage system
greenhouse, kitchen garden and living
sculptures add to the attraction.
Spectacular waterfall cascades over
large rock slabs and magically
disappears below the terrace. A
garden not to be missed. Assistance
available on request over gravel
entrance.

Willows

Visit a garden in your own time – look out for the ☎

113 WHITE BARN
Woodend Road, Crow Hill,
Ringwood BH24 3DG. Marilyn &
Barrie Knight, 01425 473527,
bandmknight@btinternet.com. *2m
SE of Ringwood. From Ringwood
take B3347 towards Winkton and
Sopley. After 1m turn L immed after
petrol stn into Moortown Lane,
proceed 1m, Woodend Rd, gravel rd
on L.* Coffee & biscuits a.m. Home-
made teas p.m. Elderflower cordial.
Adm £3, chd free. Weds 18, 25
May; Weds 1, 8, 15, 22, 29 June;
Weds 6, 13, 20, 27 July (10.30-5).
Visitors also welcome by appt.
Tranquil ³/₄-acre plant lover's garden
with harmonious colour and form.
250+ clematis and many roses attract
birds, butterflies, bees. Hollyhocks
abound. Shapes and structures blend
with the house and surrounding
views. Successional flowering
provides a different picture throughout
the season, and some visitors
returning several times. New Forest
Nat Park, pond, rose arches,
catenary, topiary, lovely views,
unusual plants and trees, relaxing
seating, greeting cards featuring
garden. Featured in Dorset Country
Gardener.

114 WHITE GABLES
Breach Lane, Sherfield-on-Loddon
RG27 0EU. Terry & Brian
Raisborough. *5m N of Basingstoke.
From Basingstoke follow A33 towards
Reading for approx 5m. Breach Lane
is unmade lane immed before
Sherfield-on-Loddon r'about on R.
Limited parking for disabled by house.
Main parking in 2 free signed car
parks in main village. Short walk to
garden.* Home-made teas. **Adm £3,**

chd free. Sun, Mon 1, 2 May; Sun 3
July (1-5).
A plantaholic's paradise! Consisting of
many sections, this garden provides a
host of inspirations and ideas towards
visitors' own gardens. Large
collections of exotic plants, hostas,
cacti and succulents and lots more -
revealing owners' passion for plants.
The winding paths take the visitor
through various themed areas on a
fascinating journey through an all-yr
garden paradise containing many life-
size statues, various arches, and
areas of sheer tranquillity.

115 WILLOWS
Pilley Hill, Boldre, nr Lymington
SO41 5QF. Elizabeth & Martin
Walker, 01590 677415,
elizabethwalker13@gmail.com,
www.willowsgarden.co.uk. *Off
A337 Lymington to Brockenhurst rd.
2m N of Lymington, 2¹/₂ m S of
Brockenhurst, turn into Rope Hill for
Pilley, Boldre and Spinners. Go 1m via
Boldre Bridge, up Pilley Hill. Garden
at school sign. Also signed from
B3054 Beaulieu to Lymington rd.
Leave M27 at J2 and follow 'Heavy
Lorry Route' to avoid traffic delays at
Lyndhurst.* Luxury cream teas. **Adm
£3, chd free.** Sats, Suns 30, 31
July; 6, 7, 20, 21, 28 Aug, Mon 29
Aug (2-5). **Also open nearby, all
dates, The Little Cottage. Visitors
also welcome by appt in Aug for
groups of 20+.**
Late summer sizzle and vibrant
exotics with a jungly mix of bananas,
bamboos, gunnera and ferns around
the tranquil pond and bog garden.
Beds ripple with vivid flower colour -
cannas, crocosmias, sedums,
helianthus, cosmos, rudbeckias and
verbenas. Sunny hot upper borders of

coleus, salvia, bedding dahlias with a
back-drop of miscanthus, grasses
and buddleia. Photographic displays
of dam and pond construction. Plans
of water catchment, storage and
distribution. Plant sales, garden plan.
Featured in Hampshire Life,
Countryside, Woman's Weekly
Gardening & Homes and Gardens
Germany.

> Small traditional
> cottage garden with
> a 'roses around the
> door' look . . .

116 1 WOGSBARNE COTTAGES
Rotherwick RG27 9BL. Mr R & Miss
S Whistler. *2¹/₂ m N of Hook. M3 J5,
M4 J11, A30 or A33 via B3349.*
Home-made teas. **Adm £3, chd free.**
Sun, Mon 10, 11 July (2-5).
Small traditional cottage garden with
a 'roses around the door' look, much
photographed, seen on calendars,
jigsaws and in magazines. Mixed
flower beds and borders. Vegetables
grown in abundance. Ornamental
pond and alpine garden. Views over
open countryside to be enjoyed whilst
you take afternoon tea on the lawn.
Small vintage motorcycle display
(weather permitting).

Enjoy a day out – look out for a Group Opening

HEREFORDSHIRE

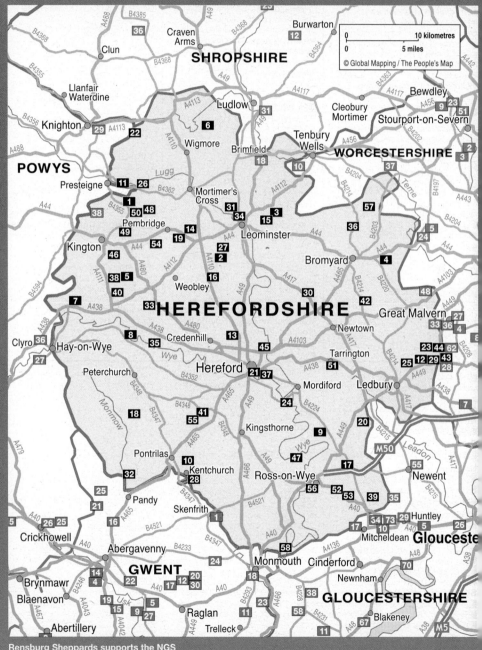

Opening Dates

February

Thursday 3
27 Ivy Croft

Thursday 10
27 Ivy Croft

Thursday 17
27 Ivy Croft

Thursday 24
27 Ivy Croft

March

Sunday 27
55 Whitfield

April

Sunday 3
39 The Old Corn Mill

Monday 4
36 Moors Meadow Gardens & Nursery

Sunday 10
30 Lower Hope

Sunday 17
16 The Great House

Friday 22
39 The Old Corn Mill

Sunday 24
2 Aulden Farm
27 Ivy Croft

Monday 25
39 The Old Corn Mill

Friday 29
25 Hope End House

Saturday 30
25 Hope End House

May

Monday 2
39 The Old Corn Mill

Saturday 7
23 The Hollies

Sunday 8
8 Brobury House Gardens
23 The Hollies
55 Whitfield

Monday 9
36 Moors Meadow Gardens & Nursery

Saturday 14
11 Bryan's Ground
28 Kentchurch Gardens
49 Titley Mill

Sunday 15
19 Hardwick House
22 Hill House Farm
28 Kentchurch Gardens

Friday 20
54 Westonbury Mill Water Garden

Sunday 22
2 Aulden Farm
6 Bridge Cottage
27 Ivy Croft
30 Lower Hope
33 Midland Farm

Friday 27
25 Hope End House

Saturday 28
25 Hope End House
35 Monnington Court

Sunday 29
14 Glan Arrow
25 Hope End House
35 Monnington Court

Monday 30
35 Monnington Court
39 The Old Corn Mill

Tuesday 31
45 The Rambles

June

Wednesday 1
8 Brobury House Gardens

Friday 3
20 Hellens

Saturday 4
18 The Griggs
20 Hellens

Sunday 5
3 Bachefield House
4 The Bannut
26 Ivy Cottage
46 Rhodds Farm

Monday 6
26 Ivy Cottage
46 Rhodds Farm

Tuesday 7
45 The Rambles

Friday 10
13 Daimor

Saturday 11
13 Daimor
32 Middle Hunt House

Sunday 12
12 Caves Folly Nursery
29 Longacre
32 Middle Hunt House
38 Newport House
41 The Old Rectory
50 Upper Tan House
51 The Vine
56 Wilton Castle on the Wye

Monday 13
36 Moors Meadow Gardens & Nursery
41 The Old Rectory
50 Upper Tan House

Tuesday 14
45 The Rambles

Friday 17
21 Hereford Cathedral Gardens

Saturday 18
31 The Marsh
34 The Mill
47 Shieldbrook
49 Titley Mill
53 Weston Mews

Sunday 19
10 The Brooks
31 The Marsh
34 The Mill
41 The Old Rectory
43 Perrycroft
47 Shieldbrook
49 Titley Mill

Monday 20
41 The Old Rectory

Tuesday 21
45 The Rambles

Saturday 25
18 The Griggs
28 Kentchurch Gardens

Sunday 26
1 Ashley Farm
26 Ivy Cottage
28 Kentchurch Gardens
33 Midland Farm
41 The Old Rectory
55 Whitfield
56 Wilton Castle on the Wye

Monday 27
1 Ashley Farm
26 Ivy Cottage
41 The Old Rectory

Tuesday 28
45 The Rambles

Wednesday 29
8 Brobury House Gardens

July

Saturday 2
57 Wolferlow House

Sunday 3
42 The Orchards

Tuesday 5
18 The Griggs
45 The Rambles

Wednesday 6
56 Wilton Castle on the Wye

Saturday 9
24 Holme Lacy House Hotel

Sunday 10
2 Aulden Farm
4 The Bannut
27 Ivy Croft
30 Lower Hope

Monday 11
36 Moors Meadow Gardens & Nursery

Tuesday 12
18 The Griggs
45 The Rambles

You are always welcome at an NGS garden

Sunday 17
22 Hill House Farm
24 Holme Lacy House Hotel
58 Woodview
Tuesday 19
45 The Rambles
Wednesday 20
56 Wilton Castle on the Wye
Sunday 24
58 Woodview
Tuesday 26
45 The Rambles
Saturday 30
23 The Hollies
Sunday 31
23 The Hollies

August

Tuesday 2
45 The Rambles
Sunday 7
44 The Picton Garden
Tuesday 9
45 The Rambles
Sunday 14
3 Bachefield House
24 Holme Lacy House Hotel
44 The Picton Garden
Monday 15
36 Moors Meadow Gardens & Nursery
Tuesday 16
45 The Rambles
Friday 19
44 The Picton Garden
Saturday 20
24 Holme Lacy House Hotel
Sunday 21
4 The Bannut
Tuesday 23
45 The Rambles
Saturday 27
44 The Picton Garden
Monday 29
44 The Picton Garden
Tuesday 30
45 The Rambles

September

Friday 2
54 Westonbury Mill Water Garden
Sunday 4
9 Brockhampton Cottage
17 Grendon Court
44 The Picton Garden
Sunday 11
2 Aulden Farm
24 Holme Lacy House Hotel
27 Ivy Croft
41 The Old Rectory
Monday 12
41 The Old Rectory

Wednesday 14
44 The Picton Garden
Saturday 17
32 Middle Hunt House
Sunday 18
10 The Brooks
32 Middle Hunt House
Thursday 29
44 The Picton Garden

October

Sunday 2
30 Lower Hope
Wednesday 5
44 The Picton Garden
Sunday 9
38 Newport House
Monday 10
44 The Picton Garden
Sunday 16
44 The Picton Garden

February 2012

By appointment only
27 Ivy Croft

Gardens open to the public

2 Aulden Farm
4 The Bannut
8 Brobury House Gardens
11 Bryan's Ground
12 Caves Folly Nursery
20 Hellens
21 Hereford Cathedral Gardens
27 Ivy Croft
32 Middle Hunt House
36 Moors Meadow Gardens & Nursery
44 The Picton Garden
48 Staunton Park
54 Westonbury Mill Water Garden

By appointment only

5 Batch Cottage
7 Brilley Court
15 Grantsfield
37 Mouse Castle
40 The Old Quarry
48 Staunton Park
52 Weston Hall

Also open by Appointment ☎

1 Ashley Farm
3 Bachefield House
14 Glan Arrow
16 The Great House
18 The Griggs

22 Hill House Farm
23 The Hollies
26 Ivy Cottage
29 Longacre
30 Lower Hope
35 Monnington Court
38 Newport House
39 The Old Corn Mill
41 The Old Rectory
42 The Orchards
43 Perrycroft
45 The Rambles
47 Shieldbrook
50 Upper Tan House
53 Weston Mews
55 Whitfield
56 Wilton Castle on the Wye
57 Wolferlow House
58 Woodview

The Gardens

1 NEW **ASHLEY FARM**
Stansbatch HR6 9LN. Roger & Jackie Pietroni, 01544 267405, jackiepietroni@hotmail.com. *2m S of Presteigne. 1m N of Titley. On B4355.* Home-made teas. **Adm £4, chd free. Sun 26, Mon 27 June (2-5).** Visitors also welcome by appt.
5-acre garden started in 2005. Designed as a series of formal rooms surrounding the house becoming more informal further away. Many places to sit and contemplate. Wonderful views. Colour themed borders, roses plentiful, orchards enchanting in blossom time. Squirrels love the nuttery, bees and butterflies think they're in heaven in the decorative and productive kitchen garden. Much more besides.
❀ ☕ ☎

2 ◆ **AULDEN FARM**
Aulden, Leominster HR6 0JT. Alun & Jill Whitehead, 01568 720129, www.auldenfarm.co.uk. *4m SW of Leominster. From Leominster take Ivington/Upper Hill Rd. ³/₄ m after Ivington Church, turn R (signed Aulden), garden 1m on R. From A4110 signed Ivington, take 2nd R (approx ³/₄ m), garden ³/₄ m on L.* Home-made: teas & ice-cream NGS days only. **Adm £3, chd free, Combined with Ivy Croft adm £5, chd free. For NGS: Suns 24 Apr; 22 May; 10 July; 11 Sept (2-5.30).** Private visits and groups welcome by appt. For other opening times and information please phone or see garden website.
Informal country garden surrounding old farmhouse. 3 acres planted with

wildlife in mind. Numerous iris incl ditch containing ensatas, sibiricas by natural pond. Hemerocallis with grasses and kniphofias for added zing. Emphasis on structure and form with hint of quirkiness. Started from scratch 1997, feels mature but still evolving. National Collection of Siberian Iris & plant nursery.

 NCCPG ☕

3 BACHEFIELD HOUSE
Kimbolton HR6 0EP. Jim & Rowena Gale, 01568 615855, rowena@jimgale.eclipse.co.uk. *3m E of Leominster. Take A4112 off A49 (signed Leysters), after 10yds 1st R (signed Stretford/Hamnish). 1st L to Grantsfield over Xrds (signed Bache), continue for approx 1m, garden on R past rd to Gorsty Hill.* Home-made teas. **Adm £3.50, chd free. Suns 5 June; 14 Aug (2-5.30). Visitors also welcome by appt May to Aug, no coach access.**
Charming traditional cottage-style garden of 1 acre. On gentle hill slope, the beds and borders bulge with beautiful blooms and foliage. Particular emphasis on roses, peonies and irises, part-walled kitchen garden, gravel beds, pond and summerhouse with fine views.

❀ ☕ ☎

4 ◆ THE BANNUT
Bringsty, Bromyard WR6 5TA. Daphne & Maurice Everett, 01885 482206, www.bannut.co.uk. *2¹/₂ m E of Bromyard. On A44 Worcester Rd, ¹/₂ m E of entrance to National Trust, Brockhampton.* **Adm £4, chd £1.50. For NGS: Suns 5 June; 10 July; 21 Aug (12.30-5). For other opening times and information, please phone or see garden website.**
3 acres of enchanting gardens with much to enjoy throughout the seasons - colourful herbaceous plants, heather gardens, interesting trees and shrubs. Garden rooms, unusual knot garden, 'secret' garden, water features, views to the Malvern Hills. Many seats around the garden. Home-made lunches and teas in award winning tea room. Featured on local radio.

♿ 🎫 ❀ ☕

5 BATCH COTTAGE
Almeley HR3 6PT. Jeremy & Elizabeth Russell, 01544 327469. *16m NW of Hereford. 2m off A438-A4111 to Kington, turn R at Eardisley.* **Adm £3.50, chd free. Visitors welcome by appt March to Oct.**
Established unregimented,

conservation-oriented garden of some 2¹/₂ acres with streams and large pond, set in a natural valley, surrounded by woodland and orchard. Over 360 labelled trees and shrubs, mixed borders, fern and bog beds, wild flower bank, stumpery, woodland walk.

♿ ❀ ☕ ☎

THE BELL AT SKENFRITH
See Gwent.

BIRTSMORTON COURT
See Worcestershire.

6 BRIDGE COTTAGE
Burrington SY8 2HT. Ray Wilkins. *5¹/₂ m SW of Ludlow. From Ludlow take B4361 S. Immed past Ludford Bridge turn R to Wigmore/Burrington. After 4m turn R to Burrington, continue 2m, cross small bridge, garden 200yds on R.* Home-made teas. **Adm £3.50, chd free. Sun 22 May (2-5.30).**
Garden surrounding old gamekeepers cottage. Mature shrubs, herbaceous planting, distinctive conifers and inspiring trees, azaleas, camellias and rhododendrons seasonally abound. Fish pond, children's vegetable patch, and arboretum. Views from elevated walkways, riverside walk. Subject to the welcoming gaze of sociable chickens and inquisitive sheep. Some steep slopes.

♿ 🎫 ❀ ☕

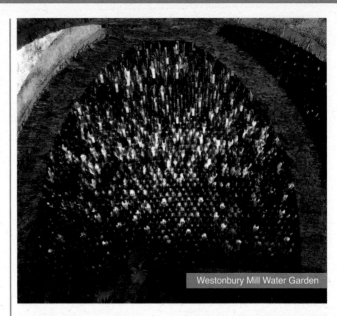
Westonbury Mill Water Garden

7 BRILLEY COURT
Whitney-on-Wye HR3 6JF. Mr & Mrs David Bulmer, 01497 831467, rosebulmer@hotmail.com. *6m NE of Hay-on-Wye. 5m SW of Kington. 1¹/₂ m off A438 Hereford to Brecon rd signed to Brilley.* **Adm £4. Visitors welcome by appt, groups & coaches. Refreshments available to pre-order.**
3-acre garden, walled, ornamental kitchen garden. Spring tulip collection, summer rose and herbaceous borders. 7-acre wild valley stream garden. Limited wheelchair access.

♿ ☕ ☎

8 ◆ BROBURY HOUSE GARDENS
Brobury by Bredwardine HR3 6BS. Keith & Pru Cartwright, 01981 500229, www.broburyhouse.co.uk. *10m W of Hereford. S off A438 signed Bredwardine & Brobury. Garden 1m L (before bridge).* Teas NGS days only. **Adm £4, chd £1. For NGS: Sun 8 May (11-5); Weds 1, 29 June (2-5). For other opening times and information, please phone or see garden website.**
9 acres of gardens, set on the banks of an exquisitely beautiful section of the R Wye, offer the visitor a delightful combination of Victorian terraces with mature specimen trees, inspiring water features, architectural planting and woodland areas. Redesign and development is ongoing. Bring a

picnic, your paint brushes, binoculars and linger awhile. Wheelchair users, strong able-bodied assistant advisable.

  ♿ 🌱 ❀ ⊨ ☕

9 BROCKHAMPTON COTTAGE
Brockhampton HR1 4TQ. Peter & Ravida Clay, 0797 456 9037, peter.clay@crocus.co.uk. *8m SW of Hereford. 5m N of Ross-on-Wye off B4224. In Brockhampton take rd signed Brockhampton Church, continue up hill for ¹/₂ m, after set of farm buildings, driveway on L over cattle grid.* **Adm £5, chd free, Combined with Grendon Court, adm £8, chd free. Sun 4 Sept (10-2).**
Created from scratch in 1999 by the owners and Tom Stuart Smith, this beautiful hilltop garden looks south and west over miles of unspoilt countryside. On one side a woodland garden and wild flower meadow, on the other side a Perry pear orchard and in valley below: lake, stream and arboretum. Picnic parties welcome by lake until 2pm. Visit Grendon Court (2-5) after your visit to us.

🌱

10 NEW THE BROOKS
Pontrilas HR2 0BL. Marion & Clive Stainton. *12m SW of Hereford. From the A465 Hereford to Abergavenny rd, turn L at Pontrilas into B4347 onto B4347, take 2nd L signed Orcop & Garway Hill. Garden 1³/₄ m on L.* Home-made teas. **Adm £3.50, chd free. Suns 19 June; 18 Sept (2-5.30).**
This 2¹/₂-acre Golden Valley garden incl part-walled enclosed vegetable garden and greenhouse (wind/solar powered), orchard, ornamental, perennial, shade and shrub borders, wildlife pond, evolving arboretum cum coppice, and meadow with stunning views. Surrounding a stone 1684 farmhouse (not open), the garden has mature elements, but much has been created since 2006, with future development plans.

❀ ☕

11 ◆ BRYAN'S GROUND
Letchmoor Lane, nr Stapleton, Presteigne LD8 2LP. David Wheeler & Simon Dorrell, 01544 260001, www.bryansground.co.uk. *12m NW of Leominster. Between Kinsham & Stapleton. At Mortimers Cross take B4362 signed Presteigne. At Combe, follow signs.* **Adm £5,**

chd £2, concessions £4.50. **For NGS: Sat 14 May (2-5). For other opening times and information, please phone or see garden website.**
Romantic Edwardian Arts and Crafts 8-acre garden. Yew and box topiary, parterres, sunken garden, formal potager, partly-walled kitchen garden. Colour-themed flower and shrub borders with 'Sulking House'. Heritage apple orchard, formal pools, belvedere, lighthouse, dovecote and Edwardian greenhouse. Arboretum. Home of Hortus, The International Garden Journal. Featured in Gardens Illustrated.

  ♿ ❀ ☕

Delightful 2 year old garden has been created to form a modern space for three generations of family . . .

12 ◆ CAVES FOLLY NURSERY
Evendine Lane, Colwall WR13 6DX. Wil Leaper & Bridget Evans, 01684 540631, www.cavesfolly.com. *1¹/₄ m NE of Ledbury. Between Malvern & Ledbury. Evendine Lane, off Colwall Green. Car parking at Caves Folly.* Home-made teas. **Combined with Longacre adm £4, chd free. For NGS: Sun 12 June (2-5). For other opening times and information please phone or see garden website.**
Organic nursery and display gardens. Specialist growers of herbaceous, alpines, grasses, vegetable and herb plants, all grown organically. This is not a manicured garden! It is full of drifts of colour and wild flowers and a haven for wildlife.

  ♿ ❀ ⊨ ☕

13 NEW DAIMOR
Burghill, Hereford HR4 7RN. Mr & Mrs R M Jenman. *3m NE of Hereford. From Hereford turn off A4103 to Burghill, after 1m fork R, garden in centre of village on L.* Home-made teas. **Adm £3, chd free. Fri 10, Sat 11 June (2-6).**
This delightful 2yr old garden, has been created to form a modern space catering for three generations of family, incl a games lawn with

cottage-style planting, lavender walk with rose swags, raised-bed vegetable and fruit gardens, tree house and greenhouse, new large pond surrounded by a wild flower meadow attracting many species of insect and bird life.

  ♿ 🌱 ❀ ☕

14 GLAN ARROW
Eardisland HR6 9BW. Christopher & Lotty James, 01544 388207, lotty@glanarrow.com. *5m W of Leominster on B4529. Cross bridge & immed turn sharp L up driveway.* Home-made teas. **Adm £3.50, chd free. Sun 29 May (2-6). Visitors also welcome by appt.**
4-acre English riverside garden with herbaceous borders, roses, bog garden leading to small lake, white garden, herringbone ha ha and potager. Gravel courtyard.

  ♿ ❀ ☕ ☎

15 GRANTSFIELD
nr Kimbolton, Leominster HR6 0ET. Colonel & Mrs J G T Polley, 01568 613338. *3m NE of Leominster. A49 N from Leominster, A4112 turn R & follow signs. No parking for coaches - drop & collect visitors in village; (minibus acceptable). A44 W to Leominster. Turn R at Drum Xrds (notice up).* Home-made teas. **Adm £3.50, chd free. Visitors welcome by appt Apr to Sept incl. Small coaches only to the house.**
Contrasting styles in gardens of old stone farmhouse; wide variety of unusual plants, trees and shrubs, old roses, climbers, herbaceous borders, superb views. 1¹/₂-acre orchard and kitchen garden with flowering and specimen trees and shrubs. Spring bulbs. Comma butterfly saved from extinction here by Emma Hutchinson in 1890s.

  ♿ ❀ ☕ ☎

16 THE GREAT HOUSE
Dilwyn HR4 8HX. Tom & Jane Hawksley, 01544 318007, greathousedilwyn@gmail.com, www.thegreathousedilwyn.co.uk. *7m W of Leominster. A44 from Leominster joining A4112 (signed Brecon). Turn L into Dilwyn village. House on RH-side opp village green.* Home-made teas. **Adm £3.50, chd free. Sun 17 Apr (2-5). Visitors also welcome by appt.**
1¹/₂-acre all-yr garden, designed and created by owners over the last 13yrs. Spring bulbs, red tulips and camassias planted in orchard,

traditional rose gardens, yew and beech hedging, raised knot garden, decorative stone and brickwork. 40ft reflecting pool and pleached hornbeams lining the drive all add interest to this country garden which is fronted by wonderful C18 wrought iron gates. Featured on Radio Hereford & Worcester. Gravel paths.

17 GRENDON COURT
Upton Bishop HR9 7QP. **Mark & Kate Edwards.** *3m NE of Ross-on-Wye. M50 J3 towards Hereford. Follow B4224 to Hereford past Moody Cow PH, down hill, up otherside, 1st gate on R. From Ross A40, B449, at Xrds, R to Upton Bishop, 100yds on L.* Home-made teas. **Adm £4, chd free. Combined with Brockhampton Cottage (morning opening), adm £8, chd free. Sun 4 Sept (2-5).**
A contemporary garden designed by Tom Stuart-Smith. Planted on 2 levels, a clever collection of mass planted perennials and grasses of different heights, textures, and colour give all-yr round interest. The upper walled garden with a sea of flowering grasses make a highlight. Views of pond and valley walk. Picnic parties welcome by lake from 1pm. Visit Brockhampton Cottage (10-2) before you visit us.

18 THE GRIGGS
Newton St Margarets HR2 0QY. **John & Bridget Biggs,** 01981 510629, www.artaura.co.uk/thegriggs. *14m SW of Hereford. Take B4348 to Vowchurch, turn L, signed Michaelchurch Escley, continue for 2¹/₂ m, then follow NGS signs. Signs will be posted locally for those approaching from Longtown & Ewyas Harold.* Home-made teas. **Adm £3.50, chd free (share to Community Action, Nepal). Sats 4, 25 June; Tues 5, 12 July (2-6). Visitors also welcome by appt May - July incl.**
Located in a remote scenic setting between the Golden Valley and the Black Mountains, a floriferous country garden of 1¹/₂ acres, managed organically and incl extensive mixed borders, over 60 old roses, wild flower meadows, wildlife pond and large productive kitchen garden. An unashamedly romantic garden in which to enjoy scrumptious teas. Partial wheelchair access.

19 HARDWICK HOUSE
Pembridge, Leominster HR6 9HE. **Mr & Mrs D J Collins.** *6m W of Leominster. Between Eardisland & Pembridge. Take A44 from Leominster, 1m before Pembridge, turn up lane signed Bearwood & Hardwick. Drive entrance 250yds up lane, over cattlegrid between stone pillars.* **Adm £3.50, chd free. Sun 15 May (11-6).**
Large garden with extensive lawns, colourful shrubberies and ornamental trees incl many rare and unusual specimens. Fine views over unspoilt countryside. Ponds with collection of waterfowl. Teas available locally.

20 ◆ HELLENS
Much Marcle, Ledbury HR8 2LY. **PMMCT,** 01531 660504, www.hellensmanor.com. *6m from Ross-on-Wye. 4m SW of Ledbury, off A449.* **Adm £2.50, chd free. For NGS: Fri 3, Sat 4 June (9-5). For other opening times and information, please phone or see garden website.**
In the grounds of Hellens Manor House, the gardens are being gently redeveloped to reflect the C17 ambience of the house. Incl a rare octagonal dovecote. 2 knot gardens and yew labyrinth, lawns, herb and kitchen gardens; short woodlands and pond walk. Longer walk to Hall Wood, site of SSSI. Some gravel paths and slopes.

21 ◆ HEREFORD CATHEDRAL GARDENS
Hereford HR1 2NG. **Dean of Hereford Cathedral,** 01432 374202, www.herefordcathedral.org. *Centre of Hereford. Approach rds to The Cathedral are signed.* **Combined adm £5, chd free (share to Homeless Charity). For NGS: Fri 17 June (11-3.45). For other opening times and information, please phone or see garden website.**
Guided tours of a collection of historic gardens: a courtyard garden; an atmospheric cloisters garden enclosed by C15 buildings; the Vicar's Choral garden, the planting having ecclesiastical connections, sloping to the R Wye; the Dean's own riverside garden; and the Bishop's garden with fine trees, vegetable and cutting garden, outdoor chapel for meditation in a floral setting. Four of these gardens are not normally open to the public. 3 of the gardens (maintained

by volunteers) awarded Level 4 - Thrive in the RHS Community Gardens Scheme. Limited wheelchair access.

HIGH VIEW
See Worcestershire.

> A true cottage garden for traditionalist or the plantaholic . . .

22 HILL HOUSE FARM
Knighton LD7 1NA. **Simon & Caroline Gourlay,** 01547 528542, simon@maryvalefarms.co.uk. *4m SE of Knighton. S of A4113 via Knighton (Llanshay Lane, 3m) or Bucknell (Reeves Lane, 3m).* Home-made teas. **Suns 15 May; 17 July (2-5.30). Visitors also welcome by appt.**
S-facing 5-acre hillside garden developed over past 40yrs with magnificent views over unspoilt countryside. Herbaceous area amongst magnificent mature oak trees, extensive lawns and paths surrounded by roses, shrubs and specimen trees. Sloping paths to Oak Pool 200ft below house. Transport available from bottom of garden if needed.

23 THE HOLLIES
Old Church Road, Colwall WR13 6EZ. **Margaret & Graham White,** 01684 540931, mandgwhite@dsl.pipex.com. *3m SW of Malvern. Take B4218 past Old Court Nursery (Picton), turn R into Old Church Rd. Hollies 400yds on R.* Home-made teas. **Adm £3, chd free. Sats, Suns 7, 8 May; 30, 31 July (2-5). Visitors also welcome by appt.**
Intensively planted ¹/₂ -acre developed over 15yrs by keen 'hardy plantsperson'. Continually evolving beds and borders containing a wide range of shrubs, bulbs and perennials which are chosen with emphasis on leaf form and colour to provide

Brobury House Gardens

Easy parking. **Adm £3, chd free.**
Suns, Mons 5, 6, 26, 27 June (2-6).
Visitors also welcome by appt May
to July, coaches permitted.
Developed over 18yrs this ¹/₂ -acre
garden is 'divided' into distinct areas
with colour co-ordination and scent in
mind. Packed with shrubs incl old and
new roses, clematis and perennials,
many unusual. Small kitchen garden,
fruit trees, wild flower areas. A true
cottage garden for traditionalist or the
plantaholic. Featured on BBC
Gardeners' World.

🌼 ☕ ☎

27 ◆ IVY CROFT
Ivington Green, Leominster
HR6 0JN. Sue & Roger Norman,
01568 720344,
www.ivycroftgarden.co.uk. *3m SW
of Leominster. From Leominster take
Ryelands Rd to Ivington. Turn R at
church, garden ³/₄ m on R. From
A4110 signed Ivington, garden
1³/₄ m on L.* **Adm £3, chd free (Feb).**
Combined with **Aulden Farm adm
£5, chd free (Suns). For NGS: Each
Thurs in Feb; (9-4); Suns 24 Apr;
22 May; 10 July; 11 Sept (2-5.30)
Private visits and groups welcome
by appt. 2012 Feb by appt. For
other opening times and
information, please phone or see
garden website.**
Garden created since 1997 surrounds
C17 cottage (not open) in 4 acres of
rich grassland. Plant lovers' garden
designed for all-yr interest. Raised
beds, mixed borders, trees, alpines,
troughs, formal vegetable garden
framed by trained fruit trees;
collections of ferns, willows and
snowdrops.

♿ 🌼 ☕

GROUP OPENING

**28 NEW KENTCHURCH
GARDENS**
Pontrilas HR2 0DB. *From Hereford
A465 to Abergavanny, at Pontrilas
turn L signed Kentchurch. After 2m
fork L, after Bridge Inn. Drive opp
church.* Home-made teas. **Combined
adm £5, chd free. Sats, Suns 14,
15 May; 25, 26 June (11-6).**

KENTCHURCH COURT 🛏
Mrs Jan Lucas-Scudamore

NEW UPPER LODGE
Jo Gregory

Kentchurch Court is sited close to the
Welsh border. The large stately home

interest throughout the yr. Small
productive fruit and vegetable garden
with raised beds. Featured on Radio
Hereford & Worcester. Limited
wheelchair access.

♿ 🏠 🌼 ☕ ☎

HOLMCROFT
See Shropshire.

**24 HOLME LACY HOUSE
HOTEL**
Holme Lacy. HR2 6LP. Warner
Leisure Hotels, 01432 870870,
www.holmelacyhouse.co.uk. *5m SE
of Hereford. From Hereford B4399,
from Gloucester B4215, then B4224,
from Ledbury A438 signed from
Holme Lacy Village.* Light
refreshments & teas. **Adm £3.
Children not permitted. Sat 9, Sun
17 July; Sun 14, Sat 20 Aug; Sun
11 Sept (10-4). For details please
phone or see garden website.**
The gardens were conceived on a
very bold scale in 'The Grand Manner'
and is Herefordshire's only surviving
example of such gardens. Battlement
gardens, ancient yew hedging, formal
Italian gardens with ponds.
Herbaceous borders, walled garden
and orchard with historic pear trees.
Gravel paths, some steep slopes.

♿ 🛏 ☕ ☎

25 HOPE END HOUSE
Hope End, Wellington Heath
HR8 1JQ. Mrs P J Maiden,
www.hopeendhouse.com. *2m NE of
Ledbury. From Ledbury A438. Signed
Bromyard, R under bridge. Take R to
Wellington Heath, 2m at top of village
junction with tree keep R into Church
Lane pass common on R &
Raycombe Lane on L. Gate house on
L over cattle grid. Take L track to
Hope End House.* Home-made teas.
**Adm £3, chd free. Fris, Sats 29, 30
Apr; 27, 28, Sun 29 May (1-4).**
5 acres of mature country house
gardens,set within 100 acre parkland
with extensive herbaceous borders,
magnificent trees, sweeping lawns
and glorious spring colours. Explore
the wild flower meadow,
rhododendron glade, and productive
gardens or extend your visit to a
fabulous bluebell wood, taking in
wonderful long-reaching views S to
Eastnor and the Malvern Hills.

🏠 🌼 🛏 ☕ ☎

26 IVY COTTAGE
Kinsham LD8 2HN. Jane & Richard
Barton, 01544 267154,
rjjebarton@btinternet.com. *12m NW
of Leominster. From Mortimers Cross
take B4362 towards Presteigne. Turn
R at Combe towards Lingen for 1m.*

(not open) dates to C11 and has been in the Scudamore family for over 1000yrs The deer park surrounding the house dates back to the Knights Hospitallers of Dinmore and lies at the heart of an estate of over 5000 acres. Historical characters associated with the house incl Welsh hero Owain Glendower, whose daughter married Sir John Scdamore. Garden partly designed by John Nash. Formal rose garden, traditional vegetable garden redesigned with colour, scent and easy access. Walled garden and herbaceous borders, rhododendrons and wild flower walk. Deer park and ancient woodland. Extensive collection of mature trees and shrubs. Stream with habitat for spawning trout. Upper Lodge is a tranquil and well established walled cottage garden situated at the centre of the main garden. Incl a wide variety of herbaceous plants, bulbs and shrubs ranging from traditional favourites to the rare and unusual. Stable Art Gallery. Kentchurch Court was recently the setting for Channel 4's Country House Party. Filmed for Country House Rescue.

LITTLE MALVERN COURT
See Worcestershire.

LLANSTEPHAN HOUSE
See Powys.

LLANTHONY AND DISTRICT GARDENS
See Gwent.

TRWYN TAL
See Gwent.

29 ▶ **LONGACRE**
Evendine Lane, Colwall Green WR13 6DT. Mr D M Pudsey, 01684 540377, davidpudsey@onetel.com. *3m S of Malvern. Off Colwall Green. Off B4218. Car parking at Caves Folly Nursery.* Home-made teas at Caves Folly. **Combined with Caves Folly adm £3.50, chd free. Sun 12 June (2-5). Visitors also welcome by appt.**
3-acre garden-cum-arboretum developed since 1970. Island beds of trees and shrubs, some underplanted with bulbs and herbaceous perennials, present a sequence of contrasting pictures and views through the seasons. There are no 'rooms' - rather long vistas lead the eye and feet, while the feeling of spaciousness is enhanced by glimpses caught between trunks and

through gaps in the planting. Over 50 types of conifer provide the background to maples, rhododendrons, azaleas, dogwoods, eucryphias etc.

30 ▶ **LOWER HOPE**
Ullingswick HR1 3JF. Mr & Mrs Clive Richards, 01432 820557, cliverichards@crco.co.uk. *5m S of Bromyard. From Hereford take A465 N to Bromyard. After 6m turn L at Burley Gate on A417 signed Leominster. Approx 2m take 3rd turning on R signed Lower Hope & Pencombe, 1/2 m on LH-side.* Home-made teas. **Adm £4, chd £1. Suns 10 Apr; 22 May; 10 July; 2 Oct (2-5). Visitors also welcome by appt min 20 visitors - for 5 days after NGS open days.**
5-acre garden facing S and W. Herbaceous borders, rose walks and gardens, laburnum tunnel, Mediterranean garden, bog gardens. Lime tree walk, lake landscaped with wild flowers; streams, ponds. Conservatories and large glasshouse with exotic species orchids incl colourful butterflies, bougainvilleas. Prizewinning herd of pedigree Hereford cattle, flock of pedigree Suffolk sheep.

31 ▶ **THE MARSH**
Eyton HR6 0AG. Peter & Jane Ramsey. *2m N of Leominster off B4361. Take B4361 to Ludlow, after 1/2 m turn L to Eyton, garden 1 1/2 m on R.* Home-made teas. **Adm £3, chd free, combined with The Mill adm £5, chd free. Sat 18, Sun 19 June (2-5).**
A developing garden based on strong formal design. Main feature is a box parterre based on the roof timbers of the medieval hall. The garden is bisected with a small stream, planted either side with marginal and herbaceous plants. Small orchard, productive vegetable plot and reed bed.

32 ◆ **MIDDLE HUNT HOUSE**
Walterstone, Hereford HR2 0DY. Trustees of Monnow Valley Arts & Rupert Otten, 01873 860359, www.monnowvalleyarts.org. *4m W of Pandy. 17m S of Hereford, 10m N of Abergavenny. A465 to Pandy, L towards Longtown, turn R at Clodock Church, 1m on R.* Disabled parking available. **Adm £5, chd £2.50.**

For NGS: Sats, Suns 11, 12 June; 17, 18 Sept (2-6). **For other opening times and information, please phone or see garden website.**
2 acre modern garden in development with outstanding views, surrounding stonebuilt farmhouse, converted gallery barn and artist's studio. A Dutch-concept garden using swathes of herbaceous plants and grasses. Sensory, vegetable and Japanese gardens, and hornbeam alley. Special features: birches under planted with irises (June) and rose borders. Also Arts and Memory, a permanant collection of contemporary carved lettering in newly landscaped Memory Field. In the sensory garden: Exhibition of Garden Benches by artists and designers. Gallery exhibitions (June) The Romantic Landscape: paintings and prints. (Sept) The History of Political Cartoons: The Jeffrey Archer Collection. Partial wheelchair access.

> Walled garden and herbaceous borders, rhododendrons and wild flower walk. Deer park and ancient woodland . . .

33 ▶ **MIDLAND FARM**
Pig Street, Norton Wood HR4 7BP. Sarah & Charles Smith. *10m NW of Hereford. From Hereford take the A480 towards Kington. 1/2 m after Norton Canon turn L towards Calver Hill. At bottom of the hill turn R into Pig St, garden 1/4 m on L.* Home-made teas. **Adm £4, chd free. Suns 22 May; 26 June (10.30-4).**
1.2 acre garden set in beautiful countryside; perennials and roses are a speciality. The garden is designed as a series of rooms consisting of a flower garden, kitchen and spring gardens.

34 THE MILL

Eyton HR6 0AD. Simon Haddock & Anna Spencer. *1¹/₂ m N of Leominster off B4361. Take B4361 to Ludlow, after ¹/₂ m turn L to Eyton, garden ¹/₂ m on L.* Teas at The Marsh. **Adm £3, chd free, combined with The Marsh adm £5, chd free.** Sat **18, Sun 19 June (2-5).**
³/₄ -acre woodland garden with trees of interest incl mature specimen of Dawn Redwood, Davidia, tulip tree, catalpa and an unusually large walnut, underplanted with acers, rhododendrons, ornamental shrubs and herbaceous plants, linked by paths and lawns.

MODEL FARM
See Worcestershire.

35 MONNINGTON COURT

Monnington-on-Wye, Hereford HR4 7NL. Mr & Mrs Bulmer, 01981 500044, www.monnington-morgans.co.uk. *9m W of Hereford. S off A438. Monnington-on-Wye. Lane to village & Monnington Court.* Home-made teas & BBQ. **Garden & display £5.50, chd £3 (share to Riding for the Disabled).** Sat **28 May to Mon 30 May (10-7). Visitors also welcome by appt all yr, groups of 10+.**
25 acres, lake, river, cider press, sculpture garden (Mrs Bulmer is sculptor Angela Conner). Famous mile-long avenue of pines and yews, favourite of Sir John Betjeman and in Kilvert's Diary. Foundation Farm of British Morgan Horse (living replicas of statues in Trafalgar Square), C13 Moot Hall, C15 and C17 house. Sculpture garden. 4pm Horse and Carriage display. New innovations each yr.

36 ◆ MOORS MEADOW GARDENS & NURSERY

Collington, Bromyard HR7 4LZ. Ros Bissell, 01885 410318, www.moorsmeadow.co.uk. *4m N of Bromyard, on B4214. ¹/₂ m up lane follow yellow arrows.* **Adm £4, chd £1. For NGS: Mons 4 Apr; 9 May; 13 June; 11 July; 15 Aug (11-5). For other opening times and information, please phone or see garden website.**
Imaginative 7-acres full of inspiration and ideas show you how to work with nature. Meandering paths lead through shrubberies, fernery, grass garden, dingles, past pools,
herbaceous borders and into kitchen garden. Intriguing features and sculptures. Voted Most Romantic garden in Central England. Contact for other charity events. Artist Blacksmiths. All plants for sale are propagated from the garden. Featured in Period Living Magazine, Herefordshire Society Magazine, German Garden Magazine, & on BBC TV Gardeners World & local radio.

37 NEW MOUSE CASTLE

Old Eign Hill, Hereford HR1 1TU. Ian & Jill Reynolds, 01432 269111. *From A438 E through Hereford turn R onto B4224 (Eign Rd), take 6th turning on L into Old Eign Hill, garden on R just before Haford /Vineyard Xrds.* **Adm £3, chd free. Visitors welcome by appt.**
30 year collection of plants by over-the-top plantaholic. Many unusual types and varieties of mainly small trees and shrubs, approx 150 acer cultivars. Garden approx 2¹/₂ acres with a strong bias to uncommon and exotic species.

38 NEWPORT HOUSE

Almeley HR3 6LL. David & Jenny Watt, jenny.watt@btconnect.com. *5m S of Kington. 1m from Almeley Church, on rd to Kington. From Kington take A4111 to Hereford. After 4m turn L to Almeley, continue 2m, garden on L.* Home-made teas. **Adm £3, chd free.** Suns **12 June; 9 Oct (11-5). Visitors also welcome by appt.**
20 acres of garden, woods and lake (with walks). Formal garden set on 3 terraces with large mixed borders framed by formal hedges, in front of Georgian House (not open). 2¹/₂ acre walled organic garden in restoration since 2009.

39 THE OLD CORN MILL

Aston Crews. Ross-on-Wye HR9 7LW. Mrs Jill Hunter, 01989 750059. *5m E of Ross-on-Wye. A40 Ross to Gloucester. Turn L at I-lights at Lea Xrds onto B4222 signed Newent. Garden ¹/₂ m on L.* Parking for disabled down drive. Home-made teas. **Adm £2.50, chd free.** Sun **3, Fri 22, Mon 25 Apr; Mons 2, 30 May (11-5). Visitors also welcome by appt all yr for individuals & small groups, coaches permitted, photographers & artists most welcome.**
Surrounding the award winning converted C18 Mill (not open), this valley garden has been designed to merge into the surrounding fields. Massed banks and borders provide colour all yr while streams, ponds, meadows and native trees support a variety of wildlife. Wild daffodils, common spotted orchids and primulas are spring highlights. Featured in GGG & on BBC Radio Hereford & Worcester.

40 THE OLD QUARRY

Almeley Road, Eardisley HR3 6PR. John & Anne Davis, 01544 327264, old.quarry@virgin.net. *16m NW of Hereford. ³/₄ m off A438 - A4111 to Kington, turn R at Eardisley.* Home-made teas. **Adm £3, chd free. Visitors welcome by appt May to Sept incl.**
Gently-sloping garden of 2¹/₂ acres, laid out in the 1930s now being renovated and developed for yr-round interest. Terraces and old quarry gardens with rhododendrons and mature trees, parterre, vegetable garden and herbaceous beds. Far-reaching views of Black Mountains and Hay Bluff.

41 THE OLD RECTORY

Thruxton HR2 9AX. Mr & Mrs Andrew Hallett, 01981 570401, ar.hallett@gmail.com. *6m SW of Hereford. A465 to Allensmore. At Locks (Shell) garage take B4348 towards Hay-on-Wye. After 1¹/₂ m turn L towards Abbey Dore & Cockyard. Car park signed 150yds.* Home-made teas. **Adm £3, chd free.** Suns, Mons **12, 13, 19, 20, 26, 27 June; 11, 12 Sept (2-5.30). Visitors also welcome by appt, individuals and groups are welcome.**
1¹/₂ acre plantsman's garden with outstanding panoramic views. Extensive borders stocked with

Wild daffodils, common spotted orchids and primulas are spring highlights . . .

shrubs, unusual perennials and old shrub roses, formal gazebo and vegetable parterre. Most of our plants have been sourced locally and are labelled. Additional paddock with newly planted arboretum, old varieties of fruit trees and rare breed bantams. Some level gravel paths.

42 THE ORCHARDS
Golden Valley, Bishops Frome, nr Bromyard WR6 5BN. Mr & Mrs Robert Humphries, 01885 490273. *14m E of Hereford. A4103 turn L at bottom of Fromes Hill, through village of Bishops Frome on B4214. Turn R immed after de-regulation signs along narrow track for 250yds. Park in field by garden.* Home-made teas. **Adm £3, chd free. Sun 3 July (2-6). Visitors also welcome by appt.**
1-acre garden designed in areas on various levels. 15 water features incl Japanese water garden and tea house, Mediterranean area, rose garden with rill, aviary. Large rose, clematis, fuchsia and dahlia collections. Seating areas on all levels. New projects every yr.

ORLETON HOUSE
See Worcestershire.

THE PANT
See Gwent.

PEN-Y-MAES
See Powys.

43 PERRYCROFT
Jubilee Drive, Upper Colwall, Malvern WR13 6DN. Gillian & Mark Archer, 01684 541501, gillianarcher@live.co.uk. *Between Malvern & Ledbury. From A449 Malvern to Ledbury rd, take B4232 at British Camp (Jubilee Drive). Garden 1m on L. Park in Gardiners Quarry car park on R (pay & display), short walk to garden. No parking at house.* Home-made teas. **Adm £3, chd free. Sun 19 June (2-5). Visitors also welcome by appt.**
10-acre garden and woodland on upper slopes of Malvern Hills with magnificent views. Arts and Crafts house (not open), garden partly designed by CFA Voysey. Ongoing restoration, walled garden, yew hedges, old roses, natural wild flower meadows, ponds (unfenced), bog garden, gravel and grass walks. Some steep and uneven paths.

44 ♦ THE PICTON GARDEN
Old Court Nurseries, Colwall WR13 6QE. Mr & Mrs Paul Picton, 01684 540416, www.autumnasters.co.uk. *3m W of Malvern. On B4218 (Walwyn Rd) N of Colwall Stone. Turn off A449 from Ledbury or Malvern.* **Adm £3.50, chd free. For NGS: Sun 7, 14, Fri 19, Sat 27, Mon 29 Aug; Sun 4, Wed 14, Thur 29 Sept; Wed 5, Mon 10, Sun 16 Oct (12-5). For other opening times and information, please phone or see garden website.**
1½ acres W of Malvern Hills. Interesting perennials and shrubs in Aug. In Sept and Oct colourful borders display the National Plant Collection of Michaelmas daisies; backed by autumn colouring trees and shrubs. Many unusual plants to be seen, incl bamboos, ferns and acers. Features raised beds and silver garden. Huge range of asters for sale incl many rare. Also other late season perennials. Featured in The English Autumn and, Blooms Best Perennials and Grasses by Adrian Bloom.

 NCCPG

PONT FAEN HOUSE
See Powys.

45 THE RAMBLES
Shelwick, Hereford HR1 3AL. Shirley & Joe Fleming, 01432 357056, joe.eff@live.co.uk. *2m E of Hereford. E of Hereford, at the A4103/A465 r'about take the Sutton St Nicholas/Bodenham rd, after 1m and under a railway bridge, turn L signed Shelwick, under another railway bridge. The Rambles is behind 1st house on L.* **Adm £3, chd free. Every Tues 31 May to 30 Aug (2-5). Visitors also welcome by appt, clubs welcome.**
Plantaholics ⅓ acre garden packed with a wide range of interesting plants, colour themed borders, large covered shade area and water feature. Many pots with tender plants. Large collection of oriental poppies in June.

46 RHODDS FARM
Lyonshall HR5 3LW. Richard & Cary Goode, 01544 340120, cary.goode@russianaeros.com, www.rhoddsfarm.co.uk. *1m E of Kington. From A44 take small turning S just E of Penrhos Hotel, 1m E of Kington. Continue 1m garden straight*

ahead. Teas (Sun only). **Adm £4, chd £1. Sun 5 (2-6), Mon 6 June (10-6).**
The garden began in 2004 and is still a work in progress. The site is challenging with steep banks rising to overhanging woodland but has wonderful views. Formal garden leads to new dovecote, mixed borders have interest throughout the year with the double herbaceous borders of hot colours being particularly good in summer. Incl a courtyard gravel garden, several ponds, wild flower meadow and woodland walks with wonderful bluebells in spring.

Stream runs through the garden and there are many secret corners. it is a magical garden for children . . .

THE ROCK HOUSE
See Powys.

47 SHIELDBROOK
Kings Caple HR1 4UB. Sue & Oliver Sharp, 01432 840670, susansharp95@btinternet.com, www.shieldbrooksculpturegarden.co.uk. *7m S of Hereford. Take A49 from Hereford or Ross. Take 1st rd signed to Hoarwithy (there are 3). Go past New Harp PH on R, then next R over R Wye. Up the hill take 2nd R into Kings Caple, down hill over Xrds then Shieldbrook ½ m on L.* Home-made teas. **Adm £5, chd free. Sat 18, Sun 19 June (2-5). Visitors also welcome by appt June - Sept, small coach permitted.**
1-acre informal country garden planted for yr-round interest featuring grasses, shrubs and perennials. Rose garden and orchard, healing garden with pond and rockery. An exhibiton of sculpture in the garden of local sculptor's work, is of special interest. Stream runs through the garden and there are many secret corners. it is a magical garden for children. Garden managed organically. Music. Art Exhibition in studio and The Sculpture Exhibition. Some gravel and grass paths.

SHUTTIFIELD COTTAGE
See Worcestershire.

48 ◆ STAUNTON PARK
Staunton-on-Arrow HR6 9LE.
Susan Fode, 01544 388556,
www.stauntonpark.co.uk. *3m N of
Pembridge. From Pembridge (on A44)
take rd signed Presteigne, Shobdon.
After 3m look out for red phone box
on R. Staunton Park is 150yds on L.
Do not go to Staunton-on-Arrow.*
Adm £3.50, chd free. For opening
times and information please
phone or visit garden website.
Visitors welcome by appt.
10-acre garden and grounds incl drive
with stately wellingtonias, rose
garden, separate kitchen garden,
large, very colourful mixed borders
and Victorian rock garden, lake and
lakeside walk with views. Specimen
trees incl mature monkey puzzle,
gigantic liriodendron, *Davidia
involucrata, Ginkgo bilobas* and
several ancient oaks. Featured in
Herefordshire Life.
& 🏡 ❀ ☎

TAWRYN
See Powys.

Romantic 3-acre garden . . . grass walks through remains of orchards . . .

49 NEW TITLEY MILL
Lyonshall, Kington HR5 3RX.
Christopher Goode & Michael
Fraser. *2¹/₂ m NE of Kington. From
Kington take B4355 to Presteigne,
after 2m turn R (before Stag Inn), take
1st R, cross river bridge, garden on L
after 300 metres.* Home-made teas.
Adm £5, chd free. Sats 14 May; 18,
Sun 19 June (2-5).
Romantic 3-acre garden. Grass walks
through remains of orchards with, in
the spring, tulips in grass, hellebores,
narcissi, camassia and in the summer
cascading roses, honeysuckles and
clematis in the trees. Double
herbaceous borders with small formal
knot garden, circular euphorbia beds
within clipped yews. Cutting and
vegetable gardens between old barns
and meadows, bog garden with iris,
primula, astilbes and cirsiums, hosta
and rogersias.
❀ ☕

50 UPPER TAN HOUSE
Stansbatch HR6 9LJ. James &
Caroline Weymouth, 01544 260574,
james@uppertanhouse.com,
www.uppertanhouse.com. *4m W of
Pembridge. Off A44 in Pembridge,
signed Shobdon & Presteigne.* Home-
made teas. Adm £4, chd free. Sun
12, Mon 13 June (2-5). Visitors also
welcome by appt, and groups.
S-facing garden sloping down to
Stansbatch brook in idyllic spot. Deep
herbaceous borders with informal and
unusual planting, pond and bog
garden, formal vegetable garden
framed by yew hedges and espaliered
pears. Reed beds, wild flower
meadow with orchids in June. Good
late summer colour and diverse
wildlife.
❀ ☕ ☎

51 THE VINE
Tarrington HR1 4EX. Richard Price.
*Between Hereford & Ledbury on
A438. Follow signs from Tarrington
Arms on A438. Park as directed.
Disabled parkng only at house.*
Home-made teas. Adm £4, chd free.
Sun 12 June (2-5.30).
Mature, traditional garden in peaceful
setting with stunning views of the
surrounding countryside. Consisting
of various rooms with mixed and
herbaceous borders. Secret garden in
blue/yellow/white, croquet lawn with
C18 summer house, temple garden
with ponds, herb and nosegay
garden, vegetable/cutting/soft fruit
garden around greenhouse on the
paddock.
& ☕

THE WALLED GARDEN
See Powys.

52 WESTON HALL
Weston-under-Penyard HR9 7NS.
Mr P & Miss L Aldrich-Blake,
01989 562597, aldrich-
blake.weston@lineone.net. *1m E of
Ross-on-Wye. On A40 towards
Gloucester.* Adm £4, chd free.
Visitors welcome by appt May -
July, for groups of 10+.
6 acres surrounding Elizabethan
house (not open). Large walled garden
with herbaceous borders, vegetables
and fruit, overlooked by Millennium
folly. Lawns with both mature and
recently planted trees, shrubs with
many unusual varieties. Ornamental
ponds and small lake. Traditional
country house garden, but evolving
after 4 generations in the family.
& ☎

53 WESTON MEWS
Weston-under-Penyard HR9 7NZ.
Ann Rothwell & John Hercock,
01989 563823. *2m E of Ross-on-
Wye. Going towards Gloucester on
A40, continue approx 100yds past
the Weston Cross PH and turn R into
grey brick-paved courtyard.* Light
refreshments & wine. Adm £3, chd
free. Sat 18 June (11-5). Visitors
also welcome by appt mid May to
mid Aug.
Walled ex-kitchen garden divided by
yew and box hedges. Traditional in
style and planting with large
herbaceous beds and borders at
different levels. Broad range of plants
incl roses. Enclosed garden with
sundial. Large vine house.
& ☕ ☎

**54 ◆ WESTONBURY MILL
WATER GARDEN**
Pembridge HR6 9HZ. Mr & Mrs
Richard Pim, 01544 388650,
www.westonburymillwatergardens.
com. *8m W of Leominster. On A44
1¹/₂ m W of village of Pembridge,
L into signed drive.* Adm £4, chd
free. For NGS: Fris 20 May; 2 Sept
(11-5). For other opening times and
information, please phone or see
garden website.
3¹/₂ -acre water mill garden situated
amid fields and orchards. Colourful
waterside plantings of bog and
moisture-loving plants around a
tangle of streams and ponds,
together with a natural bog garden in
the area of the Old Mill pond.
Adjacent wild flower meadow has
stream side walk. Follies which incl a
stone tower with water wheel
spouting gargoyles and fern dome
made of sparkling bottles.
& 🏡 ❀ ☕

55 WHITFIELD
Wormbridge HR2 9BA. Mr & Mrs
Edward Clive, 01981 570 202,
tboyd@globalnet.co.uk,
www.whitfield-hereford.com. *8m
SW of Hereford. On A465 Hereford to
Abergavenny rd.* Home-made teas.
Adm £4, chd free. Suns 27 Mar;
8 May (2-5); Sun 26 June (2-6).
Visitors also welcome by appt.
Parkland, wild flowers, ponds, walled
garden, many flowering magnolias
(species and hybrids), 1780 ginkgo
tree, 1¹/₂ m woodland walk with 1851
redwood grove. Picnic parties
welcome. Partial wheelchair access.
& 🏡 ❀ ☕ ☎

56 **WILTON CASTLE ON THE WYE**

Ross-on-Wye HR9 6AD. Alan & Suzie Parslow, 01989 565759, sue@wiltoncastle.co.uk, www.wiltoncastle.co.uk. *¹/₂ m NW of Ross on R Wye. Take the Ross rd at Wilton r'about on M50/A40/A449 trunk rd. Immed turn L opp garage, down lane. Castle entrance behind Castle Lodge Hotel.* Home-made teas. **Adm £4, chd free. Suns 12, 26 June; Weds 6, 20 July (12-5). Visitors also welcome by appt.** The romantic ruins of a restored C12 castle and C16 manor house (ruin) form the perfect backdrop for herbaceous borders, roses entwined around mullion windows, an abundance of sweetly scented old fashioned roses, gravel gardens and shrubberies. The 2-acre gardens are surrounded by a dry moat which leads down to the R Wye with swans, ducks, kingfishers etc. Guided tours. No access into dry moat area, a few steps into towers, disabled WC.

&. ⚘ ☕ ☎

Midland Farm

57 **WOLFERLOW HOUSE**

Wolferlow, nr Upper Sapey HR7 4QA. Stuart & Jill Smith, 01886 853311, hillheadfm@aol.com. *5m N of Bromyard. Disabled parking at the house. Off B4203 or B4214 between Upper Sapey & Stoke Bliss.* Home-made cakes & teas. **Adm £3.50, chd free. Sat 2 July (10.30-5). Visitors also welcome by appt for groups.** Surrounded by farmland this former Victorian Rectory is set within formal and informal gardens with planting to attract wildlife. Walks through the old orchard and ponds to sit by, space to relax and reflect taking in the views of borrowed landscape. Fruit, vegetable and cutting garden and wild flower meadow. Homemade cakes & teas. Plant stall. Gardening club visits and catering available immed after NGS opening. Gravel paths.

&. ⚘ ⊨ ☕ ☎

58 **WOODVIEW**

Great Doward, Whitchurch HR9 6DZ. Janet & Clive Townsend, 01600 890477. *6m SW of Ross-on-Wye, 4m NE of Monmouth. A40 Ross/Monmouth. At Whitchurch follow signs to Symonds Yat West. Then signs to Dowards Park Campsite. Take Forestry Rd (or follow NGS signs from Whitchurch), 1st L, garden 2nd on L. Parking at house.* Light refreshments & home-made teas. **Adm £3.50, chd free. Sun 17, 24 July (1-6). Visitors also welcome by appt June to Aug inclusive. No access for coaches - minibus OK.** Formal and informal gardens approx 2 acres in woodland setting. Herbaceous borders, hosta collection, mature trees, shrubs and seasonal bedding. Gently sloping lawns. Statuary and found sculpture, local limestone, rockwork and pools. Woodland garden, wild flower meadow and indigenous orchids. Collection of vintage tools and memorabilia. Croquet, clock golf and garden games. Featured in local press 'The drive here is as good as some gardens' - Mike George, BBC Hereford & Worcester.

&. 🞲 ⚘ ☕ ☎

Herefordshire County Volunteers

County Organiser
Rowena Gale, Bachefield House, Kimbolton, Leominster HR6 0EP, 01568 615855, rowena@jimgale.eclipse.co.uk

County Treasurer
Michael Robins, Newsholme, 77 Bridge Street, Ledbury HR8 2AN, 01531 632232

Publicity
Sue Evans, The Nest, Moreton, Eye, nr Leominster HR6 0DP, 01568 614501, s.evans.gp@btinternet.com
Gill Mullin, The White House, Lea, Ross-on-Wye HR9 7LQ, 01989 750593, gill@longorchard.plus.com

County Booklet
Chris Meakins, Yew Tree Cottage, Huntington, Kington HR5 3PF, 01544 370215, christinemeakins@btinternet.com

Assistant County Organisers
Andy Hallett, The Old Rectory, Thruxton HR2 9AX, 01981 570401, ar.hallett@googlemail.com
David Hodgson, Phelps Cottage, Coddington, nr Ledbury HR8 1JH, 01531 640622, hodgson@ukf.net
Sue Londesborough, Brighton House, St Margarets, Vowchurch HR2 0JU, 01981 510148, slondesborough138@btinternet.com
Penny Usher, Old Chapel House, Kimbolton, Leominster HR6 0HF, 01568 611688, pennyusher@btinternet.com

Sign up to our eNewsletter for news and updates

HERTFORDSHIRE

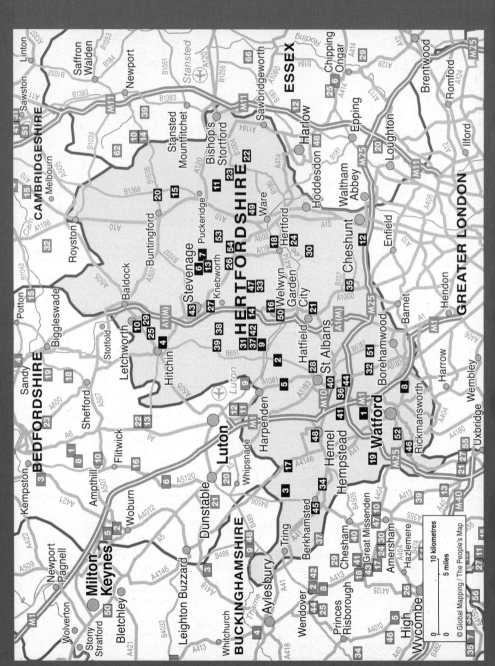

Opening Dates

March

Saturday 26
21 Hatfield House West Garden

April

Sunday 3
39 St Paul's Walden Bury
51 The Walled Garden
Sunday 17
2 Amwell Cottage
Wednesday 27
38 Rustling End Cottage

May

Sunday 1
1 The Abbots House
34 Patchwork
Sunday 8
39 St Paul's Walden Bury
48 9 Tannsfield Drive
Sunday 15
28 19 Lancaster Road
30 The Manor House Bayford
Friday 20
38 Rustling End Cottage (Evening)
Sunday 22
11 Bromley Hall
38 Rustling End Cottage
Monday 23
11 Bromley Hall
Sunday 29
17 15 Gade Valley Cottages
19 Great Sarratt Hall
24 Jenningsbury Gardens
31 The Manor House, Ayot St Lawrence
35 Queenswood School
45 St Michael's Croft

June

Sunday 5
3 Ashridge
8 47 Bournehall Avenue
9 Bride Hall
40 St Stephens Avenue Gardens
42 Shaw's Corner
49 Thundridge Hill House
53 The White House
Monday 6
53 The White House (Evening)
Saturday 11
37 2 Ruins Cottage
Sunday 12
14 Danesbury Park Gardens
29 Letchworth Gardens
37 2 Ruins Cottage

Friday 17
2 Amwell Cottage (Evening)
Sunday 19
13 Croft Cottage
25 Keys Heath
41 Serge Hill Gardens
54 Woodhall Park
Wednesday 22
13 Croft Cottage
Friday 24
36 The Royal National Rose Society (Evening)
Sunday 26
6 Benington Lordship
15 Dassels Bury
33 106 Orchard Road
47 Swan Hill Barn
52 Waterdell House

July

Friday 1
22 Hoglands and The Henry Moore Foundation grounds (Evening)
Saturday 2
26 Kingfishers
Sunday 3
26 Kingfishers
Sunday 10
17 15 Gade Valley Cottages
28 19 Lancaster Road
50 84 Valley Road
Sunday 17
7 Benington Park
Sunday 24
32 Oakridge Avenue Gardens
44 14 Spooners Drive
Friday 29
4 22a The Avenue (Evening)
Saturday 30
48 9 Tannsfield Drive
Sunday 31
16 35 Digswell Road

August

Sunday 7
5 Beesonend Gardens
20 Great Stones
48 9 Tannsfield Drive
Friday 12
10 44 Broadwater Avenue (Evening)
Sunday 14
10 44 Broadwater Avenue
18 8 Gosselin Road
Sunday 21
34 Patchwork
43 Southend Farm
Wednesday 24
43 Southend Farm

October

Saturday 15
12 Capel Manor Gardens
Sunday 16
12 Capel Manor Gardens
18 8 Gosselin Road
Sunday 23
16 35 Digswell Road

Gardens open to the public

6 Benington Lordship
12 Capel Manor Gardens
21 Hatfield House West Garden
22 Hoglands and The Henry Moore Foundation grounds
23 Hopleys
27 Knebworth House Gardens
36 The Royal National Rose Society
39 St Paul's Walden Bury
42 Shaw's Corner
51 The Walled Garden

By appointment only

46 Stresa

Also open by Appointment ☎

1 The Abbots House
11 Bromley Hall
16 35 Digswell Road
25 Keys Heath
33 106 Orchard Road
34 Patchwork
44 14 Spooners Drive
48 9 Tannsfield Drive
49 Thundridge Hill House
52 Waterdell House
53 The White House

The Gardens

1 THE ABBOTS HOUSE
10 High Street, Abbots Langley
WD5 0AR. Peter & Sue Tomson,
01923 264946,
peter.tomson@btinternet.com. *5m
NW of Watford. Exit J20 on M25.
Take A4251 signed Kings Langley. R
at 1st r'about (Home Park Industrial
Estate). R at T-junction. Follow rd,
under railway bridge and the yellow
signs will become apparent. Free
parking in village car park.* Home-
made teas in our Tithe Barn which
is in the garden. Adm £3.50, chd free
(share to Friends of St Lawrence
Church). Sun 1 May (2-5). Visitors
also welcome by appt.

Visit the website for latest information

1³/₄-acre garden with unusual trees, shrubs, mixed borders with interesting colour combinations, scented garden, sunken garden, pond, conservatory and a bed with many Himalayan plants. A garden of 'rooms' with different styles and moods. Many half-hardy plants. Plants propagated from the garden are for sale. Probably the only Oast House or Maltings in Hertfordshire. Teas in a Barn called a 'Tithe Barn'. This is the final opening of The Abbots House after twenty years. Level garden, gravel paths.

♿ ❀ ☕ ☎

2 **AMWELL COTTAGE**
Amwell Lane, Wheathampstead
AL4 8EA. Colin & Kate Birss. ¹/₂ m S of Wheathampstead. From St Helens Church, Wheathampstead turn up Brewhouse Hill. At top L fork (Amwell Lane), 300yds down lane, park in field opp. Home-made teas. L'ailolive - gourmet food suppliers will be selling light supper snacks at evening opening. **Adm £3.50, chd free. Sun 17 Apr (2-5). Evening Opening wine, Fri 17 June (6-9).** Informal garden of approx 2¹/₂ acres around C17 cottage (not open). Large orchard of mature apples, plums and pear laid out with paths. Extensive lawns with borders, framed by tall yew hedges and old brick walls. A large variety of roses, stone seats with views, woodland pond, greenhouse and recently designed fire-pit area. Depending on season and harvest there may be honey and plants for sale. Art Gallery with work by Central St Martin's art students.

♿ 🔫 ❀ ☕

3 **ASHRIDGE**
Berkhamsted HP4 1NS. Ashridge (Bonar Law Memorial Trust), www.ashridge.org.uk. 3m N of Berkhamsted. A4251, 1m S of Little Gaddesden. Cream Teas. **Adm £4, chd £2.50. Sun 5 June (2-6).** The gardens cover 190 acres forming part of the Grade II Registered Landscape of Ashridge Park. Based on designs by Humphrey Repton in 1813 modified by Jeffry Wyatville. Small secluded gardens, as well as a large lawn area leading to avenues of trees. The House is open for guided tours for five weeks over July-August. Please visit the website for details. Cream teas are available for purchase. Gravel paths and main areas are accessible.

♿ 🔫 ☕

4 **NEW** **22A THE AVENUE**
Hitchin SG4 9RL. Martin Woods. Half a mile east of town centre. Opposite St Mary's Church take Windmill Hill, continue to top into Wymondley Road. The Avenue is the 1st turning on left. **Adm £3, chd free. Evening Opening wine, Fri 29 July (6-9).** Contemporary town garden. Creative use of herbaceous plants and grasses. Modern landscaping, pond, potager, pots and more . . .

GROUP OPENING

5 **BEESONEND GARDENS**
Harpenden AL5 2AN. 1m S of Harpenden. Take A1081 S from Harpenden, after 1m turn R into Beesonend Lane, bear R into Burywick to T-junction. Follow signs to Barlings Rd & The Deerings. Home-made teas. **Combined adm £3.50, chd free. Sun 7 Aug (2-5.30).**

2 BARLINGS ROAD
Liz & Jim Machin

17 THE DEERINGS
Mr & Mrs Thompson.

Within walking distance of each other these two gardens demonstrate how plots of a similar size have been developed to reflect their owners' individual gardening interests and needs. 2 Barlings Road is packed with unusual plants. Sculptures (not for sale) are placed around the garden. Previous winner of St Albans and Harpenden in Bloom. 17 The Deerings has been designed bearing in mind the need for family parties. Winner of Harpenden in Bloom - Best Back Garden 2010. A flautist will entertain while you enjoy afternoon tea and cake at 17 The Deerings.

☕

The remains of earthwork terraces from C17 make this one of the best archaeological gardens of its date . . .

6 ♦ **BENINGTON LORDSHIP**
nr Stevenage SG2 7BS. Mr & Mrs R R A Bott, www.beningtonlordship.co.uk. 5m E of Stevenage. In Benington Village, signs off A602. Next to church. Light Refreshments at Parish hall next to the garden entrance. **Adm £4, chd free. For NGS: Sun 26 June (12-6). For other opening times and information please visit garden website.** 7-acre garden incl historic buildings, kitchen garden, lakes, roses. Spectacular herbaceous borders, unspoilt natural views.

☕

7 **NEW** **BENINGTON PARK**
Bennington SG2 7BU. Marcus & Debbie Taverner. 5m E of Stevenage. Off A602 between Stevenage and Hertford through Aston Village into Benington R at village green follow signs. Home-made teas. **Sun 17 July (2-5).** The garden and landscape have something for all. The remains of earthwork terraces from early C17 make this one of the best archaeological gardens of its date. Alongside is a beautiful modern garden created by Debbie Taverner and Amanda Brown with lovely views of surrounding countryside.

☕

8 **47 BOURNEHALL AVENUE**
Bushey WD23 3AU. Caroline & Jim Fox, carolinefox@f2s.com. 1m S of Watford. Bushey Village A411, Falconer Rd, Herkomer Rd, 2nd on Left is Bournehall Ave. Map on www.jamespfox.co.uk. Light refreshments & home-made teas. **Adm £3, chd free. Sun 5 June (2-5).** Medium sized village garden on 3 levels designed and built by owners. Garlanded planters overlook sunken garden with acers and pond. A wisteria and vine covered pergola leads to a fruited potager. Step up to sculpted lawn edged by small trees, shrubs and sumptuous perennials. Featured in Optima magazine.

❀ ☕

9 **NEW** **BRIDE HALL**
Ayot St Lawrence, Welwyn AL6 9DB. Mr & Mrs Danny Desmond. 4 m W of Welwyn. From A1(M)J4 take A6129. At r'bout take 3rd exit B197, next r'bout 3rd exit B653 for 3¹/₂ m. R into Codicote Rd, L into Bride Hall Lane. House ¹/₂ m on L. Home-made teas. **Adm £5, chd**

free. **Sun 5 June (2-5.30).**
Bride Hall overlooks a forecourt
between two magnificent listed barns
with a central lawn and borders. The
garden is divided into formal spaces,
rills run into a lily pond designed by
International Landscape Architects
Cloustons. A sheltered herb garden
linking into the informal gardens;
billowing with a mass of prairie
planting all created some 25 years
ago by the in-house gardening team.
limited wheelchair access.

10 44 BROADWATER AVENUE
Letchworth Garden City SG6 3HJ.
Karen & Ian Smith. *½ m SW
Letchworth town centre. A1(M) J9
signed Letchworth. Straight on at 1st
three r'abouts, 4th r'about take 4th
exit then R into Broadwater Ave.*
Home-made teas. **Adm £3, chd free.
Sun 14 Aug (1-5). Evening
Opening wine, Fri 12 Aug (6-9).**
Town garden in the Letchworth
Garden City conservation area that
successfully combines a family
garden with a plantswoman's garden.
Out of the ordinary, unusual
herbaceous plants and shrubs.
Attractive front garden designed for
yr-round interest. Finalist in
Letchworth in Bloom. Featured in
Amateur Gardening.

11 BROMLEY HALL
Standon, Ware SG11 1NY. Julian &
Edwina Robarts, 01279 842 422,
edwina.robarts@btinternet.com,
www.bromley-hall.co.uk. *6m W of
Bishop's Stortford. On Standon to
Much Hadham rd.* Home-made teas.
**Adm £4.50, chd free. Sun 22
(2-5.30), Mon 23 May (11-5).**
Visitors also welcome by appt.
Groups of 10+ Coaches welcome,
£5. Home-made tea available.
4½ acres surrounding C16
farmhouse. Some elements are
traditional - formal hedging, Irish
yews, and mixed borders, vegetables,
mown paths through long grass.
Others are modern, a grove of white
poplars surrounding cranes and a
modern formal garden on the site of
the old tennis court. Everywhere there
are places to sit, view and
contemplate. Featured in GGG.

7 BYNG ROAD
See London.

Thundridge Hill House

12 ◆ CAPEL MANOR GARDENS
Bullsmoor Lane, Enfield, Middlesex
EN1 4RQ. Capel Manor Charitable
Corporation, 08456 122122,
www.capelmanorgardens.co.uk.
*2m from Cheshunt. 3 mins from J25
of the M25/A10.Nearest train station
is Turkey Street, 20 minutes walk to
Capel Manor Gardens.* **Adm £5.50,
chd £2.50.**
For NGS: **Sat 15, Sun 16 Oct
(10-5.45). For other opening times
and information, please phone or
see garden website.**
A beautiful 30 acre estate providing a
colourful & scented oasis surrounding
a Georgian Manor House & Victorian
Stables. Be inspired by prize winning
themed, model & historical gardens
including the latest additions the Old
Manor House Garden & the Family
Friendly Garden (Chelsea Flower
Show Gold Medal Winner). Picnic by
the lake. Free parking. Events and
activities run throughout the year.

CLAVERING GARDENS
See Essex.

13 CROFT COTTAGE
9 Church Green, Benington
SG2 7LH. Richard Arnold-Roberts
& Julie Haire. *4m E of Stevenage.
A1M J7. A602 Hertford, L at 6th
r'bout, down short hill to mini r'about,
straight across (Broadwater Lane).
Through Aston to Xrds (1½ m).*
*Straight across. Cottage on R after
1½ m opp church.* **Adm £3, chd
free. Sun 19, Wed 22 June (1-5).**
C16 cottage with small, extensively
planted garden divided into several
areas. Many variegated and colourful-
leafed shrubs and perennials. Mixed
border in pastel shades. Euphorbia
and hosta collection. Pool with fish,
waterspout and seat. Rose and
clematis shaded arbour with view
over fields. Japanese maple garden
with pool overlooking C13 church.
Gravel paths.

GROUP OPENING

14 NEW DANESBURY PARK GARDENS
Welwyn AL6 9QB. *From South, leave
A1(M) at J6, cross 2 r'bouts, turn L
on to B656 towards Codicote.Take
1st R, then 3rd R. Park in Blakes Way
for Nathan's Close or at 17
Danesbury Park Mews (limited
parking).* Home-made teas at 17
Danesbury Park Mews. **Adm £4, chd
free. Sun 12 June (2-5.30).**

NEW **17 DANESBURY PARK
MEWS**
Francoise Austin

1 NATHANS CLOSE
Margaret & Roger Bardell

Two contrasting gardens within easy
walking distance: start at either

garden. 1 Nathan's Close: Constantly evolving plant-enthusiasts garden, with island beds, densely planted borders, pond and gravel areas. Much wildlife interest amid many unusual plants.17 Danesbury Park Mews: Long mixed borders within a walled garden, featuring roses, peonies and many cottage garden favourites. Enjoy a 15 minute stroll through Danesbury Nature Reserve, which lies between the two gardens. Plant sale at 1 Nathan's Close.

15 NEW DASSELS BURY
Dassels, Braughing SG11 2RW. Martin and Kate Slack. *2m SE of Buntingford; 1m N of Braughing on B1368. B1368 runs to the East of the A10. Parking in field on the East of the B1368 at the South end of Dassels.* Home-made teas. **Adm £4, chd free. Sun 26 June (2-5.30).**
Garden was created by present owners in 2003. Clever terracing gives stunning views. Double herbaceous border with inspired planting; kitchen garden including soft fruit and asparagus in raised beds; wildlife pond; woodland garden; a fine glasshouse; and orchard with rare breed chickens. Fine views over Quin valley with grazing alpacas. Visitors are welcome to walk through the wild flower meadows and woodland areas. Gravel paths and steep paths.

16 35 DIGSWELL ROAD
Welwyn Garden City AL8 7PB. Adrian & Clare de Baat, 01707 324074, **adrian.debaat@ntlworld.com.** *½ m N of Welwyn Garden City centre. From the Campus r'about in centre of City take N exit just past public library into Digswell Rd. Over the White Bridge, 200yds on L.* Home-made teas July only. **Adm £3.50, chd free. Sun 31 July (2-5.30); Sun 23 Oct (2-5).** Visitors also welcome by appt, June to Oct, £5 incl tea & cake.
Town garden of around 1/3 acre. Piet Oudolf-inspired naturalistic borders with herbaceous plants and grasses surround the lawn. Beyond are island beds packed with perennials, linked by grass paths. The contemporary planting gives way to the exotic, including succulent bed and lush jungle garden with bamboos, bananas and tree ferns. Plants for sale at July opening. Featured in BBC

Open Gardens and in Garden News Magazine. Grass paths, gentle slopes.

DOCWRA'S MANOR
See Cambridgeshire.

EAST BARNET GARDENS
See London.

54 FERNDOWN
See London.

17 NEW 15 GADE VALLEY COTTAGES
Dagnall Road, Great Gaddesden, Hemel Hempstead HP1 3BW. Bryan Trueman. *3 m N of Hemel Hempstead. Follow A4146 N from Hemel Hempstead. Past Water End. Go past turning for Great Gaddesden. Gade Valley Cottages on RH- side. Park in village hall car park.* Light refreshments & teas. **Adm £3, chd free. Sun 29 May; Sun 10 July (1.30-5.30).**
165 x 30 ft sloping plant enthusiasts garden.Patio,lawn,borders and pond lead through woodland area emerging by wildlife pond. Sunny border. Raised seating offering views accross the Gade valley. Many Hostas,Acers, Ferns,Hemerocallis and Heuchera. Some unusual trees and shrubs e.g. Styrax, Clethra, Heptacodium and Stewartia. Plants for sale propagated by owner. gravel paths and some steps.

> Fine views over Quin valley with grazing alpacas . . . walk through the wild flower meadows and woodland areas . . .

18 NEW 8 GOSSELIN ROAD
Bengeo, Hertford SG14 3LG. Annie Godfrey & Steve Machin, www.daisyroots.com. *Take B158 from Hertford signed to Bengeo. Gosselin Rd 2nd R after White Lion PH (phone box on corner).* **Adm £3, chd free. Sun 14 Aug (12-5.30); Sun 16 Oct (12-4.30).**
Owner of Daisy Roots nursery, garden

has been redesigned and completely replanted since it last opened in 2006. Lawn replaced by a wide gravel path, flanked by deep borders packed with perennials and grasses. Pelargonium collection in pots. New sunken area surrounded by plants chosen for scent. Small front garden with lots of foliage interest.

45 GREAT NORTH ROAD
See London.

19 GREAT SARRATT HALL
Sarratt, Rickmansworth WD3 4PD. Mr H M Neal. *5m N of Rickmansworth. From Watford N via A41 (or M1 J5) to Kings Langley; left (W) to Sarratt; garden is 1st on R after village sign.* Home-made teas. **Adm £5, chd free (share to The Courtauld Institute of Art). Sun 29 May (2-6).**
4 acres. Herbaceous and mixed shrub borders; pond, moisture-loving plants and trees; walled kitchen garden; rhododendrons, magnolias, camellias; new planting of specialist conifers and rare trees.

20 GREAT STONES
Hare Street, near Buntingford SG9 0AD. Mr & Mrs J Edwards. *1½ m E of Buntingford. From Buntingford take B1038 signed Hare Street - Newport. 1½ m garden on R. From Hare Street Village turn L in village signed Buntingford B1038. Garden on L ½ m from junction.* Cream Teas. **Adm £3.50, chd free. Sun 7 Aug (2-5).**
Approximately 2 acre informal garden, featuring herbaceous perennials of vibrant colour. A lavender walk, a wooded area, large display of hosta and large pond with marginal planting to allow visitors to enjoy different vistas of the garden. Small orchard, vegetable garden and greenhouses. Ample parking on site. Photographic exhibition. Grass paths.

13 GREENHILL PARK
See London.

21 ◆ HATFIELD HOUSE WEST GARDEN
AL9 5NQ. The Marquess of Salisbury, 01707 287010, **www.hatfield-house.co.uk.** *Opp Hatfield Stn, 21m N of London, M25 J23. 7m A1(M) J4 signed off A414 & A1000.* **Adm £6, chd free.**

For NGS: Sat 26 Mar (2-5). For other opening times and information, please phone or see garden website.
Special early opening for NGS - 2011. Dating from C17, the garden at Hatfield House has evolved into a gardeners' paradise. Enjoy the peaceful west garden's scented garden and fountains. View the famous knot garden adjoining the Tudor Old Palace. Delightful formal gardens planted for yr round colour and interest.

22 NEW ◆ **HOGLANDS AND THE HENRY MOORE FOUNDATION GROUNDS**
Perry Green, Much Hadham SG10 6EE. Henry Moore Foundation, 01279 843 333, www.henry-moore.org. *Centre of Perry Green, 1 m from Much Hadham. or see our website.* Pimms will be served in Aisled Barn. **Adm £5, chd free. For NGS: Evening Opening wine, Fri 1 July (6-8). For other opening times and information, please phone or see garden website.**
Artist Henry Moore and his wife Irina came to live at Hoglands, in 1940. Irina worked with passion to create a garden that graduates gently from vivid herbaceous borders to the grassed areas on the estate displaying Moore's sculptures. Here Irina created island beds filled with trees and shrubs, complementing orchards and fields beyond. Evening opening for NGS, with Pimm's served on the lawn The Aisled Barn, at the heart of the gardens and sculpture grounds. The Hoops Inn open for dinner. Featured in BBC's The Culture Show, BBC Newsnight, The Guardian Review, The Daily Telegraph, The Spectator, Elle Decoration, Harper's Bazaar, Country Life, Le Figaro.
&

23 ◆ **HOPLEYS**
High Street, Much Hadham SG10 6BU. Aubrey & Jan Barker, 01279 842509, www.hopleys.co.uk. *5m W of Bishop's Stortford. On B1004. M11 (J8) 7m or A10 (Puckeridge) 5m via A120. 50yds N of Bull PH in centre of Much Hadham.* **For opening times and information please phone or visit garden website.**
4 acres laid out in informal style with island beds. The garden has become a useful collection of stock plants and

trial ground for many new plants collected over the years. The frogs and toads in the pond bring natural pest control to the garden and nursery! The nursery production area is hidden by an avenue of fastigiate hornbeams.

HORNBEAMS
See London.

THE HYDE WALLED GARDEN
See Bedfordshire.

GROUP OPENING

24 **JENNINGSBURY GARDENS**
Hertford Heath SG13 7NS. *1m SE of Hertford on B1197 towards Hertford Heath. From A414 between A10 & Hertford take B1197, to Hertford Heath & Haileybury College, (Foxholes r'about, Lancaster Mercedes garage) 1/2 m on RH-side at post and rail fencing Park in field beside Daisy Roots Plant Nursery.* Home-made teas. **Combined adm £5, chd free. Sun 29 May (2-5.30).**

FAR END BARN
Mr & Mrs Richard Conyers

JENNINGSBURY
Barry & Gail Fox

THE STABLES
Mr & Mrs Christopher Abbiss

Three varied gardens in secluded development. Jenningsbury is a 3 acre plantsman's garden surrounded by an ancient moat with extensive wild flower meadow beyond. The Stables is a small stylish courtyard garden, full of unusual ideas. Far End Barn is a family garden with lawns meandering through mixed borders leading to the moat at the end of the garden. Daisy Roots nursery (award winner RHS) www.daisyroots.com is open next door to Jenningsbury.

---

25 NEW **KEYS HEATH**
Cambridge Road, Rosehill, Hitchin SG40JU. Mark & Janet Whitby, 07831 232046, mark@mark-whitby.com. *between Hitchin & Letchworth. Immediately opp the Hitchin Garden Centre on A505.* Light refreshments & teas. **Adm £4.50, chd free. Sun 19 June (10-5.30). Visitors also welcome by appt.**
A 3-acre informal garden to a 1930s house with large chaotic borders

inspired by Penelope Hobhouse and Christopher Lloyd, orchard, vegetable area, established 'pinetum', pool and dell, together with new yew hedges and sculpture, that is undergoing a transformation. Set in 18 acres of wildlife meadow and copice and walnut plantation with a free standing solar pv array. Beehives. Wheelchair access to meadows subject to weather.

Set in 18 acres of wildlife meadow and copice and walnut plantation with a free standing solar pv array . . .

26 **KINGFISHERS**
49a High Street, Watton at Stone SG14 3SX. Sheron & Derek Deards. *6m N of Hertford. From A602 between Hertford & Stevenage follow signs to Watton at Stone. Garden is on R going N in High St.* Home-made teas. **Adm £3, chd free. Sat 2, Sun 3 July (1.30-5).**
Long, narrow garden 1/3 acre. Pond by terrace, bordered by mixed beech hedge. Mixed cottage-style border, planted for year round interest. Clematis and rose arbour. Herb wheel, gazebo. Mediterranean bed, surrounded by white and 'hot' borders. Greenhouse and raised vegetable beds. Beyond, a wildlife friendly area slopes down to country views and River Beane where kingfishers often seen.

27 ◆ **KNEBWORTH HOUSE GARDENS**
Knebworth SG1 2AX. The Hon Henry Lytton Cobbold, www.knebworthhouse.com. *28m N of London. Direct access from A1(M) J7 at Stevenage. Stn, Stevenage 3m. For opening times and admission costs please see our website.* **For other opening times and information, please see garden website.**
Knebworth's magnificent gardens were laid out by Lutyens in 1910. Lutyens' pollarded lime avenues, Gertrude Jekyll's herb garden, the restored maze, yew hedges, roses

47 Bournehall Avenue

and herbaceous borders are key features of the formal gardens with peaceful woodland walks beyond. Gold garden, green garden, brick garden and walled kitchen garden.

  ♿ ✿ ☕

28 **19 LANCASTER ROAD**
St Albans AL1 4EP. Pauline & Michael Foers. ¹/₂ m N of St Albans city centre. From city centre take A1081 towards Harpenden then B651 towards Sandridge, after 100yds turn R into Sand Pit Lane, take 5th on L into Lancaster Rd. Home-made teas. **Adm £3, chd free. Suns 15 May; 10 July (2-5.30).** Winding paths give access to all parts of our medium-sized garden. Unusual trees and shrubs together with richly-planted herbaceous borders give year-round colour. In May, late tulips compete with a tulip tree; azaleas, rhododendron and a Judas tree enhance the display. In July, phlox complement heucheras. A plantsperson's garden. Small terrace with pots. Winners St Albans in Bloom.

✿ ☕

GROUP OPENING

29 **NEW** **LETCHWORTH GARDENS**
SG6 3LB. *A1(M) J9 signed to Letchworth on A505. At 2nd r'about turn L towards Hitchin, still on A505. After 1m house on L between Muddy Lane & Letchworth Lane.* Light refreshments & home-made teas served at Scudamore, Ploughmans lunches at 324 Norton Way South. **Adm £5, chd free (share to Garden House Hospice). Sun 12 June (1-6).**

NEW **324 NORTON WAY SOUTH**
Roger & Jill Thomson

SCUDAMORE
1 Baldock Road. Michael & Sheryl Hann

Two contrasting gardens within easy walking distance. Scudamore 1/3 acre garden a family garden of mature trees, mixed borders, pond and stream, wet bed, wild garden and orchard/vegetable area. Many sculptures add interest to the garden.

324 Norton Way Sth a mature 1/5 acre organic garden with David Harbur armillary as the lawn focal point surrounded by rockery, scree beds flower borders and summerhouse. Structural tree planting,a productive kitchen garden and greenhouse increase the interest. Family quiz at Scudamore.

  ♿ ✿ ☕

46 LINCOLN ROAD
See London.

30 **THE MANOR HOUSE BAYFORD**
Bayford SG13 8PU. Mr & Mrs David Latham. *3 m SW of Hertford, off B158.* Home-made teas. **Adm £4, chd free. Sun 15 May (2-5).** Large old established garden immaculately maintained. Natural ornamental lake, many specimen trees and unusual shrubs. Walled garden, spring bulbs. 900 year old John of Gaunt oak. Gravel paths.

  ♿ ☕

Be tempted by a plant from a plant stall

31 NEW THE MANOR HOUSE, AYOT ST LAWRENCE
Welwyn AL6 9BP. Rob & Sara Lucas. *4m W of Welwyn. 20 mins from J4 of the A1(M). Take B653 to Wheathampstead.Turn into Codicote Road follow signs to Shaw's Corner. Parking in the village field, short walk from the garden.* Home-made teas. **Adm £4, chd free. Sun 29 May (11-5).**
A 6 acre garden set in mature landscape around Elizabethan Manor House (not open). 1 acre walled garden incl glasshouses, fruit and vegetables, double herbaceous borders, rose and herb beds. Herbaceous perennial island beds, topiary specimens. Parterre and temple pond garden surround the house. Gates and water features by Arc Angel. Garden designed by Julie Toll.

MONTANA
See Buckinghamshire.

GROUP OPENING

32 OAKRIDGE AVENUE GARDENS
Radlett WD7 8EW. *1m N of central Radlett. Off A5183, Watling St. From S, through Radlett Village last turning on L.* Home-made & cream teas. **Combined adm £3.50, chd free. Sun 24 July (2-6).**

47 OAKRIDGE AVENUE
Sylvia Lickorish

45 OAKRIDGE AVENUE
Leonora & Edgar Vaughan

Two varied interconnecting gardens in attractive village near St Albans. Both have lovely views over open countryside. The main features of 45 Oakridge Avenue are the plants, carefully chosen to combine the use of colour throughout the year. The garden is in 2 halves approx 150ft by 60ft on 3 levels of terracing, looping around to the back for vegetables and soft fruits. 47 Oakridge Avenue is a spacious and mature garden, approx 1 acre, beautifully maintained. Large pond with gold fish, small orchard. Local brook runs along one side of the garden, on the edge of a working farm.

33 106 ORCHARD ROAD
Tewin AL6 0LZ. Linda Adams, 01438 798147, alannio@btinternet.com, www.tewinvillage.co.uk. *3m N of Welwyn Garden City. From B1000 between Hertford & WGC, signed Tewin. Pass the Rose & Crown PH, to Upper Green Road towards Burnham Green. Pass Plume of Feathers PH and Tewin Orchard.* Home-made teas. **Adm £3.50, chd free. Sun 26 June (2-5.30).** Visitors also welcome by appt May to end Sept incl.
Spacious 1 acre organic garden behind listed modern movement house (not open). Elements of 1935 garden - large island beds amid lawns, with lily fishpond and unusual trees and shrubs,topiary, labyrinth, and productive fruit and vegetable cage. Orchard part of the Hertfordshire Millennium orchard. Rabbit-resistant plants feature. Light Years' Dance group from Hertford (average age 67) will make guest appearances.

34 PATCHWORK
22 Hall Park Gate, Berkhamsted HP4 2NJ. Jean & Peter Block, 01442 864731. *3m W of Hemel Hempstead. Entering E side of Berkhamsted on A4251, turn L 200yds after 40mph sign.* Light refreshments & home-made teas. **Adm £3, chd free. Suns 1 May; 21 Aug (2-5).** Visitors also welcome by appt. March to Oct, groups welcome.
$^{1}/_{4}$ -acre garden with lots of yr-round colour, interest and perfume, particularly on opening days. Sloping site with background of colourful trees, rockeries, two small ponds, patios, shrubs and trees, spring bulbs, herbaceous border, roses, bedding, fuchsias, dahlias, patio pots and tubs galore and hanging baskets. Seating and cover from the elements.

35 QUEENSWOOD SCHOOL
Shepherds Way, Brookmans Park, Hatfield AL9 6NS. *3m N of Potters Bar. From S: M25 J24 signed Potters Bar. In $^{1}/_{2}$ m at lights turn R onto A1000 signed Hatfield. In 2m turn R onto B157. School is $^{1}/_{2}$ m on R. From N: A1000 from Hatfield. In 5m turn L onto B157.* Light refreshments & teas. **Adm £4, chd free. Sun 29 May (11-6).**
120 acres of informal gardens and

woodlands. Rhododendrons, fine specimen trees, shrubs and herbaceous borders. Glasshouses. Fine views to Chiltern Hills. Picnic area.

ROSE COTTAGE
See Buckinghamshire.

36 NEW ◆ THE ROYAL NATIONAL ROSE SOCIETY
Chiswell Green Lane, St Albans AL2 3NR. The Secretary, www.rnrs.org. *Follow brown signs, access off Chiswell Green Lane.* **Adm £5, chd free. For NGS: Evening Opening wine, Fri 24 June (6-9).** For other opening times and information, please see garden website.
Recently, redesigned by Michael Balston, the gardens contain a huge variety of roses including the newly replanted Queen Mother garden. Roses are grown in garden settings showing different styles of planting. The use of other plants associating well with roses increases the season of interest. Model gardens give inspiration for growing roses in small spaces.

> Light Years' Dance group from Hertford (average age 67) will make guest appearances . . .

37 2 RUINS COTTAGE
Ayot St Lawrence AL6 9BU. Sally Trendell. *4m W of Welwyn. A1(M) J6 follow signs to Welwyn, Codicote (B656) then Ayot St Lawrence (Shaws Corner NT).* Cream teas. **Adm £3, chd free (share to Ayot St Lawrence Old Church Preservation Trust). Sat 11 (2-7), Sun 12 June (2-6).**
Enter through adjacent romantic church ruins, this cottage garden has an eccentric twist with unusual architectural pieces and featuring a unique tree deck with stunning views

and an impressive summer house. Natural pond, koi pond, rose garden and luscious fernery, reflecting owner's eclectic taste. 'A hidden gem!' 'surreal! incredibly beautiful'. Ayot St Lawrence annual Art Show in nearby Palladian Church 11, 12, 13 June. Annette Busse will play classical piano pieces over the weekend. Full details on ngs website. Cream teas and licensed bar serving wine. wheelchair access only to lower levels, gravel paths.

38 **RUSTLING END COTTAGE**
Rustling End, nr Codicote SG4 8TD. Julie & Tim Wise, www.rustlingend.com. *1m N of Codicote. From B656 turn L into 3 Houses Lane' then R to Rustling End. House is 2nd on L.* Light refreshments & home-made teas. **Adm £4, chd free. Wed 27 Apr (2-5.30); Sun 22 May (6-11am). Evening Opening wine, Fri 20 May (6-9).**
Meander through our wild flower meadow to a cottage garden with contemporary planting. Behind lumpy hedges explore a simple box parterre, topiary and reflecting pool.Late flowering borders feature blue Camassia in the spring. Naturalistic planting includes the use of wildflowers with perennials and grasses. Hens and vegetables abound. Featured in RHS The Garden magazine.

45 **NEW** **ST MICHAEL'S CROFT**
Durrants Lane, Woodcock Hill, Berkhamsted HP4 3TR. Sue and Alan O'Neill. *1m W of Berkhamsted town centre. Leave A41 at A416 Chesham turn. Follow sign to Berkhamsted. After 500 metres go straight on to Shootersway (not sharp R) 1m further turn R into Durrants Lane. Garden 1st on L.* Light refreshments & home-made teas. **Adm £3.50, chd free. Sun 29 May (2-6).**
1-acre south facing garden with variety of densely planted borders surrounded by mature trees. Rhododendrons, azaleas, hostas, ferns, alliums, palms, cordylines and bananas. Water features and waterfall from lock gate. Pergolas with clematis and climbers, vegetable beds, 2 greenhouses. Working beehives. Easy access for wheelchairs. Seating and cover. Home produced honey for sale.

39 ◆ **ST PAUL'S WALDEN BURY**
Hitchin SG4 8BP. Simon & Caroline Bowes Lyon, 01438 871218, www.stpaulswaldenbury.co.uk. *5m S of Hitchin. On B651; ¹/₂ m N of Whitwell village. From London leave A1(M) at junction 6 for Welwyn (not Welwyn Garden City). Pick up signs to Codicote, then Whitwell.* Teas with homemade cakes. **Adm £4, chd £1. Sun 12 June 2-7. For NGS: Suns 3 Apr; 8 May (2-7).**
Spectacular formal woodland garden, Grade 1 listed, laid out 1720. Long rides lined with clipped beech hedges lead to temples, statues, lake and a green terraced theatre. Seasonal displays of snowdrops, daffodils, cowslips, irises, magnolias, rhododendrons, lilies. Wild flowers are encouraged. Birthplace and childhood home of the late Queen Mother. Summer theatre - see website for details.

Meadow to a cottage garden with contemporary planting . . .

GROUP OPENING

40 **ST STEPHENS AVENUE GARDENS**
St Albans AL3 4AD. *1¹/₂ m S of St Albans City Centre. From A414 former M10 r'about take A5183 Watling St. At double mini-r'about by St Stephens Church/King Harry PH take B4630 Watford Rd. St Stephens Ave is 1st R.* Home-made teas. **Combined adm £3.50, chd free. Sun 5 June (2-6).**

20 ST STEPHENS AVENUE
Heather & Peter Osborne

30 ST STEPHENS AVENUE
Carol & Roger Harlow

Two gardens of similar size and aspect, developed in totally different ways. 20 St Stephens Avenue is designed for yr-round flowers, foliage, texture and scent. Winding paths lead through densely planted colour co-ordinated borders. Arches and fences are festooned with fragrant honeysuckle, roses and clematis.

Wildlife pond, ornamental trees and shrubs, unusual hardy plants, patio containers, hostas, succulents and conservatory. 30 St Stephens Avenue has an informal gravel front garden, the Mediterranean style planting is tolerant of very dry conditions and poor soil. The back garden is divided into sections by clipped box and hornbeam to provide a formal framework for herbaceous planting.

GROUP OPENING

41 **SERGE HILL GARDENS**
WD5 0RY. *¹/₂ m E of Bedmond. In Bedmond, turn into Serge Hill Lane by white tin church. Follow signs which will take you down the drive to Serge Hill. From Chiswell Green, take Chiswell Green Lane by the Three Hammers PH. Follow signs to Bedmond. The gardens are ¹/₂ m up hill after crossing M1.* Home-made & cream teas. **Combined adm £6, chd free. Sun 19 June (2-5).**

THE BARN
Tom Stuart-Smith & family

SERGE HILL
Serge Hill Lane, Kate Stuart-Smith

Two very diverse gardens. At its entrance the Barn has an enclosed courtyard, with tanks of water, herbaceous perennials and shrubs tolerant of generally dry conditions. To the north there are views over the five acre wild flower meadow, and the West Garden is a series of different gardens overflowing with bulbs, herbaceous perennials and shrubs. Serge Hill is originally a Queen Anne House (not open), beautifully remodelled by Busby (Architect of Brighton and Hove) in 1811. It has wonderful views over the ha ha to the park; a walled vegetable garden with a large greenhouse, roses, large shrubs and perennials leading to a long mixed border. At the front of the house there is an outside stage used for family plays and a ship. Featured in The Telegraph 'Why I took the Telegraph Garden Home' by Cassandra Jardine.

42 ◆ **SHAW'S CORNER**
Ayot St Lawrence AL6 9BX. National Trust, 01438 820307, www.nationaltrust.org.uk/shawscor

ner. *2m NE of Wheathampstead. At SW end of village, approx 2m from B653 (A1 J4 - M1 J10). Signed from B653 (Shaw's Corner/The Ayots).* **Adm £6, chd free. For NGS: Sun 5 June (12-5.15). For other opening times and information, please phone or see garden website.** Approx 3½ acres with richly planted borders, orchard, small meadow, wooded areas and views over the Hertfordshire countryside. Historical garden, belonging to George Bernard Shaw from 1906 until his death in 1950. Hidden among the trees is the revolving writing hut where Shaw retreated. Ionian Singers performing in the garden.

43 NEW SOUTHEND FARM
Stevenage SG1 3HS. Janet Tyndale & Peter Craig. *Approx 1½ m from J8 A1(M). From S A1(M) J7, From N A1(M) J8, take A602, follow signs to Old Town.15 min walk Stevenage Railway Station. Garden on corner of Church Lane.* Home-made teas. **Adm £3.50, chd free. Sun 21, Wed 24 Aug (2-5).**
An oasis in the heart of Stevenage Old Town. Plantswoman's informal garden surrounding a Grade 2* Listed Medieval Wealden Farmhouse. Approx ⅓ acre with mixed borders, traditional cottage garden style planting, dry shade border, white border, raised pond and patio with pots. Belgian mechanical organs providing musical entertainment. Small garden railway operating, weather permitting.

44 14 SPOONERS DRIVE
St Albans AL2 2HL. Richard & Lynne Wilson, richardwilson30@yahoo.co.uk. *2m S of St Albans. From M1 South J8/7 take A414, at r'about take 3rd exit A5183 signed Radlett, 2nd R into Park St Lane and continue into Tippendell Lane & then L into Spooners Drive.* Home-made teas. **Adm £2.50, chd free. Sun 24 July (2-5.30). Visitors also welcome by appt.**
Mature trees/shrubs/deep borders/tall perennials/climbers/grasses and many interesting and more unusual plants surround this suburban garden of around 150'x30'. Features a large patio with an eclectic mix of planted tubs. The jungle/gravel area is fascinating and with a 3000 gal koi pond, water features/chickens/wild

flower garden - a must! Large patio, deep borders, gravel/jungle area. Wild British flowers, water features, chicken aviary and run. Some unusual plants for sale - not to be missed! Featured in Herts Advertiser.

For no. 45 see St Michael's Croft

A modern country garden, south facing, designed in harmony with the house by Julie Wise . . .

46 STRESA
126 The Drive, Rickmansworth WD3 4DP. Roger Trigg, 01923 774293, roger@triggmail.org.uk. *1m NW of Rickmansworth. From M25 J18 take A404 toward Rickmansworth at 200yds turn R into The Clump, then first L into The Drive. From Rickmansworth take A404 toward Amersham, first L into Nightingale Rd, sharp bend to R; becomes The Drive, follow 400yds, Stresa on the L just before x-road.* . Available for groups by arrangement: morning coffee, afternoon tea; evening wine. **Adm £3, chd free. Visitors welcome by appt late May - early September. Groups (ideally 12+) - catering available on request.**
Approx half acre plantsman's garden. Front garden part-gravel area; alpines, borderline-hardiness plants, dogwoods & grasses. Small woodland area leads to rear garden with continually evolving borders of perennials and shrubs incl hostas, heucheras, rhododendrons & shade-loving plants. Astilbes and phlox highlight summer display; Conservatory. Featured in Garden News; Optima Magazine.

47 NEW SWAN HILL BARN
75 Burnham Green Road, Burnham Green, Welwyn AL6 0NH. Peter & Helen Lowe. *500yards on R from Burnham Green Xrds in the direction of Datchworth. Set back off road behind white cottage.* Home-made teas. **Adm £3, chd free. Sun 26 June (2-5.30).**

A modern country garden, south facing, designed in harmony with the house by Julie Wise. Featuring semi formal flower beds, a rectangular pool and a vegetable garden with oak raised beds. The garden also includes a wisteria and clematis clad pergola which provides privacy from a public footpath alongside the property.

48 9 TANNSFIELD DRIVE
Hemel Hempstead HP2 5LG. Peter & Gaynor Barrett, 01442 393508, tterrabjp@ntlworld.com. *1m NE of Hemel Hempstead town centre. Approx 2m W of J8 on M1.From J8 straight across r'about on to A414 dual carriageway to Hemel Hemstead. Pass under footbridge and straight across r'about, then 1st R across the dual carriageway into Leverstock Green Rd. Continue straight on into High St Green, then L into Ellingham Rd. R into Orchard Close, L into Tannsmore Close which leads into Tannsfield Drive.* Home-made teas. Open days only. **Adm £2.50, chd free. Sun 8 May; Sat 30 July; Sun 7 Aug (2-5.30). Visitors also welcome by appt, 9 May to mid Sept, £3 per adult (home made teas not available for by appt).**
A truly interesting small town garden. The 50ft x 25ft plot has been imaginatively laid out and creatively planted. Narrow paths give the visitor many options of how to discover the garden. A good variety of grasses, ferns, clematis, fuchsias, honeysuckles and ornamental trees feature in densely planted flower beds. Shade and gravel planting along with a mini orchard and water features can also be seen. Featured in Garden News.

49 THUNDRIDGE HILL HOUSE
Cold Christmas Lane, Ware SG12 0UE. Mr & Mrs Christopher Melluish, 01920 462500, c.melluish@btopenworld.com. *2m NE of Ware from The Sow & Pigs PH off the A10 down Cold Christmas Lane, crossing new bypass.* Cream Teas. **Adm £4, chd free. Sun 5 June (2-5.30). Visitors also welcome by appt.**
Well-established garden of approx 2½ acres; good variety of plants, shrubs and roses, attractive hedges. We are at present creating an unusual yellow-only bed. Several delightful places to sit. Wonderful views in and out of the garden especially down to

the Rib Valley. 'A most popular garden to visit'. A delightful short walk down to the ruined Thundridge old church. Featured in The Hertfordshire Mercury in 2010.

 ♿ 🐱 💆 ☎

TREETOPS
See London.

50 NEW 84 VALLEY ROAD
Welwyn Garden City AL8 7DP.
Marion Jay. *West side of Welwyn Garden City. Turn R off Great North Road at Lemsford r'bout, go under the bridge then 2nd turning next r'bout. 200 yds on L.* Home-made & cream teas. **Adm £3, chd free. Sun 10 July (2-5.30).**
A dramatic garden rising steeply from the back of the house, using an 'amphitheatre' of stone wall terracing to accommodate the slope. Planting is largely in the modern perennial style, mixing drifts of drought-tolerant herbaceous plants with a variety of grasses. Three ponds, rose/clematis arch, tree-seat, pergola and acers. Plants for sale.

🐾 💆

51 ♦ THE WALLED GARDEN
Radlett Lane, Shenley WD7 9DW.
Shenley Park, 01923 852629,
www.shenleypark.co.uk. *5m S of St Albans. 2m S of M25 J22, 1m E of Radlett on Radlett to Shenley rd. At the edge of Shenley Village.* **Adm £3, chd free. For NGS: Sun 3 Apr (12-5).** For other opening times and information, please phone or see garden website.
2 acre C16 walled garden. Uniquely designed ornamental garden with terracing on 3 levels, and amphitheatre. Mature planting,

ancient fruit trees, interesting features. Fine views over adjacent countryside. 3 working Victorian greenhouses with plants sales.

 ♿ 🐱 🐾 💆

52 WATERDELL HOUSE
Little Green Lane, Croxley Green WD3 3JH. **Mr & Mrs Peter Ward,** 01923 772775,
peterward31@yahoo.com. *1¹/₂ m NE of Rickmansworth. M25, J18, direction Rickmansworth to join A412 towards Watford. From A412 turn L signed Sarratt, along Croxley Green, fork R past Coach & Horses, cross Baldwins Lane into Little Green Lane, then L at top.* Home-made teas. **Adm £4, chd free. Sun 26 June (2-5.30).** Visitors also welcome by appt. Spring visits enjoyable.
1¹/₂ -acre walled garden systematically developed over more than 50yrs by present owner/gardener: mature and young trees, topiary holly hedge, herbaceous borders, modern island beds of shrubs, old-fashioned roses, grasses and pond garden.

 ♿ 🐾 💆 ☎

Planting is largely in perennial style, mixing drifts of drought-tolerant herbaceous plants, with a variety of grasses . . .

53 NEW THE WHITE HOUSE
Munden Road, Dane End, Ware SG12 0LP. **Sally & Jonathan Pool,** 01920 438733. *5m N of Hertford. 2m W of Watton-at-Stone. Off A602 turn N to Dane End.* Home-made teas (Sun), wine (Mon). **Adm £4, chd free. Sun 5 June (2-5). Evening Opening wine, Mon 6 June (6-9).** Visitors also welcome by appt May, June & Sept.
26 year-old 1¹/₂ -acre country garden, designed by owner, surrounding 1830s dower house (not open) to incl vegetables, orchard, hedges, shrubs, herbaceous plants and conservatory.

 ♿ 🐾 💆 ☎

WIMPOLE HALL
See Cambridgeshire.

54 WOODHALL PARK
Watton-at-Stone, Hertford SG14 3NF. **Mr & Mrs Ralph Abel Smith,** www.woodhallestate.co.uk. *4m N of Hertford. 6m S of Stevenage, 4m NW of Ware. Main lodge entrance to Woodhall Park is on A119, Hertford to Stevenage, between villages of Stapleford & Watton-at-Stone.* Home-made teas. **Adm £5, chd free. Sun 19 June (12-5.30).**
Mature 4-acre garden created out of surrounding park when C18 stable block was converted in 1957(not open). Special features: courtyard, climbing and shrub roses, herbaceous and mixed borders, kitchen garden and areas to sit with unspoilt views. Grassland park full of mature and ancient trees traversed by river and lake. Visitors welcome to walk and picnic in the Park. Plants, home-made jam and free-range eggs for sale. Featured in Hertfordshire Mercury.

 ♿ 🐾 💆

Hertfordshire County Volunteers

County Organiser
Julie Wise, Rustling End Cottage, Rustling End, Nr Codicote SG4 8TD, 01438 821509, juliewise@f2s.com

County Treasurer
Peter Barrett, 9 Tannsfield Drive, Hemel Hempstead HP2 5LG, 01442 393508, tterrabip@ntworld.com

Publicity
Pauline Rhodes, 24 The Ridings, Hertford SG14 2AP, 01992 550 379, hjnprhodes@tiscali.co.uk

Booklet co-ordinator
Edwina Robarts, Bromley Hall, Standon, Ware SG11 1NY, 01279 842422, edwina.robarts@btinternet.com

Assistant County Organisers
Michael Belderbos, 6 High Elms, Hatching Green, Harpenden AL5 2JU, 01582 712612
Gail Fox, Jenningsbury, London Road, Hertford SG13 7NS, 01992 583978, foxgail@fox06.wanadoo.co.uk
Rösli Lancaster, Manor Cottage, Aspenden, Buntingford SG9 9PB, 01763 271711
Sarah Marsh,15 Hangmans Lane, Welwyn AL6 0TJ, 01438 714956, sarahkmarsh@hotmail.co.uk
Christopher Melluish, Thundridge Hill House, Cold Christmas Lane, Ware SG12 0UF, 01920 462500, c.melluish@btinternet.com
Virginia Newton, South Barn, Kettle Green, Much Hadham SG10 6AE, 01279 843232, vnewton@southbarn.net
Karen Smith, 44 Broadwater Avenue, Letchworth Garden City SG6 3HJ, 01462 673133, hertsgardeningangel@googlemail.com

Serge Hill

ISLE OF WIGHT

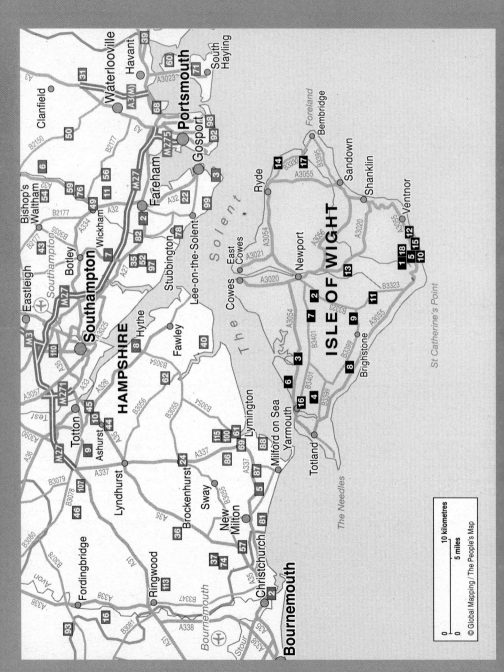

Opening Dates

February
Saturday 19 & Sunday 20
6 Highwood - **Snowdrop Days,**
by appointment only

May
Sunday 22
2 Badminton
Sunday 29
7 Meadowsweet
18 Whitwell Gardens Group

June
Sunday 12
4 Dog Kennel Cottage
11 The Old Rectory
14 Salterns Cottage
Saturday 18
10 Northern Star
Sunday 19
13 Rookley Manor
16 Thorley Manor
Sunday 26
8 Mottistone Manor Garden

July
Saturday 2
1 Ashknowle House
Sunday 3
1 Ashknowle House
Sunday 24
12 Pelham House

August
Sunday 14
15 The Shute
Sunday 21
3 Crab Cottage
Thursday 25
17 West Meades
Sunday 28
9 Northcourt Garden

Gardens open to the public
8 Mottistone Manor Garden

By appointment only
5 Haddon Lake House

Also open by Appointment
6 Highwood
9 Northcourt Garden
11 The Old Rectory
13 Rookley Manor

The Gardens

1 ASHKNOWLE HOUSE
Whitwell PO38 2PP. Mr & Mrs K Fradgley. *4m W of Ventnor. From Ventnor rd turn for Ashknowle Lane next to Old Rectory. Lane is unmade. Car parking in village but field parking available, except when wet.* Home-made teas. **Adm £3.50, chd free.** Sat 2, Sun 3 July (1-5).
A variety of features to explore in the grounds of this Victorian house. Informative woodland walks, borders, wildlife pond and other water features. Ongoing development of ornamental areas. The well-maintained kitchen garden is highly productive and boasts a wide range of fruit and vegetables grown in cages, tunnels, glasshouses and raised beds. New orchard site.
❀ ☕

2 BADMINTON
Clatterford Shute, Carisbrooke, Newport PO30 1PD. Mr & Mrs G S Montrose, 01983 526143. *1½ m SW of Newport. Free parking in Carisbrooke Castle car park. Public footpath to Millers Lane in corner of car park leads down to garden, approx 200yds. Parking for disabled can be arranged; please phone prior to opening.* Home-made teas. **Adm £3, chd free.** Sun 22 May (2-5).
One-acre garden on sheltered S- and W-facing site with good vistas. Planted for all-yr interest with many different shrubs, trees and perennials to give variety, structure and colour. Natural stream and pond being developed alongside kitchen garden.
🏡 ❀ ☕

3-acre garden with a panoramic view of Yarmouth and the Western Solent . . .

3 CRAB COTTAGE
Mill Road, Shalfleet PO30 4NE. Mr & Mrs Peter Scott. *4½ m E of Yarmouth. Turn past New Inn into Mill Rd. Please park before going through NT gates. Entrance 1st on L, less than 5 mins walk.* Home-made teas. **Adm £3, chd free.** Sun 21 Aug (11-5).
1¼ acres on gravelly soil. Part glorious views across croquet lawn over Newtown Creek and Solent leading to wild flower meadow, woodland walk and hidden water lily pond. Part walled garden protected from westerlies, with mixed borders, leading to terraced sunken garden with ornamental pool and pavilion, planted with exotics, tender shrubs and herbaceous perennials.
♿ 🏡 ❀ ☕

4 NEW DOG KENNEL COTTAGE
Broad Lane, Thorley, Yarmouth PO41 0UH. Malcolm & Helen Peplow. *2m SE of Yarmouth. On B3401. Turn R at Thorley Xrds 100yds before Thorley Church into Broad Lane. 8m W of Newport on B3401 via Calbourne, Newbridge and Wellow to Thorley. Turn L 100yds after Thorley Church, and proceed 800yds up Broad Lane.* Home-made teas. **Adm £3, chd free.** Sun 12 June (11.30-5).
3-acre garden with a panoramic view of Yarmouth and the Western Solent. Featuring a gravel garden, large rockery, climbing old roses, clematis, small stream, copse and kitchen garden. Some gravel paths.
♿ 🏡 ❀ ☕

5 HADDON LAKE HOUSE
Old Park Road, St Lawrence PO38 1XR. Phillippa & Stephen Lambert, 01983 855151, www.lakehousedesign.co.uk. *2m SW of Ventnor. Turn off Undercliff Drive (A3055) into Old Park Rd and follow signs for 'IOW Glass Studio'. Garden opp IOW Glass car park. Park off rd in front of Haddon Lake House.* **Adm £5.** Visitors welcome by appt Aug evenings and Sat pm for groups of 6-20, chd 12+yrs. Guided tour only.
Newly-restored Victorian garden dating from 1820, formerly part of the Old Park estate. A site of contrasts with contemporary borders contrasting with formal walled potager. Major features are ⅓ -acre lake with gravity-fed fountain and gravelled perimeter path. Featured in Dream Gardens of England.
☎

Crab Cottage

Get involved with the NGS – volunteer your time

6 ▶ HIGHWOOD

Cranmore Avenue, Cranmore PO41 0XS. Mr & Mrs Cooper, 01983 760550. *2m E of Yarmouth on A3054. 2m from Yarmouth, turning on LH-side, opp bus shelter, unmade rd (hoping to be made up).* **Adm £3, chd free.** Snowdrops Days, by appointment only, Sat 19, Sun 20 Feb. **Visitors also welcome by appt all year for groups, max 12.**

We welcome visitors all yr to our unforgiving clay garden (boots necessary in inclement weather!). Approx 2¹/₂ acres of garden on a 10-acre S-facing slope, incl pond, borders of shrubs and perennials and oak copse full of interesting 'woodlanders'. During June, the wild flower area has orchids incl Dactylorhiza fuchsii, followed by corky water dropwort, which is well worth visiting.

✿ ☎

A real treat for plant lovers and people who appreciate relaxed, considered spaces with horticultural interest . . .

7 ▶ MEADOWSWEET

5 Great Park Cottages, off Betty-Haunt Lane, Carisbrooke PO30 4HR. Gunda Cross. *4m SW of Newport. From A3054 Newport to Yarmouth rd turn L at crossroads Porchfield-Calbourne into Betty-Haunt Lane, over bridge and into lane on R. Parking along L side on grass verge, past Meadowsweet.* Home-made teas. **Adm £3, chd free.** Sun 29 May (11-4.30).

From windswept barren 2-acre cattle field to developing tranquil country garden. Natural, mainly native, planting and wild flowers. Cottagey front garden, herb garden, orchard, fruit cage and large pond. The good life and haven for wildlife!

♿ ✿ ☕

8 ▶ ◆ MOTTISTONE MANOR GARDEN

Mottistone PO30 4ED. National Trust, 01903 714302, www.nationaltrust.org.uk. *8m SW Newport on B3399 between Brighstone & Brook.* **Adm £3.80, chd £1.90, family £9.50.** For NGS: Sun 26 June (11-5). **For other opening times and information, please phone or see garden website.**

Set in a sheltered valley, this magical garden is full of surprises with shrub-filled banks, hidden pathways and colourful herbaceous borders. Surrounding an Elizabethan manor house (not open) this C20 garden is experimenting with a Mediterranean-style planting scheme to take advantage of its southerly location.

♿ 🐕 ✿ ✇ ☕

9 ▶ NORTHCOURT GARDEN

Main Road, Shorwell PO30 3JG. Mr & Mrs J Harrison, 01983 740415, john@northcourt.info. *4m SW of Newport. On entering Shorwell from Carisbrooke, entrance on R, immed after rustic footbridge.* Home-made teas. **Adm £4.50, chd free.** Sun 28 Aug (12.30-5). **Visitors also welcome by appt, groups of 8+ welcome.**

15-acre garden surrounding large C17 Manor House (not open), incl walled kitchen garden, chalk stream, terraces, magnolias and camellias. Subtropical planting. New broadwalk along jungle garden. Very large range of plants enjoying the different microclimates. Late summer beds of dahlias, cannas, grasses and bananas. The terraces rise 80ft behind the house with collection of hydrangeas. Picturesque wooded valley around the stone manor house. Bath house and snail mount leading to terraces. 200yd chalk stream. Featured in The English Garden.

♿ 🐕 ✿ 🛏 ☕ ☎

10 ▶ NORTHERN STAR

Hunts Road, St Lawrence, Ventnor PO38 1XT. Richard & Hazel Russell. *2m W of Ventnor. From Ventnor take A3055. Follow signs for glassworks down Old Park Rd, turn R into Hunts Rd. Limited parking in Hunts Rd & Old Park Rd.* Home-made teas. **Adm £3, chd free.** Sat 18 June (11-5).

Situated in the heart of Undercliff, gardens of approx 1 acre within sylvan setting. Mixed borders with shrubs, perennials and annuals,

planted within garden rooms. Inspiration has been drawn from Christopher Lloyd's plantings. Small vegetable plot and fruit area.

✿ ☕

11 ▶ THE OLD RECTORY

Kingston Road, Kingston PO38 2JZ. Derek & Louise Ness, 01983 551701, louiseness@gmail.com, www.kingstonrectorygarden.co.uk. *8m S of Newport. Entering Shorwell from Carisbrooke, take L turn at mini r'about towards Chale (B3399). Follow rd until Kingston sign, house 2nd on L after this. Park in adjacent field.* Home-made teas. **Adm £3, chd free.** Sun 12 June (2-5). **Visitors also welcome by appt in June only for small groups.**

Constantly evolving romantic country garden. Areas of interest include the walled kitchen garden, orchard, formal and wildlife ponds and a wonderfully scented collection of old and English roses.

🐕 ✿ ☕ ☎

12 ▶ PELHAM HOUSE

Seven Sisters Road, St Lawrence, Ventnor PO38 1UY. Steve & Dee Jaggers. *1¹/₂ m W of Ventnor. A3055 Undercliff Drive from Ventnor to Niton, ¹/₂ m past Botanical Gardens, on R, Seven Sisters Rd & St Lawrence Village Hall (free parking opp), house 3rd on R.* Home-made teas at Village Hall. **Adm £3, chd free.** Sun 24 July (11-5).

1 acre hidden away in the heart of the Undercliff. Stunning sea views, access into Pelham Woods. Planted for yr-round interest with trees, shrubs, perennials and unusual palms. Fish pond and sloping lawns lead to tropical hut and swimming pool surrounded by exotic plants and tree ferns. Vegetable garden with raised beds and greenhouse. New woodland area and echium walk. Wheelchair access to most parts but some steep slopes and steps.

♿ ✿ ☕

13 ▶ ROOKLEY MANOR

Niton Road, Rookley PO38 3NR. Mr M Eastwood & Mr M von Brasch, 01983 721991, mike@aristia.co.uk. *Enter Niton Rd from Rookley village. Manor is 8th house on R.* **Adm £3.50, chd free.** Sun 19 June (11-4). **Visitors also welcome by appt.**

Beautiful, mature 1-acre garden surrounding a Georgian manor house (not open). A romantic, well maintained garden with many old roses, rare plants and trees. Features incl a pond and views to open fields. A real treat for plant lovers and people who appreciate relaxed, considered spaces with horticultural interest. Art exhibition by artist Marius von Brasch. Live music: Harp with Anna Sacchini.

14 SALTERNS COTTAGE
Salterns Road, Seaview PO34 5AH. Susan & Noël Dobbs. *Enter Seaview from W via Springvale, Salterns Rd links the Duver Rd with Bluett Ave.* Home-made teas. **Adm £3, chd free. Sun 12 June (11-5).** Salterns Cottage is a listed building from 1640. It has a small garden, full of surprises, hidden behind the low terracotta roof and whitewashed walls. Salt was made here. The film rights of Dracula (written by Noël's great grandfather) paid for the original conversion in 1934. Susan retired in 2005, and sold her kindergarten. She was able to build a beautiful greenhouse and potager and turned what was a beach into borders filled with exotic plants.

15 THE SHUTE
Seven Sisters Road, St. Lawrence, Ventnor PO38 1UZ. Mr & Mrs C Russell. *Half way along Seven Sisters Rd, opp bottom of St Lawrence Shute. Parking in Fishers Rd or Twining Rd, or nr village hall in Undercliff Drive (steep but pleasant walk).* Home-made teas. **Adm £3, chd free. Sun 14 Aug (11-4).** About ½ acre, formerly part of a large Victorian garden. Views from the terrace across the lawn and newly planted borders to the sea. In the lower area we mix herbaceous planting with fruit and vegetables. Annuals complement the dahlias, agapanthus etc for a show of late summer colour.

16 THORLEY MANOR
Yarmouth PO41 0SJ. Mr & Mrs Anthony Blest. *1m E of Yarmouth. From Bouldnor take Wilmingham Lane. House ½ m on L.* Home-made teas. **Adm £3, chd free. Sun 19 June (2.30-5).** Delightful informal gardens of over 3 acres surrounding Manor House (not open). Garden set out in a number of walled rooms incl herb garden with water feature, perennial borders, sweeping lawn and shrub borders, plus unusual island croquet lawn. Venue renowned for excellent home-made teas and the eccentric head gardener.

Gardens which surround the revamped Art Deco style house . . . full to bursting with perennials, shrubs, clematis and climbing roses . . .

17 NEW WEST MEADES
West Green, St Helens PO33 1XA. Patsy & Jack Thompson. *3m SE of Ryde. Approach village from W along Carpenters Rd (B3330). On entering village take 1st L. House borders West Green overlooking Culver Down.* Home-made teas. **Adm £3, chd free. Thur 25 Aug (11-5).** The gardens which surround the revamped Art Deco style house have been almost completely re-designed and planted during the last 7 yrs. It is full to bursting with perennials, shrubs, clematis and climbing roses which lead to an enclosed vegetable garden. The plan is to provide a

garden of surprise and delight throughout the year. Garden accessible by wheelchair but gravel paths may be bumpy.

GROUP OPENING

18 WHITWELL GARDENS GROUP
Whitwell PO38 2PP. *4m W of Ventnor. Close to villages of Godshill and Niton. Parking in Kemming Rd, Bannock Rd & Strathwell Crescent. Entry tickets available at any of the open gardens. Village map given to all visitors.* Home-made teas. **Combined adm £4, chd free. Sun 29 May (12-5).**

NEW 3 BANNOCK ROAD
Richard & Frances Moore

SAXONS
Rhys & Nicola Nigh

13 STRATHWELL CRESCENT
George & Margaret Cole

WATERDINE
David & Penny Denness

Whitwell was probably named after the white (pure) well that was visited by many on pilgrimages during medieval times. Now a well dressing and blessing occurs every summer. Six more old water stands can be seen around the village. The lovely Church of St Mary and St Radegund dates back to the C12. Many buildings date back to the C15 and The White Horse Inn claims to be the oldest inn on the Island. Whitwell has many bridleways and footpaths and is frequented by many walkers. Amongst the garden delights are water features (incl a newly constructed stream), unusual plants, highly manicured borders, natural plantings and much more. The gardens are quite close together, so moving your car will not really be necessary. Do enjoy our colourful village, many times winner of the Best Kept Village Award.

Isle of Wight County Volunteers

County Organiser
Jennie Fradgley, Ashknowle House, Ashknowle Lane, Whitwell, Ventnor, Isle of Wight PO38 2PP, 01983 730805, jenniemf805@yahoo.co.uk

Assistant County Organisers
Sukie Hillyard, Spithead House, Seaview Lane, Seaview, Isle of Wight PO34 5DG, 01983 565093
Sally Parker, Beach House, The Duver, Seaview, Isle of Wight PO34 5AJ, 01983 612495, sallyparkeriow@btinternet.com

The Old Rectory

KENT

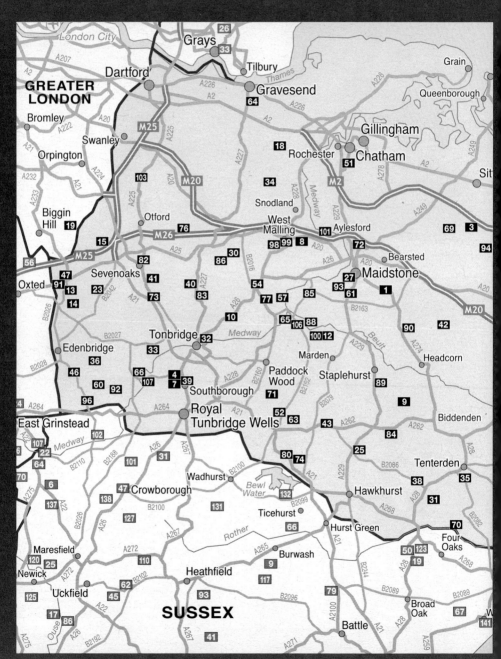

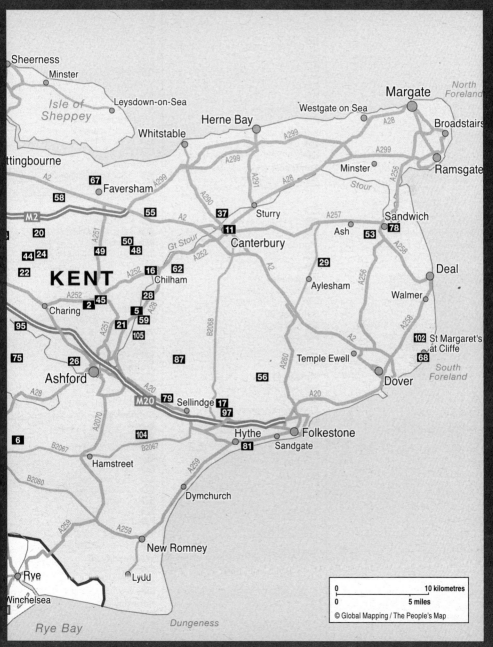

Sheerness

Minster

Isle of
Sheppey

Leysdown-on-Sea

ttingbourne

A2

67 Faversham

58

M2

20

44 **24**

22 **KENT**

A252

Charing **2** **45**

95

75

26

Ashford

A28

6

B2067

Hamstreet

B2080

A259

Rye

Winchelsea

Rye Bay

Lydd

New Romney

Dungeness

Whitstable

Herne Bay

A299

A299

A290

A2

55

A251

50
48

49

A252 **16** **62**
Chilham

A252

A251 **21**

28

5
59

105

104

B2067

Dymchurch

A259

A259

A20

M20 **79** Sellindge **17**
97

Hythe **81**

Sandgate

A20

A291

A28

A299

Westgate on Sea

A28

Minster

Stour

A257

Ash

37 Sturry

11

Canterbury

A252

A2

B2068

87

A260

29

Aylesham

Temple Ewell

56

Folkestone

Margate

North
Foreland

Broadstairs

A299

A256

Ramsgate

Sandwich

53 **78**

A258

A256

Deal

Walmer

A258

102 St Margaret's
at Cliffe

68

South
Foreland

Dover

Sandgate

| 0 | | | | 10 kilometres |
| 0 | | 5 miles | | |

© Global Mapping / The People's Map

Opening Dates

February

Sunday 6
90 Spring Platt

Sunday 13
54 Mere House

Thursday 17
10 Broadview Gardens

Sunday 20
54 Mere House
88 Southover

Wednesday 23
107 Yew Tree Cottage

Saturday 26
107 Yew Tree Cottage

Sunday 27
107 Yew Tree Cottage

March

Sunday 6
30 Great Comp Garden
90 Spring Platt

Wednesday 9
107 Yew Tree Cottage

Saturday 12
107 Yew Tree Cottage

Sunday 13
30 Great Comp Garden
91 Squerryes Court
107 Yew Tree Cottage

Sunday 20
29 Goodnestone Park Gardens
30 Great Comp Garden
92 Stonewall Park

Wednesday 23
107 Yew Tree Cottage

Saturday 26
107 Yew Tree Cottage

Sunday 27
26 Godinton House & Gardens
30 Great Comp Garden
54 Mere House
89 Spilsill Court
107 Yew Tree Cottage

Tuesday 29
78 The Secret Gardens of
Sandwich at The Salutation

April

Sunday 3
26 Godinton House & Gardens
28 Godmersham Park
37 Highlands

Tuesday 5
41 Knole

Saturday 9
107 Yew Tree Cottage

Sunday 10
29 Goodnestone Park Gardens
50 Luton House
55 Mount Ephraim
65 Parsonage Oasts
107 Yew Tree Cottage

Wednesday 13
38 Hole Park
107 Yew Tree Cottage

Friday 15
84 Sissinghurst Castle

Sunday 17
18 Cobham Hall
63 Orchard End
68 The Pines Garden
81 Sea Close

Wednesday 20
60 Old Buckhurst

Saturday 23
60 Old Buckhurst
107 Yew Tree Cottage .

Sunday 24
6 Boldshaves
22 Eagleswood
24 Frith Old Farmhouse
48 Longacre
72 11 Raymer Road
107 Yew Tree Cottage

Monday 25
48 Longacre
54 Mere House

Wednesday 27
60 Old Buckhurst
107 Yew Tree Cottage

Saturday 30
60 Old Buckhurst
74 Rogers Rough

May

Sunday 1
39 Honnington Farm
48 Longacre
70 Potmans Heath House
74 Rogers Rough
77 St Michael's Gardens

Monday 2
39 Honnington Farm
48 Longacre
74 Rogers Rough

Wild flower
meadow
surrounding the
fire pit . . . and a
pebble-dashed
Morris Minor . . . !

Tuesday 3
9 1 Brickwall Cottages
39 Honnington Farm
41 Knole

Saturday 7
9 1 Brickwall Cottages
61 Old Orchard

Sunday 8
9 1 Brickwall Cottages
45 Laurenden Forstal
60 Old Buckhurst
61 Old Orchard
92 Stonewall Park
107 Yew Tree Cottage

Tuesday 10
9 1 Brickwall Cottages
73 Riverhill Himalayan Gardens

Wednesday 11
44 Larch Cottage
66 Penshurst Place
107 Yew Tree Cottage

Saturday 14
9 1 Brickwall Cottages
60 Old Buckhurst
107 Yew Tree Cottage

Sunday 15
6 Boldshaves
9 1 Brickwall Cottages
13 Charts Edge
24 Frith Old Farmhouse
37 Highlands
48 Longacre
50 Luton House
94 Torry Hill

Tuesday 17
9 1 Brickwall Cottages

Wednesday 18
38 Hole Park
60 Old Buckhurst

Thursday 19
80 Scotney Castle

Saturday 21
79 Sandown

Sunday 22
2 Beech Court Gardens
5 Bilting House
20 Doddington Place
43 Ladham House
60 Old Buckhurst
68 The Pines Garden
77 St Michael's Gardens
79 Sandown
85 Smiths Hall
107 Yew Tree Cottage

Tuesday 24
9 1 Brickwall Cottages

Wednesday 25
52 Marle Place
88 Southover
107 Yew Tree Cottage

Saturday 28
11 Canterbury Cathedral Gardens
74 Rogers Rough

Boundes End

79 Sandown
101 Wickham Lodge
107 Yew Tree Cottage

Sunday 29
11 Canterbury Cathedral Gardens
19 Cottage Farm
33 Hall Place
48 Longacre
71 Puxted House
74 Rogers Rough
79 Sandown

Monday 30
19 Cottage Farm
48 Longacre
58 Norton Court
74 Rogers Rough
79 Sandown
106 The Yalding Gardens

Tuesday 31
9 1 Brickwall Cottages
58 Norton Court

June

Wednesday 1
19 Cottage Farm

Saturday 4
17 Churchfield
60 Old Buckhurst
97 West Court Lodge
104 Wyckhurst

Sunday 5
17 Churchfield
19 Cottage Farm
22 Eagleswood
24 Frith Old Farmhouse
57 Nettlestead Place
59 Olantigh
67 Pheasant Barn
86 Sotts Hole Cottage
95 Tram Hatch
97 West Court Lodge
98 West Malling Early June Gardens
104 Wyckhurst

Monday 6
58 Norton Court

Tuesday 7
41 Knole
58 Norton Court

Wednesday 8
19 Cottage Farm
31 Great Maytham Hall
38 Hole Park
60 Old Buckhurst
73 Riverhill Himalayan Gardens
107 Yew Tree Cottage

Saturday 11
12 Chainhurst Cottage Gardens
44 Laroh Cottage
74 Rogers Rough
79 Sandown
104 Wyckhurst
107 Yew Tree Cottage

Sunday 12
4 Bidborough Gardens
5 Bilting House
6 Boldshaves
12 Chainhurst Cottage Gardens
13 Charts Edge
19 Cottage Farm
25 Goddards Green
34 Haydown
74 Rogers Rough
77 St Michael's Gardens
79 Sandown
94 Torry Hill
99 West Malling Mid June Gardens
104 Wyckhurst
107 Yew Tree Cottage

Wednesday 15
19 Cottage Farm
60 Old Buckhurst
96 Upper Pryors (Day & Evening)

Saturday 18
60 Old Buckhurst
63 Orchard End
79 Sandown
83 Shipbourne Gardens
100 Whitehurst

Sunday 19
15 Chevening
19 Cottage Farm
28 Godmersham Park
33 Hall Place
42 Knowle Hill Farm (Evening)
45 Laurenden Forstal
62 The Orangery
63 Orchard End
70 Potmans Heath House
76 St Clere
79 Sandown

83 Shipbourne Gardens
100 Whitehurst
103 The World Garden at
Lullingstone Castle
105 Wye Gardens

Monday 20
23 Emmetts Garden
100 Whitehurst

Wednesday 22
19 Cottage Farm
52 Marle Place
100 Whitehurst
107 Yew Tree Cottage

Friday 24
26 Godinton House & Gardens

Saturday 25
67 Pheasant Barn
79 Sandown
107 Yew Tree Cottage

Sunday 26
19 Cottage Farm
20 Doddington Place
32 115 Hadlow Road
56 Mounts Court Farmhouse
82 Sevenoaks Allotments
85 Smiths Hall
89 Spilsill Court
102 Windy Ridge
107 Yew Tree Cottage

Monday 27
58 Norton Court

Tuesday 28
58 Norton Court

Wednesday 29
19 Cottage Farm

Thursday 30
49 Lords

You are always welcome at an NGS garden

July

Saturday 2
74 Rogers Rough
79 Sandown

Sunday 3
49 Lords
72 11 Raymer Road
74 Rogers Rough
79 Sandown

Tuesday 5
41 Knole

Friday 8
44 Larch Cottage

Saturday 9
79 Sandown
107 Yew Tree Cottage

Sunday 10
27 The Godlands
79 Sandown
94 Torry Hill
107 Yew Tree Cottage

Wednesday 13
14 Chartwell
52 Marle Place
60 Old Buckhurst
107 Yew Tree Cottage

Thursday 14
40 Ightham Mote

Friday 15
84 Sissinghurst Castle
95 Tram Hatch (Evening - **Must be pre-booked by 1 July**)

Saturday 16
60 Old Buckhurst
79 Sandown

Sunday 17
3 Bexon Manor
13 Charts Edge
18 Cobham Hall
56 Mounts Court Farmhouse
60 Old Buckhurst
64 58A Parrock Road
81 Sea Close
95 Tram Hatch

Thursday 21
78 The Secret Gardens of Sandwich at The Salutation

Saturday 23
1 Ashley
60 Old Buckhurst
63 Orchard End
79 Sandown
107 Yew Tree Cottage

Sunday 24
1 Ashley
3 Bexon Manor
20 Doddington Place
32 115 Hadlow Road
37 Highlands
63 Orchard End
79 Sandown
86 Sotts Hole Cottage
107 Yew Tree Cottage

Wednesday 27
107 Yew Tree Cottage

Friday 29
16 Chilham Castle (Evening)

Saturday 30
16 Chilham Castle
60 Old Buckhurst
79 Sandown

Sunday 31
60 Old Buckhurst
62 The Orangery
79 Sandown

August

Tuesday 2
41 Knole

Wednesday 3
60 Old Buckhurst

Saturday 6
47 Little Gables
60 Old Buckhurst
75 Rose Farm Studio
79 Sandown

Sunday 7
7 Boundes End
42 Knowle Hill Farm
46 Leydens
47 Little Gables
60 Old Buckhurst
68 The Pines Garden
75 Rose Farm Studio
79 Sandown

Wednesday 10
107 Yew Tree Cottage

Saturday 13
79 Sandown
107 Yew Tree Cottage

Sunday 14
2 Beech Court Gardens
79 Sandown
95 Tram Hatch
107 Yew Tree Cottage

Sunday 21
45 Laurenden Forstal

Wednesday 24
91 Squerryes Court
107 Yew Tree Cottage

Saturday 27
35 Heronden
107 Yew Tree Cottage

Can you find the tree house in the Sequoia . . . ?

Sunday 28
32 115 Hadlow Road
35 Heronden
48 Longacre
107 Yew Tree Cottage

Monday 29
48 Longacre

September

Saturday 3
60 Old Buckhurst

Sunday 4
60 Old Buckhurst

Wednesday 7
60 Old Buckhurst

Friday 9
44 Larch Cottage

Saturday 10
60 Old Buckhurst
63 Orchard End
107 Yew Tree Cottage

Sunday 11
20 Doddington Place
29 Goodnestone Park Gardens
60 Old Buckhurst
63 Orchard End
102 Windy Ridge
107 Yew Tree Cottage

Wednesday 14
107 Yew Tree Cottage

Friday 16
84 Sissinghurst Castle

Sunday 18
8 Bradbourne House and Gardens
86 Sotts Hole Cottage

Sunday 25
55 Mount Ephraim
57 Nettlestead Place

October

Sunday 2
42 Knowle Hill Farm
45 Laurenden Forstal
100 Whitehurst

Monday 3
100 Whitehurst

Tuesday 4
100 Whitehurst

Wednesday 5
100 Whitehurst

Saturday 8
78 The Secret Gardens of Sandwich at The Salutation

Sunday 9
38 Hole Park

Sunday 16
22 Eagleswood

Sunday 23
54 Mere House

Sunday 30
2 Beech Court Gardens

February 2012

Sunday 19
54 Mere House
Saturday 25
107 Yew Tree Cottage
Sunday 26
107 Yew Tree Cottage
Wednesday 29
107 Yew Tree Cottage

Gardens open to the public

2 Beech Court Gardens
10 Broadview Gardens
13 Charts Edge
14 Chartwell
16 Chilham Castle
18 Cobham Hall
20 Doddington Place
23 Emmetts Garden
26 Godinton House & Gardens
29 Goodnestone Park Gardens
30 Great Comp Garden
36 Hever Castle & Gardens
38 Hole Park
40 Ightham Mote
41 Knole
52 Marle Place
55 Mount Ephraim
60 Old Buckhurst
66 Penshurst Place
68 The Pines Garden
73 Riverhill Himalayan Gardens
78 The Secret Gardens of Sandwich at The Salutation
80 Scotney Castle
84 Sissinghurst Castle
91 Squerryes Court
103 The World Garden at Lullingstone Castle
106 The Yalding Gardens

By appointment only

21 Downs Court
51 190 Maidstone Road
53 Marshborough Farmhouse
69 Placketts Hole
87 South Hill Farm
93 Timbers

Also open by Appointment ☎

1 Ashley
5 Bilting House
0 Boundes End
7 Boundes End
9 1 Brickwall Cottages
12 1 & 3 Chainhurst Cottages, Chainhurst Cottage Gardens
19 Cottage Farm
22 Eagleswood

24 Frith Old Farmhouse
25 Goddards Green
27 The Godlands
32 115 Hadlow Road
34 Haydown
39 Honnington Farm
42 Knowle Hill Farm
44 Larch Cottage
48 Longacre
49 Lords
50 Luton House
54 Mere House
56 Mounts Court Farmhouse
58 Norton Court
61 Old Orchard
62 The Orangery
63 Orchard End
65 Parsonage Oasts
67 Pheasant Barn
71 Puxted House
74 Rogers Rough
79 Sandown
81 Sea Close
88 Southover
90 Spring Platt
94 Torry Hill
104 Wyckhurst
107 Yew Tree Cottage

The Gardens

1 **ASHLEY**
White Horse Lane, Otham, Maidstone ME15 8RQ. Susan & Roger Chartier, 01622 861333, susanchartier@hotmail.com. *4m SE of Maidstone. From A20 or A274 follow signs for Otham or Stoneacre, garden located between White Horse PH and Simmonds Lane.* **Adm £2.50, chd free (share to Kent Autistic Trust). Sat 23, Sun 24 July (2-5).** Visitors also welcome by appt. Front garden developed into a parterre, leading to surprisingly large rear garden with many unusual perennials. Pond with bridge, kitchen garden. New dry garden and collection of over 50 pelargoniums. Small garden railway layout.
  ❀ 🐾 ❀ ☎

BARNARDS FARM
See Essex.

BATEMAN'S
See Sussex.

2 ♦ **BEECH COURT GARDENS**
Canterbury Road, Challock, nr Ashford TN25 4DJ. Mr & Mrs Vyvyan Harmsworth, 01233 740735, www.beechcourtgardens.co.uk. *5m N of Ashford, Faversham 6m,*

Canterbury 9m. W of Xrds A251/A252, off the Lees. **Adm £5, chd £1. For NGS: Suns 22 May; 14 Aug; 30 Oct (10.30-5). For other opening times and information, please phone or see garden website.**
Informal woodland garden surrounding medieval farmhouse (not open). Spring bulbs, rhododendrons, azaleas and viburnums give superb spring colour; climbing roses, summer borders and hydrangeas follow; fine collection of trees incl acers give autumn colour. Extensive lawns, meandering paths and surprising vistas. Picnic area.
  ♿ ❀ ☕

3 **BEXON MANOR**
Hawks Hill Lane, Bredgar ME9 8HE. Mr & Mrs Robert Reeves. *3m S of Sittingbourne. B2163 at Bredgar, turn into Bexon Lane at church. Approx 1m turn R into Hawks Hill Lane.* Home-made & cream teas. **Adm £3, chd free (share to Guide Dogs). Suns 17, 24 July (1.30-5).**
2-acre garden. Formal ornamental walled kitchen garden planted in boxed squares with organic vegetables, herbs and flowers, plus a water feature. Several individual, well-stocked small gardens incl iris beds, magnolias and camellias surround picturesque house (not open). Mature trees fringe a spacious lawn edged by beds of roses, lavender and unusual annuals grown by owner. 5-acre woodland walk. Paths slippery when wet.
  ♿ 🐾 ❀ ☕

Pond with bridge, kitchen garden. New dry garden and collection of over 50 pelargoniums. Small garden railway layout . . .

Boldshaves

GROUP OPENING

4▶ BIDBOROUGH GARDENS
Bidborough, Tunbridge Wells
TN4 0XB. *3m N of Tunbridge Wells,
between Tonbridge and Tunbridge
Wells W off A26. Take B2176
Bidborough Ridge signed to
Penshurst. Take 1st L into Darnley
Drive, then 1st R into St Lawrence
Ave.* Home-made teas. **Combined
adm £3, chd free (share to Hospice
in the Weald). Sun 12 June (11-5).**

BOUNDES END
2 St Lawrence Avenue. Carole &
Mike Marks
(See separate entry)

1 ST LAWRENCE AVENUE
Mr & Mrs C Mauduit

The Bidborough gardens are situated
in a small village at the heart of which
are the Hare & Hounds PH (book in
advance for lunch), St Lawrence
Church and village store and primary
school. It is a thriving community with
many well-supported clubs, incl a
very active Garden Association! There
is a recreation ground where cricket
and stoolball matches are regularly
played, a bowling green, tennis court
and children's play area. In the
surrounding countryside there are
several local walks. The 2 gardens are
owner-designed and very different,
reflecting personal taste, ideas and
uses. Enjoy a variety of formal and
informal features incl a pebble bed,
terraces and pergolas as well as a
selection of unusual herbaceous and
tropical plants. Boundes End featured
in Amateur Gardening, Kent Life and
Kent & Sussex Courier. Some
wheelchair access.

  ⏶ 🐾 ❀ ☕

5▶ BILTING HOUSE
nr Ashford TN25 4HA. Mr John
Erle-Drax, 01233 812253,
jdrax@marlboroughfineart.com.
*5m NE of Ashford. A28, 9m from
Canterbury. Wye 1½ m.* **Adm £3.50,
chd free. Suns 22 May; 12 June
(1.30-5.30). Visitors also welcome
by appt.**
6-acre garden with ha-ha set in
beautiful part of Stour Valley. Wide
variety of rhododendrons, azaleas
and ornamental shrubs. Woodland
walk with spring bulbs. Mature
arboretum with new planting of
specimen trees. Rose garden and
herbaceous borders. Conservatory.

  ⏶ ❀ ☕ ☎

6▶ BOLDSHAVES
Woodchurch, nr Ashford
TN26 3RA. Mr & Mrs Peregrine
Massey, 01233 860302,
masseypd@hotmail.co.uk. *Between
Woodchurch & High Halden. From
A28 towards Ashford, turn R at village
green in High Halden. 2nd R,
Redbrook St, towards Woodchurch,
before R on unmarked lane. After
½ m R through brick entrance. Ignore
oast house on L, follow signs to car
park.* Home-made teas & light
refreshments in C18 barn. **Adm £5,
chd free (share to Kent Minds).
Suns 24 Apr; 15 May (2-6); Sun
12 June (2-8). Visitors also
welcome by appt for groups of 8+.**
7-acre garden with a number of new
features being developed. Partly
terraced, S-facing, with ornamental
trees and shrubs, walled garden,
Italian Garden, Diamond Jubilee
Garden in making for 2012,
herbaceous borders (including flame
bed and red borders), bluebell walks,
woodland and ponds. Featured in
GGG & Kent Life. Grass paths.

  ⏶ ❀ 🛏 ☕ ☎

7▶ BOUNDES END
2 St Lawrence Avenue,
Bidborough, Tunbridge Wells
TN4 0XB. Carole & Mike Marks,
01892 542233,
carole.marks@btinternet.com,
www.boundesendgarden.co.uk.
*Between Tonbridge and Tunbridge
Wells off A26. Take B2176
Bidborough Ridge signed to
Penshurst. Take 1st L into Darnley
Drive, then 1st R into St Lawrence
Ave.* Home-made teas. **Adm £2.50,
chd free (share to Hospice in the
Weald). Sun 7 Aug (11-5). Also
open 12 June with Bidborough
Gardens. Visitors also welcome by**

appt, afternoon or evening visits in July & Aug for groups of up to 20.
Garden, designed by owners, on an unusually-shaped ¹/₃ -acre plot formed from 2 triangles of land. Front garden features raised beds, and the main garden divided into a formal area with terrace, pebble bed and 2 pergolas, an informal area in a woodland setting with interesting features and specimen trees. Plenty of places to sit and enjoy the garden. Featured in Amateur Gardening, Kent Life and Kent & Sussex Courier. Some uneven ground in lower garden.

The geums which make up the National Collection occur throughout the garden . . .

8 BRADBOURNE HOUSE AND GARDENS
New Road, East Malling ME19 6DZ. East Malling Trust, www.bradbournehousekent.co.uk. *4m NW of Maidstone. Entrance is E of New Rd, which runs from Larkfield on A20 S to E Malling.* Home-made teas. **Adm £3.50, chd free. Sun 18 Sept (2-5).**
Demonstration fruit plantings within a walled former kitchen garden. Apple and pear trees pruned into 25 different forms incl pyramid, goblet, le bateau, fan, arch, arcure, espalier, table, vase etc. Examples of 47 varieties of apple, 28 varieties of pear and individuals of medlar, nectarine, peach and fig. Staff on hand for questions. Viewing of Bradbourne House, scientific exhibits, plant and produce sales, children's quiz, music and refreshments.

9 1 BRICKWALL COTTAGES
Frittenden, Cranbrook TN17 2DH. Mrs Sue Martin, 01580 852425, sue.martin@talktalk.net, www.geumcollection.co.uk. *6m NW of Tenterden. E of A229 between Cranbrook & Staplehurst & W of A274 between Biddenden & Headcorn. Park in village & walk along footpath opp school.* Cream Teas. **Adm £3,**

chd free. Tue 3 May (11-4), Sat 7, Sun 8 May (2-5.30), Tue 10 May (11-4), Sat 14, Sun 15 May (2-5.45), Tues 17, 24, 31 May (11-4). Visitors also welcome by appt.**
Small cottage garden intensively planted with mixed borders containing a wide range of hardy perennials, trees and shrubs. More formal structures incl box hedges, pergolas with climbing plants, pleached limes and a small pond, contrast with this exuberant planting. The geums which make up the National Collection occur throughout the garden.

10 ◆ BROADVIEW GARDENS
Hadlow College, Hadlow TN11 0AL, www.broadviewgardens.co.uk. *4m NE of Tonbridge. On A26 9m SW of Maidstone.* Entry to the gardens free but guided tours at 11am & 2pm £3 per person. For NGS: Thur 17 Feb (10-5). For other opening times and information, please see garden website.
10 acres of ornamental planting in attractive landscape setting; 100m double mixed border, island beds with mixed plantings, lakes and water gardens; series of demonstration gardens incl Italian, oriental and Sutton's vegetable garden. National Collections of *Anemone japonica* and hellebores. Tour & exhibition of National Collection of hellebores.

GROUP OPENING

11 CANTERBURY CATHEDRAL GARDENS
Canterbury CT1 2EP, www.canterbury-cathedral.org. *Canterbury Cathedral Precincts. Enter Precincts by main Christchurch gate.* **No access for cars: please use park & ride and public car parks.** Gardens will be signed within Precincts. Light Refreshments & home-made teas at 15 The Precincts. **Saturday: Combined Cathedral & NGS gardens ticket £13,** concessions £12. Precinct pass holders £5, chd free. Sunday: NGS gardens ticket £5, chd free. Sat 28 May (11-5.00), Sun 29 May (2-5.30).

ARCHDEACONRY 29 THE PRECINCTS
The Archdeacon, Sheila Watson

THE DEANERY
The Dean

15 THE PRECINCTS
Canon & Mrs E Condry

19 THE PRECINCTS
Canon Irvine

22 THE PRECINCTS
Canon Clare Edwards

A unique opportunity to visit five Canonical gardens, all within the historic Precincts of magnificent Canterbury Cathedral. Enjoy the large Deanery garden with its 'wild area', small orchard, unusual medlar tree, herbaceous and vegetable borders. The Archdeaconry includes the ancient mulberry tree, contrasting traditional and modern planting. The three further Precinct gardens, varied in style, offer sweeping herbaceous banks, delightful enclosed spaces, or areas planted to attract birds and insects. Step back in time amongst the monastic dormitory ruins and see the herb garden, which reflects the monastic use of herbs for medicinal purposes in the Middle Ages. The walled Memorial garden has wonderful wisteria, formal roses, mixed borders and the stone war memorial at its centre.

GROUP OPENING

12 CHAINHURST COTTAGE GARDENS
Chainhurst, Marden TN12 9SU. *6m S of Maidstone, 3m N of Marden. From Marden proceed along Pattenden Lane; at T-junction turn L, follow signs to Chainhurst. In Chainhurst take 2nd turning on L. From Maidstone take A229. At Stile Bridge Inn fork R, then 1st R until NGS signs appear.* Home-made teas. **Combined adm £4.50, chd free. Sat 11, Sun 12 June (2-5.30).**

1 CHAINHURST COTTAGES
Audrey & John Beeching
Visitors also welcome by appt June only.
01622 820654
audrey1945@aol.com

3 CHAINHURST COTTAGES
Heather & Richard Scott
Visitors also welcome by appt June only.
01622 820483
heatherscott@waitrose.com

Two cottage gardens open in this peaceful rural hamlet surrounded by arable farmland. The informal cottage garden at 1 Chainhurst Cottages leads from the front gravel area with mixed grasses and water feature alongside a blue, white and yellow border to the meadow enclosed by a hedge of native species. At the rear, the garden opens to a terrace, mixed borders, lily pond, vegetable beds and flowers for cutting. Featured in 'Country Living', the garden of the Kent peg-tiled cottage at No.3 has a small herb garden at the front, edged with clipped box, with side steps leading down to borders with silver and burgundy planting. The rear garden provides a profusion of scent and colour with a rose garden and rose and wisteria covered pergola. And don't forget the potting shed! Over the garden wall are wonderful views of surrounding farmland.

& ⊛ ☕

Springs rising in this garden from the source of the East Stour. Two large areas are home to wildfowl and fish . . .

THE CHALET
See Surrey.

13 ◆ **CHARTS EDGE**
Westerham TN16 1PL. Mr & Mrs J Bigwood, 07833 385169, www.chartsedgegardens.co.uk. ½ m S of Westerham, 4m N of Edenbridge. On B2026 towards Chartwell. **Adm £4, chd free. For NGS: Suns 15 May; 12 June; 17 July (2-5).** For other opening times and information, please phone or see garden website.
8-acre hillside garden being updated by present owners. Large collection of rhododendrons, azaleas and magnolias; among specimen trees, 2 copper beech recorded as the tallest in UK. Majority of plants labelled, rock garden, water gardens, rainbow borders and rill. Fine views over N Downs. New for 2011: the origin of plants from around the world. Charts Edge honey from our own hives.

& 🦮 ⊛ ☕

14 ◆ **CHARTWELL**
nr Westerham TN16 1PS. National Trust, 01732 868381, www.nationaltrust.org.uk. 4m N of Edenbridge. 2m S of Westerham. Fork L off B2026 after 1½ m. Light Refreshments. **Adm £6, chd £3. For NGS: Wed 13 July (11-5).** For other opening times and information, please phone or see garden website.
Informal gardens on hillside with glorious views over Weald of Kent. Water garden and lakes together with red-brick wall built by Sir Winston Churchill, former owner of Chartwell. Avenue of golden roses runs down the centre of a productive kitchen garden. Chat to our NGS Careership-trained gardeners, Giles, Matt and Jamie. Some steep slopes.

& 🦮 ⊛ ☕

CHAUFFEUR'S FLAT
See Surrey.

15 ◆ **CHEVENING**
Chevening, nr Sevenoaks TN14 6HG. The Board of Trustees of the Chevening Estate, www.cheveninghouse.com. 4m NW of Sevenoaks. Turn N off A25 at Sundridge T-lights on to B2211; at Chevening Xrds 1½ m turn L. Home-made teas. **Adm £4, chd £1. Sun 19 June (2-5).**
27 acres with lawns and woodland garden, lake, maze, formal rides, parterre. Gentle slopes, gravel paths.

& ⊛ ☕

16 ◆ **CHILHAM CASTLE**
Chilham CT4 8DB. Mr & Mrs Wheeler, 01227 733100, www.chilham-castle.co.uk. 6m SW of Canterbury. Follow signs for car park through main gates of Chilham Square. Pimm's on 29 July, Teas on 30 July. **Adm £4, chd free. For NGS: Evening Opening Fri 29 July (5.30-8.30). Sat 30 July (2.30-5.30).** For other opening times and information, please phone or see garden website.
The garden surrounds Jacobean house 1616 (not open). C17 terraces with herbaceous borders comprehensively restored by Mary Keen and Pip Morrison 2003-4. Topiary frames the magnificent views with lake walk below. Extensive kitchen and cutting garden beyond spring bulb filled Quiet Garden. Established trees and ha-ha lead onto park.

🦮 ⊛ ☕

17 NEW **CHURCHFIELD**
Pilgrims Way, Postling, Hythe CT21 4EY. Mr & Mrs C Clark. 2m NW of Hythe. From M20 J11 turn S onto A20. 1st L after ½ m on bend take rd signed Lyminge. 1st L into Postling. Home-made & cream teas in village hall. **Combined adm with adjacent garden West Court Lodge £5, chd free. Single garden entry £3, chd free. Sat 4, Sun 5 June (1-5).**
Springs rising in this garden from the source of the East Stour. Two large areas are home to wildfowl and fish and have been naturally planted. The rest of the 5-acre garden is a Kent cobnut platt and vegetable garden, large grass areas and naturally planted borders. Village church open. Areas around water may be slippery. Children must be carefully supervised.

🦮 ⊛ ☕

18 ◆ **COBHAM HALL**
Cobham DA12 3BL. Mr D Standen (Bursar), bracej@cobhamhall.com, www.cobhamhall.com. 5m W of Rochester. 8m E of M25 J2. Take A2 to exit signed Cobham, Shorne, Higham. Disregard Sat Nav directions to Lodge Lane; entrance to Cobham Hall on Brewers Rd 100m S of A2. **Adm £5.50, chd free. For NGS: Suns 17 Apr; 17 July (2-5).** For other opening times and information, please email or see garden website.
c1584 brick mansion and gardens of historical importance, now a boarding and day school for girls. Herbaceous borders, formal parterres, C17 garden walls, yew hedges and lime avenue. Humphry Repton design parkland, veteran trees with many wild flowers. Organic woodland areas returned to glades with parkland vistas.

🦮 ⊛ ☕

COLUMCILLE
See London.

19 **COTTAGE FARM**
Cacketts Lane, Cudham TN14 7QG. Phil Baxter, 01959 532 506, cottagefarmturkeys@googlemail.com, www.cottagefarmgardens.com. 5m NW of Sevenoaks, 4m SW of Orpington. Sign for Cudham from Green-Street-Green r'about on A21. 3m into village, turn L past garage. 2nd block cottages on R. Entrance through working farmyard. Cream Teas. **Sun 19 June opening followed at 5pm by BBQ, extra £5.50, chd £3. Adm £4.50, chd free (share to**

Harris Hospiscare). Sun 29, Mon 30 May; Weds, Suns 1, 5, 8, 12, 15, 19, 22, 26, 29 June (1.30-5). Visitors also welcome by appt May to July, coaches permitted.

Cottage garden. No lawns! Intimate and individual style. Approx 1 acre. Self-sufficient vegetable and fruit gardens, with raised beds growing vegetables for exhibition. Tropical garden, cut flower garden, fernery, greenhouses with tender and tropical fruits and flowers; rose-covered pergolas and wildlife ponds. Created and maintained by owner.

20 ◆ DODDINGTON PLACE
nr Sittingbourne ME9 0BB. Mr & Mrs Richard Oldfield, 01795 886385, www.doddingtonplacegardens.co. uk. *6m SE of Sittingbourne. From A20 turn N opp Lenham or from A2 turn S at Teynham or Ospringe (Faversham), all 4m.* **Adm £5, chd £1. For NGS: Suns 22 May; 26 June; 24 July; 11 Sept (2-5). For other opening times and information, please phone or see garden website.**

10-acre garden, landscaped with wide views; trees and clipped yew hedges; woodland garden with azaleas and rhododendrons; Edwardian rock garden recently renovated (not wheelchair accessible); formal garden with mixed borders. Gothic folly. Falconry display 3pm on open days.

BRAEKENAS
See Surrey.

21 DOWNS COURT
Church Lane, Boughton Aluph, Ashford TN25 4EU. Mr & Mrs Bay Green, 07984 558945, bay@baygee.com. *4m N of Ashford. From A28 Ashford or Canterbury, after Wye Xrds take next turn W to Boughton Aluph Church. Fork R at pillar box, garden next drive on R.* **Adm £4. Visitors welcome by appt at any time for any number. Coaches can park in field on firm ground.**

Three-acre downland garden on alkaline soil with fine trees, mature yew and box hedges, mixed borders with many unusual plants. Shrub roses and rose arch pathway, small parterre. Sweeping lawns and lovely views over surrounding countryside.

22 EAGLESWOOD
Slade Road, Warren Street, Lenham, Maidstone ME17 2EG. Mike & Edith Darvill, 01622 858702, mike-eagles@supanet.com. *Going E on A20 nr Lenham, L into Hubbards Hill for approx 1m then 2nd L into Slade Rd. Garden 150yds on R.* Light refreshments & home-made teas. **Adm £3.50, chd free (share to Demelza House). Suns 24 Apr; 5 June; 16 Oct (11-5). Visitors also welcome by appt.**

1½ -acre plantsman's garden situated high on N Downs, developed over the past 23yrs. Wide range of trees and shrubs (many unusual), herbaceous material and woodland plants grown to give yr-round interest including autumn colour.

23 ◆ EMMETTS GARDEN
Ide Hill TN14 6AY. National Trust, 01732 868381, www.nationaltrust.org.uk. *5m SW of Sevenoaks. 1½ m S of A25 on Sundridge-Ide Hill Rd. 1½ m N of Ide Hill off B2042.* **Adm £6.50, chd £2. For NGS: Mon 20 June (11-5). For other opening times and information, please phone or see garden website.**

5-acre hillside garden, with the highest tree top in Kent, noted for its fine collection of rare trees and flowering shrubs. The garden is particularly fine in spring, while a rose garden, rock garden and extensive planting of acers for autumn colour extend the interest throughout the season.

A riot of plants growing together as if in the wild. No neat edges or formal beds. Special interest in bulbs and woodland plants . . .

24 FRITH OLD FARMHOUSE
Frith Road, Otterden, Faversham ME13 0DD. Drs Gillian & Peter Regan, 01795 890556, peter.regan@virgin.net. *½ m off Lenham to Faversham rd. From A20 E of Lenham turn up Hubbards Hill, follow signs to Eastling. After 4m turn L signed Newnham, Doddington. From A2 in Faversham, turn S towards Brogdale and continue through Painters Forstal and Eastling. Turn R 1½ m beyond Eastling.* Home-made teas. **Adm £3.50, chd free. Suns 24 Apr; 15 May; 5 June (11-5). Visitors also welcome by appt Apr to Oct.**

A riot of plants growing together as if in the wild, developed over 30yrs, containing a very wide range of unusual plants. No neat edges or formal beds, but many interesting perennials, together with trees and shrubs chosen for yr-round appeal. Special interest in bulbs and woodland plants. Visitor comments 2010 - 'reminiscent of East Lambrook', 'more different plants than Sissinghurst'. Featured on Radio Kent.

25 GODDARDS GREEN
Angley Road, Cranbrook TN17 3LR. John & Linde Wotton, 01580 715507. *½ m SW of Cranbrook. On W of Angley Rd. at junction with High St.* Light refreshments & teas. **Adm £5, chd free. Sun 12 June (12.30-4.30). Visitors also welcome by appt.**

Garden of about 2 acres, surrounding beautiful 500yr-old clothier's hall (not open), laid out in 1920s and redesigned over past 15yrs to combine traditional and modern planting schemes. Fountain, rill and water garden, borders with bulbs, herbaceous plants, shrubs and exotics, birch grove, grass border, pond, kitchen garden and mature mixed orchard.

26 ◆ GODINTON HOUSE & GARDENS
Godinton Lane, Ashford TN23 3BP. Godinton House Preservation Trust, 01233 643854, www.godinton house gardens.co.uk. *1½ m W of Ashford. M20 J9 to Ashford. Take A20 towards Charing and Lenham, then follow brown tourist signs.* **Adm £5, chd free. For NGS: Suns 27 Mar; 3 Apr (2-5.30); Fri 24 June (11-8). For**

other opening times and information, please phone or see garden website.
13 acres complement the magnificent Jacobean house. Terraced lawns lead through herbaceous borders, rose garden and formal lily pond to intimate Italian Garden and large walled garden with delphiniums, potager, cut flowers and iris border. March/April the Wild Garden is a mass of daffodils, fritillaries, other spring flowers. June 24 NGS day during Delphinium Festival Week.

Conducted tours of the garden showing the many varieties of wild orchids . . .

27 **THE GODLANDS**
Straw Mill Hill, Tovil, Maidstone ME15 6XB. The Kent Fire & Rescue Service, 01622 692121, media.mailbox@kent.fire-uk.org, www.kent.fire-uk.org/about us. *1m S of Maidstone. From Maidstone town centre follow signs to Tovil, turn L after Woodbridge Drive up Straw Mill Hill, towards Kent Fire HQ (2nd on L).* Home-made teas. **Adm £3, chd free (share to Kent Kids, Miles of Smiles). Sun 10 July (12.30-5.30).** Visitors also welcome by appt, groups of 15+ welcome, coaches permitted.
3 acres of grounds laid out in the 1890s around an Arts and Crafts style house (not open). Substantial replanting and work over the last 5 yrs. Mature specimen trees and shrubs. Terrace, rockery and woodland paths with rock features. Gravel paths and steep grassed slopes. Woodland paths not wheelchair accessible.

28 **GODMERSHAM PARK**
Godmersham CT4 7DT. Mr John B Sunley. *5m NE of Ashford. Off A28, midway between Canterbury & Ashford.* Home-made teas. **Adm £4, chd free (share to Godmersham Church). Suns 3 Apr; 19 June (1-5).**

24 acres restored wilderness and formal gardens set around C18 mansion (not open). Topiary, rose garden, herbaceous borders and recently renovated walled kitchen garden. Superb daffodils in spring and roses in June. Historical association with Jane Austen. Also visit the Heritage Centre. Deep gravel paths in walled garden.

29 ♦ **GOODNESTONE PARK GARDENS**
Wingham CT3 1PL. Margaret, Lady FitzWalter, 01304 840107, www.goodnestoneparkgardens.co.uk. *6m SE of Canterbury. Village lies S of B2046 from A2 to Wingham. Brown tourist signs off B2046.* **Adm £5.50, chd (6-16) £1, concessions £5. For NGS: Suns 20 Mar; 10 Apr; 11 Sept (12-5). For other opening times and information, please phone or see garden website.**
10-12 acres with good trees, woodland garden, snowdrops, spring bulbs and walled garden with old-fashioned roses. Connections with Jane Austen who stayed here. 2 arboretums planted in 1984 and 2001, gravel garden. Picnics allowed.

30 ♦ **GREAT COMP GARDEN**
Comp Lane, Platt, nr Borough Green, Sevenoaks TN15 8QS. Great Comp Charitable Trust, 01732 885094, www.greatcompgarden.co.uk. *7m E of Sevenoaks. A20 at Wrotham Heath, take Seven Mile Lane, B2016; at 1st Xrds turn R; garden on L ¹/₂ m.* **Adm £5.50, chd £1, concessions £5. For NGS: Every Sun in March (11-4). For other opening times and information, please phone or see garden website.**
Skilfully designed 7-acre garden of exceptional beauty. Spacious setting of well-maintained lawns and paths lead visitors through plantsman's collection of trees, shrubs, heathers and herbaceous plants. Good autumn colour. Early C17 house (not open). Magnolias, hellebores and snowflakes (leucojum), hamamelis and winter flowering heathers are great feature in spring. A great variety of perennials in summer incl salvias, dahlias and crocosmias. Nursery featured in Mail on Sunday.

31 **GREAT MAYTHAM HALL**
Maytham Road, Rolvenden, Tenterden TN17 4NE. The Sunley Group. *3m from Tenterden. Maytham Rd off A28 at Rolvenden Church, ¹/₂ m from village on R.* **Adm £4, chd free. Wed 8 June (2-5). Also open Hole Park.**
Lutyens-designed gardens famous for having inspired Frances Hodgson Burnett to write 'The Secret Garden' (pre-Lutyens). Parkland, woodland with bluebells. Walled garden with herbaceous beds and rose pergola. Pond garden with mixed shrubbery and herbaceous borders. Interesting specimen trees. Large lawned area, rose terrace with far-reaching views.

32 **115 HADLOW ROAD**
Tonbridge TN9 1QE. Mr & Mrs Richard Esdale, 01732 353738. *1¹/₂ m N of Tonbridge stn. Take A26 from N end of High St signed Maidstone, house 1m on L in service rd.* **Adm £3, chd free. Suns 26 June; 24 July; 28 Aug (2-6). Visitors also welcome by appt.**
Almost ¹/₂ -acre unusual terraced garden with large collection of modern roses, island herbaceous border, many clematis, hardy fuchsias, heathers, grasses, hostas, phormiums, and ferns, shrub borders, alpines, annuals, kitchen garden and pond; well labelled.

33 **HALL PLACE**
Leigh TN11 8HH. The Lady Hollenden. *4m W of Tonbridge. From A21 Sevenoaks to Tonbridge, B245 to Hildenborough, then R onto B2027 through Leigh & on R.* **Adm £6, chd £2.50. Suns 29 May; 19 June (2-6).**
Large outstanding garden with 11-acre lake, lakeside walk crossing over picturesque bridges. Many rare and interesting trees and shrubs.

HARCOURT HOUSE
See London.

34 **HAYDOWN**
Great Buckland, nr Cobham DA13 0XF. Dr & Mrs I D Edeleanu, 01474 814329. *6m W of Rochester. 4m S of A2. Take turning for Cobham, at war memorial straight ahead down hill, under railway bridge to T-junction. Turn R, after 200yds take L fork, follow narrow lane for 1¹/₂ m. Entrance on L.* Light refreshments, wine &

home-made teas. **Adm £4, chd free (share to Rotary Club of Northfleet). Sun 12 June (11-5). Visitors also welcome by appt April to Aug, no coaches, groups of 12 max.**
9-acre garden on North Downs created over the past 38yrs. Formerly scrubland, it now incl woodland of indigenous and unusual trees, orchard, ponds, vineyard (wine available) and meadowland with many varieties of wild orchids. Haven for wildlife, incl badgers. Conducted tours of the garden showing the many varieties of wild orchids etc.

Goodnestone Park Gardens

35 HERONDEN
Smallhythe Road, Tenterden TN30 7LN. Peter & Vicky Costain. *From Tenterden High St, take B2082 Rye rd. Leave Tesco on L and take next R, lane marked to potato shop, Morghew. Entrance 1st R in lane.* **Home-made & cream teas. Adm £4, chd free (share to Tenterden & District Day Centre). Sat 27, Sun 28 Aug (2-5).**
Old walled garden consisting of spring, summer herbaceous and autumn borders. Centre of walled garden redesigned and prairie planted in April 2009 with mixed grasses and flowers. Remaining garden mixed shrubs incl hydrangeas. House and garden set in park. Grass paths, ramp to walled garden.

36 ◆ HEVER CASTLE & GARDENS
nr Edenbridge TN8 7NG. Broadland Properties Ltd, 01732 865224, www.hevercastle.co.uk. *3m SE of Edenbridge. Between Sevenoaks & East Grinstead off B2026. Signed from J5 & J6 of M25, A21, A264.* **For opening times and information please phone or see garden website.**
Romantic double moated castle, the childhood home of Anne Boleyn, set in 30 acres of formal and natural landscape. Topiary, Tudor herb garden, magnificent Italian gardens with classical statuary, sculpture and fountains. 38-acre lake, yew and water mazes. Walled rose garden with over 3000 roses, 110 metre-long herbaceous border. Rose Week 20-26 June, a colourful celebration of all that is in the summer garden.

37 HIGHLANDS
Hackington Close, St Stephen's, Canterbury CT2 7BB. Dr & Mrs B T Grayson. *1m N of Canterbury. At the foot of St Stephen's Hill, 200yds N of Archbishops School, on rd to Tyler Hill & Chestfield. Car parking on St Stephen's Hill Rd or Downs Rd, opp Hackington Close, or nearby side streets.* **Home-made teas. Adm £4 (April & May), £5 (July), chd free. Suns 3 Apr; 15 May (2-5); Sun 24 July (11-5).**
2-acre peaceful garden, set in S-facing bowl, with sweeps of narcissus in spring and island beds of herbaceous perennials, roses, azaleas, acers, hydrangeas, hebes and other shrubs. Many conifer and broad-leafed trees, incl plantation of ornamental trees. Two ponds, small alpine bed and hanging gardens feature.

38 ◆ HOLE PARK
Rolvenden, Cranbrook TN17 4JB. Mr & Mrs E G Barham, 01580 241344, www.holepark.com. *4m SW of Tenterden. Midway between Rolvenden & Benenden on B2086.* **Adm £6, chd 50p. For NGS: Weds 13 Apr; 18 May; 8 June; 9 Oct (11-6). Also open 8 June Great Maytham Hall. For other opening times and information, please phone or see garden website.**
First opened in 1927. 15-acre garden surrounded by parkland with beautiful views, yew hedges, large lawns and specimen trees. Walled gardens, pools and mixed borders combine with bulbs, rhododendrons and azaleas. Massed bluebells in woodland walk, standard wisterias, orchids in flower meadow and glorious autumn colours make this a garden for all seasons. Wheelchair for free hire subject to availability, may be prebooked.

Enjoy a day out – look out for a Group Opening

39 ▸ HONNINGTON FARM

Vauxhall Lane, Southborough, Tunbridge Wells TN4 0XD. Mrs Ann Tyler, 07780 800790, sianburgess@gmail.com, www.honningtonfarmgardens.co.uk. *Between Tonbridge and Tunbridge Wells. A21 to A26. Signed Honnington Equestrian Centre. Enter at Honnington and cottages.* Home-made soup and roll, light refreshments & home-made teas. **Adm £4, chd free. Sun 1, Mon 2, Tue 3 May (11-4). Visitors also welcome by appt groups of 5+.**
6-acre garden, with heavy clay soil enriched yearly and producing a wide range of habitats, incl water and bog gardens, primrose and bluebell walks. Wildlife promotion a priority. Natural swimming pool in wild flower meadow. Rose walkways, rockery, lakes and water features. Large herbaceous beds, some with New Zealand influence. Wonderful views. Sculptures exhibited by our local sculptor. Large plant sale. Featured in Kent Life Magazine. Steep slopes and gravel drives.

Home-made soup
and roll, light
refreshments &
home-made teas . . .

40 ▸ ◆ IGHTHAM MOTE

Ivy Hatch, Sevenoaks TN15 0NT. National Trust, 01732 810378, www.nationaltrust.org.uk. *6m E of Sevenoaks. Off A25, 2¹/₂ m S of Ightham. Buses from rail stns Sevenoaks or Borough Green to Ivy Hatch, ¹/₂ m walk to Ightham Mote.* **Adm £11.50, chd £5.75. For NGS: Thur 14 July (10.30-5). For other opening times and information, please phone or see garden website.**
14-acre garden and moated medieval manor c1320, first opened for NGS in 1927. North lake and woodland gardens, ornamental pond and cascade created in early C19. Orchard, enclosed, memorial, vegetable and cutting gardens all contribute to the famous sense of tranquillity. Free guided tours of garden (donations to NGS welcome). Garden team on hand for tips and advice.

41 ▸ ◆ KNOLE

Sevenoaks TN15 0RP. The Lord Sackville & The National Trust, 01732 462100, www.nationaltrust.org.uk. *¹/₂ m SE of Sevenoaks. Foot: Park entrance at S end of Sevenoaks town centre, opposite St. Nicholas's Church. Road: M25 J5 (A21). Train: Sevenoaks 1¹/₂ m.* **Adm £5, chd £2.50. For NGS: Tues 5 Apr; 3 May; 7 June; 5 July; 2 Aug (11-4). For other opening times and information, please phone or see garden website.**
Lord Sackville's private garden at Knole commands the most beautiful view of the house. An impressive display of bluebells can be seen in Apr and May. Towards the end of May and throughout June, the magnificent wisteria wall provides the most glorious and delicately scented backdrop to the garden. Wheelchair guide to garden.

42 ▸ KNOWLE HILL FARM

Ulcombe ME17 1ES. The Hon Andrew & Mrs Cairns, 01622 850240, elizabeth.cairns@btinternet.com. *7m SE of Maidstone. From M20 J8 follow A20 towards Lenham for 2m. Turn R to Ulcombe. After 1¹/₂ m, 1st L, ¹/₂ m 2nd R Windmill Hill. Past Pepper Box PH, ¹/₂ m 1st left. R at T-junction.* Wine (June), home-made teas (Aug), teas (Sept). **Adm £4, chd free. Evening Opening £4, wine, Sun 19 June (5-8). Sun 7 Aug (2-6); Sun 2 Oct (2-5). Visitors also welcome by appt May to Sept.**
1¹/₂ -acre garden created over last 25 yrs on S-facing slope of N Downs with spectacular views. Mixed borders: Mediterranean and tender plants, roses, lavenders, verbenas, salvias and grasses, which flourish on the light soil. Pool and rill enclosed in small walled garden planted mainly with white flowers. Ribbon planting around entrance. Mini vegetable and herb garden.

43 ▸ LADHAM HOUSE

Goudhurst TN17 1DB. Mr Guy Johnson. *8m E of Tunbridge Wells. On NE of village, off A262. Through village towards Cranbrook, turn L at The Chequers PH. 2nd R into Ladham Rd, main gates approx 500yds on L.* Light Refreshments & teas. **Adm £4, chd £1. Sun 22 May (2-5).**
10 acres with rolling lawns, fine specimen trees, rhododendrons, camellias, azaleas, shrubs and magnolias. Arboretum. Spectacular twin mixed borders; ha-ha; fountain and bog gardens. Fine view. Edwardian rockery, inaccessible to wheelchairs.

212 LANGLEY WAY

See London.

44 ▸ LARCH COTTAGE

Seed Road, Otterden, nr Doddington ME9 0NN. Tony & Lesley Bellew, 01795 886061, lesleybellew@yahoo.co.uk. *2¹/₂ m S of Doddington, 9m S of Sittingbourne. From A20 nr Lenham, go up Hubbards Hill, L at the Harrow and follow signs for Newnham. Go along Slade Rd, turn R at end into Seed Rd. From A2 turn off for Newnham, go L by church into Seed Rd. Go 2¹/₂ m to end of rd.* Home-made teas. **Adm £3.50, chd free. Wed 11 May; Sat 11 June; Fris 8 July; 9 Sept (12-4). Visitors also welcome by appt.**
Three-acre garden on the N Downs. Rhododendrons and woodland, colour-themed borders, knot garden, rose pergola, secret gardens, orchard walks. Plenty of seating. New landscaping continues.

45 ▸ LAURENDEN FORSTAL

Blind Lane, Challock TN25 4AU. Mrs M Cottrell, 01233 740310, 2collies@quicknet.me.uk. *6m N of Ashford. Close to junction of A251 & A252, access and signed from both. All parking in field off village hall car park behind house.* Home-made teas in medieval barn. **Adm £3, chd free. Suns 8 May; 19 June; 21 Aug; 2 Oct (2-5).**
2-acre garden with woodland and rhododendrons, around part C14 house (not open). Rose walk and yew hedging framing lawns and borders. Partly walled rose garden overlooking wildlife pond; courtyard white garden. Vegetable garden with raised beds, living willow shelter overlooking pond. A sea of bulbs and blossom in May, wonderful scented roses in June, autumn colours and magnificent berries. Rare breed chickens. Nursery selling plants, stalls selling gardenalia some open days. Featured in Kent Life & Period House.

46 LEYDENS
Hartfield Road, Edenbridge
TN8 5NH. Roger Platts,
www.rogerplatts.com. *1m S of
Edenbridge. On B2026 towards
Hartfield (use Nursery entrance & car
park).* Home-made teas. **Adm £3.50,
chd free. Sun 7 Aug (12-5). Also
open Old Buckhurst.**
Small private garden of garden
designer, nursery owner and author
who created NGS Garden at Chelsea
in 2002, winning Gold and Best in
Show, and in 2010 Gold and People's
Choice for the M&G Garden.
Constant development with wide
range of shrubs and perennials incl
late summer flowering perennial
border adjoining wild flower hay
meadow. New kitchen garden. Plants
clearly labelled and fact sheet
available.

47 LITTLE GABLES
Holcombe Close, Westerham
TN16 1HA. Peter & Elizabeth
James. *Centre of Westerham. Off E
side of London Rd A233, 200yds
from The Green. Please park in public
car park.* Home-made teas. **Adm £3,
chd free. Sat 6, Sun 7 Aug (2-5).**
¾-acre plant lover's garden
extensively planted with a wide range
of trees, shrubs, perennials etc, incl
many rare ones. Collection of climbing
and bush roses and clematis. Large
pond with fish, water lilies and bog
garden. Fruit and vegetable garden.
Large greenhouse.

48 LONGACRE
Selling ME13 9SE. Dr & Mrs G
Thomas, 01227 752254. *5m SE of
Faversham. From A2 (M2) or A251
follow signs for Selling, passing White
Lion on L. 2nd R & immed L, continue
for ¼ m. From A252 at Chilham, take
turning signed Selling at Badgers Hill
Garden Centre. L at 2nd Xrds, next R,
L & then R.* Home-made teas. **Adm
£3, chd free. Suns, Mons 24, 25,
Apr; 1, 2 May, Sun 15 May, Suns,
Mons 29, 30 May; 28, 29 Aug (2-5).
Visitors also welcome by appt Apr
to Aug, no coaches.**
Plantsman's garden with wide variety
of interesting plants, gravel garden
and vegetables in raised tubs for
cultivation from a wheelchair. We aim
to have colour and interest
throughout spring and summer using
bulbs, annuals, gravel garden and
many containers with cannas,
eucomis, *Arundo donax*, etc.

Conservatory displays range of tender
plants.

49 LORDS
Sheldwich, Faversham ME13 0NJ.
Jane Wade, 01795 536900. *4m S of
Faversham. From A2 or M2 take
A251 towards Ashford. ½ m S of
Sheldwich church find entrance lane
on R side adjacent to wood. (3½ m
N of Challock Xrds).* Light
refreshments. **Adm £4, chd free.
Thur 30 June; Sun 3 July (2-5.30).
Visitors also welcome by appt in
early July for groups of 10+.**
C18 walled garden with organic
vegetables, Mediterranean herb
terrace, rose walk and flowery mead
under fruit trees. Elsewhere old
specimen trees incl 100ft tulip tree,
yew hedges, lawns, old cherry
orchard grazed by Jacob sheep, fern
glade, ponds and woodland walk.

Depending on the
weather, those
interested in
camellias, early
trees and bulbs
may like to visit in
late March/early
April before first
opening date . . .

50 LUTON HOUSE
Selling ME13 9RQ. Sir John & Lady
Swire. *4m SE of Faversham. From A2
(M2) or A251 make for White Lion,
entrance 30yds E on same side of rd.*
**Adm £3.50, chd free. Suns 10 Apr;
15 May (2-5). Visitors also welcome
by appt, small groups of up to 20 in
spring. Please apply in writing.**
6 acres; C19 landscaped garden;
ornamental ponds; trees
underplanted with azaleas, camellias,
woodland plants. Hellebores, spring
bulbs, magnolias, cherries, daphnes,
halesias, maples, Judas trees and
cyclamen. Depending on the weather,
those interested in camellias, early
trees and bulbs may like to visit in late
Mar/early Apr before first opening
date.

51 190 MAIDSTONE ROAD
Chatham ME4 6EW. Dr M K
Douglas, 01634 842216. *1m S of
Chatham on A230.* **Adm £2, chd
free. Visitors welcome by appt.**
Informal ¼-acre garden; herbaceous
borders on either side of former tennis
court; scree garden and pool; many
snowdrops and other spring bulbs.
Doll's house (¹/₁₂ scale model of
house) may also be viewed.

52 ♦ MARLE PLACE
Marle Place Road, Brenchley, Near
Tonbridge TN12 7HS. Mr & Mrs
Gerald Williams, 01892 722304,
www.marleplace.co.uk. *8m SE of
Tonbridge. From A21 Lamberhurst
bypass, at Forstal Farm r'about follow
brown tourism signs B2162
Horsmonden direction. From A21
Kippings Cross r'about B2160 to
Matfield.R at crossroads to
Brenchley,and follow brown tourist
signs.* **Adm £5.50, chd £1. For NGS:
Weds 25 May; 22 June; 13 July
(10-5). For other opening times and
information, please phone or see
garden website.**
Victorian gazebo, plantsman's shrub
borders, walled scented garden,
Edwardian rockery, herbaceous
borders, bog and kitchen gardens.
Woodland walks, mosaic terrace,
artists' studios and gallery with
contemporary art. Autumn colour.
Restored Victorian 40ft greenhouse
with orchids.C17 listed house (not
open). Collection of interesting
chickens,. Potting shed shop with a
wide range of new and period
collectables. Our own eggs and
vegetables in season. Featured in
Gardens Illustrated. Gardening for
Wildlife Gold Award winner.

**53 NEW MARSHBOROUGH
FARMHOUSE**
Farm Lane, Marshborough,
Sandwich CT13 0PJ. David & Sarah
Ash, 01304 813679. *1½ m W of
Sandwich, ½ m S of Ash. From
Canterbury take A257 to Sandwich.
After Wingham turn R to Ash.
Through Ash, take R fork approx
200yds after War Memorial to
Woodnesborough. After 1m, sign to
Marshborough, take 1st L at white
thatched cottage on unmade rd.
Garden 100yds on L.* Refreshments
on request. **Adm £4. Visitors
welcome by appt 1 May to
30 Sept, max 20.**

Orchard End

Fascinating 2¹/₂-acre plantsman's garden, developed enthusiastically over 13yrs. Original lawns are rapidly shrinking, giving way to meandering paths around informal island beds with many unusual shrubs, trees and perennials creating yr-round colour and interest. Herbaceous border, pond, rockery, raised dry garden, vegetables and tender pot plants. WC nearby.

 ♿ ❀ ☕ ☎

54 MERE HOUSE

Mereworth ME18 5NB. Mr & Mrs Andrew Wells, andrewwells@mere-house.co.uk, www.mere-house.co.uk. *7m E of Tonbridge. From A26 turn N on to B2016 & then into Mereworth village. 3¹/₂ m S of M20/M26 J, take A20, then B2016 to Mereworth.* Home-made teas. **Adm**

£3.50, chd free. **Suns 13, 20 Feb (2-5); Sun 27 Mar; Mon 25 Apr; Sun 23 Oct (2-5.30). Sun 19 Feb 2012. Visitors also welcome by appt, groups of 15+.**
6-acre garden with C18 lake. Snowdrops, daffodils, lawns, herbaceous borders, ornamental shrubs and trees with foliage contrast and striking autumn colour. Woodland walk and major tree planting and landscaping. Park and lake walk. Featured in Country Life.

 ♿ 🏡 ❀ ☕ ☎

55 ◆ MOUNT EPHRAIM

Hernhill, Faversham ME13 9TX. Mr & Mrs E S Dawes & Mr W Dawes, 01227 751496, www.mountephraimgardens.co.uk. *3m E of Faversham. From end of M2, then A299 take slip rd 1st L to*

Hernhill, signed to gardens. **Adm £5, chd £2.50 (reduced entry for wheelchairs). For NGS: Suns 10 Apr; 25 Sept (11-5). For other opening times and information, please phone or see garden website.**
Herbaceous border; topiary; daffodils and rhododendrons; rose terraces leading to small lake. Rock garden with pools; water garden; young arboretum. Rose garden with arches and pergola planted to celebrate the Millennium. Magnificent trees. Grass maze. Superb views over fruit farms to Swale estuary.

 🏡 ❀ ☕

56 MOUNTS COURT FARMHOUSE

Acrise, nr Folkestone CT18 8LQ. Graham & Geraldine Fish, 01303 840598, graham.s.fish@btinternet.com. *6m NW of Folkestone. From A260 Folkestone to Canterbury rd, turn L at Swingfield (Densole) opp Black Horse Inn, 1¹/₂ m towards Elham & Lyminge, on N side.* Home-made teas. **Adm £3.50, chd free. Sun 26 June; Sun 17 July (2-5). Visitors also welcome by appt, coaches permitted.**
1¹/₂ acres surrounded by open farmland; variety of trees, shrubs, grasses and herbaceous plants; pond and bog garden. 20,000 gallon rainwater reservoir waters garden and keeps pond topped up; compost heats to 170° for fast turnover.

 ♿ ❀ ☕

57 NETTLESTEAD PLACE

Nettlestead ME18 5HA. Mr & Mrs Roy Tucker, www.nettlesteadplace.co.uk. *6m W/SW of Maidstone. Turn S off A26 onto B2015 then 1m on L, next to Nettlestead Church.* Home-made teas. **Adm £5, chd free. Sun 5 June (2-5.30); Sun 25 Sept (2-5).**
C13 manor house in 10-acre plantsman's garden. Large formal rose garden. Large herbaceous garden of island beds with rose and clematis walkway leading to garden of China roses. Fine collection of trees and shrubs; sunken pond garden, terraces, bamboos, glen garden, acer lawn. Young pinetum adjacent to garden. Sculptures. Wonderful open country views. Featured in Gardens Illustrated. Gravel paths. Sunken pond garden not wheelchair accessible at water level.

 ♿ 🏡 ☕

58 NEW **NORTON COURT**
Teynham, Sittingbourne ME9 9JU.
Tim & Sophia Steel, 01795 522941.
Off A2 between Teynham &
Faversham. J6 M2 onto A251
Faversham, L onto A2 direction
Sittingbourne. Through Ospringe,
over small r'about, approx 1½ m turn
L at Texaco garage into Norton Lane.
1st L into Provender Lane, then L
signed to Church for car park. Home-
made teas. **Adm £4, chd free.**
Mons, Tues 30, 31 May; 6, 7, 27,
28 June (2-6). Visitors also
welcome by appt.
10-acre garden within parkland
setting. Mature trees, topiary, wide
lawns and clipped yew hedges.
Orchard with mown paths through
wild flowers. Walled garden with
mixed borders and climbing roses.
Pine tree walk. Formal box and
lavender parterre. Tree house in the
Sequoia. Featured on Radio Kent.
Gravel paths.

59 **OLANTIGH**
Olantigh Road, Wye TN25 5EW. Mr
& Mrs J R H Loudon. *10m SW of*
Canterbury, 6m NE of Ashford. Turn
off A28 to Wye. 1m from Wye on
Olantigh rd towards Godmersham.
Adm £3, chd free. Sun 5 June (2-5).
Edwardian garden in beautiful 20-acre
setting; wide variety of trees; river
garden; rockery; shrubbery;
herbaceous border; extensive lawns;
tree sculpture and woodland walks.
This is, quite simply, a beautiful
garden. Sorry, no teas, but available in
Wye.

60 ◆ **OLD BUCKHURST**
Markbeech, nr Edenbridge
TN8 5PH. Mr & Mrs J Gladstone,
01342 850825,
www.oldbuckhurst.co.uk. *4m SE of*
Edenbridge. B2026, at Queens Arms
PH turn E to Markbeech. In approx
1½ m, 1st house on R after leaving
Markbeech. Parking in paddock if dry.
Adm £3, chd free. For NGS: Weds,
Sats 20, 23, 27, 30 Apr; Sun 8, Sat
14, Wed 18, Sun 22 May; Sats,
Weds 4, 8, 15, 18 June; Wed 13
July, Sats, Suns 16, 17, 23, 30, 31
July; Wed 3, Sat 6, Sun 7 Aug; Sat,
Sun 3, 4, Wed 7, Sat, Sun 10, 11
Sept (all dates 11-5, last entry
4.30). Also open 7 Aug Leydens.
For other opening times and
information, please phone or see
garden website.
1-acre partly-walled cottage garden
around C15 farmhouse with catslip

roof (not open). Comments from
Visitors' Book: 'perfect harmony of
vistas, contrasts and proportions.
Everything that makes an English
garden the envy of the world'. 'The
design and planting is sublime, a
garden I doubt anyone could forget'.
Mixed borders with roses, clematis,
wisteria, poppies, iris, peonies,
lavender, July/Aug a wide range of
day lilies. Parking and picnics in
paddock if dry. Groups welcome by
arrangement. WC. Featured in Garten
Idee.

61 **OLD ORCHARD**
56 Valley Drive, Loose, Maidstone
ME15 9TL. Mike & Hazel Brett,
01622 746941,
mandh.brett@tiscali.co.uk. *2½ m*
S of Maidstone. From Maidstone on
A229, turn R into Lancet Lane, 1st
L into Waldron Drive then 1st R into
Valley Drive. Garden at end of cul-de-
sac. Access also from Old Loose Hill
via footpath between bus stop and
allotments. Home-made teas. **Adm**
£2.50, chd free (share to National
Talking Newspapers & Magazines).
Sat 7, Sun 8 May (11-5). Visitors
also welcome by appt Apr to June
for groups, coaches permitted.
Secluded garden with S-facing rear
acre overlooking conservation area.
Meandering grass paths around
informal island beds containing usual
and unusual trees, shrubs and
perennials. Numerous alpines, bulbs,
dwarf irises, and dwarf shrubs in
extensive rockeries, screes, raised
beds and troughs with woodland
plants in shadier areas. Small
arboretum for foliage, form and
colour.

62 **THE ORANGERY**
Mystole, Chartham, Canterbury
CT4 7DB. Rex Stickland & Anne
Prasse, rex@mystole.fsnet.co.uk.
5m SW of Canterbury. Turn off A28
through Shalmsford Street. After
1½ m at Xrds turn R down hill. Keep
straight on, ignoring rds on L
(Pennypot Lane) & R. Ignore drive on
L signed 'Mystole House only' & at
sharp bend in 600yds turn L into
private drive signed Mystole Farm.
Home-made teas. **Adm £3, chd free**
Suns 19 June; 31 July (1-6).
Visitors also welcome by appt.
1½ -acre gardens around C18
orangery, now a house (not open).
Front gardens, established well-
stocked herbaceous border and large

walled garden with a wide variety of
shrubs and mixed borders. Splendid
views from terraces over ha-ha and
paddocks to the lovely Chartham
Downs. Water features and very
interesting collection of modern
sculptures set in natural surroundings.

Orchard with mown
paths through wild
flowers. Walled
garden with mixed
borders and
climbing roses . . .

63 **ORCHARD END**
Cock Lane, Spelmonden Road,
Horsmonden TN12 8EQ. Mr & Mrs
Hugh Nye, 01892 723118,
nye.richard@yahoo.co.uk. *8m E of*
Tunbridge Wells. From A21 going S
turn L at r'about towards
Horsmonden on B2162. After 2m turn
R into Spelmonden Rd, ½ m to top of
hill, R into Cock Lane. Garden 50yds
on R. Light refreshments & home-
made teas. **Adm £3.50, chd free.**
Sun 17 Apr (11-4); Sats, Suns 18,
19 June; 23, 24 July; 10, 11 Sept
(11-5). Visitors also welcome by
appt.
Classically English garden on
1½ -acre sloping site, landscaped
15yrs ago by owners' garden
designer son. Divided into rooms with
linking vistas. Incl hot borders,
cottage and white gardens, exotics
with pergola, raised summerhouse
overlooking lawns and drive planting.
Formal fish pond with bog garden.
Ornamental vegetable and fruit areas.
Wildlife orchard. Display and sale of
art and cards by local artists.

64 NEW **58A PARROCK ROAD**
Gravesend DA21 1QH. Mr Barry
Bowen. *200yds N of Echo Square*
r'about car park. Light refreshments &
teas. **Adm £3, chd free. Sun 17 July**
(10-5) with music from jazz trio.
Beautiful well-established town
garden, approx 120ft x 40ft,
comprising mature trees, pond and
water features. Enjoys a luscious
collection of hostas, a variety of

succulents, hanging baskets, bonsai trees, a few Mediterranean plants, with patio to lawn. All tenderly nurtured by the owner over the last 50 yrs.

✿ ☕

65 **PARSONAGE OASTS**
Hampstead Lane, Yalding ME18 6HG. Edward & Jennifer Raikes, 01622 814272. *6m SW of Maidstone. On B2162 between Yalding village & stn, turn off at Anchor PH over canal bridge, continue 100yds up lane. House and car park on L.* Home-made teas. **Adm £2.50, chd under 11 free. Sun 10 Apr (2.30-5.30).** Visitors also welcome by appt, best April early May, not suitable for coaches. ³/₄ -acre riverside garden with walls, shrubs, daffodils, spectacular magnolia. Unfenced river bank. Gravel paths and a few shallow steps.

& ☕ ☎

43 CLEVEDON ROAD
See London.

26 KENILWORTH ROAD
See London.

PENNS IN THE ROCKS
See Sussex.

66 **♦ PENSHURST PLACE**
Penshurst TN11 8DG. Viscount De L'Isle, 01892 870307, www.penshurstplace.com. *6m NW of Tunbridge Wells. SW of Tonbridge on B2176, signed from A26 N of Tunbridge Wells.* **Adm £7.80, chd £5.80. For NGS: Wed 11 May (10.30-6).** For other opening times and information, please phone or see garden website. 10 acres of garden dating back to C14; garden divided into series of rooms by over a mile of clipped yew hedge; profusion of spring bulbs: herbaceous borders; formal rose garden; famous peony border. Woodland trail. All-yr interest. Toy museum.

& ✿ ☕

PERRYHILL FARMHOUSE
See Sussex.

67 **PHEASANT BARN**
Church Road, Oare ME13 0QB. Paul & Su Vaight, 01795 591654, paul.vaight@btinternet.com. *2m NW of Faversham. Entering Oare from Faversham, turn R at Three Mariners PH towards Harty Ferry. Garden*

400yds on R, before church. Parking on roadside. **Adm £3.50, chd free. Sun 5 June, Sat 25 June (12-5).** Visitors also welcome by appt. Series of smallish gardens around award-winning, recently converted farm buildings in beautiful situation overlooking Oare Creek. Main area is nectar-rich planting in formal design with a contemporary twist inspired by local landscape. Also vegetable garden, parterre, water features, wild flower meadow and labyrinth. Kent Wildlife Trust Oare Marsh Bird Reserve within 1m. Two village inns serving lunches.

✿ ☎

Beautiful well-established town garden . . . enjoys a luscious collection of hostas . . .

68 **♦ THE PINES GARDEN**
Beach Road, St Margaret's Bay CT15 6DZ. The Bay Trust, 01304 851737, www.pinesgarden.co.uk. *4¹/₂ m NE of Dover. Approach village of St Margaret's-at-Cliffe off A258 Dover/Deal rd. Continue through village centre & down Bay Hill. Signed just before beach.* **Adm £3, chd 50p. For NGS: Suns 17 Apr; 22 May; 7 Aug (9-5).** For other opening times and information, please phone or see garden website. Adjacent to cliff walks and beach, this mature garden offers a mixture of open undulating parkland, trees, shrubs and secluded areas. Lake, waterfall, grass labyrinth, roundhouse shelter, famous Oscar Nemon statue of Winston Churchill. Sustainability trail and award-winning chalk-constructed conference & wedding venue with grass-covered roof. Museum with local history and information on Noel Coward and Ian Fleming. Tearoom.

& ✿ ☕

69 **PLACKETTS HOLE**
Bicknor, nr Sittingbourne ME9 8BA. Allison & David Wainman, 01622 884258, aj@aj-wainman.demo.co.uk. *5m S of Sittingbourne. W of B2163. Bicknor is signed from Hollingbourne Hill & from A249 at Stockbury Valley. Placketts*

Hole is midway between Bicknor & Deans Hill. Light refreshments & home-made teas. **Adm £5, chd free. Visitors welcome by appt May to end Sept.** Mature 3-acre garden in Kent Downland valley incl herbaceous borders, rose and formal herb garden, small, walled kitchen garden and informal pond intersected by walls, hedges and paths. Many unusual plants, trees and shrubs provide colour and interest from spring to autumn.

& ✿ ☕ ☎

153 PORTLAND ROAD
See London.

70 **POTMANS HEATH HOUSE**
TN30 7PU. Dr Alan & Dr Wilma Lloyd Smith. *1¹/₂ m W of Wittersham. Between Wittersham and Rolvenden, 1m from junction with B2082. 200yds E of bridge over Potmans Heath Channel.* Home-made teas. **Adm £4.50, chd free (share to Friends of the Earth). Suns 1 May; 19 June (2-6).** Large, colourful and easily explored compartmentalised country garden. Large collection of climbing roses. Specimen trees, apple and cherry orchards, part-walled vegetable garden. Adjoins open farmland (meadows) with views over Wittersham Levels which encourages a rich variety of wild birds. Spectacular blossom in spring. Public WC at Wittersham Church.

& ✿ ☕

71 **PUXTED HOUSE**
Brenchley Road, Brenchley TN12 7PB. Mr P J Oliver-Smith, 01892 722057, pjospux@aol.com. *6m SE of Tonbridge. From A21, 1m S of Pembury turn N onto B2160, turn R at Xrds in Matfield signed Brenchley. ¹/₄ m from Xrds stop at 30mph sign at village entrance.* Cream teas. **Adm £3, chd free. Sun 29 May (2-6).** Visitors also welcome by appt. 1¹/₂ acres, planted with scented and coloured foliage shrubs selected to ensure yr-long changing effects. Meandering gravel paths lead from the alpine garden via herbaceous borders and croquet lawn with its thyme terrace to formal rose garden and thereafter swing amongst oriental woodland plants and bamboos about a lily pond. Large glasshouse protects many Australasian shrubs and cacti.

& ✿ ☕ ☎

72 **11 RAYMER ROAD**
Penenden Heath, Maidstone
ME14 2JQ. Mrs Barbara Badham.
*From M20 J6 at Running Horse
r'about take Penenden Heath exit
along Sandling Lane, direction Boxley,
Bearsted. At T-lights turn into
Downsview Rd and follow signs.*
Home-made teas. **Adm £3, chd free.
Suns 24 Apr; 3 July (11-4).**
Barbara's garden has lovely views of
the N Downs. Divided into different
areas and intensely planted for
maximum use of an average-sized
plot. Cottage garden border, secret
woodland garden created under the
canopy of a strawberry tree. Organic
fruit and vegetables in raised beds
and containers, oriental themed pond,
mini orchard underplanted with wild
flowers.

73 ◆ **RIVERHILL HIMALAYAN
GARDENS**
Sevenoaks TN15 0RR. The Rogers
Family, 01732 459777,
www.riverhillgardens.co.uk. *2m S of
Sevenoaks on A225.* **Adm £6.25,
chd £3.95, concessions £5.60. For
NGS: Tue 10 May; Wed 8 June
(10.30-5). For other opening times
and information, please phone or
see garden website.**
Beautiful hillside garden, privately
owned by the Rogers family since
1840, with extensive views across the
Weald of Kent. Spectacular
rhododendrons, azaleas, fine
specimen trees and roses. Bluebell
and natural woodland walks.
Children's play area. Featured on C4
Country House Rescue. Unsuitable
for wheelchairs but users may have
free access to the tea terrace, on the
level and with views across the
garden.

74 **ROGERS ROUGH**
Chicks Lane, Kilndown, Cranbrook
TN17 2RP. Richard & Hilary Bird,
01892 890554, rb3042@gmail.com.
*10m SE of Tonbridge. From A21 2m
S of Lamberhurst turn E into
Kilndown; take 1st R down Chick's
Lane until rd divides.* Home-made
teas. **Adm £4, chd free. Sat 30 Apr;
Sun, Mon 1, 2 May, Sat, Sun, Mon
28, 29, 30 May; Sats, Suns 11,
12 June: 2, 3 July (11-5.30).
Visitors also welcome by appt May
to July, coaches welcome.**
Garden writer's 1¹⁄₂ -acre garden,
divided into many smaller gardens
containing herbaceous borders, rock

gardens, shrubs, small wood and
pond. Very wide range of plants, incl
many unusual or rare ones. Featured
in GGG.

75 **NEW** **ROSE FARM STUDIO**
Rose Farm Road, Pluckley, Ashford
TN27 0RG. Mel & Lizzi Smith. *4m W
of Ashford. 1m S of Pluckley village,
turn off Smarden rd into Rose Farm
Rd.* Cream teas & light refreshments.
**Adm £4, chd free. Sat 6, Sun 7 Aug
(12-5).**
An artist's small garden within the
grounds of our home and studio,
completely organic, built using
reclaimed materials. Incl many potted
plants, roof meadow, wild flower
meadow surrounding the fire pit,
raised vegetable beds, herbaceous
beds, polytunnel and a pebble-
dashed Morris Minor! Featured in the
Wealden Times.

76 **ST CLERE**
Kemsing, Sevenoaks TN15 6NL. Mr
& Mrs Simon & Eliza Ecclestone.
*6m NE of Sevenoaks. Take A25 from
Sevenoaks toward Maidstone; 1m
past Seal turn L signed Heaverham &
Kemsing. In Heaverham take rd to R
signed Wrotham & W Kingsdown; in
75yds straight ahead marked private
rd; 1st L & follow rd to house.* Home-
made teas. **Adm £4, chd 50p. Sun
19 June (2-5.30).**
4-acre garden, full of interest. Formal
terraces surrounding C17 mansion
(not open), with beautiful views of the
Kent countryside. Herbaceous and
shrub borders, productive kitchen and
herb gardens, lawns and rare trees.

GROUP OPENING

77 **ST MICHAEL'S GARDENS**
Roydon Hall Road, East Peckham,
East Peckham TN12 5NH. *5m NE of
Tonbridge, 5m SW of Maidstone. On
A26 at Mereworth r'about take R exit
(A228 Paddock Wood). After 1¹⁄₂ m
turn L into Roydon Hall Rd. Gardens
¹⁄₂ m up hill on L. From Paddock
Wood A228 towards West Malling.
1m after r'about with Wheelbarrow
turn R into Roydon Hall Rd.* Home-
made teas. **Combined adm £4, chd
free (share to Friends of St
Michael's Church, Roydon).
Sun 1 May (2-4), Suns 22 May;
12 June (2-5).**

ST MICHAEL'S COTTAGE
Mr Peter & Mrs Pauline Fox

ST MICHAEL'S HOUSE
Mrs W Magan

A Victorian house and cottage garden
come together to provide colour,
scent and inspiration in April, May and
June in this rural village. The year
unfolds at the grey stone old vicarage
with a lovely display of tulips in spring,
followed by irises, then a mass of
roses from red hot to old soft colours,
all complemented by yew topiary
hedges and wonderful views from the
meadow. The traditional cottage
garden, with a wildlife area, was
designed so it cannot be seen all at
once. Explore and enjoy the collection
of lavenders, hostas, clematis, ferns
and heathers. Sheep and chickens.
Meadow walk.

> An artist's small
> garden, completely
> organic, built
> with reclaimed
> materials . . . roof
> meadow . . .

78 ◆ **THE SECRET GARDENS
OF SANDWICH AT THE
SALUTATION**
Knightrider Street, Sandwich
CT13 9EW. Mr & Mrs Dominic
Parker, 01304 619919, www.the-
secretgardens.co.uk. *In the heart of
Sandwich. Turn L at Bell Hotel and
into Quayside car park. Entrance on
far R-hand corner of car park.* **Adm
£6.50, chd free. For NGS: Tue 29
Mar (10-4); Thur 21 July (10-5); Sat
8 Oct (10-4). For other opening
times and information, please
phone or see garden website.**
3¹⁄₂ acres of ornamental and formal
gardens designed by Sir Edwin
Lutyens and Gertrude Jekyll in 1911
surrounding Grade I listed house.
Designated historic park and garden,
lake, white, yellow, spring, woodland,
rose, kitchen, vegetable and
herbaceous gardens. Designed to
provide yr-round changing colour.
Traditional tearoom, gift shop.
Unusual plants for sale.

79 SANDOWN
Plain Road, Smeeth, nr Ashford TN25 6QX. Malcolm & Pamela Woodcock, 01303 813478, pmw@woodcock.mail1.co.uk. *4m SE of Ashford. Exit M20 J10 onto A20. At Smeeth Xrds turn L. At Woolpack PH turn R, past garage on L, past next L, garden on L. Park in lay-by on R up hill.* **Adm £2.50. Regret no children. Sats, Suns 21, 22, 28, 29 May, Mon 30 May; Sats, Suns 11, 12, 18, 19, 25 June; Sats, Suns 2, 3, 9, 10, 16, 23, 24, 30, 31 July; Sats, Suns 6, 7, 13, 14 Aug (1-4). Visitors also welcome by appt for groups of 10+.**
Our small and compact Japanese-style garden and Koi pond has a Japanese arbour, tea house/veranda, small waterfall and stream with places to sit and contemplate. Acers (May-June), bamboos and others, cloud trees, wisterias (June), hostas, Japanese anemone, campsis, brugmansia datura, agapanthus (July) and 'mind your own business' for ground cover. WC available. Regret no children owing to deep pond.

❀ ☎

80 ◆ SCOTNEY CASTLE
Lamberhurst TN3 8JN. National Trust, 01892 893820, www.nationaltrust.org.uk. *6m SE of Tunbridge Wells. On A21 London-Hastings, brown tourist signs. Bus: (Mon to Sat) Tunbridge Wells-Wadhurst, alight Lamberhurst Green.* **Garden only adm £9, chd £5.50. For NGS: Thur 19 May (11-4.30). For other opening times and information, please phone or see garden website.**
Victorian country house set in 'Picturesque' landscape garden, created by the Hussey family. The romantic ruins of a medieval castle and moat are the focal point of the celebrated gardens which feature spectacular displays of rhododendrons and azaleas in May.

♿ ❀ ☕

81 SEA CLOSE
Cannongate Road, Hythe CT21 5PX. Major & Mrs R H Blizard, 01303 266093. *1/2 m from Hythe. Towards Folkestone (A259), on L, signed. Cold drinks and cakes in the garden. Teas available in Hythe.* **Adm £3, chd free (share to Royal Signals Benevolent Fund). Suns 17 Apr; 17 July (2-5). Visitors also welcome by appt.**
34th year of opening. A distinguished

Arts & Crafts period house (not open) on prime site overlooking the Channel, set in a one-acre very personal garden, designed, developed and maintained by present owners over 40yrs. Kind seaboard climate allows interesting and tender plants and shrubs. Together offer unique experience. Regret not suitable for wheelchairs; very steep hill and steps to reach the top.

❀ ☕ ☎

ALLOTMENTS

82 SEVENOAKS ALLOTMENTS
Allotment Lane, off Quaker Hall Lane, Sevenoaks TN13 3TX. Sevenoaks Allotment Holders Assn, www.sevenoaksallotments.co.uk. *Quaker Hall Lane off A225, St John's Hill. Site directly behind St John's Church. Light refreshments & home-made teas.* **Adm £3, chd free. Sun 26 June (10-5).**
The Association self-manages 11½ acres of productive allotment gardens situated in the heart of the town. A wide cross-section of allotment owners grow a massive variety of flowers, fruit and vegetables using a number of different techniques. Gardeners cite healthy produce, exercise and relaxation in a beautiful open space as reasons to rent a plot. Featured on BBC Radio Kent publicity & in Sevenoaks Festival brochure. Main paths concrete with some steep slopes.

♿ 🐕 ❀ ☕

GROUP OPENING

83 NEW SHIPBOURNE GARDENS
Shipbourne, nr Tonbridge TN11 9PL. *Off A227 between Tonbridge and Borough Green. Gardens and car parking signed. See below for detailed directions to each garden. Combined group ticket and map available at each garden.* **Coffee, home-made & cream teas at the Village Hall. Combined adm £5, chd free. Sat 18, Sun 19 June (11-5).**

NEW 3 GRANGE COTTAGES
The Green. Richard & Sally Worby.
Near Village Hall

GREAT OAKS HOUSE ⌐
Puttenden Road.
Mr & Mrs M Cohen.

Turn R on leaving Plantation House (see directions below). After 200yds turn R into Claygate Lane. At end of lane, turn L for Great Oaks House

HOOKWOOD HOUSE
Puttenden Road. Mr & Mrs Nicholas Ward.
Turn R on leaving Plantation House (see directions below). After 200yds turn R into Claygate Lane. At end of lane, turn R for Hookwood House

PLANTATION HOUSE
Reeds Lane. Viv Packer & Don Williamson.
From A227 turn across Green into Upper Green Rd opp The Chaser PH. Straight on for 3/4 m, garden on R

YEW TREE COTTAGE
The Green. Susan & Ian Bowles.
Adjoining Village Hall

Shipbourne is a small picturesque village centred around one of the largest village greens in Kent which becomes a wild flower meadow in June. The village is a popular walking centre for the Greensand Way and as it is an AONB and predominantly a Conservation Area. Enjoy five different gardens, varying in size and design and reflecting the owners' interests and houses. Two are in the middle of the village green and the other three a very short car distance apart. Lunches at the two Shipbourne PHs, The Chaser (01732 810360) and The Kentish Rifleman (01732 810727). Coffee and home-made teas at the Village Hall on the Green. Studio of wildlife artist Ian Bowles open at Yew Tree Cottage. Limited wheelchair access.

♿ ☕

> Small picturesque village centred around one of the largest village greens in Kent which becomes a wild flower meadow in June . . .

84 ◆ **SISSINGHURST CASTLE**
Sissinghurst TN17 2AB. National Trust, 01580 710700, www.nationaltrust.org.uk. *16m E of Tunbridge Wells. On A262 1m E of village. Bus: Arriva Maidstone-Hastings, alight Sissinghurst 1¼ m.* **Adm £11, chd £5.50. For NGS: Fris 15 Apr; 15 July; 16 Sept (10.30-5). For other opening times and information, please phone or see garden website.** Garden created by Vita Sackville-West and Sir Harold Nicolson. Spring garden, herb garden, cottage garden, white garden, rose garden. Tudor building and tower, partly open to public. Moat. Vegetable garden and estate walks.
&. ⊛ ⊨ ☕

85 **SMITHS HALL**
Lower Road, West Farleigh ME15 0PE. Mr S Norman. *3m W of Maidstone. A26 towards Tonbridge, turn L into Teston Lane B2163. At T-junction turn R onto Lower Rd B2010. Opp Tickled Trout PH.* Light refreshments & home-made teas. **Adm £4.50, chd free (share to Dandelion Time). Suns 22 May; 26 June (11-5).** Delightful 3-acre gardens surrounding a beautiful Queen Anne House (not open). Lose yourself in this wonderful garden incl sunken water garden, iris beds, scented old fashioned rose walk, formal rose garden, peonies, magnificent herbaceous borders and specimen trees. Woodland walk, 9-acre park with huge variety of young native and American trees and meandering walk around the wild flower meadow with fine views. Sale of plants, home-made cakes, jams & chutneys.
&. 🍴 ⊛ ☕

86 **SOTTS HOLE COTTAGE**
Crouch Lane, Borough Green TN15 8QL. Mr & Mrs Jim Vinson. *7m E of Sevenoaks. Crouch Lane runs SE from A25 between Esso garage & Black Horse PH, garden at bottom of 2nd hill, approx ¾ m.* Home-made & cream teas. **Adm £4, chd free (share to Heart of Kent Hospice). Sun 5 June; Sun 24 July; Sun 18 Sept (11-6).** 6 acres of landscaped cottage garden relying entirely on the threat of visitors to motivate the owners to maintain it. We look forward to seeing you.
&. ☕

Squerryes Court

87 **SOUTH HILL FARM**
Tamley Lane, Hastingleigh TN25 5HL. Sir Charles Jessel, 01233 750325, sircjj@btinternet.com. *4½ m E of Ashford. Turn off A28 to Wye, go through village & ascend Wye Downs. In 2m turn R at Xrds marked Brabourne & South Hill, then 1st L. From Stone St (B2068) turn W opp Stelling Minnis, follow signs to Hastingleigh. Continue towards Wye & turn L at Xrds marked Brabourne & South Hill, then 1st L.* **Adm £4, incl guided tour. Visitors welcome by appt mid to end June preferred, groups of 4 to 30, coaches permitted.** 2 acres high up on N Downs, C17/18 house (not open). Old walls, ha-ha, formal water garden; old and new roses, unusual shrubs, perennials and foliage plants.
&. ☕ ☎

88 **SOUTHOVER**
Grove Lane, Hunton, Maidstone ME15 0SE. David & Anke Way, 01622 820876, anke@away2.wanadoo.co.uk. *6m S of Maidstone. Turn W from A229 to B2163. At Xrds past Coxheath turn L* down Hunton Hill, past church to school, then R into Grove Lane. Or from Yalding War Memorial follow Vicarage Rd into Hunton to school, then L into Grove Lane. Light refreshments. **Adm £3.50, chd free (share to St Mary's Church, Hunton). Sun 20 Feb; Wed 25 May (11-4). Visitors also welcome by appt. Snowdrop visitors welcome by appointment from 5 Jan.** Plant enthusiasts' 0.5ha garden in a rural setting with good countryside views. A garden of gardens which surround the C15 house. Many varied features creating diversity and contrast and providing homes for a wide range of plants incl small bulbs, extensive and diverse snowdrop collection. Also many unusual perennials. St Mary's churchyard will also be open for snowdrops on 20 Feb. Plants sometimes available. Featured in Kent Life, article on snowdrops and garden. 5th Gold Award for Wildlife Gardening from Kent Wildlife Trust.
&. ⊛ ☕ ☎

89 SPILSILL COURT

Frittenden Road, Staplehurst
TN12 0DJ. Mrs Doonie Marshall.
*8m S of Maidstone. To Staplehurst on
A229 (Maidstone to Hastings). From
S enter village, turn R immed after
garage on R & just before 30mph
sign, into Frittenden Rd; garden ½ m
on L. From N go through village to
40mph sign, immed turn L into
Frittenden Rd.* Teas in March, Cream
teas in June. **Adm £2.50, chd 50p.
Suns 27 Mar; 26 June (11-5).**
Approx 4 acres of garden, orchard
and paddock; series of gardens incl
blue, white and silver; roses; lawns;
shrubs, trees and ponds. Small
private chapel. Jacob sheep and
unusual poultry.

♿ ❖ ☕

Unusual hardy
plants, annuals
and shrubs
designed with
flower arranger's
eye . . .

90 SPRING PLATT

Boyton Court Road, Sutton Valence
ME17 3BY. Mr & Mrs John Millen,
01622 843383,
carolyn.millen1@btinternet.com.
*5m SE of Maidstone. From Maidstone
on A274 turn L into Chartway Street;
take 1st R, then straight over next
Xrds, house 1st on R. From S on
A274 turn R into Heniker Lane, bear L
into Boyton Court Road, house on L.*
Soup, bread and teas, all home-
made. **Adm £3.50, chd free. Suns 6
Feb; 6 Mar (12-4). Visitors also
welcome by appt, Feb & Mar for
individuals and groups.**
1-acre garden under development
with panoramic views over the Weald.
Raised beds with over 120 varieties of
snowdrops, borders with spring
bulbs, extensive rockeries and a
croquet lawn. Some steep slopes and
steps.

♿ ❖ ☕ ☏

91 ♦ SQUERRYES COURT

Westerham TN16 1SJ. Mrs John
Warde, www.squerryes.co.uk. *½ m
W of Westerham. Signed from A25.*
**Adm £5, chd free. For NGS: Sun
13 Mar (11.30-4); Wed 24 Aug
(11.30-4.30). For other opening
times and information, please see
garden website.**
15 acres of garden, lake and
woodland surrounding beautiful C17
manor house. Lovely throughout the
seasons from the spring bulbs to
later-flowering borders. Cenotaph
commemorating General Wolfe.
Lawns, yew hedges, ancient trees,
parterres, azaleas, roses and borders
add to the peaceful setting. House
not open for Mar 13 opening, but
tearoom and dining room open.

♿ ⚐ ❖ ☕

92 STONEWALL PARK

Chiddingstone Hoath, nr
Edenbridge TN8 7DG. The Fleming
Family. *4m SE of Edenbridge. Via
B2026. Halfway between Markbeech
& Penshurst.* Home-made teas. **Adm
£4, chd free (share to Sarah
Matheson Trust & St Mary's
Church). Suns 20 Mar; 8 May
(1.30-5).**
Romantic woodland garden in historic
setting featuring species
rhododendrons, magnolias, azaleas, a
range of interesting trees and shrubs,
wandering paths and lakes. Historic
parkland with cricket ground,
Victorian walled garden with
herbaceous borders and vegetable
garden backed by 100 yr-old espalier
pear trees. Sea of wild daffodils in
March.

⚐ ☕

93 TIMBERS

Dean Street, East Farleigh, nr
Maidstone ME15 0HS. Mrs Sue
Robinson, 01622 729568,
suerobinson.timbers@gmail.com.
*2m S of Maidstone. From Maidstone
take B2010 to East Farleigh. Opp The
Bull turn into Vicarage Lane, then L
into Forge Lane and L into Dean St.
Garden 50yds on R, park through
gates in front of house.* Home-made
teas. **Adm £3.50, chd free. Visitors
welcome by appt Apr to July for
individuals & groups, coaches
permitted, also evening visits.**
5-acre garden, well stocked with
unusual hardy plants, annuals and
shrubs designed with flower
arranger's eye. Formal areas
comprising parterre, pergola,
herbaceous, vegetables, fruit, lawns

and mature specimen trees
surrounded by 100 yr-old Kentish
cobnut plat, wild flower meadows and
woodland. Beautiful valley views and
great diversity of wildlife. Featured in
Kent Life's 25 Gardens to Visit in
Kent. Silver Award Kent Wildlife Trust.

♿ ❖ ☕ ☏

TITSEY PLACE GARDENS

See Surrey.

94 TORRY HILL

Frinsted/Milstead ME9 0SP. The
Lord & Lady Kingsdown, 01795
830258,
lady.kingsdown@btinternet.com.
*5m S of Sittingbourne. From M20 J8
take A20 (Lenham). At r'about by
Ramada Inn turn L Hollingbourne
(B2163). Turn R at Xrds at top of hill
(Ringlestone Rd). Thereafter Frinsted-
Doddington (not suitable for
coaches), then Torry Hill & NGS signs.
From M2 J5 take A249 towards
Maidstone, first L and L again
(Bredgar-Milstead), then NGS signs.*
Home-made teas. **Adm £4, chd free
(share to St Dunstan's Church
May/June, The Caldecott
Foundation July). Suns 15 May;
12 June; 10 July (2-5). Visitors also
welcome by appt Apr to Sept, max
30.**
8 acres; large lawns, specimen trees,
flowering cherries, rhododendrons,
azaleas and naturalised daffodils; the
walled gardens with lawns, shrubs,
herbaceous borders, rose garden incl
shrub roses, wild flower areas and
vegetables. Extensive views to
Medway and Thames estuaries.
Some shallow steps. No wheelchair
access to rose garden but can be
viewed from pathway.

♿ ❖ ☕ ☏

95 TRAM HATCH

Charing Heath, Ashford TN27 0BN.
Mrs P Scrivens, 01233 713373,
tramhatch@aol.com,
www.tramhatchgardens.co.uk. *10m
NW of Ashford. A20 turn towards
Charing railway stn. Continue on
Pluckley Rd over motorway, 1st R
signed Barnfield to end. Turn L, follow
lane past Barnfield, Tram Hatch on L.*
Home-made teas. **Adm £4, chd free
(share to RNLI). Suns 5 June;
17 July; 14 Aug (1.30-5.30).
Evening Opening Fri 15 July
(7-10.30). Adm £12 (regret no
children) with Hog Roast & wine.
Must be pre-booked by 1 July.**
C14 manor house with tithe barn (not
open) set in 3 acres of formal garden

with the Great River Stour edging its boundary. Large vegetable and fruit garden, orchard, rose garden, gravel garden and 2 large ponds. Large variety of plants and trees, some unusual. Organic methods used where possible.

96 UPPER PRYORS
Butterwell Hill, Cowden TN8 7HB. Mr & Mrs S G Smith. *4¹/₂ m SE of Edenbridge. From B2026 Edenbridge-Hartfield, turn R at Cowden Xrds & take 1st drive on R.* Home-made teas. **Adm £4, chd free. Wed 15 June, open Day (1-6pm, £4) & Evening (6-9pm £5 with wine).**
10 acres of country garden surrounding C16 house with herbaceous colour, magnificent lawns, water gardens and wooded/field areas.

97 WEST COURT LODGE
Postling Court, The Street, Postling, nr Hythe CT21 4EX. Mr & Mrs John Pattrick. *2m NW of Hythe. From M20 J11 turn S onto A20. Immed 1st L. After ¹/₂ m on bend take rd signed Lyminge. 1st L into Postling.* Home-made & cream teas. **Combined adm with adjacent garden Churchfield £5, chd free. Single garden entry £3, chd free. Sat 4, Sun 5 June (1-5).**
S-facing 1-acre walled garden at the foot of the N Downs, designed in 2 parts: main lawn with sunny borders and romantic woodland garden planted with woodland plants and bulbs, mostly flowering in spring. C11 Postling Church open next door.

GROUP OPENING

98 WEST MALLING EARLY JUNE GARDENS
West Malling ME19 6NE. *On A20, nr J4 of M20 and near A26. Free car parking opposite Bull PH on Town Hill or behind Tesco in High St. Railway stn has parking charges. Tickets and map available at each open garden.* Light lunches & home-made teas at Diome House from 12 to 5.30pm. **Combined adm £5, chd free (share to St Mary's Church, West Malling). Sun 5 June (12-6).**
West Malling is an attractive small market town with some fine buildings and 7 gardens to enjoy. Abbey

Brewery House, Swan Street: railed corner garden with climbing roses and box hedging. Courtyard garden with water feature. Astwell, 254 London Road: nature-friendly garden incl 10 terraces leading down to a tranquil spot by Leybourne Stream. Bantams, pond, tree stump Hobbit House. Belmont, 104 High Street: courtyard garden with pond and shady seating with alpine planting in rockery around pond. Brome House, 148 High Street: lawns, trees and mainly colour-themed herbaceous borders. Ornamental vegetable garden incl fruit arch. Gundulfs Meadow, 181 Offham Road: charming country garden with colourful borders, shady deep pond, 2 nut plats and extensive cutting garden. Lucknow, 119 High Street: small walled garden, pretty borders and wall planting. Town Hill Cottage, 58 Town Hill: long part-walled garden with winding path, many interesting plants. See NGS website for longer descriptions of gardens. For further information please phone 01732 521268/07525 365459 or see NGS website.

GROUP OPENING

99 NEW WEST MALLING MID JUNE GARDENS
West Malling ME19 6LW. *On A20, nr J4 of M20. Park in West Malling for Little Went & Went House. Follow directions to New Barns Cottages. Maps and combined ticket at each garden.* Home-made teas at New Barns Cottages. **Combined adm £5, chd free. Sun 12 June (12-6).**

LITTLE WENT
106 High Street. Anne Baring. *In middle of West Malling, opp car park*

NEW NEW BARNS COTTAGES
Lavenders Road. Mr & Mrs Anthony Drake. *From West Malling High St, past shops, 1st L after car park into Water Lane. To far end, then R up Lavenders Rd. At top bear L over bypass, garden on L after sharp R bend*

NEW WENT HOUSE
83 Swan Street. Alan & Mary Gibbins. *Opp Abbey and cascade*

West Malling is an attractive small market town with some fine buildings.

Enjoy three lovely gardens that are entirely different from each other and cannot be seen from the road. In the middle of the town, Little Went's long narrow secret garden has fish ponds, an aviary with love birds, conservatory, gravel garden and parterre, lavender garden and statues, as well as an exhibition of paintings. Went House is a Queen Anne house surrounded by a secret garden with a stream, specimen trees, old roses, mixed borders, attractive large kitchen garden, fountain and parterre. Approx ¹/₂ m S of the town, New Barns Cottages, developed over 30yrs from a blank site, is a 2¹/₂ -acre garden and paddock surrounded by orchards and woodland. From the parking area, the garden is approached via a meadowed pathway leading to a romantic roomed garden explored via serpentine paths inviting surprise and discovery.

Meadowed pathway leading to a romantic roomed garden . . .

100 WHITEHURST
Chainhurst, Marden TN12 9SU. John & Lyn Mercy, www.rosalindmercy.co.uk. *6m S of Maidstone, 3m N of Marden. From Marden stn turn R into Pattenden Lane & under railway bridge; at T-junction turn L; at next fork bear R to Chainhurst, then 2nd turning on L.* Home-made teas. **Adm £4, chd £1. Sat, Sun, Mon 18, 19, 20 June, Tue 22 June; Sun 2 Oct to Wed 5 Oct incl (2-5).**
1¹/₂ acres of romantic, rather wild garden with many delightful and unexpected features. Victorian spiral staircase leads to a treetop walk; water tumbles down stone steps to a rill and on to several ponds; tunnels of yew and dogwood; walled rose garden; courtyards and lawns. Ever-popular and changing exhibition of root dwellings and miniature porcelain, also demonstrations and sales, donations to NGS.

Wyckhurst

country and sea. Island beds of shrubs and perennials (many rare). Large collection of penstemon and salvia. Wildlife pond. Gravel seating area and viewpoint. Additional ²/₃ -acre extension to garden incl shrub and kniphofia border. Small specialist nursery.

103 ◆ **THE WORLD GARDEN AT LULLINGSTONE CASTLE**
Eynsford DA4 0JA. Guy Hart Dyke, www.lullingstonecastle.co.uk. *1m from Eynsford. M25 J3, signs to Brands Hatch then Eynsford. In Eynsford turn R at church over ford bridge. Follow lane under viaduct, with Lullingstone Roman Villa on R, to private rd sign, follow signs for World Garden via Gatehouse. Also an entrance via A225 which has more parking.* **Adm £7, chd free. For NGS: Sun 19 June (11-5). For other opening times and information, please see garden website.**
Interactive world map of plants laid out as a map of the world within a walled garden. The oceans are your pathways as you navigate the world in 1 acre. You can stroll around Mt Everest, sip water from an Asian waterfall, see Ayers Rock and walk alongside the Andes whilst reading intrepid tales of plant hunters. Discover the origins of plants - you'll be amazed where they come from! Plant nursery and Lullingstone World Garden seeds for sale. Wheelchairs available upon request.

&. ⊛ ☕

104 **WYCKHURST**
Mill Road, Aldington, Ashford TN25 7AJ. Mr & Mrs Chris Older, 01233 720395, mx3p2old@waitrose.com. *4m SE of Ashford. Leave M20 at J10, on A20 travel 2m to Aldington turning; turn R at Xrds; proceed 1¹/₂ m to Aldington village hall. Turn R and immed L by Walnut Tree. Take rd down Forge Hill signed to Dymchurch, after ¹/₄ m turn R into Mill Rd.* Home-made & cream teas. **Adm £3.50, chd free. Sats, Suns 4, 5, 11, 12 June (11-7). Visitors also welcome by appt in June only.**
C16 cottage (not open). 1-acre cottage garden in romantic setting with unusual topiary; extensive views across Romney Marsh; continually developing garden. Featured in Kent Life. Some gentle slopes.

&. ☕ ☎

101 **WICKHAM LODGE**
The Quay, High Street, Aylesford ME20 7AY. Cherith & Richard Bourne, www.wickhamlodge.co.uk. *3m NW of Maidstone. Off High St on riverbank, turning into The Quay by Chequers PH. Park in village car park.* Light refreshments & cream teas served 11am to 4pm. **Adm £4, chd free. Sat 28 May (10-5).**
Every corner of this walled and terraced ¹/₂ -acre plot has been used to create 14 inspirational small gardens that could be picked up and recreated anywhere. Journey from productive kitchen gardens to formal Tudor, from Japanese to funky banana foliage. Endless surprises are here in abundance. Featured in Kent

Life, Winner Amateur Garden of the Year.

102 **WINDY RIDGE**
Victory Road, St Margarets-at-Cliffe CT15 6HF. Mr & Mrs D Ryder, 01304 853225, www.gardenplants-nursery.co.uk. *4¹/₂ m NE of Dover. From Duke of York r'about on A2 N of Dover follow A258 signed Deal. Take 3rd rd on R (Station Rd), then 3rd rd on L (Collingwood Rd). Continue onto unmade track & follow signs (approx ¹/₂ m). Telephone for map.* Home-made teas. **Adm £3, chd free. Suns 26 June; 11 Sept (2-6).**
Plantsman's garden on top of chalk hill, with extensive views over open

GROUP OPENING

105 WYE GARDENS
TN25 5BJ. *3m NE of Ashford. From A28 take turning signed Wye. From Ashford to Canterbury via Wye. Train: Wye. Collect map at the Church.* Home-made teas at Wye Church. **Combined adm £4.50, chd free. Sun 19 June (2-6).**

3 BRAMBLE CLOSE
Bramble Lane. Dr M & Mrs D Copland

CUMBERLAND COURT
Church Street. Mr & Mrs F Huntington

MISTRAL
Oxenturn Road. Dr & Mrs G Chapman

NEW YEW TREES
Scotton Street. Ian & Elizabeth Coulson

Start at the centre of this historic village to visit four unusual gardens. 3 Bramble Close is a unique experience, a very wild garden with meadow, pond and ditches, mown paths and hedges buzzing with wildlife. A water feature and unusual artefacts complement the exciting courtyard garden at Cumberland Court, once an asphalt car park now densely planted with a wide range of unusual plants and many pots. Look out for the recently added secret garden too. 250 species of botanical interest (all labelled) flourish at Mistral,

once part of an old hard tennis court, incl white and alpine gardens. Also centre stage, see a mini outdoor theatre! Opening for the first time is Yew Trees, a large traditional garden divided into 3 distinct and secluded areas with lawns, a naturalised wildlife area with a pond, mature trees and wide borders planted with shrubs, grasses and herbaceous perennials and an enclosed potager.

106 ◆ THE YALDING GARDENS
Benover Road, nr Maidstone ME18 6EX. Samantha & Paul Smith, 01622 814650, www.yaldinggardens.org. *6m SW of Maidstone, 1/2 m S of Yalding, on B2162. Buses from Maidstone & Tonbridge, railway stn 2m.* **Adm £5, chd £2.50, concessions £3.50. Family Fun Pack £12 (2 adults and up to 5 children). For NGS: Mon 30 May (9-5), guided tours at 11am and 2pm. For other opening times and information, please phone or see garden website.** Explore the history of gardening through 18 beautiful gardens set in 5 acres of Kent countryside. From the C13 apothecary's garden to a Victorian artisan's glasshouse and even a modern day vegetable plot, discover how organic gardening methods produce stunning results achieved by nurturing nature. Featured on Radio Kent.

From the C13 apothecary's garden to a Victorian artisan's glasshouse . . .

107 YEW TREE COTTAGE
Penshurst TN11 8AD. Mrs Pam Tuppen, 01892 870689. *4m SW of Tonbridge. From A26 Tonbridge to Tunbridge Wells, join B2176 Bidborough to Penshurst rd. 2m W of Bidborough, 1m before Penshurst.* Utterly unsuitable for coaches. Please phone if needing advice for directions. Light refreshments. **Adm £2, chd free. Weds, Sats & Suns: 4th week of Feb, then 2nd and 4th week of each month, Mar to Aug incl and 2nd week of Sept (all 12-5pm). Please see diary section for exact dates. Also 25, 26, 29 Feb 2012. Visitors also welcome by appt.** Small, romantic, hillside cottage garden with steep entrance. Lots of seats and secret corners, many unusual plants - hellebores, spring bulbs, old roses, many special perennials. Small pond; something to see in all seasons. Created and maintained by owner, a natural garden full of plants.

Kent County Volunteers

County Organiser
Felicity Ward, Hookwood House, Shipbourne TN11 9RJ, 01732 810525, hookwood1@yahoo.co.uk

County Treasurer
Stephen Moir, Little Worge Barn, Willingford Lane, Brightling, E Sussex TN32 5HN, 01424 838136, moirconsult@btinternet.com

Publicity
Claire Tennant-Scull, Wellington House, Oaks Road, Tenterden TN30 6RD, 01580 766694, claire.tennantscull@gmail.com

Radio
Jane Streatfeild, The Bungalow, Hoath House, Chiddingstone Hoath, Edenbridge TN8 7DB, 01342 850362,
  jane@hoath-house.freeserve.co.uk

Booklet distribution
Susan Moir, Little Worge Barn, Willingford Lane, Brightling, E Sussex TN32 5HN, 01424 838136, spmoir@btinternet.com

Assistant County Organisers
Jacqueline Anthony, 44 Cambridge Street, Tunbridge Wells TN2 4SJ, 07793 671240, jacquelineanthony7@googlemail.com
Marylyn Bacon, Ramsden Farm, Stone-cum-Ebony, Tenterden TN30 7JB, 01797 270300, streakybacon@kent.uk.net
Clare Barham, Hole Park, Rolvenden, Cranbrook TN17 4JB, 01580 241386, clarebarham@holepark.com
Virginia Latham, Stowting Hill House, Ashford TN25 6BE, 01303 862881, vjlatham@hotmail.com
Caroline Loder-Symonds, Denne Hill Farm, Womenswold, Canterbury CT4 6HD, 01227 831203, cloder_symonds@hotmail.co.uk
Ingrid Morgan Hitchcock, 6 Brookhurst Gardens, Southborough, Tunbridge Wells TN4 0NA, 01892 528341,
  ingrid@morganhitchcock.co.uk

LANCASHIRE
Merseyside & Greater Manchester

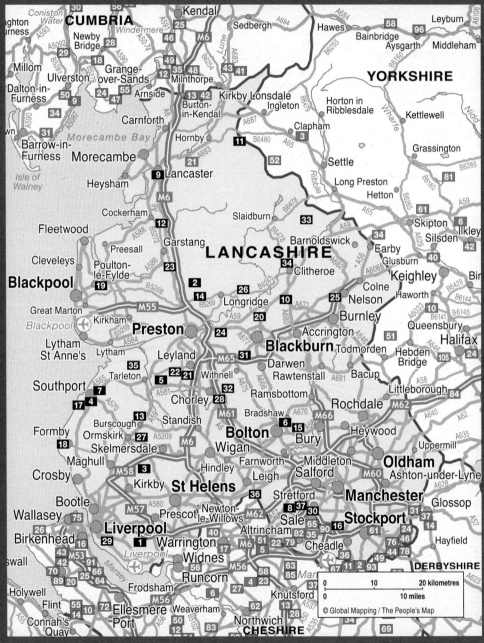

Opening Dates

February

Sunday 13
36 Weeping Ash
Sunday 20
36 Weeping Ash
Sunday 27
36 Weeping Ash

April

Saturday 9
14 Dale House Gardens
Sunday 10
14 Dale House Gardens
Sunday 17
36 Weeping Ash

May

Sunday 1
6 Bridge House
28 The Ridges
Monday 2
6 Bridge House
Sunday 15
13 Crabtree Lane Gardens
23 Little Stubbins
Monday 16
23 Little Stubbins
Saturday 28
21 Le Jardin
Sunday 29
4 Birkdale Village Gardens
5 Bretherton Gardens
11 Clearbeck House
21 Le Jardin
34 Waddow Lodge Garden
Monday 30
11 Clearbeck House

June

Saturday 4
3 Barrow Nook Gardens
25 Montford Cottage
26 New Row Cottage Gardens
Sunday 5
3 Barrow Nook Gardens
12 Clifton Hill Gardens
25 Montford Cottage
26 New Row Cottage Gardens
Saturday 11
9 Carr House Farm
24 Mill Barn
Sunday 12
9 Carr House Farm
10 Casa Lago
13 Crabtree Lane Gardens
24 Mill Barn

Sunday 19
5 Bretherton Gardens
11 Clearbeck House
16 Didsbury Gardens
17 Foxbury
19 Green Farm Cottage
Saturday 25
24 Mill Barn
31 Stockclough
35 Wedgwood
Sunday 26
11 Clearbeck House
24 Mill Barn
27 New Wood
29 Sefton Park Gardens
31 Stockclough
35 Wedgwood
37 Wroxham Gardens

July

Saturday 2
15 Davenport Farm
20 Greenacre & St Peter's Garden Trail
Sunday 3
4 Birkdale Village Gardens
15 Davenport Farm
20 Greenacre & St Peter's Garden Trail
Saturday 9
2 The Barn on the Green
30 Southlands
32 The Stones & Roses Garden
Sunday 10
18 Freshfield Gardens
30 Southlands
32 The Stones & Roses Garden
Sunday 17
4 Birkdale Village Gardens
5 Bretherton Gardens
8 Brookfield
Sunday 24
7 4 Brocklebank Road
Sunday 31
34 Waddow Lodge Garden

August

Sunday 7
1 24 Abbeyvale Drive
22 Leyland Gardens
Sunday 28
28 The Ridges

September

Sunday 4
5 Bretherton Gardens

February 2012

Sunday 12
36 Weeping Ash

Sunday 19
36 Weeping Ash
Sunday 26
36 Weeping Ash

Gardens open to the public

5 Hazelwood, Bretherton Gardens
28 The Ridges

By appointment only

33 Varley Farm

Also open by Appointment ☎

1 24 Abbeyvale Drive
18 37 Brewery Lane, Freshfield Gardens
7 4 Brocklebank Road
8 Brookfield
10 Casa Lago
13 Crabtree Lane Gardens
14 Dale House Gardens
17 Foxbury
20 Greenacre, Greenacre & St Peter's Garden Trail
5 Hazel Cottage, Bretherton Gardens
21 Le Jardin
23 Little Stubbins
4 Maple Tree Cottage, Birkdale Village Gardens
4 10 Meadow Avenue, Birkdale Village Gardens
24 Mill Barn
26 1 New Row Cottages, New Row Cottage Gardens
4 14 Saxon Road, Birkdale Village Gardens
30 Southlands
32 The Stones & Roses Garden
35 Wedgwood

The Gardens

1 24 ABBEYVALE DRIVE
Bellevale L25 2NL. Mrs Karen Lewis, 07946 725272, nevetssiwel@gmail.com. *4m SE of Liverpool. L at Liverpool end of M62 onto A5058, Queens Dr. At 1st r'about, take 1st exit onto B5178. Pass Bellevale shopping centre then L at T-lights into Naylors Rd. Then 1st L & 2nd L. Home-made teas.* **Adm £2.50, chd free. Sun 7 Aug (12-5). Visitors also welcome by appt max 20, no coaches.**
Inspirational one-off small estate garden packed with plants and colour. Garden pond with newts,

Visit the website for latest information

frogs and toads attracting dragonflies and a host of other wildlife. Sitting areas, garden features and vegetables create a growing oasis in the city. Featured on local radio and in local press.

2 THE BARN ON THE GREEN
Silk Mill Lane, Inglewhite PR3 2LP. Arthur & Vivienne Massey-Fairhurst, www.thebarnonthegreen.co.uk. *9m N of Preston, 6.2m E of Garstang. From M55, take A6 towards Garstang for 2½ m. At Roebuck PH turn R into Bilsborrow Lane for 2½ m to hamlet of Inglewhite. 1st R just before The Green. Garden on immed R next to Green Man PH where you can park, parking also available at Inglewhite Chapel just past PH & garden. Teas at Inglewhite village church.* **Adm £4, chd £2 under 5 free (share to Rotary). Sat 9 July (11-4).** This delightful 1¼ acre garden, overlooking stunning scenery, guides the visitor through a series of rooms, some secluded and secretive others allowing panoramic views. A vast array of plants, trees, bushes, bulbs, roses, hostas, water lilies, vegetables, pond, river bed and much more. Too much for you to miss. Wheelchair access, please see a steward.

GROUP OPENING

3 BARROW NOOK GARDENS
Bickerstaffe L39 0ET. *5m SW of Ormskirk. From M58, J3 to Southport (A570) to T-lights at Stanley Gate PH, turn L into Liverpool Rd, then 1st L into Church Rd, then Hall Lane, approx 1m into Barrow Nook Lane.* Cream Teas. **Combined adm £3.50, chd free. Sat 4, Sun 5 June (1-5).**

BARROW NOOK FARM
Cynthia & Keith Moakes

18 BARROW NOOK LANE
Paul & Sheila Davies

26 BARROW NOOK LANE
Gary Jones

Barrow Nook Gardens are 3 neighbouring gardens of very different styles within a short walking distance, set in rural surroundings. Barrow Nook Farm is a peaceful country garden planted in cottage garden style to attract birds, bees, butterflies and much more. The large wildlife

---

pond is an attractive feature. Pergola leads to orchard with soft and stoned fruit. Homemade jams for sale. 18 Barrow Nook Lane is a small diverse garden with herbaceous borders, pergola, gravel paths, rockery, water feature, herbs, island beds, fruit trees and raised vegetable beds. 26 Barrow Nook Lane is a low maintenance garden for people with limited time and budget who appreciate outdoor living, dining and relaxing. Cream teas and plant sales. Home made jams for sale. Featured in Lancashire Magazine.

The beautiful Birkdale Village Gardens are not to be missed . . .

GROUP OPENING

4 BIRKDALE VILLAGE GARDENS
Birkdale, Southport PR8 2AX. *1m S of Southport. Off A565 Southport to Liverpool rd. 4th on L after r'about, opp St James Church. By train short walk from Birkdale Stn, exit L for Saxon Rd. Maps available at each location.* Light refreshments & home-made teas. **Combined adm £4, chd free (share to Claire House Hospice). Suns 29 May; 3, 17 July (10.30-5.30).**

NEW 23 ASHTON ROAD
John & Jennifer Mawdsley. *¾ m S from village along Liverpool Rd, turn R into Sandon Rd (church on corner) 2nd L Ashton Rd*

FOXBURY
47 Westbourne Road. Pam & Richard James
(See separate entry)

MAPLE TREE COTTAGE
22 Hartley Crescent. Sandra & Keith Birks. *½ m from village, S along Liverpool Rd, turn R into Richmond Rd, 1st R Hartley Rd, then 1st R Hartley Crescent Not open 3 July*
Visitors also welcome by appt, June, July & Aug, groups of 10+. 01704 567182 sandie.b@talktalk.net

---

10 MEADOW AVENUE
John & Jenny Smith. *S on A5267 through Birkdale Village, L at T-lights, continue past 1 zebra Xing, just before next turn R into Warwick St, then 2nd L*
Visitors also welcome by appt June & July groups of 10+. 01704 543394

14 SAXON ROAD
Margaret & Geoff Fletcher
Visitors also welcome by appt May - Aug groups of 10+. 01704 567742 geoffwfletcher@hotmail.co.uk

An expanding group of gardens within walking distance of the attractive Victorian village of Birkdale, some opening on all 3 dates others less. Gardens feature a ½-acre inspirational cottage garden, a quirky large family garden full of reclaimed materials and surprises. A low lying suburban garden inland from the dunes with mixed beds and mature shrubs, a walled garden with an increasing array of tender plants amongst informal island beds and finally a garden of different rooms with a wonderful fruit and vegetable plot. Maps are available at all gardens and refreshments available at most gardens. 'The beautiful Birkdale Village Gardens are not to be missed', a very popular tourist attraction - 'Lancashire Life'. Featured in The Lancashire Magazine.

GROUP OPENING

5 BRETHERTON GARDENS
PR26 9AN. *8m SW of Preston. Between Southport & Preston, from A59, take B5247 towards Chorley for 1m. Gardens off North Rd (B5248) & South Rd (B5247).* Home-made teas at Bretherton Congregational Church. Light lunches July. **Combined adm £4.50 (May, July & Sept) £4 (June) child free (share to Queenscourt Hospice). Suns 29 May; 19 June; 17 July; 4 Sept (12-5).**

HAZEL COTTAGE
6 South View. John & Kris Jolley
Visitors also welcome by appt. 01772 600896 jolley@johnjolley.plus.com

♦ HAZELWOOD
North Road. Jacqueline Iddon & Thompson Dagnall
For other opening times and

---

information please phone, or visit garden website. 01772 601433 www.jacquelineiddonhardy plants.co.uk

OWL BARN
South Road. Donald & Joan Waterworth

NEW▶ **PEAR TREE COTTAGE**
Eyes Lane. John & Gwenifer Jackson.
off South Rd, turn at war memorial **Not open June 17.**

Four contrasting gardens spaced across 2m in an attractive village with conservation area. New this year, Pear Tree Cottage garden blends seamlessly into its rural setting with informal displays of ornamental and edible crops, water and mature trees, against a backdrop of open views to the West Pennine Moors. Owl Barn has a model kitchen garden, harmonious formal borders and fountains complementing an historic listed building (not open). Hazelwood Garden, Nursery and Sculpture Gallery cover 1½ acre of mature orchard, with a beautifully integrated range of habitats showing the finest plants for every situation, from moist shade to well-drained sun. Hazel Cottage garden has evolved from one-third acre Victorian subsistence plot to encompass a series of themed spaces packed with plants to engage the senses and the mind. Demonstrations of flower arranging, wood carving, live music, 1pm and 2pm at Hazelwood.

& ✿ ☕

6▶ BRIDGE HOUSE
Bolton Road, Bradshaw, Bolton BL2. Glenda & Graham Ostick. *2m NE of Bolton. On A676 to Ramsbottom, 2m from centre of Bolton. In Bradshaw half way between 'Latino Lounge' Restaurant & Ashoka Restaurant.* Cream teas. **Adm £2.50, chd free (share to The Michael Williams Trust (Bolton). Sun 1, Mon 2 May (1.30-5).**
An impressive and beautiful garden of more than 1 acre created by 2 dedicated gardeners over many years. Spring interest in bulbs, azaleas and some unusual shrubs and trees, 2 ponds. Summer, herbaceous borders, challenging 'wild area'. Views across meadow and brook, extensive lawns and prolific vegetable garden. Garden for all seasons, not to be missed. Wild area inaccessible to wheelchairs.

& ✿ ☕

7▶ 4 BROCKLEBANK ROAD
Southport PR9 9LP. Alan & Heather Sidebotham, 01704 543389. *1¼ m N of Southport. Off A565 Southport to Preston Rd, opp North entrance to Hesketh Park.* Home-made teas. **Adm £3, chd free. Sun 24 July (11-5). Visitors also welcome by appt May to Aug. Groups 10+.**
The garden consists of a series of separate areas and water features, each with different planting. Whenever possible the landscaping materials used are from reclamation materials from historic sites in the Southport area. Thus creating a garden of interest to compliment the planting schemes.

✿ ☕ ☎

8▶ BROOKFIELD
11 Irlam Road, Flixton M41 6JR. Bob & Beryl Wheeler, 0161 748 6985, rcpwheeler@aol.com. *2½ m SW of Urmston. From J10 on M60 go S through 2 r'abouts to T-lights, turn R into Moorside Rd. At next r'about take 2nd rd signed Lymm, after next T-lights take 5th rd on R Irlam Rd.* Light refreshments. **Adm £2.50, chd free. Sun 17 July (1-5). Visitors also welcome by appt min groups of 10.**
⅓-acre suburban garden on a triangular plot divided into sections with several pathways. Large selection of plants in herbaceous beds and borders with mature trees and shrubs planned for year round

effect. Raised beds, rockery, pond and water features, shade areas, patio with troughs and containers. Greenhouse and cold frames.

✿ ☕ ☎

9▶ NEW▶ CARR HOUSE FARM
Carr House Lane, Lancaster LA1 1SW. Robin & Helen Loxam. *SW of Lancaster City. From A6 Lancaster city centre turn at hospital, past B&Q and 1st R, straight under railway bridge into farm.* Cream teas. **Adm £4, chd free (share to Fairfield Flora & Fauna Assoc). Sat 11, Sun 12 June (10.30-4.30).**
A hidden gem in historic City of Lancaster. Farmhouse gardens incl Mediterranean, rustic and cottage flowers and trees intertwined beautifully with 2 ponds fed naturally by 'Lucy Brook' attracting all manner of wildlife. Apple, pear, plum, lemon and orange trees mix well within the scene. See rare breed cattle and enjoy nature walk in adjoining fields. Slope towards pond.

& ✿ ☕

10▶ CASA LAGO
1 Woodlands Park, Whalley BB7 9UG. Carole Ann & Stephen Powers, 01254 824903, livingwithnature@tiscali.co.uk. *2½ m S of Clitheroe. From M6 J31, take A59 to Clitheroe. 9m take 2nd exit at r'about for Whalley. After 2m reach village and follow yellow signs. Parking in village car parks or nearby.*

4 Brocklebank Road

Home-made teas. **Adm £2.50, chd free. Sun 12 June (1-5). Visitors also welcome by appt.** S.M.A.L.L. at Casa Lago is: Secluded. Myriad of variety. All seasons. Lovingly tendered. Lazy summer days. Two koi ponds, tree ferns, ferns from around the world, acers, bamboos, grasses, bananas and a succulent garden. Interesting features incl. black limestone wall, oak pergolas, fruit patio and conversion of a traditional driveway into an appealing planted space. Teeming with inspirational ideas. Featured in BBC Gardeners World, Radio Lancashire Gardening Programme and Lancashire Magazine. ✿ ☕ ☎

11 CLEARBECK HOUSE
Mewith Lane, Higher Tatham via Lancaster LA2 8PJ. Peter & Bronwen Osborne, www.clearbeckgarden.org.uk. *13m NE of Lancaster. Signed from Wray (M6 J34, A683, B6480) & Low Bentham.* Light refreshments & teas. **Adm £3, chd free. Sun 29, Mon 30 May; Suns 19, 26 June (11-5).** 'A surprise round every corner' is the most common response as visitors encounter fountains, streams, ponds, sculptures, boathouses and follies: (Rapunzel's tower, temple, turf maze, giant fish made of CDs, walk-through pyramid). 2-acre wildlife lake attracts many species of insects and birds. Planting incl herbaceous borders, grasses, bog plants and many roses. Artist's studio open in garden. Children's quiz available. Featured in Country Life BBC 2 Alan's Secret Gardens, GGG*, featured in Up to a Point, book on pyramids. Grassy slopes may be difficult in wet weather. ♿ 🐾 ✿ ☕

GROUP OPENING

12 NEW CLIFTON HILL GARDENS
Stony Lane, Forton PR3 0AR. *10m S of Lancaster. From M6 J33, S to Garstang along A6 for approx 2m. Turn R up School Lane just past 'Zumos'. Follow through Forton Village past cricket pitch on L - signs onto Stony Lane. Approaching on A6 in N direction, turn L into School Lane, just after the Mammoth Onion. Parking in front of the house and on lane.* Home-made teas.

Combined adm £3, chd free. Sun 5 June (1-5).

NEW **THE CHAPEL**
Joan & Jim Brindle

NEW **GILLOW GARDEN**
Lynn & Graham Jones

The house and chapel at Clifton Hill were built in 1811 by Robert Gillow (of Waring and Gillows). The adjoining gardens enjoy uninterrupted views of Bleasdale and Nicky Nook. The gardens consist of a formal garden with raised pond, and a charming packed cottage garden, conservatory. Artist's studio. Small woodland area bursting with English bluebells and wild garlic. Wild pond recently rescued and renovated. Artists studio open, large paddock suitable for picnics and for children to run around, paintings and book stall available. Chickens roam freely through the gardens. ♿ ✿ ☕

Small woodland area bursting with English bluebells and wild garlic . . .

GROUP OPENING

13 CRABTREE LANE GARDENS
Burscough L40 0RW, 01704 893713, peter.curl@btinternet.com. *3m NE of Ormskirk. Follow A59 Preston - Liverpool rd to Burscough. From N before 1st bridge turn R into Redcat Lane - brown sign Martin Mere. From S pass through village over 2nd bridge, then L into Redcat Lane, after 3/4 m turn L into Crabtree Lane. Gardens by level Xing.* Home-made teas. **Combined adm £3.50, chd free. Sun 15 May; Sun 12 June (1-5). Visitors also welcome by appt May to July.**

79 CRABTREE LANE
Sandra & Peter Curl

81 CRABTREE LANE
Prue & Barry Cooper

2 very diverse gardens 79 Crabtree Lane a 3/4 acre yr-round garden comprising many established and

contrasting hidden areas. Colour themed herbaceous beds recently replanted. Rose garden, fish pond and wildlife pond, Large rockery, pergola covered by wisteria. Spring and woodland garden, alpine garden and late summer hot bed. A 'derelict, dry stone bothy' and a recently completed slate roofed potting shed with an exotic garden surrounded by stone walls. 81 Crabtree Lane has water features, old fashioned rockery, vine covered pergola, trompe l'oeils. Central gazebo with climbers. Herbaceous plants. Arches with clematis and roses. Featured in Ormskirk Advertiser and on Radio Lancashire. ♿ ✿ ☕ ☎

CRAIGSIDE
See Derbyshire.

14 NEW DALE HOUSE GARDENS
off Church Lane, Goosnargh, Preston PR3 2BE. Caroline & Tom Luke, 01772 862464, tomlukebudgerigars@hotmail.com. *21/2 m E of Broughton. M6 J32 signed Garstang Broughton, T-lights turn R onto Whittingham Lane, 21/2 m to Whittingham & Goosnargh at r'about turn L onto Church Lane, garden between No's 17 & 19.* Home-made teas. **Adm £3, chd free (share to Bushell House Charity). Sat 9, Sun 10 Apr (10-4). Visitors also welcome by appt evenings, groups 10+.** 1/2 -acre tastefully landscaped gardens comprising of limestone rockeries, well stocked herbaceous borders, raised alpine beds, well stocked Koi pond, lawn areas, greenhouse and polytunnel, patio areas, specialising in alpines rare shrubs and trees, large collection unusual bulbs. All year round interest. Large budgerigar aviary. 300+ budgies to look at. Gravel path, lawn areas. ♿ ✿ ☕ ☎

15 NEW DAVENPORT FARM
Arthur Lane, Ainsworth, Bolton BL2 5PW. Mr & Mrs Hankins. *2m W of Bury, 2m E of Bolton. Take B619 from Bury. Follow to & through Ainsworth Village. Watch for Arthur Lane Garden Nursery, garden opp the nursery.* Home-made teas. **Adm £3, chd free. Sat 2, Sun 3 July (2-6).** No more pigs and chickens! Farmyard redeveloped into 11/2 -acre garden. Now we have lawns, trees, shrubs

and glorious herbaceous borders. Climber strewn walkway to lily pond and deck area. Newly planted orchard and raised bed vegetable plot. York stone patios. 'Old stone folly' planned for spring 2011.

GROUP OPENING

16 DIDSBURY GARDENS
Didsbury, South Manchester
M20 6TQ. *5m S of Manchester City Centre. From M60 J5 follow signs to Northenden. Turn R at T-lights onto Barlow Moor Rd to Didsbury. From M56 follow A34 to Didsbury.* Home-made & cream teas at Moor Cottage. **Combined adm £5, chd free. Sun 19 June (12-5).**

68 BROOKLAWN DRIVE
Mrs A Britt

23 CRANMER ROAD
Christine Clarke.
Off Wilmslow Rd, then Fog Lane

NEW ESTHWAITE
52 Barlow Moor Road. Margaret Crowther

16 GRANGE LANE
Mr Peter Jordan.
Entrance on Gillbrook Rd

18 GRANGE LANE
Simon Hickey.
Entrance on Gillbrook Rd

NEW 6 GRENFELL ROAD
Malcolm Allum

GROVE COTTAGE
8 Grenfell Road. Sue & David Kaberry
NEW 30 LIDGATE GROVE
Mary Powell.
off Grenfell Road

MOOR COTTAGE
Grange Lane. William Godfrey.
Off Wilmslow Rd

Didsbury is an attractive South Manchester suburb, which retains its village atmosphere and has interesting shops, cafes and restaurants. Our 9 suburban gardens range from 2 beautifully designed courtyard gems to the larger country-style walled garden of a 200yr old cottage. There are three new gardens this year as well as our now established favourites. A completely new garden of 100ft x 14ft, designed and planted in 2009 has a cottage garden ambience. An informally planted garden of 1acre has rare

mature trees and shrubs with a magnificent conservatory full of exotic plants. The third garden is tiny and planted with an artist's eye. There is much to see here, each garden is packed with plants and features. Plants on sale at Moor Cottage, Grove Cottage and 52 Barlow Moor Rd.Tea and cakes at Moor Cottage and Cranmer Rd. Featured in Garden News, Grove Cottage was garden of the week. Cranmer Road won 1st prize in the Manchester Garden Competition.

17 FOXBURY
47 Westbourne Road, Birkdale, Southport PR8 2HY. Pam & Richard James. *2m S of Southport. Off A565 Southport to Liverpool Rd. After r'about at end of Lord St, proceed towards Liverpool, at 2nd T-lights turn R into Grosvenor Rd. Turn L at end.* Home-made teas. **Adm £2.50, chd free. Sun 19 June (11-5).** Also open with Birkdale Gardens Suns 3, 17 July. Visitors also welcome by appt June & July, groups of 10+.
1/2 acre suburban garden just inland from dunes and famous golf course of Birkdale. Very low lying. Mature pine tree shelters water feature. Mixed beds and newly planted trees are interspersed through a well maintained lawn. Mature shrubs and hedges shelter this developing garden from off-shore winds, giving a peaceful atmosphere. Featured in The Lancashire Magazine.

GROUP OPENING

18 FRESHFIELD GARDENS
L37 1PB. *6m S of Southport. From A565 (Crosby to Southport Rd) take B5424 signed Formby. At Grapes PH mini r'about turn R into Green Lane, Woodlands is 500yds on R. Brewery Lane (off West Lane) is within walking distance. For Victoria Rd & Gorse Way (off Larkhill Lane), drive over Freshfield level xing towards beach.* Home-made teas. **Combined adm £3.50, chd free. Sun 10 July (10.30-4.30).**

37 BREWERY LANE
Mr & Mrs P Thornton
Visitors also welcome by appt July & Aug. 01704 873107

2 GORSE WAY
Brenda & Ray Doldon

THE SQUIRRELS
67 Victoria Road. Kathleen & Andrew Train

WOODLANDS
46 Green Lane. Ken & Rita Carlin

4 suburban gardens on sandy soil near to Formby sand dunes & NT nature reserve, home to the red squirrel. 2 Gorse Way completely redesigned by the present owners. This split level garden features a sunken garden, pergola, pond, beach area and colour themed beds. Woodlands has a leafy shady front garden, mature trees, cottage style colourful borders and plenty of seating areas to relax and view. The Squirrels is a plant collector's well stocked garden, primarily to attract wildlife. Unusual tender plants in containers and interesting collection of cacti. 37 Brewery Lane. A compact garden with grasses, pergola, dry stone wall and interesting conifers. 'Twenty shades of green' contrast with bright summer bedding and architectural plants.

19 NEW GREEN FARM COTTAGE
42 Lower Green, Poulton-le-Fylde FY6 7EJ. Sharon McDonnell & Eric Rawcliffe. *500yds from Poulton-le-Fylde Village. M55 J3 follow A585 Fleetwood. T- lights turn L. Next lights bear L A586. Poulton 2nd set of lights turn R Lower Green. Cottage on L.* Light refreshments & teas. **Adm £3, chd free. Sun 19 June (10-5).**
1/3 -acre well established formal cottage gardens. Feature Koi pond, paths leading to different areas. Lots of climbers and rose beds. Packed with plants of all kinds. Many shrubs and trees. Themed colour borders. Well laid out lawns. Said by visitors to be 'a real hidden jewel'.

Themed colour borders. Well laid out lawns. Said by visitors to be 'a real hidden jewel' . . .

14 Saxon Road

Visitors also welcome by appt day or evening, June & July.
A well established garden with mature herbaceous borders and shrubs. Floral designers garden with several themed areas incl a collection of hostas. A continually evolving plant collector's garden with emphasis on colour form and texture. In essence a simple and spontaneous garden containing a naturally harmonious ambience as featured in Lancashire Life.

❀ ☕ ☎

GROUP OPENING

22 LEYLAND GARDENS
PR25 1HL. *Leave M6 at J28, both gardens off A49 for Deerhurst follow B5248. Kasauli 1/2 m from J28 on B5256 (signed Chorley). Maps available at each garden.* Light refreshments & teas at Kasauli.
Combined adm £3, chd free.
Sun 7 Aug (1-5).

DEERHURST
10 Forestway. Julia Harwood-Geall & Fred Bell

KASAULI
32 Lancaster Lane, Clayton-Le-Woods. William & Barbara Joyce

Two very interesting suburban gardens 2m apart with something for everyone. Deerhurst is a medium sized garden and has been developed over many years and is now well-stocked with unusual perennials and vegetable plot. Kasauli is a varied garden incl formal area with lawns and well filled, colour themed herbaceous borders. Small secluded area with ponds leading to artist's studio. Informal areas, interesting structures and places to sit.

❀ ☕

GROUP OPENING

20 NEW GREENACRE & ST PETER'S GARDEN TRAIL
Clayton-Le-Dale, Blackburn BB1 9HT. *3 1/2 m N of Blackburn. Leave M6 J31 take A59 towards Clitheroe. In 7m at T-lights turn R towards Blackburn on B6245. Ribchester Road Gardens 1/2 m on RH-side and Memorial Hall 3/4 m on RH-side.* Home-made lunches & teas at Salesbury Memorial Hall.
Combined adm £4.50, chd free (weekend ticket). Sat 2 (11-5), Sun 3 July (1-5).

NEW 8 ALBANY DRIVE
Copster Green. John & Shelagh Beaghan

NEW 6 ALBANY DRIVE
Copster Green. Barrie & Margaret Stones

GREENACRE
157 Ribchester Road. Dorothy & Andrew Richards
Visitors also welcome by appt May, June & late Aug, groups of 14 to 25. 01254 249694
andrewfrichards@talk21.com

NEW MAYFIELD COACH HOUSE
Ribchester Road. Ken & Anne Haselden

NEW WHITECROFT
Lovely Hall Lane. Keith & Kathleen Sowerbutts
Our gardens are in a semi-rural area

with St Peter's Church and the Memorial Hall at the hub. There are stunning views over the Ribble Valley and Pendle Hill, excellent local eateries and the Ribble Valley food trail is nearby. The Ribchester Road neighbours are 1/4 m and the Salesbury three are 3/4 m from the Church.Albany Drive gardens are small gems packed with plants and colour. Whitecroft faces the lovely Copster Green and this medium size and mature garden feels homely with wisteria and honeysuckle. Mayfield Coach House has 3/4 -acre designer garden made to blend with the landscape. The 1-acre Greenacre garden incl a brimming potager set in a mature orchard, beds packed with interesting plants and signature yellow foliage. Maps and tickets can be purchased at the Memorial Hall and the gardens. Plant sale at Greenacre, also guided tours at 2pm and 3.30pm. Powerpoint presentation of NGS Lancashire gardens in the Memorial Hall at 1pm and 4pm.

♿ ❀ ☕

21 LE JARDIN
12 Crocus Field, Leyland PR25 3DY. Margaret & David Moore, 01772 456616,
davidsmoore@talktalk.net. *7m S of Preston. From M6, J28 take B5256 towards Leyland, 1st r'about take 1st exit, next r'about 2nd exit (B5248) in 600yds L into Beech Avenue, T-junction turn R.* Cream teas. **Adm £3, chd free. Sat 28, Sun 29 May (1-5).**

23 LITTLE STUBBINS
Stubbins Lane, Claughton-on-Brock, Preston PR3 0PL. Margaret & Mick Richardson, 01995 640376,
littlestubbins@aol.com,
www.littlestubbins.co.uk. *2m S of Garstang. Leave M6 at J32. Follow signs for Garstang 6m, turn R onto B6340, 2nd on R, Stubbins Lane 1/2 m on R.* Tea & Home-made teas.
Adm £3, chd free. Sun 15 (1-5.30), Mon 16 May (11-4.30). Visitors also welcome by appt.

³/₄ -acre, split between front·and rear lawned gardens with paved patio areas. Mixed borders containing a large selection of herbaceous, shrubs, roses and bulbs giving all-yr interest and colour. 90+ varieties of hostas mainly in pots. Newly constructed patio area by the stream. Featured in Lancashire Living and Design.

  ⬤ 🏵 ⊛ 🛏 ☕ ☎

24 MILL BARN

Goosefoot Close, Samlesbury PR5 0SS. Chris Mortimer, 01254 853300, chris@millbarn.net. *6m E of Preston. From M6 J31 2¹/₂ m on A59/A677 B/burn. Turn S. Nabs Head Lane, then Goosefoot Lane.* Home-made teas. **Adm £3, chd free. Sats, Suns 11, 12, 25, 26 June (1-5).** Visitors also welcome by appt mid May to mid July, min group donation £30.

Tranquil terraced garden along the banks of R Darwen. A garden on many levels, both physical and psychological. A sense of fun and mystique is present and an adventurous spirit may be needed to negotiate the various parts. Flowers, follies and sculptures engage the senses, moving up from the semi formal to the semi wild where nature is only just under control. A grotto dedicated to alchemy, a suspension bridge over the R Darwen 20m wide at this point, and a tower on the far bank above the 'Lorelei' rocks where a princess might wait for her lover. Wheelchair visitors have not been disappointed in the past.

  ⬤ 🏵 ⊛ 🛏 ☕ ☎

25 MONTFORD COTTAGE

Cuckstool Lane, Fence-in-Pendle BB12 9NZ. Craig Bullock & Tony Morris, www.montfordcottagegarden. talktalk.net. *4m N of Burnley. From J13 M65, take A6068 (signed Fence), in 2m turn L onto B6248 (signed Brierfield). Proceed down hill for ¹/₂ m (past Barocco's, formerly Forest PH). Entrance to garden on L, with limited car park further down hill.* Light refreshments & cream teas. **Adm £3.50, chd free. Sat 4, Sun 5 June (11-5).**

Artist's garden in Pendle Hill country. The synthesis between cottage garden planting, garden buildings, statuary and follies evokes atmosphere which you are encouraged to soak up - by relaxing and using the plentiful seating areas in the garden. Visitors comment that

they lost all sense of time and place - is it the magic of the witch country that casts its spell over this one-and-a-half acre plot?

  ⬤ 🏵 ⊛ ☕

GROUP OPENING

26 NEW ROW COTTAGE GARDENS

Clitheroe Road, Knowle Green, Longridge PR3 2YS, 01254 878447, hjcpnewrow1@talktalk.net. *8m W of Clitheroe, 8m E of Preston. From S leave M6 J31a. Follow B6243 for approx 6m, New Row on L. From N leave M6 J32 follow B5269 to Longridge, join B6243 to New Row.* Cream teas. **Combined adm £4, chd free. Sat 4, Sun 5 June (11-5).** Visitors also welcome by appt Groups of 10+.

LONG VIEW
6 New Row Cottages. Mr & Mrs R Dixon

3 NEW ROW COTTAGES
Pat Barlow

1 NEW ROW COTTAGES
Clitheroe Road. Harry & Jean Procter
Visitors also welcome by appt Groups10+.01254 878447 hjcpnewrow1@talktalk.net

TILLYCLIFFE COTTAGE
Cliff & Tilly Carefoot

Four typical old Lancashire handloom weavers cottage gardens in glorious countryside. Emphasis on peaceful relaxing seating areas from which to admire the rolling scenery and overflowing herbaceous borders. Plant stall. Featured in BBC Gardener's World with Carol Klein.Featured in Lancashire Magazine and Longridge News.

  ⬤ 🏵 ⊛ ☕ ☎

27 NEW NEW WOOD

Castle Lane, Lathom, Ormskirk L40 5UH. Mrs L McNeill. *2m E of Ormskirk. J3 M58. Follow signs to Ormskirk & at r'about take the 2nd exit. Turn L on A577. Turn R at The Halton Castle into Castle Lane. New Wood is 1m ahead on L at the junction with Lathom Lane & Sandy Lane.* Cream teas. **Adm £4, chd free. Sun 26 June (11-5).** Only 5yrs old, providing diversity within 1 acre of gardens and paddock created from a blank canvas surrounded by a rural landscape. A

structured garden with ancillary breeze house, stumpery and dry stone folly merges harmoniously with the paddock that incl a large wildlife pond and water edge planting.

  ⬤ ☕

Stumpery and dry stone folly merges harmoniously with the paddock . . .

28 ◆ THE RIDGES

Weavers Brow, (cont. of Cowling Rd), Limbrick, Chorley PR6 9EB. Mr & Mrs J M Barlow, 01257 279981, www.bedbreakfast-gardenvisits.com. *2m SE of Chorley town centre. M6 J27, M61 J8 follow signs for Chorley A6, then Cowling & Rivington. At Morrison's up Brook St. to Mini r'about. Take Cowling Brow, garden on RH-side after Spinners Arms.* **Adm £3.50, chd free. For NGS: Sun 1 May; Sun 28 Aug (11-5). For other opening times and information, please phone or see garden website.**

3 acres, incl old walled orchard garden, cottage-style herbaceous borders and perfumed rambling roses through the trees. Living arch leads to large formal lawn, surrounded by natural woodland, shrub borders and trees with contrasting foliage. New woodland walks and dell. Natural looking stream and wildlife ponds. Walled feature with Italian influence and area planted with scented roses and herbs. Classical music played. Featured in Lancashire Life. A few gravel paths.

  ⬤ 🏵 ⊛ 🛏 ☕

GROUP OPENING

29 SEFTON PARK GARDENS

Liverpool, Liverpool L8 3SL. *3m S of Liverpool city centre. From end of M62 take A5058 Queens Drive ring rd through Allerton to Sefton Park and follow signs. Park roadside in Sefton Park. Maps and tickets at all gardens except York House.* Light refreshments & home-made teas. **Combined adm £5, chd free. Sun 26 June (12-5).**

PARKMOUNT
38 Ullet Road. Jeremy Nicholls

SEFTON PARK ALLOTMENTS
Greenbank Drive. Sefton Park
Allotments Society.
*Next door to Sefton Park cricket
club*

SEFTON VILLA
14 Sefton Drive.
Patricia Williams

**VICE CHANCELLOR'S
GARDEN**
12 Sefton Park Road. University
of Liverpool, Vice-Chancellor
Sir Howard & Lady Sheila
Newby

NEW ➤ **34 YORK HOUSE**
Croxteth Drive. Jean Niblock &
Arena Homes

An inspirational communal tower
block garden is joining the group this
year which includes two large, one
small, interesting city gardens and
nearly 100 allotments. This 3 year old
tower block garden has a backbone
of beech and privet hedging, shrubs
and herbaceous borders, colourful
containers and large greenhouse.
Rare and unusual plants for sale,
musical entertainment at the Vice
Chancellor's garden. Some surprises
and many rare plants in one of
Liverpool's old merchant house
gardens overlooking Sefton Park with
Paddy Christian's beautiful plants for
sale. Visit the new Children's
Allotment among the nearly 100
individually tended plots with a wide
variety of produce at Sefton Park
Allotments. The small walled Victorian
garden at Sefton Villa is secluded and
tranquil, with rare plants and
interesting features incl an enclosed
Japanese garden. The Vice-
Chancellor's Lodge features an
historic and traditional rose garden,
beautiful terrace and sweeping
shrubberies with a string quartet
providing musical entertainment. New
34 York ouse is an inspirational
communal tower block is joining the
group this year which incls two large
and one small... Bonsai
demonstration by Geoff Brown at 12
Sefton Drive at 11am.
⊗ ☕

---

30 ➤ **SOUTHLANDS**
12 Sandy Lane, Stretford M32 9DA.
Maureen Sawyer & Duncan
Watmough, 0161 283 9425,
moe@southlands12.com,
www.southlands12.com. *3m S of
Manchester. Sandy Lane (B5213) is
situated off A5181 (A56) ¼ m from
M60 J7.* Home-made teas. **Adm £3,**

chd free. **Sat 9, Sun 10 July (1-6).
Visitors also welcome by appt. 1
June to end Aug. Guided tour for
groups of 10+.**
Artist's inspirational south facing
garden unfolding into a series of
beautiful garden 'rooms' each with its
own theme incl courtyard,
Mediterranean, ornamental and
woodland garden. Organic kitchen
garden with large glasshouse
containing vines and tomatoes.
Extensive herbaceous borders,
stunning containers of exotics,
succulents and annuals, 2 ponds and
water feature. Live jazz twice daily
(weather permitting). Exhibition of art
work derived from the garden.
Featured in All Things Bright and
Beautiful, Manchester Evening News,
Gardens Monthly.

---

31 ➤ NEW ➤ **STOCKCLOUGH**
Stockclough Lane, Feniscowles,
Blackburn BB2 5JR. David &
Kathleen Paintin. *3m SW of
Blackburn town centre. Leave M65
J3. Follow A674 to Blackburn. At T-
lights continue for 1m. Turn R at
Feilden Arms. Turn R at r'about to
Tockholes sharp R onto Stockclough
Lane.* Light refreshments & home-
made teas. **Adm £3, chd free. Sat
25, Sun 26 June (12-5).**
Over 1 acre of established garden
surrounding a renovated large stone
cottage. The garden has four parts.
Firstly an entertaining patio area with
planting, water feature and converted
stone building containing seating
beside a fire. Developing courtyard
garden. Secondly large lawned area
surrounded by mature trees,
herbaceous beds and garden room
with fig trees. Thirdly for the more
adventurous, a wild garden with pond
and fern lined woodland walk. Finally
vegetable beds and greenhouse with
interesting varieties and vines. Partial
wheelchair access.
⅋ ⊗ ☕

---

32 ➤ **THE STONES & ROSES
GARDEN**
White Coppice Farm, White
Coppice, Chorley PR6 9DF.
Raymond & Linda Smith,
www.stonesandroses.org. *3m NE of
Chorley. J8 M61. A674 to Blackburn.
3rd R to Heapey & White Coppice.
Parking next to garden.* Cream Teas.
**Adm £3, chd free. Sat 9, Sun 10
July (2-5). Visitors also welcome by
appt from late June, min 15.**
Still developing 3-acre garden where

the cows used to live. Sunken
garden, with loads of Stonework and
Roses (500). Fountains, streams,
waterfall, cascade, rockery,
herbaceous, all with colour themed
planting. Stumpery, fruit tree walk
down to small lake with jetty, with
wildflower planting. Formal kitchen
garden built with the last of the
inherited stone. Set in the beautiful
Hamlet of White Coppice with
stunning cricket field, voted in the top
four most beautiful in the country.
Lovely Pennine walks.
⅋ 🐕 ⊗ ☕ ☎

For the more
adventurous, a wild
garden with pond
and fern lined
woodland walk . . .

---

33 ➤ **VARLEY FARM**
Anna Lane, Forest Becks, Bolton-
by-Bowland, Clitheroe BB7 4NZ.
Mr & Mrs B Farmer, 0788 763 8436,
varleyforestbecks@btinternet.com.
*7m N of Clitheroe. 9m S of Settle.
7 m E of Clitheroe. Leave A59 at
Sawley & follow signs to Settle, take
the second left after the Copy Nook
Pub onto Settle Rd, turn left onto
Anna Lane at the black & white road
sign (Settle 9m Clitheroe 7m) Follow
the Lane to a sharp right hand turn.
Varley farm is on the left.* Home-made
teas. Drinks and Scones, cakes incl in
admission price. **Adm £5, chd free.
Visitors welcome by appt, groups
of 10+.**
1½ -acre garden that's been
developing from 2004. Varley Farm is
700ft above sea level with views
across the Forest of Bowland and
Pendle. Herbaceous lawned cottage
garden, flagged herb garden and
walled gravel garden, steps to
orchard and organic kitchen garden.
Stream and Pond area planted in
2009 still maturing with a grassed
walk through natural meadow.
☕ ☎

---

34 ➤ NEW ➤ **WADDOW LODGE
GARDEN**
Clitheroe Road, Waddington,
Clitheroe BB7 3HQ. Liz Dean &
Peter Foley,
www.gardentalks.co.uk. *1½ m N of
Clitheroe. From M6 J31 take A59*

(Preston-Skipton). A671 to Clitheroe then B6478. 1st house on L in village. Parking available on rd; blue badges in drive parking area on gravel. Home-made teas. **Adm £3.50, chd free. Suns 29 May; 31 July (1-5).**
Inspirational 2-acre organic garden for all seasons surrounding Georgian house (not open) with views to Pendle and Bowland. An enthusiast's collection of many unusual plants with herbaceous borders, large island beds, shrubs, rhododendrons, small mature wooded area, old fashioned and hybrid roses. Extensive kitchen garden of vegetables and soft fruit, interesting heritage apple orchard, herbs, alpines and greenhouse plus developing wildlife meadow. Many colourful containers. Featured on BBC Radio Lancashire and in Lancashire Magazine. Some gravel paths.

35 WEDGWOOD
Shore Road, Hesketh Bank PR4 6XP. Denis & Susan Watson, 01772 816509, heskethbank@aol.com, www.wedgwoodgarden.com. *10m SW of Preston. From Preston Take A59 towards Liverpool. Turn R at T-lights for Tarleton. Through Tarleton & Hesketh Bank, 2¹/₂ m straight down Hesketh Lane/Station Rd. Bear L onto Shore Rd. Garden 1.3m. Parking on rd.* Home-made teas. **Adm £3, chd free. Sat 25, Sun 26 June (10-5). Visitors also welcome by appt June & July only.**
1-acre country garden containing gravel garden with pots, formal pond, 2 lawns surrounded by extensive herbaceous borders in sun or shade, with mature trees, 50ft glasshouse, patio leading to 90ft parterre with

colour themed beds, archways pergolas and rose covered gazebo, wild flower meadow, fruit trees.

36 WEEPING ASH
Bents Garden & Home, Warrington Road, Glazebury WA3 5NS. John Bent, www.bents.co.uk. *15m W of Manchester. Located next to Bents Garden & Home, just off the East Lancs Rd A580 at Greyhound r'about near Leigh. Follow brown 'Garden Centre' signs.* Light refreshments & teas at The Fresh Approach Restaurant which is located within Bents Garden & Home, adjacent to Weeping Ash. **Adm £2, chd free. Suns 13, 20, 27 Feb (11-3.30); Sun 17 Apr (11-4.30); 2012 Suns 12, 19, 26 Feb .**
Created by retired nurseryman and photographer John Bent, Weeping Ash is a garden of all-year interest with a beautiful display of early snowdrops. Broad sweeps of colour lend elegance to this beautiful garden, which is currently undergoing an extensive re-design. The new work will retain an eclectic mix of foliage, flowers and form.

GROUP OPENING

37 WROXHAM GARDENS
Davyhulme, Manchester, Davyhulme M41 5TE. *1m SW of Urmston. From J10 on M60 follow Urmston signs to 2nd r'about, take 3rd exit and immed 1st R into Davyhulme Rd. Gardens situated behind St Mary's Church.* Home-made teas. **Combined adm £3, chd free. Sun 26 June (12-5).**

12 BOWERS AVENUE
Mel & Phil Gibbs
1 WROXHAM AVENUE
Liz Auld
2 WROXHAM AVENUE
Margaret & Bren Kinnucane
9 WROXHAM AVENUE
Jonathan & Katrina Myers
11 WROXHAM AVENUE
Alan Slack
These ever popular gardens have something for everyone and are often appreciated because they represent the more 'average' urban garden, offering plenty of interesting planting styles and ideas for the visitors to take away. Varied in size, shape and aspect, they demonstrate contrasting styles, from cottage garden to contemporary, formal garden to town garden. Key features include, various sized ponds and water features, vegetable and herb plots of different types and sizes, a range of herbaceous borders, cottage style planting, selection of lawn shapes and sizes, several alpine and succulent collections, tasteful decking areas and homes for visiting wildlife. Nice garden-party style atmosphere, good selection of plants for sale, home-made refreshments and stall organised by the Wroxham Gardens younger generation! Will suit all the family looking for a good afternoon out.

Will suit all the family looking for a good afternoon out . . .

LEICESTERSHIRE & RUTLAND

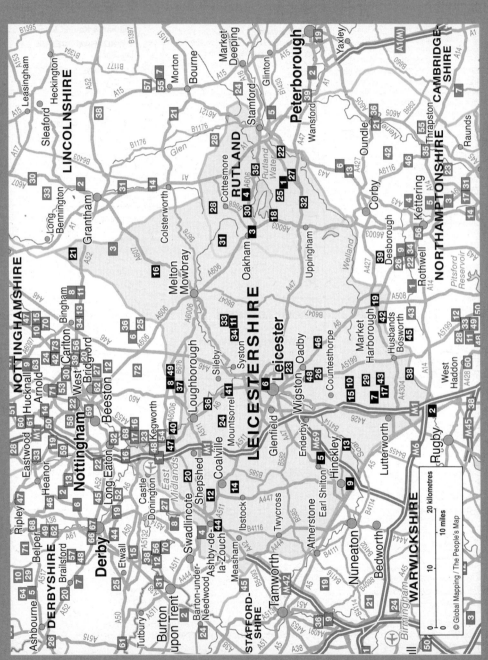

Opening Dates

February

Sunday 27
9 Burbage Gardens
46 Westview

March

Sunday 6
4 Barnsdale Gardens
21 The Homestead

Sunday 27
19 Hammond Arboretum
32 The Park House

April

Sunday 3
18 Gunthorpe Hall

Sunday 10
11 Copper Coin
33 Parkside

Sunday 17
28 The Old Hall

May

Sunday 1
3 Barleythorpe Gardens
7 Bents Farmhouse
17 The Grange

Monday 2
7 Bents Farmhouse
17 The Grange

Saturday 14
24 Long Close

Sunday 15
6 Belgrave Hall Museum & Gardens
24 Long Close
26 Mill House
30 The Old Vicarage, Burley
47 Whatton Gardens

Wednesday 18
42 Thorpe Lubenham Hall

Saturday 21
16 Goadby Marwood Hall

Sunday 22
13 Dairy Cottage
31 The Old Vicarage, Whissendine
49 Wymeswold Gardens

Wednesday 25
37 Ridgewold Farm

Sunday 29
9 Barracca
9 Burbage Gardens
27 North Luffenham Hall
40 Tebutts Farm

Monday 30
38 South Kilworth Gardens

June

Wednesday 1
39 Stoke Albany House

Sunday 5
36 Quorn Orchard Gardens

Wednesday 8
39 Stoke Albany House

Saturday 11
14 Donington Le Heath Manor House

Sunday 12
8 109 Brook Street
29 The Old Stables
35 Prebendal House
43 Walton Gardens

Wednesday 15
26 Mill House (Evening)
39 Stoke Albany House
43 Walton Gardens

Saturday 18
38 South Kilworth Gardens
48 Wigston Magna Gardens

Sunday 19
48 Wigston Magna Gardens

Wednesday 22
25 Lyndon Gardens (Evening)
37 Ridgewold Farm (Evening)
39 Stoke Albany House

Saturday 25
38 South Kilworth Gardens

Sunday 26
10 Coldor
13 Dairy Cottage
15 Farmway
22 Ketton Gardens
44 Warwick Glen
46 Westview

Wednesday 29
7 Bents Farmhouse (Evening)
17 The Grange (Evening)
39 Stoke Albany House

July

Saturday 2
14 Donington Le Heath Manor House

Sunday 3
7 Bents Farmhouse
17 The Grange
32 The Park House

Wednesday 6
39 Stoke Albany House

Saturday 9
48 Wigston Magna Gardens

Sunday 10
1 Acre End
5 Barracca
20 Hill Park Farm
40 Tebutts Farm
47 Whatton Gardens
48 Wigston Magna Gardens

Wednesday 13
39 Stoke Albany House

Sunday 17
26 Mill House
29 The Old Stables
44 Warwick Glen

Wednesday 20
39 Stoke Albany House

Sunday 24
23 27 Linden Drive

Wednesday 27
39 Stoke Albany House

Sunday 31
10 Coldor
15 Farmway

August

Sunday 7
45 2 Welford Road

Friday 19
45 2 Welford Road (Evening)

Sunday 21
41 7 The Crescent

Saturday 27
45 2 Welford Road

Sunday 28
2 Avon House

September

Sunday 4
46 Westview

Sunday 11
45 2 Welford Road

October

Sunday 9
19 Hammond Arboretum

Sunday 23
4 Barnsdale Gardens

Gardens open to the public

4 Barnsdale Gardens
6 Belgrave Hall Museum & Gardens
14 Donington Le Heath Manor House
47 Whatton Gardens

Fruit trees, chickens, bees and garden ponds all tucked away behind a country cottage . . .

You are always welcome at an NGS garden

By appointment only

12 The Dairy
34 Pine House

Also open by Appointment

1 Acre End
2 Avon House
5 Barracca
7 Bents Farmhouse
8 109 Brook Street
10 Coldor
38 Croft Acre, South Kilworth Gardens
15 Farmway
48 28 Gladstone Street, Wigston Magna Gardens
16 Goadby Marwood Hall
20 Hill Park Farm
21 The Homestead
24 Oak Tree House
24 Long Close
26 Mill House
28 The Old Hall
30 The Old Vicarage, Burley
31 The Old Vicarage, Whissendine
32 The Park House
33 Parkside
37 Ridgewold Farm
38 South Kilworth Gardens
39 Stoke Albany House
40 Tebutts Farm
45 2 Welford Road
46 Westview
48 1 Wellhouse Close, Wigston Magna Gardens

The Gardens

1 **ACRE END**
The Jetties, North Luffenham
LE15 8JX. Jim & Mima Bolton,
01780 720906, mmkb@mac.com.
*7m SE of Oakham. Via Manton &
Edith Weston, 7m SW of Stamford via
Ketton. 2m off A47 through Morcott
village.* Home-made teas at North
Luffenham Community Centre. **Adm
£4, chd free.** Sun 10 July (11-5).
Visitors also welcome by appt mid-
June to mid August; groups
welcome.
1-acre garden, imaginatively
designed, intensively planted, incl
knot garden, oriental courtyard
garden, mixed borders, circular lawn
with island beds, herb and scented
garden. Working fruit and vegetable
garden, long herbaceous border,
woodland garden. Many unusual
trees, shrubs, herbaceous perennials,

tender exotics in containers. All
organically managed to encourage
wildlife. Paintings, cards, crafts. (share
to NGS). Wildlife wood carvings.
Challenging Quiz. Featured in GGG.
Mainly grass paths and lawns, some
gravel.
⟶ ⊛ 🍵 ☎

**ARTHINGWORTH OPEN
GARDENS**
See Northamptonshire.

2 **AVON HOUSE**
4 Rugby Road, Catthorpe,
Lutterworth LE17 6DA. David &
Julia King, 01788 860346,
avonhouse4@btinternet.com. *3m
NE Rugby. 1m SW M1, A14, M6
Junctions. ½ m NE A5.* Light
refreshments & teas at Manor Farm
Shop (nearby). **Adm £2.50, chd free**
(share to LOROS). Sun 28 Aug
(11-5). Visitors also welcome by
appt for small groups March to
Sept.
A surprising ½ -acre garden in the
heart of the village with varied interest.
Large vegetable plot, mixed borders
of late season interest, fruit trees,
chickens, bees and garden ponds all
tucked away behind a country
cottage. Ideas of storage and use of
produce from the garden. Small
gravelled area.
⟶ 🍵 ☎   -

GROUP OPENING

3 **BARLEYTHORPE GARDENS**
Barleythorpe, nr Oakham
LE15 7EQ. *1m from Oakham on
A6006 towards Melton Mowbray. Car
park in Pasture Lane 1st turn L in
Barleythorpe by post box. Please park
in field on L not on lane.* Home-made
teas. **Combined adm £4, chd free**
(share to East Midlands Immediate
Care Scheme). Sun 1 May (2-5).

DAIRY COTTAGE
Mr & Mrs W Smith

THE LODGE
Dr & Mrs T J Gray

8 MANOR LANE
Richard Turner

Visit 3 beautiful gardens in this
Rutland village. **Dairy Cottage** -
Cottage-style garden at rear with
interesting and unusual shrubs and
spring bulbs. Paved/walled garden to
front (with pond) and lime hedge.
Separate semi-formal orchard. Gravel
access from car park. **The Lodge** -

Mixed flowers within walled garden,
½ lawn and part-walled kitchen
garden. Small stretch of gravel path
between lawned area and vegetable
garden. **8 Manor Lane**- Water and
woodland. Flowering shrubs, large
weeping trees, small lake and
woodland walk. Children must be
supervised at all times.
⊛ 🍵

4 ♦ **BARNSDALE GARDENS**
The Avenue, Exton, Oakham
LE15 8AH. Nick Hamilton, 01572
813200,
www.barnsdalegardens.co.uk. *3m
E of Oakham. Turn off A606, between
Oakham and Stamford, at Barnsdale
Lodge Hotel then 1m on left.* Light
Refreshments. **Adm £6.50, chd £2.**
Donation to NGS. For NGS: Suns 6
Mar; 23 Oct (10-4). For other
opening times and information,
please phone or see garden
website.
Consisting of 38 individual gardens
and features laid out within an 8 acre
garden, most of which were originally
developed and used by the late Geoff
Hamilton for BBC TV Gardeners'
World. Wide variety of ideas and
garden designs for yr-round interest.
Enjoyed by gardeners and non-
gardeners alike. The gardens have
lots of easy-to-make homemade
features. Organic and peat-free
vegetable plants and produce for sale
at various times of the year.
⟶ ⊛ 🍵 ☎

5 **NEW** **BARRACCA**
Ivydene Close, Earl Shilton
LE9 7NR. Mrs & Mrs John & Sue
Osborn, 01455 842609,
susan.osborn1@btinternet.com.
*10m W of Leicester. From A47 after
entering Earl Shilton, Ivydene Close
can be located as the 4th on L from
Leicester side of A47.* Home-made
teas. **Adm £3, chd free.** Suns 29
May; 10 July (11-5). Visitors also
welcome by appt, groups 10+.
1-acre garden with lots of different
areas, a silver birch walk, wildlife pond
with seating, apple tree garden,
Mediterranean planted area and
lawns surrounded with herbaceous
plants and shrubs. Patio area with
climbing roses and wisteria. There is
also a utility garden with greenhouse,
vegetables in beds, herbs and
perennial flower beds, lawn and fruit
cage.
⊛ 🍵 ☎

Pine House

◆ BELGRAVE HALL MUSEUM & GARDENS

Church Road off Thurcaston Road, Belgrave, Leicester LE4 5PE. Leicester City Council, www.leicester.gov.uk/museums. 1½ m N of Leicester. From A6/A563 junction at Redhill roundabout take A6030 Loughborough Rd towards city, signed Outdoor Pursuits Centre. Turn R at 1st T-lights and L at Talbot PH. **Adm £3, chd free. For NGS: Sun 15 May (1-4).** For opening times and information please visit website or telephone.
Historic Grade II listed garden. House and walled garden date from 1709. Incl formal garden, herbaceous garden, rose walks, Victorian evergreen garden, rock and water garden, botanic beds, herb border, woodland garden. Alpine, temperate and tropical glasshouses with wide collection of plants incl banana. The handkerchief tree, Davida Involucrata usually produces a spectacular display of white bracts in May.

  ♿ ☕

BELVOIR CASTLE

See Lincolnshire.

⓻ BENTS FARMHOUSE

Church Drive, Gilmorton LE17 5PF. Mrs Jill Mackenzie, 01455 558566, fourseasons@harborough.uk.com, www.fourseasonsgardendesign.com. 2m N of Lutterworth. **Combined adm with The Grange £3, chd free. Sun & Mon 1, 2 May; Sun 3 July (11-6) Evening Opening Wed 29 June (2-8).** Visitors also welcome by appt June & July.
Georgian farmhouse walled garden created by RHS medal winning designer owner over 20 years and still being developed. Formal beds with large collection of roses and informal cottage style planting. Small potager and some interesting features. Lavender walk, areas for wildlife, wisteria covered pergola and sculptures. Gravel paths.

  ♿ ⚘ ❀ ⛺ ☎

BISHOPS COTTAGE

See Nottinghamshire.

BLUEBELL ARBORETUM AND NURSERY

See Derbyshire.

⓼ 109 BROOK STREET

Wymeswold LE12 6TT. Maggie & Steve Johnson, 01509 880866, sameuk@tiscali.co.uk. 4m NE of Loughborough. From A6006 Wymeswold turn S onto Stockwell, then E along Brook Street. Road side parking along Brook Street. Steep drive with limited disabled parking at house. Tea & Light Refreshments. **Adm £2.50, chd free. Sun 12 June (2-6).** Visitors also welcome by appt June & July only.
·S-facing ¾-acre gently sloping garden with views to open country. Mature garden much improved recently. Patio with roses and clematis, wildlife, fish ponds, mixed borders, vegetable garden, orchard, hot garden, woodland garden plus more. David Austin roses and wide selection of shrubs and perennials. Demonstration of rain water harvesting on limited budget. Access from special parking area over gravel drive.

  ♿ ⚘ ❀ ☕ ☎

GROUP OPENING

⓽ BURBAGE GARDENS

LE10 2LR. 1m S of Hinckley. From M69 J1, take B4109 signed Hinckley. 1st L after 2nd r'about into Sketchley Manor Estate then 1st R, 1st L. All gardens within walking distance. Light refreshments at 7 Hall Rd (Feb) & home-made teas at 6 Denis Rd (May). **Combined adm £3 (Feb) & £3.50 (May), chd free. Suns 27 Feb (11-4); 29 May (11-5).**

7 HALL ROAD
Don & Mary Baker

13 HALL ROAD
Mr & Mrs G A & A J Kierton.
(Not open Sun 27 Feb)

6 DENIS ROAD
Mr & Mrs D A Dawkins

A pleasant West Leicestershire village. 6 Denis Road, small garden designed to look much larger. Wide range of plants incl ferns, hostas and special clematis. Alpines in sinks and large collection of snowdrops. 7 Hall Road, medium sized garden with mixed borders and a good mix of shrubs. Foliage plants, hellebores, spring bulbs, hardy geraniums and unusual perennials. 13 Hall Rd, decorative, medium sized flower garden incl pool and waterfall. Central lawn, herbaceous borders, pergola, summerhouse, greenhouse and small fountain.

  ♿ ❀ ☕

Look out for the gardens with the ☎ – enjoy a private visit . . .

CALKE ABBEY
See Derbyshire.

10 COLDOR
4 Arnesby Lane, Peatling Magna,
Leicester LE8 5UN. Colin & Doreen
Shepherd, 01162 478407. *9m S of
Leicester. 2m W of Arnesby on
A5199. Arnesby Lane is opp Cock
Inn. Garden is on private drive 100yds
from Cock Inn. Parking on Main St.*
Home-made teas at Coldor (June) &
Light refreshments at Farmway (July).
**Adm £2, combined adm with
Farmway £3, chd free. Suns 26
June; 31 July (11-5).** Visitors also
welcome by appt June to mid
August. Max 30 visitors.
$^1/_4$ -acre garden with immaculate
lawns, mixed herbaceous and shrub
borders. Small pond and water
features. Patio with many plants in
containers, alpine rockery. Garden
nursery, plants for sale.

The separate
rooms of the
garden create
surprises around
every corner . . .

11 NEW COPPER COIN
Cross Street, Gaddesby LE7 4WD.
Mrs J Watson. *8m NE of Leicester.
From A607 Rearsby by-pass. L at
Cheney Arms, L at Cross St. (approx
200yrds) garden on L.* **Combined
adm with Parkside £3, chd free.
Sun 10 Apr (11-5).**
Small S-facing garden in centre of
village. Developed on heavy clay, the
garden contains trees and shrubs
together with mixed borders and
centre beds. Small water feature and
several seating areas. Winter aconites
and snowdrops give way to daffodils,
tulips and bluebells.

THE COTTAGE
See Derbyshire.

12 THE DAIRY
Moor Lane, Coleorton LE67 8FQ.
Mr & Mrs J B Moseley, 01530
834539. *2m E of Ashby De La Zouch.
Moor Lane is off A512 200yds W of
Peggs Green roundabout.* **Adm £3,
chd free.** Visitors welcome by appt
June, July & Aug only, groups of
10+, coaches permitted.
Refreshments available on request.
Approx $^1/_2$ acre of mature trees,
shrubs and herbaceous borders
containing many unusual and
architectural plants. Herb garden,
fragrant roses, pergola, Japanese
garden and dry area with grasses and
agaves. The separate rooms of the
garden create surprises around every
corner. Summer flowering plants
create a riot of colour in June and
July. Plant sale Sat 30 April (10-5)
Adm £1 with shared proceeds to the
NGS/St Marys Church. Please note
the garden will not be open.

13 NEW DAIRY COTTAGE
15 Sharnford Road, Sapcote
LE9 4JN. Mrs Norah Robinson-
Smith. *9m SW of Leicester. Follow
NGS signs from centre of Sapcote.*
Home-made teas. **Adm £3, chd free.
Suns 22 May; 26 June (11-4).**
Old cottage garden set in $^3/_4$ acre,
extensively planted with a wide range
of bulbs, shrubs and perennials. With
over 60 varieties of clematis and
many roses climbing over arches,
ropes and trees. Walled garden with
pergola. Garden extends into a
potager.

**14 NEW ♦ DONINGTON LE
HEATH MANOR HOUSE**
Manor Road, Donington Le Heath,
Coalville LE67 2FW. Leicestershire
County Council, 01530 831259,
www.leics-gov-uk/Donington. *7m
from Ashby. Signed off A511 near M1
J22 or A42 J12 with A511.* **Adm
£2.50, chd free. For NGS: Sats
11 June; 2 July (11-4).** For other
opening times and information,
please phone or see garden
website.
C13 Manor House showed how
people lived in Medieval Tudor and
Stuart times. The adjoining stone barn
houses a tea room. Surrounding the
Manor House are period gardens and
woodland planted as part of the
development of the National Forest.

The gardens re-created in a C17 style
incl flower and herb gardens, an
ornamental maze and an orchard.
Awarded Learning Outside the
Classroom quality badge. VAQAS
award as an accredited museum.
Limited access for people with
disabilities to gardens & ground floor
of Manor House. Virtual tour available
showing upper floor.

ELM HOUSE
See Nottinghamshire.

15 FARMWAY
Church Farm Lane, Willoughby
Waterleys LE8 6UD. Eileen
Spencer, 0116 2478321,
eileenfarmway9@msn.com. *9m S of
Leicester. From Leicester take A426.
L at t-lights at Dunton Bassett x-rds.
Follow signs to Willoughby. From M1
J20 take A426 through Lutterworth.
R at t-lights at Dunton Bassett x-rds.
Park in main street.* Light
Refreshments at Willoughby Village
Hall. 31st July only. **Adm £2,
combined adm with Coldor, £3,
chd free. Suns 26 June; 31 July
(11-5).** Visitors also welcome by
appt end of June to mid August.
Groups, Max 20.
W-facing, $^1/_4$ -acre garden on gentle
slope with views across
Leicestershire. Mature plant lover's
garden, closely planted with a wide
variety of shrubs, herbaceous
perennials, roses and clematis. Many
varieties of lavender. Two ponds,
vegetable garden, herbs and
extensive collection of containers.
Good for late summer colour.
Willoughby Embroidery displayed at
village hall 31st. July. Featured in BBC
East Midlands TV & in Garden News.

**16 NEW GOADBY MARWOOD
HALL**
Goadby Marwood, Melton
Mowbray LE14 4LN. Mr & Mrs
Westropp, 01664 464202. *4 miles
NW of Melton Mowbray, between
Waltham on the Wolds & Eastwell.*
Home-made teas. **Adm £4, chd free
(share to the local Air Ambulance).
Sat 21 May (11-4).** Visitors also
welcome by appt anytime, except
end July - mid Aug.
Redesigned in 2000 by the owner
based on C18 plans. A chain of 5
lakes and several walled gardens all
interconnected. Limited wheelchair
access.

17 NEW THE GRANGE
Kimcote, Lutterworth LE17 5RU.
Shaun & Mary Mackaness,
www.thegrangekimcote.co.uk. *12m
S of Leicester. 4m from J20 of M1.
Proceed through Lutterworth town
centre turn R at police station. Follow
signs to Kimcote. From Leicester
follow A426 towards Lutterworth. At
Dunton Bassett turn L towards
Gilmorton and Kimcote. From A5199
towards Bruntingthorpe then via
Walton.* Home-made teas at All Saints
Church (1 May, 3 July). No teas
2 May). **Combined adm with Bents
Farmhouse£3, chd free (share to
LORUS). Sun 1, Mon 2 May; Sun
3 July (11-6) Evening Opening
Wed 29 June (2-8), teas/wine.**
Newly designed and renovated
English country garden hidden behind
original brick walls of beautiful Grade
II listed Queen Anne house. 3/4 -acre
garden with immaculate expanses of
lawn, interesting features, parterre,
pond, croquet lawn and stone
terraces. Herbaceous borders with
collection of Old English roses. Green
oak structures and hand-forged
gazebo and rose arches. Walkways
through wild woodland areas with
mature trees, pleached hornbeams
and naturalised bulbs.
🛏 ☕

GREENWAY
See Northamptonshire.

18 NEW GUNTHORPE HALL
Gunthorpe, nr Oakham LE15 8BE.
Tim Haywood. *1m S of Oakham.
A6003, up drive, past lodges.* Home-
made teas. **Adm £3.50, chd free.
Sun 3 Apr (2-5).**
Large garden in a most beautiful
country setting with extensive views
across the Rutland landscape. A
great deal of recent re-design and
new plantings have transformed this
garden (which opened regularly for
the NGS some years ago). The new
spring bulbs and shrubs are once
again spectacular.
🚾 🌱 ☕

19 HAMMOND ARBORETUM
The Robert Smyth School, Burnmill
Road, Market Harborough
LE16 7JG. Hammond Arboretum.
*From the High Street, follow signs to
The Robert Smyth School via
Bowden Lane to Burnmill Road. Park
in the first entrance on the left.* Home-
made teas. **Adm £3, chd free. Suns
27 Mar; 9 Oct (2-5).**
A site of 2.4-acres containing an

unusual collection of trees and
shrubs, many from Francis
Hammond's original planting dating
from 1913 to 1936 whilst headmaster
of the school. Species from America,
China and Japan with malus and
philadelphus walks and a moat.
Proud owners of 4 'champion' trees
identified by national specialist.
Guided walks and walk plans
available. Some steep paths.
♿ 🐕 ☕

20 HILL PARK FARM
Dodgeford Lane, Belton,
Loughborough LE12 9TE. John &
Jean Adkin, 01530 222208. *6m W of
Loughborough. Dodgeford Lane off
B5324 bet Belton & Osgathorpe.*
Home-made teas. **Adm £2.50, chd
free. Sun 10 July (2-6). Visitors also
welcome by appt in June & July
only, coaches permitted.**
Medium-sized garden to a working
farm. Herbaceous borders, rock
garden; many planted stone troughs
and pergola with clematis and roses.
❁ ☕ ☎

HOLYWELL HALL
See Lincolnshire.

21 THE HOMESTEAD
Normanton-by-Bottesford
NG13 0EP. John & Shirley Palmer,
01949 842745. *8m W of Grantham.
From A52. In Bottesford turn N,
signed Normanton; last house on R
before disused airfield. From A1, in
Long Bennington follow signs S to
Normanton, 1st house on L.* **Adm £2,
chd free. Sun 6 Mar (1-5). Visitors
also welcome by appt, single &
groups.**
3/4 -acre informal plant lover's garden.
Vegetable garden, small orchard,
woodland area, many hellebores,
growing collection (about 100) of
snowdrops and some single peonies
and salvias. Collections of hostas and
sempervivums. National Collection of
heliotropes.
🐕 ❁ NCCPG ☎

Large garden in a
most beautiful
country setting with
extensive views
across the Rutland
landscape . . .

GROUP OPENING

22 NEW KETTON GARDENS
Ketton, Stamford PE9 3RD. *4m W
of Stamford. On A6121.* Home-made
teas at The Old Vicarage. **Combined
adm £3.50, chd free. Sun 26 June
(2-6).**

NEW ORCHARD HOUSE
Desforges. Malcolm &
Rosemary

THE OLD VICARAGE
Dick & Jenny Bell

Two different styles of garden in this
beautiful Rutland village where the
houses are built of local stone with
Collyweston roofs. **Orchard House** is
on the High St next to the Northwick
Arms PH. This small garden was once
a walled farmyard, it is now randomly
planted. A pond, water features,
summerhouse, gravel garden and
variety of potted plants are
surrounded by extensive climbing
roses, clematis and honeysuckles.
The Old Vicarage snuggles in a
quiet corner between the ancient
Church of St Mary's and the bubbling
R. Chater. Stone walls and mature
hedging divide this 1 1/2 -acre garden
into areas with different functions and
form. Lawns are bordered by
herbaceous and shrub planting. A
swimming pool garden leads to the
river and a tranquil area incl a
fountain and several specimen trees.
Children must be supervised at all
times. Wheelchair access but some
gravel.
❁ ☕

KILSBY GARDENS
See Northamptonshire.

23 27 LINDEN DRIVE
Evington LE5 6AJ. Marlene & John
Revis. *3m S of Leicester. From
Leicester take A6 (London Rd) turn L
at sign A6030 'Ring Rd East' after 1m
turn R at T-lights into Evington Lane.
50yds L into Linden Drive.* Home-
made teas. **Adm £2, chd free.
Sun 24 July (2-5).**
Small town garden designed by
the current owners in 2007 with
mixed borders and interesting
features.
❁ ☕

Orchards

24 LONG CLOSE
Main St, Woodhouse Eaves
LE12 8RZ. John Oakland, 01509
890376. *4m S of Loughborough.
Nr M1 J23. From A6, W in Quorn.*
Home-made teas. **Adm £4, chd 50p.**
Sat 14 (2-5), Sun 15 May (11-4).
Visitors also welcome daily Tues to
Sun & BH weekends, April to July &
Sept to mid Oct. Group visits by
appt only.
5 acres spring bulbs, rhododendrons,
azaleas, camellias, magnolias, many
rare shrubs, mature trees, lily ponds;
terraced lawns, herbaceous borders,
potager in walled kitchen garden,
penstemon collection, wild flower
meadow walk. Winter, spring,
summer and autumn colour, a garden
for all seasons. Plants for sale. Partial
disabled access only.
&. ✿ ☕ ☎

GROUP OPENING

25 LYNDON GARDENS
Post Office Lane, Lyndon, Oakham
LE15 8TZ. *S Shore of Rutland water.
Between Oakham & Uppingham
(A6003), S Shore of Rutland water,
¹/₂ m off Manton/Edith Weston Rd.*
Combined adm £3.50, chd free
(share to Riding for the Disabled).
Evening Opening wine, Wed 22
June (5-8.30).

NEW▶ **PARK COTTAGE**
Gill & Mike Walsh

PARSONS ORCHARD
Sarah & Mike Peck

THE POST HOUSE
Pauline & Clive Pitts

Three adjoining gardens in the
delightful and secluded village of
Lyndon, largely owned by the Conant
family, who have occupied Lyndon
Hall since it was built in 1667. The
village is one of the few in Rutland
that are s-facing and is mainly
traditional stone-built. Small C12
church will be open; and visit the
developing Community Kitchen
Garden on the way. **Parson's
Orchard**, a ¹/₂ -acre S-facing village
garden in a beautiful setting. Mixed
borders, shrubs, herbaceous,
scented/old fashioned roses,
integrated herb and vegetable
garden, peaceful corners. **The Post
House** is a small, stylish and
contemporary garden with rural views
to rear of recently constructed stone
cottage. Planting designed with
emphasis on foliage and yr-round
interest. Some gravel. **Park Cottage** a
delightful small old-fashioned cottage
garden, well planned and full of
colour, which enjoys the same
wonderful southerly aspect.
&. ✿

THE MALTINGS
See Northamptonshire.

26 MILL HOUSE
118 Welford Road, Wigston,
Leicester LE18 3SN. Mr & Mrs P
Measures. *4m S of Leicester. 1m
S of Wigston, on A5199 (old A50).*
Home-made teas & Light
Refreshments. **Adm £2, chd free.**
Suns 15 May; 17 July (11-5)
Evening Opening Wed 15 June
(3-7). Visitors also welcome by
appt June & July. Groups of 10+.
Walled town garden; extensive plant
variety. Unusual and interesting
design features incorporating
planting, bygones and memorabilia.
A genuine journey back in time.
Featured in BBC East Midlands
Today.
✿ ☕

27 NORTH LUFFENHAM HALL
Church Street, North Luffenham
LE15 8JR. Roger & Mary Canham.
*5m from Stamford A1, 2m from A47
Morcott. In the heart of the village
next to the church.* Home-made teas.
Adm £3.50, chd free (share to
Mary's Meals). Sun 29 May
(11-4.30).
This is only the second time the Hall
gardens have opened for the NGS.
7 acres of beautiful gardens against
the backdrop of a C16 hall. Wonderful
collection of imaginatively designed
gardens within a garden incl working
fruit and vegetable garden, pond,
meadow wildlife haven,
Mediterranean olive grove, with folly
and pergola plus much more.
&. ✿ ☕

28 THE OLD HALL
Main Street, Market Overton
LE15 7PL. Mr & Mrs Timothy Hart,
01572 767145,
stefa@hambleton.co.uk. *6m N of
Oakham. Beyond Cottesmore; 5m
from A1 via Thistleton. 10m E from
Melton Mowbray via Wymondham.*
Home-made teas. **Adm £4, chd free
(share to Rutland MacMillan
Cancer Support). Sun 17 Apr (2-6).
Visitors also welcome by appt.**
Garden is set on a southerly ridge
overlooking Catmose Vale. Garden
now on 4 levels with stone walls and
yew hedges dividing the garden up
into enclosed areas with herbaceous
borders, shrubs, and young and
mature trees. In 2006 the lower part
of garden was planted with new
shrubs to create a walk with mown
paths. Terrace and lawn give a great
sense of space, enhancing the view.
Neil Hewertson has been involved in
the gardens design since 1990s.
Gravel and steep grass paths.

Mixed borders,
planted to
encourage wildlife,
including pond,
and provide a
family friendly
environment . . .

**THE OLD RECTORY, CLIFTON
CAMPVILLE**
See Staffordshire Birmingham &
part of West Midlands.

29 THE OLD STABLES
Bruntingthorpe LE17 5QL. Gordon
& Hilary Roberts. *10m S of
Leicester. From Leicester A5199, R at
Arnesby, follow signs for
Bruntingthorpe. At end of village R
towards Peatling Parva, 200 yds on
R. From M1, J20 for Lutterworth
A426. In town R front of police
station, follow signs for
Bruntingthorpe. Additional parking in*

*village and approach through
churchyard.* Home-made teas. **Adm
£3, chd free. Suns 12 June; 17 July
(11-5).**
Plant-lovers' 1-acre country garden
where the different parts combine to
make a delightful whole. Wide grass
walks set off the large herbaceous
borders packed with a variety of
perennials and shrubs. Many mature
trees, wild-life area with pond; striking
views to Leicester. Rockery, raised
alpine beds, tender plants in
containers. Featured in Leicestershire
& Rutland Life magazine. Gravel at
entrance.

**30 NEW THE OLD VICARAGE,
BURLEY**
Church Road. LE15 7SU. Jonathan
& Sandra Blaza, 01572 770588,
sandra.blaza@btinternet.com. *1m
NE of Oakham. Just off B668
between Oakham and Cottesmore.
Church Rd opp village green, garden
1st L off Church Rd.* Home-made
teas. **Adm £3.50, chd free (share to
Eden Valley Hospice). Sun 15 May
(2-5.30). Visitors also welcome by
appt. Coaches permitted.**
3-acre country garden, planted for yr-
round interest incl walled garden (with
vine-house) producing fruit, herbs,
vegetables and cut flowers. Formal
lawns and borders, lime walk, rose
gardens and a rill through avenue of
standard wisteria. Wildlife garden with
pond, 2 orchards and ancient beech
woodland. Wheelchair access to
most of garden via grassy paths,
some gravel, slopes & steps.

**31 THE OLD VICARAGE,
WHISSENDINE**
LE15 7HG. Prof Peter & Dr Sarah
Furness, 01664 474549,
shfdesign@pathology.plus.com. *5m
N of Oakham. Whissendine village is
signed from A606 between Melton
Mowbray & Oakham. Head for church
- very visible tower. The Old Vicarage
is adjacent, higher up the hill. Main
entrance on opp side, 1st L on
Station Rd; alternative entrance from
churchyard. Maps available on
website.* Home-made teas served in
the church. **Adm £3, chd free. Sun
22 May (2-5.30). Visitors also
welcome by appt. Please book well
in advance.**
²/₃ -acre packed with variety. Walled
terrace with mature olive trees, formal
fountain and raised beds backed by
small gothic orangery burgeoning with

tender plants. Herbaceous borders
surround main lawn. Wisteria tunnel
leads to orchard filled with naturalised
bulbs, home to two beehives. Hidden
'white walk' overflowing with unusual
plants. Much more... Plant Stall.
Featured in GGG.

32 THE PARK HOUSE
Glaston Park, Spring Lane, Glaston
LE15 9BW. Sheila & Stuart
Makings, 01572 821214,
sheilamakings@btconnect.com. *6m
S of Oakham on A47. 2m E of A6003
Uppingham roundabout travelling on
A47 towards Peterborough.* Home-
made teas at Glaston Village Hall.
**Adm £3.50, chd free. Sun 27 Mar
(1-5); Sun 3 July (2-6). Visitors also
welcome by appt for groups 20+.
No teas for private visits.**
4 acres approx of historic parkland,
formerly part of grounds of Glaston
Hall. Informal walks incl extensive lime
arbour. Serpentine yew hedge,
mature trees, medieval ha-ha and fish
ponds. Herbaceous borders,
traditional rose garden. Rural views,
wildlife friendly. Wild wood walk.
Carpets of spring bulbs, hellebores
and shrubs. Children welcome but
must be supervised at all times.
Ornamental wildfowl. Adjacent
parking, some gravel and bark,
sloping grounds, unfenced water.

33 PARKSIDE
6 Park Hill, Gaddesby LE7 4WH.
Mr & Mrs D Wyrko, 01664 840385,
david.wyrko1@btopenworld.com.
*8m NE of Leicester. From A607
Rearsby bypass turn off for
Gaddesby. L at Cheney Arms. Garden
400yds on R.* Home-made teas. **Adm
£3, chd free. Sun 10 Apr (11-5).
Also opening with Copper Coin
10 April. Visitors also welcome by
appt April to September. Any size
group welcome.**
1¹/₄ -acre garden and woodland
evolving from original planting. Mature
trees and shrubs, together with
informal mixed borders, planted to
encourage wildlife, including pond,
and provide a family friendly
environment. Vegetable and fruit area
together with new greenhouse and
cold frame. Many spring bulbs and
hellebores in a woodland setting.

PIECEMEAL
See Nottinghamshire.

34 PINE HOUSE

Gaddesby LE7 4XE. Mr & Mrs T Milward, 01664 840213. *8m NE of Leicester. From A607, turn off for Gaddesby*. Home-made teas. **Adm £3.50, chd free.** Visitors welcome by appt available april to october groups welcome.

2-acre garden with fine mature trees, woodland walk, and water garden. Herb and potager garden and wisteria archway to Victorian vinery. Pleached lime trees, mixed borders with rare and unusual plants. Wide variety of tender plants in gravel garden and terracotta pot garden. Interesting topiary hedges and box trees. A wonderful handkerchief tree, Wellingtonia and large copper beech. Yew hedge shaped as a large dragon.

☕ ☎

35 PREBENDAL HOUSE

Empingham LE15 8PS. Mr J Partridge. *5m E of Oakham. 5m W of Stamford.* On A606. Home-made teas. **Adm £3.50, chd free.** Sun 12 June (2-5.30).

House (not open) built in 1688; summer palace for the Bishop of Lincoln. 4-acre garden incl herbaceous borders, water garden, topiary and kitchen gardens.

🏡 ❀ ☕

> 3 neighbours with a common interest in creating a beautiful garden in their own individual style . . .

GROUP OPENING

36 NEW QUORN ORCHARD GARDENS

Barrow Road, Quorn LE12 8DH. *2m S of Loughborough. From A6 take exit signed Woodhouse, Quorn & Great Central Railway. At 1st set T-lights go straight on towards Quorn village centre. At small r'about turn L into Barrow Road. Parking often congested, additional parking available in school field at far end of road. Some SatNavs do not recognise Barrow Road as no through road.* Home-made teas at 45 Barrow Road. **Combined adm £2.50, chd free.** Sun 5 June (11-5).

NEW 35 BARROW ROAD
Sally Ash

NEW 45 BARROW ROAD
Mr & Mrs Cox

NEW 37 BARROW ROAD
Jacqui Fowler & Pat Manning

Quorn is a large village, close to the National Forest, that retains many of the qualities of a rural settlement, with generous green spaces and countryside walks. Features of local interest incl St Bartholomew's Church dating back to 1153, the Great Central Railway, many restaurants and PHs. These 3 neighbours with a common interest in creating a beautiful garden in their own individual style, would like to invite you to share their interest for an afternoon. Typical of 1930s urban properties, these gardens have generous proportions and are created upon an old orchard.

❀ ☕

37 RIDGEWOLD FARM

Burton Lane, Wymeswold, Loughborough LE12 6UN. Robert & Ann Waterfall, 01509 881689. *5m SE of Loughborough. Off Burton Lane between A6006 & B676.* Home-made teas. **Adm £2.50, chd free.** Evening Openings Weds 25 May, 22 June (3-9). Visitors also welcome by appt June & July, max 40 visitors, coaches permitted.

2½-acre outstanding garden around a new farmhouse set in rural landscape. Approached by a sweeping drive through an arboretum. Special interests incl clematis pergola, wisteria, cytisus battandiere, spring-flowering shrubs, ivy cloister, rose garden, herbaceous borders, water feature with a large natural fish pond, kitchen garden, fruit and native plantation with woodland walks. All achieved during last 9 years. Treasure hunt for children. Gravel paths.

♿ 🏡 ❀ ☕ ☎

GROUP OPENING

38 SOUTH KILWORTH GARDENS

Nr Lutterworth LE17 6DX. *15m S of Leicester. From M1 J20, take A4304 towards Market Harborough. At Walcote turn R, signed South Kilworth.* Home-made teas at Croft Acre. **Adm £3, combined adm £3.50, chd free.** Mon 30 May; Sats 18, 25 June (11-5). Visitors also welcome by appt.

CROFT ACRE
Colin & Verena Olle
Visitors also welcome by appt June to mid July.
01858 575791
colin.olle@tiscali.co.uk

OAK TREE HOUSE
Pam & Martin Shave.
Not open Mon 30 May. Visitors also welcome by appt please contact Croft Acre.

South Kilworth (or South Kynelingworth as it was known in 1186) is a small village tucked away in the SW corner of Leicestershire, with excellent views over the Avon valley and Hemploe hills. The restored Church of Norman origin, which will be open, features 3 original Norman arches and a C13 font. Come and view two gardens of different styles. 1-acre garden with formal and informal rooms for quiet contemplation. Patio, wildlife ponds and stream, informally planted herbaceous and perennial borders. Summerhouse, rose and wisteria clothed pergolas. Circular rose and rope garden with unusual water sculpture. Vegetable garden. New formal front driveway, garden and water feature. Enjoy delicious tea and cake in sumptuous setting. ⅔ acre garden with newly designed upper lawn, with stone circle and sculpture to complement the formal layout. Large, colourful herbaceous borders, ornamental vegetable plots. Pond and greenhouse. Patios with numerous pots and baskets. Arched pergolas with roses and clematis. Many benches to sit and admire the views! Surrounded by mature trees.

♿ ❀ ☕ ☎

39 STOKE ALBANY HOUSE

Desborough Road, Stoke Albany LE16 8PT. Mr & Mrs A M Vinton, 01858 535227. *4m E of Market Harborough. Via A427 to Corby, turn to Stoke Albany, R at the White Horse (B669) garden ½ m on L.* **Adm £3.50, chd free (share to Marie Curie Cancer Care).** Weds, 1 June to 29 June; (2-4.30). Visitors also welcome by appt, June, Tues & Weds only.

4-acre country-house garden; fine

trees and shrubs with wide herbaceous borders and sweeping striped lawn. Good display of bulbs in spring, roses June and July. Walled grey garden; nepeta walk arched with roses, parterre with box and roses. Mediterranean garden. Heated greenhouse, potager with topiary, water feature garden and sculptures. Featured on Radio Northampton Green Wellie Show. Wheelchair users avoiding rough paths can see most of the garden.

40 NEW TEBUTTS FARM
Butt Lane, Normanton-on-Soar LE12 5EE. **Helen & Peter Lister,** 01509 843340, **helen.lister10@btinternet.com.** *12m N of Leicester. Butt Lane is opposite The Plough in Normanton. Tebutts Farm is up the hill, past railway bridge on R.* Home-made teas. **Adm £3, chd free. Suns 29 May; 10 July (1-6). Visitors also welcome by appt throughout May, June, July & Aug. Any size group. Coaches permitted.**
Country garden with memorable field views across the Soar Valley, with rose beds, shrubberies and ponds. Herbaceous border and cutting garden with variety of flowers and herbs, many grown from seed. Large orchard is home to hens and 12m wind turbine. Several areas for sitting. Courtyard in bloom in July. Vegetable garden. Someone will availble to talk about renewable energy.

41 NEW 7 THE CRESCENT
Rothley LE7 7RW. **Mrs Fiona Dunkley.** *Off Montsorrel Lane, Rothley. Parking available in Montsorrel Lane.* Home-made teas. **Adm £2, chd free. Sun 21 Aug (1-5).**
Small, well designed garden with interesting and unusual plants, incl many grasses and bamboos. Water features.

42 THORPE LUBENHAM HALL
Lubenham LE16 9TR. **Sir Bruce & Lady MacPhail.** *2m W of Market Harborough. From Market Harborough take 3rd L off main rd, down Rushes Lane, past church on L, under old railway bridge and straight on up private drive.* Cream Teas. **Adm £3, chd free. Wed 18 May (10-4.30).**
15 acres of formal and informal

garden surrounded by parkland and arable. Many mature trees. Traditional herbaceous borders and various water features. Rose and lavender beds circling large pond. Walled pool garden with raised beds. Ancient moat area along driveway. Gravel paths, some steep slopes and steps.

GROUP OPENING

43 WALTON GARDENS
LE17 5RP. *4m NE of Lutterworth. M1 J20 and, via Lutterworth follow signs for Kimcote and Walton, or from Leicester take A5199. After Shearsby turn R signed Bruntingthorpe. Follow signs.* Home-made teas. **Adm £4, chd free. Sun 12, Wed 15 June (11-5).**

THE MEADOWS
Mr & Mrs Falkner

ORCHARDS
Mr & Mrs G Cousins

SANDYLAND
Martin & Linda Goddard

TOAD HALL
Sue Beardmore

Small village set in beautiful south Leicestershire countryside. The four gardens at walton are in such contrasting sizes and styles that; together, they make the perfect garden visit. There is a plantsman's garden filled with gorgeous rare plants; a Modernist garden where all the leaves are green (no variegated, gold or purple foliage) featuring the extensive use of grasses and a lovely view across the surrounding landscape; a traditional and very pretty country garden with an excellent vegetable plot; last but not least, a really delightful enclosed cottage garden.

Large orchard is home to hens and 12 metre wind turbine . . .

44 NEW WARWICK GLEN
Willesley Road, Willesley, Ashby de la Zouch LE65 2QA. **Alison & Alan Cross.** *1m SE of Ashby de la Zouch. At J12 of A42 take Ashby/Willesley rd towards Ashby de la Zouch. After 1m turn L into Willesley Rd past golf club. Warwick Glen 200yrds on L.* Light refreshments & teas. **Adm £2, chd free. Suns 26 June; 17 July (11-5).**
$^1/_4$ acre packed with plant and design variety. Large frontage incl small and mature trees, perennial areas and 20 square metres of raised vegetable borders. Rear garden consists of patio, gravel and grass area, rockery, small tropical feature, perennial area and children's woodland walk. Large summerhouse and new additions incl octagonal greenhouse and hen house.

45 NEW 2 WELFORD ROAD
Sibbertoft LE16 9UJ. **Geoff Smith & Sue Garman,** 01858 880215, **geoffsmith269@gmail.com.** *6m SW of Market Harborough.* Home-made teas. Also catering in village hall Suns. **Adm £2.50, chd free. Sun 7, Sat 27 Aug; Sun 11 Sept (11-6) Evening Opening Fri 19 Aug (6-9). Visitors also welcome by appt all of Aug, minimum group size 10, max 30.**
$^1/_3$ acre of mixed herbaceous beds, shrubs and a collection of some 70 different clemetis that have been planted over the last 2yrs. Easily accessible gravel drive.

46 WESTVIEW
1 St Thomas's Rd, Great Glen LE8 9EH. **Gill & John Hadland,** 0116 2592170, **gill@hadland.wanadoo.co.uk.** *7m S of Leicester. Take either r'about from A6 into Great Glen. In village centre (War Memorial) follow NGS signs towards Burton Overy.* Home-made teas. **Adm £2, chd free. Sun 27 Feb (11-4); Sun 26 June; Sun 4 Sept (11-5). Visitors also welcome by appt.**
Small walled cottage-style garden with yr-round interest. Interesting and unusual plants, many grown from seed. Formal box parterre herb garden, courtyard, small wildlife pond, greenhouse, vegetable and fruit area. Auricula display. Small collection of Galanthus (snowdrops). Featured in Leicestershire and Rutland Life magazine.

Visit a garden in your own time – look out for the ☎

A hidden treasure and a truly relaxing experience for all the family . . .

churches, All Saints and St Wistans. It also has a unique Frameworks Knitters Museum (open Sundays) Two small but very interesting gardens. Wollhouse Close is designed to attract birds and bees with herbaceous borders and many varieties of hosta. Gladstone Street is designed to look larger with perennials, containers, pond and unusual shade house.

47 ◆ **WHATTON GARDENS**
Kegworth, Loughborough
LE12 5BG. Lord & Lady Crawshaw, whattho@tiscali.co.uk. *4m NE of Loughborough. On A6 between Hathern & Kegworth; 2¹/₂ m SE of J24 on M1.* **Adm £3.50, chd free. For NGS: Suns 15 May; 10 July (11-6). For opening times and information please email.**
A wonderful extensive 15 acre 19th century country house garden. Arboretum with many fine trees, large herbaceous borders, traditional rose garden, ornamental ponds, flowering shrubs and many spring bulbs. Nooks and crannies to explore. A hidden treasure and a truly relaxing experience for all the family. Featured in local television coverage of a reunion of War Babies. Gravel paths.

GROUP OPENING

48 NEW **WIGSTON MAGNA GARDENS**
Wigston Magna LE18 1AE. *4m Sof Leicester. Off Wigston bypass (A5199) follow signs off r'aboutfor Gladstone St. & t'lights for Wellhouse Close.* Home-made teas. **Adm £3, chd free.** Sats 18 June, 9 July (11-5); Suns 19 June, 10 July (1-5).

> NEW **28 GLADSTONE STREET**
> Chris & Janet Huscroft
> Visitors also welcome by appt June & July.
> 0116 2886014
> chris.huscroft@tiscali.co.uk

> NEW **1 WELLHOUSE CLOSE**
> Barry & Mary Haywood
> Visitors also welcome by appt, anytime.
> 0116 2884018
> maryehayward@googlemail.com

Wigston Magna is an ancient borough 4m S of Leicester. It has a mix of old and new buildings, incl 2 medieval

GROUP OPENING

49 NEW **WYMESWOLD GARDENS**
Loughborough LE12 6TU. *3m NE of Longborough. On A6006 between Melton and Kegworth.* Home-made teas at Cradock Cottage. **Combined adm £3, chd free.** Sun 22 May (1-5).

> NEW **88 BROOK STREET**
> Adrian & Ita Cooke

> NEW **CRADOCK COTTAGE**
> Mike & Carol Robinson

Wymeswold is an attractive village on the Leicestershire/Nottinghamshire border, midway between the cities of Nottingham and Leicester. Both these gardens are owner maintained and almost adjacent to each other on the South side of Brook Street. Although designed in contrasting styles, both gardens provide fine views of the village and surrounding countryside. Display & stall by garden retailers - The Worm That Turned.

Leicestershire & Rutland County Volunteers

Sign up to our eNewsletter for news and updates

Oak Tree House

Be tempted by a plant from a plant stall ⊗

LINCOLNSHIRE

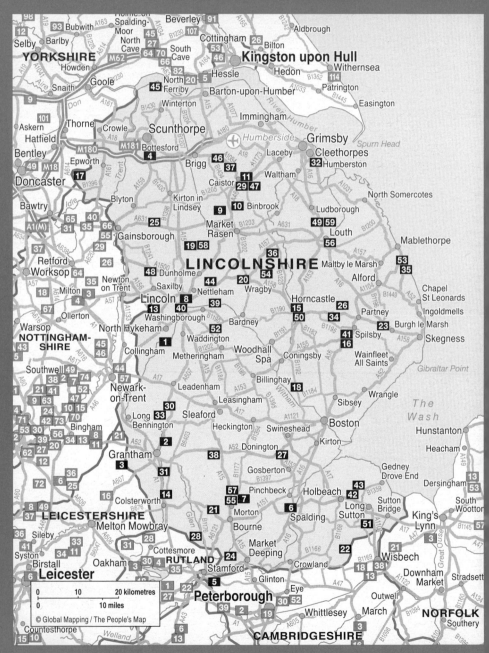

Opening Dates

February

Saturday 12
31 Little Ponton Hall
Sunday 13
31 Little Ponton Hall
Thursday 17
20 Goltho House
Friday 18
20 Goltho House
Saturday 26
7 21 Chapel Street
Sunday 27
7 21 Chapel Street

March

Sunday 20
13 Doddington Hall Gardens
Sunday 27
46 Pinefields

April

Saturday 2
19 The Garden House
58 West Barn
Sunday 3
19 The Garden House
58 West Barn
Saturday 9
5 Burghley House Private South Gardens
Sunday 10
5 Burghley House Private South Gardens
32 1 Lomond Grove
Sunday 17
21 Grimsthorpe Castle
32 1 Lomond Grove
41 The Old Rectory
Friday 22
14 Easton Walled Gardens
Sunday 24
59 Woodlands

May

Sunday 1
35 Marigold Cottage
Saturday 14
2 Belton House
Sunday 22
16 Fen View
41 The Old Rectory
52 Station House
Wednesday 25
13 Doddington Hall Gardens

Saturday 28
34 Manor House
57 10 Wendover Close
Sunday 29
27 The Hawthorns
57 10 Wendover Close
59 Woodlands
Monday 30
20 Goltho House

June

Saturday 4
55 Walters Cottage
Sunday 5
18 Frog Hall Cottage
39 Mulberry Croft
54 The Walled Garden
55 Walters Cottage
Sunday 12
8 The Coach House
10 Corner House
22 Guanock House
30 Les Allees
40 Multum in Parvo
50 Sir Joseph Banks Tribute Garden
Monday 13
3 Belvoir Castle
Tuesday 14
28 Holywell Hall
Thursday 16
21 Grimsthorpe Castle
Sunday 19
27 The Hawthorns
38 The Moat
Monday 20
3 Belvoir Castle
Saturday 25
4 Bottesford Gardens
35 Marigold Cottage
53 Sutton on Sea Gardens
Sunday 26
1 Aubourn Hall
4 Bottesford Gardens
33 The Long House
42 The Old Vicarage
43 Old White House
49 Shepherds Hey
52 Station House
59 Woodlands

July

Saturday 2
36 2 Mill Cottage
Sunday 3
10 Frog Hall Cottage
29 Hope House
37 Mill Farm
45 Pegasus House
47 Ramada
Sunday 10
9 Cobwebs Nursery & Garden

48 73 Saxilby Road
50 Sir Joseph Banks Tribute Garden
Wednesday 13
56 68 Watts Lane
Saturday 16
6 39 Cathedral Drive
Sunday 17
6 39 Cathedral Drive
Saturday 23
2 Belton House
17 Field House Farm
51 South Holland House
Sunday 24
17 Field House Farm
51 South Holland House
Saturday 30
17 Field House Farm
Sunday 31
17 Field House Farm
23 Gunby Hall
52 Station House
59 Woodlands

August

Sunday 7
26 Harrington Hall
56 68 Watts Lane
Sunday 14
9 Cobwebs Nursery & Garden
11 The Crocosmia Gardens
50 Sir Joseph Banks Tribute Garden
Sunday 21
56 68 Watts Lane
Sunday 28
29 Hope House
47 Ramada
Monday 29
34 Manor House

September

Saturday 3
25 Hall Farm
Sunday 4
25 Hall Farm
Sunday 11
35 Marigold Cottage

Look out for the gardens with the ☎ enjoy a private visit . . .

Friday 16
24 The Hall Cottage
Saturday 17
2 Belton House
Saturday 24
19 The Garden House
58 West Barn
Sunday 25
19 The Garden House
58 West Barn
59 Woodlands

October
Saturday 1
51 South Holland House
Sunday 2
48 73 Saxilby Road
51 South Holland House

February 2012
Saturday 25
7 21 Chapel Street
Sunday 26
7 21 Chapel Street

Gardens open to the public
2 Belton House
3 Belvoir Castle
5 Burghley House Private South Gardens
13 Doddington Hall Gardens
14 Easton Walled Gardens
19 The Garden House
20 Goltho House
21 Grimsthorpe Castle
23 Gunby Hall
25 Hall Farm

By appointment only
15 15 Elmhirst Road
44 Overbeck

Also open by Appointment ☎
1 Aubourn Hall
6 39 Cathedral Drive
7 21 Chapel Street
11 The Crocosmia Gardens
22 Guanock House
24 The Hall Cottage
28 Holywell Hall
32 1 Lomond Grove
34 Manor House
57 Marigold Cottage, Sutton on Sea Gardens
38 The Moat
41 The Old Rectory
42 The Old Vicarage

45 Pegasus House
48 73 Saxilby Road
55 Walters Cottage
56 68 Watts Lane
57 10 Wendover Close
59 Woodlands

The Gardens

ASKHAM GARDENS
See Nottinghamshire.

1 ◆ AUBOURN HALL
Harmston Road, Aubourn, nr Lincoln LN5 9DZ. Mr & Mrs Christopher Nevile, 01522 788224, ginny@aubournhall.co.uk or andrew@aubournhall.co.uk. *7m SW of Lincoln. Signed off A607 at Harmston & off A46 at Thorpe.* Home-made teas & light refreshments. **Adm £4, chd free.** Sun 26 June (2-5.30). Visitors also welcome by appt throughout the season. Contact Andrew Widd, Head Gardener.
Approx 5 acres. Lawns, mature trees, shrubs, roses, mixed borders, new rose garden, wild garden and topiary, spring bulbs and ponds. C11 church adjoining.
  ♿ ⚘ ☕ ☎

BANK FARM
See Norfolk.

THE BEECHES
See Nottinghamshire.

2 ◆ BELTON HOUSE
Grantham NG32 2LS. National Trust, 01476 566116, www.nationaltrust.org.uk. *3m NE of Grantham. On A607 Grantham to Lincoln rd. Easily reached & signed from A1 (Grantham N junction).* **Adm £9, chd £5. For NGS: Sats 14 May; 23 July; 17 Sept (10.30-5.30).** For other opening times and information, please phone or see garden website.
The 35-acre gardens at Belton House are a yr-round inspiration. Formal gardens with orangery by Sir Jeffrey Wyatville, iconic fountain and timeless topiary lead on to informal woodland areas, lakeside and boathouse. Wheelchair users please ask for access map of grounds. Most areas of garden accessible but there are gravel paths & some steps preclude the ornagery.
  ♿ ⚘ ☕ ☎

3 ◆ BELVOIR CASTLE
Grantham NG32 4DQ. The Duke & Duchess of Rutland, 01476 871002, www.belvoircastle.com. *9m from Grantham. Follow brown heritage signs for Belvoir Castle on A52, A1, A607.* **Adm £5, chd £3. For NGS: Mons 13, 20 June (11-5).** For other opening times and information, please phone or see garden website.
English Heritage Grade 2 garden. Secluded in steep woodland ½ m from castle. A haven of tranquillity created around original moss house. Magical hillside setting in natural amphitheatre with fresh water springs. Many mature specimen trees and shrubs ensure all-yr colour. Rhododendrons, azaleas, naturalised daffodils, primroses and bluebells. Tallest bird cherry (90ft) and yew tree (93ft) in British Isles. Flat shoes essential. Rose garden with sculpture exhibition. Steep slopes.
  ♿ ☕ ☎

> A haven of tranquillity created around original moss house. Magical hillside setting in natural amphitheatre . . .

GROUP OPENING

4 BOTTESFORD GARDENS
Bottesford, Scunthorpe DN17 2QY. *S of Scunthorpe. A159 Scunthorpe to Messingham Rd.* Home-made teas. **Combined adm £3, chd free. Sat & Sun 25, 26 June (1-5).**

280A MESSINGHAM ROAD
Mrs Ann Brumpton

NEW 278 MESSINGHAM ROAD
Mr Gerry Dawson

Two large gardens set in the village of Bottesford. 280a Messingham Rd. Well tendered lawns are surrounded by summer bedding, garden ornaments, vibrant pots and fountain.

Follow us on Facebook and Twitter

Thatched gazebo covering ornamental pond and waterfall. 278 Messingham Rd. Split level garden with elevated sections. Acer trees, bedding plants and shrubs, archway with clematis and climbers, enclosed upper garden with greenhouse and potting shed. Why not top your visit off with a lovely home-made tea. Bottesford is a small town on S side of Scunthorpe adjoining open countryside. Bottesford Beck walks, C12 St Peters-ad-Vinicula Church, Templars Bath spring and St Johns Ragwell; Bulls Field with its mature trees. Featured in local press and on local radio.

---

5 ◆ **BURGHLEY HOUSE PRIVATE SOUTH GARDENS**
Stamford PE9 3JY. Burghley House Preservation Trust, 01780 752451, www.burghley.co.uk. *1m E of Stamford. From Stamford follow signs to Burghley via B1443.* **Adm £3.50, chd £2.** For NGS: Sat & Sun 9, 10 Apr (11-4). **For other opening times and information, please phone or see garden website.**
On 9th and 10th April the Private South Gardens at Burghley House will open for the NGS with spectacular spring bulbs in parklike setting with magnificent trees and the opportunity to enjoy Capability Brown's famous lake and summerhouse. Entry to the Private South Gardens via Orangery. The Garden of Surprises, Sculpture Garden and house are open as normal. Regular admission prices apply.

---

6 **39 CATHEDRAL DRIVE**
Spalding PE11 1PQ. Mr & Mrs John Mepham, 01775 725291. *1m W of Spalding. Take A151 towards Bourne. Turn R onto Park Rd immed after railway Xing. Then 1st L onto Pennygate, 1st R into Woolram Wygate, 2nd R into Lincoln Way, R into Cathedral Drive.* Light refreshments & teas. **Adm £2.50, chd free.** Sat & Sun 16, 17 July (1-5). **Visitors also welcome by appt 18 to 31 July only, max 20.**
Medium-sized town garden filled with perennials and annuals to supply a rainbow of colours. Ornamental trees, path leading to second garden and patio. New for 2010 Japanese Garden. Featured in 'The Guardian' and local press.

21 Chapel Street

7 **21 CHAPEL STREET**
Hacconby, Bourne PE10 0UL. Cliff & Joan Curtis, 01778 570314. *3m N of Bourne. A15, turn E at Xrds into Hacconby, L at village green.* Home-made teas. **Adm £2, chd free.** Sat & Sun 26, 27 Feb; (11-5); 25, 26 Feb 2012 (11-5). **Visitors also welcome by appt.**
Cottage garden overflowing with plants for yr-round interest; early openings for large collection of unusual snowdrops, hellebores with numerous other spring plants and bulbs. Autumn large borders of asters and dahlias accompanied by other herbaceous plants and shrubs for interest.

8 **THE COACH HOUSE**
1A Hereward Street, Lincoln LN1 3EW. Jo & Ken Slone, www.bruntswoldcoachhouse.co.uk *Central Lincoln. Coming off the A46 N circular take B1226 to Newport. 150yds from Radio Lincs turn into Rasen Lane, then take1st R into Hereward St. Parking at Lord Tennyson PH on Raven Lane.* Home-made teas. **Combined adm with Multum in Parvo £3, chd free.** Sun 12 June (11-5).
Small courtyard garden behind Victorian town house, 5mins walk from historic quarter of Lincoln. Brimming with unusual plants, climbers and sculpture. Many plants grown in containers for versatility, complemented by summer bedding. Featured in Sunday Mail supplement. Small gravel area.

9 COBWEBS NURSERY & GARDEN
Moor Road, North Owersby, Market Rasen LN8 3PR. Ms Pauline Gass, www.simplesite.com/cobwebsnursery. $4^1/_2$ m N of Market Rasen. Turn off A46 at North Owersby sign. Garden 200yds on R. Home-made teas. **Adm £3, chd free.** Suns 10 July; 14 Aug (11-5). **Also open The Crocosmia Gardens 14 Aug.**
Mature cottage garden extending to two thirds of an acre set amid open countryside. Many large herbaceous borders crammed with unusual and colourful perennials and grasses. Steps leading to patio and pergola clothed in clematis and wisteria. Wildlife pond.Nursery offering many of the plants grown in the garden. Featured in The Journal.

10 NEW CORNER HOUSE
Pelham Road, Claxby, nr Market Rasen LN8 3YR. Penny & Trevor Lyle. *4m N of Market Rasen. Off A46 follow rd signs to Claxby, garden at junction St Marys Lane & Pelham Rd. Ample parking in adjoining field.* Home-made teas. **Adm £2.50, chd free.** Sun 12 June (11-5).
Informal $3/_4$ -acre mature country garden situated at foot of the Wolds, woodland area with walkways, water feature newly designed, small wild flower area, pergolas with clematis and roses. Rhododendron bushes, summerhouse, herbaceous borders, mature specimen trees, seating areas. Gravel drive alongside grass area.

11 THE CROCOSMIA GARDENS
9 North Street, Caistor LN7 6QU. Mr M A Fox, 01472 859269, thecrocosmiagardens@live.co.uk, thecrocosmiagardens.net. *On Caistor High St, follow signs for Town Hall car park. Garden next to car park, free parking.* Home-made & cream teas. **Adm £2.50, chd free.** Sun 14 Aug (10-5). **Also opening Cobwebs 14 Aug.** Visitors also welcome by appt. Small groups welcome.
Small terraced cottage garden full of some unusual cottage garden plants plus the Plant Heritage National Collection of Crocosmia and the National Collection of Schizostylis. Plants for sale.
NCCPG

13 ◆ DODDINGTON HALL GARDENS
Doddington, Lincoln LN6 4RU. Claire & James Birch, 01522 812510, www.doddingtonhall.com. *5m W of Lincoln. Signed clearly from A46 Lincoln bypass & A57, 3m.* **Adm £5, chd £2.75. For NGS: Sun 20 Mar (11-4); Wed 25 May (11-5). For other opening times and information, please phone or see garden website.**
5 acres of romantic walled and wild gardens. Naturalised spring bulbs and scented shrubs from Feb to May. Spectacular iris display late May/early June in box-edged parterres of West Garden. Sumptuous herbaceous borders throughout summer; ancient chestnut trees; turf maze; Temple of the Winds. Fully productive, walled kitchen garden. Award winning Farm Shop & Cafe. Stunning Elizabethan family home. Gravel paths and ramps. Free buggy available. Please phone to book.

14 ◆ EASTON WALLED GARDENS
Easton NG33 5AP. Sir Fred & Lady Cholmeley, 01476 530063, www.eastonwalledgardens.co.uk. *7m S of Grantham. 1m off A1. 6m S of Granthm. Follow village signposts via B6403.* **Adm £6, chd £1.50. For NGS: Fri 22 Apr (11-4). For other opening times and information, please phone or see garden website.**
12 acres of 400 yr old forgotten gardens undergoing extensive renovation. Set in parkland with dramatic views. C16 garden with Victorian embellishments. Italianate terraces; yew tunnel; snowdrops and cut flower garden. David Austin roses, iris, daffodil and sweet pea collections. Cottage and vegetable gardens. Please wear sensible shoes suitable for country walking. Featured in The English Garden & BBC Gardeners World. Tearoom, shop & upper gardens all accessible. No access to lower gardens for wheelchair users.

15 15 ELMHIRST ROAD
Horncastle LN9 5AT. Sylvia Ravenhall, 01507 526014, john.ravenhall@btinternet.com. *From A158 Lincoln Rd turn into Accommodation Rd, go to end, turn L into Elmhirst Rd. No 15 approx 80yds on L.* Light refreshments & teas. **Adm**

£2.50, chd free. Visitors welcome by appt 28th May to 24th July. Individuals, groups and coaches. Evening visits welcome.
Plantswoman's long and narrow town garden with beds and borders of mainly herbaceous plants with climbers, shrubs and small trees. A wide range of hostas grown in containers and in the ground. Winding paths with shallow steps give access to all areas.

Sculptures in various materials on display in the garden . . .

16 FEN VIEW
Fen Lane, East Keal PE23 4AY. Mr & Mrs Geoffrey Wheatley. *2m SW of Spilsby. Park at The Old Rectory, path to Fen View.* Teas at The Old Rectory. **Combined adm with The Old Rectory £3.50, chd free. Sun 22 May (1.30-4.30).**
Sloping secluded $1/_2$ -acre garden planted to reflect the owners interest in gardening for wildlife. Designed around a number of different themed areas, ponds, vistas, sculptures and plenty of seating.

THE FERNS
See Nottinghamshire.

17 FIELD HOUSE FARM
Field Lane, Wroot DN9 2BL. Sue Dare & Joan Wilson. *5m W of Epworth. M180 J2, S on A161 to Epworth.* Home-made teas. **Adm £3, chd free. Sats & Suns 23, 24, 30, 31 July (11-4).**
1-acre garden designed by garden designer Sue Dare. Paths lead around exuberant herbaceous borders overflowing with colourful perennials and grasses. Features incl willow dome, reclining turf figures, pond, productive organic vegetable garden, prairie style planting, small woodland area, sculpture trail, art exhibition, many places to sit and relax. Sculptures in various materials on display in the garden. Paintings & small ceramics in house. Gravel paths, steep slope in front garden.

FROG HALL COTTAGE
Langrick Road, New York LN4 4XH.
Kathy Wright. *B1192 2m S of New
York Xrds. 3½ m N of Langrick
Bridge.* Home-made teas. **Adm
£2.50, chd free. Suns 5 June;
3 July (2-5).**
¾-acre garden. Patio with many
unusual plants, stream, courtyard-
style patio, large gravelled area with
raised beds and an arbour, again
planted for interest. Lawned area with
large island beds, unfenced pond.
Classic-style garden planted with
roses, shrubs and perennials, small
paved terrace, small newly planted
picnic area. Featured in GGG.
⊕ ☕

19 ◆ **THE GARDEN HOUSE**
Saxby, Lincoln LN8 2DQ. Chris
Neave & Jonathan Cartwright,
01673 878820,
www.thegardenhousesaxby.co.uk.
8m N of Lincoln; 2¼ m E of A15.
Light Refreshments. **Adm £4, chd
free. For NGS: Sats & Suns 2,
3 Apr; 24, 25 Sept (10-5).** For other
opening times and information,
please phone or see garden
website.
8-acre landscaped garden packed
with interest. Yew hedging and walls
enclose magical garden rooms full of
roses and herbaceous plants. Long
terrace, Dutch, pergola and obelisk
gardens link to a lavender walk. Large
natural damp garden. Dry garden
leading onto hillside planted with rarer
trees overlooking a large reflective
pond. Native woodland areas, prairie
and wild flower meadow planted with
massed bulbs. Wonderful views.
Adjacent to C18 classical church.
& ⊕ ☕ ☎

GOADBY MARWOOD HALL
See Leicestershire & Rutland.

20 ◆ **GOLTHO HOUSE**
Goltho LN8 5NF. Mr & Mrs S
Hollingworth,
www.golthogardens.com. *10m E of
Lincoln. On A158, 1m before Wragby.
Garden on LH-side (not in Goltho
Village).* **Adm £5, chd free. For NGS:
Thur & Fri 17, 18 Feb (10-3); Mon
30 May (10-4).** For other opening
times and information, please
phone or see garden website.
4½-acre garden started in 1998 but
looking established with long grass
walk flanked by abundantly planted
herbaceous borders forming a focal
point. Paths and walkway span out to
other features incl nut walk, prairie

border, wild flower meadow, rose
garden and large pond area.
Snowdrops, hellebores and shrubs for
winter interest.
& ⊕ 🛌

21 ◆ **GRIMSTHORPE CASTLE**
Bourne PE10 0LY. Grimsthorpe &
Drummond Castle Trust, 01778
591205, www.grimsthorpe.co.uk.
*3m NW of Bourne. 8m E of A1 on
A151 from Colsterworth junction.*
Lunches & light refreshments. **Adm
£5, chd £2. For NGS: Sun 17 Apr;
Thur 16 June (11-6).** For other
opening times and information,
please phone or see garden
website.
15 acres of formal and woodland
gardens incl bulbs and wild flowers.
Formal gardens encompass fine
topiary, roses, herbaceous borders
and unusual ornamental kitchen
garden.
& ☕ ☎

Native woodland areas, prairie and wild flower meadow planted with massed bulbs. Wonderful views . . .

GRINGLEY GARDENS
See Nottinghamshire.

22 **GUANOCK HOUSE**
Guanock Gate, Sutton St Edmund
PE12 0LW. Mr & Mrs Michael
Coleman, 07799 463437. *16m SE of
Spalding. From village church turn R,
cross rd, then L Guanockgate.
Garden at end of rd, RH-side.* Home-
made teas. **Adm £3, chd free. Sun
12 June (2-5.30).** Visitors also
welcome by appt May to Aug.
Group size 5 to 30 visitors.
Garden designed by Arne Maynard.
5 acres. Herbaceous border, knot
garden, rose garden and lime walk.
Orchard, walled kitchen garden,
Italian garden. Guanock House is a
C16 manor house built in the flat fens
of S Lincs. Plant stall.
& ⊕ ☕ ☎

23 ◆ **GUNBY HALL**
Spilsby PE23 5SS. National Trust,
01526 342 543,
www.nationaltrust.org.uk. *2½ m
NW of Burgh-le-Marsh. 7m W of
Skegness. On A158. Signed off
Gunby roundabout.* **Adm £4, chd £2.
For NGS: Sun 31 July (11-5).** For
other opening times and
information, please phone or see
garden website.
7 acres of formal and walled gardens;
old roses, herbaceous borders; herb
garden; kitchen garden with fruit trees
and vegetables. Greenhouses, carp
pond and sweeping lawns.
Tennyson's 'Haunt of Ancient Peace'.
House built by Sir William
Massingberd 1700. Gravel paths but
access for wheelchairs on lawns.
& 🐕 ⊕ ☕ ☎

24 **THE HALL COTTAGE**
Greatford PE9 4QA. Mr & Mrs D
Lygo, 01778 560061,
francielygo@btinternet.com. *4m E of
Stamford. At T-junction in village nr.
Hare & Hounds public house, take
route to Carlby and Braceborough.
Garden is 2nd on L.* Home-made teas.
Adm £4, chd free. Fri 16 Sept (2-6).
Visitors also welcome by appt.
Lovely ½ -acre village garden
overlooking St Thomas' church.
Situated on the R Glen, original water
wheel and open, unfenced mill pond.
Informal planting of shrubs,
herbaceous borders around the lawn
and formal parterre garden of fruit and
vegetables to the south. Large decking
with seating area and prairie planting.
Open water areas not suitable for
unsupervised children. Duck Race!
& ⊕ ☕ ☎

25 ◆ **HALL FARM**
Harpswell Lane, Harpswell
DN21 5UU. Pam & Mark Tatam,
01427 668412,
hfnursery@hallfarm.co.uk. *7m E of
Gainsborough. On A631. 1½ m W of
Caenby Corner.* Light Refreshments.
**Adm £3.50, chd free. For NGS: Sat
& Sun 3, 4 Sept (10-5).** For other
opening times and information,
please phone or see garden
website.
1½ -acre garden with mixed borders
of trees, shrubs, old roses and
unusual perennials. Sunken garden,
pond, courtyard garden, walled gravel
garden and orchard garden. Short
walk to old moat and woodland. Free
seed collecting in garden on open
days. Large plant nursery.
& ⊕ ☕ ☎

26 **HARRINGTON HALL**

Harrington, Spilsby PE23 4NH.
Mr & Mrs David Price. *6m NW of
Spilsby. Turn off A158 (Lincoln-
Skegness) at Hagworthingham, 2m to
Harrington.* Home-made teas. **Adm
£3, chd free. Sun 7 Aug (2-5).**
Approx 6-acre Tudor and C18 walled
gardens, incl 3 walled gardens;
herbaceous borders, croquet lawn
leading to viewing terrace, Tennyson's
High Hall Garden in 'Maud'. Organic
kitchen garden, shrub borders, roses,
wildlife pond and step garden.

27 **THE HAWTHORNS**

Bicker Road, Donington PE11 4XP.
**Colin & Janet Johnson, 01775
822808, colinj04@hotmail.com.**
*¹/₂ m NW of Donington. Bicker Rd is
directly off A52 opp Church Rd.
Roadside parking available in Church
Rd or in village centre car park.*
Home-made teas. **Adm £3.50, chd
free. Suns 29 May; 19 June (11-4).**
Traditional garden, newly created
from fallow land with extensive
herbaceous borders, pond, large old
English rose garden, vegetable and
fruit areas with feature greenhouse.
Cider orchard and area housing rare
breed animals incl pigs, sheep and
chickens.

HOLMES VILLA
See Nottinghamshire.

28 **HOLYWELL HALL**

Holywell PE9 4DT.
**Mr & Mrs R Gillespie,
podgillespie@hotmail.com.** *8m N of
Stamford. From A1 signed Clipsham.
Through Clipsham then turn R to
Holywell. Entrance to Hall 2m on L.*
**Adm £4, chd free. Tue 14 June
(2-6). Visitors also welcome by
appt.**
The beautiful gardens at Holywell are
among the most handsome and
historically interesting in S
Lincolnshire. Nestled in a vale they are
laid out on a broad S-facing slope
overlooking C18 lake. Numerous
water features, walled vegetable
garden, stunning herbaceous
borders, chapel, fishing temple and
orangery. Wild flower meadow.
Colourful flower garden created by
Head Gardener Brian Oldman.

THE HOMESTEAD
See Leicestershire & Rutland.

29 **NEW HOPE HOUSE**

15 Horsemarket, Caistor LN7 6UP.
Sue Neave. *Caistor is off A46
between Lincoln & Grimsby. Garden
off Market Place down hill.* Home-
made teas. **Combined adm with
Ramada £3, chd free. Suns 3 July;
28 Aug (1-5.30).**
Country garden in the town. Small
walled garden attached to an
interesting Georgian house. Climbing
roses, perenials, shrubs, trees, fruit
and small raised vegetable area.
Wildlife pond and formal water trough
in the dining area. All round colour
and interest in a tranquil space.

30 **LES ALLEES**

12 Frieston Road, Caythorpe
NG32 3BX. **Alan & Marylyn Mason.**
*8m N of Grantham. From Grantham
A607 towards Lincoln. L turn to
Caythorpe village, immed L again into
Frieston Rd. No 12 300yds ahead.*
Home-made teas. **Adm £3.50, chd
free. Sun 12 June (2-6).**
Plantsman's garden created by Alan
Mason, TV gardener and garden
designer. Ornamental potager,
woodland walk, specimen trees and
shrubs, Avenue of Italian cypresses.
200 year old Olive tree. Pond; large
mixed borders; tree house;
subtropical border. A garden of
different styles and atmospheres
which link seamlessly. Avenues and
allées lead round the garden.

31 **LITTLE PONTON HALL**

Grantham NG33 5BS. **Mrs Alastair
McCorquodale.** *2m S of Grantham.
¹/₂ m E of A1 at S end of Grantham
bypass.* Home-made teas. **Adm £4,
chd free. Sat & Sun 12, 13 Feb
(11-4).**
3 to 4-acre garden. Massed
snowdrops and aconites in Feb.
Stream, spring blossom and
hellebores, bulbs and river walk.
Spacious lawns with cedar tree over
200yrs old. Formal walled kitchen
garden and listed dovecote, with
recently developed herb garden.
Victorian greenhouses with many
plants from exotic locations. Featured
in Dream Gardens of England -
100 Inspirational Gardens. Special car
park for disabled visitors. Good
access on all hard surfaces,
unsuitable on grass.

32 **NEW 1 LOMOND GROVE**

Humberston, Grimsby DN36 4BD.
**Mike Ireland, 01472 319579,
m.ireland1@ntlworld.com.** *1m S of
Cleethorpes. From A16 Peaks
Parkway turn onto A1098 Hewitts Av.
Turn R at r'about onto A1031
Grimsby Rd. 3rd R turn into Derwent
Dr. 2nd R into Lomond Grove.
Parking on Grimsby Rd. & nearby
streets. Short walk to garden.* **Adm
£2.50, chd free. Suns 10, 17 Apr
(11-3). Visitors also welcome by
appt.**
Small S-facing garden for alpines,
bulbs, dwarf conifers and other
interesting genera which grow
alongside alpines. Acers grown from
seed provide shade. Trillium,
corydalis, primula, pulsatilla, crocus,
fritillaria, anemone, lapageria and
sanguinaria are just some of the
species grown. Also raised tufa bed in
alpine house.

33 **THE LONG HOUSE**

Gelston NG32 2AE. **Dr Lisanne
Radice.** *5m N of Grantham. 16m S of
Lincoln. Between Hough-on-the-Hill &
Marston.* Home-made teas. They're
delicious! **Adm £3, chd free. Sun 26
June (2-5).**
2-acre garden with extensive views
over the Vale of Belvoir. There are
roses in abundance, a knot garden,
an informal arrangement of borders
and a newly designed pond to
encourage wildlife. Work in progress
includes an extended grass bed
together with a new shade garden to
incorporate the existing phormium
and bamboo border. Book stall and
plants for sale.

Avenue of Italian
cypresses . . .
200 year old Olive
tree . . .

34 **NEW** **MANOR HOUSE**
Hagworthingham, Spilsby
PE23 4LN. Gill Maxim & David
O'Connor, 01507 588530. *5m E of
Horncastle. S of A158 in
Hagworthingham, turn into Bond
Hayes Lane downhill, becomes
Manor Rd. Parking available.* Home-
made teas. **Adm £3, chd free (share
to Holy Trinity Hagworthingham).**
Sat 28 May; Mon 29 Aug (2-5).
Visitors also welcome by appt.
2-acre garden on S-facing slope,
partly terraced and well protected by
established trees and shrubs.
Redeveloped over 10yrs with natural
and formal ponds. Shrub roses,
laburnum walk, hosta border, gravel
bed and other areas mainly planted
with hardy perennials.

35 **MARIGOLD COTTAGE**
Hotchin Road, Sutton-on-Sea
LN12 2NP. Stephanie Lee and
John Raby,
www.marigoldcottage.webs.com.
*From High St facing sea, turn R at
Corner House Café, along Furlong's
Rd past playing fields, round bend,
into Hotchin Rd. Garden 2nd on L.*
Home-made teas. **Adm £3, chd free.**
Sun 1 May; Sat 25 June; Sun 11
Sept (11-4).
This plantswoman's seaside garden
has doubled in size with the aquisition
of adjacent land. New vegetable plot,
greenhouse, summerhouse, gravel
garden and raised beds providing
more planting and design
opportunities. Oriental influence from
years spent in the Far East.

36 **NEW** **2 MILL COTTAGE**
Barkwith Road, South Willingham,
Market Rasen LN8 6NN. Mrs Jo
Rouston. *5m E of Wragby. On A157,
turn R at PH in East Barkwith then
immed L to South Willingham. Cottage
1m on L.* Home-made teas. **Adm
£2.50, chd free.** Sat 2 July (12-5).
New garden of several defined
spaces, packed with interesting
features, unusual plants and well
placed seating areas, created by
garden designer Jo Rouston over the
last 3yrs. Original engine shed, a
working well, raised beds using local
rock with small pond. Clipped box,
alpines, roses, summerhouses and
water feature. Box and lavender
hedge to greenhouse and herb
garden.

Holywell Hall

37 **MILL FARM**
Grasby DN38 6AQ. Mike & Helen
Boothman. *3m NW of Caistor on
A1084. Between Brigg & Caistor on
A1084. From Cross Keys PH head
towards Caistor for approx 200yrds.*
Home-made teas. **Adm £3, chd free.**
Sun 3 July (11-5).
3½ -acre hill-top garden with
panoramic views. Development
began circa 2005. New beds and
features still evolving, whilst the older
beds are now maturing. New rill,rose
and peony beds now completed.
Remains of windmill adapted into a
fernery. A plantsman garden with a
wealth of shrubs and perennials,
wildlife ponds, veg beds & woodland
area with specimen trees.

38 **THE MOAT**
Newton NG34 0ED. Mr & Mrs Mike
Barnes, 01529 497462. *Off A52
halfway between Grantham &
Sleaford. In Newton village, opp
church. Please park sensibly in village.*
Home-made teas. **Adm £3, chd free.**
Sun 19 June (11-5). **Visitors also
welcome by appt.**
2½ -acre country garden,
established 9 years. Island beds,
featuring many unusual perennials,
natural pond, courtyard garden,
interestingly planted ha-ha. Also
features numerous specimen
trees.

39 **MULBERRY CROFT**
Nelson Road, Fiskerton LN3 4ER.
John & Marilyn Howard. *3½ m
E of Lincoln. Signed from A158
Lincoln to Skegness road. Nelson
Rd is between Carpenters Arms &
village church.* Home-made teas.
Adm £2.50, chd free. Sun 5 June
(10-4).
Garden started in 2005. Plants
chosen to attract wildlife, minimum
chemical use. Front gravelled drive
with perennials, shrubs, sorbus and
mulberry trees. S-facing rear garden,
colourful mixed borders and beds,

mainly perennials. Good range of irises and peonies. Recently planted trees incl quince, olives and various sorbus.

40 NEW MULTUM IN PARVO
58 Willis Close, Lincoln LN1 3LG. Sarah Scarlett. *Central Lincoln. From A46 Lincoln bypass take B1226 (signed Historic Lincoln) to Newport. Turn R into Raven Lane, straight on at T-lights to Upper Long Leys Rd. Willis Close is 2nd L.* Home-made teas. **Combined adm with The Coach House £3, chd free.** Sun 12 June (11-5).
Enclosed courtyard garden with raised lily pool, small pergola and clipped box. Evergreen shrubs, ferns and ivies. Small collection of bonsai and Japanese water feature. Front garden with clipped yew, roses and clematis. A calm green oasis yards from the city centre.

41 THE OLD RECTORY
East Keal, Spilsby PE23 4AT. Mrs Ruth Ward, 01790 752477, rfjward@btinternet.com. *2m SW of Spilsby. Off A16. Turn into Church Lane by PO.* Home-made teas. **Sun 17 Apr, adm £3; Sun 22 May combined adm with Fen View £3.50, chd free (1.30-4.30). Visitors also welcome by appt. Group or individuals.**
Beautifully situated, with fine views, rambling cottage garden on different levels falling naturally into separate areas, with changing effects and atmosphere. Steps, paths and vistas to lead you on, with seats well placed for appreciating special views or relaxing and enjoying the peace. Dry garden, vegetable garden, orchard, woodland walk. some plants for sale. wildlife friendly, children enjoy exploring, owner available for questions.

42 THE OLD VICARAGE
Low Road, Holbeach Hurn PE12 8JN. Mrs Liz Dixon-Spain, 01406 424148, lizds@ukonline.co.uk. *2m NE of Holbeach. Turn off A17 N to Holbeach Hurn, past post box in middle of village, 1st turn R into Low Rd. Old Vicarage on R approx 400yds.* Home-made teas at at the Old White House. **Combined adm with Old White House £4.50, chd free.** Sun 26 June (12-5). Visitors also welcome by appt

April to September. Please phone or email.
2 acres of gardens with mature trees, old grass tennis court and croquet lawns surrounded by borders of shrubs, roses, herbaceous plants;shrub roses & herb garden in old paddock surrounded by informal areas with pond and bog garden, wild flowers, grasses and bulbs, fruit and veg gardens. Wild life garden, environmentally maintained with many butterflies, birds,hedgehogs,montjac and chickens all resident.

43 OLD WHITE HOUSE
Holbeach Hurn PE12 8JP. Mr & Mrs A Worth. *2m N of Holbeach. Turn off A17 N to Holbeach Hurn, follow signs to village, go straight through, turn R after Rose & Crown at Baileys Lane.* Home-made teas. **Combined adm with The Old Vicarage £4.50, chd free.** Sun 26 June (1-5).
1½ acres of mature garden, featuring herbaceous borders, roses, patterned garden, herb garden and walled kitchen garden.

44 OVERBECK
46 Main Street, Scothern LN2 2UW. John & Joyce Good, 01673 862200, jandjgood@btinternet.com. *4m E of Lincoln. Scothern is signed from A46 at Dunholme & A158 at Sudbrooke. Overbeck is at E end of Main Street.* Light refreshments & teas. **Adm £2.50, chd free. Visitors welcome by appt. Individuals, groups or coaches. May to August. Evening visits welcome.**
Approx ½ -acre garden in quiet village. Long herbaceous borders and colour-themed island beds with some unusual perennials. Hosta border, gravel bed with grasses, fernery, trees, numerous shrubs and climbers and large prolific vegetable and fruit area. Featured in Garden News.

45 NEW PEGASUS HOUSE
DN15 9LH. Andrew & Karen Clifford and Pat & Terry Silcock, 07917 202692, amclifford@btinternet.com. *10m N of Scunthorpe. 11m W of Humber Bridge. Follow signs for West Halton & Whitton from A1077. 1st house on L after Village Hall, adjacent to church.* Home-made teas in Village Hall. **Adm £2.50, chd free. Sun 3 July (1-5). Visitors also welcome by appt 30 May - 31 Aug. Max group 20 people.**

Approx 2-acres of family garden with magnificent panoramic views over the R Humber. This relatively new evolving garden has developed over the last 4yrs, with large mixed borders, an ornamental pond and pergola walk, large wildlife pond and chickens. Plenty of seating areas to sit quietly and take in the views.

A calm green
oasis yards from
the city centre . . .

46 PINEFIELDS
Smithy Lane, Bigby, Barnetby DN38 6ER. Reg & Madeleine Hill. *Bigby is on A1084. 5m Caistor, 4m Brigg. Turn into Bigby Village off A1084. House at top of Smithy Lane junction with Main St.* Home-made teas. **Adm £2.50, chd free.** Sun 27 Mar (1-5).
¾ -acre country garden with lots of interest. A paved terrace leads on to shrub/herbaceous beds packed with plants, many unusual. Clipped box and gravel area, half circle pergola and wildlife garden. Early spring starts with hellebores incl many Ashwood doubles and anemone centred varieties. One step up to garden.

PRIMROSE COTTAGE
See Nottinghamshire.

47 NEW RAMADA
17 Horsemarket, Caistor, Market Rasen LN7 6UP. Peter & Gwyn Thompson. **Combined adm with Hope House £3, chd free.** Suns 3 July; 28 Aug (1-5.30).
Hillside garden with terraced herbaceous borders filled with perenials. Vegetable garden, natural spring and small pond.

ROSELEA
See Nottinghamshire.

48 **73 SAXILBY ROAD**
Sturton by Stow LN1 2AA. Charles
& Tricia Elliott, 01427 788517. *9m
NW of Lincoln. On B1241. Halfway
between Lincoln & Gainsborough*.
Home-made teas. **Adm £2.50, chd
free. Suns 10 July; 2 Oct (11-5)**.
Visitors also welcome by appt.
Extensively cultivated plot planted in a
cottage garden style and mainly
devoted to a wide selection of
summer and autumn flowering
perennials and late season grasses.
Shrub borders with some unusual
shrubs and small trees chosen to give
early interest in leaf colour and shape
and to produce good autumn colour.
Large display of tender fuchsias.
Small hardy plant nursery. Small art
exhibition and handcrafted card stall.

49 **NEW** **SHEPHERDS HEY**
Peppin Lane, Fotherby, Louth
LN11 0UW. Roger & Barbara
Chester. *2m N of Louth. Leave A16
to Fotherby. Peppin Lane is no-
through rd running E from village
centre. Please park on RH verge opp
allotments*. Home-made teas at
Woodlands. **Combined adm with
Woodlands £3.50, chd free. Sun
26 June (11-5)**.
Small garden less than 5yrs old, still
being developed and packed with
unusual and interesting perennials.
Open frontage gives visitors a warm
welcome with a small pond. Terraced
border and steep bank side to a small
stream. Rear garden takes advantage
of the panoramic views over open
countryside. Limited access to rear
garden. Front garden can be view
from road.

50 **NEW** **SIR JOSEPH BANKS
TRIBUTE GARDEN**
Bridge Street, Horncastle LN9 5HZ.
Sir Joseph Banks Society. *8m S of
Wragby. From Horncastle Market
Square 100yrds along Bridge St.
Garden is on LHS, entrance through
shop*. Home-made teas. **Adm £2.50,
chd free. Suns 12 June; 10 July;
14 Aug (2-5)**.
Sir Joseph Banks (1743 - 1820)
Tribute Garden is a courtyard
providing an attractive oasis in a busy
market town. It features 70 different
species of plants, many collected on
his voyage with Capt. Cook on HMS
Endeavour. Interpretation material
available. Level gravel path.

51 **NEW** **SOUTH HOLLAND
HOUSE**
PE12 9AP. Jenny Cox. *2m S of Long
Sutton. From A17 middle Long
Sutton r'about take B1390 signed
Sutton St James. Spendla's Lane is
off to L*. Home-made teas. **Adm
£2.50, chd free. Sats & Suns 23,
24 July; 1, 2 Oct (10-4)**.
Two acre garden in rural setting
incorporating areas of very different
styles. Traditional English garden,
large natural pond, swamp garden,
woodland, gravel garden, orchard,
vegetable garden and poly tunnel.
Huge variety of plants collected by
owner over many yrs. Spectacular
displays of day lilies, heleniums, cone
flowers, fuchsias and hydrangeas.
Gravel paths.

SQUIRREL LODGE
See Nottinghamshire.

52 **STATION HOUSE**
Station Road, Potterhanworth,
Lincoln LN4 2DX. Carol Harvey.
*6m S of Lincoln. B1178 immed on L
under railway bridge before reaching
Potterhanworth village*. Light
refreshments. **Adm £2.50, chd free.
Suns 22 May; 26 June; 31 July
(1-5)**.
Old Station Master's house in ¼ acre
gardens by railway embankment, a
haven for wildlife. Very informal style
with mixed borders, lawns and 2 tiny
ponds. New flower beds created and
other features incorporated.
Collection of old memorabilia and
'quirky' accessories. Garden owner
keen ornithologist.

GROUP OPENING

53 **SUTTON ON SEA
GARDENS**
Sutton on Sea LN12 2HE. *16m N of
Skegness on A52. 7m E of Alford on
A1111*. Home-made teas at Orchard
House. **Adm £3, chd free. Sat 25
June (11-4)**.

CHARIS
Carol Thomas and Richard Foy

THE COTTAGE
R C Lightsey & C N Edwards

MARIGOLD COTTAGE
Stephanie Lee & John Raby
Visitors also welcome by appt
all year.
01507 442151

marigoldlee@btinternet.com
www.marigoldcottage.webs.
com

ORCHARD HOUSE
Chris & Steve Calcott

Quiet, old-fashioned seaside village,
clean shady beaches - a classic hardy
plant environment! Four very different
gardens will be open. On the High
Street, Orchard House, a modern
garden with innovative features
designed to give a calming influence.
Next door, The Cottage is packed
with quirky features and recycling
ideas. In the area called the Park,
Charis, a stylish cottage garden incl a
summerhouse and secret garden.
Marigold Cottage, a plantswoman's
seaside garden with oriental
influences. Raised borders, secret
paths and a productive kitchen
garden add to the interest.

THISTLE FARM
See Nottinghamshire.

54 **NEW** **THE WALLED
GARDEN**
Panton, nr Wragby, Market Rasen
LN8 5LQ. David & Jenny Eckford.
*5m NE of Wragby. Turn off A157 at
E Barkwith. From E turn off B1225 to
Benniworth. Garden on Benniworth to
Panton Rd*. Home-made teas. **Adm
£3, chd free. Sun 5 June (11-5)**.
Atmospheric 2-acre C18 walled
garden in woodland setting. Rescued
from dereliction and lovingly restored
by present owners. Informal planting
within a formal framework. Long
herbaceous borders with gravel
paths. Many unusual plants and trees.
Panoramic view from the roof terrace.
Limited wheelchair access due to
varying levels of gravel, step leading
to garden.

Seaside village,
clean shady
beaches - a classic
hardy plant
environment . . . !

55 WALTERS COTTAGE

6 Hall Road, Hacconby, nr Bourne
PE10 0UY. Ivan & Sadie Hall, 01778
571859. *3m N of Bourne A15. Turn E
at Xrds to Hacconby. Turn R at Hare &
Hounds PH.* Home-made teas. **Adm
£3, chd free. Sat & Sun 4, 5 June
(12-5).** Visitors also welcome by
appt in June only. 10+ people.
Country cottage garden of over
1/4 acre developed over the past 7yrs.
Various themed areas. Walled garden
with hornbeam allée, topiary and rill.
Woodland area with wildlife pond and
plants. Sunken garden. Long
herbaceous borders, lawns and
collection of hostas. Garden is well-
stocked with many interesting and
rare plants with added features.
Featured in The English Garden.
Finalist in Daily Mail Garden
Competiton.

56 68 WATTS LANE

Louth LN11 9DG. Jenny & Rodger
Grasham, 01507 601004 or 07977
318145. *1/2 m S of Louth town centre.
Watts Lane off B1200 Louth to
Mablethorpe rd. Turn by pedestrian
lights and Londis shop.* Home-made
teas. **Adm £2, chd free** (share to
Louth and District Hospice). **Wed
13 July (11-5); Suns 7, 21 Aug
(12-5).** Visitors also welcome by
appt July & Aug, coaches by
arrangement.
Blank canvas of 1/8acre in early 90's.
Developed to lush, colourful, exotic to
traditional plant-packed haven. A
whole new world on entering from
street. Generous borders, raised
exotic island, long hot exotic border,

ponds, stumpery, developing prairie
style border. Conservatory, grapevine.
Intimate seating areas along garden's
journey. Featured in Garden News
and Lincolnshire Today. Grass
pathways.

57 10 WENDOVER CLOSE

Rippingale PE10 0TQ. Chris & Tim
Bladon, 01778 440499,
timbla7@btinternet.com. *51/2 m N of
Bourne. Rippingale is signed on the
A15. On entering village at the
Rippengale / Kirby Underwood Xrd,
Wendover Close is 1st turning on L.
Garden at end of the close.* Home-
made teas. **Adm £2.50, chd free.
Sat & Sun 28, 29 May (11-5).**
Visitors also welcome by appt June
& July. 10+ people.
Peaceful village garden of approx
1/2 acre containing usual and unusual
herbaceous plants, shrubs and trees
of general and specialist interest in a
secluded situation. Approx 30yds
from main entrance to garden is
gravel.

♿ ❀ ☕ ☎

58 WEST BARN

Saxby, Lincoln LN8 2DQ. Mrs E
Neave. *8m N of Lincoln; 21/4 m E of
A15.* **Combined adm with The
Garden House £4, chd free. Sats &
Suns 2, 3 Apr; 24, 25 Sept (10-5).**
Formal walled courtyard garden with
loggia, box hedging, shrub roses,
climbers and herbaceous planting.
Water feature and pots with seasonal
planting. Gravel paths, some steps.

♿ ❀ ☕

59 WOODLANDS

Peppin Lane, Fotherby, Louth
LN11 0UW. Ann & Bob Armstrong,
www.woodlandsplants.co.uk. *2m
N of Louth. On A16. Leave bypass
(A16) signed Fotherby. Woodlands is
situated nr far end of Peppin Lane, a
no through rd, running E from village
centre. No parking at garden. Please
park on RH verge opp allotments and
walk (approx 250yds) to garden.*
Home-made teas. **Adm £2.50, £3.50
(June), chd free. Suns 24 Apr;
29 May; 26 June; 31 July; 25 Sept
(11-5).** Visitors also welcome by
appt.
A lovely mature woodland garden with
many unusual plants set against a
backdrop of an ever changing
tapestry of greenery. A peaceful
garden where wildlife is given a
chance to thrive. The nursery gives
visitors the opportunity to purchase
plants seen in the garden. Award
winning professional artist's
studio/gallery open to visitors. Plant
nursery featured in RHS Plantfinder.
Easter Egg hunt on Easter Day. Some
gravel and bark paths.

♿ 🐾 ❀ ☕

*A peaceful garden
where wildlife is
given a chance to
thrive . . .*

Lincolnshire County Volunteers

County Organiser
Susie Dean, The Orchards, Old Somerby, Grantham NG33 4AG, 01476 565456, susie@dean0.plus.com

County Treasurer
Peter Sandberg, Croft House, Ulceby DN39 6SW, 01469 588330, peter.sandberg@btinternet.com

Publicity
Erica McGarrigle, Corner House Farm, Little Humby, Grantham NG33 4HW, 01476 585909, colinmcgarrigle@tiscali.co.uk

Leaflet Coordinator
Sylvia Ravenhall, 15 Elmhirst Road, Horncastle LN9 5AT, 01507 526014, john.ravenhall@btinternet.com
Vic Atkinson, Belvedere, 36 Elmhirst Road, Horncastle LN9 5AT, 01507 522205, vic.atkinson@btconect.com

Assistant County Organisers
Helen Boothman, The Farmhouse, Mill Farm, Grasby, Barnetby, N.Lincolnshire, 01652 628424, the.boothmans@btinternet.com
Sally Grant, Holly House, Fishtoft Drove, Boston PE22 7ES, 01205 750486. sallygrant50@btinternet.com
Stephanie Lee, Marigold Cottage, 77 Church Lane, Sutton-on-Sea, Lincolnshire, LN12 2JA, 01507 442151,
    marigoldlee@btinternet.com
Lizzie Milligan-Manby, Wykeham Hall Farm, East Wykeham, Ludford, Market Rasen LN8 6AU, 01507 313286,
    lizzie@milliganmanby.plus.com
Chris Neave, The Garden House, Saxby, Market Rasen LN8 2DQ, 01673 878820, jonland@btinternet.com
Margaret Sandberg, Croft House, Ulceby DN39 6SW, 01469 588330, margaret.sandberg@btinternet.com

---

Support the NGS – eat more cake! ☕

Guanock House

LONDON

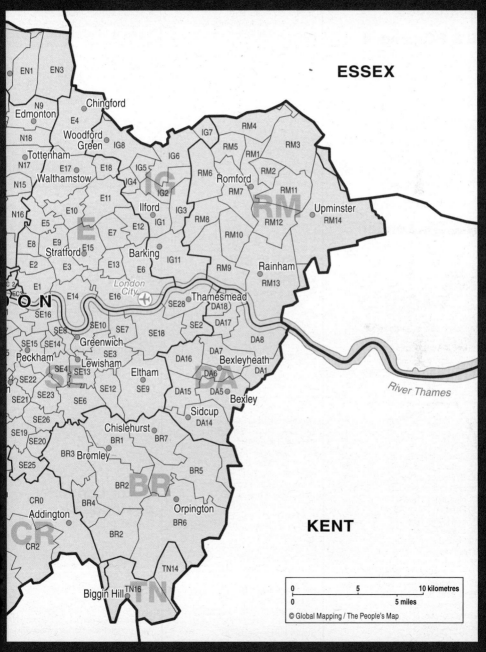

ESSEX

KENT

River Thames

0   5   10 kilometres
0   5 miles
© Global Mapping / The People's Map

London gardens listed by postcode

Inner London postcodes

E & EC London

Lower Clapton Gardens, E5
42 Latimer Road, E7
London Fields Gardens, E8
17a Navarino Road, E8
12 Bushberry Road, E9
128 Cadogan Terrace, E9
64 Thornhill Road, E10
17 Greenstone Mews, E11
12 Western Road, E13
47 Maynard Road, E17
87 St Johns Road, E17
Waltham Forest Register Office, E17
Amwell Gardens Group, EC1
Charterhouse, EC1
The Inner Temple Garden, EC4

N & NW London

29 Canonbury Park North, N1
De Beauvoir Gardens, N1
Gardening on a Shoestring, N1
The Happy Triange Garden, N1
Islington Gardens, N1
King Henry's Walk Garden, N1
Malvern Terrace Gardens, N1
5 Northampton Park, N1
St Mary's Grove Gardens, N1
66 Abbots Gardens, N2
79 Church Lane, N2
269 Creighton Avenue, N2
East Finchley Cottage Gardens, N2
2 Stanley Road, N2
18 Park Crescent, N3
51 Cholmeley Crescent, N6
7 The Grove, N6
Linear House, N6
2 Millfield Place, N6
3 The Park, N6
Southwood Lodge, N6
16 Furlong Road, N7
90 St George's Avenue, N7
1a Hungerford Road, N7
62 Hungerford Road, N7
30 Redston Road, N8
5 Cecil Road, N10
46 Dukes Avenue, N10
19 Hillfield Park, N10
6 Methuen Park, N10
66 Muswell Avenue, N10
Princes Avenue Gardens, N10
12 Rookfield Avenue, N10
131 Rosebery Road, N10
5 St Regis Close, N10
27 Wood Vale, N10
33 Wood Vale, N10

29 Woodberry Crescent, N10
15 Creswick Walk, NW11
Golf Course Allotments, N11
Hampstead Garden Suburb Gardens, NW11
51 Northway, NW11
21 Wroxham Gardens, N11
5 Russell Road, N13
15 Norcott Road, N16
94 Marsh Lane Allotments, N17
Alexandra Park Gardens N22
Railway Cottages, N22
Gloucester Crescent Group, NW1
The Holme, NW1
4 Park Village East, NW1
Royal College of Physicians Garden, NW1
10 Hoveden Road, NW2
58A Teignmouth Road, NW2
208 Walm Lane, The Garden Flat, NW2
Whixall House Garden, NW2
180 Adelaide Road, NW3
Fenton House, NW3
Frognal Gardens, NW3
Little House A, NW3
116 Hamilton Terrace, NW8
4 Asmuns Hill, NW11
113 Corringham Road, NW11
5 Hillcrest Avenue, NW11
86 Willifield Way, NW11

S, SE & SW London

Garden Barge Square at Downings Roads Moorings, SE1
The Garden Museum, SE1
28 Morden Road, SE3
Camberwell Grove Gardens, SE5
35 Camberwell Grove, SE5
24 Grove Park, SE5
Roots and Shoots, SE11
41 Southbrook Road, SE12
Choumert Square, SE15
5 Lyndhurst Square, SE15
94a Lyndhurst Way, SE15
Walworth Garden Farm, SE17
The 'Lived in' Garden, SE18
13 Gipsy Hill, SE19
21a Waldegrave Road, SE19
Penge Gardens, SE20
Ash Cottage, SE21
Dulwich Village: Two Gardens, SE21
14 Frank Dixon Way, SE21
32 Lovelace Road, SE21
174 Peckham Rye, SE22
4 Piermont Green, SE22
22 Scutari Road, SE22
86 Underhill Road, SE22
20 Dacres Road, SE23
Tewkesbury Lodge Garden Group, SE23
5 Burbage Road, SE24
30 Half Moon Lane, SE24
South London Botanical Institute, SE24
Stoney Hill House, SE26

24 Chestnut Road, SE27
Cadogan Place South Garden, SW1
Eccleston Square, SW1
Brixton Water Lane Gardens, SW2
15 Criffel Avenue, SW2
93 Palace Road, SW2
Chelsea Physic Garden, SW3
51 The Chase, SW4
Clapham Manor Street Gardens, SW4
17 Crescent Lane, SW4
The Hurlingham Club, SW6
Natural History Museum Wildlife Garden, SW7
225a Brixton Road, SW9
6 Cornford Grove, SW12
28 Old Devonshire Road, SW12
2 Western Lane, SW12
12 Westmoreland Road, SW13
5 Garden Close, SW15
66 Woodbourne Avenue, SW16
20 Eatonville Road, SW17
18 Littleton Street, SW18
36 Melrose Road, SW18
28 Multon Road, SW18
61 Arthur Road, SW19
97 Arthur Road, SW19
55 Grasmere Avenue, SW19
11 Lauriston Road, SW19
19 Lauriston Road, SW19
101 Pitt Crescent, SW19
123 South Park Road, SW19
Southside House, SW19
Paddock Allotments & Leisure Gardens, SW20

W London

4 Cumberland Park, W3
Mill Hill Road Gardens, W3
41 Mill Hill Road, W3
65 Mill Hill Road, W3
Zen Garden, W3
Chiswick Mall Gardens, W4
The Orchard, W4
All Seasons, W5
Edwardes Square, W8
7 Upper Phillimore Gardens, W8
57 St Quintin Avenue, W10
29 Addison Avenue, W11
12 Lansdowne Road, W11
8 Lansdowne Walk, W11
27 St James Avenue, W13

Outer London postcodes

Harcourt House, Bromley, BR1
153 Portland Road, Bromley, BR1
36 Downs Hill, Beckenham, BR3
212 Langley Way, West Wickham, BR4
Columcille, Chislehurst, BR7
Elm Tree Cottage, South Croydon, CR2
55 Warham Road, South Croydon, CR2
17 Valley View Gardens, Purley, CR8
East Barnet Gardens, East Barnet, EN4
West Lodge Park, Hadley Wood, EN4

7 Byng Road, High Barnet, EN5
45 Great North Road, Barnet, EN5
13 Greenhill Park, Barnet, EN5
54 Ferndown, Northwood Hills, HA6
46 Lincoln Road, Northwood Hills, HA6
Treetops, Northwood, HA6
Hornbeams, Stanmore, HA7
20 Goldhaze Close, Woodford Green,
     IG8
4 Stradbroke Grove, Buckhurst Hill, IG9
The Watergardens, Kingston-upon-
     Thames, KT2
The Wych Elm Public House, Kingston-
     upon-Thames, KT2
Badgers Retreat, New Malden, KT3
65 Farm Way, Worcester Park, KT4
52A Berrylands Road, Surbiton, KT5
Fishponds House, Surbiton, KT6
Little Lodge, Thames Ditton, KT7
10 Arnison Road, East Molesey, KT8
Hampton Court Palace, East Molesey,
     KT8
12 Vine Road, East Molesey, KT8
239a Hook Road, Chessington, KT9
7 St George's Road, Twickenham,
     TW1
Osterley Park and House, Isleworth,
     TW7
Kew Green Gardens, Kew, TW9
Old Palace Lane Allotments,
     Richmond, TW9
Richmond Riverside, Richmond, TW9
355 Sandycombe Road, Kew, TW9
31 West Park Road, Kew, TW9
Ham House and Garden, Richmond,
     TW10
Ormeley Lodge, Richmond, TW10
Petersham House, Petersham, TW10
Petersham Lodge, Richmond, TW10
St Michael's Convent, Richmond,
     TW10
Hampton Hill Gardens, Hampton Hill,
     TW12
30 St James's Road, Hampton Hill,
     TW12

Opening Dates

March

Wednesday 30
Hampton Court Palace (Evening -
     Pre-booking essential)

April

Sunday 3
Chelsea Physic Garden, SW3
Sunday 10
7 The Grove, N6
17a Navarino Road, E8
St Michael's Convent
Sunday 17
Edwardes Square, W8
Malvern Terrace Gardens, N1
7 Upper Phillimore Gardens, W8

Wednesday 27
51 The Chase, SW4 (Evening)
Hampton Court Palace (Evening -
     Pre-booking essential)

May

Sunday 1
5 Burbage Road, SE24
Cadogan Place South Garden, SW1
51 The Chase, SW4
36 Downs Hill
5 Russell Road, N13
5 St Regis Close, N10
64 Thornhill Road, E10
The Watergardens
Monday 2
Petersham Lodge
Saturday 7
The Garden Museum, SE1
Sunday 8
6 Cornford Grove
Elm Tree Cottage
The Inner Temple Garden, EC4
2 Millfield Place, N6
Natural History Museum Wildlife
     Garden, SW7
The Orchard, W4
Petersham House
Southwood Lodge, N6
Saturday 14
Hampton Hill Gardens
Zen Garden, W3
Sunday 15
66 Abbots Gardens, N2
Hampton Hill Gardens
8 Lansdowne Walk, W11
Princes Avenue Gardens, N10
Stoney Hill House, SE26
West Lodge Park
33 Wood Vale, N10
Zen Garden, W3
Wednesday 18
8 Lansdowne Walk, W11
     (Evening)
Saturday 21
The Hurlingham Club, SW6
Walworth Garden Farm, SE17
Sunday 22
Brixton Water Lane Gardens, SW2
Eccleston Square, SW1
14 Frank Dixon Way, SE21
30 Half Moon Lane, SE24
Kew Green Gardens
Little Lodge
36 Melrose Road, SW18
15 Norcott Road, N16
22 Scutari Road, SE22
Walworth Garden Farm, SE17
Wednesday 25
12 Lansdowne Walk, W11
Roots and Shoots, SE11 (Evening)
Saturday 28
212 Langley Way

Sunday 29
Chiswick Mall Gardens, W4
212 Langley Way
18 Littleton Street, SW18
4 Park Village East, NW1
64 Thornhill Road, E10
86 Underhill Road, SE22
29 Woodberry Crescent, N10
Monday 30
212 Langley Way
18 Littleton Street, SW18

June

Sunday 5
Choumert Square, SE15
East Finchley Cottage Gardens, N2
20 Eatonville Road, SW17
Elm Tree Cottage
55 Grasmere Avenue, SW19
7 The Grove, N6
Hampstead Garden Suburb Gardens,
     NW11
10 Hoveden Road, NW2
Islington Gardens, N1
11 Lauriston Road, SW19
46 Lincoln Road
Lower Clapton Gardens, E5
28 Old Devonshire Road, SW12
Osterley Park and House
3 The Park, N6
174 Peckham Rye, SE22
Penge Gardens, SE20
Petersham House
4 Piermont Green, SE22
7 St George's Road
2 Stanley Road, N2
2 Western Lane, SW12
12 Western Road, E13
Wednesday 8
Little Lodge
Thursday 9
Fenton House, NW3 (Evening)
Saturday 11
Richmond Riverside (Evening)
Tewkesbury Lodge Garden Group,
     SE23 (Evening)
Sunday 12
61 Arthur Road, SW19
97 Arthur Road, SW19
Ash Cottage, SE21
35 Camberwell Grove, SE5
79 Church Lane, N2
Clapham Manor Street Gardens, SW4
Columcille
17 Crescent Lane, SW4
15 Criffel Avenue, SW2
De Beauvoir Gardens, N1
East Barnet Gardens
Fishponds House
16 Furlong Road, N7
13 Greenhill Park
5 Hillcrest Avenue, NW11
239a Hook Road
1a Hungerford Road, N7
62 Hungerford Road, N7

Little House A, NW3
90 St George's Avenue, N7
4 Stradbroke Grove
Tewkesbury Lodge Garden Group, SE23
21 Wroxham Gardens, N11
Tuesday 14
Charterhouse, EC1 (Evening)
15 Criffel Avenue, SW2 (Evening)
Wednesday 15
5 Hillcrest Avenue, NW11 (Evening)
239a Hook Road (Evening)
65 Mill Hill Road, W3 (Evening)
2 Millfield Place, N6 (Evening)
28 Old Devonshire Road, SW12 (Evening)
St Mary's Grove Gardens, N1 (Evening)
Saturday 18
5 Northampton Park, N1 (Evening)
12 Rookfield Avenue, N10 (Evening)
7 St George's Road (Evening)
Zen Garden, W3
Sunday 19
Amwell Gardens Group, EC1
20 Dacres Road, SE23
Dulwich Village Two Gardens, SE21
Frognal Gardens, NW3
46 Lincoln Road
London Fields Gardens, E8
17a Navarino Road, E8
Ormeley Lodge
101 Pitt Crescent, SW19
30 Redston Road, N8
131 Rosebery Road, N10
355 Sandycombe Road
123 South Park Road, SW19
41 Southbrook Road, SE12
Southwood Lodge, N6
17 Valley View Gardens
12 Vine Road
31 West Park Road
12 Westmoreland Road, SW13
Whixall House Garden, NW2
Zen Garden, W3
Thursday 23
113 Corringham Road, NW11 (Evening)
Saturday 25
4 Cumberland Park, W3 (Evening)
The Holme, NW1
Sunday 26
4 Asmuns Hill, NW11
Badgers Retreat
12 Bushberry Road, E9
Camberwell Grove Gardens, SE5
5 Cecil Road, N10
269 Creighton Avenue, N2
15 Creswick Walk, NW11
65 Farm Way
The Holme, NW1
5 Lyndhurst Square, SE15
94a Lyndhurst Way, SE15
18 Park Crescent, N3
5 St Regis Close, N10

South London Botanical Institute, SE24
208 Walm Lane, The Garden Flat, NW2
Wednesday 29
Badgers Retreat (Evening)

July

Saturday 2
87 St Johns Road, E17 (Evening)
Sunday 3
Elm Tree Cottage
5 Garden Close, SW15
93 Palace Road, SW2
27 St James Avenue, W13
87 St Johns Road, E17
Wednesday 6
King Henry's Walk Garden, N1 (Evening)
Roots and Shoots, SE11
Friday 8
28 Morden Road, SE3 (Evening)
Saturday 9
Ham House and Garden
27 Wood Vale, N10
Sunday 10
29 Canonbury Park North, N1
Garden Barge Square at Downings Roads Moorings, SE1
Gardening on a Shoestring, N1
13 Gipsy Hill, SE19
Gloucester Crescent Group, NW1
The Happy Triangle Garden, N1
19 Lauriston Road, SW19
32 Lovelace Road, SE21
Mill Hill Road Gardens, W3
Railway Cottages, N22
57 St Quintin Avenue, W10
58A Teignmouth Road, NW2
27 Wood Vale, N10
33 Wood Vale, N10
66 Woodbourne Avenue, SW16
Wednesday 13
Hampton Court Palace (Evening - **Pre-booking essential**)
Saturday 16
Hampton Hill Gardens
Paddock Allotments & Leisure Gardens, SW20
87 St Johns Road, E17 (Evening)
Sunday 17
180 Adelaide Road, NW3
52A Berrylands Road
128 Cadogan Terrace, E9
79 Church Lane, N2
Hampton Hill Gardens
The 'Lived in' Garden, SE18
47 Maynard Road, E17
66 Muswell Avenue, N10
87 St Johns Road, E17
Wednesday 20
30 St James's Road (Evening)
Saturday 23
42 Latimer Road, E7

Sunday 24
29 Addison Avenue, W11
10 Arnison Road
20 Goldhaze Close
42 Latimer Road, E7
Linear House, N6
47 Maynard Road, E17
51 Northway, NW11
57 St Quintin Avenue, W10
5 St Regis Close, N10
86 Willifield Way, NW11
Saturday 30
87 St Johns Road, E17 (Evening)
Sunday 31
45 Great North Road
19 Hillfield Park, N10
47 Maynard Road, E17
87 St Johns Road, E17
Treetops
29 Woodberry Crescent, N10
The Wych Elm Public House

August

Sunday 7
180 Adelaide Road, NW3
Alexandra Park Gardens, N22
All Seasons, W5
10 Arnison Road (Evening)
Elm Tree Cottage
Gloucester Crescent Group, NW1
94 Marsh Lane Allotments, N17
47 Maynard Road, E17
55 Warham Road
Saturday 13
The Holme, NW1
212 Langley Way
Sunday 14
20 Goldhaze Close
Harcourt House
The Holme, NW1
212 Langley Way
41 Mill Hill Road, W3 (Evening)
Old Palace Lane Allotments
153 Portland Road
Royal College of Physicians Garden, NW1
Sunday 21
Columcille
54 Ferndown
Sunday 28
225a Brixton Road, SW9 (Day & Evening)
28 Multon Road, SW18

September

Friday 2
86 Underhill Road, SE22 (Evening)
Sunday 4
7 Byng Road
24 Chestnut Road, SE27 (Evening)
Elm Tree Cottage
Golf Course Allotments, N11
24 Grove Park, SE5
5 Russell Road, N13

Wednesday 7
Hampton Court Palace (Evening -
  Pre-booking essential)
Sunday 18
6 Cornford Grove

October

Sunday 2
64 Thornhill Road, E10
Sunday 16
The Watergardens
Sunday 30 •
West Lodge Park

Gardens open to the public

Chelsea Physic Garden, SW3
Fenton House
The Garden Museum, SE1
Ham House and Garden
Hampton Court Palace
Natural History Museum Wildlife
  Garden, SW7
Osterley Park and House
Roots and Shoots, SE11

By appointment only

51 Cholmeley Crescent, N6
46 Dukes Avenue, N10
17 Greenstone Mews, E11
116 Hamilton Terrace, NW8
Hampton Court Palace
Hornbeams
6 Methuen Park, N10
The Roof Terrace, 21a Waldegrave
  Road, SE19
Waltham Forest Register Office, E17

Also open by Appointment ☎

66 Abbots Gardens, N2
180 Adelaide Road, NW3
10 Arnison Road
4 Asmuns Hill, NW11
Badgers Retreat
1 Battlebridge Court, Islington
  Gardens, N1
225a Brixton Road, SW9
5 Burbage Road, SE24
12 Bushberry Road, E9
7 Byng Road
35 Camberwell Grove, SE5
51 The Chase, SW4
The Coach House, Tewkesbury Lodge
  Garden Group, SE23
Columcille
158 Culford Road, De Beauvoir
  Gardens, N1
4 Cumberland Park, W3
2 & 4 Dorset Road, Railway Cottages,
  N22
36 Downs Hill

207 East Barnet Road, East Barnet
  Gardens
Elm Tree Cottage
16 Eyot Gardens, Chiswick Mall
  Gardens, W4
65 Farm Way
54 Ferndown
69 & 70 Gloucester Crescent,
  Gloucester Crescent Group, NW1
45 Great North Road
7 The Grove, N6
Harcourt House
5 Hillcrest Avenue, NW11
19 Hillfield Park, N10
239a Hook Road
1a Hungerford Road, N7
26 Kenilworth Road, Penge Gardens,
  SE20
71 Kew Green, Kew Green Gardens
212 Langley Way
61 Lansdowne Drive, London Fields
  Gardens, E8
8 Lansdowne Walk, W11
46 Lincoln Road
Little Lodge
The 'Lived in' Garden, SE18
5 Lyndhurst Square, SE15
94a Lyndhurst Way, SE15
36 Malvern Road, London Fields
  Gardens, E8
53 Mapledene Road, London Fields
  Gardens, E8
94 Marsh Lane Allotments, N17
7 Maynard Road, E17
41 Mill Hill Road, W3
65 Mill Hill Road, W3
28 Mutton Road, SW18
66 Muswell Avenue, N10
17a Navarino Road, E8
5 Northampton Park, N1
21 Northchurch Terrace, De Beauvoir
  Gardens, N1
94 Oakwood Road, Hampstead
  Garden Suburb Gardens, NW11
28 Old Devonshire Road, SW12
93 Palace Road, SW2
4 Park Village East, NW1
3 The Park, N6
4 Piermont Green, SE22
101 Pitt Crescent, SW19
Redwing, Mill Hill Road Gardens, W3
Royal College of Physicians Garden,
  NW1
58 Rushmore Road, Lower Clapton
  Gardens, E5
7 St George's Road
1 St Helena Terrace, Richmond
  Riverside
87 St Johns Road, E17
57 St Quintin Avenue, W10
5 St Regis Close, N10
Southwood Lodge, N6
2 Stanley Road, N2
4 Stradbroke Grove
64 Thornhill Road, E10
2 Western Lane, SW12
12 Western Road, E13
33 Wood Vale, N10

The Gardens

66 ABBOTS GARDENS, N2
East Finchley, London N2 0JH.
Stephen & Ruth Kersley,
gardens.kersley@virgin.net. *Tube:
East Finchley, 6 mins walk from rear
exit along the Causeway (pedestrian)
to East End Rd, 2nd L into Abbots
Gdns. Buses: 143 stop at Abbots
Gdns on East End Rd. 102, 263 &
234 stop on East Finchley High Rd.*
Light refreshments & home-made
teas. **Adm £3, chd free. Sun 15 May
(2-5.30). Visitors also welcome by
appt.**
Designed for tranquillity and all-yr
interest, this 6yr old S-facing garden
(20m x 10m) uses plant form, colour,
texture and strong underlying
asymmetrical geometry (inspired by
Thomas Church) to create a calming
yet dramatic environment with
grasses, herbaceous perennials,
ornamental shrubs and trees, water
features and a discreet vegetable plot
enhanced by hanging fused glass
'amphoras' and a mosaic created by
glass artist Ruth. Circular, N-facing
front garden. Stephen studied garden
design at Capel Manor.

29 ADDISON AVENUE, W11
London W11 4QS. David & Shirley
Nicholson. *No entry for cars from
Holland Park Ave, approach via
Norland Square & Queensdale Rd.
Tube: Holland Park & Shepherds
Bush. Buses: 31, 94, 148, 295.* **Adm
£2.50, chd free. Sun 24 July (2-6).
Also open nearby 57 St Quintin
Ave.**
An ancient pear tree dominates the
lawn with unusual foliage plants and
late-flowering clematis in the side
borders. Raised beds of phlox,
monarda, salvia, agastache and
eupatorium produce a rich long-
lasting colour scheme in purple, blue
and pink (no yellow allowed!). Plenty
of ideas for those who think their
gardens are finished by the end of
June.

180 ADELAIDE ROAD, NW3
Swiss Cottage, London NW3 3PA.
Simone Rothman, 07817 060206,
simonerothman@ukonline.co.uk.
*Tube: Swiss Cottage, 100yds. Buses:
13, 46, 82, 113 on Finchley Rd; 31 &
C11 on Adelaide Rd. 50yds from
Marriott Hotel, Winchester Rd.* Home-
made teas. **Adm £2.50, chd free.
Suns 17 July; 7 Aug (3-5). Visitors**

also welcome by appt.
Enchanting S-facing walled garden
25ft x 30ft, with numerous densely
planted large containers on gravel,
profuse and colourful. Roses,
clematis and topiary. Stylish front
garden with lawn, shrubs, topiary and
many herbaceous plants.

In spring
woodland walks,
filled with bulbs,
flowering shrubs
and ferns . . .

GROUP OPENING

**ALEXANDRA PARK GARDENS,
N22**
London N22 7BG. *Tube: Bounds
Green or Wood Green, then bus 15
mins. Mainline: Alexandra Palace 3
mins. Buses: 184, W3 alight at
junction of Alexandra Park Rd &
Palace Gates Rd.* Home-made teas &
wine. **Combined adm £3.50, chd
free. Sun 7 Aug (2-6).**

    **272 ALEXANDRA PARK
    ROAD**
    Clive Boutle & Kate Tattersall

    **279 ALEXANDRA PARK
    ROAD**
    Gail & Wilf Downing

    **289 ALEXANDRA PARK
    ROAD**
    Julie Littlejohn

    **300 ALEXANDRA PARK
    ROAD**
    Paul Cox & Bee Peak

On the site of the original Alexandra
Park estate are four gardens to enjoy:
the surprisingly long rear garden of a
1920s house backing onto deer
enclosure and four exuberant
contrasting front gardens. The back
garden retains many pre-war features
incl an Anderson Shelter rock garden,
crazy paving and venerable trees as
well as a tree house, greenhouse and
wildlife-friendly eclectic planting. The
four front gardens all provide colour
and interest for the community and
are inspiring examples of how much
can be achieved in a very small
space. There is a profusion of colour
in pots, while tall plants hide a secret
hidden from the street. One steeply-
sloping front garden has a semi-
tropical theme, with a rill running
through a riverbed rockery,
disappearing under the path and
dropping into a pool surrounded by
beautiful stones, another is a modern
re-creation of a cottage country
garden. Folk music and dancing,
party atmosphere. Group winners
Conservation Society Green Corners
award, 'On the Move' category.

ALL SEASONS, W5
97 Grange Road, Ealing, London
W5 3PH. Dr Benjamin & Mrs Maria
Royappa. *Tube: walking distance
Ealing Broadway.* Light refreshments
& home-made teas. **Adm £3, chd
free. Sun 7 Aug (11-6.30).**
Garden designed and planted by
owners, with changes and new,
interesting planting for 2011. Features
incl ponds, pergolas, Japanese
gardens, tropical house for orchids
and exotics, aviaries, recycled
features, composting and rain water
harvesting, orchard, kiwi, grape vines,
architectural and unusual plants,
collections incl ferns, bamboos,
conifers and cacti.

GROUP OPENING

**AMWELL GARDENS GROUP,
EC1**
South Islington, London EC1R 1YE.
*Tube: Angel, 5 mins walk. Buses: 19,
38 to Rosebery Ave; 30, 73 to
Pentonville Rd.* Home-made teas at
11 Chadwell St. **Combined adm £5,
chd free. Sun 19 June (2-5.30).**

    11 CHADWELL STREET
    Mary Aylmer & Andrew Post

    24 MYDDELTON SQUARE
    Professor Diana Leonard

    27 MYDDELTON SQUARE
    Sally & Rob Hull

    LLOYD SQUARE
    Lloyd Square Garden
    Committee.
    Through gate opp 7 Lloyd Square

    NEW RIVER HEAD
    The Nautilus Building,
    Myddelton Passage. The
    Residents

The Amwell Gardens Group is in a
secluded corner of Georgian
Clerkenwell. Contrasting gardens
include Lloyd Square, a mature space
with drifting borders in the centre of
the Lloyd Baker Estate, and the
nearby gardens surrounding the
historic New River Head, where a
stylish fountain and pergola have
replaced the outer pond, which
distributed fresh water to London. In
Myddelton Square is a rooftop oasis
with views towards St Paul's
contrasts with small, lushly planted
gardens in this elegant terraced
setting. Some wheelchair access.

10 ARNISON ROAD
East Molesey KT8 9JJ. David
Clarke, 07984 011223. *¹/₂ m from
Hampton Court. Towards East
Molesey via Bridge Rd, Arnison Rd
3rd on R.* Teas July, wine Aug. **Adm
£2.50, chd free. Sun 24 July (1-6).
Evening Opening £3.50, wine, Sun
7 Aug (7-10.30).** Visitors also
welcome by appt in July & Aug,
with good prior notice.
Medium-sized, ever-evolving garden
with natural planting designed to
attract wildlife and insects. Large
collection of fragrant lilies. Restful koi
pond with waterfall: sit and
contemplate and possibly feed the
fish. Borders and island beds packed
with colour, and a shade area for
plants that like these conditions.
African lodge with artefacts. A garden
to tickle the senses and a new
experience around every corner.
Evening opening features lights and
candles in profusion with background
music to suit the mood of the garden.

NEW   **61 ARTHUR ROAD, SW19**
Wimbledon, London SW19 7DN.
Daniela McBride. *Tube: Wimbledon
Park, then 8mins walk. Mainline:
Wimbledon, 18mins walk.* Light
refreshments & home-made teas.
**Adm £3.50, chd free. Sun 12 June
(2-6). Also open 97 Arthur Rd .**
In spring, the main features of this
steeply sloping garden are the
woodland walks, filled with bulbs,
flowering shrubs and ferns. In early
summer the focus moves to the many
roses grown around the garden, then
later the autumn colour is provided by
trees and shrubs. Steep slopes.

97 ARTHUR ROAD, SW19
Wimbledon, London SW19 7DP.
Tony & Bella Covill. *Wimbledon Park tube, then 200yds up hill on R. Light refreshments.* **Adm £3, chd free. Sun 12 June (2-6). Also open 61 Arthur Rd.**
1/3 -acre garden of an Edwardian house. Garden established for more than 20yrs and constantly evolving with a large variety of plants and shrubs. It has grown up around several lawns with pond and fountains. Abundance of wildlife and a bird haven. A beautiful place with much colour, foliage and texture.

12 Vine Road

NEW ASH COTTAGE, SE21
1B Court Lane, Dulwich Village, London SE21 7DH. Brigid Gardner. *Rail: N Dulwich (6 mins walk). Bus: P4 & 37. Tube: Brixton & P4. Parking nearby. Light refreshments & home-made teas.* **Adm £2.50, chd free. Sun 12 June (2-5.30).**
The garden aims to show that even a 100ft x 40ft plot can provide intriguing vistas and unexpected surprises. It is divided into: a paved garden with traditional scented flowers; an orchard with treehouse, hammock and swing; a long, thin herb and vegetable garden. These are separated by hedges and climber-covered trellis, intersected with narrow linking archways.

4 ASMUNS HILL, NW11
Hampstead Garden Suburb NW11 6ET. Peter & Yvonne Oliver, 020 8455 8741. *Close to Finchley Rd & N Circular. Tube: Golders Green, then buses 82,102 or 460 to Temple Fortune, then 2 mins walk along Hampstead Way, Asmuns Hill 2nd on L.* **Adm £3, chd free. Sun 26 June (2-6). Also open 15 Creswick Walk. Visitors also welcome by appt.**
Award-winning Arts & Crafts cottage garden in artisan's quarter of Hampstead Garden Suburb. Many clematis and other climbers, both front and back. Succulents, acers and other plants in pots and containers. Pond, patio, herbaceous bed, shade area. Sculptures and objets trouvés.

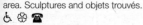

BADGERS RETREAT
39 Motspur Park, New Malden, Kingston KT3 6PS. Peter & Jenny Barham, 020 8949 3733, jennym@orchidconsultancy.co.uk. *3m N Kingston town centre. Buses:*

213 from Kingston or Sutton; K9 from Epsom. 7-10 mins walk Motspur Park railway stn. By car: A3 to New Malden/Worcester Park underpass. Take Malden Rd to Worcester Park, then 3rd rd on L. Parking in Wendover Drive & Blakes Ave. *Home-made teas (Sun), wine (Wed).* **Adm £3.50, chd free (share to Wildlife Aid). Sun 26 June (2-6). Evening Opening £4, wine, Wed 29 June (6-8.30). Also open 26 June 65 Farm Way. Visitors also welcome by appt, individuals and small groups.**
Inspirational garden designed by owner for foliage effect with lots of large pots. Exotic plants incl grasses, tree ferns, banana, bamboo and echium. Small waterfall running off patio onto rockery with alpines into fish pond. Wildlife pond with bridge, mini jungle area leading to path with mirrors. Decking with summerhouse giving Japanese effect. Lots of focal points and seats.

52A BERRYLANDS ROAD
Surbiton KT5 8PD. Dr Tim & Mrs Julia Leunig. *A3 to Tolworth; A240 (towards Kingston) for approx 1m, then R into Berrylands Rd (after Fire Stn). 52A on R after Xrds. Home-made teas.* **Adm £2.50, chd free. Sun 17 July (2.30-5.30).**
Professionally designed T-shaped garden. Lawn and patio surrounded

by cypress, lavender, magnolia, cistus, albizia, tetrapanax, myrtle, lobelia tupa, roses, ginger, interesting hydrangeas and clipped hebe parviflora. Natural wooded area under copper beech arranged around pond, stream and waterfall with eucalyptus, bamboo, tree fern and gunnera. Featured in local press.

225A BRIXTON ROAD, SW9
London SW9 6LW. Deborah Nagan & Michael Johnson, 07773 816622, deborah@naganjohnson.co.uk. *Tube: Oval or Brixton. Buses: 3, 59, 133, 159. Brixton Rd is the A23; 225a is on E side, next to Mostyn Rd. Home-made teas.* **Adm £3, chd free. Day & Evening Opening, wine, Sun 28 June (2-8). Also open 28 Multon Rd. Visitors also welcome by appt for groups and individuals, afternoon tea by arrangement.**
Architects' home with productive vegetable garden in modern raised beds in the front garden. To the rear are fruit and mostly perennial flowers in a rusty palette. Lower level calm garden with fish pond. Modern urban oasis with unusual materials but designed for maximum floral effect. Sale of specialist plants from Plaxtol Nursery; garden-grown lemon verbena tea and home-made cakes. Remains open into the evening (wine available).

GROUP OPENING

 BRIXTON WATER LANE GARDENS, SW2
Brixton, London SW2 1QB. *Tube: Brixton. Mainline: Herne Hill, both 10 mins.* Buses: 3, 37, 196 or 2, 415, 432 along Tulse Hill. Home-made teas. **Combined adm £5, chd free. Sun 22 May (2-5.30).**

> **NEW** **60 BRIXTON WATER LANE**
> Caddy & Chris Sitwell

> **NEW** **62 BRIXTON WATER LANE**
> Daisy & Nicholas Pearson

Two 90ft gardens backing onto Brockwell Park with original apple trees from the old orchard. No. 60 has a large farmhouse garden with bee hives and hens wandering through ornamental grasses. Mature wisteria covers the house wall and strong colour comes from laburnum, mimosa and lilac. No. 62 is a country garden with exuberant borders of soft colours, a productive greenhouse and a mass of pots on the terrace. Plenty of spring colour from lilac, apple blossom and a magnolia.

5 BURBAGE ROAD, SE24
Dulwich, London SE24 9HJ. Crawford & Rosemary Lindsay, 020 7274 5610, rl@rosemarylindsay.com, www.rosemarylindsay.com. *Nr junction with Half Moon Lane. Herne Hill and N Dulwich mainline stns, 5 mins walk.* Buses: 3, 37, 40, 68, 196, 468. Home-made teas. **Adm £3, chd free. Sun 1 May (2-5). Visitors also welcome by appt.**
Garden of member of The Society of Botanical Artists. 150ft x 40ft with large and varied range of plants. Herb garden, herbaceous borders for sun and shade, climbing plants, pots, terraces, lawns. Gravel areas to reduce watering. See our website for what the papers said.

12 BUSHBERRY ROAD, E9
Hackney, London E9 5SX. Molly St Hilaire, 020 8985 6805. *Overground stn: Homerton, then 5 mins walk.* Buses: 26, 30, 388, alight last stop in Cassland Rd. Light refreshments & home-made teas. **Adm £1.50, chd free. Sun 26 June (2-5). Visitors**

also welcome by appt.
Petite courtyard garden with water feature. Rambling roses, jasmine, vine and clematis cover the overarching pergola.

7 BYNG ROAD
High Barnet EN5 4NW. Mr & Mrs Julian Bishop, 020 8440 2042. *Tube: High Barnet. Stn: Hadley Wood or New Barnet. Buses: 107, 263, 384 alight Ravenscroft Park or The Spires.* Home-made teas. **Adm £3, chd free (share to Barnet Hospital Special Care Baby Unit). Sun 4 Sept (2-5). Visitors also welcome by appt.**
Six different borders all in one London garden. Each one different: one filled with tropical plants, another 'hot' border, two with cooler coloured perennials. Lots of rare and unusual varieties with a modern design twist. Owner a Chelsea Flower Show producer for the past 10 yrs. Emphasis on salvias, rudbeckias, persicarias, anything creating a 'wow' factor!

Two 90ft gardens backing onto Brockwell Park with original apple trees from the old orchard . . .

CADOGAN PLACE SOUTH GARDEN, SW1
Sloane Street, London SW1X 9PE. *Entrance to garden opp 97 Sloane St.* **Adm £3.50, chd free. Sun 1 May (10-5).**
Many surprises and unusual trees and shrubs are hidden behind the railings of this large London square. The first square to be developed by architect Henry Holland for Lord Cadogan at the end of C18, it was then called the London Botanic Garden. Mulberry trees planted for silk production at end of C17. Cherry trees, magnolias and bulbs are outstanding in spring, when the fern garden is unfurling. Hans Sloane Garden first exhibited at the Chelsea Flower Show 2004. Feel free to bring a picnic.

128 CADOGAN TERRACE, E9
Hackney, London E9 5HP. William Dowden. *Overground stn: Hackney Wick. Cadogan Terrace runs parallel to A102M, along edge of Victoria Park, enter by St Mark's Gate.* Cream Teas. **Adm £3, chd free. Sun 17 July (2-6).**
A tranquil yet exotic garden. Your journey begins at the Regent's Canal. You enter the upper level with its gazebo surrounded by roses, hibiscus and lavatera. You move through the middle level with its shrub borders, and finally enter the courtyard with its sunken pool. Journey's end. Adjacent nursery.

GROUP OPENING

NEW **CAMBERWELL GROVE GARDENS, SE5**
Camberwell, London SE5 8JE. *5 mins from Denmark Hill mainline stn.* Buses: 12, 36, 68, 148, 171, 176, 185, 436. Entrance through garden room at rear. Home-made teas. **Combined adm £5, chd free. Sun 26 June (2-6).**

> **NEW** **81 CAMBERWELL GROVE**
> Alex & Jane Maitland Hudson

> **83 CAMBERWELL GROVE**
> John Hall & Robert Hirschhorn

Neighbouring walled gardens behind C18 houses in this beautiful tree-lined street. At number 81 the owners are 3 yrs into restructuring and replanting the garden around existing features: a large Japanese maple, a tall trachycarpus palm and York stone paving. Borders filled with herbaceous perennials, roses, clematis and shade-loving ground cover. Newly planted hornbeam hedge and newly built garden house. Pots of all sizes filled with a wide variety of planting including a collection of hostas. Number 83 is a 90ft x 18ft beautifully designed plant-lovers' garden developed over the last 10 yrs. The emphasis is on yr-round interest, with abundant unusual planting within a formal structure of box hedging to provide varied and interesting areas of peace and privacy. Contemporary garden room, gravel and York stone paths and seating areas, lovely views of parish church.

35 CAMBERWELL GROVE, SE5
London SE5 8JA. Lynette Hemmant & Juri Gabriel, 020 7703 6186, juri@jurigabriel.com. *From Camberwell Green go down Camberwell Church St. Turn R into Camberwell Grove.* Juice & biscuits available. **Adm £3, chd free (share to St Giles Church restoration fund). Sun 12 June (12-7). Visitors also welcome by appt for groups of 10+ only, max 30 (£100 min for tour groups).**
120ft x 20ft garden with backdrop of St Giles Church. Evolved over 26yrs into romantic country-style garden brimming with colour and overflowing with pots. In June spectacular roses swamp the artist's studio and festoon an old iron staircase. Artist's studio open.

29 CANONBURY PARK NORTH, N1
London N1 2JZ. Jamie Longstaff, www.29cpn.com. *Between Upper St and St Paul's Rd. Tube: Highbury & Islington. Buses: 19, 73, 277.* **Adm £3, chd free. Sun 10 July (12-4). Also open 55 and 58 Canonbury Park North.**
Bold foliage and Christopher Lloyd inspired planting combine with formal landscaping in this urban garden which evokes Venice and the N of Italy. This compact 4yr-old garden demonstrates that you don't need acres of space to create an oasis in the heart of the city.

Candle lit evening opening with fire pit ensures a warm welcome for all . . .

CAPEL MANOR GARDENS
See Hertfordshire.

5 CECIL ROAD, N10
Muswell Hill, London N10 2BU. Ben Loftus. *Off Alexandra Park Rd. Buses: 102, 299 from E Finchley or Bounds Green, alight St Andrew's Church.* **Adm £2.50, chd free. Sun 26 June (2-5). Teas & plant sale at 5 St Regis Close, also open.**
Garden designer's sloping garden

featured in several magazines. Spectacular, well planted large pots (irrigated), interesting small raised pond, unusual small trees, shrubs and perennials with much emphasis on foliage and shape. Stylish garden office with green roof of bulbs, thymes etc.

CHARTERHOUSE, EC1
Charterhouse Square, London EC1M 6AN, www.thecharterhouse.org. *Buses: 4, 55. Tube: Barbican. Turn L out of stn, L into Carthusian St & into square. Entrance through car park.* **Adm £5, chd free. Evening Opening, wine, Tue 14 June (6-9).**
Enclosed courtyard gardens within the grounds of the historic Charterhouse, which dates back to 1347. 'English Country Garden' style featuring roses, ancient mulberry trees and small pond. Various garden herbs found here are still used in the kitchen today. Buildings not open.
&

CHARTS EDGE
See Kent.

51 THE CHASE, SW4
London SW4 0NP. Mr Charles Rutherfoord & Mr Rupert Tyler, 020 7627 0182, mail@charlesrutherfoord.net, www.charlesrutherfoord.net. *Off Clapham Common Northside. Tube: Clapham Common. Buses: 137, 452.* Light Refreshments. **Adm £3, chd free. Evening Opening Wed 27 Apr (6-8). Sun 1 May (2-6). Visitors also welcome by appt.**
Member of the Society of Garden Designers, Charles has created the garden over 20yrs using 15 different species of trees. Spectacular in spring, 1500 tulips bloom among irises and tree peonies. Narrow paths lead to a mound surrounded by acanthus and topped by a large steel sculpture. Rupert's geodetic dome shelters seedlings, succulents and subtropicals.

CHAUFFEUR'S FLAT
See Surrey.

◆ CHELSEA PHYSIC GARDEN, SW3
66 Royal Hospital Road, London SW3 4HS. Chelsea Physic Garden self-funding charity, 020 7352 5646, www.chelseaphysicgarden.co.uk. *Tube: Sloane Square (10 mins). Bus:*

170. Parking Battersea Park (charged). Entrance in Swan Walk (except wheelchairs). **Adm £5. For NGS: Sun 3 Apr (12-6). For other opening times and information, please phone or see garden website.**
Oldest Botanic Garden in London. 3³/₄ acres with medicinal and herb garden, perfumery border, family order beds, historical walk, glasshouses. Cool fernery and Robert Fortune's tank pond. Guided and audio tours.

24 CHESTNUT ROAD, SE27
West Norwood, London SE27 9LF. Paul Brewer & Anne Rogerson. *Stns: West Norwood or Tulse Hill. Buses: 2, 68, 196, 322, 432, 468. Off S end of Norwood Rd, nr W Norwood Cemetery.* **Adm £3, chd free (share to Sound Minds). Evening Opening wine, Sun 4 Sept (5-9).**
Front garden with telekia and mixed borders. Compact rear garden with a jungly feel. Lush planting of vintage ferns, acer griseum, bamboos, banana, grape, fig and lots of pots. Relax by the pond or in the SE Asian style gazebo (from recycled wood). Shed with green roof. Penguin. Candle lit evening opening with fire pit ensures a warm welcome for all. Featured in House Beautiful magazine.

CHEVENING
See Kent.

GROUP OPENING

CHISWICK MALL GARDENS, W4
Chiswick, London W6 9TN. *Tube: Stamford Brook or Turnham Green. Buses: 27, 190, 267 & 391 to Young's Corner from Hammersmith, through St Peter's Sq under A4 to river. By car to Hogarth r'about, A4 westbound turn off at Eyot Gdns S, then R into Chiswick Mall.* Home-made teas at 16 Eyot Gardens. **Adm £2 each garden, chd free. Sun 29 May (2-6).**

EYOT COTTAGE
Mrs Peter Trumper

16 EYOT GARDENS
Ms Dianne Farris.
At R-angle to Chiswick Mall where Hammersmith Terrace starts **Visitors also welcome by appt, max 30 visitors.** 020 8741 1370

Southwood Lodge, N6

the eye to a hidden pond, through a rustic archway into a shady fernie glen. Here the greenhouse sits alongside David's 'man sanctuary' shed! Visitors enter through the 'catatorium', an open air conservatory created for feline frolics, full of plants and catwalks, giving wild birds the freedom of the haven beyond. Trialists for Thompson and Morgan plants. Guest bee keeper available for info on bee keeping. London correspondents for Garden News 'From where I'm gardening'.

GROUP OPENING

NEW ▶ **CLAPHAM MANOR STREET GARDENS, SW4**
Clapham Old Town, London SW4 6DZ. *Tube: Clapham Common. Off Clapham High St.* Light refreshments, home-made teas & wine. **Combined adm £5, chd free. Sun 12 June (3-6).**

> **NEW** ▶ **40 CLAPHAM MANOR STREET**
> Mrs Nina Murdoch

> **NEW** ▶ **44 CLAPHAM MANOR STREET**
> Mrs Annette Marchini

Two creatively inspired secret, romantic walled gardens. No.40 is a large garden divided by trained arches of apple trees. It contains a cobbled courtyard, a stream, ferns and ivy garden, 2 ponds and many climbers. No.44 has the emphasis on lush green planting with white flowers, creating a soft, organic counterpoint to the contemporary extension. Perfect habitats for breeding birds, especially sparrows.

LINGARD HOUSE
Rachel Austin

SWAN HOUSE
Mr & Mrs George Nissen

A unique group of riverside houses and gardens situated in an unspoilt quiet backwater. Eyot Cottage has two interconnecting gardens, one an old walled garden with many unusual white plants, the other a terrace garden with imaginative use of old stones and pavers. The garden at 16 Eyot Gardens has been redesigned and replanted for its 21st yr of opening for the NGS, and with the help and inspiration of Anthony Noel has taken on a new lease of life. Lingard House's walled garden is divided into a brick courtyard and terrace with huge acacia tree; formal lawn with miniature pond and water-spout and wild garden with ancient apple trees, climbing roses and beehive. At Swan House see an informal walled garden, herbaceous border, fruit trees, small vegetable garden and a tiny greenhouse. Also a small wild flower area, 2 ponds, a rill and a new knot garden.

---

51 CHOLMELEY CRESCENT, N6
Highgate, London N6 5EX. Ernst Sondheimer, 020 8340 6607, ernst@sondheimer.fsnet.co.uk. *Between Highgate Hill & Archway Rd, off Cholmeley Park. Tube: Highgate.* **Adm £2, chd free. Visitors welcome by appt.**
Approx 1/6 -acre garden with many alpines in screes, peat beds, tufa,

troughs and greenhouse; shrubs, rhododendrons, camellias, magnolias, pieris, ceanothus etc. Clematis, bog plants, roses, primulas, tree ferns. Water features. Terraced garden with steps and slopes.

CHOUMERT SQUARE, SE15
London SE15 4RE. The Residents. *Via wrought iron gates off Choumert Grove. Peckham Rye mainline stn is visible from the gates, & buses galore (12, 36, 37, 63, 78, 171, 312, 345) less than 10 mins walk. Car park 2 mins.* Light refreshments & home-made teas. **Adm £3, chd 50p (share to St Christopher's Hospice). Sun 5 June (1-6).**
About 46 mini gardens with maxi-planting in Shangri-la situation that the media has described as a 'Floral Canyon', which leads to small communal 'secret garden'. Art, craft and home-made produce stalls and live music. Delicious refreshments. Gardens and village fête in one!

79 CHURCH LANE, N2
London N2 0TH. Caro & David Broome. *Tube: E Finchley, then East End Rd for 3/4 m, R into Church Lane. Buses: 143 to Five Bells PH, 3 min walk; 263 to E Finchley Library, 5 min walk.* Home-made teas. **Adm £2.50, chd free. Suns 12 June; 17 July (2-6).**
Garden writer's cottage garden with a twist. Foliage of shrubs, tumbling roses and grasses enhance interesting perennials, creating a colour co-ordinated palette that leads

COLUMCILLE
9 Norlands Crescent, Chislehurst BR7 5RN. Nancy & Jim Pratt, 020 8467 9383, nancyandjim@btinternet.com. *Off A222 turn into Cricket Ground Rd, then 1st R into Norlands Cres, approx 1/2 m from Chislehurst BR stn. Buses: 162 or 269, Susan Wood stop.* Home-made teas. **Adm £3, chd free (share to St Nicholas Church). Sun 12 June; Sun 21 Aug (1-5). Visitors also welcome by appt.**
Small garden featuring Japanese sanctuary, influenced by Zen tradition, incl water feature, lanterns, traditional

Japanese plants and garden shed transformed into a tea house. Also cottage garden section with colourful display of roses, digitalis, lupins, peonies and delphiniums, especially in June; lilies July, dahlias Aug and Sept.

NEW 6 CORNFORD GROVE, SW12
London SW12 9JF. Susan Venner & Richard Glassborow. *Tube & mainline Balham, then 3 min walk.* Home-made teas. **Adm £2.50, chd free (share to Trees for Cities). Suns 8 May; 18 Sept (2-6).**
This medium sized garden is an integral extension of sustainable low carbon living. The guiding principles within the garden combine aesthetic values with productivity, biodiversity and low maintenance. Technically an orchard, 20 fruiting trees and forest berries merge with herbaceous planting and two working bee hives. Featured in Sunday Telegraph.

113 CORRINGHAM ROAD, NW11
Hampstead Garden Suburb, London NW11 7DL. Veronica Clein. *Tube: Golders Green, then 10mins walk. Entrance to courtyard between 101 & 117 Corringham Rd (Hampstead Way end). Buses: 13, 82, 102, 113, 460 to Golders Green.* Light refreshments & wine. **Adm £5, chd free. Evening Opening Thur 23 June (5.30-9).**
Garden designer and plantswoman's atmospheric garden created since 2005. Profusely planted with perennials, shrubs and annuals in Persian carpet colours. Dry shade woodland garden, wildlife pond, potager, greenhouse and sculptured figure. Terrace with lavishly planted containers. Live jazz music. Featured in Gardens Monthly, GGG & Hampstead & Highgate Express.

COTTAGE FARM
See Kent.

NEW 269 CREIGHTON AVENUE, N2
East Finchley, London N2 9BP. David Godny. *Buses: 102, 143 to E Finchley Tube. Short walk up hill, turn R at HSS hire shop. Bus 263 stops opp Creighton Ave.* Light refreshments. **Adm £2.50, chd free. Sun 26 June (2-5.30).**
A sense of the wild has been created in this lush 90ft garden where the

tropical and exotic has been imaginatively blended with the traditional by its artist owner. Meandering paths wind their way from a lush open arena crammed with roses, camellias, tree peonies and hydrangeas to the secluded jungle woodland of bamboos, eucalyptuses, phormiums and tree ferns. Rare and unusual plants abound. Nature photography.

A good example of what can be achieved in a small space in a short time . . .

17 CRESCENT LANE, SW4
London SW4 9PT. Sue Phipps and Paddy Sumner. *Near junction of Abbeville Rd and Crescent Lane, NOT in one-way part of Crescent Lane.* Home-made teas. **Adm £3, chd free. Sun 12 June (3-6).**
Pretty, tranquil garden, which starts with a long lawn, edged with borders, and opens out into a large square lawn, surrounded by roses, shrubs and trees, with a pond, backed by a yew hedge. The design and size are unusual for this part of London.

NEW 15 CRESWICK WALK, NW11
Hampstead Garden Suburb, London NW11 6AN. Ian Shelley. *Tube: Golders Green, then buses 82, 102 or 460 to Henlys Corner/Addison Way stop. Cross rd to Addison Way, 1st R Creswick Walk.* Home-made teas. **Adm £3, chd free. Sun 26 June (2-5.30). Also open 4 Asmuns Hill.**
Modern-style garden with simplicity of line and sculptural quality. At the back, form follows function to create an outdoor room with a wide patio leading to a minimalist space. Four topiaried holly balls are set in a line of box-edged squares, counterbalanced by an impeccable lawn. The front garden has a more relaxed feel, Strong, asymmetrical design underpins the lush planting. Cottage garden plants are repeated throughout the beds giving rhythm and movement to the design.

NEW 15 CRIFFEL AVENUE, SW2
Streatham Hill, London SW2 4AY. Jane and Michael Ovens. *Mainline: Streatham Hill, 5 mins walk. Buses: 59, 133, 137, 159 to Telford Ave.* Light refreshments & teas (Sun). **Adm £3, chd free. Sun 12 June (3-6). Evening Opening, wine, Tue 14 June (6-9).**
Cottage-style 70ft x 30ft garden with 200 yr-old oak tree. Herbaceous, shrubs and old roses with a hint of formality. A tranquil oasis in the midst of London rush. Seeds and cuttings for sale.

4 CUMBERLAND PARK, W3
Acton, London W3 6SY. Sarah Hamilton-Fairley & Richard Crofton, 020 8992 2360, richcro@hotmail.co.uk. *E of Ealing. Tube & mainline: Acton Central & Acton Main Line stns 5 mins walk. First house N of Woodhurst Rd, on W side of Cumberland Park.* **Adm £5, chd free. Evening Opening £5, chd free, wine & light refreshments, Sat 25 June (6-8). Visitors also welcome by appt from 2-26 June, max 6 visitors.**
A luscious, sensuous town house back garden. The deck looks over a terrace with shrubs, pots and sinks; a pergola laden with rose and clematis, lawn, more shrubs, a summerhouse. The perfect place to chill with a glass of wine as the evening sun backlights the foliage.

NEW 20 DACRES ROAD, SE23
Forest Hill, London SE23 2NW. Andrew & Julie McMurtrie. *Off S Circular (A205). From Forest Hill stn turn S onto Perry Vale. Dacres Rd 1st main turning on R. Buses: 176, 185, 197, 356 pass close by.* Home-made teas. **Adm £3, chd free. Sun 19 June (2-5.30).**
Front garden features a native hedge and wildlife pond. Rear garden (40ft x 170ft) surrounded by mature trees, has a 'naturalistic' feel. A scented courtyard area overlooks the lawn, surrounded by imaginative planting and rambling roses. Woodchip paths lead to the henhouse and 'secret' woodland area with working bee hives and log cabin. Laying hens.

GROUP OPENING

DE BEAUVOIR GARDENS, N1
N1 4HU. *Haggerston Station, London Overground (East London line); Highbury & Islington tube then 30 or 277 bus; Angel tube then 38, 56 or 73 bus. Street parking available.* Home-made teas at 158 Culford Road. **Combined adm £5 or £2 each garden, chd free. Sun 12 June (2-6).**

158 CULFORD ROAD
Gillian Blachford
Visitors also welcome by appt.
020 7254 3780
gmblachford@btopenworld.com

114 DE BEAUVOIR ROAD
Nancy & Richard Turnbull

21 NORTHCHURCH TERRACE
Ms Nancy Korman
Visitors also welcome by appt in June & July only, max 6, no coaches.
020 7249 4919
nancylkorman@hotmail.co.uk

Three gardens to explore in De Beauvoir, a leafy enclave of Victorian villas next to Islington. The area boasts some of Hackney's keenest gardeners, many having resuscitated their gardens from neglect and sensitively restored them to glory. 158 Culford Road's long narrow garden has a romantic feel. A path winds through full borders with shrubs, small trees, perennials and many unusual plants. The family garden at 114 De Beauvoir Road was designed to be wildlife-friendly and low maintenance. Decorative borders contain echinacea, penstemons, astelia and grasses. The walled garden at 21 Northchurch Terrace has a more formal feel, with deep herbaceous borders, pond, fruit trees, pergola, patio pots and herb beds.

36 DOWNS HILL
Beckenham BR3 5HB. Marc & Janet Berlin, 020 8650 9377, janetberlin@hotmail.com. *1m W of Bromley. 2 mins from Ravensbourne mainline stn nr top of Foxgrove Rd.* Home-made teas. **Adm £2.50, chd free. Sun 1 May (2-5). Visitors also welcome by appt, groups welcome.** Long, ²/₃ -acre E-facing, award-winning garden sloping steeply.

Ponds, water courses and several varied patio areas. Many tender unusual plants and hundreds of pots. Wooded paths, dense planting of trees, shrubs and flowers, raised beds and new gravel areas. Alpine house, bulbs in pots and a display of auriculas. Featured in Garden News.

46 DUKES AVENUE, N10
Muswell Hill, London N10 2PU. Judith Glover, judith@judithglover.com, www.judithglover.com. *Short walk from main Muswell Hill r'about. Tube: Highgate then bus 43 or 134 to Muswell Hill Broadway or bus 7 from Finsbury Park.* Refreshments available by arrangement. **Visitors welcome by appt.** Designer and botanical illustrator's country-style garden described as being 'just on the right side of controlled chaos'. Organic, curvy beds with foxgloves, aquilegias, irises and valerian anchored with clipped evergreens. Topiary, grasses and cloud-pruned Ilex crenata from the medal-winning garden Judith designed for the Chelsea Flower Show in 2003. Owner's studio open to visitors, refreshments provided.

GROUP OPENING

DULWICH VILLAGE TWO GARDENS, SE21
London SE21 7BJ. *Rail: N Dulwich or W Dulwich then 10-15 mins walk. Tube: Brixton then P4 bus passes the gardens. Street parking.* Home-made teas. **Combined adm £4.50, chd free (share to Macmillan, local branch). Sun 19 June (2-5).**

103 DULWICH VILLAGE
Mr & Mrs N Annesley

105 DULWICH VILLAGE
Mr & Mrs A Rutherford

2 Georgian houses with large gardens, 3 mins walk from Dulwich Picture Gallery and Dulwich Park. 103 Dulwich Village is a 'country garden in London' with a long herbaceous border, lawn, pond, roses and fruit and vegetable garden. 105 Dulwich Village is a very pretty garden with many unusual plants, lots of old-fashioned roses, fish pond and water garden.

GROUP OPENING

NEW EAST BARNET GARDENS
East Barnet EN4 8QS. *M25 J24 then A111 to Cockfosters. Tube: High Barnet or Cockfosters. Buses: 184, 307 & 326.* Delicious home-made teas and plants for sale at 207 East Barnet Rd. **Combined adm £3, chd free. Sun 12 June (2-5).**

NEW 33A BROOKHILL ROAD
Barbara Perry

207 EAST BARNET ROAD
Margaret Chadwick
Visitors also welcome by appt.
020 8440 0377
magg1ee@hotmail.com

Two interesting courtyard gardens, developed in different styles, within easy walking distance of each other. Both are designed not to reveal themselves all at once. The garden at 33a Brookhill Road is secluded and has an interesting collection of shrubs and clematis. Fences are covered with wisteria and trees grow in pots - a good example of what can be achieved in a small space in a short time. 207 East Barnet Road has high fences covered with clematis, honeysuckle and passion flowers. Roses and a vine scramble over an arch above a seat, specimen plants are grown in containers, and a small pond sustains goldfish, frogs and water plants. Clever use of mirrors lends added dimensions to the pretty garden.

The guiding principles within the garden combine aesthetic values with productivity, biodiversity and low maintenance . . .

GROUP OPENING

EAST FINCHLEY COTTAGE GARDENS, N2
East Finchley, London N2 8JJ.
*Tube: East Finchley 12 mins walk.
Bus: 263 to library, turn L into Church
Lane, R into Trinity Rd. Car: turn into
Trinity Rd from Long Lane, off Church
Lane.* Combined adm £3, chd free.
Sun 5 June (2-5). Teas & plant sale
at 2 Stanley Rd, also open.

22 TRINITY ROAD
J Maitland

20 TRINITY ROAD
Jane Meir

Two very different cottage gardens,
creating intimate spaces filled with
exuberant planting. In one, cottage
garden plants mingle happily with
elegant ferns and grasses. A majestic
black bamboo towers over pots of
dainty annuals and a giant
trachycarpus palm falls over a
feathery tamarix. In the other, a mass
of unusual perennials and shrubs
spills over hard landscaping. A host of
pots display a wide spectrum of plant
shapes, colours and textures.

20 EATONVILLE ROAD, SW17
Tooting Bec, London SW17 7SL.
Gethyn Davies & Pamela Johnson.
*Stns: Tooting Bec 5 min walk,
Wandsworth Common 10 min walk.
Buses: 219 & 319 on Trinity Rd.*
Home-made teas. Adm £2.50, chd
free. Sun 5 June (2-6). Also open
28 Old Devonshire Rd & 2 Western
Lane.
Garden designer's experiment in
planting combinations with unusual
perennials, shrubs and fragrant
climbers next to culinary herbs and
salad leaves. Garden on two levels
with small water feature and lawn.

ECCLESTON SQUARE, SW1
London SW1V 1NP. Roger Phillips
& the Residents,
roger.phillips@rogersroses.com,
www.rogerstreesandshrubs.com.
*Off Belgrave Rd nr Victoria stn,
parking allowed on Suns.* Home-
made teas. Adm £4, chd free. Sun
22 May (2-5).
Planned by Cubitt in 1828, the 3-acre
square is subdivided into mini-
gardens with camellias, iris, ferns and
containers. Dramatic collection of
tender climbing roses and 20 different

forms of tree peonies. National
Collection of ceanothus incl more
than 70 species and cultivars.
Notable important additions of tender
plants being grown and tested.
Wisteria arbour and mosaic/brick
patio. Children's play area.

 NCCPG

EDWARDES SQUARE, W8
South Edwardes Square,
Kensington, London W8 6HL.
Edwardes Square Garden
Committee. *Tube: Kensington High
St & Earls Court. Buses: 9, 10, 27,
28, 31, 49 & 74 to Odeon Cinema.
Entrance in South Edwardes Square.*
Cream Teas, cakes & light
refreshments. Adm £4, chd free. Sun
17 Apr (1-5). Also open 7 Upper
Phillimore Gardens.
One of London's prettiest secluded
garden squares. 3½ acres laid out
differently from other squares, with
serpentine paths by Agostino
Agliothe, Italian artist and decorator
who lived at No.15 from 1814-1820,
and a beautiful Grecian temple which
is traditionally the home of the
gardener. Romantic rose tunnel winds
through the middle of the garden.
Good displays of bulbs and blossom.
Very easy wheelchair access.

ELM TREE COTTAGE
85 Croham Road, South Croydon
CR2 7HJ. Wendy Witherick &
Michael Wilkinson, 020 8681 8622,
elmtreecottage@sky.com. *2m S of
Croydon. Off B275 from Croydon, off
A2022 from Selsdon, bus 64.* Adm
£3. Suns 8 May; 5 June; 3 July;
7 Aug; 4 Sept (1-4.30). Also open
7 Aug 55 Warham Road. Visitors
also welcome by appt.
Be inspired by our much-written-about
Mediterranean-style garden, planted
with palms, olives, phlomis, figs,
lavender, grasses and much more.
Agaves and cacti complement the
hard landscaping that runs throughout
the garden. Be surprised at every turn
then sit and enjoy the views. Featured
in BBC Gardeners' World Magazine.
Steep garden, unsuitable for those
unsteady on their feet.

65 FARM WAY
Worcester Park KT4 8SB. Mr & Mrs
A Rutherford, 020 8296 9806. *Stn:
Worcester Park. Bus: 213.* Light
refreshments & home-made teas.
Adm £3, chd free. Sun 26 June
(1-5). Also open Badgers Retreat.

Visitors also welcome by appt June
to Aug.
Plant lover's 3yr-old garden with wide
mixed borders bursting with colour
and plants of different textures and
interest, incl shrubs, roses and
perennials. Assorted pots of
vegetables, raised beds. Paved and
decked, plenty of seating areas.

◆ FENTON HOUSE, NW3
Hampstead Grove, London
NW3 6RT. National Trust,
www.nationaltrust.org.uk. *300yds
from Hampstead tube. Entrances: top
of Holly Hill & Hampstead Grove.*
For NGS: Evening Opening £4, chd
£2, wine, Thur 9 June (6.30-8.30).
For other opening times and
information, please see garden
website.
Timeless 1½ -acre walled garden, laid
out on three levels, containing
imaginative plantings concealed by
yew hedges. The herbaceous borders
give yr-round interest while the brick-
paved sunken rose garden provides a
sheltered hollow of scent and colour.
The formal lawn area contrasts with
the rustic charm of the kitchen garden
and orchard. Vine house. In spring,
good borders and underplanted
orchard.

54 FERNDOWN
Northwood Hills HA6 1PH. David &
Ros Bryson, 020 8866 3792,
davidbryson@sky.com. *Tube:
Northwood Hills 5 mins walk. R out of
stn, R down Briarwood Drive then 1st
R.* Light refreshments & teas. Adm
£3, chd free. Sun 21 Aug (11-5).
Visitors also welcome by appt.
Subtropical escapism in suburbia.
Intensely planted with a shoehorn,
this garden contains more than meets
the eye. Many rare species incl
several 'champion' species of palm
trees along with countless species of
ferns, succulents and other unusual
plants. Unusual collection of exotics,
cacti and Australasian and South
African plants.

FISHPONDS HOUSE
Fishponds Park, 219 Ewell Road,
Surbiton KT6 6BE. Robert Eyre-
Brook. *1m from Tolworth A3 junction
towards Kingston on A240. House
behind main pond in middle of The
Fishponds, a public park bordered by
Ewell Rd, Browns Rd, King Charles
Rd & Hollyfield Rd. House is behind*

the main pond. Park in neighbouring rds. No vehicle access to park other than for disabled; disabled access from Fwell Rd. Home-made teas. **Adm £2.50, chd free. Sun 12 June (2-5).**
Large garden, part formal, part terrace, with adjoining woodland overlooking a large duck pond. Designed in 2002 by Andy Sturgeon, 'Best in Show' winner at the 2010 Chelsea Flower Show, and filled with structural plants and grasses. Visitors could visit the park for a picnic before garden opening.

14 FRANK DIXON WAY, SE21
Dulwich, London SE21 7ET. Sally & Michael Bridgeland. *Mainline: W Dulwich. From Dulwich Village pass Dulwich Gallery on R, Frank Dixon Way (private rd) 500m on L.* Home-made teas. **Adm £3, chd free. Sun 22 May (2-5). Also open 30 Half Moon Lane.**
Large, friendly, family garden of lawns surrounded by mature trees and shrubs, with annual plantings giving interest and colour. There is a spectacular playhouse, a rope bridge and a sit-on railway for children's rides around the garden!

GROUP OPENING

FROGNAL GARDENS, NW3
Hampstead, London NW3 6UY. *Tube: Hampstead. Buses: 46, 268 to Hampstead High St. Frognal Gardens 2nd R off Church Row from Heath St.* Home-made teas. **Combined adm £3.50, chd free. Sun 19 June (2-5).**

5 FROGNAL GARDENS
Ruth & Brian Levy

5A FROGNAL GARDENS
Ian & Barbara Jackson

Two neighbouring gardens divided by path lined with trellises of cascading roses and clematis, underplanted with carpets of flowers. At No. 5, the long narrow structured garden is romantically planted with soft colours and a profusion of unusual climbers and cottage perennials. The small, beautifully landscaped garden at 5A is a garden to enjoy and relax in with lawn, colourful flower beds and containers. 4 inch step from patio doors.

NEW **16 FURLONG ROAD, N7**
Islington, London N7 8LS. Charles & Ingrid Maggs. *3 mins Highbury & Islington tube, & overground between Holloway Rd and Liverpool Rd.* **Adm £3, chd free. Sun 12 June (2-6).**
Flowery borders and trellises of roses, surrounding lawn, a pond, pergola and rock garden. Exceptional aspect as garden backs onto churchyard with church steeple giving a feeling of being in the country rather than just off the Holloway Road.

Imaginative use of magical 'flower trees' enables plants to take advantage of available sunlight . . .

GARDEN BARGE SQUARE AT DOWNINGS ROADS MOORINGS, SE1
31 Mill Street, London SE1 2AX. Mr Nick Lacey. *Close to Tower Bridge & Design Museum. Mill St off Jamaica Rd, between London Bridge & Bermondsey stns, Tower Hill also nearby. Buses: 47, 188, 381, RV1.* Home-made teas. **Adm £3, chd free (share to RNLI). Sun 10 July (2-5).**
Series of 7 floating barge gardens connected by walkways and bridges. Gardens have an eclectic range of plants for year round seasonal interest. Marine environment: suitable shoes and care needed. Not suitable for small children.

5 GARDEN CLOSE, SW15
London SW15 3TH. Vivien Fowler. *¹/₂ m E of Roehampton. Off Portsmouth Rd, 15 mins walk from the Green Man PH, via Wildcroft Rd, Putney Hill.* **Adm £3, chd free. Sun 3 July (11-5).**
¹/₄-acre walled garden which serves as backdrop to architect's all-glass house. Oriental inspiration with black bamboos, and swathes of box, hebe, lavender and rhododendrons. Ponds and timber decks surround house. House and garden open.

◆ **THE GARDEN MUSEUM, SE1**
Lambeth Palace Road, London SE1 7LB, 020 7401 8865. *www.gardenmuseum.org.uk. E side of Lambeth Bridge. Tube: Lambeth North, Vauxhall, Waterloo. Buses: 507 Red Arrow from Victoria or Waterloo mainline & tube stns, also 3, 77, 344.* **Adm £6, chd free (share to Garden Museum) For NGS: Sat 7 May (10.30-3). For other opening times and information, please phone or see garden website.**
Reproduction C17 knot garden with period plants, topiary and box hedging. Wild garden in front of graveyard area; drought planting at front entrance; themed installation planting on front border. Historic tools, information displays, changing exhibitions, shop and café housed in former church of St-Mary-at-Lambeth.

NCCPG

NEW **GARDENING ON A SHOESTRING, N1**
55 Canonbury Park North, Islington, London N1 2JU. Lina Pini. *Tube: Highbury & Islington, 10 mins. Canonbury overground, 3 mins. Buses: 19, 30, 73, 277.* **Combined adm with The Happy Triangle Garden (58 Canonbury Park North) £3.50, chd free. Sun 10 July (12-4). Also open 29 Canonbury Park North.**
Surrounded by mature trees, a N-facing garden cheats nature, having colour and interest all yr. Imaginative use of containers and magical 'flower trees' enables plants to take advantage of available sunlight. Sustainable planting using seeds, cuttings and 'rescued' plants. Vegetables and herbs flourish among hydrangeas, oleanders, rhododendrons, lilies, fuchsias and pelargoniums. A romantic gem in the heart of Canonbury.

13 GIPSY HILL, SE19
Crystal Palace, London SE19 1QG. Jon & Eils Digby-Rogers. *Stn: Gipsy Hill. Bus: 322 from Clapham Junction via Herne Hill goes up Gipsy Hill, Crystal Palace buses within walking distance.* Light refreshments, home-made teas & Pimm's. **Adm £3, chd free. Sun 10 July (2-7). Also open 32 Lovelace Rd.**
Secluded town garden, 17m x 17m, protected by high brick wall and steep shrub covered bank. York stone terracing, many coloured glazed and terracotta pots. Wide variety of shrubs, climbers and perennials for

---

yr-round colour. Wisteria-covered oak pergola, summerhouse, large blown glass/copper fountain, making outside rooms for the home.

☕

1A Hungerford Road, N7

GROUP OPENING

GLOUCESTER CRESCENT GROUP, NW1
Camden Town, London NW1 7EG. *Tube: Camden Town 2 mins, Mornington Crescent 10 mins. Limited metered parking in Oval Rd.* **Combined adm £3.50, chd free. Suns 10 July; 7 Aug (2-5.30).**

69 GLOUCESTER CRESCENT
Sandra Clapham
Visitors also welcome by appt.
020 7485 5764
set69@gloscres.fsnet.co.uk

70 GLOUCESTER CRESCENT
London. Lucy Gent & Malcolm Turner
Visitors also welcome by appt.
020 7485 6906
l-gent@tiscali.co.uk

Two neighbouring gardens (both welcoming visitors at other times by appointment) in a street well-known for its literary and musical connections. Ursula Vaughan Williams lived at no. 69 and Mrs Charles Dickens at no.70. Unexpected oases of calm and plant interest, 1 min from Camden Lock. 69 Gloucester Crescent is an ingenious and welcoming cottage garden, a treat behind front wall and gate. Roses, perennials, annuals and a bed of tomatoes, plus the odd self-seeder. 70 Gloucester Crescent meets the challenges of space and shade constraints, plus a warm microclimate, with by versatile planting. All-yr interest, with a climax of colour in August, incl a miniature pomegranate.

❀

NEW 20 GOLDHAZE CLOSE
Woodford Green IG8 7LE. Jenny Richmond. *By car, along A406 to Charlie Brown's r'about, L onto Chigwell Rd to T-lights. L to Broadmead Rd, 1st R Underwood Rd, L into Goldhaze Close. Tube: Woodford. Buses: 14 from South Woodford tube stn, 275 from Walthamstow Central stn.* Home-made teas. **Adm £2.50, chd free. Suns 24 July; 14 Aug (12-5).**

The 100ft L-shaped garden is bursting with over 100 plants grown in different types of conditions. A huge 25yr-old eucalyptus resembles a mature oak with beautiful bark. Paths lined with plants such as a strawberry tree, roses, campsis, penstemons, crocosmia and vegetables (in pots grown from seed in a greenhouse) lead to a secret decked garden for relaxation.

❀ ☕

ALLOTMENTS

GOLF COURSE ALLOTMENTS, N11
Winton Avenue, London N11 2AR. GCAA/Haringey, www.gcaa.pwp.blueyonder.co.uk. *Tube: Bounds Green approx 1km. Buses: 102, 184, 299 to Sunshine Garden Centre, Durnsford Rd. Then Bidwell Gardens (on foot through park) to Winton Ave. Gate opp junction with Blake Rd.* Home-made teas. **Adm £2.50, chd free. Sun 4 Sept (1-4.30). Also open 5 Russell Rd.**

Large, long-established allotment with over 200 plots maintained by culturally diverse community growing a wide variety of flowers, fruit and vegetables - some working towards organic cultivation. Picturesque corners and charming sheds. Autumn Show, prizewinning displays of produce, cakes and jams. Children's section. Tours of best plots. Location

for BBC TV Nigel Slater's Simple Suppers. Gravel and some uneven paths, but good access for all. WC.
♿ 🏡 ❀ ☕

NEW 55 GRASMERE AVENUE, SW19
Merton Park, London SW19 3DY. Glen Burnell & Roger Blanks. *1m S of Wimbledon. Tube: Morden, then 5 mins walk. Turn R out of stn, Grasmere Ave 2nd on R. By car, close to Morden Town Centre, just off one way system, Baptist Church on corner of Grasmere Ave.* Light refreshments. **Adm £2.50, chd free. Sun 5 June (11-2).**

An oasis of calm in suburbia. Rich lush foliage, sculptured with tropical planting, sets off a subtle palette of cooling purple and white in a little haven of tranquillity in this 70ft rear garden of a 1930s London semi. Piped classical music playing softly.
☕

45 GREAT NORTH ROAD
Barnet EN5 1EJ. Ron & Miriam Raymond, 07880 500617, ron.raymond91@yahoo.co.uk. *1m S of Barnet High St, 1m N of Whetstone. Buses 34, 263, 326, 634 alight at Lyonsdown Rd, 45 Great North Rd at junction of Cherry Hill, midway between High Barnet and Totteridge & Whetstone Stns, 20 mins walk.* Home-made teas. **Adm £2.50, chd free. Sun 31 July (2-6). Visitors also welcome by appt.**

Designed to give a riot of colour in July, the large front garden is packed with interesting perennials. Three tiered stands line the side with over 64 pots displaying hostas, ferns, fuchsias, heucheras. The rear garden incl over 50 tubs and hanging baskets plus a small pond surrounded by tiered beds. Children's fun trail (for 3-8yr olds), prizes. Adult garden quiz, also with prizes.

13 GREENHILL PARK
Barnet EN5 1HQ. Sally & Andy Fry. *1m S of High Barnet. ½ m S of High Barnet tube stn. Take 1st L after Odeon Cinema, Weaver PH on corner. Buses: 34, 84, 234, 263, 326.* Home-made teas. **Adm £2.50, chd free. Sun 12 June (2-5.30).** An oasis in suburbia. Approx ¼ acre. Colourful herbaceous borders, wildlife pond, summerhouse, Victorian plant house and shady fern garden. Series of rustic arches link main garden to path through wildlife-friendly secret garden, incorporating tree fern collection, stumpery, Japanese themed area and hidden courtyard vegetable garden with rare breed chickens.

17 GREENSTONE MEWS, E11
London E11 2RS. Mr & Mrs S Farnham, 07761 476651, farnhamz@yahoo.co.uk. *Tube: Snaresbrook or Wanstead, 5 mins walk. Bus: 101, 308 to Wanstead High St.* Light refreshments & home-made teas. **Adm £2.50, chd free. Visitors welcome by appt for groups of 4+.** Tiny 20ft x 17ft garden. Mature strawberry tree and plants grown from cuttings. Thames driftwood and a buried bath used as a fishpond provide interest. Evergreen climbers and vegetables clothe fences. Especially pretty in spring. Spring bulbs and summer vegetables flourish, cultivated with tools stored in a shed on castors. A visit could provide encouragement and ideas for small city gardening with low maintenance. Book sale on open days.

NEW 24 GROVE PARK, SE5
Camberwell, London SE5 8LH. Clive Pankhurst. *Chadwick Rd end of Grove Park. Stns: Peckham Rye or Denmark Hill, both 10 mins walk.* Good street parking. **Adm £2.50, chd**

free. Sun 4 Sept (2-5.30). Subtropical style planting of a 100ft x 35ft walled Victorian back garden in Camberwell with pond and sunken contemporary terrace. Bold planting with dramatic castor oil plants, banana trees and tetrapanax. Plantsman's garden with lots of different hardy exotics and unusual plants incl a greenhouse with carnivorous plants.

7 THE GROVE, N6
Highgate Village, London N6 6JU. Mr Thomas Lyttelton, 07713 638161. *The Grove is between Highgate West Hill & Hampstead Lane. Tube: Archway or Highgate. Buses: 143, 210, 271 to Highgate Village from Archway, 214 from Camden Town.* Home-made teas. **Adm £3, chd free (share to North London Hospice). Suns 10 Apr; 5 June (2-5.30). Visitors also welcome by appt.** ½ acre designed for max all-yr interest with its variety of conifers and other trees, ground cover, water garden, vistas, 19 paths, surprises. Exceptional camellias and magnolia in Mar/April. Wheelchair access to main lawn only; some very narrow paths.

NEW 30 HALF MOON LANE, SE24
Herne Hill, London SE24 9HY. Paul & Janet Barry. *Stn: Herne Hill 5 mins. Buses: 3, 37, 68, 196, 322. Close to Herne Hill shops between Stradella & Winterbrook Rds.* **Adm £3, chd free. Sun 22 May (12-5). Also open 14 Frank Dixon Way.** Designed by Ian Smith and Debbie Roberts, a lush green oasis in a busy urban environment. A bubbling urn and pond bring movement and nature to the garden. There is a rich palette of foliage and texture to create an oasis of calm. Part of Great London Garden Trail 2010. Gravel drive to access garden.

♦ HAM HOUSE AND GARDEN
Ham, Richmond TW10 7RS. National Trust, 020 8940 1950, www.nationaltrust.org.uk. *Mid-way between Richmond & Kingston. W of A307 on Surrey bank of R Thames. Follow NT signs.* **Adm £3.65, chd £2.45, family £9.75. For NGS: Sat 9 July (11-5).** For other opening times and information, please phone or see garden website.

The beautiful C17 gardens incl Cherry Garden, featuring lavender parterres flanked by hornbeam arbours; S terrace with clipped yew cones, hibiscus and pomegranate trees; eight grass plats; maze-like wilderness; C17 orangery with working kitchen garden and licensed café and terrace.

A bubbling urn and pond bring movement and nature to the garden . . .

116 HAMILTON TERRACE, NW8
London NW8 9UT. Mr & Mrs I B Kathuria, 020 7625 6909, gkathuria@hotmail.co.uk. *Tube: Maida Vale, 5 mins walk, St John's Wood, 10 mins walk. Buses: Maida Vale 16, 98, Abbey Rd 139, 189, Finchley Rd 13, 113.* **Adm £3, chd free (share to St. Mark's Church). Visitors welcome by appt.** Lush front garden full of dramatic foliage with a water feature and tree ferns. Large back garden of different levels with Yorkshire stone paving, many large terracotta pots and containers, water feature and lawn. Wide variety of perennials, many unusual, and subtropical plants, succulents, acers, ferns, hebes, climbers, roses, fuchsias and prizewinning hostas. Packed with colour and rich foliage of varied texture.

GROUP OPENING

NEW HAMPSTEAD GARDEN SUBURB GARDENS, NW11
Hampstead, London NW11 6YJ. *1m N of Golders Green. Tube: Golders Green then H2 bus stops on request a few yds from all the gardens in Meadway, Northway, Erskine Hill and Willifield Way. Map available with ticket.* Home-made teas at 91 Willifield Way. **Combined adm £8 or £2.50 each garden, chd free. Sun 5 June (2-6).**

48 ERSKINE HILL
Marjorie & David Harris

5 HEATHGATE
Patricia Larsen

94 OAKWOOD ROAD
Michael Franklin
Visitors also welcome by appt in June & July only, max 10.
020 8458 5846
mikefrank@onetel.com

91 WILLIFIELD WAY
Mrs Karen Grant

Hampstead's enchanting Garden Suburb is internationally renowned for its Lutyens churches and stylish architecture. The rich and famous have always been attracted here; you will see many blue plaques commemorating former residents. 5 Heathgate has lavishly planted herbaceous borders and some interesting contemporary features. 94 Oakwood Road is a romantic cottage garden with many unusual plants in a beautiful woodland setting. 48 Erskine Hill is a bird-friendly organic garden with old and new cottage favourites, a terrace adorned with beautifully planted containers, raised beds for vegetables and herbs, fruit trees and a greenhouse with plants for sale. 91 Willifield Way is a charming re-creation of an Elizabethan parterre, with box-edged beds filled with scented roses, sweet peas, honeysuckle and jasmine. A white dovecote and topiary framed windows complete the effect. Tea is served on the lawn. No wheelchair access at 91 Willifield Way, some steps at 48 Erskine Hill and 5 Heathgate.

◆ **HAMPTON COURT PALACE**
East Molesey KT8 9AU. Historic Royal Palaces, 0870 751 5175, www.hrp.org.uk. Adm £8, with wine. For NGS: Pre-booking essential Wed 30 Mar; Wed 27 April; Wed 13 July; Wed 7 Sept (6.15-8). Special evening tours with specialist talks. Please visit www.ngs.org.uk for information & bookings, or phone 01483 211535. For other opening times and information, please phone or see garden website.
The finest surviving Anglo-Dutch gardens in Europe, best demonstrated by the restored Privy Garden and the Orangery Gardens. As well as these garden reconstructions, visitors can enjoy a riot of colour all spring and summer. Take this rare opportunity to join four very special NGS private tours - in the

peace of the evening, after the gardens have closed to the public. Experience **Spring at Hampton Court Palace** on 30 March and enjoy the wonderful displays of bulbs. On 27 April explore **The Heart of it All**, enjoying privileged access to the nursery where thousands of bedding plants are being nurtured and learn about the 'melon ground'. On July 13, enjoy **The Glory of the Garden** and learn how the gardens team takes care of the gardens in high summer. Join the **Time Travellers** on 7 September, and hear the stories the gardens call tell of kings, queens, courtiers and gardeners. With specialist talks, and the chance to go behind the scenes, come and learn about the 500 year history of these royal gardens and find out what goes into creating and maintaining them.

GROUP OPENING

HAMPTON HILL GARDENS
Hampton Hill TW12 1DW. *4m from Twickenham/Kingston-upon-Thames. Between A312 (Uxbridge Rd) and A313 (Park Rd). Bus: 285 from Kingston stops at end of rd. Stn: Fulwell 15 mins walk. Tickets from 18 Cranmer Rd only.* Home-made teas at 30 St James's Rd on all open days, wine at 76 Park Rd on 16, 17 July. **Combined adm May £4, July £5, chd free. Sats, Suns 14, 15 May; 16, 17 July (2-5).**

18 CRANMER ROAD
Bernard Wigginton

76 PARK ROAD
Mrs Margaret Gawler.
On the corner of Park Rd and Cranmer Rd, 5 mins from 18 Cranmer Rd

30 ST JAMES'S ROAD
Ms Jean Burman
(See separate entry)

Three gardens of diverse interest in an attractive West London suburb. With the backdrop of St James's Church spire, 18 Cranmer Road is a colourful garden with herbaceous and exotic borders and a WW2 air raid shelter transformed as rockery and water garden with azaleas, helianthemums and foliage plants. 76 Park Road is an imaginative and surprising grand Victorian garden with a tiered fountain, large glasshouse and rondaval. York stone paths lead to a magnificent Lebanese cedar, weeping

willow, rambling roses and exotic border planting. The SE-facing garden at 30 St James's Road is subdivided into 5 rooms. Decking with seating leads to ponds surrounded by grasses and shrubs and an African-themed thatched exterior 'sitting room'. Partial wheelchair access.

A charming re-creation of an Elizabethan parterre . . .

NEW ▶ **THE HAPPY TRIANGLE GARDEN, N1**
58 Canonbury Park North, Islington, London N1 2JT. Amanda & Susie. *Buses: 19, 30, 73, 277. Tube: Highbury & Islington, 10 mins. Canonbury overground, 3 mins. At E end of Canonbury Pk N.* **Combined adm with Gardening on a Shoestring (55 Canonbury Park North) £3.50, chd free. Sun 10 July (12-4). Also open 29 Canonbury Park North.**
Contemporary modern garden with a back patio surrounded by ferns and ivy, with a Spanish tapas feel.

HARCOURT HOUSE
Grasmere Road, Bromley BR1 4BB. Freda Davis, 07958 534074, fredagdavis@aol.com, www.fredasgarden.co.uk. *1½ m W of Bromley. WD buses 208, 227 is junction of Highland Rd.* Home-made teas. **Adm £3, chd free. Sun 14 Aug (2-5). Also open 153 Portland Road. Visitors also welcome by appt June to Sept, coaches or groups of 10+.**
Colourful Victorian garden wrapped around large Victorian house. Winding pathways, fern garden, Hercules secret garden, water features, many statues, unusual objects incl French antique lamp-posts placed among planted areas. Dozens of pots, many hanging baskets and large conservatory in Victorian style. London Gardens Society Certificate of Excellence, Highly Commended. Kent Life: runner up Amateur Garden of the Year.

6 Methuen Park, N10

5 HILLCREST AVENUE, NW11

London NW11 0EP. Mrs R M Rees, 020 8455 0419, ruthmrees@aol.com. *1m N of Golders Green. Buses: 82, 102, 460 to Temple Fortune. Tube: Golders Green. Walk down Bridge Lane, Hillcrest Ave off Bridge Lane.* Light refreshments & home-made teas (Sun). **Adm £2.50, chd free (share to Alzheimer's Society). Sun 12 June (2-6). Evening Opening £3.50, wine, Wed 15 June (5-9). Visitors also welcome by appt.**
Small labour-saving traditional back garden with rockery, fish pond, conservatory, tree ferns, and secluded patio. Urban jungle front garden with drought-resistant plants. Stairlift in back from decking to main garden.

NEW **19 HILLFIELD PARK, N10**
London N10 3QT. Mr Zaki & Ruth Elia, 020 8883 2782, zaki@2plusltd.com. *Off Muswell Hill Boulevard. Buses: W7, 43, 102, 144, 134, 234. Tube: Highgate, E Finchley, Finsbury Park.* Light refreshments. **Adm £2.50, chd free. Sun 31 July (2-6). Visitors also welcome by appt, small groups.**
A Moorish garden in Edwardian Muswell Hill. Created by owner/designer, inspired by the original Orientalist features within the house. Three tiled terraces unfold around a traditional fountain. A bespoke

Eastern-style shed crowns the top terrace, while dramatic planting by Declan Buckley cocoons visitors in lush seclusion.

THE HOLME, NW1

Inner Circle, Regents Park, London NW1 4NT. **Lessee of The Crown Commission.** *5 mins from Baker St in Regents Park. Opp Rose Garden. Tube: Regents Park or Baker St, over York bridge then L at Inner Circle. Buses 13, 18, 27, 30, 74, 82, 113, 139, 159, 274.* **Adm £3.50, chd free. Sats, Suns 25, 26 June; 13, 14 Aug (2.30-5.30). Also open 14 July Royal College of Physicians Garden.**
4-acre garden filled with interesting and unusual plants. Sweeping lakeside lawns intersected by islands of herbaceous beds. Extensive rock garden with waterfall, stream and pool. Formal flower garden with unusual annual and half hardy plants, sunken lawn, fountain pool and arbour. Teas available in nearby Rose Garden café. Gravel paths.

239A HOOK ROAD

Chessington KT9 1EQ. Mr & Mrs D St Romaine, 020 8397 3761, derek@gardenphotolibrary.com. *4m S of Kingston. A3 from London, turn L at Hook underpass onto A243 Hook Rd. Garden approx 300yds on L. Parking opp in park. Buses: K4, 71, 465 from Kingston & Surbiton to North Star PH.* Home-made teas.

Adm £2.50, chd free (share to St Catherine of Siena Church). Sun 12 June (2-6). Evening Opening £4, wine, Wed 15 June (8.30-10.30). Visitors also welcome by appt.
Garden photographer's garden. Contemporary flower garden with entertaining area, gravel garden, colour-themed herbaceous borders, fernery, pond and rose tunnel. Traditional potager with over 15 varieties of fruit and 50+ varieties of vegetables and herbs. Special late night opening to show how over 500 candles and lighting, used in imaginative ways with containers and architectural foliage, can effectively transform areas of a garden at night.

HORNBEAMS

Priory Drive, Stanmore HA7 3HN. Dr & Mrs R B Stalbow, 020 8954 2218, barbara@bstalbow.co.uk. *5m SE of Watford. Tube: Stanmore. Priory Drive private rd off Stanmore Hill (A4140 Stanmore-Bushey Heath Rd).* Refreshments available by arrangement. **Visitors welcome by appt.**
Garden designed by owner for yr-round interest. Carpets of aconites, snowdrops and anemones underplant winter-flowering shrubs, Tulipa sprengeri naturalised throughout, Banksian rose clipped hard a special feature. Kitchen garden extended with pots on the terrace, incl potatoes and carrots. Soft fruit, cherries, plums, peaches, Muscat grape shading the conservatory, tomatoes and cucumbers in the green house all nourished by compost produced in three large bins. A fig and vines outside. Oh yes, we also have summer flowers!

10 HOVEDEN ROAD, NW2

London NW2 3XD. Ian Brownhill & Michael Hirschl. *Tube: Kilburn or Willesden Green. Buses: 16, 32, 189, 226, 245, 260, 266 & 316 to Cricklewood Broadway, then consult A-Z.* Light refreshments & wine. **Adm £3, chd free. Sun 5 June (4-8).**
70ft x 25ft award-winning urban garden. Stylish deck with pergola and fish pond leads into attractive circular paved area surrounded by box hedging and deeply planted borders, extensively redesigned and replanted in the last yr. Shade area at the end of the garden features gazebo. No access for wheelchairs or prams.

Be tempted by a plant from a plant stall ✿

1A HUNGERFORD ROAD, N7

London N7 9LA. David Matzdorf, davidmatzdorf@blueyonder.co.uk. *Tube: Caledonian Rd, 6 mins walk. Buses: 29 & 253 to Hillmarton Rd stop in Camden Rd; 17, 91 & 259 to last stop in Hillmarton Rd; 10 to York Way at Market Rd & 274 to junction of Market Rd & Caledonian Rd.* **Adm £2, chd free (share to Terrence Higgins Trust). Sun 12 June (12-6). Also open 62 Hungerford Rd. Visitors also welcome by appt. Entirety of green roof accessible by private appointment.**

Unique eco-house with walled, lush front garden planted in modern-exotic style. Front garden densely planted with palms, acacia, ginger lilies, brugmansias, bananas, euphorbias, yuccas and bamboo. Floriferous 'green roof' resembling scree slope planted with agaves, aloes, cacti, bromeliads, alpines, sedums, mesembryanthemums, bulbs, grasses, Mediterranean shrubs and aromatic herbs. Access via ladder to part of roof (for safety reasons, can also be seen from below). Garden and roof each 50ft x 18ft.

3-acre garden between the Thames and Fleet Street . . .

62 HUNGERFORD ROAD, N7

N7 9LP. John Gilbert & Lynne Berry. *Directions as 1a Hungerford Rd.* **Adm £2.50, chd free. Sun 12 June (2-6). Also open 1a Hungerford Rd.**

Densely planted mature town garden at rear of Victorian terrace house which has been designed to maximise space for planting and create several different sitting areas, views and moods. Arranged in a series of paved rooms with a good range of perennials, shrubs and trees. Professional garden designer's own garden.

THE HURLINGHAM CLUB, SW6

Ranelagh Gardens, Fulham, London SW6 3PR, 020 7471 8209, ellen.wells@hurlinghamclub.org.uk, www.hurlinghamclub.org.uk. *Main gate at E end of Ranelagh Gardens. Tube: Putney Bridge (110yds). Light Refreshments.* **Adm £5, chd free. Sat 21 May (11-4).**

Rare opportunity to visit this 42-acre

jewel with many mature trees, 2-acre lake with water fowl, expansive lawns and a river walk. Capability Brown and Humphry Repton were involved with landscaping. The gardens are renowned for their roses, herbaceous and lakeside borders, shrubberies and stunning bedding displays. The riverbank is a haven for wildlife with native trees, shrubs and wild flowers. Guided tour at 2pm.

THE INNER TEMPLE GARDEN, EC4

Crown Office Row, Inner Temple, London EC4Y 7HL. The Honourable Society of the Inner Temple. *Use Tudor St gate on Tudor St, wheelchair access via disabled entrance. Tea & biscuits.* **Adm £3.50, chd free. Sun 8 May (12.30-4).**

A 3-acre garden between the Thames and Fleet St with sweeping lawns, unusual trees, and charming woodland areas. The grand herbaceous border shows off a multitude of tulips, and a quilt of them flows like a river along the War of the Roses border. Peonies flourish around the mulberry lawn. The famous C12 Temple church and courtyards are adjacent. Featured in GGG, House & Garden and Gardens Illustrated.

GROUP OPENING

ISLINGTON GARDENS, N1

London N1 1BE. *Tube: King's Cross or Angel. Buses: 17, 91, 259 to Caledonian Rd. Home-made & cream teas.* **Combined adm £6, or £2 each garden, chd free. Sun 5 June (2-6).**

BARNSBURY WOOD
Islington Council.
Off Crescent Street, N of Thornhill Square

1 BATTLEBRIDGE COURT
Wharfdale Road. Mike Jackson
Visitors also welcome by appt.
michaeljackson215@
blueyonder.co.uk

44 HEMINGFORD ROAD
Peter Willis & Haremi Kudo

36 THORNHILL SQUARE
Anna & Christopher McKane

Walk through Islington's Georgian streets to these contrasting gardens. At Barnsbury Wood flower borders lead to Islington's hidden secret: a place of peace and relaxation, the

borough's only site of mature woodland and one of London's smallest nature reserves. 44 Hemingford Road is a surprisingly lush, country-style garden with interesting trees, shrubs, perennials, lawns and pond in a very small space. 36 Thornhill Square's 120ft long garden has old roses, hardy geraniums and clematis in curved beds giving a country garden atmosphere; also a small bonsai collection and many unusual perennials for sale. The use of sun and shade are maximised at the 35ft x 17ft plantsman's garden at 1 Battlebridge Court with its peat block terracing. Look out for the naturalised terrapins living between the nearby houseboats, a peaceful oasis only 2 mins from Kings Cross. Wildlife gardening advice and information available at Barnsbury Wood.

GROUP OPENING

KEW GREEN GARDENS
Kew, London TW9 3AH. *NW side of Kew Green. Tube: Kew Gardens. Mainline stn: Kew Bridge. Buses: 65, 391. Entrance via towpath.* Home-made teas at 67 Kew Green. **Combined adm £5, chd free. Sun 22 May (2-6).**

65 KEW GREEN
Giles & Angela Dixon

69 KEW GREEN
John & Virginia Godfrey

71 KEW GREEN
Mr & Mrs Jan Pethick
Visitors also welcome by appt.
linda@bpethick.me.uk

73 KEW GREEN
Sir Donald & Lady Elizabeth Insall

Four long gardens behind a row of C18 houses on the Green, close to the Royal Botanic Gardens. These gardens feature the profusely planted and traditional borders of a mature English country garden, and contrast formal gardens, terraces, lawns, laid out around tall old trees, with wilder areas and woodland and wild flower planting. One has an unusual architect-designed summerhouse, while another offers the surprise of a modern planting of espaliered miniature fruit trees.

NEW KING HENRY'S WALK GARDEN, N1
London N1 4NX. Friends of King Henry's Walk Garden, www.khwgarden.org.uk. *Buses incl: 30, 56, 277, 381. Behind adventure playground on KHW, off Balls Pond Rd.* **Adm £5, chd free. Evening Opening with string quartet, light refreshments & wine, Wed 6 July (6-9).**
Vibrant ornamental planting welcomes the visitor to this hidden oasis and leads you into a verdant community garden with secluded woodland area, bee hives, wildlife pond, wall-trained fruit trees, and plots used by local residents to grow their own fruit and vegetables. Winner Community Garden, London in Bloom. Featured on Plus 1 Living (Japan).

Verdant community garden, winner Community Garden, London in Bloom . . .

212 LANGLEY WAY
West Wickham BR4 0DU. Fleur, Cliff & William Wood, fleur.wood@ntlworld.com. *1¹/₂ m SW of Bromley. At junction of A232 (Croydon to Orpington Rd) with B265 T-lights, turn N into Baston Road. At mini r'about junction with B251 turn L into Pickhurst Lane. Follow rd to Pickhurst PH, then 1st L into Langley Way.* Light refreshments, home-made teas & wine. **Adm £3, chd free (share to National Hospital Development Foundation). Sat, Sun, Mon 28, 29, 30 May; Sat, Sun 13, 14 Aug (11-5.30). Visitors also welcome by appt for groups of 10+, coaches permitted, lunches by arrangement.**
Not your average suburban back garden! Enter through old oak door under brick arch into cool white courtyard garden. In contrast, fiery Mediterranean terrace with marble fountain and fish, and pergola with vines. Natural cottage garden, a tree house in jungle garden, vegetable area with raised beds, greenhouses, fruit trees and chickens. Everything

grown organically with emphasis on wildlife. London Gardens Society Certificate of Excellence. Narrow paths, rear of garden not wheelchair accessible.

12 LANSDOWNE ROAD, W11
London W11 3LW. The Lady Amabel Lindsay. *Turn N off Holland Park Ave nr Holland Park stn or W off Ladbroke Grove halfway along. Buses: 12, 88, GL 711, 715. Bus stop & tube: Holland Park, 4 mins.* Light refreshments. **Adm £3, chd free. Wed 25 May (3-7).**
Medium-sized garden with a 200yr-old mulberry tree as a centrepiece. It includes densely planted borders in mostly soft colours. A large terrace with massed pots and a greenhouse of climbing geraniums.

8 LANSDOWNE WALK, W11
London W11 3LN. Nerissa Guest, 020 7727 2660, nmguest@waitrose.com. *Tube: Holland Park, then 2 mins walk N. Buses: 94, 148.* Home-made teas (Sun only). **Adm £3, chd free. Sun 15 May (2.30-6). Evening Opening wine, Wed 18 May (4-7.30). Visitors also welcome by appt.**
Medium-sized garden owned by plantaholic with a penchant for the exotic! All year interest: specialist collection of camellias, winter and spring; choice salvias in autumn. Emphasis on foliage, texture and scent with unusual and eclectic mix of exotic and herbaceous, entwined with many clematis. Containers incl pseudopanax and woodwardia.

42 LATIMER ROAD, E7
Forest Gate, London E7 0LQ. Janet Daniels. *8 mins walk from Forest Gate or Wanstead Park stn. From Forest Gate cross to Sebert Rd, then 3rd rd on L.* Home-made teas. **Adm £2.50, chd free. Sat, Sun 23, 24 July (11-4.30).**
Plantaholic's garden, 90ft x 15ft, behind terraced house, with every planting opportunity maximised through a colourful abundance of baskets, climbers, shrubs and fruit trees. Raised koi carp pond. 4 steps down to secret garden, 70ft x 40ft, with exuberant mixed borders, wildlife pond with gunnera and small green oasis lawn with arbour.

NEW 19 LAURISTON ROAD, SW19
Wimbledon, London SW19 4TJ. Simon and Belinda Leathes. *Mainline & tube: Wimbledon then 20mins walk. Buses: 200 to Ridgway (end of rd) or 93, 493 to Wimbledon village & short walk.* Home-made teas. **Adm £3, chd free. Sun 10 July (2-6).**
Newly designed garden created in 2010, based around the combination of a geometric framework and naturalistic planting incorporating herbaceous perennials, grasses, wild flower area, vegetable plot and hornbeam columns. Existing mature planting merges with the new additions.

11 LAURISTON ROAD, SW19
Wimbledon, London SW19 4TJ. Patrick Wilson. *Mainline & tube: Wimbledon, then 20 mins (hilly) walk. Buses: 200 to Ridgway (end of road) or 93, 493 to Wimbledon Village and short walk.* Home-made teas. **Adm £3, chd free. Sun 5 June (2-6).**
105ft x 66ft family garden designed by Andrew Wilson (award-winning designer and RHS Chief Assessor), planted in 2008. The garden revolves around an elliptical lawn and main border flanked by borders defined by clipped yew hedges providing structure and compartments for the wide variety of planting. Terrace with reflecting pool. Vegetable garden. The terrace and gravel pathways are paved in basalt and the reflecting pool is filtered through decorative reeds. Featured in The Great London Garden Trail & Gardens Illustrated.

46 LINCOLN ROAD
Northwood Hills HA6 1LD. Philip Simpson & Sharon Foster, 01923 450639. *10 mins walk from Northwood Hills tube stn in Joel St (B472), turn into Norwich Rd, then 3rd turning on R, 2nd last house on R at top of hill.* Light refreshments & home-made teas. **Adm £2.50, chd free. Suns 5, 19 June (1-6). Visitors also welcome by appt in June & July for small groups.**
95ft x 25ft professional gardener's suburban garden with a quirky personality. Planted primarily for foliage effect and filled to bursting with over 400 hosta and 150 acer varieties, combined with rare and unusual plants. Vintage treasures, herbaceous border, 2 ponds, water

features, 2 planted pergolas, summerhouse and seating areas. Featured in House Beautiful.

NEW **LINEAR HOUSE, N6**
70 Southwood Lane, Highgate, London N6 5DY. Mr Patrick Deane. *Tube: Highgate, 4 mins walk. Buses 43, 134, 263. Between Highgate tube & Highgate Village.* **Adm £3.50, chd free. Sun 24 July (2-6).** Discreetly located in the Highgate Conservation Area, this garden encloses the award-winning Linear House (not open) with two planted green roofs providing an added dimension. Features incl woodland area with naturalised stream and mini-lake, formal area, ornamentals, exotics, specimen trees and kitchen garden. Approx ¾ acre, an oasis in N London. Electric wheelchair ramp allows access to terrace area; other areas inaccessible owing to steps, slopes and narrow paths.

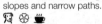

LITTLE HOUSE A, NW3
16A Maresfield Gardens, Hampstead, London NW3 5SU. Linda & Stephen Williams. *5 mins walk Swiss Cottage or Finchley Rd tube. Off Fitzjohn's Ave and 2 doors away from Freud Museum (signed).* Home-made teas. **Adm £3, chd free. Sun 12 June (2-6).** 1920s Arts & Crafts house (not open) built by Danish artist Arild Rosenkrantz. Award-winning front and rear garden set out formally with water features, stream and sculpture. Unusual shrubs and perennials, many rare, incl *Paeonia rockii* and *Dicksonia fibrosa*. Wide collections of hellebores, roses, hostas, toad lilies, acers, clematis and astrantia.

LITTLE LODGE
Watts Road, Thames Ditton KT7 0BX. Mr & Mrs P Hickman, 020 8339 0931, julia.hickman@virgin.net. *2m SW of Kingston. Mainline stn Thames Ditton 5 mins. A3 from London; after Hook underpass turn L to Esher; at Scilly Isles turn R towards Kingston; after 2nd railway bridge turn L to Thames Ditton village; house opp library after Giggs Hill Green.* **Adm £3, chd free (share to Cancer Research UK). Sun 22 May (11.30-5.30); Wed 8 June (2-6). Visitors also welcome by appt.** Partly walled informal flower garden

filled with shrubs and herbaceous plants that create an atmosphere of peace. Small secret garden; terracotta pots; stone troughs and sinks; roses; clematis; topiary; very productive parterre vegetable garden.

18 LITTLETON STREET, SW18
London SW18 3SY. Ian & Cathy Shaw. *Stn: Earlsfield, 10 mins walk. Buses: 44, 77, 270 along Garratt Lane.* Home-made teas. **Adm £2.50, chd free. Sun 29 (11.30-5), Mon 30 May (11.30-3).** Not the typical terrace garden, S facing, though shady places, allowing us to grow a wide spectrum of plants. Thousands of rose blooms in summer supported by many perennials and flowering shrubs in cottage garden riot of colour and scent. Small pool with sunbathing frogs, other wildlife visitors too.

Contemporary design meets ornamental and edible plants alongside chickens, rabbits and a multitude of wildlife . . .

NEW **THE 'LIVED IN' GARDEN, SE18**
93 Shrewsbury Lane, Shooters Hill, London SE18 3JW. Susan Saint Ledger, 07905 110966, s.saint-ledger@ntlworld.com. *From Shooters Hill/Dover Road (A270) turn at The Bull. DLR to Woolwich Arsenal, then bus 244 which stops outside house (The Old Fire Station stop on Shrewsbury Lane). Or Jubilee Line to N Greenwich, then bus 468 to The Bull, then 5 mins walk, or bus 244 for 2 stops.* Home-made teas. **Adm £2.50, chd free. Sun 17 July (2-5.30). Visitors also welcome by appt June to Sept.** Contemporary design meets a plethora of ornamental and edible plants alongside chickens, rabbits, guinea pigs, goldfish and a multitude of wildlife. House and garden set out on 6 levels, each with areas to sit and enjoy, with panoramic views of

London. Every part of the garden is used and a relaxed design subtly runs throughout. Surrounded by trees, providing a variety of microclimates. Steep steps. Difficult for pushchairs.

GROUP OPENING

LONDON FIELDS GARDENS, E8
Hackney, London E8 3LS. *Short walk from Haggerston stn, London Overground (E London Line); train from Liverpool St to London Fields stn; or tube to Bethnal Green, then buses 106, 254 or 388 towards Hackney.* Home-made teas. **Combined adm £5, chd free. Sun 19 June (2-5).**

61 LANSDOWNE DRIVE
Chris Thow & Graham Hart
Visitors also welcome by appt.
020 7249 4550
chris.thow@blueyonder.co.uk

84 LAVENDER GROVE
Anne Pauleau

36 MALVERN ROAD
Kath Harris
Visitors also welcome by appt.
020 7923 3481
daveharris27@btinternet.com

53 MAPLEDENE ROAD
Tigger Cullinan
Visitors also welcome by appt.
020 7249 3745
tiggerine8@blueyonder.co.uk

NEW **84 MIDDLETON ROAD**
Penny Fowler

A diverse group of five gardens in London Fields, an area which takes its name from fields on the London side of the old village of Hackney. New this year, a large long wildlife and sculpture garden, which complements a fascinating plantsman's garden, lush tropical plantings, a scented cottage garden, and a serene designer garden filled with the sound of running water. Unexpected havens from Hackney's hustle and bustle, these are densely packed city plots with an exciting variety of colours, scents and design, from courtyards to wilder areas and bananas to showers of roses and clematis. There is even a pond with water lilies and giant Gunnera manicata which is home to frogs, newts and damselflies.

32 LOVELACE ROAD, SE21

London SE21 8JX. Nick & Jane Perkins. *Stns: midway between W Dulwich & Tulse Hill.* Buses: 2, 3 & 68. Home-made teas. **Adm £3.50, chd free. Sun 10 July (2-6). Also open 13 Gipsy Hill.**
40m x 10m inclined garden divided into 5 sections starting with contemporary terrace with potted olive trees and finishing with timber deck looking back down over garden, having passed formal lawn with pleached hornbeam and 'wild' planted area. Also includes water features and many areas to sit and relax.

Unique allotment exuding peace and tranquillity . . .

GROUP OPENING

LOWER CLAPTON GARDENS, E5

Hackney, London E5 0RL. *Tube: Bethnal Green, then buses 106, 254, or Manor House, then buses 253, 254, alight Lower Clapton Rd. Pleasant 10 min walk from Hackney Central or Hackney Downs stns.* Home-made teas. **Combined adm £5, chd free. Sun 5 June (2-6).**

8 ALMACK ROAD
Philip Lightowlers

NEW▶ 16 POWERSCROFT ROAD
Elizabeth Welch

58 RUSHMORE ROAD
Annie Moloney.
If driving entrance is only by Millfields Rd or Atherton Rd. Visitors also welcome by appt. 07989 803196 anniemoloney58@yahoo.co.uk

Lower Clapton is an area of mid Victorian terraces sloping down towards the R Lea. This varied group of gardens reflects their owners' tastes and interests. New this year is 16 Powerscroft Road, which features a lawn bordered by an old brick path, and a semi-formal planting of shrubs and flowers. A backdrop of mature trees give peace and privacy. 58 Rushmore Road is a small S-facing Mediterranean-style patio

garden on two levels: the lower has pots and a water feature; the upper, reached by a spiral staircase, has subtropical plants. 8 Almack Road is a long walled garden in 2 rooms: the first has a grass, roses and shrubs, tree fern and water feature; a winding path leads to a second area with a warm sunny feel with tropical foliage, succulents and a potted agave named Audrey.

5 LYNDHURST SQUARE, SE15

London SE15 5AR. Martin Lawlor & Paul Ward, 020 7771 0823, martin.lawlor@sky.com. *Stn: Peckham Rye (reduced service on Suns), 5 mins walk NW. Buses: 36 from Oval tube or 171 from Waterloo. Free parking in Lyndhurst Square.* Light refreshments & home-made teas. **Adm £3, chd free (share to Terrence Higgins Trust). Sun 26 June (1.30-5). Also open 94a Lyndhurst Way.** Visitors also welcome by appt.
Charming and unusual garden in this early Victorian Gothic garden square in the heart of Southwark. The 90ft x 50ft secret garden has a mix of traditional and unusual herbaceous plants and shrubs. The design combines Italianate and Gothic themes and offers a secluded green vista.

94A LYNDHURST WAY, SE15

London SE15 5AQ. Susan Collier, 020 7820 3628, susan@colliercampbell.com. *Stn: Peckham Rye. Buses: P13 to Streatham, also 36 & 171.* Home-made teas. **Adm £2.50, chd free. Sun 26 June (2-6). Also open 5 Lyndhurst Square.** Visitors also welcome by appt May to Sept for groups of 10 to 12.
Step up from the hot Mediterranean terrace to the newly-terraced small square London garden, designed for relaxation, sociability and wildlife. Shallow pond with shingle 'beach', raised vegetable bed (based on a French medieval model), a good collection of newly-planted trees and perennial plants chosen with an artist's eye for contrasting colour and form or simply for their delightful perfume, incl the unmistakeable scent of clematis uncinata. Jersey Tiger Moth in the wisteria. Hand-painted & hand-made cards for sale.

GROUP OPENING

MALVERN TERRACE GARDENS, N1

N1 1HR. *Approach from S via Pentonville Rd into Penton St, then into Barnsbury Rd. From N via Thornhill Rd opp Albion PH. Tube: Angel, Highbury & Islington, Kings Cross. Buses: 4, 19, 30 to Upper St, Town Hall or 17, 91 from Kings Cross to Caledonian Rd (Richmond Ave).* Home-made teas. **Combined adm £3.50, chd free. Sun 17 Apr (2-5.30).**
Group of unique 1830s London terrace houses built on the site of Thomas Oldfield's dairy and cricket field. Cottage-style gardens in cobbled cul-de-sac. Music and plant stall.

ALLOTMENTS

NEW▶ 94 MARSH LANE ALLOTMENTS, N17

Marsh Lane, Tottenham, London N17 0HY. Chris Achilleos, 07903 211715, a_c_h1964@yahoo.co.uk. *Opp Northumberland Park stn, on the corner of Marsh Lane & Marigold Rd. Buses: W3, 318, 341, 476.* Home-made teas. **Adm £2.50, chd free. Sun 7 Aug (2-6).** Visitors also welcome by appt June to Sept.
An oasis in the city, a unique allotment exuding peace and tranquillity. An exuberant collection of decorative, edible and exotic plants. Gravel plants lined with potted tender specimens. Established herbaceous border, mini orchard of Mediterranean and native fruit trees. Central gazebo, wildlife pond, sculptures - something for everyone.

47 MAYNARD ROAD, E17

Walthamstow, London E17 9JE. Don Mapp, 020 8520 1565, don.mapp@gmail.com, www.donsgarden.co.uk. *10 mins walk from Walthamstow (central stn). Bus to Tesco on Lea Bridge Rd then walk through Barclay Path, or bus W12 to Addison Rd. Turn R to Beulah Path.* Light refreshments & home-made cream teas. **Adm £2.50, chd free. Suns 17, 24, 31 July; 7 Aug (11-6).** Visitors also welcome by appt after mid June.
Plant collector's paradise. An eclectic mix of exotic and other

ornaments in a 40ft x 16ft space, entered via a densely planted front garden. The front garden will again be 'Food, Fruits and Herbs' showcasing how much food can be grown in a small space. Painting, drawings (mainly botanical) and Pergamano by Hazel Pettifer, and photographic and other displays. Best Garden, London in Bloom Walthamstow Village competition. Access for wheelchairs via standard doors.

36 MELROSE ROAD, SW18

London SW18 1NE. John Tyrwhitt. *¼ m E of A3 Wandsworth. Tube: East Putney, exit R. Take first R, Keswick Rd. Take 2nd L Portinscale Rd. Over lights into West Hill Rd. *After ¼ mile when rd bends L, fork R on to Viewfield Rd. Keep grass triangle on your R. Last house on L, on the corner of Melrose Rd. By car: coming from A3 northbound, turn R at lights into West Hill Rd & follow above directions from *. Home-made teas.* **Adm £3, chd free. Sun 22 May (3-6).** Unusual walled and paved garden on 2 levels, created in 11 yrs. Densely planted for sun and shade and yr-round interest with shrubs, climbers, architectural plants and creative pot arrangements.

6 METHUEN PARK, N10

Muswell Hill, London N10 2JS. Yulia Badian, 07850 756784, yulia@gardenshrink.com. *Tube: Highgate, then bus 43, 134 to Muswell Hill Broadway, 3rd on L off Dukes Ave or Finsbury Park tube then W7 bus.* **Adm £2.50, chd free. Visitors welcome by appt, refreshments provided.** Contemporary family garden designed by Chelsea medal winner, featuring a moat with frogs and darting fish, and sonic installation with 5 Perspex speakers singing about love and the mysteries of life. Formal hardwood decking contrasts with flowing curves and unique planting to create an enchanting peaceful space.

GROUP OPENING

MILL HILL ROAD GARDENS, W3

Acton, London W3 8JE. *Tube: Acton Town, turn R, Mill Hill Rd 3rd on R off Gunnersbury Lane. Home-made teas.* **Combined adm £6, chd free. Sun 10 July (2-6).**

The Roof Terrace, 21A Waldegrave Road, SE19

41 MILL HILL ROAD

Marcia Hurst
(See separate entry)

65 MILL HILL ROAD

Anna Dargavel
(See separate entry)

REDWING

69 Mill Hill Road. Mr & Mrs M Temple
Visitors also welcome by appt.
020 8993 6514

Three gardens in one road encourage wildlife with ponds, a mound and a huge range of plants to attract insects. The owner at 41 Mill Hill Road describes herself as a compulsive plantaholic. The 120ft x 40ft garden features a newly created paved area with semi-circular vegetable plot. Lawn with herbaceous border and lavender hedge and a raised terrace with topiary. 65 Mill Hill Road is a typically long narrow London garden, paved, with borders and planted with fruit trees and shrubs. It is wildlife-friendly with ponds and flowers to which bees and other insect are attracted. Frogs and dragonflies abound. Visit Redwing for a secluded, contemplative wildlife-friendly garden with its 'Lavender Hall' pavilion. 41 Mill Hill Rd also open 14 Aug 6-8 & 65 Mill Hill Rd 15 June 6-8.

41 MILL HILL ROAD, W3

Acton, London W3 8JE. Marcia Hurst, 020 8992 2632, marcia.hurst@sudbury-house.co.uk. *Tube: Acton Town, turn R, Mill Hill Rd 3rd on R off Gunnersbury Lane.* **Adm £3, chd free (share to Thrive). Evening Opening, wine & light refreshments, Sun 14 Aug (6-8). Also opening with Mill Hill Road Gardens Sun 10 July. Visitors also welcome by appt.** 120ft x 40ft garden. Newly created paved area with semi-circular vegetable plot. Lawn bordered by 50ft herbaceous border on one side and lavender hedge on the other. Raised terrace with topiary. Owner compulsive plantaholic.

65 MILL HILL ROAD, W3

Acton, London W3 8JF. Anna Dargavel, 020 8992 1723, annadargavel@mac.com. *Tube: Acton Town, turn R, Mill Hill Rd 3rd on R off Gunnersbury Lane.* **Adm £2.50, chd free. Evening Opening, wine & light refreshments, Wed 15 June (6-8). Also opening with Mill Hill Road Gardens Sun 10 July. Visitors also welcome by appt in June & July only.** Garden designer's own garden. Secluded and tranquil with fruit trees, topiary, borders and paved areas with subtle changes of level leading to a partly hidden studio at the end. Planting and ponds demonstrate the possibility that an organic and wildlife-friendly environment can exist with design, outdoor dining and interesting planting. Ealing in Bloom 1st prize for best improved garden.

2 MILLFIELD PLACE, N6

London N6 6JP. *Off Highgate West Hill, E side of Hampstead Heath. Buses: C2, C11 or 214 to Parliament Hill Fields.* Home-made teas (Sun only). **Adm £3, chd free. Sun 8 May (2-6). Evening Opening £4, chd free, wine, Wed 15 June (5.30-9).** 1½ -acre spring and summer garden with camellias, rhododendrons, many flowering shrubs and unusual plants. Spring bulbs, herbaceous borders, small orchard, spacious lawns. Wheelchair assistance available, please ask at gate if needed.

NEW 28 MORDEN ROAD, SE3

London SE3 0AA. Mr & Mrs R Taylor. *Stn: Blackheath BR (10 mins walk). Buses: 89, 108, 202 to Blackheath village. Street parking available (with permit obtainable at gate).* **Adm £4, chd free. Evening Opening, wine, Fri 8 July (6-8).** Formal front garden leads to open back garden, surrounded by mature trees with interesting planting near terrace and 2 small ponds. Lower garden emphasis on planting for shade, incl ferns and hostas. Modern sculptures dotted throughout garden. Partial wheelchair access to terrace, with good view of garden.

28 MULTON ROAD, SW18

Wandsworth, London SW18 3LH. Victoria Orr, v.summerley@independent.co.uk, www.victoriasbackyard.co.uk. *Mainline: 10 mins walk from Earlsfield or Wandsworth Common. Buses: 219, 319 along Trinity Rd.* Home-made teas. **Adm £3, chd free. Sun 28 Aug (2-6). Also open 225a Brixton Rd.** Visitors also welcome by appt.
'The planting here is strong and modern: bananas, gorgeous tetrapanax, a tree fern... and the biggest phormium I've ever seen. Vast paddle leaves of bananas splay out against a background of bamboo' (Anna Pavord). 70ft x 40ft subtropical suburban oasis, designed to defy global warming, garden pests and

kids without recourse to carbon emissions, chemicals or cranial damage. Design is contemporary but not minimalist, there is lots of seating, and ponds with frogs and goldfish.

NEW 66 MUSWELL AVENUE, N10

London N10 2EL. Kay Thomson & Nick Wood-Glover, 07872 952959, kaythomson@valox.demon.co.uk. *1st L into Muswell Ave from Alexandra Park Rd. Tube: Bounds Green or E Finchley then buses 102 or 299, alight Colney Hatch.* Home-made teas. **Adm £2.50, chd free. Sun 17 July (2-6). Visitors also welcome by appt.**
Echoes of Cornish roots resonate in Edwardian suburban back garden. Mediterranean planted terrace with oleander, jasmine, grape vine, herbs and vegetables. Lawn area leads through archway to pond with abundant wildlife and native planting, pebble beach, boat and small patio. Mallard ducks visit. Three different atmospheres, three different environments.

◆ NATURAL HISTORY MUSEUM WILDLIFE GARDEN, SW7

Cromwell Road, London SW7 5BD, 020 7942 5011, www.nhm.ac.uk/garden. *Tube: South Kensington, 5 mins walk.* **Adm by donation. For NGS: Sun 8 May (12-5). For other opening times and information, please phone or see garden website.**
Set in the Museum grounds, the Wildlife Garden has provided a lush and tranquil habitat in the heart of London since 1995. It reveals a varied range of British lowland habitats, incl deciduous woodland, meadow and ponds. With over 2000 plant and animal species, it beautifully demonstrates the potential for wildlife conservation in the inner city. Spring wildlife displays and workshops. Princess Alice Alice Countess of Athlone Award for the Environment.

NEW 17A NAVARINO ROAD, E8

London E8 1AD. Ben Nel, 07734 773990, benjamin123nel@googlemail.com. *Situated between Dalston & Hackney. Buses 30, 38, 242 or 277 alight Graham Rd. Short walk from Hackney Central or London Fields stns.* Light refreshments & teas. **Adm £3, chd**

free. Suns 10 Apr (2-5); 19 June (2-6). Visitors also welcome by appt.
Established Italian and Japanese water garden reborn under new ownership. Features a square pond with Corinthian fountain, topiary yew border, lilies and Mediterranean trees. Leading to Japanese garden with pond, bridge and stream cutting the Soleirolia soleirolii landscape, with acer, cypress, ferns & bamboo, overlooked by a beautiful tea house.

15 NORCOTT ROAD, N16

Stoke Newington, London N16 7BJ. Amanda & John Welch. *Buses: 67, 73, 76, 106, 149, 243, 393, 476. Clapton & Rectory Rd mainline stns. One way system: by car approach from Brooke Rd which crosses Norcott Rd, garden in S half of Norcott Rd.* **Adm £2.50, chd free. Sun 22 May (2-6).**
Largish (for Hackney) walled back garden developed by present owners over 30yrs, with pond, long-established fruit trees, abundantly planted with a great variety of herbaceous plants and front garden recently released from concrete. We are opening in May, hopefully to catch the bearded irises.

Echoes of Cornish roots resonate in Edwardian suburban back garden . . .

5 NORTHAMPTON PARK, N1

Islington, London N1 2PP. Andrew Bernhardt & Anne Brogan, 020 7503 4735, bernhardt8@gmail.com. *3 mins walk from Canonbury stn, 10 mins from Highbury.* Light refreshments & wine. **Adm £4, chd free. Lamplit Evening Opening Sat 18 June (6.30-10). Visitors also welcome by appt.**
S-facing walled garden, 160 yrs old, saved from neglect and developed over the last 20 yrs. The use of arches with box and yew hedging creates contrasting areas of interest which are evolving from cool North European blues, whites and greys to 'hot' splashes of Mediterranean influence.

NEW▶ 51 NORTHWAY, NW11
Hampstead Garden Suburb,
London NW11 6PB. **Tessa & Larry
Levine.** *Tube: Golders Green, then
bus H2 to Northway. Plenty of parking
in local rds.* **Adm £3, chd free.
Sun 24 July (2-5.30). Also open,
with teas, 86 Willifield Way.**
This mature, secluded garden, with
the backdrop of an ancient wood, is
crammed with a diverse and colourful
selection of hydrangeas, clematis,
roses, perennials, grasses and
shrubs. At the back, a path meanders
through a woodland area with shade-
loving hostas, ferns and foxgloves.

**28 OLD DEVONSHIRE ROAD,
SW12**
London SW12 9RB. **Georgina Ivor,
020 8673 7179,
georgina@balhambandb.co.uk.**
*Tube and mainline rail: Balham,
5 mins walk.* Cream Teas (Sun). **Adm
£2.50, chd free (share to Trinity
Hospice). Sun 5 June (2-5.30).
Evening opening £3.50, with
Pimm's or Prosecco, Wed 15 June
(6-8.30). Also open 20 Eatonville
Rd & 2 Western Lane. Visitors also
welcome by appt.**
Walk past the Mediterranean-style
front garden to a tranquil oasis at the
back. A cool eucalyptus reaches for
the house-tops whilst a well-
established pear tree looks down on a
walled garden full to bursting with
planting both familiar and surprising.
On the balustraded wooden balcony
there are herbs in troughs and a
vibrant orange trumpet vine.

ALLOTMENTS

**OLD PALACE LANE
ALLOTMENTS**
Old Palace Lane, Richmond
TW9 1PG. **Old Palace Lane
Allotment Group.** *Next to White
Swan PH, through gate in wall.
Mainline and tube: Richmond. Parking
on meters in lane or round Richmond
Green, or in Old Deer Park car park,
entrance on A316 Twickenham Rd.*
Home-made teas. **Adm £3, chd free.
Sun 14 Aug (2-5).**
Secret garden in the heart of
Richmond. 33 allotments on the site
of Old Richmond Palace, squeezed
between an ancient wall and a railway
viaduct midway between Richmond
Green and the river. Some resemble
cottage gardens where sunflowers

and sweet peas mingle haphazardly
with sweetcorn and zucchini, while
others sport raised beds, regimented
rows of runner beans and gleaming
greenhouses.

THE ORCHARD, W4
40A Hazledene Road, London W4
3JB. **Vivien Cantor.** *10 mins walk
from Chiswick mainline &
Gunnersbury tube. Close to junction
of A4 & Sutton Court Rd, off
Fauconberg Rd.* Home-made teas.
**Adm £3.50, chd free. Sun 8 May
(2-6).**
Informal, romantic ¹/₄ -acre garden
with mature flowering trees, incl a
spectacular Paulownia, shrubs and
imaginative planting in flowing
herbaceous borders. Climbers, water
features with ponds, bridge and
waterfall and fern planting in this ever-
evolving garden.

Secluded, peaceful,
restorative . . .

ORMELEY LODGE
Ham Gate Avenue, Richmond
TW10 5HB. **Lady Annabel
Goldsmith.** *From Richmond Park, exit
at Ham Gate into Ham Gate Ave. 1st
house on R. From Richmond, A307;
after 1¹/₂ m, past New Inn on R, at T-
lights turn L into Ham Gate Ave.* **Adm
£4, chd free. Sun 19 June (3-6).**
Large walled garden in delightful rural
setting on Ham Common. Wide
herbaceous borders and box hedges.
Walk through to orchard with wild
flowers. Vegetable garden, knot
garden, aviary. Trellised tennis court
with roses and climbers.

♦ OSTERLEY PARK AND HOUSE
Jersey Road, Isleworth TW7 4RB.
National Trust, 020 8232 5055,
www.nationaltrust.org.uk. *4m N of
Richmond. Tube: Osterley, turn L on
leaving stn, 1m walk. Access via
Thornbury Rd on N side of A4
between Gillette Corner & Osterley
tube stn. Follow brown tourist signs.*

Car Park £3.50. **Adm £4, chd £2.
For NGS: Sun 5 June (11-5). For
other opening times and
information, please phone or see
garden website.**
C18 garden created by the Child
family, owners of Osterley Park
House, in late 1700s. Currently being
restored to its former glory following
much research incl the discovery of
documents in America showing lists
of plants purchased for the garden in
1788. Highlights incl a Robert Adam
designed Garden House, the Great
Meadow and Mrs Child's Flower
Garden.

ALLOTMENTS

**PADDOCK ALLOTMENTS &
LEISURE GARDENS, SW20**
51 Heath Drive, Raynes Park
SW20 9BE. **Paddock Horticultural
Society.** *Stn: Raynes Park, then 10
min walk or bus 163 via Grand Drive.
Buses: 57, 131, 200 to Raynes Park
stn; 152 to Bushey Rd, 7 min walk via
Grand Drive; 413, 5 min walk from
Cannon Hill Lane via Parkway. Street
parking close by.* Home-made teas.
Adm £3, chd free. Sat 16 July (12-5).
With over 150 plots, set in 5¹/₂ acres,
situated on Cannon Hill Common and
surrounded by trees. Some plots
resemble English cottage gardens
while others are typical allotments.
Many varieties of flowers, fruit and
vegetables grown. Surplus produce
may be available for sale. London in
Bloom award, Best Allotment in
London. Grass paths, mainly level.

93 PALACE ROAD, SW2
London SW2 3LB. **Charlotte &
Matthew Vaight,
charlieandmatt@tiscali.co.uk.** *Stn:
Tulse Hill. Buses: 2, 68, 322, 432,
468.* Home-made teas. **Adm £3, chd
free. Sun 3 July (12-5). Visitors also
welcome by appt.**
This 80ft contemporary cottage
garden is set over 3 levels. The main
focus is the curvy lawn wrapped by a
boardwalk. Strong lines of hard
landscaping are softened by
overflowing borders containing a mix
of trees, shrubs and perennials.
Features incl sculpture, planted
terraces, wildlife pond, vegetable
garden and glasshouse.

Be tempted by a plant from a plant stall ⊛

123 South Park Road, SW19

contrasting foliage. Unusual plants are combined with old favourites. It remains easy-care and child-friendly. Garden originally designed by Jude Sharpe.

GROUP OPENING

PENGE GARDENS, SE20
SE20 7QG. *Nr junction A213 & A234. Short walk from Kent House mainline stn. Buses: 176, 227, 356 & 358. Tram: Beckenham Rd.* Home-made teas. **Combined adm £5, chd free. Sun 5 June (2-6).**

43 CLEVEDON ROAD
Elizabeth Parker

26 KENILWORTH ROAD
Mhairi & Simon Clutson
Visitors also welcome by appt, groups of 10+. 020 8402 9035
mhairi@grozone.co.uk

Two gardens, one contemporary, the other a cottage garden, within easy walking distance of each other. The 50ft x 22ft cottage garden at 43 Clevedon Road has unusual trees and shrubs which incl snake-bark maple, sorbus cashmiriana and itea ilicifolia. Enjoy also the abundant rambler roses, incl Félicité Perpétue, colourful mixed borders and pots on the terrace. 26 Kenilworth Road offers a garden designer's inspirational contemporary garden which maximises the use of a small area and forms an extension to the living space. Planting is bold and architectural with a diverse selection of drought-tolerant Mediterranean plants incl olives, cistus, pine, arbutus and phlomis. There is a low maintenance front garden with a sedum-roofed recycling unit.

◆ **PENSHURST PLACE**
See Kent.

PETERSHAM HOUSE
Petersham TW10 7AA. Francesco & Gael Boglione. *Stn: Richmond, then 65 bus to Dysart PH. Entry to garden off Petersham Rd, through nursery. Parking very limited on Church Lane.* Light Refreshments & teas at Petersham Nurseries. **Adm £3.50, chd free. Suns 8 May; 5 June (11-4).** Broad lawn with large topiary, generously planted double borders. Productive vegetable garden with chickens.

NEW **18 PARK CRESCENT, N3**
Finchley, London N3 2NJ. Rosie Daniels. *Tube: Finchley Central. Buses: 82 to Essex Park, also 125, 460, 626, 683.* Home-made teas. **Adm £2.50, chd free (share to North London Hospice). Sun 26 June (2-6).**
Charming small garden designed and densely planted by owner. Roses, clematis, heuchera and lots more. Mini pond, tub water feature and bird haven. Stepped terrace with lots of pots. Glass installation and sculpture by owner. Garden extension is work in progress. Hidden seating with view through garden. Secluded, peaceful, restorative.

4 PARK VILLAGE EAST, NW1
Regents Park, London NW1 7PX. Eveline Carn, 020 7388 1113, eveline@carnfamily.co.uk. *Tube: Camden Town 7 mins, Mornington Crescent 10 mins. Bus: C2 and 274, 3 mins. Garden diagonally opp The York & Albany, just off junction of Parkway/Prince Albert Rd/Gloucester Gate.* Home-made teas. **Adm £3, chd free. Sun 29 May (2-5.30). Visitors also welcome by appt.**
A terraced garden on four levels around a Nash villa (c 1828) on the edge of Regents Park. Three terraces lead down to where once flowed the Regents Canal. A green garden of bold textures with an evolving area of ferns and woodland planting behind a

maze of yew hedging below the old canal walls. Sculpture, working bee hives, trees, ponds and many steps. Featured in Ruth Pavey's Gardening column in the Ham & High.

3 THE PARK, N6
off Southwood Lane, London N6 4EU. Mr & Mrs G Schrager, 020 8348 3314, bunty@schredds.com. *3 mins from Highgate tube, up Southwood Lane. The Park is 1st on R. Buses: 43, 134, 143, 263.* Home-made teas. **Sun 5 June (2.30-6). Visitors also welcome by appt.**
Large garden with pond and frogs, fruit trees and eclectic planting. Interesting plants for sale. Children especially welcome. Home made jam for sale.

174 PECKHAM RYE, SE22
London SE22 9QA. Mr & Mrs Ian Bland. *Stn: Peckham Rye. Buses: 12, 37, 63, 197, 363. Overlooks Peckham Rye Common from Dulwich side. Reached by alley to side of house.* Home-made teas. **Adm £2.50, chd free (share to St Christopher's Hospice). Sun 5 June (2.30-5.30). Also open 4 Piermont Green.**
Visitors call our garden an oasis of calm in Peckham. Every year the garden changes and matures. It is densely planted with a wide variety of

PETERSHAM LODGE
River Lane, Richmond TW10 7AG.
Princess J C Loewenstein. *Stn: Richmond, then Bus 65 to Dysart PH.* **Adm £3.50, chd free. Mon 2 May (11-4).**
3½-acre garden around the Georgian House, with formal borders and a knot garden with Rosa *banksiae* covering the SW facade. Numerous paths lead to semi-formal areas: small lake with Chinese bridge, temple, bluebell glade and large specimen trees. Also potager and vegetable garden.

 4 PIERMONT GREEN, SE22
East Dulwich, London SE22 0LP.
Janine Wookey, 020 8693 1015, j.wookey@btinternet.com. *Triangle of green facing Peckham Rye at the Honor Oak end. Stns: Peckham Rye & Honor Oak. Buses: 63 (passes the door) & 12. No parking on green but free parking on side st nearby.* Home-made teas. **Adm £3, chd free. Sun 5 June (2-5).** Also open **174 Peckham Rye. Visitors also welcome by appt May to July for small groups.**
A small front garden where box parterres and a lollipopped olive tree give a formal feel, softened by roses and clematis. To the rear, a dining terrace leads to a gravel garden opening out to a lawn framed by herbaceous planting and a gnarled and much-loved apple tree, entwined with white clematis. Tucked away vegetable garden, greenhouse and compost heap. Enthusiasm sometimes outruns orderliness in this garden journalist's garden!

101 PITT CRESCENT, SW19
London SW19 8HR. Karen Grosch, 020 8893 3660, daytime only, info@whettonandgrosch.co.uk, www.karensgarden.org.uk. *Tube: Wimbledon Park 10 mins walk. Bus: 156 along Durnsford Rd. Limited parking in Pitt Crescent.* Home-made teas. **Adm £2.50, chd free. Sun 19 June (2-6).** Also open **123 South Park Rd. Visitors also welcome by appt, June only.**
Secluded terraced garden packed with well structured subtle plant combinations, great design ideas for long sloping garden overlooked by busy railway. Top walled terrace with greenhouse, garden studio, mature

trees, scented climbers and atmospheric seating areas. Creative use of reclaimed and donated materials and sculptural features. Featured in GGG & see www.victoriasbackyard.blogspot.com /2010_07_01_archive.html.

153 PORTLAND ROAD
Bromley BR1 5AY. Lucia & Simon Parnell. *Off Burnt Ash Lane between Sundridge Park and Grove Park BR stns. From Burnt Ash Lane, turn into New Street Hill, beside Toyota showroom, go to end of rd. L into Portland Rd.* Home-made teas & Pimm's. **Adm £3, chd free. Sun 14 Aug (2-6).** Also open **Harcourt House, 5 mins drive.**
Following the success of our opening last year, you are invited to return to this beautiful garden which interests the visitor from every angle. Enjoy Pimm's, tea and delicious cakes in the company of a guitarist and review the progress of replanting. Pergola, wisteria, pond and greenhouse. Raised beds of hostas. 4 large composters continually nourish this charming garden.

GROUP OPENING

PRINCES AVENUE GARDENS, N10
Muswell Hill, London N10 3LS.
Buses: 43 & 134 from Highgate tube; also W7, 102, 144, 234, 299. Ave opp M&S in Muswell Hill Broadway, or John Baird PH in Fortis Green. Home-made teas. **Combined adm £3.50, chd free. Sun 15 May (2-6).**

28 PRINCES AVENUE
Ian & Viv Roberts

15 PRINCES AVENUE
Eliot & Emma Glover

In a beautiful Edwardian avenue in the heart of Muswell Hill Conservation Area, two very different gardens reflect the diverse life-styles of their owners. The large S-facing family garden at No. 15 has been designed for entertaining and yr-round interest. White and blue themed beds with alliums and a wide variety of perennials and shrubs frame an *exceptional* lawn. A Wendy house and hidden wooden castle provide delight for children of all ages. No. 28 is a well-established traditional garden reflecting the charm typical of

the era. Mature trees, shrubs, mixed borders and rose beds create an oasis of calm just off the bustling Broadway.

GROUP OPENING

RAILWAY COTTAGES, N22
Alexandra Palace, London N22 7SL. *Tube: Wood Green, 10 mins walk. Stn: Alexandra Palace, 3 mins. Buses: W3, 184, 3 mins. Free parking in Bridge Rd, Buckingham Rd, Palace Gates Rd, Station Rd, Dorset Rd.* Home-made teas at 2 Dorset Rd. **Combined adm £3.50, chd free. Sun 10 July (2-5.30).**

 2 DORSET ROAD
 Jane Stevens
 Visitors also welcome by appt. janestevens_london@yahoo.co.uk

  4 DORSET ROAD
 Mark Longworth
 Visitors also welcome by appt. 07792 170755 mail@marklongworthhart.com

 14 DORSET ROAD
 Cathy Brogan

 22 DORSET ROAD
 Mike & Noreen Ainger

Two front gardens of a row of historical railway cottages and two railway cottage back gardens. The two front gardens at 14 & 22 Dorset Road show a variety of interesting planting, incl aromatic shrubs and herbs, jasmine, flax, fig, fuchsia, vines and a climbing rose, with an emphasis on sustainability and organic methods. The tranquil country-style garden at 2 Dorset Road is on 3 sides of the house and is full of interest. Topiary and clipped box hedges contrast with climbing roses, clematis, jasmine and honeysuckle. Trees incl mulberry, quince, fig, apple and a mature willow that creates an opportunity for an interesting shady corner. A pond transforms an old Anderson shelter and a gravel garden is slowly maturing. New to the group, and accessed through the rear of No. 2, is the pretty secluded woodland garden at No. 4 which sets off the sculptor owner's figurative and abstract work among acers, sambucus nigra, species shrubs and old fruit trees.

NEW **30 REDSTON ROAD, N8**
Crouch End, London N8 7HJ. Mr
Brian Bowles. *Redston Rd off Priory
Rd at bottom of Muswell Hill, 100yds
from Xrds leading into Alexandra
Palace. Buses: W3, W7, 144.* Home-
made teas. **Adm £2.50, chd free.
Sun 19 June (2-6).**
Former Kew Gardens' designer,
Stuart Robbins, created this garden
on the diagonal to cheat the eye and
maximise width. Features: a lawn,
decking and pergola overhanging a
pond and a variety of sun and shade
borders with shrubs, perennials and
annuals. The garden slopes gently
down a series of terraces. Stairs
down from the veranda: unsuitable for
the less mobile.

Gnarled and much-
loved apple
tree, entwined with
white clematis . . .

GROUP OPENING

RICHMOND RIVERSIDE
Friars Lane, Richmond TW9 1NR.
*Tube & mainline stn: Richmond, then
5 mins walk via Richmond Green, on
Friars Lane 50yds from river, just
beyond car park. Access only from
towpath, tickets to both gardens only
from 1 St Helena Terrace.* **Combined
adm £5, chd free. Evening
Opening, wine, Sat 11 June (6-8).**

1 ST HELENA TERRACE
Christina Gascoigne
Visitors also welcome by appt,
max 10.
020 8940 3894
christina@christinagascoigne.
com

SARAH'S GARDEN,
TRUMPETERS HOUSE
Mrs Pamela Franklyn

Two very different hidden gardens on
Richmond Riverside with direct
access from the towpath. 1 St Helena
Terrace is a small secret studio
garden on 3 levels of brick terraces,
around 35ft curving fish pond with a
5ft waterfall tumbling over natural

rocks. Sarah's garden (Trumpeters'
House) has a gravel garden with
eucalyptus and drought resistant
plants, poppies and aquilegia,
parterre, aviary with doves and small
orchard. Partial wheelchair access.

---

12 ROOKFIELD AVENUE, N10
Muswell Hill, London N10 3TS.
Andrew Barr & Johanna Ryan.
*Bottom of Muswell Hill. Tube:
Highgate, 1m lovely walk through
Queen's Wood. Bus: W7 from
Finsbury Park stn or Muswell Hill
Broadway to top of Park Rd, then
walk up Etheldene Ave.* **Adm £3, chd
free. Evening opening, wine, Sat
18 June (5-8).**
Naturalistic garden to complement
our 1910 Arts and Crafts cottage,
enclosing it on three levels, within a
rural estate (itself worth investigation).
Incl 33ft x 12ft herbaceous border,
densely planted to limit excavations
by our Springer Spaniel. Opening in
June only this year for display of many
old varieties of rose, all fragrant.
Strictly organic and fuchsia-free. We
produce our own flower remedies and
propagate (from seed) many
perennials for sale. To feature, with
RHS Wisley, in 'Garden Dreams' on
Finnish TV.

◆ **ROOTS AND SHOOTS, SE11**
Walnut Tree Walk, Kennington,
London SE11 6DN. Trustees of
Roots and Shoots, 020 7587 1131,
www.rootsandshoots.org.uk. *Tube:
Lambeth North. Buses: 3, 59, 159,
360. Just S of Waterloo Stn, off
Kennington Rd, 5 mins from Imperial
War Museum. No car parking on site.*
Light Refreshments. **Adm £2, chd
free. For NGS: Evening Openings
Weds 25 May, 6 July (6-8.30). For
other opening times and
information, please phone or see
garden website.**
½ -acre wildlife garden run by
innovative charity providing training
and garden advice. Summer
meadow, observation beehives,
2 large ponds, hot borders,
Mediterranean mound, old roses and
echiums. Learning centre with
photovoltaic roof, solar heating,
rainwater catchment, three planted
roofs, one brown roof. Wildlife garden
study centre exhibition with photo,
video and other wildlife interpretation
materials. Winner City of London
Sustainable Cities Award & Evening

Standard Green Corners initiative.
Featured 365th in London Guide
Book '1000 things to do in London'!

NEW **131 ROSEBERY ROAD,
N10**
Muswell Hill, London N10 2LD.
Kirsty Monaghan. *Tube: Highgate,
then bus 43 or 134 to Muswell Hill
Broadway. Bus W7 from Finsbury
Park Tube. Walk down Dukes Ave or
bus 102, 299 alight Rosebery Rd.*
Home-made teas. **Adm £3, chd free.
Sun 19 June (2-6).**
Garden designer's family garden based
on circles and fluid curves with full
luxurious planting. Circular layout and
attention to fine detail reflects Kirsty's
past career in jewellery design. The
sinuous path, laid in sandstone sets,
divides two lawns. Planting designed
to provide interesting foliage, textures
and colour combinations incl roses,
clematis, hardy geraniums and
honeysuckles, with tall perennials and
grasses for height and movement.
Three seating areas.

ROYAL COLLEGE OF
PHYSICIANS GARDEN, NW1
11 St Andrews Place, London
NW1 4LE. Royal College of
Physicians of London,
020 7034 4901,
paula.croisier@rcplondon.ac.uk,
www.rcplondon.ac.uk/garden.
*Outer Circle, SE corner of Regents
Park. Tube: Regents Park turn R, go
100yds, L to Outer Circle, 150yds on
R.* Light refreshments & teas. **Adm
£3, chd free. Sun 14 Aug (10-5).
Visitors also welcome by appt.
Guided tours can be given to
groups by appt on weekdays. Also
open 14 Aug The Holme.**
1000 different plants used in
conventional and herbal medicines
around the world during the past
3000 yrs; plants named after
physicians and plants with medical
implications. The plants are labelled,
and arranged by continent. Garden
tours with explanations about the
past and present medicinal uses of
the plants.

5 RUSSELL ROAD, N13
Bowes Park, London N13 4RS.
Angela Kreeger. *Close to N Circular
Rd and Green Lanes. Tube: Bounds
Green, 10 mins walk. Mainline: Bowes
Park, 3 mins walk. Numerous bus
routes. Off Whittington Rd.* **Adm**

£2.50, chd free. Suns 1 May;
4 Sept (2-6). Also open 4 Sept Golf
Course Allotments.
A 'poem for the eyes', the garden has
structure, full generous, romantic
planting. Billowing, overflowing,
balanced by flat, open lawn in first
half, and airy, dreamy planting in
second half, a pebble garden marks
the border. This is not a manicured
garden. Simple, unfussy with a
contemporary feel, calm, quiet and
peaceful. Many spring plants and
bulbs, some in pots. Autumn is rusty,
even looser and soft. A different
pleasure. Golden in sunlight.

90 ST GEORGE'S AVENUE, N7
Tufnell Park, London N7 0AH. Ms J
Chamberlain & Mr R Hamilton.
*Tube: Tufnell Park, or bus 4 to Tufnell
Park Rd, alight Dalmeny Rd.* Adm £3,
chd free. Sun 12 June (2-6).
A long narrow garden divided into
2 distinct sections by a pergola
covered with clematis, a bed of
evergreen shrubs and a beautiful acer
griseum. Climbers on the fences,
mixed planting in the borders, and a
side patio filled with pots containing
hostas, camellias, fatsia and
hydrangeas complete the picture.
Islington in Bloom Silver Award for
Front Garden.

Lovely inspirational
garden for others
like me who have
small spaces . . .

7 ST GEORGE'S ROAD
St Margarets, Twickenham
TW1 1QS. Richard & Jenny
Raworth, 020 8892 3713,
jraworth@googlemail.com,
www.raworthgarden.com. *1½ m
SW of Richmond. Off A316 between
Twickenham Bridge & St Margarets
roundabout.* Home-made teas (Sun).
Adm £4, chd 50p. Sun 5 June
(11-5). Evening Opening £5, wine,
Sat 18 June (6-8). Visitors also
welcome by appt.
Exuberant displays of Old English
roses and vigorous climbers with
unusual herbaceous perennials.
Massed scented crambe cordifolia.
Pond with bridge converted into
child-safe lush bog garden. Large N-
facing luxuriant conservatory with rare
plants and climbers. Pelargoniums a

speciality. Sunken garden and knot
garden. Pergola covered with
climbing roses and clematis. Featured
in Period Living, Inspirational Gardens
by Pamela Westland and GGG.

27 ST JAMES AVENUE, W13
Ealing, London W13 9DL. Andrew &
Julie Brixey-Williams. *Uxbridge Rd
(A206) to West Ealing; Leeland
Terrace leads to St James Ave.*
Home-made teas. Adm £3.50, chd
free. Sun 3 July (2-5.30).
Inspired by our love of the Far East and
Jim Thompson's Bangkok 'jungle', the
garden comprises a stepping stone
path leading to two stone circles
surrounded by lush, diverse planting. A
stone bridge crosses a butterfly-
shaped pond to a mini jungle with 30ft
bamboo, tetrapanax papyrifera rex,
bananas and lomatia ferruginea,
amongst other rarities.

30 ST JAMES'S ROAD
Hampton Hill TW12 1DQ. Jean
Burman. *Between A312 (Uxbridge
Rd) and A313 (Park Rd).* Bus: 285
from Kingston stops at end of rd (15
mins walk). Stn: Fulwell (20 mins
walk). Adm £2.50, chd free. Evening
Opening, cheese & wine, Wed 20
July (7-10.30).
Lovely SE-facing garden (35ft x 90ft)
with tasteful features throughout,
subdivided into 5 rooms of interest.
Decking with seating leads to ponds,
surrounded by grasses and shrubs
and an African-themed thatched
exterior 'sitting room'. Fairy lights and
candles make this perfect for a
magical evening's visit.

87 ST JOHNS ROAD, E17
London E17 4JH. Andrew Bliss,
07790 230053,
blisshand@yahoo.co.uk. *From
Walthamstow tube 15 mins walk
through the charming old village of
Walthamstow or 275 or 212 bus from
bus stn opp tube stn. Alight stop just
after Texaco/Somerfield on L, St
Johns Rd on corner.* Light
refreshments & home-made teas
(Suns). Adm £2.50, chd free. Suns
3, 17, 31 July (1-5). Evening
Openings £5, with welcome drink
and canapés, Sats 2, 16, 30 July
(7.00-10.30). Visitors also welcome
by appt.
To entice you, comments from my
Visitors Book of 2010: 'Beautiful &
immaculate. Keep noticing new things
hidden away'. 'Lovely inspirational

garden for others like me who have
small spaces'. 'Fantastic display of
plants. So much to see and ALL in
pots and containers'. 'Such a
delicate, detailed delightful garden'. 'A
hidden gem in E17'. The host is an
artist creating great variety of quirky
objets d'art, mirrors, furniture and wall
art, all for sale.

GROUP OPENING

NEW ST MARY'S GROVE GARDENS, N1
Islington, London N1 2NT. *Tube:
Highbury & Islington 6 mins. Access
from St Paul's Rd via Compton Rd
and Prior Bolton St to 36 St Mary's
Grove (access from yard at rear
between 8 & 10 St Mary's Grove to
other terrace gardens).* Light
refreshments & wine. Combined adm
£4.50, chd free. Evening Opening,
wine, Wed 15 June (6.30-9).

NEW 20 ST MARY'S GROVE
B J Capel

NEW 22 ST MARY'S GROVE
Marcus Richter

NEW 32 ST MARY'S GROVE
Jackie Roe

NEW 36 ST MARY'S GROVE
Mary Francis

St Mary's Grove Gardens are in the
heart of the leafy Canonbury
conservation area and close to
Canonbury Square and the historic
Canonbury tower. A 'plantswoman's
obsession', no. 36 has been recently
redesigned and replanted (unusual
cultivars), and also features green
roofs and ponds, composting a
speciality. The much smaller gardens
of 3 neighbouring terrace houses
each individually create oases of calm
and plant interest. Islington in Bloom
Silver Awards for all St Mary's Grove
front gardens. Wheelchair access to
no. 36 only.

ST MICHAEL'S CONVENT
56 Ham Common, Ham, Richmond
TW10 7JH. Community of the
Sisters of the Church. *2m S of
Richmond. From Richmond or
Kingston, A307, turn onto the
common at the Xrds nr New Inn,
100yds on the R adjacent to
Martingales Close. Mainline trains to
Richmond & Kingston also tube to*

Richmond, then bus 65 from either stn to Ham Common. **Adm £3, chd free. Sun 10 Apr (2-5).**
4-acre organic garden comprises walled vegetable garden, orchards, vine house, ancient mulberry tree, extensive borders, meditation and Bible gardens. Spring blossom and bulbs a feature. Some gravel paths.

57 ST QUINTIN AVENUE, W10
London W10 6NZ. Mr H Groffman, 020 8969 8292. 1m from Ladbroke Grove or White City tube. Buses: 7, 70 from Ladbroke Grove stn; 220 from White City, all to North Pole Rd. Home-made teas. **Adm £2.50, chd free. Suns 10, 24 July (2-6). Also open 24 July 29 Addison Ave. Visitors also welcome by appt in July only, no limit to group size.**
30ft x 40ft walled garden; wide selection of plant material incl evergreen and deciduous shrubs for foliage effects. Patio area mainly furnished with bedding material, colour themed. Focal points throughout. Refurbished with new plantings and special features. For 2011: 'Where have all the flowers gone?', a special display of foliage - leaf shapes, colours and textures. 3 awards Brighter Kensington & Chelsea Scheme, 2 awards Kensington Gardeners Club.

5 ST REGIS CLOSE, N10
Alexandra Park Road, London N10 2DE. Ms S Bennett & Mr E Hyde, 020 8883 8540, suebearlh@gmail.com. 2nd L in Alexandra Park Rd from Colney Hatch Lane. Tube: Bounds Green or E Finchley then bus 102 or 299. Alight at St Andrew's Church on Windermere Rd. Bus: 43 or 134 to Alexandra Park Rd. Home-made teas. **Adm £3, chd free. Suns 1 May; 26 June; 24 July (2-7). Also open 26 June 5 Cecil Rd. Visitors also welcome by appt, groups 6-60 welcome, incl coach parties (convenient parking), catering by arrangement.**
A cornucopia of sensual delights! Artists' garden renowned for unique architectural features and delicious cakes. Baroque temple, pagodas, oriental raku-tiled mirrored wall conceals plant nursery. Compost heap with medieval pretensions alongside American Gothic shed. Maureen Lipman's favourite garden, combining colour, humour and

trompe l'oeil with wildlife-friendly ponds, waterfalls, weeping willow and lawns. Imaginative container planting and abundant borders incl exotic and native species, creating an inspirational and re-energising experience. Open studio with ceramics and prints. Horticultural advice from knowledgeable helpers. Collecting broken or unwanted hand tools for 'Tools Shed' project. Featured on BBC TV Gardeners' World & ITV Britain's Best Back Gardens.

355 SANDYCOMBE ROAD
Kew, Richmond TW9 3PR. Henry Gentle & Sally Woodward Gentle. 200m S of Kew Gardens Stn. Garden entrance between house nos. 351 & 353 Sandycombe Road. Home-made teas. **Adm £3, chd free. Sun 19 June (2-5). Also open 31 West Park Road.**
Unexpectedly large urban garden on two levels. Terracing with wooden sleepers, bricks and decking provide distinct areas of interest incl lavenders, olives, grasses, euphorbias and other plants for sandy soils and shady areas. A garden for adults and children alike.

Collecting broken or unwanted hand tools for 'Tools Shed' project . . .

22 SCUTARI ROAD, SE22
East Dulwich, London SE22 0NN. Sue Hillwood-Harris & David Hardy. S side of Peckham Rye Park. B238 Peckham Rye/Forest Hill Rd, turn into Colyton Rd (opp Herne Tavern). 3rd on R. Bus: 63. Stn: East Dulwich. Home-made teas. **Adm £2.50, chd free. Sun 22 May (2-6).**
Our inspirational labour of love, created from boring scratch 6yrs ago, is still evolving. It has a cottagey area, water, trees, ferns and many attractive maturing shrubs. Palatially-housed chickens produce eggs (on sale for NGS funds, subject to feathery whim) which are used in tea and cakes of

memorable standard. Steps and narrow paths may make access difficult for less mobile visitors.

SOUTH LONDON BOTANICAL INSTITUTE, SE24
323 Norwood Road, London SE24 9AQ, www.slbi.org.uk. Mainline stn: Tulse Hill. Buses: 68, 196, 322 & 468 stop at junction of Norwood & Romola Rds. Home-made teas. **Adm £2.50, chd free (share to South London Botanical Institute). Sun 26 June (2-5).**
London's smallest botanical garden, densely planted with over 500 labelled species grown in a formal layout of themed borders. Wild flowers and native plants flourish alongside traditional medicinal herbs. Carnivorous, scented and shade-tolerant plants are featured, growing among rare trees and shrubs. The pond is home to frogs, newts and wetland plants. New garden mosaic and exhibition of botanical art. Tours of our historic building and herbarium. Unusual plants, herbs and botanically inspired jewellery for sale.

123 SOUTH PARK ROAD, SW19
Wimbledon, London SW19 8RX. Susan Adcock. Mainline & tube: Wimbledon, 10 mins; S Wimbledon tube 5 mins. Buses: 57, 93, 131, 219 along High St. Entrance in Bridges Rd (next to church hall) off South Park Rd. Cream Teas. **Adm £2.50, chd free. Sun 19 June (2-6). Also open Pitt Crescent.**
A high deck in the trees looks over the main area of lawn, water, patio and pots. This small, harmonious L-shaped garden contains a courtyard with raised vegetable beds and pergola, and a hot tub!

41 SOUTHBROOK ROAD, SE12
Lee, London SE12 8LJ. Barbara & Marek Polanski. Off Sth Circular at Burnt Ash Rd. Mainline stns: Lee & Hither Green, both 10 mins walk. Home-made teas. **Adm £3, chd free. Sun 19 June (2-5).**
Large suburban garden in rural setting. Formal paving and pond to the rear divided from the main garden by a parterre with climbing roses and arbours. Large lawn with deep herbaceous borders. Sunny terrace close to house.

SOUTHWOOD LODGE, N6
33 Kingsley Place, Highgate,
London N6 5EA. Mr & Mrs C
Whittington, 020 8348 2785,
suewhittington@hotmail.co.uk.
*Tube: Highgate then 5 min walk up
Southwood Lane. 4 min walk from
Highgate Village along Southwood
Lane. Buses: 143, 210, 214, 271.*
Home-made teas. **Adm £3, chd free.
Suns 8 May; 19 June (2-5.30).
Visitors also welcome by appt,
refreshments by arrangement.**
Secret garden hidden behind C18
house (not open), laid out last century
on steeply sloping site, now densely
planted with wide variety of shrubs,
climbers and perennials. Ponds,
waterfall, frogs and newts. Many
unusual plants are grown and
propagated for sale - rare
pelargoniums a speciality. Toffee hunt
for children, Lucky Dip for fathers on
Fathers' Day (19 June).

SQUERRYES COURT
See Kent.

2 STANLEY ROAD, N2
East Finchley, London N2 0NB.
Tudor & Hilary Spencer, 020 8883
7301, tudorspencer@hotmail.com.
*Tube: East Finchley, then 10 mins
walk. Bus: 143, or any bus to High
Rd, then 5 mins walk.* Home-made
teas. **Adm £2, chd free. Sun 5 June
(2-6).** Also open **East Finchley
Cottage Gardens. Visitors also
welcome by appt.**
Densely planted front and rear
gardens of an Edwardian semi with
8 distinct areas incl colourful
vegetable plot, alpine bed, ferns,
bamboos and perennials. Boundaries
softened with varied climbers for
scent and foliage. Landscaping
incorporates a koi pond, centre circle
and viewing platform. Designed to be
completely wheelchair-friendly without
aesthetic compromise in hard
landscape or planting. A garden for
year-round enjoyment.

STONEY HILL HOUSE, SE26
Rock Hill, London SE26 6SW.
Cinzia & Adam Greaves. *Stn:
Sydenham Hill, steep climb, exits in
Rock Hill. Buses: to Crystal Palace or
363 along Sydenham Hill, house at
end of cul-de-sac on L.* Home-made
teas. **Adm £3, chd free. Sun 15 May
(2-5).**
Garden and woodland of approx 1 acre
providing a secluded green oasis in

the city. Mature trees and shrubs are
offset by pieces of contemporary
sculpture and the informal and natural
planting is designed to attract wildlife
and insects.

4 STRADBROKE GROVE
Buckhurst Hill IG9 5PD. Mr & Mrs T
Brighten, 020 8505 2716,
carol@cbrighten.fsnet.co.uk.
*Between Epping & Woodford, 5m
from M25 J26. Tube: Buckhurst Hill,
turn R cross rd to Stradbroke Grove.*
Home-made teas. **Adm £2, chd free.
Sun 12 June (2-6). Visitors also
welcome by appt.**
Secluded garden, designed to
enhance its strong sloping aspect.
Central gravelled bed with grasses,
shells, pots and succulents. Rose-
screened vegetable and fruit garden.
Large lawn with good herbaceous
borders and pergola to disguise
conifer hedge. Featured in Garden
News magazine.

**NEW ▶ 58A TEIGNMOUTH ROAD,
NW2**
Cricklewood, London NW2 4DX.
Drs Elayne & Jim Coakes. *Tube:
Willesden Green. Buses: 16, 32, 260,
266, 332, 460. Middle of Teignmouth
Rd, nr junction with Dawlish Rd.* **Adm
£5, chd free. Sun 10 July (2-7) with
wine & light refreshments.**
New front and back gardens recently
created by plant fiend with eclectic

schemes including colour co-
ordinated beds, pergola with climbing
roses and clematis, 2 ponds, water
features and lawn replaced by
grasses with prairie-style planting.
Rainwater harvesting with integral
watering system and organic
treatment means a home for many
creatures and a wildlife hotel for frogs
and bees.

GROUP OPENING

**TEWKESBURY LODGE GARDEN
GROUP, SE23**
Forest Hill, London SE23 3DE. *Off
S Circular (A205) behind Horniman
Museum & Gardens. Stn: Forest Hill,
10 mins walk. Buses: 176, 185, 312,
P4. Tickets and plants to be
purchased centrally at junction of
Horniman Drive and Liphook
Crescent.* Home-made teas (Sun) at
53 Ringmore Rise. **Combined adm
£7, chd free** (share to St
Christopher's Hospice and the
Marsha Phoenix Trust). **Evening
Opening, wine, Sat 11 June (6-9).
Sun 12 June (2-6).**

THE COACH HOUSE
3 The Hermitage. Pat Rae
Visitors also welcome by appt.
pat@patrae.co.uk

27 HORNIMAN DRIVE
Rose Agnew

4 Stradbroke Grove

28 HORNIMAN DRIVE
Frankie Locke

53 RINGMORE RISE
Valerie Ward

NEW 25 WESTWOOD PARK
Beth & Steph Falkingham-Blackwell

30 WESTWOOD PARK
Jackie McLaren

Six very different gardens within a short walk of each other on a steep hill. Their often challenging locations include spectacular views over London and the North Downs and conditions ranging from full sun to deep shade. There is a sculptor's courtyard, crammed full of unusual plants and the artist's ceramics. A garden designer's own country-style garden (featured in national magazines) delights the eye with lovely plant combinations. Other owners offer a front garden inspired by Beth Chatto's dry garden; herbaceous planting that complements a modern house extension; and deep informal flower borders under mature trees. A love of vegetable growing is evident with greenhouses, raised beds, fruit cage and chicken run. The new garden is a peaceful organic haven with a gravelled bed, summerhouse and newly-planted red garden. Wildlife flourishes too, with areas to encourage interest and diversity. Steep slopes, unfenced ponds, regret no pushchairs. Art, sculpture and plants for sale.

Ping pong and bamboo . . . !

64 THORNHILL ROAD, E10
Leyton, London E10 5LL. Mr P Minter & Mr M Weldon, 020 8558 5895, paul@paulminter.co.uk. *Tube: Leyton, 10 mins walk. Off Oliver Rd, nr Leyton Orient football ground*. Home-made teas May, light refreshments Oct. **Adm £3, chd £1.50. Suns 1, 29 May (1-5); Sun 2 Oct (2-5). Visitors also welcome by appt.**
Re-opening after a 3yr break, a theatrical and elegant formal town garden gradually dissolves into informal woodland in this most unexpected 165ft x 30ft plot. This deeply atmospheric and well-designed garden is packed with architectural and botanical interest and would well repay the effort of a longer journey. Tulips in early May, massive climbing roses in late May and fabulous autumn colour in October.

NEW TREETOPS
Sandy Lane, Northwood HA6 3ES. Mrs Carole Kitchner. *Opp Northwood HQ. Tube: Northwood, 10 mins walk. Bus 8 stops at the bottom of lane. Parking in Lane*. Light refreshments & home-made teas. **Adm £3.50, chd free. Sun 31 July (2-6).**
Nestling in quiet lane in Northwood conservation area, sloping garden with long terrace and large pots. Rose-covered pergola, water feature, small lawn, wide variety of unusual shrubs incl magnolia grandiflora, paulownias, trochodendron. Peaking in high summer, heleniums, agapanthus, lobelias, eryngiums, crocosmias present a vibrant vision - well worth a visit!

NEW 86 UNDERHILL ROAD, SE22
East Dulwich, London SE22 0QU. Claire & Rob Goldie. *Between Langton Rise & Melford Rd. Stn: Forest Hill. Buses: P13 & 63 pass close by*. Home-made teas May, wine & light refreshments Sept. **Adm £3, chd free. Sun 29 May (2-6). Evening Opening £3.50, wine, Fri 2 Sept (6-9).**
A colourful family garden. Blue limestone terrace leading to a gravel garden with raised beds. Ping pong and bamboo! A mixture of the traditional and naturalistic - modern and quirky with a summerhouse built on reclaimed tyres!

7 UPPER PHILLIMORE GARDENS, W8
London W8 7HF. Mr & Mrs B Ritchie. *From Kensington High St take Phillimore Gdns or Campden Hill Rd; entrance Duchess of Bedford Walk*. Home-made teas. **Adm £2.50, chd free. Sun 17 Apr (2-6). Also open (1-5) Edwardes Square.**
Well-planned, mature garden on different levels, creating areas of varied character and mood. Colourful bulbs brighten this pretty garden in spring.

17 VALLEY VIEW GARDENS
Kenley, Purley CR8 5BR. Mr & Mrs Tassera. *2m S of Purley on A22 Eastbourne Rd. Parking for 500yds on either side of A22 in bays provided & on pavement. House below A22 behind hedges. Ignore final L or R turn on Sat Nav as restricted access*. Home-made teas. **Adm £3, chd free. Sun 19 June (1-5).**
Eclectic mix of plants and recycled materials are cleverly combined to make this multi-levelled plot as much a theatrical piece as a garden. Drama and humour abound in equal measure in this long, narrow garden.

12 VINE ROAD
East Molesey KT8 9LA. Peter & Esmé Auer. *1/2 m from Hampton Court stn, towards E Molesey via Bridge Rd. Turn down Palace Rd, L at end by church. House on corner of 1st Xrds*. **Adm £3.50, chd free. Sun 19 June (2-5).**
Formal topiary front garden with shaded planting of hostas, ferns and martagon lilies under large magnolia tree. S-facing back garden bordered by mature trees. Planted with traditional borders of roses and perennials, lavender terrace, sweet peas up tall obelisks, spouting water tank, small potager with step-over apples and a tiny greenhouse.

THE ROOF TERRACE, 21A WALDEGRAVE ROAD, SE19
London SE19 2AL. Suzie Gibbons, suzie@flowerpowerpictures.com, www.flowerpowerpictures.com. *Off Anerley Rd, 1min from Crystal Palace mainline stn. Turn L outside stn then L onto Anerley Rd, next R*. Light Refreshments. **Adm £2.50, chd free. Visitors welcome by appt July to Sept.**
Urban roof terrace, 60ft x 30ft, with Mary Poppins views, central rusty water feature and sedum roof. Simply planted with trees, grasses and verbena bonariensis. A calm oasis in the sky. Access via 2 flights of stairs, regret not suitable for small children. View photos in portfolio on garden website.

208 WALM LANE, THE GARDEN FLAT, NW2

London NW2 3BP. Miranda & Chris Mason, www.thegardennw2.co.uk. *Tube: Kilburn. Garden at junction of Exeter Rd & Walm Lane. Buses: 16, 32, 189, 226, 245, 260, 266, 316 to Cricklewood Broadway, then consult A-Z.* Light refreshments, home-made teas & wine. **Adm £3, chd free. Sun 26 June (1-7).**
Large S-facing oasis of green with big sky. Meandering lawn with island beds, fishpond with fountain, curved and deeply planted borders of perennials and flowering shrubs. Shaded mini woodland area of tall trees underplanted with rhododendrons, ferns and hostas with winding path from oriental-inspired summerhouse to secluded circular seating area. Woodwind quartet, Latin guitar duo, plant sale & raffle prizes.

WALTHAM FOREST REGISTER OFFICE, E17

106 Grove Road, Walthamstow E17 9BY. Garden Curator, Teresa Farnham, 07761 476651, farnhamz@yahoo.co.uk. *On corner of Grove Rd & Fraser Rd. Bus to Lea Bridge Rd, Bakers Arms & 5 mins walk up Fraser Rd. Separate gates to front and rear garden.* **Adm £2.50, chd free. Visitors welcome by appt.**
Front and rear gardens of former Victorian vicarage in Walthamstow. Plants grown from cuttings and seed for dry shallow soil are chemical-free. Mixed borders include an oak, Judas tree, strawberry tree which form background for photographs. Wildlife proliferates in this green oasis. Advice on taking cuttings. Featured in The Retirement Show Magazine & Hardy Plant Society Journal.

WALWORTH GARDEN FARM, SE17

Braganza Street/Manor Place, Kennington, London SE17 3BN. Trustees of Walworth Garden Farm. *Tube: Kennington, 500yds down Braganza St, corner of Manor Place.* **Adm £2, chd free. Sat 21, Sun 22 May (10-4).**
Walworth Garden Farm is an oasis of green in Southwark. From a derelict site this charity has created a productive garden full of organically grown fruit and vegetables surrounded by colourful flowerbeds. It is a working garden with greenhouses, a large newly constructed apiary, bee hives, ponds (a haven for wildlife) and a vital part of the local community providing training and development. Plants and honey for sale.

55 WARHAM ROAD

South Croydon CR2 6LH. Shanthee Siva. *Off A23, S of central Croydon. Mainline stn: S Croydon, or E Croydon then buses 119, 405, 455.* Light refreshments & home-made teas. **Adm £3, chd free. Sun 7 Aug (2-6). Also open Elm Tree Cottage.**
Large suburban garden with wide lawn edged by sweeping borders. Planted for maximum colour with wide variety of plants, surrounded by mature trees and shrubs interspersed with some semi-tropical planting.

THE WATERGARDENS

Warren Road, Kingston-upon-Thames KT2 7LF. The Residents' Association. *1m E of Kingston. From Kingston take A308 (Kingston Hill) towards London; after approx ¹/₂ m turn R into Warren Rd.* **Adm £3, chd £1. Suns 1 May; 16 Oct (2-4.30).**
Japanese landscaped garden originally part of Coombe Wood Nursery, planted by the Veitch family in the 1860s. Approx 9 acres with ponds, streams and waterfalls. Many rare trees which, in spring and autumn, provide stunning colour. For the tree-lover this is a must-see garden. Gardens attractive to wildlife. Some steep slopes and steps.

WEST LODGE PARK

Cockfosters Road, Hadley Wood EN4 0PY. Beales Hotels. *2m S of Potters Bar. On A111. J24 from M25 signed Cockfosters.* Tea, coffee & biscuits available at entrance to Arboretum. Afternoon cream teas (not for NGS) are available in the hotel, booking in advance advisable on Open Days. **Adm £4, chd free. Sun 15 May (2-5); Sun 30 Oct (1-4).**
35-acre Beale Arboretum consists of over 800 varieties of trees and shrubs, incl National Collection of Hornbeam cultivars, with a good selection of conifers, oaks, maples and mountain ash. A network of paths has been laid out, and most specimens are labelled. 2 rare Wollemi pines.

31 WEST PARK ROAD

Kew, Richmond TW9 4DA. Anna Anderson. *By Kew Gardens Stn, on E side of railway line.* **Adm £3, chd free. Sun 19 June (2-5). Teas at 355 Sandycombe Road, also open.**
Modern botanical garden with an oriental twist. Emphasis on foliage and an eclectic mix of plants, reflecting pool and rotating willow screens which provide varying views or privacy. Dry bed, shady beds, mature trees and a private paved dining area with dappled light and shade.

National Collection of Hornbeam cultivars, conifers, oaks, maples and mountain ash . . .

2 WESTERN LANE, SW12

London SW12 8JS. Mrs Anne Birnhak, annebirnhak@castlebalham.fsnet.co.uk. *Tube: Clapham South or Balham. Wandsworth Common mainline stn. Please park in Nightingale Lane.* **Adm £3, chd free. Sun 5 June (3-4.30). Also open 20 Eatonville Rd & 28 Old Devonshire Rd. Visitors also welcome by appt, groups of 10+.**
Weather permitting, Anne's eponymous floribunda rose should be flowering on 5 June. Features incl a circular wooden pergola, 12 towering metal obelisks and pots stacked in tiers. Mature trees thrive in vast containers. 250 clematis scramble through 2000 species plants. Sensational walled patio garden (28ft x 22ft), a horticultural 'jungle' of scented flowers and textured plants. A rose, named after the garden owner, featured on cover of Amateur Gardening. No wheelchair, pram or bicycle access.

NEW▶ 12 WESTERN ROAD, E13

Plaistow, London E13 9JF. Elaine & Kevin Fieldhouse, 020 8470 3681, fhouse@btinternet.com. *Stn: Upton Park, 3 min walk. Buses: 58, 104, 330, 376.* Home-made teas. **Adm £2.50, chd free. Sun 5 June (2-6). Visitors also welcome by appt 5 to 30 June only, for 4+.**

79 Church Lane, N2

Urban oasis, 85ft garden designed and planted by owners. Relying more heavily on evergreen, ferns, foliage and herbaceous planting. Rear of garden leads directly onto a 110ft allotment - part allotment, part extension of the garden - featuring topiary, medlar tree, mulberry tree, 2 ponds, small fruit trees and small iris collection.

12 WESTMORELAND ROAD, SW13

London SW13 9RY. Mrs Norman Moore. *Buses: 33, 72, 209, 283 to the Red Lion from Hammersmith.* **Adm £3, chd free (share to Myeloma UK). Sun 19 June (3-6).** S-facing raised terrace planted with wisteria, vine, scented roses, jasmine, sweet peas and decorative herbs. Two lower lawns, flanked by densely planted borders and divided by pretty gazebo with clematis, roses and golden hop overlooked by charming bower seat. Tranquil shady lawn with trickling water in huge urn, ferns, hydrangeas, day lilies and a mulberry tree. Secret potting area with children's Mini Gardens and Bug House.

⚘

NEW▶ WHIXALL HOUSE GARDEN, NW2

Exeter Road, London NW2 4SD. Maureen Amar & Richard Jenkins. *Tube: Kilburn, 8 mins walk along Exeter Rd. Parallel to A5 between Mapesbury Road and Walm Lane. 20 metres N of junction with St Gabriels Rd. House between 32 & 34 Exeter Rd.* Home-made teas. **Adm £3, chd free. Sun 19 June (1-6).** Caged, raised vegetable beds, soft fruit borders, espaliered fruit trees enclosing geometrical herb garden; octagonal pond and fountain at focus of an intense herbaceous bowl; shrubberies, wildlife pond, two-storey heated glasshouse, and several other original and functional constructions. Three-stage composting system. A haven for birds, bees, butterflies, and the owners.

⚘ ☕

86 WILLIFIELD WAY, NW11

Hampstead Garden Suburb, London NW11 6YJ. Diane Berger. *1m N of Golders Green. Tube: Golders Green, then H2 bus to Willifield Way. Or buses 82, 102, 460 to Temple Fortune, walk along Hampstead Way, turn L at The Orchard.* Home-made teas. **Adm £3, chd free. Sun 24 July (2-6). Also open 51 Northway.** A cottage garden with a contemporary twist with colour-themed herbaceous borders designed for yr-round interest, wildlife pond, gazebo, rose and clematis-clad pergola and interesting, mature shrubs and perennials. Teas served on communal lawns in front of this historic Arts & Crafts cottage.

☕

27 WOOD VALE, N10

London N10 3DJ. Mr & Mrs A W Dallman. *Muswell Hill 1m. A1 to Woodman PH; signed Muswell Hill. From Highgate tube, take Muswell Hill Rd, sharp R into Wood Lane leading to Wood Vale.* Home-made teas. **Adm £3, chd free. Sat, Sun 9, 10 July (1.30-6). Also open 10 July 33 Wood Vale.** One of the most enduringly popular gardens in London, maintained to prize-winning standards. 300ft long, ³/₄ acre, child-friendly, seating over 90 in sun or shady arbours. An unexpected adventure unfolds through herbaceous borders, winding paths with water features, to lawn with orchard, vegetable garden and greenhouses. Enjoy home made tea and celebrate our 25th year of opening. We would love to see you! London Garden Society Cup for Best Large Garden, Silver Medal for Containers and Bronze Medal for Front Garden. Winner Highgate Hort Society Best Small Greenhouse competition.

⚘ ☕

33 WOOD VALE, N10

Highgate, London N10 3DJ. Mona Abboud, 020 8883 4955, monaabboud@hotmail.com. *Tube: Highgate, 10 mins walk. Buses: W3, W7 to top of Park Rd.* **Adm £2, chd free. Suns 15 May; 10 July (2-6). Also open 10 July with teas, 27 Wood Vale. Visitors also welcome by appt.** Very long garden entered via steep but safe staircase. A living roof of succulent plants now covers the greenhouse. A new raised herbaceous border of soft-textured greys, blues and pinks of grasses and perennials complements the unusual trees and Mediterranean shrubs. The mood of the garden becomes increasingly informal as it meanders away from the house. A bog garden and camomile seat are being established.

☎

29 WOODBERRY CRESCENT, N10

Muswell Hill, London N10 1PJ.
Edwina Roberts. *Tube: Finsbury
Park, Highgate, East Finchley. Buses:
W7, 43, 102, 134. Off Muswell Hill
Broadway, diagonally opp PO.* Home-
made teas. **Adm £2.50, chd free.
Suns 29 May; 31 July (2-7).**
Town garden with country feel. Mixed
planting with trees, shrubs,
herbaceous and climbers creating
privacy and hidden spaces. Large
pond with variety of fish, pond plants
and marginals. Trompe l'oeil mirrors
and sunny terrace. Lots of places to
sit, contemplate and enjoy vistas from
many angles. Container herb garden
harmonises with container planting
throughout the garden.

66 WOODBOURNE AVENUE, SW16

London SW16 1UT. **Brian Palmer &
Keith Simmonds.** *Enter from Garrads
Rd by Tooting Bec Common (by car
only).* Home-made teas. **Adm £2.50,
chd 50p. Sun 10 July (1-6).**
A popular garden (17th year of
opening) that is constantly evolving.
Cottage-style front garden 40ft x 60ft
containing roses and herbaceous
plants with a subtropical twist with
bananas and palms. Rear garden
approx 40ft x 80ft with recently added
features, rare shrubs, trees and
gazebo, creating a tranquil oasis in an
urban setting. Take-away service for
our renowned home made cakes.

THE WORLD GARDEN AT LULLINGSTONE CASTLE

See Kent.

NEW▶ 21 WROXHAM GARDENS, N11

London N11 2AY. **Mrs L Coleman.**
*Buses: 102, 184, 299 from Bounds
Green stn, alight Albert Rd. Walk up
Wroxham Gardens, beside Sunshine
Garden Centre.* Home-made teas.
Adm £3, chd free. Sun 12 June (2-7).
Artist's garden delights with lush
planting and winding paths revealing
sculpture and pottery amidst fragrant
herbaceous borders filled with
scented flowers and rambling roses.
Wildlife is nurtured, with areas of
natural planting, a pond, active
beehive and insect hotel, while fruit
trees benefit all the residents of this
lovely organic garden. Information
about keeping honey bees and
encouraging wildlife.

THE WYCH ELM PUBLIC HOUSE

93 Elm Road, Kingston-upon-
Thames KT2 6HT. **Janet Turnes,**
www.thewychelm.co.uk. *Stn:
Kingston, 10min walk. 8min walk
Kingston Gate, Richmond Park.* Light
refreshments, teas & BBQ. **Adm
£2.50, chd free. Sun 31 July (12-6).**
Prize-winning floriferous garden
famed for its brilliant colourful display
from eaves to pavement. Back
garden features pampered exotic
plants creating a Mediterranean
atmosphere. Many unusual species

lovingly tended by plantaholic
licensee. Cool, shady corner and hot
colours on the terrace. Pergola,
festooned with exotic climbers,
protects banana and other tender
plants. Winner Kingston in Bloom,
London Gardens Society award.

Borders filled with scented flowers and rambling roses . . .

ZEN GARDEN, W3

55 Carbery Avenue, Acton, London
W3 9AB. Three Wheels Buddhist
Centre, www.threewheels.co.uk.
*Tube: Acton Town 5 mins walk,
200yds off A406.* Home-made teas &
Japanese green tea with sweet. **Adm
£3, chd free. Sats, Suns 14,
15 May; 18, 19 June (2-5.30).**
Pure Japanese Zen garden (so no
flowers) with 12 large and small rocks
of various colours and textures set in
islands of moss and surrounded by a
sea of grey granite gravel raked in a
stylised wave pattern. Garden
surrounded by trees and bushes
outside a cob wall. Oak-framed wattle
and daub shelter with Norfolk reed
thatched roof. Japanese Tea
Ceremony demonstration and talks by
designer/creator of the garden.
Buddha Room open to visitors.

London County Volunteers

County Organiser
Penny Snell, Moleshill House, The Fairmile, Cobham, Surrey KT11 1BG, 01932 864532, pennysnellflowers@btinternet.com

County Treasurer
Richard Raworth, 7 St George's Road, St Margarets, Twickenham TW1 1QS, 07831 476088, raworth.r@blueyonder.co.uk

Assistant County Organisers
Outer W London Rita Armfield, 45 Tudor Road, Hampton TW12 2NG, 020 8941 3315, rita@tudor45.plus.com
NW London Susan Bennett & Earl Hyde, 5 St Regis Close, Alexandra Park Road, Muswell Hill, London N10 2DE,
    020 8883 8540, suebearlh@yahoo.co.uk
SW London Joey Clover, 13 Fullerton Road, London SW18 1BU, 020 8870 8740, joeyclover@dsl.pipex.com
Hampstead Garden Suburb Anne Crawley, 116 Willifield Way, London NW11 6YG, 020 8455 7618, annecrawley@waitrose.com
SE London Gillian Davies, 32 Chestnut Road, London SE27 9LF, 020 8670 8916, cag.davies@btinternet.com
E London Teresa & Stuart Farnham, 17 Greenstone Mews, London E11 2RS, 020 8530 6729, farnhamz@yahoo.co.uk
Hampstead Ruth Levy, 5 Frognal Gardens, London NW3 6UY, 020 7435 4124, ruthlevy@tiscali.co.uk
Hackney Philip Lightowlers, 8 Almack Road, London E5 0RL, 020 8533 0052, plighto@btinternet.com
Islington Nell Darby Brown, 26 Canonbury Place, London N1 2NY, 020 7226 6880, pendarbybrown@blueyonder.co.uk
    Gill Evansky, 25 Canonbury Place, London N1 2NY, 020 7359 2484
SE & Outer London Sue Phipps, 17 Crescent Lane, London SW4 9PT, 020 7622 7230, sue@crescentlane.co.uk
W London, Barnes & Chiswick Jenny Raworth, 7 St George's Road, St Margarets, Twickenham TW1 1QS, 020 8892 3713,
    jraworth@googlemail.com
Highgate, St John's Wood & Holland Park Sue Whittington, Southwood Lodge, 33 Kingsley Place, London N6 5EA,
    020 8348 2785, suewhittington@hotmail.co.uk

NORFOLK

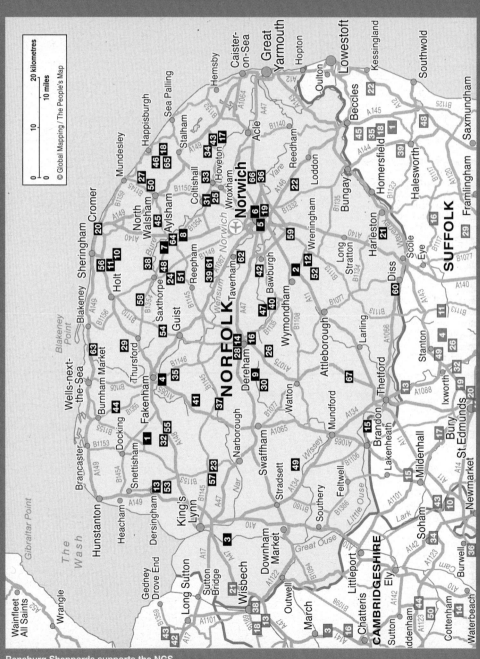

Opening Dates

February

Sunday 13
37 Lexham Hall

Sunday 20
1 Bagthorpe Hall

Saturday 26
31 Horstead House

March

Sunday 6
11 Chestnut Farm

Sunday 27
36 Lake House
66 16 Witton Lane

April

Sunday 3
12 The Conifers
15 Desert World Gardens
29 Hindringham Hall
38 Mannington Hall

Sunday 10
12 The Conifers

Saturday 16
18 East Ruston Old Vicarage

Sunday 17
9 Bradenham Hall
57 Spinney Lodge

Sunday 24
67 Wretham Lodge

Monday 25
67 Wretham Lodge

May

Sunday 1
13 Croft House
36 Lake House

Monday 2
36 Lake House

Sunday 8
52 Sallowfield Cottage

Sunday 15
43 The Mowle

Thursday 19
33 Hoveton Hall Gardens

Saturday 21
42 4 Mill Road

Sunday 22
34 How Hill Farm
37 Lexham Hall
42 4 Mill Road
46 The Old Rectory, Ridlington
56 Sheringham Park
65 West View

Monday 23
37 Lexham Hall

Sunday 29
30 Holme Hale Hall
48 Oulton Hall
63 Warborough House

Monday 30
8 Bolwick Hall

June

Wednesday 1
10 Chaucer Barn (Evening)

Sunday 5
4 5 Batterby Green
50 Rivermount
56 Sheringham Park
60 Sundown

Friday 10
38 Mannington Hall (Evening)

Saturday 11
21 Furze House

Sunday 12
17 The Dutch House
21 Furze House
44 North Creake Gardens
59 Summer Cottage

Sunday 19
23 Gayton Hall
25 Heggatt Hall
40 Manor Farm, Coston
49 Oxburgh Hall

Monday 20
23 Gayton Hall

Wednesday 22
28 Hill Farm, Gressenhall (Evening)

Sunday 26
6 Bishop's House
12 The Conifers
20 Felbrigg Hall
24 The Grange
26 High House Gardens
41 Manor House Farm, Wellingham
47 The Old Rectory, Brandon Parva

Wednesday 29
26 High House Gardens

July

Saturday 2
5 The Bear Shop

Sunday 3
2 Banhams Barn
5 The Bear Shop
15 Desert World Gardens
32 Houghton Hall Walled Garden
39 Manor Farm House
61 Swannington Manor

Sunday 10
3 Bank Farm
51 Salle Park

Saturday 16
7 Blickling Hall

Sunday 17
30 Holme Hale Hall

33 Hoveton Hall Gardens
35 6 Jarvis Drive
42 4 Mill Road
49 Oxburgh Hall
64 West Lodge

Tuesday 19
42 4 Mill Road

Sunday 24
9 Bradenham Hall
14 Dale Farm
55 Sharane

Sunday 31
19 The Exotic Garden

August

Sunday 7
16 Dunbheagan
54 Severals Grange

Saturday 20
21 Furze House

Sunday 21
11 Chestnut Farm
21 Furze House

September

Sunday 4
20 Felbrigg Hall

Saturday 10
22 The Garden in an Orchard

Sunday 11
22 The Garden in an Orchard
30 Holme Hale Hall

Sunday 18
26 High House Gardens
62 The Urban Jungle Gardens

Wednesday 21
26 High House Gardens
37 Lexham Hall

Sunday 25
9 Bradenham Hall

October

Saturday 8
18 East Ruston Old Vicarage

Saturday 15
7 Blickling Hall

Gardens open to the public

7 Blickling Hall
9 Bradenham Hall
18 East Ruston Old Vicarage
19 The Exotic Garden
20 Felbrigg Hall
32 Houghton Hall Walled Garden
33 Hoveton Hall Gardens
38 Mannington Hall
49 Oxburgh Hall
53 Sandringham Gardens
54 Severals Grange

Support the NGS – eat more cake!

56 Sheringham Park
58 Stody Lodge
62 The Urban Jungle Gardens

By appointment only

27 Hill Cottage
45 The Old Cottage

Also open by Appointment

4 5 Batterby Green
5 The Bear Shop
8 Bolwick Hall
11 Chestnut Farm
12 The Conifers
14 Dale Farm
15 Desert World Gardens
16 Dunbheagan
17 The Dutch House
21 Furze House
22 The Garden in an Orchard
23 Gayton Hall
27 Hill Cottage
28 Hill Farm, Gressenhall
30 Holme Hale Hall
35 6 Jarvis Drive
36 Lake House
42 4 Mill Road
43 The Mowle
45 The Old Cottage
47 The Old Rectory, Brandon Parva
52 Sallowfield Cottage
57 Spinney Lodge
60 Sundown
65 West View

The Gardens

1 **BAGTHORPE HALL**
Bagthorpe PE31 6QY. Mr & Mrs D
Morton. 3¹/₂ m N of East Rudham, off
A148. At King's Lynn take A148 to
Fakenham. At East Rudham (approx
12m) turn L opp The Crown, 3¹/₂ m
into hamlet of Bagthorpe. Farm
buildings on L, wood on R, white
gates set back from road, at top of
drive. Home-made teas. **Adm £3.50,
chd free. Sun 20 Feb** (11-4).
Snowdrops carpeting woodland walk.
🐦 ❀ 🛏 ☕

2 **BANHAMS BARN**
Browick Road, Wymondham
NR18 9RB. Mr C Cooper & Mrs J
Harden. 1m E of Wymondham. A11
from Attleborough, exit signed
Mulbarton. R at r'about, cross bridge
over A11. Immed take farm track on R
opp rd signed E Carleton/
Ketteringham. A11 from Norwich, exit
signed Mulbarton, L at r'about, then

as above. Home-made teas. **Adm
£3.50, chd free. Sun 3 July** (11-5).
1-acre lawned garden with all-yr
round interest. Specimen trees,
parterre, well stocked borders, large
pond and kitchen garden are the main
features. In July hemerocallis, roses,
lavender and an extensive
herbaceous border are at their best.
A paddock and woodland walk lie
beyond the wildlife pond. Enjoy home
made teas on the walled terrace.
Plants from the garden, and home
made produce for sale.
🔶 ❀ ☕ ☎

Wood turning
demonstration by
professional wood
turner . . .

3 **NEW** **BANK FARM**
Fallow Pipe Road, Saddlebow,
Kings Lynn PE34 3AS. Mr & Mrs
Alan Kew. 3m S of Kings Lynn. Turn
off Kings Lynn southern bypass (A47)
via slip rd signed St Germans. Cross
river in Saddlebow village. 1m fork R
into Fallow Pipe Rd. Farmhouse ¹/₄ m
by River Great Ouse. Home-made
teas. **Adm £3, chd free. Sun 10 July**
(11-5).
³/₄ -acre windswept garden was
created from a field in 1994. A low
maintenance garden of contrasts,
filled with trees, shrubs and newly
planted perennials. Many features
include large fish pond, small
vegetable garden with greenhouse.
Splashes of colour from annuals.
Walks along the banks of Great Ouse.
Dogs on leads. Wood turning
demonstration by professional wood
turner. Short gravel entrance.
🔶 🐦 ❀ ☕

4 **5 BATTERBY GREEN**
Hempton, Fakenham NR21 7LY.
Maureen Rose, 01328 862264. 1m
S of Fakenham. From A148 at
Fakenham take A1065 towards
Swaffham. 1st rd on R signed Byway
to Shereford. Down Shereford rd. 1st
L into Batterby Green. Parking at
Banhams on A1065 signed. Home-
made teas. **Adm £3, chd free. Sun 5
June** (11-5). **Visitors also welcome
by appt. No coaches.**

Enclosed small cottage garden
packed with plants, many surprises
and unusual treasures. A plantsman's
garden very colourful with yr-round
interest. Pond, arches with roses and
clematis, patio with pots, courtyard
area. 2 small front gardens. Some
gravel paths. Member of Norfolk
Cottage Garden Society, Hardy Plant
Society and Plant Heritage NCCPG.
🔶 ❀ ☕ ☎

5 **THE BEAR SHOP**
Elm Hill, Norwich NR3 1HN. Robert
Stone, 01603 766866,
enquiries@bearshops.co.uk.
Norwich City Centre. From St
Andrews, L to Princes St, then L to
Elm Hill. Garden at side of shop
through large wooden gate and along
alleyway. **Adm £3, chd free. Sat,
Sun 2, 3 July** (11-4.30). **Visitors
also welcome by appt.**
Considered to be based on a design
by Gertrude Jekyll, a small terraced
garden behind a C15 house in the
historic Cathedral Quarter of Norwich.
Enjoy the tranquillity of the riverside.
🐦 ❀ ☎

6 **BISHOP'S HOUSE**
Bishopgate, Norwich NR3 1SB. The
Bishop of Norwich. City centre.
Entrance opp Law Courts on
Bishopgate on N side of Cathedral
(not through The Close). Through
Archway on R. Public car parking
nearby. No parking at garden. Home-
made teas. **Adm £3, chd free. Sun
26 June** (1-5).
4-acre walled garden dating back to
C12. Extensive lawns with specimen
trees. Borders with many rare and
unusual shrubs. Spectacular
herbaceous borders flanked by yew
hedges. Rose beds, meadow
labyrinth, kitchen garden, woodland
walk and long border with hostas and
bamboo walk. Popular plant sales.
🔶 ❀ ☕

7 **◆ BLICKLING HALL**
Aylsham NR11 6NF. National Trust,
01263 738030,
www.nationaltrust.org.uk/blickling.
15m N of Norwich. 1¹/₂ m NW of
Aylsham on N side of B1354. **Adm
£7.50, chd £4.. For NGS: Sats
16 July; 15 Oct** (10-5.30). **For other
opening times and information,
please phone or see garden
website**
Large garden, orangery, crescent
lake, azaleas, rhododendrons,
herbaceous borders. Historic
Jacobean house. New wilderness

area project taking shape. Kitchen garden open. 3 x powered mobility vehicles (subject to availability), gravel paths.

8 BOLWICK HALL

Marsham NR10 5PU. Mr & Mrs G C Fisher, 01263 732131. *¹/₂ m S of Aylsham. On A140 towards Aylsham, take 1st R past Plough PH at Marsham, then next R onto private rd to front of Hall.* **Adm £3.50, chd free.** Mon 30 May (1-5). **Visitors also welcome by appt.**
Landscaped gardens and park, attributed to Humphry Repton, surrounding late Georgian hall (not open) and stable block. Collection of mature trees, woodland walks around stream and mill pond, as well as more recently planted borders and working vegetable garden.

9 ◆ BRADENHAM HALL

Bradenham, Thetford IP25 7QP. Chris & Panda Allhusen, 01362 687279, www.bradenhamhall.co.uk. *6m E of Swaffham. 5m W of East Dereham off A47. Turn S signed Wendling & Longham. 1m turn S signed Bradenham, 2m.* Home-made teas. **Adm £4, chd free.** For NGS: Suns 17 Apr; 24 July; 25 Sept (2-5.30). **For other opening times and information, please phone or see garden website.**
A garden for all seasons. Flower gardens, formally designed and richly planted, formal rose gardens, paved garden, unusual climbers, herbaceous and shrub borders, traditional kitchen gardens with 2 glasshouses. Arboretum of over 800 different trees, all labelled. Massed daffodils in spring. A delight and an education.

10 CHAUCER BARN

NR11 8RL. James Mermagen. *3m S of Sheringham. Turn off A149 nr junction of A149 & A1082 signed Gresham/E Beckham. Turn L at T-junction. 1st building in Gresham. 1st gravel drive on L of sharp L bend.* Tea. **Adm £3.50, chd free.** Evening Opening wine, Wed 1 June (2-7). 5-acre garden created by owner over 20 years in ruins of farmyard. Uphill drive flanked by topiary leads to award winning barn conversion. Knot/herb garden leads to lawn flanked by walled herbaceous borders

and pergola leading through contemporary topiary garden to stunning views over rolling hills to woodland. Woodland path leads downhill to wild flower meadow and young arboretum. Some steep slopes.

11 CHESTNUT FARM

Church Road, West Beckham NR25 6NX. Mr & Mrs John McNeil Wilson, 01263 822241, john@mcneil-wilson.freeserve.co.uk. *2¹/₂ m S of Sheringham. Mid-way between Holt & Cromer. 1m S off the A148 at the Sheringham Park entrance. Sign post indicates 'By Rd to W Beckham'. Chestnut Farm located behind the village sign. Lots of free parking, WC.* Light refreshments & home-made teas. **Adm £4, chd free.** Suns 6 Mar; 21 Aug (11-5). **Visitors also welcome by appt Feb to Sept, for groups of 45 max, coaches permitted.**
See garden and small arboretum at two distinct periods. February 70+ varieties of snowdrops, snowdrop walk and drifts of single and double snowdrops. Very early spring flowering shrubs, hellebores, crocus and heavenly scented Daphne 'Jacqueline Postill'. August: new and exciting plants, shrubs and bulbs abound, herbaceous border, and small interesting collection of Aroids

and Pinellias. Featured in Eastern Daily Press & North Norfolk News. Wheelchair access weather permitting.

12 THE CONIFERS

NR16 1AT. Sue Sayers & Barry Layton, 01508 489654, sue.sayers@yahoo.co.uk. *7m S of Norwich. 4m E Wymondham. From A11 follow signs to Mulbarton, 2nd R turn to Pennys Green, R at T-junction, R into Wymondham Road. From Norwich A140 - B1113, turn R at Bird in Hand PH, 2nd R into Wymondham Road. 300 yds on R.* Home-made teas. **Adm £3 (April) £3.50 (June) chd free.** Suns 3, 10 Apr (11-3); Sun 26 June (11-5). **Visitors also welcome by appt April to July.**
1¹/₂ -acre garden with 3 ponds and bog garden, herbaceous and shrub borders, rose pergolas and statuary. Informal area featuring many trees incl walnut, medlar,larch, birch and oak.In Spring blossom and massed planting of daffodils and narcissi.

13 CROFT HOUSE

111 Manor Road, Dersingham PE31 6YW. Walter & Jane Blaney. *8m NE of King's Lynn. Take A149 N from King's Lynn then B1440 into Dersingham. At T-lights turn R into Chapel Rd. In ¹/₂ m bear R into Manor Rd. Croft House opp church car park.*

Dale Farm

Visit a garden in your own time – look out for the ☎

Park in adjacent rds & church hall car park. Cream Teas at adjacent church hall. **Adm £4, chd free. Sun 1 May (1-5).**
In this 2¹/₂-acre garden, adjacent to Sandringham Estate, paths meander through shady woodland containing secluded gardens in clearings, each with its special character and hidden surprises. Lawns are punctuated by formal shrub and herbaceous beds. Ponds, water features, statuary, and many unusual plants make this a special and memorable garden. Plants for sale by Gold Medal winning nursery.

♿ ❀ ☕ ☎

🔢14 DALE FARM
Sandy Lane, Dereham NR19 2EA. Graham & Sally Watts, 01362 690065, grahamwatts@dsl.pipex.com. *16m W of Norwich. 12m E of Swaffam. Off A47 take B1146 signed to Fakenham, turn R at T-junction, ¹/₄ m turn L into Sandy Lane (before pelican crossing).* Home-made teas. **Adm £3.50, chd free. Sun 24 July (11-5).** Visitors also welcome by appt May to Aug in groups of 10+.
2 acre plant lover's garden with spring fed lake. Over 700 plant varieties featured in exuberantly planted borders and waterside gardens. Kitchen garden, orchard, naturalistic planting areas and wood sculptures. Garden completely redesigned in 2007. Gravel drive and some grass paths. Wide range of plants for sale.

❀ ☕ ☎

🔢15 DESERT WORLD GARDENS
Thetford Road (B1107), Santon Downham IP27 0TU. Mr & Mrs Barry Gayton, 01842 765861. *4m N of Thetford. On B1107 Brandon 2m.* Light refreshments & teas. **Adm £3.50, chd free. Suns 3 Apr; 3 July (10-5).** Visitors also welcome by appt.
1¹/₄ acres plantsman's garden, specialising in tropical and arid plants. Hardy succulents - sempervivums, hanging gardens of Babylon (plectranthus). Main garden - bamboos, herbaceous primula theatre, spring/summer bulbs, particularly lilies. Over 70 varieties of magnificent magnolias. View from roof garden. Radio Cambridge gardener. Glasshouses cacti/succulents 12500, viewing by appt only on a different day. Plant identifications. Will give any demos if asked. Country Wide Gardener's Question Road Show.

❀ ☕ ☎

🔢16 DUNBHEAGAN
Dereham Road, Westfield NR19 1QF. Jean & John Walton, 01362 696163, jandjwalton@btinternet.com. *2m S of Dereham. From Dereham take A1075 towards Shipdham. Turn L at Premier Food Store/Vauxhall garage (Westfield Rd). At staggered Xrds continue straight ahead down narrow lane. Garden 4th on L. Disabled parking in drive.* Home-made teas. **Adm £3.50, chd free. Sun 7 Aug (12.30-5.30).** Visitors also welcome by appt June to Aug.
NEW beds/planting for 2011. 1.4 acres of flower garden richly planted for year round interest Still providing masses of colour into late summer. Rare/unusual plants, ponds, rockery, island beds, exotic bed, 'Heaven and Hell', gravel beds, carnivorous bog. Paths/stepping stones invite you to walk through many beds. Shady corner. Beautiful music from Reepham ensemble (2-4pm). Featured in Norfolk Magazine. Dereham Times. Radio Norfolk. Gravel driveway. Access to 90% of garden.

♿ 🎲 ❀ ☕ ☎

Look out for the gardens with the ☎ – enjoy a private visit . . .

🔢17 THE DUTCH HOUSE
Ludham NR29 5NS. Mrs Peter Seymour, 01692 678225. *5m W of Wroxham. B1062 Wroxham to Ludham 7m. Turn R by Ludham village church into Staithe Rd. Garden ¹/₄ m from village.* Home-made teas. **Adm £3.50, chd free. Sun 12 June (2-5).** Visitors also welcome by appt June/July only, groups 10+.
Long, narrow garden of approx 2¹/₂ acres leading through marsh and wood to Womack Water. Designed and planted originally by the painter Edward Seago and recently replanted by the present owner. Access to Womack Water limited due to steep bridge and uneven paths. Further re-planting in hand. Uneven paths. Disabled access possible but not easy.

♿ ☕ ☎

🔢18 ◆ EAST RUSTON OLD VICARAGE
East Ruston NR12 9HN. Alan Gray & Graham Robeson, 01692 650432, www.eastrustonoldvicaragegardens.co.uk. *3m N of Stalham. Turn off A149 onto B1159 signed Bacton, Happisburgh. After 2m turn R 200yds N of East Ruston Church (ignore sign to East Ruston).* **Adm £7, chd £1. For NGS: Sats 16 Apr; 8 Oct (2-5.30).** For other opening times and information, please phone or see garden website.
20-acre exotic coastal garden incl traditional borders, exotic garden, desert wash, sunk garden, topiary, water features, walled and Mediterranean gardens. Many rare and unusual plants, stunning plant combinations, wild flower meadows, old-fashioned cornfield, vegetable and cutting gardens.

♿ ❀ ☕

EUSTON HALL
Thetford. See Suffolk.

🔢19 ◆ THE EXOTIC GARDEN
126 Thorpe Road, Thorpe, Norwich NR1 1UL. Mr Will Giles, 01603 623167, www.exoticgarden.com. *Off A47. New entrance & car park via side entrance of Alan Boswell Insurance 126 Thorpe Rd next to DEFRA. Approx ¹/₂ m from Thorpe railway stn.* **Adm £4.60, chd free. For NGS: Sun 31 July (1-5).** For other opening times and information, please phone or see garden website.
Exotic city garden covering approx 1 acre on a S-facing hillside incl ¹/₂-acre bamboo garden with the largest tree house in Norfolk. In high summer the garden is a riot of colour among towering architectural plants such as cannas, bananas, aroids, palms etc giving the garden a truly subtropical feel, especially with its use of houseplants as bedding. New xerophytic garden (desert garden). Open every Sun 19 June to 23 Oct 1-5.

❀ ☕

🔢20 ◆ FELBRIGG HALL
Felbrigg NR11 8PR. National Trust, 01263 837444, www.nationaltrust.org.uk. *2¹/₂ m SW of Cromer. S of A148; main entrance from B1436.* **Adm £4.30, chd £1.90. For NGS: Suns 26 June; 4 Sept (11-5).** For other opening times and information, please phone or see garden website.

Large pleasure gardens; mainly lawns and shrubs; orangery with camellias; large walled garden restored and restocked as fruit, vegetable, herb and flower garden; vine house; dovecote; dahlias; National Collection of *Colchicum*; wooded parks. 1 electric and 2 manual wheelchairs available.

♿

> Cottage style planting in profusion. Lawned paths flow around many new island beds . . .

21 NEW FURZE HOUSE

Harleston Road, Rushall, Diss IP21 4RT. **Philip & Christine Greenacre, 01379 852375, philip@furzehouse.com.** *2m W of Harleston. A140 to Dickleburgh Village, turn R at church, then 3m on L. A143 Harleston r'about to Diss. Turn R Upper Harman's Lane, turn L at T-junction, 1st house ½ m on R.* Light refreshments & home-made teas. **Adm £3.50, chd free. Sats, Suns 11, 12 June; 20, 21 Aug (10-6). Visitors also welcome by appt.**
2-acre plantsman's garden comprising herbaceous and shrub borders with cottage style planting in profusion. Lawned paths flow around many new island beds, incorporating established specimen trees, intensively planted with unusual shrubs, special perennials. Established, informal wildlife pond, large alpine scree area with water feature flowing through. 2 Haygrove polytunnels protecting tender and special specimens. Rose pergola, vegetable, fruit gardens.

♿ 🍺 ♨

22 THE GARDEN IN AN ORCHARD

Mill Road, Bergh Apton NR15 1BQ. **Mr & Mrs R W Boardman, 01508 480322.** *6m SE of Norwich. Off A146 at Hellington Corner signed to Bergh Apton. Down Mill Rd 300yds.* **Adm £3, chd free. Sat 10, Sun 11 Sept (11-5). Visitors also welcome by appt.**
3½ -acre garden created by the

owners set in old orchard. Many rare plants set out in an informal pattern of wandering paths. ½ acre of wild flower meadows, many bamboos, species roses and Michaelmas daisies. 9 species of eucalyptus. A plantsman's garden. Garden sculpture. Embroidery Exhibition.

♿ 🍺 ♨

23 GAYTON HALL

Gayton PE32 1PL. **The Earl & Countess of Romney, 01553 636259, ciciromney@tiscali.co.uk.** *6m E of King's Lynn. On B1145; R on B1153. R down Back St 1st entrance on L.* Home-made teas. **Adm £4, chd free. Sun 19 (1-5.30), Mon 20 June (2-5).** Visitors also welcome by appt.
20-acre water garden, with over 2 miles of paths. Lawns, woodland, lakes, streams and bridges. Many unusual trees and shrubs. Spring bulbs and autumn colour. Traditional and waterside borders. Primulas, astilbes, hostas, lysichitums, gunneras and magnificent rambling roses through trees and yews.

♿ 🍺 ♨

24 THE GRANGE

Heydon, Norwich NR11 6RH. **Mrs T Bulwer-Long.** *13m N of Norwich. 7m from Holt off B1149 signed Heydon 2m, on entering village, 1st drive on R, signed The Grange.* Home-made teas. **Adm £3.50, chd free. Sun 26 June (2-5).**
Set in the historic village of Heydon, 3 acre garden in a romantic setting. Rose and herbaceous borders surrounded by old walls with views to Parkland. Pond with fountain. Ancient yew topiary. A new walk of malus. Music, flower and plants stalls, sculpture. Featured on Radio Norfolk.

♿ ♨

25 HEGGATT HALL

Horstead NR12 7AY. **Mr & Mrs Richard Gurney.** *6m N of Norwich. Take B1150 North Walsham rd out of Norwich go for N 6m. R at small Xrds signed Heggatt Hall. Turn L at T-junction house 400yds on L.* Home-made teas. **Adm £3.50, chd free. Sun 19 June (2-5).**
Elizabethan house (not open) set in large gardens surrounded by parkland with ancient chestnut trees. Herbaceous border, sunken garden. Walled knot/rose garden leading into kitchen garden with wisteria walk and further flower beds.

♨

26 HIGH HOUSE GARDENS

Blackmoor Row, Shipdham, Thetford IP25 7PU. **Mr & Mrs F Nickerson.** *6m SW of Dereham. Take the airfield or Cranworth Rd off A1075 in Shipdham. Blackmoor Row is signed.* Home-made teas. **Adm £4, chd free. Suns, Weds 26, 29 June; 18, 21 Sept (2-5.30).**
Plantsman's garden with colour-themed herbaceous borders with extensive range of perennials. Box-edged rose and shrub borders. Woodland garden, pond and bog area. Newly planted orchard and vegetable garden. Wildlife area. Glasshouses.

♿ ♨ ♨

27 HILL COTTAGE

School Road, Edingthorpe NR28 9SY. **Shirley Gilbert, 01692 403519, shirley@flandershouse.demon.co.uk.** *3m NE of North Walsham. Off B1150 halfway between North Walsham and Bacton, leave main rd at Edingthorpe Green and continue straight towards Paston for ¾ m. Cottage on L at top of hill. Parking in adjacent field.* Light refreshments by arrangement. **Adm £3.50, chd free.** Visitors welcome by appt, incl small groups, no coaches.
Cottage garden, approx ¼ acre, surrounding former farm workers' cottages. Organically cultivated, never watered and densely planted with both traditional and unusual varieties of drought resistant climbers, shrubs, perennials and annuals. Fruit, vegetable and herb gardens, greenhouse and pond. A real butterfly and wildlife paradise. Small nursery. Member of Norfolk Cottage Garden Society. Photos may be taken with owner's permission. A Year in the Cottage Garden, a series of practical Garden Workshops see website for full details or phone Shirley Gilbert 01692403519 £45 inc lunch.

♿ ♨ ♨ ♨

28 NEW HILL FARM, GRESSENHALL

Hill Farm, Gressenhall, East Dereham NR19 2NR. **Mr and Mrs John Bullard, 01362 699186, john.bullard@identrust.com.** *2 m W of East Dereham. Rd4 to East Dereham. Exit Dereham on old A47, heading West, down past George Hotel. 2nd R into Rushmeadow Rd. 1m. Entrance to drive on R.* Light refreshments. **Adm £3.50, chd free.** Evening Opening Wed 22 June

(4-9). **Visitors also welcome by appt June & July, max 30 people.**
3 acres, set in mature parkland, includes water features, statues/ stones, lily pond, varied rose gardens, yew hedging, vegetable garden, lawns with floodlighting for mature trees. Areas of garden still under construction. Wheelchair access only to patio and paved areas but not good on gravel paths.

29 HINDRINGHAM HALL
Blacksmiths Lane, Hindringham NR21 0QA. Mr & Mrs Charles Tucker. *7m from Holt/Fakenham/Wells. Off A148 Thursford signed Hindringham. After village hall L into Holme Lane (after the church). Follow signs to parking.* Light refreshments & home-made teas at Hindringham Pavilion Wells Rd. **Adm £4, chd free. Sun 3 Apr (10-4).**
Tudor Manor House with complete 13thC. moat containing Victorian Nut Walk, formal beds and Wild Garden. Surrounding the Moat are thousands of Narcissi (32 varieties), a working Walled Vegetable Garden and Stream Garden ablaze with Hellibore and Primula. Plants at the gate. Featured in Country Life.

30 HOLME HALE HALL
Holme Hale IP25 7ED. Mr & Mrs Simon Broke, 01760 440328, simon.broke@hotmail.co.uk. *6m E of Swaffham, 8m W Dereham. Exit A47 King's Lynn/Norwich rd at Necton Garden Centre. Continue through Necton village and Holme Hale village approx 1½ m. At T-junction turn L, Hall gates on L immed after Low Common Rd.* Light refreshments & home-made teas. **Adm £4.50, chd free. Suns 29 May; 17 July; 11 Sept (11-5). Visitors also welcome by appt, individuals & groups.**
The garden is noted for its spring display of over 5000 tulips, historic wisteria plus mid and late summer flowering. Contemporary walled kitchen garden and front garden designed and planted in 2000 by Chelsea winner Arne Maynard. The garden incorporates large herbaceous borders, trained fruit, vegetables and traditional greenhouse.

31 NEW HORSTEAD HOUSE
Mill Road, Horstead, Norwich NR12 7AU. Mr & Mrs Matthew Fleming. *6m NE of Norwich. B1150 Norwich to North Walsham rd. Turn down Mill Road at mini r'about by Recruiting Sargeant PH. House at far end of Mill Rd by Mill Pond.* Home-made teas. **Adm £3.50, chd free. Sat 26 Feb (11-4).**
Millions of beautiful snowdrops carpet the woodland setting, which has also been recently planted with scented winter flowering shrubs. A stunning feature are the dogwoods growing on a small island in R Bure, which flows through the garden. Small walled garden. River Bure. Wheel chair access to main snowdrop area.

32 ◆ HOUGHTON HALL WALLED GARDEN
New Houghton, King's Lynn PE31 6UE. The Cholmondeley Gardens Trust, 01485 528569, www.houghtonhall.com. *11m W of Fakenham. 13m E of King's Lynn. Signed from A148.* **Adm £6, chd £2.50. For NGS: Sun 3 July (11.30-5.30). For other opening times and information please phone or visit garden website.**
Superbly laid-out award-winning 5-acre walled garden divided by clipped yew hedges into 'garden rooms', incl large mixed kitchen garden. Magnificently colourful 120m double herbaceous border. Rose parterre with over 120 varieties. Fountains, incl 'Waterflame' by Jeppe Hein, glasshouse, statues, rustic temple and croquet lawn. Plants on sale. Gravel and grass paths. Electric buggies available for use in the walled garden.

33 ◆ HOVETON HALL GARDENS
nr Wroxham NR12 8RJ. Mr & Mrs Andrew Buxton, 01603 782798, www.hovetonhallgardens.co.uk. *8m N of Norwich. 1m N of Wroxham Bridge. Off A1151 Stalham Rd - follow brown tourist signs.* **Adm £6.50, chd £3. For NGS: Thur 19 May; Sun 17 July (10.30-5). For other opening times and information, please phone or see garden website.**
15-acre gardens and grounds taking you through the seasons. Featuring daffodils, azaleas, rhododendrons and hydrangeas in woodland. Mature walled herbaceous garden, and redesigned walled kitchen garden. Tearooms open serving light lunches and afternoon tea. Plant sales also available. Newly opened rare restored C19 Iron Glasshouse. Children's nature trails available.

34 HOW HILL FARM
Ludham NR29 5PG. Mr P D S Boardman. *2m W of Ludham. On A1062; then follow signs to How Hill. Farm garden S of How Hill.* Home-made teas. **Adm £3, chd free. Sun 22 May (1-5).**
2 pretty gardens around house, 3rd

Salle Park

Follow us on Facebook and Twitter

started 1968 leading to 3-acre Broad dug 1978 with views over R Ant and Turf Fen Mill. About 12 acres incl Broad, 4 ponds, site of old Broad with 5ft Tussock sedges, about an acre of indigenous ferns under oak and alder. Paths through rare conifers, rhododendrons, azaleas, ornamental trees, shrubs, bamboos and herbaceous plants. Collection of holly species and varieties. Good vistas.

35 6 JARVIS DRIVE
Colkirk NR21 7NG. Geoff Clark & Jenny Filby, 01328 853153, geoffclark@btinternet.com. *2m S of Fakenham. From Fakenham take B1145 towards Dereham. Through Pudding Norton then 1st R (signed Byway to Colkirk). Follow lane into village, Jarvis Drive is opp The Crown PH. Drop-off & pick-up only in Jarvis Drive (narrow cul-de-sac). Please park in field opp or if wet, surrounding rds or The Crown PH (Sun lunch bookable).* Home-made teas. **Adm £3.50, chd free. Sun 17 July (1-5). Visitors also welcome by appt for groups.**
Secret paths and enticing viewpoints lead visitors through the many colour-packed mixed borders in this 0.4 acre organic garden. Over 300 varieties of shrubs and perennials, some rare, provide many ideas for planting schemes in both full sun and full shade. Large vegetable and fruit garden, white-stemmed birch grove, hosta display, sculptural features and spectacular driftwood plus some surprises! Full planting plans. Renowned for our cakes! Short gravel access drive.

36 LAKE HOUSE
Postwick Lane, Brundall NR13 5LU. Mrs Janet Muter, 01603 712933. *5m E of Norwich. On A47; take Brundall turn at r'about. Turn R into Postwick Lane at T-junction.* **Adm £4, chd free. Sun 27 Mar (2-5); Sun 1, Mon 2 May (11-5). Combined with 16 Witton Lane adm £5.50, 27 March. Visitors also welcome by appt Feb to Nov.**
In the centre of Brundall Gardens, a series of ponds descends through a wooded valley to the shore of a lake. Steep paths wind through a variety of shrubs and flowers in season, which attract every kind of wildlife. Light refreshments by arrangement.

37 LEXHAM HALL
nr Litcham PE32 2QJ. Mr & Mrs Neil Foster. *2m W of Litcham. 6m N of Swaffham off B1145.* Light refreshments & home-made teas. **Adm £4.50, chd free. Sun 13 Feb (11-4); Sun 22, Mon 23 May; Wed 21 Sept (11-5).**
Fine C17/C18 Hall (not open). Parkland with lake and river walks. Formal garden with terraces, yew hedges, roses and mixed borders. Traditional kitchen garden with crinkle crankle wall. Extensive collection of scented, winter flowering shrubs and woods, carpeted with snowdrops. 3-acre woodland garden with azaleas, rhododendrons, camellias, spring bulbs, and fine trees. A major new planting scheme commences in the walled garden autumn 2009. Dogs on leads welcome Feb only.

38 ◆ MANNINGTON HALL
nr Saxthorpe/Corpusty NR11 7BB. The Lord & Lady Walpole, 01263 584175, www.manningtongardens.co.uk. *18m NW of Norwich. 2m N of Saxthorpe via B1149 towards Holt. At Saxthorpe/Corpusty follow sign posts to Mannington.* **Adm £5, chd free, concessions £4. For NGS: Sun 3 Apr (12-5); Evening Opening Fri 10 June (6-9). For other opening times and information, please phone or see garden website.**
20 acres feature shrubs, lake, trees and roses. Heritage rose and period gardens. Borders. Sensory garden. Extensive countryside walks and trails. Moated manor house and Saxon church with C19 follies. Wild flowers and birds. Gravel paths, slopes, ask at entrance for special parking.

39 MANOR FARM HOUSE
Swannington NR9 5NR. Mr John Powles. *7m NW of Norwich. From Swannington Manor Drive or via Romantic Garden Nursery.* Teas. **Adm £4, chd free. Sun 3 July (12-5). Also opening with Swannington Manor 3rd July.**
Garden under re-development incl knot garden planted spring 06 with a Brian Turner fountain as centre piece, terrace built autumn 06 with large pots of agapanthus and lavender, and small rose garden planted spring 08. Access to the Romantic Garden Nursery, which ajoins the garden.

40 MANOR FARM, COSTON
Coston Lane, Coston, nr Barnham Broom NR9 4DT. Mr & Mrs J O Hambro. *10m W of Norwich. Off B1108 Watton Rd. Take B1135 to Dereham at Kimberley. After approx 300yds sharp L bend, go straight over down Coston Lane.* Light refreshments & home-made teas. **Adm £4, chd free. Sun 19 June (11-5).**
Approx 3 acre country garden, several small garden rooms with both formal and informal planting. Walled kitchen garden, white, grass and late summer gardens, roses, herbaceous and shrub borders. Wild flower areas with ponds. Many interesting plants. Local arts and crafts, plant sale,.

Secret paths and enticing viewpoints lead visitors through the many colour-packed mixed borders . . .

41 MANOR HOUSE FARM, WELLINGHAM
PE32 2TH. Robin & Elisabeth Ellis, www.manor-house-farm.co.uk. *7m from Fakenham. 8m from Swaffham. 1/2 m off A1065 N of Weasenham. Garden is beside the church.* Home-made teas. **Adm £4, chd free. Sun 26 June (2-5.30).**
Charming 4-acre garden surrounds an attractive farmhouse. Many interesting features. Formal quadrants with obelisks. 'Hot Spot' with grasses and gravel. Small arboretum with specimen trees, pleached lime walk, vegetable parterre and rose tunnel. Unusual 'Taj' garden with old-fashioned roses, tree peonies, lilies and pond. Small herd of Formosan Sika deer. Featured in Local press and on front cover of Yellow Book 2010.

42 4 MILL ROAD
Marlingford NR9 5HL. Mrs Jean Austen, 01603 880396, jeanausten101@btinternet.com. *6m W of Norwich. A47 to B1108 Watton Rd junction, 3rd on R. Bear R past mill & garden on R after village hall, (parking) before The Bell. From*

Easton, signed opp Des Amis. Home-made teas. **Adm £3, chd free. Sat 21, Sun 22 May; Sun 17, Tue 19 July (11-5).** Visitors also welcome by appt May to July, max 25 visitors.
This small peaceful 7yr-old garden has a modern interpretation of the classic garden, designed to draw your eye past the formality of the box-edged rooms and linking paths to the water meadows beyond. Colour-themed borders, Japanese garden, wisteria arch, pleached limes, fruit, vegetables and wildlife pond. Several new features for 2011. Plenty of places to sit and enjoy. Children's trail. Featured on BBC Radio Norfolk. Two shallow steps, handrail.

A plaque commemorates that this was the scene of the only major wartime incident to occur in North Creake . . .

43 **THE MOWLE**
Staithe Road, Ludham NR29 5NP. Mrs N N Green, 1692678213, ann@mowlegreen.fsnet.co.uk. *5m W of Wroxham. B1062 Wroxham to Ludham 7m. Turn R by Ludham village church into Staithe Rd. Garden ¹/₄ m from village.* Home-made teas. **Adm £4, chd free. Sun 15 May (1.30-5.30).** Visitors also welcome by appt.
Approx 2¹/₂ acres running down to marshes. The garden incl several varieties of catalpa. Japanese garden and enlarged wildlife pond with bog garden. A special border for gunnera as in Aug 2008 we were given full National Collection status. New boardwalk into wild area completed in 2009.

GROUP OPENING

44 **NEW** **NORTH CREAKE GARDENS**
Fakenham NR21 9LG. *2m S of Burnham Market & 5m NW of Fakenham on B1355. From Fakenham A148 W then 1st R on*

B1355, Creake House 1st drive on R in Wells Rd & The Old Bakehouse garden is 1st drive on L. The Red House 200yds N past the church. Home-made teas at Creake House. **Combined adm £5, chd free. Sun 12 June (12-5).**

NEW **CREAKE HOUSE**
Wells Road, North Creake. Mr & Mrs J Powell

NEW **THE OLD BAKEHOUSE**
4 Burnham Road, entry from Wells Road. Mr & Mrs Richard Faire

NEW **THE RED HOUSE**
Church Street. Dr & Mrs J Stabler

Three very diverse gardens Creake House is a 2-acre, part walled garden with yr round interest, low maintenance in mind. It has a range of shrubs, roses and trees with some herbaceous plants and an informal pond, The Old Bakehouse a small informal garden with mixed planting, on the bank of R Burn, designed by owners to accommodate inherited garden ornaments. A plaque on the gate commemorates that this garden was the scene of the only major wartime incident to occur in North Creake. The Red House garden was created over 25 years by the present owners. Thickly planted with the aim of looking good throughout the year. Many unusual and doubtfully hardy plants, with a stream, shell garden and area specifically planted to attract butterflies. Plants for sale at The Red House.

45 **THE OLD COTTAGE**
Colby Corner, nr Aylsham NR11 7EB. Stuart Clarke, 01263-734574, enchanting@talktalk.net, www.enchantinggardens.co.uk. *14m N of Norwich. Take B1145 from Aylsham to N Walsham. After 3¹/₂ m turn L opp Banningham Bridge Inn Garage onto Bridge Rd. Pass Colby school on R & continue straight, following Colby Corner sign. Garden on the L, parking by the poly tunnel.* Tea. **Adm £5, chd free.** Visitors welcome by appt. Hopefully by 'appointment only' will encourage keen gardeners to see The Old Cottage.
A 2 acre garden set in a beautiful and peaceful location. Extended in two phases over the last ten years to contain a range of mini gardens relevant to smaller plots. Containing a

wide range of plant types covering all the seasons.In 2010 40% of the herbacious border will have been replanted so the garden in 2011 will open by appointment only. No plants for sale but spares are given free and cuttings are encouraged.

46 **THE OLD RECTORY, RIDLINGTON**
Ridlington, Nr North Walsham NR28 9NZ. Peter & Fiona Black. *4m E of North Walsham 4m N of Stalham. Take B1149 Stalham to Bacton Rd, turn left at By Way to Foxhill sign continue to Xrds turn R past farm continue for ¹/₂ m house on R.* Home-made teas. **Combined with West View adm £5, chd free. Sun 22 May (12-5).**
A tranquil 2 acre garden around a former rectory. Established trees and some topiary. Mixed borders of shrubs, perennials, roses and bulbs, raised vegetable beds. A peaceful spot for a cup of tea! Grass paths may be difficult if wet.

47 **THE OLD RECTORY, BRANDON PARVA**
Stone Lane, Brandon Parva NR9 4DL. Mr & Mrs S Guest, 01362 858317, guest63@btinternet.com. *9m W of Norwich. Leave Norwich on B1108 towards Watton, turn R at sign for Barnham Broom. L at T-junction, stay on rd approx 3m until L next turn to Yaxham.L at Xrds.* Home-made teas. **Adm £4, chd free. Sun 26 June (11-4).** Visitors also welcome by appt June & July.
4-acre, mature garden with over 70 types of trees, more than 60 types of shrubs and a variety of perennials displayed in different settings - a walled garden, large formal lawns and borders, small flower and shrub gardens, shady walkways under covered pergolas, woodland and pond garden. Featured on Radio Norfolk 'Treasure Quest'.

48 **OULTON HALL**
Oulton, Aylsham NR11 6NU. Clare & Bolton Agnew. *4m W of Aylsham. From Aylsham take B1354. After 4m Turn L for Oulton Chapel, Hall ¹/₂ m on R. From B1149 (Norwich/Holt rd) take B1354, next R, Hall ¹/₂ m on R.* Light refreshments & home-made teas. **Adm £5, chd free. Sun 29 May (11-5).**

C18 manor house (not open) and clocktower set in 6-acre garden with lake and woodland walks. Chelsea designer's own garden - herbaceous, Italian, bog, water, wild, verdant, sunken and parterre gardens all flowing from one tempting vista to another. Developed over 15yrs with emphasis on structure, height and texture, with a lot of recent replanting in the contemporary manner.

49 ♦ OXBURGH HALL
Oxborough PE33 9PS. National Trust, 01366 328258, www.nationaltrust.org.uk. *7m SW of Swaffham. At Oxborough on Stoke Ferry rd.* **For NGS: Suns 19 June; Sun 17 July (11-5). For other opening times and information please phone or visit garden website.**
Hall and moat surrounded by lawns, fine trees, colourful borders; charming parterre garden of French design. Orchard and vegetable garden. Woodland walks. A garden steward is on duty on open days to lead 4 free tours throughout the day. Events for next year not decided, I will notify by end Sept. Gravel paths, steep slopes by the side of the moat.

50 RIVERMOUNT
Hall Lane, Knapton NR28 9SW. Mrs E Purdy. *2m NE North Walsham. B1150 through North Walsham towards Bacton. Follow signs for Pigney's Wood. 2nd turning on L after Blue Bell PH & pond. Ample parking.* Home-made teas. **Adm £3, chd free. Sun 5 June (2-5).**
Traditional style garden. Brick terrace to woodland garden. Herbaceous borders enclosed by climbing rose trellis. Paved kitchen garden with herbs and old-fashioned roses. Wild flower and woodland walk with some bluebells. Art Exhibition.

51 SALLE PARK
Salle, Norwich NR10 4SF. Sir John White, www.salleestategardens.com. *1m N of Reepham. Off B1145, between Cawston & Reepham.* Home-made teas. **Adm £4, chd free. Sun 10 July (12-5).**
Very varied estate gardens consisting of delightful, fully productive Victorian kitchen garden with original vine houses, double herbaceous borders, display glasshouse, ice house,

Sharane

orchard and wild flowers. Formal Georgian pleasure gardens with yew topiary, rose gardens, all-yr round interest shrubs beds, lawns, specimen trees and exotically planted orangery.

52 ♦ SALLOWFIELD COTTAGE
Wattlefield Road, Wymondham NR18 9NX. Caroline Musker, 01953 605086, caroline.musker@tesco.net, www.sallowfieldcottage.co.uk. *2m S of Wymondham. Leave A11 signed Wymondham & Spooner Row. Turn R for Spooner Row, into village straight over Xrds at Boars PH. At T-junction take L, after 1½ m, grey barrels on L. Disabled parking near the house.* **Adm £3.50, chd free. Sun 8 May (11-5). Visitors also welcome by appt.**
1-acre garden with large pond, lots of clematis, old roses, herbaceous plants and wooded area. Views toward Wymondham Abbey across what used to be Wymondham deer park. Tulips, daffodils and other spring flowering woodland plants.

53 ♦ SANDRINGHAM GARDENS
Sandringham PE35 6EN. Her Majesty The Queen, 01553 612908/772675, www.sandringhamestate.co.uk. *6m NW of King's Lynn. By gracious permission, the House, Museum & Gardens at Sandringham will be open.* **Adm £7.50, chd £4, concessions £6.50. For opening times and information, please phone or see garden website.**
60 acres of formal gardens, woodland and lakes, with rare plants and trees. Donations are given from the Estate to various charities. Gravel paths, long distances - please tel or visit garden website for details.

54 ♦ SEVERALS GRANGE
Holt Road, Wood Norton NR20 5BL. Jane Lister, www.hoecroft.co.uk. *8m S of Holt, 6m E of Fakenham. 2m N of Guist on LH-side of B1110. Guist is situated 5m SE of Fakenham on A1067 Norwich rd.* **Adm £3, chd free. For NGS: Sun 7 Aug (2-5). For other opening times and information please visit website.**
The gardens surrounding Severals Grange and the adjoining nursery Hoecroft Plants are a perfect example of how colour, shape and form can be created by the use of foliage plants, from large shrubs to small alpines. Movement and lightness is achieved by interspersing these plants with a wide range of ornamental grasses, which are at their best in late summer.

Visit the website for latest information

55 SHARANE

Lynn Road, West Rudham PE31 8RW. Eileen & Michael Barratt. *6¹/₂ m W of Fakenham. 16m E of Kings Lynn. From Kings Lynn take A148 to Fakenham. At West Rudham village take 1st R Lynn Fields for parking. From Fakenham take A148 to Kings Lynn. Continue past West Rudham village green, past garden take 1st L for parking. All parking in Lynn Fields past 30mph sign, LH-side only. Garden directions from parking area.* Home-made teas. **Adm £3, chd free. Sun 24 July (11-5).**

¹/₃ acre plantsman's garden, created over several years by enthusiastic owners. Densely planted colourful borders of perennials, hostas, ferns, roses, iris, some exotic plants and grasses, with a collection of over 150 dazzling day lilies. Other features of interest, small pond with wildlife, raised vegetable beds, greenhouses and fruiting bushes and trees.

🌂 ⊛ ☕

56 ◆ SHERINGHAM PARK

Upper Sheringham NR26 8TL. National Trust, 01263 820550, www.nationaltrust.org.uk/ sheringham. *2m SW of Sheringham. Access for cars off A148 Cromer to Holt Rd, 5m W of Cromer, 6m E of Holt, signs in Sheringham town.* **Adm £4.50, chd free. For NGS: Suns 22 May; 5 June (8-8). For other opening times and information, please phone or see garden website.**

50 acres of species rhododendron, azalea and magnolia. Also numerous specimen trees incl handkerchief tree. Viewing towers, waymarked walks, sea and parkland views. Special walkway and WCs for disabled. Park open dawn to dusk all year.

♿ 🌂 ⊛ ☕

57 SPINNEY LODGE

Winch Road, Gayton, King's Lynn PE32 1QP. Mr & Mrs Peter Grant, 01553 636165, peterjgrant@tesco.net. *6m E of King's Lynn on B1145. R at Winch Rd, 200yds on R past Back St junction. Blue badge parking only, all others at Bardie House, Winch Rd as signed.* Home-made teas. **Adm £3.50, chd free. Sun 17 Apr (11-4.30). Visitors also welcome by appt limited to March to May.**

Approx 2-acre smallholding transformed by owners in past 11 yrs into landscaped gardens with existing unusual trees and shrubs. Bounded with stream and divided into formal and informal areas with shrubbery, boardwalk with large wildlife pond, naturalistic woodland walk and a Victorian raised bed vegetable garden featured in gardening magazine 2010. Essentially a Spring Garden with snowdrops, bluebells, wood aneomes and flowering shrubs. Featured in 'Grow It' magazine February 2010.

♿ ⊛ ☕ ☎

A collection of over 150 dazzling day lilies . . .

58 ◆ STODY LODGE

Melton Constable NR24 2ER. Mrs AJ MacNicol, 01263 860572, www.stodyestate.co.uk. *16m NW of Norwich, 3m S of Holt. Off B1354. Signed from Melton Constable on Holt Rd.* **Adm £4.50, chd under 12 free. For opening times and information please phone or see garden website. Donations to NGS.**

Spectacular gardens having one of the largest concentrations of rhododendrons and azaleas in East Anglia. Created in the 1920's, the gardens also feature many ornamental trees, shrubs, late daffodils, tulips and bluebells. Expansive lawns and magnificent yew hedges. Lovely walks to woodland Japanese Water Gardens. Picnic area, delicious home-made teas and plant stall, parking. Gravel paths to water gardens, some uneven ground. Open Suns in May, BH Mon 30 May.

♿ 🌂 ⊛ ☕

59 SUMMER COTTAGE

High Common, Swardeston NR14 8DL. Richard & Deidre Cave. *4m S of Norwich. Take B1113 out of Norwich, turn R at Swardeston Village sign, down Short Lane, then L round bend on unmade rd to High Common. Park on edge of cricket pitch or by village hall.* Home-made teas. **Adm £3, chd free. Sun 12 June (11-5).**

A 'Tardis' created from an old apple orchard in 2000, behind a pink cottage. 5 small gardens in ¹/₃ -acre linked by brick, grass and gravel paths, featuring wild flowers with pond and summerhouse. Formal English borders, intimate sundial retreat, ornamental kitchen garden and walled area with bamboos. Possible cricket match on High Common.

🌂 ☕

60 SUNDOWN

Hall Lane, Roydon, Diss IP22 5XL. Liz Bloom, 01379 642074, liza.bloom@virgin.net. *2m W of Diss. From Diss take A1066 Thetford Rd, after Roydon White Hart PH, turn R into Hall Lane. From Thetford on A1066, approx 1m after Blooms of Bressingham, turn L into Hall lane.* Home-made teas. **Adm £3, chd free. Sun 5 June (11-5). Visitors also welcome by appt for groups 20+.**

1-acre plantsman's garden established over 40yrs ago. Densely planted with wide variety of unusual perennials, shrubs and trees for colour and foliage yr-round. Woodland walk with rhododendrons and other woodland favourites. Recently developed areas incl ornamental kitchen garden and terrace area with water features.

♿ 🌂 ⊛ ☕ ☎

61 SWANNINGTON MANOR

Norwich NR9 5NR. Caroline & David Prior. *7m NW of Norwich. Almost ¹/₂ way between A1067 (to Fakenham) & B1149 (to Holt). In village look for black wrought iron gates opp post box in church wall.* Home-made teas. **Adm £4, chd free. Sun 3 July (12-5). Also open Manor Farm House.**

The C17 manor house (not open) creates a stunning backdrop to this romantic garden which is framed by extensive 300yr old hedges, thought to be unique in this country. Mixed shrub and herbaceous borders, water garden, sunken rose and knot gardens, specimen trees and sloping lawns combine to make this garden both delightful and unusual.

♿ 🌂 ☕

62 NEW ◆ THE URBAN JUNGLE GARDENS

Ringland Lane, Old Costessey NR8 5BG. Urban Jungle, 01603 744997, www.urbanjungle.uk.com. *5m W of Norwich. From Norwich: on A1074 Dereham Rd. After 3m turn R at Longwater Rd, at T-junction turn L into West End for 1m, turn R into Ringland Lane. Garden 200yds on R. From A1067 Fakenham Rd: turn L*

into Sandy Lane, then on to Towerham Lane and down to T-junction, turn R into Ringland Lane. Garden 200yds on R. **Adm £3, chd free. For NGS: Sun 18 Sept (10-4). For other opening times and information please phone or visit garden website.**
Rare collector's species with the best of traditional plants, displayed in garden compositions that demonstrate a wide range of styles and climate zones. Vertical gardens. New 'Edible Jungle', a flamboyant garden combining exotic flowers, fruits and vegetables.

63 WARBOROUGH HOUSE
Wells Road, Stiffkey NR23 1QH. **Mr & Mrs J Morgan.** *13m N of Fakenham, 4m E of Wells Next The Sea. On A149 in centre of Stiffkey Village, opp Post Office and Stores. Coasthopper bus stop outside garden. Follow signs at garden entrance for parking. No parking on main rd. Very narrow and will cause congestion.* Home-made teas. **Adm £3.50, chd free. Sun 29 May (1-6).**
7 acre garden on a steep chalk slope, surrounding C19 house (not open) with views across the Stiffkey valley and to the coast. Woodland walks, formal terraces, shrub borders, lawns and walled garden create a garden of contrasts. Garden is on a slope which is steep in parts. Paths are gravel, bark chip or grass and may be uneven.

64 WEST LODGE
Aylsham NR11 6HB. **Mr & Mrs Jonathan Hirst.** *1/4 m NW of Aylsham. Off B1354 Blickling Rd out of Aylsham, turn R down Rawlinsons Lane, garden on L.* Home-made teas. **Adm £3.50, chd free. Sun 17 July (12-5).**

9-acre garden with lawns, splendid mature trees, rose garden, well-stocked herbaceous borders, ornamental pond, magnificent C19 walled kitchen garden (maintained as such). Georgian house (not open) and outbuildings incl a well-stocked tool shed (open) and greenhouses.

65 NEW WEST VIEW
Youngmans Lane, East Ruston, nr Stalham NR12 9JN. **Chris & Bev Hewitt,** 01692 650514. *3 m N of Stalham. Take B1149 Stalham to Bacton Rd turn R after East Ruston Church, continue 3/4 m turn R by Butchers Arms PH (Oak Lane), turn R into Youngmans Lane, 1st house on L.* **Combined with The Old Rectory, Ridlington adm £5, chd free. Sun 22 May (12-5).** Visitors also welcome by appt April - July. No Coaches.
1 acre plantsmans garden incl borders with trees and shrubs underplanted with carpets of hellebores and bulbs, pergolas with roses and clematis, greenhouse with many interesting plants, a summer border with mixed perennials, vegetable parterre, tropical border, orchard and pond. Gravel Paths.

WHITE HOUSE FARM
See Suffolk.

Trees and shrubs underplanted with carpets of hellebores and bulbs . . .

66 16 WITTON LANE
Little Plumstead NR13 5DL. **Sally Ward & Richard Hobbs.** *5m E of Norwich. From B1140 Norwich to Acle rd after railway xing, turn R at 2nd Xrds, signed Little Plumstead next to Brick Kilns PH. Take 2nd L into School Lane, then 2nd R into Witton Lane. From A47 Norwich to Yarmouth rd take L signed Witton Green & Great Plumstead just pass pylons. Then 1st R into Witton Lane keep going for 1 1/2 m, garden on L.* Home-made teas. **Adm £2.50, chd free; Combined with Lake House adm £5.50. Sun 27 Mar (11-4).**
An 'Aladdin's Cave' for the alpine and woodland plant enthusiast. Tiny garden with wide range of rare and unusual plants will be of great interest with its species tulips, daffodils, scillas, dog violets, many more bulbous plants and an abundance of trilliums and wood anemones. A garden indeed for the plant specialist. National Collection of Muscari. Featured in Norfolk & Suffolk Life Magazine & on BBC Radio Norfolk.

67 WRETHAM LODGE
East Wretham IP24 1RL. **Mr Gordon Alexander.** *6m NE of Thetford. A11 E from Thetford, L up A1075, L by village sign, R at Xrds then bear L.* Teas in Church. **Adm £3.50, chd free. Sun 24, Mon 25 Apr (12-5).**
In spring masses of species tulips, hellebores, fritillaries, daffodils and narcissi; bluebell walk. In June hundreds of old roses. Walled garden, with fruit and interesting vegetable plots. Mixed borders and fine old trees. Double herbaceous borders. Wild flower meadows.

Norfolk County Volunteers

County Organisers
Fiona Black, The Old Rectory, Ridlington, North Walsham NR28 9NZ, 01692 650247, blacks7@email.com
Anthea Foster, Lexham Hall, King's Lynn PE32 2QJ, 01328 701341, antheafoster@lexhamestate.co.uk

County Treasurer
Neil Foster, Lexham Hall, King's Lynn PE32 2QJ, 01328 701288, neilfoster@lexhamestate.co.uk

Publicity
Graham Watts, Dale Farm, Sandy Lane, Dereham NR19 2EA, 01362 690065, grahamwatts@dsl.pipex.com

Assistant County Organisers
Panda Allhusen, Bradenham Hall, Bradenham, Thetford IP25 7QP, 01362 687243/687279, panda@bradenhamhall.co.uk
Jenny Dyer, Orchard Barn, 4 Lacey's Farm, Long Lane, Colby, NR11 7EF, 01263 761811, jandrdyer@btinternet.com
Stephanie Powell, Creake House, Wells Road, North Creake, Fakenham NR21 9LG, 01328 730113, stephaniepowell@creake.com
Jan Saunt, Plovers Hill, Buckenham Road, Strumpshaw NR13 4NL, 01603 714587, jamessaunt@hotmail.com

NORTHAMPTONSHIRE

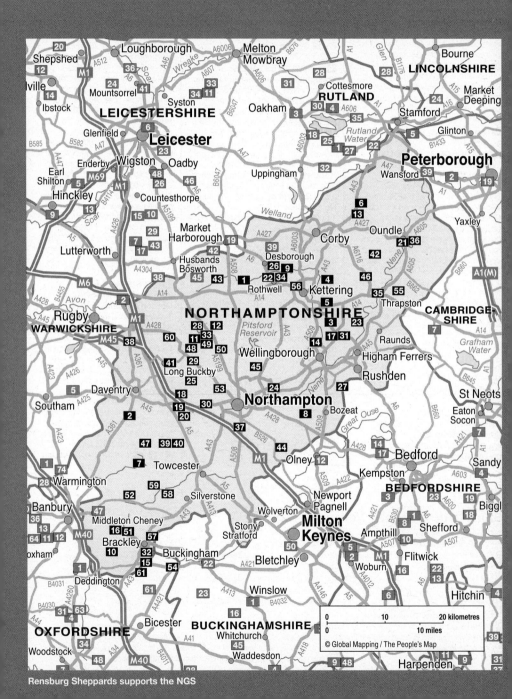

Opening Dates

February

Sunday 20
3 Beech House

Sunday 27
4 Boughton House
14 Dolphins
49 Rosemount

March

Sunday 6
3 Beech House
27 Greywalls

Sunday 13
46 The Old Rectory, Sudborough

April

Sunday 17
5 Briarwood
12 Cottesbrooke Hall Gardens
20 Flore Spring Gardens
40 Litchborough Spring Gardens

Saturday 23
43 The Maltings

Sunday 24
43 The Maltings

Monday 25
23 Great Addington Manor
43 The Maltings

May

Sunday 1
15 Evenley Wood Garden
25 Great Brington Gardens

Monday 2
15 Evenley Wood Garden

Tuesday 3
11 Coton Manor Garden

Sunday 8
35 Islip Gardens
50 Spratton Gardens

Saturday 14
28 Guilsborough Spring Gardens

Sunday 15
26 Greenway
28 Guilsborough Spring Gardens

Sunday 22
36 Jericho
51 Steane Park

Wednesday 25
13 Deene Park

Thursday 26
26 Greenway (Evening)

Sunday 29
10 Charlton Gardens
54 Tile House Farm
57 Turweston Gardens

Monday 30
21 Foxtail Lilly
54 Tile House Farm
55 Titchmarsh House

June

Sunday 5
17 Finedon Gardens
24 Great Billing Village
34 Hostellarie
37 Karell House
39 Litchborough Gardens
42 Lyveden New Bield
47 Preston Capes Gardens

Thursday 9
31 67-69 High Street

Saturday 11
55 Titchmarsh House

Sunday 12
2 Badby and Newnham Gardens
16 Farthinghoe Gardens
30 Harpole Gardens
38 Kilsby Gardens
56 Top Lodge
58 Wappenham Gardens

Thursday 16
31 67-69 High Street (Evening)

Friday 17
43 The Maltings (Evening)

Saturday 18
7 Canons Ashby House
19 Flore Gardens
43 The Maltings

Sunday 19
9 Cedar Farm
19 Flore Gardens
41 Long Buckby Gardens
43 The Maltings
46 The Old Rectory, Sudborough
52 Sulgrave Gardens
59 Weedon Lois & Weston Gardens

Thursday 23
31 67-69 High Street (Evening)

Saturday 25
60 West Haddon Gardens (Evening)

Sunday 26
17 Finedon Gardens
18 Flore Fields
44 The Menagerie
60 West Haddon Gardens

July

Sunday 3
1 Arthingworth Open Gardens
6 Bulwick Gardens
34 Hostellarie
45 Moulton (west)

Sunday 10
8 Castle Ashby Gardens
48 Ravensthorpe Gardens

Friday 29
43 The Maltings (Evening)

Saturday 30
43 The Maltings

Sunday 31
22 Froggery Cottage
43 The Maltings

August

Sunday 14
33 Hollowell Gardens

Sunday 21
37 Karell House

September

Sunday 4
7 Canons Ashby House

Saturday 10
29 Haddonstone Show Gardens

Sunday 11
29 Haddonstone Show Gardens
54 Tile House Farm

October

Sunday 30
4 Boughton House

February 2012

Sunday 26
36 Jericho

Gardens open to the public

4 Boughton House
7 Canons Ashby House
8 Castle Ashby Gardens
11 Coton Manor Garden
12 Cottesbrooke Hall Gardens
13 Deene Park
15 Evenley Wood Garden
29 Haddonstone Show Gardens
42 Lyveden New Bield
44 The Menagerie
46 The Old Rectory, Sudborough
51 Steane Park

Look out for the gardens with the ☎ – enjoy a private visit . . .

By appointment only

32 Hill Grounds
53 Thimble Hall
61 Woodchippings

Also open by Appointment ☎

3 Beech House
9 Cedar Farm
28 Dripwell House, Guilsborough Spring Gardens
21 Foxtail Lilly
26 Greenway
27 Greywalls
31 67-69 High Street
33 Ivy Cottage, Hollowell Gardens
36 Jericho
60 Lime House, West Haddon Gardens (Evening)
43 The Maltings
41 Mill House, Long Buckby Gardens
19 The Old Bakery, Flore Gardens
20 The Old Bakery, Flore Spring Gardens
59 Old Barn, Weedon Lois & Weston Gardens
48 Ravensthorpe Nursery, Ravensthorpe Gardens
49 Rosemount
55 Titchmarsh House
56 Top Lodge
99 Townley Barn, West Haddon Gardens (Evening)

The Gardens

GROUP OPENING

1 **NEW** **ARTHINGWORTH OPEN GARDENS**
Arthingworth, nr Market Harborough LE16 8LA. *6m S of Market Harborough. From Market Harborough via A508 after 4m take L to Arthingworth. From Northampton, A508 turn R just after Kelmarsh.* Home-made teas & light refreshments. **Combined adm £5, chd free. Sun 3 July (2-6).**

NEW **2 AGRICULTURAL COTTAGES**
Mr & Mrs A Knott

NEW **BOSWORTH HOUSE**
Mr & Mrs Irving-Swift

NEW **THE GATE HOUSE**
Mr & Mrs J Maybank

NEW **THE LAURELS**
Mr & Mrs D Newton

NEW **ORCHARD HOUSE**
Mr & Mrs Mike Osgood

NEW **11 OXENDON ROAD**
Nr & Mrs B Cunningham

NEW **THE WILLOWS**
Mr & Mrs J Nikel

Arthingworth is a small village off the beaten track. It has a C12 church, village hall, manor, PH and nearly 225 villagers, 14 of which are welcoming you into their gardens. Many others will help on the day with the cakes, cream teas, coffee and parking. The 7 open gardens are very different, from classical to post modernist, from sweeping views to hidden corners, from walled to open windswept, from 2 acres plus to less than a ¼, from established to new and from being tended by weathered gardeners to the new generation. You will see herbaceous borders, potager, rose pergolas with clematis, orchard, little spinney, hens, chickens, geese, koi carp, even a swimming pool with a glass wall. Wheelchair access not available at all gardens.

♿ ❀ ☕

AVON DASSETT GARDENS
See Warwickshire.

AVON HOUSE
See Leicestershire & Rutland.

GROUP OPENING

2 **BADBY AND NEWNHAM GARDENS**
Daventry NN11 3AR. *3m S of Daventry. E side of A361. Maps provided for visitors.* Home-made teas at At Badby and Newnham Churches. **Combined adm £4, chd free. Sun 12 June (2-6).**

NEW **THE BANKS**
Daventry Road, Newham.
Sue Styles & Geoff Chester
www.suestyles.co.uk

HILLTOP
Church Street, Newham.
David & Mercy Messenger

THE LILACS
School Lane, Badby.
Matthew and Ruth Moser

SHAKESPEARES COTTAGE
Church Hill, Badby. Sarah & Jocelyn Hartland-Swann

NEW **SOUTHVIEW COTTAGE**
Bunkers Hill, Badby.
Mr & Mrs Alan & Karen Brown

TRIFIDIA
Church Hill, Badby
Colin & Shirley Cripps

Six gardens in two small villages with attractive old houses of golden-coloured Hornton stone set around their Village greens. In Badby, three such houses, one opening for the first time, show differing styles of cottage gardens. A wisteria-clad thatched cottage with modern sculptures, a terraced garden with vegetables and orchard and a newly developed garden with views over the Village. The fourth garden with pond, conservatory, glasshouses and vegetables has unusual plants and aims for year-round interest. In Newnham, there is a 3-acre organic garden around a picturesque C17 thatched cottage with lawns, densely planted borders, vegetable and cutting garden and paddocks with feature trees and, also opening for the first time, the garden of a garden designer with pools, herbaceous borders, vegetables and herbs developed as rooms among mature trees. Nearby Badby Wood is renowned for its spectacular bluebells, and has many Saxon footpaths favoured by walkers.

🐕 ☕

3 **BEECH HOUSE**
73 Church Street, Burton Latimer NN15 5LU. Mr & Mrs Nicholas Loake, 01536 723593, gloake@mac.com. *4m S of Kettering. From High St turn into Church St by War Memorial, Beech House on L 100yds past church.* Home-made teas. **Adm £3, chd free. Sun 20 Feb; Sun 6 Mar (10-4). Visitors also welcome by appt, minimum group 8.** Semi-formal garden with winter/spring interest. Clipped box and yew hedging frame borders containing over 150 cultivars of snowdrops plus hellebores etc.

♿ ☕ ☎

Why not visit a group garden opening and really make a day of it . . .

BENTS FARMHOUSE
See Leicestershire & Rutland.

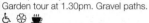 **NEW ◆ BOUGHTON HOUSE**
Geddington, Kettering NN14 1BJ.
Duke of Buccleuch & Queensberry.
3m E of Kettering. From A14, 2m along A43 Kettering to Stamford, turn R in to Geddington, House entrance 1¹/₂ m on R. Home-made teas. **Adm £4.50 (£2.50 to NGS), chd free. Suns 27 Feb; 30 Oct (11-3).**
Boughton gardens incl a striking historic walled garden incl a beautiful herbaceous border, sensory and wildlife garden. The Rose Garden provides views of the village like proportions of the house and visitors can explore the gardens of Sir David Scott, presently under restoration. Garden tour at 1.30pm. Gravel paths.
♿ ✿ ☕

5 NEW BRIARWOOD
4 Poplars Farm Road, Barton Seagrave, Kettering NN15 5AF.
Elaine Christian & William Portch.
1¹/₂ m SE of Kettering town centre. J10 off A14 - turn onto Barton rd towards Wicksteed Park. R into Warkton Lane, after 200m R into Poplars Farm Road. Home-made teas. **Adm £2.50, chd free. Sun 17 Apr (10-3).**
A garden in two parts with quirky original sculptures and many faces: firstly, a S-facing lawn and borders with spring bulbs and blossom trees, mature hedging, palms, climbers, fish and lily pond, patio with potted bulbs; secondly, a secret garden with summerhouse, small orchard, raised bed potager, greenhouse and water feature. Children's creative activities, craft & plant sales. Unfenced pond.
♿ ✿ ☕

GROUP OPENING

6 BULWICK GARDENS
Bulwick NN17 3DZ. *10m SW of Stamford. ¹/₂ m off A43.* Home-made teas Bulwick Hall. **Adm £3, chd free. Sun 3 July (2-5).**

BULWICK HALL
Mr & Mrs G T G Conant

19 CHURCH LANE
David Haines

THE SHAMBLES
12 Main Street. Roger Glithero

Unspoilt Northamptonshire stone

Coton Manor Garden

conservation village. Interesting C14 church and PH. Bulwick Hall is a formal terraced 8-acre walled garden leading to river and island,50 metre double herbaceous borders, topiary, walled kitchengarden. C17 wrought iron gates, C19 orangery and C17 arcade.Peacocks and rare breed hens. 19 Church Lane is a small cottage garden with courtyard and water feature.The Shambles has an original village well, lawns, hedges and stone walls. MS Stall. Dave the Fuchsia Man Plant Stall.
♿ ✿ ☕

7 ◆ CANONS ASHBY HOUSE
Daventry NN11 3SD. National Trust, 01327 860044, www.nationaltrust.org.uk. *12m NE of Banbury, 9m S of Daventry. On unclassified rd between B4525 and A5. Follow NT signs.* **Adm £2, chd free. For NGS: Sat 18 June; Sun 4 Sept (11-5). For other opening times and information, please**

phone or see garden website.
Home of the Dryden family since C16. C18 London and Wise style garden enclosed by walls with fine topiary, paths and terraces. Garden restoration project in progress including fernery, reinstated beds and borders to the 1880 designs of Sir Henry Dryden. National Trust shop selling locally grown plants and other garden items. Garden Tearoom. Portable ramp to access garden, gravel paths,.
♿ ✿ ☕ ☎

8 ◆ CASTLE ASHBY GARDENS
Northampton NN7 1LQ.
Earl Compton,
www.castleashbygardens.co.uk.
6m E of Northampton. 1¹/₂ m N of A428; turn off between Denton & Yardley Hastings. **Adm £5, chd £4.50. For NGS: Sun 10 July (10-5.30). For other opening times and information, please see garden website.**

Be tempted by a plant from a plant stall ✿

25 acres within a 10,000 acre estate of both formal and informal gardens, incl Italian gardens with orangery and arboretum with lakes, all dating back to the 1860s.

9 CEDAR FARM
Copelands Road, Desborough NN14 2QD. Mr & Mrs R Tuffen, 01536 763992, thetuffenfamily@aol.com. *6m N of Kettering, 5m S of Market Harborough, from A6. Signed from centre of Desborough on NGS open day only. Home-made teas.* **Adm £3.50, chd free. Sun 19 June (1-6). Visitors also welcome by appt.** 3-acre garden plus 7 acre beautiful walks through an arboretum containing many unusual trees leading to wildlife ponds,new avenue of quercus coccinea, vegetable garden,a mature avenue of lime trees, garden underplanted with spring bulbs, great autumn colour. Main garden large colour planted borders, Secret Garden with roses and clematis and a large mirror pond,many rare fowl. Featured in English Garden, Homes & Antiques, GGG & many other publications.

GROUP OPENING

10 CHARLTON GARDENS
Banbury OX17 3DR. *7m SE of Banbury, 5m W of Brackley. From B4100 turn off N at Aynho, or from A422 turn off S at Farthinghoe. Off road parking.* Home-made teas at The Cottage. **Combined adm £5, chd free. Sun 29 May (2-6).**

> NEW **8 CARTWRIGHT ROAD**
> Miss Valerie Trinder
>
> **THE COTTAGE**
> Lady Juliet Townsend
>
> NEW **THE CROFT**
> Mr & Mrs R D Whitrow
>
> **HOLLY HOUSE**
> Miss Alice Townsend
>
> **HOME FARM HOUSE**
> Mrs N Grove-White
>
> **WALNUT HOUSE**
> Sir Paul & Lady Hayter

Well preserved stone village with a selection of gardens, large and small including a woodland walk, stream and lakes and a small, mainly dry gravel garden developed from new over the past 5yrs with bamboos and grasses. Walled garden with beautiful views, paved courtyard with tubs, containers and climbers and a large garden behind a C17 farmhouse with colour themed borders and beech and yew hedges.

Large drifts of snowdrops. Abundant hellebores, shrubs and trees for winter interest . . .

COLDOR
See Leicestershire & Rutland.

11 ◆ COTON MANOR GARDEN
Guilsborough, Northampton NN6 8RQ. Mr & Mrs Ian Pasley-Tyler, 01604 740219, www.cotonmanor.co.uk. *10m N of Northampton, 11m SE of Rugby. From A428 & A5199 follow tourist signs.* **Adm £6, chd £2. For NGS: Tue 3 May (12-5.30). For other opening times and information, please phone or see garden website.** 10-acre garden set in peaceful countryside with old yew and holly hedges, extensive herbaceous borders containing many unusual plants, rose, water, herb and woodland gardens, famous bluebell wood, wild flower meadow. Adjacent specialist nursery with over 1000 plant varieties propagated from the garden.

12 ◆ COTTESBROOKE HALL GARDENS
Cottesbrooke NN6 8PF. Mr & Mrs A R Macdonald-Buchanan, 01604 505808, www.cottesbrookehall.co.uk. *10m N of Northampton. Signed from J1 on A14. Off A5199 at Creaton, A508 at Brixworth.* **Adm £5.50, chd £2.50. For NGS: Sun 17 Apr (2-5.30). For opening times and information please visit website or telephone.** Award winning gardens by Geoffrey Jellicoe, Dame Sylvia Crowe, James Alexander Sinclair and more recently Arne Maynard. Formal gardens and terraces surround Queen Anne house with extensive vistas onto the lake

and C18 parkland containing many mature trees. Wild and woodland gardens, which are exceptional in Spring, a short distance from the formal areas.

13 ◆ DEENE PARK
Corby NN17 3EW. Mr E Brudenell & The Hon Mrs Brudenell, 01780 450278, www.deenepark.com. *6m N of Corby. Off A43 between Corby & Stamford.* **For NGS: Wed 25 May (2-5), last admission 4pm. For other opening times and information, please phone or see garden website.** Interesting garden set in beautiful parkland. Large parterre with topiary designed by David Hicks echoing the C16 decoration on the porch stonework, long mixed borders, old-fashioned roses, Tudor courtyard and white garden. Lake and waterside walks with rare mature trees in natural garden. Wheelchair access available to main features of garden.

14 DOLPHINS
Great Harrowden NN9 5AB. Mr & Mrs R C Handley. *2m N of Wellingborough. 5m S of Kettering on A509.* **Adm £3, chd free. Sun 27 Feb (10-4).** 2-acre country garden surrounding old stone house (not open). Large drifts of snowdrops and several smaller groups in variety. Abundant hellebores, shrubs and trees for winter interest. Very free draining with beech hedges and firm gravel paths.

15 ◆ EVENLEY WOOD GARDEN
Evenley, Brackley NN13 5SH. Timothy Whiteley, 07776 307849, www.evenleywoodgarden.co.uk. *¾ m S of Brackley. Turn off at the Evenley r'about on the A43 and go straight through the village towards Mixbury before taking the 1st turn L.* **Adm £5, chd £1. For NGS: Sun & Mon 1, 2 May (11-5). For other opening times and information, please phone or see garden website.** This 60-acre woodland is a plantsman's garden with a huge variety of plants all of which are labelled. Mainly trees, shrubs, bulbs and lilies. Many magnolias, azaleas, rhododendrons and camellias. All paths are grass.

FARMWAY
See Leicestershire & Rutland.

GROUP OPENING

 FARTHINGHOE GARDENS
Farthinghoe, Brackley NN13 5NZ.
3m NW of Brackley. A422 between Brackley and Banbury. Home-made teas. **Combined adm £3.50, chd free. Sun 12 June (2-6).**

FOLLY COTTAGE
Mary Scarff

THE OLD RECTORY
Mr & Mrs David Montagu-Smith

THE OLD RECTORY STABLE HOUSE
Simon Cox

WINDY RIDGE
Mr & Mrs M Phipps

Group of 4 gardens each with its own character and interest in a pretty stone built village.

GROUP OPENING

 FINEDON GARDENS
NN9 5JN. *2m NE of Wellingborough. 6m SE Kettering, A6/A510 junction.* Home-made teas 67-69 High Street. **Adm £2.50, chd free. Sun 5, 26 June (2-6).**

24 ALBERT ROAD
Ray & Honor Parbery

67-69 HIGH STREET
Mary & Stuart Hendry

11 THRAPSTON ROAD
John & Gillian Ellson

The village has a varied history dating from Roman times and evolving through farming, ironstone mining, shoe and leather manufacturing. An ancient parish church with a collection of 'green men' and many other historical buildings. All three gardens are very different - everything from vegetables to flowers on show. **24 Albert Road** has an array of pots, containers and border plants and many cacti, boasting a period dolls house, gypsy caravan, patio and summerhouse. **67-69 High Street** is an ever evolving rear garden of ¹/₃acre of C17 cottage (not open). Mixed borders, many obelisks and containers. Planting for varied interest Spring to Autumn [see separate entry at 67-69 High Street].

11 Thrapston Road has a super cottage garden with mixed vegetable plot, soft fruit and apple trees, summer house and tree house. Large selection of home-raised plants for sale - all proceeds for NGS.

Many of our gardens offer delicious home-made teas. Look for the ☕ symbol and enjoy a slice of cake or two . . . !

 FLORE FIELDS
NN7 4JX. Lady Morton. *1m N of Flore. 2m E of Weedon. On A45 midway between Northampton & Daventry. From Flore take Brockhall Rd 1m. Lodge at end of drive.* **Adm £4, chd free. Sun 26 June (2-5.30).**
3¹/₂-acre gardeb in glorious setting. Extensive lawns, specimen trees, shrubs, part walled garden with several herbaceous borders, roses, peonies.

GROUP OPENING

 FLORE GARDENS
Flore NN7 4LQ. *7m W of Northampton. 5m E of Daventry on A45. Garden map provided at official free car park, signed.* Lunches & home-made teas. **Combined adm £5, chd free (share to Flore Flower Festival). Sat 18, Sun 19 June (11-6).**

BERTHA'S PATCH
Claire and Gary Ryan

BLISS LANE NURSERY
Geoff & Chris Littlewood

24 BLISS LANE
John & Sally Miller

NEW 20 BROCKHALL ROAD
Alan & Jane Rouse

17 THE CRESCENT
Edward & Lindsey Atkinson

THE CROFT
John & Dorothy Boast

THE GARDEN HOUSE
Edward & Penny Aubrey-Fletcher

THE OLD BAKERY
John Amos & Karl Jones
Visitors also welcome by appt April - end Aug.
01327 349080
cortaderia@ukonline.co.uk

NEW RUSSELL HOUSE
Peter Pickering & Stephen George

STONE COTTAGE
John & Pat Davis

10 interesting, diverse and constantly developing gardens open in association with the long established Flower Festival in this Northamptonshire village overlooking the Nene Valley. Incl formal and informal designs, vegetables, fruit and herb gardens. Many unusual trees and shrubs, lots of roses and clematis. Much herbaceous planting incl exotic and unusual, many for sunny areas as well as shady woodland. Variety of garden buildings, structures, patios, courtyard, barbecue and seating areas affording the opportunity to sit and rest whilst admiring the gardens. There is a former walled kitchen garden, a C19 gazebo with a unique collection of Queen-Empresses, swags of wisteria, archways of hornbeam and archways clothed in roses and other climbers for both sun and shade, alpines, ponds and other water features, small and large. Gardens open in association with Flore Flower Festival. Wheelchair access available at some gardens. Dogs permitted in some gardens.

GROUP OPENING

 FLORE SPRING GARDENS
Flore NN7 4LQ. *7m W of Northampton. 5m E of Daventry on A45. Garden map provided at the official free car park, signed.* Home-made teas at Chapel School Room. **Combined adm £4, chd free. Sun 17 Apr (2-6).**

BLISS LANE NURSERY
Chris & Geoff Littlewood

24 BLISS LANE
John & Sally Miller

THE CROFT
John & Dorothy Boast

3 MEADOW FARM CLOSE
Eric & Jackie Ingram

THE OLD BAKERY
Johnnie Amos & Karl Jones
Visitors also welcome by appt
April - end of Aug.
01327 349080
yeolbakery@aol.com

5 gardens of varying size and design. Planting for yr-round interest with mixtures of flowers, fruit, herbs and vegetables. Colourful displays of unusual shrubs and early flowering perennials. Lots of spring bulbs in pots as well as drifts in borders. Shade tolerant plants in a woodland setting and colourful spring displays.
🏡 ☕

---

21 FOXTAIL LILLY
41 South Road, Oundle PE8 4BP. Tracey Mathieson, 01832 274593, tracey@mathieson4727.freeserve. co.uk, www.foxtail-lilly.co.uk. *1m town centre. From A605 at Barnwell Xrds take Barnwell Rd, 1st R to South Rd.* Home-made teas. **Adm £3, chd free. Mon 30 May (11-5).** Visitors also welcome by appt.
A cottage garden where perennials and grasses are grouped creatively together amongst gravel paths, complementing one another to create a natural look. Some unusual plants and quirky oddities create a different and colourful informal garden. Lots of flowers for cutting, shop in barn. New meadow pasture turned into new cutting garden. Featured in Country Living magazine & Sunday Telegraph gardening section.
🏡 ❀ ☕ ☎

Evenley Wood Garden

---

22 FROGGERY COTTAGE
85 Breakleys Road, Desborough NN14 2PT. Mr John Lee. *6m N of Kettering, 5m S of Market Harborough. Signed off A6 & A14.* Light refreshments & teas. **Adm £2.50, chd free. Sun 31 July (11.30-6).** ³/₄-acre plantsman's garden full of rare and unusual plants. NCCPG Collection of 435 varieties of penstemons incl dwarfs and species. Artefacts on display incl old ploughs and garden implements. Featured in Garden Answers.
 🏡 ❀ **NCCPG** ☕

THE GRANGE
See Leicestershire & Rutland.

23 GREAT ADDINGTON MANOR
Great Addington NN14 4BH. Mr & Mrs Geoffrey Groome. *7m SE of Kettering. J11, A510 exit off A14 signed Finedon & Wellingborough. Take 2nd L to the Addingtons.* Home-made teas in Village Hall. **Adm £4, chd £2. Mon 25 Apr (2-5).** 5 acre manor gardens with terrace, lawns, mature trees, mulberry, yew hedges, pond and spinney, wild garden and spring daffodils.
🏡 ❀ ☕

GROUP OPENING

24 NEW GREAT BILLING VILLAGE
NN3 9HA. *3m E of Northampton. off A4500.* Home-made teas 22 Standing Stones & 20 Elwes Way. Combined adm £4, chd free. Sun 5 June (2-6).

> NEW 20 ELWES WAY
> Cindy & John Evitt

> NEW FIELD VIEW
> Anner Fehnert

> NEW PLANTATION HOUSE
> Freddie Rayner

> NEW 20 STANDING STONES
> Janet & John James

> NEW 22 STANDING STONES
> Mr & Mrs D Vaughan

The village is listed in the Domesday Book and parts still retain the old atmosphere with the C12 church of St Andrew and the old rectory. At one time the Elwes family owned almost the whole village. They lived in Billing Hall, sadly demolished in 1956. Today the only tangible links are The Elwes Arms, Elwes Way and Lady

Winefride's Walk. One garden is in the conservation area, which is predominately stone-built. A short walk away, across open parkland by the church; the other gardens are in a recent development, in the grounds of the old Hall. Behind conventional facades lie unexpected delights. In one you could imagine being on a beach, another is formal, with clipped hedges and a cricket pavilion. One has a series of garden rooms around old farm buildings. A warm welcome awaits. Regret no wheelchair access at Plantation House.

GROUP OPENING

25 GREAT BRINGTON GARDENS
Great Brington NN7 4JJ. *7m NW of Northampton. Off A428 Rugby Rd. 1st L turn past main gates of Althorp. Free parking. Programmes & maps available.* Home-made teas at parish church, lunches in the Reading Room. **Adm £3.50, chd free. Sun 1 May (11-5).**

> **8 BEDFORD COTTAGES**
> Anne & Bob Billingsby
>
> **BRINGTON LODGE**
> Peter & Jenny Cooch
>
> **THE OLD RECTORY**
> Mr & Mrs R Thomas
>
> **ROSE COTTAGE**
> David Green & Elaine MacKenzie
>
> **THE STABLES**
> Mrs A George

The village is renowned for its warm welcome with dozens of parish volunteers helping on the day. A particularly picturesque, predominately stone and thatch village which is well worth a visit in its own right. The C12 church rated as one of Simon Jenkins' 1000 Best and connections with Spencers of Althorp & George Washington ensure a memorable day. 5 gardens this yr of immense variety from small cottage garden with a summer house to a 3-acre formal garden complete with extensive vegetable patch and orchard. Many continue to evolve each yr; several have unique water features; most are planned and maintained by their owners. Local history exhibition & plant sale.

26 GREENWAY
Pipewell Road, Desborough NN14 2SN. Robert Bass, 01536 760934. *6m NW of Kettering, 5m SE of Market Harborough. On B576. 150 metres E of Pipewell Rd railway bridge and Travis Perkins builders' yard.* Home-made teas. **Adm £2.50, chd free. Sun 15 May (2-6); Evening Opening, wine, Thur 26 May (6-9). Visitors also welcome by appt May only.**
Constantly evolving arboretum style garden set in ¹/₃ acre with over 90 acers (Japanese maple cultivars) in containers and open planting. Many garden structures, water features, statuary, sculptures and containers to provide yr-round interest. Recent additions include gothic folly with fernery. Covered seating areas for contemplation.

27 GREYWALLS
Farndish NN29 7HJ. Mrs P M Anderson, 01933 353495. *2¹/₂ m SE of Wellingborough. A609 from Wellingborough, B570 to Irchester, turn to Farndish by cenotaph. House adjacent to church.* Tea & Light Refreshments. **Adm £3, chd free. Sun 6 Mar (12-4). Visitors also welcome by appt March only. 10+ visitors.**
2-acre mature garden surrounding old vicarage (not open). Over 100 varieties of snowdrops, drifts of hardy cyclamen and hellebores. Alpine house and raised alpine beds. Water features and natural ponds with views over open countryside. Rare breed hens.

Many garden
structures, water
features, statuary,
sculptures and
containers. Recent
additions include
gothic folly with
fernery . . .

GROUP OPENING

28 GUILSBOROUGH SPRING GARDENS
Guilsborough NN6 8PT. *10m NW of Northampton. 10m E of Rugby. Between A5199 & A428. J1 off A14. Car parking in field at Guilsborough House. Maps provided.* Lunches available at village shop & PH. Home-made teas. **Combined adm £5, chd free. Sat & Sun 14, 15 May (2-6).**

> **DRIPWELL HOUSE**
> Mr J W Langfield & Dr C Moss
> Visitors also welcome by appt.
> 01604 740140
> cattimoss@aol.com
>
> **FOUR ACRES**
> Mark & Gay Webster
>
> **THE GATE HOUSE**
> Mike & Sarah Edwards
>
> **GUILSBOROUGH HOUSE**
> Mr & Mrs John McCall
>
> **NORTOFT GRANGE**
> Sir John & Lady Lowther
>
> **OAK DENE**
> Mr & Mrs R A Darker
>
> **THE OLD HOUSE**
> Richard & Libby Seaton Evans
>
> **THE OLD VICARAGE**
> John & Christine Benbow

Eight varied village gardens in attractive rural setting. Two small cottage-style gardens, one belonging to a keen flower arranger, the other a secret walled garden crammed with fruit, flowers and vegetables. The remaining gardens are much larger, ranging from a magical woodland garden on a very steep site to formal gardens with sweeping lawns, mature trees and beautiful views. There is plenty of room to sit and relax. Walled kitchen gardens and a potager are an important part of our gardening. Plants for sale will incl both the rare and unusual from our plantsmen's gardens, a true highlight here. Dripwell House, open for the NGS since 1986, was originally an individual garden as was Nortoft Grange. There is thus a lot to see and visitors find that they need the whole afternoon. Featured in Local press, Radio Northampton.

29 ◆ HADDONSTONE SHOW GARDENS
The Forge House, Church Lane, East Haddon, Northampton NN6 8DB. Haddonstone Ltd, 01604 770711, www.haddonstone.com. *7m NW of Northampton. Brown tourism signs from A428. Located in centre of village opp school.* Teas. **Adm by donation. For NGS: Sat & Sun 10, 11 Sept (10-5).** For other opening times and information, please phone or see garden website.
See Haddonstone's classic garden ornaments in the beautiful setting of the walled Manor gardens inc planters, fountains, statuary, bird baths, sundials, balustrading and landscape follies. Garden is on different levels with shrub roses, conifers, clematis and climbers. Jubilee Garden inc pavilion, temple, gothic grotto and new contemporary garden. Haddonstone seconds available for purchase from Brixworth Manufactory (Saturday 10 Sept only). Plants for sale. Featured in Period Living.
&. ⊛ ☕ ☎

HAMMOND ARBORETUM
See Leicestershire & Rutland.

GROUP OPENING

30 HARPOLE GARDENS
Harpole NN7 4BX. *4m W Northampton. On A45 towards Weedon. Turn R at The Turnpike Hotel into Harpole. Village maps given to all visitors.* Home-made teas at The Close. **Combined adm £4, chd free. Sun 12 June (1-6).**

BRYTTEN-COLLIER HOUSE
James & Lucy Strickland

THE CLOSE
Michael Orton-Jones

NEW 30 HIGH STREET
Martin & Stephanie Farley

19 MANOR CLOSE
Caroline & Andy Kemshed

MILLERS
Mr & Mrs M Still

THE OLD DAIRY
David & Di Ballard

NEW ORCHARD COTTAGE
David & Joan Spencer

Attractive Northamptonshire village, well known for its annual scarecrow festival (2nd weekend September).

Enjoy a lovely farmhouse garden with an acre of lawn, mixed borders, mature trees, views overlooking the farm and strawberry field. Visit a partly walled S-facing garden with herbaceous borders, many climbing roses and clematis and a beautiful tree house. See two completely different cottage gardens (one open for the first time), and find an abundance of quirky features amongst the cottage garden planting. Our second new opening contains a newly designed cottage garden, a well stocked vegetable area and an orchard with geese, chickens and ducks. View a smaller garden (40x10yds) belonging to a more recently constructed house. This is a flower arranger's garden of interesting design with water features and mixed borders. Take tea in an old-fashioned country garden with large lawns, herbaceous borders and mature trees. An interesting and varied afternoon is guaranteed with a warm welcome to all.
&. ⊛ ☕

31 67-69 HIGH STREET
Finedon NN9 5JN. Mary & Stuart Hendry, 01933 680414, sh_archt@hotmail.com. *6m SE Kettering, J A6 & A510.* **Adm £3, chd free. Evening Opening, wine, Thurs 9, 16, 23 June (5-9).** Visitors also welcome by appt February to September, groups 4+, min charge £20. Coaches welcome.
Constantly evolving, ¹⁄₃-acre rear garden of C17 cottage (not open). Mixed borders, many obelisks and containers, kitchen garden and herb bed, rope border. Spring garden with snowdrops, bluebells and hellebores; Summer borders rose/clematis pergolas; All giving varied interest from Feb through to Oct. Large selection of home-raised plants for sale - all for NGS. Featured on BBC Radio Northampton.
&. ⊛ ☎

32 HILL GROUNDS
Evenley NN13 5RZ. Mr & Mrs C F Cropley, 01280 703224, cropleyhg@hotmail.co.uk. *1m S of Brackley. On A43, turn L into Evenley. R off Church Lane.* **Adm £4.50 inc coffee/biscuits, chd free. Visitors welcome by appt,** groups & individuals. Large coaches must park in village requiring a walk of ¹⁄₃ m.
Plantsman's garden of 2 acres,

surrounded by C19 200yd yew hedge. Planted for yr-round interest with bulbs at all seasons, terrace with pots, 4 pergolas, one laden with roses, many late clematis and double herbaceous borders. Millenium arborette encouraging colonies of British flora. Stone paths slippery when wet.
&. 🐕 ☕ ☎

HILLESDEN HOUSE
See Buckinghamshire.

An interesting and varied afternoon is guaranteed with a warm welcome to all . . .

GROUP OPENING

33 NEW HOLLOWELL GARDENS
Hollowell NN6 8RR. *8m N of Northampton. ¹⁄₂ m off A5099, turn off at Creaton.* Home-made teas at Village Hall. **Combined adm £3.50, chd free. Sun 14 Aug (11-5).**

NEW HILLVIEW
Jan & Crawford Craig

NEW IVY COTTAGE
Rev John & Mrs Wendy Evans
Visitors also welcome by appt May to Sept.
01604 743878
revjohnwenevans@yahoo.co.uk

ROSEMOUNT
Mr & Mrs J Leatherland

Small village with church built approx 150yrs ago using sandstone from Duston Quarry and the Village Hall was the local school until its closure about 40yrs ago. The gardens open are **Rosemount** with its collections of clematis, mimulas and salvias. **Ivy Cottage** is a semi-wildlife garden with orchard, vegetable garden and model railway. **Hillview** is a traditional country agrden incl a lily pond dating from the 1930s. Church & Village Hall open.
&. 🐕 ⊛ ☕

NEW HOSTELLARIE
78 Breakleys Road, Desborough
NN14 2PT. Stella & Stan Freeman.
*6m N of Kettering. 5m S of Market
Harborough. Signed from centre of
Desborough.* Home-made teas incl
gluten free. **Adm £2.50, chd free.
Suns 5 June; 3 July (2-6).**
Long town garden, divided into rooms
of different character, courtyard,
cottage garden, Japanese walk, fruit
and vegetable area, all linked by
lawns and grass paths. Ponds, water
features and a collection of over 35
different hostas, of all sizes, in beds
and containers.

GROUP OPENING

35 ISLIP GARDENS
Islip, nr Kettering NN14 3JY. *1m
from A14 J12. Leave A14 at J12, join
A6116. Follow signs for Islip Village &
NGS signs.* Home-made teas in the
Village Hall. **Combined adm £4, chd
free. Sun 8 May (12-5).**

> **NEW HEADMASTERS
> HOUSE**
> Julie & Bob Lymn
>
> **30 LOWICK ROAD**
> Mrs D Eyles
>
> **8 LOWICK ROAD**
> Dawn & Richard Scrutton
>
> **MANOR FARM**
> Roy & Carol Martin

4 lovely gardens, from ever-changing
front and rear gardens with colourful
mix of shrubs to a split level garden
with apple and pear trees.
Plantsman's small garden to the rear
of a late Georgian cottage with a
collection of clematis, hellebore, hardy
geraniums and Japanese acers, a
variety of sculptural plants in raised
beds, incl pots and borders. Charming
collection of C17/18 stone cottages
under thatched, pantiles and slate
roofs. C15 church. Islip is listed in the
Domesday Book and has prehistoric,
Roman & Anglo Saxon sites.

36 NEW JERICHO
42 Market Place, Oundle PE8 4AJ.
Stephen & Pepita Aris,
01832 275416,
stephenaris@btinternet.com. *From
Oundle Market Place, find Jericho
Pottery, go through blue door and
down yard to garden.* Home-made

teas & light refreshments. **Adm £3,
chd free. Suns 22 May (12-5);
26 Feb 2012 (12-4).** Visitors also
welcome by appt any time by prior
arrangement.
Inspired by Vita Sackville-West 50
years ago, the 100 metre, S-facing,
walled garden is divided into a series
of 'secret' spaces. House (not open)
is clothed in wisteria, clematis and
roses. Massive hornbeam hedge also
clipped box and lavender, long
herbaceous border. Over 50 labelled
species roses. Herb garden.
Snowdrops & crocuses fabulous at
the Feb opening.

37 NEW KARELL HOUSE
NN4 0PB. Jenny & Jim Redmond.
*1.9m E J15 M1 Northamptonshire.
Exit J15 of M1, head towards
Northampton on A508, pass Hilton
Hotel on L. Follow sign to Collingtree
Park Golf Course, L onto winding
Brook Lane, 3rd R onto Turnberry
Lane, 1st R onto Belfrey Lane.* **Adm
£3, chd free. Suns 5 June; 21 Aug
(12-5).**
Constantly evolving garden adjacent
to the Collingtree Park Golf Course
with Wootten Brook at the bottom of
the garden which consists of mixed
borders full of hostas, tree peonies
and many old favourites also some
rare and unusual plants surrounded
by well manicured lawns. River bank
not suitable for wheelchairs.

GROUP OPENING

38 KILSBY GARDENS
Kilsby Village CV23 8XP. *5m SE of
Rugby. 6m N of Daventry on A361.
From Rugby on A428 turn R onto
B4038. From J18 on M1 take A428
towards Rugby. At junction with A5
going S turn L. Entrance to Kilsby on
R just after 30mph sign.* Home-made
teas at Kilsby Village Hall. **Adm £3.50,
chd free. Sun 12 June (1-5).**

> **NEW 6A ESSEN LANE**
> Phil & Lilian Francis
>
> **MOATHOUSE FARM**
> Mrs C Walker
>
> **PYTCHLEY HOUSE**
> Mr & Mrs T F Clay
>
> **RAINBOW'S END**
> Mr & Mrs J Madigan
>
> **5 THE LAWNS**
> Charles Smedley

Kilsby is a stone and brick village with
historic interest, home of St Faith's
Church dating from the C12 and
2 PH. The village was the site of one
of the first skirmishes of the Civil War
in 1642 and also gave its name to
Stephenson's nearby lengthy rail
tunnel built in the 1830s. 5 attractive
gardens within the village with very
different characters. In one a C19
reservoir was discovered during
creation of a new herbaceous bed.
Some of the gardens open alternate
yrs ensuring variety. New garden
opening for the first time this yr, so
there is always something new to see
and always plants for sale. Visitors
have commented on the friendly
welcome so come and see us.
Embroidery Exhibition in the Kilsby
Room at the Village Hall. Village
Heritage Trail leaflets available.

Four lovely gardens,
from ever-changing
front and rear
gardens with
colourful mix of
shrubs to a split
level garden with
apple and pear
trees . . .

GROUP OPENING

39 LITCHBOROUGH GARDENS
Litchborough NN12 8JQ. *10m SW
of Northampton, nr Towcester. Please
use car park nr village green. Maps
provided.* Home-made teas in Villlage
Hall. **Combined adm £4, chd free.
Sun 5 June (2-6).**

> **BRUYERE COURT**
> Mr M Billington
>
> **4 KILN LANE**
> Roger & Angela Linnell
>
> **THE LIME HOUSE**
> Mr & Mrs L Skinner

ORCHARD HOUSE
Mr & Mrs B Smith

NEW **41 TOWCESTER ROAD**
Ian & Vanessa Lowery

51 TOWCESTER ROAD
Mr Norman Drinkwater

A small attractive ironstone village within conservation area, listed buildings and C13 church. 6 gardens of diverse size and interest. Lawns, ornamental lakes with rhododendrons and azaleas. Cottage garden with well, summerhouse and walled herb garden. 300yr-old cottage with modern cottage garden developed over the past 10yrs, landscape architects' country garden designed for low maintenance, mixed terrace garden with some work still in progress. Wildlife pond and patio with pots and containers and a small garden with shrubs, rockery and productive vegetable garden. *

 ♿ 🏡 ✿ ☕

GROUP OPENING

40 **LITCHBOROUGH SPRING GARDENS**
NN12 8JF. Home-made teas in the Village Hall. **Combined adm £4, chd free. Sun 17 Apr (2-6).**

BRUYERE COURT
Mr M Billington

NEW **4 KILN LANE**
Roger & Angela Linnell

ORCHARD HOUSE
Mr & Mrs B Smith

THE HALL
Mr & Mrs A R Heygate

Small attractive ironstone village within conservation area, listed buildings and C13 Church. 4 gardens of diverse size and interest. Large garden with parkland views and woodland walk with lovely bulbs. Landscape architect's garden planted for low maintenance and large garden with ornamental lakes with rhododendrons and azaleas. 300yr-old cottage with modern cottage garden featuring wildlife pond, summerhouse, patio with pots and containers, ornamental shrubs and borders.

♿ 🏡 ✿ ☕

GROUP OPENING

41 **LONG BUCKBY GARDENS**
NN6 7RE. 8m NW of Northampton, midway between A428 & A5. 4 gardens in village close to Square, WC and parking. Mill House at junction of A428 and Long Lane, 1m distant with plenty of parking. Maps at each garden. Home-made teas 45 Brington Road. **Adm £4, chd free. Sun 19 June (1-6).**

ASHMORE HOUSE
Mike Greaves & Sally Sokoloff

45 BRINGTON ROAD
Derick & Sandra Cooper

SAXIGOE
Mr and Mrs R J Burt

MILL HOUSE
Ken and Gill Pawson
Visitors also welcome by appt
Mid June to Mid July.
01604 770103
gill@gpplanning.co.uk

TORESTIN
June Ford

Four village gardens, with a variety of layout and planting, one on a sloping site. One fully organic garden, constructed using reclaimed materials. Selection of water features, pergolas and other garden structures. Variety of planting, incl annuals, herbaceous and shrubs. One large garden in the countryside, with large fruit and vegetable plot, wildlife areas, orchard, borders, wooded area, wildflower plot and pond, with foundations of East Haddon windmill; owner is a Heritage Seed Guardian. Plant sales.

♿ 🏡 ✿ ☕

Look out for the gardens with the ☎ – enjoy a private visit . . .

42 ♦ **LYVEDEN NEW BIELD**
Oundle PE8 5AT. National Trust, 01832 205358, www.nationaltrust.org.uk. *5m SW of Oundle, 3m E of Brigstock. Signed off A427 & A6116.* **Adm £5, chd free. For NGS: Sun 5 June (10.30-5).** For other opening times and information, please phone or see garden website.
One of England's oldest garden landscapes, abandoned in 1605 after family involvement in the Gunpowder Plot, Lyveden still retains original terraces, prospect mounts, canals and the impressive garden lodge built to symbolise the Treshams Catholic faith. Recently replanted 5-acre orchard of pre-C17 tree varieties. Garden tour 2pm.

 ♿ 🏡 ☎

43 **THE MALTINGS**
10 The Green, Clipston LE16 9RS. Mr & Mrs Hamish Connell, 01858 525336, j.connell118@btinternet.com. *4m S of Market Harborough, 9m W of Kettering, 10m N Northampton. From A14 take junction 2, A508 N. After 2m turn L for Clipston. 2 houses away from Old Red Lion.* Home-made teas. **Adm £3, chd free. Sat 23 (2-6), Sun & Mon 24, 25 Apr; (11-6); Sats & Suns 18, 19 June; 30, 31 July (2-6) Evening Openings wine, Fris 17 June; 29 July (5-8.30). Visitors also welcome by appt. Groups 10+ all year.**
³/₄ acre sloping plantsman's garden designed for all year interest by the present owner. Many unusual plants, shrubs, old and new trees. Over 60 different clematis, wild garden walk, spring bulb area, over 20 different species roses, 2 ponds connected by a stream, bog garden. Home made cake stall. Swing and slide for children. Featured in Harborough Mail, Radio Northampton. Partial wheelchair access.

 ♿ ☕ ☎

44 ♦ **THE MENAGERIE**
Newport Pagnell Road, Horton NN7 2BX. Mr A Myers, 01604 870957, www.themenageriehorton.co.uk. *6m S of Northampton. 1m S of Horton. On B526, turn E at lay-by, across field.* **Adm £8, chd £4, concessions £4. For NGS: Sun 26 June (2-6). For other opening times and information, please phone or see garden website.**
Newly developed gardens set around

C18 folly, with 2 delightful thatched arbours. Recently completed large formal walled garden with fountain, used for vegetables, fruit and cutting flowers. Recently extended exotic bog garden and native wetland area. Also rose garden, shrubberies, herbaceous borders and wild flower areas.

MIDDLETON CHENEY GARDENS
See Oxfordshire.

GROUP OPENING

45 NEW MOULTON (WEST)
West side of Mouton village, Moulton, Northampton NN3 7SW. *2 miles N of Northampton. Parking to rear of Moulton College, accessed from A508 at Boughton. Also off A43 at r'about along Overstone Rd to village centre. Follow yellow signs.* Teas at coffee shop at college & home-made teas in village. **Adm £5, chd free. Sun 3 July (11-5).**

NEW BAYTREE COTTAGE
Ian Longstaff

NEW 10 BOUGHTON ROAD
David & Athene Butcher

NEW 8 BOUGHTON ROAD
Chris and Barry Homer

NEW 33 BOUGHTON ROAD
Christoph Bouerke

NEW GALLERY WEST STREET
Sue Brooks
www.jgallery.org.uk

NEW MOULTON ALLOTMENT ASSOCIATION
Helen Dobbs

NEW MOULTON COLLEGE
Moulton College
www.moulton.ac.uk

THE NYMPH'S ROSE GARDEN
Peter Hughes, Mary Morris, Irene Kay

NEW 9 PARADE BANK
Mr and Mrs D J Sanders

Moulton is a typical Northamptonshire village, with many interesting old buildings in local stone. This yr's gardens are on the west side of the village, where we are celebrating gardening in many guises. At the Gallery are paintings and sculpture in a garden seting. We have topiary, a Mediterranean garden, a traditional cottage, acers grown from seed, a vegeatble enthusiast, a group of allotments and the horticultural department of Moulton College. Here are students' show gardens, an arboretum planted in 2000, plantings maintained by the students and a garden centre. In 2010 we welcomed over 1000 visitors to a different group of Moulton gardens. The C13th chuch will be open for visiting.The gallery is planning a garden themed exhibition. Featured in local press, BBC local radio.

The Old Rectory, Sudborough

46 ◆ THE OLD RECTORY, SUDBOROUGH
NN14 3BX. Mr & Mrs A Huntington, 01832 733247, www.oldrectorygardens.co.uk. *8m NE of Kettering. Exit 12 off A14. Village just off A6116 between Thrapston & Brigstock.* **Adm £4.50, chd free. For NGS: Suns 13 Mar (2-6); 19 June (10-6) in conjunction with Marie Curie Cancer Care. For other opening times and information, please phone or see garden website.**
Classic 3-acre country garden with extensive herbaceous borders of unusual plants. Magnolias and cornus in spring, containers of bulbs and large plantings of tulips and daffodils, early rare hellebores. Formal rose circle and box edged potager designed by Rosemary Verey, woodland walk and pond alongside Harpers Brook. Featured in Dream Gardens of England, 100 Inspirational Gardens.

THE OLD STABLES
See Leicestershire & Rutland.

GROUP OPENING

47 PRESTON CAPES GARDENS
Daventry NN11 3TF. *6m SW of Daventry. 13m NE of Banbury. 3m N of Canons Ashby.* Home-made teas at Old West Farm. Homemade light lunches served 12-2, cakes and teas all day. **Adm £4, chd free. Sun 5 June (12-5).**

CITY COTTAGE
Mr & Mrs Gavin Cowen

LADYCROFT
Mervyn & Sophia Maddison

LANGDALE HOUSE
Michael & Penny Eves

NORTH FARM
Mr & Mrs Tim Coleridge

OLD WEST FARM
Mr & Mrs Gerard Hoare
Little Preston
3/4 m E of Preston Capes

VILLAGE FARM
Trevor & Julia Clarke

WEST ORCHARD FARM HOUSE
Mr & Mrs Nick Price

Seven varied gardens in a beautiful south Northamptonshire ironstone village mostly with wonderful views. Gardens range from small contemporary to large extensive with woodland walk and ponds. Unspoilt rural village in the Northamptonshire uplands. Local sandstone houses and cottages. Norman Church.

February opening features our collection of nearly 200 different snowdrops . . .

GROUP OPENING

48 ► RAVENSTHORPE GARDENS
Ravensthorpe NN6 8ES. *7m NW of Northampton. Signed from A5199 and the A428. Mill House im'med on R as you turn off A428 down Long Lane. 1m from village.* Home-made teas at Village Hall. **Adm £4, chd free. Sun 10 July** (1-5).

MILL HOUSE
Ken and Gill Pawson

THE OLD FORGE HOUSE
Bryan & Anna Guest

QUIET WAYS
Russ & Sally Barringer

RAVENSTHORPE NURSERY
Mr & Mrs Richard Wiseman
Visitors also welcome by appt.
01604 770548
ravensthorpenursery@hotmail.com

NEW ► TREETOPS
Ros and Gordon Smith

Attractive villlage in Northamptonshire uplands near to Ravensthorpe reservoir and Top Ardles Wood Woodland Trust which have bird watching and picnic opportunities.

---

5 very different established and developing gardens set in beautiful countryside displaying a wide range of plants, many of which are available from the Nursery, offering inspirational planting, quiet contemplation, beautiful views, gardens encouraging wildlife, fruit and vegetable gardens owned by Heritage Seed Library Guardian, rose garden and woodland walk.

---

49 ► ROSEMOUNT
Church Hill, Hollowell NN6 8RR. Mr & Mrs Leatherland, 01604 740354. *10m NW of Northampton, 5m S junction 1 A14. Between A5199 and A428.* Parking at village hall. Light refreshments & teas at village hall. **Adm £3, chd free. Sun 27 Feb** (11-3). Visitors also welcome by appt 1 March to 31 Aug. Groups 10+.
February opening features our collection of nearly 200 different snowdrops many hellebores and usual spring bulbs, some for sale. Limited wheelchair access.

SOUTH KILWORTH GARDENS
See Leicestershire & Rutland.

CROFT ACRE
See Leicestershire & Rutland.

GROUP OPENING

50 ► SPRATTON GARDENS
Spratton NN6 8HL. *6¹/₂ m NNW of Northampton. From Northampton on A5199 turn L at Holdenby Rd for Spratton Grange Farm, after ¹/₂ m turn L up long drive. For other gardens turn R at Brixworth Rd. Car park signed. Car parking in village well signed with close access to first garden. Maps given to all visitors.* Tea & Light Refreshments at St Andrew's Church. **Combined adm £5, chd free. Sun 8 May** (11-5).

DALE HOUSE ⊨
Fiona & Chris Cox

FORGE COTTAGE
Daniel Bailey & Jo Lawrence

THE GRANARY
Stephanie Bamford & Mark Wilkinson

11 HIGH STREET
Philip & Frances Roseblade

MULBERRY COTTAGE
Michael & Morley Heaton

SPRATTON GRANGE FARM
Dennis & Christine Yardy

THE STABLES
Pam & Tony Woods

NEW ► VIRGINIA COTTAGE
Ellis & Valentina Potter

WALTHAM COTTAGE
Norma & Allan Simons

The old part of the picturesque village has many late C17 stone built houses and turn of the C19/20 brick-built ones. These line the route between the eight inner village gardens, which are of a very varied nature. One is more formal with courtyard, walled garden and orchard, another a natural stream and pond, one has a 300yr old Holm (evergreen) oak. 3 gardens are cottage-style, with one well-stocked with tulips. Many interesting shrubs with good use of foliage colour. 3 gardens show how much can be made of a small area and the new one is under development. Several gardens have fine views over rolling agricultural countryside. The garden outside of the village centre was created from a farm and at 2-acres is the largest. Natural pond, bog garden and beautiful courtyard where once cows stood. One of the gardens will be hosting a massive plant sale. Attractive village with C12 Grade I Norman church which is a very fine example and its many interior features can be admired whilst enjoying some light refreshments. Disabled access to most gardens.

---

51 ► ◆ STEANE PARK
NN13 6DP. Lady Connell, 01280 705899. www.steanepark.co.uk. *2m from Brackley towards Banbury. On A422, 6m E of Banbury.* **Adm £4.50, chd free under 5. For NGS: Sun 22 May** (11-5). For other opening times and information please visit website or telephone. Beautiful trees in 80 acres of parkland, old waterway and fishponds, 1620 church in grounds. The gardens are constantly being remade and redesigned in sympathy with old stone house and church. Limited access for wheelchairs.

STOKE ALBANY HOUSE
See Leicestershire & Rutland.

Why not visit a
group garden
opening and
really make a day
of it . . . !

GROUP OPENING

52 SULGRAVE GARDENS
Banbury OX17 2RP. *8m NE of
Banbury. Just off B4525 Banbury to
Northampton rd, 7m from J11 off
M40.* Home-made teas at Asby
House. **Combined adm £4, chd
free.** Sun 19 June (2-6).

> **THE HERB SOCIETY
> GARDEN AT SULGRAVE
> MANOR**
> The Herb Society
>
> **MILL HOLLOW BARN**
> David Thompson
>
> **RECTORY FARM**
> Mr & Mrs C Smyth-Osborne
>
> **NEW▶ SULGRAVE
> ALLOTMENTS**
> Mrs Janet Smith
>
> **SUNNYMEAD**
> Bob & Jean Bates
>
> **THREEWAYS**
> Alison & Digby Lewis
>
> **THE WATERMILL**
> Mr & Mrs A J Todd

Small historic village with lovely stone
houses. C14 church and C16 manor
house, home of George Washington's
ancestors. Award winning community
owned and run village shop. Seven
gardens opening, incl 2 new this year
- the re-started village allotments and
a 1-acre garden established over last
5yrs with attractively planted water rill
and pools. All gardens have been
sympathetically and excitingly planted
for a wide range of sites incl a small
old cottage garden with container
grown vegetable, a mature ¼-acre
garden complete with rescue
chickens, contemporary garden
designed by Alexander-Sinclair set
around C17 water mill and pond,
extensive 7-acre garden incl an
arboretum and ponds. Lastly the
National Garden of Herb Society
based at the Manor has grown a
range of herbs that the Founding
Fathers would have taken to America.
Small historic village with lovely stone
houses, C14 church and C16 manor
house, home of George Washington's
ancestors. Award winning community
owned and run village shop.
🐾 ✿ 🍵

53▶ THIMBLE HALL
601 Harlstone Road. NN5 6NU. Mrs
Maureen Basford, 01604 751208.
*4m W of Northampton on A428.
1½ m from Lower Harlestone, 3½ m
Althorp.* Tea & Light Refreshments.
**Adm £2, chd free. Regret, no
children under 12yrs. Visitors
welcome by appt.** Open daily
15 May - 31 July.
Small garden divided into small rooms
with some unusual plants. Wildlife
pond, barn owls on display, garden
shop.
✿ 🍵 ☎

THORPE LUBENHAM HALL
See Leicestershire & Rutland.

54▶ TILE HOUSE FARM
Fulwell Rd, Finmere MK18 4AS.
Peter & Buzzy Lepper,
01280 848358,
tilehouseplants@fsmail.net,
www.tilehouseplants.co.uk. *4m E
Brackley, 4m W of Buckingham. From
A421 through Finmere on Fulwell Rd
to Westbury. From A422 towards
Finmere follow daisy sign.* Home-
made teas. **Adm £3.50, chd free.
Sun & Mon 29, 30 May; Sun
11 Sept (2-6). Visitors also
welcome by appt.**
³⁄₄ -acre individual farmhouse garden
bursting with colour and interesting
ideas. Fun element to the garden
planted to encourage birds and
wildlife. Raised beds, avery and
hidden features included within
pond, kitchen and gravel gardens.
Adjacent nursery. Partial wheelchair
access.
♿ ✿ 🍵 ☎

55▶ TITCHMARSH HOUSE
Chapel Street. NN14 3DA. Sir Ewan
& Lady Harper, 01832 732439,
jenny.harper@church-schools.com.
*2m N of Thrapston. 6m S of Oundle.
Exit A14 at A605 J, Titchmarsh
signed as turning to E.* Home-made
teas at Village Fete on 30th May &
Community Shop 11 June. **Adm £3,
chd free. Mon 30 May (2-6); Sat 11
June (12-5). Visitors also welcome
by appt April to mid June.**
4½ acres extended and laid out since
1972. Cherries, magnolias,
herbaceous, irises, shrub roses,
range of unusual shrubs, walled
borders and ornamental vegetable
garden.
♿ 🍵 ☎

56▶ TOP LODGE
Violet Lane, Glendon, nr Kettering
NN14 1QL. Glenn & Anne Burley,
01536 511784,
glennburley@btconnect.com.
*3m NW of Kettering. Take A6003
to Corby, off r'about W of Kettering
turn L onto Glendon Rd, signed at
T-lights, approx 2m L into Violet Lane.*
Cream Teas. **Adm £3, chd free.
Sun 12 June (1.30-5). Visitors also
welcome by appt May to July,
coaches welcome.**
1½ -acre garden which is full of
pleasant surprises around every
corner. Large collection of plants,
some rare and unusual shrubs plus a
good selection of climbing roses and
clematis. Woodland area, pond with
stream and waterfalls, gravel,
secluded garden and a children's
garden.
♿ ✿ 🍵 ☎

GROUP OPENING

57▶ TURWESTON GARDENS
Brackley NN13 5JY. *A43 from M40
J10. On Brackley bypass turn R on
A422 towards Buckingham, ½ m turn
L signed Turweston.* Home-made
teas at Versions Farm. **Combined
adm £4.00, chd free.** Sun 29 May
(2-5.30).

> **OATLEYS HALL**
> Caroline & Ralph Grayson
>
> **TURWESTON HOUSE**
> Mr & Mrs C Allen
>
> **TURWESTON MILL**
> Mr & Mrs Harry Leventis
>
> **VERSIONS FARM**
> Mrs E T Smyth-Osbourne

Charming unspoilt stone built village
in a conservation area. 3 quite large
beautiful gardens. The Mill with
bridges over the river and a
spectacular waterfall, wildlife pond
and newly designed kitchen garden.
A 3-acre plantsman's garden with old
stonewalls and terraces, pergola,
pond and small water garden. 5-acre

garden with woodland and pond. Formal terrace and swimming pool area designed by James Alexander-Sinclair in 2008.

WALTON GARDENS
See Leicestershire & Rutland.

GROUP OPENING

58 **WAPPENHAM GARDENS**
NN12 8SJ. *4m W of Towcester, 6m N of Brackley, 8m E of Banbury. Maps available for all visitors.* Home-made teas. **Combined adm £4, chd free.** Sun 12 June (2-5.30).

HOME FARM
Mr & Mr Robert Tomkinson

NEW **THE LAURELS**
Mr Colin Bullock

PITTAMS FARM
Hilary and John Wickham

STONE COTTAGE
Diane & Brian Watts

WAPPENHAM MANOR
Mr & Mrs Fordham

Unspoilt rural stone, brick built village. Interesting church with C13 tower and unusual C17 clock. Village includes several Gilbert Scott buildings.

WARMINGTON VILLAGE GARDENS
See Warwickshire.

GROUP OPENING

59 **WEEDON LOIS & WESTON GARDENS**
NN12 8PJ. *7m W of Towcester. 7m N of Blackley. Off A43.* Cream teas. **Combined adm £4.50, chd free.** Sun 19 June (2-5.30).

HOME CLOSE
Clyde Burbidge

LOIS WEEDON HOUSE
Sir John & Lady Greenaway

OLD BARN
Mr & Mrs John Gregory
Visitors also welcome by appt in June & July.
01327 860577
irisgregory@tiscali.co.uk

Hill Grounds

NEW **RIDGEWAY COTTAGE**
Jonathan & Elizabeth Carpenter

THE WILDE HOUSE GARDEN
Mrs Sara Wilde

Two adjacent villages in S Northants with a handsome medieval church in Weedon Lois. The extension churchyard contains the graves of the poets Dame Edith Sitwell and her brother Sacheveral who lived in Weston Hall. Weston has some fine stone houses incl Armada House, Weston Hall and a cluster of village centre farmhouses. Large beautiful garden with magnificent trees, a plantsmans garden, newly designed award winning garden and a charming cottage garden opening for the first time. Wheelchair access at The Wilde House Garden, Ridgeway Cottage & Lois Weedon House only.

2 WELFORD ROAD
See Leicestershire & Rutland.

Snowdrops, hellebores and woodland garden in spring. Vibrant perennials in hot borders in summer . . .

GROUP OPENING

60 **WEST HADDON GARDENS**
NN6 7AP. *10m NW of Northampton. Off A428 between Rugby & Northampton, 4m E of M1 J18. Village now bypassed. Tickets and maps at all gardens.* Home-made teas in Village Hall. **Combined adm £4, chd free. Evening Opening £5, Sat 25 June (7-10); Sun 26 June (2-6).**

CLOVER COTTAGE
Helen & Stephen Chown

THE CROWN COURTYARD
Mark Byrom

16 FIELD CLOSE
Andy & Bev French

NEW **11 FIELD CLOSE**
Paul & Diana Butcher

LIME HOUSE
Lesley & David Roberts
Visitors also welcome by appt May, June and July.
01788 510437
lesley.c.roberts@btinternet.com

TOWNLEY BARN
Kate & Richard Tilt
Visitors also welcome by appt May June August.
01788 540658
katerichard.tilt@btinternet.com

WESLYAN COTTAGE
Arnie & Gillean Stensones

A traditional village, predominantly brick but some local stone and thatch, plus modern housing estates. A few shops, PH with restaurants, and a well preserved church and chapel. Interesting mix of small and large gardens. Walled cottage garden with terraces, decking and sheltered area with a lemon tree and orange bush, and PH courtyard with C16 outbuildings. Small, low maintenance

---

garden with numerous shrubs and small pond, and walled garden with rockeries, shrubbery, croquet lawn, rose and herbaceous borders, garden statues and ornaments. Organic garden with wild flower meadow and peaceful inner courtyard, a garden with a number of separate areas, incl enclosure with roses, a beach garden, vegetable and soft fruits area, and a small low maintenance garden with decking, pots and shrubs. 25 June, 4 gardens open, live Blues and Jazz. Refreshments available. Tickets can be re-used to visit on 26 June. Featured in Local press.

61 **WOODCHIPPINGS**
Juniper Hill NN13 5RH. Richard Bashford & Valerie Bexley, 01869 810170. *3m S of Brackley, 3m N J10 M40. Off A43, S of Croughton r'about take L turn, 1/2 m to Juniper Hill.* **Adm £4, chd free. Visitors welcome by appt** from Feb to mid July, **individuals & groups welcome.** 1/3 -acre plantsman's garden surrounding stone cottage. Densely and abundantly planted for colour and scent. Snowdrops, hellebores and woodland garden in spring. Vibrant perennials in hot borders in summer. Planting especially for insects. Narrow paths may be unsuitable for infirm or very young. Small nursery.

> ### For Northumberland please see North East page 398

Northamptonshire County Volunteers

County Organisers
David Abbott, Wroxton Lodge, Church Hill, Finedon, Wellingborough NN9 5NR, 01933 680363, d_j_abbott@btinternet.com
Annabel Smyth-Osbourne, Versions Farm, Turweston, Brackley NN13 5JY, 01280 702412, annabelso@aol.com
Gay Webster, Four Acres, The Green, Guilsborough NN6 8PT, 01604 740203, egwebster16@hotmail.com

County Treasurer & Publicity
Michael Heaton, Mulberry Cottage, Yew Tree Lane, Spratton NN6 8HL, 01604 846032, ngs@mimomul.co.uk

Assistant County Organisers
Joy Haywood, 29 Welford Road, Creaton NN6 8NH, 01604 505458
Philippa Heumann, The Old Vicarage, Broad Lane, Evenley, Brackley NN13 5SF, 01280 702409, philippaheumann@andreas-heumann.com
Geoff Sage, West Cottage, West End, West Haddon NN6 7AY, 01788 510334, geoffsage@aol.com

---

Visit a garden in your own time – look out for the ☎

NORTH EAST

County Durham, Northumberland, Teesside & Tyne and Wear

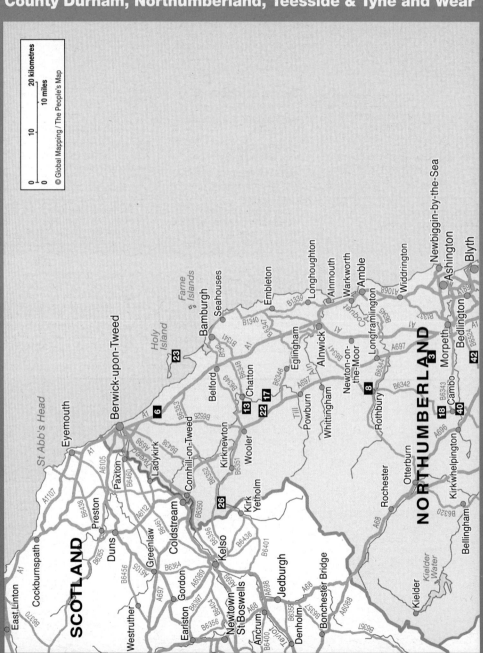

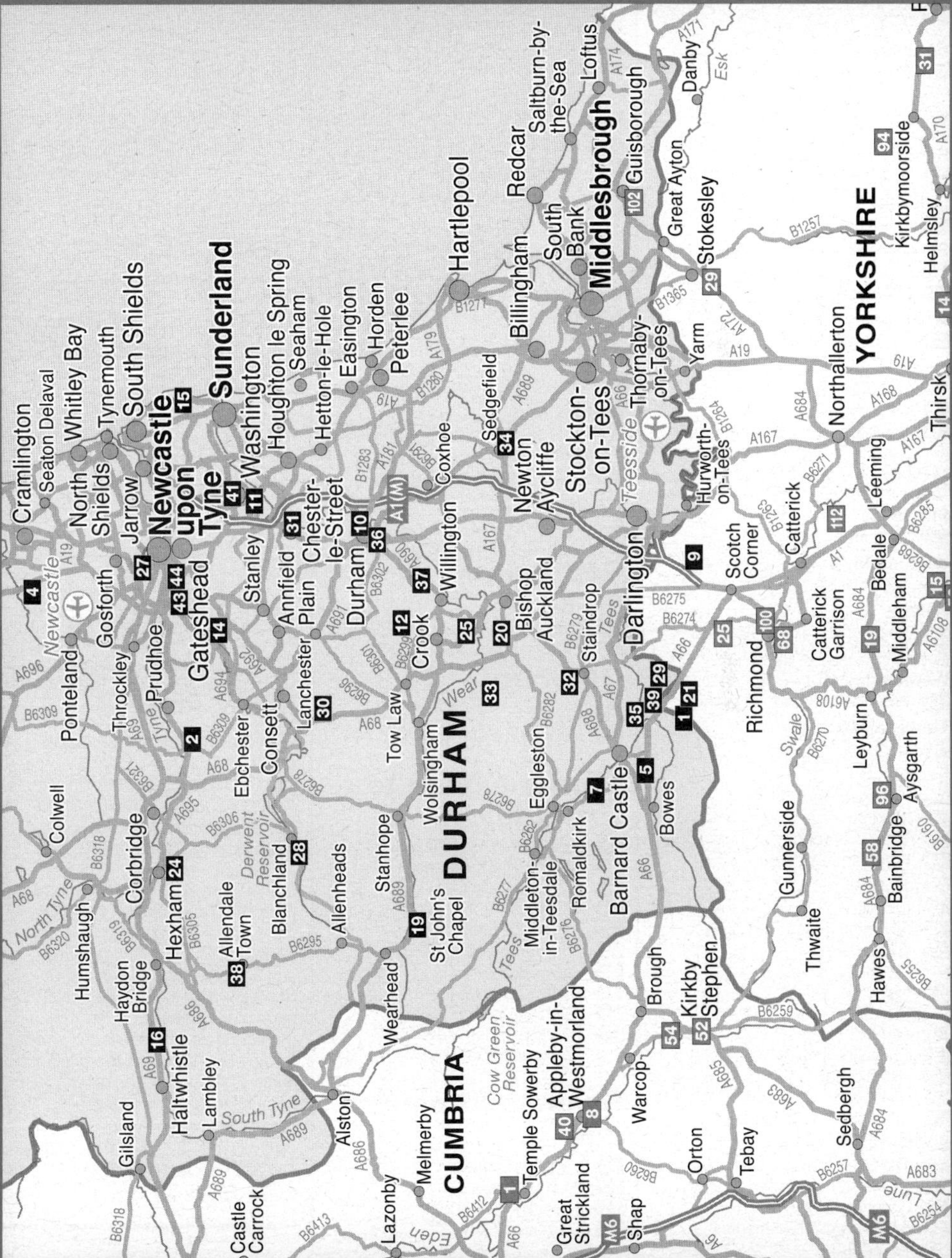
Cramlington
Seaton Delaval
Whitley Bay
Tynemouth
North Shields
South Shields
Jarrow
Newcastle upon Tyne
Gateshead
Sunderland
Washington
Houghton le Spring
Seaham
Hetton-le-Hole
Easington
Horden
Peterlee
Hartlepool
Billingham
Redcar
Saltburn-by-the-Sea
Loftus
South Bank
Middlesbrough
Guisborough
Great Ayton
Stokesley
Danby
Esk
Stockton-on-Tees
Thornaby-on-Tees
Yarm
Teesside
Hurworth-on-Tees
Darlington
Sedgefield
Newton Aycliffe
Coxhoe
Chester-le-Street
Durham
Willington
Bishop Auckland
Staindrop
Crook
Tow Law
Wolsingham
Stanhope
St John's Chapel
Wearhead
Allenheads
Annfield Plain
Stanley
Lanchester
Consett
Ebchester
Blanchland
Derwent Reservoir
Allendale Town
Hexham
Corbridge
Prudhoe
Throckley
Ponteland
Gosforth
Newcastle
Colwell
Humshaugh
North Tyne
Haydon Bridge
Haltwhistle
Lambley
South Tyne
Gilsland
Castle Carrock
Alston
Lazonby
Melmerby
Temple Sowerby
Cow Green Reservoir
Appleby-in-Westmorland
Great Strickland
Shap
Warcop
Brough
Kirkby Stephen
Orton
Tebay
Sedbergh
Lune
Eden
Tees
Wear
Tyne
Swale
Middleton-in-Teesdale
Romaldkirk
Eggleston
Barnard Castle
Bowes
Richmond
Scotch Corner
Catterick
Catterick Garrison
Leyburn
Middleham
Bedale
Leeming
Northallerton
Thirsk
Helmsley
Kirkbymoorside
Aysgarth
Bainbridge
Hawes
Thwaite
Gunnerside
DURHAM
CUMBRIA
YORKSHIRE

Opening Dates

March

Sunday 27
27 Moorbank Botanic Garden

April

Saturday 23
3 Bide-a-Wee Cottage

May

Sunday 1
29 The Old Vicarage, Hutton Magna

Saturday 7
41 Washington Old Hall

Sunday 15
22 Lilburn Tower
40 Wallington

Wednesday 18
27 Moorbank Botanic Garden (Evening)

Sunday 22
4 Blagdon
36 Sledwich

June

Sunday 5
9 Croft Hall

Wednesday 8
10 Crook Hall & Gardens

Sunday 12
1 Barningham Village Gardens
30 Oliver Ford Garden

Wednesday 15
44 Woodland Cottage (Evening)

Thursday 16
18 Herterton House

Sunday 19
16 Henshaw Barn
26 Mindrum
39 Thorpe Gardens
44 Woodland Cottage

Sunday 26
5 Browside
13 Fowberry Mains Farmhouse
15 Glebe Farm

July

Sunday 3
6 Cheswick House
19 High Hill Top
21 Ivy House
42 Whalton Manor Gardens

Sunday 10
2 The Beacon
7 Cotherstone Village Gardens
24 Loughbrow House
34 St Margaret's Allotments
40 Wallington

Thursday 14
18 Herterton House

Saturday 16
8 Cragside

Sunday 17
11 111 Fatfield Park
28 Newbiggin House

Sunday 24
12 The Fold

Monday 25
23 Lindisfarne Castle Garden

Saturday 30
3 Bide-a-Wee Cottage

Sunday 31
43 Whickham Hermitage Community Garden
44 Woodland Cottage

August

Wednesday 3
27 Moorbank Botanic Garden (Evening)

Sunday 7
33 Ravensford Farm

Sunday 14
17 Hepburn Bell

Thursday 18
18 Herterton House

Sunday 21
38 Thornley House

September

Saturday 3
14 Gibside

October

Sunday 23
27 Moorbank Botanic Garden

Gardens open to the public

3 Bide-a-Wee Cottage
10 Crook Hall & Gardens
8 Cragside
14 Gibside
18 Herterton House
23 Lindisfarne Castle Garden
32 Raby Castle
40 Wallington
41 Washington Old Hall
43 Whickham Hermitage Community Garden

By appointment only

20 2 Hillside Cottage
25 10 Low Row
31 25 Park Road South
37 4 Stockley Grove

Also open by Appointment ☎

6 Cheswick House
11 111 Fatfield Park
12 The Fold
19 High Hill Top
24 Loughbrow House
28 Newbiggin House
33 Ravensford Farm
38 Thornley House
42 Whalton Manor Gardens
44 Woodland Cottage

This garden has been created over the last 12 years and illustrates how to make a garden, with lots of interest at different levels, on a steep site . . .

The Gardens

GROUP OPENING

1 BARNINGHAM VILLAGE GARDENS
DL11 7DW. *6m SE of Barnard Castle. 9m W of Scotch Corner turn S off A66 at Greta Bridge, or from A66 motel via Newsham.* Home-made teas & lunch time sandwiches at Barningham Village Hall. **Combined adm £4, chd free. Sun 12 June (12-5).**
Six interesting and varied gardens, and one private nursery in the beautiful village of Barningham on the edge of the Yorkshire dales. The gardens are intimate reflections of their owners style and character, the nursery has a collection of rarer cornus, holly, maple and conifer species www.plantsmancorner.co.uk. All are in a delightful setting. Featured in North East Life magazine.
♿ 🐕 🌐 ☕

2 NEW **THE BEACON**
10 Crabtree Road, Stocksfield
NE43 7NX. Mr & Mrs G Hodgson.
*12m W of Newcastle upon Tyne.
From A69, Stocksfield turn off, into
village.Pass cricket ground, station on
L. Either park in station carpark (cross
road to signed path) or turn next R -
Cadehill Rd; next R.* Home-made
teas. **Adm £3, chd free. Sun 10 July
(2-6).**
This garden has been created over
the last 12 years and illustrates how
to make a garden, with lots of interest
at different levels, on a steep site.
Water gently runs through it, and it is
planted with acers, apple and lilac
trees, roses, rhododendron and
herbaceous perennials. There are
quiet, tranquil places to sit.

3 ◆ **BIDE-A-WEE COTTAGE**
Stanton, Morpeth NE65 8PR. Mr M
Robson, 01670 772238,
www.bideawee.co.uk. *7m NNW of
Morpeth. Turn L off A192 out of
Morpeth at Fairmoor. Stanton is 6m
along this rd.* **Adm £2.50, chd free.
For NGS: Sat 23 Apr (1.30-4.30);
Sat 30 July (1.30-5). For other
opening times and information,
please phone or see garden
website.**
Unique secret garden created over
the last 26yrs out of a small
sandstone quarry, it features rock and
water. Unusual perennials are woven
within a matrix of ferns, trees and
shrubs. The garden contains the
National Collection of centaurea, and
many other plants seldom seen.

4 **BLAGDON**
Seaton Burn NE13 6DE. The Hon
Matt Ridley,
www.blagdonestate.co.uk. *5m S of
Morpeth on A1. A1 N of Newcastle
8m, turn on to B1318 towards Seaton
Burn then L at r'about (Holiday Inn)
and follow signs to Blagdon. Entrance
to parking area signed.* Home-made
teas. **Adm £3.50, chd free. Sun 22
May (1-5).**
Unique 27 acre garden
encompassing formal garden with
Lutyens designed 'canal', Lutyens
structures and walled kitchen garden.
Valley with stream and various follies,
quarry garden and woodland walks.
Large numbers of ornamental trees
and shrubs planted over many
generations. National Collections of
Acer, Alnus and Sorbus.

Blagdon

5 **BROWSIDE**
Boldron, Barnard Castle, Co
Durham DL12 9RQ. Mr & Mrs R D
Kearton. *3m S of Barnard Castle. On
A66 3m W of Greta Bridge, turn R to
Boldron, then proceed 1/2 m, entrance
opp junction. From Barnard Castle
take A67 to Bowes, after 2m turn L
to Boldron.* Home-made teas. **Adm
£2.50, chd free. Sun 26 June
(1-5.30).**
1 1/4 acres with unusual water features
and large collection of conifers and
acers, wide range of plants and
imaginative stone objects.
Wonderfully tranquil seating areas.
Live music from Northumbrian Pipers.

6 **CHESWICK HOUSE**
Cheswick TD15 2RL. Mr & Mrs P
Bennett, 01289 387387,
info@cheswickhouse.co.uk,
www.cheswickhouse.co.uk. *4m S
of Berwick upon Tweed. Turn E from
A1 signed Goswick/Cheswick.* Home-
made & cream teas. **Adm £3, chd
free. Sun 3 July (1-5.30). Visitors
also welcome by appt.**
A large Gothic Victorian garden
undergoing a restoration programme
including new herbaceous borders,
and water features. Romantic walled
garden and newly created garden
rooms each with a distinctive
character. Former Curling rink
converted into a Mediterranean gravel

garden with raised beds and circular pond. Magnificent views of cheviots and coast and varied woodland walks. Plant stall, teas. Tennis court. Limited wheelchair access.

GROUP OPENING

7 COTHERSTONE VILLAGE GARDENS
Contact. Ian/Sandra Moorhouse, 01833650730. DL12 9PQ. *4m NW of Barnard Castle. On B6277 Middleton-in-Teesdale to Barnard Castle road.* Light refreshments & home-made teas. **Combined adm £4, chd free. Sun 10 July (11-5).**
A warm welcome awaits you in one of the best 20 villages in the country. Very picturesque at the confluence of the Rivers, Tees and Balder. A variety of country gardens and allotments, small medium, large, Edwardian, Wooded and a Naturalists. Some areas weaving in local and natural history. Make your visit more memorable by joining us for lunch and tea, served in interesting locations, take part in a gardens Treasure Hunt or buy and browse at the plant stalls.

8 ◆ CRAGSIDE
Rothbury NE65 7PX. National Trust, 01669 620333, www.nationaltrust.org.uk. *13m SW of Alnwick. (B6341); 15m NW of Morpeth (A697).* **Adm £7.50, chd £4.80. For NGS: Sat 16 July (10.30-7).** For other opening times and information, please phone or see garden website.
3 acre formal garden in the 'High Victorian' style created by the 1st Lord Armstrong. Restored Italian terrace, orchard house, carpet bedding, dahlia walk and fernery. 4¹/₂ acre rock garden with its restored cascades. Extensive grounds of over 1000 acres famous for rhododendrons in June, beautiful lakeside walks and woodland.

9 NEW CROFT HALL
Croft-on-Tees DL2 2TB. Mr & Mrs Trevor Chaytor Norris. *3m S of Darlington. On A167 to Northallerton, 6m from Scotch Corner. Croft Hall is 1st house on R as you enter village from Scotch Corner.* Home-made teas. **Adm £4, chd free. Sun 5 June (2-6).**

A lovely lavender walk leads to a Queen Anne fronted house (not open) surrounded by a 5-acre garden, comprising a stunning herbaceous border, large fruit and vegetable plot, two ponds and wonderful topiary arched wall. New pretty rose garden and mature box Italianate parterre are beautifully set in this garden offering peaceful, tranquil views of open countryside. Some gravel paths.

10 ◆ CROOK HALL & GARDENS
Sidegate, Durham City DH1 5SZ. Maggie Bell, 0191 384 8028, www.crookhallgardens.co.uk. *Centre of Durham City. Crook Hall is short walk from Durham's Market Place. Follow the tourist info signs. Parking available at entrance.* **Adm £6, chd 3-16yrs £5, concessions £5.50. For NGS: Wed 8 June (11-5).** For other opening times and information, please phone or see garden website.
Described in Country Life as having 'history, romance and beauty'. Intriguing medieval manor house surrounded by 4 acres of fine gardens. Visitors can enjoy magnificent cathedral views from the 2 walled gardens. Other garden 'rooms' incl the silver and white garden, orchard, moat, pool and maze.

New pretty rose garden and mature box Italianate parterre are beautifully set offering peaceful, tranquil views . . .

11 111 FATFIELD PARK
Washington NE38 8BP. Gillian & Peter Lund, 0191 4167923, gill.lund@btinternet.com. *1¹/₂ m SE of Washington Town Centre. Take Washington exit on A1(M) Junction 64. Follow A195 for approx 2m. 3rd exit on 2nd O into Biddick Lane following brown signs for Art Centre in Biddick Lane. 85yds after Art Centre turn R into Fatfield Park and follow yellow signs to garden.* Home-made teas. **Adm £2.50, chd free. Sun 17 July (12-4.30).** Visitors also welcome by appt.

Inspirational, developing garden full of yr-round colour and interest. Many plants grown from seed and cuttings to produce a large variety of interesting plants. Wildlife friendly pond and bog garden.Large herbaceous borders with cottage style planting. Gravel garden with grasses and perenials.

12 NEW THE FOLD
High Wooley, Stanley, Crook DL15 9AP. Mr & Mrs G Young, 01388 768412, gfamyoung@madasafish.com. *3m N of Crook. On A690 S from Durham turn R at Brancepeth X-rds (signed to Castle), after 3¹/₂ m follow yellow signs. From A1 going N on A68 take B6299 to Tow Law after approx 2m follow yellow signs.* Cream teas. **Adm £3, chd free. Sun 24 July (2-5).** Visitors also welcome by appt.
Large rural cottage-style garden, approx ¹/₃ -acre at 700ft. Splendid views of surrounding countryside. Herbaceous borders and island beds. Ponds and numerous mature trees. Small roof garden. Award of Merit in Beautiful Durham.

13 FOWBERRY MAINS FARMHOUSE
Wooler NE71 6EN. Mr & Mrs A F McEwen. *2m W of Chatton, 3m E of Wooler. Signed between Wooler & Chatton on B6348.* Home-made teas. **Adm £3.50, chd free (share to Holy Cross Chatton & St Peters Chillingham). Sun 26 June (2-5.30).**
Artistically and lovingly created colourful 1-acre garden. Relaxed country style featuring informal beds with hardy perennials, roses and shrubs, well stocked mixed herbaceous borders. Pretty gravel beds with grasses and drought tolerant plants. Productive vegetable garden. Small wild area with trees, shrubs and bog-loving plants. Beautiful views.

14 NEW ◆ GIBSIDE
nr Rowlands Gill, Tyne and Wear NE16 6BG. National Trust, 01207 541820, www.nationaltrust.org.uk. *6m SW of Gateshead. Entrance on B6314 between Burnopfield & Rowlands Gill. Follow brown signs from A1 exit N of Metro Centre. Bus service from Newcastle upon Tyne.* **Adm £6.50, chd £4. For NGS: Sat 3 Sept (10-6).** For other opening

times and information please phone or visit garden website.
C18 landscape park designed by Stephen Switzer for one of the richest men in Georgian England, George Bowes, and his celebrated grand-daughter Mary Eleanor. Inner pleasure grounds with tree lined avenue and productive walled garden, plus miles of woodland and riverside walks in the Derwent Valley. New for 2011: restoration of a historic garden walk that once connected Gibside Chapel and hall via the elegant greenhouse and ice house dene. Designed to captivate the senses, its planting displays guide you through areas of dark and light, offering views and gorgeous scents. 'Meet the Gardener' - our head gardener will be on hand to chat about Gibside's garden restoration. Mobility vehicle available.
& 🏠 ⊗ ☕

15 **NEW** **GLEBE FARM**
Moor Lane, Whitburn, Sunderland SR6 7JP. John & Kathryn Moor. *2m N of Sunderland. From junction of A19 & A184, follow A184 E through W & E Bolden. After passing Dog Track on L turn L at r'about onto A1018 towards South Shields. Take 2nd R (after 1m) onto Moor Lane. Farm & parking on R on entering village.* Home-made teas. **Adm £3, chd free. Sun 26 June (1-5).**
This lovely garden is on the edge of the picturesque village of Whitburn. Its ³/₄ acre has a range of colours, moods and styles - lawned and gravelled areas surrounded by herbaceous borders with David Austin roses, a wide variety of shrubs and herbaceous perennials. Ornamental trees, herb garden and small woodland. Views of the sea, and the North York Moors (on a good day).
⊗ ☕

16 **HENSHAW BARN**
Henshaw, Hexham NE47 7EN. Pauline Ellis & John Rutherford. *14m W of Hexham on A69. 1st R after garage. 1st L into village. Following rd round, car park through field gate.* Cream teas. **Adm £2.50, chd free. Sun 19 June (2-6).**
Nicely maturing wildlife friendly garden begun 2007/08, innovatively designed in a relaxed style. Distinctive willow arches and screens. Local stone retaining walls incorporating a rill, pond and rockery. Old roses, clematis, mixed herbaceous borders, grasses, clipped box, laburnum walk and embryonic woodland garden.

Productive allotment with flowers, fruit and vegetables. Magnificent views. Plant stall. Very limited wheelchair access.
& ⊗ ☕

17 **NEW** **HEPBURN BELL**
Chillingham, Alnwick NE66 4EF. Camilla Davidson. *6m SE of Wooler. Follow signs for Chillingham. Garden will be signed from Chillingham Castle.* Home-made teas. **Adm £3.50, chd free. Sun 14 Aug (2-5).**
Walled garden designed by Justin Spink within an old farm steading. Different areas incl a potager, and flower garden. On different levels, the garden incl steps.
☕

18 ◆ **HERTERTON HOUSE**
Cambo, Hartington NE61 4BN. Mr Frank Lawley, 01670 774278. *12m W of Morpeth. 23m NW of Newcastle. 2m N of Cambo on the B6342 signed to Hartington. Brown signs.* **Adm £3.50, chd free. For NGS: Thurs 16 June; 14 July; 18 Aug (1.30-5.30). For other opening times and information, please phone.**
1 acre of formal garden in stone walls around C16 farmhouse (not open). Incl small topiary garden, physic garden, flower garden, fancy garden, gazebo and nursery garden.
⊗

19 **HIGH HILL TOP**
St John's Chapel DL13 1RJ. Mr & Mrs I Hedley, 01388 537952. *7m W of Stanhope. On A689. Turn L into Harthope Rd after Co-op shop in St John's Chapel. Up hill for ¹/₂ m past the Animal Hotel. Garden next house on L.* Home-made teas. **Adm £3, chd free. Sun 3 July (10-4). Visitors also welcome by appt.**
See what can be achieved in an exposed garden at 1200ft. Mixed planting incl wonderful collection of sorbus, hostas, ferns, eucalyptus and candelabra primulas. Magnificent backdrop of North Pennines. More of this lovely garden was made accessible in 2010.
⊗ ☕ 🕿

20 **NEW** **2 HILLSIDE COTTAGE**
Low Etherley, Bishop Auckland DL14 0EZ. Mrs M Smith, 01388 832727, mary@maryruth.plus.com. *3m W of Bishop Auckland. From Bishop Auckland take B6282 to Etherley. Turn R opp no. 63 Low*

Etherley into Heritage Railway Trail (signed). From A68 take B6282 for ¹/₂ m, then turn L as above. Light refreshments. **Adm £3. Visitors welcome by appt.**
Very interesting year round colourful garden with many unusual plants, trees, shrubs and wide variety of perennials. Two ponds which attract a myriad of wildlife. Small meadow full of cowslips and fritillarias. Raised vegetable beds, greenhouse and fruit area. Small gravel and bog garden.
☕ 🕿

A small patio and flat grassed terrace invite you to walk up the gentle slope . . .

21 **NEW** **IVY HOUSE**
Newsham, Richmond DL11 7RD. Mr & Mrs J Ord. *6m E of Barnard Castle. From Scotch Corner on A1 take A66 W for 7m. Turn L at A66 Motel to Newsham, after 1¹/₄ m garden is last house in village on L. Parking in village hall.* Home-made teas at village hall. **Adm £3, chd free. Sun 3 July (12-5).**
This²/₃ -acre garden is on a sloping site and stocked with a huge variety of plants, mature trees and lovely garden pond with a small waterfall. Two large Wellingtonia trees give a good backdrop to this pretty garden with island beds and beautifully made stone walls. A small patio and flat grassed terrace invite you to walk up the gentle slope. Limited wheelchair access.
& 🏠 ☕

22 **LILBURN TOWER**
Alnwick NE66 4PQ. Mr & Mrs D Davidson. *3m S of Wooler. On A697.* Home-made teas. **Adm £3.50, chd free. Sun 15 May (2-6).**
10 acres of walled and formal gardens incl conservatory and large glasshouse. Approx 30 acres of woodland with walks and pond garden. Rhododendrons and azaleas. Also ruins of Pele Tower, and C12 church. Steps to main garden. Woodland garden accessible.
& 🏠 ⊗ ☕

Support the NGS – eat more cake! ☕

Fowberry Mains Farmhouse

23 NEW ◆ **LINDISFARNE CASTLE GARDEN**
Holy Island, Lindisfarne TD15 2SH. National Trust, 01289 389244, www.nationaltrust.org.uk. *Located on Lindisfarne (Holy Island). On approching the castle the garden can be seen 500 metres across the field to the L.* Adm £1.50, chd free. For NGS: Mon 25 July (1-5). For other opening times and information please phone or see garden website. In 1911 Gertude Jekyll designed this garden as a summer garden for the then owner of the castle, Edward Hudson. Containing large drifts of hardy annuals (incl a fine show of sweet peas) the garden is a riot of colour in the height of summer. Guided talk by the gardener 1.30pm, 3pm and 4.30pm.

24 **LOUGHBROW HOUSE**
Hexham NE46 1RS. Mrs K A Clark, 01434 603351, patriciaclark351@btinternet.com. *1m S of Hexham. Take B6306 from Hexham, signed Blanchland, after ¹/₄ m take RH-fork. After a further ¹/₄ m you come to another fork, lodge gates are in intersection. Garden ¹/₂ m up the drive.* Home-made teas. Adm £3, chd free. Sun 10 July (2-5). Visitors also welcome by appt May to July.
Woodland garden with rhododendrons, azaleas and hosta bed in the quarry. Bog garden with pond. Old-fashioned roses, 3 herbaceous borders, large area of lawns. Extensive kitchen garden and paved courtyard. Developing wild flower meadow with specimen

trees. Home-made jams & chutneys for sale.
🐕 ❀ 🛏 ☕ ☎

25 **10 LOW ROW**
North Bitchburn, Crook DL15 8AJ. Mrs Ann Pickering, 01388 766345. *3m NW of Bishop Auckland. From Bishop Auckland take A689 (N) to Howden Le Wear. R up Bank before petrol stn, 1st R in village at 30mph sign.* Refreshments at The Red Lion in the village. Adm £2. Visitors welcome by appt all year (not Tues).
Quirky original garden with 90% grown from seeds and cuttings. Extensive views over the Wear valley. An amazing garden created without commercially bought plants or expense. Totally organic and

environmentally friendly. A haven for wildlife. Beautiful through the year from snowdrops to autumn leaves. Featured in Amateur Gardening.

26 MINDRUM

nr Cornhill on Tweed & Yetholm TD12 4QN. Mrs V Fairfax, www.mindrumgarden.co.uk. *6m SW of Coldstream, 9m NW of Wooler. 4m N of Yetholm. 5m from Cornhill on Tweed on B6352.* Cream Teas. **Adm £3.50, chd free. Sun 19 June (2-6).** Superbly varied garden with old-fashioned roses; rock and water garden; shrub borders. Wonderful views along Bowmont Valley. Approx 3 acres, or more if you like to wander by the river. Plants galore. Many and varied plants for sale.

27 MOORBANK BOTANIC GARDEN

Claremont Road, Newcastle upon Tyne NE2 4NL. University of Newcastle. *³/₄ m from Newcastle Haymarket. W end of Claremont Rd, just E of Cat & Dog Shelter. Shared entrance with Town Moor Superintendents Farm (blue gate). 12 mins walk up Claremont Rd from Exhibition Park entrance r'about. No parking in garden.* Wine (May). **Adm £3, chd free (share to Friends of Moorbank Garden). Sun 27 Mar (2-5); Evening Openings wine, Weds 18 May; 3 Aug (5-8); Sun 23 Oct (1-4).**
3 acre university botanic garden with collections of rare conifers, rhododendrons, sorbus, pond, perennials, herb garden, meadow. Extensive plantings under glass with tropical plants, succulents, insectivorous plants. Many original collections, originally from Kilbryde Gardens, Corbridge. Outside plantings maintained with volunteer help. Guided walks around the garden.

28 NEWBIGGIN HOUSE

Blanchland DH8 9UD. Mrs A Scott-Harden, 01434 675005. *12m S of Hexham. From Blanchland village take Stanhope Rd. ¹/₂ m along narrow rd follow yellow signs up tarmac drive into car park.* Cream teas. **Adm £4, chd free. Sun 17 July (2-5.30). Visitors also welcome by appt May, June & July, coaches permitted.**
5-acre landscaped garden at 1000ft, started in 1996 and maturing

beautifully. Old-fashioned herbaceous border, peonies, shrubs, roses, bog and wild garden incl wild rose walk. Magnificent collection of unusual trees and shrubs. Limited wheelchair access.

3 acres, or more if you like to wander by the river . . . plants galore . . .

29 THE OLD VICARAGE, HUTTON MAGNA

nr Richmond, N Yorkshire DL11 7HJ. Mr & Mrs D M Raw. *8m SE of Barnard Castle. 6m W of Scotch Corner on A66, Penrith direction. Signed Hutton Magna R. Continue to, and through, village. Garden 200yds past village on L, on corner of T-junction.* Home-made teas. **Adm £3, chd free. Sun 1 May (2-5.30).**
S-facing garden, elevation 450ft. Plantings, since 1978, now maturing within original design contemporary to 1887 house (not open). Cut and topiary hedging, old orchard; rose and herbaceous borders featuring hellebores in profusion, with tulips and primulas. Large and interesting plant sale.

30 OLIVER FORD GARDEN

Longedge Lane, Rowley, Consett DH8 9HG. Bob & Bev Tridgett, www.gardensanctuaries.co.uk. *5m NW of Lanchester. From Castleside approx 1m S on A68 turn L to Lanchester ¹/₂ m on L. From Lanchester B6296 signed Satley approx 2m turn R at Woodlea Manor, garden 2.9m on R.* Light refreshments & teas. **Adm £3, chd free. Sun 12 June (1-5).**
Spectacular 1¹/₂ -acre woodland garden that includes rare Acers,

Stewartia, Betula and Prunus. Stream, wildlife pond and bog garden. Japanese maple and dwarf Rhododendron garden. 80 square metre rock garden containing a significant collection of dwarf conifers. Insect nectar bar. Orchard and 1¹/₂ acre upland meadow. Annual wildflower area.

31 25 PARK ROAD SOUTH

Chester le Street DH3 3LS. Mrs A Middleton, 0191 388 3225. *4m N of Durham. A167 N towards Chester le Street. L at r'about (Durham Rd) to town centre. 1st R for parking and rear access to garden only. S from A1 - 3rd r'about then R as above.* **Adm £2.50, chd chd free. Visitors welcome by appt, 15 May to 30 Aug.**
Plantswoman's garden with all-yr round interest, colour, texture and foliage. Unusual perennials, grasses, shrubs and container planting. Cool courtyard garden using foliage only. Small front gravel garden. New planting and gazebo for 2010.

32 ◆ RABY CASTLE

Staindrop, Nr Darlington DL2 3AH. Lord Barnard, 01833 660202, www.rabycastle.com. *12m NW of Darlington, 1m N of Staindrop. On A688 8m NE of Barnard Castle.* **For opening times and information, please phone or see garden website.**
C18 walled gardens set within the grounds of Raby Castle. Designers such as Thomas White and James Paine have worked to establish the gardens, which now extend to 5 acres, displaying herbaceous borders, old yew hedges, formal rose gardens and informal heather and conifer gardens.

33 RAVENSFORD FARM

Hamsterley DL13 3NH. Mr & Mrs J Peacock, 01388 488305, peacock@ravensford.eclipse.co.uk. *7m W of Bishop Auckland. From A68 at Witton-le-Wear turn off W to Hamsterley. Go through village & turn L just before tennis courts at far end.* Home-made teas. **Adm £3, chd free. Sun 7 Aug (2.30-5). Visitors also welcome by appt, groups of 10+ but please no coaches.**
A late summer date for this garden of varied areas and moods containing a true plant-lover's range of ornamental

trees and shrubs - nearly all labelled - and flowers galore. There are 2 ponds (one with ducks), an orchard with children's play area, a secret sunken garden and plenty more to enjoy. Live music in the background. Some gravel, so assistance will be needed.

ALLOTMENTS

34 **ST MARGARET'S ALLOTMENTS**
Margery Lane, Durham DH1 4QG. *From A1 take A690 to city centre/Crook. Straight ahead at T-lights after passing 4 r'abouts. Pedestrians walk up Sutton St from big roundabout at viaduct. Allotments L in Margery Lane.* Home-made teas at Antioch House, Crossgate. **Combined adm £2.50, chd free.** Sun 10 July (2-5).
5 acres of 82 allotments against the spectacular backdrop of Durham Cathedral. This site has been cultivated since the middle ages, and was saved from development 20yrs ago, allowing a number of enthusiastic gardeners to develop their plots which display a great variety of fruit, vegetables and flowers. Display relating to the Save Our Allotments campaign of 1988-90.

35 **SEDGEFIELD GARDENS**
TS21 2AE. Mrs S Hannan. *12m SE of Durham. Off A689 Bishop Auckland to Hartlepool rd, 2½ m E of junction 60 of A1(M). From Teeside take A19 N & then follow signs for A689 to Bishop Auckland. Collect a route map from Ceddesfeld Hall, Rectory Row, TS21 2AE.* Cream teas in Ceddesfeld Hall, Rectory Row. **Adm £4, chd free.** Sun 19 July (1-5).
Selection of 8-10 gardens in beautiful village featuring water gardens, cottage planting and oriental display. Sedgefield boasts magnificent C13 church set on traditional village green. Winner Best Small Town - Northumbria in Bloom. Limited wheelchair access.

36 **NEW** **SLEDWICH**
Whorlton, Barnard Castle DL12 8UU. Capt N Pease. *3m E of Barnard Castle. 1m from Whorlton Village. From Barnard Castle, pass Bowes Museum towards Whorlton.*

3m turn R into Sledwich. Home-made teas. **Adm £3, chd free.** Sun 22 May (2-5.30).
A beautiful Elizabethan Manor House (not open) is hidden behind a large border of azaleas and rhododendrons. Lovely woodland walk through daffodils and bluebells to a small lake. Walled garden contains a variety of shrubs. Large herbaceous border. Good views towards R Tees from a large S facing paved courtyard.

Places to sit out and enjoy a picnic or afternoon tea. Excellent home-made teas . . .

37 **NEW** **4 STOCKLEY GROVE**
Brancepeth DH7 8DU. Mr & Mrs Bainbridge, 07944 523551, fabb63@waitrose.com. *5m W of Durham City. Take A690 from Durham to Brancepeth, through village and last turning on L after X-rds signed to 'To Castle'. Follow yellow NGS signs into Stockley Grove.* **Adm £3.** **Visitors welcome by appt,** no coaches.
Stunning ½ -acre garden packed with interesting and unusual plants, shrubs and trees incl 25 acers. Beautifully landscaped incl wildlife pond. Large patio with two ponds linked by a small stream with rockery area. Limited wheelchair access.

38 **THORNLEY HOUSE**
Thornley Gate, Allendale, Northum NE47 9NH. Ms Eileen Finn, 01434 683255, enquiries@thornleyhouse.co.uk, www.thornleyhouse.co.uk. *1m W of Allendale. From Allendale town, down hill from Hare & Hound to 5th rd junction, 1m Thornley House is big house in field in front.* Light refreshments & home-made teas. **Adm £3.50, chd free (share to Brooke charity for Working Animals).** Sun 21 Aug (2-5). **Visitors also welcome by appt open any time.**
Unusual 1-acre garden consisting of

woodland, stream, pond, vegetable and fruit garden, rose avenue and mixed planting. A feline theme is evident throughout this child-friendly garden. Seek and find quiz is available for family fun. Maine Coon cats and ornamental animals enhance this garden. Live classical music.

GROUP OPENING

39 **THORPE GARDENS**
DL12 9TU. *5m SE of Barnard Castle. 9m from Scotch Corner W on A66. Turn R at Peel House Farm Shop signed Wycliffe and Whorlton, 1m from A66.* Home-made teas at Thorpe Cottages. **Combined adm £3, chd free.** Sun 19 June (2-5).
Thorpe is a charming hamlet where there are three very different cottage gardens. One has 2 ponds linked by a small waterfall which attracts wildlife and contains some large fish. There is a greenhouse and vegetable garden along with flower borders and stunning views over open countryside. Another has a colourful large herbaceous bed and concealed seating area at the top of a small slope where there is a mature, prolific cherry tree. The third mature garden has many unusual plants and is gardened in a typical cottage garden manner. Also open is Thorpe Hall, a large interesting formal garden still in the course of development and now opened is a magnificent walled kitchen garden. Wood carving demonstration.

40 ◆ **WALLINGTON**
Cambo NE61 4AR. National Trust, 01670 774389, www.nationaltrust.org.uk. *12m W of Morpeth. From N B6343; from S via A696 from Newcastle, 6m W of Belsay, B6342 to Cambo.* **Adm £7.50, chd £3.50. For NGS: Suns 15 May; 10 July (10-7).** For other opening times and information, please phone or see garden website.
Walled, terraced garden with fine herbaceous and mixed borders; Edwardian conservatory; 100 acres woodland and lakes. House dates from 1688 but altered, interior greatly changed c1740; exceptional rococo plasterwork by Francini brothers.

41 NEW ◆ **WASHINGTON OLD HALL**
The Avenue, Washington Village NE38 7LE. National Trust, 0191 416 6879, www.nationaltrust.org.uk. *7m SE of Newcastle upon Tyne. Exit A1 J64 onto A195. From A19 & other routes take A1231 & follow brown signs to Washington Old Hall in Washington Village, next to church on the hill.* Adm £2, chd free. For NGS: Sat 7 May (11-3). For other opening times and information, please phone or see garden website.
The picturesque stone manor house and its gardens provide a tranquil oasis in an historic setting. It contains a formal Jacobean garden with box hedging borders around evergreens and perennials, vegetable garden, wild flower nut orchard. Places to sit out and enjoy a picnic or afternoon tea. Excellent home-made teas provided by the Friends of Washington Old Hall.

42 ◆ **WHALTON MANOR GARDENS**
Whalton NE61 3UT. Mr & Mrs T R P S Norton, 01670 775205, norton@whaltonmanor.fsnet.co.uk, www.whaltonmanor.co.uk. *5m W of Morpeth. On the B6524, the house is at the east end of the village and will be signed.* Adm £3.50, chd free. Sun 3 July (2-5.30). Visitors also welcome by appt, from end May to Sept for groups of 15 - 50.
The historic Whalton Manor, altered by Sir Edwin Lutyens in 1908, is surrounded by 3 acres of magnificent walled gardens, designed by Lutyens with the help of Gertrude Jekyll. The gardens have been developed by the Norton family since the 1920s and incl extensive herbaceous borders, 30yd peony border, rose garden, listed summerhouses, pergolas and walls, festooned with rambling roses and clematis. Partial wheelchair access. some stone steps.

43 NEW ◆ **WHICKHAM HERMITAGE COMMUNITY GARDEN**
Hermitage Lane, Front Street, Whickham NE16 4JL. Whickham Community Centre, 0785 4438187, www.whickhamhermitagegarden. co.uk. *SW of Newcastle. Follow B6317 (Whickham Highway from East/Swalwell Bank from West). Garden in Hermitage Lane behind Community Centre. Public parking opp Community Centre in Back Row, behind Bridle Path PH, or in West car park. No parking on site.* Adm £3, chd free. For NGS: Sun 31 July (10-4). For other opening times and information, please phone or see garden website.
This tucked away tranquil gem of a 1-acre garden was rescued from dereliction and has been created into a modern Victorian garden, solely through the work of volunteers. Wildlife pond and box garden, fruit and vegetable garden. This award winning garden has been extensively planted with trees, flowers and shrubs of many varieties. President's Award, Northumbria in Bloom.

44 ◆ **WOODLAND COTTAGE**
Duckpool Lane, off Market Lane, Whickham, Gateshead NE16 4TH. Mrs B Savage, 01914 960678, woodlandcott@aol.com. *2m S of Newcastle. On A1, climb ramp to Metro Centre but drive opp direction on local rd signposted Dunston/Whickham - bear L follow rd for 1/2 m. Duckpool Lane is off Market Lane. Opp Poachers Pocket PH (park in car park).* Adm £3, chd free (share to Multiple Sclerosis). Evening Opening Wed 15 June (6-8); Sun 19 June (12.30-4); Sun 31 July (2-4). Visitors also welcome by appt, small groups, max 10.
This is a flower arranger's garden full of vibrant early summer colour. Most plants have been chosen for their garden merit, interesting texture and colour. Small yet packed with perennials, small ornamental trees and evergreens carefully planted along pathways, transforms a small family garden into a layout with stylish design.

> 1-acre garden was rescued from dereliction and has been created into a modern Victorian garden, solely through the work of volunteers . . .

North East County Volunteers

County Organisers
County Durham Shanah Smailes, The Stables, Chapman's Court, Catterick Village, North Yorkshire DL10 7UE, 01748 812887, shanah@talktalk.net
Northumberland and Tyne and Wear Maureen Kesteven, No. 2 Ferndene, Holburn Lane Court, Ryton NE40 3PN, 0191 4135937, maureen@patrickkesteven.plus.com

County Treasurers
County Durham Shanah Smailes, The Stables, Chapman's Court, Catterick Village, North Yorkshire DL10 7UE. 01748 812887, shanah@talktalk.net
Northumberland and Tyne and Wear David Oakley, david@chesterswalledgarden.fsnet.co.uk

Publicity
County Durham Kay Duggan, Braeside, Barningham, Richmond, North Yorkshire DL11 7DW, 01833 621455, kay@kayduggan.fsnet.co.uk
Northumberland and Tyne and Wear Susie White, 07941 077595, susie@susie-white.co.uk

Assistant County Organisers
County Durham Elizabeth Carrick, Green House, Stone Man Lane, Gayles, nr Richmond, North Yorkshire DL11 7JB, 01833 621199
County Durham Gill Naisby, 44 Whitebridge Drive, Darlington DL1 3TY, 01325 381324, gillnaisby@tiscali.co.uk
Northumberland and Tyne and Wear Patricia Fleming, Wooperton Hall, Alnwick NE66 4XS 01668 217009
Northumberland and Tyne and Wear Natasha McEwen, Fowberry Mains Farmhouse, Wooler NE71 6EN, 01668 282092

NOTTINGHAMSHIRE

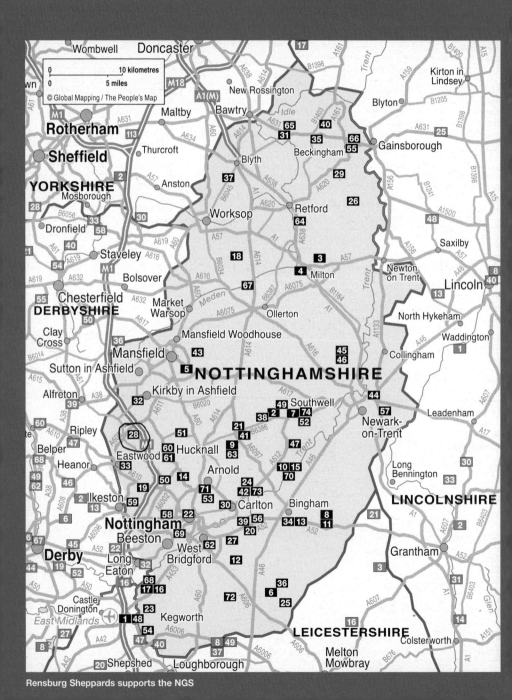

Opening Dates

February

From 5 Feb to 28 Feb
37 Hodsock Priory Gardens
Sunday 27
4 The Beeches

March

From 1 Mar to 6 Mar
37 Hodsock Priory Gardens
Sunday 6
39 Holme Pierrepont Hall
Sunday 13
4 The Beeches

April

Sunday 10
10 Capability Barn
Sunday 17
25 Elm House
28 Felley Priory
Sunday 24
44 Lumless House
Monday 25
47 Old Mill House

May

Sunday 1
2 Ashdene
4 The Beeches
9 Calverton House
12 Charnwood
21 Crows Nest Cottage
22 Darby House
23 Davryl
47 Old Mill House
Monday 2
12 Charnwood
Sunday 15
10 Capability Barn
24 Dumbleside
42 61 Lambley Lane
64 Squirrel Lodge
Saturday 21
7 Bishops Manor
Sunday 22
7 Bishops Manor
9 Calverton House
13 13 Cherry Street
15 Church House
34 Granby House
46 Norwell Nurseries
63 Smithy Cottage
70 West Farm House
Sunday 29
51 Papplewick Hall
72 The White House
73 Woodpeckers

Monday 30
38 Holbeck Lodge
40 Holmes Villa
49 The Old Vicarage
73 Woodpeckers

June

Wednesday 1
72 The White House
Sunday 5
1 25 Ashby Road
41 Home Farm Cottage
Sunday 12
14 The Chimes
23 Davryl
29 The Ferns
50 20 The Paddocks
Wednesday 15
10 Capability Barn
50 20 The Paddocks (Evening)
Saturday 18
7 Bishops Manor
Sunday 19
3 Askham Gardens
6 Bishops Cottage
7 Bishops Manor
22 Darby House
36 Hall Farm Cottage
38 Holbeck Lodge
49 The Old Vicarage
Wednesday 22
3 Askham Gardens (Evening)
56 Riseholme, 125 Shelford Road (Evening)
Saturday 25
8 5 Burton Lane
11 Cedarwood
54 Piecemeal
Sunday 26
9 Calverton House
32 Gardeners Cottage
35 Gringley Gardens
44 Lumless House
45 Norwell Gardens
46 Norwell Nurseries
71 6 Weston Close
Wednesday 29
32 Gardeners Cottage (Evening)
35 Gringley Gardens (Evening)
45 Norwell Gardens (Evening)
46 Norwell Nurseries (Evening)

July

Friday 1
20 Cornerstones (Evening)
Saturday 2
67 Thoresby Hall Hotel & Spa
Sunday 3
31 Gable Cottage
53 48 Penarth Gardens
55 Primrose Cottage
65 Sunnyside Cottage

66 Thistle Farm
71 6 Weston Close
Saturday 9
67 Thoresby Hall Hotel & Spa
Sunday 10
5 335 Berry Hill Lane
20 Cornerstones
30 Fuchsia View
49 The Old Vicarage
59 Sandown, 41 Church Lane
68 Thrumpton Hall
72 The White House
Wednesday 13
53 48 Penarth Gardens (Evening)
72 The White House
Thursday 14
30 Fuchsia View (Evening)
Saturday 16
18 Clumber Park Walled Kitchen Garden
54 Piecemeal
67 Thoresby Hall Hotel & Spa
Sunday 17
63 Smithy Cottage
Saturday 23
67 Thoresby Hall Hotel & Spa
74 The Workhouse
Wednesday 27
1 25 Ashby Road
Thursday 28
30 Fuchsia View (Evening)
Saturday 30
67 Thoresby Hall Hotel & Spa
Sunday 31
26 The Elms
27 Elms Farm
30 Fuchsia View
48 The Old Police House

August

Sunday 7
20 Cornerstones
33 Gorene
58 55 Russell Avenue
60 78 Sandy Lane
61 96 Sandy Lane
62 The Small Exotic Garden
69 University of Nottingham Gardens
Sunday 14
14 The Chimes
43 29 Lime Grove
52 Park Farm
64 Squirrel Lodge
Sunday 21
13 13 Cherry Street
34 Granby House
62 The Small Exotic Garden
Saturday 27
54 Piecemeal

Visit a garden in your own time – look out for the ☎

September

Wednesday 14
7 Bishops Manor
49 The Old Vicarage
Sunday 18
35 Gringley Gardens

October

Sunday 9
44 Lumless House
Sunday 16
46 Norwell Nurseries

January 2012

Sunday 22
4 The Beeches

Gardens open to the public

18 Clumber Park Walled Kitchen Garden
28 Felley Priory
37 Hodsock Priory Gardens
39 Holme Pierrepont Hall
46 Norwell Nurseries
74 The Workhouse

By appointment only

16 54 Church Lane
17 59 Church Lane
19 7 Collygate
57 Roselea

Also open by Appointment ☎

1 25 Ashby Road
2 Ashdene
4 The Beeches
8 5 Burton Lane
10 Capability Barn
11 Cedarwood
13 13 Cherry Street
15 Church House
20 Cornerstones
22 Darby House
24 Dumbleside
26 The Elms
27 Elms Farm
30 Fuchsia View
32 Gardeners Cottage
33 Gorene
34 Granby House
35 Gringley Hall, Gringley Gardens
38 Holbeck Lodge
40 Holmes Villa
41 Home Farm Cottage
44 Lumless House
47 Old Mill House
48 The Old Police House

50 20 The Paddocks
52 Park Farm
53 48 Penarth Gardens
54 Piecemeal
55 Primrose Cottage
56 Riseholme, 125 Shelford Road
60 78 Sandy Lane
62 The Small Exotic Garden
65 Sunnyside Cottage
70 West Farm House
71 6 Weston Close
73 Woodpeckers

The lawn is awash with crocus, fritillarias, anemones, narcissi and cyclamen . . .

The Gardens

1 NEW **25 ASHBY ROAD**
25 Ashby Road, Kegworth
DE74 2DH. Richard & Leigh
Woods, 01509 674732,
liliesandchillies@btinternet.com.
*10m S of Nottingham. 6m N of
Loughborough. From A6 into
High st. (opp Boots, next to Flying
Horse PH). Follow for 500m into
Ashby Rd.* Tea & biscuits. **Adm
£2.50, chd free. Sun 5 June (11-5);
Wed 27 July (2-7). Visitors also
welcome by appt June, July &
August. Max group 15.**
Plant lover's garden, packed with
traditional, rare and unusual plants.
Mixed borders throughout this
relatively small garden (8m x 40m)
giving flower, foliage, colour and
interest all yr. Also several specimen
trees incl oak, liquidambar and
liriodendron. No lawn to speak of, just
a bit of grass! Formal pond and
seating areas to relax and enjoy
something refreshing.
❀ ☕ ☎

2 **ASHDENE**
Radley Road, Halam NG22 8AH.
Glenys & David Herbert, 01636
812335. *1m W of Southwell. From
B6386 in Halam village 300yds past
church.* Home-made teas. **Adm £3,
chd free. Sun 1 May (1-5.30).
Visitors also welcome by appt.**
Many mature trees incl magnificent
walnut (200yrs), paulownia (50yrs)
and mulberry. Japanese-style garden
incl mature spiral yew. Species and

scented rose and woodland gardens.
Many clematis, hebes. Newly-planted
Bible garden.
♿ ☕ ❀ ☕ ☎

GROUP OPENING

3 **ASKHAM GARDENS**
Markham Moor NG22 0RP. *6m S of
Retford. On A638, in Rockley village
turn E to Askham.* Home-made teas.
**Combined adm £3.50, chd free.
Sun 19 June (2-6) Evening
Opening, wine, Wed 22 June (6-9).**

DOVECOTE COTTAGE
Mrs C Slack

FERN LEA
Mr G Thompson & Miss N Loy

NURSERY HOUSE
Mr & Mrs D Bird

STONE LEA
Mr & Mrs J Kelly

Variety of pleasant English village
gardens, with a flower festival in
church. Nursery House is a
plantsman's garden, secluded and
very private, with every plant
meticulously labelled; waterfall and
well-stocked pond. Fern Lea is a
small, ornamental garden with lawns
and borders at different levels. Stone
Lea has an interesting sequence of
gardens surrounding the house.
Dovecote Cottage is a small English
garden nr the church.
❀ ❀ ☕

STON GARDENS
Aston. See Yorkshire.

4 **THE BEECHES**
The Avenue, Milton, Tuxford,
Newark NG22 0PW. Margaret & Jim
Swindin, 01777 870828. *1m S A1
Markham Moor. Exit A1 at Markham
Moor, take Walesby sign into village
(1m). From Main Street, L up The
Avenue.* Home-made teas. **Adm £3,
chd free. Suns 27 Feb (11-4);
13 Mar; 1 May (2-5); 22 Jan 2012
(11-4). Visitors also welcome by
appt.**
1-acre garden full of colour and
interest to plant enthusiasts looking
for unusual and rare plants. Spring
gives some 250 named snowdrops
together with hellebores and early
daffodils. The lawn is awash with
crocus, fritillarias, anemones, narcissi
and cyclamen. Large vegetable
garden on raised beds. Lovely views
over open countryside. Newcastle

Mausoleum (adjacent) open. Featured in Daily Telegraph, The Times, other local publications & local radio. Limited access. Some slopes & steps which can be avoided.

BELVOIR CASTLE
See Lincolnshire.

 335 BERRY HILL LANE
Berry Hill Lane, Mansfield
NG18 4JB. Sheila Whalley. *2m S of Mansfield. Berry Hill Lane joins A60 Nottingham Road and goes through to A614 Southwell Road opposite the Oak Tree PH.* Home-made teas. **Adm £2.50, chd free. Sun 10 July (1-5).**
A 'Tardis Garden' with herbaceous borders, water features, statuary, mature trees. Features incl Greek Gods, Balinese wood carvings etc. Terraced steps lead down to large patio and summerhouse. New additions for 2011. Marquees will be erected if wet.

 BISHOPS COTTAGE
89 Main Street, Kinoulton
NG12 3EL. Ann Hammond. *8m SE of West Bridgford. Kinoulton is off A46 just N of intersection with A606. Into village, pass school & village hall. Garden on R after bend on Main St.* Home-made teas. **Combined adm with Hall Farm Cottage £3.50, chd free. Sun 19 June (2-5).**
This large mature cottage garden with mixed herbaceous borders, old fruit trees, two ponds - one formal with fish, one natural. Old varieties of roses round the door and everywhere else. Vegetable patch to the rear of the property. Open views across the countryside.

 BISHOPS MANOR
Bishops Drive, Southwell
NG25 0JR. The Rt Rev & Mrs P Butler. *Centre of Southwell, end of Bishops Dr on S side of Minster. Close to War Memorial Park.* Home-made teas. **Adm £3, chd free. Sats & Suns 21, 22 May; 18, 19 June; (1-5); Wed 14 Sept (2-5).**
Mature Edwardian gardens surrounding the medieval walls of the Archbishops of York Palace. Delightful enclosed garden within the ruined walls incl a herb knot garden overlooked by Southwell Minister and the Great Hall. Woodland walks. Gravel paths.

Cornorstones

109 BROOK STREET
See Leicestershire & Rutland.

 NEW **5 BURTON LANE**
5 Burton Lane, Whatton in the Vale
NG13 9EQ. Mr & Mrs Faulconbridge, 01949 850942, jpfalconbridge@hotmail.co.uk. *3m E of Bingham.* Follow signs to Whatton from A52 between Bingham & Elton. Garden nr Church in old part of village. Will be signed. Home-made teas at the Village Hall. **Combined adm with Cedarwood £4, chd free. Sat 25 June (1-6). Visitors also welcome by appt for small groups only.**
Medium sized, organic, wildlife-friendly garden. Attractive fruit and vegetable areas at front and side. Back has romantic atmosphere. Scented plants and seating. Large beds have stepping stone paths with great variety of plants, incl rarities, climbers, wild flowers and herbs. Also features hot gravel garden, pond, shade planting and trained fruit. Historic church & local history display in village hall.

 NEW **CALVERTON HOUSE**
8 Main Street, Calverton
NG14 6FQ. Isabel & Iain Dodson. *7m NE of Nottingham. On Main St 100yds E of church.* Home-made teas, ploughmans lunch available 22 May (1-2). **Adm £3 Suns 1, 22 May; 26 June (1-5). Combined adm with**

Smithy Cottage 22 May £4, chd free.
A mature, peaceful acre surrounding an elegant Georgian house. Topiaried, open, formal areas relax into a variety of gardens and moods, from sun-trap courtyard to a narcissus planted grove of silver birch. Paths wander through shrubberies, wilderness and orchard all planted with colour, texture, scent and atmosphere in mind.

 CAPABILITY BARN
Gonalston Lane, Hoveringham
NG14 7JH. Malcolm & Wendy Fisher, 01159 664322. *8m NE of Nottingham. A612 from Nottingham through Lowdham. Take 1st R into Gonalston Lane. 1m on L.* Home-made teas. **Adm £3, chd free. Suns 10 Apr; 15 May; Wed 15 June (1-5). Visitors also welcome by appt.**
Escape into an oasis of calm in this large country garden set in one of Nottinghamshire's prettiest riverside villages. Mature trees give this continually evolving garden an established feel. Plantsman's garden with carefully placed plants according to their needs. Daffodils, hostas, ornamental grasses and begonias star in their seasons. Featured on BBC East Midlands News & Nottingham Evening Post. Some gravel areas and bark paths.

11 NEW CEDARWOOD

Burton Lane, Whatton in the Vale NG13 9EQ. Louise Bateman, 01949 850227, louise.bateman@hotmail.co.uk. *3m E of Bingham. Cedarwood is in the old part of Whatton, just around the corner from the church. Cedarwood is a cedarwood bungalow set back off the rd.* Teas in the Village Hall. **Combined adm with 5 Burton Lane £4, chd free. Sat 25 June (1-6). Visitors also welcome by appt. Please ring to discuss your requirements.**
Cedarwood is a ¹/₃ acre plantswoman's garden developed over 6yrs where flowers dominate; incl a rose garden, formal pond, bog garden, raised alpine bed and beautiful mixed plantings. Majority of plants are grown from seed by the owner and this enables frequent experiments with planting combinations. Historic church & local history display in village hall.

12 CHARNWOOD

120 Cotgrave Lane, Tollerton, Nottingham NG12 4FY. Kate and Peter Foale, www.katescuttings.net. *5m SE Nottingham. From Wheatcroft r'about, A606 Melton, turn L at 2nd set T-lights signed Cotgrave. After 1m turn L. From A46 take A606. After 5m turn R at T-lights.* Home-made teas. **Adm £3, chd free. Sun & Mon 1, 2 May (2-5).**
One-acre garden developed over 23 yrs with many mature trees and shrubs by obsessive plantswoman and patient husband. Bulbs, blossom and woodland planting, early perennials, large well-established pond with jetty. Seaside gravel garden, unusual sculptures, 'secret' bamboo garden. Come and get lost in the tranquility of this plant-lover's garden. Some grassy slopes & bark paths.

13 13 CHERRY STREET

13 Cherry Street, Bingham NG13 8AJ. Jayne Green, 01949 875802. *8m E of Nottingham. From A52 or A46 follow sign to Bingham. Follow NGS signs to garden.* Home-made teas. **Combined admission with Granby House adm £4, chd free. Suns 22 May; 21 Aug (2-5). Visitors also welcome by appt. Please call to make arrangments.**
In just 3yrs this ¹/₃ -acre suburban

garden has been transformed from a neglected space into a delightful, tranquil retreat. Featuring secluded seating areas with extensive yr-round planting that is especially colourful. Unusual mature trees add a unique feature to provide shape and character whilst the informal pond is a haven for wildlife.

14 NEW THE CHIMES

37 Glenorchy Crescent, Heronridge NG5 9LG. Stan & Ellen Maddock. *4m N of Nottingham. Take A611 towards Hucknall, onto Bulwell Common, turn R at Tesco, Top Valley, up to island, turn L, 100yds. 1st L, then 2nd L onto Glenorchy Crescent, down to bottom.* Cream teas. **Adm £2.50, chd free. Suns 12 June; 14 Aug (1-5).**
We would like to invite you to visit our small but well stocked garden. Full of roses, peonies, lilies and much more. We have a small pond and plenty of pots and baskets.

15 CHURCH HOUSE

Gonalston Lane, Hoveringham NG14 7JH. Alex & Sue Allan, 01159 664982. *6m NE of Nottingham. Signed from A612 Nottingham to Southwell Rd. Just on Southwell side of Lowdham.* Light refreshments & teas at Village Hall. **Adm £4, chd free. Sun 22 May (1-5). Also opening West Farm House. Visitors also welcome by appt. Groups of 10+.**
Small, charming cottage-style garden with herbaceous borders, auricula theatre and vegetable plot. Relax in the Japanese area, spot the magic toadstools in the stumpery and meet our resident chickens. Featured in Nottingham Evening Post.

16 54 CHURCH LANE

Thrumpton, Nottingham NG11 0AW. Carol & Mike Staves, 01159 830720, stavesmc@btinternet.com. *7m SW of Nottingham. Thrumpton is off A453 between Nottingham & J24 of M1. From Nottingham 1st R signed Thrumpton approx 2m after Crusader PH in Clifton. In ¹/₂ m R, No 54 is ¹/₂ m on R. From M1 approx 3m along A453 turn L just after power station. 1st R then L in ¹/₂ m. No 54 is ¹/₂ m on R.* Light refreshments & teas. **Combined adm with 59 Church Lane £3.50, chd free. Visitors**

welcome by appt. Groups or individuals.
Herbaceous borders overflowing with shrubs, perennials and many different types of roses wandering through trees, fences and shrubs. Larger front garden is tiered on two levels and has patio area at front. Back garden has beautiful views stretching for miles, with two further patio areas, plus water feature.

Come and get lost in the tranquility of this plant-lover's garden . . .

17 59 CHURCH LANE

Thrumpton, Nottingham NG11 0AW. Valerie & John Collins, 01159 830533/01159 830720. *7m SW of Nottingham. See 54 Church Lane for directions.* Light Refreshments. **Combined adm with 54 Church Lane £3.50, chd free. Visitors welcome by appt. Groups or individuals.**
Two styles: naturalistic grasses and perennials ablaze with colour in Aug/Sept, plus pond and waterfall; herbaceous perennials, shrubs and trees best in June/July and arranged with an eye for gentle colour and form. Small wild flower meadow and woodland with a rural landscape beyond complete this 'garden with a view'.

18 ◆ CLUMBER PARK WALLED KITCHEN GARDEN

Clumber Park, Worksop S80 3AZ. National Trust, 01909 476592, www.nationaltrust.org.uk. *4m S of Worksop. From main car park follow directions to the Walled Kitchen Garden.* **Adm £3, chd free. £5.50 parking charge applies. For NGS: Sat 16 July (10-6).** For other opening times and information, please phone or see garden website.
Beautiful 4-acre walled kitchen garden, growing unusual and old varieties of vegetables, fruits, herbs and ornamentals, incl the magnificent recently extended 400ft long double herbaceous borders. 450ft long glasshouse, with grape vines,

peaches, nectarines and figs. Museum of gardening tools. New soft fruit garden and rose garden. Featured in local publications regularly.

⌖ ▣ ☎

COBWEBS NURSERY & GARDEN
See Lincolnshire.

19 ▶ 7 COLLYGATE
Swingate, Kimberley NG16 2PJ. Doreen Fahey & John Arkinstall, 01159 192690. *6m W of Nottingham. From M1 J26 take A610 towards Nottingham. L at next island on B600 into Kimberley. At Sainsbury's mini island take L. L at top. Park on this rd in 500yds. Collygate on R.* **Adm £2.50, chd free. Visitors welcome by appt** May, June, July. Coaches permitted.
Delightful garden created by serious plant addicts tucked away at the end of a short narrow lane in Swingate. It greets you with an impact of unexpected colour and delights you with the variety and sensitivity of the planting. A peaceful backwater in an urban setting.

⌖ ❀ ☎

7 COLLYGATE
See Nottinghamshire.

20 ▶ CORNERSTONES
15 Lamcote Gardens, Radcliffe-on-Trent, Nottingham NG12 2BS. Judith & Jeff Coombes, 01158 458055, judith.coombes@ntlworld.com, www.cornerstonesgarden.co.uk. *4m E of Nottingham. From A52 take Radcliffe exit at the RSPCA junction, then 2nd L just before hairpin bend.* Home-made teas & light refreshments. **Adm £3, chd free. Suns 10 July; 7 Aug (1.30-5.30) Evening Opening £4, wine, Fri 1 July (6-9). Visitors also welcome by appt,** groups of 10+ during July & August. Coaches permitted.
Plant lover's garden, approaching ¹/₂ acre. Flowing herbaceous borders, containing rare, exotic and unusual plants, provide a wealth of colour and interest, whilst an abundance of produce is grown in the unique vegetable and fruit garden. Bananas, palms, olive border, fernery, fish pond, bog garden, summerhouse, greenhouse and areas for relaxation.

⌖ ❀ ☕ ☎

THE COTTAGE
See Derbyshire.

21 ▶ CROWS NEST COTTAGE
Forest Road. NG25 0SZ. Joan Arnold & Tom Heinersdorff. *From B6386 turn R into Oxton village (Blind Lane). At T-junction turn R into Forest Rd. Garden is approx 200yds on R.* Home-made teas & light refreshments. **Adm £3, chd free. Sun 1 May (12-5).**
Bird friendly, mature garden wrapped around the cottage with large wildlife ponds, streams and waterfalls. Yr-round interest with winter-flowering shrubs and a wealth of spring bulbs following snowdrops. Colourful tulips and green herbaceous shoots appearing. Planted pots and the promise of bluebells, azaleas and summer colour to come.

❀ ☕

THE DAIRY
See Leicestershire & Rutland.

22 ▶ DARBY HOUSE
10 The Grove, Southey Street, Nottingham NG7 4BS. Jed Brignal, 07960 065042, www.jedbrignal.co.uk. *³/₄ m NE of city centre take A610, turn R into Bentinck Rd, turn R at lights into Southey St.* **Adm £2, chd free. Suns 1 May; 19 June (2-5). Visitors also** welcome by appt.
Unusual city garden designed and developed by artist owner is a tranquil oasis in unlikely location. Victorian walled garden with ponds, gazebos and fairy-tale shady area surrounded by mature trees. House (1849) and garden provide temporary home and sanctuary for actors, writers, dancers and other creative visitors. Rare plant nursery & bespoke craft stalls. Featured on BBC East Midlands TV.

▣ ❀ ☕ ☎

23 ▶ NEW ▶ DAVRYL
9 The Green, Kingston-on-Soar NG11 0DA. David & Beryl Elliott. *10m SW of Nottingham. From J24 of M1, A6 to Loughborough, then 1st turning L signed Kingston. From Nottingham, SE on A453, turn L, through Ratcliffe on Soar, then 1st L under railway. Opp village green, 4th cottage from church, path by telephone box.* Home-made teas. **Adm £2.50, chd free. Suns 1 May; 12 June (2-6).**
Located in small peaceful village, garden borders filled with colourful perennials, annuals and bulbs as well as mature trees and shrubs. Lawn runs down to brook and small pond. Plenty of secluded seating for teas.

The home-made teas are Beryl's speciality and are an absolute must.

☕

DODDINGTON HALL GARDENS
See Lincolnshire.

24 ▶ DUMBLESIDE
17 Bridle Road, Burton Joyce NG14 5FT. Mr P Bates, 01159 313725. *5m NE of Nottingham. In Burton Joyce turn off A612, Nottingham to Southwell Rd into Lambley Lane. Bridle Rd is an impassable looking rd to the R off Lambley Lane. Car parking easiest beyond garden.* **Combined with 6 Lambley Lane adm £4, chd free. Sun 15 May (2-6). Visitors also** welcome by appt any day Feb - April (bulbs in grass) & Aug - Oct (Cyclamen & late border flowers). 2 acres of varied habitat. Natural spring and stream planted with primulas, fritillaries and fine specimen shrubs. A small meadow is being developed with large variety of bulbs and wild flowers planted and seeded into grass. 60yd mixed border. Ferns are an important feature in spring, cyclamen in Aug and Sept and through the winter. Steep slopes towards stream.

⌖ ▣ ❀ ☎

It delights you with the variety and sensitivity of the planting . . .

25 ▶ NEW ▶ ELM HOUSE
Main Street, Hickling, Melton Mowbray LE14 3AJ. Mr David Chambers, 07775 507569, davidpacific462@aol.com. *12m E of Nottingham. 7m W of Melton Mowbray. From Nottingham take A606 E. After crossing A46 turn L at Bridgegate Lane signed Hickling. In village turn R at T-junction. Elm House is last on R.* **Adm £3, chd free. Sun 17 Apr (1-5).**
Large interesting garden (1.8 acres) with many different areas. Lovely in spring with more than 25 varieties of magnolia and many spring bulbs. Other features incl a railway garden, seaside garden, small walled garden, woodland area and pond with fish. Featured on BBC TV East Midlands Today. Level garden with some gravel.

⌖ ❀ ☕ ☎

Be tempted by a plant from a plant stall ❀

The White House

29 THE FERNS
Low Pasture Lane, North Wheatley, Retford DN22 9DQ. Keith & Flicky Hebdon. *Off A620 between Retford & Gainsborough. Enter N Wheatley at Sun Inn PH. Follow Low Street for ¹/₂ m. L into Low Pasture Lane, at end go through gates to park at adjoining property.* Home-made teas. **Sun 12 June (12-5).**
Cottage garden of 1-acre, retrieved from woodland 12yrs ago. Sloping site incl pond, stream, ferns and bog garden. Model train set meanders through 'rooms'. Rose garden, statuary, oriental poppies and paeonies in borders. Gentle slopes, some gravel access.
 ♿ ⚘ ☕

FIELD HOUSE FARM
See Lincolnshire.

FIRVALE ALLOTMENT GARDEN
See Yorkshire.

30 FUCHSIA VIEW
9 Winster Avenue, off Cromford Avenue, Carlton NG4 3RW. Mr & Mrs J Thorp, 01159 872069, www.fuchsiaview.co.uk. *4m N of Nottingham. Follow the Carlton Rd into Carlton. Turn L at Tesco past police stn. Over the mini island, pass the cemetery up Cavendish Rd. R into Cromford Ave. 1st L into Winster Ave or from Mapperley, down Westdale Lane & R onto Cavendish Road & L onto Cromford or Buxton Ave where parking is advisable.* Light refreshments & cream teas. **Adm £2.50, chd free. Suns 10, 31 July (11-5) Evening Openings £4, wine, Thurs 14, 28 July (6-9).** Visitors also welcome by appt.
The abundance of colour in this garden is achieved by the dense planting of roses and 150 varieties of fuchsia's supported by mixed perennials, penstemons and hanging baskets, 5 patio areas give a panoramic view over Carlton while enjoying a strawberry scone or home-made cake. Visit the secret garden with a fish pond. In the evening enjoy a glass of wine with the chef's canapés. Disabled access to patio only. Steps to rest of garden.
♿ ⚘ ☕ ☎

26 THE ELMS
Main Street, North Leverton DN22 0AR. Tim & Tracy Ward, 01427 881164, Tracy@wardt2.fsnet.co.uk. *5m E of Retford, 6m SW of Gainsborough. From Retford town centre take the rd to Leverton for 5m, into North Leverton with Habblesthorpe.* Adm £2.50, **Sun 31 July, combined adm with Squirrel Lodge Suns 15 May; 14 Aug £3, chd free.** Visitors also welcome by appt.
This small garden is very different, creating an extension to the living space. Inspiration comes from tropical countries, giving a Mediterranean feel. Palms and bananas, along with other exotics, create drama, and yet make a statement true to many gardens, that of peace and calm. North Leverton Windmill will be open for visitors. All the garden can be viewed without having to use the steps.
♿ ⚘ ☕ ☎

27 ELMS FARM
Bassingfield, Nottingham NG12 2LG. Philip & Jane Parker, 01159 814899. *2m SE of Trent Bridge, Nottingham. Off A52 Lings Bar Rd to Tollerton, Bassingfield 1st*
L. Home-made teas. **Adm £2.50, chd free. Sun 31 July (2-5).** Visitors also welcome by appt.
Garden of approx 2-acres developed in the last 18yrs. Unusual trees, shrubs, herbaceous plants in island beds and borders. Wide selection of flowering annuals. Large pond and stream. Plenty of seating areas.
♿ ⚅ ⚘ ☕ ☎

28 ♦ FELLEY PRIORY
Underwood NG16 5FJ. Miss Michelle Upchurch, 07763 189771. *8m SW of Mansfield. Off A608 ¹/₂ m W M1 J27.* **Adm £3, chd free. For NGS: Sun 17 Apr (10-4). For other opening times and information, please phone.**
Garden for all seasons with yew hedges and topiary, snowdrops, hellebores, orchard of daffodils, herbaceous borders and old-fashioned rose garden. There are pergolas, a medieval garden, a small arboretum and borders filled with unusual trees, shrubs, plants and bulbs. The grass-edged pond is planted with primulas, bamboo, iris, roses and eucomis. Mini plant fair.
♿ ⚘ ☕ ☎

31 NEW GABLE COTTAGE
High Street, Everton DN10 5AR. Mr & Mrs David Slater. *7m N of Retford. 3m S of Bawtry. Everton on the Bawtry to Gainsborough Rd A631. L to High St opp Sun Inn. Garden 2nd*

on R opp hairdressers. Home-made teas in Village Hall. **Combined adm Sunnyside Cottage, Primrose Cottage & Thistle Farm £3, chd free. Sun 3 July (2-6).**
Long narrow garden to the front of the property, developed 3yrs ago from a tarmacadam driveway to create a low maintenance all yr-round interest garden, consisting of trees, shrubs, buxus hedges and herbaceous plants.

Masterclass in the positioning and management of plants which have to move if they don't behave! . . .

32> GARDENERS COTTAGE
Rectory Lane, Kirkby in Ashfield NG17 8PZ. Martin & Chris Brown, 01623 489489. *1m W of Kirkby. From the A38, take the B6018 towards Kirkby in Ashfield. Straight across mini island. Rectory Lane (no parking) is at the side of St Wilfrid's Church, on Church St.* Home-made teas. **Adm £3.50, chd free. Sun 26 June (1-5) Evening Opening £4.50, wine, Wed 29 June (6-9). Visitors also welcome by appt.**
Just 10-yrs ago we looked at a steeply sloping old orchard and had a dream to create our unique and special garden. Now reaching maturity, full of plants and shrubs sought out from far and wide, which enhance the distinctive features and unusual trees gathered in this dream of a garden. Outstanding homemade cakes and Yorkshire tea.

33> GORENE
20 Kirby Road, Beauvale Estate, Newthorpe NG16 3PZ. Irene Middleton, 01773 788407. *5m NE of Nottingham. From M1 J26 take A610 (Eastwood & Kimberley bypass) exit Langley Mill (not Eastwood). At island turn R to Eastwood to 1st set of T-lights. Keep L down Mansfield Rd, turn R at bollards (Greenhills Rd).Turn R at the 7th rd - Kirby Rd.* Light

refreshments & teas. **Adm £2, chd free. Sun 7 Aug (1-4). Visitors also welcome by appt June to Aug. Groups of 4 to 40 max.**
The garden is always a delight to garden lovers who go away with many new ideas for their own garden. The garden is abundant in the summer with water feature, secret garden, palms, Japanese maples and perennials.

34> GRANBY HOUSE
8 Long Acre, Bingham NG13 8BG. Maureen & John Gladwin, 01949 836340. *8m E of Nottingham. From A46 or A52 follow signs for Bingham. Follow NGS signs to garden.* **Adm £4, chd free. Suns 22 May; 21 Aug (2-5). Visitors also welcome by appt. Please call to make arrangments.**
Town centre garden of just under ⅓ acre, previously a thriving nursery. Lots of nooks and crannies, borders with wide variety of shrubs and plants. Formal pond, woodland plant area and bog garden. Wisteria in bloom May as shown in Garden News. Featured in Garden News.

GROUP OPENING

35> GRINGLEY GARDENS
Gringley-on-the-Hill, Doncaster DN10 4QT. *5m E of Bawtry. Gringley is midway between Bawtry & Gainsborough on A631. Folow NGS signs off by-pass into village.* Home-made teas. **Combined adm £4, chd free. Suns 26 June (1-5); 18 Sept (2-5) Evening Opening Wed 29 June (5-9).**

NEW ELLICAR HOUSE
Will & Sarah Murch

GRINGLEY HALL 🛏
Ian & Dulce Threlfall
Visitors also welcome by appt.
01777 817262
dulce@gringleyhall.fsnet.co.uk

THE SUMMER HOUSE 🛏
Helena Bishop
Not open Sun 18 Sept.

Gringley on the Hill hides in the corner of 3 counties and is one of the most attractive villages in this region. With panoramic views to the Vale of York in the North and The Dukeries in the South, this unspoilt Beacon village retains the character of a bygone age.

Three large but diverse gardens in different settings; large Regency house with 1½ -acre walled garden now being redesigned to be more formal with parterre, rose tunnel and new pool in rose garden; also containing several mixed borders bursting with plants. The Summer House sits on a splendid S-facing site with a less formal garden containing large pond with stream, many roses, terrace with pergola, wildflower meadow and delightful views. Ellicar House has an extensive garden with a wealth of treasures recently planted by the owner, who is a garden designer. The extensive potager provides a haven for bees, insects, beetles, toads, hedgehogs and more; a garden for children to enjoy. Also cows/calves, pigs, sheep, hens and ponies. The very large new natural pool is of great interest. Please note that The Summer House will not be open 18 Sept.

36> HALL FARM COTTAGE
Hall Lane, Kinoulton NG12 3EF. Mrs Bel Grundy. *8m SE of West Bridgford. Kinoulton is off A46 just N of intersection with A606. Into village to T-junction with PH on L. Cottage at end of lane on L.* **Combined adm with Bishops Cottage £3.50, chd free. Sun 19 June (2-5).**
Plantaholic's small cottage garden. Masterclass in the positioning and management of plants which have to move if they don't behave! Grower of Brugmansia 'Angels Trumpets'. Highly-fragrant exotic plants. Also Aeoniums in Black & Green. Collection of home-grown bonsai demonstrates attention to detail and the quality of 'plants for sale' ensures that Bel has no escape from her addiction.

HILL PARK FARM
See Leicestershire & Rutland.

37> ◆ HODSOCK PRIORY GARDENS
Blyth, Worksop S81 0TY. Sir Andrew & Lady Buchanan, 01909 591 204, www.snowdrops.co.uk. *2m from A1(M) at Blyth. 4m N of Worksop off B6045, Blyth-Worksop rd approx 2 miles from A1. Well signed locally.* **Adm £5, chd £1. For NGS: Daily Sat 5 Feb to Sun 6 Mar; (10-4). For other opening times and**

information, please phone or see garden website.

Top 10 Snowdrop Garden. The opening of The Courtyard at Hodsock allows visitors to stay for short breaks in one of our 10 beautiful self catering suites. Enjoy exploring our estate and nearby attractions. Visitors to the Snowdrops at Hodsock can enjoy a leisurely walk through the gardens and woods. Millions of Snowdrops, Woodland Walk, Tearoom, Gift Shop, Plant Sales, Bonfire, Victorian Beehives. Featured on BBC TV, A Garden in Snowdonia. Some gravel paths, steep slopes and wood paths soft if wet.

38 HOLBECK LODGE
Manor Fields, Halam From B6386. Paul & Jane Oakley, 01636 813896, pauloakley07@btinternet.com. *1½ miles west of Southwell. From B6386 in Halam village 350yds past church, R into Manor Fields. Parking on Radley Rd.* Light refreshments at Old Vicarage. **Adm £4.50, chd free. Mon 30 May; Sun 19 June (1-5). Also opening with The Old Vicarage, Halam. Visitors also welcome by appt. June only.**
Lovely garden created from scratch to complement house buit in 2001, this ½ -acre area has been selectively planted to blend in with open countryside and bordering beck. Wild plants, herbaceous beds, shrubs, Cornus Kousa, ferns,containers, vegetable garden, rose pergolas, spectacular Constance Spry, Maigold and the Generous Gardener.

39 ◆ HOLME PIERREPONT HALL
Holme Pierrepont, Nottingham NG12 2LD. Mr & Mrs Robin Brackenbury, 0115 933 2371, www.holmepierreponthall.com. *5m E of Nottingham. From Nottingham A52 E-bound, follow signs for National Watersports Centre. Continue 1m past main entrance. House on L next to church. Park outside church.* **Adm £3, chd £1. For NGS: Sun 6 Mar (2-5). For other opening times and information, please phone or see garden website.**
Hellebore Sunday. Snowdrops may still be flowering, shot through with crocus tomasinianus, and early daffodils and tulips making their presence felt. Sweet-scented shrubs such as daphne bholua and

hamamelis are in flower, all set round the clipped yew avenue. The courtyard garden and box hedge will be awakening. Featured in Nottingham Evening Post.

Each corner of this magical cottage garden offers a new and exciting experience . . .

40 HOLMES VILLA
Holmes Lane, Walkeringham, nr Gainsborough DN10 4JP. Peter & Sheila Clark, 01427 890233, clarkshaulage@aol.com. *4m NW of Gainsborough. A620 from Retford or A631 from Bawtry/Gainsborough & A161 to Walkeringham then towards Misterton. Follow yellow signs for last mile.* Home-made teas. **Adm £2, chd free. Mon 30 May (1-5). Visitors also welcome by appt.**
1¾ -acre plantsman's interesting and inspirational garden; surprises around every corner with places to sit and ponder, gazebos, arbours, ponds, hosta garden, unusual perennials and shrubs for flower arranging. Lots of ideas to copy. Old tools, ornamental ducks and scarecrows. Plant stall, cake stall, driftwood. Featured in Lincolnshire Today & Yorkshire Post.

41 HOME FARM COTTAGE
Blind Lane, Oxton NG25 0SS. Pauline Hansler, 01159 655860, jhansler410@btinternet.com. *From B6386 turn into Oxton village (Blind Lane). Home Farm Cottage is on L opp Green Dragon PH, immed before T-junction.* **Adm £3, chd free. Sun 5 June (12-5). Visitors also welcome by appt.**
Each corner of this magical cottage garden offers a new and exciting experience. At every turn, from the hidden alpine garden, through the imaginative stumpery and woodland grotto to the selection of unusual plants, it reveals a horticultural heaven.

THE HOMESTEAD
See Leicestershire & Rutland.

42 NEW 61 LAMBLEY LANE
61 Lambley Lane, Burton Joyce NG14 5BG. Mr Richard Powell. *6m N of Nottingham. In Burton Joyce turn off A612 (Nottingham to Southwell Rd) into Lambley Lane.* **Combined adm with Dumbleside £4, chd free. Sun 15 May (2-6).**
Approx ¾ -acre of spring flowering shrubs, plants and bulbs. Mixed borders, greenhouse and terrace. Cacti, vegetable garden, fruit trees, colourful display of azaleas and camelias. Steep drive to entrance.

43 29 LIME GROVE
Forest Town, Mansfield NG19 0HR. Laurence & Margaret Brown. *2m E Mansfield. On B6030 through Forest Town on Clipstone Road West.Lime Grove R turn immediately before Shell filling station. (Caution-narrow entry) Parking in field adjacent no. 20 on R.* Home-made teas. **Adm £2.50, chd free. Sun 14 Aug (1-5).**
Beautifully laid out plant lovers' garden of 1.3 acres. Large neat front garden with topiary and many varieties of colourful perennials all year round. Rear garden is a gardener's joy with lawn, irregular colourful herbaceous borders, beds and koi pond. All varieties of planting with specimen trees leading through to nursery and vegetable beds.

LONG CLOSE
See Leicestershire & Rutland.

44 NEW LUMLESS HOUSE
77 Gainsborough Road, Winthorpe, Newark NG24 2NR. Mr Steven Jackson, 01636 671377. *3½ m NE of Newark. Turn off A1133 into Winthorpe, drive through village past Lord Nelson PH and church (approx 1m) the rd slopes downhill. 77 is at bottom of hill on L set back from rd.* Home-made teas. **Adm £3, chd free (share to Winthorpe Parish Church from the proceeds of Sun 24 April open day). Suns 24 Apr; 26 June; 9 Oct (11-5). Visitors also welcome by appt May, June & July only. Groups 10+.**
Walled garden of approx 2-acres which slopes down slightly from N to SW and is divided into garden 'rooms' - Japanese garden, Italianate etc; incorporating 2 formal and one natural pond on an old garden well (circa: 1771). Many decorative trees, conifers, shrubs and flowers. There are also clematis and laburnum walks.

Museum of Commemoratives 1793 - 2010. Featured on TV show Bargain Hunt & local radio.

GROUP OPENING

45▶ NORWELL GARDENS
NG23 6JX. *6m N of Newark. Off A1 at Cromwell turning, take Norwell Rd at bus shelter.* Home-made teas in Village Hall 26 June & Norwell Nurseries 29 June. **Combined adm £4, chd free. Sun 26 June (1.30-5) Evening Opening £4, wine, Wed 29 June (6.30-9).**

> **NEW▶ 4 MOORLANDS CLOSE**
> Jackie Musgrove

> **NORWELL ALLOTMENT PARISH GARDENS**
> Norwell Parish Council

> **NORWELL NURSERIES**
> Andrew & Helen Ward
> (See separate entry)

> **NEW▶ THE OLD FORGE**
> Adam & Hilary Ward

> **THE OLD MILL HOUSE, NORWELL**
> Mr & Mrs M Burgess

Range of different, very appealing gardens all making superb use of the beautiful backdrop of a quintessentially English Village and countryside. They incl an outstanding plantsman's garden with over 2,500 different plants radiating from a 'Monet' pond to provide yr-round interest. 32 allotments of different sizes are tended by gardeners from 10 to 90 yrs-old. Recently a couple gave up a day of their holiday to garner tips for their vegetable patch. They were spotted an hour after official closing still chatting away. Also walled gardens, water features, sun and shade gardens, knot gardens, gardens where innovative features abound with lush and colourful plantings incl roses, perennials and grasses. A tiny quirky garden shows what can be done when space is restricted but ideas are not and the developement of a family garden will allow visitors to follow the evolution of a garden over the next few yrs. Beautiful Medieval church of St Lawrence will be open especially to show the grass labyrinth & summer flower meadow.

46▶ ◆ NORWELL NURSERIES
Woodhouse Road, Norwell NG23 6JX. Andrew & Helen Ward, 01636 636337, **www.norwellnurseries.co.uk.** *6m N of Newark. Turn off A1 at Cromwell turning, take rd to Norwell at bus stop.* **Adm £2.50. Combined with Norwell Gardens adm £4, chd free. For NGS: Suns 22 May; 16 Oct (2-5); as part of Norwell Gardens, 26 June (1.30-5); Evening Opening Wed 29 June (6.30-9).** For other opening times and information, please phone or see garden website.
Jewel box of over 2,500 different, beautiful and unusual plants sumptuously set out in a ³/₄ -acre plantsman's garden incl shady garden with orchids, woodland gems, cottage garden borders, alpine and scree areas. Pond with opulently planted margins. Extensive herbaceous borders and effervescent colour themed beds. New borders every year. Evening opening features UK's largest collection of hardy chrysanthamums available and asters. Featured in Nottingham Evening Post. Gravel drive.

A pretty garden with lots of seats to sit and enjoy homemade cakes and a cuppa . . .

47▶ OLD MILL HOUSE
Goverton, nr Bleasby NG14 7FN. Mr & Mrs Langley, 01636 830215, **tonitsmith@tiscali.co.uk.** *11m SW of Newark. Taking A612 from Nottingham (towards Southwell) enter Thurgarton Village, R signed Bleasby. Garden up lane on L, approx 1m out of Thurgarton.* Home-made teas. **Adm £3, chd free. Mon 25 Apr; Sun 1 May (2-5). Visitors also welcome by appt in Spring. Contact for details.**
Relaxing or stimulating - you choose! Rest awhile under shady copses contemplating glorious Trent Valley

---

views or ponder, in our meditation hut, on the history behind the ancient Bramley orchard, feature yews and original Victorian Hothouse. Conversely, take the gardeners' quiz and be inspired by the large working kitchen garden, topiary and spring colour bursting everywhere. An eclectic mix!Slopes slippery when wet-Disabled parking at house. Plant sales. Local craft & produce for sale. Agility display on request (donations).

48▶ THE OLD POLICE HOUSE
69 Derby Road, Kegworth DE74 2EN. Val & Paul Blyth, 01509 670565. *10m S of Nottingham. 6m N of Loughborough. From A453 on M1 J24 r'about take 1st exit signed A6 Loughborough/Kegworth. ¹/₂ m from J24 on R opp Londis garage. A6 from Loughborough, through village on L opp garage.* Home-made teas. **Adm £2, chd free. Sun 31 July (1-5). Visitors also welcome by appt June & August only.**
A very warm welcome awaits you. Our patio is filled with annuals in some unusual containers. The garden slopes gently and is in 4 sections with many shrubs incl hydrangeas, and hidden areas. Plenty of colour in old-fashioned urns. A pretty garden with lots of seats to sit and enjoy homemade cakes and a cuppa.

49▶ THE OLD VICARAGE
Halam Hill, Halam Village, nr Southwell NG22 8AX. Mrs Beverley Perks. *1m W of Southwell. On approach to Halam village down hill on LH-side or from A614 through Farnsfield & Edingley villages over Xrds in Halam, last house on RH-side.* Home-made teas available except for 14 Sept. **Adm £4.50 May & June), £3 (July & Sept), chd free. Mon 30 May; Suns 19 June; 10 July (1-5); Wed 14 Sept (2-5). Also opening with Holbeck Lodge, Halam May 30th, June 19th only.**
Plantsman's garden designed on hillside for year-round beauty, peaceful rooms, woodland setting, borrowed views farming countryside. Clematis and roses tumble freely, balanced with texture, colour and fragrance. Children's haven. Swimming pool planting matured to soften this hidden suntrap. Productive kitchen garden. Aga baking to add to enjoyment on new terraces. C11 Norman Church with rare C14 window. Abundantly planted

Visit the website for latest information

churchyard open only short walk away to complete a peaceful, interesting visit. Featured in Newark Advertiser. Garden used for international company advertisement.

  ♿

50 20 THE PADDOCKS
Nuthall NG16 1DR. Mr & Mrs Bowness-Saunders, 01159 384590. *5m NW of Nottingham. From M1 J26, A610 towards Nottingham. At 1st roundabout take B600 towards Kimberley. Paddocks is 2nd rd on L after Three Ponds PH. Parking in cul-de-sac restricted, please park on main rd or on L as you enter The Paddocks.* Home-made teas. **Adm £3, chd free. Sun 12 June (1-5) Evening Opening £3.50, wine, Wed 15 June (6-9). Visitors also welcome by appt.**
Fun garden shared with children and dogs which unlike oil and water do mix in this unusual combination of interesting gardens. Many inspirational ideas incl beach, well, living willow structures, ponds, mature trees, herbaceous borders and vegetables. A gardener's playground not to be missed (200 x 80ft).

 ♿

> Fun garden shared with children and dogs which unlike oil and water do mix . . . a gardener's playground not to be missed . . .

51 PAPPLEWICK HALL
Blidworth Waye, Papplewick NG15 8FE. Mr & Mrs J R Godwin-Austen, www.papplewickhall.co.uk. *7m N of Nottingham. N end of Papplewick village on B683, off the A60.* Parking at Hall. Home-made teas. **Adm £3, chd free. Sun 29 May (2-5).**
This historic, mature, 8-acre garden, mostly shaded woodland, abounds with rhododendrons, hostas, ferns, and spring bulbs. Gravel paths.

 ♿

52 PARK FARM
Crink Lane, Southwell NG25 0TJ. Dr & Mrs Ian Johnston, 01636 812195. *1m SE of Southwell. A612 out of Southwell towards Newark, take rd to Fiskerton and 200yds up hill turn R into Crink Lane.* Home-made teas. **Adm £3, chd free. Sun 14 Aug (2-5). Visitors also welcome by appt.**
3-acre garden for gardeners and nature lovers. Extensive borders with large varieties of plants, shrubs and trees planned to excite the eye. Woodland garden, oak arches with roses, long flower borders, large wild flower meadow, pond and ha-ha complement the garden with spectacular views across fields to The Minster Cathedral.

 ♿

PARKSIDE
See Leicestershire & Rutland.

53 48 PENARTH GARDENS
Sherwood Vale, Nottingham NG5 4EG. Josie & Geoff Goodlud, 01159 609067. *Approx 2½ m N of Nottingham city centre off B684 (Woodborough Rd). From city centre, take B684 Woodborough Rd, turn L after Autopark Garage into Woodthorpe Rd, turn L again into Penarth Rise, L again into Penarth Gardens.* Home-made teas. **Adm £2.50, chd free. Sun 3 July (12-5) Evening Opening £4, chd free, wine, Wed 13 July (6-9). Visitors also welcome by appt.**
One of Nottingham city's hidden gems is to be found in the unlikely setting of the old Nottingham Brickwork Quarry. The landscape has been transformed with pathways, steps and a summer house. Clever planting with trees, fences, bamboos, palms and specimen shrubs, lead to flowing herbaceous borders which provide colour and interest with many unusual plants. Featured in 'Garden News'.

 ♿

54 PIECEMEAL
123 Main Street, Sutton Bonington, Loughborough LE12 5PE. Mary Thomas, 01509 672056, admet123@btinternet.com. *2m SE of Kegworth (M1 J24). 6m NE of Loughborough. Almost opp St Michael's Church.* **Adm £2.50, chd free. Sats 25 June; 16 July; 27 Aug (2-6.30). Visitors also welcome by appt June to August inclusive. Small groups only.**
Shelter of plant enthusiast's tiny walled garden enables amazing collection to thrive in around 500 pots. Huge variety, many unusual and not fully hardy. Busy herbaceous borders. Plants with distinctive foliage and colour combinations provide interest from spring to autumn. Conservatory. Fern-filled well. A jungle by late summer. Featured in Garden News as 'Garden of the Week', Nottingham Evening Post, Loughborough Echo and on BBC Radio Nottingham.

 ♿

55 PRIMROSE COTTAGE
16 Bar Road North, Beckingham DN10 4NN. Terry & Brenda Wilson, 01427 848852. *8m N of Retford. Off A631, main island off Beckingham bypass into village, L to village green, L to Bar Road.* Light refreshments & teas. **Combined adm with Sunnyside Cottage, Thistle Farm & Gable Cottage £3, chd free. Sun 3 July (1-5). Visitors also welcome by appt June & July.**
Old fashioned cottage garden. Walled herbaceous border, well stocked shrubbery. Many old roses, feature pergola, vegetable garden, summerhouse.

 ♿

QUORN ORCHARD GARDENS
See Leicestershire & Rutland.

RIDGEWOLD FARM
See Leicestershire & Rutland.

56 RISEHOLME, 125 SHELFORD ROAD
Radcliffe on Trent NG12 1AZ. John & Elaine Walker, 01159 119867. *4m E of Nottingham. From A52 follow signs to Radcliffe. In village centre take turning for Shelford (by Co-op). Approx ¾ m on LH-side.* **Evening Opening £4, wine, chd free, Wed 22 June (6-9). Visitors also welcome by appt groups of 10+.**
Just under ½ acre designed for colour, texture and movement. Many unusual varieties, hardy perennials, grasses. Formal front garden with packed borders incl hot/cool colour-themed beds and prairie-style borders. Back garden has flowing curves with informal planting, gazebo, pond and jungle area with turf dragon. Colour and interest all yr. A stunning garden, Monty Don. Back garden is truly spectacular, Prof David Stevens. Decorated mirrors around garden and for sale.

 ♿

57 ROSELEA

40 Newark Road, Coddington NG24 2QF. Bruce & Marian Richmond, 01636 676737, richmonds.roselea@tiscali.co.uk. *1¹/₂ m E of Newark. Leave A1 signed Coddington, 100yds from junction S; 300yds from junction N.* Home-made teas. **Adm £2, chd free (share to Parkinson's Society). Visitors welcome by appt** all year, groups or individuals.

Picturesque plantsman's garden. Mixed borders, shrubs, roses, clematis and geraniums. Many unusual plants. Hostas and ferns in pots. Small alpine area. Pergolas covered with climbers. Compost area. Places to sit and ponder. Come and enjoy home-made cakes and teas.

58 55 RUSSELL AVENUE

Wollaton NG8 2BN. John Munns & Janet Wood. *2m W of Nottingham. From Nottingham city centre take A609 towards Ilkeston. Approx 2m turn R at Wheelhouse PH then bear left onto Russell Ave.* Light refreshments & teas. **Adm £2.50, chd free. Sun 7 Aug (2-5.30).**

Small S-facing town garden with a cottage feel. Backed by mature trees, colourful borders of well-matched annual and perennial plants fill the flower garden. Grasses and hostas are displayed with flair in a gravel area.

59 SANDOWN, 41 CHURCH LANE

Cossall Village NG16 2RW. Barrie & Kath Spittal. *3m W of Nottingham. J26 M1 take A610 (W). 1st L, A6096 then Awsworth - Cossall. L to Cossall village. Or from A609 Trowell, take lane signed Cossall.* Home-made teas. **Adm £2.50, chd free. Sun 10 July (1-5).**

A cottage garden with secluded front garden set with colourful perennials and shrubs. Rear garden has curved lawn paths, mixed borders and beds immaculately planted. Lovely displays of geraniums, crocosmia and day lilies. A conveniently placed summerhouse for viewing the garden and a small vegetable patch fits in nicely.

60 78 SANDY LANE

Hucknall NG15 7GP. Alan & Linda Foster, 01159 534609. *7m N of Nottingham. On Hucknall by-pass*

Piecemeal

A611 from Nottingham 1st turn R then 4th turn L. From Mansfield 1st L then 4th R.* Home-made teas at 96 Sandy Lane. **Combined adm with 96 Sandy Lane £3, chd free. Sun 7 Aug (1-5). Visitors also welcome by appt,** June to Sept, parties of 2 - 30.

¹/₄ -acre plant lovers' garden bursting with perennials, shrubs and grasses. From pinks and blues in early summer changing to hotter colours for late summer. Every corner is crammed with plants and features incl shade loving plants, two frog friendly ponds and chickens housed in their own special run. Grass paths, 2 small slopes.

61 96 SANDY LANE

Hucknall NG15 7GP. Helen Rose. *7m N of Nottingham. From Nottingham take Hucknall by-pass A611, take 1st R then 4th L. From Mansfield take 1st L then 4th R.* Home-made teas. **Combined adm with 78 Sandy Lane £3, chd free. Sun 7 Aug (1-5).**

Medium sized, low maintenance, child-friendly garden with steps down to lawned and planted area with summerhouse. Wheelchair access only to patio area.

73 SAXILBY ROAD

See Lincolnshire.

62 NEW THE SMALL EXOTIC GARDEN

26 Selby Road, West Bridgford NG2 7BL. Tim & Jenny Martin, 01159 813657. *2m SE of Nottingham city centre. Off A52 Ring Rd between A606 (Melton Rd) & Musters Rd.* **Adm £2.50, chd free. Suns 7, 21 Aug (1-5). Visitors also welcome by appt** in Aug. Max group 10.

Small green oasis hidden behind an ordinary suburban semi, planted mainly for foliage effect. Patio with exotic potted plants leads down (3 steps) to gravel beds with unusual plants from Mediterranean climates. Beyond a 'mini jungle' features big leaved giants, a secluded 'jungle hut' and wildlife pond, all enriched by meandering bark paths.

63 ▶ NEW ▶ **SMITHY COTTAGE**
18 Main Street, Calverton
NG14 6FQ. Richard & Ronnie Ogier.
*6m NE of Nottingham. From A60 N
from Nottingham take A614 & then
turn R B6386 signed to Southwell.
After Golf Club turn R and follow road
into the village. House is 2nd L after
church. Parking on road. Please do
NOT use unpaved private road
opposite.* **Adm £2.50. Combined
adm with Calverton House 22 May
£4 (incl Church Opening), chd free.
Suns 22 May, 17 July (1-5).**
Our garden has been developed over
5 years as a medium sized 'cottage'
garden with a strong emphasis on
perennial planting. We have an
intimate courtyard planted with herbs
and the back garden features a pond
with a planted waterfall together with
raised vegetable beds, greenhouse
and fruit cage. One step down to
lawn area.

&. ✿ ☕

Beyond a 'mini
jungle' features big
leaved giants, a
secluded 'jungle
hut' and wildlife
pond . . .

64 ▶ **SQUIRREL LODGE**
2 Goosemoor Lane, Retford
DN22 7JA. Peter & Joan
Whitehead. *1m S of Retford.
Travelling S out of Retford on A638,
last R turn before railway bridge.*
Home-made teas. **Combined adm
with The Elms £3, chd free. Suns
15 May; 14 Aug (2-5).**
Journey a little further north in the
County and you will be rewarded by a
garden that has been skilfully crafted
into a corner plot. Some is in deep
shade but the variety will both delight
and please as will the welcome and
the teas. Venture into Mr McGregors
garden and find Peter Rabbit!
Occasional artist at work. Sometimes
pedigree rabbits for handling.
Featured in Garden News &
Nottinghamshire Life.

&. 🐕 ✿ ☕

65 ▶ **SUNNYSIDE COTTAGE**
High Street, Everton DN10 5AU.
Mrs Anne Beeby, 01777 817170,
anne.beeby@sky.com. *7m N of
Retford. 3m S of Bawtry. Everton - on
the Bawtry to Gainsborough Rd
A631. L to High Street opposite Sun
Inn. Garden opposite village hall on
High Street.* Home-made teas in
Village Hall. **Combined adm
Primrose Cottage, Thistle Farm &
Gable Cottage £3, chd free. Sun 3
July (1-5). Visitors also welcome by
appt.**
¹/₃ -acre S-facing secluded cottage
garden designed to incorporate
areas of different planting schemes
and features which include roses,
perennials. acers, a pond and some
unusual foliage plants and trees.
New this year small wild flower
garden.

&. ✿ ☕ ☎

TEBUTTS FARM
See Leicestershire & Rutland.

66 ▶ **THISTLE FARM**
Beckingham DN10 4PS. Jayne &
Russell Hanson. *8m N of Retford.
Off A631, main island off Beckingham
bypass into village. House at junction
of Low St & The Green.* Light
Refreshments in Village Hall.
**Combined adm Primrose Cottage,
Sunnyside Cottage & Gable
Cottage £3, chd free. Sun 3 July
(1-5).**
This garden gem is entered via a
small shrubbery and day garden.
Rambling roses and old wisteria lead
into French-style parterre with clipped
box, roses and herbs.

&. ☕

67 ▶ **THORESBY HALL
HOTEL & SPA**
Thoresby Park, nr Ollerton
NG22 9WH. Warner Leisure Hotels,
01623 821000,
www.warnerleisurehotels.co.uk.
*N of Nottingham. Exit A1signed A614
Nottingham - Leicester. After 4m at
the r'about take exit signed Thoresby
Hall Hotel. Entrance 1m on L.* **Adm
£3.50 (sorry no children). Sat 2, 9,
16, 23, 30 July (10-4).**
Thoresby Hall gardens are famous for
their beauty. Set in 30-acres of Sir
Humphry Repton designed gardens,
featuring a Grade 1 listed victorian
rose garden with rare species. Gravel
paths.

&. ☕

68 ▶ **THRUMPTON HALL**
Thrumpton NG11 0AX. Miranda
Seymour, www.thrumptonhall.com.
*7m S of Nottingham. M1 J24 take
A453 towards Nottingham. Turn L to
Thrumpton Village & continue to
Thrumpton Hall.* Home-made teas.
**Adm £3, chd free. Sun 10 July
(2-5).**
Two acres lawns, rare trees, lakeside
walks, flower borders, rose-garden
and box-bordered sunken herb
garden, all enclosed by C18 ha-ha
and encircling a Jacobean house.
Garden is surrounded by an C18
landscaped park and is bordered by a
river. Rare opportunity to visit
Thrumpton Hall (separate ticket).
Jacobean mansion, unique carved
staircase, Great Saloon, State
Bedroom, Priest's Hole.

&. 🐕 ✿ ☕

69 ▶ **UNIVERSITY OF
NOTTINGHAM GARDENS**
University Park, Nottingham
NG7 2RD. Desmond O'Grady,
www.nottingham.ac.uk/estate/
grounds.htm. *1¹/₂ m W of
Nottingham city centre. Suggest
visitors use University Park's North
Entrance on A52 adjacent to Queens
Medical Centre roundabout.
Millennium Garden well signed on
campus.* Tea & Light Refreshments.
**Adm £2.50, chd free. Sun 7 Aug
(12-5).**
University Park has many beautiful
gardens including the award-
winning Millennium Garden with its
dazzling flower garden, timed
fountains and turf maze, the huge
Lenton Firs rock garden, the dry
garden and Jekyll garden. During
summer the walled garden will be
alive with exotic plantings. In total,
300 acres of landscape and
gardens. Cafeteria available for
refreshments. Short tours. Minibus
available for visiting gardens around
the campus.

&. 🐕 ✿ ☕

70 ▶ **WEST FARM HOUSE**
Gonalston Lane, Hoveringham
NG14 7JH. Dr R S & Mrs C D Torr,
01159 664771, richard-
torr1@tiscali.co.uk. *6m NE of
Nottinghamshire. Signed from A612
Nottingham to Southwell Rd. Just on
Southwell side of Lowdham.* Light
refreshments & teas at Village Hall.
**Adm £4, chd free. Sun 22 May
(1-5). Also opening with Church
House. Visitors also welcome by
appt. Groups of 10+.**

¹/₂ -acre cottage style garden in a beautiful village setting bordering open countryside. Fine herbaceous borders featuring hardy geraniums, hostas, delphiniums and wide range of shrubs and other herbaceous perennials. Extensive greenhouse collection of cacti and succulents, with over 1000 plants on display, at the peak of flowering May and June. Featured in Nottingham Evening Post.

Plant-lovers' garden featured in many magazines; twice televised. Now maturing after complete transformation . . .

71▶ 6 WESTON CLOSE
Woodthorpe NG5 4FS. Diane & Steve Harrington, 01159 857506, di.harrington@o2.co.uk. *3m N of Nottingham city centre. From city centre, A60 Mansfield Road. After Sherwood shops turn R at T-lights by Woodthorpe Park into Woodthorpe Drive. 2nd L into Grange Road. R into The Crescent, R into Weston Close. Park in The Crescent.* Home-made teas. **Adm £2.50, chd free. Suns 26 June; 3 July (1-5). Visitors also welcome by appt mid June to end July, min group 6+.**
Medium sized densely planted garden created over 18yrs from bare plot, taking advantage of a

substantial upward slope to create a full, varied yet relaxed display in 3 separate areas. Mixed borders, scented roses, clematis, hostas, fuchsias, summer bedding in pots, small vegetable plot.

WHATTON GARDENS
See Leicestershire & Rutland.

72▶ THE WHITE HOUSE
Nicker Hill, Keyworth NG12 5EA. Tony & Gillian Hill, gillygardenplantsenqs@gmail.com. *8m SE of Nottingham. From A606 at Stanton-on-the-Wolds turn into Browns Lane beside petrol station. Follow rd 1¹/₂ m into Stanton Lane becoming Nicker Hill.* Home-made teas. **Adm £2.50, chd free. Suns 29 May; 10 July; Weds 1 June; 13 July (2-5).**
³/₄ -acre plant-lovers' garden featured in many magazines; twice televised. Now maturing after complete transformation featuring new extensive dry garden and sensory, secret garden. Pond, plant-smothered archways, arbour, pergolas and trellises. Intensively planted and constantly refreshed for yr-round colour incl many rarities often available from specialist nursery on site open days only.

73▶ WOODPECKERS
35 Lambley Lane, Burton Joyce NG14 5BG. Lynn Drake & Mark Carr, 01159 313237, info@woodpeckersdining.co.uk. *6m N of Nottingham. In Burton Joyce, turn off A612 (Nottm/Southwell rd) into Lambley Lane, garden on L.* Home-made teas. **Adm £3, chd free. Sun & Mon 29, 30 May (12-5).**

Visitors also welcome by appt.
4 acres of mature woodland and formal gardens with spectacular views over the Trent Valley. Over 500 rhododendrons and azaleas. Balustraded terrace for teas or pimms. Glade with 200 yr-old cedars overlooking ponds, waterfalls and croquet lawn. Bog garden and sunken area below ha-ha, created in 2009 and planted to tempt the eye onwards towards ancient well.

74▶ ◆ THE WORKHOUSE
Upton Road, Southwell NG25 0PT. Rachel Harrison, 01636 817260, www.nationaltrust.org.uk. *1m E of Southwell on A612. Signed from centre of Southwell.* **House and Garden Adm £6.75, chd £3.40. For NGS: Sat 23 July (12-4). For other opening times and information, please phone or see garden website.**
Originally started in 1825 to provide food and labour for the pauper inmates, the north side was cultivated to provide potatoes, and the south was used to grow vegetables and a pasture for two cows. Volunteers have been recreating the kitchen garden using traditional techniques and heirloom varieties of produce. Tours of garden explainig its historical significance & later developments available. Wheelchair accessible garden & ground floor of main property.
&

WYMESWOLD GARDENS
See Leicestershire & Rutland

OXFORDSHIRE

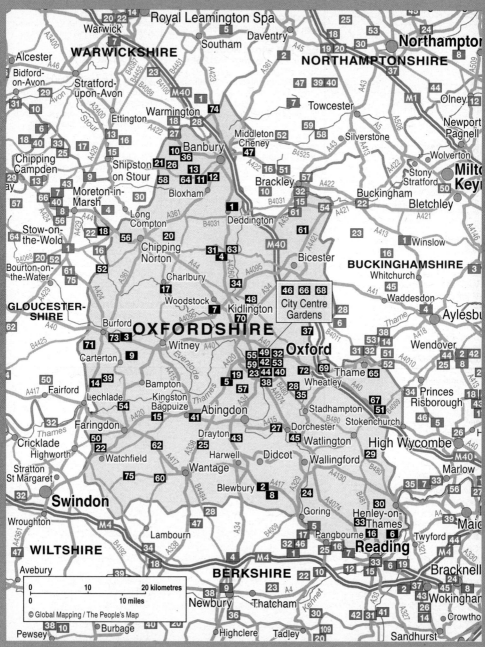

Opening Dates

March

Sunday 20
68 Wadham College
Sunday 27
41 Kingston Bagpuize House
66 Trinity College

April

Sunday 3
2 Ashbrook House
26 Epwell Mill
48 Monks Head
Sunday 10
15 Buckland Lakes
50 The Old Rectory, Coleshill
Sunday 17
21 Church Farm Field
28 Garsington Manor
37 Horton Cum Studley Gardens
43 Lime Close
44 Magdalen College
69 Waterperry Gardens
74 Wildwood
Wednesday 20
75 Woolstone Mill House
Monday 25
10 Brook Cottage
39 Kencot Gardens
Wednesday 27
75 Woolstone Mill House

May

Sunday 1
12 Broughton Grange
17 Charlbury Gardens
Wednesday 4
75 Woolstone Mill House
Sunday 8
57 The Sheiling
Wednesday 11
75 Woolstone Mill House
Sunday 15
42 Lady Margaret Hall
Wednesday 18
74 Wildwood
75 Woolstone Mill House
Saturday 21
5 36 Bertie Road
19 14 Chawley Lane
Sunday 22
31 The Grove
Wednesday 25
33 Hearns House
75 Woolstone Mill House
Friday 27
33 Hearns House

Sunday 29
4 Barton Abbey
27 Evelegh's
56 Salford Gardens
Monday 30
60 Sparsholt Manor

June

Wednesday 1
75 Woolstone Mill House
Saturday 4
34 Hill Court
Sunday 5
9 Brize Norton Gardens
21 Church Farm Field
25 East Hanney Gardens
26 Epwell Mill
32 Headington Gardens
34 Hill Court
43 Lime Close
63 Steeple Aston Gardens
65 Thame Gardens
Wednesday 8
75 Woolstone Mill House
Sunday 12
3 Asthall Manor
38 Iffley Gardens
51 The Old Vicarage
Tuesday 14
30 Greys Court
Wednesday 15
6 Binfield Heath Gardens
74 Wildwood
75 Woolstone Mill House
Saturday 18
6 Binfield Heath Gardens
Sunday 19
1 Adderbury Gardens
8 Blewbury Gardens
12 Broughton Grange
16 Chalkhouse Green Farm
28 Garsington Manor
54 Radcot House
58 Sibford Gower Gardens
71 Westwell Manor
Wednesday 22
75 Woolstone Mill House
Thursday 23
29 Greenfield Farm (Evening)
Saturday 25
7 Blenheim Palace
Sunday 26
13 Broughton Grounds Farm
45 Manor House
47 Middleton Cheney Gardens
72 Wheatley Gardens
73 Whitehill Farm
Wednesday 29
47 Middleton Cheney Gardens (Evening)
75 Woolstone Mill House

July

Sunday 3
23 Corpus Christi College
Wednesday 6
75 Woolstone Mill House
Saturday 9
49 North Oxford Gardens
Sunday 10
14 Broughton Poggs & Filkins Gardens
18 Chastleton House
24 The Cutting Garden
59 Somerville College
68 Wadham College
Wednesday 13
75 Woolstone Mill House
Wednesday 20
74 Wildwood
75 Woolstone Mill House
Sunday 24
11 Broughton Castle
46 Merton College Oxford Fellows' Garden
66 Trinity College
Wednesday 27
75 Woolstone Mill House
Sunday 31
12 Broughton Grange

August

Wednesday 3
75 Woolstone Mill House
Wednesday 10
75 Woolstone Mill House
Wednesday 17
75 Woolstone Mill House
Sunday 21
54 Radcot House
Wednesday 24
75 Woolstone Mill House
Monday 29
10 Brook Cottage
Wednesday 31
75 Woolstone Mill House

September

Sunday 4
2 Ashbrook House
50 The Old Rectory, Coleshill
Wednesday 7
75 Woolstone Mill House
Sunday 11
25 East Hanney Gardens
26 Epwell Mill
Wednesday 14
75 Woolstone Mill House
Sunday 18
28 Garsington Manor
54 Radcot House
69 Waterperry Gardens

You are always welcome at an NGS garden

Wednesday 21
75 Woolstone Mill House
Monday 26
41 Kingston Bagpuize House
Wednesday 28
75 Woolstone Mill House

Look out for the
gardens with the ☎
– enjoy a private
visit . . .

Gardens open to the public
7 Blenheim Palace
10 Brook Cottage
11 Broughton Castle
18 Chastleton House
30 Greys Court
41 Kingston Bagpuize House
44 Magdalen College
46 Merton College Oxford Fellows' Garden
69 Waterperry Gardens

By appointment only
20 Chivel Farm
22 Clock House
35 Home Close
36 Home Farm
40 10 Kennett Road
52 The Old Vicarage, Bledington
53 40 Osler Road
55 9 Rawlinson Road
61 Springhill House
62 Stansfield
64 Tadmarton Manor
67 Upper Chalford Farm
70 Wayside

Also open by Appointment ☎
2 Ashbrook House
72 Breach House Garden, Wheatley Gardens
8 Carpenters, Blewbury Gardens
16 Chalkhouse Green Farm
21 Church Farm Field
24 The Cutting Garden

26 Epwell Mill
29 Greenfield Farm
33 Hearns House
6 Heath Cottage, Binfield Heath Gardens
43 Lime Close
56 Manor Farm, Salford Gardens
45 Manor House
72 The Manor House, Wheatley Gardens
48 Monks Head
56 Old Rectory, Salford Gardens
51 The Old Vicarage
32 40 Osler Road, Headington Gardens
54 Radcot House
72 The Studio, Wheatley Gardens
63 Touchwood, Steeple Aston Gardens
73 Whitehill Farm
56 Willow Tree Cottage, Salford Gardens
75 Woolstone Mill House

The Gardens

GROUP OPENING

1 **ADDERBURY GARDENS**
Adderbury OX17 3LS. *3m S of Banbury. J10 M40, onto A43 signed Northampton, then A4260 to Adderbury, or A4260 S from Banbury. Maps with garden descriptions given to all visitors.* Home-made teas at Adderbury Parish Institute. **Combined adm £5, chd free (share to Katharine House Hospice).** Sun 19 June (2-6).

CROSSHILL HOUSE
Mr & Mrs Gurth Hoyer Millar

HOLLY BANK
Malcolm & Erica Brown

THE OLD VICARAGE
Christine & Peter Job

PLACKETTS
Dr D White

SORBROOK MANOR
Mr & Mrs Robin Thistlethwayte

Attractive Ironstone village, with 5 gardens ranging from quite small to very large. Crosshill House 4-acre classic Victorian walled garden and grounds with ha-ha. Holly Bank ⅓acre. Interesting redevelopment. Island beds with variety of plants, many unusual varieties. The Old Vicarage walled front garden, large rear garden stretching from ha ha to small lake and flood meadows. Unusual plants and trees. Japanese

maple plantation. Placketts 0.2 acre walled garden with sheltered gravel courtyard, main garden exposed, with views. Plethora of colourful plants throughout the yr with late summer colour. Sorbrook Manor 3-acres. Trees and shrubs sloping down to Sor Brook. Wheelchair access at Holly Bank & Sorbrook Manor only. Dogs allowed at The Old Vicarage, Crosshill House & Sorbrook Manor.
  ♿ 🐕 ❀ ☕

2 **ASHBROOK HOUSE**
Blewbury OX11 9QA. Mr & Mrs S A Barrett, 01235 850810, janembarrett@me.com. *4m SE of Didcot. Turn off A417 in Blewbury into Westbrook St. 1st house on R. Follow yellow signs for parking in Boham's Road.* **Adm £3, chd free.** Suns 3 Apr; 4 Sept (2-6). Visitors also welcome by appt.
The garden where Kenneth Grahame read Wind in the Willows to local children and where he took inspiration for his description of the oak doors to Badger's House. Come and see - you may catch a glimpse of Toad and friends in this 3½-acre chalk and water garden in a beautiful spring-line village. In spring the banks are a mass of daffodils and in late summer the borders are full of unusual plants. Plant sale, April only.
  ♿ 🐕 ❀ ☕ ☎

3 **ASTHALL MANOR**
Asthall, nr Burford OX18 4HW. Rosanna Pearson, www.onformsculpture.co.uk. *3m E of Burford. At r'about between Witney & Burford on A40, take turning to Minster Lovell. Turn immed L (signed to Asthall). At bottom of hill, follow avenue of trees and look for car park signs.* Home-made teas in the village. **Adm £5, chd free.** Sun 12 June (2-6).
6-acres of garden surround this C17 manor house (not open) once home to the Mitford family and overlooking the Windrush Valley. The gardens, designed by I & J Bannerman in 1998, offer 'a beguiling mix of traditional and contemporary'. Exuberant scented borders, sloping box parterres, wild flowers, a turf sculpture and a hidden lake are all part of the mix. The Ballroom, converted from a barn into a music room and library by the Mitfords, will be open. Featured in Gardens Illustrated & Country Life. Limited wheelchair access.
  ♿ ❀ ☕

AVON DASSETT GARDENS
See Warwickshire.

 BARTON ABBEY
Steeple Barton OX25 4QS. Mr &
Mrs P Fleming. *8m E of Chipping
Norton. On B4030, ¹/₂ m from junction
of A4260 & B4030.* Home-made teas.
Adm £4, chd free. Sun 29 May
(2-5).
15-acre garden with views from
house (not open) across sweeping
lawns and picturesque lake. Walled
garden with colourful herbaceous
borders, separated by established
yew hedges and espalier fruit,
contrasts with more informal
woodland garden paths with vistas of
specimen trees and meadows.
Working glasshouses and fine display
of fruit and vegetables.

 NEW 36 BERTIE ROAD
36 Bertie Road, Cumnor OX2 9PS.
Esther & Neil Whiting. *3¹/₂ m W of
Oxford. Take W rd out of Oxford,
through Botley and continue up hill.
At car showrooms turn R. Park in
Bertie/Norreys Rd.* Teas at 14
Chawley Lane. **Combined adm with
14 Chawley Lane £4, chd free.** Sat
21 May (2-5.30).
Professionally designed developing
garden planted in 2007 in pleasant
suburban setting. Structured layout,
relaxed planting, incl ornamental
grasses. Small area of gravel path.

GROUP OPENING

**6 NEW BINFIELD HEATH
GARDENS**
Binfield Heath RG9 4ED. *3¹/₂ m S of
Henley-on-Thames. Off A4155 Henley
to Reading Rd. Heathfield Ave opp
PO in centre of village. Kiln Lane lies
behind, 5 min walk away.* Cream teas.
Combined adm £4, chd free.
Wed 15, Sat 18 June (2-5).

NEW HEATH COTTAGE
6 Heathfield Avenue. Noreen
Walsh
Visitors also welcome by appt
June only. 01189 478839
noreenandhope@aol.com

NEW HOMESIDE
Kiln Lane. Paul & Wendy
Robinson

NEW TWO JAYS
Heathfield Avenue. Mrs Susan
Smmerland

NEW VERONICA
13 Heathfield Avenue. Robin &
Christine Head

Four different and interesting gardens
in the quiet village of Binfield Heath,
which lies 3¹/₂ m S of Henley-on-
Thames. Three gardens in Heathfield
Ave are similar sized (long and
narrow) but delightfully different.
Maintained to create loads of interest
in planting and design using exotic
and unusual plants to attract and
inspire. The 4th garden in Kiln Lane
has interesting features with many
different areas and spectacular views
over the South Oxfordshire
countryside. Cream teas and plants
available here. Locally made garden
artefacts will be displayed around the
gardens and a percentage of sales
will go to NGS. Locally produced
garden artefacts and paintings will be
displayed in the gardens,
refreshments area in next door
garden. Wheelchair access at
Veronica & limited access at Two Jays
& Homeside.

Asthall Manor

7 ◆ BLENHEIM PALACE
Woodstock OX20 1PX. His Grace
the Duke of Marlborough, 01993
810530, www.blenheimpalace.com.
*8m N of Oxford. Bus: S3 Oxford-
Chipping Norton, alight Woodstock.*
Adm £4, chd £2. For NGS: Sat 25
June (10-6). **For other opening
times and information, please visit
website or telephone.**
Blenheim Gardens, originally laid out
by Henry Wise, include the formal
Water Terraces and Italian Garden by
Achille Duchêne, Rose Garden,
Arboretum, and Cascade. The Secret
Garden, opened in 2004, offers a
stunning garden paradise in all
seasons. Blenheim Lake, created by
Capability Brown and spanned by
Vanburgh's Grand Bridge, is the focal
point of over 2,000 acres of
landscaped parkland. The Pleasure
Gardens complex includes the Herb
and Lavender Garden and Butterfly
House. Other activities incl the
Marlborough Maze, putting greens,
adventure play area, giant chess and
draughts. Dogs allowed in park only.
Some gravel paths.

GROUP OPENING

8 ▶ BLEWBURY GARDENS
Blewbury OX11 9QB. *4m SE of
Didcot. On A417. Follow yellow signs
for car parks.* Tea & Light
Refreshments in various locations.
Adm £4, chd free. Sun 19 June
(2-6).

ABNERS
Joyce Gilbert

BROOKS END
Jean & David Richards

CARPENTERS
Nick & Melanie Longhurst
Visitors also welcome by appt.
melanie_longhurst@hotmail.com

CHAPMANS ⊨
Jenny Craig

GREEN BUSHES
Phil Rogers

HALL BARN
Malcolm & Deirdre Cochrane

STOCKS
Norma & Richard Bird

As celebrated by Rachel de Thame in
Gardener's World. Seven gardens in
charming downland village. Abners:
The view from the gate draws you into
this natural cottage garden.
Brooks End: a 1960s bungalow,
newly designed garden with colour
themed beds, damp border, hidden
garden, small orchard, greenhouse
and vegetable garden. Carpenters:
Surrounds C16 thatched cottage.
Mature trees, mixed borders of
herbaceous plants, roses and shrubs,
shade areas and vegetable garden.
Chapmans: a ½-acre garden with
listed house. Informal beds with new
and established herbaceous planting
with some unusual plants. Green
Bushes: Created by plant lover Rhon
(decd 2007) around C16 cottage.
Colour themed borders, ponds and
poolside planting, alpine troughs,
ferns, pleached limes and roses. Hall
Barn: Extends over 4 acres and incl
traditional herbaceous borders,
kitchen garden and a croquet lawn.
C16 dovecote, thatched cob wall and
clear chalk streams. Stocks: an early
cruck-constructed thatched cottage
surrounded by densely planted, lime-
tolerant herbaceous perennials
offering tiers of colour yr-round. Plant
Stall in car park. Regret no wheelchair
access at Abners & Carpenters.
& ⊛ ☕

GROUP OPENING

9 ▶ BRIZE NORTON GARDENS
Brize Norton OX18 3NN, 01993
846386. *3m SW of Witney. Brize
Norton village, S of A40, between
Witney & Burford. Parking at various
locations in the village.* Home-made
teas at Elderbank Hall. **Adm £4, chd
free.** Sun 5 June (1-6).

BARNSTABLE HOUSE
Mr & Mrs P Butcher

10 CHICHESTER PLACE
David & Claire Harrison

CHURCH FARM HOUSE
Philip & Mary Holmes

NEW▶ THE COTTAGE
G & J A Griffin

16 DAUBIGNY MEAD
Bob & Margaret Watts

GAYLYN
Mrs B Wallace

GRANGE FARM
Mark & Lucy Artus

MIJESHE
Mr & Mrs M Harper

PAINSWICK HOUSE
Mr & Mrs T Gush

ROSEDALE
Mr & Mrs S Finlayson

95 STATION ROAD
Mr & Mrs P A Timms

STONE COTTAGE
Mr & Mrs K Humphris

Pretty village on the edge of the
Cotswold's offering 12 gardens open
for your enjoyment. You can see a
wide variety of planting incl a bog
garden, ornamental trees,
herbaceous borders, ornamental
grasses and traditional fruit and
vegetable gardens. Features incl a
Mediterranean style patio, courtyard
garden, water features, C14 dovecote
plus many gardens where you can
just sit and relax. Visit the pretty
Norman Church of St Britius, which
will be holding a flower festival of
outstanding beauty. Coaches
welcome but should telephone first to
arrange parking.
& ✿ ⊛ ☕

10 ▶ ◆ BROOK COTTAGE
Well Lane, Alkerton OX15 6NL. Mrs
David Hodges, 01295 670303,
www.brookcottagegarden.co.uk.

*6m NW of Banbury. ½ m off A422.
Follow signs in village.* **Adm £5, chd
free.** For NGS: Mons 25 Apr;
29 Aug (9-6). For other opening
times and information, please
phone or see garden website.
4-acre hillside garden formed since
1964. Wide variety of trees, shrubs
and perennials in areas of differing
character. Water gardens, gravel
garden, colour coordinated borders.
Over 200 shrub and climbing roses.
Many clematis; magnificent trees,
interesting throughout season. Open
Easter Mon to end Oct, Mon - Fri (9-
6) Not for NGS.
& ✿ ⊛ ☎

The view from the gate draws you into this natural cottage garden . . .

11 ▶ ◆ BROUGHTON CASTLE
nr Banbury OX15 5EB. The Lord
Saye & Sele, 01295 276070,
www.broughtoncastle.com. *2½ m
SW of Banbury. On Shipston-on-
Stour rd (B4035).* **Adm £3, chd £3.**
For NGS: Sun 24 July (2-5). For
other opening times and
information please visit website or
telephone.
1 acre; shrubs, herbaceous borders,
walled garden, roses, climbers seen
against background of C14-C16
castle surrounded by moat in open
parkland. House also open, extra
charge.
& ✿ ⊛ ☕ ☎

12 ▶ BROUGHTON GRANGE
Wykham Lane, Broughton
OX15 5DS. *¼ m out of village. From
Banbury take the B4035 to village of
Broughton. At the Seye & Sele Arms
PH turn L up Wykham Lane (one
way). Follow rd out of village along
lane for ¼ m. Entrance on R.* **Adm
£6, chd free.** Suns 1 May; 19 June;
31 July (10-5).
An impressive 25 acres of gardens
and light woodland in an attractive
Oxfordshire setting. The centrepiece
is a large terraced walled garden
created by Tom Stuart-Smith in 2001.
Vision has been used to blend the
gardens into the countryside. Good

early displays of bulbs followed by outstanding herbaceous planting in summer. Formal and informal areas combine to make this a special site incl newly laid arboretum with many ongoing projects.

13 BROUGHTON GROUNDS FARM

North Newington OX15 6AW. Mr & Mrs Andrew Taylor. *3m from Banbury. 3m off B4035 through North Newington. Leave Banbury on Shipston Rd, B4035. Turn R to N Newington, follow rd signed Shutford. On L ³/₄ m signed B & B.* Home-made teas. **Adm £3, chd free. Sun 26 June (2-5).**
One of the first farms to achieve recognition under the High Level Stewardship Scheme. You will see rare wild flowers, grasses and wildlife in an area set in an 18-acre meadow. Also incl an old mill race and views of the deserted (1914) village of Hazelford. An area which is species rich. Featured in BBC South Today.

GROUP OPENING

14 BROUGHTON POGGS & FILKINS GARDENS

GL7 3JH. *3m N of Lechlade. 5m S of Burford. Just off A361 between Burford & Lechlade.* Home-made teas in Filkins village hall. **Combined adm £4.50, chd free. Sun 10 July (2-5.30).**

BROUGHTON HALL
Karen & Ian Jobling

BROUGHTON POGGS MILL
Charles Payne & Avril Inglis

FIELD COTTAGE
Peter & Sheila Gray

FILKINS HALL
Filkins Hall Residents

LITTLE PEACOCKS
Colvin & Moggridge

NO 1 COACH HOUSE
David & Jaine Mylam

NEW PEACOCK FARMHOUSE
Pauline & Peter Care

NEW PIGEON COTTAGE
Lynn Savage

PIP COTTAGE
G B Woodin

ST PETER'S HOUSE
John Cambridge

NEW STONE HOUSE
Jackie & Roland Callum

TAYLOR COTTAGE
Ian & Ronnie Bailey

WILLOW COTTAGE
Sue Logan

13 gardens in these beautiful and vibrant Cotswold stone twin villages. Scale and character vary from the grand landscape setting of Filkins Hall and the equally extensive but more intimate Broughton Hall, to the small but action-packed Pigeon Cottage and Taylor Cottage. Broughton Poggs Mill has a rushing mill stream with an exciting bridge, Little Peacocks is a serene composition of spaces (Brenda Colvin's own garden) and Pip Cottage combines topiary, box hedges and a fine rural view. In these and the other equally exciting gardens horticultural interest abounds and vegetables are well represented. Legendary teas at the Village Hall. Visit the community-run shop, the Swinford Museum of Cotswold tools and artefacts, and Cotswold Woollen Weavers. Maps available. Demonstration of beekeeping (no flying bees) by County lecturer. Plant stall by professional local nursery. Most gardens are suitable for wheelchair access. Some gardens do not welcome dogs.

You will see rare wild flowers, grasses and wildlife in an area set in an 18-acre meadow . . .

15 BUCKLAND LAKES

nr Faringdon SN7 8QR. The Wellesley family. *3m NE of Faringdon. Signed to Buckland off A420, lane between two churches. Minibus shuttle available between car park and hall.* Home-made teas at Memorial Hall. **Adm £3.50, chd free. Sun 10 Apr (2-5).**
Six acres of parkland surround the

lakeside walk, designed by Richard Woods; fine trees; daffodils; shrubs. Norman church adjoins garden. C18 icehouse; thatched boathouse; exedra. Children must be supervised due to large expanse of open water which is unfenced.

BURROW FARM
See Buckinghamshire.

16 CHALKHOUSE GREEN FARM

nr Kidmore End RG4 9AL. Mr & Mrs J Hall, 01189 723631. *2m N of Reading, 5m SW of Henley-on-Thames. Situated between A4074 & B481. From Kidmore End take Chalkhouse Green Rd. Follow yellow signs.* Home-made teas. **Adm £3, chd free. Sun 19 June (2-6). Visitors also welcome by appt.**
1-acre garden and open traditional farmstead. Herbaceous borders, herb garden, shrubs, old-fashioned roses, trees incl medlar, quince and mulberries, walled ornamental kitchen garden. New cherry orchard. Rare breed farm animals incl an ancient breed of British White cattle, Suffolk Punch & Percheron horses, donkeys, Berkshire pigs, piglets, chickens, ducks and turkeys. Vintage farm machinery displays. Farm trail and donkey rides, vintage tractor trailer rides, WW 2 Air Raid shelter, plant stall, horse logging demonstration, bee keeping display, jams & honey for sale. Featured on BBC Radio Berkshire & Oxford. Areas of loose gravel; assistance available if requested at ticket sale table.

GROUP OPENING

17 CHARLBURY GARDENS

OX7 3PP. *6m SE of Chipping Norton. Large Cotswold village on B4022 Witney-Enstone Rd.* Teas at Charlbury Memorial Hall. **Combined adm £5, chd free. Sun 1 May (2-5.30).**

GOTHIC HOUSE
Mr & Mrs Andrew Lawson

THE PRIORY GARDEN
Dr D El Kabir & Colleagues

NEW TAMARIN HOUSE
Jo & Gerard Appadoo

3 varied gardens in the centre of this large Cotswold village, in the context of traditional stone houses. Gothic

House. 1/3 -acre walled garden designed with sculpture and colour in mind. New area of planted squares replaces lawn. False perspective, pleached lime walk, trellis, terracotta containers. The Priory Garden has 1acre of formal terraced topiary gardens with Italianate features. Foliage colour schemes, shrubs, parterres with fragrant plants, old roses, water features, sculpture and inscriptions aim to produce a poetic, wistful atmosphere. Arboretum of over 3 acres. Borders R Evenlode. Incl wildlife garden and pond. Tamarin House is a 2-acre mature garden with mixed borders, restored over the last 12 yrs with a new formal approach adopted in 2007. Organic, raised vegetable beds to rear.

CHARLTON GARDENS
See Northamptonshire.

18 ◆ **CHASTLETON HOUSE**
Chaselton, Moreton-in-Marsh
GL56 0SU. National Trust,
www.nationaltrust.org.uk. *Follow brown signs for Chastleton House from A44 between Morton in Marsh & Chipping Norton.* **Adm £2.50, chd free.** For NGS: Sun 10 July (2-6). **For other opening times and information please visit website.** Chastleton is a historic Jacobean garden. Made up of various rooms, it still shows how certain areas were accessed only depending on your status in the househod. The garden has a variety of topiaries, shrubs, fruit, vegetables, trees and herbaceous planting with an ancient feel. It has 2 croquet lawns and is home of croquet. Plant sales, garden tools, bee keeping stand & advice, information on fruit keeping/growing etc. Steep slopes & gravel paths.

19 NEW **14 CHAWLEY LANE**
14 Chawley Lane, Cumnor
OX2 9PX. Paul & Alice Munsey.
3m W of Oxford. From Oxford, at top of Cumnor Hill, turn R by Lexus garage into Chawley Lane. Garden is 50m on R. Parking in Norreys and Bertie Road. **Home-made teas.** **Combined adm with 36 Bertie Road £4, chd free.** Sat 21 May (2-5.30).
Plantsman's 1/2 - acre garden with wide and interesting range of plants, many unusual. Owner has a particular interest in alpines and woodland plants. Lovely views over valley and Wytham Woods. One slight slope. Small step to WC.

20 **CHIVEL FARM**
Heythrop OX7 5TR. Mr & Mrs
J D Sword, 01608 683227,
rosalind.sword@btinternet.com.
4m E of Chipping Norton. Off A361 or A44. **Adm £4, chd free.** Visitors welcome by appt.
Beautifully designed country garden, with extensive views, designed for continuous interest. Colour-schemed borders with many unusual trees, shrubs and herbaceous plants. Small formal white garden. Conservatory.

21 **CHURCH FARM FIELD**
Church Lane, Epwell OX15 6LD.
Mr V D & Mrs D V D Castle, 01295
788473. *71/2 m W of Banbury on N side of Epwell.* **Adm £2, chd free.** Suns 17 Apr; 5 June (2-6). **Also open Epwell Mill.** Visitors also welcome by appt.
Woods; arboretum with wild flowers (planting started 1992); over 150 different trees and shrubs in 41/2 acres. Paths cut through trees for access to various parts.

22 **CLOCK HOUSE**
Coleshill SN6 7PT. Denny Wickham & Peter Fox, 01793 762476,
denny.andrews@virgin.net. *31/2 m SW of Faringdon. On B4019.* **Adm £3, chd free.** Visitors welcome by appt, max group size 20, no coaches.
Rambling garden on hilltop overlooking NT parkland and Vale of the White Horse. On the site of Coleshill House, burnt down in 1952, the floor plan has been laid out as a garden with lavender and box 'walls' and gravel 'rooms' full of self-sown

Broughton Castle

butterfly-attracting flowers. Exuberant, not too tidy, garden with unusual plants; walled garden; vegetables.

23 CORPUS CHRISTI COLLEGE
Merton Street, Oxford OX1 4JF. Mr C Holmes, Domestic Bursar. *Entrance from Merton St.* **Adm £2, chd free. Sun 3 July (3-7).**
David Leake, the College gardener since 1979, eschewing chemicals and sprays, has created a marvellous 'wild' garden by blending a huge range of wild and cultivated flowers into a vivid, yet harmonious, landscape. In amongst beautiful buildings and with wonderful views of Christ Church meadows from the mound beside the ancient city wall, the Corpus garden is a real treasure. One slope.

CUDDINGTON GARDENS
See Buckinghamshire.

24 NEW THE CUTTING GARDEN
Little Stoke, Wallingford OX10 6AX. Rachel Siegfried, 07977 445041, info@greenandgorgeousflowers. co.uk, www.greenandgorgeousflowers.co. uk. *3m S of Wallingford. Off B4009 between N & S Stoke; follow single track road down to farm.* Home-made teas. **Adm £3, chd free. Sun 10 July (12-5).** Visitors also welcome by appt.
3-acre working flower farm next to R Thames. Organically grown cut flowers (many unusual varieties) in large plots and polytunnels, planted with combination of annuals, bulbs, perennials, roses and shrubs, plus some herbs, vegetables and fruit to feed the workers! Flowers selected for scent, novelty, nostalgia and naturalistic style. Floristry demonstrations. Featured in Country Homes & Interiors, Amateur Gardening & on BBC Gardeners' World. Short grass paths, large concrete areas.

DAYLESFORD HOUSE
See Gloucestershire North & Central.

GROUP OPENING

25 EAST HANNEY GARDENS
East Hanney OX12 0HJ. *3m out of Wantage on A338 towards Oxford. Turn into E Hanney off A338 opp La Fontana Restaurant, keep red telephone box on L & continue 200yds down road, turn L into Halls Lane. Philberds & free car park on R.* Home-made teas at Philberd's Manor (June & Sept) and Lower Mill (June only). **Combined adm £5, chd free (share to Sobell House Hospice). Suns 5 June; 11 Sept (2-5).**

JASMINE COTTAGE
Gill & David Parry
Not open Sun 11 Sept.

LOWER MILL
Robert & Maryrose Hodgson

PHILBERD'S MANOR
Robert & Maryrose Hodgson

Visit 3 gardens in this character filled village with many thatched and timber framed cottages. Ancient church with Norman features and monumental brasses (W Hanney) and good village PH. Pretty walk between the gardens along the willow-lined bank of the Letcombe Brook, with timeless views over water meadows. Jasmine Cottage: ¹/₅ -acre, developed by a plantaholic and willing helper. Cordon fruit trees, vegetable patch and terrace. Lower Mill: atmospheric garden designed by Jinny Blom, planted in silt from the Letcombe Brooke, which borders it. Philberd's Manor: 1¹/₂ -acres of peaceful garden surrounding beautiful C17 manor house (not open). Perennial borders, herb garden and restored terrace.

Pretty walk between the gardens along the willow-lined bank of the Letcombe Brook . . .

---

26 EPWELL MILL
nr Banbury OX15 6HG. Mrs William Graham & Mrs David Long, 01295 788242, caroline.long@talk21.com. *7m W of Banbury. Between Shutford & Epwell, ¹/₂ m outside Epwell.* Home-made teas. **Adm £2.50, chd free. Suns 3 Apr; 5 June; 11 Sept (2-6).** Also open Church Farm Field (5 June only). Visitors also welcome by appt.
Medium-sized peaceful garden, interestingly landscaped in open country, based around former watermill with terraced pools. Spring bulbs in April, azaleas in May and early autumn colour in September. White double border; productive vegetable garden; a haven for wild birds.

27 EVELEGH'S
High Street, Long Wittenham, nr Abingdon OX14 4QH. Dr & Mrs C S Ogg. *3m NE of Didcot. Evelegh's is next to The Plough PH, Long Wittenham.* Home-made teas in village hall. **Adm £3.50, chd free. Sun 29 May (2-6).**
³/₄ -acre garden leading through areas of different characters to River Thames. Well stocked with many unusual shrubs, bulbs and perennials, incl collections of old bush roses, delphiniums, tree and herbaceous peonies and iris. Steep slope to river.

EVENLEY WOOD GARDEN
See Northamptonshire.

FARTHINGHOE GARDENS
See Northamptonshire.

28 GARSINGTON MANOR
28 Southend, Garsington OX44 9DH. Mrs R Ingrams, newbritishlandscapes@hotmail.com. *3m SE of Oxford. N of B480. 1¹/₂ m S of Wheatley.* Home-made teas. **Adm £4.50, chd free. Suns 17 Apr; 19 June; 18 Sept (2-5).** Visitors also welcome by appt Apr-Sept. Email Head Gardener for futher details.
C17 Manor house of architectural, literary and musical interest (not open). Early monastic fish ponds, water garden, dovecote c1700. Lake and flower parterre, Italianate terrace and loggia and Italian statues laid out by Philip and Lady Ottoline Morrell c1915-1923. Pottery stall at spring opening. Gravel paths, steps, steep slopes.

29 GREENFIELD FARM

Christmas Common, nr Watlington OX49 5HG. Andrew & Jane Ingram, 01491 612434, abingram@hotmail.co.uk. *4m from J5 of M40, 7m from Henley. J5 M40; A40 towards Oxford for ¹/₂ m; turn L signed Christmas Common. ³/₄ m past Fox & Hounds. Turn L at Tree Barn sign.* Adm £3, chd free (share to Farming & Wildlife Advisory Group). Evening Opening Thur 23 June (6-8). Visitors also welcome by appt during the summer except July. Groups only please, no individual visitors.

10-acre wild flower meadow, surrounded by woodland, established 14 yrs ago under the Countryside Stewardship Scheme. Traditional Chiltern chalkland meadow in beautiful peaceful setting with 100 species of perennial wild flowers, grasses and 5 species of orchids. ¹/₂ m walk from parking area to meadow. Opportunity to return via typical Chiltern beechwood. Guided walk at 6.15, or walk round at your own pace at any time during opening.

30 ♦ GREYS COURT

Rotherfield Greys, Henley-on-Thames RG9 4PG. National Trust, 01491 628529, www.nationaltrust.org.uk. *2m W of Henley-on-Thames. Signed from Nettlebed taking B481. Direct route from Henley-on-Thames town centre (unsigned for NT): follow signs to Badgemore Golf Club towards Rotherfield Greys, about 3m out of Henley.* Light Refreshments. Adm £4, chd £2. For NGS: Tue 14 June (2-4.30). For other opening times and information, please phone or see garden website.
The tranquil gardens cover 9 acres and surround a Tudor house with many alterations, as well as a Donkey Wheel and Tower. They incl lawns, a maze and small arboretum. The highlights are the series of enchanting walled gardens, a colourful patchwork of interest set amid medieval walls. Meet the gardeners and volunteers who look after the gardens.

31 THE GROVE

North Street, Middle Barton, Chipping Norton OX7 7BZ. Ivor & Barbara Hill. *7m E Chipping Norton. On B4030, 2m from junction A4260 & B4030, opp Carpenters Arms PH. Parking in street.* Home-made teas.

Adm £3, chd free. Sun 22 May (2-5).
Mature informal plantsman's garden. ¹/₃ acre planted for all year interest around C19 Cotswold Stone cottage (not open). Numerous borders with wide variety of unusual shrubs, trees and hardy plants; several species weigela, syringa viburnum and philadelphus. Pond area, well-stocked greenhouse. Plant list available. Homemade preserves and crafts for sale. Artweek site locally in same and neighbouring village.

Beautiful peaceful setting with 100 species of perennial wild flowers . . .

GROUP OPENING

32 HEADINGTON GARDENS

Old Headington OX3 9BT. *2m E from centre of Oxford. After T-lights, centre of Headington, towards Oxford, 2nd turn on R into Osler Rd. Gardens at end of rd in Old Headington.* Teas at Ruskin College. Combined adm £4, chd free (share to Ruskin College). Sun 5 June (2-5).

37 ST ANDREWS ROAD
Judith & David Marquand

THE COACH HOUSE
Mr & Mrs David Rowe

40 OSLER ROAD
Nicholas & Pam Coote
07804 932748
Visitors also welcome by appt.

35 ST ANDREWS ROAD
Mrs Alison Soskice

NEW WHITE LODGE
Denis & Catharine Macksmith and Roger & Frances Little

Headington was an Anglo-Saxon settlement at the centre of a large royal domain inhabited by Mercian kings and situated high above the Cherwell and Thames. The village pre-dates Oxford, which was a fortified borough created in 912 to defend a crossing of the Thames from the Danes. Today Headington village

---

is centred round a Norman church (est.1142) and is remarkable for its high stone walls, mature trees, narrow lanes and distinctive terraced cottages. The five open gardens provide a rare glimpse behind the walls, and demonstrate how one garden can 'borrow' interest from its neighbours' backdrop of trees, and the extra-ordinary differences in levels within the village. Three adjoin what is known locally as the 'Berlin wall' (after long-term resident Sir Isaiah Berlin). New this year, is White Lodge which offers a privileged vision of a Regency mansion set in 2 acres of mature grounds.

33 HEARNS HOUSE

Gallows Tree Common RG4 9DE. John & Joan Pumfrey, 0118 972 2848, joanpumfrey@lineone.net. *5m N of Reading, 5m W of Henley. From A4074 turn E at Cane End.* Home-made teas. Adm £3.50, chd free. Wed 25, Fri 27 May (10-5). Visitors also welcome by appt.
2-acre garden provides yr-round interest with pergolas, crinkle-crankle walls, sculpture, ponds. Inspirational variety of indigenous and exotic planting. Some self-sown plants are allowed to flourish where they enhance the original design. The nursery is full of wonderful plants propagated from the garden. National Collections of brunnera and omphalodes. Special plant fairs will be held on open days. Music suppers and teas, exhibitions and study days possible; please contact owners for details.

34 HILL COURT

Tackley OX5 3AQ. Mr & Mrs Andrew C Peake. *9m N of Oxford. Turn off A4260 at Sturdy's Castle.* Home-made teas. Adm £2.50, chd free. Sat & Sun 4, 5 June (2-6).
Walled garden of 2 acres with yew cones at top of terrace as a design feature by Russell Page in the 1960s. Terraces incl silver, pink and blue plantings, white garden, herbaceous borders, shrubberies, orangery. Many rare and unusual plants. Entry incl History Trail with unique geometric fish ponds (1620), C17 stables, pigeon house, C18 lakes, ice house (not suitable for wheelchairs). Plants and Local Crafts for sale. Music in the garden on Sunday only.

HILL GROUNDS
See Northamptonshire.

HILLESDEN HOUSE
See Buckinghamshire.

35 HOME CLOSE
Southend, Garsington OX44 9DH.
Ms M Waud & Dr P Giangrande,
01865 361394. *3m SE of Oxford.
Southend. N of B480. Opp
Garsington Manor.* **Adm £3.50, chd
free.** Visitors welcome by appt
1 April to 30 September.
2-acre garden with listed house (not
open) and granary. Trees, shrubs and
perennials planted for all-yr effect.
Terraces, walls and hedges divide the
garden into ten distinct areas to
reflect a Mediterranean interest.

36 HOME FARM
Balscote OX15 6JP. Mr Godfrey
Royle, 01295 738194. *5m W of
Banbury. 1/2 m off A422.* **Adm £3,
chd free.** Visitors welcome by
appt, **Apr - Oct.**
Formerly a plant lover's peaceful
garden, but now redesigned as a
gravel garden by Zizi 3D garden
design, with flowering shrubs and
mature trees and a unique Balscote-
sur-Mer theme. Two lawns give a
feeling of spaciousness, and a small
terrace has views of surrounding
countryside.
&

GROUP OPENING

37 NEW HORTON CUM STUDLEY GARDENS
Horton Cum Studley OX33 1BU.
*6m NE of Oxford. From Headington/
Green Rd r'about on Oxford ring rd,
take Bayswater rd signed Barton and
Crematorium. After 1m, turn R and
immed L at staggerd X-roads,
following signs to Horton cum
Studley. Cont straight to village.* Teas
in Village Church. **Combined adm
£4, chd free.** Sun 17 Apr (2-6).

> **NEW HILL TOP COTTAGE**
> Mrs Sarah Rogers

> **NEW UPPER GREEN**
> Susan & Peter Burge

> **NEW YEW TREE COTTAGE**
> Richard & Rachel Hawes

Explore 3 contrasting gardens in this
Otmoor village with almshouses
(1636) and church designed by

William Butterfield (1867) **Upper
Green** is a 1/2 -acre garden with views
to the Chilterns. Incl gravel garden,
mixed borders, small potager, bog
area and pond (great crested newts in
residence). Old apple trees. In spring
the garden is a carpet of colour with
marsh marigolds, primroses,
hellebores, euphorbias, fritillaries and
other bulbs. **Hilltop Cottage** a large
cottage garden with productive
vegetable plot and soft fruit. Beds incl
herbaceous, shrubbery and prairie-
look. Informal planting of shrubs,
bulbs, perennials and grasses. Small
trees e.g. acer griseum. many spring
bulbs, primulas, anemones, less usual
hellebores and dogwoods. **Yew Tree
Cottage** Splendid 1-acre garden with
wonderful views over Otmoor.
Created in 2001 it has evolved with
large herbaceous and small beds,
2 ponds, a well stocked formal
vegetable garden, secluded
woodland grove, many spring bulbs
and climbing plants. Wheelchair
access at Upper Green & Yew Tree
Cottage.
&

Look out for the
gardens with the ☎
– enjoy a private
visit . . .

GROUP OPENING

38 IFFLEY GARDENS
Iffley Village OX4 4ET. *2m S of
Oxford. Within Oxford's ring rd, off
A4158 from Magdalen Bridge to
Littlemore roundabout.* Map provided
at each garden. Home-made teas.
Combined adm £4, chd free.
Sun 12 June (2-6).

> **15 ABBERBURY ROAD**
> Allen & Boglarka Hill

> **65 CHURCH WAY**
> Jacqueline Woodfill

> **86 CHURCH WAY**
> Helen Beinart & Alex Coren

> **122 CHURCH WAY**
> Sir John & Lady Elliott

6 FITZHERBERT CLOSE
Tom & Eunice Martin

THE MALT HOUSE
Mrs Helen Potts

THE THATCHED COTTAGE
Martin & Helen Foreman

Visit 7 gardens ranging in variety and
style from an English cottage garden
with Californian plants to a small
professionally designed Japanese
style garden, with maples and
miniature pines. Varied planting
throughout the gardens incl
herbaceous borders and shade loving
plants, roses, fine specimen trees and
plants in terracing. Features incl water
features, formal gardens, small lake
and riverbank. Secluded old village
with renowned Norman church,
featured on cover of Pevsner's Oxon
guide.
❀ ☕

KEMPSFORD MANOR
See Gloucestershire North &
Central.

GROUP OPENING

39 KENCOT GARDENS
Kencot, nr Lechlade GL7 3QT. *5m
NE of Lechlade. E of A361 between
Burford & Lechlade.* Village maps
available. Home-made teas in Village
Hall. **Combined adm £4, chd free.**
Mon 25 Apr (2-6).

> **THE ALLOTMENTS**
> Amelia Carter Trust

> **DE ROUGEMONT**
> David & Susan Portergill

> **GABLE END**
> Norman & Sallie Baylis

> **HILLVIEW HOUSE**
> John & Andrea Moss

> **IVY NOOK**
> Gill & Wally Cox

> **KENCOT HOUSE**
> Tim & Kate Gardner

> **MANOR FARM**
> Jane & Jonathan Fyson

> **PINNOCKS**
> Joy & John Coxeter

> **WELL HOUSE**
> Gill & Ian Morrison

8 gardens and the allotments are
open and the fine Norman Church will
be beautifully decorated with Easter

flowers. Springtime in Kencot is a magical time. Gardens abound with naturalised, varied daffodils and narcissi, hellebores, wood anemones, primrose, primulas and fritillaries. Many unusual trees incl a 150yr old apple tree at Ivy Nook, an ancient ginko at Kencot House, medlar, mulberry, a pleached lime walk and 2 C19 clipped yew balls at Manor Farm, a rare Japanese plum tree and red oak at Gable End and a miniature woodland glade at Well House. Vegetables are not forgotten with walled kitchen gardens and the allotments where the emphasis is on organic gardening. To complete this village idyll - geese, chickens and 2 alpacas. Plant sale at Manor Farm. Wheelchair access to all gardens except Gable End & The Allotments.

---

40 10 KENNETT ROAD
Headington OX3 7BJ. Linda & David Clover, 01865 765881, lindaclover@yahoo.co.uk. *2m E of Oxford. South side of London Rd in Headington.* Adm £3, chd free. Visitors welcome by appt. Please e-mail, telephone or write to arrange visit.
Small (20' x 90') densely-planted suburban oasis. Created for yr-round interest it includes a sheltered patio, mixed shrub and herbaceous planting, succulents and cactus, secluded fernery, small unfenced wildlife pond and an unparalled view of 'Untitled 1986' Headington's world-famous roof top sculpture.

41 ◆ KINGSTON BAGPUIZE HOUSE
Kingston Bagpuize, nr Abingdon OX13 5AX. Mrs Francis Grant, 01865 820259, www.kingstonbagpuizehouse.com. *5m W of Abingdon. In Kingston Bagpuize just off A415, ¼ m S of A415/A420 and accessed from Rectory Lane.* Light Refreshments. Adm £5, chd free. For NGS: Sun 27 Mar (12-5); Mon 26 Sept (1-6). For other opening times and information, please phone or see garden website.
Notable collection of unusual trees, incl magnolias, shrubs, perennials snowdrops and other bulbs, providing yr-round interest and colour. Large mixed borders, interesting summer flowering trees and shrubs. New for 2011: The Mattock Rose Garden with

a large collection of Silk Road Hybrids is being established. Roses and other plants for sale in the Mattock Rose Garden. Gravel and grass paths.

42 LADY MARGARET HALL
Norham Gardens, Oxford OX2 6QA. Principal & Fellows of Lady Margaret Hall. *1m N of Carfax. From Banbury Rd, R at T-lights into Norham Gdns.* Home-made teas. Adm £3, chd free. Sun 15 May (2-5.30).
Beautiful college garden, full of interesting plants, wonderful buildings and riverside walk.

43 LIME CLOSE
35 Henleys Lane, Drayton, Abingdon OX14 4HU. M C de Laubarede, mail@mclgardendesign.com. *2m S of Abingdon. Henleys Lane is off main rd through Drayton.* Home-made teas. Adm £4, chd free. Suns 17 Apr; 5 June (2-5). Visitors also welcome by appt up to end June & Autumn, groups 10+.
3-acre mature plantsman's garden with rare trees, shrubs, perennials and bulbs. Mixed borders, raised beds, pergola, unusual topiary and shade borders. Herb garden designed by Rosemary Verey. Listed C16 house (not open). New cottage garden designed by MCL Garden Design, focusing on colour combinations and an iris garden with over 100 varieties of tall bearded irises. Many winter bulbs, hellebores and shrubs.

LORDS WOOD
See Buckinghamshire.

LYDIARD PARK WALLED GARDEN
See Wiltshire.

44 ◆ MAGDALEN COLLEGE
Oxford OX1 4AU. Magdalen College, 01865 276000, www.magd.ox.ac.uk. *Entrance in High St.* Adm £4, chd £3. For NGS: Sun 17 Apr (1-6). For opening times and information please visit website or telephone.
60 acres incl deer park, college lawns, numerous trees 150-200yrs old, notable herbaceous and shrub plantings; Magdalen meadow, where purple and white snake's-head fritillaries can be found, is surrounded by Addison's Walk, a tree-lined circuit by the R Cherwell developed since

the late C18. Ancient herd of 60 deer. Sculpture commissioned to celebrate 550th anniversary. It is by Turner prize-winning artist Mark Wallinger and is called Y. Made of steel, 10m high, in the form of a tree, it is situated in Bat Willow Meadow. Wheelchair users please ring bell at Porters' Lodge. Some uneven ground. Not all areas are accessible.

Spacious lawn leading to riverside copse of towering black poplars from which there are fine views of Dorchester Abbey . . .

45 MANOR HOUSE
Manor Farm Road, Dorchester-on-Thames OX10 7HZ. Mr & Mrs S H Broadbent, 01865 340101. *8m SSE of Oxford. Off A4074, signs from village centre. Parking at Bridge Meadow 400m. Disabled parking at house.* Home-made teas at Abbey Tea Room (open 3-5). Adm £3.50, chd free. Sun 26 June (2-5.30). Visitors also welcome by appt.
2-acre garden in beautiful setting around Georgian house (not open) and medieval abbey. Spacious lawn leading to riverside copse of towering black poplars from which there are fine views of Dorchester Abbey. Terrace with rose and vine covered pergola around lily pond. Colourful herbaceous borders, small orchard and vegetable garden. Gravel paths.

THE MANOR HOUSE, HAMBLEDEN
See Buckinghamshire.

MARYFIELD
See Buckinghamshire.

46 ◆ MERTON COLLEGE OXFORD FELLOWS' GARDEN
Merton Street, Oxford OX1 4JD. *Merton Street runs parallel to High Street.* Adm £3.50, chd free. For NGS: Sun 24 July (2-5).

Ancient mulberry, said to have associations with James I. Specimen trees, long mixed border, recently-established herbaceous bed. View of Christ Church meadow. Steps to garden. Limited wheelchair access.

Gothic House

GROUP OPENING

47 MIDDLETON CHENEY GARDENS

Middleton Cheney OX17 2NP. *3m E of Banbury. From M40 J11 follow A422, signed Middleton Cheney. Map available at all gardens.* Home-made teas at Peartree House. **Combined adm £5, chd free.** Sun 26 June (1-6) Evening Opening £4, wine, Wed 29 June (6-9).

CHURCH COTTAGE
David & Sue Thompson

8 CHURCH LANE
Mr & Mrs Style

38 MIDWAY
Margaret & David Finch

PEARTREE HOUSE
Roger & Barbara Charlesworth

14 QUEEN STREET
Brian & Kathy Goodey

NEW 46 STANWELL LEA
Brian & Joan Darbon

NEW 1 THE MOORS DRIVE
Charles & Anne Woolland

Large village with 7 gardens (2 new for 2011) diverse in styles ranging from traditional English cottage gardens, cottage gardens with a Mediterranean influence to a family garden with rooms. Planting includes yellow and white themed borders, vegetable and fruit areas, orchard areas, mixed borders. Water features incl ponds, streams and waterfalls await the visitor. Also open, late C13 church with Pre-Raphaelite stained glass and William Morris ceiling (Sun 26 June only). Wheelchair access difficult at some gardens.

48 MONKS HEAD

Weston Road, Bletchingdon OX5 3DH. Sue Bedwell, 01869 350155. *Approx 4m N of Kidlington. From A34 take B4027 to Bletchingdon, turn R at Xrds into Weston Rd.* Home-made teas. **Adm £3, chd free.** Sun 3 Apr (2-5). Visitors also welcome by appt

throughout the year. Plantaholics' garden for all-yr interest. Bulb frame and alpine area, greenhouse.

GROUP OPENING

49 NORTH OXFORD GARDENS

Oxford OX2 6UZ. *³/₄ m N of Oxford City Centre. Within Oxford ring rd, ¹/₄ m S of Summertown on E side of Banbury Rd A4165.* Home-made teas at Bishop's House. **Adm £3.50, chd free** (share to HIV/AIDs project Kimberly/Kuruman, South Africa). Sat 9 July (2-5).

13 BELBROUGHTON ROAD
Oxford. Dr Jennie Turner

BISHOPS HOUSE
27 Linton Road. Mrs Wendy Pritchard

Two interesting but very different gardens dating from the 1920s within the North Oxford conservation area.

13 Belbroughton Road is a mature garden with a sunken area which is part of the original 1920s garden. It is well stocked with a range of unusual and interesting plants and incl an ornamental vegetable garden. **Bishop's House**, is a large mature garden currently being restored. It is divided into different rooms and features well stocked herbaceous borders, an Italian garden, a bamboo forest with walkway, a woodland area and an orchard with vegetable garden.

THE OLD RECTORY FARNBOROUGH
See Berkshire.

50 THE OLD RECTORY, COLESHILL

Highworth SN6 7PR. Sir George & Lady Martin. *3m SW of Faringdon. Coleshill (NT village) is on B4019.* Home-made teas. **Adm £3, chd free.** Suns 10 Apr; 4 Sept (2-5).

Be tempted by a plant from a plant stall �

Medium-sized garden; lawns and informal shrub beds; wide variety shrubs, incl old-fashioned roses, 60yr-old standard wisteria. Distant views of Berkshire and Wiltshire Downs. House (not open) dates from late C14.

51 THE OLD VICARAGE
Aston Rowant, Watlington OX49 5ST. Julian & Rona Knight, 01844 351315, jknight652@aol.com. *Between Chinnor and Watlington. From M40 J6, take B4009 towards Chinnor and Princes Risborough. After 1m L signed 'Aston Rowant village only'.* Home-made teas. **Adm £3, chd free.** Sun 12 June (2-5.30). **Visitors also welcome by appt, groups 10+.**
Romantic, 1³/₄ -acre vicarage garden lovingly rejuvenated and enjoyed by the present family. Centered around a croquet lawn surrounded by beds brimming with shrubs and herbaceous plants, hot bed and roses. Lushly planted pond leading through a pergola overflowing with roses and clematis to a tranquil green garden. Small vegetable and cutting garden.

52 THE OLD VICARAGE, BLEDINGTON
Main Road, Bledington, Chipping Norton OX7 6UX. Sue & Tony Windsor, 01608 658525, tony.windsor@tiscali.co.uk. *6m SW of Chipping Norton. 4m SE of Stow-on-the-Wold. On the main st, B4450, through Bledington. NOT next to church.* **Adm £3, chd free.** Visitors welcome by appt Apr to July, single visitors or coaches.
1¹/₂ -acre garden around a late Georgian (1843) vicarage (not open). Borders and beds filled with hardy perennials, shrubs and trees. Informal rose garden with 350 David Austin roses. Small pond and vegetable patch. Paddock with trees, shrubs and herbaceous border. Planted for yr-round interest. Gravel driveway and slope which can be difficult for wheelchair users.

53 40 OSLER ROAD
Oxford OX3 9BJ. Nicholas & Pam Coote, 07804 932748, nicholas@coote100.freeserve.co.uk. *2m E from centre of Oxford. Off London Rd, ³/₄ m inside ring rd. After T-lights in centre of Headington*

towards Oxford, 2nd turn on R, Osler Rd. Teas at Ruskin College, Dunstan Rd. **Adm £4, chd free. Also open with Headington Gardens** Sun 5 June (2-5). **Visitors welcome by appt at other times.**
Richly planted ²/₃ acre garden, now into its fourth decade, surrounding a unique 1920's house with whitewashed walls and shutters. Clear structure with box and yew hedges (currently being rejuvenated), majestic trees and shrubs, abundant flowers, trompe l'oeil paths, mosaic water-feature, cypresses and a multitude of pots borrowing the 'panache' of Italy.

Lushly planted pond leading through a pergola overflowing with roses . . .

54 RADCOT HOUSE
Radcot OX18 2SX. Robin & Jeanne Stainer, 01367 810231, rstainer@radcothouse.co.uk, www.radcothouse.com. *1¹/₄ m S of Clanfield. On A4095 bet Witney & Faringdon, 300yds N of Radcot bridge.* Cream teas. **Adm £5, chd free.** Suns 19 June; 21 Aug; 18 Sept (2-6). **Visitors also welcome by appt.**
Approx 2¹/₂ acres of dramatic yet harmonious planting in light and shade, formal pond, fruit and vegetable cages. Convenient seating at key points enables relaxed observation and reflection. Extensive use of grasses and unusual perennials and interesting sculptural surprises. Featured on BBC Radio Oxford & Oxford Times magazine.

55 9 RAWLINSON ROAD
Oxford OX2 6UE. Rani Lall, 01865 559614, ranilall@hotmail.com. *³/₄ m N of Oxford Centre. Rawlinson Rd runs between Banbury & Woodstock Rds midway between Oxford City Centre & Summertown shops.* **Adm £3, chd free.** Visitors welcome by appt anytime.

Small town garden with structured disarray of roses. Terrace of stone inlaid with brick and enclosed by Chinese fretwork balustrade, chunky brick and oak pergola covered with roses, wisteria and clematis; potted topiary. Until autumn, garden delightfully replete with aconites, lobelias, phloxes, daisies and meandering clematis.

GROUP OPENING

56 SALFORD GARDENS
Salford OX7 5YN. *2m W of Chipping Norton. Off A44 Oxford-Worcester Rd.* Home-made teas in Salford village hall. **Combined adm £4, chd free.** Sun 29 May (2-6).

MANOR FARM
Mrs P G Caldin
Visitors also welcome by appt.
01608 642597
rachel_caldin@lawtext.com

OLD RECTORY
Mr & Mrs N M Chambers
Visitors also welcome by appt.
01608 643969
sallchambers@gmail.com

WILLOW TREE COTTAGE
Mr & Mrs J Shapley
Visitors also welcome by appt.
01608 642478
john.shapley@virgin.net

Visit 3 gardens in this small attractive Cotswold village with church. Gardens range from small family ones to village gardens. There are also walled gardens, of differing sizes. Planting incl cottage-style herbaceous borders, old roses, vegetables, many clematis and a large alpine garden. This village has a lot going for it - there is interest for all.

57 THE SHEILING
OX1 5JE. Sue & Tony Shepherd. *3m S of Oxford. From S ring rd A4142 at J with A34 follow signs to Wootton & Boars Hill. 1m turn R into Berkley Rd signed Old Boars Hill & Scout Camp. At bend turn into Bedwells Heath. Garden ¹/₄ m on L.* Home-made teas. **Adm £3, chd free.** Sun 8 May (2-5.30).
Delightful N-facing hillside garden set amongst mature Scots pines, oaks and silver birch. Spring garden of ²/₃ acre planted with unusual rhododendrons, azaleas, magnolias,

camellias, pieris, hellebores and spring bulbs. Stream cascading to naturalised pond surrounded by acers. Parking Berkley Rd, Jarn Way & Ridgeway. No wheelchair access to lower part of garden.

GROUP OPENING

58 SIBFORD GOWER GARDENS

Sibford Gower OX15 5RX. *7m W of Banbury. Nr the Warwickshire border, S of B4035, in centre of village nr Wykham Arms PH.* Home-made teas. **Combined adm £4, chd free.** Sun 19 June (2-6).

BUTTSLADE HOUSE
Mrs Diana Thompson
01295 788818
janthompson50@hotmail.com

CARTER'S YARD
Sue & Malcolm Bannister

GOWERS CLOSE
Judith Hitching & John Marshall
01295 780348
j.hitching@virgin.net

NEW GREEN ACRES
Paul & Margaret Hobson

THE MANOR HOUSE
Michael Donovan & Alison Jenkins

Charming small village off the beaten track, with thatched stone cottages. Four gardens open, all different, all very interesting. The cottage gardens complement the ancient houses they surround. Masses of roses, wisteria and clematis clamber over walls and pergolas. Box parterres, clipped yew hedges, herb gardens, bosky borders in pinks and purples plus productive kitchen gardens. Some new and innovative planting with unusual plants. Old established garden surrounds the intriguing thatched Manor House and Indian runner ducks walk up from the village pond to greet the visitor. New this year is a woodland walk.

59 SOMERVILLE COLLEGE

Woodstock Road, Oxford OX2 6HD. Somerville College. *½ m E of Carfax Tower. Enter from the Woodstock Rd, S of the Radcliffe Infirmary.* **Adm £2.50, chd free (share to Friends of Oxford Botanic Garden).** Sun 10 July (2-6). Approx 2 acres, robust college garden planted for yr-round interest. Formal bedding, colour-themed and vibrant old-fashioned mixed herbaceous borders.

60 SPARSHOLT MANOR

nr Wantage OX12 9PT. Sir Adrian & Lady Judith Swire. *3½ m W of Wantage. Off B4507 Ashbury Rd.* Home-made teas in adjacent village hall. **Adm £3, chd free.** Mon 30 May (2-6).
Lakes and wildfowl; ancient boxwood, wilderness and summer borders. Wheelchair access to most of garden.

61 SPRINGHILL HOUSE

Main Street, Hethe OX27 8ES. Mrs Penny Jacoby, 01869 277971, robin.jacoby@psych.ox.ac.uk. *4m N of Bicester. L off A4421 N from Bicester. Follow signs to Hethe.* **Adm £3, chd free.** Visitors welcome by appt May to Sept.
A secret 1¾ -acre garden cascading down a slope to a delightfully planted extensive pond. The walled garden area is heavily planted with many varieties of plants. There are over 200 roses, a Mediterranean garden incl many tender and exotic plants (no wheelchair access), a vegetable garden and small arboretum. True plantswoman's garden. Hot border good in Jul & Aug. Mediterranean garden difficult for wheelchair users.

Lime Close

Follow us on Facebook and Twitter

62 STANSFIELD
49 High Street, Stanford-in-the-Vale SN7 8NQ. Mr & Mrs David Keeble, 01367 710340. *3¹/₂ m SE of Faringdon. Park in street.* Home-made teas. **Adm £3, chd free.** Visitors welcome by appt available all year. Max group size 50 persons. Please call to arrange visits.

1¹/₄ -acre plantsman's garden on alkaline soil. Wide variety of unusual trees, shrubs and hardy plants. New labelling system almost completed. Scree, damp garden, copse underplanted with woodlanders. Flower arrangers' and drought resistant plants. Guided tours if wished.

STEANE PARK
See Northamptonshire.

63 STEEPLE ASTON GARDENS
Steeple Aston OX25 4SP. *14m N of Oxford, 9m S of Banbury. ¹/₂ m E of A4260.* Home-made teas. **Combined adm £5, chd free.** Sun 5 June (1-6).

ACACIA COTTAGE
Jane & David Stewart

KRALINGEN
Mr & Mrs Roderick Nicholson

THE LONGBYRE
Mr Vaughan Billings

THE POUND HOUSE
Mr & Mrs R Clarke

PRIMROSE COTTAGE
Richard & Daphne Preston

TOUCHWOOD
Gary Norris
Visitors also welcome by appt.
01869 347112

WILLOW COTTAGE
Mrs Joy Vivian

Acacia Cottage Approx ¹/₂ -acre garden within high stone walls. Herbaceous border, decked and paved area around Edwardian summerhouse and old stone barns. Box edged parterre with white planting in a courtyard setting. **Kralingen** 1 hectare informal garden created over many yrs by present owners. Great variety of interesting trees and shrubs and mixed borders lead down to tranquil woodland/water/bog garden, with candelabra primulas, bluebells, golden saxifrage, fernery etc. Newly created rose garden on old tennis court. **The Longbyre** Hornton stone house (not open) in ¹/₄ acre. Garden constructed in old orchard. Water feature, mixed perennials, shrubs and tubs on different levels **The Pound House** Approx ³/₄ -acre garden on an old village pound. Developed over 30yrs from a children's play area and a pony paddock to a new tranquil haven of peace and quiet. Substantial trees, wildlife pond and newly developed glasshouse, raised parterre and vegetable beds. **Primrose Cottage** Former walled kitchen garden of approx 1 acre on southerly elevations. Shrubs, herbaceous borders, ponds and glass. Many features designed and constructed by the owners. Garden offering interest throughout the yr. **Touchwood** Cottage garden with ponds on 2 levels. Truly astonishing array of plants and colour in this small space, with view to lovely countryside beyond. A must for koi lover's **Willow Cottage** Closely planted ¹/₂ -acre garden evolved over 25yrs with many mature specimen trees giving a canopy of interwoven foliage, colour and texture. Discretely interlinked garden rooms, fish pond and many pots. Wheelchair access is available at The Pound House, The Longbyre, Kralingen & Acacia Cottage only.

64 TADMARTON MANOR
Upper Tadmarton OX15 5TD. Mr & Mrs R K Asser, 01295 780212. *5m SW of Banbury. On B4035.* **Adm £3, chd free.** Visitors welcome by appt June and August.

Old-established 2¹/₂ -acre garden; beautiful views of unspoilt countryside; great variety of perennial plants and shrubs; tunnel arbour; C15 barn and C18 dovecote. Agapanthus bed (Aug); bank of autumn cyclamen; stilted hornbeam hedge; two large tree sculptures.

There is a chance to enjoy a quirky and unique garden with an amazing range of plants . . .

65 THAME GARDENS
Thame OX9 3LA. *¹/₂ m E of Thame centre. From M40 J7/8 follow signs to Thame.* Home-made teas 18 Willow Road. **Combined adm £4, chd free** (share to Thame Scouts & Guides). Sun 5 June (2-6).

143 CHINNOR ROAD
Mrs D Metcalf.
On B4445 Chinnor Rd, close to dog-leg over bridge on outskirts of Thame

7 NEWBARN CLOSE
Mary & Brian Dover.
Thame town centre take B4445 Chinnor Rd, turn R by post box into Newbarn Close. Limited parking. Suggest using Station Approach

12 PARK TERRACE
Maggie & Colin Sear.
From centre of Thame follow signs for Chinnor (B4445). At junction with Postcombe Rd (B4012) Park Terrace is on R, opp B.P garage. Parking on Station Approach

NEW THE STABLES
Pam & Roger Smith.
Bell Lane, next to Waitrose entrance

18 WILLOW ROAD
Mrs K M Pease.
In Thame, park in public car park opp entrance to Waitrose. Up Lashlake Rd, opp Waitrose. Willow Rd 2nd R, down end of rd on R

Five gardens set in the market town of Thame, incl a heavily planted, natural garden with mature shrubs, perennials and a pond and with a restful seating area designed around a large walnut tree; a keen plantswoman's garden where the easily maintained main garden creates a restful oasis alongside the fine grass and gravel front garden; there is a chance to enjoy a quirky and unique garden with an amazing range of plants in pots and baskets where children will love to hunt the animals; in marked contrast is a very modern bungalow with a small cottage-style garden and borders brimming with perennials, shrubs and climbers and, new this year, a very attractive well-planted town garden showing what can be done in 3 yrs.

TILE HOUSE FARM
See Northamptonshire.

66 TRINITY COLLEGE
Oxford OX1 3BH. Dr C R Prior,
Garden Master,
www.trinity.ox.ac.uk. *Central Oxford.
Entrance in Broad St*. Home-made
teas. **Adm £2.50, chd free. Suns
27 Mar; 24 July (2-5).**
Historic main College Gardens with
specimen trees incl aged forked
catalpa, spring bulbs, fine long
herbaceous border and handsome
garden quad originally designed by
Wren. President's Garden surrounded
by high old stone walls, mixed
borders of herbaceous, shrubs and
statuary. Fellows' Garden: small
walled terrace, herbaceous borders;
water feature formed by Jacobean
stone heraldic beasts. Award-winning
lavender garden and walk-through
rose arbour.

TURWESTON GARDENS
See Northamptonshire.

TURWESTON HOUSE
See Northamptonshire.

TURWESTON MILL
See Northamptonshire.

VERSIONS FARM
See Northamptonshire.

TYTHROP PARK
See Buckinghamshire.

67 UPPER CHALFORD FARM
between Sydenham & Postcombe
OX39 4NH. Mr & Mrs Paul
Rooksby, 01844 351320. *4¹/₂ m SE
of Thame. M40 J6, then A40. At
Postcombe turn R signed Chalford
(turn L if on A40 from Oxford
direction). After 1 mile on LH-side at
1st telegraph pole. (House is ¹/₂ -way
Sydenham to Postcombe).* **Adm
upon application** (share to M.S
Research). **Visitors welcome by
appt** April - early Aug. June & July
are the best months to visit. Any
size group welcome but sorry no
coaches.
Jacobean farmhouse garden, old
roses, shrubs and perennials. Unusual
trees and an ancient black pine.
Hidden gardens with different
plantings and peaceful places to sit.
Spring-fed pond and stream with
damp planted banks leading to
reclaimed woodland with treehouse.
Short access over gravel drive.

68 WADHAM COLLEGE
Parks Road, Oxford OX1 3PN. The
Warden & Fellows. *Central Oxford.
Parks Road*. **Adm £2, chd free
(share to Michael Sobell House).
Suns 20 Mar; 10 July (2-5).**
5 acres, best known for trees, spring
bulbs and mixed borders. In Fellows'
main garden, fine ginkgo and
Magnolia acuminata; bamboo
plantation; in Back Quadrangle very
large *Tilia tomentosa* 'Petiolaris'; in
Mallam Court white scented garden
est 1994; in Warden's garden an
ancient tulip tree; in Fellows' private
garden, Civil War embankment with
period fruit tree cultivars, recently
established shrubbery with unusual
trees and ground cover amongst
older plantings.
&

*Hidden gardens
with different
plantings and
peaceful places
to sit . . .*

**WARMINGTON VILLAGE
GARDENS**
See Warwickshire.

69 ◆ WATERPERRY GARDENS
Waterperry, Wheatley OX33 1JZ.
Mrs Susie Hunt, 01844 339226,
www.waterperrygardens.co.uk. *9m
E of Oxford. M40 J8 from London
(turn off Oxford-Wheatley, first L to
Wheatley, follow brown rose symbol).
J8a from Birmingham (turn R Oxford-
Wheatley over A40, first R Wheatley,
follow brown rose symbol. We are
2¹/₂ m N of Wheatley. Light
Refreshments*. **Adm £6.10, chd free.
For NGS: Suns 17 Apr (10-5);
18 Sept (10-5.30). For opening
times and information please visit
website or telephone.**
Waterperry Gardens are an
inspiration. 8 acres of landscaped
gardens incl rose and formal knot
garden, water lily canal, riverside walk
and one of the country's finest purely
herbaceous borders. There's also a
plant centre, garden shop, teashop,

art gallery, museum and Saxon
church. National Collection of
Kabschia Saxifrages. Fritillaries
looking fantastic for April opening.
Michaelmas Daisy Weekend (Sept)
Visit the border and country food
fair.

70 WAYSIDE
82 Banbury Road, Kidlington
OX5 2BX. Margaret & Alistair
Urquhart, 01865 460180,
alistairurquhart@ntlworld.com. *5m
N of Oxford. On the RH-side of
A4260 travelling N through Kidlington*.
**Adm £3, chd free. Visitors
welcome by appt.**
¹/₄ -acre garden with wide variety of
plants and mature trees; mixed
borders with hardy geraniums,
clematis and bulbs. Conservatory,
greenhouse and fern house with
tender plants. Woodland garden with
unusual species of tree ferns and
extensive collection of hardy ferns;
drought resistant planting in gravel
garden.
❀ ☎

71 WESTWELL MANOR
nr Burford OX18 4JT. Mr Thomas
Gibson. *2m SW of Burford. From
A40 Burford-Cheltenham, turn L ¹/₂ m
after Burford roundabout on narrow
rd signed Westwell. Unspoilt hamlet
with delightful church.* **Adm £5, chd
free (share to St Marys Church,
Westwell). Sun 19 June (2.30-6).**
6 acres surrounding old Cotswold
manor house (not open), knot garden,
potager, shrub roses, herbaceous
borders, topiary, earth works,
moonlight garden, rills and water
garden, new auricula ladder.
❀

GROUP OPENING

72 WHEATLEY GARDENS
Wheatley OX33 1XX. *5m E of
Oxford. Leave A40 at Wheatley, turn
into High St. Gardens at W end of
High St. Access from the High St, the
original Oxford to London Rd, before
it climbs onto the Shotover plain*.
Cream teas. **Combined adm £4.50,
chd free. Sun 26 June (2-6).**

BREACH HOUSE GARDEN
Liz Parry
Visitors also welcome by appt.
01865 876278
liz.parry@dial.pipex.com

Visit the website for latest information

THE MANOR HOUSE
High Street, Wheatley. Mrs Edward Hess
Visitors also welcome by appt. 01865 875022
ehess@harcourtchambers.law.co.uk

THE STUDIO
S & A Buckingham.
Access via The Manor house
Visitors also welcome by appt. 01365 876526
stanleybuckingham@sky.com

Three adjoining gardens in the historic coaching village of Wheatley. Breach House Garden has an established main area with extensive shrubs and perennials, also a more contemporary reflective space with a wild pond. The Manor House is a 1½-acre garden surrounding an Elizabethan manor house (not open). Formal box walk, herb garden, cottage garden with rose arches and a shrubbery with old roses. A romantic oasis in this busy village. The Studio is a cottage-style walled garden developed from what was once a farm yard. Herbaceous borders, climbing roses and clematis, shrubs, vegetable plot and fruit trees. All in all a lovely little collection of gardens set in the busy village of Wheatley. Various musical events.

WHICHFORD & ASCOTT GARDENS
See Warwickshire.

WHITEHILL FARM
Widford nr Burford OX18 4DT. Mr & Mrs Paul Youngson, 01993 823218, a.youngson@virgin.net. *1m E of Burford. From A40 take turn signed Widford. Follow signs to Whitehill Farm Nursery.* Home-made teas. Adm £3, chd free. Sun 26 June (2-6). Visitors also welcome by appt June to August. Groups welcome.
2 acres of hillside gardens and woodland with spectacular views overlooking Burford and Windrush valley. Informal plantsman's garden being continuously developed in various areas. Herbaceous and shrub borders, ponds and bog area, old-fashioned roses, ground cover, ornamental grasses, bamboos and hardy geraniums.

WHITEWALLS
See Buckinghamshire.

74 WILDWOOD
Farnborough OX17 1EL. Mr & Mrs M Hart. *5m N of Banbury, 8m S of Southam. On A423 at Oxon/Warwicks border. Next to Farnborough Garden Centre.* Home-made teas. Adm £2.50, chd free. Sun 17 Apr; Weds 18 May; 15 June; 20 July (2-5).
Delightful ½-acre garden in the country set amongst mature trees and shrubs providing a haven for wildlife. Garden is stocked with many unusual plants and shrubs and also contains interesting rustic garden features, many of which are made by the owner. Country craft demonstrations and items for sale.

WOODCHIPPINGS
See Northamptonshire.

WOOLLEY PARK
See Berkshire.

75 WOOLSTONE MILL HOUSE
Woolstone, nr Faringdon SN7 7QL. Mr & Mrs Anthony Spink, 01367 820219, spinkos@btinternet.com. *7m W of Wantage. 7m S of Faringdon. Woolstone is a small village off B4507 below Uffington White Horse Hill.* Home-made teas. Adm £4, chd free. Weds, 20 Apr to 28 Sept; (2-5). Visitors also welcome by appt.
2-acre garden in pretty hidden village. Stream runs through garden. Large mixed herbaceous and shrub circular border bounded by yew hedges. Small gravel, cutting, kitchen and bog gardens. Topiary. Medlars and old-fashioned roses. Tree house with spectacular views to Uffington White Horse and White Horse Hill. C18 mill house and barn, not open. Partial wheelchair access.

Two acres of hillside gardens and woodland with spectacular views . . .

Support the NGS – visit a garden near you

Broughton Grange

SHROPSHIRE

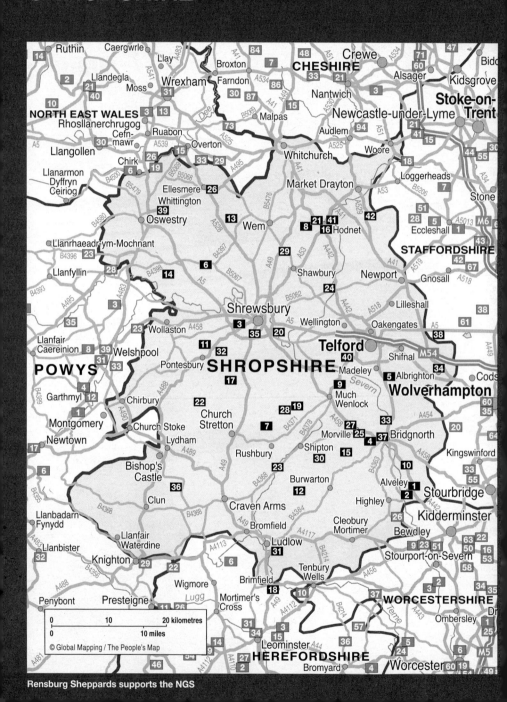

Opening Dates

April
Friday 8
37 8 Westgate Villas (Evening)
Sunday 10
37 8 Westgate Villas
Saturday 16
29 Preston Hall
Sunday 17
24 Moortown
Monday 25
28 Preen Manor

May
Sunday 1
17 Holly Grove
Monday 2
23 Millichope Park
Friday 6
41 Wollerton Old Hall
Saturday 14
10 Dudmaston Hall Gardens
Sunday 15
1 Ancoireán
26 Oteley
Sunday 22
8 The Citadel
20 Longner Hall
22 Marehay Farm
34 Swallow Hayes
Thursday 26
28 Preen Manor
Friday 27
41 Wollerton Old Hall
Sunday 29
36 Walcot Hall
Monday 30
36 Walcot Hall

June
Friday 3
42 Woodeaves Garden Plants
Sunday 5
33 Stanley Hall
Wednesday 8
11 Edge Villa
Thursday 9
30 Ruthall Manor
Saturday 11
30 Ruthall Manor
Sunday 12
9 The Cottage
25 Morville Hall Gardens
30 Ruthall Manor
Thursday 16
9 The Cottage

Saturday 18
5 Brockton Court
39 Whittington Village Gardens
Sunday 19
14 Hall Farm Nursery
16 Hodnet Hall Gardens
39 Whittington Village Gardens
Thursday 23
28 Preen Manor
Friday 24
40 Windy Ridge
Sunday 26
2 Applecross House
15 Heath House
18 Holmcroft
27 Poplar Cottage Farm
31 Secret Garden

July
Wednesday 6
38 Weston Park
Sunday 10
21 Marchamley House Garden
40 Windy Ridge
Sunday 17
1 Ancoireán
3 Bowbrook Allotment Community
Thursday 21
28 Preen Manor
Sunday 24
19 Jessamine Cottage
35 Valducci Flower & Vegetable Gardens
Sunday 31
32 Sibberscote Manor

August
Friday 5
42 Woodeaves Garden Plants
Sunday 7
40 Windy Ridge
Sunday 14
7 Cardington Gardens
15 Heath House
Sunday 21
11 Edge Villa
Sunday 28
19 Jessamine Cottage

Wide variety of styles and plants from formal terraces to woodland paths . . .

September
Sunday 4
40 Windy Ridge
Sunday 25
2 Applecross House

October
Sunday 2
28 Preen Manor

Gardens open to the public
10 Dudmaston Hall Gardens
19 Jessamine Cottage
38 Weston Park
41 Wollerton Old Hall

By appointment only
4 Bridgwalton House
6 Brownhill House
12 Field House
13 Gate Cottage

Also open by Appointment ☎
1 Ancoireán
2 Applecross House
9 The Cottage
11 Edge Villa
17 Holly Grove
18 Holmcroft
22 Marehay Farm
23 Millichope Park
26 Oteley
28 Preen Manor
29 Preston Hall
30 Ruthall Manor
34 Swallow Hayes
35 Valducci Flower & Vegetable Gardens
40 Windy Ridge
42 Woodeaves Garden Plants

The Gardens

ABERNANT
See Powys.

1 ANCOIREÁN
24 Romsley View, Alveley
WV15 6PJ. Judy & Peter Creed,
01746 780504,
peter@creedpd.freeserve.co.uk.
6m S Bridgnorth off A442 Bridgnorth to Kidderminster rd. N from Kidderminster, turn L just after Royal Oak PH, S from Bridgnorth turn R after Squirrel PH. Take 3rd turning R into Romsley View after 50yds bear R

Get involved with the NGS – volunteer your time

& follow NGS signs to bottom of rd, last house in the corner on R. Home-made teas. **Adm £3, chd free. Suns 15 May; 17 July (1-5). Visitors also welcome by appt May to Sept. Min 20.**
Natural garden layout on several levels, developed over 30yrs, with a large variety of plants and shrubs. Water features, wooded area with bog garden containing numerous varieties of ferns and hostas. Features incl chickens in wooded area, and new ornamental grass border. Large selection of plants and bird and insect boxes for sale. Close to Severn Valley Park and Dudmaston Hall NT. Featured in Shropshire Magazine, and on Shropshire Radio.

✿ ☕ ☎

Nest boxes, bat boxes and insect shelters abound . . .

 APPLECROSS HOUSE
Alveley, Bridgnorth WV15 6NB. Mary & Colin Wells, 01746 780313, mary@marywells.com. *6m S of Bridgnorth. Alveley off A442 Bridgnorth to Kidderminster rds. N from Kidderminster, turn L just after the Royal Oak PH. S from Bridgnorth, turn R after the Squirrel PH follow NGS signs.* Home-made teas. **Adm £3.50, chd free. Suns 26 June; 25 Sept (1-5). Visitors also welcome by appt for 20+.**
2 acre garden divided into several small areas described by Shropshire Life as 'A Well-Sculpted Garden' because of the contemporary sculpture collection. Other features incl ponds, pergolas, dovecote, orchard and vegetable garden. Large range of trees, shrubs and herbaceous plants. This garden is still developing so please come again. Some gravel paths.

♿ ✿ ☕ ☎

BIRCH TREES
See Staffordshire Birmingham & part of West Midlands.

ALLOTMENTS

 NEW **BOWBROOK ALLOTMENT COMMUNITY**
Mytton Oak Road, Shrewsbury SY3 5BT, www.bowbrookallotments.co.uk. *1/2 m from Royal Shrewsbury Hospital. From A5 Shrewsbury bypass take B4386 following signs for hospital. Allotments situated 1/2 m along B4386. (Mytton Oak Rd) on R.* **Combined adm £3, chd free. Sun 17 July (1-5).**
The 4-acre site which opened in Spring 2009 has 68 productive plots displaying wide-ranging cultivation methods. Organic techniques incl companion planting and attracting natural predators are encouraged. Green spaces throughout the site are designed to attract wildlife and encourage community involvement. Nest boxes, bat boxes and insect shelters abound. The site features an interest trail, 2 orchards, picnic area, wild flowers, wildlife areas and 'Gardens of the Seasons'. Local environmental groups and schools welcomed. The community has a website(see above) and regular newsletters for members. Children enjoy the trail, willow den and tunnel, turf maze and sensory garden. The site boasts a compost toilet and information hut. Surplus produce is delivered weekly to the local hospice. Interest Trail Leaflet. Children's quiz sheets. Natural England Big Wildlife Garden Silver Award & Heart of England in Bloom RHS It's Your Neighbourhood Awards received Level 4 'Thriving'.

♿ ☕

 BRIDGWALTON HOUSE
Telegraph Lane, Morville WV16 5NP. Mary Bower, 01746 714401. *1m from Bridgnorth. Off A458 Shrewsbury to Bridgnorth, nr Morville.* Home-made teas. **Adm £3.50. Visitors welcome by appt Jan to July.**
1¼ acres plantsman's award winning garden with many unusual trees and shrubs. Collections of daphnes and peonies with oriental design at the garden. Wonderful views. All year interest with garden rooms, exuberant planting of herbaceous shrubs and bulbs, highly praised by Roy Lancaster. Featured in Shropshire magazine.

♿ ✿ ☕ ☎

BROCKTON COURT
Brockton TF11 9LZ. Mr & Mrs H Meynell. *5m S Telford. From Shifnal A4169 Bridgnorth rd for 2m then B4379 for 1m. In Brockton fork R for Coalport. From Bridgnorth A442 for Telford 8m Sutton Maddock Garage, continue on A442 towards Telford for 1/2 m, turn R signed Brockton. Brockton Court is 1st house on L.* Home-made teas. **Adm £3, chd free. Sat 18 June (2.30-5).**
Approx 2 acres herbaceous and mixed borders, bedding, roses, hanging and ornamental tubs, shrubs, arboretum, fruit and vegetables. Cascade water feature with flower/shrub border surround. Cottage garden with greenhouses and cacti. Gravel paths.

♿ ✿ ☕

 BROWNHILL HOUSE
Ruyton XI Towns SY4 1LR. Roger & Yoland Brown, 01939 261121, brownhill@eleventowns.co.uk, www.eleventowns.co.uk. *10m NW of Shrewsbury. On B4397.* Home-made teas. **Adm £3.50, chd free. Visitors welcome by appt any number welcome mid April-Aug.**
"Has to be seen to be believed". A unique hillside garden (over 700 steps) bordering R Perry. Wide variety of styles and plants from formal terraces to woodland paths, plus large kitchen garden. Kit cars on show. Featured in Shropshire Magazine.

✿ 🛏 ☕ ☎

BRYAN'S GROUND
See Herefordshire.

GROUP OPENING

 CARDINGTON GARDENS
nr Church Stretton SY6 7JZ, www.cardington.org.uk. *5m NE of Church Stretton. From Shrewsbury, take A49 S, turn L at Leebotwood just past The Pound Inn for Cardington. From Ludlow/Church Stretton, turn R off A49 at T-lights on to B4371 turn L at Wall for Cardington. From Much Wenlock, take B4371 turn R at Longville for Cardington.* Light refreshments & home-made teas at Gulley Green, refreshments & home-made teas at village hall, smoked salmon & champagne at New Inn House. **Combined adm £4, chd free. Sun 14 Aug (1-6).**
Cardington is a Conservation Village

and one of the prettiest in the county, nestling with its outlying hamlets under Caer Caradoc in the beautiful upland hill country of S Shropshire in an area of Outstanding Beauty. We have an enthusiastic band of gardeners ready to welcome you to one of the most attractive group of openings in the Marches. A typical quote from last year: 'The whole day was a lovely experience wandering through the pretty village and being treated to marvellous gardens with splendid tea and cakes'. The TEN gardens which will delight and inspire you include: Immaculate cottage gardens and topiary. Vicarage garden with magnificent views and sweeping lawns. Vegetable and fruit gardens. Formal gardens and water gardens. Romantic roomed garden with annual wild flower meadow. 10 acre conservation garden, natural ponds and wonderful planting. Butterfly meadow. Tickets: Village Hall and outlying gardens. Featured in Shropshire Magazine, national & local press & on Shropshire radio & national websites. Limited wheelchair access.

 ♿ ✂ ❀ ☕

CARTREF
See Powys

CIL Y WENNOL
See Powys.

8️⃣ NEW THE CITADEL
Weston-under-Redcastle SY4 5JY. Mr Beverley & Mrs Sylvia Griffiths, www.thecitadelweston.co.uk. *12m N of Shrewsbury. On A49. At Xrds turn for Hawkstone Park, through village of Weston-under-Redcastle, 1/4 m on R beyond village.* Home-made teas. **Adm £3, chd free. Sun 22 May (2-6).**
Imposing castellated house (not open) stands in 4 acres. Mature garden, with fine trees, rhododendrons, azaleas, acers and camellias. Herbaceous borders; walled potager and Victorian thatched summerhouse provide added interest. Paths meander around and over sandstone outcrop at centre.

♿ ✂ ⌆ ☕

9️⃣ THE COTTAGE
2 Farley Dingle, Much Wenlock TF13 6NX. Mr & Mrs P D Wight, 01952 727568, pdwight@btinternet.com. *2m E of Much Wenlock. On A4169 Much Wenlock to Telford rd. At the end of the dead end lane, opp the road signed Wyke. Parking is limited.* Light refreshments & home-made teas. **Adm £3.50, chd free. Sun 12 (11-5), Thur 16 June (3-7). Visitors also welcome by appt June-July only, min 20**
2-acre valley garden where formal beds merge into woodland. Paths and steps abound with many seating and viewing areas. A natural stream meanders through the garden making it a 'Hosta Heaven' with ferns, ornamental trees, perennials and shrubs offering a plantman's paradise. The garden has been described as a 'feat of engineering surrounded by lush planting'. I Spy challenge for children finding 20 different wooden animals in the garden. Featured on Shropshire Radio's Gardening Programme.

✂ ☕ ☎

> The whole day was a lovely experience wandering through the pretty village and being treated to marvellous gardens with splendid tea and cakes . . .

CWM-WEEG
See Powys.

CYFIE FARM
See Powys.

DINGLE NURSERIES & GARDEN
See Powys.

DOROTHY CLIVE GARDEN
See Staffordshire Birmingham & part of West Midlands.

🔟 ◆ DUDMASTON HALL GARDENS
Quatt, nr Bridgnorth WV15 6QN. National Trust, 01746 780866, www.nationaltrust.org.uk. *4m SE of Bridgnorth. On A442, between Bridgnorth & Kidderminster.* **Adm £3, chd free. For NGS: Sat 14 May (12-6). For other opening times and information, please phone or see garden website.**
9 acres featuring terraced lawn leading to lakeside and woodland walks. Unique modern sculpture dots the landscape. Wide range of species incl Cornus kousa, magnolia, rhododendron, azalea. Rose border, herbaceous border and bog garden. Access to top terrace with views across whole garden.

♿ ✂ ☕

11️⃣ EDGE VILLA
Edge, nr Yockleton SY5 9PY. Mr & Mrs W F Neil, 01743 821651, bill@billfneil.fsnet.co.uk. *6m SW of Shrewsbury. From A5 take either A488 signed to Bishops Castle or B4386 to Montgomery for approx 6m then follow NGS signs.* Light refreshments (Wed), home-made teas (Sun). **Adm £3, chd free. Wed 8 June (10-1); Sun 21 Aug (2-5). Visitors also welcome by appt, small coaches only.**
Two acres nestling in South Shropshire hills. Self-sufficient vegetable plot. Chickens in orchard foxes permitting. Large herbaceous borders. Dewpond surrounded by purple elder, irises, candelabra primulas and dieramas. Large selection of fragrant roses. Comprehensive plant stall. Teas in sheltered courtyard. Some gravel paths.

♿ ✂ ⌆ ☕ ☎

THE ELMS
See Staffordshire Birmingham & part of West Midlands.

12️⃣ FIELD HOUSE
Clee St Margaret SY7 9DT. Dr & Mrs John Bell, 01584 823242, bellbrownclee@aol.com. *8m NE of Ludlow. Turning to Stoke St Milborough & Clee St Margaret, 5m from Ludlow, 10m from Bridgnorth along B4364. Through Stoke St Milborough to Clee St Margaret. Ignore R turn to Clee Village. Field House on L.* **Visitors welcome by appt June & July only, no coaches as approach too narrow.**
1-acre garden created since 1982 for yr-round interest. Mixed borders; rose walk; pool garden; herbaceous borders. Lovely views, in a tranquil rural setting with donkeys and sheep.

♿ ✂ ☎

13️⃣ GATE COTTAGE
Cockshutt SY12 0JU. G W Nicholson & Kevin Gunnell, 01939 270606. *10m N of Shrewsbury. On A528. At Cockshutt take rd signed English Frankton. Garden 1m on R. Parking in adjacent field.* **Visitors welcome by appt.**

2 acres of informal mixed plantings of trees, shrubs, herbaceous plants of interest to flower arrangers and plantsmen. Pool, rock garden and informal pools. Large collection of hostas; old orchard with roses, incl items of unusual growth or colour. New plantings of arum lilies together with gravel garden and prairie planted grasses.

GLANSEVERN HALL GARDENS
See Powys.

14 NEW HALL FARM NURSERY
Vicarage Lane, Kinnerley, Oswestry SY10 8DH. Christine & Nick Ffoulkes Jones, www.hallfarmnursery.co.uk. *2 m off A5 mid-way between Shrewsbury & Oswestry turn off A5 at Wolfshead Island onto B4396, take 1st L towards Kinnerley.* Home-made teas. **Adm £3, chd free. Sun 19 June (10-4).**
Nursery display beds with a wide range of herbaceous plants. Raised beds with scree plants. Creative container plantings. Organic herb stall with culinary and peat free ornamental herbs from the cottage herbery.

15 HEATH HOUSE
Lightwood WV16 6UL. Margaret Bill. *5m W of Bridgnorth. From Bridgnorth bypass take B4364 to Ludlow, fork R after 1.2m, signpost 'Middleton Priors', garden 2.9m on L.* Home-made teas. **Adm £3, chd free. Suns 26 June; 14 Aug (2-5).**
Over 1-acre, natural pond with primulas, iris and lilies, secret garden with rill. Mixed herbaceous and shrub borders, orchard and vegetable garden. Long border with mixed planting leading to country views. Described as 'one of the best plant collections in the county' by Shropshire Magazine.

HEATH HOUSE
See Staffordshire Birmingham & part of West Midlands.

16 HODNET HALL GARDENS
Hodnet, nr Market Drayton TF9 3NN. Mr & The Hon Mrs Heber-Percy, 01630 685786 (Secretary), www.hodnethallgardens.org. *5½ m SW of Market Drayton. 12m NE Shrewsbury. At junction of A53 & A442.* Light refreshments & home-made teas. **Adm £5, chd £2.50.**

Sun 19 June (12-5).
60-acre landscaped garden with series of lakes and pools; magnificent forest trees, great variety of flowers, shrubs providing colour throughout season. Unique collection of big-game trophies in C17 tearooms. Kitchen garden. For details please see website.

17 HOLLY GROVE
Church Pulverbatch SY5 8DD. Peter & Angela Unsworth, 01743 718221, angela.unsworth@btinternet.com. *6m S of Shrewsbury. Midway between Stapleton & Church Pulverbatch. From A49 follow signs to Stapleton & Pulverbatch.* Home-made teas. **Adm £4, chd free. Sun 1 May (2-6). Visitors also welcome by appt coaches welcome.**
3-acre garden set in S Shropshire countryside. Yew and beech hedges enclosing 'rooms', box parterres, pleached limes, vegetable garden, rose and herbaceous borders containing many rare plants. Arboretum, lake and wild flower meadows. Opportunity to see rare White Park cattle and Soay sheep. Featured in BBC Gardening Through the Centuries.

18 HOLMCROFT
Wyson Lane, Brimfield, nr Ludlow SY8 4NW. Mr & Mrs Michael Dowding, 01584 711743, caroleandmike@ anenglishcottageonline.com, www.anenglishcottageonline.com. *4m S of Ludlow. 6m N of Leominster. From Ludlow or Leominster leave A49 at the Salway Arms PH, turn into lane signed Wyson Only. From Tenbury Wells cross the A49 opp the Salway Arms into Wyson Lane.* Home-made teas. **Adm £3.50, chd free. Sun 26 June (2-5.30). Visitors also welcome by appt June & July, coaches only.**
C17 thatched cottage (not open), set in ³/₄ -acre garden with views of Mortimer Forest and Clee Hill. Sunken, terraced and gravel gardens with willow tunnel that takes you to long borders. Rose walk leads through orchard to the kitchen garden and on to woodland walk with fern bank and stumpery.

HUNTERS END
See Worcestershire.

19 ◆ JESSAMINE COTTAGE
Kenley SY5 6NS. Lee & Pamela Wheeler, 01694 771279, www.stmem.com/jessamine-cottage. *6m W of Much Wenlock. Signed from B4371 Much Wenlock to Church Stretton rd and from A458 Shrewsbury to Much Wenlock rd at Harley.* **Adm £3.50, chd £1.For NGS: Suns 24 July; 28 Aug (2-6). For other opening times and information, please phone or see garden website.**
'A slice of heaven' and 'inspirational': typical comments from visitors to this 3-acre garden which incl mature wildlife pond, mixed island beds, lime avenue, large kitchen garden; parterre; stream and woodland. All-season colour is provided by a rose garden and ornamental trees, large range of attractive perennials and shrubs. Groups by appt.

20 LONGNER HALL
Atcham, Shrewsbury SY4 4TG. Mr & Mrs R L Burton. *4m SE of Shrewsbury. From M54 follow A5 to Shrewsbury, then B4380 to Atcham. From Atcham take Uffington rd, entrance ¹/₄ m on L.* Home-made teas. **Adm £4, chd free. Sun 22 May (2-5).**
A long drive approach through parkland designed by Humphry Repton. Walks lined with golden yew through extensive lawns, with views over Severn Valley. Borders containing roses, herbaceous and shrubs, also ancient yew wood. Enclosed walled garden containing mixed planting, garden buildings, tower and game larder. Short woodland walk around old moat pond. Some gravel paths and gentle slopes. Woodland walk not suitable for wheelchairs.

MAESFRON HALL AND GARDENS
See Powys.

21 MARCHAMLEY HOUSE GARDEN
Marchamley, nr Hodnet SY4 5LE. Mr & Mrs A Davies. *6m SW of Market Drayton. At Hodnet on A53 between Market Drayton & Shrewsbury take rd opp the Bear Hotel to Marchamley & follow NGS signs for parking.* Home-made teas. **Adm £3, chd free. Sun 10 July (1.30-5.30).**
2-acre garden set in the Shropshire countryside with stunning views. Lily

Windy Ridge

Enjoy a day out – look out for a Group Opening

Preen Manor

Be tempted by a plant from a plant stall ⊕

pond and herb garden with shrub and herbaceous perennial borders, fruit trees and vegetable garden. Sloping lawn leads down to a large pond with mature trees, with a meadow walk beyond.

22 MAREHAY FARM

Gatten, Ratlinghope SY5 0SJ. Stuart & Carol Buxton, 01588 650289. *6¹/₂ m W of Church Stretton. 6m S of Pontesbury, 9m NNE of Bishops Castle. 1¹/₂ m from 'The Bridges' Xrds & the intersection of the Longden, Pulverbatch & Bishops Castle rd and the minor rd from Church Stretton to the Stiperstones.* Home-made teas. **Adm £3, chd free. Sun 22 May (11-6). Visitors also welcome by appt mid May to mid July.**

In 1982 a building society surveyor reported 'there is no garden and at this height (1100ft), elevation and aspect there never will be!' Since 1990, on heavy boulder clay a 1¹/₂ acre woodland/water garden evolved, with primulas, hostas, iris, damp/shade tolerant perennials. Rhododendrons, azaleas, various conifers, trees, roses and shrubs complementing the location. Woodland walk. Wheelchairs with assistance, some gravel.

MILL COTTAGE

See Powys.

23 MILLICHOPE PARK

Munslow SY7 9HA. Mr & Mrs L Bury, 01584 841234, sarah@millichope.com. *8m NE of Craven Arms. From Ludlow (11m) turn L off B4368, ³/₄ m out of Munslow.* Home-made teas. **Adm £4, chd free. Mon 2 May (2-6). Visitors also welcome by appt.**

13-acre garden with lakes, woodland walks, fine specimen trees, wild flowers and herbaceous borders, good autumn colour. Recently restored cascades.

24 MOORTOWN

nr Wellington TF6 6JE. Mr David Bromley. *8m N of Telford. 5m N of Wellington. Take B5062 signed Moortown 1m between High Ercall & Crudgington.* Home-made teas. **Adm £4, chd £1. Sun 17 Apr (2-5.30).**

Approx 1-acre plantsman's garden. Here may be found the old-fashioned, the unusual and even the oddities of plant life, in mixed borders of 'controlled' confusion.

GROUP OPENING

25 MORVILLE HALL GARDENS

nr Bridgnorth WV16 5NB. *3m W of Bridgnorth. On A458 at junction with B4368.* Home-made teas in church. **Combined adm £5, chd free (share to Morville Church). Sun 12 June (2-5).**

THE COTTAGE
Mr & Mrs Begg

THE DOWER HOUSE
Dr Katherine Swift

MORVILLE HALL
Dr & Mrs J C Douglas & National Trust

SOUTH PAVILION
Mr & Mrs B Jenkinson

2 THE GATE HOUSE
Mrs G Medland

1 THE GATE HOUSE
Mr & Mrs Rowe

An interesting group of gardens that surround a beautiful Grade 1 listed mansion (not open). The Cottage is a pretty, walled cottage garden with good climbers and a fruit and vegetable area. The Dower House is a horticultural history lesson about Morville Hall which incl a turf maze, cloister garden, Elizabethan knot garden, C18 canal garden, Edwardian kitchen garden and more. It is the site of Katherine Swift's bestselling 2008 book 'The Morville Hours', and the 2011 sequel 'The Morville Year'. 1 & 2 The Gate House are cottage-style gardens with colourful borders, formal areas, lawns and wooded glades. The 4-acre Morville Hall (NT) garden has a parterre, medieval stew pond, shrub borders and large lawns, all offering glorious views across the Mor Valley. The courtyard garden of South Pavilion has many hebes, cistus and roses.

A series of 'rooms' inspired by Chelsea Flower Show . . .

MOSS COTTAGE

See Staffordshire Birmingham & part of West Midlands.

26 OTELEY

Ellesmere SY12 0PB. Mr & Mrs R K Mainwaring, 01691 622514. *1m SE of Ellesmere. Entrance out of Ellesmere past Mere, opp Convent nr to A528/495 junction.* Home-made teas. **Adm £3, chd free. Sun 15 May (1-5). Visitors also welcome by appt for groups of 10+, coaches permitted.**

10 acres running down to Mere, incl walled kitchen garden; architectural features; many interesting trees, rhododendrons and azaleas, incl wild woodland walk, views across Mere to Ellesmere Church. Gravel paths - only suitable for wheelchairs if dry.

PEN-Y-MAES
See Powys

FAEN HOUSE
See Powys

27 POPLAR COTTAGE FARM

Morville, nr Bridgnorth WV16 4RS. Elizabeth & Barry Bacon. *³/₄ m NW of Morville. On A458.* Home-made teas. **Adm £2.50, chd free. Sun 26 June (2-6).**

¹/₃ -acre flower arranger's garden with yr-round interest. Varied planting in a series of 'rooms' inspired by the small gardens at Chelsea Flower Show over the last 10 yrs. Restored gipsy caravans to view.

POWIS CASTLE GARDEN
See Powys.

28 PREEN MANOR

Church Preen SY6 7LQ. Mrs Ann Trevor-Jones, 01694 771207. *6m W of Much Wenlock. Signed from B4371.* Home-made teas. **Adm £4, chd 50p. Mon 25 Apr (2-5); Thurs 26 May; 23 June; 21 July (2-6); Sun 2 Oct (2-5). Visitors also welcome by appt June & July only, groups of 10+.**

6-acre garden on site of Cluniac monastery and Norman Shaw mansion. Kitchen, chess, water and wild gardens. Fine trees in park; woodland walks. Developed for over 30yrs with changes always in progress. Easter produce stall (Apr). Harvest Produce stall & Thanksgiving 4.30 in church adjacent to garden (Oct).

29 PRESTON HALL

Preston Brockhurst SY4 5QA. C C & L Corbet, 01939 220312, corbetleil@btinternet.com. *8m N of Shrewsbury. On A49.* **Adm £4, chd free. Sat 16 Apr (5-7) with hot soup. Visitors also welcome by appt.**

Lovely spring garden around Cromwellian house (not open). Flowering trees and shrubs, spring flowers, courtyard garden. Walled garden with a newly restored 1911 Cricket Pavilion (open), meadow walk. Grass paths, courtyard has steps.

Children's trail including Yew Tree Cottage, grotto and horrible face . . .

THE ROCK HOUSE
See Powys.

ROWAN
See Powys.

ROWLEY HOUSE FARM
See Staffordshire Birmingham & part of West Midlands.

30 RUTHALL MANOR

Ditton Priors, Bridgnorth WV16 6TN. Mr & Mrs G T Clarke, 01746 712608, clarke@ruthall.orangehome.co.uk. *7m SW of Bridgnorth. Ruthall Rd signed nr garage in Ditton Priors.* Home-made teas at Oak Farm (Thurs & Sat), in village (Sun). **Adm £3, chd free. Thur 9, Sat 11 (2-6), Sun 12 June (12-6). Visitors also welcome by appt.**

1-acre garden with ha-ha and old horse pond planted with candelabra primulas, iris and bog plants. Rare specimen trees. Designed for easy maintenance with lots of ground cover and unusual plants. Gravel art garden and other areas for low maintenance incl stumpery. New features being added year by year. Featured in 'Shropshire' Magazine.

31 NEW SECRET GARDEN

21 Steventon Terrace, Steventon New Road, Ludlow SY8 1JZ. Mr & Mrs Wood. *Park & ride available, bus 702. No parking in Steventon Terrace.*

Home-made teas & coffee. **Adm £3, chd free. Sun 26 June (12-5).** 1/2 -acre of very secret S-facing garden, divided into different sections, roses, herbaceous borders, lawn and summer house. Developed over 30yrs by present owners. Terraced vegetable garden and greenhouses. 1/4 -acre project started in 2010 - poly tunnel, vegetable plot, chickens, completed in 2011. Semi finalist in Shropshire Star last 3yrs.

32 SIBBERSCOTE MANOR

Lea Cross, Shrewsbury SY5 8JF. Lady Kingsland. *5m S of Shrewsbury. Take A488 S off Shrewsbury bypass, 4m take L turn in Lea Cross to Arscott.* Home-made teas. **Adm £4, chd free. Sun 31 July (2-6).**

Garden created to complement C16 timbered farmhouse (not open). Lovely views over 4-acre lake and S Shropshire hills. Artistically planted with roses, herbaceous and shrub borders, interesting topiary and showing a collection of sculpture. Teas in renovated farm buildings. Mown walk round lake with nesting swans and much wildlife. Wheelchair access on gravel and grass.

33 STANLEY HALL

Bridgnorth WV16 4SP. Mr & Mrs M J Thompson. *1/2 m N of Bridgnorth. Leave by N gate; B4373; turn R at Stanley Lane.* Home-made teas. **Combined adm £4, chd free. Sun 5 June (2-6).**

Drive 1/2 m with rhododendrons, azaleas, fine trees and chain of pools. Restored ice-house. Also open **The Granary** (Mr & Mrs Jack Major) Charming small trellis garden - 5yrs old. Profusion of flowers in hanging baskets and herbaceous borders.

34 SWALLOW HAYES

Rectory Road, Albrighton WV7 3EP. Mrs P Edwards, 01902 372624, patedwards70@btinternet.com. *7m NW of Wolverhampton. M54 J3. Rectory Rd to R, 1m towards Wolverhampton off A41 just past Wyevale Garden Centre.* Teas. **Adm £3.50, chd free. Sun 22 May (1-5). Visitors also welcome by appt.**

2 acres planted with emphasis on all-yr interest and ease of maintenance. National Collection of *Hamamelis*. Nearly 3000 different plants. Trees, shrubs, herbaceous, bulbs,

groundcover and ferns. Children's trail incl Yew Tree Cottage, grotto and horrible face, (map on leaflet). Mature magnolias and rhododendrons. Some gravel paths.

TAN-Y-LLYN
See Powys.

35 VALDUCCI FLOWER & VEGETABLE GARDENS

Vicarage Road Site, Meole Brace SY3 9EV. Luigi Valducci, 07921 368968, valducci@uwclub.net. *2m W of Shrewsbury. Meole Brace Garden & Allotment Club. On A5 exit at Dobbies r-about, direction Shrewsbury. Follow sign for Nuffield Hospital, opp hospital Stanley Lane, follow Stanley Lane until you reach Vicarage Rd. Car park on R, garden on L.* Light refreshments & home-made teas. **Adm £3.50, chd free. Sun 24 July (12-5). Visitors also welcome by appt any day and number of people.**

An Italian style of gardening focusing on unusual vegetables and flowers. The Valducci Horticultural site has been featured in many national and regional magazines and ITV Midland Today. Visited by 16 international judges (Europe, USA, Canada). The National Collection of *Brugmansias* has won 7 golds in shows.

36 WALCOT HALL

Lydbury North SY7 8AZ. Mr & Mrs C R W Parish, www.walcothall.com. *4m SE of Bishop's Castle. B4385 Craven Arms to Bishop's Castle, turn L by Powis Arms, in Lydbury North.* Light refreshments & home-made teas. **Adm £3.50, chd free. Sun 29, Mon 30 May (1.30-5.30).**

Arboretum planted by Lord Clive of India's son, Edward. Cascades of rhododendrons, azaleas amongst specimen trees and pools. Fine views of Sir William Chambers' Clock Towers, with lake and hills beyond. Walled kitchen garden; dovecote; meat safe; ice house and mile-long lakes. Outstanding ballroom where excellent teas are served. Russian wooden church, grotto and fountain now complete and working; tin chapel. Beautiful borders and rare shrubs.

37 **8 WESTGATE VILLAS**
Salop Street, Bridgnorth
WV16 4QX. Bill & Marilyn
Hammerton. *From A458 Bridgnorth
bypass, take rd into Bridgnorth at
Ludlow Rd r'about signed town
centre. At T-junction (pay & display
parking at B/N council offices here)
turn R, garden 100 yds on L just past
entrance to Victoria Rd.* Home-made
teas. **Adm £3.50, chd free. Evening
Opening £5, canapés & wine, Fri 8
Apr (7-9.30); Sun 10 Apr (2-5.30).**
Town garden having formal Victorian
front garden with box hedging and
water feature to complement house.
Back garden has shade border, lawn,
small knot garden and orchard
together with a strong oriental
influence, incl Japanese style
teahouse and zen garden, and path in
Chinese style. Music and garden
lighting at evening opening. Featured
in local press, 'Czek' magazine, book
'Garden Styles an Essential Guide' by
Freda Cox.

38 ◆ **WESTON PARK**
Weston-under-Lizard, Shifnal
TF11 8LE. The Weston Park
Foundation, 01952 852100,
www.weston-park.com. *6m E of
Telford. Situated on A5 at Weston-
under-Lizard. J12 M6 & J3 M54.* **Adm
£5, chd £3, concessions £4.50. For
other opening times and
information, please phone or see
garden website. For NGS: Wed 6
July (11-6).**
Capability Brown landscaped gardens
and parkland. Formal gardens
restored to original C19 design, rose
garden and long border together with
colourful adjacent Broderie garden.
Orchard in the walled garden.
Disabled route map available on
request.

GROUP OPENING

39 **WHITTINGTON VILLAGE
GARDENS**
nr Oswestry SY11 4EA. *2½ m NE of
Oswestry. Daisy Lane & Top St,
Whittington. Turn off B5009 150yds
NW of church into Top St. Car parking
at Whittington Castle (charge) & Top
St.* Home-made teas at Greystones,
Daisy Lane. **Combined adm £3, chd
free. Sat 18, Sun 19 June (12-5).**
Opening off Daisy Lane, adjacent and
local gardens of variety, colour and
interest. Ranging from cottage gardens
maximising smaller spaces, to larger,
well established gardens with mature
trees, woodland and wild meadow
planting. Several vegetable plots,
ponds and plenty of wildlife interest.

THE WICKETS
See Staffordshire Birmingham &
part of West Midlands.

40 **WINDY RIDGE**
Church Lane, Little Wenlock,
Telford TF6 5BB. George & Fiona
Chancellor, 01952 507675,
fionachancellor@btinternet.com,
www.gardenschool.co.uk. *2m S of
Wellington. Follow signs for Little
Wenlock from the north (junction7,
M54) or east (off A5223 at Horsehay).
Look for parking signs. Do not rely on
Sat Nav.* Home-made teas. **Adm £4,
chd free. Fri 24 June; Suns 10 July;
7 Aug; 4 Sept (12-5). Visitors also
welcome by appt.**
'Stunning' and 'inspirational' are how
visitors frequently describe this multi-
award-winning ²/₃ -acre village
garden. The strong design and
exuberant colour-themed planting
(over 1000 species, mostly labelled)
offer a picture around every corner,

---

while the new contemporary gravel
garden has proved to be a great hit.
Awarded a star in GGG.

41 ◆ **WOLLERTON OLD HALL**
Wollerton, Market Drayton
TF9 3NA. Lesley & John Jenkins,
01630 685760,
www.wollertonoldhallgarden.com.
*4m SW of Market Drayton. On A53
between Hodnet & A53-A41 junction.
Follow brown signs.* **Adm £5.50, chd
£1. For NGS: Fris 6, 27 May (12-5).
For other opening times and
information, please phone or see
garden website.**
4-acre garden created around C16
house (not open). Formal structure
creates variety of gardens each with
own colour theme and character.
Planting is mainly of perennials, the
large range of which results in
significant collections of salvias,
clematis, crocosmias and roses.
Lunches provided.

42 **NEW** **WOODEAVES
GARDEN PLANTS**
Sydnall Lane, Woodeaves, Market
Drayton TF9 2AS. Mrs Jean
Haywood, 01630 653161. *2m S of
Market Drayton. Just off A529
between Market Drayton & Hinstock.*
Home-made teas. **Adm £3, chd free.
Fris 3 June; 5 Aug (1-5). Visitors
also welcome by appt.**
2-acre unique nursery of a different
concept. Display sections,
herbaceous, ponds, herbs,
collections of lavender, rosemary and
thyme. Arbour seating, willow fences,
60ft willow tunnel planted with plants
(modern, traditional, rare and unusual)
for all seasons. Model railway with
rides so you can view more.

Shropshire County Volunteers

County Organiser
Chris Neil, Edge Villa, Edge, Yockleton, Shrewsbury SY5 9PY, 01743 821651, bill@billfneil.fsnet.co.uk ,

County Treasurer
Melinda Laws, 50 Sheinton Street, Much Wenlock TF13 6HU, 01952 727237, melinda@mlaws.freeserve.co.uk

Publicity
David Brown, Pelham Grove, Cound, Shrewsbury SY5 6AL, 01743 761636, pelham_grove@breathe.com
Allison Walter, Holly Cottage, Great Argoed, Mellington, nr Church Stoke SY15 6TH, allison.walter2@btinternet.com

Leaflet Coordinator
Fiona Chancellor, Windy Ridge, Little Wenlock, Telford TF6 5BB, 01952 507675, fionachancellor@btinternet.com

Assistant County Organisers
Christine Brown, Pelham Grove, Cound, Shrewsbury SY5 6AL, 01743 761636
Bill Neil, Edge Villa, Edge, Yockleton, Shrewsbury SY5 9PY, 01743 821651
Penny Tryhorn, The Granary, Folley Road, Ackleton WV6 7JL, 01746 783931

SOMERSET, BRISTOL AREA & SOUTH GLOUCESTERSHIRE incl Bath

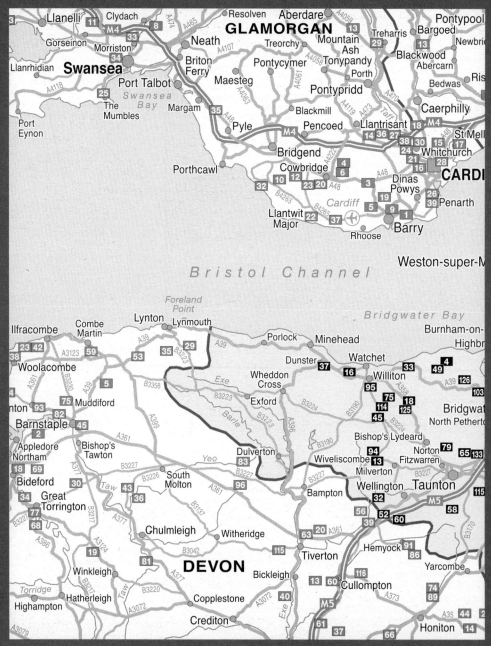

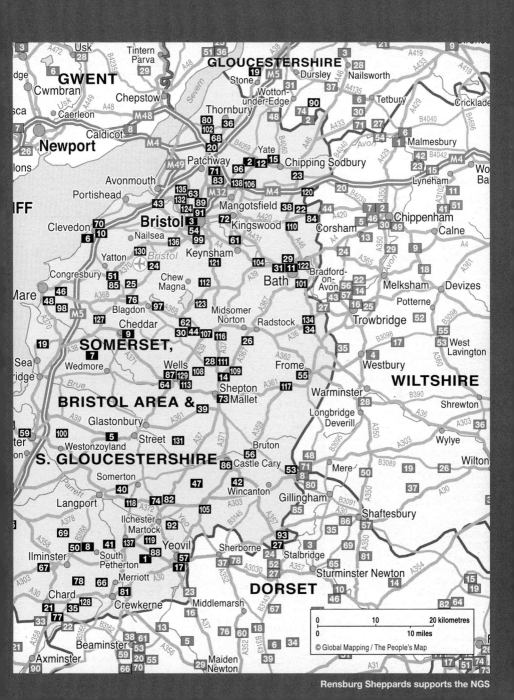

Opening Dates

January

Sunday 30
`102` Rock House

February

Sunday 6
`41` East Lambrook Manor Gardens
`102` Rock House
Sunday 13
`107` Sherborne Garden
Monday 14
`107` Sherborne Garden
Wednesday 16
`90` Newark Park

March

Tuesday 1
`65` Hestercombe Gardens
Sunday 13
`107` Sherborne Garden
Sunday 27
`104` Saltford Farm Barn
Monday 28
`82` Lytes Cary Manor

April

Sunday 3
`35` Cricket House and Gardens
`49` Fairfield
`128` Wayford Manor
Sunday 10
`30` Coley Court & Rose Cottage
Tuesday 12
`11` Bath Priory Hotel
`45` Elworthy Cottage
Saturday 16
`8` Barrington Court
Sunday 17
`60` Hangeridge Farmhouse
Wednesday 20
`109` Somerfoss
`127` Watcombe
Friday 22
`120` Tormarton Court
Saturday 23
`131` Westbrook House
Sunday 24
`128` Wayford Manor
Monday 25
`45` Elworthy Cottage
`97` The Organic Garden at Holt Farm
`128` Wayford Manor
Wednesday 27
`109` Somerfoss
Saturday 30

`24` The Caves
`78` Little Garth

May

Sunday 1
`17` 1 Braggchurch
`24` The Caves
`67` The Hollies
`128` Wayford Manor
Monday 2
`17` 1 Braggchurch
`60` Hangeridge Farmhouse
`67` The Hollies
`128` Wayford Manor
Saturday 7
`9` Bartley Cottage
Sunday 8
`33` Court House
`81` Lower Severalls
`101` Prior Park Landscape Garden
Friday 13
`79` Little Yarford Farmhouse
Saturday 14
`41` East Lambrook Manor Gardens
`78` Little Garth
`79` Little Yarford Farmhouse
Sunday 15
`60` Hangeridge Farmhouse
`79` Little Yarford Farmhouse
`87` Milton Lodge
`112` Stanton Court Nursing Home
`127` Watcombe
Monday 16
`79` Little Yarford Farmhouse
Wednesday 18
`73` Kilver Court
Thursday 19
`53` Forest Lodge
Saturday 21
`66` Hinton St George Gardens
Sunday 22
`6` 6 Ashton Close
`18` 4 Brendon View
`66` Hinton St George Gardens
`74` Kingsdon Nursery Garden
`95` Orchard Wyndham
Tuesday 24
`45` Elworthy Cottage
Thursday 26
`70` Jasmine Cottage
Saturday 28
`78` Little Garth
`84` Marshfield Gardens
Sunday 29
`13` 3 Beech Tree Close
`18` 4 Brendon View
`47` Esotera
`62` Harptree Court
`84` Marshfield Gardens
`86` The Mill House
`92` The Old Rectory
`94` Olive Cottage

`128` Wayford Manor
Monday 30
`13` 3 Beech Tree Close
`47` Esotera
`86` The Mill House
`92` The Old Rectory
`94` Olive Cottage
`128` Wayford Manor
Tuesday 31
`45` Elworthy Cottage
`129` Wellfield Barn

June

Thursday 2
`4` Ash Cottage
`70` Jasmine Cottage
Saturday 4
`9` Bartley Cottage
`38` Dyrham Gardens
`57` 190 Goldcroft
`69` Isle Abbotts Gardens
`135` 18 Woodgrove Road
Sunday 5
`28` Church Farm House
`38` Dyrham Gardens
`57` 190 Goldcroft
`69` Isle Abbotts Gardens
`87` Milton Lodge
`89` 16 Montroy Close
`103` 13 Rydon Crescent
`125` Vellacott
`126` The Walled Gardens of Cannington
`138` Yonder Cottage
Monday 6
`57` 190 Goldcroft (Evening)
`61` Hanham Court
Tuesday 7
`65` Hestercombe Gardens
Wednesday 8
`121` Tranby House
Thursday 9
`4` Ash Cottage
`70` Jasmine Cottage
Saturday 11
`31` 45A Combe Park
`67` The Hollies
`78` Little Garth
`91` 26 Northumberland Road
`105` Self Realization Meditation Healing Centre Garden
Sunday 12
`5` Ashcott Gardens
`6` 6 Ashton Close
`12` Beech House
`28` Church Farm House
`44` Eastwood Manor
`46` 14 Eskdale Close
`50` Farndon Thatch
`63` 4 Haytor Park
`67` The Hollies
`80` Littleton-on-Severn Gardens
`91` 26 Northumberland Road

123 Truffles
127 Watcombe
132 159 Westbury Lane
136 The Wycke
Monday 13
50 Farndon Thatch
123 Truffles
Wednesday 15
28 Church Farm House
Thursday 16
70 Jasmine Cottage
110 Special Plants
125 Vellacott
Saturday 18
25 Cedar House
81 Lower Severalls
88 Montacute House
119 Tintinhull
131 Westbrook House
Sunday 19
25 Cedar House
28 Church Farm House
35 Cricket House and Gardens
58 Goosehill
74 Kingsdon Nursery Garden
81 Lower Severalls
100 Penwood Farm
111 Spindle Cottage
114 Stogumber Gardens

Look out for the
gardens with the ☎
– enjoy a private
visit . . .

Tuesday 21
45 Elworthy Cottage
Thursday 23
53 Forest Lodge
70 Jasmine Cottage
Friday 24
120 Tormarton Court
Saturday 25
3 22 Ambra Vale
9 Bartley Cottage
66 Hinton St George Gardens
78 Little Garth
135 18 Woodgrove Road
Sunday 26
1 Abbey Farm
3 22 Ambra Vale
6 6 Ashton Close
13 3 Beech Tree Close
55 Frome Gardens
58 Goosehill
66 Hinton St George Gardens
94 Olive Cottage
98 3 Palmer's Way

99 22 Parson Street
100 Penwood Farm
137 Yews Farm
Monday 27
1 Abbey Farm
Thursday 30
70 Jasmine Cottage

July

Saturday 2
22 Cadwell Hill Barn
81 Lower Severalls
Sunday 3
14 The Beeches
22 Cadwell Hill Barn
51 Fernbank
52 Fernhill
60 Hangeridge Farmhouse
72 28 Kensington Road
76 Langford Court
85 Middlecombe Nursery
130 43 West Town Road
Wednesday 6
52 Fernhill
Thursday 7
70 Jasmine Cottage
Saturday 9
20 Brook Farm
67 The Hollies
68 Holly Trees
74 Kingsdon Nursery Garden
78 Little Garth
84 Marshfield Gardens
Sunday 10
19 Brent Knoll Gardens
20 Brook Farm
34 Cranbrook
36 Daggs Allotments
41 East Lambrook Manor Gardens
50 Farndon Thatch
67 The Hollies
68 Holly Trees
72 28 Kensington Road
87 Milton Lodge
98 3 Palmer's Way
99 22 Parson Street
117 Sunny Bank
134 White Cross Garden
Monday 11
50 Farndon Thatch
Tuesday 12
43 Easton-in-Gordano Gardens
Thursday 14
70 Jasmine Cottage
121 Tranby House
Sunday 17
28 Church Farm House
37 Dunster Castle Gardens
39 East Burford House
60 Hangeridge Farmhouse
96 Organic Blooms
99 22 Parson Street
73 Sole Retreat

118 Sutton Hosey Manor
Monday 18
39 East Burford House
Tuesday 19
43 Easton-in-Gordano Gardens
Thursday 21
70 Jasmine Cottage
110 Special Plants
Friday 22
82 Lytes Cary Manor
Saturday 23
8 Barrington Court
16 Binham Grange Gardens
26 The Chalet
78 Little Garth
Sunday 24
48 22 Exeter Road
54 1 Frobisher Road
71 Jen's Gardyn
83 Mandy's Garden
Tuesday 26
16 Binham Grange Gardens
43 Easton-in-Gordano Gardens
Thursday 28
10 Barum
70 Jasmine Cottage
Friday 29
71 Jen's Gardyn (Evening)
Saturday 30
9 Bartley Cottage
Sunday 31
23 Camers
32 Cothay Manor Gardens
48 22 Exeter Road
71 Jen's Gardyn
83 Mandy's Garden

August

Wednesday 3
116 Ston Easton Park
Thursday 4
10 Barum
70 Jasmine Cottage
Sunday 7
52 Fernhill
59 Grove Rise
60 Hangeridge Farmhouse
Wednesday 10
52 Fernhill
Thursday 11
10 Barum
70 Jasmine Cottage
Saturday 13
67 The Hollies
78 Little Garth
Sunday 14
21 20 Bubwith Road
56 Gants Mill & Garden
59 Grove Rise
67 The Hollies
77 Lift The Latch
109 Somerfoss

You are always welcome at an NGS garden

Monday 15
21 20 Bubwith Road
77 Lift The Latch
Thursday 18
11 Bath Priory Hotel
110 Special Plants
Sunday 21
18 4 Brendon View
28 Church Farm House
42 Eastfield
50 Farndon Thatch
121 Tranby House
Monday 22
42 Eastfield
50 Farndon Thatch
Wednesday 24
109 Somerfoss
Saturday 27
78 Little Garth
Sunday 28
21 20 Bubwith Road
77 Lift The Latch
Monday 29
21 20 Bubwith Road
45 Elworthy Cottage
77 Lift The Latch

September

Sunday 4
12 Beech House
103 13 Rydon Crescent
109 Somerfoss
124 University of Bristol Botanic Garden
126 The Walled Gardens of Cannington
Saturday 10
78 Little Garth
Sunday 11
15 Beechwell House
33 Court House
112 Stanton Court Nursing Home
Thursday 15
110 Special Plants
Saturday 17
113 Stoberry Garden
Sunday 18
54 1 Frobisher Road
113 Stoberry Garden
Tuesday 20
113 Stoberry Garden
Wednesday 21
113 Stoberry Garden
Friday 23
113 Stoberry Garden
Saturday 24
113 Stoberry Garden
Sunday 25
113 Stoberry Garden
Tuesday 27
113 Stoberry Garden

Wednesday 28
113 Stoberry Garden
Friday 30
113 Stoberry Garden

October

Saturday 1
113 Stoberry Garden
Sunday 2
113 Stoberry Garden
Monday 3
82 Lytes Cary Manor
Thursday 20
110 Special Plants
Saturday 22
35 Cricket House and Gardens
Sunday 23
35 Cricket House and Gardens

February 2012

Sunday 5
41 East Lambrook Manor Gardens
102 Rock House
Sunday 12
102 Rock House

Gardens open to the public

8 Barrington Court
16 Binham Grange Gardens
32 Cothay Manor Gardens
37 Dunster Castle Gardens
41 East Lambrook Manor Gardens
45 Elworthy Cottage
56 Gants Mill & Garden
61 Hanham Court
65 Hestercombe Gardens
73 Kilver Court
81 Lower Severalls
82 Lytes Cary Manor
87 Milton Lodge
88 Montacute House
90 Newark Park
97 The Organic Garden at Holt Farm
101 Prior Park Landscape Garden
107 Sherborne Garden
110 Special Plants
116 Ston Easton Park
119 Tintinhull
124 University of Bristol Botanic Garden
126 The Walled Gardens of Cannington

By appointment only

2 Algars Manor
7 Badgers' Acre
27 Cherry Bolberry Farm
29 9 Church Road

40 East End Farm
64 Henley Mill
75 Knoll Cottage
93 35 Old Station Gardens
106 Serridge House
115 Stoke St Mary Gardens
122 8 Trossachs Drive
133 Whales Farm

Also open by Appointment ☎

1 Abbey Farm
6 6 Ashton Close
9 Bartley Cottage
10 Barum
14 The Beeches
17 1 Braggchurch
23 Camers
25 Cedar House
28 Church Farm House
31 45A Combe Park
19 Copse Hall, Brent Knoll Gardens
43 Easton-in-Gordano Gardens
50 Farndon Thatch
52 Fernhill
53 Forest Lodge
57 190 Goldcroft
59 Grove Rise
60 Hangeridge Farmhouse
63 4 Haytor Park
66 Hooper's Holding, Hinton St George Gardens
70 Jasmine Cottage
71 Jen's Gardyn
72 28 Kensington Road
74 Kingsdon Nursery Garden
76 Langford Court
77 Lift The Latch
78 Little Garth
79 Little Yarford Farmhouse
89 16 Montroy Close
92 The Old Rectory
94 Olive Cottage
98 3 Palmer's Way
99 22 Parson Street
100 Penwood Farm
102 Rock House
30 Rose Cottage, Coley Court & Rose Cottage
105 Self Realization Meditation Healing Centre Garden
109 Somerfoss
111 Spindle Cottage
118 Sutton Hosey Manor
120 Tormarton Court
123 Truffles
127 Watcombe
129 Wellfield Barn
130 43 West Town Road
131 Westbrook House
132 159 Westbury Lane
137 Yews Farm

The Gardens

Yonder Cottage

 ABBEY FARM

Montacute TA15 6UA. Mr & Mrs G Jenkins, 01935 823572, abbeygj@dsl.pipex.com. *4m from Yeovil. Follow A3088, take slip rd to Montacute, turn L at T-junction into village. Turn R between Church & King's Arms (no through rd).* Home-made teas in church. **Adm £3.50, chd free. Sun 26, Mon 27 June (2-5). Visitors also welcome by appt.**
2¹/₂ acres of mainly walled gardens on sloping site, provide the setting for Cluniac medieval Priory gatehouse. Interesting plants incl roses, shrubs, grasses, clematis. Herbaceous borders, white garden, gravel garden. Small arboretum. Pond for wildlife - frogs, newts, dragonflies. Fine mulberry, walnut and monkey puzzle trees. Seats for resting. Gravel area & one steep slope.

 🚻 ⊕ ☕ ☎

 ALGARS MANOR

Station Road, Iron Acton BS37 9TB. Mrs B Naish, 01454 228372, bnaish@googlemail.com. *9m N of Bristol. 3m W of Yate/Chipping Sodbury. Turn S off Iron Acton bypass B4059, past village green, 200yds, then over level Xing (Station Rd).* **Adm £4, chd free. Visitors welcome by appt for groups of 10+.**
2 acres of woodland garden beside R Frome, mill stream, native plants mixed with collections of 60 magnolias and 70 camellias, eucalyptus and other unusual trees and shrubs. Mar/Apr camellias, magnolias; Apr/May/June rhododendrons, azaleas; Oct autumn colours. Limited wheelchair access, gravel paths, some steep slopes.

 🚻 ☎

3 **22 AMBRA VALE**

Clifton Wood, Bristol BS8 4RW. Joyce Poole. *Off A4 Hotwells Rd nr Holy Trinity Church.* Very limited parking. Entrance in Ambrose Rd next to Ambrose Villas. Light refreshments. **Adm £3.50, chd free. Sat 25, Sun 26 June (1-6).**
Part-walled small town garden with romantic feel. Informal planting incl grasses, ferns, exotics, fig and vine. Lots of interesting features incl statues, mosaics and secluded seating areas. 2 wildlife ponds with water features, fish and frogs. Plenty of hidden corners for bird watching and restive contemplation with a glass of wine.

☕

4 **ASH COTTAGE**

Shurton, Bridgwater TA5 1QF. Barbara & Peter Oates. *8m W of Bridgwater. From A39 nr Holford, follow signs to Stogursey then to Shurton. From A39 at Cannington follow signs to Hinkley Point then Shurton.* Cream teas. **Adm £3.50, chd free. Thurs 2, 9 June (2-5.30).**
Tranquil cottage garden in rural area, approx ²/₃ acre, wrapping around 3 sides of early C16 cottage (not open). Colour-themed borders and flowerbeds incl recently-created island bed, with raised 40ft border reached by steps from either end. Natural stream with planted banks runs through garden. Children must be supervised at all times. Some gravel paths.

🚻 ⊕ ☕

GROUP OPENING

5 **ASHCOTT GARDENS**

TA7 9QB. *3m W of Street on A39. Turn opp Ashcott Inn into Middle St. At T-junction turn R to car park at village hall.* Home-made teas in Village Hall. **Combined adm £5, chd free. Sun 12 June (2-5.30).**

NEW **9 KINGS LANE**
Mary & Brian Prettejohn

NEW **LITTLE KIMBLE**
Fulpitts Lane. Simon & Elaine Hayne

MANOR HOUSE
11 Middle Street. Peter & Daphne Willis

NEW **3 MIDDLE STREET**
Sally Kelland

MILLGREEN
3 Station Road. Ruth & Gus Wans

THE NORMANS
22 Middle Street. Mary & David Adkins

A pleasant and friendly village situated in the Polden Hills. Magnificent views. 6 interesting and varied gardens ranging in size from the small colourful garden to an acre reclaimed from a field, now nicely mature. Bog areas with hardy and tender exotics, several ponds and 2 waterfalls. 4 vegetable gardens, fruits. Enjoy the wildlife-friendly garden with its lily/fish pond, the gravel garden planted with grasses and the shrub, perennial and rose beds. We look forward to welcoming visitors to our NGS Open Gardens. Wheelchair access to 3 gardens, gravel entrance at The Normans.

🚻 ⊕ ☕

6 6 ASHTON CLOSE

Clevedon BS21 7UT. Helen & Roy Goodchild, 01275 874547. *12m W of Bristol. M5 J20. Follow ring rd L onto Southern Way. Past sports centre on R, next turning on R (Westerleigh Rd), Ashton Close on R at end.* Home-made teas. **Adm £2.50, chd free. Sun 22 May; Sun 12, 26 June (2-5).** Visitors also welcome by appt May/June/July.
Japanese inspired creation representing your progress through life. Emphasis on varied use of rocks and planting which conveys reminders of places visited. Acers, flowering shrubs and trees are designed to form a continuing series of pictures with yr-round interest. Old clay pit provides wildlife-friendly pond. Gravel paths.

🎋 ☕ ☎

7 BADGERS' ACRE

New Road, Stone Allerton BS26 2NW. Lucy Hetherington & Jim Mathers, 01934 713159, lucyhetherington@btinternet.com. *3m SW of Cheddar.* Home-made teas. **Adm £3, chd free.** Visitors welcome by appt 1 April to 31 July incl. Please call for directions.
1-acre garden. Colour-themed mixed shrub and herbaceous borders. Secret Walk with shade-loving plants. Pond and colourful rockery. Semi-circular tulip and allium bed surrounded by box hedge and pergola with climbing roses, clematis and pyracantha. Vegetable potager with raised brick beds and pergola draped in rambling roses and clematis.

🎋 ❀ ☕ ☎

8 ◆ BARRINGTON COURT

Barrington, Ilminster TA19 0NQ. National Trust, 01460 241938, www.nationaltrust.org.uk. *5m NE of Ilminster. In Barrington village on B3168.* **Adm £9.50, chd £4.15. For NGS: Sats 16 Apr; 23 July (11-5).** For other opening times and information, please phone or see garden website.
Well known garden constructed in 1920 by Col Arthur Lyle from derelict farmland (the C19 cattle stalls still exist). Gertrude Jekyll suggested planting schemes for the layout. Paved paths with walled rose and iris, white and lily gardens, large kitchen garden.

♿ ❀ ☕ ☕

9 NEW BARTLEY COTTAGE

Birch Hill, Cheddar BS27 3JP. Mr & Mrs S Cleverdon, 01934 740387/07737 132214. *Cheddar town centre. Parking in public car park next to Riverside Inn at bottom of Cheddar Gorge. Follow yellow signs on foot to garden. 5 minute walk.* Cream teas. **Adm £2, chd free. Sats 7 May; 4, 25 June; 30 July (12-5).** Visitors also welcome by appt for groups of 12+ May, June, July.
Small garden filled with over 100 very rare and unusual conifers which will surprise our visitors with differing colours, shapes and textures. Large koi pond. Tranquil oriental-style garden with large outdoor bonsai. Shaded greenhouse with over 100 phalaenopsis orchids. Spectacular views of Cheddar Gorge. Sorry, no children.

❀ ☕ ☎

Colour, light and perfume are abundant in this densely-planted artist's garden . . .

10 BARUM

50 Edward Road, Clevedon BS21 7DT. Marian & Roger Peacock, 01275 341584, barum@blueyonder.co.uk, www.barum.pwp.blueyonder.co.uk. *12m W of Bristol. M5 J20, follow signs to pier, continue N, past Walton Park Hotel, turn R at St Mary's Church. Up Channel Rd, over Xrds, turn L into Edward Rd at top.* **Adm £2.50, chd free. Thurs 28 July; 4, 11 Aug (2-5).** Visitors also welcome by appt for groups of 10+.
Informal 1/3 acre plantsman's garden, reclaimed by the owners from years of neglect. Now crammed with shrubs and perennials from around the world, incl tender and exotic species using the clement coastal climate and well-drained soil. The vegetable patch uses a no-tread bedding system growing several tender crops.

❀ ☎

11 BATH PRIORY HOTEL

Weston Road, Bath BA1 2XT. Jane Moore, Head Gardener, www.thebathpriory.co.uk. *Close to centre of Bath. From Bath centre take Upper Bristol Rd, turn R at end of Victoria Park & L into Weston Rd.* Home-made teas. **Adm £2.50, chd free. Tues 12 Apr; Thur 18 Aug (2-5).**
3-acre walled garden. Main garden has croquet lawn, herbaceous borders and dell with snowdrops and spring bulbs in April. Adjoining garden has summer meadow and woodland borders with specimen trees. Formal pool surrounded by roses leads to stone gazebo overlooking the vegetable garden which supplies the restaurant. Late summer colour August. Gravel paths and grass.

♿ ❀ ☕

12 BEECH HOUSE

Yate Road, Iron Acton BS37 9XX. John & Hazel Williams. *9m N of Bristol, 3m W of Yate. From A432, Badminton Rd, turn into B4059 - Stover Rd. Garden opp entrance to Beeches Industrial Estate. From B4059, Iron Acton bypass exit at r'about for Yate Station.* Cream Teas. **Adm £3.50, chd free. Suns 12 June; 4 Sept (1-5).**
Well laid-out garden of approx 1 acre. Many level paths intertwine between borders of mixed shrubs, roses, herbaceous and rockery areas. Fish pond, mini arboretum, kitchen garden, orchard with chickens and beehive, fernery, herbs and productive greenhouse adapted from Victorian pigsty, 1/2 m walk through wild life meadow along R Frome. Interesting garden features made from scrap wood and metal to amuse and admire. Landshare allotments selling fresh produce. Featured in local press.

♿ ❀ 🛏 ☕

13 NEW 3 BEECH TREE CLOSE

Wiveliscombe TA4 2PE. Clare Duvergier. *11m W of Taunton. From Taunton A358/B3227 to Wiveliscombe. At T-lights, L on B3187 to Wellington. Garden 1st on R opp Kingsmead School.* Home-made teas. **Adm £2.50, chd free. Sun 29, Mon 30 May; Sun 26 June (2-6).** Also open **Olive Cottage, Langley Marsh.**
Colour, light and perfume are abundant in this densely-planted artist's garden which has a wide

variety of herbaceous perennials, shrubs, clematis and roses. Partly bounded by high old estate wall, it offers a broad range of habitats and a tranquil aspect west over farmland and valley. Art exhibition in summerhouse incl original oils, watercolours, prints and cards. Partial wheelchair access only.

&. ⊗ ☕

14 NEW THE BEECHES
High Street, Oakhill BA3 5AS. Wendy Hounsfield, 01749 841776. *2¹/₂ m N of Shepton Mallet. From Oakhill Church, turn into High St, ¹/₄ m on L (parking on High St).* Home-made teas. **Adm £3.50, chd free. Sun 3 July (2-5). Visitors also welcome by appt July only for groups of 10+, no coaches.** ³/₄ -acre. Magical, peaceful garden brimming with colour. Walled garden, rose walk, formal vegetable garden. Terraced garden with many places to sit and linger. A flower arranger's delight.

⊗ ☕ ☎

15 BEECHWELL HOUSE
51 Goose Green, Yate BS37 5BL. Tim Wilmot, www.beechwell.com. *10m NE of Bristol. From centre of Yate (Shopping & Leisure Centre) or Station Rd B4060, turn N onto Church Rd. After ¹/₂ m turn L onto Greenways Rd then immed R onto continuation of Church Rd. Goose Green starts after 200yds. After 100yds take R-fork, garden 100yds on L. Limited parking.* Home-made teas. **Adm £3, chd free. Sun 11 Sept (1-5).**
Enclosed, level, subtropical garden created over last 19 yrs and filled with exotic planting, incl palms (over 12 varieties), tree ferns, yuccas, agaves and succulent bed, phormiums, bamboos, bananas, aroids and other architectural planting. Wildlife pond and koi pond. C16 40ft deep well. Rare plant raffle every hour. Featured in Inspirational Gardens Around the World book.

&. ☕

16 ◆ BINHAM GRANGE GARDENS
Old Cleeve, Minehead TA24 6HX. Stewart & Marie Thomas, 01984 640056, mariethomas@btconnect.com. *4m E of Dunster. Take A39 for Minehead, R at Xrds after Washford to Blue Anchor, past Old Cleeve, garden on L.* **Adm £3, chd free, concessions**

£2. For NGS: Sat 23, Tue 26 July (2-6). Open daily (10-5.30) except Feb.
Established garden set in 300 acres of farmed Somerset countryside with extensive views. Parterre garden to the front of house, Italian-style garden, pergola, island beds, cutting and vegetable garden. Plants for the senses working with the seasons. Gravel paths.

&. ⊗ ☕ ⊨ ☕

17 1 BRAGGCHURCH
93 Hendford Hill, Yeovil BA20 2RE. Veronica Sartin, 01935 473841/471508. *Walking distance of Yeovil centre. Approaching Yeovil on A30 from The Quicksilver Mail PH r'about, go halfway down Hendford Hill, 1st driveway on R. Roadside parking at Southwoods (next R down hill) and Public Car Park at bottom of Hendford Hill.* Home-made teas. **Adm £3, chd free. Sun 1, Mon 2 May (2-6). Visitors also welcome by appt.**
Old garden of undulating lawns and mature trees evolving, since May 2002, to semi-wild, nature-friendly, woodland garden with a few surprises within the new planting - refurbished tree house, dancing figures, Anderson shelter, pond, more willow weaving, retreat with poetry, medlar tree enclosure, rhododendron hideaway and courtyard curios.

⊗ ☕ ☎

18 4 BRENDON VIEW
Crowcombe TA4 4AG. Chris Hayes. *9m NW of Taunton. Off A358 signed Crowcombe. Garden opp turning for Hagleys Green.* **Adm £2.50, chd free. Suns 22, 29 May; 21 Aug (2-5.30).**
Plantsman's garden, S-facing with views of the Quantock Hills. Subtropical planting, mixed herbaceous borders. Vegetables. Over 600 species of cacti and other succulents in 2 greenhouses, many in flower in May & June.

⊗

GROUP OPENING

19 BRENT KNOLL GARDENS
TA9 4DF. *2m N of Highbridge. Off A38 & M5 J22.* Cream teas at Copse Hall. **Combined adm £5, chd free. Sun 10 July (2-6).**

COPSE HALL
Mrs S Boss & Mr A J Hill

Visitors also welcome by appt. 01278 760301 susan.boss@gmail.com

DOLPHIN COTTAGE
Church Lane. Colin Townsend

NEW LOWER WICK FARM
Wick Lane, Lympsham. Ms Elaine Coles & Mr Nigel Bishop

The distinctive hill of Brent Knoll, an iron age hill fort, is well worth climbing 449ft for the 360 degree view of surrounding hills, incl Glastonbury Tor and levels. Lovely C13 church renowned for its bench ends. Copse Hall: S-facing Edwardian house (not open) on lower slopes of the Knoll. Front garden newly designed with curving slopes and paths. The ha-ha, wild area and kitchen garden remain. Views to Quantock & Polden Hills. Dolphin Cottage: old cottage garden under restoration. Lower Wick Farm: farmhouse garden with interesting areas. Pond area with waterfall feature and gazebo. Summerhouse and herb garden, orchard, large rockery. Beehive and honey for sale. Wheelchair access in all gardens, some restricted.

&. ☕ ⊗ ☕

Magical, peaceful garden brimming with colour . . .

20 BROOK FARM
Lower Tockington Rd, Tockington BS32 4LE. Dr & Mrs James Mulvein. *2m NW of Almondsbury. Off A38, N of Almondsbury, down Fernhill, signed Olveston and Tockington. Garden on R after 30mph sign at entrance to Tockington. Parking available.* Home-made teas. **Combined adm £4, chd free. Sat 9, Sun 10 July (2-5). Combined with Holly Trees.**
¹/₂ -acre garden beside Tockington Rhine, partially walled, with herbaceous borders, roses, shrubs and trees. Patio area beside small pond and bog garden.

&. ☕ ☕

Cedar House

parking signs, do not park in rd. Home-made teas. **Adm £3.50, chd free. Sat 30 Apr; Sun 1 May (2-5.30).** Woodland garden created from 2-acre field and inhospitable infill bank. Many unusual trees and shrubs. Wildlife areas incl large pond with stream wandering down from rocky outcrop. Summerhouse overlooks herbaceous borders in upper garden. Meandering paths thread through heavily planted bank. Purple toothwort on one of the willows and many other spring flowers - badger permitting. Featured in Mendip Times and Somerset Gardener and on local radio.

25 CEDAR HOUSE
High Street, Wrington BS40 5QD. Jenny Denny, 01934 863375. *12m S of Bristol on A38. Follow sign for Wrington after airport & on reaching village, garage on L. T-junction turn R up hill. House on L. Parking in village (or at house by arrangement).* Home-made teas. **Sat 18, Sun 19 June (11-5). Visitors also welcome by appt 18 June to 15 July.**
Large formal garden with mature trees, lawns, herbaceous border, roses, hostas and hydrangea beds. In complete contrast, a gate leads through into an old orchard with sculpture and stunning wild flowers. Paths lead through long grass towards a pond fed by warm springs. Exhibition of art, ceramics and sculpture. Sculpture trail for children. Plant sales.

21 20 BUBWITH ROAD
Chard TA20 2BN. Paul & Barbara Blackburn. *A30 or A358 to Chard. At T-lights surrounded by 2 churches, school and garage, take Axminster rd (A358), L at mini r'about into Milfield Rd, next R. Garden on L before 2nd R turn. From Axminster, pass police stn on L before mini r'about, R into Milfield Rd.* **Adm £2, chd free. Suns, Mons 14, 15, 28, 29 Aug (1-5). Also open Lift The Latch, Chard.**
Surprising oasis for a small young garden now in its 6th yr. Full of perennials, shrubs, herbaceous plants, trees, lawn area, deck, arches and containered acers. To the rear, gently winding paths lead you to a surprise round every corner. At front, unusual parking incorporated into cottage-style planting. Winner Chard Best Small Garden. Featured in House Beautiful & Garden News.

22 CADWELL HILL BARN
West Littleton, Chippenham SN14 8JE. Mrs E Edwards. *8m N of Bath. M4 J18 or from Bath A46, R after Dyrham Park. 2nd L signed West Littleton. 1/2 m on R. then turning signed W Littleton as above.* Home-made teas. **Adm £2.50, chd free. Sat 2, Sun 3 July (2-5).**
Created 16yrs ago. Dry stone walls surround distinct areas linked together by lawn and gravel walkways. Raised terrace overlooking

circular Italianate garden with clipped box hedges and topiary mini maze. Herbaceous border and pleached lime walk.

23 CAMERS
Old Sodbury BS37 6RG. Mr & Mrs A G Denman, 01454 322430, dorothydenman@camers.org, www.camers.org. *2m E of Chipping Sodbury. Entrance in Chapel Lane off A432 at Dog Inn.* Home-made teas. **Adm £4, chd free. Sun 31 July (2-5.30). Visitors also welcome by appt groups of 20+.**
Elizabethan farmhouse (not open) set in 4 acres of garden and woodland with spectacular views over Severn Vale. Garden full of surprises, formal and informal areas planted with very wide range of species to provide yr-round interest. Parterre, topiary, Japanese garden, bog and prairie areas, waterfalls, white and hot gardens, woodland walks. Some steep slopes.

24 THE CAVES
Downside Rd, Backwell, Bristol BS48 3DH. Sylvia & Graham Guest, 01275 472393, gandsguest@btinternet.com. *9m S of Bristol. Mid distance along rd joining A38 and A370, Brockley Combe, alongside Bristol Airport and next to Coombe Garage. Follow*

26 THE CHALET
52 Charlton Road, Midsomer Norton BA3 4AH. Sheila & Chris Jones. *1/2 m from centre of Midsomer Norton. Just off A367. Past the White Post Inn towards Radstock, turn L immed after next mini r'about into Charlton Rd. Disabled parking only at house.* Home-made teas. **Adm £3, chd free. Sat 23 July (2-5).**
Covering 1 acre, garden contains lots of interest with plenty of lawns, mixed borders, vegetable garden and 80yr-old rotating cedar shingle summerhouse. Topiary is slowly becoming a feature. A quiet, relaxing garden next to a busy rd, it is shared by Orchard Lodge (52a), the next generation of the family.

27 CHERRY BOLBERRY FARM

Furge Lane, Henstridge BA8 0RN.
Mrs Jenny Raymond,
01963 364321,
cherrybolberryfarm@tiscali.co.uk.
*6m E of Sherborne. In centre of
Henstridge, turn R at small Xrds
signed Furge Lane. Continue straight
on to farm.* Home-made teas by
arrangement. **Combined with 35 Old
Station Gardens adm £4, chd free.
Visitors welcome by appt June
only for groups of 10+, coach
parties welcome. Please book
early.**
35 yr-old, owner-designed 1-acre
garden planted for yr-round interest
with wildlife in mind. Colour-themed
island beds, shrub and herbaceous
borders, unusual perennials and
shrubs, old roses and specimen
trees. Vegetable and flower cutting
garden, greenhouses, nature ponds.
Wonderful extensive views.

28 CHURCH FARM HOUSE

Turners Court Lane, Binegar,
Radstock BA3 4UA. Susan & Tony
Griffin, 01749 841628,
smgriffin@beanacrebarn.co.uk,
www.beanacrebarn.co.uk. *4m NE of
Wells. On A37 Binegar (Gurney
Slade), at George Inn, follow sign to
Binegar. 1m past PH and church to
Xrds at Binegar Green, turn R,
300metres, turn R. From Wells
B3139, 4m turn R signed Binegar. 1m
to Xrds. Turn L, 300metres turn R.*
**Adm £3.50, chd free. Suns 5, 12
June, Wed, Sun 15, 19 June; Suns
17 July; 21 Aug (11-5). Visitors also
welcome by appt
May/June/July/Aug only.**
Attitude at altitude atop the Mendips!
Green Man's Throne of living willow
oversees 2 walled gardens and prairie
patch and creeping gravel planting in
old farmyard. Colourist design incl
unusual perennials in deep borders
giving interest throughout season.
Grass is remorselessly giving way to
provide yet more planting
opportunities. Featured in Somerset
Life. Gravel forecourt, 2 shallow
steps.

29 9 CHURCH ROAD

Weston, Bath BA1 4BT. Jane &
Bernard Rymer, 01225 427277,
bernard@rymer99.fsnet.co.uk. *2m
NW of city centre. Follow signs for
Royal United Hospital in Weston.
Continue N for 1/4 m, R just before
zebra crossing into Weston High St,*
*L at war memorial. Next L just before
Lucklands Rd/Old Crown PH. No
parking in Church Rd.* Home-made
teas. **Adm £3, chd free. Visitors
welcome by appt.**
1/3 -acre informal garden tucked away
in city suburb. Colour-themed shrubs
and herbaceous plants, ferns and
annual planting which can be viewed
from numerous sitting areas and
paths meandering through the
borders. Walled garden with pond
and waterfall surrounded by grasses
and mixed planting with adjacent rose
garden and alpine bed.

Attitude at altitude atop the Mendips . . . !

GROUP OPENING

30 COLEY COURT & ROSE COTTAGE

Coley/East Harptree. *5m N of Wells,
15m S of Bristol.* Home-made teas at
Rose Cottage, cream teas at New
Manor Farm Shop, N Widecombe.
**Combined adm £4.50, chd free.
Sun 10 Apr (2-5).**

COLEY COURT

Coley. Mrs M J Hill.
*From A39 at Chewton Mendip
take B3114 for 2m. Well before E
Harptree turn R at sign Coley and
Hiton Blewitt. From E Harptree, R
at bottom of High St onto B3114
towards Chewton Mendip for 1m.
Turn L at sign to Coley*

ROSE COTTAGE

East Harptree. Bev & Jenny
Cruse.
*From B3114 turn into High St in
East Harptree. L at Clock Tower
and immed R into Middle St,
continue up hill for 1m. From
B3134 take East Harptree turning
opp Castle of Comfort, continue
for 1 1/2 m. Car parking in field opp
cottage*
**Visitors also welcome by appt
April/June only.**
01761 221627
bandjcruse@gmail.com
2 contrasting gardens. Coley Court:
early Jacobean house (not open).
1-acre garden, stone walls, spring
bulbs; 1-acre old mixed orchard.
Rose Cottage: 1-acre hillside cottage
garden with panoramic views over the
Chew Valley. Garden is carpeted with
primroses, spring bulbs and
hellebores and is bordered by stream
and established mixed hedges.
Wildlife area and pond in corner of car
park field. Rose Cottage featured in
Garden Answers, also award winner
Bath in Bloom.

31 45A COMBE PARK

Weston, Bath BA1 3NS. Stephen
Brook, 01225 428288,
stephenbrook4@tiscali.co.uk.
*1 1/2 m W of city centre. Follow signs
for Royal United Hospital in Weston.
Garden 10metres from main hospital
entrance.* Light refreshments & teas.
**Adm £3, chd free. Sat 11 June
(1-5). Visitors also welcome by
appt.**
Walled town garden creatively
landscaped on 3 levels with raised
borders of colour-schemed
perennials. Grasses, phormiums,
acers and vine-covered pergola lead
to fernery with large tree ferns. Pond
with wooden walkway, small central
lawn and secluded seating areas.
Bath in Bloom winner for best large
rear garden.

32 ◆ COTHAY MANOR GARDENS

Greenham, nr Wellington TA21 0JR.
Mr & Mrs Alastair Robb, 01823
672283, www.cothaymanor.co.uk.
*5m SW of Wellington. At M5 J26 or
27 take A38. Approx 4m follow
Cothay Brown sign. After 1m follow
brown signs and finger posts. In lane
always keep L.* **Adm £7, chd £3.50.
For NGS: Sun 31 July (2-5). For
other opening times and
information, please phone or see
garden website.**
Few gardens are as evocatively
romantic as Cothay. Laid out in 1920s
and replanted in 1990s within the
original framework, Cothay
encompasses a rare blend of old and
new. Plantsman's paradise set in 12
acres of magical gardens. Sculpture,
antique shop, garden shop. House
open. Featured on C4 Country House
Rescue and in numerous
publications. Gravel paths.

33 COURT HOUSE

East Quantoxhead TA5 1EJ. East Quantoxhead Estate (The Late Lady Luttrell). *12m W of Bridgwater. Off A39; house at end of village past duck pond. Enter by Frog Lane (Bridgwater/Kilve side from A39).* Cream teas in Village Hall. **Adm £4, chd free. Suns 8 May; 11 Sept (2-5).**
Lovely 5-acre garden; trees, shrubs, many rare and tender; herbaceous and 3-acre woodland garden with spring interest and late summer borders. Traditional kitchen garden (all chemical free). Views to sea and Quantocks.

34 NEW CRANBROOK

Mackley Lane, Norton St Philip BA2 7LJ. Anne & David Wharton. *8m SE of Bath. From Bath on B3110 through village past George Inn to 1st R turn signed Laverton. 2nd house in lane. Refreshments and parking in Fleur de Lys PH.* **Combined adm £4, chd free. Sun 10 July (2-5). Combined with White Cross Garden.**
Plant lover's garden divided into rooms. Large collection of roses, clematis, perennial geraniums and herbaceous plants. Vegetable garden incl heritage varieties. Mature walnut, mulberry, quince and apple trees. Small children's play area.

35 CRICKET HOUSE AND GARDENS

Nr Chard TA20 4DD. Warner Leisure Hotels. *3m E of Chard. On A303, Cricket St Thomas Wildlife Park signed from M3, M4, M5.* Home-made teas. **Adm £3.50. Suns 3 Apr; 19 June (2-5); Sat 22, Sun 23 Oct (12-5).**
The grounds were designed by a student of Capability Brown. Mixture of mature trees in beautiful setting along valley. Recently-planted rose gardens and selection of borders. New 2nd phase garden reclamation. Worth visiting at any time of yr. Sorry, no children. Some gravel paths and steep slopes.

36 DAGGS ALLOTMENTS

High Street, Thornbury BS35 2AW, www.thornburyallotments.com. *Park in free car park off Chapel St.* Home-made & cream teas. **Adm £3, chd free. Sun 10 July (2-5).**
Thornbury is a historic town and a

Britain in Bloom RHS Gold Award Winner in 2009. 105 plots, all in cultivation, many organic, including vegetables, soft fruit, herbs and flowers for cutting. Narrow, steep, grass paths between plots. Many plot holders will be available to answer any questions you may have about the plots, cultivation techniques and varieties grown. Story-telling under shady tree, plant and produce stall and cream teas with home-made cakes available.

> Story-telling under shady tree, produce stall and cream teas . . .

37 ◆ DUNSTER CASTLE GARDENS

Dunster TA24 6SL. National Trust, 01643 821314, www.nationaltrust.org.uk. *3m SE of Minehead. NT car park approached direct from A39 Minehead to Bridgwater rd, nr to A396 turning. Car park charge to non-NT members.* **Adm £9, chd £4.40, family £21.50. For NGS: Sun 17 July (10-5). For other opening times and information, please phone or see garden website.**
Hillside woodland garden surrounding fortified mansion, previously home to the Luttrell family for 600yrs. Terraced areas, interlinked by old carriage drives and paths, feature tender plants. Fine views over old lawns and landscape with C18 features. New winter interest border, more plantings planned for 2010. Dream garden. Lots of dahlias. Gravel paths and steep slopes.

GROUP OPENING

38 NEW DYRHAM GARDENS

Dyrham SN14 8ER. *12m E of Bristol, 8m N of Bath. From M4, J18: 2m S on A46, R at sign to Dyrham and Hinton. From Bath: 1st L after Tollgate Teashop. From A4174 ring rd:* through Pucklechurch & R before Hinton. *Follow signs to Dyrham village. Parking only in designated car park. Maps given to all.* Home-made teas & light refreshments. **Combined adm £5, chd free. Sat 4, Sun 5 June (1-5).**

NEW BAYTREE COTTAGE
Lower Street. Nicolette Hayward

NEW THE COTTAGE
Upper Street. Dr David Lockey & Mrs Kate Lockey

◆ DYRHAM PARK
Bath. National Trust
For other opening times and information, please phone or see garden website.
01179 371331
www.nationaltrust.org.uk/dyrhampark

NEW THE GARDEN HOUSE
Upper Street. Stephen & Penny Ross

NEW HINDS COTTAGE
Edward & Joanna Walsh

NEW LONG VIEW HOUSE
Old Home Farm. Roy & Bryony Smedley

NEW WYNTER HOUSE
Upper Street. Elizabeth Karlsen & Stephen Woolley

Dyrham is on W of lower Cotswold Escarpment and is mentioned in the Domesday Book. Its houses were once the estate houses of Dyrham Park. Baytree Cottage: wonderful cottage garden surrounding pretty C16 house, developed over past 3 yrs. The Cottage: deep borders and bulbs. Perennials, a mass of white foxgloves, peonies and alliums. Dyrham Park: fine C17 mansion house with restored garden, 270 acres of parkland and adjacent parish church dating back to C13. The Garden House: mature 2-acre garden. Topiary garden, lily pond, prunus-malus avenues, wild water woodland, vegetable and fruit garden. Hinds Cottage: sheltered, mature gardens around house dating from late C17 to C21. Long View House: flower-filled haylofts and baskets decorate the courtyard of this converted cow barn. Uninterrupted view of the Boyd Valley and the Mendips. Wynter Garden: sloping garden leading up from the R Boyd, incl. walled kitchen garden.

Be tempted by a plant from a plant stall ⊛

NEW EAST BURFORD HOUSE
Summer Hill Lane, West Compton, Pilton BA4 4PA. Christopher & Lindsay Bond. *3m W of Shepton Mallet. At Xrds at bottom of hill in Pilton on A361 go uphill between PH and shop for* $^1/_2$ *m to bottom of valley, black gates on L.* Home-made teas. **Adm £4, chd free. Sun 17, Mon 18 July (11-5).**
Garden full of surprises, 3 acres surround fine country house (not open) set in isolated Mendip valley. Formal walled and wild gardens, different areas incl herbaceous, bog, woodland, gravel, wisteria pergola, desert and raised strawberry beds, lake with shell beach, rills, pagoda, pavilion, sculptures and children's playground. Plants incl roses, hostas, cactus, citrus and bamboos. Only 5mins to hanging valley woodland, an ideal place for a 'bring your own' picnic lunch. Wheelchair access limited to walled garden and part of wild garden only.

40 EAST END FARM
Pitney, Langport TA10 9AL. Mrs A M Wray, 01458 250598. *Please telephone for directions.* **Adm £2.50, chd free. Visitors welcome by appt June only.**
Timeless small garden of old roses in herbaceous borders set amongst ancient farm buildings.

41 ◆ EAST LAMBROOK MANOR GARDENS
East Lambrook TA13 5HH. Mike & Gail Werkmeister, 01460 240328, www.eastlambrook.com. *2m N of South Petherton. Off A303 at South Petherton. Follow brown East Lambrook Manor Gardens and flower signs from A303 or Martock.* **Adm £5.50, chd free, concessions £5. For NGS: Sun 6 Feb; Sat 14 May; Sun 10 July (10-5); 2012 Sun 5 Feb. For other opening times and information please phone or visit garden website.**
One of England's best loved privately owned gardens created by the late Margery Fish. Old-fashioned and contemporary plants in a relaxed and informal manner, creating an extraordinary garden of great charm. Grade I listed, renowned as the premier example of the English cottage gardening style and noted for its specialist collections of snowdrops and hardy geraniums. Snowdrops

Feb. Art exhibitions in Malthouse Gallery: Kay Parmenter in May, Moish Sokal July. Featured in The Daily Telegraph. Partial wheelchair access only, narrow paths and steps.

42 EASTFIELD
Pound Lane, Yarlington, Wincanton BA9 8DQ. Lucy McAuslan-Crine. *3m W of Wincanton. A303 Wincanton exit, follow A371 to Castle Cary, Shepton Mallet, L on bend to Yarlington (2m). 2nd or 3rd R to Yarlington. At Xrds follow lane past front of Stags Head to end, entrance and parking at rear of Eastfield.* **Adm £3, chd free. Sun 21, Mon 22 Aug (2-5).**
Approx $^1/_2$ acre made up of small gardens each with a different planting style. Mixture of tender and hardy herbaceous plants and shrubs incl olive trees, palms, agapanthus. A hint of the Mediterranean in Somerset. Ponds, roof garden, organic kitchen garden, young orchard, greenhouse, conservatory with beds filled with tropical plants.

GROUP OPENING

43 EASTON-IN-GORDANO GARDENS
Easton-in-Gordano BS20 0NB, 01275 372698, i.crichton@talktalk.net. *5m W of Bristol. M5 J19 Gordano Services, exit Bristol. 1st L for Easton-in-Gordano, past King's Arms PH. Park in church hall car park by football field and follow directions in car park BS20 0PR.* Home-made teas. **Adm £3.50, chd free. Tue 12, 19, 26 July (2-5). Visitors also welcome by appt July only.**

36 CHURCH ROAD
Mr & Mrs I Crichton

16 GORDANO GARDENS
Mr & Mrs Milsom.
From car park, walk through field directly behind scout hut

2 beautiful gardens, well worth a visit. 36 Church Road: $^1/_4$ -acre garden developed around ancient dewpond. Unusual secret garden incl large pond with fish, waterfall, and bridge built by local school. Herbaceous borders contain many flower arrangers' plants. Limited wheelchair access.16 Gordano Gardens: Cottage-style garden 80ft long with many pretty and

unusual features incl decked area, natural pond with waterfall, grasses and herbaceous plants.

Garden full of surprises, set in isolated Mendip valley . . .

44 NEW EASTWOOD MANOR
East Harptree BS40 6AH. *8m N of Wells. S of A368 in Chew Valley. W of A37, 1m S of East Harptree village centre.* **Adm £3.50, chd free. Sun 12 June (2-5).**
Victorian Manor House with large restored formal gardens overlooking Chew Valley lake. Lime tree avenue, herbaceous borders, lavender parterre, enclosed gardens, mature trees, terraces. Spiral mound. Partial wheelchair access, some steps, slopes and gravel.

45 ◆ ELWORTHY COTTAGE
Elworthy, Taunton TA4 3PX. Mike & Jenny Spiller, 01984 656427, www.elworthy-cottage.co.uk. *12m NW of Taunton. On B3188 between Wiveliscombe & Watchet.* **Adm £3, chd free. For NGS: Tue 12 Apr; Mon 25 May; Tues 24, 31 May; 21 June; Mon 29 Aug (11-5).**
1-acre plantsman's garden in tranquil setting. Island beds, scented plants, clematis, unusual perennials and ornamental trees and shrubs to provide yr-round interest. In spring, pulmonarias, hellebores and more than 100 varieties of snowdrops. Planted to encourage birds, bees and butterflies, lots of birdsong. Wild flower areas, decorative vegetable garden, living willow screen. Stone ex privy and pigsty feature. Adjoining nursery. Also open Thurs only Apr-Aug incl (10-4) or by appt.

46 ▶ 14 ESKDALE CLOSE
Weston-Super-Mare BS22 8QG.
Janet & Adrian Smith. 1½ m E of
WSM town centre. J21 M5, 1½ m
(B3440) towards WSM town centre.
L at chevrons into Corondale Rd, 1st
R into Garsdale Rd. Park halfway
along and take footpath beside no.
37. From town centre take B3440
towards Bristol. After 1½ m keep
straight on at mini r'about then 1st R
into Corondale Rd. Home-made teas.
**Adm £3, chd free. Sun 12 June
(1-5).**
Interestingly-planned, natural style
cottage garden with all-yr interest.
Fish pond with seating areas, lawn,
patio, rockery with conifers, Heidi
playhouse with secrets. Wisteria
archway leading to productive
vegetable, herb and fruit garden.

Aim to cover every inch with a variety of plants . . .

47 ▶ ESOTERA
Foddington, nr Babcary TA11 7EL.
Andrew & Shirley Harvey. 6m E of
Somerton, 6m SW of Castle Cary.
Signs to garden off A37 Ilchester to
Shepton Mallet and B3153 Somerton
to Castle Cary. (Old) A303 from
Sparkford. Cream teas. **Adm £3.50,
chd free. Sun 29, Mon 30 May
(11-5).**
2-acre established informal country
garden housing 3 wildlife ponds.
Large prairie border. Contemporary
new potting shed with shrubs and
herbaceous planting. Mature trees,
boxed topiary, courtyard and meadow
walk leading to shepherd hut.
Children must be supervised at all
times.

48 ▶ 22 EXETER ROAD
Weston-super-Mare BS23 4DB.
Mrs P A Williams. Weston-super-
Mare. M5 J21, A370 towards town
centre, L into Drove Rd (by
gasholders). Over rail bridge, R into
Quantock Rd, R into Malvern Rd then
R then R. Use rear entrance between
nos 20 & 21. Home-made teas. **Adm**

£2.50, chd free. **Sun 24, 31 July
(10-4).**
Small rear garden behind Victorian
terraced house. Jungle-like
appearance, packed with plants,
some unusual or exotic - palms,
bananas, elephant ears, bamboo,
Australian tree fern & olive tree.

49 ▶ FAIRFIELD
nr Stogursey TA5 1PU. Lady
Acland Hood Gass, 01278 732251.
7m E of Williton. 11m W of
Bridgwater. From A39 Bridgwater to
Minehead rd turn N; garden 1½ m
W of Stogursey on Stringston rd. No
coaches. For directions please phone
01278 732251. Teas. **Adm £3.50,
chd free. Sun 3 Apr (2-5).**
Woodland garden with bulbs, shrubs
and fine trees; paved maze. Views of
Quantocks and sea.

50 ▶ FARNDON THATCH
Puckington, Ilminster TA19 9JA.
Bob & Jane St John Wright, 01460
259845, bobstjw@yahoo.co.uk. 3m
N of Ilminster. From Ilminster take
B3168 to Langport. Through
Puckington village, last house on L.
No parking at house, directions on
arrival. Home-made teas. **Adm £3,
chd free. Suns, Mons 12, 13 June;
10, 11 July; 21, 22 Aug (12-6).
Visitors also welcome by appt.**
With panoramic views to die for, this
1-acre plantaholic's garden comes
complete with C16 thatched cottage.
Banks and borders brimming with
shrubs and perennials. Planted for yr-
round interest. Terrace and courtyard
with pots; sculptures, vegetable
garden, fine trees and lawns and
areas of natural tranquility.

51 ▶ FERNBANK
High Street, Congresbury
BS49 5JA. Simon & Julia Thyer.
Midway between Weston-super-Mare
and Bristol. From t-lights on A370 at
Ship & Castle, turn into High St
(B3133). Garden 100yds on R, park in
side streets or car park N of river.
**Combined adm £4, chd free.
Sun 3 July (10.30-5). Combined
with Middlecombe Nursery.**
⅓ acre haven for wildlife tucked
away behind Victorian house (not
open). Patio with hundreds of potted
plants incl bamboos, hostas, trees
and even gunnera. Conservatory,
kitchen garden with picturesque
greenhouse and potting shed, mature

copper beech, 2 ponds and a tiny
'courtyard' with Wendy house.
Narrow paths, free-range bantams.

52 ▶ FERNHILL
nr Wellington TA21 0LU. Peter &
Audrey Bowler, 01823 672423,
peter@bowler1934.fsnet.co.uk. 3m
W of Wellington. On A38, White Ball
Hill. Past Beam Bridge Hotel stay on
A38 at top of hill, follow signs on L
into garden & car park. Home-made
teas. **Adm £3, chd free. Suns, Weds
3, 6 July; 7, 10 Aug (2-5). Visitors
also welcome by appt July/Aug
only.**
Mature wooded garden in approx
2 acres with rose, herbaceous, shrub
and mixed borders, all unique in
colour and content. Interesting
octagonal pergola; alpine and bog
garden with waterfalls and pools
leading to shady arbour, banks of
hydrangeas mid-summer. Fine views
over ha-ha to Blackdowns and
Mendips.

53 ▶ FOREST LODGE
Pen Selwood BA9 8LL. Mr & Mrs
James Nelson, 01747 841283,
lucyn2002@aol.com. 1½ m N of
A303, 3m E of Wincanton. Leave
A303 at B3081 (Wincanton to
Gillingham rd), up hill to Pen Selwood,
L towards church. ½ m, garden on L.
Home-made teas. **Adm £3.50, chd
free. Thurs 19 May; 23 June (2-5).
Visitors also welcome by appt.**
3-acre mature garden with many
camellias and rhododendrons in May.
Lovely views towards Blackmore Vale.
Part formal with pleached hornbeam
allée and rill, part water garden with
lake. Unusual trees. Wonderful roses
in June.

FOSSLEIGH
See Devon.

54 ▶ 1 FROBISHER ROAD
Bristol BS3 2AU. Karen Thomas.
2m SW of city centre. Bristol City FC
on R, next R Duckmoor Rd, 5th
turning L before bollards. **Adm £2.50,
chd free. Suns 24 July; 18 Sept
(2-5).**
Compact and interesting inner city
garden with mature trees and shrubs.
Aim to cover every inch with a variety
of plants, some from seed.
Comments from visitors 'amazing',
'a gem', 'a treasure'. Featured in local
press.

GROUP OPENING

Hanham Court

55 NEW FROME GARDENS
Frome BA11 4HR. *15m S of Bath.
Town centre W towards Shepton
Mallet (A361). At Sainsbury's r'about
turn R, follow lane for ¹/₂ m, L into
Critchill Rd, over Xrds then 1st L for
9 Catherston Close, Bastion garden
in town centre.* Teas at Bastion
Garden. **Adm £3, chd free.
Sun 26 June (12-5).**

> **NEW THE BASTION
> GARDEN**
> Mrs Karen Harvey.
> *Access to garden via Zion Path -
> next to Catherine House Nursing
> Home, Cork St*
> www.bastiongarden.com

> **NEW 9 CATHERSTON
> CLOSE**
> Dave & Prue Moon

2 varied gardens. Bastion Garden:
restored early in C18, garden features
reveted banks, raised platforms, yew
hedges and pond. Emphasis on
shape and form, not extensive floral
planting. Colourful 50-metre curved
border of David Austin roses with low
box hedging. 9 Catherston Close:
¹/₃ -acre town garden. Colour-themed
shrub and herbaceous borders, pond,
patios, pergolas and wild meadow
areas, with extensive views of
countryside. Productive vegetable
and fruit garden with greenhouse.
Exhibition of garden photography by
owner displayed in summerhouse. 9
Catherston Close 5 times gold winner
Frome in Bloom.

56 ◆ GANTS MILL & GARDEN
Gants Mill Lane, Bruton BA10 0DB.
Alison & Brian Shingler, 01749
812393, www.gantsmill.co.uk.
*¹/₂ m SW of Bruton. From Bruton
centre take Yeovil rd, A359, under
railway bridge, 100yds uphill, fork R
down Gants Mill Lane.* Mill & garden
adm £6, chd £1, garden only adm
£4, chd £1. For NGS: Sun 14 Aug
(2-5).
³/₄ -acre garden. Clematis, rose
arches and pergolas; streams, ponds,
bog garden. Sculptures, riverside
walk to top weir; tulips, iris,
delphiniums, day lilies, 100+ dahlia
varieties; also vegetable, soft fruit and
cutting flower garden. The garden is
overlooked by the historic watermill,
also open on NGS day. Guided tours

of historic watermill. Also open 2nd
Suns May - Sept (2-5). Several
shallow steps, gravel paths.

57 190 GOLDCROFT
Yeovil BA21 4DB. Eric & Katrina
Crate, 01935 475535,
eric@ericcrate.orangehome.co.uk.
*Take A359 from r'about by Yeovil
College, then 1st R.* Home-made
teas. **Adm £2.50, chd free. Sat 4,
Sun 5 June (2-5) Evening Opening
wine, Mon 6 June (4-8). Visitors
also welcome by appt, any group
size, coaches welcome.**
¹/₄ acre. Colour-themed shrub and
herbaceous borders and island beds,
rose garden, raised pond, seaside
deck, fernery, hosta walk, arbour
surrounded by silver bed, vegetable
garden designed for the visually
impaired and greenhouse. Many
mature shrubs and trees and sensory
features. Featured on West Country
TV.

58 GOOSEHILL
Sellicks Green TA3 7SA. Marina &
Chris Lane. *3¹/₂ m SW of Taunton.
On rd between Blagdon Hill and
Pitminster.* Cream teas. **Adm £3, chd
free. Suns 19, 26 June (2-6).**
Pretty 2-acre country garden
surrounding C15 thatched house (not
open) with extensive views of
Blackdown and Brendon Hills.
Traditional cottage garden with listed
moon gate, potager, orchard,

vegetable plot and exotic courtyard
garden. Mature trees and hedges
provide structure. New planting since
last opening in 2008.

59 GROVE RISE
Downhall Drive, Wembdon,
Bridgwater TA6 7RT. Chris &
Dianne McKinley, 01278 421675.
*2m NW of Bridgwater. From
Wembdon Rd, R into Church Rd then
immed L up private rd. Car parking at
village church car park.* **Adm £2.50,
chd free. Suns 7, 14 Aug (1-5).
Visitors also welcome by appt.**
Small, mature garden created over
25yrs. On steep hillside terraced to
create an interesting design with
variety of shrubs, mature trees,
climbers and flowers. Seating areas
with distant views of Quantock Hills.

60 HANGERIDGE FARMHOUSE
Wrangway, Wellington TA21 9QG.
Mrs J M Chave, 01823 662339,
hangeridge@hotmail.co.uk. *2m S of
Wellington. 1m off A38 bypass signed
Wrangway. 1st L towards Wellington
Monument over mway bridge 1st R.*
Home-made teas. **Adm £3, chd free.
Sun 17 Apr; Mon 2, Suns 15 May;
0, 17 July; 7 Aug (11-5). Visitors
also welcome by appt.**
Informal, relaxing, mature family
garden set under Blackdown Hills.
Seats to enjoy views across Somerset
landscape. Atmospheric mix of
herbaceous borders and this lovely-

designed and still-evolving garden contains wonderful flowering shrubs, heathers, mature trees, rambling climbers and seasonal bulbs. Content and design belie its 1-acre size. Garden not to be missed. Winner of Wellington in Bloom.

& ⊛ ⊨ ☕ ☎

61 ◆ HANHAM COURT
Ferry Rd, Hanham Abbots BS15 3NT. Julian & Isabel Bannerman, www.hanhamcourt.co.uk. *5m E of Bristol centre. Old Bristol Rd A431 from Bath, through Wilsbridge, L down Court Farm Rd for 1m. Drive entrance on L.* Adm £6.50, chd free. For NGS: Mon 6 June (2.30-5). The garden designers Julian & Isabel Bannerman are still developing this rich mix of bold formality, water, woodland, orchard, meadow and kitchen garden with emphasis on scent, structure and romance, set amid a remarkable cluster of manorial buildings between Bath and Bristol. Tree peonies, wisteria and witch hazels in May; hot borders of dahlias etc in Sept. Also open 8 May to 8 Aug. Regret no picnics. Featured in Country Living, Gardens Illustrated, Saturday Telegraph, Homes & Gardens and Cotswold Life Magazine.

62 HARPTREE COURT
East Harptree BS40 6AA. Mrs Richard Hill & Mr & Mrs Charles Hill, www.harptreecourt.co.uk. *8m N of Wells. A39 Bristol rd to Chewton Mendip, then B3114 to E Harptree, gates on L. From Bath, A368 Weston-super-Mare rd to W Harptree.* Cream teas. Adm £3.50, chd free. Sun 29 May (2-6). Spacious garden designed when the house was built in 1797. Two ponds linked by a romantic waterfall and a stream, flanked by large trees. Lily pond and formal garden. Pleached limes. Walled garden with herbaceous borders, fruit trees and other fruits.

& ♫ ⊛ ⊨ ☕

63 4 HAYTOR PARK
BS9 2LR. Mr & Mrs C J Prior, 01179 856582, p.l.prior@gmail.com. *Edge of Coombe Dingle. From A4162 Inner Ring Rd between A4 Portway & A4108 Falcondale Rd, take turning into Coombe Bridge Ave, Haytor Park is 1st turning L. No parking in Haytor Park.* Home-made teas at 159 Westbury Lane. Combined adm £5, chd free. Sun 12 June (2-6).

Combined with **159 Westbury Lane. Visitors also welcome by appt Apr to Sept only.** Lose yourself in this tranquil oasis. Seemingly never-ending, packed with plants for every niche and season. Winding paths entice under flower-bejewelled arches. Nooks and crannies abound, here an unusual plant, there a sculpture. Ponds, pots and wildlife too but please do not disturb the sleeping dragon.

⊛ ☎

64 HENLEY MILL
Wookey BA5 1AW. Peter & Sally Gregson, 01749 676966, millcottageplants@gmail.com. *2m W of Wells. Off A371. Turn L into Henley Lane, driveway 50yds on L through white pillars to end of drive.* Adm £3, chd free. Visitors welcome by appt May to Sept, coaches permitted. 2½ acres beside R Axe. Scented garden with roses, hydrangea borders, shady 'folly garden' and late summer borders with grasses and perennials. New zig-zag boardwalk at river level. Ornamental kitchen garden. Rare Japanese hydrangeas.

& ⊛ ☎

Winding paths entice under flower-bejewelled arches . . .

65 ◆ HESTERCOMBE GARDENS
Cheddon Fitzpaine TA2 8LG. Mr P White, Hestercombe Gardens Trust, 01823 413923, www.hestercombe.com. *4m N of Taunton. Follow tourist signs.* Adm £8.60, chd £3.25 (under 5 free), concessions £8. For NGS: Tues 1 Mar; 7 June (10-5.30). For other opening times and information, please phone or see garden website. Georgian landscape garden designed by Coplestone Warre Bampfylde, Victorian terrace/shrubbery and

---

stunning Edwardian Lutyens/Jekyll formal gardens together make up 40 acres of woodland walks, temples, terraces, pergolas, lakes and cascades. Gravel paths, steep slopes.

& ♫ ⊛ ☕

GROUP OPENING

66 HINTON ST GEORGE GARDENS
TA17 8SA. *3m N of Crewkerne. N of A30 Crewkerne-Chard; S of A303 Ilminster Town Rd, at r'about signed Lopen & Merriott, then R to Hinton St George.* Home-made teas at Hooper's Holding. Combined adm £5, chd free. Sats, Suns 21, 22 May; 25, 26 June (2.30-5.30).

ARKARINGA
69 West Street. Bel Annetts.
Access through passage on L not open 21, 22 May

END HOUSE
West Street. Helen Newman

HOOPER'S HOLDING
45 High Street. Ken & Lyn Spencer-Mills
Visitors also welcome by appt up to mid-Aug.
01460 76389
kenlyn@devonrex.demon.co.uk

THE OLD RECTORY
Church St. Robert & Caroline Duval.
Adjacent to churchyard

RUSSETS
Lopen Road. Jean & Eric Burgess.
Not open 25/26 June.

5 cottage gardens varying in size and style in beautiful hamstone village. C15 church. Country seat of the Earls of Poullett for 600yrs until 1973. Visit Hooper's Holding with its developing garden mosaics and the secluded wildlife and bird-friendly Russets. The Old Rectory has mature trees and shrubs with herbaceous borders and wide lawns. End House has sweeping lawns, gravel gardens and interesting trees and shrubs (approx ½ acre). Arkaringa is a narrow sloping garden full of colour, texture and shape throughout the yr. Wheelchair access to 3 gardens.

& ♫ ⊛ ☕

HOLCOMBE COURT
See Devon.

67 NEW THE HOLLIES
3 Paulls Lane, Horton, Ilminster
TA19 9SA. Allison & Steve Mason.
2¹/₂ m NW of Ilminster. From
A303/358 r'about at Ilminster take
A358 in direction of Chard. 2nd R,
continue approx 1m then 5th R into
Pound Rd. At 5 Dials Xrds take 1st R
into Trotts Lane to bottom Paulls
Lane. Home-made teas. Adm £3,
chd free. Sun 1, Mon 2 May; Sats,
Suns 11, 12 June; 9, 10 July; 13,
14 Aug (2-6).
Corner house with small interesting
garden. Front uses flowing curves,
adding interest to the aspect. Rear
garden is structured to incorporate
pond, split level lawn surrounded by
herbaceous beds with abundance of
planting and secret potager.
☕

68 NEW HOLLY TREES
Alveston Road, Old Down,
Tockington BS32 4PH. Vicki &
Tracy Watkeys. 2m S of Thornbury.
Off A38 N of Almondsbury down Fern
Hill, into Tockington, 1st R after Swan
PH, 1st L up Old Down Hill then 1st
R, garden approx 300yds on L.
Combined adm £4, chd free. Sat 9,
Sun 10 July (2-5). Combined with
Brook Farm.
Large garden, approx 1 acre
cultivated, partitioned with yew
hedges into separate rooms.
Landscaping started 1999, still
ongoing! Sunken patio, herbaceous
borders, small orchard, vegetable
garden and more. Gravel paths.
&

GROUP OPENING

**69 NEW ISLE ABBOTTS
GARDENS**
Isle Abbotts, nr Ilminster TA3 6RH.
4m N of Ilminster. B3168 from
Ilminster towards Curry Rivel. 1st L
after going over A303 flyover and
immed R. A378 from Taunton, R in
Fivehead just before garage and
follow signs. Car parking at Thimble
Hall next to garden, signed from
village centre. Home-made teas in
village hall. Combined adm £5, chd
free. Sat 4, Sun 5 June (2-6).

> **NEW LAUREL COTTAGE**
> Ann & Peter Cottell
>
> **NEW 8 MANOR ROAD**
> Wendy & Mike Webb
>
> **NEW MONKS ORCHARD**
> Maureen & David Bradshaw

Historic village dating from Saxon
times, located on edge of Somerset
Levels with many thatched stone
cottages. C13 Grade I listed church is
described as 'The Jewel in the Crown
of Somerset Churches'! ³/₄ m steam-
operated miniature ride-on railway line
through scenic route hopefully
operating. Open church tower - have
a go at bell-ringing. 3 well-established
unique gardens with many exquisite
herbaceous borders. Laurel Cottage:
¹/₂ -acre cottage garden developed
over 23 yrs. Paths weave through
herbaceous borders where plants are
encouraged to self-seed. Productive
vegetable and nursery area.
Monks Orchard: ³/₄ -acre garden
developed over 7 yrs. Many large
mixed borders with lots of unusual
plants. Stunning views. 8 Manor
Road: Award-winning garden.
Perennials, roses, clematis and much
more. Stunning views. 1st prize
Yarlington Housing Group Best
Overall Garden competition.
Wheelchair access to 2 gardens.
& ✿ ☕

70 JASMINE COTTAGE
26 Channel Road, Clevedon
BS21 7BY. Margaret & Michael
Redgrave, 01275 871850,
margaret@bologrew.net,
www.jasminecottage.bologrew.net.
12m W of Bristol. M5 J20. From
Clevedon seafront travel N (0.8m), via
Wellington Terrace follow winding rd
to St Mary's Church, R into Channel
Rd, approx 100yds on L. Bus stop nr
church - X25 & X26. Adm £3, chd
free. Every Thurs 26 May to
11 Aug (11-4). Visitors also
welcome by appt.
Cottage garden with a difference.
¹/₃ acre with intriguing layout, incl
sweet pea tunnel and mini potager.
Unusual plants, grown for sale and
displayed in beds and borders, incl
Dicentra macrocapnos, rhodochiton
and many, many others. From July
varieties of 50-strong salvia grow,
begin to bloom and continue their
display until frosts come. Featured in
Somerset Country Gardener &
Somerset Life. RHS Recommended
Garden.
✿ ☎

71 JEN'S GARDYN
4 Wroxham Drive, Little Stoke
BS34 6EJ. Jennifer & Gary
Ellington, 01454 610317,
jenniferearl@hotmail.com,
jensgardyn.moonfruit.com. 5m N of
Bristol city centre. From Cribbs

Causeway r'about go S on A38. Over
next r'about, L into Stoke Lane, 4th L
into Braydon Ave, 1st L into Wroxham
Dr. Light Refreshments & teas incl
home grown herbal teas. Adm £3,
chd free. Suns 24, 31 July (2-5)
Evening Opening £4.50, wine,
Fri 29 July (6-9). Also open
Mandy's Garden Suns 24th, 31st
July. Visitors also welcome by appt
July/Aug max 8.
Only 15ft x 31ft but very tall! The
sky's the limit in our World Jungle.
Passionately planted. Bamboo,
grasses, palms, bananas from all
corners of the earth. Fernery, grotto,
wildlife stream, goldfish ponds.
Extensive collection of rare, healing
and aromatic herbs. Inspirational,
innovative, intimate. The smallest
jungle in the world... probably!
Organic home-grown herbs, plants &
seeds for sale. Herb tasting and info.
Rare plant/herb raffle every hr.
Featured in Amateur Gardening
magazine & local press.
✿ ☕ ☎

The smallest jungle in the world . . . probably . . . !

72 28 KENSINGTON ROAD
St George, Bristol BS5 7NB. Mr
Grenville Johnson & Mr Alan Elms,
0117 9496788,
victorianhouse@blueyonder.co.uk,
www.victorianhousegarden.pwp.
blueyonder.co.uk. 2¹/₂ m E of Bristol
City centre. Take A420 in direction of
St George towards Kingswood &
Chippenham Rd. At Bell Hill St
George, turn into Kensington Rd.
Entrance to garden in Cromwell Rd at
side of house. Adm £4, chd free.
Open Suns 3, 10 July (2-5) by
appointment only. Visitors also
welcome by appt on other days,
please contact us to check
availability.
Award-winning, small courtyard town
house garden on two levels with
classical features and statuary
incorporating a temple folly ruin in an
Italianate setting, exotic and
S-hemisphere garden, Woodland
garden, stumpery, grotto and wildlife
pond. Featured in 100 Dream

University of Bristol Botanic Garden

Gardens of England & Big Gardens in Small Spaces and on television and local radio. Winners of Bristol in Bloom.

73 ◆ **KILVER COURT**
Kilver St, Shepton Mallet BA4 5NF. Roger Saul, 01749 340410, www.kilvercourt.com. *Directly off A37, opp Gaymer Cider factory.* **Adm £3.50, chd free. For NGS: Wed 18 May (10-4). For other opening times and information, please phone or see garden website.**
Created in 1800s and restored in 1960s by the Showering family, who commissioned George Whiteleg to recreate his gold medal winning Chelsea garden. Millpond, boating lake, herbaceous borders and parterre with the most stunning feature being the Grade II listed viaduct built for the Somerset and Dorset railway. Featured in local press. Wheelchair access to main features.

74 **KINGSDON NURSERY GARDEN**
Kingsdon, Somerton TA11 7LE. Patricia Marrow, 01935 840232. *2m SE of Somerton. Off B3151 Ilchester rd. From Ilchester r'about on A303 follow NT signs to Lytes Cary; L opp gates, ½ m to Kingsdon. Drive through village, nursery signs on L gate.* Home-made teas. **Adm £3.50, chd free. Suns 22 May; 19 June; Sat 9 July (2-6). Visitors also welcome by appt all yr, coaches permitted.**
2-acre plantsman's garden with lovely plants to see. Large nursery. Selection of trees, shrubs and herbaceous and rock plants for sale. Knowledgeable gardener to help with new or established gardens.

75 **KNOLL COTTAGE**
Stogumber TA4 3TN. Elaine & John Leech, 01984 656689, john@leech45.com, www.knoll-cottage.co.uk. *3m SE of Williton. From Taunton take A358 towards*

Minehead. After 11m turn L to Stogumber. In centre of Stogumber, R towards Williton. After ⅓ m, R up narrow lane, follow signs for parking. **Adm £3, chd free. Visitors welcome by appt.**
2-acre garden started from fields in 1998. Extensive mixed beds with shrubs, perennials and annuals. Over 80 different roses. Woodland area incl many different rowans, hawthorns and birches. Pond, vegetable and fruit area.

76 **LANGFORD COURT**
Langford BS40 5DA. Sir David & Lady Wills, 01934 862338, ladywills@langfordcourt.co.uk. *11½ m S of Bristol. 150yds S of A38 Bristol to Bridgwater rd. 1½ m N of Churchill T-lights. Signed Upper Langford.* Home-made teas. **Adm £3.50, chd free. Sun 3 July (2-5). Visitors also welcome by appt.**
3½ acres. Lawns and trees. Topiary with Thyme Walk. New formal garden designed by Nicky Rylance. Pleasant setting and outlook. Water garden and woodland walk. Orangerie.

77 **LIFT THE LATCH**
Blacklands Lane, Forton, Chard TA20 2NF. Pauline & David Wright, 01460 64752, davidwright@ltlpublishing.freeserve.co.uk. *1½ m S of Chard. Blacklands Lane is off B3162 at E end of Forton from Chard.* Home-made teas. **Adm £2.50, chd free. Suns, Mons 14, 15, 28, 29 Aug (1-5). Also open 20 Bubwith Rd, Chard. Visitors also welcome by appt all yr incl groups up to 50.**
Pretty cottage garden bordered by small stream. Large wildlife pond and raised fish pond. Wide variety of evergreens, giving yr-round interest. Particularly colourful rhododendrons, azaleas and acers in spring and vivid autumn colours from many trees and shrubs such as rhus, liquidambar and cornus, but interesting 365 days of the yr.

78 **LITTLE GARTH**
Dowlish Wake, Ilminster TA19 0NX. Roger & Marion Pollard, 01460 52594. *2m S of Ilminster. Turn R off Ilminster to Crewkerne rd at Kingstone Cross, then L, follow Dowlish Wake sign. Turn L at Glebe Cottage (white cottage) before reaching church. Turn R following*

signs. Speke Hall car park in front of nearby church may be used. Cream teas. **Adm £3, chd free. Sats 30 Apr; 14, 28 May; 11, 25 June; 9, 23 July; 13, 27 Aug; 10 Sept (10-5.30). Visitors also welcome by appt.** 1/2 -acre plantsman's garden for all seasons with many interesting and unusual perennials. Although essentially cottage style, emphasis is placed on the artistic arrangement of plants, using foliage, grasses and colour themes. Cream teas, plants for sale and public toilets at nearby Cider Mill.

79 LITTLE YARFORD FARMHOUSE
Yarford, Kingston St Mary TA2 8AN. Brian Bradley, 01823 451350, yarford@ic24.net. 3 1/2 m N of Taunton. From Taunton on Kingston St Mary rd. At 30mph sign turn L at Parsonage Lane. Continue 1 1/4 m W, to Yarford sign. Continue 400yds. Turn R up concrete rd. Park on L. Cream teas and light refreshments. **Adm £4, chd free. Fri 13 May (11-5), Sat 14, Sun 15 May (2-6), Mon 16 May (11-5). Visitors also welcome by appt.**
This unusual garden embraces a C17 house (not open) overgrown with a tapestry of climbing plants. The 3 ponds exhibit a wide range of aquatic gems. The special interest is an array of unusual and rare trees all differing in shape and colour (especially weeping and fastigiate). The 3 acres are a delight to both artist and plantsman. Some slopes.

GROUP OPENING

80 NEW LITTLETON-ON-SEVERN GARDENS
Littleton-on-Severn BS35 1NT. 10m N of Bristol, 3 1/2 m SW of Thornbury. From old Severn Bridge on M48 take B4461 to Alveston. In Elberton, 1st L to village. **Combined adm £5, chd free. Sun 12 June (1-5).**

NEW HAYWOOD HOUSE
Andrew & Kath Bealing. 1st house on R before entering village

THE LINTELS
Mr & Mrs Ernest Baker. 4th house 100yds past Field Lane

SUNNYSIDE COTTAGE
Harold & Hesta Knapp.

Through village past the Old School. Opp Evangelical Church

3 contrasting gardens. Haywood House: approx 1 1/2 acres with panoramic views. Lawns, mixed borders, koi pond, small arboretum, rockeries. The Lintels: Small cottage-type garden in front of house with good variety of herbaceous plants. Main attraction Japanese garden at rear with waterfall, koi carp, stream, teahouse. Sunnyside Cottage: Approx 1/2 acre of mixed perennial borders, water feature, shrubs, vegetables, also far-reaching views. Over 60 different roses and 30 clematis, several wisterias and a Blue Atlas cedar. Wheelchair access to 2 gardens.

A lovely place to sit and stare . . .

81 ◆ LOWER SEVERALLS
Crewkerne TA18 7NX. Mary Pring, 01460 73234, www.lowerseveralls.co.uk. 1 1/2 m NE of Crewkerne. Signed off A30 Crewkerne to Yeovil rd or A356 Crewkerne to A303. **Adm £3, chd free. For NGS: Suns, Sats 8 May; 18, 19 June; 2 July (Sats 10-5, Suns 2-5). For other opening times and information please visit website or telephone.**
3-acre plantsman's garden beside early Hamstone farmhouse. Herbaceous borders and island beds with collections of unusual plants, shrubs and interesting features incl dogwood basket, wadi, scented garden. Green roofed building. Nursery specialises in herbs, and herbaceous perennials. Featured in Camping & Caravanning.

82 ◆ LYTES CARY MANOR
Kingsdon TA11 7HU. National Trust, 01458 224471, www.nationaltrust.org.uk. 3m SE of Somerton. Signed from Podimore r'about at junction of A303, A37, take A372. **Adm £5.75, chd £2.95. For NGS: Mon 28 Mar; Fri 22 July; Mon 3 Oct (11-5). For other opening times and information, please phone or see garden website.**
Garden laid out in series of rooms with many contrasts, topiary, mixed borders and herbal border based on famous C16 Lytes Herbal, which can be seen in house. Garden and Behind the Scenes tours at 12pm and 2.30pm.

83 MANDY'S GARDEN
70 Silver Birch Close, Little Stoke BS34 6RN. Nora McMullen. 5m N of Bristol. From M5 J16 take A38/Gloucester Rd towards Filton. Over next r'about, L into Stoke Lane, 3rd L into Braydon Ave, 3rd R into Silver Birch Cl. **Adm £2.50, chd free. Suns 24, 31 July (2-5). Also open Jen's Gardyn.**
Small back garden which owners have turned, over 23 yrs, into colourful oasis. A lovely place to sit and stare. Mature trees and shrubs. Roses, many clematis, some over arches. Hanging baskets. Annual and perennial plants provide colour throughout the season.

GROUP OPENING

84 MARSHFIELD GARDENS
Marshfield SN14 8LR. 7m NE of Bath. From Bath A46 to Cold Ashton r'about, turn R onto A420. Marshfield 2m. From M4 J18, turn R onto A46 and L at Cold Ashton r'about. May - light lunches & home-made teas at 111 High Street; flowers, music and teas in St Mary's Church. July - teas at Marshfield Chapel, 98 High St. **Combined adm £5 May, £3.50 July, chd free. Sat 28, Sun 29 May; Sat 9 July (1-5). Not open May - 3 Tanners Walk; not open July - 4 Old School Court & 111 High St.**

4 OLD SCHOOL COURT
Mrs Jenny Wilkinson Not open 9 July.

WEIR COTTAGE
Weir Lane. Ian & Margaret Jones. Opp Old School Court

43 HIGH STREET
Linda & Denis Beazer.
Continue on from Weir Cottage, entrance from Weir Lane

111 HIGH STREET
Joy & Mervyn Pierce.
Bristol end of village
Not open 9 July.

NEW▶ 42 HIGH STREET
Mary & Simon Turner.
Access from back lane

NEW▶ 3 TANNERS WALK
June & John Haynes
Not open 28/29 May.

6 gardens in large, interesting village. May - late spring gardens with newly-planted vegetable plots; July - summer interest with maturing vegetable plots (with luck). 4 Old School Court: Small courtyard garden packed full of plants in cottage garden style. Weir Cottage: Planted to give colour through the yr and to withstand the extremes of the Marshfield weather. 43 High Street: Walled garden with terraced potager. New for 2011, waterfall, pebble beach and bog garden. 111 High Street: Quiet, relaxing garden split into many areas. Pond, summerhouse, many seating places. 42 High Street: Well-established garden set in traditional burgage plot. 3 Tanners Walk: Small, enclosed garden incl roses, clematis in pots and raised beds. Circular footpath, gravel area. 28 May 10.30am - guided walk by Chief Cotswold Warden around access trail of Marshfield starting in Market place; 29 May 11am - guided walk by Chairman Marshfield & District Local History Society (01225 891229/ian@weircott.plus.com for more info).

85▶ MIDDLECOMBE NURSERY
Wrington Rd, Congresbury BS49 5AN. Nigel J North, www.middlecombenursery.co.uk. *Midway Bristol/Weston-super-Mare. On the edge of Congresbury, on the Bristol side, turn to Wrington along the Wrington Rd off the A370 Weston to Bristol rd. Garden 200yds on L.* Home-made teas. **Combined adm £4, chd free. Sun 3 July (10.30-5). Combined with Fernbank.**
Series of gardens, lovely country setting, woods bordering 3-acre nursery site. Different styles and features, excellent shrub borders and beds in sweeping lawn area alongside delightful fish pond. Surrounding patio gardens and water features ensure an enjoyable visit with a chance to see many of the nursery plants fully grown. Dogs on leads.

> Terraced sloping
> garden, with stream
> and waterfalls.
> Emphasis on
> natural look . . .

86▶ THE MILL HOUSE
Torbay Road, Castle Cary BA7 7DR. Peter Davies. *Do not go into Castle Cary Town Centre, but follow signs to Torbay Rd Industrial Estate (W). Entrances to Trading Estate on L. Park on Trading estate rds.* Home-made teas. **Adm £3.50, chd free. Sun 29, Mon 30 May (2-5).**
Approx 1-acre terraced sloping garden, with stream and waterfalls. Emphasis on natural look. Many interesting plants mingled with native flora. Bog garden with selection of candelabra and farina primulas, rodgersias and hostas; vegetable plot. Partial wheelchair access.

87▶ ◆ MILTON LODGE
Wells BA5 3AQ. Simon Tudway Quilter, 01749 672168, www.miltonlodgegardens.co.uk. *½ m N of Wells. From A39 Bristol-Wells, turn N up Old Bristol Rd; car park first gate on L.* **Adm £5, chd under 14 free. For NGS: Suns 15 May; 5 June; 10 July (2-5).**
Mature Grade II listed terraced garden with outstanding views of Wells Cathedral and Vale of Avalon. Mixed borders, roses, fine trees. Separate 7-acre arboretum. Open Tues, Weds, Suns, BHs, Easter - 31 Oct (2-5).

88▶ ◆ MONTACUTE HOUSE
Montacute TA15 6XP. National Trust, 01935 823289, www.nationaltrust.org.uk. *4m W of Yeovil. NT signs off A3088 & A303.* **Adm £6, chd £3. For NGS: Sat 18 June (11-5).** For other opening times and information, please phone or see garden website.
Magnificent Elizabethan house with contemporary garden layout. Fine stonework provides setting for informally planted mixed borders and old roses; range of garden features illustrates its long history. 80% wheelchair access.

89▶ 16 MONTROY CLOSE
Henleaze, Bristol BS9 4RS. Sue & Rod Jones, 0117 9624599. *3½ m N of Bristol city centre. On B4056 continue past all shops, R into Rockside Dr (opp Eastfield Inn). Up hill, across Xrds into The Crescent, Montroy Close is 3rd turning on L.* Home-made teas. **Adm £2.50, chd free. Sun 5 June (2-6).** Visitors also welcome by appt afternoons/eves in June.
Large SW-facing town garden on corner plot. 20ft stream, informal pond with pebble beach, pergola and seats. Lawn with curving flower beds incl fernery, shrubs, perennials, climbers, small rock gardens, unusual partitioned greenhouse with alpine bench. Hanging baskets and many pots of fuchsias etc. New for 2011: 8 ft wide arch with climbers. Width of gateway: 79cm.

90▶ NEW▶ ◆ NEWARK PARK
Ozleworth GL12 7PZ. National Trust, 01453 842644, www.nationatrust.org.uk. *2m E of Wotton-under-Edge. Follow signs off A4135 to Ozleworth.* **Adm £6.25, chd £3.15. For NGS: Wed 16 Feb (11-4.30).** For other opening times and information, please phone or see garden website.
Wild woodland garden with good display of snowdrops. Wonderful views to the South. Limited wheelchair access, garden on slope.

91▶ 26 NORTHUMBERLAND ROAD
Redland BS6 7BB. Gwendoline Todd. *Bristol. 5 mins walk from Redland Stn, close to and parallel with Cranbrook Rd.* Home-made teas at No 24 on Sat and opp at No 31 on

Sun. **Adm £3, chd free. Sat 11, Sun 12 June (11-6).**
Fragrant country cottage garden in middle of city. Delightful small garden packed with wide range of plants and climbers with emphasis on perfume. Patio full of pots. New hothouse for exotic plants. Shady front garden has jungle effect and is home to ferns, palms, hellabores, cordylines and a wonderful Dicksonia antarctica.

92 NEW THE OLD RECTORY
Church St, Limington, nr Yeovil BA22 8EQ. John Langdon, 01935 840127, jdlpv@aol.com. *2m E of Ilchester. From A303 exit on A37 to Yeovil/Ilchester. At 1st r'about L to Ilchester/Limington. 2nd R to Limington. Continue 1½ m.* Home-made teas. **Adm £3.50, chd free. Sun 29, Mon 30 May (2-6).** Visitors also welcome by appt May/June & Aug/Sept only, max 10, no coaches.
Romantic walled gardens of 1½ acres. Formal parterres, herbaceous borders. Many unusual shrubs and trees incl 200 yr-old lucombe oak, liriodendron, paulownia, davidia, laburnocytisus, leycesteria and poncirus. Extensive planting of bulbs incl galanthus, anemone blanda, winter aconites, tulips and alliums. Gravel drive, one short slope.

93 35 OLD STATION GARDENS
Henstridge, Templecombe BA8 0PU. Mary McLean, 01963 364321, marysmclean@btinternet.com. *6m E of Sherborne, 9m W of Shaftesbury on A30. Signage from A30 T-lights at Henstridge and at rd end.* Home-made teas if required. **Combined adm £4, chd free. Combined with Cherry Bolberry Farm.** Visitors welcome by appt June only for groups of 10+, coach parties welcome, please book early.
Small owner-designed plantaholic's garden. Many exotics mixed with roses, clematis and herbaceous. Raised beds, pergolas, patio and pond. Floriferous and abundant planting with added spring underplanting of bulbs to give extra interest. Bonsai collection of native and exotic trees. Very limited access to back garden patio, paths not suitable for wheelchairs/pushchairs.

94 OLIVE COTTAGE
Langley Marsh, Wiveliscombe TA4 2UJ. Frankie Constantine, 01984 624210, frankieconstantine@hotmail.co.uk. *1m NW of Wiveliscombe. From Taunton take B3227 to Wiveliscombe. Turn R at T-lights. At Square turn R past White Hart & continue 1m. Olive Cottage on R before Three Horseshoes PH.* Home-made teas. **Adm £3, chd free (share to St Margarets Hospice). Sun 29, Mon 30 May; Sun 26 June (2-6).** Visitors also welcome by appt, May, June, July only.
An informal cottage garden of about ⅔ acre created by the owner for over 30yrs. Small pond, bog garden and new rockery, together with shrubs, perennials, climbers and trees create colour and interest throughout the yr. Productive kitchen garden and 2 greenhouses where many of the plants are raised. Exhibition of local arts and crafts. Gravel paths, short slopes, unfenced pond, overhanging shrubs.

95 ORCHARD WYNDHAM
nr Williton TA4 4HH. The Trustees. *7m SE of Minehead, 16m from Taunton. 16m Taunton. In Williton take A39 towards Minehead and immed L opp agricultural machines showroom signed Bakelite Museum, follow lane past church to lodge, long drive to house.* **Adm £3, chd free. Sun 22 May (2-5.30).**
Garden of historic house (not open on NGS days) in parkland setting: woods, interesting old trees, borders, rose walk, small lake, wild garden.

96 ORGANIC BLOOMS
Latteridge Lane, Latteridge, Bristol BS37 9TS. Jo & Chris Wright, www.organicblooms.co.uk. *5m W of Yate. 6 miles from Junction 16 of the M5, on the B4059 that runs between the A38 and Iron Acton, South Gloucestershire.* Tea & Light Refreshments. Home made cakes. **Adm £2.50, chd free. Sun 17 July (11-4).**
We are a working cut flower nursery. We specialise in growing traditional cut flower crops from sweet williams and anemone to zinnias, dahlias and sweetpeas. Flowers are grown using organic principles. We are opening our new site exclusively to NGS visitors this year! Site tours with explanation of organic cut flower

growing and demonstration of hand-tied bunches. Plants and cut flowers for sale. Light refreshments. Featured in The English Garden. Woodchip paths.

97 ◆ THE ORGANIC GARDEN AT HOLT FARM
Bath Road, Blagdon BS40 7SQ. Mr & Mrs Tim Mead, 01761 461650, holtfarm-gardens@yeovalley.co.uk, www.theorganicgardens.co.uk. *12m S of Bristol. Off A368 Weston-super-Mare to Bath rd, between Blagdon & Ubley. Entrance to Holt Farm approx ½ m outside Blagdon, on LH-side.* **Adm £4, chd free. For NGS: Mon 25 Apr (2-5). For other opening times and information, please phone or see garden website.**
One of a handful of organic ornamental gardens as certified by the Soil Association, 5 acres of contemporary planting, quirky sculptures, purple palace, glorious meadows, autumnal fireworks, posh vegetable patch. Great views, green ideas and most importantly sinful teas in the tea room. Featured in The English Garden, The Somerset Gardener & Western Daily Press.

Exhibition of local arts and crafts . . .

98 3 PALMER'S WAY
Hutton, Weston-super-Mare BS24 9QT. Mary & Peter Beckett, 01934 815110, macbeckett@tiscali.co.uk. *3m S of Weston-super-Mare. From A370 (N or S) follow signs to Hutton. L at PO, 1st L into St Mary's Rd, 2nd R to car park. Very limited disabled parking at garden.* Home-made teas. **Adm £3, chd free. Sun 26 June; Sun 10 July (2-5.30). Visitors also welcome by appt Weds in June and July.**
Average small suburban plot - no long

vistas or chance for your Sunday constitutional, but densely mixed planting includes 11 fruit trees, unusual perennials, grasses, box hedging, small ponds, hardy geraniums. Described as 'a plantman's garden' and 'an informal tapestry'. Plant list names 200 varieties. Lots of plants for sale. Chutneys, jams and jellies from own-grown produce. Cards and beadwork for sale. Some steps. Wheelchair access more limited if wet.

♿ ⚛ ☕ ☎

99 22 PARSON STREET

Bedminster BS3 5PT. Andrew Tyas, 0117 966 3553. *2m S of Bristol City centre. From Redcliffe area, take A38 through Bedminster into West St, L into Parson St, over bridge towards T-lights. Garden just before junction with Bedminster Rd and Parson St, nr Mansfield St.* Cream Teas. **Adm £2.50, chd free. Suns 26 June; 10, 17 July (10-4). Visitors also welcome by appt.**
Stunning, compact cottage-style garden with rich and versatile planting. Herbaceous perennials, unusual shrubs, exotic perennials such as echiums, banksia and protea. Tropical polytunnel containing many unusual exotic plants. Inspiration for the garden drawn from foreign travel. Front garden: rose garden with yew hedging. Featured in Amateur Gardening magazine and Country Gardener.

♿ ⚛ ☕ ☎

PEN MILL FARM
See Dorset.

100 PENWOOD FARM

Parchey, Chedzoy, nr Bridgwater TA7 8RW. Mr & Mrs E F W Clapp, 01278 451631, clapppauline@aol.com. *3¹/₂ m E of Bridgwater. Take A39 from Bridgwater. Bridge over M5, turn sharp R into Chedzoy Lane. At T-junction in village turn L. Pass church approx ³/₄ m. Penwood Farm facing sharp LH-bend. From Stawell off Glastonbury rd, cross bridge over King's Sedgemoor Drain (Parchey River). 1st house on L.* Home-made teas. **Adm £2.50, chd free. Suns 19, 26 June (2-5). Visitors also welcome by appt 14 June to 1 July only, coaches permitted, groups 10-48 persons.**
Plant lover's garden approx ³/₄ acre. Terrace, patio, pergola, gravel, rock, water and kitchen gardens. Hundreds

of different roses - old, 'new' English and modern; collections of clematis, hosta, penstemon, shrubs and herbaceous perennials, unusual plants and trees. Japanese-style bridge over sunken garden with water lilies. Blue garden, vegetable and cutting garden. Swallows nest in tractor shed tearoom.

⚛ ☕ ☎

101 ◆ PRIOR PARK LANDSCAPE GARDEN

Ralph Allen Drive, Bath BA2 5AH. National Trust, 01225 833422 www.nationaltrust.org.uk. *1m S of Bath. Visitors are advised to use public transport as there is no parking at Prior Park or nearby, except for disabled visitors. Telephone for 'How to get there' leaflet.* Light Refreshments situated by the lakes. Tea Kiosk open 11.30am - 4.30pm. **Adm £5.50, chd £3.50. For NGS: Sun 8 May (11-5.30). For other opening times and information, please phone or see garden website.**
Beautiful and intimate C18 landscape garden created by Bath entrepreneur Ralph Allen (1693-1764) with advice from the poet Alexander Pope and Capability Brown. Sweeping valley with magnificent views of city, Palladian bridge and lakes. Wilderness restoration, completed in 2007, involved reinstating the Serpentine Lake, Cascade and Cabinet to their former glory. See drifts of wild garlic carpeting the woodlands. Pick your own wild garlic leaves to experiment with the recipes we supply. The wilderness and view point are fully accessible. The rest of the garden is steep and uneven.

 ☕

102 ROCK HOUSE

Elberton BS35 4AQ. Mr & Mrs John Gunnery, 01454 413225. *10m N of Bristol. 3¹/₂ m SW Thornbury. From Old Severn Bridge on M48 take B4461 to Alveston. In Elberton, take 1st turning L to Littleton-on-Severn & turn immed R.* **Adm £2.50, chd free (share to St Johns Church, Elberton). Suns 30 Jan; 6 Feb 2011; 5, 12 Feb 2012 (11-4). Visitors also welcome by appt.**
1-acre walled garden undergoing improvement. Pond and old yew tree, mixed borders, cottage garden plants and developing woodland with many snowdrops.

⚛ ☎

103 13 RYDON CRESCENT

Cannington, Bridgwater TA5 2JT. John & Maureen Hudson. *4m W of Bridgwater. Off A39 Bridgwater to Minehead rd. Into Cannington 2nd turning R into Lonsdale Rd, 1st R into Rydon Cres.* **Adm £2, chd free. Suns 5 June; 4 Sept (10-5). Also open The Walled Gardens of Cannington.**
Downsized from The Mill, Cannington, which we opened for 18yrs. Small bungalow garden 42ft x 45ft at back and ¹/₃ of that at front. Designed and planted in last 3 yrs. Plantaholics' garden with 14 climbing roses and 60 clematis. Small vegetable and fruit garden, glasshouse and summerhouse. All on horrid clay soil.

♿

Garden of reflection depicting owner's life in New Zealand and England . . .

104 SALTFORD FARM BARN

565a Bath Road, Saltford BS31 3JS. Eve Hessey, 012225 873380, eve.hessey@blueyonder.co.uk. *6m W of Bath. On A4 between Bath & Bristol, Saltford Farm Barn is at Bath end of village. Parking arrangements will be signed - busy A4 not suitable for parking.* Home-made teas. **Adm £3, chd free. Sun 27 Mar (2-5.30). Visitors also welcome by appt.**
1-acre garden with 5 main separate gardens. Ornamental vegetable garden with trained fruit trees contained within scented hedges of lavender, rosemary and box. Woodland garden with seasonal shrubs and trees underplanted with spring bulbs, hellebores, ferns, foxgloves and alpine strawberries. Garden of reflection depicting owner's life in New Zealand and England, labyrinth, meadow, orchard and Mediterranean garden. Crafts.

⚛ ☕ ☎

105 SELF REALIZATION MEDITATION HEALING CENTRE GARDEN

Laurel Lane, Queen Camel BA22 7NU. SRMH Charitable Trust, 01935 850266, www.selfrealizationcentres.org. *6m NE of Yeovil. A359 S from Sparkford r'about (on A303) to Queen Camel. Garden 100yds off High St, R after school and before Hair Studio. Park opp school in field, disabled parking at SRMH centre. Follow signs for other car parking.* **Adm £3, chd free. Sat 11 June (2-5). Visitors also welcome by appt.**
Peaceful 3-acre garden with varied vistas, trees, lawns and Mediterranean area, surrounding spiritual retreat and training centre. Stunning herbaceous borders and fragrant old roses around C17 farmhouse (not open). Wildflower tumps, pond, waterfall, maze, herb beds and meditation room garden. Oriental garden and koi pond by arrangement only.

106 SERRIDGE HOUSE

Henfield Road, Coalpit Heath BS36 2UY. Mrs J Manning, 01454 773188. *9m N of Bristol. On A432 at Coalpit Heath T-lights (opp church), turn into Henfield Rd. R at PH, 1/2 m small Xrds, house with iron gates on corner.* **Adm £4 incl cream tea, chd free. Visitors welcome by appt July/Aug only, groups of 10+.**
2½ -acre garden with mature trees, heather and conifer beds, island beds mostly of perennials, woodland area with pond. Colourful courtyard with old farm implements. Lake views and lakeside walks. Unique tree carvings.

SHAPCOTT BARTON ESTATE

See Devon.

107 ◆ SHERBORNE GARDEN

nr Litton, Norton-Radstock BA3 4PP. Mr & Mrs John Southwell, 01761 241220. *15m S of Bristol. 15m W of Bath, 7m N of Wells. On B3114 Chewton Mendip to Harptree rd, 1/2 m past The Kings Arms. Car park in field.* **Adm £3.50, chd free. For NGS: Sun 13, Mon 14 Feb; Sun 13 Mar (11-4), groups welcome by appointment. For other opening times and information, please phone or see garden website.**
4½ -acre gently sloping garden with small pinetum, holly wood and many unusual trees and shrubs. Cottage garden leading to privy. 3 ponds linked by wadi and rills with stone and wooden bridges. Hosta walk leading to pear and nut wood. Rondel and gravel gardens with grasses and phormiums. Collections of daylilies, rambling and rose species. Good labelling. Plenty of seats.

108 SOLE RETREAT

Haydon Drove, West Horrington, nr Wells BA5 3EH. Jane Clisby, www.soleretreat.co.uk. *3m NE of Wells. From Wells take B3139 to the Horringtons. After 3m, L for Sole Retreat Reflexology, garden 50yds on L.* Home-made teas. **Adm £3, chd free. Sun 17 July (11-5).**
It is a challenge to garden at almost 1000ft on the Mendip Hills AONB, close to the cathedral city of Wells. Peaceful garden full of old garden favourites set in 1/3 acre. Cottage garden style within dry stone walls and raw face bedrock. 9 differing areas incl sun terrace and swimming pool, water feature and pool, therapy garden, hidden contemplation garden, fernery and vegetable plot.

Ston Easton Park

Featured on BBC Radio Somerset. Some gravel.

109 SOMERFOSS

Bath Road, Oakhill BA3 5AG. Ewan & Rosemary Curphey, 01749 840542, ecurphey@aol.com. *3m N of Shepton Mallet. From Oakhill School 1/4 m N on A367. Parking in lay-by on R.* Home-made teas. **Adm £4, chd free. Weds 20, 27 Apr; Sun 14, Wed 24 Aug; Sun 4 Sept (2-6). Visitors also welcome by appt April, May, May, Aug, for groups of 10+, small coaches only.**
2-acre garden in peaceful valley planted for year round interest. Banks of primroses, cowslips, violets and daffodils in April. In August island beds full of grasses, prairie plants and perennials. New crevice garden. Untouched meadow areas grow spring wild flowers with a stand of wild orchids flowering in June. Abundant insect life. Have teas and enjoy the view over the garden from our large decks. Steep slopes, steps and uneven ground.

110 ♦ **SPECIAL PLANTS**
Greenways Lane, Nr Cold Ashton
SN14 8LA. Derry Watkins, 01225
891686, www.specialplants.net. *6m
N of Bath on A46. From Bath on A46,
turn L into Greenways Lane just
before r'about with A420.* **Adm £4,
chd free. For NGS: Thurs 16 June;
21 July; 18 Aug; 15 Sept; 20 Oct
(11-5). For other opening times and
information, please phone or see
garden website.**
Architect-designed ³/₄ -acre hillside
garden with stunning views. Started
autumn 1996. Exotic plants. Gravel
gardens for borderline hardy plants.
Black and white (purple and silver)
garden. Vegetable garden and
orchard. Hot border. Lemon and lime
bank. Annual, biennial and tender
plants for late summer colour. Spring-
fed ponds. Bog garden. Woodland
walk. Allium alley. Free list of plants in
garden.

111 ▶ **SPINDLE COTTAGE**
Binegar Green, Binegar, Nr Wells
BA3 4UE. Angela & Alban Bunting,
01749 840497,
angela@spindlecottage.co.uk,
www.spindlecottage.co.uk. *15m S
of Bath, 5m N of Wells. Binegar
Green, parking on the Green only for
disabled, other parking in nearby field.*
Light ploughman's lunch &
homemade cream teas. **Adm £3, chd
free. Sun 19 June (11.30-5.30).
Visitors also welcome by appt
small or large groups.**
Unique, magical cottage garden with
3 period playhouses: Ruth's Cottage,
Gothic; Tom's Lodge, Elizabethan;
Charlotte's Post Office, Victorian.
Gazebo, jousting tent, hedgehog
house, potting shed, wildlife pond,
well, loggia, Owl and Pussycat garden
and a Norman tower. Productive
organic vegetable garden. Places to
sit with your cream tea. Live music.
Featured in local press and on Radio
Bristol & BBC Gardeners' World.

112 ▶ **STANTON COURT NURSING
HOME**
Stanton Drew BS39 4ER. Pam
Townsend. *5m S of Bristol. From
Bristol on A37, R onto B3130 signed
Chew Magna. 1.4m, L at old thatched
toll house into Stanton Drew, 1st
property on L.* Light lunches and
cream teas. **Adm £2.50, chd free.
Sun 15 May; Sun 11 Sept (1-4).**
2 acres of tranquil gardens around
gracious Georgian House (grade II

listed). Mature trees, extensive
herbaceous borders with many
interesting plants and spring bulbs.
Large vegetable garden, fruit trees
and soft fruit bushes; raised beds
planted by local primary school.
Gardener Judith Chubb Whittle keeps
this lovely garden interesting in all
seasons. Prehistoric stone circle can
be seen from the garden. Featured in
Somerset Country Gardener and local
press.

113 ▶ **STOBERRY GARDEN**
Stoberry Park, Wells BA5 3LD.
Frances & Tim Young, 01749
672906, stay@stoberry-park.co.uk.
*¹/₂ m N of Wells. From Bristol - Wells
on A39, L into College Rd and immed
L through Stoberry Park.* **Adm £3.50,
chd free. Sats, Suns, Tues, Weds,
Fris 17, 18, 20, 21, 23, 24, 25, 27,
28, 30 Sept; Sat 1, Sun 2 Oct
(11.30-5).**
With breathtaking views over Wells
and the Vale of Avalon, this 6-acre
family garden planted sympathetically
within its landscape provides a
stunning combination of vistas
accented with wildlife ponds, water
features, sculpture, 1¹/₂ -acre walled
garden, sunken garden, gazebo,
potager, lime walk. Colour and
interest in every season; spring bulbs,
irises, roses, acer glade, salvias.
Stoberry will host local sculptors
showing their work as part of this
glorious garden during Somerset Arts
Week. Incl ceramics, water features,
stainless steel work, knitted wire
sculpture, range of steel, copper and
wire sculptures and more. Featured in
Sunday Times and Historic Gardens
of Somerset.

*Owl and Pussycat
garden and a
Norman tower . . .*

GROUP OPENING

114 ▶ **STOGUMBER GARDENS**
Stogumber TA4 3SZ. *11m NW of
Taunton. On A358. Sign to
Stogumber, W of Crowcombe. Maps
given to all visitors.* Home-made teas
in Village Hall. **Combined adm £4,
chd free. Sun 19 June (2-6).**

> **BRAGLANDS BARN**
> Simon & Sue Youell
> www.braglandsbarn.com
>
> **BROOK HOUSE**
> Brook Street. Dr & Mrs J
> Secker-Walker.
> *Next to car park*
>
> **CRIDLANDS STEEP**
> Mrs A M Leitch
>
> **FAIRLANDS**
> 3 Hill St. Mrs B Simms
>
> **KNOLL COTTAGE**
> Elaine & John Leech
> (See separate entry)
> www.knoll-cottage.co.uk
>
> **POUND HOUSE**
> Mr & Mrs B Hibbert

6 delightful and very varied gardens in
picturesque village at edge of
Quantocks. There are small and not-
so-small, densely-planted cottage
gardens in village centre, a semi-wild
garden, and a couple of 2-acre
gardens on outskirts of village, with
many rare and unusual plants. The
conditions range from waterlogged
clay to well-drained sand. Ponds, bog
gardens, vegetable and fruit gardens,
collection of over 80 different roses,
even a cider-apple orchard. Fine
views of surrounding countryside.
Disabled access to all gardens, dogs
on leads allowed in 4 gardens.

GROUP OPENING

115 ▶ **STOKE ST MARY GARDENS**
TA3 5BY, 01823 442556,
stepcroc@btinternet.com. *2¹/₂ m SE
of Taunton. From M5 J25 take A358
S towards Ilminster. Turn 1st R after
1¹/₂ m. 1st R in Henlade then 1st L
signed Stoke St Mary. Car parking in
village hall car park, no parking at
either garden.* Home-made teas.
**Combined adm £5, chd free.
Visitors welcome by appt** May to
Sept incl, groups of 10+.

FYRSE COTTAGE
Miss S Crockett
01823 442556
stepcroc@btinternet.com

TUCKERS FARMHOUSE
Rebecca Pow & Charles Clark
01823 443816
rebecca@powproductions.tv

Village nestles below beautiful backdrop of Stoke Hill. C13 church (with stained glass windows by the renowned Patrick Reyntiens), popular Half Moon Inn, playground at nearby Village Hall. Fyrse Cottage: secluded cottage garden with oriental flavour. ¹/₂ acre of lush planting with stream, pond, pergola, lots of sculptures and Chinese pots. Birch avenue leading to ¹/₂ -acre wildlife area. Gravel and flower gardens. Oil paintings and cards for sale. Tuckers Farmhouse: family garden in lovely rural location. Formal/cottage-style extending to natural with wildlife. Jekyll-style border and 'busy persons' gravel/grass border. Topiary, exotic planting in courtyard, pear tree avenue. Fruit garden, raised bed vegetable garden, a very small smallholding. Tuckers Farmhouse featured in Amateur Gardening. Wheelchair access to Tuckers Farmhouse.

---

116 ◆ **STON EASTON PARK**
Ston Easton BA3 4DF, 01761 241631, www.stoneaston.co.uk. *On A37 between Bath & Wells. Entrance to Park from main rd (A37) in centre of village, opp bus shelter.* **Adm £3.50, chd free. For NGS: Wed 3 Aug (10.30-4). For other opening times and information, please phone or see garden website.**
A hidden treasure in the heart of the Mendips. Walk through the historic 30 acres of Repton landscape alongside R Norr to the productive, walled, Victorian kitchen garden. Also visit octagonal rose garden, stunning herbaceous border, numerous colourful flowerbeds, fruit cage and orchard. Gravel paths, steep slopes.

117 NEW **SUNNY BANK**
High Street, Nunney, Frome BA11 4LZ. Mr & Mrs S Thomas. *3m S of Frome. 50 metres from market square, 1m from Nunney Catch Services off A361.* Home-made teas. **Adm £3, chd free. Sun 10 July (11-5).**
Bamboo and herbaceous borders

divide this ¹/₂ -acre garden from 2 subtropical houses containing cacti, succulents and unusual plants to a dappled fern area, raised pond and kitchen garden. In shade, provided by a mature acer, is a collection of hostas, tree ferns and woodland plants. Slight incline from rd at garden entrance. One subtropical house not accessible.

> Winding paths, ponds and waterfalls . . . an interesting garden . . .

118 ▶ **SUTTON HOSEY MANOR**
Long Sutton TA10 9NA. Roger Bramble, 0207 3906700, rbramble@bdbltd.co.uk. *2m E of Langport, on A372. Gates N of A372 at E end of Long Sutton.* Home-made teas. **Adm £3.50, chd £2. Sun 17 July (2.30-6). Visitors also welcome by appt after mid July.**
3 acres, of which 2 walled. Lily canal through pleached limes leading to amelanchier walk past duck pond; rose and juniper walk from Italian terrace; Judas tree avenue; Ptelea walk. Ornamental potager. Drive-side shrubbery. Music by players from The Sinfonia of Westminster.

119 ◆ **TINTINHULL**
nr Yeovil BA22 8PZ. National Trust, 01935 823289, www.nationaltrust.org.uk. *5m NW of Yeovil. Tintinhull village. Signs on A303, W of Ilchester.* **Adm £5.90, chd £2.90. For NGS: Sat 18 June (11-5). For other opening times and information, please phone or see garden website.**
C17 and C18 house (not open). Famous 2-acre garden in compartments, developed 1900 to present day, influenced by Hidcote; many good and uncommon plants.

120 **TORMARTON COURT**
Church Road, Tormarton GL9 1HT. Noreen & Bruce Finnamore, 07896 482468, na1young@yahoo.co.uk. *3m E Chipping Sodbury, off A46 J to M4. Follow signs to Tormarton, opp Tormarton Church.* Home-made teas. **Adm £5, chd free. Fri 22 Apr; Fri 24 June (10-4). Visitors also welcome by appt Weekdays April - July only.**
11 acres of formal and natural gardens in stunning Cotswold setting. Features incl roses, herbaceous, kitchen garden, Mediterranean garden, mound and natural pond. Extensive walled garden, spring glade and meadows with young and mature trees.

121 **TRANBY HOUSE**
Norton Lane, Whitchurch BS14 0BT. Jan Barkworth. *5m S of Bristol. ¹/₂ m S of Whitchurch. Leave Bristol on A37 Wells Rd, through Whitchurch village, 1st turning on R signed Norton Malreward.* Home-made teas. **Adm £3, chd free. Wed 8 June; Thur 14 July (1-4); Sun 21 Aug (2-5).**
1¹/₄ -acre well-established informal garden, designed and planted to encourage wildlife. Wide variety of trees, shrubs and herbaceous plants; ponds and wild flower meadow.

122 **8 TROSSACHS DRIVE**
Bathampton, Bath BA2 6RP. Sheila Batterbury, 01225 447864, sheila@batterbury88.co.uk, www.sheilabatterbury.co.uk. *1m E of Bath. On A36. From Bath, 2nd R up Warminster Rd (A36) into Trossachs Drive. From Warminster, 3rd L on entering Bathampton.* Teas on request. **Adm £5, chd free. Visitors welcome by appt May and June. Roses featured in June. Max 12. Small coaches permitted. Teas on request.**
Terraced garden with views over Bath. Winding paths, ponds and waterfalls. Unusual plants and shrubs, rockeries, bog garden, herbaceous perennials, old roses, sitting areas with fine views over the countryside. An interesting garden with the benefit of National Trust woods as backdrop. A haven for wildlife. A plantswoman's garden. Featured on BBC Radio. Partial wheelchair access.

Ash Cottage

pollination/flowering plant evolution. Glasshouses, home to Giant Amazon Waterlily, tropical fruit and medicinal plants, orchids and cacti. Unique sacred lotus collection. Bristol Annual Honey Festival - exhibits, stands, demonstrations and live hives. Featured on BBC TV. Assistance required for wheelchair users through evolutionary dell. Glasshouses negotiable with care.

♿ ⦿ ☕

125 VELLACOTT
Lawford, Crowcombe TA4 4AL. **Kevin & Pat Chittenden.** *9m NW of Taunton. Off A358, signed Lawford. For directions phone 01984 618249.* Home-made teas. **Adm £2.50, chd free. Sun 5, Thur 16 June (11-5).** Large S-facing cottage garden with splendid panoramic views. Wide range of plants and trees. Ornamental vegetable garden and other interesting features - ruin still under construction!

⦿ ☕

126 ◆ THE WALLED GARDENS OF CANNINGTON
Bowling Green (Church St), Cannington TA5 2HA. **Bridgwater College, 01278 655042, www.canningtonwalledgardens.co. uk.** *3m NW of Bridgwater. On A39 Bridgwater-Minehead rd - at 1st r'about in Cannington 2nd exit, through village. War memorial, 1st L into Bowling Green (Church St) then 1st L, car park on R.* **Adm £3.50, chd free, concessions £2.50. For NGS: Suns 5 June; 4 Sept (10-5). Also open 13 Rydon Crescent. For other opening times and information, please phone or see garden website.**
Lying within the grounds of medieval priory, the gardens have undergone extensive redevelopment over last few yrs. Features, both classic and contemporary, incl hot herbaceous border, stunning blue garden, sub-tropical walk, Victorian-style fernery and large botanical glasshouse. Some gravel paths. One mobility scooter available.

♿ ⦿ ☕

127 WATCOMBE
92 Church Road, Winscombe BS25 1BP. **Peter & Ann Owen, 01934 842666, peter.o@which.net.** *2m NW of Axbridge. From Axbridge, A371 to A38 N. Turn R up hill then next L into Winscombe Hill. After 1m reach The Square. Pink house on L*

123 TRUFFLES
Church Lane, Bishop Sutton BS39 5UP. **Sally Monkhouse, 01275 333665.** *10m N of Wells. On A368 Bath to Weston-Super-Mare rd take rd opp Bishop Sutton PO/stores towards Hinton Blewett. 1st R into Church Lane.* Home-made teas. **Adm £3, chd free. Sun 12, Mon 13 June (2-6). Visitors also welcome by appt.**
2 acres, intriguing and surprising garden set in countryside. Formal and semi-formal planting linked with meandering paths. Secret Sylvan valley and small stream, amphitheatre, wildlife pond, wild flower bed and meadow. 1/4 -acre kitchen garden with long, large waist-high raised beds, new herb and new rose garden. Ceramic exhibits. Partial access, gravel and grass paths, some steep slopes.

♿ ✉ ☕ ☎

124 ◆ UNIVERSITY OF BRISTOL BOTANIC GARDEN
Stoke Park Road, Stoke Bishop, Bristol BS9 1JG, 0117 3314906, **www.bris.ac.uk/Depts/ BotanicGardens.** *1/4 m W of Durdham Downs. By car from city centre, proceed across Downs towards Stoke Bishop, crossing T-lights at edge of Downs. Stoke Park Rd, 1st turning R off Stoke Hill. Parking opp in Churchill Hall Car Park.* **Adm £4.50, chd free. For NGS: Sun 4 Sept (10-4.30). For other opening times and information, please phone or see garden website.**
Exciting contemporary Botanic Garden with organic flowing network of paths which lead visitors through collections of Mediterranean flora, rare natives, useful plants (incl European and Chinese herbs) and those that illustrate plant evolution. Large floral displays illustrating

after further 150yds down hill. Cream teas. **Adm £3, chd free. Wed 20 Apr; Sun 15 May; Sun 12 June (2-5.30). Visitors also welcome by appt Apr to July incl, coaches welcome.**
³/₄ -acre mature Edwardian garden with colour-themed, informally planted mixed borders. Topiary, box hedging, lime walk, pleached hornbeams, orchard, vegetable plot, 2 small formal ponds, many unusual trees and shrubs. Featured in GGG & The English Garden. Shallow steps nr house.

Overgrown quarry transformed, poultry, cider orchard with sorbus and silver birch collections . . .

128 WAYFORD MANOR
Wayford, Crewkerne TA18 8QG. Mr & Mrs Robin Goffe. *3m SW of Crewkerne. Turning N off B3165 at Clapton; or S off A30 Chard to Crewkerne rd.* Cream teas. **Adm £4, chd free. Suns 3, 24, Mon 25 Apr; Suns, Mons 1, 2, 29, 30 May (2-5).**
The mainly Elizabethan manor (not open) mentioned in C17 for its 'fair and pleasant' garden was redesigned by Harold Peto in 1902. Formal terraces with yew hedges and topiary have fine views over W Dorset. Steps down between spring-fed ponds past mature and new plantings of magnolia, rhododendron, maples, cornus and, in season, spring bulbs, cyclamen, arum lily, gunnera around lower ponds.

129 WELLFIELD BARN
Walcombe Lane, Wells BA5 3AG. David & Virginia Nasmyth, 01749 675129, david.nasmyth@talktalk.net. *¹/₂ m N of Wells. From A39 Bristol to Wells rd turn R at 30mph sign into Walcombe Lane. Entrance at 1st cottage on R, parking signed.* Home-made teas. **Adm £3.50, chd free. Tue 31 May (11-6). Visitors also welcome by**

appt, coaches up to 29 seats permitted on site.
1¹/₂ -acre gardens, made by owners over the past 14yrs from concrete farmyard. Ha-ha, wonderful views, pond, lawn, mixed borders, formal sunken garden, grass walks and interesting young trees. Structured design integrates house and garden with landscape. New areas under development. Featured in Saga magazine. Steepish slopes.

130 43 WEST TOWN ROAD
Backwell, N Somerset BS48 3HG. Jane & Derek Farr, 01275 464957. *7m S of Bristol on A370 (Weston-super-Mare rd). From Bristol after 2 sets of T-lights, alongside Methodist chapel. Steep slope to driveway, rear gate entry only. Park on rd or nr shops on Rodney Rd.* Home-made teas. **Adm £2.50, chd free. Sun 3 July (2-5). Visitors also welcome by appt, no groups please.**
Medium-sized garden and walled courtyard garden. Herbaceous borders, lovely wisterias, phormiums, ferns, hostas, bamboo, roses. Pond, pergola, decked area, gravel garden. Raised vegetable plot. Mature shrubs, clematis, lawns on 2 levels, sunken garden. Container plants in cottage courtyard incl camellias, skimmias, pieris. Old stone walls. Creatively landscaped garden.

131 WESTBROOK HOUSE
West Bradley BA6 8LS. Keith Anderson and David Mendel, 01458 850604, andersonmendel@aol.com. *4m E of Glastonbury. From A361 at W Pennard follow signs to W Bradley (2m).* **Adm £3, chd free (share to West Bradley Church). Sats 23 Apr; 18 June (11-5). Visitors also welcome by appt.**
1¹/₂ acres of formal gardens with mixed shrub/herbaceous borders; 2 acres of newly-planted orchard and meadows with spring flowers and species roses.

132 159 WESTBURY LANE
Coombe Dingle BS9 2PY. Maureen Dickens, 0117 9043008, jmd159@blueyonder.co.uk. *2m from J18 M5. L A4162/Sylvan Way, B4054/Shirehampton Rd, R to Westbury Lane. 1st house on R.* Home-made teas. **Combined adm £5, chd free. Sun 12 June (2-6).**

Combined with **4 Haytor Park.** **Visitors also welcome by appt Apr to Sept.**
Gently sloping garden. Large patio at rear, walled beds, pond and many other features. Some common and unusual plants with successional planting to give colour throughout yr. Closely planted in owner's style. From patio, garden is seen through rambler and other climber-covered wooden archways. Garden now coming into shape and changing rapidly as plants fill out. Wheelchair access to front garden and back patio only.

133 WHALES FARM
Gotton Lane, Gotton TA2 8LL. Janet & Richard Smith, 01823 412418. *3¹/₂ m N of Taunton off Bridgwater rd. At Monkton Heathfield turn into Meadway, follow signs to Hestercombe and into Gotton Lane.* **Adm £2.50, chd free. Visitors welcome by appt Mar to Oct.**
4 acres of mixed gardens, overgrown quarry transformed, poultry, cider orchard with sorbus and silver birch collections, bees, pond. Listed with Somerset Private Nature Reserves. Several lawns and grass paths in orchard. Some steps.

134 NEW WHITE CROSS GARDEN and CRANBROOK
Bath Road, Norton St Philip BA2 7LP. Robert & Jane Standen. *8m SE of Bath. From centre of NSP B3110 towards Hinton Charterhouse. Garden at very edge of village on L opp farm lane. No parking at house, park in village.* Refreshments and parking in Fleur de Lys PH. **Combined adm £4, chd free. Sun 10 July (2-5). Combined with Cranbrook.**
Garden has 2 distinct parts: Ornamental garden consisting of mature trees and shrubs, lawn, terrace with perennial plants, topiary parterre, informal pond, backed by views towards village. Productive garden with vegetable plots, fruit trees and soft fruit. Ancient village with C14 church. Village mead with playground facilities. Wheelchair access to ornamental garden only.

135 18 WOODGROVE ROAD
Henbury BS10 7RE. Peter & Ruth Whitby. *4m N of Bristol. M5 J17, follow B4018, R at 4th r'about signed Blaise Castle. R opp Blaise Castle car*

park - rd next to Avon riding centre. Home-made teas. **Adm £2.50, chd free**. Sats 4, 25 June (2-5). Medium-sized garden divided into 3 sections. Traditional flower garden with Bonsai display and small wildlife pond. Cottage garden with greenhouse and plant sale area. Small orchard with dwarf fruit trees and small vegetable garden.

136 THE WYCKE
61 Long Ashton Road, Long Ashton BS41 9HW. John & Linda Leigh. *3m SW of Bristol. A370 from Bristol then B3128 (Clevedon). After 0.6m, L into Long Ashton Rd. Follow for 0.9m.* Home-made teas. **Adm £3, chd free. Sun 12 June (2-6).** 1/2 -acre, partly-walled private garden with varied planting incl flowering shrubs, sprawling perennials and clipped evergreens. Pergola and arches adorned with roses and clematis. Attractive to both adults and children with ceramic sculptures and ponds. Organic kitchen garden.

One acre of theatrical planting in large walled garden . . .

137 YEWS FARM
East Street, Martock TA12 6NF. Louise & Fergus Dowding, 01935 822202, louise@louisedowding.co.uk. *Midway between Yeovil & Langport. Turn off main str through village at Market House, onto East Str, past PO, garden 150yds on R between Nag's Head and White Hart.* Home-made teas by arrangement. **Adm £4, chd free. Sun 26 June (2-6). Visitors also welcome by appt for groups of 20+ June/July.** 1 acre of theatrical planting in large walled garden. Outsized plants in jungle garden. Sculptural planting for height, shape, leaf and texture. Self-seeded gravel garden, box and bay ball border, espalier apples, cloud

pruning. Working organic kitchen garden. Hens, pigs and orchard. Mostly wheelchair access.

138 YONDER COTTAGE
72 Church Road, Winterbourne Down BS36 1BY. Rowan & Helen Isaac. *6m NE of Bristol. From A4174 ring rd take A432 signed Yate. Approx 1m after crossing M4 L signed Winterbourne Down, 3rd L opp Cross Hands PH into Church Rd then immed R, 3rd house on L.* Home-made teas at All Saints Village Hall, Church Rd (200 yards). **Adm £2.50, chd free. Sun 5 June (2-5.30).** Informal 1/3 -acre garden with interesting mix of herbaceous planting complementing established framework of trees and shrubs. The sloping site also incl woodland walk, allium glade, pond, summerhouse, dry-stone walls and pergola. Rural landscape beyond garden completes this garden with a view.

Follow us on Facebook and Twitter

Wayford Manor

STAFFORDSHIRE

Birmingham & West Midlands

Opening Dates

March

Saturday 19
18 Dorothy Clive Garden
Sunday 20
52 23 St Johns Road

April

Sunday 10
37 Millennium Garden
Sunday 24
49 Pereira Road Gardens
Monday 25
28 Heath House
57 Stonehill Quarry Garden

May

Sunday 1
25 Hall Green Gardens
67 Yew Tree Cottage
Saturday 7
22 Four Seasons
Sunday 8
15 Courtwood House
22 Four Seasons
Monday 9
16 12 Darges Lane
Wednesday 11
27 89 Harts Green Road
Saturday 14
22 Four Seasons
Sunday 15
3 The Beeches
19 Dorset House
22 Four Seasons
63 Wits End
Friday 20
52 23 St Johns Road (Evening)
Saturday 21
35 The Magic Garden
56 Small But Beautiful
Sunday 22
11 Castle Bromwich Hall Gardens
53 The Secret Garden
Wednesday 25
2 Bankcroft Farm
Saturday 28
44 The Old Dairy House
Sunday 29
26 Hamilton House
44 The Old Dairy House
67 Yew Tree Cottage
Monday 30
9 Bridge House
28 Heath House

June

Wednesday 1
2 Bankcroft Farm
43 The Mount, Great Bridgeford
Thursday 2
64 The Wombourne Wodehouse
Friday 3
12 Coley Cottage
53 The Secret Garden
Saturday 4
21 10 Fern Dene
Sunday 5
5 Birch Trees
23 The Garth
32 Inglenook
38 Mitton Manor
Wednesday 8
2 Bankcroft Farm
Saturday 11
20 The Elms
Sunday 12
36 Middleton Hall
59 91 Tower Road
60 19 Waterdale
Wednesday 15
2 Bankcroft Farm
27 89 Harts Green Road
Saturday 18
8 The Brambles
Sunday 19
3 The Beeches
8 The Brambles
35 The Magic Garden
49 Pereira Road Gardens
Wednesday 22
2 Bankcroft Farm
Saturday 25
24 Grafton Cottage (Evening)
Sunday 26
1 Ashcroft
6 Blackwood House Farm
12 Coley Cottage
23 The Garth
37 Millennium Garden
40 Moseley Gardens South
42 The Mount, Coton, Gnosall
51 Rowley House Farm
53 The Secret Garden
55 Silverwood
58 Tanglewood Cottage
Wednesday 29
2 Bankcroft Farm

July

Friday 1
66 Yarlet House
Saturday 2
47 The Old Vicarage
Sunday 3
24 Grafton Cottage

28 Heath House
30 High Trees
34 Lilac Cottage
38 Mitton Manor
46 The Old Rectory, Mavesyn Ridware
47 The Old Vicarage
63 Wits End
Saturday 9
35 The Magic Garden
56 Small But Beautiful
65 Woodleighton Grove Gardens
Sunday 10
5 Birch Trees
10 37 Brookfields Road
13 Colour Mill
17 4 Dene Close
25 Hall Green Gardens
32 Inglenook
39 Moorfield
61 The Wickets
65 Woodleighton Grove Gardens
67 Yew Tree Cottage
Friday 15
52 23 St Johns Road
Saturday 16
4 Biddulph Grange Garden
31 133 Hillfield Lane
58 Tanglewood Cottage
Sunday 17
24 Grafton Cottage
31 133 Hillfield Lane
41 Moss Cottage
43 The Mount, Great Bridgeford
Sunday 24
7 The Bowers
19 Dorset House
50 8 Rectory Road
Sunday 31
3 The Beeches
20 The Elms
29 Hidden Gem
62 Windy Arbour

August

Friday 5
12 Coley Cottage
53 The Secret Garden
Saturday 6
35 The Magic Garden (Evening)
Sunday 7
24 Grafton Cottage
44 The Old Dairy House
62 Windy Arbour
63 Wits End
Saturday 13
31 133 Hillfield Lane
Sunday 14
31 133 Hillfield Lane
Friday 19
58 Tanglewood Cottage (Evening)

You are always welcome at an NGS garden

Saturday 20
26 Hamilton House (Evening)
35 The Magic Garden (Evening)
Sunday 28
5 Birch Trees
Monday 29
5 Birch Trees
9 Bridge House

September

Sunday 4
3 The Beeches
Saturday 17
4 Biddulph Grange Garden
56 Small But Beautiful (Evening)

October

Sunday 2
57 Stonehill Quarry Garden
Sunday 16
33 John's Garden
Sunday 23
21 10 Fern Dene

Gardens open to the public

4 Biddulph Grange Garden
11 Castle Bromwich Hall Gardens
14 Consall Hall Landscape Garden
18 Dorothy Clive Garden
36 Middleton Hall

By appointment only

45 The Old Rectory, Clifton Campville
48 Paul's Oasis of Calm
54 9 Shepherds Fold

Also open by Appointment ☎

3 The Beeches
5 Birch Trees
6 Blackwood House Farm
8 The Brambles
9 Bridge House
10 37 Brookfields Road
25 16 & 37 Burnaston Road, Hall Green Gardens
12 Coley Cottage
15 Courtwood House
16 12 Darges Lane
17 4 Dene Close
19 Dorset House
20 The Elms
25 36 Ferndale Road, Hall Green Gardens
23 The Garth
24 Grafton Cottage
27 89 Harts Green Road

28 Heath House
29 Hidden Gem
65 Karibu, Woodleighton Grove Gardens
35 The Magic Garden
39 Moorfield
41 Moss Cottage
42 The Mount, Coton, Gnosall
43 The Mount, Great Bridgeford
45 The Old Rectory, Clifton Campville
48 Paul's Oasis of Calm
49 50 Pereira Road, Pereira Road Gardens
51 Rowley House Farm
25 120 Russell Road, Hall Green Gardens
52 23 St Johns Road
53 The Secret Garden
54 9 Shepherds Fold
58 Tanglewood Cottage
61 The Wickets
62 Windy Arbour
63 Wits End
64 The Wombourne Wodehouse
67 Yew Tree Cottage

The Gardens

1 **NEW** **ASHCROFT**
1 Stafford Road, Eccleshall
ST21 6JP. Peter & Gillian Bertram.
7m W of Stafford. J14 M6. At Eccleshall end of A5013 the garden is 100 metres from the junction of A5013. On street parking nearby.
Home-made teas. **Adm £3, chd free.**
Sun 26 June (1.30-5.30).
3 mins walk from the historic town of Eccleshall, weeping limes hide a 1 acre oasis of green tranquillity. From the small pond to the covered courtyard with water feature, take tea then explore. Sunken herb bed, treillage, Victorian style green house, pergola and gravel beds. Wildlife friendly boundaries run down to the woodland, look for the stone carvings. Garden on N facing slope - 90% is accessible by wheelchair.
♿ ❀ ☕

Wildlife friendly boundaries run down to the woodland, look for the stone carvings . . .

2 **BANKCROFT FARM**
Tatenhill, Burton-on-Trent
DE13 9SA. Mrs Penelope Adkins.
2m SW of Burton-on-Trent. Take Tatenhill Rd off A38 Burton-Branston flyover. 1m, 1st house on L approaching village. Parking on farm.
Adm £3, chd free. Weds 25 May to 29 June (2-5).
Lose yourself for an afternoon in our 1½ -acre organic country garden. Arbour, gazebo and many other seating areas to view ponds and herbaceous borders, backed with shrubs and trees with emphasis on structure, foliage and colour. Productive fruit and vegetable gardens, wildlife areas and adjoining 12 acre native woodland walk. Picnics welcome. Winner of Gold Award Staffs Brighter Borough Premier gardens. Gravel paths.
♿

3 **THE BEECHES**
Mill Street, Rocester ST14 5JX. Ken & Joy Sutton, 01889 590631,
joy@joy50.orangehome.co.uk. *5m N of Uttoxeter. On B5030, turn R into village by JCB factory. By Red Lion PH & mini r'about take rd for Marston Montgomery. Garden 250yds on R.*
Home-made teas. **Adm £3, chd free.**
Suns 15 May; 19 June; 31 July; 4 Sept (1.30-5). Also open Windy Arbour 31 July. Visitors also welcome by appt May to Aug.
Stroll along the sweeping driveway containing island beds planted with mixed shrubs and perennials, before entering a stunning plant lover's garden of approx ²/₃ acre, enjoying views of surrounding countryside. Formal box garden, vibrant colour-themed herbaceous borders, shrubs incl rhododendrons, azaleas (looking good in May), pools, roses, fruit trees, clematis and climbing plants, late flowering perennials (good in Sept), yr-round garden. Cottage garden planting with a surprise round every corner, also small raised bed vegetable and soft fruit garden.
♿ ❀ ☕ ☎

4 **♦ BIDDULPH GRANGE GARDEN**
Grange Road, Biddulph ST8 7SD.
National Trust, 01782 517999,
www.nationaltrust.org.uk/biddulph grange. *3½ m SE of Congleton. 7m N of Stoke-on-Trent off the A527. Congleton to Biddulph rd.* **Adm £6.68, chd free.** For NGS: Sats 16 July; 17 Sept (10.30-5). For other opening times and information, please

phone or see garden website.
Amazing Victorian garden created by
Darwin contemporary and
correspondent James Bateman as an
extension of his beliefs, scientific
interests and collection of plants. Visit
the Italian terrace, Chinese inspired
garden, dahlia walk and the oldest
surviving golden larch in Britain
brought from China by the great plant
hunter Robert Fortune.

5 ▶ BIRCH TREES

Copmere End, Eccleshall, Stafford
ST21 6HH. Susan & John Weston,
01785 850448,
johnweston123@btinternet.com.
*1¹/₂ m W of Eccleshall. On B5026,
turn at junction signed Copmere End.
After ¹/₂ m straight across Xrds by
Star Inn.* Home-made teas. **Adm £3,
chd free.** Suns 5 June; 10 July; Sun
28, Mon 29 Aug (1.30-5.30).
Visitors also welcome by appt.
Peaceful country garden with ample
seating to allow visitors to enjoy the
views over the 'borrowed
landscape'of the surrounding
countryside. Plant enthusiasts'
garden, with rare and unusual
varieties. Herbaceous borders and
island beds, water features and
vegetable plot. Cedar alpine house
with permanent planting. Featured in
BBC2 Open Gardens, Staffordshire
Life and Express and Star.

6 ▶ BLACKWOOD HOUSE FARM

Horton ST13 8QA. Anne & Adam
James, 01538 306605,
blackwood.house@hotmail.co.uk.
*4m W of Leek. 6m N of Stoke-on-
Trent. A53 Stoke to Leek turn off at
Black Horse PH in Endon, go to
T-junction, turn R into Gratton Lane.
Take 4th L (approx 2¹/₂ m) signed
Lask Edge, over ford up bank, farm
on L.* Home-made teas. **Adm £4, chd
free.** Sun 26 June (2-5). **Visitors
also welcome by appt.**
1¹/₂ acre country cottage garden with
spectacular views. Large mixed
borders, rockery, natural stream and
koi carp pond. Grass and gravel
paths through shrubs and trees.
Lovely colourful wildlife garden
packed with plants and topiary!

7 ▶ THE BOWERS

Church Lane, Standon, nr
Eccleshall ST21 6RW. Maurice &
Sheila Thacker,
metbowers@aol.com. *5m N of*

Birch Trees

*Eccleshall. Take A519 & at Cotes
Heath turn L signed Standon. After
1m turn R at Xrds by church, into
Church Lane ¹/₂ m on L.* Home-made
teas. **Adm £3, chd free.** Sun 24 July
(1-5).
Romantic multi-roomed cottage
garden set in ¹/₃ -acre quiet rural
location. Strong colour-themed
borders planted with rare and unusual
perennials. with 200 clematis, height
and blossom in abundance. Water
feature, collections of hardy
geraniums and hostas. A colourful
tranquil oasis.

8 ▶ NEW ▶ THE BRAMBLES

Lancaster Avenue, Fulford, Stoke-
on-Trent ST11 9LP. John & Evelyn
Hooley, 01782 393554. *4m NE of
Stone. B5066 Meir to Hilderstone Rd,
Spotacre Xrds sign to Fulford. 6th L
turn into Meadow Lane. 50yds turn R.
2nd Avenue on L.* Home-made teas.
Adm £3, chd free. Sat 18, Sun 19
June (1-5). **Visitors also welcome
by appt anytime.**
A village garden, with colour and
interest. Roses, perennials and
annuals give a traditional feel and a

medley of pots and hanging baskets
provide a riot of colour. Several
features incl a small bridge over water
and hostas thriving in the shaded
stumpery. Teas served in the
conservatory.

9 ▶ BRIDGE HOUSE

Dog Lane, Bodymoor Heath
B76 9JF. Mr & Mrs J Cerone,
01827 873205,
janecerone@btinternet.com. *5m S
of Tamworth. From A446 at the Belfry,
head 1 mile N on A4091, R at sign
into Bodymoor Heath Lane. ³/₄ m into
village, R into Dog Lane. Immed after
hump back bridge.* Home-made teas.
Adm £3, chd free. Mons 30 May;
29 Aug (2-5.30). **Visitors also
welcome by appt from May to end
Sept.**
1-acre garden surrounding converted
public house divided into smaller
areas with a mix of shrub borders,
azalea and fuchsia, herbaceous and
bedding, orchard, kitchen garden and
wild flower meadow. Pergola walk,
wisteria, formal fish pool, pond and
lawns.

10 37 BROOKFIELDS ROAD
Ipstones ST10 2LY. Pat & Pam Murray, 01538 266224. *7m SE of Leek. From N on A523 turn on to B5053 southwards at Green Man Pub, Bottomhouse. From S on A52 turn N on to B5053 at Froghall. In the centre of Ipstone Village tight turn opp Trading Post shop into Brookfields Rd.* Home-made teas. **Adm £3, chd free.** Sun 10 July (2-6). Also open **Colour Mill. Visitors also welcome by appt.**
1-acre organic garden with splendid views over Churnet Valley. Established white garden, wildlife pond, herbaceous borders and long cut flower bed. Large vegetable garden with raised beds surrounded by native hedging. Winding willow tunnel leads down to wild flower meadow, woodland and stream with bridge and stepping stones. Entire garden including hedge laying, dry stone walls and stone buildings created by owners in last 13yrs to harmonise with the surrounding village conservation area.
🐕 😊 ☕ ☎

11 ◆ CASTLE BROMWICH HALL GARDENS
Chester Road, Castle Bromwich, Birmingham B36 9BT. Castle Bromwich Hall Gardens Trust, 0121 749 4100, www.cbhgt.org.uk. *4m E of Birmingham. 1m J5 M6 (exit N only).* **Adm £4, chd £1.** For NGS: Sun 22 May (1.30-5.30). For other opening times and information, please phone or see garden website.
Restored C18 formal walled gardens provide visitors with the opportunity to see a unique collection of historic plants, shrubs, medicinal and culinary herbs and fascinating vegetable collection. Intriguing holly maze. Orchards, Espalier and Cordons. Guided tours, gift shop, coffee shop, plant and produce sales. Dogs allowed on short leads.
♿ 🐕 😊 ☕

12 COLEY COTTAGE
Coley Lane, Little Haywood ST18 0UU. Yvonne Branson, 01889 882715, yvonnebranson0uu@btinternet.com. *5m SE of Stafford. A51 from Rugeley or Weston signed Lt Haywood. 1/2 m from Seven Springs. A513 Coley Lane from Red Lion PH past Back Lane, 100yds on L opp red Post Box.* Home-made teas. **Adm £2.50, chd free.** Fri 3, Sun 26 June;

Fri 5 Aug (11-4). Also open **The Secret Garden all 3 dates, The Garth & Tanglewood 26 June. Visitors also welcome by appt.**
A plant lover's cottage garden, full of subtle colours and perfume, every inch packed with plants. Clematis and old roses covering arches, many hostas and agapanthus, a wildlife pool, all designed to attract birds and butterflies. This garden has been created in 4yrs from a blank canvas, shrubs and small trees are maturing.
🐕 😊 ☕ ☎

> Set beside the
> delightful river
> Hamps frequented
> by kingfisher and
> dipper . . .

13 NEW COLOUR MILL
Winkhill, Leek ST13 7PR. Bob & Jackie Pakes. *7m E of Leek. From Leek follow A523 to Ashbourne on entering Winkhill look for red telephone box on L. Colour Mill is 200yds past telephone box on R. Turning is immed before 50mph sign beside a building.* Home-made teas. **Adm £3, chd free.** Sun 10 July (1.30-5.30). Also open **37 Brookfields Road.**
3/4 acre south facing garden, created in the shadow of a former iron foundry, set beside the delightful river Hamps frequented by kingfisher and dipper. Informal planting in a variety of rooms surrounded by beautiful 7ft beech hedges. Large organic vegetable patch complete with greenhouse. Maturing trees provide shade for the interesting seating areas.

14 ◆ CONSALL HALL LANDSCAPE GARDEN
Wetley Rocks, Stoke on Trent ST9 0AG. William Podmore, 01782 551947, www.consallgardens.co.uk. *7m from Stoke-on-Trent, Leek & Cheadle. A52 after Cellarhead Xrds. Turn L on to A522, after 1/4 m turn R to Consall & straight on through village. Garden entrance 3/4 m on R.* Ample free car park. **Adm £5.50, chd £1.50.** For opening times and information,

please phone or see garden website.
Designed and created over 50 years by William Podmore, this 70-acre landscape with its breathtaking views, is set in four valleys with six lakes, enhanced with pack-horse bridges, numerous follies and summerhouses to form a series of enchanting vistas throughout the year. Open Weds, Suns & BH Apr to Oct (10-5). Steep slopes.
♿ 🐕 😊 ☕

15 COURTWOOD HOUSE
Court Walk, Betley CW3 9DP. Mike & Edith Reeves, 01270 820715. *6m S of Crewe. On A531 going toward Keele & Newcastle-u-Lyme or from J16 of the M6 pick up the A531 off the A500 on the Nantwich rd. In Betley Village into courtyard by sign 'Betley Court'.* Home-made teas. **Adm £3, chd £1.50.** Sun 8 May (1.30-5.30). Visitors also welcome by appt May to Aug, small coaches permitted. Max group 20, incls evening visits (after 8pm) to see the coloured lights.
Small L-shaped, walled garden, which is designed as a walk-through sculpture. Many creations, structures and water features, with hidden spaces and seating areas, with strong shapes and effects utilising a wide range of materials incl a synthetic inner lawn. Night-time illumination with hidden coloured spotlights. Small art gallery within this secluded oasis. Small display of acrylic paintings on canvas by the owner. Cards & Book Stall (in aid of St Lukes Hospice).
☕ ☎

16 12 DARGES LANE
Great Wyrley WS6 6LE. Mrs A Hackett, 01922 415064, annofdarges@orange.net. *2m SE of Cannock. From A5 take A34 towards Walsall. Darges Lane is 1st turning on R (over brow of hill). House on R on corner of Cherrington Drive.* Light refreshments & teas. **Adm £3, chd free.** Mon 9 May (12-4). Visitors also welcome by appt.
1/4 -acre well-stocked enthusiastic plantsman's garden on two levels. Foliage plants are a special feature which, together with shrubacceous borders containing rare and unusual plants, give all-yr interest. National Collection of lamiums. Collection of 95 clematis. Features are constantly updated and refurbished. Display of owners paintings and artwork.
😊 NCCPG ☕ ☎

17 4 DENE CLOSE
Penkridge ST19 5HL. David & Anne
Smith, 01785 712580. *6m S of
Stafford. On A449 from Stafford. At
far end of Penkridge turn L into
Boscomoor Lane, 2nd L into Filance
Lane, 3rd R Dene Close. Please park
with consideration in Filance Lane.
Disabled only in Dene Close.* Home-
made teas. **Adm £3, chd free.** Sun
10 July (11-5). **Visitors also
welcome by appt July & Aug,
coaches permitted.**
A medium-sized garden of many
surprises. Vibrant colour-themed
herbaceous areas incl a long 'rainbow
border'. Many different grasses and
bamboos creating texture and interest
in the garden. Large oak tree provides
conditions for hostas and ferns and
other shade loving plants. Water
feature. Summerhouse and quiet
seating areas within the garden.
Featured in Express & Star & local
press.

**18 ◆ DOROTHY CLIVE
GARDEN**
Willoughbridge, Market Drayton
TF9 4EU. Willoughbridge Garden
Trust, 01630 647237,
www.dorothyclivegarden.co.uk. *3m
SE of Bridgemere Garden World.
From M6 J15 take A53 W bound,
then A51 N bound midway between
Nantwich & Stone, near Woore.* **Adm
£6, chd free. For NGS: Sat 19 Mar
(10-5.30). For other opening times
and information, please phone or
see garden website.**
12 informal acres, incl superb
woodland garden, alpine scree, gravel
garden, fine collection of trees and
spectacular flower borders.
Renowned in May when woodland
quarry is brilliant with rhododendrons.
Creative planting has produced
stunning summer borders. Much to
see, whatever the season. Plant
sales. Featured in North Staffordshire
Magazine.

19 DORSET HOUSE
68 Station Street, Cheslyn Hay
WS6 7EE. Mary & David Blundell,
01922 419437,
david.blundell@talktalk.net. *2m SE
of Cannock. J11 M6. A462 towards
Willenhall. L at island, follow rd to next
island. R into one-way system (Low
St), at T-junction L into Station St. A5
Bridgetown L over M6 toll rd to
island, L into Coppice Rd. At T-
junction R into Station St.* **Adm £3,**

chd free. Suns 15 May; 24 July
(12-5). **Visitors also welcome by
appt, May - July, groups of 10+,
coaches permitted.**
Inspirational $\frac{1}{2}$ -acre plantaholic's
country garden giving all-yr interest.
Many unique features, wealth of
unusual rhododendrons, acers,
shrubs and perennials, planted in
mixed borders. Clematis-covered
arches, intimate seating areas, hidden
corners, water features, stream, all
creating a haven of peace and
tranquillity. New features, incl wildlife
pond. Featured in The Journal.

DOVE COTTAGE
See Derbyshire.

20 THE ELMS
Post Office Road, Seisdon,
Wolverhampton WV5 7HA. Mr Alec
Smith & Ms Susan Wilkinson,
01902 893482,
scw365@googlemail.com. *6m W of
Wolverhampton. A454 B'north rd.
After Lealans Nurseries on R, turn L at
Fox PH into Fox Rd. 1m T-junction. L
at Seven Stars PH into Ebstree Rd.
Take 2nd L into Post Office Rd (after
narrow bridge). Garden on R through
large walled entrance.* Home-made
teas. **Adm £3.50, chd free.** Sat 11
June; Sun 31 July (2-5). **Visitors
also welcome by appt, small
groups of 10 -25.**
4-acre country garden, set around
Georgian villa. Kitchen herb garden
with topiary and pots. Tropical style
walled garden enclosing swimming
pool. Variety of borders and lawns.
Ha-ha leading to open lawned area
with new and ancient trees. Victorian
bandstand, re-located from
Ilfracombe pier. 50m shrubbery
designed and planted 2010.Over 100
roses, most named.

Ha-ha leading to
open lawned area
with new and
ancient trees.
Victorian
bandstand, re-
located from
Ilfracombe pier . . .

21 10 FERN DENE
Madeley, Crewe CW3 9ER. Martin
& Stella Clifford-Jones. *10m W of
Newcastle under Lyme. Madeley is on
A525 between Keele/ Woore. Enter
Moss Lane next to Madeley Pool. 2nd
R, Charles Cotton Drive. At end turn
R then L into the Bridle Path, 1st R to
Fern Dene.* Home-made teas. **Adm
£3, chd free.** Sat 4 June (2-5); Sun
23 Oct (1.30-4.30).
1 acre garden on sloping site with
natural springs designed to
encourage wildlife. There are 5 ponds,
woodland walk and a new stumpery.
We are always on the look out for
interesting plants and are
redeveloping areas of the garden.
Enjoy homemade cakes and unwind
on the patio, decking or the new
conservatory.

22 FOUR SEASONS
26 Buchanan Road, Walsall
WS4 2EN. Marie and Tony Newton,
www.fourseasonsgarden.co.uk.
*Adjacent to Walsall Arboretum. M6
J7 take A34 Walsall. At double island
take 3rd exit A4148 onto Ring Rd.
Over 2 islands, at large junction turn R
A461 (signed Lichfield). At 1st island
take 3rd exit Buchanan Ave, R into
Buchanan Rd.* Extensive parking in rd
or ave. **Adm £3, chd free.** Sats,
Suns 7, 8, 14, 15 May (10-5).
Stunning tapestry of colour. S-facing
$\frac{1}{3}$ acre, suburban garden, gently
sloping to arboretum, some steps.
200 acers, 350 azaleas, bright
clipped conifers and shrubs. Many
'rooms' and themes including
contrast of red, blue and yellow.
Jungle, oriental pagoda, bridges,
water features and stone ornaments.
Interesting tree barks. Steps down to
garden. WC at garden level. Featured
in Daily Mail, Garden Answers, China-
Flower News, BBC2 Gardeners'
World half-hour special, Garden News
Overall Gardeners of the Year.

23 THE GARTH
2 Broc Hill Way, Milford, Stafford
ST17 0UB. Mr & Mrs David Wright,
01785 661182,
anitawright1@yahoo.co.uk,
www.anitawright.co.uk. *4½ m SE of
Stafford. A513 Stafford to Rugeley rd;
at Barley Mow turn R (S) to Brocton;
L after ½ m.* Cream teas. **Adm £3,
chd free.** Suns 5, 26 June (2-6).
**Also open Coley Cottage, The
Secret Garden, Tanglewood
Cottage 26 June. Visitors also**

Dorothy Clive Garden

25 HALL GREEN GARDENS
Birmingham B28 8DG. *Off A34, 3m city centre, 6m from M42 J4. Take A34 to Hall Green, turn into Colebank Rd where S Birmingham College is situated, turn 1st R into Southam Rd, 1st L into Burnaston Rd.* Home-made teas. **Combined adm £3.50, chd free.** Suns 1 May; 10 July (2-5.30).

16 BURNASTON ROAD
Howard Hemmings & Sandra Hateley
Visitors also welcome by appt May to July. 0121 624 1488 howard.hemmings@blueyonder.co.uk

37 BURNASTON ROAD
Mrs Carolyn Wynne-Jones
Visitors also welcome by appt May to July. 0121 608 2397

36 FERNDALE ROAD
Mrs A A Appelbe & Mrs E A Nicholson
Visitors also welcome by appt all year. 0121 777 4921

120 RUSSELL ROAD
Mr David Worthington
Visitors also welcome by appt June to Aug. 0121 624 7906

A group of 4 suburban gardens, each unique in style. They include a S-facing formal lawn and border garden with an unusual log display. A small garden with well stocked borders and miniature stream running into wildlife ponds, and a tranquil garden with curving borders, shade areas, fruit, vegetables and a surprise! There are also a florist's large garden and plantsman's garden both sub-divided, with many unusual plants and containers. No wheelchair access to 120 Russell Rd.
&. ⊕ ☕ 🐾

welcome by appt May to Sept, min 15.
¹/₂ -acre garden of many levels on Channock Chase AONB. Acid soil loving plants. Series of small gardens, water features, raised beds. Rare trees, island beds of unusual shrubs and perennials, many varieties of hosta and ferns. Ancient sandstone caves. Featured in GGG & on BBC Radio Stoke.
🎇 ⊕ ☕ ☎

24 GRAFTON COTTAGE
Barton-under-Needwood DE13 8AL. Margaret & Peter Hargreaves, 01283 713639, marpeter@talktalk.net. *6m N of Lichfield. Leave A38 for Catholme S of Barton, follow sign to Barton Green, ¹/₄ m on L.* Home-made teas. **Adm £3, chd free** (share to Alzheimer's Research Trust).

Evening Opening £4, wine, Sat 25 June (6.30-9). Suns 3 (11.30-5), 17 July (1.30-5); Sun 7 Aug (11.30-5). **Visitors also welcome by appt min £60 per group, coaches permitted.** Our 20th year of opening. Step into an idyllic cottage garden with winding paths, and scent from old fashioned roses, dianthus, sweet peas, phlox, lilies and more. Delphiniums form backdrop to herbaceous borders followed by clematis which clothe trellises. Textured plants, artemisia, atrepex, heuchera form the basis of colour themed borders. Cottage garden annuals add to tranquillity. Garden designed and maintained by owners. Particular interest viticella clematis. Small vegetable plot. Plants propagated for sale. Featured in RHS The Garden, Country Life & Garden Style.
⊕ ☕ ☎

26 HAMILTON HOUSE
Roman Grange, Roman Road, Little Aston Park B74 3GA. Philip & Diana Berry. *3m N of Sutton Coldfield. Follow A454 (Walsal Rd) & enter Roman Rd, Little Aston Pk. Roman Grange is 1st L after church but enter rd via pedestrian gate.* Home-made teas (May), wine & canapes (Aug). **Adm £3.50, chd free.** Sun 29 May (2-5). Evening Opening wine, Sat 20 Aug (7.30-10.30). ¹/₂ -acre N facing English woodland garden in tranquil setting, making the

most of challenging shade, providing haven for birds and other wild life. Large pond with stone bridge, pergolas, water features, box garden with a variety of roses and herbs. Interesting collection of rhododendrons, hostas,ferns and old English roses. 29 May A String Quartet, Pimms punch & home made cakes to die for! 20 Aug our English country garden by candlelight. Summer is still here. A string quartet,wine & canapés. Featured in local press.

27 **89 HARTS GREEN ROAD**
Harborne B17 9TZ. Mrs Barbara Richardson, 0121 427 5200. *3m SE of Birmingham. Off Fellows Lane-War Lane.* **Adm £2.50, chd free.** Weds 11 May; 15 June (2-5). **Visitors also welcome by appt.**
Wildlife-friendly split-level garden protected by mature trees. Extensively planted with unusual herbaceous perennials, shrubs and climbers. Herbs and edible flowers border a path through the rockery. Large display of plants in containers featuring half hardy perennials and shade plants. Pond and vegetable garden.

28 **HEATH HOUSE**
Offley Brook, nr Eccleshall ST21 6HA. Dr D W Eyre-Walker, 01785 280318. *3m W of Eccleshall. Take B5026 towards Woore. At Sugnall turn L, after 1¹/₂ m turn R immed by stone garden wall. After 1m straight across Xrds.* Home-made teas. **Adm £3, chd free (share to Adbaston Church).** Mons 25 Apr; 30 May; Sun 3 July (2-5.30). **Visitors also welcome by appt.**
1¹/₂ -acre country garden of C18 miller's house in lovely valley setting, overlooking mill pool. Plantsman's garden containing many rare and unusual plants in borders, bog garden, woodland, alpine house, raised bed and shrubberies and incl slowly expanding collection of hardy terrestrial orchids.

29 **HIDDEN GEM**
15 St Johns Road, Pleck, Walsall WS2 0TJ. Maureen & Sid Allen, 07825 804670, hsallen@virginmedia.com, 15 St Johns Road. *2m W of Walsall. Off J10 M6. Head for Walsall on A454 Wolverhampton Rd. Turn R into Pleck*

Rd A4148 then 4th R into St Johns Rd. **Adm £3, chd free.** Sun 31 July (1-5). **Visitors also welcome by appt mid June to late Aug, coaches welcome.**
Situated between two busy motorway junctions, come and visit our 'Hidden Gem' what a suprise. A long narrow pretty garden, lovely foliage in June, pretty perennials, shrubs, trees, lush tropical plants July onwards. Japanese area with stream. Shady walk with ferns, into pretty gravel garden lots of wild life. Very relaxing atmosphere. WHAT A GEM. Featured on BBC Gardeners World and in local press.

30 **HIGH TREES**
18 Drubbery Lane, nr Longton Park ST3 4BA. Peter & Pat Teggin. *5m S of Stoke-on-Trent. Off A5035, midway between Trentham Gardens & Longton. Opp Longton Park.* Cream Teas. **Adm £3, chd free.** Sun 3 July (2-5).
A garden designer's personal, very pretty, garden with co-ordinating design features. Colourful herbaceous borders planted with many unusual plants highlighting colour, texture and form for all-yr interest. An ideas garden offering inspiration, where roses intermingle with clematis, and the coolness of hosta and ferns contrasts with lush summer planting.

31 **133 HILLFIELD LANE**
133, Hillfield Lane, Stretton, Burton-on-Trent DE13 0BL. Clive & Margaret Smith. *Exit A38 at Clay Mills Junction onto A5121 Derby Rd, 1st R into Hillfield Lane.* Tea & Home-made teas. **Adm £3, chd free.** Sat 16, Sun 17 July; Sat 13, Sun 14 Aug (1.30-5).
Award winning ¹/₃ -acre suburban garden with water features, raised beds and vegetable garden. Many innovative features. Gold Medal winner in East Staffs in Bloom Premier Division.

32 **INGLENOOK**
20 Waxland Road, Halesowen B63 3DW. Ron & Anne Kerr. *¹/₄ m from Halesowen town centre. M5, J3 take A456 to Kidderminster, R at 1st island, 1st L into Dogkennel Lane. Waxland Rd 2nd L.* 2 car parks in town centre, limited roadside parking. Home-made teas. **Adm £3, chd free.** Suns 5 June; 10 July (1-5).

Charming garden featuring waterfalls which cascade over rocks down to ponds set within a woodland area. A path meandering through the trees brings you back to the lawn and patio. Hidden area hosts greenhouses, vegetable plots, asparagus beds and mixed borders. Enjoy panoramic views from the raised decked area with its semi-tropical planting overlooking terraces which display a wide variety of low-growing conifers.

A String Quartet, Pimms punch & home made cakes to die for . . . !

33 **JOHN'S GARDEN**
Ashwood Lower Lane, Ashwood, nr Kingswinford DY6 0AE. John Massey, www.ashwoodnurseries.com. *5m S of Wolverhampton. 1m past Wall Heath on A449 turn R to Ashwood along Doctors Lane. At T-junction, turn L, park at Ashwood Nurseries.* Home-made teas in adjacent tea rooms at Ashwood Nurseries. **Adm £4, chd free.** Sun 16 Oct (10.30-4).
A plantsman's garden bordered by the Staffordshire and Worcestershire canal, incorporating many innovative design features in a natural setting. The garden contains a huge plant collection, where flowers and foliage blend in perfect harmony. October sees the development of many autumn tints, and colourful fruits on the malus walk.

34 **LILAC COTTAGE**
Chapel Lane, Gentleshaw, nr Rugeley WS15 4ND. Mrs Sylvia Nunn, www.lilaccottagegarden.co.uk. *5m NW of Lichfield. Approx midway between Lichfield & Rugeley on A51 at Longdon, turn W into Borough Lane signed Cannock Wood & Gentleshaw. Continue 1m to T-junction. L for 1¹/₂ m to Gentleshaw. From Burntwood, A5190 head N on Rugeley Rd at Burntwood Swan*

island; turn L at Xrds approx ¹/₂ m past Nags Head PH, over Xrds to Gentleshaw. Parking only at village hall. Roadside disabled & elderly parking only at Lilac Cottage. Home-made teas. **Adm £3, chd free. Sun 3 July (11.30-5).**
Be inspired! Colour-themed mixed borders, unusual trees, shrubs, perennials and English roses providing all yr interest. Relish the vibrant 'hot' border, shady walks, tranquil seating areas, sweeping lawns, wildlife pond, lush bog garden. At 750ft this plantswoman's 1-acre horticultural heaven offers glorious views over the Trent Valley and beyond.Some gravel paths.Unusual perennials for sale. Close to ancient Iron Age Fort 'Castle Ring' on Cannock Chase and Gentleshaw Common (SSSI). Willow craft demonstration. Featured in Woman's Weekly, Staffordshire Life, The Magazine, Express & Star and other local press. Some gravel paths.

  ♿ ❀ ☕

35▶ THE MAGIC GARDEN
43 Broad Lane, Bradmore, Wolverhampton WV3 9BW. Bob Parker & Greg Kowalczuk, 01902 332228,
roboparker@blueyonder.co.uk. *2m SW of Wolverhampton. 2m from town centre on SW side. Follow signs for Bantock House, adjacent to Bantock Park. Broad Lane is part of B4161. 200yds from Bradmore Arms T-light.* Home-made teas. **Adm £3, chd free. Sat 21 May; Sun 19 June; Sat 9 July (1.30-5.30). Evening Openings £5, wine & chocolates, Sats 6, 20 Aug (7.30-10.30). Visitors also welcome by appt June to Aug, for groups of 15+.**
Escape busy urban surroundings and enter an Aladdin's cave, full of the unexpected. Candles flicker and lanterns glow in the evening. Next to the moon and the stars, this is the best sight to see in the dark. Daylight is no less enchanting: a designer's garden, but different. Numerous sculptures, water features and found objects. Evening openings, chandeliers, lanterns, flares, candles and other lights.New features added each year. Featured in 'Dream Gardens Of England 'published by Merrell. The Weekend Telegraph.

  ☕ ☎

MAXSTOKE CASTLE
See Warwickshire.

36▶ ♦ MIDDLETON HALL
Tamworth B78 2AE. Middleton Hall Trust, 01827 283095,
www.middleton-hall.org.uk. *4m S of Tamworth, 2m N J9 M42. On A4091 between The Belfry & Drayton Manor.* **Adm £3, chd £1. For NGS: Sun 12 June (1-5). For other times and information please phone or visit garden website.**
Two walled gardens set in 40 acres of grounds surrounding GII Middleton Hall, the C17 home of naturalists Sir Francis Willoughby and John Ray. Large colour themed herbaceous borders radiating from a central pond, restored gazebo, pergola planted with roses and wisteria. Courtyard garden with raised beds. SSSI Nature Trail, craft centre, music in Hall.

  ♿ 🐕 ❀ ☕

Look out for the gardens with the ☎ – enjoy a private visit . . .

37▶ MILLENNIUM GARDEN
London Road, Lichfield WS14 9RB. Carol Cooper. *1m S of Lichfield. Off A38 along A5206 towards Lichfield ¹/₄ m past A38 island towards Shoulder of Mutton PH. Park in field on L.* Home-made teas. **Adm £3.50, chd free. Suns 10 Apr; 26 June (1-5).**
2-acre garden with many flower beds, host of golden daffodils in March. Millennium bridge over landscaped water garden, leading to attractive walks along rough mown paths through maturing woodland, and seasonal wild flowers, Uneven surfaces and gravel paths.

  ♿ ☕

38▶ MITTON MANOR
Mitton ST19 5QW. Mrs E A Wilson. *2m W of Penkridge. At Texaco island on A449 in Penkridge turn W into Bungham Lane. Turn R at end then immed L. Keep R at the fork after single file bridge. House is 1¹/₂ m from bridge on R. Car park at rear, 2nd entrance on R.* Cream Teas. **Adm £4, chd free. Suns 5 June; 3 July (11-5).**

Started 10yrs ago, this 7 acre country garden is developing from an overgrown wilderness into a gem. The garden surrounds a Victorian manor house (not open) and contains rooms of different styles, formal box/topiary, prairie planting and natural woodland bordered by a stream. Contains striking water features and sculpture. Live music. Gravel paths and slopes. May not be suitable for wheelchairs.

  ☕

39▶ MOORFIELD
Post Lane, Endon, Stoke-on-Trent ST9 9DU. Ian & June Sellers, 01782 504096. *4m W of Leek. 6m from Stoke-on-Trent A53. Turn into Station Rd over railway line, canal bridge with lights, 1st on L opp Endon Cricket Club.* Home-made teas. **Adm £3, chd free. Sun 10 July (1.30-5). Visitors also welcome by appt.**
Flower arrangers delight situated in ¹/₃ acre. This colourful garden has a variety of different styles ranging from herbaceous borders to areas with a Mediterranean feel, the garden incls many structural features such as unusual wooden tree stumps to a spacious summerhouse. Wide variety of unusual plants. Featured in & on national press & radio.

  ♿ 🐕 ❀ ☕ ☎

GROUP OPENING

40▶ MOSELEY GARDENS SOUTH
Birmingham B13 9TF. *3m city centre. Halfway between Kings Heath and Moseley village. From A435 turn at the main Moseley T-lights on to St Mary's Row/Wake Green Rd. 1st R, Oxford Rd, then 1st R, School Rd. Prospect Rd is 3rd on L, Ashfield Rd is 4th on R.* Home-made teas. **Combined adm £3.50, chd free. Sun 26 June (2-6).**

7 ASHFIELD ROAD
Hilary Bartlett

14 PROSPECT ROAD
Jan Birtle & Mark Wilson

16 PROSPECT ROAD
Andy Horn

19 PROSPECT ROAD
Tony White

65 SCHOOL ROAD
Wendy Weston

NEW 51 VALENTINE ROAD
Clare Goulder

NEW ▶ WILD ROSE COTTAGE
34 Woodfield Road. Rosemary Chatfield

Explore these urban gardens to the front and rear of inter-war and Victorian houses set in a quiet, leafy suburb of Birmingham. Enjoy wildlife and ornamental fish ponds, water features, easy maintenance design and planting, outdoor artwork, vegetable plots and chickens! We also feature a garden inspired by famous artists' gardens and a garden with an Oriental meditation theme. Moseley looks at its best at this time of year, thanks to Moseley in Bloom, Gold Award winners of Heart of England in Bloom. There are hanging baskets, road-side tubs and boxes plus floral displays by residents and local businesses. Extra attractions on Open Day include treasure trails for children, tea and cakes and a stall selling plants, preserves and floral art photography in aid of Prostate Cancer Charities. Featured in B13 Magazine - a local interest publication.

41 ▶ MOSS COTTAGE
Moss Lane, Madeley CW3 9NQ. Liz & Alan Forster, 01782 751366, Lizcforster@aol.com. *7m W of Newcastle-under-Lyme. Madeley is on A525 between Keele/Woore. Enter Moss Lane next to Madeley pool.* Home-made teas. **Adm £3, chd free. Sun 17 July (1.30-5). Visitors also welcome by appt.**
1/3 acre secluded, colourful cottage garden with mixed beds and herbaceous borders. Small wildlife pond with wildlife planting. Small rock garden with water feature. Many places to sit, relax and enjoy the flowers. A garden with interest for the whole year. Britain in Bloom Silver Award Garden 2010.

42 ▶ THE MOUNT, COTON, GNOSALL
Gnosall ST20 0EQ. Andrew & Celia Payne, 01785 822253, ac.payne@waitrose.com. *8m W of Stafford. 4m E of Newport. From Stafford take A518 W towards Newport/Telford. Go through Gnosall, over canal. Garden on edge of Gnosall Village, on LH-side of A518.* Parking approx 200yds signed up lane. Home-made teas. **Adm £3, chd free. Sun 26 June (2-5.30). Visitors also welcome by appt June & July.**

Established ³/₄ acre colourful country garden divided into garden rooms. Wildlife friendly with wildflower meadow, small pond and bog area. Over 80 different varieties of hosta, huge Kiftsgate rose, interesting and colourful containers, attractive trees, unusual perennials and raised vegetable beds, there is something for everyone.

43 ▶ THE MOUNT, GREAT BRIDGEFORD
33 Newport Road, Great Bridgeford, Stafford ST18 9PR. Adrian Hubble, 01785 282423, crocus88@btinternet.com. *2m NW of Stafford. From J14 M6 take A5013 to Great Bridgeford. Turn L on to B5405. Park at village hall on L, or with consideration in Jasmine Rd on R. Short walk to last house in 40mph limit in Newport Rd.* Home-made teas. **Adm £3, chd free. Wed 1 June; Sun 17 July (2-5). Visitors also welcome by appt June & July, groups (min 20), no coaches.**
1/3 acre garden created from scratch over the last 6yrs by former chairman of Staffs group Hardy Plants Society. Mixed borders of rare and choice plants with outstanding colour associations designed for all-yr interest, incl water feature and alpine bed.

> Extra attractions on Open Day include treasure trails for children, tea and cakes and a stall selling plants, preserves and floral art photography . . .

44 ▶ THE OLD DAIRY HOUSE
Trentham Park, Stoke-on-Trent ST4 8AE. Philip & Michelle Moore. *S edge of Stoke-on-Trent. Behind Trentham Gardens on rd to Trentham Church and Trentham Park Golf Club. From A34 turn into Whitmore Rd B5038. 1st L and follow NGS signs. Please use Church car park.* Home-made & cream teas. **Adm £3, chd free. Sat 28, Suns 29 May; 7 Aug (1-5).**

Grade 2 listed house (not open) designed by Sir Charles Barry forms backdrop to this 2-acre garden in parkland setting. Shaded area for rhododendrons, azaleas plus expanding hosta and fern collection. Mature trees, 'cottage garden' and long borders. Narrow brick paths in vegetable plot. Large courtyard area for teas. Visitors are requested to park in the church car park.

45 ▶ THE OLD RECTORY, CLIFTON CAMPVILLE
B79 0AP. Martin & Margaret Browne, 01827 373533, MBrowne526@aol.com. *6m N of Tamworth. 2m W of M42 J11, in centre of Clifton Campville. Village signed off B5493 from Statfold or No Man's Heath. Entrance to garden on S side of Main St at top of hill, between bus shelter and school.* Home-made teas. Refreshments tailored to group requirements. **Adm £3.50, chd free. Visitors welcome by appt incl group visits tailored to your needs.**
Tranquil 2-acre garden around historic former Rectory developed over 29yrs by the present owners. Established trees enhanced by a diverse range of plants. Enjoy a garden on an ancient site, full of colour and interest in all seasons. Gravel and bark paths give easy access to lawns, borders, fruit and vegetables. Small walled garden and gravel areas. Opportunity to visit one of the Midland's finest Grade I listed medieval churches.

46 ▶ THE OLD RECTORY, MAVESYN RIDWARE
Church Lane, Mavesyn Ridware, nr Rugeley WS15 3QE. Sandra & Riach Ryder, sandra@oldrectory-mavesyn.co.uk. *5m N of Rugeley. Off B5014 - Lichfield to Abbots Bromley Rd, signed Church & Mavesyn Ridware - follow arrows.* Cream teas. **Adm £3.50, chd free. Sun 3 July (1-5).**
Approx 1¹/₂ acres S-facing and bounded by the Mill Stream. Herbaceous borders flank lawn that leads to a Victorian water fountain, surrounded by rose garden. Many water-loving plants can be seen along Mill stream bank. Living arbour along E-side of garden past the potting shed and kennels; Italian garden linked to main garden with laburnum walk. In the front wild roses growing the height of the old tithe barn and in

the courtyard mature trees along the boundary. Entrance through C17 Tythe barn. Church open - founded 1140. Cream teas, plants for sale and cake stall.

47 THE OLD VICARAGE
Fulford, nr Stone ST11 9QS. Mike & Cherry Dodson. *4m N of Stone. From Stone A520 (Leek). 1m R turn to Spot Acre and Fulford, turn L down Post Office Terrace, past village green/PH, take 2nd L. Good parking.* Home-made teas. Adm £3.50, chd free. Sat 2, Sun 3 July (2-5.30). Victorian house on sloping site of established shrubs conifers, and island beds. Wildlife friendly pond. Raised bed organic vegetables, fruit cage, greenhouse, summerhouse. Take a pleasant walk around the maturing, ongoing restoration of marl pit with jetty, fishing hut, interesting trees and informal waterside planting to encourage wildlife.

♿ ☕

48 NEW PAUL'S OASIS OF CALM
18 Kings Close, Kings Heath, Birmingham B14 6TP. Mr Paul Doogan, 0121 444 6943. *4m from city centre. 5m from the M42 J4. Take A345 to Kings Heath High Street then B4122 Vicarage Rd. Turn L onto Kings Rd then R to King Close.* Adm £2.50, chd free. Visitors welcome by appt May to Aug, coaches permitted, max group 15.
Garden cultivated from nothing into a little oasis. Measuring 18ft wide and 70ft long. It's small but packed with interesting and unusual plants, water features and 7 seating areas. It's my piece of heaven.

GROUP OPENING

49 PEREIRA ROAD GARDENS
Harborne, Birmingham B17 9JN. *Between Gillhurst Rd & Margaret Grove, 1/4 m from Hagley Rd or 1/2 m from Harborne High St.* Combined adm; April £2.50, June £3.50, chd free. Suns 24 Apr; 19 June (2-5).

14 PEREIRA ROAD
Mike Foster

48 PEREIRA ROAD
Rosemary Klem
Not open 24 April.

50 PEREIRA ROAD
Peg Peil
Visitors also welcome by appt. 07905 892831 (after 6.30pm)

55 PEREIRA ROAD
Emma Davies & Martin Commander
Not open 24 April.

A group of 4 different urban gardens. No.14 a well established suburban garden with mixed herbaceous and shrub borders and small fruit vegetable area. Wildlife friendly with 2 ponds. Ongoing alterations provide new area of interest each year. No. 48 south facing sloping, tiered garden with mature shrubs and koi pond. No.50 plantaholic's paradise with over 1000 varieties, many rare, incl fruits, vegetables, herbs, grasses and large bed of plants with African connections. Over 100 varieties on saleÖ see how they grow. No.55 sloping garden, incl gravelled beds with mixed planting, grasses and a small pond; all backing onto the Chad Brook.

♿

50 8 RECTORY ROAD
Solihull B91 3RP. Nigel & Daphne Carter. *Town centre. From M42 J5 follow directions toward town centre. 1st L after St Alphage Church into Rectory Road.* Home-made teas. Adm £3, chd free. Sun 24 July (12.30-5.30).
Stunning town garden divided into areas with different features. Unusual decking on entrance, surrounded by a variety of mixed planting. Steps down into lower garden, exotically planted and with summerhouse; past soft fruit plot and dry river bed theme and onto pond feature. Unusual plants throughout garden.

It's small but packed with interesting and unusual plants, water features and seven seating areas. It's my piece of heaven . . .

51 ROWLEY HOUSE FARM
Croxton, Stafford ST21 6PJ. Tony & Beryl Roe, 01630 620248. *4m W of Eccleshall. Between Eccleshall & Loggerheads on B5026. At Wetwood xrds turn for Fairoak. Take 1st L turn & continue for 3/4 m.* Home-made teas. Adm £3.50, chd free. Sun 26 June (2-5). Visitors also welcome by appt June & July only, coaches permitted.
Quiet country garden, part reclaimed from farm rick-yard. Shrub roses in orchard, soft fruits, vegetables and water feature incl. Extensive views towards the Wrekin and Welsh hills from adjacent land at 570ft, with plantings of 95 varieties of 7 species of ilex, various corylus and specimen trees.

52 23 ST JOHNS ROAD
Rowley Park, Stafford ST17 9AS. Colin & Fiona Horwath, 01785 258923, fiona_horwath@yahoo.co.uk. *1/2 m S of Stafford Town Centre. Just a few minutes from J13 of the M6. Off the A449 just after Rising Brook. Through entrance into private park, therefore please park considerately.* Home-made teas. Adm £3, chd free. Sun 20 Mar; Evening Opening £4, wine, Fri 20 May (6-9); Fri 15 July (2-5). Visitors also welcome by appt.
Pass through the black-and-white gate of this Victorian house into a part-walled gardener's haven, encouraging birds and other wildlife with an organic approach. Bulbs and shady woodlanders in Spring, many herbaceous plants and climbers. Sit and enjoy home-made cakes, by pond or Victorian-style greenhouse. Gardener is keen Hardy Planter and sows far too many seeds so always something good for sale!

♿ ☕ ☎

53 THE SECRET GARDEN
Little Haywood ST18 0UL. Derek Higgott & David Aston, 01889 883473. *5m SE of Stafford. A51, from Rugeley or Weston signed Little Haywood 1/2 m from Seven Springs. A513 Coley Lane from public house's at Back Lane, R into Coley Grove. Entrance to garden in Coley Grove.* Light refreshments & cream teas. Adm £3, chd free. Suns, Fris 22 May; 3, 26 June; 5 Aug (11-4). Also open Coley Cottage last 3 dates, The Garth, Tanglewood. 26 June. Visitors also welcome by appt June to Aug.

Wander past the other cottage gardens and through the evergreen arch and there before you a fantasy for the eyes and soul. Stunning garden approx 1/2 acre, created over the last 25yrs. Strong colour theme of trees and shrubs, underplanted with perennials, 1000 bulbs and laced with clematis; other features incl water, laburnum and rose tunnel and unique buildings. Is this the jewel in the crown? Raised gazebo with wonderful views over untouched meadows and Cannock Chase, also new features to be discovered. Hardy Plant Society sale in village hall Sun 22 May. Featured in Daily Telegraph (50 best small gardens to visit). Some slopes.

Heath House

54 9 SHEPHERDS FOLD
Wildwood, Stafford ST17 4SF. Peter & Alison Jordan, 01785 660819, alison.jordan2@btinternet.com. *3m S of Stafford. Follow A34 out of Stafford towards Connock 2nd R onto Wildwood estate. Follow ring rd, Shepherds Fold is 5th turning on L.* Home-made teas. **Adm £2.50, chd free. Visitors welcome by appt March to July.**
S-facing steep garden on heavy clay soil. Informal cottage planting, range of bulbs and perennials. No chemicals used on garden. Far reaching views over Penk Valley flood plain. Many interesting nooks and crannies. Owners get a lot of help in the garden from guide dog puppies.

55 SILVERWOOD
16 Beechfield Road, Trentham ST4 8HG. Aki & Sarah Akhtar. *3m S of Stoke on Trent. From A34 Trentham Gardens r'about take A5035 Longton Rd. After Nat West Bank take R turn into Oaktree Rd. From Longton (A50) follow A5035 into Trentham. After PH take L turn into Oaktree Rd, which becomes Beechfield Rd. Parking limited.* Home-made teas. **Adm £3, chd free (share to Breast Cancer Campaign). Sun 26 June (2-5).**
Designed for tranquillity and all year interest, this is a small, secluded town garden for plant collectors - brimming with colour and overflowing with pots. Plants for shade, cornus kousa, bamboos, almost a national collection of brunneras and an unusual water feature.

56 SMALL BUT BEAUTIFUL
6 Fishley Close, Bloxwich WS3 3QA. John & Julie Quinn. *1m NE of Bloxwich. Turn at side of Bloxwich Golf Club on A34, L at island, L at Costcutter into Fishley Lane, park on Saddlers PH (garden 5 mins walk away).* Home-made teas. **Adm £2.50, chd free. Sats 21 May; 9 July (10-5). Evening Opening £3, light refreshments, Sat 17 Sept (7-10).**
This beautiful garden is an inspiration to anyone who is looking to make the most of limited space. Every corner is used to its best potential and clever planting incorporates mature Japanese maples, stunning water feature, oriental bridge and stone ornaments. The evening opening enhances the garden beauty with masses of candles and coloured lights creating a truly magical atmosphere - sheer bliss. Featured in Daily Telegraph (Top 50 small gardens to visit), local press & on Midlands TV & local radio.

57 STONEHILL QUARRY GARDEN
Great Gate, Croxden, nr Uttoxeter ST10 4HF. Mrs Caroline Raymont. *6m NW of Uttoxeter. A50 to Uttoxeter. Take B5030 to JCB Rocester, L to Hollington & Croxden Abbey. Third R into Keelings Lane & Croxden Abbey. At Great Gate, T-junction L to Stonehill.* Tea & Coffee. **Adm £3. Mon 25 Apr; Sun 2 Oct (2-5).**
6-acre quarry garden incorporating numerous ornamental trees and shrubs (magnolias, acers, catalpa, Davidia, peonies, azaleas) underplanted with unusual Asiatic and American woodlanders (lilies, trillium, erythroniums, paris, podophyllum, arisaemas, hellebores), bamboo 'jungle', rock garden, mixed borders. Spring bulbs and hellebores. Autumn colour of particular interest with new winter bark feature to give a 'zing' to dreary days. C12 Cistercian Abbey ruins (adm free) 1/2 kilometre away. Churnet Valley walks & Alton Towers 10mins away. Featured in Historic

Gardens of England (Staffordshire) by Mowle & Barre. Regret NOT suitable for children.

58 TANGLEWOOD COTTAGE
Crossheads, Colwich ST18 0UG. Dennis & Helen Wood, 01889 882857, shuvitdog@hotmail.com. *5m SE of Stafford. A51 from Rugeley or Weston, signed Colwich, into village - Main Rd. Past church on L and school on R, under bridge & up hill, immed on R turn into Railway Lane (Crossheads) keep rail track to R & Abbey on L, approx 1/4 m (it does lead somewhere). Park on grass as signposted.* Home-made, cream teas & glass of wine. **Adm £3, chd free.** Sun 26 June (11-4); Sat 16 July (1-5). Evening Opening £4, wine, Fri 19 Aug (7-10). **Also open The Garth, Secret Garden and Coley Cottage (with separate admission) 26 June. Visitors also welcome by appt.**
A large country cottage garden, divided into smaller areas of interest. Mixed borders, koi carp pool, tranquil seated areas, vegetables and fruit, chickens and aviary. Exotics and unusual perennials incl abutilons, daturas, dicksonias and palms. Plant lover's garden. Winners of Haywoods Private Garden.

59 91 TOWER ROAD
Sutton Coldfield B75 5EQ. Heather & Gary Hawkins. *3m N Sutton Coldfield. From A5127 at Mere Green*

Island, turn into Mere Green Rd, L at St James, L again. Cream teas. **Adm £2.50, chd free.** Sun 12 June (1.30-5.30).
This 163ft S-facing garden with sweeping borders and island beds is planted with an eclectic mix of shrubs and perennials. The fishpond, cast iron water feature and hiding griffin enhance your journey around the garden. The ideal setting for sunbathing, hide and seek and lively garden parties. Featured in Sutton Observer.

60 NEW 19 WATERDALE
Compton, Wolverhampton WV3 9DY. Mr & Mrs Bailey. *1 1/2 m W of Wolverhampton city centre. From Wolverhampton Ring Rd take A454 towards Bridgnorth. Turn L into Waterdale off A545 Compton Rd West. Car park available at Compton Grange on R of Compton Rd W, opp Linden Lea - 5 mins walk. Limited parking for less able in Waterdale.* Home-made teas. **Adm £3, chd free.** Sun 12 June (1.30-5).
A secluded town garden which gradually unfolds from the sunny terrace and upper garden, through a shady fernery to the summerhouse garden and on to a Japanese teahouse, hidden by towering bamboo. Densely planted, in spite of dry conditions, incl many unusual perennials and shrubs, shell grotto project in progress.

61 THE WICKETS
47 Long Street, Wheaton Aston ST19 9NF. Tony & Kate Bennett, 01785 840233, ajtonyb@tiscali.co.uk. *8m W of Cannock, 10m N of Wolverhampton. From M6 J12 turn W towards Telford on A5; across A449 Gailey r'about; A5 for 1 1/2 m; turn R signed Stretton, 150yds turn L signed Wheaton Aston; 2 1/2 m turn L; 1/2 m over canal bridge; garden on R. Or Bradford Arms Wheaton Aston 2m.* **Adm £3, chd free.** Sun 10 July (1.30-5). **Visitors also welcome by appt.**
This garden is full of ideas, being made up of 20 different rooms and features including a pond, dry stream, clock golf, fernery, scree beds and many hanging baskets and containers. Following on from last year's enthusiastic reception, we will be showing our new model railway and diorama. Popular and pleasant walks along the Shropshire Union Canal just 25 metres away.

62 WINDY ARBOUR
Hollis Lane, Denstone ST14 5HP. Dave & Gill Brown, 01889 591013, stay@windyarbour.co.uk. *5m N of Uttoxeter, 3m S of Alton Towers. From A50 in Uttoxeter, follow Alton Towers signs on B5030. Turn L by JCB factory on B5031 for Denstone. Take 4th L into College Rd. Continue into Hollis Lane (no through rd) up hill into narrow farm track.* Home-made teas. **Adm £3, chd free.** Sun 31 July; Sun 7 Aug (1-5). **Also open The Beeches 31 July. Visitors also welcome by appt.**
Peaceful farmhouse retreat with panoramic views over surrounding countryside, designed to extend around converted outbuildings. Mixed and herbaceous borders, rockeries, herb garden, vegetable garden, rose arch, alpines, grasses, small fish pond, water features and arbours. Plenty of seating and large conservatory in which to enjoy afternoon tea.

63 WITS END
59 Tanworth Lane, Shirley B90 4DQ. Sue Mansell, 0121 744 4337, wits-end@hotmail.co.uk. *2m SW of Solihull. Take B4102 from Solihull, 2m. R at island onto A34. After next island (Sainsbury's) Tanworth Lane is 1st L off A34.* Home-made teas. **Adm £2.50, chd free.** Suns 15 May; 3 July; 7 Aug (2-5). **Visitors also**

Four Seasons

Visit the website for latest information

welcome by appt, groups of 10+. Interesting all-yr-round plantaholic's cottage-style garden. Hundreds of perennials, alpines and shrubs, many unusual in various shaped beds (some colour co-ordinated) plus spectacular late summer border. Gravel area, alpine sinks, rockery, small waterfall, river and bog. Millennium Wheel of sleepers and crazy paving in woodland setting and extensive shade.

Fascinating approaches to design, layout and planting, and according to their Visitors Book, have inspired and given many people ideas for their own gardens . . .

64 THE WOMBOURNE WODEHOUSE

Wolverhampton WV5 9BW. Mr & Mrs J Phillips, 01902 892202. *4m S of Wolverhampton. Just off A449 on A463 to Sedgley.* Home-made teas. **Adm £5, chd free.** Thur 2 June (2-5.30). Visitors also welcome by appt May to July.
18-acre garden laid out in 1750. Mainly rhododendrons, herbaceous border, woodland walk, water garden and over 170 different varieties of tall bearded irises in walled kitchen garden. Partial wheelchair access.

GROUP OPENING

65 WOODLEIGHTON GROVE GARDENS

Woodleighton Grove, Uttoxeter ST14 8BX. *SE area of Uttoxeter. From Uttoxeter take B5017 (Marchington). Go over Town Bridge, turn L, then R into Highwood Road, pass turning to Racecourse. After ¹/₄ mile turn R.* Home-made & cream teas. **Combined adm £3.50, chd free.** Sat 9 (11-5), Sun 10 July (1.30-5.30).

APOLLONIA
Helen & David Loughton

KARIBU
Graham & Judy White
Visitors also welcome by appt, prefer mid June to mid July, other dates on request.
01889 563930
cityofgold@lineone.net

These adjacent gardens demonstrate varied and fascinating approaches to design, layout and planting, and according to their Visitors Book, have inspired and given many people ideas for their own gardens. Appollonia is a plantaholics garden, strong structure on several levels. Summer house, greenhouse, laburnum arch, natural stream, some steep steps. Unusual and interesting planting including bamboos, tree ferns, bananas, hostas and agaves. A place to relax and enjoy. Karibu is a distinctive and intriguing garden with a number of absorbing features. Informally planted on two levels, with a natural stream, summerhouse, folly and gazebo. Archways, bridges, steps and a boardwalk lead to a selection of tranquil resting places. The garden discreetly houses a number of interesting artefacts. The greenhouse contains over 350 different cacti and succulents. An Artefacts Quiz and

Garden Search is available for any of our younger visitors who might be looking bored!

66 YARLET HOUSE

Yarlet, Stafford ST18 9SU. Mr & Mrs Nikolas Tarling. *2m S of Stone. Take A34 from Stone towards Stafford, turn L into Yarlet School and L again into car park.* Light refreshments & home-made teas. **Adm £4, chd free (share to Staffordshire Wildlife Trust).** Fri 1 July (2.30-6.30).
4 acre garden with extensive lawns, walks, lengthy herbaceous borders and traditional Victorian box hedge. Water gardens with fountain and rare lilies. Sweeping views across Trent Valley to Sandon. Victorian School Chapel. 9 hole putting course. Boules pitch. Yarlet School Art Display.

67 YEW TREE COTTAGE

Podmores Corner, Long Lane, White Cross, Haughton ST18 9JR. Clive & Ruth Plant, 01785 282516, pottyplantz@aol.com. *4m W of Stafford. Take A518 W Haughton, turn R Station Rd (signed Ranton) 1m, then turn R at Xrds ¹/₄ m on R.* Home-made teas. **Adm £3, chd free.** Suns 1, 29 May; 10 July (2-5). Visitors also welcome by appt.
Plantsman's garden brimming with unusual plants. Planted to give all year round interest but at present special interest in meconopsis, trillium, arisaema and dierama. ¹/₂ -acre incl pond, gravel gardens, herbaceous borders and vegetable garden for award winning vegetable, and plant sales area. Courtyard with oak timbered vinery to take tea in if the weather is unkind, and seats in the garden for lingering on sunny days.

Staffordshire County Volunteers

County Organisers
Susan & John Weston, Birch Trees, Copmere End, Eccleshall, Stafford ST21 6HH, 01785 850448, johnweston123@btinternet.com

County Treasurer
John Weston, Birch Trees, Copmere End, Eccleshall, Stafford ST21 6HH, 01785 850448, johnweston123@btinternet.com

Publicity
Bob Parker & Greg Kowalczuk, Magic Garden, 43, Broad Lane, Wolverhampton WV3 9BW. roboparker@blueyonder.co.uk

Assistant County Organiser
Pat Teggin, High Trees, 18 Drubbery Lane, Stoke-on-Trent ST3 4BA, 01782 318453, pat.teggin@btinternet.com

See more garden images at www.ngs.org.uk

SUFFOLK

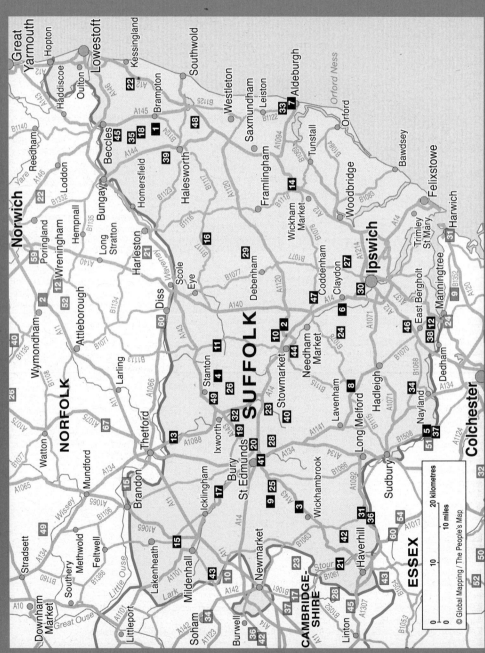

Opening Dates

February

Sunday 20
6 Blakenham Woodland Garden
18 Gable House

March

Saturday 26
47 Woodwards
Sunday 27
26 Langham Hall Gardens
47 Woodwards

April

Every Tue, Wed & Thur
48 Woottens
Sunday 3
4 The Beeches
Sunday 10
6 Blakenham Woodland Garden
21 Great Thurlow Hall
39 Rydal Mount
Sunday 17
6 Blakenham Woodland Garden
11 Corner Cottage
12 East Bergholt Place - The Place for Plants
Sunday 24
38 Rosemary
Saturday 30
27 Larks Hill

May

Every Tue, Wed & Thur
48 Woottens
Monday 2
5 Bevills
Sunday 8
12 East Bergholt Place - The Place for Plants
Saturday 14
49 Wyken Hall
Sunday 15
43 Street Farm
49 Wyken Hall
Sunday 22
28 The Lucy Redman School of Garden Design
34 The Priory
37 Rosedale
46 Windmill Cottage
Monday 23
48 Woottens
Friday 27
48 Woottens
Saturday 28
27 Larks Hill
48 Woottens

Sunday 29
31 Orchard House
41 South Hill
48 Woottens
Monday 30
48 Woottens

June

Every Tue, Wed & Thur
48 Woottens
Friday 3
48 Woottens
Saturday 4
48 Woottens
Sunday 5
10 Columbine Hall
15 The Former Rectory
18 Gable House
20 Great Barton Outskirts
48 Woottens
Monday 6
48 Woottens
Friday 10
48 Woottens
Saturday 11
45 White House Farm
Sunday 12
23 Hessett House
47 Woodwards
Saturday 18
25 Ickworth House Park & Gardens
Sunday 19
1 Barracks Cottage
14 The Firs
21 Great Thurlow Hall
29 Monksfield House
30 428 Norwich Road
40 Smallwood Green Gardens
Saturday 25
27 Larks Hill
Sunday 26
7 Brick Kiln Cottage
22 Henstead Exotic Garden
32 Pakenham Gardens
33 Priors Oak
39 Rydal Mount
44 Valley Farm Barn

July

Every Tue, Wed & Thur
48 Woottens
Sunday 3
16 Frythe Barn
24 2 High View
42 Southleigh
Sunday 10
35 Redisham Hall
36 Riverside House
48 Woottens
Monday 11
48 Woottens
Sunday 17
2 Bays Farm

47 Woodwards
48 Woottens
Monday 18
48 Woottens
Saturday 23
27 Larks Hill
Sunday 24
9 Cobbs Hall
48 Woottens
Monday 25
48 Woottens
Sunday 31
37 Rosedale

August

Every Tue, Wed & Thur
48 Woottens
Saturday 20
27 Larks Hill
Sunday 21
3 Beech Hall
47 Woodwards
Sunday 28
29 Monksfield House

September

Every Tue, Wed & Thur
48 Woottens
Sunday 4
11 Corner Cottage
16 Frythe Barn
19 Great Barton Gardens
Saturday 17
27 Larks Hill
Sunday 18
47 Woodwards
Sunday 25
17 Fullers Mill

Gardens open to the public

6 Blakenham Woodland Garden
12 East Bergholt Place - The Place for Plants
13 Euston Hall
25 Ickworth House Park & Gardens
48 Woottens
49 Wyken Hall

By appointment only

8 The Coach House

Also open by Appointment ☎

2 Bays Farm
3 Beech Hall
7 Brick Kiln Cottage

9 Cobbs Hall
11 Corner Cottage
32 Fen House, Pakenham Gardens
14 The Firs
18 Gable House
22 Henstead Exotic Garden
27 Larks Hill
28 The Lucy Redman School of Garden Design
30 428 Norwich Road
33 Priors Oak
37 Rosedale
38 Rosemary
39 Rydal Mount
40 Smallwood Farmhouse, Smallwood Green Gardens
40 Smallwood House, Smallwood Green Gardens
41 South Hill
44 Valley Farm Barn
45 White House Farm
46 Windmill Cottage
47 Woodwards

The Gardens

1 ▶ BARRACKS COTTAGE
Bacons Green Road, Westhall, Halesworth IP19 8RA. Maggie & Adrian Simpson-James. *4m NE of Halesworth. From Bungay & Halesworth take A144. Turn E at Spexhall Xrds follow signs. From Beccles take A145, turn W at Brampton Dog follow signs. From A12 take A145 to Beccles, turn L at Brampton Church onto B1124 follow signs.* Home-made teas. **Adm £3, chd free. Sun 19 June (12-6).**
This old cottage (not open) and garden nestles in the peaceful heart of Suffolk. A series of different 'rooms', incl cottage garden, rose pergola, natural pond, secret patio, potager and grass garden with surprise view. A must for rose lovers, with over 60 roses. The perfect place to sit and relax on a summer's afternoon. Sale of home produce. Firm gravel and bark paths with slight slope.
&♿ ⊕ ☕

2 ▶ NEW ▶ BAYS FARM
Forward Green, Earl Stonham IP14 5HU. Richard & Stephanie Challinor, 01449 711286, stephanie@baysfarmsuffolk.co.uk, www.baysfarmsuffolk.co.uk. *3¹/₂ m E of Stowmarket. J50 A14, take A1120 direction Stowupland. Proceed through Stowupland on A1120 for 1m, at sharp L bend turn R signed Broad Green. 1st house on R.* Home-made teas. **Adm £3, chd free. Sun 17 July (1-6). Visitors also welcome by appt max 10**

visitors.
2-acre garden with formal areas designed by Xa Tollemache. Shady borders, scented and sun-loving beds, with woodland and butterfly planting. Enclosed extensive kitchen garden with greenhouse and flower cutting beds. Wide-ranging orchard newly planted and new herb garden (2011). Gardens continue to be developed each year. Gravel paths.
&♿ ⊕ ┅ ☕ ☎

3 ▶ NEW ▶ BEECH HALL
Depden IP29 4BU. Mrs J Bolton, 01284 850220. *Midway between Bury St Edmunds & Haverhill on A143, take 1st R turn after Chedburgh.* Home-made teas. **Adm £3, chd free. Sun 21 Aug (1-5). Visitors also welcome by appt groups of 20+.**
9 acres of beautiful gardens with herbaceous borders and mixed variety of mature trees. New woodland walk with pond and various shrubs. Two summerhouses are situated in the garden together with large pond with Monet-style bridge. Partial wheelchair access.
&♿ 🐕 ☕ ☎

4 ▶ THE BEECHES
Grove Road, Walsham-le-Willows IP31 3AD. Dr A J Russell. *11m E of Bury St Edmunds. From A143 to Diss take turning to village.* Home-made teas. **Adm £3.50, chd free. Sun 3 Apr (2-5).**
150yr-old, 3-acre garden, which incl specimen trees, pond, potager, memorial garden, lawns and variety of beds. Stream area landscaped. New Mediterranean bed and camellia bed. Main drive gravel.
&♿ 🐕 ☕

5 ▶ BEVILLS
Sudbury Road, Bures CO8 5JW. Mr & Mrs G T C Probert. *4m S of Sudbury. Just N of Bures on the Sudbury rd B1508.* Light refreshments & home-made teas. **Adm £3, chd free. Mon 2 May (2-6).**
A beautiful house (not open) overlooking the Stour Valley with parkland trees, hills and woodland. The gardens are formal and Italianate in style with hedges and lawns flanked by Irish yews and mature specimen trees. Terraces, borders, ponds, vistas and woodland walks. Spring bulbs and bluebell wood. Some steep slopes.
&♿ 🐕 ☕

6 ▶ ♦ BLAKENHAM WOODLAND GARDEN
Little Blakenham, Ipswich IP8 4LZ. Lord Blakenham, 07760 342131, www.blakenhamwoodlandgarden. org.uk. *4m NW of Ipswich. Follow signs at Little Blakenham, 1m off B1113.* No teas 17 April. **Adm £3, chd £1.50. For NGS: Suns 20 Feb; 10, 17 Apr (10-5). For other opening times and information, please phone or see garden website.**
Beautiful 6-acre woodland garden with variety of rare trees and shrubs. Chinese rocks and a landscape sculpture. Especially lovely in spring with daffodils, camellias, magnolias and bluebells followed by roses in early summer. Snowdrop festival 20 Feb, special magnolia opening 10 Apr. Featured in Suffolk Norfolk Life.
&♿ ☕

Two summerhouses are situated in the garden together with large pond with Monet-style bridge . . .

7 ▶ BRICK KILN COTTAGE
Warren Hill Lane, Aldeburgh IP15 5QB. Sally Irvine & Rosemary Carter, sally.bkc@btinternet.com. *¹/₂ m from Aldeburgh. At Aldeburgh r'about turn L on to Leiston Rd. Warren Hill Lane unmade, no through rd on R after ¹/₂ m.* Light refreshments. **Adm £3, chd free. Sun 26 June (2-6). Also open Priors Oak. Visitors also welcome by appt July only, max 10, no coaches.**
2 acres by RSPB reserve with views to sea and Aldeburgh. Interesting varying levels and terracing, courtyard with hostas. Mixed shrubberies, wooded dell with walkway through ferns, kitchen garden, rose and lavender slope and specimen trees. New planting for 2011 following external house works. Accessible for wheelchairs with care, some slopes and grass.
&♿ ☕ ☎

BYNDES COTTAGE
See Essex.

CHIPPENHAM PARK
See Cambridgeshire.

8 THE COACH HOUSE

Hall Road, Chelsworth IP7 7HX. Susan & Elio de Sabata, 01449 740334, edesabata@aol.com. *From centre of village over hump back bridge opp Peacock PH, 2nd house on RH-side.* Home-made teas. **Adm £3.50, chd free. Visitors welcome by appt**, groups.

The $\frac{1}{3}$-acre garden benefits from having been part of Chelsworth Park, with its magnificent trees and borrowed landscaped across the river to the village church. A typical English garden with an Italian influence incl ancient gnarled olives. The garden incl fruit and vegetable plots, ponds, many roses and wild flower area. There will also be a small exhibition of local artists and shops, incl drawings, jewellery, greeting cards, garden furniture and iron work'.

9 COBBS HALL

Great Saxham IP29 5JN. Dr & Mrs R H Soper, 01284 850678, soperdoc@gmail.com. *4½ m W of Bury St Edmunds. A14 exit to Westley. R at Westley Xrds. L fork at Little Saxham signed Hargrave & Chevington. Approx 1½ m to sign on R turn. Mustard-coloured house 300yds on L.* Home-made teas. **Adm £3.50, chd free (share to St Andrews Church, Gt Saxham). Sun 24 July (2-6). Visitors also welcome by appt.**

2 acres of lawns and borders, ornamental trees, large fish/lily pond. Parterre, folly, walled kitchen garden, grass tennis court and pretty courtyard.

10 COLUMBINE HALL

Stowupland IP14 4AT. Hew Stevenson & Leslie Geddes-Brown, www.columbinehall.co.uk. *1½ m NE of Stowmarket. Turn N off A1120 opp Shell garage across village green, then R at T-junction into Gipping Rd. Garden on L just beyond derestriction sign.* Home-made teas. **Adm £4, chd free. Sun 5 June (2-6).**

George Carter's formal garden and herb garden surround moated medieval manor (not open). Outside the moat, vistas, stream, ponds and bog garden, Mediterranean garden, colour-themed vegetable garden, cutting garden, orchards and parkland. Gardens developed since 1994 with constant work-in-progress, incl transformed farm buildings and eyecatchers.

11 CORNER COTTAGE

Rickinghall Road, Gislingham IP23 8JJ. Trevor & Pauline Cox, 01449 781379. *5m W of Eye. On B1113 approx 9m N of Stowmarket or approx 2½ m S of Rickinghall.* **Adm £3, chd free. Suns 17 Apr; 4 Sept (11-5). Visitors also welcome by appt April to Sept.**

Our $\frac{3}{4}$-acre garden has informal borders with shrubs (many unusual) underplanted with perennials and in spring, naturalised snakes head fritillaries, anemones and cowslips. Around the house (not open) are paved and gravelled areas with raised beds planted with shrubs and alpines.

12 ◆ EAST BERGHOLT PLACE - THE PLACE FOR PLANTS

East Bergholt CO7 6UP. Mr & Mrs Rupert Eley, www.placeforplants.co.uk. *On B1070 towards Manningtree, 2m E of A12. Situated on the edge of East Bergholt.* **Adm £4, chd free. For NGS: Sun 17 Apr (10-5); Sun 8 May (10-5.30). For other opening times and information please see garden website**

20-acre garden originally laid out at the beginning of the century by the present owner's great grandfather. Full of many fine trees and shrubs, many seldom seen in East Anglia. A fine collection of camellias, magnolias and rhododendrons, topiary, and the National Collection of deciduous Euonymus.

NCCPG

13 ◆ EUSTON HALL

Thetford IP24 2QW. His Grace The Duke of Grafton, 01842 766366, www.eustonhall.co.uk. *12m N of Bury St Edmunds. 3m S of Thetford on A1088.* **Adm £7, chd £3. For opening times and information, please tel or see garden website.**

Terraced lawns, herbaceous borders, rose garden, C17 pleasure grounds, lake and watermill. C18 house open; famous collection of paintings. C17 church; temple by William Kent. Shop and teas.

14 THE FIRS

Church Road, Marlesford, Woodbridge IP13 0AT. Paul & Lesley Bensley, 01728 747152, lesleybensley@gmail.com. *2m E of Wickham Market. On A12 travelling N from Wickham Market take L turn signed Parham. Drive past village signpost, take next L. Parking at Village Hall next door.* Light Refreshments. Lunches and teas. **Adm £3.50, chd free. Sun 19 June (11-5). Visitors also welcome by appt.**

Garden in grounds of Edwardian House (not open). 2-acre country

Great Thurlow Hall

garden with open views encompassing the Edwardian themes of formal yew hedging, herbaceous borders and informal woodland planting. Includes vegetable plot and small orchard. Paddock is registered with Suffolk Wildlife Trust and being developed as a private nature reserve. Families with children most welcome.

15 NEW THE FORMER RECTORY
The Street, Eriswell, Brandon IP27 9BH. Bernard & Marian Ransome. *3m NE of Mildenhall. From Fiveways r'about at Barton Mills on A11 take A1065 towards Brandon, after approx 2m turn L onto B1112. On approaching Eriswell Village garden on L of War Memorial next to church.* Home-made teas. **Adm £3, chd free** (share to Action for ME). **Sun 5 June** (2-6).
1 acre consisting of shrub and perennial borders surrounded by lawned area containing specimen trees offering many different aspects. Unusual features incl cathedral style pergola with clock tower and water fountain. The well stocked vegetable garden has raised and garden beds divided by grass paths.

16 NEW FRYTHE BARN
Wilby Road, Stradbroke, Eye IP21 5JP. Don & Carol Darling. *11m SE of Diss, 10m N of Framlingham. From Framlingham B1118 to Stradbroke through Wilby, after ³/₄ m sharp LH bend (Neaves Lane on R) then 2nd driveway on R. Frythe Barn to R of drive. From Diss B1118 to Stradbroke. Centre of village R at church, immed L, Wilby Rd (B1118) ³/₄ m out of village, sharp LH bend, driveway on L 50yds after bend.* Cream teas July, home-made teas Sept. **Adm £4, chd free. Suns 3 July; 4 Sept** (11-5).
Still evolving garden of 2 acres. Incl natural pond with constructed stream, solar powered. Mediterranean-style patio with unusual water feature. Herbaceous and shrub borders, large grass beds, many lovely roses. Willow tunnel leading to wild flower meadow and spinney with path to bee hives - very placid bees! Picnickers welcome. No wheelchair access to spinney garden.

17 FULLERS MILL
West Stow IP28 6HD. Fullers Mill Trust. *6m NW of Bury St Edmunds. Off A1101 Bury to Mildenhall rd, signed West Stow.* **Adm £4, chd free. Sun 25 Sept** (2-5).
An enchanting 7 acre garden on the banks of R Lark. Combining a beautiful site of light, dappled woodland with a plantsman's paradise of rare and unusual shrubs, perennials and marginals planted with great natural charm. Euphorbias and lilies are a particular feature. A garden with interest in every season. In late Sept colchicums in flower incl outstanding white variety. Also yellow crocus-like Sternbergia should be in bloom. Gravel and grass paths, difficult when wet.

> Willow tunnel leading to wild flower meadow with path to bee hives . . . very placid bees! Picnickers welcome . . .

18 GABLE HOUSE
Halesworth Road, Redisham, Beccles NR34 8NE. John & Brenda Foster, 01502 575298. *5m S of Beccles. From Bungay A144 to Halesworth for 5m, turn L at St Lawrence School, 2m to Gable House. From A12 Blythburgh take A145 to Beccles, at Brampton X-roads L to Station Rd. 3m on at junction is Gable House.* Light Refreshments & home-made teas. Soup Lunches on Snowdrop Day; Salad Lunches on 5 June. **Adm £3.50, chd free. Sun 20 Feb** (11-4); **Sun 5 June** (11-5). **Visitors also welcome by appt.**
1-acre plantsman's garden of all-year interest. Vast collection of snowdrops, cyclamen, hellebores etc for the winter opening. The June open day brings colour and variety from shrub roses, perennials and interesting trees and shrubs. Greenhouses contain rare bulbs and tender plants. Featured in Garden News and The Garden.

GROUP OPENING

19 NEW GREAT BARTON GARDENS
Great Barton IP31 2PL. *NE of Bury St Edmunds. Take J43 A14, A143 exit to Bury St Edmunds/Diss. At r'about 1st exit onto Compiegne Way (A143), at next r'about 3rd exit stay on Compiegne Way. Through village then R onto Thurston Rd, just past L turning to Pakenham (tall pale green house).* Teas. **Sun 4 Sept** (12-5).

> NEW THE ARBORETUM
> School Lane. Mr & Mrs S Dancer

> NEW THE LILACS
> Thurston Road. Rob Hale & Jane Hamblin www.landarmydesigns.co.uk

> NEW WINBURN
> Thurston Road. Chris & Jennie Simpkin

Great Barton is of Saxon origin close to the historic town of Bury St Edmunds and noteworthy villages such as Lavenham, Cavendish, Clare and Ickworth. Three very lovely gardens: The Arboretum part of former Gt Barton Hall estate with a 2¹/₂ -acre walled garden has topiary with formal lawns and Japanese area with huge bamboos. The Lilacs, just 2yrs old, a garden of yr-round interest and easy maintenance with a kitchen and cutting garden. A garden for relaxing and entertaining. Winburn is a semi tropical surprise with a variety of exotic plants incl tree ferns, palms, bananas, bamboos, succulents and ferns overlooked by our jungle tree house with a woodland backdrop.

GROUP OPENING

20 NEW GREAT BARTON OUTSKIRTS
Great Barton IP31 2QU. *2m E of Bury St Edmunds. Leave A14 J45 at Routham Industrial Site, ¹/₂ m along Sow Lane to T-junction at Battlies Corner. Take L towards Bury St Edmunds for 1m along Mount Rd.* Home-made teas at Barton Mere. **Combined adm £4, chd free. Sun 5 June** (2-5).

> BARTON MERE
> Thurston Road. Mr & Mrs C O Stenderup

WALLOW
Mount Road. Linda & Mike Draper
www.thewallow.co.uk

Two very different gardens within 1½ m of each other close to historic Bury St Edmunds. Barton Mere, C16 house (not open) with later Georgian façade, set in parkland overlooking lake (The Mere). Mainly walled gardens with roses, herbaceous borders, shrubs, large vegetable garden and conservatory. Gravel paths. The Wallow 2 acres with wild flower meadows, potager, herbaceous borders plus raised vegetable beds with companion planting. Ongoing woodland planting (productive plants), wild area around large natural pond. Chickens and bees, things planned and things natural live very closely together.

21 GREAT THURLOW HALL
Haverhill CB9 7LF. Mr & Mrs George Vestey. *12m S of Bury St Edmunds, 4m N of Haverhill. Great Thurlow village on B1061 from Newmarket; 3½ m N of junction with A143 Haverhill/Bury St Edmunds rd.* Tea. **Adm £4, chd free. Sun 10 Apr; Sun 19 June (2-5).**
River walk newly restored and trout lake with extensive display of daffodils and blossom. Spacious lawns, shrubberies and roses. Walled kitchen garden.

22 HENSTEAD EXOTIC GARDEN
Yew Cottage, Church Road, Henstead NR34 7LD. Andrew Brogan, 07751 876606, absuffolk@hotmail.co.uk, www.hensteadexoticgarden.co.uk. *Equal distance between Beccles, Southwold & Lowestoft approx 5m. 1m from A12 turning after Wrentham (signed Henstead) very close to B1127.* **Adm £4, chd free. Sun 26 June (11-4). Visitors also welcome by appt.**
1-acre exotic garden featuring 80 large palms, 20+ bananas and 200 bamboo plants. 2 streams, 20ft tiered walkway leading to Thai style wooden covered pavilion. Mediterranean and jungle plants around 3 large ponds with fish. 'Suffolk's most exotic garden. Signed copies of garden owner's book for sale 'The History of the making of 'Henstead Exotic Garden'.

23 NEW HESSETT HOUSE
Drinkstone Road, Beyton, Bury St Edmunds IP30 9AH. Mr & Mrs Richard Hoet. *5m E of Bury St Edmunds. 1m up Drinkstone Rd, from Beyton on R.* Home-made teas. **Adm £3, chd free. Sun 12 June (2-6).**
Large country garden with S-facing lawns, looking over the ha ha to parkland planted with native mature trees and a young copse. The rose garden is set in 16 formal beds of mature old fashioned roses backed by a pergola of roses and clematis. Shrub beds border the lawns. Swimming pool and tennis court gardens with hedges of yew and viburnum and beech hedge of impressive size. A gate leads through to young arboretum and beds of hydrangea. Gravel paths, grassed areas.

Raised vegetable plots, apple and pear archway, woodland nature area . . .

24 NEW 2 HIGH VIEW
Derrick Hill, Willisham, Ipswich IP8 4SG. Mr & Mrs Hill. *6m NW of Ipswich. Just off Barking Rd between Bramford (B1113) and Barking (B1078).* Home-made teas. **Adm £3.50, chd free. Sun 3 July (11-5).**
Garden divided into rooms on elevated ³/₄ -acre site with unique and stunning views across valley towards Offton. Traditional cottage garden with herbaceous borders. Parterre with kitchen herb garden. Raised vegetable plots, apple and pear archway, woodland nature area. Summerhouse with tropical plants and grasses. Rockery with water feature.

25 ◆ ICKWORTH HOUSE PARK & GARDENS
Horringer IP29 5QE. National Trust, 01284 735819, www.nationaltrust.org.uk. *2m SW of Bury St Edmunds. Ickworth is in the village of Horringer on the A143 Bury to Haverhill Road, 2 miles from Bury St Edmunds.* **Adm £4.50, chd free. For NGS: Sat 18 June (10-4). For other opening times and**

information, please phone or see garden website.
70 acres of garden. South gardens restored to stylised Italian landscape to reflect extraordinary design of the house. Fine orangery, with agapanthus and geraniums. North gardens informal; wild flower lawns with wooded walk; the *Buxus* Collection, great variety of evergreens and Victorian stumpery. New planting of cedars. Parkland and woodland walks. Plant sales (not Buxus) and restaurant. Dogs not allowed in Italianate garden elsewhere on leads only.

KIRTLING TOWER
See Cambridgeshire.

26 LANGHAM HALL GARDENS
Bury St Edmunds IP31 3EF. Mr & Mrs Charles Blackwell, www.langhamherbs.co.uk / www.alpinecampanulas.co.uk. *Equidistant between Ixworth & Walsham-Le-Willows. 2m from A143 or 2m from A1088.* Home-made teas & cream teas. **Adm £3.50, chd free. Sun 27 Mar (2-5).**
Georgian gem set in 8 acres of gardens incl an historic 3.7 acres walled garden housing a National Collection of Alpine Campanulas and a fully working herb and fruit garden. Large variety of daffodils and other spring bulbs. Lovely trees and shrubs - a beautiful time of yr for this diverse garden. gravel paths.

27 LARKS HILL
Tuddenham St Martin IP6 9BY. Mr John Lambert, 01473 785248. *3m NE of Ipswich. From Ipswich take B1077 to Westerfield. Turn R for Tuddenham St Martin at Xrds, signed with NGS arrows to Clopton Rd & Larks Hill.* Home-made teas. **Adm £4, chd free. Sats 30 Apr; 28 May; 25 June; 23 July; 20 Aug; 17 Sept (1-5). Visitors also welcome by appt.**
The gardens of 8 acres comprise woodland, field and more formal areas, and fall away from the house to the valley floor. A hill within a garden and in Suffolk at that! Hilly garden with a modern castle keep with an interesting and beautiful site overlooking the gentle Fynn valley and the village beyond.

LODE GARDENS
See Cambridgeshire.

Support the NGS – eat more cake!

28 THE LUCY REDMAN SCHOOL OF GARDEN DESIGN

6 The Village, Rushbrooke, Bury St Edmunds IP30 0ER. Lucy Redman & Dominic Watts, 01284 386 250, lucy@lucyredman.co.uk, www.lucyredman.co.uk. *3m E of Bury St Edmunds. From A14 Bury St Edmunds E Sudbury exit, proceed towards town centre. After 50yds, 1st L exit from r'about and immed R. ³/₄ m to T-junction, turn L, follow rd for 2m. Before church turn R between white houses, past brick well, thatched house on L.* Home-made teas. **Adm £3, chd free. Sun 22 May (2-5).** ● **Visitors also welcome by appt.**
Thatched cottage surrounded by ³/₄ -acre quirky plantsman's family garden with impressive colour-coordinated borders containing unusual shrubs, roses, grasses and perennials. Stone parterre, turf tree seat, sculptures, sedum roofed pavilion. Unusual bulb and rhizome garden, willow tunnel. 'Palais de Poulet' and decorative vegetable garden. 20m Celtic Race track sculpture topped with 250 Sedum and Sempervivium. Highest garden accolade - garden visited by Beth Chatto. Church open. Featured in Sunday Telegraph August (front cover and article in Life section) Good Garden Guide 2010/11Dream Gardens of England book by Barbara Baker - photos by Jerry and Marcus Harpur. Planting by Diarmuid Gavin and Terence Conran.

&. ⚘ ☕ ☎

29 MONKSFIELD HOUSE

The Green, Monk Soham IP13 7EX. Kay & Richard Lacey, www.k-plants.co.uk. *3m E of Debenham. 4m W of Framlingham. Off A1120 between Framsden & Earl Soham, drive through Ashfield cum Thorpe. Follow rd for 3m, turn R signed Monk Soham. Fork L at Y-junction, garden on L after ³/₄ m.* Cream Teas. **Adm £4, chd free. Suns 19 June; 28 Aug (11-5).**
2-acre plantsman's garden comprising herbaceous and shrub borders with cottage style planting, parterre, meadow with native orchids. Japanese style area with unusual acers and prairie borders with large variety of specimen grasses. Natural pond. Bog garden with alpine planting and water feature. Woodland with tranquil walks. Exotic plant collection. Visit in June to see the native orchids in flower. Landscaping nursery open for plant sales.

&. 🔫 ⚘ ☕

30 428 NORWICH ROAD

Ipswich IP1 5DU. Robert & Gloria Lawrence, 01473 743673, globoblaw@talktalk.net. *1¹/₂ m W of Ipswich town centre. On A1156 Norwich Rd garden is 200yds W of railway bridge.* Home-made teas. **Adm £2.50, chd free. Sun 19 June (2-5). Visitors also welcome by appt from 19 June to 31July.**
¹/₃ - acre garden with sunken terrace and small pond leading up to lawn with rose beds and herbaceous border and dry stone garden. Lawn leads to bog garden, island mixed bed and on to orchard (15 fruit trees), asparagus bed, small vegetable plot with composting area.

⚘ ☕ ☎

31 NEW ORCHARD HOUSE

22 Nethergate Street, Clare CO10 8NP. Gillian & Geoffrey Bray. *100yds from centre of Clare. On L of Nethergate St (A1092) from direction of Stoke-by-Clare. Limited on-street parking. Please use Country Park car park off Well Lane.* Home-made teas. **Adm £3, chd free. Sun 29 May (2-5.30).**
A surprisingly large garden for a town house. We redesigned, re-landscaped and replanted it in 2007/08 and maintain it entirely by ourselves. The long formal garden is divided into areas of different interest, which incl a tranquil pond garden, herb garden, colour-themed borders and productive kitchen garden. Wild area with newly planted trees and meadow flowers. Gravel drive on slight slope, before hard paths reached.

&. ☕

GROUP OPENING

32 NEW PAKENHAM GARDENS

Pakenham IP31 2LP. *5m NE of Bury St Edmunds. Off A143, 11m NW of Stowmarket A14 & A1088. 11m S of Thetford A1088 & A143.* Cream teas at Squires Gate. **Combined adm £3.50, chd free. Sun 26 June (11-5).**

> **NEW FEN HOUSE**
> Lynn & Glynn Patterson-Evans. *On entering Great Barton approx 1m, take R turn at Bunbury Arms signed Thurston/Pakenham. Turn L towards Pakenham through village, L past Agri Centre signed Watermill. Garden ¹/₄ m on R* **Visitors also welcome by appt**

May to Aug, groups 10 max. No coaches. 01359 234968 glynn.evans@hotmail.co.uk

> **NEW PELAMBECH**
> Mr & Mrs A Jacobi

> **NEW SQUIRES GATE**
> Rip & Mary Kirby

Three quite different gardens in picturesque village with a working watermill and windmill. Fen House is a beautiful ¹/₂ -acre garden created on two levels accessed via steps or slope. Large pond with waterfall, numerous beds, incl collection of hostas, mature trees, shrubs, pergola and folly, small courtyard garden complete with red telephone box. Squires Gate is a garden of many parts. In a secluded area covered in vines and creepers is a garden pond containing 16,000 gallons of water with a range of fish. The rear terraced gardens are planted with many flowers and shrubs, complemented by waterfall, bridge, pond and hosta house. Pelambech - a delight to wander around this pretty cottage garden of approx ²/₃ -acre built on two levels. Interesting and colourful at most times of the year. This established garden has various water features and many attractive trees. RSPB Micklemere Bird Sanctuary (hide). Watermill and tea rooms open to public. No wheelchair access to Squires Gate.

&. ☕

Three quite different gardens in picturesque village with a working watermill and windmill . . .

33 PRIORS OAK

Leiston Road, Aldeburgh IP15 5QE. Mrs Trudie Willis, 01728 452580, trudie.willis@dinkum.free-online.co.uk. *1m N of Aldeburgh on B1122. Garden on L opp RSPB Reserve.* Light refreshments, teas & wine. **Adm £3, chd free. Sun 26 June (2-6). Also open Brick Kiln Cottage. Visitors also welcome by appt.**
10-acre wildlife and butterfly garden. Ornamental salad and vegetable gardens with companion planting.

Herbaceous borders, ferns and Mediterranean plants. Pond and wild flower acid grassland with a small wood. Interesting trees and over 30 varieties of buddleia. Very tranquil and fragrant garden with grass paths and yearly interest.

 ♿ ✿ ☕ ☎

Rosemary

34▶ THE PRIORY
Stoke-by-Nayland CO6 4RL. Mr & Mrs H F A Engleheart. *5m SW of Hadleigh. Entrance on B1068 to Sudbury (NW of Stoke-by-Nayland).* Home-made teas. **Adm £3.50, chd free.** Sun 22 May (2-5).
Interesting 9-acre garden with fine views over Constable countryside; lawns sloping down to small lakes and water garden; fine trees, rhododendrons and azaleas; walled garden; mixed borders and ornamental greenhouse. Wide variety of plants. Gravel paths, some slopes.

 ♿ 🐕 ✿ ☕ 🍺

35▶ REDISHAM HALL
nr Beccles NR34 8LZ. The Palgrave Brown Family. *5m S of Beccles. From A145, turn W on to Ringsfield-Bungay rd. Beccles, Halesworth or Bungay, all within 5m.* Home-made teas. **Adm £3.50, chd free.** Sun 10 July (2-6).
C18 Georgian house (not open). 5-acre garden set in 400 acres parkland and woods. Incl 2-acre walled kitchen garden (in full production) with peach house, vinery and glasshouses. Lawns, herbaceous borders, shrubberies, ponds and mature trees.

 ♿ 🍺

36▶ RIVERSIDE HOUSE
Stoke Road, Clare, Sudbury CO10 8NS. Mr & Mrs A C W Bone, www.clare.bulbs.co.uk/garden. *On Haverhill side of Clare on A1092, 500yds from town centre.* Teas available in town centre (500yds). **Adm £3.50, chd free.** Sun 10 July (12-5.30).
Peaceful walled country garden leading down to the R Stour. Fine lawns, trees, shrubs and mixed herbaceous beds. A splash of summer annuals completes the picture. Home of the Clare Bulb Company. Winner Best Garden in Suffolk, 1-acre category.

 🐕 🍺

ROOKWOODS
See Essex.

37▶ ROSEDALE
40 Colchester Road, Bures CO8 5AE. Mr & Mrs Colin Lorking, 01787 227619, rosedale40@btinternet.com. *6m SE of Sudbury. 9m NW of Colchester on B1508. As you enter the village of Bures, garden on L. From Sudbury follow signs through village towards Colchester, garden on R as you leave village.* Home-made teas. **Adm £3, chd free.** Sun 22 May; Sun 31 July (12-5.15). Visitors also welcome by appt.
Approx ¹/₃-acre plantsman's garden; many unusual plants, herbaceous borders, pond, woodland area,for the May opening come & see an impressive display of Peonies including a superb Joseph Rock & for the Aug opening you can enjoy a stunning collection of approx 60 agapanthus in full flower.

 ✿ 🍺 ☎

38▶ ROSEMARY
Rectory Hill, East Bergholt CO7 6TH. Mrs N E M Finch, 01206 298241. *9m NE of Colchester. Turn off A12 onto B1070 to East Bergholt, 1st R Hadleigh Rd, bear L at end of rd. At junction with Village St turn R, pass Red Lion PH, post office & church. Garden 100yds down from church on L.* Home-made teas. **Adm £3.50, chd free.** Sun 24 Apr (2-5.30). Visitors also welcome by appt.
This romantic garden, which appeals particularly to artists, has been developed over 35yrs. Planted to reveal paths and vistas. Many flowering trees and shrubs, much admired 'tapestry' bed with mixed hellebores, bulbs and appropriate ground cover. 2 bog beds, and unusual trees. Planted for all seasons.

 ♿ 🐕 ✿ 🛏 ☕ 🍺 ☎

39 RYDAL MOUNT

Grays Lane, Wissett IP19 0JP. Mr & Mrs A Witherby, 01986 873339. *2m W of Halesworth. From A12 exit onto A144 signed Halesworth/Bungay. Turn R into Halesworth, straight over 3 r'abouts then 1st L into Wissett Rd. Follow rd to Wissett, past church in Wissett, Grays Lane is next turning on R. Garden 1st house on L.* Home-made teas. **Adm £4, chd free. Suns 10 Apr; 26 June (11-5).** Visitors also welcome by appt April & June only, min 10, no max.

Fine vistas of daffodils shown off by flowering cherries, and ornamental trees. Primroses and cowslips in abundance. Roses predominate in June with many beds, climbers and ramblers are supported by superb pergolas. 2 ponds, fine shrubbery, young orchard with orchids, chickens and geese, kitchen garden, polytunnel, and soft fruit. New Victorian greenhouse.

  ♿ 🏵 ⊗ ☕ ☎

SHRUBS FARM

See Essex.

GROUP OPENING

40 NEW SMALLWOOD GREEN GARDENS

Bradford St George IP30 0AJ. *¹/₂ m from Bradford Woods. On main rd between Hessett & Felsham.* Home-made teas at Martins Nursery. **Combined adm £3, chd free. Sun 19 June (10-4).**

> #### NEW SMALLWOOD FARMHOUSE
> Widget & Tim Finn
> Visitors also welcome by appt. 01449 736358
> widget.finn@gmail.com

> #### NEW SMALLWOOD HOUSE
> Richard & Susan Martin
> Visitors also welcome by appt coaches welcome, parking available.
> 01449 737698
> martinsnurseries@btconnect. com

Two adjacent gardens with different styles of herbaceous gardening in the hamlet of Smallwood Green. Smallwood House has a relatively new garden full of herbaceous perennials with two distinctive styles of gardening on view. Smallwood Farmhouse, a C16 farmhouse is a backdrop to a romantic mature 3-acre garden with old roses, clematis,

honeysuckle rambling through trees, paths winding through ancient meadow to Ruby dome. With a variety of habitats. Smallwood Farmhouse featured in Dream Gardens of England & Country Living.

♿ 🏵 ⊗ ☕

---

41 SOUTH HILL

42 Southgate Street, Bury St Edmunds IP33 2AZ. Professor & Mrs S Gull, segull@btconnect.com. *Exit A14 J44, take 3rd exit off 2nd r'about into Southgate St, follow yellow signs. Opp Government offices in Southgate St, car park St Mary's Sq.* Home-made teas. **Adm £3, chd free. Sun 29 May (11-6).** Visitors also welcome by appt.

Town garden where Mr Pickwick landed in a gooseberry bush. Free-draining soil, divided into compartments in 1993, incl small maze, woodland path, herb garden and herbaceous borders. Productive compost heap and dye plants.

♿ ⊗ ☕ ☎

3-acre garden with old roses, clematis, honeysuckle rambling ancient meadow to Ruby dome . . .

---

42 SOUTHLEIGH

Valley Wash, Hundon CO10 8EJ. Paula Halson & Mike Laycock, www.southleighhouse.co.uk. *3¹/₂ m NW of Clare. 5m NE of Haverhill, 10m S of Bury St Edmunds. A143 out of Haverhill, turn R at Grey's Lane to Barnardiston/Hundon. Follow rd into village, ¹/₂ m past R turn to Chimney St or Clare Rd to Hundon, garden immed past 2nd R turn to Stradishall & Bury St Edmunds.* Home-made teas. **Adm £3, chd free. Sun 3 July (10.30-4).**

Secluded ¹/₂ -acre cottage garden surrounding thatched cottage (not open) dating from 1640, situated on outskirts of village. Garden restored in recent yrs to incl both cottage-style planting and more formal borders.

Exhibition by local artists. Quiet incidental musical entertainment. Gravel pathways. Shallow steps up to main garden. Assistance willingly offered.

♿ 🏵 ⊗ ☕

SPENCERS

See Essex.

43 STREET FARM

North Street, Freckenham IP28 8HY. David & Clodagh Dugdale. *3m W of Mildenhall. From A11 exit at Kennett to Chippenham. Through Chippenham and take 1st R then 1st R to Freckenham. North St on L by village cross, Street Farm 2nd on L.* Light Refreshments & teas. **Adm £4, chd free. Sun 15 May (10-5).**

Approx 1 acre of landscaped garden, with several mature trees. The garden incl a water cascade, pond with island and a number of bridges. Formal box garden, rose pergola, herbaceous borders and hornbeam walk. Gravel paths wth steps and slopes.

☕

TUDOR ROOST

See Essex.

44 VALLEY FARM BARN

Combs Lane, Combs Ford IP14 2NL. Lynn & Robin Lloyd, 01449 614670, lynn.lloyd@pprune.com. *¹/₂ m W of Stowmarket. Just outside village of Combs Ford on SW corner of Stowmarket. Follow signs to Combs Ford once on Combs Lane the Barn is 400m W of village.* Home-made teas. **Adm £3.50, chd free. Sun 26 June (11-5).** Visitors also welcome by appt.

Classic C16 Suffolk barn on gently sloping site of approx ³/₄ acre surrounded by countryside. Formal areas, herbaceous and shrub borders, landscaped water feature with stream and 2 ponds, areas of wild flower meadow with grass pathways meandering through. Chicken run with fruit and vegetable beds. Ponds with koi, rudd, carp etc. Small entertaining flock of fancy fowl and visiting ducks. Live music and original botanical art for sale.

♿ 🏵 ⊗ ☕ ☎

45 WHITE HOUSE FARM

Ringsfield, Beccles NR34 8JU. James & Jan Barlow, 07795 170892. *2m SW of Beccles. From*

Be tempted by a plant from a plant stall ⊗

Beccles take B1062 towards Bungay, after 1½ m turn L, signed Ringsfield. Continue for 1m passing Ringsfield Church. Garden 300yds on L over small white railed bridge. Parking opp church. Home-made teas & cream teas. **Adm £3.50, chd free. Sat 11 June (10.30-4.30). Visitors also welcome by appt.**
Tranquil park-type garden approx 30 acres, bordered by farmland and with fine views. Comprising formal areas, copses, natural pond, ornamental pond, woodland walk, vegetable garden and orchard. Picnickers welcome. NB The ponds and beck are unfenced.

46 WINDMILL COTTAGE
Mill Hill, Capel-St-Mary, Ipswich IP9 2JE. Mr & Mrs G A Cox, 01473 311121, gaandemcox@lineone.net. *3m SW of Ipswich. Turn off A12 at Capel-St-Mary. At far end of village on R after 1¼ m.* Home-made teas. **Adm £3, chd free. Sun 22 May (2-5). Visitors also welcome by appt.**
½ -acre plantsman's cottage-style garden. Island beds, pergolas with clematis and other climbers. Many trees and shrubs, wildlife ponds and vegetable plot.

47 WOODWARDS
Blacksmiths Lane, Coddenham, Ipswich IP6 9TX. Marion & Richard Kenward, 01449 760639. *7m N of Ipswich. From A14 turn onto A140, after ¼ m take B1078 towards Wickham Market, Coddenham is on route. Ample parking for coaches.*

Home-made teas. **Adm £2.50, chd free. Sat 26, Sun 27 Mar; Suns 12 June; 17 July; 21 Aug; 18 Sept (10-6). Visitors also welcome by appt.**
Award winning S-facing gently sloping garden of 1½ acres, overlooking the rolling Suffolk countryside. Designed and maintained by owners for yr-round colour and interest, lots of island beds, well stocked with 1000s of bulbs, shrubs and perennials, vegetable plot, numerous hanging baskets for spring and summer. Well maniured lawns, with large mature trees. More than 16000 bulbs have been planted over the last 2yrs, for our spring display.

More than 16000 bulbs have been planted over the last 2 years, for our spring display . . .

48 ◆ WOOTTENS
Blackheath Road, Wenhaston IP19 9HD. Mr M Loftus, 01502 478258, www.woottensplants.co.uk. *18m S of Lowestoft. On A12 & B1123, follow*

signs to Wenhaston. **Adm £2, chd free. For NGS: Tues, Weds, Thurs, 01 April to 30 Sept (The Garden), Mons, Tues, Weds, Thurs, Fris, Sats, Suns, 23 May to 10 June (The Bearded Iris Field), Mons, Suns, 10 July to 25 July (The Hemerocallis Field). For other opening times and information, please phone or see garden website.**
Small romantic garden, redesigned in 2003. Species and Scented-leafed pelargoniums, violas, cranesbills, lilies, salvias, penstemons, primulas, etc. 2 acres of bearded iris, 1 acre of hemerocallis. A nursery with the largest range of Herbaceous plants in East Anglia. Featured in Mail on Sunday and Sunday Telegraph, and on BBC Gardeners Question Time.

49 ◆ WYKEN HALL
Stanton IP31 2DW. Sir Kenneth & Lady Carlisle, www.wykenvineyards.co.uk. *9m NE of Bury St Edmunds. Along A143. Follow signs to Wyken Vineyards on A143 between Ixworth & Stanton.* **Adm £4, chd free. For NGS: Sat 14, Sun 15 May (2-6). For other opening times and information, please see garden website.**
4-acre garden much developed recently; knot and herb garden; old-fashioned rose garden, wild garden, nuttery, pond, gazebo and maze; herbaceous borders and old orchard. Woodland walk, vineyard. Restaurant, shop.

Suffolk County Volunteers

County Organisers
East Kay & Richard Lacey, Monksfield House, Monk Soham, Woodbrdge IP13 7EX 01728 628449 kplants@btinternet.com
West Jenny Reeve, 6a Church Walk, Mildenhall IP28 7ED, 01638 715289, j.reeve05@tiscali.co.uk

County Treasurers
East Geoffrey Cox, Windmill Cottage, Mill Hill, Capel St. Mary, Ipswich, Suffolk IP9 2JE, 01473 311121, gaandemcox@lineone.net
West David Reeve, 6a Church Walk, Mildenhall, Bury St. Edmunds IP28 7ED, 01638 715289, j.reeve05@tiscali.co.uk

Publicity
Dick Soper, Cobbs Hall, Cobbs Hall Lane, Great Saxham, Bury St Edmunds, IP29 5JN, 01284 850678, soperdoc@gmail.com

Booklet Coordinator
Catherine Horwood Barwise, Richmond House, 20 Nethergate Street, Clare, Sudbury CO10 8NP, 01787 279315

Assistant County Organisers:
East Patricia Short, 7 Joseph Close, Hadleigh, Suffolk IP7 5FH, 01473 823639
East Jobie West, The Millstone, Friars Road, Hadleigh IP7 6DF, 01473 823154
West Julie King, Chestnuts, Church Road, Great Barton, Bury St Edmunds IP31 2QR, 01284 788236, jckingst@hotmail.co.uk
West Yvonne Leonard, Crossbills, Field Road, Mildenhall IP28 7AL, 01638 712742, yj.leonard@btinternet.com

Sign up to our eNewsletter for news and updates

SURREY

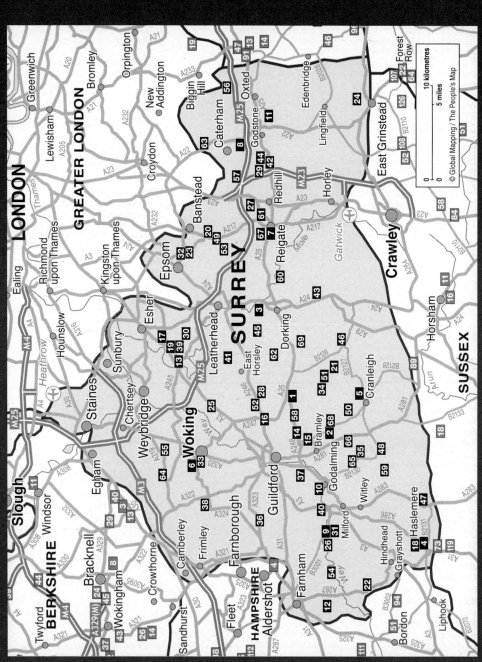

Opening Dates

February

Sunday 20
27 Gatton Park

Wednesday 23
27 Gatton Park

March

Saturday 12
11 Chauffeur's Flat

Sunday 13
11 Chauffeur's Flat

Sunday 20
1 Albury Park

Sunday 27
8 The Chalet
16 Clandon Park
55 Timber Hill
59 Vann

Monday 28
59 Vann

Tuesday 29
59 Vann

Wednesday 30
59 Vann

Thursday 31
59 Vann

April

Friday 1
59 Vann

Saturday 2
59 Vann
66 Wintershall Manor

Sunday 3
8 The Chalet
59 Vann

Sunday 10
7 Caxton House
21 Coverwood Lakes

Thursday 14
68 Woodhill Manor - **Pre-booking essential**

Friday 15
68 Woodhill Manor - **Pre-booking essential**

Sunday 17
21 Coverwood Lakes
49 41 Shelvers Way
55 Timber Hill
58 Vale End
65 Winkworth Arboretum

Sunday 24
13 Chestnut Lodge

Monday 25
21 Coverwood Lakes

Thursday 28
25 Dunsborough Park

May

Sunday 1
22 Crosswater Farm
43 The Old Croft
63 57 Westhall Road

Monday 2
21 Coverwood Lakes
22 Crosswater Farm
43 The Old Croft
59 Vann
62 Walton Poor House
63 57 Westhall Road

Tuesday 3
59 Vann

Wednesday 4
59 Vann

Thursday 5
59 Vann

Friday 6
59 Vann

Saturday 7
17 Claremont Landscape Garden
59 Vann
64 Westways Farm
66 Wintershall Manor

Sunday 8
14 Chilworth Manor
21 Coverwood Lakes
28 Hatchlands Park
59 Vann
64 Westways Farm

Friday 13
47 Ramster

Sunday 15
21 Coverwood Lakes
37 Loseley Park

Saturday 21
29 The Woodland Trail at the Hawthorns School
56 Titsey Place Gardens

Sunday 22
34 Knowle Grange
51 Spurfold

Wednesday 25
20 The Copse Lodge

Sunday 29
12 Chestnut Cottage
19 The Coach House
20 The Copse Lodge
23 Culverkeys
38 Memoirs
39 Moleshill House
43 The Old Croft
63 57 Westhall Road

Monday 30
19 The Coach House
39 Moleshill House
43 The Old Croft
63 57 Westhall Road

Tuesday 31
20 The Copse Lodge (Evening)

June

Sunday 5
9 Chandlers
24 Dormans Park Safari
31 Hideaway House
59 Vann
62 Walton Poor House

Monday 6
59 Vann

Tuesday 7
59 Vann

Wednesday 8
5 Barhatch Farm
59 Vann

Thursday 9
59 Vann

Friday 10
58 Vale End (Evening)
59 Vann

Saturday 11
54 Tilford Cottage
59 Vann

Sunday 12
5 Barhatch Farm
30 Heathside
36 Longer End Cottage
48 The Round House
54 Tilford Cottage
57 Tollsworth Manor
59 Vann

Wednesday 15
48 The Round House
58 Vale End

Friday 17
3 Ashleigh Grange (Evening)
54 Tilford Cottage (Evening)

Saturday 18
4 Bardsey
54 Tilford Cottage
56 Titsey Place Gardens

Sunday 19
3 Ashleigh Grange
4 Bardsey
10 Charterhouse
15 Chinthurst Lodge
18 Cleeves
25 Dunsborough Park
36 Longer End Cottage
54 Tilford Cottage
69 Wotton House

Wednesday 22
3 Ashleigh Grange
15 Chinthurst Lodge
52 Stuart Cottage (Evening)

Saturday 25
44 The Old Rectory
60 Vicarage Cottage
63 57 Westhall Road

Sunday 26
6 Birch Cottage
7 Caxton House
33 Horsell Allotments
60 Vicarage Cottage
63 57 Westhall Road

You are always welcome at an NGS garden

July

Sunday 3
13 Chestnut Lodge

Saturday 9
43 The Old Croft
67 Woodbury Cottage

Sunday 10
40 Norney Wood
43 The Old Croft
45 Polesden Lacey
48 The Round House
62 Walton Poor House
67 Woodbury Cottage
69 Wotton House

Wednesday 13
26 Foxhill
48 The Round House

Thursday 14
26 Foxhill

Friday 15
26 Foxhill

Saturday 16
56 Titsey Place Gardens

Sunday 17
23 Culverkeys
49 41 Shelvers Way

Thursday 21
68 Woodhill Manor - **Pre-booking essential**

Friday 22
68 Woodhill Manor - **Pre-booking essential**

Saturday 23
2 Appletrees

Sunday 24
2 Appletrees
52 Stuart Cottage

Friday 29
2 Appletrees (Evening)

Saturday 30
53 35 Tadorne Road

Sunday 31
32 29 Higher Green
53 35 Tadorne Road
61 Walnut House

August

Wednesday 3
61 Walnut House (Evening)

Saturday 6
43 The Old Croft

Sunday 7
42 Odstock
43 The Old Croft

Saturday 20
46 Pratsham Grange
56 Titsey Place Gardens

Sunday 21
46 Pratsham Grange
49 41 Shelvers Way

Sunday 28
41 Norwood Farm
52 Stuart Cottage

September

Saturday 3
67 Woodbury Cottage

Sunday 4
67 Woodbury Cottage

Wednesday 7
67 Woodbury Cottage

Sunday 11
34 Knowle Grange

Sunday 18
13 Chestnut Lodge
25 Dunsborough Park

October

Sunday 2
1 Albury Park
65 Winkworth Arboretum

Sunday 9
17 Claremont Landscape Garden

Sunday 16
21 Coverwood Lakes
28 Hatchlands Park

February 2012

Sunday 12
27 Gatton Park

Gardens open to the public

16 Clandon Park
17 Claremont Landscape Garden
22 Crosswater Farm
27 Gatton Park
28 Hatchlands Park
37 Loseley Park
45 Polesden Lacey
47 Ramster
56 Titsey Place Gardens
59 Vann
65 Winkworth Arboretum

By appointment only

35 Lodkin
50 Smithwood House
68 Woodhill Manor

Also open by Appointment ☎

2 Appletrees
3 Ashleigh Grange
4 Bardsey
5 Barhatch Farm
7 Caxton House
15 Chinthurst Lodge
20 The Copse Lodge

23 Culverkeys
30 Heathside
32 29 Higher Green
36 Longer End Cottage
39 Moleshill House
42 Odstock
48 The Round House
49 41 Shelvers Way
51 Spurfold
52 Stuart Cottage
54 Tilford Cottage
55 Timber Hill
58 Vale End
59 Vann
61 Walnut House
62 Walton Poor House
64 Westways Farm
67 Woodbury Cottage

The Gardens

1 **ALBURY PARK**
Albury GU5 9BH. Trustees of Albury Estate. *5m SE of Guildford. From A25 take A248 towards Albury for ¼ m, then up New Rd, entrance to Albury Park immed on L.* Home-made teas. Adm £3.50, chd free. Suns 20 Mar; 2 Oct (2-5). 14-acre pleasure grounds laid out in 1670s by John Evelyn for Henry Howard, later 6th Duke of Norfolk. ¼ m terraces, fine collection of trees, lake and river. Albury Park Mansion gardens also open (by kind permission of Historic House Retirement Homes Ltd. House not open). Gravel path and slight slope.
&. ☕

23 ANGLESEY ROAD
See Hampshire.

2 **APPLETREES**
Stonards Brow, Shamley Green GU5 0UY. Mr & Mrs A Hodgson, 01483 898779, thodgson@uwclub.net. *5m SE of Guildford. A281 Guildford to Horsham rd, turn L at Shalford on B2128 via Wonersh to Shamley Green. Turn R before Red Lion PH, then R into Sweetwater Lane. At top of lane turn R into Stonards Brow or follow signs to car park when entering village. From Ewhurst/Cranleigh turn L at village stores, proceed down Hullbrook Lane following signs to Longacre School car park.* Adm £3.50, chd free. Sat 23 July (12-4 with lunchtime BBQ & cream teas), Sun 24 July (2-6 with cream teas). Evening Opening with music from Rigaudon string duo, wine & cheese £6, chd free, Fri 29 July (6-9). Visitors also welcome by appt.

Knowle Grange

¹/₄ -acre garden with many interesting features. Several small water features incl koi pond. Summerhouse, greenhouses, raised railway sleeper beds, pergolas. Shrub and perennial borders. Patio and gravel area with several colourful containers. Raised vegetable beds; jungle beds with bananas and an elevated walkway; new secret garden and white water garden. Obelisks and clematis, all on a sandy loam soil. An ideas garden. Limited wheelchair access. Parking for disabled reserved outside house.

3 ▶ ASHLEIGH GRANGE
off Chapel Lane, Westhumble RH5 6AY. Clive & Angela Gilchrist, 01306 884613, ar.gilchrist@btinternet.com. *2m N of Dorking. From A24 at Boxhill/Burford Bridge follow signs to Westhumble. Through village & L up drive by ruined chapel (1m from A24)*. Home-made teas. **Adm £3, chd free (share to Barnardo's). Evening Opening £4.50, wine, Fri 17 June (6-8). Sun 19 June, Wed 22 June (2-5.30). Visitors also welcome by appt May to July, visitors warmly welcomed.**
Sloping chalk garden on 3¹/₂ -acre site in charming rural setting with delightful views. Many areas of interest incl rockery and water feature, raised ericaceous bed, prairie-style bank, foliage plants, woodland walk, fernery and folly. Large mixed herbaceous and shrub borders planted for dry alkaline soil and widespread interest.

4 ▶ BARDSEY
11 Derby Road, Haslemere GU27 1BS. Maggie & David Boyd, 01428 652283, maggie.boyd@live.co.uk, www.bardseygarden.co.uk. *¹/₄ m N of Haslemere stn. Turn off B2131 (which links A287 to A286 through town) 400yds W of stn into Weydown Rd, 3rd R into Derby Rd, garden 400yds on R*. Home-made teas. **Adm £3.50, chd free. Sat 18, Sun 19 June (11-5). Visitors also welcome by appt in June for groups of 15+.**
Relax in this 2-acre garden in the heart of Haslemere. Wander through fragrant herb and rose parterres bordered by lavender and box. Enjoy the herbaceous borders, raised vegetable beds and caged fruit

garden. In the lower garden watch Aylesbury ducks, dragonflies and newts in the natural ponds. Classic MGs on view.

5 ▶ BARHATCH FARM
Barhatch Lane, Cranleigh GU6 7NG. Mr & Mrs P M Grol, 01483 277968, tina.grol@btconnect.com. *2m N of Cranleigh. A281 from Guildford, L at B2128 to Cranleigh, through village, take Ewhurst Rd for 1m, turn L into Barhatch Rd which becomes Barhatch Lane. Garden 1st on R after Cranleigh Golf & Leisure Club*. Home-made teas. **Adm £4, chd free. Wed 8, Sun 12 June (11-5). Visitors also welcome by appt in June only for groups of 20+ only.**
Romantic 6-acre garden surrounding listed Tudor farmhouse. Spring and summer herbaceous borders with an abundance of old roses; well-established rose tunnel; tropical walk along 'Smugglers Lane'; pet sanctuary nestled amidst yew tree grove; wild flower and allium meadow with Tasmanian fern walk; walled pond and ornamental pond; wildlife pond attracting many insects and dragonflies. Zen garden converted from 017 cock-fighting pit, new boxed white garden. Happily, many repeat visitors! Partial wheelchair access, some gravel paths and steps.

BEECHENWOOD FARM
See Hampshire.

6 ▶ BIRCH COTTAGE
5 High Street, Horsell, Woking GU21 4XA. Celia & Mel Keenan. *Entrance on High St opp Bullbeggars Lane*. Home-made teas. **Combined adm with Horsell Allotments £3.50, chd free. Sun 26 June (11-4).**
Created since 1999, smallish garden designed to reflect the 400yr old Grade II listed cottage. Knot-style box garden in front; at the rear, courtyard with planted pots and hanging baskets, rill water feature, gravel garden, active dovecote, archway with climbing roses through to the kitchen garden, with greenhouse. Shrubs and perennials throughout.

BOXWOOD HOUSE
See Berkshire.

7 ▶ CAXTON HOUSE
67 West Street, Reigate RH2 9DA. Bob Bushby, 01737 243158. *¹/₄ m W of Reigate. On A25 towards Dorking, approx ¹/₄ m W of Reigate on L. Parking on rd*. Home-made teas. **Adm £3, chd free. Suns 10 Apr; 26 June (2-5). Visitors also welcome by appt April to Sept for groups of 10+.**
Lovely large April garden with a wildlife wood which is now nicely maturing. There are 2 well-stocked ponds and a large collection of hellebores and carpets of spring

flowers. On the terrace there are pots planted with colourful spring and summer displays and interesting plants can be seen in the conservatory. Small gothic folly built by owner. Herbaceous borders and new bed with grasses, perennials and spring bulbs. Sunken garden, parterre.

&. 🏵 ⊕ ☕ ☎

8 **THE CHALET**
Tupwood Lane, Caterham CR3 6ET. Miss Lesley Manning & Mr David Gold. *1/2 m N of M25 J6. Exit J6 of M25 onto A22 going N. After 1/2 m take sharp 1st L, Tupwood Lane. 1st house on R after 1/4 m. Or follow signs from centre of Caterham Valley.* Home-made teas. **Adm £3, chd free (share to St Catherine's Hospice). Suns 27 Mar; 3 Apr (11-4.30).**
55 acres. Carpets of tens of thousands of daffodils; lakes, ornamental ponds, koi pond and waterfall. Ancient woodlands, grass lands and formal garden. Large planted terraces. Beautiful Victorian mansion (not open). Woodland and garden trail. Partial wheelchair access, some steep slopes. 3 large unfenced ponds.

&. 🏵 ☕

Original stewponds integrated with new Japanese-themed garden and woodland garden . . .

9 **CHANDLERS**
Lower Ham Lane, Elstead GU8 6HQ. Mrs Kim Budge. *From A3 Milford take B3001 to Elstead. Entering village turn 2nd R signed EVTC (tennis club). From Farnham, B3001 through village, then L after tel box signed EVTC. Park on Burford Lea recreation ground. Disabled parking use Hideaway House, Lower Ham Lane (off Broomfield).* Home-made teas at Hideaway House. **Combined adm with Hideaway House £3.50, chd free. Sun 5 June (1-5).**
Come and enjoy a stroll around this 1/2 -acre garden brimming with

exciting planting combinations, many unusual shrubs, trees, grasses, perennials and bulbs. Divided into rooms incl a picturesque potager with step-over apple trees and companion planting, woodland, and mixed borders radiating from a semi-circular slate, multi-level patio and pergola. Some woodland paths inaccessible to wheelchairs.

&. 🏵 ⊕ ☕

10 **CHARTERHOUSE**
Hurtmore Road, Godalming GU7 2DF. *1/2 m N of Godalming town centre at top of Charterhouse Hill. Follow signs for Charterhouse from A3 & Godalming town centre.* Light refreshments & home-made teas. **Adm £4, chd free. Sun 19 June (2.30-5).**
Extensive grounds with mature trees and mixed borders around beautiful old buildings. Two historical borders planted with species available prior to 1872, based on the writings of William Robinson; several enclosed individual gardens. Headmaster's garden, originally designed by Gertrude Jekyll, with long herbaceous border, pergola, mixed borders, Lutyens summerhouse and double dry stone wall.

&. ⊕ ☕

CHARTS EDGE
See Kent.

CHARTWELL
See Kent.

11 **CHAUFFEUR'S FLAT**
Tandridge Lane, Tandridge RH8 9NJ. Mr & Mrs Richins. *2m E of Godstone. Turn off A25 for Tandridge. Take drive on L past church. Follow arrows to circular courtyard.* Light refreshments. **Adm £3, chd free. Sat 12, Sun 13 Mar (10.30-4.30).**
With a special early spring opening for 2011, sure-footed visitors enter a 1-acre magical garden with magnificent views. Spring bulbs, structures, textures and imaginative use of recycled materials create an inspired variety of ideas.

☕

12 **CHESTNUT COTTAGE**
15 Jubilee Lane, Boundstone, Farnham GU10 4SZ. Mr & Mrs David Wingent. *2 1/2 m SW of Farnham. From A31 r'bout take A325 to Petersfield, 1/2 m bear L. At mini r'about into School Hill, 1/2 m over*

staggered Xrds, into Sandrock Hill Road, 4th turn R after PH. Home-made teas. **Adm £3, chd free. Sun 29 May (2-5.30).**
1/2 -acre garden created by owners on different levels. Rhododendrons, azaleas, acers and conifers. Long pergola with wisteria and roses, attractive gazebo copied from the original at NT Hunting Lodge in Odiham. Peaceful setting.

☕

13 **CHESTNUT LODGE**
Old Common Road, Cobham KT11 1BU. Mr R Sawyer. *From A3 take A245 towards Cobham bearing L at 2nd r'about onto A307. Just after Dagenham Motors turn L into Old Common Rd, Chestnut Lodge at very end.* Home-made teas. **Adm £5. Regret no children under 15 admitted. Suns 24 Apr; 3 July; 18 Sept (11-5).**
Very interesting 5-acre garden surrounding late Georgian house (not open) offering unrivalled opportunity to enjoy fine specimen trees, wonderful wisteria, shrubs and rare and exotic plants at close quarters. Areas near house formally planted, while opposite is large naturalised pond, home to many waterfowl incl flamingos. Formal areas planted round rectangular pools are complemented by bonsai and topiary which lead to an aviary walk with many fine tropical birds. Some gravel paths.

&. ☕

14 **CHILWORTH MANOR**
Halfpenny Lane, Chilworth, Guildford GU4 8NN. Mia & Graham Wrigley. *3 1/2 m SE of Guildford. From centre of Chilworth village turn into Blacksmith Lane. 1st drive on R on Halfpenny Lane.* Home-made teas. **Adm £5, chd free. Sun 8 May (11-5).**
Extensive grounds of lawns and mature trees around C17/C18 manor on C11 monastic site. Substantial C18 terraced walled garden laid out by Sarah, Duchess of Marlborough, with herbaceous borders, topiary and fruit trees. Original stewponds integrated with new Japanese-themed woodland garden and walk. Paddock home to alpacas. Ongoing restoration project aims to create a contemporary and practical garden sensitive to its historic context. Guided walks at 11.30, 12.30, 1.30 and 2.30.

☕

15 CHINTHURST LODGE
Wonersh Common Road, Wonersh
GU5 0PR. Mr & Mrs M R
Goodridge, 01483 535108,
michaelgoodridge@ymail.com. *4m
S of Guildford. From A281 at Shalford
turn E onto B2128 towards Wonersh.
Just after Wonersh sign, before
village, garden on R.* Home-made
teas. **Adm £3.50, chd free. Sun 19,
Wed 22 June (12-5.30). Visitors
also welcome by appt in June, July
& Aug.**
1-acre yr-round enthusiast's
atmospheric garden, divided into
rooms. Herbaceous borders, white
garden, specimen trees and shrubs,
gravel garden with water feature,
small kitchen garden, fruit cage,
2 wells, ornamental ponds, herb
parterre and millennium parterre
garden. Some gravel paths, which
can be avoided.
&♿ ❀ ☕ ☎

16 ♦ CLANDON PARK
West Clandon, Guildford GU4 7RQ.
National Trust, 01483 222482,
www.nationaltrust.org.uk. *3m E of
Guildford on A247. From A3 follow
signs to Ripley to join A247 via
B2215.* **Garden only adm £4.20,
chd £2. For NGS: Sun 27 Mar
(11-5). For other opening times and
information, please phone or see
garden website.**
Garden around the house laid out
informally, apart from parterre beneath
S front. To the S a mid C18 grotto.
Principal front faces parkland, laid out
in the style of Capability Brown
around 1770. Created in 1901, Dutch
garden modelled on the pond garden
at Hampton Court Palace. Large bulb
field looks stunning in spring.
♿ ☕

**17 ♦ CLAREMONT
LANDSCAPE GARDEN**
Portsmouth Road, Esher
KT10 9JG. National Trust, 01372
467806, www.nationaltrust.org.uk.
*1m SW of Esher. On E side of A307
(no access from A3 bypass).* **Adm
£6.80, chd £3.40. For NGS: Sat 7
May; Sun 9 Oct (10-6). For other
opening times and information,
please phone or see garden
website.**
One of the earliest surviving English
landscape gardens, begun by
Vanbrugh and Bridgeman before 1720
and extended and naturalized by Kent
and Capability Brown. Lake, island
with pavilion; grotto and turf
amphitheatre; viewpoints and avenues.
♿ ☕

18 NEW CLEEVES
Weydown Rd, Haslemere
GU27 1DT. Peter & Sue Morgan.
*Just over 1/2 m from Haslemere Stn. R
out of stn, under railway bridge, R into
Weydown Rd, approx 1/2 m up on R.*
Home-made teas. **Adm £3.50, chd
free. Sun 19 June (11-5).**
Listed Edwardian house (not open),
striking conservatory, 2-acre garden
designed by John Brookes. Acid soil.
Seven sectors: natural front garden;
upper lawn, border, terrace; lower
lawn, border, shrubbery, specimen
trees; pool area, rose and vine
pergola, tree house; copse; orchard;
lower garden by Susan Gernaey,
vegetable parterre, flower garden.
♿ ☕

19 THE COACH HOUSE
The Fairmile, Cobham KT11 1BG.
Peter & Sarah Filmer. *2m NE of
Cobham. On A307 Esher to Cobham
rd next to free car park by A3 bridge,
at entrance to Waterford Close.* Light
refreshments & Pimm's. **Combined
with Moleshill House £6, chd free
(share to Otakar Kraus Music
Trust). Sun 29 May with Music in
the Garden at Moleshill House
(2-5). Mon 30 May with Opera
Singers in the Garden at The
Coach House (2-5).**
Walled garden evolving to meet the
challenge of light sandy soil and dry
summers. Colourful borders with
mixed shrubs and herbaceous
planting, tulips and alliums.
Productive vegetable plot, newly-
restored original greenhouse, parterre,
terrace with pots, many climbers and
wall-trained fruit trees plus newly built
arbour.
❀ ☕

20 THE COPSE LODGE
Brighton Road, Burgh Heath
KT20 6BL. Marian & Edward
Wallbank,. 01737 361084,
marian.wallbank@sky.com. *6m S of
Sutton. On A217. 200yds past T-
lights at junction with Reigate Rd.
Turn L into Heathside Premier Lodge,
park in hotel car park courtesy of
hotel. Walk 80yds to garden.* Disabled
parking at garden. Home-made teas.
**Adm £3.50, chd free. Wed 25, Sun
29 May (2-6). Evening Opening, £4,
wine, Tue 31 May (6-9). Visitors
also welcome by appt late May &
June only, for groups of 15+.**
Very unusual 1-acre garden with
architectural features and exciting
planting. Large Japanese garden
abounds with acers, bamboo,

wisteria and bonsai. Wander through
the tea house and emerge refreshed
to enjoy the contrast of exotic
planting and beautiful tender
specimens. Kitchen garden, cactus
house.
♿ ❀ ☕ ☎

All have beautiful gardens tended by passionate owners . . . make a day out, with tea, coffee and cakes in 3 gardens . . .

21 COVERWOOD LAKES
Peaslake Road, Ewhurst GU6 7NT.
The Metson Family,
www.coverwoodlakes.co.uk. *7m
SW of Dorking. From A25 follow signs
for Peaslake; garden 1/2 m beyond
Peaslake on Ewhurst rd.* Home-made
teas. **Adm £5, chd £2. Suns 10,
17 Apr, Mon 25 Apr; Mon 2 May,
Suns 8, 15 May (2-6); Sun 16 Oct
(11-4.30).**
14-acre landscaped garden in
stunning position high in the Surrey
Hills with 4 lakes and bog garden.
Extensive rhododendrons, azaleas
and fine trees. 31/2 -acre lakeside
arboretum. Marked trail through the
working farm with Hereford cows and
calves, sheep and horses, extensive
views of the surrounding hills.
♿ 🛏 ☕

22 ♦ CROSSWATER FARM
Crosswater Lane, Churt, Farnham
GU10 2JN. Mrs E G Millais &
Family,
sales@rhododendrons.co.uk,
www.rhododendrons.co.uk. *6m S
of Farnham, 6m NW of Haslemere.
From A287 turn E into Jumps Rd
1/2 m N of Churt village centre. After
1/4 m turn acute L into Crosswater
Lane & follow signs for Millais
Nurseries.* **Adm £3, chd free. For
NGS: Sun 1, Mon 2 May (10-5).
For other opening times and
information, please email or see
garden website.**
Idyllic 6-acre woodland garden.

Plantsman's collection of rhododendrons and azaleas, incl rare species collected in the Himalayas, hybrids raised by the owners. Everything from alpine dwarfs to architectural large-leaved trees. Ponds, stream and companion plantings incl sorbus, magnolias and Japanese acers. Trial gardens of new varieties. Plant Centre stocks the widest range of rhododendrons in the country. Mail order throughout Europe. RHS Rothschild Cup for best display of Rhododendrons, International Rhododendron Symposium. Grass paths can be soft after rain.

&. ⊛

23 CULVERKEYS
20A Longdown Lane North, Ewell, Epsom KT17 3JQ. Anne & Geoff Salt, 020 8393 6861. *1m E of Epsom, 1m S of Ewell Village. Leave Ewell bypass (A24) by Reigate Rd (A240) to pass Nescot on L. Turn R in ¹/₄ m.* **Adm £3, chd free. Suns 29 May; 17 July (2-5).** Visitors also welcome by appt.
A romantic somewhat secret garden on the edge of Epsom Downs. Meandering paths pass borders planted to capacity with interesting and unusual plants. Arches smothered in climbers reveal secluded corners and running water soothes the spirit. Designed for yr-round interest, shrubs and trees play host to many clematis.

☎

GROUP OPENING

24 NEW DORMANS PARK SAFARI
Dormans Park, East Grinstead RH19 2NB. *Between Lingfield and East Grinstead. Two entrances to Dormans Park: from East Grinstead, on A264 turn L after hospital down road to Dormansland, entrance on L after 1m. Or from A22 to Lingfield, follow rd at 2nd r'about to Felcourt, bear L into Blackberry Lane then turn L and follow signs. Entrance nr Dormans stn. Please buy a ticket and collect a map (showing directions and parking) at one of the 2 entrances to the Park.* Home-made teas Lake House, Castanas & Bentley Lodge. **Combined adm £6, chd free. Sun 5 June (10.30-5).**

NEW BENTLEY LODGE
Andrew Simpson & Annabel Morgan

BRAEKENAS
Ann Lindfield

NEW CASTANAS
Mrs A Brown

NEW LAKE HOUSE
The Rousell family

NEW LOENWOOD
Maria Osmore

NEW TULGEY WOOD
Charles Cater

NEW WYLDER LODGE
Margaret & Eric Richardson

Foxhill

First year of this Safari. 7 gardens have been chosen to take part and all gardens offer something quite different, combining to make a unique experience. Dormans Park dates back to 1887 and originally comprised 218 acres of farmland and coppiced woodland. Following the arrival of the railway, plots were sold off for development by the Bellaggio Estate. Today the Park offers an interesting variety of houses old and new. Some have architectural interest and history, but all have beautiful gardens tended by passionate owners. There will be gardens where picnics are allowed (and WCs) so possibility to make a day out, buying tea, coffee and cakes in 3 gardens. Wheelchair access to most gardens (not Tulgey Wood).

⊛ ☕

25 DUNSBOROUGH PARK
Ripley GU23 6AL. Baron & Baroness Sweerts de Landas Wyborgh, www.dunsboroughpark.com. *6m NE of Guildford. Entrance across Ripley Green via The Milkway opp Wylie & Mar.* Home-made teas. **Adm £5, chd free. Thur 28 Apr (4-7.30); Suns 19 June; 18 Sept (2-6).** Extensive walled gardens of 6 acres redesigned by Penelope Hobhouse and Rupert Golby. Good structure with much box hedging creating many different garden rooms. Exciting long herbaceous borders with beautiful standard wisterias. Unusual 70ft ginkgo hedge and ancient mulberry tree. Atmospheric water garden recently redesigned and restored. Fabulous display of tulips in April with 10,000 bulbs and large cut flower garden. Festival of Tulips (not NGS) 17, 21, 29 April, 1 May (4-7.30pm, adm £5).

&. ⊛ ☕

ELM TREE COTTAGE
See London.

26 FOXHILL
Farnham Road, Elstead GU8 6LE. Alison & Mike Welton. *5m W of Godalming, 3¹/₂ m E of Farnham. From A3 take B3001 towards Farnham. Garden 1m past Elstead village on R opp Donkey PH. From Farnham take B3001 towards Godalming, garden 3¹/₂ m on L opp PH.* Home-made teas. **Adm £5, chd free. Wed 13, Thur 14, Fri 15 July (2-5).**

Over 4 acres incl formal gardens and a developing woodland garden with rhododendrons, azaleas and primulas. The formal garden incl herbaceous and mixed planting and was partly designed by Gertrude Jekyll in 1923 with hard landscaping and an interesting water feature.

FROGMORE HOUSE GARDEN
See Berkshire.

Newly-created garden in the style of Gertrude Jekyll . ..

FROYLE GARDENS
See Hampshire.

THE GARDEN LODGE
See Berkshire.

27 ◆ GATTON PARK
Rocky Lane, Merstham RH2 0TW. Royal Alexandra & Albert School, 01737 649068,
www.gattonpark.com. *3m NE of Reigate. 5 mins from M25 J8 (A217) or from top of Reigate Hill, over M25 then follow sign to Merstham. Entrance is off Rocky Lane accessible from Gatton Bottom or A23 Merstham.* **Adm £4, chd free. For NGS: Sun 20 Feb (11-4), Wed 23 Feb (12-4); Sun 12 Feb 2012 (11-4). For other opening times and information, please phone or see garden website.**
Formerly home to the Colman family (of mustard fame), now the grounds of the Royal Alexandra and Albert School. Hidden gardens within historic Capability Brown parkland. 1910 Edwardian Japanese garden restored for Channel 4's 'Lost Gardens'. Dramatic 1912 Pulham rock garden, walled gardens, lakeside trail. Restoration of gardens ongoing and maintained by volunteers. Ivan Hick's children's trail behind main lake. Massed snowdrops in Feb and Mar. Free activities for children. Limited wheelchair access.

HANGING HOSTA GARDEN
See Hampshire.

28 ◆ HATCHLANDS PARK
East Clandon, Guildford GU4 7RT. National Trust, 01483 222482, www.nationaltrust.org.uk. *4m E of Guildford. Off A246. A3 from London, follow signs to Ripley to join A247 & via W Clandon to A246. From Guildford take A25 then A246 towards Leatherhead at W Clandon.* **Garden only adm £4, chd £2. For NGS: Suns 8 May (10-6); 16 Oct (11-6). For other opening times and information, please phone or see garden website.**
Garden and park designed by Repton in 1800. Follow one of the park walks to the stunning bluebell wood in spring (40 mins walk, rough and sometimes muddy ground). In autumn enjoy the changing colours on the long walk. S of the house a small parterre designed by Gertrude Jekyll in 1913 to flower in early June.

29 NEW THE WOODLAND TRAIL AT THE HAWTHORNS SCHOOL
Pendell Road, Bletchingley RH1 4QJ. The Hawthorns School. *1m N of Bletchingley. Turn off A25 by Red Lion in Bletchingley along Little Common Lane. School over Xrds at bottom of hill.* **Adm £3, chd free. Sat 21 May (1-5).**
Not a garden as you might expect! Opened 2010 by Roy Lancaster, this self-guided Woodland Trail takes visitors through several hundred years of history. Numbered posts lead past ancient hedgerows, through newly planted orchard and into remnants of Victorian arboretum created by Sir George Macleay. All practical work has been done, by hand, by pupils. Trail incl a stile and uneven ground.

30 HEATHSIDE
10 Links Green Way, Cobham KT11 2QH. Miss Margaret Arnott & Mr Terry Bartholomew, 01372 842459,
m.a.arnott@btinternet.com. *1½ m E of Cobham. Off A245 Cobham to Leatherhead rd. From Cobham take 4th turning L after Esso Garage into Fairmile Lane. Straight on at mini-r'about into Water Lane for ½ m. Links Green Way 3rd on L.* Home-made teas. **Adm £3, chd free. Sun 12 June (11-5). Visitors also welcome by appt at any time.**
⅓ -acre terraced garden planted for yr-round interest, beautiful in any season. Spring bulbs and alpines,

herbaceous borders, roses and clematis in summer, leaf colour and berries in autumn and winter, all set off by harmonious landscaping with pergola, parterre, ponds, obelisks and urns. Many inspirational ideas.

31 HIDEAWAY HOUSE
Lower Ham Lane, Elstead GU8 6HQ. Mr & Mrs C Burridge. *For directions see entry for Chandlers.* Home-made teas. **Combined adm with Chandlers £3.50, chd free. Sun 5 June (1-5).**
¾ -acre Italianate garden with large rolling lawn interspersed with follies, ornaments and unusual architectural plants, designed for easy maintenance. Also incl woodland area, rockery, formal and natural pond. Many exceptional pots with annual and specimen displays. Large patio area for teas.

32 NEW 29 HIGHER GREEN
Epsom KT17 3BB. Marie Rajendra, 020 8393 3057,
st.anthony@btopenworld.com. *2m E of Epsom. From Ewell bypass, turn L onto Reigate Rd (A240). Turn R into Longdown Lane N. Higher Green 3rd turn on R.* Cakes and Indian snacks with tea or coffee. **Adm £3, chd free. Sun 31 July (10-5). Visitors also welcome by appt June to Aug.**
An attractive front and back garden with unusual plants throughout the year. Herbaceous and annuals in summer give colour to the garden. A striking fernery together with acers and hostas adds further interest.

239A HOOK ROAD
See London.

ALLOTMENTS

33 HORSELL ALLOTMENTS
Bullbeggars Lane, Horsell, Woking GU21 4SQ. Horsell Allotments Association,
www.windowonwoking.org.uk/sites /haa. *1½ m W of Woking. From Woking follow signs to Horsell, along High St, Bullbeggars Lane at Chobham end of Village. Disabled parking only at Allotments.* Light Refreshments & teas at Birch Cottage. **Combined adm with Birch Cottage £3.50, chd free. Sun 26 June (11-4).**
With over 100 individual plots growing

a variety of flowers, fruit and vegetables, showcasing a mixture of modern, well-known, heritage and unusual vegetables, many not seen in supermarkets. Two working beehives with informative talks. Vegetable and herb plants for sale. Featured in Chairman's weekly column on allotment life in the Woking News and Mail & on Radio 4 Today programme.

KIMPTON HOUSE
See Hampshire.

34 KNOWLE GRANGE
Hound House Road, Shere GU5 9JH. Mr P R & Mrs M E Wood. *8m S of Guildford. From Shere (off A25), through village for ³/₄ m. After railway bridge, continue 1¹/₂ m past Hound House on R (stone dogs on gatepost). After 100yds turn R at Knowle Grange sign, go to end of lane.* Home-made teas. **Adm £5, chd free. Suns 22 May; 11 Sept (11-5).**
80-acre idyllic hilltop position. Extraordinary and exciting 7-acre gardens, created from scratch since 1990 by Marie-Elisabeth Wood, blend the free romantic style with the strong architectural frame of the classical tradition. Walk the rural one-mile Bluebell Valley Unicursal Path of Life and discover its secret allegory. Deep unfenced pools, high unfenced drops.

LEYDENS
See Kent.

LITTLE GABLES
See Kent.

LITTLE LODGE
See London.

35 LODKIN
Lodkin Hill, Hascombe GU8 4JP. Mr & Mrs W N Bolt, 01483 208323, willibolt2@aol.com. *3m S of Godalming. Just off B2130 Godalming to Cranleigh rd, on outskirts of Hascombe; take narrow lane marked Lodkin Hill.* Refreshments by arrangement. **Adm £3.50, chd free** (share to St Peter's Church). **Visitors welcome by appt for groups of up to 60. Coaches permitted but narrow lane.**
4-acre country garden on many levels in a rural valley, Lodkin has been developed and greatly enlarged since 1976. 110ft of greenhouses, extensive flower borders, kitchen garden and orchard augment the flowering trees, thousands of bulbs

and the wild garden stream, pond and bog area. Plants sometimes for sale. Garden very steep in parts, so limited wheelchair access.

36 LONGER END COTTAGE
Normandy Common Lane, Normandy GU3 2AP. Ann & John McIlwham, 01483 811858, jmcilwham@hotmail.com. *4m W of Guildford on A323. At War Memorial Xrds in Normandy turn R into Hunts Hill Rd then 1st R into Normandy Common Lane.* Home-made teas. **Adm £3.50, chd free. Suns 12, 19 June (1-6). Visitors also welcome by appt, June only for groups of 20+.**
1¹/₂ -acre garden divided into rooms with wide variety of plants, shrubs and trees incl roses, delphiniums, tree ferns, gunnera, grasses etc. Knot garden, laburnum walk, wild flower meadow, folly and small stumpery add to the attraction of the garden. Featured in GGG. Uneven drive.

Not a garden as you might expect! This self-guided Woodland Trail takes visitors through several hundred years of history . . .

37 ◆ LOSELEY PARK
Guildford GU3 1HS. Mr & Mrs M G More-Molyneux, 01483 304440, www.loseley-park.com. *4m SW of Guildford. Leave A3 at Compton S of Guildford, on B3000 for 2m. Signed. Guildford stn 2m, Godalming stn 3m. If using SatNav, type in Stakescorner Rd, not postcode.* **Adm £4.50, chd £2.25. For other opening times and information, please phone or see garden website. For NGS: Sun 15 May (11-5).**
Delightful 2¹/₂ -acre walled garden based on design by Gertrude Jekyll. Award-winning rose garden (over 1,000 bushes, mainly old-fashioned varieties), extensive herb garden, fruit/flower garden, white garden with fountains, and spectacular organic

vegetable garden. Magnificent vine walk, herbaceous borders, moat walk, ancient wisteria and mulberry trees. Wild flower meadow. Featured in Radio Times, Sunday Telegraph & local press.

LOWDER MILL
See Sussex.

38 MEMOIRS
Stafford Lake, Queen's Road, Bisley GU24 9AY. Mr Ted Stephens. *Approx 6m N of Guildford. A322 Guildford to Bagshot rd to Bisley, then L into Queens Rd at T-lights after Fox PH. Follow Queens Rd for just under 1m then L into unmarked track (footpath sign) and follow NGS signs.* Home-made teas. **Adm £3.50, chd free. Sun 29 May (1.30-5.30).**
Interesting and varied 8-acre organic garden created by owners. Formal lawn and borders, stream, ponds, bog garden, kitchen garden, terrace garden, wildlife areas, woodland, orchard and fields with rare-breed sheep, goats, chicken and ducks. Small museum of gardening and agricultural tools. Hand made jewellery sale.

39 MOLESHILL HOUSE
The Fairmile, Cobham KT11 1BG. Penny Snell, 01932 864532, pennysnellflowers@btinternet.com, www.pennysnellflowers.co.uk. *2m NE of Cobham. On A307 Esher to Cobham Rd next to free car park by A3 bridge, at entrance to Waterford Close.* Home-made teas. **Combined with The Coach House £6, chd free. Sun 29 May with Music in the Garden at Moleshill House (2-5). Mon 30 May with Opera Singers in the Garden at The Coach House (2-5). Visitors also welcome by appt for groups of 10+. £6 a head incl refreshments.**
Romantic garden. Short woodland path leads from dovecote to beehives. Informal planting contrasts with formal topiary box and garlanded cisterns. Colourful courtyard and pots, conservatory, fountains, bog garden. Pleached avenue, new circular gravel garden replacing most of the lawn. Some vegetables, chickens permitting! Garden 5 mins from Claremont Landscape Garden, Painshill Park & Wisley. Also adjacent excellent dog-walking woods. Featured in Gardens Illustrated.

40 **NEW** **NORNEY WOOD**
Elstead Road, Shackleford,
Godalming GU8 6AY. Richard &
Jean Thompson. *5m SW of
Guildford. At Xrds of Elstead rd &
Shackleford rd, ¹/₂ m towards Elstead
from A3 Hurtmore/Shackleford
junction.* Home-made teas. **Adm £4,
chd free. Sun 10 July (11-5).**
Newly-created garden in the style of
Gertrude Jekyll set against a
backdrop of mature trees and
rhododendrons. The formal lawn
terrace garden is surrounded by rose
and herbaceous borders. Gertrude
Jekyll's love of garden structures has
been recreated with a garden house
and paths linking the upper lawn
terrace with the lower formal water
garden. Recently planted pleached
lime path leads off to woodland
walks. New aspects of the garden
under construction.

Woodbury Cottage

41 **NEW** **NORWOOD FARM**
Effingham Common Road,
Effingham, Leatherhead KT24 5JF.
Judith & Mervyn Gardner. *Approx
5m from J10, M25. 800yds SE of
Effingham Junction stn, towards
Effingham.* Home-made teas. **Adm
£5, chd free. Sun 28 Aug (11-5).**
C15 listed Hall house and 100ft long
listed barn surrounded by over 10
acres of immaculate gardens. There
are extensive, well-stocked
herbaceous borders and shrubberies,
a formal area with fish pond and a
white garden. Two duck ponds linked
by a stream, woodland walk and a
large area planted with specimen
trees.

42 **ODSTOCK**
Castle Square, Bletchingley
RH1 4LB. Averil & John Trott, 01883
743100. *3m W of Godstone. Just off
A25 in Bletchingley. At top of village nr
Red Lion PH. Parking in village, no
parking in Castle Square. Disabled
parking by gate.* Home-made teas.
**Adm £3, chd free. Sun 7 Aug
(11-5). Visitors also welcome by
appt.**
²/₃ -acre plantsman's garden
maintained by owners and developed
for all-yr interest. Special interest in
grasses and climbers, approx 80 at
last count. Japanese features;
dahlias. No-dig, low-maintenance
vegetable garden. Children's quiz.
Short gravel drive.

OLD BUCKHURST
See Kent.

43 **THE OLD CROFT**
South Holmwood, Dorking
RH5 4NT. David & Virginia Lardner-
Burke, www.lardner-burke.org.uk.
*2m S of Dorking. From Dorking take
A24 S for 2m. Turn L at sign to Leigh-
Brockham into Mill Road. ¹/₂ m on L,
2 free car parks in NT Holmwood
Common. Follow signs for 500yds
along woodland walk.* **Disabled and
elderly: for direct access tel 01306
888224.** Home-made teas. **Adm £4,
chd free. Suns, Mons 1, 2, 29, 30
May; Sats, Suns 9, 10 July; 6, 7
Aug (2-6).**
Remarkable 5-acre garden with many
diverse areas of exquisite natural
beauty, giving a sense of peace and
tranquillity. Stunning vistas incl lake,
bridge, pond fed by natural stream
running over rocky weirs, bog
gardens, roses, perennial borders,
elevated viewing hide, tropical
bamboo maze, curved pergola of
rambling roses, unique topiary
buttress hedge, many specimen trees
and shrubs. Visitors return again and
again.

44 **THE OLD RECTORY**
Sandy Lane, Brewer Street,
Bletchingley RH1 4QW. Mr & Mrs A
Procter. *3m W of Godstone. Just off
A25 in Bletchingley. At top of village nr
Red Lion PH, turn R into Little*
*Common Lane then R at Cross Rd
into Sandy Lane. Parking near house,
disabled parking in courtyard.* Home-
made teas. **Adm £4, chd free. Sat
25 June (11-5).**
Georgian Manor House (not open).
Quintessential Italianate topiary
garden, statuary and box parterres.
Courtyard with columns, water
features and antique terracotta pots.
Much of the 4-acre garden is the
subject of ongoing reclamation. This
incl the ancient moat and woodland
with fine specimen trees and walled
kitchen garden. Sunken garden under
construction. Film location for BBC
TV 'Emma'.

**OLD THATCH & THE
MILLENNIUM BARN**
See Hampshire.

45 **♦ POLESDEN LACEY**
Great Bookham, Dorking RH5 6BD.
National Trust, 01372 452048,
www.nationaltrust.org.uk. *Nr
Dorking, off A246 Leatherhead to
Guildford rd. 1¹/₂ m S of Great
Bookham, well signed.* **Garden only
adm £7.40, chd £3.70. For NGS:
Sun 10 July (10-5). For other
opening times and information,
please phone or see garden
website.**
Originally the home of Edwardian
socialite and hostess Margaret
Greville, the beautiful gardens offered
a spectacular backdrop to lavish

house parties. Perched on a ridge of the N Downs, overlooking breathtaking countryside, Mrs Greville's rose garden is the epitome of the Edwardian country house rose garden.

  🕭 🏵 ☕

46 NEW **PRATSHAM GRANGE**
Tanhurst Lane, Holmbury St Mary RH5 6LZ. Alan & Felicity Comber. *12m SE of Guildford, 10m SW of Dorking. From A25 take B2126. 1¹/₂ m after Holmbury church turn L into Tanhurst Lane. House 2nd on L after ¹/₄ m. From A29 take B2126. Before Forest Green turn R on B2126 signed Holmbury. After ¹/₄ m turn R into Tanhurst Lane.* Home-made teas. **Adm £4, chd free. Sat 20, Sun 21 Aug (12-5).**
4-acre garden around late Victorian house (not open) with excellent views of Surrey Hills. The garden has been created over the last 5yrs and is surrounded by mature oaks, laurels, rhododendrons and paddocks. New features incl herbaceous borders, ponds, knot garden, rose beds and kitchen garden. Some slopes and gravel paths. Deep ponds.

  🕭 🏵 ☕

10 acres of immaculate gardens . . . two duck ponds linked by a stream . . .

47 ◆ **RAMSTER**
Chiddingfold GU8 4SN. Mr & Mrs Paul Gunn, rosie@ramsterevents.com, www.ramsterweddings.co.uk. *1¹/₂ m S of Chiddingfold. On A283 1¹/₂ miles S of Chiddingfold; large iron gates on R.* **Adm £5, chd free. For NGS: Fri 13 May (10-5). For other opening times and information, please email or see garden website.**
A stunning, mature woodland garden set in over 30 acres, famous for its rhododendron and azalea collection and carpets of bluebells. Enjoy a peaceful wander down the meandering woodland walk, explore the bog garden with stepping stones or relax in the tranquil enclosed Tennis Court Garden. Ramster Textile Art and

Embroidery Exhibition 8-21 April. Tea house, WC & some paths suitable for wheelchairs.

  🕭 🏵 ☕

48 **THE ROUND HOUSE**
Dunsfold Road, Loxhill GU8 4BL. Mrs Sue Lawson, 01483 200375, suelaw.law@btinternet.com. *4m S of Bramley. Off A281, at Smithbrook Kilns turn R to Dunsfold. Follow to T-junction. Go R (B2130). After 1.2m Park Hatch on R, enter park, follow drive to garden.* Home-made teas. **Adm £3.50, chd free. Suns, Weds 12, 15 June; 10, 13 July (2-5.30). Visitors also welcome by appt.**
2¹/₂ -acre walled Victorian garden with far-reaching views from the top of the garden. Continuing renewal programme since 2002. Colourful mixed beds with perennials, roses and interesting statuary. Water cascades. Apple and plum orchard. Serpentine paths between shrubs and wild flowers. 75 metre lavender walk. Ornamental fish pond. Gravel paths and steep slopes.

  🕭 🏵 ☕ ☎

SANDY SLOPES
See Hampshire.

SHALFORD HOUSE
See Sussex.

49 **41 SHELVERS WAY**
Tadworth KT20 5QJ. Keith & Elizabeth Lewis, 01737 210707, kandelewis@cwcom.net. *6m S of Sutton off A217. 1st turning on R after Burgh Heath T-lights heading S on A217. 400yds down Shelvers Way on L.* Home-made teas. **Adm £3, chd free. Suns 17 Apr; 17 July; 21 Aug (2-5.30). Visitors also welcome by appt at any time of year for groups of 10+.**
Just under ¹/₂ -acre back garden of dense and detailed planting, interesting at all seasons, starting with a mass of spring bulbs with over 100 varieties of daffodils. In one part, beds of choice perennials are interlaced by paths and backed by unusual shrubs and mature trees; in the other, cobbles and shingle support grasses and special plants for dry conditions.

  🏵 ☕ ☎

50 **SMITHWOOD HOUSE**
Smithwood Common Road, Cranleigh GU6 8QY. Barbara Rubenstein, 01483 267969, bsrubenstein@aol.com. *2m N of Cranleigh. From Cranleigh turn R at*

cricket ground passing Cranleigh School. 1¹/₂ m N of school, 1st house on L past Winterfold turn. From Guildford A281, 1m S of Bramley turn L onto B2128. At r'about R then immed L into Smithwood Common Rd, 2nd house on R. **Adm £3, chd free. Visitors welcome by appt, last 2 weeks in May, first 2 weeks in June only.**
3-acre park-like garden surrounding listed Georgian farmhouse (not open) with formal and informal areas. Many mature specimen trees and shrub borders. Sculpture walk with musical theme and water features. Formal yew walk with topiary and garden temple. Natural pond with waterfall and ornamental planting and secluded seating areas. Featured on BBC TV Open Gardens.

  🕭 ☎

51 **SPURFOLD**
Peaslake GU5 9SZ. Mr & Mrs A Barnes, 01306 730196, spurfold@btinternet.com. *8m SE of Guildford. A25 to Shere. Turn R through Shere village & up hill. Over railway bridge, 1st L to Peaslake. In Peaslake turn L after village stores Radnor Rd. Approx ¹/₂ m up single track lane to car park.* Home-made teas. **Adm £4, chd free. Sun 22 May (12-6). Visitors also welcome by appt May to Aug for groups of 15+. Home-made teas or wine and nibbles by arrangement.**
4 acres, large herbaceous and shrub borders, formal pond with Cambodian Buddha head, sunken gravel garden with topiary box and water feature, terraces, beautiful lawns, mature rhododendrons and azaleas, woodland paths, and gazebos. Garden contains unique collection of Indian elephants and other objets d'art. New topiary garden created 2010.

  🏵 ☕ ☎

SQUERRYES COURT
See Kent.

STONEWALL PARK
See Kent.

52 **STUART COTTAGE**
Ripley Road, East Clandon GU4 7SF. Mr & Mrs J M Leader, 01483 222689. *4m E of Guildford. Off A246 or from A3 through Ripley until r'about, turn L and continue through West Clandon until T-lights, then L onto A246. East Clandon 1st L.*

Home-made teas (Suns). **Adm (Suns) £3, chd free. Evening Opening with music £6, wine and home-made canapés, Wed 22 June (6.30-8.30). Suns 24 July; 28 Aug (2-6).** Visitors also welcome by appt for groups of 20+.
¹/₂ -acre partly walled garden using some traditional box shapes and hedging to offer formality in the otherwise informal garden of this C16 cottage. Wisteria and rose/clematis walks give shade to the S/W aspect while rosemary and lavender edge the brick paths. Unusual herbaceous plants vie for attention among cottage garden favourites. From decorative organic kitchen garden pass to 4 large potted brugmansia plants to a small chequerboard mown orchard. Talented harpist, Naomi Harling, will play on 22 June.

SUNNINGDALE PARK
See Berkshire.

53 ▶ 35 TADORNE ROAD
Tadworth KT20 5TF. Dr & Mrs J R Lay. *6m S of Sutton. On A217 to large r'about, 3m N of M25 J8. Take B2220 signed Tadworth. Tadorne Rd 2nd on R.* Home-made teas. **Adm £3, chd free** (share to Tadworth Walton Overseas Aid Trust). **Sat 30, Sun 31 July (2-5.30).**
Colourful, curvaceous garden with hardly a straight line. We have bright herbaceous borders, shrubby island beds, flower-covered pergolas, secluded seating areas, potager-style vegetable plot, pebble patch, wild woodland corner and varied patio display - all in ¹/₃ acre! Home -made teas served in plant-filled conservatory. Gravel drive at entrance.

54 ▶ TILFORD COTTAGE
Tilford Road, Tilford GU10 2BX. Mr & Mrs R Burn, 01252 795423, rodburn@tiscali.co.uk, www.tilfordcottagegarden.co.uk. *3m SE of Farnham. From Farnham stn along Tilford Rd. Tilford Cottage opp Tilford House. Parking by village green.* Teas Sats & Suns. **Adm £5.50, chd free. Sat 11, Sun 12 June (10.30-4.30). Evening Opening £6.50, wine, Fri 17 June (6.30-9). Sat 18, Sun 19 June (10.30 1.30).** Visitors also welcome by appt all year, for groups of 6+, max 100.
Artist's garden designed to surprise, delight and amuse. Formal planting, herb and knot garden. Numerous

examples of topiary combine beautifully with the wild flower river walk. Japanese and water gardens, hosta beds, rose, apple and willow arches, treehouse and fairy grotto all continue the playful quality especially enjoyed by children. Pam Burn's Holistic Centre and Rod Burn's art studio will be open for viewing during open days. Some gravel paths and steep slopes.

Treehouse and fairy grotto all continue the playful quality . . .

55 ▶ TIMBER HILL
Chertsey Road, Chobham GU24 8JF. Mr & Mrs Nick Sealy, 01932 873635, nicksealy@chobham.net. *4m N of Woking. 2¹/₂ m E of Chobham and ¹/₃ m E of Fairoaks aerodrome on A319 (N side). 1¹/₄ m W of Ottershaw, J11 M25.* Delicious refreshments & teas served in lovely old Surrey Barn. **Adm £3.50, chd free. Suns 27 Mar; 17 Apr (11-4.30).** Visitors also welcome by appt in Jan/Feb for witch hazels and snowdrops, early May for bluebells and azaleas. Min charge of £50 applies.
Beautifully situated 15-acre garden, woodland garden and park, sheep grazing and views to N Downs. Fine specimens of oaks, liquidambar and liriodendron. Early witch hazel walk (by appt), new plantings of oaks, beech, cherry and acers. Many camellias and magnolias shelter behind banks of rhododendron ponticum. Drifts of narcissi, daffodils and spring bulbs; shrub and ground-cover borders. Bluebells and azaleas in early May (by appt). Good help for disabled and wheelchair users.

56 ◆ TITSEY PLACE GARDENS
Titsey Hill, Oxted RH8 0SD. The Trustees of the Titsey Foundation, 01273 715359, www.titsey.org. *3m N of Oxted. A25 between Oxted & Westerham. Follow brown signs to Titsey Estate from A25 at Limpsfield or see website directions.* Tearooms open on NGS days. **Adm £4.50, chd £1. For NGS: Sats 21 May; 18 June; 16 July; 20 Aug (12.30-5).** For other opening times and information, please phone or see garden website.

One of the largest surviving historic estates in Surrey. Magnificent ancestral home and gardens of the Gresham family since 1534. Walled kitchen garden restored early 1990s. Golden Jubilee rose garden. Etruscan summer house adjoining picturesque lakes and fountains. 15 acres of formal and informal gardens in idyllic setting within the M25. Dogs allowed in park only. Partial wheelchair access.

57 ▶ TOLLSWORTH MANOR
Rook Lane, Chaldon, Caterham CR3 5BQ. Carol & Gordon Gillett. *2m W of Caterham. From Caterham-on-the-Hill, take B2031 through Chaldon. 300yds out of Chaldon take concrete farm track on L. Parking in farmyard beyond house.* Home-made teas. **Adm £3.50, chd free. Sun 12 June (11-5).**
Surrounding a C14 rose/clematis covered house, an old-fashioned country garden, created from derelict site over 28yrs by present owners. Well-stocked herbaceous borders with old-fashioned roses, peonies, delphiniums. Wildlife pond and duck pond with ducks. Lovely views over surrounding farmland. Shetland pony. Friendly atmosphere with lovely home made teas. Sue Broadhead ceramic sculptures, mosaic pottery, Maytree cards featuring wildlife and Tollsworth Manor. Some uneven paths.

58 ▶ VALE END
Chilworth Road, Albury GU5 9BE. Mr & Mrs John Foulsham, 01483 202594, daphne@dfoulsham.freeserve.co. uk. *4m SE of Guildford. From Albury take A248 W for ¹/₄ m.* Home-made teas. **Adm £3, chd free. Sun 17 Apr (2-5). Evening Opening with harpist £5, chd free, wine, Fri 10 June (6-8.30). Wed 15 June (2-5).** Visitors also welcome by appt.
1-acre walled garden arranged on many levels in idyllic setting overlooking mill pond. Spring garden and wild flower meadow give way to borders richly planted with roses, shrubs, perennials and annuals. Formal clipped yew walk with rope swags festooned with wisteria, roses and vines. Attractive hidden courtyard, gravel garden and steps by pantiled cascade lead up to fruit, vegetable and sunken herb garden. Delightful stream, lake and woodland walk from garden on public footpaths.

59 ◆ **VANN**
Hambledon GU8 4EF. Mrs M Caroe,
01428 683413, mary@caroe.com,
www.vanngarden.co.uk. *6m S of
Godalming. A283 to Wormley. Turn L
at Hambledon. Follow yellow Vann
signs for 2m (NGS days only), or see
website for directions. Park in field,
not in road.* **Home-made teas Mon
2 May only. Adm £4.50, chd free.
For NGS: Sun 27 Mar to Sun 3 Apr
incl (10-6); Mon 2 May (2-6); Tue 3
May to Sun 8 May incl; Sun 5 June
to Sun 12 June incl (10-6).** Visitors
also welcome by appt for groups &
individuals, Feb to July. For other
opening times and information,
please phone or see garden
website.
5-acre English Heritage registered
garden surrounding Tudor and William
and Mary house (not open) with Arts
and Crafts additions by W D Carôe
incl a Bargate stone pergola. At the
front, brick-paved original 'cottage'
garden; to the rear, 1/4 -acre pond,
yew walk with rill and Gertrude Jekyll
water garden. Snowdrops and
hellebores, spring bulbs, Fritillaria
meleagris in March. Island beds,
crinkle crankle wall, orchard with wild
flowers, Centenary garden and
woodland. Planted for easy
maintenance by owner with 3 days'
help a week. Deep water. Water
garden paths not suitable for
wheelchairs, but many others are.
Please ring prior to visit to request
disabled parking.

60 **VICARAGE COTTAGE**
Brockham Green, Betchworth
RH3 7JS. Mr & Mrs R Harman.
*2m E of Dorking. Take signed rd from
A25 between Dorking and Reigate,
then 1/2 m to Brockham Green. No
parking on Green, considerate
parking on rd please.* **Ploughman's
lunches & home-made teas. Adm £3,
chd free. Sat 25, Sun 26 June
(11-5).**
1/2 -acre cottage garden situated on
the Green, next to church and in one
of Surrey's most beautiful villages.
Designed to complement the 400yr-
old cottage. Gently curving borders
surround a central ancient yew tree,
with a mix of flowers, shrubs and
roses. Pond, stumpery, small wild
flower meadow and kitchen garden.
This year featuring Wind in the
Willows. The little houses where the
characters lived on the riverbank will
be set around the pond area, only
visible from the woodland path. All will

be created using natural materials.
Lovely river walk to Betchworth
Village.

WALBURY
See Hampshire.

61 **WALNUT HOUSE**
Gatton Close, Reigate RH2 0HG.
Inger & Dirk Laan, 01737 241081,
dlaan@talktalk.net. *1m N of Reigate.
M25 J8, then S on A217. After Esso
garage, L into Raglan Rd, at Xrds L
into Gatton Rd. After 500yds Gatton
Close on L. Or from A242 into Raglan
Rd, 1st R into Gatton Rd, follow
signs. Please park in Gatton Rd.
Disabled parking in Gatton Close.*
**Home-made teas & waffles (Sunday).
Adm £3.50, chd free. Sun 31 July
(12-5). Evening Opening £5.50,
wine & canapés, Wed 3 Aug
(5.30-8.30).** Visitors also welcome
by appt, coaches permitted.
1/3 garden of contrasting moods,
created by owners, leading the visitor
through a shady fernery into large
water garden, with 2 fountains,
reflecting light from open skies.
Romantic flower garden with unusual
plants and old favourites. Charming
and comfortable seating areas afford
various vistas of the garden and,
beyond, to Reigate Hill. Pergola,
greenhouse, raised decorative
vegetable/flower beds. Featured in
Surrey Life. Steep access slope.

62 **WALTON POOR HOUSE**
Ranmore RH5 6SX. Prue Calvert,
01483 282273. *6m NW of Dorking.
From Dorking take rd to Ranmore,
continue for approx 4m, after Xrds in
dip 1m on L. From A246 at East
Horsley go S into Greendene, 1st L
Crocknorth Rd, 1m on R.* **Home-
made & cream teas. Adm £3, chd
free. Mon 2 May; Suns 5 June;
10 July (12-5).** Visitors also
welcome by appt.
Tranquil, almost secretive, 4-acre
mostly wooded garden in N Downs
AONB, planted to show contrast
between colourful shrubs and mature
trees. Paths wind through garden to
pond, hideaway dell and herb garden,
planted to show the use of aromatic
plants and shrubs. Specialist nursery
with wide variety of herbs, shrubs and
aromatic plants. Talks on history,
cultivation and culinary use of herbs,
together with recipe leaflet. Grass
paths.

63 NEW **57 WESTHALL
ROAD**
Warlingham CR6 9BG. Robert &
Wendy Baston. *Approx 3m from
M25, J6. Travelling N on A22 at
r'about in centre of Whyteleafe turn
R onto B270 towards Warlingham.
Sharp R after going under railway
bridge. Parking on roads above no.
57.* **Home-made teas. Adm £3, chd
free (share to Warlingham
Methodist Church). Suns, Mons 1,
2, 29, 30 May; Sat 25, Sun 26 June
(2-5).**
Reward for the sure-footed - many
steep steps to 3 levels! Swathes of
tulips and alliums. Mature kiwi and
grape vines. Mixed borders. Raised
vegetable beds. Box, bay, cork oak
and yew topiaries. 'Amphitheatre' of
potted plants on lower steps.
Stunning views of Caterham and
Whyteleafe from top garden.

64 **WESTWAYS FARM**
Gracious Pond Road, Chobham
GU24 8HH. Paul & Nicky Biddle,
01276 856163,
nicolabiddle@rocketmail.com. *4m
N of Woking. From Chobham Church
proceed over r'about towards
Sunningdale, 1st Xrds R into Red Lion
Rd to junction with Mincing Lane.*
**Home-made teas. Adm £3.50, chd
free. Sat 7, Sun 8 May (11-5).**
Visitors also welcome by appt.
Open 6-acre garden surrounded by
woodlands planted in 1930s with
mature and some rare rhododendrons,
azaleas, camellias and magnolias,
underplanted with bluebells,
erythroniums, lilies and dogwood;
extensive lawns and sunken pond
garden. Working stables and
sandschool. Lovely Queen Anne
House (not open) covered with listed
Magnolia grandiflora. Victorian design
glasshouse.

WHEATLEY HOUSE
See Hampshire.

WHISPERS
See Hampshire.

65 ◆ **WINKWORTH
ARBORETUM**
Hascombe Road, Godalming
GU8 4AD. National Trust, 01483
208477, www.nationaltrust.org.uk.
*2m SE of Godalming on B2130. By
rd: nr Hascombe, 2m SE of
Godalming on E side of B2130. By
bus: 42/44 Guildford to Cranleigh*

(stops at Arboretum). **Adm £6.20, chd £3.10 (under 5 free), family £15.50. For NGS: Suns 17 Apr; 2 Oct (10-5). For other opening times and information, please phone or see garden website.**
This dramatic hillside Arboretum perfectly demonstrates what Dr Fox, the Arboretum's creator, described as 'using trees and shrubs to paint a picture'. Impressive displays of daffodils, bluebells and azaleas await in spring. Picnic by the lake in summer. Don't miss the stunning autumnal display created by maples, cherries and tupelos. Light lunches & home-made cakes served in friendly tearoom. Steep slopes.

66 WINTERSHALL MANOR
Bramley GU5 0LR. Mr & Mrs Peter Hutley. *3m S of Bramley Village. On A281 turn R, then next R. Wintershall Drive next on L. Bus: AV33 Guildford to Horsham, alight Palmers Cross, 1m.* Home-made teas. **Adm £3.50, chd free (share to St Anna's Children's Home, Ghana). Sats 2 Apr; 7 May (2-5).**
2-acre garden and 200 acres of park and woodland. Bluebell walks in spring, wild daffodils, rhododendrons, specimen trees. Lakes and flight ponds; superb views. Chapel of St Mary, stations of Cross, Rosary Walk and St Francis Chapel.

67 WOODBURY COTTAGE
Colley Lane, Reigate RH2 9JJ. Shirley & Bob Stoneley, 01737 244235. *1m W of Reigate. M25 J8, A217 (direction Reigate). Immed before level Xing turn R into Somers Rd, cont as Manor Rd. At very end turn R into Coppice Lane & follow signs to car park. Garden is 300yds walk from car park. Approach from*

A25 not recommended. Home-made teas. **Adm £3, chd free. Sats, Suns 9, 10 July; 3, 4 Sept (Sats 2-5, Suns 11-5); Wed 7 Sept (2-5). Visitors also welcome by appt in early Sept for groups of 10+.**
Cottage garden of just under ¼ acre, made and maintained by owners. Garden is stepped on a slope, enhanced by its setting under Colley Hill and N Downs Way. We grow a rich diversity of plants, incl perennials, annuals and tender ones, with many plants in pots. The garden is colour-themed, and still looking great in Sept. Featured in Surrey Life.

68 WOODHILL MANOR
Woodhill Lane, Shamley Green GU5 0SP, 01483 891004, stephanie@smithkingdom.com, www.woodhillmanor.com. *5m S of Guildford. Directions on application when booking visit.* Home-made teas. **Adm £4.50, regret no children owing to deep ponds and steep steps. Pre-booked visitors welcome, STRICTLY BY APPT ONLY Thur 14, Fri 15 Apr; Thur 21, Fri 22 July (10.30-4.30). Pre-booking for all dates essential. No coaches.**
Georgian manor house (not open) with glorious mix of traditional and formal gardens with views towards the S Downs. Dramatic display of tulips and spring bulbs in April. Box parterres, large and varied colourful herbaceous beds, cut flower beds, courtyards with scented lavender and roses in July with strategically placed seating throughout. Wild flower meadow walks, extensive parkland with mature trees incl mulberry, tulip tree, monkey puzzles. Established wildlife ponds. Delightful auricula theatre and sales.

Dunsborough Park

69 WOTTON HOUSE
Guildford Road, Dorking RH5 6HS. Principal Hayley. *3m W of Dorking. On A25 towards Guildford. Gravel driveway (signed), adjacent to Wotton Hatch PH.* Cream teas (not NGS). **Adm £3, chd free. Suns 19 June; 10 July (11-4).**
For 2011, a continuing programme of restoration is still taking place by the new garden team. The 20 acres of parkland were created in 1640 by George Evelyn and his brother John, the eminent diarist and designer. A full garden history, featuring a terraced mount, classical garden temple, statuary, tortoise house (uninhabited), and grottoes.

Surrey County Volunteers

County Organiser
Gayle Leader, Stuart Cottage, East Clandon, Surrey GU4 7SF, 01483 222689

County Treasurer
Roger Nickolds, Old Post House, East Clandon, Surrey GU4 7SE, 01483 224027, rogernickolds@gmail.com

Publicity
Mary Farmery, Fairlawn, Camilla Drive, Westhumble, Surrey RH5 6BU, 01306 640225, maryfarmery@hotmail.com

Assistant County Organisers
Anne Barnes, Spurfold, Radnor Road, Peaslake, Guildford, Surrey GU5 9SZ, 01306 730196
Maggie Boyd, Bardsey, 11 Derby Road, Haslemere, Surrey GU27 1BS, 01428 652283
Keith Lewis, 41 Shelvers Way, Tadworth, Surrey KT20 5QJ, 01737 210707
Shirley Stoneley, Woodbury Cottage, Colley Lane, Reigate, Surrey RH2 9JJ, 01737 244235
Averil Trott, Odstock, Castle Square, Bletchingley, Surrey RH1 4LB, 01883 743100

SUSSEX

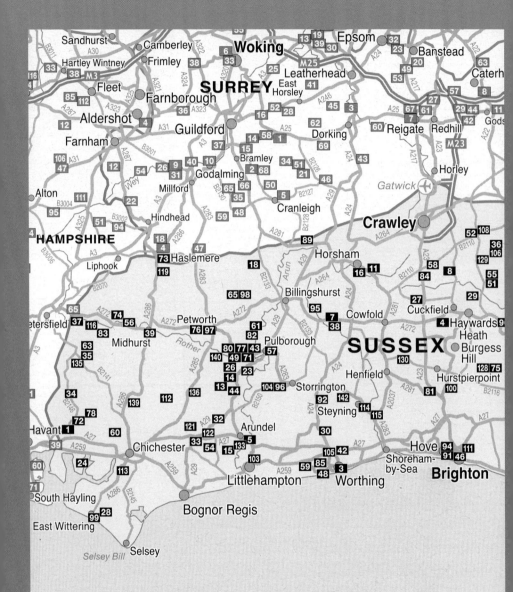

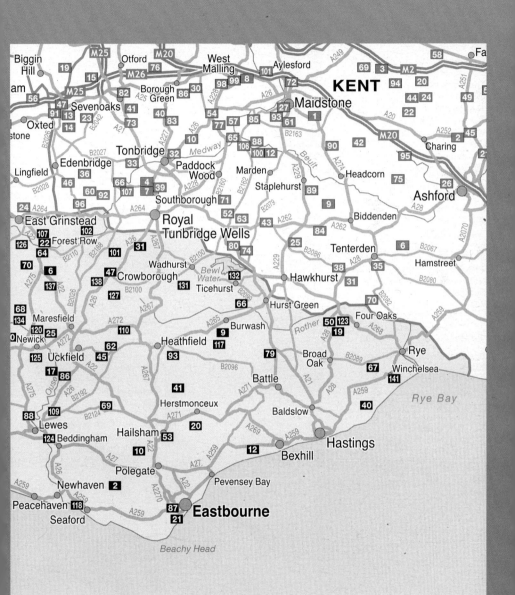

Opening Dates

February

Sunday 6
76 The Manor of Dean

Tuesday 15
100 Pembury House

Wednesday 16
100 Pembury House

Thursday 17
100 Pembury House

Tuesday 22
100 Pembury House

Wednesday 23
100 Pembury House

Thursday 24
100 Pembury House

March

Sunday 13
1 Aldsworth House

Wednesday 16
1 Aldsworth House

Sunday 20
49 The Grange
76 The Manor of Dean

Sunday 27
46 The Garden House
101 Penns in the Rocks

April

Saturday 2
20 Butlers Farmhouse
72 Lordington House
116 Sandhill Farm House

Sunday 3
20 Butlers Farmhouse
41 Fineoaks
72 Lordington House
105 6 Plantation Rise
116 Sandhill Farm House

Wednesday 6
14 Bignor Park
105 6 Plantation Rise

Saturday 9
84 Nymans

Sunday 10
61 Horsebridge House
81 Newtimber Place
96 Parham House & Gardens

Wednesday 13
14 Bignor Park

Saturday 16
76 The Manor of Dean
113 Rymans

Sunday 17
49 The Grange
76 The Manor of Dean
113 Rymans

Wednesday 20
14 Bignor Park

Friday 22
17 Bradness Gallery

Saturday 23
17 Bradness Gallery

Sunday 24
17 Bradness Gallery
18 Bradstow Lodge
66 King John's Lodge
110 Rose Cottage
138 Warren House

Monday 25
17 Bradness Gallery
65 Kiln Copse Farm
66 King John's Lodge

Wednesday 27
14 Bignor Park
65 Kiln Copse Farm

May

Sunday 1
15 4 Birch Close
34 Dormers
35 Down Place
52 Grove Farm House
74 Malt House
88 Offham House

Monday 2
15 4 Birch Close
35 Down Place
74 Malt House
138 Warren House

Tuesday 3
120 Sheffield Park and Garden

Wednesday 4
9 Bateman's
43 Fittleworth House
87 Ocklynge Manor

Saturday 7
89 The Old Farmhouse
102 Perryhill Farmhouse
127 Stone Cross House

Sunday 8
4 Ansty Gardens
6 Ashdown Park Hotel
25 Clinton Lodge
34 Dormers
45 Framfield Grange
56 Hammerwood House
74 Malt House
89 The Old Farmhouse
102 Perryhill Farmhouse
127 Stone Cross House

Wednesday 11
43 Fittleworth House

Saturday 14
55 Ham Cottage

Sunday 15
7 Bakers House
55 Ham Cottage
56 Hammerwood House
70 Legsheath Farm

76 The Manor of Dean
79 Mountfield Court
89 The Old Farmhouse
119 Shalford House
138 Warren House

Wednesday 18
8 Balcombe Gardens
43 Fittleworth House

Thursday 19
137 Vachery Forest Garden

Friday 20
22 Caxton Manor
68 Latchetts
107 2 Quarry Cottages

Saturday 21
21 51 Carlisle Road
22 Caxton Manor
29 Copyhold Hollow
55 Ham Cottage
68 Latchetts
107 2 Quarry Cottages
129 Stonehurst

Sunday 22
1 Aldsworth House
21 51 Carlisle Road
29 Copyhold Hollow
55 Ham Cottage
58 High Beeches
109 Ringmer Park
128 Stonehealed Farm

Monday 23
139 West Dean Gardens

Wednesday 25
1 Aldsworth House
43 Fittleworth House
125 Sparrow Hatch

Thursday 26
125 Sparrow Hatch

Saturday 28
36 Duckyls Holt
73 Lowder Mill
106 The Priest House

Sunday 29
16 Blue Jays
28 Cookscroft
36 Duckyls Holt
59 Highdown Gardens
66 King John's Lodge
73 Lowder Mill
110 Rose Cottage
133 Torton Top
136 Upwaltham Barns

Monday 30
16 Blue Jays
28 Cookscroft
36 Duckyls Holt
66 King John's Lodge
73 Lowder Mill
77 Manvilles Field
133 Torton Top
136 Upwaltham Barns
138 Warren House

Be tempted by a plant from a plant stall ✿

June

Wednesday 1
- **43** Fittleworth House

Thursday 2
- **19** Brickwall
- **135** Uppark

Friday 3
- **105** 6 Plantation Rise (Evening)

Saturday 4
- **83** Nyewood House
- **116** Sandhill Farm House

Sunday 5
- **25** Clinton Lodge
- **53** Hailsham Grange
- **83** Nyewood House
- **88** Offham House
- **116** Sandhill Farm House
- **142** Wiston House

Wednesday 8
- **43** Fittleworth House

Thursday 9
- **59** Highdown Gardens

Friday 10
- **17** Bradness Gallery

Saturday 11
- **13** Bignor Mill
- **17** Bradness Gallery
- **42** 83 First Avenue
- **63** Kent House
- **64** Kidbrooke Park
- **75** Malthouse Farm
- **89** The Old Farmhouse
- **113** Rymans

Sunday 12
- **12** Bexhill Gardens
- **13** Bignor Mill
- **17** Bradness Gallery
- **32** Dale Park House
- **39** 54 Elmleigh
- **54** Halfpenny Cottage
- **60** 4 Hillside Cottages
- **63** Kent House
- **67** Knellstone House
- **82** North Springs
- **89** The Old Farmhouse
- **95** Palmers Farm
- **113** Rymans
- **134** Town Place

Monday 13
- **39** 54 Elmleigh

Tuesday 14
- **39** 54 Elmleigh

Wednesday 15
- **2** Alfriston Clergy House
- **43** Fittleworth House
- **47** Ghyll Road Gardens

Thursday 16
- **109** Ringmer Park
- **122** Slindon Gardens
- **134** Town Place

Friday 17
- **46** The Garden House (Evening)
- **68** Latchetts
- **98** Parsonage Farm (Day & Evening)

Saturday 18
- **8** Balcombe Gardens
- **17** Bradness Gallery (Evening)
- **35** Down Place
- **47** Ghyll Road Gardens
- **68** Latchetts
- **91** 64 Old Shoreham Road
- **92** The Old Vicarage

Sunday 19
- **7** Bakers House
- **35** Down Place
- **76** The Manor of Dean
- **85** Oak Grove & Palatine Gardens
- **89** The Old Farmhouse
- **90** Old Scaynes Hill House
- **92** The Old Vicarage
- **93** The Old Vicarage
- **109** Ringmer Park
- **122** Slindon Gardens

Monday 20
- **25** Clinton Lodge

Tuesday 21
- **109** Ringmer Park

Wednesday 22
- **40** Fairlight End
- **43** Fittleworth House

Thursday 23
- **134** Town Place

Friday 24
- **92** The Old Vicarage

Saturday 25
- **11** 4 Ben's Acre
- **36** Duckyls Holt
- **92** The Old Vicarage
- **106** The Priest House
- **118** Seaford & Bishopstone Gardens
- **141** Winchelsea's Secret Gardens

Sunday 26
- **3** Ambrose Place Back Gardens
- **4** Ansty Gardens
- **10** Bates Green
- **25** Clinton Lodge
- **36** Duckyls Holt
- **37** Durford Mill House
- **110** Rose Cottage
- **134** Town Place

Two large ponds are home to wild ducks, kingfisher, dragonflies and frogs . . .

Wednesday 29
- **43** Fittleworth House
- **125** Sparrow Hatch

Thursday 30
- **125** Sparrow Hatch

July

Saturday 2
- **41** Fineoaks
- **69** Laughton Gardens

Sunday 3
- **53** Hailsham Grange
- **85** Oak Grove & Palatine Gardens
- **134** Town Place

Monday 4
- **25** Clinton Lodge

Wednesday 6
- **43** Fittleworth House

Thursday 7
- **135** Uppark

Saturday 9
- **48** Goring Gardens
- **90** Old Scaynes Hill House
- **73** Ridge House
- **126** Standen

Sunday 10
- **48** Goring Gardens
- **99** 33 Peerley Road
- **73** Ridge House
- **119** Shalford House
- **126** Standen
- **134** Town Place

Wednesday 13
- **43** Fittleworth House

Friday 15
- **68** Latchetts
- **115** St Mary's House Gardens

Saturday 16
- **42** 83 First Avenue
- **68** Latchetts
- **115** St Mary's House Gardens

Sunday 17
- **109** Ringmer Park
- **114** Saffrons

Wednesday 20
- **43** Fittleworth House
- **114** Saffrons

Friday 22
- **86** The Oast House (Evening)

Sunday 24
- **62** The Hundred House
- **86** The Oast House

Monday 25
- **25** Clinton Lodge
- **62** The Hundred House

Wednesday 27
- **43** Fittleworth House

Sunday 31
- **111** Round Hill Gardens

August

Monday 1
25 Clinton Lodge
Friday 5
68 Latchetts
Saturday 6
68 Latchetts
112 Roundhill Cottage
Sunday 7
101 Penns in the Rocks
112 Roundhill Cottage
Monday 8
25 Clinton Lodge
84 Nymans
Saturday 13
20 Butlers Farmhouse
57 Heatherbank
Sunday 14
20 Butlers Farmhouse
57 Heatherbank
76 The Manor of Dean
Wednesday 17
27 Colwood House
Sunday 21
27 Colwood House
86 The Oast House
Saturday 27
11 4 Ben's Acre
Sunday 28
89 The Old Farmhouse
Monday 29
89 The Old Farmhouse

September

Saturday 3
123 South Grange
Sunday 4
6 Ashdown Park Hotel
123 South Grange
Wednesday 7
9 Bateman's
Saturday 10
113 Rymans
Sunday 11
76 The Manor of Dean
98 Parsonage Farm
113 Rymans
124 Southerham Gardens
128 Stonehealed Farm

Look out for the
gardens with the
☎ – you are
guaranteed a
friendly
welcome . . .

Saturday 17
71 Little Poynes
130 Sussex Prairies
Sunday 18
10 Bates Green
71 Little Poynes
109 Ringmer Park
119 Shalford House
130 Sussex Prairies
Saturday 24
116 Sandhill Farm House
117 Sarah Raven's Cutting Garden
Sunday 25
58 High Beeches
116 Sandhill Farm House

October

Tuesday 4
120 Sheffield Park and Garden
Wednesday 5
14 Bignor Park

February 2012

Tuesday 14
100 Pembury House
Wednesday 15
100 Pembury House
Thursday 16
100 Pembury House
Tuesday 21
100 Pembury House
Wednesday 22
100 Pembury House
Thursday 23
100 Pembury House

Gardens open to the public

2 Alfriston Clergy House
5 Arundel Castle & Gardens - The Collector Earl's Garden
9 Bateman's
10 Bates Green
25 Clinton Lodge
33 Denmans Garden
50 Great Dixter House & Gardens
53 Hailsham Grange
58 High Beeches
59 Highdown Gardens
66 King John's Lodge
84 Nymans
96 Parham
106 The Priest House
115 St Mary's House Gardens
117 Sarah Raven's Cutting Garden
120 Sheffield Park and Garden
126 Standen
130 Sussex Prairies
135 Uppark
139 West Dean Gardens

By appointment only

23 Champs Hill
24 Chidmere Gardens
26 Coates Manor
30 46 Cross Lane
31 Crown House
38 Durrance Manor
44 Five Oaks Cottage
51 Great Lywood Farmhouse
78 Mitchmere Farm
80 New Barn
94 Overstrand
97 6 Park Terrace
103 Pindars
104 Pine Cottage
121 Sherburne House
131 Tidebrook Manor
132 Tinkers Bridge Cottage
140 Westacre

Also open by Appointment ☎

7 Bakers House
111 1 Belton Close, Round Hill Gardens
11 4 Ben's Acre
15 4 Birch Close
16 Blue Jays
17 Bradness Gallery
20 Butlers Farmhouse
21 51 Carlisle Road
48 Channel View, 52 Brook Barn Way, Goring Gardens
27 Colwood House
28 Cookscroft
29 Copyhold Hollow
32 Dale Park House
34 Dormers
35 Down Place
118 Driftwood, Seaford & Bishopstone Gardens
36 Duckyls Holt
43 Fittleworth House
46 The Garden House
124 The Granary, Southerham Gardens
49 The Grange
55 Ham Cottage
56 Hammerwood House
60 4 Hillside Cottages
63 Kent House
67 Knellstone House
68 Latchetts
70 Legsheath Farm
72 Lordington House
74 Malt House
75 Malthouse Farm
76 The Manor of Dean
83 Nyewood House
85 Oak Grove College
86 The Oast House
87 Ocklynge Manor
89 The Old Farmhouse
90 Old Scaynes Hill House

The Gardens

33 Peerley Road

1 ALDSWORTH HOUSE
Emsworth Common Road,
Aldsworth PO10 8QT. Tom & Sarah
Williams. *6m W of Chichester. From
Havant follow signs to Stansted
House until Emsworth Common Rd.
Stay on this rd to reach Aldsworth.
From Chichester take B2178; go
straight on at Funtington, house 1st
on R in Aldsworth (not in Emsworth).*
Light refreshments, home-made &
cream teas. **Adm £3.50, chd free.**
**Suns, Weds 13, 16 Mar; 22, 25 May
(11-5).**
6-acre Victorian family garden being
adapted to modern needs by
plantaholic owners, with enthusiastic
help from a terrier and spaniel.
Unusual trees, shrubs, perennials incl
hellebores, old apple trees,
magnolias, roses, 130 clematis and 2
lions. Great views. Carpets of spring
bulbs, particularly crocus, daffodils
and fritillaries. Gravel and walled
gardens. 2 small arboretums.
  👤 🌼 ☕

**2 ◆ ALFRISTON CLERGY
HOUSE**
Alfriston BN26 5TL. National Trust,
01323 870001,
www.nationaltrust.org.uk. *4m NE of
Seaford. Just E of B2108, in Alfriston
village, adjoining The Tye & St
Andrew's Church. Bus: RDH 125
from Lewes, Autopoint 126 from
Eastbourne & Seaford.* **Adm £4.75,
chd £2.40.** For NGS: Wed 15 June
(10.30-4.30). For other opening
times and information, please

phone or see garden website.
Enjoy the scent of roses and pinks in
a tranquil setting with views across
the River Cuckmere. Visit this C14
thatched Wealden hall house, the first
building to be acquired by the
National Trust in 1896. Our gardener
will be available to talk to you about
this peaceful cottage garden.

GROUP OPENING

**3 AMBROSE PLACE BACK
GARDENS**
Richmond Road, Worthing
BN11 1PZ. *Worthing Town Centre.*
'...a horticultural phenomenon'
The Telegraph 2005, *'...ordinary
people - extraordinary back
gardens'* The Times 2008, *'...rivals
Chelsea'* GMTV 2008. Winners NGS
Exceptional Service Award 2009.
Afternoon teas & cakes at 'Way-In
Café', Worthing Tabernacle Church,
Chapel Rd, by £2 prepaid ticket only
from 10 Ambrose Place or entry
points. **Gardens combined adm £5,
chd under 14 free. Sun 26 June
(11-1 & 2-5).**

1 AMBROSE PLACE
Mrs M M Rosenberg

3 AMBROSE PLACE
Tim & Fiona Reynoldson

4 AMBROSE PLACE
Mark & Caroline Robson

5 AMBROSE PLACE
Pat & Sue Owen

6 AMBROSE PLACE
Catherine Reeve

7 AMBROSE PLACE
Mark & Susan Frost

8 AMBROSE PLACE
Claire & Steve Hughes

9 AMBROSE PLACE
Anna & Derek Irvine

10 AMBROSE PLACE
Alan & Marie Pringle

11 AMBROSE PLACE
Mrs M Stewart

12 AMBROSE PLACE
Peter & Nina May

13 AMBROSE PLACE

AMBROSE VILLA
Mark & Christine Potter

The highly acclaimed back gardens of
Ambrose Place are indeed a
'horticultural phenomenon' in their
rich panoply of styles, plantings and
layouts. Behind a classic Regency
Terrace, itself the architectural jewel of
Worthing, the gardens draw
inspiration from such exotic diversity
as Morocco, Provence and the
Alhambra to the more traditional
sources of the English Cottage and

Victorian gardens. All within the typically limited space of a terrace (NB seriously restricted disabled access), a variety of imaginative water features add to the charm and attraction for all gardeners and prove that small can be beautiful. Do come and enjoy our special spaces!

Ansty's gardens offer interesting contrast and gentle exercise . . .

GROUP OPENING

4 ANSTY GARDENS
Haywards Heath RH17 5AW. *3m W of Haywards Heath on A272. 1m E of A23.* Home-made teas at The Barn House (May) & Whydown Cottage (June). **Combined adm £5, chd free. Suns 8 May; 26 June (1.30-6).**

APPLE TREE COTTAGE
Mr & Mrs G J Longfield

THE BARN HOUSE
Mr & Mrs Michael Dykes

NEW 3 LAVENDER COTTAGES
Derry Baillieux

NETHERBY
Mr & Mrs R Gilbert

NEW SPRINGFIELD
David & Julie Pyrah

WHYDOWN COTTAGE
Mrs M Gibson & Lance Gibson

Ansty's gardens offer interesting contrast and gentle exercise. Parking is in a field opposite Netherby, the first garden - a small but thoughtfully planted garden with some interesting features. A short walk to the second garden, Whydown Cottage, which covers an acre but seems larger, with clever planting, the occasional water feature and an atmospheric woodland full of interesting and unusual trees. Onward to pretty Apple Tree Cottage

(C16) set in 2 acres with herbaceous beds, fernery, rockery and wonderful views and excellent vegetable plot. 3 Lavender Cottages has a very neat and attractive garden to the front and brick courtyard to the rear, cottage flowers and lots of lavender. Springfield's 1 acre offers mature trees and large pond, also camellias, azaleas and rhododendrons plus herbaceous borders. The Barn House features a walled garden, a formal layout with informal planting, a pond surrounded by wild flowers, and wonderful views. The front is in a formal style with roses and clipped box. Wheelchair access to 4 gardens.

5 ◆ ARUNDEL CASTLE & GARDENS - THE COLLECTOR EARL'S GARDEN
Arundel BN18 9AB. Arundel Castle Trustees Ltd, 01903 882173, www.arundelcastle.org. *In the centre of Arundel, N of A27.* **Adm £7.50. For opening times and information please phone or visit website.**
Home of the Duke & Duchess of Norfolk. 40 acres of grounds and gardens. The Collector Earl's Garden with hot subtropical borders and wild flowers. English herbaceous borders. 2 restored Victorian glasshouses with exotic fruit and vegetables. Walled flower and organic kitchen gardens. C14 Fitzalan Chapel white garden. Featured in Country Life & The English Garden.

6 ASHDOWN PARK HOTEL
Wych Cross RH18 5JR. Mr Kevin Sweet, www.elitehotels.co.uk. *6m S of E Grinstead. Take A22, 3m S of Forest Row turn L at Wych Cross by garage, 1m on R. From M25 take M23 S, exit J10 on A264 to E Grinstead. Approach from S on A22, turn R at Wych Cross.* Teas (not for NGS). **Adm £4, chd free. Suns 8 May; 4 Sept (2-5).**
186 acres of parkland, grounds and gardens surrounding Ashdown Park Hotel. Our 'Secret Garden' is well worth a visit with many new plantings. Large number of deer roam the estate and can often be seen during the day. Enjoy and explore the woodland paths, quiet areas and views. Some gravel paths and uneven ground with steps.

7 BAKERS HOUSE
Bakers Lane, Shipley RH13 8GJ. Mr & Mrs Mark Burrell. *5m S of Horsham. Take A24 to Worthing, then A272 W, 2nd turn to Dragon's Green. L at George & Dragon PH, Bakers Lane then 300yds on L.* Home-made teas. **Adm £4, chd free (share to St Mary the Virgin, Shipley). Suns 15 May; 19 June (2-6).** Visitors also welcome by appt, please apply in writing.
Large parkland garden with great oaks, lake, laburnum tunnel, rose walks of old-fashioned roses, scented knot garden, olive and lemon walk, bog gardens and big kitchen garden with potager. Gravel paths, partial wheelchair access.

GROUP OPENING

8 BALCOMBE GARDENS
RH17 6JJ. *3m N of Cuckfield on B2036. From J10A on M23, follow B2036 S for 2¹/₂ m.* Home-made teas. **Combined adm £5, chd free. Wed 18 May; Sat 18 June (12-5).**

KRAWDEN
Victoria Road. Ann & Eddie Bryant

46 WESTUP FARM COTTAGES
Chris & Sarah Cornwell. *¹/₄ m N of stn, turn L off B2036 immed before Balcombe Primary School (signed) ³/₄ m* Visitors also welcome by appt, groups of 4+, £2.50 per visitor, min £10 per group, coaches welcome. 01444 811891

WINTERFIELD
Sue & Sarah Howe. *Just N of stn, R into Newlands, ¹/₄ m signed*

Balcombe is an ancient village with 55 listed buildings incl the C15 parish church of St Mary's. The village hall contains interesting murals on the theme of War and Peace, while nearby is the famous Ouse valley viaduct and beautiful woods, lakes, millpond and reservoir. The three gardens opening for the NGS will especially appeal to plant-lovers and are full of variety and interest. Hidden in the countryside of the High Weald, the cottage garden contains unique and traditional features linked by intimate paths through lush and subtle planting, while Winterfield contains as many trees and shrubs as can be crammed into ¹/₂ acre! There are also wild flowers, gravelled areas, alpine troughs, a secret garden, pond and borders. Krawden offers roses, herbaceous borders fruit and vegetables, a Mediterranean area with gravel and water feature and provides the venue for teas.

9 ◆ BATEMAN'S

Burwash TN19 7DS. National Trust, 01435 882302, www.nationaltrust.org.uk. *6m E of Heathfield.* $^1/_2$ *m S of A265 on rd leading S at W end of Burwash, or N from Woods Corner (B2096).* **Adm £8.60, chd £4.30. For NGS: Weds 4 May; 7 Sept (11-5). For other opening times and information, please phone or see garden website.**
Bateman's is an idyllic spot, loved by Rudyard Kipling until the end of his life. Nestled in a shallow valley, the house and garden were a joy and an inspiration to him, from the formal lawns and clipped yew hedges to the romantic meadow with the meandering river flowing through it. Discover the story of Rudyard Kipling and his 'good and peaceable place' with guided tours of the garden. Slope down to the garden from the car-park and uneven paths. Pick up and drop off point available.

10 ◆ BATES GREEN

Tye Hill Road, Arlington, Nr Hailsham BN26 6SH. Carolyn & John McCutchan, 01323 485152, www.batesgreen.co.uk. *3$^1/_2$ m SW of Hailsham and of A22. 2m S of Michelham Priory. Midway between the A22 & A27. Bates Green is in Tye Hill Rd (N of Arlington Village) 350 yds S of Old Oak Inn.* **Adm £4, chd free. For NGS: Suns 26 June; 18 Sept (11-5). For other opening times and information, please phone or see garden website.**
Plantsman's 2-acre tranquil garden with different areas of interest and colour through the seasons. Springtime incl narcissi, primroses, violets, early tulips and coloured stems of cornus. Summer progresses with alliums, hardy geraniums, kniphofias, hemerocallis, grasses, crocosmias and organic vegetables. Autumn peaks with asters, cyclamen, colchicum, dahlias, heleniums, miscanthus, and verbenas. Featured in Sussex Life & English Garden.

11 4 BEN'S ACRE

Horsham RH13 6LW. Pauline Clark, 01403 266912. *From A281 via Cowfold after Hilliers Garden Centre on L take 2nd R by restaurant into St Leonards Rd which runs into Comptons Lane. 5th R into Heron Way after mini r'about, 2nd L Grebe Crescent, 1st L Ben's Acre.* Home-made teas. **Adm £3, chd free. Sats 25 June; 27 Aug (1-5).** Visitors also welcome by appt, groups of 10+, small art groups also welcome.
'A little piece of heaven' on the edge of St Leonard's Forest and Horsham Riverside Walk, a 100ft x 45ft plant lover's garden that belies its size. Steps lined with pots of succulents, sloping gently up and away from the house, water features, summerhouse, arbour. Hidden seating. Visitors say: 'Inspirational, wonderful variety of flowers and ideas'. 'Excellence in abundance and a lovely welcome'. Tempting plants for sale. Featured in Gardens Monthly.

GROUP OPENING

12 BEXHILL GARDENS

TN39 4QB. *$^1/_2$ m W of centre of Bexhill. Proceed to Little Common r'about on A259, then see directions for each garden.* Home-made teas at 57 Barnhorn Road. **Combined adm £4, chd free. Sun 12 June (10.30-5).**

57 BARNHORN ROAD
Trevor Oldham & John Vickers.
At r'about continue on A259 (Barnhorn Rd) approx 450yds. Garden on L

NEW 89 COODEN DRIVE
Carole & Ian Woodland.
From Little Common r'about exit into Cooden Sea Rd. At Cooden Beach follow rd round to L into Cooden Drive, garden approx 1m on L

NEW ERANSLEA
17 Collington Lane East. Eric & Sue Fasey.
From Little Common r'about turn R into Cooden Sea Rd, 2nd L into Birkdale. Take 4th on L into Collington Lane East

An attractive Edwardian residential seaside town famous for its De LaWarr Pavilion arts centre. Also noted for the many enthusiastic gardeners who open to the public - and here are three gardens to prove

it! Prepare to be surprised, entertained and inspired. Two gardens are new to NGS, one a cleverly designed garden with secret areas, the other a plant lover's extravaganza. At 57 Barnhorn Road enjoy a delicious home-made tea in a spacious English garden with lawns and beds with summer flowers.

Prepare to be surprised, entertained and inspired . . .

---

13 NEW BIGNOR MILL

Bignor, Pulborough RH20 1PQ. Simone Robertson. *5m S of Petworth. $^1/_2$ m from Roman Villa at Bignor, between Bignor and Sutton.* Cream teas. **Adm £3, chd free (share to Juvenile Diabetes Research Foundation). Sat 11, Sun 12 June (10-4).**
An informal and wildlife-friendly garden with millpond, stream, orchard, paddock, and artist's studio. The millwheel, which has been incorporated into the new part of the house, will be open to the public. Limited wheelchair access over lawns and grass paths.

14 BIGNOR PARK

Pulborough RH20 1HG. The Mersey Family, www.bignorpark.co.uk. *5m S of Petworth and Pulborough. Well signed from B2138. Nearest village Sutton.* **Adm £3.50, chd free. Every Wednesday in April and October (2-5).**
11 acres of garden to explore, with magnificent views of S Downs. Interesting trees, shrubs, wild flower areas with swathes of daffodils in spring. Walled flower and vegetable gardens. Plenty of seats for contemplation, and shelter if it rains. Temple, Greek loggia, Zen pond and unusual sculptures. A peaceful garden with no traffic noise. Wheelchair access possible in shrubbery, not easy in walled gardens.

6 Plantation Rise

Visitors also welcome by appt. Delightful and tranquil mature garden with trees, scented shrubs, old roses, herbaceous borders and spring bulbs. A wooded stream flows along the bottom and two large ponds are home to wild ducks, kingfisher, dragonflies and frogs. Also raised vegetable beds, flower cutting patch, camomile lawn and planted courtyard. Original paintings and prints in gallery. Tuition days. Live gentle jazz at evening opening; bring blanket and picnic. Lower half of garden slopes to stream and ponds.

18 BRADSTOW LODGE
The Drive, Ifold RH14 0TE. Ian & Elizabeth Gregory. *1m S of Loxwood. From A272/A281 take B2133 (Loxwood). $^{1}/_{2}$ m S of Loxwood take the Plaistow Rd, after 800yds turn R into The Drive (by village shop). Follow signs. Parking in The Drive only, please park considerately.* Home-made teas. **Adm £3.50, chd free. Sun 24 Apr (2-5).**
A garden of surprises. A series of 'rooms' give a varied range of moods and plantings from a formal knot garden with associated topiary to a wild circle. Raised herbaceous and vegetable beds, ponds, bog garden, light woodland shade and many containers give form and yr-round interest.

19 BRICKWALL
Rye Road, Northiam TN31 6NL. The Frewen Educational Trust Ltd. *8m NW of Rye. S end of Northiam High St at A28/B2088 junction. Rail and bus: Rye, Northiam to Hastings service.* Home-made teas. **Adm £4, chd free. Thur 2 June (2-5).**
Listed garden surrounding a Grade I listed Jacobean Mansion (also open) and housing a school for dyslexic children. Gardens incl chess garden with topiary yew pieces and a number of Stuart characteristics: brick walls, clipped yew and beech are particular features, also small arboretum. New introductions incl vegetable allotment and conservation area. Inter-departmental scarecrow competition on show. Plants and some produce for sale. Extensive replanting. It is hoped a woodland walk will also be open. Some gravel paths, slopes and small flights of steps.

15 4 BIRCH CLOSE
Arundel BN18 9HN. Elizabeth & Mike Gammon, 01903 882722, e.gammon@toucansurf.com. *1m S of Arundel. From A27/A284 r'about at W end of Arundel take Ford Rd. Immediately turn R into Torton Hill Rd, after $^{1}/_{2}$ mile straight on into Dalloway Rd, Birch Close 2nd on L.* Home-made teas. **Adm £3, chd free. Sun 1, Mon 2 May (2-5). Visitors also welcome by appt in May.**
0.4 acre of woodland garden on edge of Arundel. Wide range of mature trees and shrubs with many hardy perennials. Emphasis on extensive selection of spring flowers and clematis (over 100 incl 11 montana). All set in a tranquil setting with secluded corners, meandering paths and plenty of seating. Featured in Sussex Life.

16 BLUE JAYS
Chesworth Close, Horsham RH13 5AL. Stella & Mike Schofield, 01403 251065. *5 mins walk SE of St Mary's Church. From A281 (East St) L down Denne Rd, L to Chesworth Lane, R to Chesworth Close. Garden at end of close with 4 disabled parking spaces. Other parking in Denne Rd car park; some spaces in Denne Rd,* Normandy and Queensway, free on Suns. Home-made teas. **Adm £3, chd free (share to The Badger Trust). Sun 29, Mon 30 May (12-5). Visitors also welcome by appt, minimum 4 adults.**
One-acre garden with rhododendrons, camellias and azaleas. Primroses, spring bulbs and candelabra primulas edge a woodland path which runs along a stream and R Arun. Cordylines, gunnera and tree ferns are set in open lawns. An arch leads to the orchard with soft fruit and vegetable plot. In the corner of the orchard large WW2 pill box. Visits inside with short talk are available. Small art show.

17 NEW BRADNESS GALLERY
Spithurst Road, Spithurst, Barcombe BN8 5EB. Michael Cruickshank & Emma Burnett, 01273 400606, emmaburnett16@btinternet.com. *5m N of Lewes. Bradness Gallery lies midway between the villages of Barcombe & Newick in Spithurst.* Home-made teas. **Adm £3.50, chd free. Fri 22 Apr to Mon 25 Apr incl; Fri 10 June to Sun 12 June incl (11-6). Evening Opening with live jazz & wine, £5, Sat 18 June (6-10).**

20 BUTLERS FARMHOUSE
Butlers Lane, Herstmonceux
BN27 1QH. Irene Eltringham-
Willson, 01323 833 770,
irene.willson@btinternet.com. *3m E
of Hailsham. Take A271 from
Hailsham, go through village of
Herstmonceux, turn R signed Church
Rd then approx 1m turn R.* Cream
Teas. **Adm £3 (April) £4 (Aug), chd
free. Sats, Suns 2, 3 Apr; 13, 14
Aug (2-5). Visitors also welcome by
appt.**
Lovely rural setting for ³/₄ -acre garden
surrounding C16 farmhouse (not
open) with views of S Downs. Pretty
in spring with primroses and
hellebores. Mainly herbaceous with
rainbow border, small pond with
dribbling frogs and Cornish-inspired
beach corners. Restored to former
glory, as shown in old photographs,
but with a few quirky twists. Recent
projects incl a grass corner, poison
garden and a secret jungle garden.
Relax and listen to live jazz in the
garden in August. Featured on
Channel 4 TV 'Four in a Bed'.
🚫 🌼 🛏 🍵 ☎

21 51 CARLISLE ROAD
Eastbourne BN21 4JR. Mr & Mrs N
Fraser-Gausden, 01323 722545,
n.fg@sky.com. *200yds inland from
seafront (Wish Tower), close to
Congress Theatre.* Home-made teas.
**Adm £3, chd free. Sat 21, Sun 22
May (2-5). Visitors also welcome by
appt.**
Walled, S-facing garden (82ft sq) with
mixed beds intersected by stone
paths and incl small pool. Profuse and
diverse planting. Wide selection of
shrubs, old roses, herbaceous plants
and perennials mingle with specimen
trees and climbers. Constantly revised
planting to maintain the magical and
secluded atmosphere.
🌼 🍵 ☎

22 CAXTON MANOR
Wall Hill, Forest Row RH18 5EG.
Adele & Jules Speelman. *1m N of
Forest Row, 2m S of E Grinstead.
From A22 take turning to
Ashurstwood, entrance on L after
¹/₃ m, or 1m on R from N.* Home-
made teas. **Adm £4, chd free. Fri
20, Sat 21 May (2-5). Also open
2 Quarry Cottages.**
Delightful Japanese-inspired gardens
planted with mature rhododendrons,
azaleas and acers, surrounding large
pond with boat house, massive
rockery and waterfall, beneath the
home of the late Sir Archibald

McIndoe (house not open).
Elizabethan-style parterre at rear of
house. New for 2011, Japanese tea
house.
🚫 🌼 🍵

Lovely rural
setting with views
of South Downs.
Pretty in spring with
primroses and
hellebores . . .

23 CHAMPS HILL
Waltham Park Road, Coldwaltham
RH20 1LY. Mr & Mrs David
Bowerman, 01798 831868,
m.bowerman@btconnect.com. *3m
S of Pulborough. On A29, turn R to
Fittleworth into Waltham Park Rd;
garden 400yds.* **Adm £4, chd free.
Visitors welcome by appt,**
preferably for groups of 10+.
27 acres of acid-loving plants around
sand pits and woodland. Superb
views. Sculptures.
🚫 🍵 ☎

CHARTS EDGE
See Kent.

CHAUFFEUR'S FLAT
See Surrey.

24 CHIDMERE GARDENS
Chidham Lane, Chidham,
Chichester PO18 8TD. Jackie &
David Russell, 01243 572287,
jackie@chidmere.com,
www.chidmere.com. *6m W of
Chichester at SE end of Chidham
Lane by pond in village.* **Visitors
welcome by appt.**
Wisteria-clad G15 house surrounded
by yew and hornbeam hedges
situated next to Chidmere pond.
Garden incl white garden, formal rose
garden, well-stocked herbaceous
borders and springtime woods. 8
acres of orchards with wide selection
of heritage and modern varieties of
apples, pears and plums incl 200yr
old varieties of Blenheim Orange and
Bramley Seedling. Chidmere Farm
apple juice produced.
☎

25 ◆ CLINTON LODGE
Fletching, Uckfield TN22 3ST. Lady
Collum, 01825 722952,
www.clintonlodgegardens.co.uk.
*4m NW of Uckfield. From A272 turn N
at Piltdown for Fletching, 1¹/₂ m. Car
park available (weather permitting) on
Suns and Mons in June.* **Adm £5,
chd free. For NGS: Sun 8 May; Sun
5, Mon 20, Sun 26 June; Mons 4,
25 July; 1, 8 Aug (2-5.30). For other
opening times and information,
please phone or see garden
website.**
6-acre formal and romantic garden,
overlooking parkland, with old roses,
William Pye water feature, double
herbaceous borders, yew hedges,
pleached lime walks, copy of C17
scented herb garden, medieval-style
potager, vine and rose allée, wild
flower garden. Canal garden, small
knot garden and shady glade.
Caroline and Georgian house, not
open. Featured in Country Life.
🌼 🍵

26 COATES MANOR
Fittleworth RH20 1ES. Mrs G H
Thorp, 01798 865356. *3¹/₂ m SW of
Pulborough. Turn off B2138 signed
Coates.* **Adm £3.50, chd free. £5
with light refreshments, by
arrangement. Visitors welcome by
appt all year.**
1 acre, mainly shrubs and foliage of
special interest, surrounding
Elizabethan house (not open). Flowing
design punctuated by clipped shrubs
and specimen trees. Paved walled
garden with interesting perennials,
clematis, scented climbers and
smaller treasures. Cyclamen, nerines,
amaryllis, berries and coloured foliage
give late season interest.
🍵 ☎

27 COLWOOD HOUSE
Cuckfield Lane, Warninglid
RH17 5SP. Mr & Mrs Patrick
Brenan, 01444 461831. *6m W of
Haywards Heath, 6m SE of Horsham.
Entrance on B2115 (Cuckfield Lane).
From E, N & S, turn off A23, turn W
towards Warninglid for ³/₄ m. From W
come through Warninglid village.* **Adm
£4, chd free (share to Warninglid
Village Hall). Wed 17 Aug, Sun 21
Aug (2-5). Visitors also welcome by
appt.**
12 acres of garden, with mature and
specimen trees from the late 1800s,
lawns and woodland edge. Formal
parterre, rose and herb gardens.
100ft terrace and herbaceous border
overlooking flower-rimmed croquet

lawn. Cut turf labyrinth and forsythia tunnel. Water features and fountains, ornaments and gazebos. Pets' cemetery. Giant chessboard. Gravel paths.

   ⛓ 🪑 ☕ ☎

28▶ COOKSCROFT
Bookers Lane, Earnley, nr Chichester PO20 7JG. Mr & Mrs J Williams, 01243 513671, williams.cookscroft@virgin.net, www.cookscroft.co.uk. *6m S of Chichester. At end of Birdham Straight A286 from Chichester, take L fork to E Wittering B2198. 1m on, before sharp bend, turn L into Bookers Lane. 2nd house on L.* Home-made teas. **Adm £3, chd free. Sun 29, Mon 30 May (2-6).** Visitors also welcome by appt, individuals and groups, coaches accommodated, all by appt please. This is a garden for all seasons which delights the visitor. Started in 1988, it features Cottage, Woodland and Japanese gardens, water features and borders of perennials, with a particular emphasis on S Hemisphere plants. Unusual plants for the plantsman to enjoy, many grown from seed. Grass paths, unfenced ponds.

   ⛓ 🪑 ✿ ☕ ☎

Emphasis on Southern Hemisphere plants. Unusual plants for the plantsman to enjoy, many grown from seed . . .

29▶ COPYHOLD HOLLOW
Copyhold Lane, Borde Hill, Haywards Heath RH16 1XU. Frances Druce, 01444 413265, yb@copyholdhollow.co.uk, www.copyholdhollow.co.uk. *2m N of Haywards Heath. Follow signs for Borde Hill Gardens. With BHG on L, over brow of hill and take 1st R signed Ardingly. Garden ½ m.* Home-made teas. **Adm £3, chd free. Sat 21, Sun 22 May (1-4).** Visitors also welcome by appt, groups of 10+.

Enchanting N-facing 2-acre cottage and woodland garden, in a steep-sided hollow surrounding C16 listed house (not open) behind 1000yr-old box hedge. Mixed borders, pond and bog garden. Mature woodland enhanced with camellias, rhododendrons, shrubs, non-native trees and bulbs. Wildlife encouraged. Newly formed oak stumpery. Crow's nest viewing platform slung between two oak trees affording far-reaching views of garden and countryside.

   ✿ 🛏 ☕ ☎

30▶ NEW 46 CROSS LANE
Findon BN14 0UG. Karen and Michael Roffey, 01903 872593, karenroffey@gmail.com. *4m N of Worthing. From Worthing A24 N towards London, after approx 2½ m signed on L into Cross Lane. Garden 500 yds on L.* Refreshments by arrangement. **Adm £3, chd free.** Visitors welcome by appt May to Sept, individuals and groups welcome.
This 95ft by 50ft garden has been developed by owners since 2006. Features incl a large selection of roses, clematis, shrubs, perennials, pergola, vegetable plot, hosta collection and small Japanese area. The garden has a number of seating areas. Enjoy the views over the Downs from the large patio.

   ☕ ☎

31▶ CROWN HOUSE
Sham Farm Road, Eridge TN3 9JU. Major L Cave (Retd), 01892 864389. *3m SW of Tunbridge Wells. Signed from A26 Tunbridge Wells to Crowborough rd, approx 400yds. Buses: 29 (½ hourly service), also 225, 228 & 229. In Eridge take Rotherfield turn S (Sham Farm Rd). 300yds take R fork, 1st R, house 1st on L, short walk from bus stop.* **Adm £4.50, chd free.** Visitors welcome by appt. Open most afternoons May to Oct for individual visits or groups of up to 50. Please phone to confirm availability of proposed date.
Situated in an AONB, 1½ acres with pools and fountain, rose garden and rose walk, herbaceous borders and heather border, herb garden. Full size croquet lawn. Laid out as a series of garden rooms in the style of Gertrude Jekyll. Panoramic views of the High Weald and Eridge Park. Rose walk not suitable for wheelchairs.

   ⛓ ✿ ☎

32▶ DALE PARK HOUSE
Madehurst BN18 0NP. Robert & Jane Green, 01243 814260, robertgreen@farming.co.uk. *4m W of Arundel. Take A27 E from Chichester or W from Arundel, then A29 (London) for 2m, turn L to Madehurst & follow red arrows.* Home-made teas. **Adm £3.50, chd free. Sun 12 June (2-5).** Visitors also welcome by appt.
Set in parkland on S Downs with magnificent views to the sea. Large walled garden with 200ft herbaceous border, mixed borders and rose garden. Gravel sunken garden. Rose and clematis arches, interesting collection of hostas, foliage plants and shrubs, orchard and kitchen garden.

   ✿ ☕ ☎

33▶ ◆ DENMANS GARDEN
Denmans Lane, Fontwell BN18 0SU. Michael Neve & John Brookes, 01243 542808, www.denmans-garden.co.uk. *5m from Chichester & Arundel. Off A27, ½ m W of Fontwell r'about.* For opening times and information, please phone or see garden website.
Denmans is a unique 4 acre garden designed for yr-round interest through use of form, colour and texture. Owned by Michael Neve and John Brookes MBE, renowned garden designer and writer. It is a garden full of ideas to be interpreted within smaller home spaces. Plant centre, award-winning café and shops.

   ⛓ ✿ ☕

DORMANS PARK SAFARI
See Surrey.

BRAEKENAS
See Surrey.

34▶ DORMERS
West Marden, Chichester PO18 9ES. Mr & Mrs John Cairns, 02392 631543. *10m NW of Chichester. On B2146. In centre of village turn up hill towards Rowlands Castle. Good tearoom in Compton, 1m.* **Adm £3, chd free. Suns 1, 8 May (2-5).** Visitors also welcome by appt in Feb for hellebores and snowdrops.
Village garden on chalk. Cottage-style planting, mainly herbaceous and bulbs, hellebores in early spring. Each area with a different colour scheme, small but productive vegetable patch. Gravel paths.

   ⛓ ✿ ☎

35 ▶ DOWN PLACE
South Harting, Petersfield
GU31 5PN. Mr & Mrs D M
Thistleton-Smith, 01730 825374.
*1m SE of South Harting. B2141 to
Chichester, turn L down unmarked
lane below top of hill.* Cream teas.
Adm £3, chd free (share to Friends
of Harting Church). Sun 1, Mon 2
May; Sat 18, Sun 19 June (2-6).
Visitors also welcome by appt Apr
to July, for 15+.
7-acre hillside, chalk garden on the N
side of S Downs with fine views of
surrounding countryside. Extensive
herbaceous, shrub and rose borders
on different levels merging into natural
wild flower meadow renowned for its
collection of native orchids. Fully
stocked vegetable garden and
greenhouses. Spring flowers and
blossom. Substantial top terrace and
borders accessible to wheelchairs.
⟨icons⟩

36 ▶ DUCKYLS HOLT
Selsfield Road, West Hoathly
RH19 4QN. Mrs Diana Hill & Miss
Sophie Hill, 01342 810282. *4m SW
of East Grinstead, 6m E of Crawley.
At Turners Hill take B2028. After 1m S
fork L to West Hoathly. Garden on R
immed beyond 30mph sign.* Home-
made teas. Adm £3.50, chd free.
Combined with The Priest House
28 May & 25 June adm £4, chd
free. Sat 28, Sun 29, Mon 30 May;
Sat 25, Sun 26 June (11-6). Visitors
also welcome by appt late May &
June.
Delightful cottage garden of approx 2
acres on many different levels. Small
herb garden, colourful formal and
informal plantings, herbaceous
borders, rose border and formal rose
garden, lots of pots and baskets - a
riot of colour. Mature azaleas and
rhododendrons in season. Limited
parking.
⟨icons⟩

37 ▶ DURFORD MILL HOUSE
West Harting, Petersfield
GU31 5AZ. Mrs John Jones. *3m E
of Petersfield. Just off A272 between
Petersfield and Rogate, signed
Durford Mill and The Hartings. Cross
medieval bridge, parking on R. From
S leave village shop (South Harting)
on L, take 1st L signed West Harting.*
Home-made teas. Adm £3, chd free.
Sun 26 June (2-5).
Come and walk around the lovely
gardens and enjoy the freshly-brewed
tea/coffee and home-made cakes.
These beautiful gardens have many

hidden charms; the meandering
millstream, large herbaceous borders
and magnificent mature trees are only
just part of these peaceful gardens.
⟨icons⟩

38 ▶ DURRANCE MANOR
Smithers Hill Lane, Shipley
RH13 8PE. Gordon & Joan Lindsay,
01403 741577,
jlindsay@dsl.pipex.com. *7m SW of
Horsham. Take A24 to A272 (S from
Horsham, N from Worthing), then turn
W towards Billingshurst. Go 1.7m to
2nd turning on L Smithers Hill Lane
signed to Countryman PH. Durrance
Manor 2nd on L.* Adm £3.50, chd
free. £5 with teas and cakes, by
arrangement. Visitors welcome by
appt preferably groups of 10+.
2-acre site surrounding medieval hall
house (not open) with Horsham stone
roof. Uninterrupted views to S Downs
and Chanctonbury Ring over ha-ha.
Many different gardens including
colourful long borders with exotic
plants, Japanese-style gardens,
shade gardens, large pond, wild
flowering meadow and orchard,
greenhouse and vegetable garden.
⟨icons⟩

39 ▶ NEW ▶ 54 ELMLEIGH
Midhurst GU29 9HA. Wendy Liddle,
01730 813845,
wendyliddle@btconnect.com.
¼ m W of Midhurst, off A272. Home-
made & cream teas. Adm £3, chd
free. Sun, Mon, Tue 12, 13, 14 June
(10-5).
Come and walk around this beautiful,
award-winning garden on the edge of
Midhurst. It has been likened to a
Tardis. Planted with majestic Scots
pines, shrubs, perennials and annuals
- a tapestry of unusual plants giving
all-season colour. Many raised beds.
A child-friendly garden, with a
competition and a reward. Garden
photo cards for sale. 1st prize
Midhurst in Bloom.
⟨icons⟩

EMSWORTH GARDENS
See Hampshire.

40 ▶ NEW ▶ FAIRLIGHT END
Pett Road, Pett, Hastings
TN35 4HB. Chris & Robin Hutt.
*From Hastings take A259 to Rye. At
White Hart Beefeater turn R into Friars
Hill. Descend into Pett village. Garden
opp village hall.* Home-made teas.
Adm £3.50, chd free. Wed 22 June
(11-5).
An exceptional garden created within

last few years. 3-acre sloping site with
just about everything: lovely views,
paved terrace, lawn and ancient
cherry tree, kitchen garden with 25
raised beds, wild flower meadow with
mown paths, expansive orchard, two
natural ponds joined by a stream and
terraced herbaceous borders. Steep
paths, unfenced ponds.
⟨icons⟩

> Child-friendly
> garden, with a
> competition and
> a reward . . .

41 ▶ NEW ▶ FINEOAKS
Hammer Lane, Cowbeech,
Heathfield TN21 9HF. Brian &
Brenda Taylor. *5m S of Heathfield,
5m N of Hailsham. From Cowbeech
1m, on LH-side side.* Light
refreshments & home-made teas.
Adm £4, chd free. Sun 3 Apr; Sat
2 July (12-5).
An immaculate 3½ -acre garden in
lovely countryside. Along the northern
boundary runs a trout stream, flowing
in spring, trickling in summer. The
lawns are punctuated with island
beds planted idiosyncratically with a
mixture of shrubs, herbaceous and
bedding plants. Further afield an
orchard, large vegetable and fruit
garden, greenhouse and woodland
(bluebell walk in April). Nearer the
house a pond, fountain and pretty
rockery. Advice given. Home-made
naturally grown jams and marmalades
for sale.
⟨icons⟩

42 ▶ 83 FIRST AVENUE
Charmandean, Worthing BN14 9NP.
Tricia & Peter Croucher. *Going E
from A27/A24 r'about towards
Brighton, take 1st L (First Avenue).*
Home-made teas. Adm £3, chd free
(share to St Barnabas Hospice).
Sat 11 June; Sat 16 July (2-5).
Secluded and peaceful, this typical
suburban garden is on different levels.
The garden backs onto the S Downs
and has mature trees, topiary, borders
planted with shrubs, perennials and

annuals, all offset by a fine lawn. A small camomile lawn and path lead through a rose arch to a delightful box-edged potager containing a variety of vegetables, salad and fruit.

⊛ ☕

43 FITTLEWORTH HOUSE

Bedham Lane, Fittleworth, Pulborough RH20 1JH. Edward & Isabel Braham, 01798 865074, www.gardenlifephotos.com. *3m SE of Petworth. Just off A283, midway between Petworth and Pulborough, 200yds along lane signed Bedham.* Adm £4, chd free. **Every Wednesday in May, June & July (2-5). Visitors also welcome by appt May to mid Aug for groups of 5+, clubs and societies welcome.**
3-acre garden with working walled kitchen garden growing a wide range of fruit, vegetables and flowers. Large glasshouse and old potting shed. Rhododendrons, roses, fountain, mixed borders. Magnificent cedar overlooks wisteria-covered Georgian house (not open) and croquet lawn. Wild garden, long grass areas, wildlife pond, spring bulbs. Head Gardener on hand to answer questions. Featured in Gardens Monthly.

♿ 🏡 ⊛ ☎

44 FIVE OAKS COTTAGE

West Burton RH20 1HD. Jean & Steve Jackman, 01798 831286, jeanjackman@hotmail.com. *5m S of Pulborough. Please ring or email for directions.* Adm £3.50, chd free. **Visitors welcome by appt. Garden especially attractive in May and June. No groups.**
A botanical watercolourists' naturalistic garden. Self-seeding and wildlife encouraged. We love to show our garden so please ring or email to agree a date to visit. We can only accommodate one car full of people at a time. Wonderful teas nearby. Plants, plant supports and botanical cards for sale.

⊛ ☎

45 FRAMFIELD GRANGE

Framfield, Uckfield TN22 5PN. Mr & Mrs Jack Gore. *3m E of Uckfield. From Uckfield take B2102 to Framfield 2½ m. Continue through Framfield on B2102. The Grange approx ¼ m E on R.* Home-made teas. Adm £5, chd free. **Sun 8 May (2-5).**
10 acres of garden with shrub borders, wild flower meadow with orchids and lakes. Woodland walks, bluebell glades. Many hybrids and species of rhododendrons and azaleas. Beautifully kept walled kitchen garden.

♿ 🏡 ⊛ ☕

Lawn and ancient cherry tree, kitchen garden with 25 raised beds, wild flower meadow with mown paths . . .

46 THE GARDEN HOUSE

5 Warleigh Road, Brighton BN1 4NT. Bridgette Saunders & Graham Lee, 07729 037182, contact@gardenhousebrighton.co.uk,. *1½ m N of sea front. 1st turning L off Ditchling Rd, heading N from sea front.* Home-made teas (Sun only). Adm £3.50, chd free. **Sun 27 Mar (1-5). Evening Opening £5.50, wine, Fri 17 June (6-8.30). Visitors also welcome by appt.**
Tucked away in the heart of the city this really is a secret garden, in Victorian times a market garden. The garden is organic and gives interest all year, supporting cut flowers, vegetables, fruit, old climbing roses and a pond. Many of the plants have been propagated by the garden owner, and the garden has unique features using many recycled materials. Garden produce and plants for sale. Featured in Gardens Monthly.

⊛ ☕ ☎

GROUP OPENING

47 GHYLL ROAD GARDENS

Crowborough TN6 1ST. *8m S of Tonbridge Wells on A26. From T-lights on A26, take London Rd towards Groombridge. Ghyll Road ½ m from lights on L. Parking in road.* Home-made teas at Trees. **Combined adm £3.50, chd free. Wed 15, Sat 18 June (2-5).**

TREES
Michael & Jacqueline Carden

WHITE ROSE
Patsy & Peter Beech

These two ⅓ -acre gardens are about 100yds apart, one on an open site divided by the meandering stream from which Ghyll Road takes its name, the other in a more level and sheltered location a little way up the hill. At White Rose, bridges connect a lawn, fish pond and bright terraced beds on one bank with grassy slopes, shrubs, woodland and fruit trees and a little greenhouse full of geraniums on the other. At Trees, narrow paths lead from a patio through a herb garden, a rose garden with a pergola, a vegetable and fruit garden, a wild area and a shady area, all with places to sit and enjoy an afternoon tea. Herbaceous borders are planted for year-round interest. Visitors who enjoyed the gardens last year will this time be able to see what they are like a little later in the season.

🏡 ⊛ ☕ ☎

GROUP OPENING

48 GORING GARDENS

Goring-by-Sea BN12 4DW. *Turn S off A259 into Parklands Ave, L at T-junction into Alinora Crescent, Brook Barn Way immed on L. Harvey Rd runs parallel to Brook Barn Way to N, 5 mins walk.* Home-made teas at 29 Harvey Road. **Combined adm £4, chd free. Sat 9, Sun 10 July (1-5).**

CHANNEL VIEW, 52 BROOK BARN WAY
Mrs J Rollings
Visitors also welcome by appt.
01903 242431
tjrollings@gmail.com

29 HARVEY ROAD
Tim & Jean Blewitt
www.goringfolly.netfirms.com

Two closely located gardens near the seafront in Goring. Each garden is a total contrast to the other. Channel View in Brook Barn Way is a mature owner-designed garden by the sea, imaginatively blending traditional Tudor cottage garden with subtropical, Mediterranean and antipodean planting. Unusually designed structures, paths, arches and pond combine dense planting with shady viewpoints and sunny patios. 29 Harvey Road is an artist's S-facing garden designed by the owner to have something of interest throughout the year. This includes a millennium folly (featured on 'Grass Roots'), a kitchen garden, koi pond and garden shrine. There are lots of ideas for the smaller garden plus geraniums, sempervivums, bonsai, koi pond and cacti. Teas at 29 Harvey Road, plants for sale at Channel View.

49 THE GRANGE
Fittleworth RH20 1EW. Mr & Mrs W Caldwell, 01798 865 384, billcaldwell@btinternet.com. *3m W of Pulborough. A283 midway Petworth-Pulborough; in Fittleworth turn S onto B2138 then turn W at Swan PH*. Home-made teas. **Adm £4, chd free.** Suns 20 Mar; 17 Apr (2-5.30). Visitors also welcome by appt Feb to June for groups of 10+. Garden of 3 acres gently sloping to R Rother. Formal areas enclosed by yew hedges comprising colour-themed beds and herbaceous borders around pretty C18 house (not open). Small potager and orchard. Large collection of hellebores and a further 7000 bulbs planted for 2011. Pond area being restored and replanted. Gravel paths.

50 ♦ GREAT DIXTER HOUSE & GARDENS
Northiam TN31 6PH. Great Dixter Charitable Trust, 01797 252878, www.greatdixter.co.uk. *8m N of Rye. ¹/₂ m NW of Northiam off A28.* **For opening times and information, please phone or see garden website.** Designed by Edwin Lutyens and Nathaniel Lloyd whose son, Christopher, officiated over these gardens for 55yrs, creating one of the most experimental and constantly changing gardens of our time. Wide variety of interest from clipped topiary, wild meadow flowers, natural ponds, formal pool and the famous long border and exotic garden. A long and varied season is aimed for. Nursery offering direct and mail order sales. Most of the plants are raised by the nursery and many can be seen in the fabric of the gardens. Descriptive catalogue and expert advice available.

51 GREAT LYWOOD FARMHOUSE
Lindfield Road, Ardingly RH17 6SW. Richard & Susan Laing, 01444 892500, splaing@btinternet.com. *2¹/₂ m N of Haywards Heath. Take B2028 for Ardingly. 2m from centre of Lindfield, turn L down single track.* Home-made teas. **Adm £6 incl tea & cake.**

Aldsworth House

Visitors welcome by appt in June & July only. Max 50 visitors, coaches permitted. Approx 1¹/₂ -acre terraced garden surrounding C17 Sussex farmhouse (not open). Lovely views to S Downs. Featuring lawns and grass walks, mixed borders, rose garden, kitchen garden and orchard, walled garden with dovecote.

52 GROVE FARM HOUSE
Paddockhurst Road, Turners Hill RH10 4SF. Mr & Mrs Piers Gibson. *¹/₄ m W of Turners Hill on B2110.* Home-made teas. **Adm £4, chd free.** Sun 1 May (2-5). 4-acre classic terraced garden with views of S Downs. The garden incl a maze, ha-ha, lime walk, herb and vegetable gardens and a brilliant hot bed.

53 ♦ HAILSHAM GRANGE
Vicarage Road, Hailsham BN27 1BL. Noel Thompson Esq, 01323 844248, noel@hgrange.co.uk. *Adjacent to church in centre of Hailsham. Turn L off Hailsham High St into Vicarage Rd, park in public car park.* **Adm £4, chd free.** For NGS: Suns 5 June; 3 July (2-5.30). For other opening times

and information, please phone or email. Formal garden designed and planted in grounds of former early C18 Vicarage (not open). Series of garden areas representing modern interpretation of C18 formality; Gothic summerhouse; pleached hedges; herbaceous borders, colour-themed romantic planting in separate garden compartments. Featured in Country Life.

54 HALFPENNY COTTAGE
Copse Lane, Walberton BN18 0QH. Sue & Dave Settle. *5m from Chichester & Arundel. Off A27 at Fontwell r'about, past petrol stn to end of village. At last mini r'about turn R onto West Walberton Lane, Copse Lane next on L.* Home-made teas. **Adm £3.50, chd free.** Sun 12 June (1-5). Delightful ¹/₂ -acre garden designed and planted in a romantic cottage style with different colour-themed areas using a palette of soft colours. Winding brick paths, rose pergola, Mediterranean garden, small but productive kitchen garden with raised beds, all created within the last 7yrs by the present owners.

55 ▶ HAM COTTAGE
Hammingden Lane, Highbrook,
Ardingly RH17 6SR. Peter & Andrea
Browne, 01444 892746,
aegbrowne@btinternet.com. *5m N
of Haywards Heath. On B2028 1m S
of Ardingly turn into Burstow Hill
Lane. Signed to Highbrook, then
follow NGS signs.* Home-made teas.
Adm £4.50, chd free. Sats, Suns
14, 15, 21, 22 May (2-5.30). Visitors
also welcome by appt.
8-acre garden created from
agricultural land by the present
owners. Formal planting around
house, pond surrounded by azaleas.
Stream fed bog garden bordered by
rhododendrons, azaleas and
camellias. Field recently planted with
trees for autumn colour. 2 areas of
woodland, one with a sandstone
outcrop and drifts of bluebells.
🏵 ⊗ ⊨ ☕ ☎

Two areas of
woodland, one
with a sandstone
outcrop and drifts
of bluebells . . .

56 ▶ HAMMERWOOD HOUSE
Iping GU29 0PF. Mr & Mrs M Lakin,
01730 815627,
amandalakin@me.com. *3m W of
Midhurst. 1m N of A272 Midhurst to
Petersfield rd. Well signed.* Adm
£4.50, chd free. Sun 8, 15 May
(1.30-5). Visitors also welcome by
appt for groups of 8+, home-made
teas can be provided.
7-acre garden comprising yew and
beech hedges giving structure to the
colourful rhododendrons, azaleas and
numerous other shrubs. The front of
the house is faced with a herbaceous
border. ¼ m walk through wild water
garden. Tea on the newly planted
terrace is a must with the most
beautiful view of the S Downs.
🕭 🏵 ⊗ ☕ ☎

57 ▶ HEATHERBANK
20 London Road, Pulborough
RH20 1AS. Colin & Dee Morley. *On
A29 opp Esso garage in Pulborough,
large eucalyptus tree in front garden.*
Home-made teas. Adm £3.50, chd
free. Sat 13 Aug (2-5.30), Sun 14
Aug (1.30-5.30).
A real oasis in a most unexpected
location. A Mediterranean-style
suburban garden (200ft x 40ft), with
interesting features and well stocked
with many unusual plants, incl several
tropical species.
⊗ ☕

58 ▶ ◆ HIGH BEECHES
Handcross, Haywards Heath
RH17 6HQ. High Beeches Gardens
Conservation Trust, 01444 400589,
www.highbeeches.com. *5m NW of
Cuckfield. On B2110, 1m E of A23 at
Handcross.* Adm £6, chd free. For
NGS: Suns 22 May; 25 Sept (1-5).
For other opening times and
information, please phone or see
garden website.
25 acres of enchanting landscaped
woodland and water gardens with
spring daffodils, bluebells and azalea
walks, many rare and beautiful plants,
wild flower meadows and glorious
autumn colours. Picnic area. National
Collection of Stewartias.
NCCPG ☕

59 ▶ ◆ HIGHDOWN GARDENS
Littlehampton Road, Goring-by-
Sea, Worthing BN12 6PG. Worthing
Borough Council, 01903 501054,
www.highdowngardens.co.uk. *3m
W of Worthing. Off A259. Stn: Goring-
by-Sea, 1m.* Adm by donation.
For NGS: Sun 29 May; Thur 9 June
(10-6). For other opening times and
information, please phone or see
garden website.
Famous garden created by Sir
Frederick Stern situated in chalk pit
and downland area containing a wide
collection of plants. Many plants were
raised from seed brought from China
by great collectors like Wilson, Farrer
and Kingdon-Ward.
♿ **NCCPG**

60 ▶ 4 HILLSIDE COTTAGES
Downs Road, West Stoke
PO18 9BL. Heather & Chris Lock,
01243 574802. *3m NW of
Chichester. From A286 at Lavant,
head W for 1½ m, nr Kingley Vale.*
Home-made teas. Adm £3, chd free.
Sun 12 June (2-5). Visitors also
welcome by appt in June, July &
Aug.

Garden 120ft x 27ft in established
rural setting, created from scratch in
1996. Densely planted with mixed
borders and shrubs, large collection
of roses, clematis and fuchsias.
Profusion of colour and scent in an
immaculately maintained small
garden.
☕ ☎

61 ▶ HORSEBRIDGE HOUSE
Fittleworth Road, Wisborough
Green RH14 0HD. J R & K D
Watson. *2½ m SW of Wisborough
Green. From Wisborough Green take
A272 towards Petworth. Turn L into
Fittleworth Rd, signed Coldharbour,
proceed 2m. At sign 'Beware low
flying owls' turn R into Horsebridge
House. From Fittleworth take Bedham
Lane, 2½ m NE.* Home-made teas.
Adm £3.50, chd free. Sun 10 Apr
(10-4.30).
Large formal garden divided into
rooms centred on 1920s croquet
lawn. Unusual hedging and shrub
planting, spring cherry, apple and
pear blossom with underplanted
daffodils. Formal vegetable garden
with box hedging; asparagus bed.
Woods and parkland. Featured in
Country Homes & Interiors.
♿ ☕

62 ▶ THE HUNDRED HOUSE
Pound Lane, Framfield TN22 5RU.
Dr & Mrs Michael Gurney. *4m E of
Uckfield. From Uckfield take B2102
through Framfield. 1m from centre of
village turn L into Pound Lane, then
¾ m on R.* Home-made teas. Adm
£4, chd free. Sun 24, Mon 25 July
(2-5).
Delightful garden with panoramic
views set in the grounds of the
historic The Hundred House. Fine
stone ha-ha. 1½ -acre garden with
mixed herbaceous borders,
productive vegetable garden,
greenhouse, ancient yew tree, pond
area with some subtropical plants,
secret woodland copse and orchard.
Beech hedge, field and butterfly walk.
♿ 🕭 ⊗ ☕

63 ▶ KENT HOUSE
East Harting, nr Petersfield
GU31 5LS. Mr & Mrs David Gault,
01730 825206. *4m SE of Petersfield.
On B2146 at South Harting take
Elsted to Midhurst rd E for ½ m. Just
W of Turkey Island, turn N up no
through road for 400yds.* Adm £3,
chd free. Sat 11, Sun 12 June (2-6).
Visitors also welcome by appt April
to July.

1½ -acre garden with fine trees, ha-ha, shade-loving plants for Apr and May, walled garden, exceptional views of the Downs from pretty Georgian house (not open). Mixed borders of unusual shrubs and herbaceous plants.

64 KIDBROOKE PARK
Priory Road, Forest Row RH18 5JA. Michael Hall School. *½ m from village centre. Approaching from N on A22: at mini r'about outside Parish Church in village, turn R down Priory Rd, then approx ½ m on L.* Light refreshments & home-made teas. **Adm £5, chd free (share to Michael Hall Steiner Waldorf School).** Sat 11 June (2-6). Kidbrook Mansion (1734) is now home to Michael Hall Steiner Waldorf School. Grounds landscaped by Humphry Repton still retain many of his original vistas, including lakes, cascades, ornamental bridges and 19th Century greenhouses. Original kitchen garden in full use as a prolific biodynamic plot. Weedy, but wonderful. Much to explore in 60 acres. Organic produce for sale, Lively 'Mansion Market' offering variety of artisan products and crafts.

65 KILN COPSE FARM
Kirdford RH14 0JJ. Bill & Pat Shere. *4m NE of Petworth.* *Take A283 from Petworth then fork R signed Kirdford & Balls Cross. Through Balls Cross, over narrow bridge then 400yds on L.* Home-made teas. **Adm £3.50, chd free.** Mon 25, Wed 27 Apr (1-5.30). 2-acre garden on clay that has gradually evolved to blend with the natural woodland setting. Many informal mixed shrub and herbaceous borders, low-maintenance conifer border, spacious lawns, vegetable garden and ponds. The wild flowers in spring are a joy, with a walk through the bluebell woods and fields giving lovely views. Partial wheelchair access.

KIMPTON HOUSE
See Hampshire.

66 ◆ KING JOHN'S LODGE
Sheepstreet Lane, Etchingham TN19 7AZ. Jill Cunningham, 01580 819232, www.kingjohnsnursery.co.uk. *2m W of Hurst Green. A265 Burwash to*

Etchingham. Turn L before Etchingham Church into Church Lane which leads into Sheepstreet Lane after ½ m. L after 1m. Teas on NGS days. **Adm £4, chd free. For NGS: Suns, Mons 24, 25 Apr; 29, 30 May (10-5). For other opening times and information, please phone or see garden website.** 4-acre romantic garden for all seasons surrounding an historic listed house (not open). Formal garden with water features, rose walk and wild garden and pond. Rustic bridge to shaded ivy garden, large herbaceous borders, old shrub roses and secret garden. Further 4 acres of meadows, fine trees and grazing sheep.

Small wood, wildlife pond and formal pool courtyard as well as a parterre for cut flowers and produce . . .

67 NEW KNELLSTONE HOUSE
Udimore, Rye TN31 6AR. Linda & Stuart Harland, 01797 222410, www.knellstonehouse.co.uk. *3m W of Rye. B2089 on R past Float Lane going towards Rye.* Home-made teas. **Adm £4, chd free.** Sun 12 June (2-5.30). **Visitors also welcome by appt, groups of 8+.** This 3½ -acre garden surrounds a beautiful C15 house (not open) within an AONB. Separate areas accommodate the sloping landscape, exploiting the stunning views across the Brede Valley to the sea. There is a small wood, wildlife pond and formal pool courtyard as well as a parterre for cut flowers and produce, hydrangea bank, plus many other features, pathways and viewing points. Limited wheelchair access, gravel paths and some slopes.

68 LATCHETTS
Freshfield Lane, Danehill, Haywards Heath RH17 7HQ. Laurence & Rebeka Hardy, 01825 790237, rebekahardy@googlemail.com. *5m NE of Haywards Heath. SW off A275. In Danehill turn into Freshfield Lane at War Memorial. 1m on R (not Latchetts Farmhouse).* Light refreshments, home-made & cream teas. **Adm £5, chd free (share to Danehill Parish Church).** Fris, Sats 20, 21 May; 17, 18 June; 15, 16 July; 5, 6 Aug (1.30-5.30). **Visitors also welcome by appt late May to 12 Aug, for groups of 20+ for ploughman's and evening visits.** 8-acre country garden full of surprises, variety and humour. Lovely lawns set off weed-free beds brimming with colour and assured planting. Ponds and water features abound, roses, dahlias, unusual plants, shrubs, prairie, vegetables. Christian walled garden, fern stumpery, water lilies in sunken garden. Wild flower meadow. Safari Hunt for children. 'Scary Path' for all ages! Renowned home made teas. Featured in Sussex Life & GGG. Some slopes in garden to avoid steps.

GROUP OPENING

69 LAUGHTON GARDENS
Laughton and Muddles Green BN8 6BL. *3m E of Ringmer. Gardens signed from Roebuck PH on B2124 in Laughton village. Map to Muddles Green available at Laughton gardens.* Home-made teas at Netherwood Lodge, Muddles Green. **Combined adm £4, chd free.** Sat 2 July (2-5).

NEW ▶ BARROWSMEAD
Ivor & Nanette Berresford. *300yds N of Roebuck Inn*

NETHERWOOD LODGE
Muddles Green. Margaret Clarke. *Via Laughton gardens, or from A22 turn opp Golden Cross PH. Go 5m to junction, 1st R at Toll House, down unmade lane, on L*

2 WOODSIDE
Dick & Kathy Boland. *300yds E of Roebuck PH* **Visitors also welcome by appt in July, max 15.** 01323 811507 k.boland01@tiscali.co.uk

Rose Cottage

The three gardens are sited in two small villages within sight of the Downs. Laughton has a C12 church, a pond and woodland walks. The garden at Woodside is a ¹/₂ acre designed for living in as soon as the sun shines. It has roses, two ponds, stream, shaded area, herbaceous borders, herbs and raised vegetable beds. Barrowsmead is a natural garden created from fields. Trees, shrubs, roses, topiary and grasses are in interlinked spaces. Courtyards have a Japanese influence. The charming hamlet of Muddles Green, 1¹/₂ m from Laughton, has Netherwood Lodge, a pretty, romantic garden with borders, roses, interesting climbers and seasonal pots designed to complement a rural retreat. Plants for sale at Woodside and Netherwood.

70 LEGSHEATH FARM
nr Forest Row RH19 4JN. Mr & Mrs M Neal, 01342 810230, legsheath@btinternet.com. *4m S of E Grinstead. 2m W of Forest Row, 1m S of Weirwood Reservoir.* Home-made teas. **Adm £5, chd free. Sun 15 May (2-5). Visitors also welcome by appt.**
Panoramic views over Weirwood reservoir. Exciting 10-acre garden with

woodland walks, water gardens and formal borders. Of particular interest, clumps of wild orchids, fine davidia, acers, eucryphia and rhododendrons. Mass planting of different species of meconopsis on the way to ponds.

LEYDENS
See Kent.

71 LITTLE POYNES
Lower Street, Fittleworth RH20 1JE. Wade & Beth Houlden. *2m W of Pulborough. Off A283, between Pulborough and Petworth. Lower Street B2138. Parking on School Lane, Village Hall car park and in lane by St Mary's Church.* Home-made teas. **Adm £3, chd free. Sat 17, Sun 18 Sept (2-6).**
Secluded ¹/₂-acre village garden created over the last 9 yrs, full of late summer colour. Sunny and shady areas, with striking combinations of contrasting foliage. Shady gravel garden, cutting beds and vegetables. Plenty of places to sit and enjoy. Featured in Homes & Gardens.

72 LORDINGTON HOUSE
Lordington, Chichester PO18 9DX. Mr & Mrs John Hamilton, 01243 375862. *7m W of Chichester. On W side of B2146, ¹/₂ m S of Walderton,*

6m S of South Harting. Home-made teas. **Adm £4, chd free. Sat 2, Sun 3 Apr (1.30-4.30). Visitors also welcome by appt May, June & July only, no coaches.**
Early C17 house (not open) and walled gardens. Clipped yew and box, lawns, borders and fine views. Vegetables, fruit and poultry in old kitchen garden. Carpet of daffodils in spring. Various trees both mature and young. Gravel paths, uneven paving, slopes.

73 LOWDER MILL
Bell Vale Lane, Fernhurst, Haslemere GU27 3DJ. Anne & John Denning, 01428 644822, www.lowdermill.com. *1¹/₂ m S of Haslemere. 6m N of Midhurst. Follow A286 out of Midhurst towards Haslemere, through Fernhurst and take 2nd R after Kingsley Green into Bell Vale Lane. Lowder Mill approx ¹/₂ m on R.* Light refreshments & home-made teas. **Adm £3.50, chd £1.50. Sat 28, Sun 29 May (11-5), Mon 30 May (1-5).**
C17 mill house and former mill set in 3-acre garden. The garden had been neglected before the present owners began restoration in 2002. Interesting assortment of container planting forming a stunning courtyard between house and mill. Streams, waterfalls, innovative and quirky container planting around the potting shed and restored greenhouse. Raised vegetable garden. Rare breed chicken and ducks, as well as resident kingfishers. Renowned for superb home-made teas, served overlooking the mill lake. Extensive and interesting plant stall with home produced plants and shrubs, garden accessories and bric a brac. Featured in English Garden, Country Living, Guildford Magazine & Chichester Observer.

74 MALT HOUSE
Chithurst Lane, Rogate GU31 5EZ. Mr & Mrs G Ferguson, 01730 821433, g.ferguson34@btinternet.com. *3m W of Midhurst. From A272, 3¹/₂ m W of Midhurst turn N signed Chithurst then 1¹/₂ m, very narrow lane; or at Liphook turn off A3 onto old A3 (B2070) for 2m before turning L to Milland, then follow signs to Chithurst for 1¹/₂ m.* Light refreshments & teas. **Adm £4, chd free. Sun 1, Mon 2, Sun 8 May (2-6). Visitors also welcome by appt.**

6 acres; flowering shrubs incl exceptional rhododendrons and azaleas, leading to 50 acres of arboretum and lovely woodland walks plus many rare plants and trees. Some steep slopes, but access easy at bottom and top of hillside.

75 NEW **MALTHOUSE FARM**
Streat Lane, Streat, Hassocks BN6 8SA. Richard & Helen Keys, 01273 890356, helen.k.keys@btinternet.com. *2m SE of Burgess Hill. From Ditchling B2116, 1m E of Westmeston, turn L signed Streat. 2m on L immed after railway bridge.* Home-made teas. **Adm £4, chd free.** Sat 11 June (2-5.30). **Visitors also welcome by appt, groups of 20+.**
Rural garden with wonderful views to the S Downs. Garden divided into rooms. Box parterre, herbaceous and shrub borders, kitchen garden. Young orchard leading to partitioned area with grass walks through field. Snail mound. Large ponds. All planted over the last 7yrs.

Rural garden with wonderful views divided into rooms. Snail mound . . .

76 **THE MANOR OF DEAN**
Tillington, Petworth GU28 9AP. Mr & Mrs James Mitford, 07887 992349, emma@mitford.uk.com. *3m W of Petworth. On A272 from Petworth to Midhurst. Pass through Tillington village. A272 then has short section of dual carriageway. Turn R at end of this section and proceed N, entrance to garden approx 1/2 m.* Home-made teas. **Adm £3.50, chd free.** Suns 6 Feb (1.30-4.30); 20 Mar; Sat 16, Sun 17 Apr; Suns 15 May; 19 June; 14 Aug; 11 Sept (2-5). **Visitors also welcome by appt for groups of 10+. No parking for coaches.**
Approx 3 acres. Traditional English

garden, herbaceous borders, a variety of early-flowering bulbs and snowdrops, spring bulbs, grass walks, walled kitchen garden with vegetables and fruit, some available for purchase. Lawns, rose garden and informal areas. Garden under a long-term programme of improvements. Recently renovated Jacobean house (not open) with views to S Downs. New for 2011, grass staircase and terrace. Children's activity walk.

77 **MANVILLES FIELD**
Bedham Lane, Fittleworth, Pulborough RH20 1JH. Mrs P Aschan & Miss C Wilson. *3m SE of Petworth. Just off A283 between Petworth and Pulborough, 400yds along lane signed Bedham.* Home-made teas. **Adm £3, chd free.** Mon 30 May (2-5.30).
2-acre established garden featuring a wonderful mix of shrubs, clematis, roses and herbaceous perennials. Established trees, orchard, lawns and lovely views. Long grass areas.

78 **MITCHMERE FARM**
Stoughton PO18 9JW. Neil & Sue Edden, 02392 631456, sue@mitchmere.ndo.co.uk. *5 1/2 m NW of Chichester. Turn off the B2146 at Walderton towards Stoughton. Farm is 3/4 m on L, 1/4 m beyond the turning to Upmarden.* **Adm £3, chd free.** Visitors welcome by appt in Feb 2011 & 2012, for groups only (snowdrops for sale Jan to Mar).
1 1/2 -acre garden in lovely downland position. Unusual trees and shrubs growing in dry gravel, briefly wet most years when the Winterbourne rises and flows through the garden. Coloured stems, catkins, drifts of snowdrops and crocuses. Small collection of special snowdrops. Free-range bantams. Wellies advisable.

79 **MOUNTFIELD COURT**
nr Robertsbridge TN32 5JP. Mr & Mrs Simon Fraser. *3m N of Battle. On A21 London-Hastings; 1/2 m from Johns Cross.* Home-made teas. **Adm £3.50, chd free.** Sun 15 May (2-5).
3-acre wild woodland garden; walkways through exceptional rhododendrons, azaleas, camellias and other flowering shrubs; fine trees and outstanding views. Small paved herb garden.

80 **NEW BARN**
Egdean, nr Petworth RH20 1JX. Mr & Mrs Adrian Tuck, 01798 865502, adetuck@aol.com. *2m SE of Petworth. 1/2 m S of Petworth turn off A285 to Pulborough, at 2nd Xrds turn R into lane. Or 1m W of Fittleworth take L fork to Midhurst off A283. 150yds turn L.* Visitors welcome by appt, **adm £3.50 plus any refreshments as agreed.**
Converted C18 barn (not open) with 2-acre garden in beautiful, peaceful farmland setting. Large natural pond and stream. Owner-maintained and planned for yr-round interest from snowdrops, camellias, spring flowers, bluebells, azaleas, water-irises, shrubs and herbaceous through to autumn colour. Trees planted for flower, bark and leaf. Seats and a swing. Fountain by Humphrey Bowden & owl sculpture by Paul Vanstone.

81 **NEWTIMBER PLACE**
Newtimber BN6 9BU. Mr & Mrs Andrew Clay, www.newtimber.co.uk. *7m N of Brighton. From A23, take A281 towards Henfield. Turn R at small Xrds signed Newtimber in approx 1/2 m.* Home-made teas. **Adm £4, chd free.** Sun 10 Apr (2-5.30).
Beautiful C17 moated house (not open). Gardens and woods full of bulbs and wild flowers in spring. In summer, roses, herbaceous border and lawns. Moat flanked by water plants. Mature trees. Wild garden, ducks, chickens and fish.

82 **NORTH SPRINGS**
Bedham, nr Fittleworth RH20 1JP. Mr & Mrs R Haythornthwaite. *Between Fittleworth and Wisborough Green. From Wisborough Green take A272 towards Petworth. Turn L into Fittleworth Rd signed Coldharbour. Proceed 1 1/2 m. From Fittleworth take Bedham Lane off A283 and proceed for approx 3m NE. Limited parking.* Home-made teas. **Adm £4, chd free.** Sun 12 June (2-6).
Hillside garden with beautiful views surrounded by mixed woodland. Focus on structure with a wide range of mature trees and shrubs. Stream, pond and bog area. Abundance of roses, clematis, hostas, rhododendrons and azaleas.

83 NYEWOOD HOUSE
Nyewood, nr Rogate GU31 5JL. Mr
& Mrs C J Wright, 01730 821563,
s.warren.wright@gmail.com. *4m E
of Petersfield. From A272 at Rogate
take South Harting rd for 1¹/₂ m. Turn
L at pylon towards South Downs
Hotel. Nyewood House 2nd on R over
cattle grid.* Cream teas. Adm £3, chd
free. Sat 4, Sun 5 June (2-6).
Visitors also welcome by appt April
to July, minibuses and groups of
12+.
Victorian country house garden with
stunning views of S Downs. 3 acres
comprising formal gardens with rose
walk and arbours, pleached
hornbeam, colour-themed
herbaceous borders, shrub borders,
lily pond and kitchen garden with
greenhouse. Wooded area featuring
spring flowers followed by wild
orchids. Featured in Chichester
Observer & West Sussex Gazette.
♿ 🎭 ❀ ☕ ☎

84 ◆ NYMANS
Handcross RH17 6EB. National
Trust, 01444 405250,
www.nationaltrust.org.uk. *4m S of
Crawley. On B2114 at Handcross
signed off M23/A23 London-Brighton
rd. Bus: 73 from Hove or Crawley &
271 from Haywards Heath.* Adm
£8.50, chd £4.50. For NGS: Sat 9
Apr (10-5); Mon 8 Aug (10-5) also
Workshop: Creating the summer
borders (see below). For other
opening times and information,
please phone or see garden
website.
In the late 1800s, an unusually
creative family bought Nymans estate
to make a home in the country. The
Messels created one of the greatest
gardens, with experimental designs
and new plants from around the
world. They entertained family and
friends, enjoyed relaxing in the garden
and walking the woods. You can now
enjoy Nymans as they did. We are
reinventing Nymans for the C21 by
working the estate in a new, greener
way. Mon 8 August (11-12.30)
Workshop: Creating the summer
borders. Join the Head Gardener
and Propagator for a workshop in
planting successful summer borders.
You will learn propagating techniques
through practical demonstrations and
have the opportunity to discuss
methods to help you plan your own
garden design at home. £10. Booking
essential 01444 405250.
♿ ❀ ☕

GROUP OPENING

**85 OAK GROVE & PALATINE
GARDENS**
Worthing BN12 6JP. *1m W of
Worthing. Turn S off A2032 at r'about
onto The Boulevard, signed Goring.
Oak Grove College entrance 1st on L
(shared entrance with Durrington High
School). For Palatine School take R
turn at next r'about into Palatine Rd.
School approx 100yds on R.* **Tickets
and entry at Palatine School.**
Lunches & teas (19 June), teas &
cakes (3 July) at Oak Grove College.
Combined adm £4, chd free. Sun
19 June (11-5); Sun 3 July (2-5).

OAK GROVE COLLEGE
The Boulevard. .
*Turn S off A2032 at r'about onto
The Boulevard, signed Goring.
School entrance 1st on L (shared
entrance with Durrington High
School)*
Visitors also welcome by appt
on most dates during term time.
01903 708870
jrollings@wsgfl.org.uk

**PALATINE SCHOOL
GARDENS**
Palatine Road. Mrs N Hawkins.
*Turn S off A2032 at r'about onto
The Boulevard, signed Goring.
Take R turn at next r'about into
Palatine Rd. School approx
100yds on R*
Visitors also welcome by appt
on most dates during term time.
01903 242835
nhawkins@wsgfl.org.uk

One price, two gardens! Two, large,
closely located, award-winning
gardens created by teachers,
volunteers and children with special
needs. An inspiring example of how
special needs children can be
transforming their school grounds into
green oases. Oak Grove College,
winners Gold and Best Special
School Garden for S of England in
Bloom 2010, has extensive and
unusual planting, with features incl
water wise, memorial and herb
gardens, large sensory courtyard,
sculptures, mosaics, and large food
growing area. Living willow, reclaimed
woodland, outdoor textiles and
chicken run. The many roomed
mature garden at Palatine School has
varied planting. Constructed by
teachers, volunteers and children with
special needs, it never ceases to
surprise visitors and features
conservation and wildlife area, large

and small ponds, bog and sea
gardens, oriental, dry and thinking
gardens, along with rockeries,
labyrinth, mosaics, echiums, orchard,
interesting tree collection and picnic
areas. Outdoor dance and musical
performances by pupils and staff
throughout the day, and guides to
show you round.
♿ ❀ ☕

Workshop:
Creating the
summer
borders . . .

86 THE OAST HOUSE
Elms Farm, Isfield TN22 5XG.
Richard & Ann Montier,
annmontier@hotmail.com. *5m NE of
Lewes. 1¹/₂ m off A26 Lewes (5m) to
Uckfield (4m). From A272 turn R at
Piltdown, take R fork after The
Peacock. Isfield 2m. Car parking at
adjacent village hall, disabled parking
only at The Oast House.* Home-made
teas (Suns). Adm £4, chd free.
Evening Opening £6, Fri 22 July
(6-8.30). Suns 24 July; 21 Aug
(2-5). Visitors also welcome by
appt July & Aug only.
A gorgeous, unusual 2-acre garden.
Using the backdrop of the S Downs,
at its centre a large pond with
herbaceous borders, a jetty walk and
prairie planting. A double helix mound
gives views of Firle and beyond. For
2011, areas of pictorial meadows and
border of 'river' planting. Featured in
Country Homes and Interiors, and on
NHK Japanese TV.
♿ ❀ ☕ ☎

87 OCKLYNGE MANOR
Mill Road, Eastbourne BN21 2PG.
Wendy & David Dugdill,
01323 734121,
ocklyngemanor@hotmail.com,
www.ocklyngemanor.co.uk. *Take
A22 (Willingdon Rd) towards old
Town, turn L into Mill Rd just before
parade of shops.* Adm £3.50, chd free. Wed 4 May
(1-6). Visitors also welcome by
appt.

Hidden oasis behind an ancient, flint wall. Informal and tranquil, $\frac{1}{2}$-acre chalk garden with sunny and shaded places to sit. Use of architectural and unusual trees. Rhododendrons, azaleas and acers in containers. Garden evolved over 20yrs, maintained by owners. Georgian house (not open), former home of Mabel Lucie Attwell.

88 OFFHAM HOUSE
Offham BN7 3QE. Mr S Goodman & Mr & Mrs P Carminger. 2m N of Lewes on A275. Cooksbridge stn $\frac{1}{2}$ m. Home-made teas. Adm £4.50, chd free. Suns 1 May; 5 June (1-5). Fountains, flowering trees, double herbaceous border, long peony bed. 1676 Queen Anne house (not open) with well-knapped flint facade. Herb garden. Walled kitchen garden with glasshouses.

OLD BUCKHURST
See Kent.

89 THE OLD FARMHOUSE
Hermongers, Rudgwick RH12 3AL. Caspian Robertson, 01403 823787, surreygardens@googlemail.com, www.surreygardens.org. Between Horsham & Cranleigh. $\frac{1}{2}$ m N of Rudgwick on B2128 at Cox Green turn R (E) into Hermongers Lane. $\frac{1}{2}$ m, parking signed. Disabled parking available. Teas & wine. Adm £5, chd free (share to Mind Music Spirit Trust). Sat, Sun 7, 8 May (2-dusk), Sun 15 May (without music, 2-dusk). Sat, Sun 11, 12 June (3-dusk), Sun 19 June (without music, 3-dusk). Sun, Mon 28, 29 Aug (2pm-dusk). Visitors also welcome by appt.
1$\frac{1}{2}$-acre traditional garden set about C16 Grade II listed farmhouse (not open) and barns. Features incl winter garden, rose garden, espalier avenue of fruit trees, water features, fine views and walks. Live music events in magnificent C17 converted barn on some open days. Wheelchair access to main garden and concert hall.

90 OLD SCAYNES HILL HOUSE
Clearwater Lane, Scaynes Hill RH17 7NF. Sue & Andy Spooner, 01444 831602. 2m E of Haywards Heath. On A272, 50yds down Sussex border path beside BP Garage shop, & opp Farmers Inn. No parking at garden (drop off only), please park

considerately in village. Home-made teas. Adm £3, chd free. Sun 19 June; Sat 9 July (2-5.30). Visitors also welcome by appt in June & July only for groups of 10+.
In memory of Sarah Robinson. Entrance archway with steps leading to peaceful 1-acre naturalistic garden on S-facing slope of clay. Mature trees and shrubs, several colourful herbaceous borders and island beds. Many roses, hemerocallis and ornamental grasses, small wild flower meadow with orchids, fruit and vegetable area and natural-looking pond.

Linked ponds, bog garden and meadow exploit the natural spring and old ditches . . .

91 64 OLD SHOREHAM ROAD
Hove BN3 6GF. Brian & Muriel Bailey, 01273 889247, baileybm@ntlworld.com. A270. On S side between Shirley Drive & Upper Drive. Home-made teas. Adm £2.50, chd free. Sat 18 June (2-5.30). Visitors also welcome by appt.
Once a playground of grass, designed, constructed and maintained by its owners into a garden of features which can be copied. Conservatory, terrace, ponds, pergola, rose arbours, bog garden, arches, trellises, vegetable garden, hexagonal greenhouse, octagonal shed, alpines, parterre, waterfall. Advice given on automatic watering and keeping hostas slug and snail free.

93 NEW THE OLD VICARAGE
School Hill, Old Heathfield TN21 9AD. Shineen Galloway. 2m E of Heathfield. Through Heathfield going E on A265. L on B2096 to Battle, next L to Old Heathfield, approx 200yds on R, 2nd driveway. 250yds down drive to house. Home-made teas. Adm £3.50, chd free. Sun 19 June (2-6).

Romantic 2-acre garden surrounding early C18 vicarage with views over unspoilt countryside. Terrace, shrubs, and herbaceous borders. Linked ponds, bog garden and meadow exploit the natural spring and old ditches. Enclosed rose garden. In the old walled garden are formal vegetable beds, trained fruit trees and Mediterranean herb garden.

92 THE OLD VICARAGE
The Street, Washington RH20 4AS. Meryl & Peter Walters. 2$\frac{1}{2}$ m E of Storrington, 4m W of Steyning. From Washington r'about on A24 take A283 to Steyning. 500yds R to Washington. Pass Frankland Arms, R to St Mary's Church. Adm £4.50, chd free. Sat 18, Sun 19 June, Fri 24, Sat 25 June (11-4).
3$\frac{1}{2}$-acre garden, set around 1832 Regency-style house (not open). Front is formally laid out with topiary, a large lawn and mixed border. To the rear some mature trees dating back to C19, herbaceous border and stunning uninterrupted 20 mile view to the N Downs.

94 OVERSTRAND
20 Shirley Road, Hove BN3 6NN. Ivor & Anne O'Mahony, 01273 554034, omahony900@btinternet.com. A270, turn N into Shirley Drive, 1st R. Home-made teas. Adm £3.50, chd free. Visitors welcome by appt 1 May to 31 Aug for groups of 4+. Clubs and societies welcome.
Large S-facing town garden with formal lawn, raised seaside planting, tropical area and many interesting, well-stocked perennial borders. Established trees, shrubs, rose-clad pergolas and bubbling water features. Lower garden with medicinal plants, fernery, tall grasses, fruit cage, vegetable area with charming vine-clad greenhouse and linear wild life pond.

95 NEW PALMERS FARM
West Chiltington Lane, Coneyhurst, Billingshurst RH14 9DN. Mr & Mrs Stephen Lowden. From A272 between Billingshurst and Coolham Garden signed to West Chiltington Lane (N), entrance after $\frac{1}{2}$ m on L. Home-made teas. Adm £4, chd free. Sun 12 June (2-6).
Approx 1$\frac{1}{2}$-acre garden surrounding Tudor farmhouse (not open). Features

incl colourful herbaceous borders, wishing well garden and walled garden with espaliered fruit and box-edged planting. Climbing roses and a mix of perennials and annuals surround the house, together with a small, productive vegetable plot, ensure plenty to see. Lots of places to sit and enjoy this peaceful garden.

☕

96 ◆ PARHAM
Parham Park, Storrington, nr Pulborough RH20 4HS. Parham Park Ltd, 01903 742021, www.parhaminsussex.co.uk. *1m W of Storrington. Main entrance on A283 Pulborough to Storrington rd.* Adm £8.50, chd £4, concessions £8, family £24 (note no free entry for RHS members at this event). For NGS: SPECIAL OPENING 'Celebration of Spring' Sun 10 Apr (11-5) to incl garden tours, a range of practical demonstrations, spring bulbs and flowers, specialist nurseries. House open. For other opening times and information, please phone or see garden website.
The spectacular 4-acre C18 garden incl a vegetable garden, orchard and 1920s Wendy House. The garden's mixed herbaceous borders and greenhouse provide flowers and plants to decorate the rooms in the house. The adjoining Pleasure Grounds leading down to the lake incl a brick and turf maze and vistas of the Downs. Featured on BBC Gardeners' World & Radio Sussex.
♿ 🏠 ⊛ ☕

97 6 PARK TERRACE
Tillington, Petworth GU28 9AE. Mr & Mrs H Bowden, 01798 343588, isabelle44bowden@gmail.com. *On A272, between Midhurst & Petworth. 1m W of Petworth, turn uphill at sign to Tillington Village, past Horseguards PH and church, No. 6 past village hall. Please do not park in residents' spaces but further up lane.* Lunches, teas & dinners for groups by arrangement. Adm £3, chd free. Visitors welcome by appt for groups of any size; no visits during Hampton Court Flower Show.
The garden has had a facelift. Terraces under ivy, wisteria, roses. Small ponds, aviary, archways, topiaries, large dome of fruit trees, clematis, roses. Sunset terrace with S Downs views. Golden pheasants and bantams pen. Herbaceous beds, shrubs, pigsty and greenhouse.

Garden designed for entertaining, providing lots of quiet retreats and eating areas, accompanied by the sound of water from fountains made by Humphrey.
🏠 ⊛ ☕ ☎

> Wishing well garden and walled garden with espaliered fruit and box-edged planting . . .

98 PARSONAGE FARM
Kirdford RH14 0NH. David & Victoria Thomas, 01403 820295. *5m NE of Petworth. From centre of Kirdford (before church) turn R, through village, past Forresters PH on R. Entrance on L, just past R turn to Plaistow.* Teas, wine in evening. Adm £4, chd free (share to Churcher's College and World Vision Ghana). Day & Evening Opening, Fri 17 June (2-9). Sun 11 Sept (2-6).
Major garden under development, now growing to maturity with fruit theme and many unusual plants. Formally laid out gardens on a grand scale, C18 walled garden with borders in apricot, orange, scarlet and crimson, topiary walk, pleached lime allée, tulip tree avenue, rose borders, vegetable garden with trained fruit, lake, turf amphitheatre, recently planted autumn shrubbery and jungle walk. Owners and Head Gardener available to give advice.
♿ ☕

99 33 PEERLEY ROAD
East Wittering PO20 8PD. Paul & Trudi Harrison. *7m S of Chichester. From A286 take B2198 to Bracklesham. Turn R into Stocks Lane then L at Royal British Legion into Legion Way & follow rd round to Peerley Rd half way along.* Adm £2.50, chd free. Sun 10 July (1-4).
Small garden 65ft x 32ft, 110yds from sea. Packed full of ideas and interesting plants using every inch of space to create rooms and places for adults and children to play. A must for

any suburban gardener. Specialising in unusual plants that grow well in seaside conditions with advice on coastal gardening.
⊛

100 PEMBURY HOUSE
Ditchling Road (New Road), Clayton, nr Hassocks BN6 9PH. Nick & Jane Baker, 01273 842805, www.pemburyhouse.co.uk. *6m N of Brighton. On B2112, approx 100yds from A273. Disabled parking at the house, otherwise parking at village green clearly signed. Garden can be reached by public transport.* Light refreshments & home-made teas. Adm £4, chd free. Tues, Weds, Thurs 15, 16, 17, 22, 23, 24 Feb (11-4). 14, 15, 16, 21, 22, 23 Feb 2012. Visitors also welcome by appt on non-NGS days in late Feb & early March, groups of 15+, small coaches permitted.
Depending on the vagaries of the season, winter-flowering shrubs, hellebores and drifts of snowdrops are at their best in Feb. Winding paths give a choice of walks through the 2+ acres of garden which is in the South Downs National Park and enjoys views to the Downs. Small 25yr old woodland. Wellies, macs and winter woollies advised. See our website for extra hellebore open days. Hellebores and snowdrops for sale. Limited disabled access in wet weather.
♿ 🏠 ⊛ ☕ ☎

101 PENNS IN THE ROCKS
Groombridge TN3 9PA. Lady Gibson, 01892 864244. *7m SW of Tunbridge Wells. On B2188 Groombridge to Crowborough rd just S of Plumeyfeather corner.* Adm £4.50, chd £1. Suns 27 Mar; 7 Aug (2.30-5.30). Visitors also welcome by appt.
Large wild garden with rocks, lake, C18 temple and old walled garden with herbaceous, roses and shrubs. House (not open) part C18. Dogs under control in park only (no shade in car park).
⊛ ☕ ☎

102 PERRYHILL FARMHOUSE
Edenbridge Road, Hartfield TN7 4JP. Mr & Mrs John Whitmore. *7m E of East Grinstead. Midway between E Grinstead & Tunbridge Wells. 1m N of Hartfield on B2026. Turn into unmade lane adjacent to Perryhill Nurseries.* Home-made teas. Adm £4, chd free. Sat 7, Sun 8 May (2-5).

1¹/₂ acres, set below beautiful C15 hall house (not open), with stunning views of Ashdown Forest. Herbaceous and mixed borders, formal rose garden and climbing rose species, water garden, parterre, pergola. Many varieties of unusual shrubs and trees. Croquet lawn (open for play). Top and soft fruit. Productive Victorian greenhouse. Featured in Sussex Life & on local radio.

103▶ PINDARS
Lyminster, nr Arundel BN17 7QF. Mr & Mrs Clive Newman, 01903 882628, pindars@tiscali.co.uk. *2m S of Arundel. Lyminster on A284 between A27 & A259. 1m S of A27 Pindars on L.* **Visitors welcome by appt** in June & July, groups of 10-25. **Adm £6 to incl home-made refreshments.**
Owner-maintained garden created over 40yrs. Many mature trees form an enclosed peaceful space with lots of seating to enjoy vistas. Interesting and ever-changing herbaceous plants, bulbs and shrubs are planted for long-lasting colour and interest. Two Burmese cats join us in giving you a warm welcome. Some gravel paths not wheelchair accessible.

Stonehealed Farm

104▶ PINE COTTAGE
Rackham, Pulborough RH20 2EU. Rob & Glenys Rowe, 01903 744115, glenysrowepc@aol.com. *4m S of Pulborough. From Pulborough take A283 to Storrington, after 4m turn into Greatham Rd. Follow Rackham signs. From Arundel take A284 then B2139 to Storrington. After Amberley turn L into Rackham St. Please park as indicated, no roadside parking. Garden entrance via public footpath adjacent to Rackham Old School and Rackham Woods.* **Adm £4. Visitors welcome by appt** 22 May to 30 June, groups of 5 to 30, coaches permitted.
4-acre garden developed in quiet harmony with the surrounding landscape of the Amberley Wildbrooks and the S Downs. 3 large ponds, one with a well-established reed bed, a bog garden, wild flower areas, an organic kitchen garden and orchard. Relaxed planting with native species encourages a wide range of wildlife. Deep water, children must be strictly supervised.

105▶ 6 PLANTATION RISE
Worthing BN13 2AH. Nigel & Trixie Hall, 01903 262206, trixiehall@btinternet.com. *2m from seafront on outskirts of Worthing. A24 meets A27 at Offington r'about. Proceed into Offington Lane. Take 1st R into The Plantation, 1st R again to Plantation Rise. Please park in The Plantation, short walk to Plantation Rise.* Home-made Teas (Sun & Wed). **Adm £3, chd free. Sun 3, Wed 6 Apr (2-4.30). Evening Opening wine, Fri 3 June (6-8.30).** Visitors also welcome by appt June, July & Aug.
An award-winning garden, our sanctuary is 70ft x 80ft, spectacularly landscaped by Nigel to give the impression of a much larger garden. Planted for all-yr interest, features incl: pond, summerhouse, pergolas, shrubs, rhododendrons, azaleas, camellias, heathers, roses and clematis in June, perennials in August. A surprise awaits you, welcome! WC available on request. Featured in Garden News & Sussex Life. Some Steps.

106▶ ◆ THE PRIEST HOUSE
North Lane, West Hoathly RH19 4PP. Sussex Archaeological Society, 01342 810479, www.sussexpast.co.uk. *4m SW of East Grinstead. Turn E to West Hoathly 1m S of Turners Hill at the Selsfield Common junction on B2028. 2m S turn R into North Lane. Garden ¹/₄ m further on.* **Adm £2, chd free. Combined adm with Duckyls Holt (also open) £4, chd free.** For NGS: **Sats 28 May; 25 June (10.30-5.30).** For other opening times and information, please phone or see garden website.
C15 timber-framed farmhouse with cottage garden on fertile acid clay. Large collection of culinary and medicinal herbs in a small formal garden and mixed with perennials and shrubs in exuberant borders. Long-established yew topiary, box hedges and espalier apple trees provide structural elements. Traditional fernery and small secluded shrubbery. Adm to Priest House Museum £1 for NGS visitors.

2 QUARRY COTTAGES
Wall Hill Road, Ashurst Wood, East Grinstead RH19 3TQ. Mrs Hazel Anne Archibald. *1m S of E Grinstead. From N turn L off A22 from E Grinstead, garden adjoining John Pears Memorial Ground. From S turn R off A22 from Forest Row, garden on R at top of hill.* Home-made teas. Adm £2.50, chd free. **Fri 20, Sat 21 May (2-5).** Also open **Caxton Manor.**
Peaceful little garden that has evolved over 40yrs in the present ownership. A natural sandstone outcrop hangs over an ornamental pond; mixed borders of perennials and shrubs with specimen trees. Many seating areas tucked into corners. Highly productive vegetable plot. Florist and gift shop in barn.

108 **RIDGE HOUSE**
East Street, Turners Hill RH10 4PU. Mr & Mrs Nicholas Daniels, 01342 715344, nickanwyn@supanet.com. *4m SW of East Grinstead. 3m E of Crawley. On B2110, 5m SE of J10 M23. Via A264 & B2028. 30yds E of Crown PH on Turners Hill Xrds. Parking at recreation ground E of Ridge House.* Home-made teas. Adm £3.50, chd free. **Sat 9, Sun 10 July (2-5.30).** Visitors also welcome by appt in June & July only.
A magical view of the High Weald greets the visitor, with all-yr interest being offered by Nigel's Garden in its quiet corner together with the mixed borders, dell with its pond and the productive vegetable garden. Large beautifully manicured bi-coloured Leylandii hedge plus other clipped shrubs. Paths lead to unexpected vistas, and the large compost heaps and Victorian greenhouse with its underground reservoir should not be missed. Mainly flat, some steep slopes.

109 **RINGMER PARK**
Ringmer, Lewes BN8 5RW. Deborah & Michael Bedford. *On A26 Lewes to Uckfield rd. 1¹/₂ m NE of Lewes, 5m S of Uckfield.* Home-made teas. Adm £4.50, chd free. **Sun 22 May; Thur 16, Sun 19, Tue 21 June; Suns 17 July; 18 Sept (2-5).**
Densely-planted 8-acre formal garden with soft edges. Emphasis is on continuous flowering from spring to Oct, with bold and dramatic blocks of colour. Features incl a striking hot

garden, rose garden, pergola covered with roses and clematis, double herbaceous borders, a new grasses garden and much more. Outstanding views of S Downs. Featured in Country Life, Sussex Life & GGG.

110 **ROSE COTTAGE**
Hall Lane, Hadlow Down TN22 4HJ. Ken & Heather Mines, 01825 830314, kenmines@hotmail.com. *6m NE of Uckfield. After entering village on A272, turn L (100yds) by phone box just after New Inn, follow signs.* Home-made teas. Adm £3.50, chd free. **Suns 24 Apr; 29 May; 26 June (2-5.30).** Visitors also welcome by appt April to July for groups of 10+, coaches permitted.
Plantsman's ²/₃ -acre garden. Old-fashioned roses, exuberant planting and luxuriance within a strong design results in a garden that visitors refer to as harmonious and tranquil and which evokes memories of childhood. Self-seeding is encouraged, so a constantly-changing garden. Collection of David Newman sculptures are integral to the design, further enhanced by Victorian church stonework. Bug hunt and fact sheet for children. Some gravel paths.

Old-fashioned roses, exuberant planting and luxuriance within a strong design . . .

GROUP OPENING

111 **ROUND HILL GARDENS**
Brighton BN2 3RY. *1¹/₂ m N of Brighton pier. On A23 pass Preston Park, cinema and fire stn. At next T-lights turn L up hill (Ditchling Rd). Princes Crescent 2nd R, Belton Rd then 1st L. Richmond Rd off Princes Crescent. Map, directions, photos and blog at* **www.roundhillgardens.co.uk.** Home-made teas & produce for sale

at 1 Belton Close. Combined adm £3, chd free. **Sun 31 July (12-5).**

1 BELTON CLOSE
Steve Bustin & John Williams. *Belton Close lies between 7 & 9 Belton Rd, off Princes Cres. No parking in Close but plenty of free on-street parking in immediate vicinity.*
Visitors also welcome by appt June to Sept for groups (up to 15). Drinks & canapés provided, £5 per person.
01273 625300
steve@vadamedia.co.uk

85 PRINCES CRESCENT
George Coleby

118 RICHMOND ROAD
Vicky Sharman & John Bridger

Three beautiful, creative and remarkably different gardens, all designed and planted by keen and knowledgeable gardeners in response to site, soil and micro-climate. All use unusual and well chosen plants to bring colour, texture and interest to late summer planting schemes. 1 Belton Close uses tropical and perennial planting to colourful effect. 85 Princes Crescent sees creative landscaping and plant selection used to overcome a steeply sloping site. 118 Richmond Road uses beech and box hedging to create a series of formal and individual garden rooms. All gardens are within 5 mins walk of each other. Featured in Amateur Gardening, BBC Sussex 'Dig It', Beige Magazine, Out There Magazine.

112 **ROUNDHILL COTTAGE**
East Dean PO18 0JF. Mr Jeremy Adams, 01243 811447, louby.adams@hotmail.co.uk. *7m NE of Chichester. Take A286 towards Midhurst. At Singleton follow signs to Charlton/East Dean. In East Dean turn R at Star & Garter Inn, Roundhill approx 100yds.* Light refreshments & cream teas. Adm £3, chd free. **Sat 6, Sun 7 Aug (2-6).** Visitors also welcome by appt.
1¹/₂ -acre country garden set in tranquil fold of the S Downs, designed in 1980 by Judith Adams whose inspiration came from French impressionists and continued by her daughter Louise, whose love of secret gardens, wild flower meadows, ponds, crumbly gothic ruins and shepherd huts all show to delightful effect in a garden full of surprises. Come and enjoy. Daily Mail National

Garden of the Year 2010 finalist. Featured in ETC magazine, Chichester Observer & West Sussex Gazette.

113 RYMANS
Apuldram, Chichester PO20 7EG. Mrs Michael Gayford, 01243 783147. *1m S of Chichester. Take Witterings rd, at 1½ m SW turn R signed Dell Quay. Turn 1st R, garden ½ m on L.* Home-made teas. **Adm £4, chd free. Sats, Suns 16, 17 Apr; 11, 12 June (2-5); 10, 11 Sept (2-4). Visitors also welcome by appt.**
Walled and other gardens surrounding lovely C15 stone house (not open); bulbs, flowering shrubs, roses, ponds, potager. Many unusual and rare trees and shrubs. In late spring the wisterias are spectacular. The heady scent of hybrid musk roses fills the walled garden in June. In late summer the garden is ablaze with dahlias, sedums, late roses, sages and Japanese anemones.

114 SAFFRONS
Holland Road, Steyning BN44 3GJ. Tim Melton & Bernardean Carey. *6m NE of Worthing. Exit r'about on A283 at S end of Steyning bypass into Clays Hill Rd. 1st R into Goring Rd, 4th L into Holland Rd. Parking in Goring Rd and Holland Rd.* Home-made teas. **Adm £3.50, chd free. Sun 17, Wed 20 July (2-5.30).**
¾ -acre garden tucked into a quiet side street, redesigned since 2001. Combining colour and texture is a theme throughout the garden. It features herbaceous beds with an emphasis on plants that thrive in sun and on free-draining soil, a long border of shrubs, trees, grasses and bamboos, mature and younger specimen trees and a kitchen garden with fruit cage and asparagus bed.

115 ◆ ST MARY'S HOUSE GARDENS
Bramber BN44 3WE. Peter Thorogood & Roger Linton, 01903 816205, www.stmarysbramber.co.uk. *1m E of Steyning. 10m NW of Brighton in Bramber Village off A283.* **Adm £4, chd free. For NGS: Fri 15, Sat 16 July (2-5.30). For other opening times and information, please phone or see garden website.**
Five acres incl charming formal topiary, ivy-clad 'Monks' Walk', large

Ginkgo biloba, and magnificent *Magnolia grandiflora* around charming timber-framed medieval house. Victorian 'Secret' gardens incl splendid 140ft fruit wall, Rural Museum, terracotta garden, delightful Jubilee Rose Garden, heated pineapple pits and English Poetry Garden.

116 SANDHILL FARM HOUSE
Nyewood Road, Rogate GU31 5HU. Rosemary Alexander, www.rosemaryalexander.co.uk. *4m SE of Petersfield. From A272 Xrds in Rogate, take rd S signed Nyewood/Harting. Follow rd for approx 1m over small bridge. Sandhill Farm House on R, over cattle grid.* Home-made teas. **Adm £3.50, chd free. Sats, Suns 2, 3 Apr; 4, 5 June; 24, 25 Sept (2-5).**
Front and rear gardens are broken up into garden rooms. Front garden incl small woodland area planted with early spring flowering shrubs and bulbs, white garden and hot dry terraced area. Rear garden has mirror borders, small decorative vegetable garden and 'red' border. Grit and grasses garden. Organic and environmentally friendly. Home of author and Principal of The English Gardening School. Flower and nature paintings for sale. Featured in Gardens Illustrated & The English Garden.

117 ◆ SARAH RAVEN'S CUTTING GARDEN
Perch Hill Farm, Willingford Lane, Brightling TN32 5HP. Sarah Raven, 01424 838000, www.sarahraven.com. *7m SW of Hurst Green. From A21 Hurst Green take A265 Heathfield Rd for 6m. In Burwash turn L by church, go 3m to Xrds at top of hill. At large green triangle, R down Willingford Lane, garden ½ m on R. Field parking, uneven ground.* **Adm £5, chd free. For NGS: Sat 24 Sept (9.30-4). For other opening times and information, please phone or see garden website.**
Sarah's inspirational, productive 2-acre working garden with different garden rooms including large cut flower garden, vegetable and fruit garden, salads and herbs area plus two ornamental gardens and a willow bed.

> The three gardens, each on chalk, are all completely different . . .

GROUP OPENING

118 NEW SEAFORD & BISHOPSTONE GARDENS
Seaford BN25 3LL. *A259 midway between Brighton & Eastbourne, both 12m. Signed off Alfriston Road, turn L by Downs Leisure Centre on A259 from Seaford Town centre, or R by Texaco Garage from Cuckmere Haven on A259. Map available at each garden.* Home-made teas at Barrack Cottage. **Combined adm £4, chd free. Sat 25 June (11-5).**

NEW BARRACK COTTAGE
Bishopstone. David & Karen Allam.
Follow signs to Bishopstone village, past the church, cottage down hill on R

NEW DRIFTWOOD
4 Marine Drive, Bishopstone. Geoff Stonebanks & Mark Glassman.
Between Seaford & Newhaven, signed on A259 close to Bishopstone stn Visitors also welcome by appt in June & July, max 15. 01323 899296 geoffstonebanks@gmail.com www.geoffstonebanks.co.uk

NEW 8 SANDGATE CLOSE
Seaford. Aideen & Denis Jones Visitors also welcome by appt June only, max 15 visitors. 01323 899450 aideenjones1@gmail.com

In the C16 Seaford was an important port. Today people come for the shops and long promenade. An added incentive in 2011 will be the NGS Seaford and Bishopstone Gardens, with 2 gardens situated in Bishopstone and one in Seaford. The three gardens, each on chalk, are all completely different. Start your trail at Sandgate Close (see group entry for

Perryhill Farmhouse

directions), a tranquil haven, with a delightful mix of trees, shrubs and perennial borders, with gazebo, water features and plenty of space to sit. Driftwood (3m away) is an award-winning exposed coastal garden with sea views and over 280 varieties of plants, cleverly combining peace with quirkiness. Barrack Cottage (½ m away) is a 5-acre garden in the heart of Bishopstone village in an AONB near the Saxon church and village green. Enjoy a partly walled garden with rooms, pergolas and arbours, roses, lavenders, vegetables, soft fruit orchard and woodland - as well as home-made cakes and tea. Seaford in Bloom: Driftwood awarded Jubilee Cup for best overall entry & 1st prize Best Back Garden; Sandgate Close, Plantsman's Cup for most original planting & 2nd in Best Back Garden. Featured widely in local press.

❀ ☕

119 SHALFORD HOUSE
Square Drive, Kingsley Green
GU27 3LW. Vernon & Hazel Ellis.
2m S of Haslemere. Just S of border with Surrey on A286. Square Drive is at brow of hill, to the E. Turn L after 0.2m and follow rd to R at bottom of hill. Home-made teas. **Adm £5, chd free.** Suns 15 May; 10 July (2-6); 18 Sept (2-5).
Highly regarded 10-acre garden designed and created from scratch over last 18 yrs. Wonderful hilly setting with terraces, streams, ponds, waterfall, sunken garden, good late borders, azaleas, walled kitchen garden, wild flower meadows with orchids. Prairie-style plantation and stumpery merging into 7-acre woodland. Further 30-acre wood with beech, rhododendrons, bluebells, ponds, Japanese-themed area and woodland walks. Children's woodland trail.

☕

120 ◆ SHEFFIELD PARK AND GARDEN
Sheffield Park TN22 3QX. National Trust, 01825 790231, www.nationaltrust.org.uk/sheffield park. *10m S of E Grinstead. 5m NW of Uckfield; E of A275.* **Adm £8.60, chd £4.30.** For NGS: Tues 3 May; 4 Oct (10.30-5.30, last entry 4.30). For other opening times and information, please phone or see garden website.
Magnificent 120 acres (40 hectares) landscaped garden laid out in C18 by Capability Brown and Humphry Repton. Further development in early yrs of this century by its owner Arthur G Soames. Centrepiece is original lakes, with many rare trees and shrubs. Beautiful at all times of the year, but noted for its spring and autumn colours. National Collection of Ghent azaleas. Garden largely accessible for wheelchairs - please call for any access information.
  ♿ ❀ **NCCPG**

121 SHERBURNE HOUSE
Eartham, nr Chichester PO18 0LP.
Mr & Mrs Angus Hewat, 01243 814261, anne.hewat@virgin.net. *6m NE of Chichester. Approach from A27 Chichester-Arundel rd or A285 Chichester-Petworth rd, nr centre of village, 200yds S of church.* **Adm £4, chd free.** Visitors welcome by appt, groups and individuals, refreshments by arrangement.
Chalk garden of approx 2 acres. Shrub and climbing roses, lime-tolerant shrubs, herbaceous, grey-leaved and foliage plants, pots, water feature, small herb garden, kitchen garden potager with octagonal pergola, fruit cage, wild flower meadow and conservatory.
  ♿ ☕ ☎

GROUP OPENING

122 SLINDON GARDENS
Slindon, nr Arundel BN18 0RE. *4m E of Arundel. From Slindon Xrds on A29 turn N into village. Follow rd up village for approx ½ m. The Well House on L just past Church Hill, park in farm opp.* Home-made teas at The Well House. **Combined adm £4, chd free.** Thur 16, Sun 19 June (2-5).

COURT COTTAGE
Mark & Clare Bacchus

THE WELL HOUSE
Sue & Patrick Foley
www.wellhousegarden.com

The National Trust village of Slindon nestles on the S side of the Downs between the Roman city of Chichester and the historic town of Arundel. Slindon has many fine listed buildings, two pretty churches and lovely walks on the Downs and through the woods. Enjoy two contrasting gardens, within a short stroll of each other. Court Cottage features 'hot' and 'cool' island borders, which have seen some changes this year, linked by an arch of roses and clematis, and a splendid, mature beech hedge. A large sunny patio is complemented by a smaller, shady area, an ideal retreat in the height of summer. Enjoy a delicious home-made tea in the delightful romantic setting of the old, walled garden at The Well House (featured in the Chichester Observer). There is much to delight incl traditional herbaceous beds stocked with mixed perennials, shrubs and roses, a small vegetable and cutting garden and side garden designed around a pool. Interesting perennials propagated from our gardens for sale. Dogs allowed at Court Cottage only. Featured in Chichester Observer and Gardening section of Daily Telegraph.

& ⊛ ☕

123 ▶ SOUTH GRANGE
Quickbourne Lane, Northiam, Rye TN31 6QY. Linda & Michael Belton, 01797 252984, belton.northiam@virgin.net. *Between A268 & A28, 1km E of Northiam. From Northiam centre follow Beales Lane into Quickbourne Lane, or Quickbourne Lane leaves A286 approx 2/3 km S of A28/A286 junction.* Light refreshments & home-made teas. **Adm £3.50, chd free. Sat 3, Sun 4 Sept (11-5).** Visitors also welcome by appt June to Sept incl for 10+ visitors, max 20.
1/2 acre with annuals, a large variety of herbaceous perennials, grasses, shrubs and trees plus raised beds and wildlife pond for yr-round colour and interest. Vegetable beds. 1/2 acre of orchard with rough grass and fruitcage with woven willow windbreak, 1/2 -acre wild wood. The whole is managed to sustain a wide range of wildlife. Water management by diverting house runoff to bulk tanks and garage runoff to pond via a rill. Some greywater use. Many home propagated plants for sale.

& ⊛ ╠═ ☕ ☎

Many lovely ornamental grasses and late summer perennials . . .

GROUP OPENING

124 NEW▶ SOUTHERHAM GARDENS
Southerham, Lewes BN8 6JN. *1/4 m SE of Lewes. From Lewes via Cuilfail Tunnel go to Southerham r'about on A27, take first exit for Eastbourne/Newhaven. Southerham sign approx 100yds on L.* Home-made teas at The Granary. **Combined adm £3.50, chd free (share to The Sussex MS Treatment Centre). Sun 11 Sept (2-5).**

NEW▶ THE GRANARY ╠═
Steve & Alison Grint
Visitors also welcome by appt for any size of group at any time.
01273 480728
ali899@hotmail.co.uk

NEW▶ OXSETTON
Peter & Jean Burges
Visitors also welcome by appt at any time, smaller groups preferred.
01273 472851

Unexpectedly nestling at the foot of the South Downs between the A27 and an industrial estate lies the peaceful hamlet of Southerham. There you will find 2 very different gardens created from old paddock and solid concrete farmyards. The Granary is a contemporary country garden with winding paths, using naturalistic a planting style with many lovely ornamental grasses and late summer perennials. Enjoy the gravel garden, fernery, tropical border, lavender, olive trees and vegetable garden as well as a large pond with a decked viewing platform and summerhouse and a newly-created stream water feature. Oxsetton's walled courtyard garden is built on an existing farmyard, featuring an ancient flint horse trough, an old well and raised beds containing a variety of interesting herbaceous plants, roses and clematis. Many containers are filled with shrubs, trees and bamboos. There is a pergola and summerhouse and seating areas to enjoy a recently acquired view of downland. Some steps to part of the garden. Local artists' work exhibited and for sale.

& ⊛ ☕

125 ▶ SPARROW HATCH
Cornwell's Bank, nr Newick BN8 4RD. Tony & Jane Welfare. *5m E of Haywards Heath. From A272 turn R into Oxbottom Lane (signed Barcombe), 1/2 m fork L into Narrow Rd, continue to T-junction & park in Chailey Lane (no parking at house).* **Adm £3, chd free. Weds, Thurs 25, 26 May; 29, 30 June (2-5).**
Delightful 1/3 -acre plantsman's cottage garden, wholly designed, made and maintained by owners. Many features incl 2 ponds, formal and wildlife, herbaceous borders, shady dell, vegetables, herbs, alpines. Planned for owners' enjoyment and love of growing plants, both usual and unusual. Plants for sale, propagated and grown by garden owner.

⊛

SQUERRYES COURT
See Kent.

126 ▶ ♦ STANDEN
West Hoathly Road, East Grinstead RH19 4NE. National Trust, 01342 323029, www.nationaltrust.org.uk/standen. *2m S of E Grinstead. Signed from B2110 Turners Hill Road and from East Grinstead town centre.* **Adm £9, chd £4.50. For NGS: Sat 9, Sun 10 July (11-5.30).** For other opening times and information, please phone or see garden website.
Approx 12 acres of hillside garden, divided into small compartments: notably a quarry garden, kitchen garden and bamboo garden with pool and cascades. Woodland walks and stunning views over the Medway and Ashdown Forest. Ongoing restoration. Plant sales area. Kitchen garden produce available to buy. Only proceeds from sales of kitchen garden produce will be donated to NGS on NGS days. Hillside garden with steps, slopes and gravel paths; wheelchair map available.

& ⊛ ☕

127 STONE CROSS HOUSE
Alice Bright Lane, Crowborough
TN6 3SH. **Mr & Mrs D A Tate.** $^1/_2$ m
S of Crowborough. At Crowborough
T-lights (A26) turn S into High St, &
shortly R into Croft Rd. Straight over
2 mini r'abouts into Alice Bright Lane.
Garden on L at next Xrds about 1$^1/_2$ m
from T-lights. Home-made teas. **Adm
£3, chd free. Sat 7, Sun 8 May
(2-5.30).**
Beautiful 9-acre country property with
gardens containing a delightful array
of azaleas, rhododendrons and
camellias, interplanted with an
abundance of spring bulbs. The very
pretty cottage garden has interesting
examples of topiary and unusual
plants. Jacob sheep graze the
surrounding pastures. Featured on
local TV & radio. Gravel drive.
&. 🐾 ☕

Ancient oak trees
and large lawn
areas interspersed
with well-stocked
flower beds and
borders . . .

128 STONEHEALED FARM
Streat Lane, Streat BN6 8SA. **Lance
& Fiona Smith,** 01273 891145,
afionasmith@hotmail.com. 2m SE of
Burgess Hill. From Ditchling B2116,
1m E of Westmeston, turn L (N)
signed Streat, 2m on R immed after
railway bridge. Home-made teas.
**Adm £3.50, chd free. Suns 22 May;
11 Sept (2-5). Visitors also
welcome by appt May & Sept for
groups of 10+.**
1$^1/_2$ acres surrounded by fields with
views to the S Downs. Terrace with
seasonal pots, hidden front garden,
shaded pond with serpentine bridge,
kitchen garden, family path, lime walk,
oak tree deck. Early-flowering shrubs,
bulbs and emerging perennial foliage
in May. Dramatic late summer colour
and grasses in Sept. New hand-
carved stepping stone 'family path'.
&. ✿ ☕ ☎

129 STONEHURST
Selsfield Road, Ardingly RH17 6TN.
Mr & Mrs M Holman. 1$^1/_4$ m N of
Ardingly. On B2028 opp Wakehurst
place. Home-made teas. **Adm £4.50,
chd free. Sat 21 May (12-5).**
Gardens of approx 12 acres designed
and laid out early in the last century
by Thomas Mawson with a wealth of
architectural brick and stone work.
Fine views across the Cob Valley and
to S Downs. Amongst established
planting is large collection incl
camellias, acers, rhododendrons and
azaleas.

130 ◆ SUSSEX PRAIRIES
Morlands Farm, Wheatsheaf Road,
Henfield BN5 9AT. **Paul & Pauline
McBride,** 01273 495902,
www.sussexprairies.co.uk. 2m E of
Henfield on B2116 Wheatsheaf Rd
(also known as Albourne Rd). **Adm
£6, chd free. For NGS: Sat 17, Sun
18 Sept (11-5). For other opening
times and information, please
phone or see garden website.**
Exciting Prairie garden of approx 6
acres planted in the naturalistic style
using 30,000 plants and 600 different
varieties. A colourful garden featuring
a huge variety of unusual ornamental
grasses. Expect layers of colour,
texture and architectural splendour.
Surrounded by mature oak trees with
views of Chanctonbury Ring and
Devil's Dyke on the S Downs.
Collection of sculptures. Spirit of the
West will provide a living exhibition of
Native American life. Rare breed
animals. Featured in The Guardian &
House & Garden. Woodchip paths
may be difficult for wheelchairs.
&. 🐾 ✿ 🛏 ☕

131 TIDEBROOK MANOR
Tidebrook, Wadhurst TN5 6PD,
07957 172949 **Ed Flint,**
caroline.tidebrook@tiscali.co.uk.
Between Wadhurst & Mayfield. From
Wadhurst take B2100 towards Mark
Cross, L at Best Beech PH, down hill,
200m past church on R. **Adm £5,
chd free. Visitors welcome by appt
for groups 10+ all year.**
Open for group visits only, but a very
special 4-acre garden with
outstanding views and set in the heart
of the Sussex countryside. Tidebrook
Manor has been lovingly and
beautifully refurbished by the owners
and their expert and cricket-mad
gardener. Large mixed borders,
lawns, meadows, hydrangea walk,
wild woodland, productive kitchen

garden - a fascinating mix of planting
styles, colours and textures providing
interest all year.
&. ☎

**132 TINKERS BRIDGE
COTTAGE**
Tinkers Lane, Ticehurst TN5 7LU.
Mrs M A Landsberg, 01580 200272.
11m SE of Tunbridge Wells. From
B2099 $^1/_2$ m W Ticehurst, turn N to
Three Leg Cross for 1m, R after Bull
Inn. House at bottom of hill. **Adm £5,
chd free. Visitors welcome by appt
Apr to July incl, max 25, no
coaches.**
12 acres landscaped; stream garden
nr house (not open) leading to
herbaceous borders, wildlife meadow
with ponds and woodland walks.
&. 🐾 ✿ ☕ ☎

133 TORTON TOP
36 Torton Hill Road, Arundel
BN18 9HL. **Barry & Lucy Hopkins.**
$^1/_2$ m W of Arundel town centre. Exit
A27 Arundel bypass at r'about next to
river, taking Ford/Climping exit into
Ford Rd. 100m turn R into Torton Hill
Rd, garden at top of hill on R. Home-
made teas. **Adm £3.50, chd free.
Sun 29, Mon 30 May (2-5.30).**
Mature gardens of $^1/_2$ acre with
ancient oak trees and large lawn
areas interspersed with well-stocked
flower beds and borders. Many
specimen shrubs, trees and
perennials incl acers, clematis, roses
and penstemons. Delightful natural
pond feature with waterfall and
wetland planting. Present owners
have redesigned the entire garden
over the past 21yrs and care for all
planting and maintenance. You are
guaranteed a very friendly welcome.
&. ☕

134 TOWN PLACE
Ketches Lane, Freshfield, nr
Sheffield Park RH17 7NR. **Mr & Mrs
Anthony McGrath,** 01825 790221,
mcgrathsussex@hotmail.com,
www.townplacegarden.org.uk. 3m
E of Haywards Heath. From A275
turn W at Sheffield Green into
Ketches Lane for Lindfield. 1$^3/_4$ m on
L. Cream Teas. **Adm £5, chd free.
Suns, Thurs 12, 16, 23, 26 June;
Suns 3, 10 July (2-6). Visitors also
welcome by appt June & July only
for groups of 20+. £10 per person
(£7 for local garden groups).**
3 acres with over 600 roses, 150ft
herbaceous border, walled herb
garden, ornamental grasses, ancient
hollow oak, orchard and potager.

6 Park Terrace

'Green' Priory Church and Cloisters. C17 Sussex farmhouse (not open). Featured in The English Garden, Magnet and Garten Traume.

135 ◆ **UPPARK**
South Harting GU31 5QR. National Trust, 01730 825415, www.nationaltrust.org.uk. *1½ m S of S Harting. 5m SE of Petersfield on B2146.* Adm £4.40, chd £2.20. For NGS: Thurs 2 June; 7 July (11.30-5). For other opening times and information, please phone or see garden website.
Intimate restored Picturesque garden nestles behind Uppark House, in contrast to the sweeping panoramic views to the South. Fine restored mansion. Gardener leads afternoon tours on NGS days.

136 **UPWALTHAM BARNS**
Upwaltham GU28 0LX. Roger & Sue Kearsey, 01798 343145. *6m S of Petworth. 6m N of Chichester on A285.* Lunches, home-made teas & wine. Adm £4, chd free (share to St Mary's Church). Sun 29, Mon 30 May (11-5.30). Visitors also welcome by appt in May, June, July, Sept & Oct, groups of 10+, coaches permitted.
Unique farm setting has been transformed into a garden of many rooms. Entrance is a tapestry of perennial planting to set off C17 flint barns. At the rear, walled terraced garden redeveloped and planted in an abundance of unusual plants. Extensive vegetable garden. Landscaping in walled garden in progress. Roam at leisure, relax and enjoy at every season, with lovely views of S Downs and C12 Shepherds Church (open to visitors). Some gravel paths.

137 ◆ **VACHERY FOREST GARDEN**
Wych Cross TN22 3HR. Conservators of Ashdown Forest, www.ashdownforest.org. *⅔ m W of A22 between Wych Cross & Nutley. Park 1½ m S of Wych Cross on A22 at Trees car park. Access along rides, across heath and down steepish bridleway. Round trip 2½ m, no facilities.* Light lunches & teas available at Llama Park at Wych Cross. Adm £3, chd free. Thur 19 May (11-5).
The Vachery Garden, a hidden gem of Ashdown Forest, is being restored. It

comprises a string of lakes, sluices and weirs with a Folly Bridge; a 'gorge' of Cheddar Gorge limestone landscaped by Gavin Jones in 1925; and fine stands of rhododendrons and native and introduced trees. Guided tours at 11am, 1pm & 3pm, starting from the Folly Bridge in the Garden (directions will be given). NB Allow 15 mins walk from car park.

138 **WARREN HOUSE**
Warren Road, Crowborough TN6 1TX. Mr & Mrs M J Hands. *1½ m SW of Crowborough Cross. From Crowborough Cross towards Uckfield A26, 4th turning on R. 1m down Warren Rd. From South 2nd L after Blue Anchor.* Home-made teas. Adm £3.50, chd free. Sun 24 Apr; Mon 2, Sun 15, Mon 30 May (2-5). Beautiful house (not open) steeped in history with 9-acre garden and views over Ashdown Forest. Series of gardens old and new, displaying wealth of azaleas, rhododendrons, impressive variety of trees and shrubs. Sweeping lawns framed by delightful walls and terraces, woodlands, ponds, ducks.

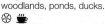

Unusual plants are maturing well in much enriched poor sandy soil. Intriguing from spring to autumn . . .

139 ◆ **WEST DEAN GARDENS**
West Dean PO18 0QZ. Edward James Foundation, 01243 818210, www.westdean.org.uk. *5m N of Chichester. On A286.* For NGS: Mon 23 May (10.30-5). For other opening times and adm , information, please phone or see garden website.
35-acre historic garden in tranquil downland setting. 300ft long Harold Peto pergola, mixed and herbaceous borders, rustic summerhouses, redeveloped water and spring garden,

specimen trees. Restored 2½ -acre walled garden contains fruit collection, 13 Victorian glasshouses, apple store, large working kitchen garden, extensive plant collection. Circuit walk (2¼ m) climbs through parkland to 45-acre St Roche's Arboretum. National Collections of *Aesculus* and liriodendron.

140 **WESTACRE**
Burton Park Road, Petworth GU28 0JS. Mrs R Charles, 01798 344467. *2m S of Petworth, off A285 (Chichester rd). Turn L past Chandlers Builders onto Burton Park Rd, garden ¼ m on L.* Refreshments by arrangement. Adm £4. Visitors welcome by appt.
Started from scratch but framed by old forest trees and with glimpses of the Downs, this 6yr-old garden now has a pond and bog gardens, a pergola leading to a potager, wall planting, terrace beds and raised shrub banks. Unusual plants are maturing well in much enriched poor sandy soil. Intriguing from spring to autumn.

GROUP OPENING

141 **WINCHELSEA'S SECRET GARDENS**
Winchelsea TN36 4EJ. *2m W of Rye, 8m E of Hastings. Follow signs for parking. Purchase ticket for all gardens at first garden visited; a map will be provided.* Home-made teas at New Hall. Combined adm £5, chd free. Sat 25 June (1-5.30).

ALARDS PLAT
1 High Street. Richard & Cynthia Feast

THE ARMOURY
Mr & Mrs A Jasper

CLEVELAND HOUSE
Mr & Mrs J Jempson

NEW **CLEVELAND PLACE**
Friars Road. Sally & Graham Rhodda

NEW **MOUNT EDGE TERRACES**
Christine & Angus Johnson

PERITEAU HOUSE
Dr & Mrs Lawrence Youlten

RYE VIEW
Howard Norton & David Page

THE WELL HOUSE
Castle Street. Alice Kenyon

NEW 1 WHITE CLOSE
Jane Sullivan

Winchelsea is a beautiful medieval town founded in 1288 by Edward I. For nearly 200 years, as a Cinque Port, it was a major trading centre. Now all that remains of that time are the medieval merchants' cellars and the old streets, built on a grid system, behind whose old walls are the Secret Gardens. The gardens open this year include a variety of styles, from formal to informal to wild. They vary in size from small town gardens to large gardens divided into themed areas.

Teas in the New Hall. Guided tours of medieval cellars at 10.30 & 11.30, £5, booking essential, 01797 229525 or cellars@winchelsea.com. Beautiful church of St Thomas open to visitors. For more town information visit www.winchelsea.com.

Victorian garden under restoration . . .

 WISTON HOUSE
Steyning Road, Wiston BN44 3DD. Mr & Mrs R H Goring. *A24 Washington r'about, take A283 to Steyning.* **Adm £5, chd free. Sun 5 June** (1.30-5.30).
Nestled at the foot of the S Downs within a landscaped park, Wiston House has a Victorian garden under restoration. Features incl a conservatory, terraced lawns with herbaceous borders, a recently discovered cascade, woodland garden, Italian parterre, a new herb garden, walled vegetable garden and Victorian greenhouses.

Sussex County Volunteers
East & Mid Sussex

County Organiser
Irene Eltringham-Willson, Butlers Farmhouse, Butlers Lane, Herstmonceux BN27 1QH, 01323 833770, irene.willson@btinternet.com

Treasurer & Publicity
Robin Lloyd, Bankton Cottage, Turners Hill Road, Crawley Down RH10 4EY, 01342 718907 (01323 870432 after July), robin.lloyd@dsl.pipex.com

ACO and Publicity Production
Sara Turner, 9 Terminus Avenue, Bexhill TN39 3LS, 01424 210716, sara.kidd@virgin.net

Assistant County Organisers
Lynne Brown, 26 Cornwall Gardens, Brighton BN1 6RJ, 01273 556439, brown.lynne@ntlworld.com
Jasmine Hart, Roundstone House, Town Littleworth, Cooksbridge BN8 4TH, 01273 400427, jasminehart111@yahoo.co.uk
Richard & Matty Holmes, Beauchamps, Float Lane, Udimore TN31 6BY, 01797 223055, mrholmes@rye.hivetelecom.net
Philippa Hopkins, Birchover Cottage, 10 Maypole Road, Ashurstwood RH19 3QN, 01342 822090, piphop@waitrose.com
Jean Kendrick, Brinkers, Brinkers Lane, Wadhurst TN5 6LS, 01892 785507, jm.kendrick@virgin.net
Susan Laing, Great Lywood Farmhouse, Lindfield Road, Ardingly RH17 6SW, 01444 892500, lainghome@btinternet.com
Rosie Lloyd, Bankton Cottage, Turners Hill Road, Crawley Down RH10 4EY, 01342 718907 (01323 870432 after July), rosie.lloyd@dsl.pipex.com
Jan Newman, Graywood House, Graywood, East Hoathly BN8 6QP, 01825 872623
Brenda Sisson, Lantern Cottage, Spring Lane, Lindfield RH16 2RF, 01444 482103, dereksisson@btinternet.com
Janet Wood, Woodhill, Cross in Hand, Heathfield TN21 0TP, 01435 868209, woodhill2uk@yahoo.co.uk

West Sussex

County Organiser
Jane Allen, Dyers House, Pickhurst Road, Chiddingfold GU8 4TG, 01428 683130, jane.allen01@talktalk.net

Treasurer
Peter Edwards, Quince Cottage, The Street, Bury, Pulborough RH20 1PA, 01798 831900, peteredwards425@btinternet.com

Assistant County Organisers
Paula Baker, 077877 23462, jp.baker@tinyworld.co.uk
Sanda Belcher, Highercombe West, Haslemere GU27 2LH, 01428 642329, sandabelcher@tiscali.co.uk
Jane Burton, Church Farmhouse, Ford Water Road, Lavant, Chichester PO18 0AL, 01243 527822
Lesley Chamberlain, Dew Cottage, Beaumont Road, Broadwater, Worthing BN14 8HG, 01903 820813, chamberlain_lesley@hotmail.com
Elizabeth Gammon, 4 Birch Close, Arundel BN18 9HN, 01903 882722, e.gammon@toucansurf.com
Joan Lindsay, Durrance Manor, Smithers Hill Lane, Shipley, Horsham RH13 8PE, 01403 741577, jlindsay@dsl.pipex.com
Jane Lywood, Battlehurst Farm, Kirdford, Billingshurst RH14 0LJ, 01403 820225, jmlywood@aol.com
Carrie McArdle, Message Cottage, Kirdford RH14 0JR, 01403 820272, carrie.mcardle@btinternet.com
Claudia Pearce, 17 Sheridan Road, Worthing BN14 8EU, 07985 648216, claudiapearce17@gmail.com
Fiona Phillips, Old Erringham Cottage, Steyning Road, Shoreham-by-Sea BN43 5FD, 01273 462285, fiona.h.phillips@btinternet.com
Susan Pinder, 30 Townfield, Kirdford RH14 0LZ, 01403 820430, nasus.rednip@virgin.net
Sue Shipway, Browns House, The Street, Sutton, nr Pulborough RH20 1PS, 01798 869206, shipway@arunvalley.net

Enjoy a day out – look out for a Group Opening

WARWICKSHIRE

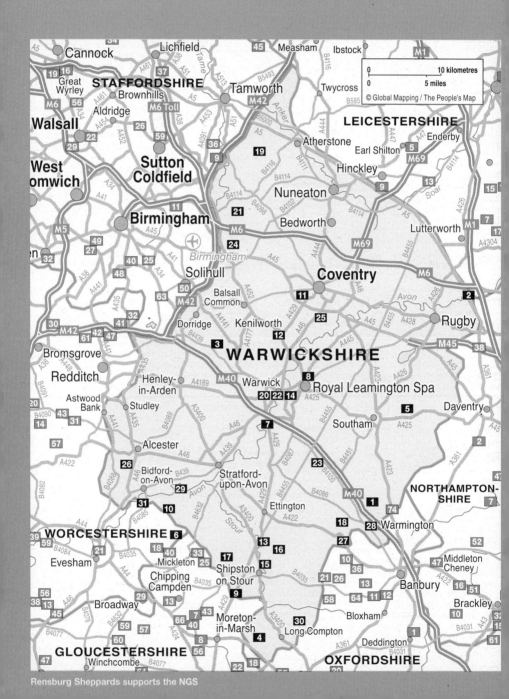

Opening Dates

February

Sunday 6
26 Ragley Hall Gardens

April

Sunday 17
18 Ivy Lodge

May

Sunday 1
25 The Quarry Garden
Monday 2
25 The Quarry Garden
Sunday 8
9 Court House
Tuesday 10
13 The Folly Lodge
Sunday 15
8 19 Church Lane
Sunday 29
4 Barton House
6 Broad Marston & Pebworth Gardens
25 The Quarry Garden
Monday 30
6 Broad Marston & Pebworth Gardens
25 The Quarry Garden

June

Sunday 5
8 19 Church Lane
12 Fieldgate
Sunday 12
10 Dorsington Gardens
17 Ilmington Gardens
21 Maxstoke Castle
Tuesday 14
13 The Folly Lodge

Sunday 19
15 Honington Village Gardens
23 The Old Rectory
28 Warmington Village Gardens
30 Whichford & Ascott Gardens
Saturday 25
19 Latimers Rest
29 Welford-on-Avon & District
Sunday 26
19 Latimers Rest
29 Welford-on-Avon & District

July

Sunday 3
16 Idlicote Gardens
24 Packington Hall
Sunday 10
1 Avon Dassett Gardens
9 Court House
Tuesday 12
13 The Folly Lodge
Thursday 28
7 5 Carter Drive

August

Open every day
5 Bridge Nursery
20 The Master's Garden
Saturday 6
19 Latimers Rest
Sunday 7
2 Avondale Nursery
19 Latimers Rest
Tuesday 9
13 The Folly Lodge
Sunday 14
3 Baddesley Clinton Hall

September

Sunday 4
12 Fieldgate
Saturday 11
2 Avondale Nursery

Tuesday 13
13 The Folly Lodge
Saturday 17
14 Hill Close Gardens
Sunday 18
26 Ragley Hall Gardens

February 2012

Sunday 19
26 Ragley Hall Gardens

Gardens open to the public

2 Avondale Nursery
3 Baddesley Clinton Hall
5 Bridge Nursery
14 Hill Close Gardens
20 The Master's Garden
22 The Mill Garden
25 The Quarry Garden
26 Ragley Hall Gardens
27 Upton House & Gardens

By appointment only

31 Woodpeckers

Also open by Appointment

4 Barton House
5 Bridge Nursery
7 5 Carter Drive
8 19 Church Lane
9 Court House
13 The Folly Lodge
19 Latimers Rest
30 Whichford House, Whichford & Ascott Gardens

Technicolor cornucopia of plants, this garden is a well-labelled reference book illustrating the unusual, exciting and even some long-lost treasures . . .

The Gardens

GROUP OPENING

1 ▶ AVON DASSETT GARDENS

CV47 2AE. *7m N of Banbury. From M40 J12 turn L & L again B4100. 2nd L into village. Park in village & at top of hill.* Home-made teas at Old Mill Cottage. **Combined adm £4, chd free (share to Myton Hospice).** Sun 10 July (2-6).

AVON HOUSE
Mrs L Dunkley

HILL TOP FARM
Mrs N & Mr D Hicks

THE LIMES
John & Diane Anderson

OLD MILL COTTAGE
Mike & Jill Lewis

THE OLD NEW HOUSE
Mr & Mrs W Allan

THE OLD RECTORY
Lily Hope-Frost

POPPY COTTAGE
Bob & Audrey Butler

Pretty Hornton Stone village sheltering in the lee of the Burton Dassett hills, well wooded and with parkland setting, The Old Rectory mentioned in Domesday Book. Wide variety of gardens incl kitchen gardens, gravel and tropical gardens. Range of plants incl alpines, herbaceous, perennials, roses, climbers and shrubs.
🏵 ⊛ ☕

2 ▶ ◆ AVONDALE NURSERY

at Russell's Nursery, Mill Hill, Baginton CV8 3AG. Mr Brian Ellis, 02476 673662,
www.avondalenursery.co.uk. *3m S Coventry. At junction of A45/A46 take slip rd to Baginton, 1st L to Mill Hill. Opp Old Mill Inn.* **Adm £3, chd free. For NGS: Suns 7 Aug; 11 Sept (11-4). For opening times and information please visit website or telephone.**
Vast array of flowers and ornamental grasses, incl potential national collection of Sanguisorba and Aster Novae-angliae. Technicolor cornucopia of plants, this garden is a well-labelled reference book illustrating the unusual, exciting and even some long-lost treasures. Adjacent nursery is a plantaholic's

delight. Visitors often remark: Why have I not visited this garden before?.
⎣ 🏵 ⊛ ☕ ☎

3 ▶ ◆ BADDESLEY CLINTON HALL

Rising Lane, Knowle B93 0DQ. National Trust, 01564 783294,
www.nationaltrust.org.uk. *7½ m NW of Warwick. ¾ m W of A4141 Warwick to Birmingham rd nr Chadwick End.* **Adm £6.50, chd £3.25. For NGS: Sun 14 Aug (11-5). For other opening times and information, please phone or see garden website.**
Medieval moated manor house little changed since1634. Walled garden and herbaceous borders, natural areas, lakeside walk, nature trail. Gravel paths around garden.
⎣ ⊛ ☎

4 ▶ BARTON HOUSE

Barton-on-the-Heath GL56 0PJ. Mr & Mrs I H B Cathie, 01608 674 303, cathie@bartonfarms.fsnet.co.uk. *2m W of Long Compton. 2m off A3400 Stratford-upon-Avon to Oxford rd. 1¼ m off A44 Chipping Norton to Moreton-in-Marsh rd.**Home-made teas. **Adm £5, chd free (share to St Lawrence Church).** Sun 29 May (2-6). Visitors also welcome by appt. Group visits 25+ £6.00 per person.
6½ acres with mature trees, azaleas, species and hybrid rhododendrons, magnolias, moutain tree peonies. National collection of arbutus. Japanese garden, catalpa walk, rose garden, secret garden and many rare and exotic plants. Victorian kitchen garden. Exotic garden with palms, cypresses and olive trees established 2002. Vineyard planted 2000 - free wine tasting. Manor house by Inigo Jones (not open). 4m high Pawlonia Fargesii seedlings, 5 new species of Arbutus.
⎣ ⊛ **NCCPG** ☕ ☎

5 ▶ ◆ BRIDGE NURSERY

Tomlow Road, Napton, nr Southam CV47 8HX. Christine Dakin & Philip Martino, 01926 812737,
www.bridge-nursery.co.uk. *3m E of Southam. Brown tourist sign at Napton Xrds on the A425 Southam to Daventry rd.* **Adm £2, chd free. For NGS: Daily Fri 1 Apr to Mon 31 Oct (10-4). Visitors welcome by appt for groups 12+. For other opening times and information, please phone or see garden website.**

Be inspired by the range of rare and unusual plants thriving in heavy clay soil. Our 1½ -acre garden is a fine example of mind over matter! Large pond and bamboo grove. Hedgerow walk, butterfly border, cutting garden. Wildlife abounds.
⎣ 🏵 ⊛ ☕ ☎

> Be inspired by the range of rare and unusual plants thriving in heavy clay soil . . .

GROUP OPENING

6 ▶ BROAD MARSTON & PEBWORTH GARDENS

Stratford-upon-Avon CV37 8XZ. *9m SW of Stratford-upon-Avon. On B439 at Bidford turn L towards Honeybourne, after 3m turn L at Xrds signed Pebworth.* Home-made teas at Pebworth Village Hall & Orchard Dene Broad Marston. **Combined adm £5, chd free.** Sun 29, Mon 30 May (2-6).

BANK FARM HOUSE
Craig & Erica Chapman

1 ELM CLOSE
Mr & Mrs G Keyte

ICKNIELD BARN
Sheila Davies

IVYBANK
Mr & Mrs R Davis

THE KNOLL
Mr & Mrs K Wood

THE MOUNT
Mr & Mrs J Ilott

NOLAN COTTAGE
Gill & Ron Thomas

NEW▶ NORTON HALL
Bridget & David Ross

ORCHARD DENE
Robert & Barbara Woodthorpe Brown

The hamlet of Broad Marston has been described as an indiscriminate scattering of houses which incl thatched cottages, a Manor and Priory, some C20 houses and a C21 conversion. Half a mile away is Pebworth, with its C13 simple country church on the top of the hill and its Manor. Some gardens are on the level but most run down the hill, leading to some interesting designs. At the bottom lies the Village Hall and Primary school with a flourishing garden where the children are enthusiastic workers. Amongst the houses at the foot of the hill are some small but very interesting gardens. Shakespeare is reputed to have visited to drink in Friday St. On the outskirts of the village is Fibrex Nursery, holder of the National Collection of Pelargoniums and Hederas. There are 9 gardens of very different styles to visit with a new garden to the group this yr with various animals, ducks and chickens.

Dorsington House

---

7 **NEW** **5 CARTER DRIVE**
Barford, Warwick CV35 8ET. Mary & David Stenning, 01926 620026, marystenning@hotmail.com. *8m NE of Stratford. From J16 on M40 take A429 Wellsbourne. Turn L sign posted to Barford. At mini r'about turn L into Church St, turn L into Kytes Lane (Barford village shop), turn L into Carter Drive.* Light refreshments & teas. Adm £3.50, chd free. Thur 28 July (2-6). Visitors also welcome by appt.
Welcome to our jewelled haven, meandering down to the banks of the Avon where bright perennials bloom. We hope you visit our unique garden soon. Mixed media artwork on display. Steps to decking on one side leading to river & gravel leading down to river.

---

8 **19 CHURCH LANE**
Lillington, Leamington Spa CV32 7RG. David & Judy Hirst, 01926 422591. *1½ m NE Leamington Spa. Take A445 towards Rugby. Church Lane on R just beyond r'about junction with B4453. Garden on corner of Hill Close. Enter via driveway in Church Lane.* Adm £2, chd free. Suns 15 May; 5 June (2-5.30). Visitors also welcome by appt Mons in Mar (for hellebores) & in April, adm £2.50.
Enjoy a plantsperson's cottage-style garden with a country atmosphere. Visitors have been intrigued by the wide range of unusual plants and their combinations, different aspects and areas. Narrow paths, may not be suitable for very young or infirm.

---

9 **COURT HOUSE**
Stretton-on-Fosse GL56 9SD. Christopher White, 01608 663811, mum@star.co.uk. *Between Moreton-in-Marsh & Shipston-on-Stour on A429. Court House in the centre of the village next to St Peter's Church.* Home-made teas. Adm £5, chd free. Suns 8 May; 10 July (2-6). Visitors also welcome by appt.
4-acre garden with yr-round interest and colour. Extensive and varied spring bulbs. Herbaceous borders, fernery, recently redesigned and restored walled kitchen garden. Rose garden, newly planted winter garden, pond area and paddocks which are gradually being established with wild flowers. Plants for sale.

GROUP OPENING

10 **DORSINGTON GARDENS**
Dorsington CV37 8AR. *6m SW of Stratford-upon-Avon. On B439 from Stratford turn L to Welford-on-Avon, then R to Dorsington.* Free shuttle bus service and map incl. Home-made & cream teas. Adm £6, chd free. Sun 12 June (12-5).

THE BARN
Mr & Mrs P Reeve

COLLETTS FARM
Mr & Mrs D Bliss

NEW **CRABTREE FARM COTTAGE**
Mr & Mrs David Boulton

DORSINGTON ARBORETUM
Mr F Dennis

DORSINGTON HOUSE
Mr & Mrs I Kolodotschko

2 DORSINGTON MANOR
Mr & Mrs C James

3 DORSINGTON MANOR
Mr & Mrs E Rusling

1 GLEBE COTTAGE
Mr & Mrs A Brough

MANOR FARM HOUSE
Mr & Mrs Coffey, Mr A Smart & Miss L Burfoot

THE OLD MANOR
Mr F Dennis

THE OLD RECTORY
Mr & Mrs Nigel Phillips

SAPPHIRE HOUSE
Mrs D Sawyer

THE WELSHMAN'S BARN
Mr F Dennis

WHITE GATES
Mr & Mrs A Carus

Dorsington is a Domesday hamlet with a secret... it is revealed one magic day in June - Midsummer Night's Dream spectacle of glorious gardens, tea and cake, plants, vintage Rolls Royces, statues and farm animals. These gardens offer an array of different styles such as at The Old Rectory with its traditional roses and herbaceous borders; restful garden rooms at 1 Glebe Cottages and fan-trained fruits at Colletts Farm. White Gates has cottage flowers and beyond at Sapphire House there are orchards and vegetables; gurgling brook runs through No.2 and No.3 Dorsington Manor. There is a two-tier plot at The Barn, with fun for the children and farm animals at Manor Farm. You can see the Rolls Royces and wander amoung the life-size statues at Welshman's Barn together with Oz Maze and Japanese garden. Highfield astonishes with aquarium, mosaic pool and 'Treasure Island' fantasies. In contrast the garden at ultra modern Dorsington House is futuristic and minimal.

♿ ❉ ☕

The mature trees, lend it an air of peace and tranquillity . . .

GROUP OPENING

11 ▶ EARLSDON GARDENS
CV5 6FS. *Turn towards Coventry at A45/A429 T-lights. Take 3rd L turn into Beechwood Ave, continue ¹/₂ m to St Barbara's Church. At X'roads with Rochester Rd. Maps & Tickets at St Barbara's Church Hall.* Light refreshments & teas at St Barbaras Church. **Combined adm £3, chd free.** Mon 2 May (11-4).

43 ARMORIAL ROAD
Gary & Jane Flanagan

3 BATES ROAD
Victor & Judith Keene

41 HARTINGTON CRESCENT
Clare Gavin & James McArthur

40 HARTINGTON CRESCENT
Viv & George Buss

114 HARTINGTON CRESCENT
Liz Campbell & Denis Crowley

36 PROVIDENCE STREET
Rachel Culley & Steve Shiner

87 ROCHESTER ROAD
Edith Lewin

54 SALISBURY AVENUE
Peter & Pam Moffit

NEW ▶ **23 SPENCER AVENUE**
Susan & Keith Darwood

8 THE SPINNEY
Professor Michael & Eleni Tovey

NEW ▶ **35 WARWICK AVENUE**
Anne-Marie Greene & Peter Gillam

Varied selection of town gardens from small to more formal with interest for all tastes incl a mature garden with deep borders bursting with spring colour, a large garden with extensive lawns and an array of rhododendrons, azaleas and large mature trees; a densely planted town garden with sheltered patio area and wilder woodland and a surprisingly large garden offering interest to all ages! There is also a pretty garden set on several levels with hidden aspects, a large peaceful garden with water features and vegetable plot and a large mature garden in a peaceful surrounding. Plantaholic's garden with a large variety of plants, clematis and small trees, some unusual and a woodland setting providing the backdrop to a garden of many

---

contrasts incl a terrace of subtropical plants. There are 2 new gardens open this year, one with a formal quadrant layout with lawns set around a central rill and a vegetable garden currently under development plus a shady semi-walled garden with cottage style herbaceous borders, gentle English hues and a mix of old and new varieties designed to work in sympathy with the 1913 red brick property.

☙ ❉ ☕

12 ▶ NEW **FIELDGATE**
Fieldgate Lane, Kenilworth CV8 1BT. Liz Watson. *At junction of A452 (Fieldgate Lane) & A429 (New Street) in Kenilworth Old Town close to Abbeyfields Park.* Home-made teas. **Adm £3, chd free.** Suns 5 June; 4 Sept (2-5).
Fieldgate is a ¹/₄ -acre town garden laid out with lawns and herbaceous borders and formal ponds. It was remodelled by the present owners in 2002 and has since matured nicely, with the borders containing a wide variety of plants. The garden is surrounded by mature trees, which lend it an air of peace and tranquillity. Free parking available in Abbey Fields car park. Additional parking on High Street & Fieldgate Lane. Kenilworth Castle is close by with pleasant walks in the Park & Millennium Walk. Gold medal & category winner, Kenilworth in Bloom.

☕

13 ▶ **THE FOLLY LODGE**
Halford CV36 5DG. Mike & Susan Solomon, 01789 740183, SS@follylodge.eclipse.co.uk. *3m NE Shipston-on-Stour. On A429 (Fosse Way). In Halford take turning to Idlicote. Garden on R past Feldon Edge.* Home-made teas. **Adm £3.50, chd free.** Tues 10 May; 14 June; 12 July; 9 Aug; 13 Sept (2-5). **Visitors also welcome by appt, groups 8+ May to September.**
Come and enjoy the sight and scent of hundreds of plants. Come and watch butterflies, bees and birds. Come and see Susan's ceramic sculptures. Come to sit and relax in this peaceful garden. Come and eat delicious home-made cake. And for the men - come and see the stripes on the lawn! Featured in Garden News.

---

14 ◆ HILL CLOSE GARDENS

Bread & Meat Close, Warwick
CV34 6HF. Hill Close Gardens Trust,
01926 493339,
www.hillclosegardens.com. *Town
centre. Entry from Friars St by Bread
& Meat Close. Car park by entrance
next to racecourse. Two hours free
parking. Disabled parking outside the
gates.* **Adm £3, chd free. For NGS:
Sat 17 Sept (11-5).** **For other
opening times and information,
please phone or see garden
website.**
Restored Grade II* Victorian leisure
gardens comprising 16 individual
hedged gardens, 8 brick
summerhouses. Herbaceous borders,
heritage apple and pear trees, 19th
century daffodils, many varieties of
asters and chrysanthemums. Heritage
vegetables. NCCPG border, auricula
theatre, Victorian style glasshouse.
Children's garden. Gardener's walk
2nd Fri in month. Plants and produce
for sale. Award winning guide book.
Children's garden trails. Featured in
Historic Gardens. Recommended
route indicated to avoid steep slopes.

GROUP OPENING

15 HONINGTON VILLAGE GARDENS

Shipston CV36 5AA. *1½ m N of
Shipston-on-Stour. Take A3400
towards Stratford-upon-Avon then
turn R signed Honington.* Home-
made teas. **Combined adm £4, chd
free (share to Honington Church).**
Sun 19 June (2.15-5.30).

> **NEW HOME FARM**
> Mr Guy Winter
>
> **HONINGTON GLEBE**
> Mr & Mrs J C Orchard
>
> **HONINGTON HALL**
> B H E Wiggin
>
> **MALT HOUSE RISE**
> Mr & Mrs M Underhill
>
> **THE OLD HOUSE**
> Mr & Mrs I F Beaumont
>
> **ORCHARD HOUSE**
> Mr & Mrs Monnington
>
> **SHOEMAKERS COTTAGE**
> Christopher & Anne Jordan
>
> **NEW STABLE COTTAGE**
> Mr Shaun de Wolf

C17 village, recorded in Domesday,
entered by old toll gate. Ornamental

---

stone bridge over the R Stour and
interesting church with C13 tower and
late C17 nave after Wren. 8 super
gardens. 2-acre plantsman's garden
consisting of rooms planted informally
with yr-round interest in contrasting
foliage, texture, lily pool and parterre.
Extensive lawns and fine mature trees
with river and garden monuments.
Small garden that is well stocked with
interesting established shrubs and
container plants and a structured
cottage garden formally laid out with
box hedging and small fountain.
Small, developing garden created by
the owners with informal mixed beds
and borders.

Why not visit a
group opening
and really make a
day of it . . . !

GROUP OPENING

16 IDLICOTE GARDENS

CV36 5DT. *3m NE of Shipston-on-
Stour.* Home-made teas at Badgers
Farm. **Combined adm £5, chd free
(share to Idlicote Church).**
Sun 3 July (2-6).

> **BADGERS FARM**
> Sir Derek & Lady Hornby
>
> **1 BICKERSTAFF COTTAGES**
> Mr & Mrs C Balchin
>
> **2 BICKERSTAFF COTTAGES**
> Mr D Amos
>
> **BICKERSTAFF FARM**
> Lady Owen
>
> **IDLICOTE HOUSE**
> Mr M Dill
>
> **THE OLD FORGE**
> Mr & Mrs J Terry
>
> **THE OLD RECTORY**
> Mr & Mrs G Thomson
>
> **WOODLANDS**
> Captain & Mrs P R Doyne

Eight gardens of varying size, design
and planting in a quiet hamlet with
spectacular views over rolling
countryside. Attractions range from
cottage flower gardens to mature
woodland bordering extensive lawns
and incl the grounds of an C18 manor
house, C13 church and neighbouring
rectory, and two substantial farm
houses. Other interesting features
comprise vegetable gardens,
greenhouses and ponds, notably the
central village pond which is
populated by ornamental ducks and
other native wildlife. In the grounds of
the manor can be found a kitchen
garden containing newly-built sunken
greenhouses overlooked by a
magnificent octagonal dovecote.
Paddock parking available in village.

GROUP OPENING

17 ILMINGTON GARDENS

Ilmington CV36 4LA. *8m S of
Stratford-upon-Avon. 8m N of
Moreton in Marsh. 4m NW of
Shipston-on-Stour off A3400. 3m
NE of Chipping Campden.* Light
refreshments & teas in village hall.
**Combined adm £5, chd free (share
to Warwickshire &
Northamptonshire Air Ambulance).**
Sun 12 June (2-6).

> **ARMSCOTE HOUSE**
> Christopher & Lana Taylor.
> *(2m East)*
>
> **THE BEVINGTONS**
> Mr & Mrs N Tustain
>
> **COMPTON SCORPION FARM**
> Mr & Mrs T Karlsen.
> *(2m South)*
>
> **CRAB MILL**
> Mr & Mrs D Brown
>
> **FOXCOTE HILL**
> Mr & Mrs Micheal Dingley
>
> **FROG ORCHARD**
> Jeremy & Diane Snowden
>
> **THE GRANGE**
> Mr & Mrs Iain Barker
>
> **ILMINGTON MANOR**
> Mr Martin Taylor

Wander through the narrow stone
paths of this ancient Cotswold village,
beside burbling streams to the **Manor
House** (next to the Red Lion PH)
with its clipped yews, rose garden,
long borders and specimen trees.
The Grange perched like an eerie on

high ground above Back Street. **Foxcote Hill**, surrounded by its orchard walks and borders with views to distant Edgehill. **Crab Mill**, in Grump Street, once home to Nobel prize winner Dorothy Hodgkin, with sloping gardens and views down to the church. **Frog Orchard** in Frog Lane, an exquisite modern cottage garden. **The Bevingtons**, once three cottages, between the manor and the church, with hedge divided gardens and hens roaming. 2m E visit an Elizabethan gem, **Armscote House** with its wonderfully revived gardens approached over a moat; recently planted borders, hot beds and enormous yew hedges. 2m S you will find **Compton Scorpion Farm** with its beautifully planted gardens in a remote hillside setting with sweeping countryside views. A beautiful day out for all to enjoy. Ancient village centred on a Cotswold stone Norman church and Elizabethan manor surrounded by clusters of stone houses and thatched cottages on the slopes of Ilmington Downs, the highest hill in Warwickshire and northernmost hill in the Cotswolds. Ilmington Morris Men will play around the village.

Baddesley Clinton Hall

 IVY LODGE
Radway CV35 0UE. Mr Martin Dunne. *12m S of Warwick. From J12 M40 take B4451 to Kineton, B4086 S for 3m to signed turning, Radway.* Home-made teas. **Adm £4, chd free.** Sun 17 Apr (2-6).
The garden planted in 1956 by the late Jim Russell and the current owner's mother Mrs Willis. They incorporated a 3-acre field to make a 4-acre garden. Large areas of bulbs and blossoming fruit trees. Grass paths wind through the wilder areas of the garden amongst the flower beds, shrubs and ornamental trees.

19 **LATIMERS REST**
Hipsley Lane, Baxterley CV9 2HS. Gerald & Christine Leedham, 01827 875526, christine_leedham@yahoo.co.uk. *3m S of Atherstone on B4116. From A5 Atherstone, at island, take Merevale Lane to Baxterley. From M42 J9 take A4097 for Kingsbury. At island follow signs to Hurley & Baxterley, garden nr church.* Home-made teas. **Adm £5, chd free.** Sats & Suns 25, 26 June; 6, 7 Aug (1-5). Visitors also welcome by appt for parties of 10+.

2½ acres of wonderful contrasts. Formal lawns and ponds with colourful flower beds and giant hanging baskets give way to hostas and ferns with medieval moat backdrop. Feature rose gardens with over 40 standard roses. Small arboretum with specimen trees, vegetable gardens, greenhouses and chickens.

20 ◆ **THE MASTER'S GARDEN**
Lord Leycester Hospital, Warwick CV34 4BH. The Governors. *W end of Warwick High St, behind ancient Hospital buildings.* **Adm £2, chd free.** Open daily Tue 19 Apr to Fri 30 Sept; (10-4.30).
Restored historic walled garden hidden behind the medieval buildings of this home for retired ex-servicemen, also open to the public. Mixed shrub and herbaceous planting with climbing roses and clematis, Norman arch, ancient Egyptian Nilometer, thatched summerhouse, gazebo, knot garden and C18 pineapple pit. Seasonal produce and plants for sale.

21 **MAXSTOKE CASTLE**
Coleshill B46 2RD. Mr & Mrs M C Fetherston-Dilke. *2½ m E of Coleshill. E of Birmingham, on B4114. Take R turn down Castle Lane, Castle drive 1¼ m on R.* Sun 12 June (11-5). Approx 5 acres of garden and grounds with herbaceous, shrubs and trees in the immed surroundings of this C14 moated castle.

22 ◆ **THE MILL GARDEN**
55 Mill Street, Warwick CV34 4HB. Julia (née Measures) Russell & David Russell, 01926 492877. *Off A425 beside castle gate, at the bottom of Mill St. Use St Nicholas car park.* **Adm £1.50, chd free with adult.** Open 1 Apr - 31 Oct (9-6).
This garden lies in a magical setting on the banks of the R Avon beneath the walls of Warwick Castle. Winding paths lead round every corner to dramatic views of the castle and ruined medieval bridge. This informal cottage garden is a profusion of plants, shrubs and trees. Beautiful all-yr. Limited wheelchair access due to narrow paths. Unsuitable for electric wheelchairs.

23 NEW **THE OLD RECTORY**
Lighthorne, Warwick CV35 0AR.
The Hon Lady Butler. *10m S of Warwick just off B4100. From village green head for Church. At lych gate turn R up lane. Entrance on R. Parking straight on.* Home-made teas. Adm £4, chd free. Sun 19 June (2-6).
An old established garden sheltered by brick walls surrounding the C17 rectory. Sloping lawns with two fine copper beeches lead down to the house. Roses adorn the house and garden walls. Adjacent pretty church will also be open. Main part of garden accessible but steep slope in part.

& 🐕 🍵

24 NEW **PACKINGTON HALL**
Meriden CV7 7HF. Lord & Lady Aylesford. *Midway between Coventry & Birmingham on A45. Entrance 400yrds from Stonebridge Island towards Coventry. Use postcode CV7 7HE for SatNav.* Home-made teas. Adm £5, chd free. Sun 3 July (2.30-6).
Packington is the setting for an elegant Capability Brown landscape. Designed from 1750 in 100 acres of parkland which sweeps down to a lake incl 1762 Japanese bridge. Mirrored terrace beds glow with perennials. Nearby is the Millennium Rose Garden planted with old fashioned roses complete with flowers, hips and haws. Garden is mainly mowed lawn. Gravel terrace. Steps from grass to terrace where teas are served.

& 🍵

25 ♦ **THE QUARRY GARDEN**
Mill Hill, Baginton CV8 3AG.
Russells Nurseries, 01926 492877, www.russelsgardencentre.co.uk. *2m S Coventry centre. ¼ m from Lunt Roman Fort, opp Old Mill PH.* Adm £3, chd £1.50. For NGS: Suns & Mons 1, 2 & 29, 30 May (10.30-4.30). For other opening times and information, please phone or see garden website.
Stunning 6-acre quarry garden with a 35ft rock face. Ponds and rock features amongst a beautiful collection of magnolias and camellias followed by a blaze of colour with azaleas and rhododendrons amongst oaks, crategus, birches, conifers, heathers. Limited wheelchair access due to steep gravel paths and slopes.

& ❀ 🍵 ☎

26 ♦ **RAGLEY HALL GARDENS**
Alcester B49 5NJ. Marquess & Marchioness of Hertford, 07917 425664, www.ragleyhall.com. *2m SW of Alcester. Off A435/A46 8m from Stratford-upon-Avon.* Garden only adm £3, chd free. For NGS: Sun 6 Feb (11-3), garden only adm £4, chd free. For other opening times and information, please phone or see garden website.
24 acres of gardens, predominantly mature broadleaved trees, within which a variety of cultivated and non-cultivated areas have been blended to achieve a garden rich in both horticulture and bio-diversity. The winter garden, spring meadows and bulbs make way for summer meadows, herbaceous borders and annual bedding. New rose garden has been planted and looks stunning from late June through to Sept. Please note we will be open on Sun 18 Sept and Sun 26 Feb (10-4.30); adm £6.50 for adults & chd. Donation of adult ticket sales from both days to NGS.

& ☎

27 ♦ **UPTON HOUSE & GARDENS**
Banbury OX15 6HT. National Trust, 01295 670266, www.nationaltrust.org.uk. *7m NW of Banbury. On A422, 1m S of Edgehill.* Adm £5.95, chd £2.90. For NGS: Wed 28 Sept (11-5). For other opening times and information, please phone or see garden website.
Extensive valley gardens with elements from medieval through to 1930s. Cascading terraces of colourful borders descend to a rare kitchen garden, with pools and a bog garden in the valley below. National Collection of Asters, splendid in the autumn. Wide lawns surround house famous for an internationally important collection of fine art and porcelain. Garden tours.

❀ NCCPG 🍵 ☎

Cascading terraces of colourful borders descend to a rare kitchen garden . . .

GROUP OPENING

28 **WARMINGTON VILLAGE GARDENS**
OX17 1BU. *5m NW of Banbury. Off B4100.* Home-made teas at Village Hall. Adm £4, chd free. Sun 19 June (2-6).

NEW **AGDON HOUSE**
Mr & Mrs P Grenet

THE MANOR HOUSE
Mr & Mrs G Lewis

1 RECTORY CLOSE
Mrs J Adams

SPRINGFIELD HOUSE 🛏
Jenny & Roger Handscombe

WESTERING
Mr & Mrs R Neale

1 THE WHEELWRIGHTS
Ms E Bunn

2 THE WHEELWRIGHTS
Mrs C Hunter

Warmington at the edge of the Cotswolds is an exceptionally attractive village with its Hornton stone houses and cottages set around the Village Green. In front of the Pond is The Manor with its Elizabethan Knot Garden, topiary and beautifully planted fruit and vegetables. The Wheelwrights, two lovely adjacent gardens of different character are examples of inspiring design and planting in a small space. Mature trees and shrubs with vegetables and a floral border are to be found at Rectory Close while Springfield House with its gravel garden and rockery is an informal terraced country garden. There are colourful borders with many interesting and unusual plants at Agdon House and Westering. Several ponds, wall gardens and chickens are also features of Warmington gardens. Do visit St. Michaels Church at the top of the village containing the Millenium Tapestry.

❀ 🍵

GROUP OPENING

29 NEW **WELFORD-ON-AVON & DISTRICT**
Welford-on-Avon CV37 8PT. *5m SW of Stratford-upon-Avon. Off B4390.* Home-made teas. Combined adm £5, chd free. Sat 25, Sun 26 June (2-6).

You are always welcome at an NGS garden

NEW ▶ ALCOVE
Anne Ramsbottom

NEW ▶ ARDENCOTE
Mike & Sally Luntley

NEW ▶ BRIDGEFIELD
Mr W D Owen

NEW ▶ THE COTTAGE
Jan & Paul Stewart

NEW ▶ THE DOVECOTES
David & Angela Brooks

ELM CLOSE
Eric & Glenis Dyer
Visitors also welcome by appt
in groups 10+. Smaller groups
welcome to join larger pre-
arranged visits. Please ring for
details.
01789 750793

NEW ▶ THE HOLLIES
Mr & Mrs Brad Plimmer

NEW ▶ PEAR TREE CLOSE
Mr & Mrs J Sugden

NEW ▶ 9 QUINEYS LEYS
Ann Raff

NEW ▶ WATERMILL COTTAGE
Martin & Sheila Greenwood

In addition to its superb position on
the river, with serene swans, dabbling
ducks and resident herons, Welford-
on-Avon has a beautiful church, an
excellent family butcher's shop, a very
convenient general store and
selection of PH's serving great food.
Just down the road is a highly popular
farm-shop where seasonal fruit and
vegetables are much in demand. With
its great variety of house styles, incl
an abundance of beautiful cottages
with thatched roofs and chocolate-
box charisma, Welford also has an
army of keen gardeners (3yr old
garden club already has over 100
members!) The gardens open for the

NGS range from a dry garden with
robotic lawnmower, a tiered riverside
garden, a plot with fantastic topiary,
herb knot and live willow weaving, to
a walled garden, an overflowing
cottage garden, gardens with fun
sculptures, flowerpot men, prairie
planting and water features, all with a
glorious array of containers and
hanging baskets. Fruit and vegetable
areas are also integral to these
gardens for all seasons.

GROUP OPENING

**30 ▶ WHICHFORD & ASCOTT
GARDENS**
CV36 5PG. *6m SE of Shipston-on-
Stour. Turn E off A3400 at Long
Compton for Whichford.* Home-made
teas at Whichford House. **Combined
adm £5, chd free.** Sun 19 June
(2-6).

ASCOTT LODGE
Charlotte Copley

BROOK HOLLOW
John & Shirley Round

THE OLD HOUSE
Terry & Barbara Maher

THE OLD RECTORY
Peter & Caroline O'Kane

WHICHFORD HOUSE
Bridget & Simon Herrtage
Visitors also welcome by appt
June only.
01608 684437
bcb@macfarlanes.com

THE WHICHFORD POTTERY
Jim & Dominique Keeling
www.whichfordpottery.com

Visit a collection of 6 beautiful and
quite different country gardens set

within a mile or so of each other in
2 peaceful Cotswold stone villages.
Visitors will also be able to see the
C13 church, internationally renowned
pottery and local PH. The gardens
offer a variety of mature trees and
shrubs as well as new plants together
with ponds, streams and other water
features. There are wonderful views of
Brailles Hill. Climbing and other roses
are abundant and there are many
wonderful borders. Visitors will also
see a courtyard and secret walled
garden. Competition for children, tell
the time on the human sun dial & their
own treats in a tree house. Featured
in Country Life magazine.

---

31 ▶ WOODPECKERS
The Bank, Marlcliff, nr Bidford-on-
Avon B50 4NT. Dr Lallie Cox &
Family, 01789 773416. *7m SW of
Stratford-upon-Avon. Off B4085
between Bidford-on-Avon & Cleeve
Prior.* **Visitors welcome by appt all
year.**
Peaceful 2½ -acre plantsman's
country garden designed and
maintained by the owners since 1965.
A garden for all seasons. Unusual
plants, hidden surprises, interesting
trees, colour-themed borders,
potager and knot garden. Wooden
sculptures of St Fiacre and The Green
Man carved by the owner. Lovely
garden buildings of framed green oak.
Featured in Period Living.

Wooden sculptures
carved by the
owner . . .

Warwickshire Volunteers

County Organiser
Julia Sewell, Dinsdale House, Baldwins Lane, Upper Tysoe, Warwick CV35 0TX, 01295 680234, sewelljulia@btinternet.com

County Treasurer
Susan Solomon, Folly Lodge, Halford, Idlicote Road, Shipston-on-Stour, Warwicks, CV36 5DG, 01789 740183,
SS@follylodge.eclipse.co.uk

Publicity
Carole Longden, Meon View, Priory Lane, Broad Marston CV37 8XZ, 02476 470382, carolelongden@longden.co.uk
Peter Pashley, Millstone, Mayfield Avenue, Stratford upon Avon CV37 6XB, 01789 294932, peter@peterpash.mail1.co.uk

Booklet Coordinator
Janet Neale, Westering, The Green, Warmington, Banbury OX17 1BU, 01295 690515, janet.neale@unity-solutions.co.uk

Assistant County Organiser
David Ainsworth, 1 Evenlode Close, Stratford-upon-Avon CV37 7EL, 01789 292487, dainsworth@btinternet.com
Keith Browne, 1a Williams Road, Radford Semele, Leamington Spa CV31 1UR, 01926 420284, keith_browne@hotmail.com
Elspeth Napier, 17 Simpson Road, Shipston-on-Stour CV36 4JT, 01608 666278, elspeth@cherryvilla.demon.co.uk

Sign up to our eNewsletter for news and updates

Ilmington Manor

WILTSHIRE

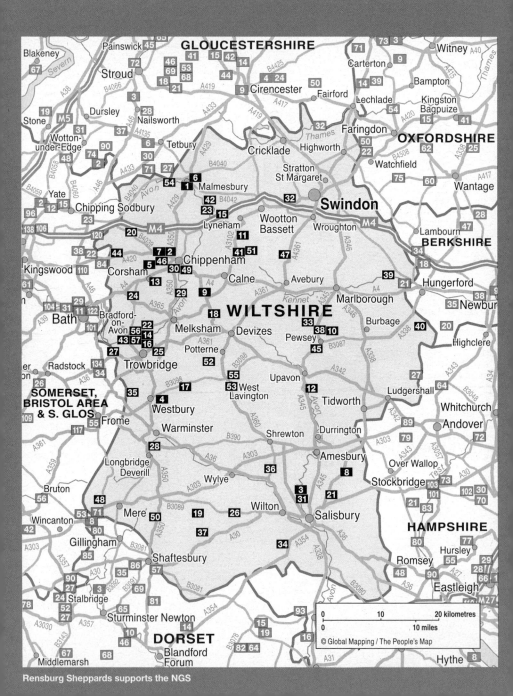

Opening Dates

February

Sunday 6
22 Great Chalfield Manor
Saturday 12
29 Lacock Abbey Gardens
Sunday 13
29 Lacock Abbey Gardens
Saturday 19
29 Lacock Abbey Gardens
Sunday 20
3 Avon Cottage
8 Boscombe Village Gardens
29 Lacock Abbey Gardens
Monday 21
8 Boscombe Village Gardens

March

Sunday 20
1 Abbey House Gardens
3 Avon Cottage
Sunday 27
8 Boscombe Village Gardens
13 Corsham Court
19 Fonthill House
36 The Mill House
Monday 28
8 Boscombe Village Gardens

April

Wednesday 6
45 Sharcott Manor
Sunday 10
44 Ridleys Cheer
45 Sharcott Manor
52 Wellaway
Wednesday 13
10 Broomsgrove Lodge
Sunday 17
3 Avon Cottage
10 Broomsgrove Lodge
27 Iford Manor
28 Job's Mill
31 Little Durnford Manor
38 Oare House
40 The Old Rectory
43 Priory House
Wednesday 20
10 Broomsgrove Lodge
Sunday 24
8 Boscombe Village Gardens
Monday 25
8 Boscombe Village Gardens

May

Sunday 1
50 Waterdale House

Wednesday 4
45 Sharcott Manor
Saturday 7
48 Stourhead Garden
Sunday 8
2 Allington Grange
Saturday 14
14 The Courts
Sunday 15
5 Biddestone Manor
44 Ridleys Cheer
Wednesday 18
18 Enfield
Thursday 19
18 Enfield
39 The Old Mill
Friday 20
55 Windmill Cottage
Sunday 22
24 Hazelbury Manor Gardens
Wednesday 25
18 Enfield
Thursday 26
18 Enfield
46 Sheldon Manor
Sunday 29
8 Boscombe Village Gardens
26 Hyde's House
Monday 30
8 Boscombe Village Gardens
21 The Grange
56 Woolley Grange Hotel
57 13 Woolley Green

June

Wednesday 1
18 Enfield
45 Sharcott Manor
Thursday 2
18 Enfield
Friday 3
55 Windmill Cottage
Saturday 4
53 West Lavington Manor
Sunday 5
9 Bowood Rhododendron Walks
13 Corsham Court
17 Edington Gardens
28 Job's Mill
31 Little Durnford Manor
37 North Cottage & Woodview Cottage
41 The Old Vicarage
42 The Pound House
51 Weavers
56 Woolley Grange Hotel
57 13 Woolley Green
Wednesday 8
18 Enfield
Thursday 9
18 Enfield

Saturday 11
33 Manor Farm
Sunday 12
11 33 Calne Road
12 Chisenbury Priory
15 Dauntsey Gardens
20 Goulters Mill Farm
24 Hazelbury Manor Gardens
33 Manor Farm
41 The Old Vicarage
51 Weavers
Wednesday 15
18 Enfield
Thursday 16
18 Enfield
Friday 17
34 Manor House (Evening)
55 Windmill Cottage
Saturday 18
23 Great Somerford Gardens
34 Manor House
37 North Cottage & Woodview Cottage
Sunday 19
7 Bolehyde Manor
16 Edgecombe, 138 Wyke Road
23 Great Somerford Gardens
25 Hilperton House
47 Silver Birches
Sunday 26
8 Boscombe Village Gardens
36 The Mill House
47 Silver Birches
Monday 27
8 Boscombe Village Gardens

July

Friday 1
55 Windmill Cottage
Sunday 3
6 Blicks Hill House
54 Whatley Manor
Wednesday 6
45 Sharcott Manor
Sunday 17
38 Oare House
Friday 22
55 Windmill Cottage
Saturday 23
4 Beggars Knoll
Sunday 24
4 Beggars Knoll
30 130 Ladyfield Road and Hungerdown Allotments
49 Sweetbriar Cottage
Sunday 31
32 Lydiard Park Walled Garden
39 The Old Mill

August

Monday 1
39 The Old Mill

Wednesday 3
45 Sharcott Manor
Sunday 7
43 Priory House
Sunday 21
35 The Mead Nursery

September

Thursday 1
39 The Old Mill
Saturday 3
14 The Courts
Wednesday 7
34 Manor House
45 Sharcott Manor
Friday 9
55 Windmill Cottage
Sunday 11
45 Sharcott Manor
52 Wellaway
Sunday 18
56 Woolley Grange Hotel

February 2012

Saturday 11
29 Lacock Abbey Gardens
Sunday 12
29 Lacock Abbey Gardens
Saturday 18
29 Lacock Abbey Gardens
Sunday 19
3 Avon Cottage
8 Boscombe Village Gardens
29 Lacock Abbey Gardens
Monday 20
8 Boscombe Village Gardens

Gardens open to the public

1 Abbey House Gardens
9 Bowood Rhododendron Walks
13 Corsham Court
14 The Courts
22 Great Chalfield Manor
27 Iford Manor
29 Lacock Abbey Gardens
32 Lydiard Park Walled Garden
35 The Mead Nursery
36 The Mill House
46 Sheldon Manor
48 Stourhead Garden
50 Waterdale House

Also open by Appointment ☎

3 Avon Cottage
4 Beggars Knoll
5 Biddestone Manor
6 Blicks Hill House
7 Bolehyde Manor

12 Chisenbury Priory
8 Cottage in the Trees, Boscombe Village Gardens
18 Enfield
25 Hilperton House
37 North Cottage & Woodview Cottage
41 The Old Vicarage
42 The Pound House
44 Ridleys Cheer
45 Sharcott Manor
49 Sweetbriar Cottage
8 Westcroft, Boscombe Village Gardens
55 Windmill Cottage

The Gardens

1 ◆ **ABBEY HOUSE GARDENS**
Malmesbury Town Centre
SN16 9AS. Ian & Barbara Pollard,
01666 822212,
www.abbeyhousegardens.co.uk.
5m N of J17 M4. Beside C12 Abbey. Parking in town centre (short stay) or follow brown signs to long stay (via steps to gardens). **Adm £6.50, chd £2.50. For NGS: Sun 20 Mar (11-5.30). For other opening times and information, please phone or see garden website.**
Beside Malmesbury's Abbey Church and straddling the R Avon, this spectacular 5-acre garden, home to The Naked Gardeners, has brought praise from around the world. Spring bulbs begin the display, as 70,000 tulips bloom from March to May.
&♿ ❀ ☕ ☎

2 **NEW** **ALLINGTON GRANGE**
Allington, Chippenham SN14 6LW.
Mrs Rhyddian Roper. *2m W of Chippenham. Take A420 W. 1st R signed Allington Village, entrance 1m on L.* Home-made teas. **Adm £3, chd free. Sun 8 May (2-5).**
Informal garden of approx 1 acre, created over the last 7yrs around C17 farmhouse (not open) with a diverse range of plants. Mixed and herbaceous borders; white garden with topiary and water fountain. Pergola lined with clematis and roses. Small walled vegetable garden. Wildlife pond with natural planting. Many spring bulbs. Ramp into walled garden.
&♿ 🎪 ❀ ☕

3 ◆ **AVON COTTAGE**
Lower Woodford, Salisbury
SP4 6NQ. Mr & Mrs Trevor Shepherd, 01722 782295,
sheila.shepherd@virgin.net. *4m N of*

Salisbury. Off Woodford Valley Rd; between A360 & A345. Home-made teas. **Adm £3, chd free. Suns 20 Feb; 20 Mar (11-3); 17 Apr (2-5); Sun 19 Feb 2012 (11-3). Visitors also welcome by appt Wednesdays and Fridays.**
Garden in a beautiful unspoilt valley featuring snowdrops along the stream and woodland with aconites, crocus, hellebores, erythroniums and other spring bulbs. Mature hedges break up the level site with early flowering, fragrant shrubs. There are lovely views over the working water meadows to the river Avon with abundant birdlife. Gravel drive and tree roots on woodland paths.
&♿ ☕ ☎

BATH PRIORY HOTEL
See Somerset & Bristol.

4 **BEGGARS KNOLL**
Newtown BA13 3ED. Colin Little & Penny Stirling, 01373 823383,
silkendalliance @talktalk.net. *1m SE of Westbury. Turn off B3098 at White Horse Pottery, up hill towards the White Horse for 1 km. Limited parking at end of drive. Overflow parking 300 yds up hill.* Home-made teas. **Adm £3, chd free. Sat 23, Sun 24 July (2-6). Visitors also welcome by appt.**
Enjoy the peace and serenity of one of the few Chinese gardens in England. Wander through decorative gateways and along zigzag pathways, examine rare Chinese plants and rest in exotic pavilions. Tour the extensive potager and visit the chickens and pigs, then take in the spectacular views towards the Mendips on the way to the secret Bamboo Garden.
❀ ☕ ☎

Enjoy the peace and serenity of one of the few Chinese gardens in England. Wander through decorative gateways and along zigzag pathways . . .

Beggars Knoll

5 ▸ BIDDESTONE MANOR

Chippenham Lane, Biddestone SN14 7DJ. Rosie Harris, Head Gardener, 01249 713211. *5m W of Chippenham. On A4 between Chippenham & Corsham turn N. From A420, 5m W of Chippenham, turn S. Use car park.* Home-made teas. **Adm £4, chd free. Sun 15 May (2-5). Visitors also welcome by appt, groups of 10+ May & June only. Coaches by prior arrangement.** Stroll through our 8 peaceful acres of wide lawns, lake and ponds, arboretum and roses. Kitchen and cutting gardens and orchard. Then join us for tea in the formal front garden. Beautiful C17 Manor House (not open) with ancient dovecote. Maybe spot the bee orchids and kingfisher. Garden photography for sale.

♿ 🐾 ❀ ☕ ☎

6 ▸ BLICKS HILL HOUSE

Blicks Hill, Malmesbury SN16 9HZ. Alan & Valerie Trotman, 01666 829669, vat@timberwright.co.uk. *½ m E of Malmesbury. On A429 Malmesbury bypass, turn off ½ way between r'abouts.* Home-made teas. **Adm £3.50, chd free. Sun 3 July (11.30-5). Visitors also welcome by appt, groups 10+ incl coaches.** Stunning, and having the wow factor is how visitors describe this garden situated on a 1-acre stepped and sloping site. Mature trees give a backdrop to the colourful beds and borders which have all been created since 2004. Unique pergola leading to a woodland glade, new water feature and stream constructed in green slate, hanging baskets, tubs and bedding plants add extra impact. Very much a plantsman's garden. Gradual slope.

♿ ❀ ☕ ☎

7 ▸ BOLEHYDE MANOR

Allington SN14 6LW. The Earl & Countess Cairns, amcairns@aol.com. *1½ m W of Chippenham. On Bristol Rd (A420). Turn N at Allington Xrds. ½ m on R. Parking in field.* Home-made teas. **Adm £3.50, chd 50p. Sun 19 June (2-5.30). Visitors also welcome by appt. May & June only. £5 per person by appointment.** Series of gardens around C16 manor house (not open), enclosed by walls and topiary. Formal framework densely planted with many interesting shrubs and climbers, especially roses. Mixed borders. Blue walk of alliums and agapanthus. Inner courtyard with troughs full of tender plants. Collection of tender pelargoniums. Vegetable/fruit garden and greenhouse. Some steps.

🐾 ❀ ☕ ☎

GROUP OPENING

8 BOSCOMBE VILLAGE GARDENS
Boscombe SP4 0AB. *7m N of Salisbury. Westcroft is on A338 from Salisbury, just past Boscombe & District Social Club, parking in field opp. For Cottage in the Trees turn L off A338, just before Social Club. Continue past church, turn R after bridge to Queen Manor, cottage on R by farmyard.* Home-made teas at Westcroft only in Feb, both gardens all other dates. **Combined adm £4.50, chd free. Suns & Mons 20, 21 Feb (11-4); 27, 28 Mar; 24, 25 Apr; 29, 30 May; 26, 27 June (2-5); 19, 20 Feb 2012 (11-4).**

COTTAGE IN THE TREES
Karen & Richard Robertson
Visitors also welcome by appt for groups of 12+, Feb to Oct, coaches permitted.
01980 610921
robertson909@btinternet.com

WESTCROFT
Lyn Miles
Visitors also welcome by appt for groups of 12+, Feb to Oct, coaches permitted.
01980 610877
lyn@resale26.demon.co.uk

There is much to discover in two contrasting gardens, approx ³/₄ m apart. **Westcroft's** ²/₃ acre of wilderness paradise is much loved by wildlife but there is an area with bind weed. Enjoy a pond, sun-baked terraces, colour-themed herbaceous planting, naturalised chalk bank with orchids and climbing roses over old fruit trees. There are specialist displays of snowdrops, hellebores, pulmonarias, grasses and other unusual plants, especially those rich in nectar. The enchanting ¹/₂ -acre cottage garden at **Cottage in the Trees** has been immaculately planted, with a water feature, raised vegetable patch, small wildlife pond and gravel garden. Spring bulbs, hellebores and pulmonarias give a welcome start to the season, with pots and baskets, roses and clematis. Mixed borders of herbaceous plants and shrubs give all-yr interest. Limited wheelchair access at Westcroft.

9 ◆ BOWOOD RHODODENDRON WALKS
Calne SN11 9PG. The Marquis of Lansdowne, 01249 812102, www.bowood.org. *3¹/₂ m SE of Chippenham. Located off Junction 17 M4 near Bath and Chippenham. Entrance off A342 between Sandy Lane & Derry Hill villages.* **Adm £6, chd free. For NGS: Sun 5 June (11-6).** For other opening times and information, please phone or see garden website.
This 60-acre woodland garden of azaleas and rhododendrons is one of the most exciting of its type in the country. From the individual flowers to the breathtaking sweep of colour formed by hundreds of shrubs, surrounded by carpets of bluebells, this is a garden not to be missed. Planting began in 1850 and some of the earliest known hybrids feature among the collection. The Rhododendron Walks are located 2 miles from Bowood House & Gardens.

10 BROOMSGROVE LODGE
New Mill, Pewsey SN9 5LE. Diana Robertson. *2m E of Pewsey. From A345 take B3087 Burbage Rd, after 1¹/₂ m L to New Mill, through village and past canal. Park in field.* Home-made teas & light refreshments. **Adm £3, chd free. Wed 13 (11-4), Sun 17 (2-5), Wed 20 Apr (11-4).** Alongside stunning views of Martinsell Hill discover the imaginatively planted herbaceous borders, in spring full of tulips and forget-me-nots. Large vegetable garden, greenhouse and tunnel. Sunken terrace full of vibrantly planted pots where tea is served and a 4-acre field to wander around to admire the views. Large field parking area where you could picnic and children play before strolling round the garden.

> Breathtaking sweep of colour formed by hundreds of shrubs, surrounded by carpets of bluebells, this is a garden not to be missed . . .

THE BUILDINGS
See Hampshire.

11 33 CALNE ROAD
Lyneham SN15 4PT. Sue & Sam Wright. *7m N of Calne. Next to RAF Lyneham entrance.* Home-made teas. **Adm £2, chd 50p. Sun 12 June (1-5).** Also open **The Old Vicarage & Weavers**, Hilmarton. Approx ³/₄ -acre informal garden comprising modest collection of hostas, clematis and roses. Small kitchen garden, pond and mature orchard with bantams, chickens, doves and dovecote. Wheelchairs only. Not mobility scooters.

CHIFFCHAFFS
See Dorset.

12 CHISENBURY PRIORY
East Chisenbury SN9 6AQ. Mr & Mrs John Manser, 07810 483984, john.manser@shaftesbury.co.uk. *3m SW of Pewsey. Turn E from A345 at Enford then N to E Chisenbury, main gates 1m on R.* Cream Teas. **Adm £3.50, chd free. Sun 12 June (2-6).** Visitors also welcome by appt.
Medieval Priory with Queen Anne face and early C17 rear (not open) in middle of 5-acre garden on chalk. Mature garden with fine trees within clump and flint walls, herbaceous borders, shrubs, roses. Moisture-loving plants along mill leat, carp pond, orchard and wild garden, many unusual plants. Front borders redesigned in 2009 by Tom Stuart-Smith.

CONHOLT PARK
See Hampshire.

13 ◆ CORSHAM COURT
Corsham SN13 0BZ. Mr James Methuen-Campbell, 01249 712214, www.corsham-court.co.uk. *4m W of Chippenham. S of A4.* **Adm £2.50, chd £1.50. For NGS: Suns 27 Mar; 5 June (2-5.30).** For opening times and information please visit website.
Park and gardens laid out by Capability Brown and Repton. Large lawns with fine specimens of ornamental trees surround the Elizabethan mansion. C18 bath house hidden in the grounds. Spring bulbs, beautiful lily pond with Indian bean trees, young arboretum and stunning collection of magnolias.

COTTAGE ROW
See Dorset.

14 ◆ **THE COURTS**
Holt, Trowbridge BA14 6RR.
National Trust, 01225 782875,
www.nationaltrust.org.uk. *2m E of
Bradford-on-Avon. S of B3107 to
Melksham. In Holt follow NT signs,
park at village hall & at overflow car
park when signed.* Adm £6.50, chd
£3.60. For NGS: Sats 14 May;
3 Sept (11-5.30). For other opening
times and information, please
phone or see garden website.
Beautifully kept but eclectic garden.
Yew hedges divide garden
compartments with colour themed
borders and organically shaped
topiary. Water garden with 2 recently
restored pools, temple, conservatory
and small kitchen garden split by an
apple allée, all surrounded by 3½
acres of arboretum with specimen
trees. Wheelchair access map
available.

GROUP OPENING

15 **DAUNTSEY GARDENS**
SN15 4HW. *5m SE of Malmesbury.
Approach via Dauntsey Rd from Gt
Somerford, 1¼ m from Volunteer Inn.*
Home-made teas. **Combined adm
£5, chd free. Sun 12 June (1.30-5).**

    THE COACH HOUSE
    Col & Mrs J Seddon-Brown

    DAUNTSEY PARK
    Mr & Mrs Giovanni Amati

    THE GARDEN COTTAGE
    Miss Ann Sturgis

    IDOVER HOUSE
    Mr & Mrs Christopher Jerram

    THE OLD POND HOUSE
    Mr & Mrs Stephen Love

This group of 5 gardens, centred
around historic Dauntsey Park Estate,
ranges from the Classical C18
country house setting of Dauntsey
Park, with spacious lawns, old trees
and views over the R Avon, to mature
country house gardens and traditional
walled gardens. Enjoy the formal rose
garden in pink and white, old
fashioned borders and duck ponds at
Idover House, and the quiet seclusion
of The Coach House with its with
thyme terrace and gazebos, climbing
roses and clematis. Here, too, mop-
headed pruned crataegus prunifolia
line the drive. The Garden Cottage

---

has a traditional walled kitchen
garden with organic vegetables, apple
orchard, woodland walk and yew
topiary. Meanwhile the 2 acres at The
Old Pond House are both clipped and
unclipped! Large pond with lilies and
fat carp, and look out for the giraffe
and turtle.

DYRHAM PARK
See Somerset & Bristol.

16 **EDGECOMBE, 138 WYKE
ROAD**
Hilperton, Trowbridge BA14 7NT.
Madeline Webb. *½ m from
Trowbridge. Through Hilperton village,
turn into Horse Rd, R at r'about into
Wyke Rd.* Cream teas. **Adm £2, chd
free. Sun 19 June (2-6). Also open
Hilperton House.**
Completely restored small garden
featuring herbaceous borders,
vegetable garden, orchard and wild
flower area.

GROUP OPENING

17 **EDINGTON GARDENS**
BA13 4QF. *4m NE of Westbury. On
B3098 between Westbury & West
Lavington. Park off B3098 in church
car park, or in car park near B3098
and Monastery Rd junction, or in
Tinhead Road for Becketts House.
Overflow parking on verge in
Monastery Road beyond the church.
Village minibus available to take
visitors from church car park to
Becketts House. Gardens map
provided.* Home-made teas in Parish
Hall. **Combined adm £4, chd free.
Sun 5 June (2-6).**

    BONSHOMMES COTTAGE
    Mr Michael Jones

    THE OLD VICARAGE
    Mr J N d'Arcy

    THE PLOUGH
    Mr & Mrs Nicholas Buckman

Three varied gardens on greensand,
many with lovely views, are open in
this historic village. From a camomile
lawn the size of a handkerchief to a
large old garden with fine views, the
gardens are full of colour, interest and
ideas. Among the highlights are an
arboretum with a growing range of
unusual trees and an avenue of
fastigiate hornbeams, herbaceous
borders, a gravel garden, roses, fruit

---

and vegetables - and even some
long-established Japanese knotweed
which has been retained as a feature.
The Old Vicarage is home to National
Collection of evening primroses, with
over 20 species. Wheelchair access
at The Old Vicarage only. Wheelchair
access at Becketts House & The Old
Vicarage.

---

*Large pond
with lilies and fat
carp, and look
out for the giraffe
and turtle . . .*

---

18 **ENFIELD**
62 Yard Lane, Netherstreet,
Bromham SN15 2DT. Graham &
Elizabeth Veals, 01380 859303,
EnfieldGarden@talktalk.net,
www.enfieldgarden.talktalk.net. *4m
NW of Devizes. E off A342 into Yard
Lane, garden ¼ m on R. Limited
parking.* Home-made teas. **Adm
£2.50, chd free. Weds, Thurs,
18 May to 16 June; (10.30-4.30).
Visitors also welcome by appt.**
The cottage garden style of planting
combines old favourites with many
plants not commonly seen in gardens
today. The ½ acre incl 4 separate
areas and over 550 species and
cultivars of herbaceous plants incl a
significant collection of foxgloves
planted in the last 5 yrs. Featured in
Wiltshire Life.

19 **FONTHILL HOUSE**
nr Tisbury SP3 5SA. The Lord
Margadale of Islay. *13m W of
Salisbury. Via B3089 in Fonthill
Bishop. 3m N of Tisbury.* **Adm £5,
chd free. Sun 27 Mar (2-6).**
Large woodland garden. Daffodils,
rhododendrons, azaleas, shrubs,
bulbs; magnificent views; formal
garden. Limited wheelchair access.

GANTS MILL & GARDEN
See Somerset & Bristol.

GILBERTS NURSERY
See Hampshire.

20 GOULTERS MILL FARM
The Gibb SN14 7LL. Mr & Mrs
Michael Harvey. *Nr Salutation Inn on
B4039. Parking at top of 300yd drive,
elderly/disabled at the Mill.* Home-
made teas. **Adm £3, chd free.**
Sun 12 June (2-5).
³/₄ -acre garden in steep sided valley
bordered by the beginnings of the
Bybrook, threaded through with
gravel paths, punctuated with topiary
and mounds of shrubs. Underplanted
with an eclectic mix of perennials and
self-sown annuals, dahlias and
salvias. Hellebores, tulips, anemones,
daphne bholua, sarçocca, and
lonicera fragrantissima and later a
heady mix of delphiniums, salvias,
eremurus, aconites and asters. The E
side of the valley is alive with
harebells, rock roses,vipers bugloss
and blue butterflies if you are lucky.
Bluebell wood a must in May, June &
July. Local TV appearance with Bob
Crampton. Limited wheelchair
access.
 ♿ ❈ ⏺ ☕

Walled fruit and
vegetable garden,
small woodland
area with teddy
bears picnic . . .

21 THE GRANGE
Gaters Lane, Winterbourne
Dauntsey SP4 6ER. Mr & Mrs
Rebdi. *4m NE of Salisbury on A338.*
Home-made teas. **Adm £3.50, chd
free. Mon 30 May (2-6).**
Spacious 6-acre garden with R
Bourne running through. Clipped box,
borders. Laburnum, rose and
clematis arched walk, lily pond,
vegetable and herb garden. Wild
natural area. Restored C17 thatched
barn open. New this yr is the
Japanese style garden with tea house
next to river. Gravel paths.
 ♿ ❈ ☕

**22 ◆ GREAT CHALFIELD
MANOR**
Melksham SN12 8NH. Mr & Mrs R
Floyd & The National Trust, 01225
782239. *3m SW of Melksham. Take
B3107 from Melksham then 1st R to
Broughton Gifford. Follow sign for
Atworth, turn L for 1m to Manor. Park
on grass outside.* **Adm £4, chd free.**
**For NGS: Sun 6 Feb (2-4.30). For
other opening times and
information, please phone.**
Garden and grounds of 7 acres laid
out 1905-12 by Robert Fuller and his
wife to Arts and Crafts designs by
Alfred Parsons, Capt Partridge and
Sir Harold Brakspear. Incl roses,
daffodils, spring flowers, topiary
houses, borders, terraces, gazebo,
orchard, autumn border. C15 moated
manor (not open) and adjoining Parish
Church. In early spring snowdrops
and aconites enhance the moat walk.
Ramp to higher level, gravel path to
lower level.
 ♿ ❈ ☎

GROUP OPENING

**23 GREAT SOMERFORD
GARDENS**
SN15 5JB. *4m SE of Malmesbury.
4m N of M4 between J16 & J17; 2m
S of B4042 Malmesbury to Wootton
Bassett rd; 3m E of A429 Cirencester
to Chippenham rd.* Home-made teas.
**Adm £4, chd free. Sat 18, Sun 19
June (1.30-5).**

 CLEMATIS
 Arthur & Iris Scott

 **GREAT SOMERFORD'S FREE
 GARDENS & ALLOTMENTS**

 1 HOLLOW STREET
 Bridget Smith

 THE MOUNT
 Mr & Mrs McGrath.

Great Somerford is a medium-sized
village, bordered by R Avon with a
lovely river walk. There is a thriving
community with school, pub, post
office and general stores. Maintained
by very active gardeners, a well-
established 3-acre garden and two
charming smaller gardens are
opening for the NGS, joined by Great
Somerford's Free Gardens and
Allotments. Endowed in 1809 by the
philanthropic village rector, these are
thought to be the oldest continuously
cultivated allotments in the country.
The gardens offer a wide range of
interest with perennials, a collection of

about 20 clematis, old wisteria, trees,
fruit, vegetables and ponds. At The
Mount is a historic barn to view and
an ancient motte area has been
sympathetically replanted and
meanders to the R Avon.
 ⚀ ❈ ☕

**24 HAZELBURY MANOR
GARDENS**
Wadswick, Box SN13 8HX. Mr L
Lacroix. *5m SW of Chippenham, 5m
NE of Bath. From A4 at Box, A365 to
Melksham; at Five Ways junction L
onto B3109, 1st L, drive immed on R.*
Home-made teas. **Adm £5, chd free.**
Suns 22 May; 12 June (2-6).
8 acres Grade II landscaped organic
gardens around C15 fortified manor
(not open). Impressive yew topiary
and clipped beeches around large
lawn, herbaceous and mixed
borders ablaze in summer, laburnum
and lime walkways, rose garden,
stone circle and rockery. Walled
kitchen garden.
 ❈ ☕

HILLTOP
See Dorset.

25 NEW HILPERTON HOUSE
The Knapp, Hilperton, Trowbridge
BA14 7RJ. Mr & Mrs Chris Brown,
01225 774137,
candros@blueyonder.co.uk. *1¹/₂ m
NE of Trowbridge. Follow R361
towards Trowbridge and turn R at
r'about signed Hilperton. House is
next door to St Michaels Church in
the Knapp off Church St.* Home-
made teas. **Adm £3.50, chd free.**
**Sun 19 June (2-6). Also open
Edgecombe. Visitors also welcome
by appt June & July only, min
group size 10, max 20.**
2¹/₂ acres well stocked borders, small
stream leading to large pond with fish,
water lilies, waterfall and fountain.
Fine mature trees incl unusual
specimens. Walled fruit and vegetable
garden, small woodland area with
teddy bears picnic and activity sheets
for children. Rose walk with roses and
clematis, 160yr old vine in
conservatory of grade II listed house
(circa 1705)(House not open). Some
gravel paths which can be by-passed
on lawns. Conservatory (to see vines)
not accessible by wheelchair.
 ♿ ❈ ☕ ☎

HODGES BARN
See Gloucestershire North &
Central.

HOOKSHOUSE POTTERY
See Gloucestershire North & Central.

 HYDE'S HOUSE
Dinton SP3 5HH. **Mr George Cruddas.** *9m W of Salisbury. Off B3089 nr Dinton Church.* Home-made teas. **Adm £4, chd free.** Sun 29 May (2-5).
3 acres of wild and formal garden in beautiful situation with series of hedged garden rooms. Numerous shrubs, flowers and borders, all allowing tolerated wild flowers and preferred 'weeds'. Large walled kitchen garden, herb garden and C13 dovecote (open). Charming C16/18 Grade I listed house (not open),with lovely courtyard. Free walks around park and lake.
& ▨ ☕

27 ◆ **IFORD MANOR**
Lower Westwood, Bradford-on-Avon BA15 2BA. **Mrs Elizabeth Cartwright-Hignett, 01225 863146, www.ifordmanor.co.uk.** *7m S of Bath. Off A36, brown tourist sign to Iford 1m. Or from Bradford-on-Avon or Trowbridge via Lower Westwood village (brown signs).* **Adm £5, chd £4.50. For NGS: Sun 17 Apr (2-5). For opening times and information please visit website or telephone.**
Very romantic award-winning, Grade I listed Italianate garden famous for its tranquil beauty. Home to the Edwardian architect and designer Harold Peto 1899-1933. The garden is characterised by steps, terraces, sculpture and magnificent rural views. (House not open.). Partial access with assistance: please call in advance.
& ▨ ☕ ☎

28 **JOB'S MILL**
Crockerton BA12 8BB. **Lady Silvy McQuiston.** *1½ m S of Warminster. Down lane E of A350, S of A36 r'about.* **Adm £3, chd free.** Suns 17 Apr (2-5); 5 June (2-6).
Surrounding an old converted water mill, a delightful medium-sized terraced garden through which R Wylye flows. Riverside and woodland walks, vegetable patch, orchard, herbaceous border and water garden.
▨ ❀

KEMPSFORD MANOR
See Gloucestershire North & Central.

29 ◆ **LACOCK ABBEY GARDENS**
Chippenham SN15 2LG. **National Trust, 01249 730459, www.nationaltrust.org.uk.** *3m S of Chippenham. Off A350. Follow NT signs. Use public car park just outside Abbey.* **Adm £4, chd £2. For NGS: Sats & Suns 12, 13, 19, 20 Feb (11-4); 11, 12, 18, 19 Feb 2012 adm £5, chd £2.50 (11-4). For other opening times and information, please phone or see garden website.**
Victorian woodland garden with pond, botanic garden and exotic tree specimens. Display of early spring flowers with carpets of aconites, snowdrops, crocuses and daffodils. C13 Abbey with C18 Gothick additions.
& ▨ ❀ ☎

30 **130 LADYFIELD ROAD AND HUNGERDOWN ALLOTMENTS**
Ladyfield Road, Chippenham SN14 0AP. **Philip & Pat Canter and Chippenham Town Council.** *1m SW of Chippenham. Between A4 Bath and A420 Bristol Rds. Signed off B4528 Hungerdown Lane which runs between the A4 & A420.* **Adm £2.50, chd free.** Sun 24 July (1.30-5.30). **Also open Sweetbriar Cottage.**
Very pretty small garden with more than 30 clematis, climbing roses and a small fish pond. Curved neat edges packed with colourful herbaceous plants and small trees. 2 patio areas with lush lawn, pagoda and garden arbour. Next to garden are allotments with 15 gardens owned by Chippenham Town Council. Wheelchair access to allotments only on main drive way due to narrow paths.
& ▨ ❀ ☕

Priory House

31 ▶ LITTLE DURNFORD MANOR
Salisbury SP4 6AH. The Earl &
Countess of Chichester. *3m N of
Salisbury. Just beyond Stratford-sub-
Castle.* Home-made teas. **Adm
£3.50, chd £1.** Suns 17 Apr; 5 June
(2-6).
Extensive lawns with cedars, walled
gardens, fruit trees, large vegetable
garden, small knot and herb gardens.
Terraces, borders, sunken garden,
water garden, lake with islands, river
walks, labyrinth walk. Some steep
slopes & gravel but mostly accessible.

**32 ▶ ♦ LYDIARD PARK WALLED
GARDEN**
Lydiard Tregoze, Swindon
SN5 3PA. Swindon Borough
Council, 01793 770401,
www.lydiardpark.org.uk. *3m W
Swindon, 1m from J16 M4.* Follow
brown signs from W Swindon. **Adm
£2.50, chd £1.** For NGS: Sun 31
July (11-5). **For opening times and
information please visit website or
telephone.**
Beautiful ornamental and flower C18
walled garden. Trimmed shrubs
alternating with individually planted
flowers and bulbs incl rare daffodils

and tulips, sweet peas, annuals and
wall-trained fruit trees. Park and
children's playground.

33 ▶ MANOR FARM
Huish SN8 4JN. Mr & Mrs J
Roberts. *3m NW of Pewsey. Huish is
signed from A345 by White Hart PH
in Oare. Follow lane for 1m into Huish,
turn R by dead-end sign.* Home-
made teas served in landscaped
farmyard. **Adm £3, chd free.**
Sat 11, Sun 12 June (2-5.30).
Fine downland views surround this
intriguing and extensive garden which
has a surprise around every corner.
Ongoing design and planting
schemes create new interest each
year. Wide variety of clematis and
roses, pleached lime walk, woodland
pond and grotto. Fusion of old and
modern areas allow for very varied
planting. This garden will appeal to all
age groups: plenty of space to run
around and strategic benches to sit
and admire the views; opp ancient
Huish church. Fun sculptures to
discover. Some paths, particularly
around pond, too narrow for
wheelchairs.

34 ▶ MANOR HOUSE
Stratford Tony, Salisbury SP5 4AT.
Mr & Mrs H Cookson,
01722 718 496,
lucindacookson@care4free.net. *4m
SW of Salisbury. Take minor rd W off
A354 at Coombe Bissett. Garden on
S after 1m.* Home-made teas. **Adm
£4, chd free.** Sat 18 June; Wed 7
Sept (2-5) **Evening Opening,** wine,
Fri 17 June (5-8).
Varied 4-acre garden with all yr
interest. Formal and informal areas.
Small lake fed from R Ebble,
waterside planting, herbaceous
borders with colour through to late
autumn. Pergola-covered vegetable
garden, formal parterre garden,
orchard, shrubberies, roses,
specimen trees, winter colour and
structure, many original contemporary
features.

MARSHFIELD GARDENS
See Somerset & Bristol.

MAYO FARM
See Dorset.

35 ▶ ♦ THE MEAD NURSERY
Brokerswood, Westbury BA13 4EG.
Mr & Mrs S Lewis-Dale,
01373 859990,
www.themeadnursery.co.uk. *3m W
of Westbury. E of Rudge. Follow signs
for Country Park at Brokerswood.
Halfway between Rudge & Country
Park.* **Adult & chd adm £3 to incl tea
& home-made cake.** For NGS: Sun
21 Aug (12-5). **For other opening
times and information, please
phone or see garden website.**
1¼-acre nursery and garden with
herbaceous borders, raised alpine
beds, sink garden and bog bed. Well-
drained Mediterranean-style raised
bed and small wildlife pond. Nursery
with extensive range of herbaceous
perennials, alpines, pot-grown bulbs
and grasses in peat free compost.
Guest stalls, garden tombola.

36 ▶ ♦ THE MILL HOUSE
Berwick St James, Salisbury
SP3 4TS. Diana Gifford Mead,
01722 790331,
www.millhouse.org.uk. *8m NW of
Salisbury. S of A303, N of A36, on
B3083, S end of village.* Cream teas
in village hall. **Adm £3, chd free.** For
NGS: Suns 27 Mar; 26 June (2-6).
**For other opening times and
information, please phone or see
garden website.**

Whatley Manor

Surrounded by the R Till, millstream and a 10-acre traditional wet water meadow, this garden of wildness supports over 300 species of old fashioned roses rambling from the many trees. It is filled with butterflies, moths and insects. Birdsong is phenomenal in spring and summer. Herbaceous borders crammed with plants of yesteryear, unforgettable scents. Glorious spring bulbs. SSSI.

&. 🎍 🛏 🍽 ☎

37▶ NORTH COTTAGE & WOODVIEW COTTAGE
Tisbury Row, Tisbury SP3 6RZ. Jacqueline & Robert Baker, Diane McBride, 01747 870019, robert.baker@pearceseeds.co.uk. *12m W of Salisbury. From A30 turn N through Ansty, L at T-junction, towards Tisbury. From Tisbury take Ansty rd. Entrance nr junction signed Tisbury Row.* Home-made teas in the barn & lunches available Sun. **Adm £3, chd free. Sun 5 (11.30-5), Sat 18 June (2-6). Visitors also welcome by appt mid May to Mid July. Groups only.**
Two homely cottage gardens with big aspirations and a 4 arce small holding nestling in the Wiltshire countryside. Gardens are constantly changing and hopefully improving. A real Country Living garden, a well kept secret we were told. So if flowers, fruit, veg, orchard, woods, water features and sculptures interest us we look forward to welcoming you. Pottery, jewellery and crafts.

❀ 🍽 ☎

38▶ OARE HOUSE
Rudge Lane, Oare, Nr Pewsey SN8 4JQ. Sir Henry Keswick. *2m N of Pewsey. On Marlborough Rd (A345).* Home-made teas. **Adm £3, chd free (share to The Order of St John). Suns 17 Apr; 17 July (2-6).**
Fine house (not open) in large garden with large trees, hedges, spring flowers, woodlands, extensive lawns and kitchen garden. Gravel paths, some too narrow for wheelchairs & motorised buggies.

&. 🎍 🍽

39▶ THE OLD MILL
Ramsbury SN8 2PN. Annabel and James Dallas, *8m NE of Marlborough. From Marlborough head to Ramsbury. At The Bell PH follow sign to Hungerford. Garden behind yew hedge on R 100yds beyond The Bell.* No teas available 19 May. **Adm £4, chd free.**

Thur 19 May; Sun 31 July; Mon 1 Aug; Thur 1 Sept (2-6). Water running through multitude of channels no longer drives the mill but provides backdrop for whimsical garden of pollarded limes, sculpture, overflowing pots and herbaceous borders bursting with colour. Paths meander by streams and over small bridges. Vistas cut through trees give dramatic views of downs beyond. Featured in 100 Dream Gardens, Wiltshire Magazine, GGG.

🍽

> ## It is filled with butterflies, moths and insects. Birdsong is phenomenal in spring and summer . . .

40▶ THE OLD RECTORY
Ham, Marlborough SN8 3QR. Mr & Mrs N Baring. *3m S of Hungerford. Take A338, bear L after 2½ m on minor rd signed Ham. Entrance 50yds from village green on N side of Inkpen Rd.* **Adm £3.50, chd free. Sun 17 Apr (2-6).**
4-acre garden incl wide expanse of lawn and yew-hedged enclosures leading to informal area with fine old trees and some recent planting of interesting shrubs. Areas of mixed bulbs, restored pond with new waterside plants. Separate cottage garden. Unfenced pond.

&. ❀ 🍽

THE OLD RECTORY, HOUGHTON
See Hampshire.

41▶ THE OLD VICARAGE
Swindon Road, Hilmarton, Calne SN11 8SB. Lesley & George Hudson, 07802 741293, lesleyhudson@hotmail.com. *4m S of Wootton Bassett on A3102 between Lynham & Calne.* Home-made teas & light refreshments. **Combined adm with Weavers £4.50, chd free. Sun 5, 12 June (11.30-5). Visitors also welcome by appt.**
7-acre plot incl a Victorian walled garden, ornamental pond, wisteria-covered pergola, blue and white herbaceous border, Italianate secret

garden, woodland garden, colourful herbaceous borders flanked by lawns and a herb garden. Adjacent to the formal garden are two paddocks incorporating a wildflower meadow (in June), orchard and kitchen garden.

❀ 🍽 ☎

PEN MILL FARM
See Dorset.

42▶ THE POUND HOUSE
Little Somerford SN15 5JW. Mr & Mrs Michael Baines, 01666 823212, squeezebaines@yahoo.com. *2m E of Malmesbury on B4024. In village turn S, leave church on R. Car park on R before railway bridge.* Home-made teas. **Adm £3, chd free. Sun 5 June (2-6). Visitors also welcome by appt May to September incl coaches.**
Large well planted garden surrounding former rectory. Mature trees, hedges and spacious lawns. Well-stocked herbaceous borders, roses, shrubs, pergola, parterre, swimming pool garden, water, ducks, chickens, alpacas and horses. Raised vegetable garden and lots of places to sit.

&. ❀ 🛏 🍽 ☎

PRIOR PARK LANDSCAPE GARDEN
See Somerset & Bristol.

43▶ PRIORY HOUSE
Market Street, Bradford-on-Avon BA15 1LH. Mr & Mrs Tim Woodall. *Town centre. Park in town centre. Take A363 signed Bath up Market St. House 500yds.* Home-made teas. **Adm £2.50, chd free. Sun 17 Apr; Sun 7 Aug (2-5.30).**
³/₄-acre town garden, mostly formal. Spring garden of narcissi, tulips and hellebores. Late summer borders of herbaceous, grasses and hydrangeas. Knot garden in front of part Georgian house is an interpretation of the sash windows. Featured in The English Garden & Wiltshire Magazine.

&. 🎍 ❀ 🍽

44▶ RIDLEYS CHEER
Mountain Bower SN14 7AJ. Mr & Mrs A J Young, 01225 891204, antonyoung@ridleyscheer.co.uk, www.ridleyscheer.co.uk. *9m W/NW of Chippenham. At The Shoe, on A420 8m W of Chippenham, turn N then take 2nd L & 1st R.* Teas & light refreshments. **Adm £4, chd free. Sun 10 Apr; Sun 15 May (2-6). Visitors also welcome by appt.**

Be tempted by a plant from a plant stall ❀

Largely informal garden; mixed borders, lawns, interesting collection of shrubs and trees incl acers, magnolias, liriodendrons, tree peonies, deutzias, daphnes, oaks, beech and hollies. Some 130 rose varieties; old-fashioned and modern shrub roses, and magnificent tree ramblers. Potager, miniature box garden, arboretum, 3-acre wild flower meadow, plus new ¹/₂ -acre meadow. Dew pond, constructed Sept 2009.

  🕓 ✿ 🛏 🍵 ☎

SANDLE COTTAGE
See Hampshire.

Magnificent tree ramblers. Woodland walk carpeted with spring bulbs . . . good autumn colour . . .

45 SHARCOTT MANOR
Pewsey SN9 5PA. Captain & Mrs D Armytage, 01672 563485. *1m SW of Pewsey. Via A345 from Pewsey towards Salisbury. Turn R signed Sharcott at grass triangle. 400yds up lane, garden on L over cattle-grid.* Home-made teas. **Adm £3.50, chd free. Weds 6 Apr; 4 May; 1 June; 6 July; 3 Aug; 7 Sept (11-5); Suns 10 Apr; 11 Sept (2-6). Visitors also welcome by appt also groups and coaches.**
6-acre plantsman's garden on greensand, planted for yr-round interest. Wide range of trees and shrubs, densely planted mixed borders, with many unusual plants and climbers. Magnificent tree ramblers. Woodland walk carpeted with spring bulbs around ¹/₂ -acre lake. Good autumn colour. Small vegetable garden, ornamental water fowl. Some gravel paths, grass slope, narrow grass paths.

  🕓 ✿ 🍵 ☎

46 ◆ SHELDON MANOR
Chippenham SN14 0RG. Kenneth & Caroline Hawkins, 01249 653120, www.sheldonmanor.co.uk. *1¹/₂ m W of Chippenham. Take A420 W. 1st L signed Chippenham RFC, entrance approx ¹/₂ m on R.* **Garden only adm £4.50, chd under 12 free. For NGS: Thur 26 May (2-4). For other opening times and information**

please visit website or telephone. Wiltshire's oldest inhabited manor house with C13 porch and C15 chapel. Gardens with ancient yews, mulberry tree and profusion of old-fashioned roses blooming in May and June. Featured in Alastair Sawday - Special Getaways.

🏡 🍵 ☎

47 NEW SILVER BIRCHES
Winterbourne Bassett SN4 9QB. Robert & Sarah Harvey. *8m NW of Marlborough. ¹/₂ m from A4361 between Avebury & Wroughton. Follow signs to White Horse PH. Park in church car park.* Home-made teas. **Adm £3, chd free. Suns 19; 26 June (2-6).**
Thoughtfully designed ¹/₂ -acre downland garden featuring Mediterranean-style courtyard, seaside garden, subtropical border, croquet lawn, herbaceous borders, pergola, wildflower meadow, stone circle, wild-life ponds, bluebell wood, fruit and vegetables, summer-house, cedar greenhouse and well-stocked conservatory. Information panels describe the making of the garden over last 5yrs. Quiz.

🕓 🍵

SNAPE COTTAGE PLANTSMAN'S GARDEN
See Dorset.

SPECIAL PLANTS
See Somerset & Bristol.

48 ◆ STOURHEAD GARDEN
Stourton, Warminster BA12 6QD. National Trust, 01747 841152, www.nationaltrust.org.uk. *3m NW of Mere on B3092. Follow NT signs.* **Adm £8.10, chd £4.40. For NGS: Sat 7 May (9-6). For other opening times and information, please phone or see garden website.**
One of the earliest and greatest landscape gardens in the world, creation of banker Henry Hoare in 1740s on his return from the Grand Tour, inspired by paintings of Claude and Poussin. Planted with rare trees, rhododendrons and azaleas over last 250yrs. Some steep slopes.

  🕓 ✿ 🛏 ☎ 🍵

49 ◆ SWEETBRIAR COTTAGE
19 Gladstone Road, Chippenham SN15 3BW. Paul & Joy Gough, 01249 656005, paulgough@btopenworld.com. *In Chippenham town centre, turn off A4 Ave La Fleche into Gladstone Rd.*

Park in Borough Parade car parks. Garden just above car park opp Angel Hotel. Home-made teas. **Adm £2.50, chd free. Sun 24 July (1.30-5.30). Also open 130 Ladyfield Road & Hungerdown Allotments. Visitors also welcome by appt.**
Over ¹/₂ acre of walled garden recently restored, planted with ornamental and fruit trees, low box-edged cottage-style planting to encourage bees and butterflies. Small wildlife pond and ornamental fish pond. Can be viewed from slate paths throughout. Organic vegetables grown in 4ft beds. A tranquil wildlife haven in a town centre.

🕓 🍵

TORMARTON COURT
See Somerset & Bristol.

8 TROSSACHS DRIVE
See Somerset & Bristol.

50 ◆ WATERDALE HOUSE
East Knoyle SP3 6BL. Mr & Mrs Julian Seymour, 01747 830262. *8m S of Warminster. N of East Knoyle, garden signed from A350. DO NOT use Sat Nav.* **Adm £4, chd free. For NGS: Sun 1 May (2-6). For other opening times and information, please phone or see garden website.**
4-acre mature woodland garden with rhododendrons, azaleas, camellias, maples, magnolias, ornamental water, bog garden, herbaceous borders. Bluebell walk. New shrub border created by storm damage mixed with agapanthus and half hardy salvias. SatNav poor.

🏡 🍵

51 NEW WEAVERS
Church Road, Hilmarton, Calne SN11 8SE. Sheron & Mel Wilkins. *A3102 between Calne & Lyneham. After passing church Weavers can be found on the L of the village School.* Home-made teas & light refreshments. **Combined adm with The Old Vicarage £4.50, chd free. Suns 5, 12 June (11-5).**
Weavers is an extremely pretty cottage garden established 5yrs ago by present owners. The garden has matured very quickly and complements the lovely cottage. Wind your way through the pergola surrounded by pretty borders in the first room then through into other 'rooms' all with well maintained and stocked herbaceous and shrub borders and areas of lawn.

🏡 🍵

52 WELLAWAY
Close Lane, Marston SN10 5SN.
Mr & Mrs P Lewis. *5m SW of Devizes. From A360, Devizes to Salisbury, R into Potterne through Worton, signed L to Marston, lane ¹/₂ m on L.* Home-made teas. **Adm £4, chd free. Suns 10 Apr; 11 Sept (2-6).**
2-acre flower arranger's garden comprising herbaceous borders, orchard, vegetable garden, ornamental and wildlife ponds, lawns and naturalised areas. Planted since 1979 for yr-round interest. Shrubberies and rose garden, other areas underplanted with bulbs or ground cover. Springtime particularly colourful with daffodils, tulips and hellebores.

53 WEST LAVINGTON MANOR
1 Church Street, West Lavington SN10 4LA. **Mr & Mrs Andrew Doman.** *6m S of Devizes, on A360. House opp White St, where parking available.* Home-made teas. **Adm £5, chd free (share to West Lavington Church). Sat 4 June (12-5).**
A 5-acre walled garden first established in C17 by John Danvers who brought Italianate gardens to the UK. Variety of formal and informal areas incl herbaceous border, Japanese garden, rose garden, orchard and arboretum with some outstanding specimen trees all centred around a trout stream and duck pond.

WESTON HOUSE
See Dorset.

54 WHATLEY MANOR
Easton Grey SN16 0RB. **Christian & Alix Landolt,** www.whatleymanor.com. *4m W of Malmesbury. From A429 at*

Malmesbury take B4040 signed Sherston. Manor 2m on L. Home-made teas. **Adm £4, chd free. Sun 3 July (2-5).**
12 acres of English country gardens with 26 distinct rooms each with a strong theme based on colour, scent or style. Original 1920s plan inspired the design and combines classic style with more contemporary touches. Specially commissioned sculptures.

WINCOMBE PARK
See Dorset.

55 WINDMILL COTTAGE
Kings Road, Market Lavington SN10 4QB. **Rupert & Gill Wade,** 01380 813527. *5m S of Devizes. Turn E off A360 1m N of West Lavington, 2m S of Potterne. At top of hill turn L into Kings Rd, L into Windmill Lane after 200yds. Limited parking.* **Adm £2.50, chd free. Fris 20 May; 3, 17 July; 1, 22 July; 9 Sept (2-5.30). Visitors also welcome by appt late May to end July, also early Sept for groups of 4+.**
1-acre cottage-style garden on greensand. Mixed beds and borders with long season of interest. Roses on pagoda, large vegetable patch for kitchen and exhibition at local shows, polytunnel and greenhouse. Whole garden virtually pesticide free for last 14yrs. Small bog garden by revamped pond. Secret glade with prairie. Some second-hand materials awaiting reuse.

56 NEW WOOLLEY GRANGE HOTEL
Woolley Green, Bradford-on-Avon BA15 1TX. Woolley Grange Hotel, 01225 864705, info@woolleygrangehotel.co.uk. *1¹/₂ m NE of Bradford-on-Avon. Just off B3105 at Woolley Green.* **Adm**

£2.50, chd free. Mon 30 May; Suns 5 June; 18 Sept (2-6). Also open Woolley Green 30 May & 5 June.
Newly refurbished 1-acre walled garden with vegetable, fruit, herbs, cut flower borders, children's play area and chicken run. Main hotel grounds (12 acres) are laid mainly to lawn with mixed borders, pond, a mown maze, new faerie garden. Lots of play areas for children. Garden staff will be available for help & advice. Some areas of the grounds have steps but otherwise mostly accessible.

> ## Springtime particularly colourful with daffodils, tulips and hellebores . . .

57 NEW 13 WOOLLEY GREEN
Woolley Green, Bradford-on Avon BA15 1TX. **Mrs S Dark.** *1¹/₂ m NE of Bradford-on-Avon. Just off B3105 at Woolley Green.* **Adm £2.50, chd free. Mon 30 May; Sun 5 June (2-6). Also open Woolley Grange Hotel where teas are available.**
C18 converted coach house with impressive gothic entrance arch in ²/₃ acre of gardens. Cottage garden with mixed herbaceous borders, shrubs, roses, set around independent terraced lawns. Mature trees, paddock and free range chickens and ducks. Also studio barn and vegetable garden with half standard fruit trees. Exhibition of drawings of buildings in Bradford-upon-Avon over last 20yrs.

Wiltshire County Volunteers

County Organisers
Sean & Kena Magee, Byams House, Willesley, Tetbury GL8 8QU, 01666 880009, spbmagee@googlemail.com

Publicity
Tricia Duncan, Chapel Cottage, Easton Royal, Pewsey SN9 5RU, 01672 810443, tricia@windward.biz

Assistant County Organisers
Cosima Armytage, Sharcott Manor, Pewsey SN9 5PA, 01672 563485
Sarah Coate, Colts Corner, Upper Woodford, Salisbury SP4 6PA, 01722 782365
Tricia Duncan, Chapel Cottage, Easton Royal, Pewsey SN9 5LY, 01672 810443, tricia@windward.biz
Jo Hankey, Mill Cottage, Burcombe, Wilton SP2 0EJ, 01722 742472, richard.hankey@virgin.net
Shirley Heywood, Monkton House, Monkton Deverill BA12 7EX, 01985 844486
Diana Robertson, Broomsgrove Lodge, New Mill, nr Pewsey SN9 5LE, 01672 810515, diana@broomsgrovelodge.co.uk
Anne Shand, Ashton House, Worton, Devizes SN10 5RU, 01380 726249, anneshand@btinternet.com

Follow us on Facebook and Twitter

WORCESTERSHIRE

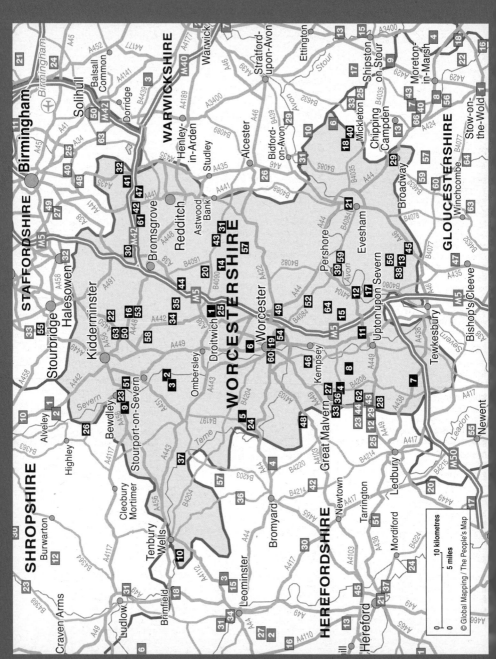

Opening Dates

February

Wednesday 23
16 Dial Park

March

Thursday 3
43 Red House Farm

Wednesday 9
14 The Cottage

Thursday 10
43 Red House Farm

Thursday 17
43 Red House Farm

Sunday 20
28 Little Malvern Court

Thursday 24
43 Red House Farm

Wednesday 30
14 The Cottage

Thursday 31
43 Red House Farm

April

Wednesday 6
11 Bylane

Thursday 7
43 Red House Farm

Thursday 14
43 Red House Farm

Saturday 16
54 The Walled Garden

Thursday 21
43 Red House Farm

Friday 22
49 Spetchley Park Gardens

Sunday 24
1 24 Alexander Avenue
40 4 Poden Cottages
58 Whitlenge Gardens

Monday 25
40 4 Poden Cottages
58 Whitlenge Gardens

Thursday 28
43 Red House Farm

Saturday 30
12 1 Church Cottage
48 Shuttifield Cottage

May

Sunday 1
12 1 Church Cottage
58 Whitlenge Gardens

Monday 2
58 Whitlenge Gardens

Wednesday 4
6 Beckett Drive Gardens (Evening)

Thursday 5
43 Red House Farm

Sunday 8
33 Model Farm

Monday 9
19 The Greyfriars

Wednesday 11
14 The Cottage
25 Hiraeth

Thursday 12
43 Red House Farm

Saturday 14
48 Shuttifield Cottage
56 Whitcombe House

Sunday 15
18 Frogs Nest
51 Toll House Cottage
56 Whitcombe House

Thursday 19
43 Red House Farm

Saturday 21
9 Bowcastle Farm

Sunday 22
26 Hunters End
33 Model Farm
57 White Cottage
64 Woodmancote

Thursday 26
43 Red House Farm

Saturday 28
12 1 Church Cottage
17 Eckington Gardens
32 74 Meadow Road

Sunday 29
3 Astley Towne House
12 1 Church Cottage
17 Eckington Gardens
29 Luggers Hall
30 Marlbrook Gardens
32 74 Meadow Road
58 Whitlenge Gardens
64 Woodmancote

Monday 30
58 Whitlenge Gardens
64 Woodmancote

June

Wednesday 1
11 Bylane

Thursday 2
43 Red House Farm

Saturday 4
5 The Barton
48 Shuttifield Cottage

Sunday 5
5 The Barton
21 Harrells Hardy Plants Nursery Garden
33 Model Farm

Wednesday 4
42 Rectory Cottage
60 68 Windsor Avenue

Thursday 9
43 Red House Farm

Saturday 11
27 Layton Avenue Gardens
47 Seechem Manor

Sunday 12
7 Birtsmorton Court
25 Hiraeth
27 Layton Avenue Gardens
39 Pershore Gardens
47 Seechem Manor
56 Whitcombe House
57 White Cottage

Thursday 16
21 Harrells Hardy Plants Nursery Garden
43 Red House Farm

Saturday 18
41 Pump Cottage

Sunday 19
2 Astley Country Gardens
26 Hunters End
29 Luggers Hall
40 4 Poden Cottages
41 Pump Cottage
45 Rose Villa

Monday 20
41 Pump Cottage

Wednesday 22
14 The Cottage

Thursday 23
43 Red House Farm

Friday 24
10 Brook Farm

Saturday 25
34 New House Farm, Cutnall Green
48 Shuttifield Cottage
54 The Walled Garden

Sunday 26
21 Harrells Hardy Plants Nursery Garden
23 High Bank
34 New House Farm, Cutnall Green
59 Wick Village
61 Withybed Green
63 The Woodlands

Wednesday 29
25 Hiraeth

Thursday 30
43 Red House Farm

July

Saturday 2
22 Harvington Hall

Sunday 3
1 24 Alexander Avenue
18 Frogs Nest
22 Harvington Hall
49 Spetchley Park Gardens
56 Whitcombe House

Tuesday 5
8 Blackmore Grange

Thursday 7
43 Red House Farm

Sunday 10
6 Beckett Drive Gardens
21 Harrells Hardy Plants Nursery Garden
30 Marlbrook Gardens
47 Seechem Manor

Wednesday 13
14 The Cottage

Thursday 14
21 Harrells Hardy Plants Nursery Garden
43 Red House Farm

Saturday 16
20 Hanbury Hall
48 Shuttifield Cottage
62 21 Woodfarm Road

Sunday 17
25 Hiraeth
51 Toll House Cottage
62 21 Woodfarm Road

Thursday 21
43 Red House Farm

Saturday 23
55 Westacres

Sunday 24
21 Harrells Hardy Plants Nursery Garden
55 Westacres
63 The Woodlands

Thursday 28
43 Red House Farm

Saturday 30
34 New House Farm, Cutnall Green

Sunday 31
3 Astley Towne House
34 New House Farm, Cutnall Green
52 The Tynings

August

Thursday 4
43 Red House Farm

Saturday 6
52 The Tynings (Evening)
54 The Walled Garden

Sunday 7
23 High Bank
24 High View

Wednesday 10
25 Hiraeth

Thursday 11
43 Red House Farm

Sunday 14
30 Marlbrook Gardens

Thursday 18
43 Red House Farm

Saturday 20
48 Shuttifield Cottage

Wednesday 24
14 The Cottage

Thursday 25
43 Red House Farm

Sunday 28
3 Astley Towne House
58 Whitlenge Gardens

Monday 29
58 Whitlenge Gardens

September

Thursday 1
43 Red House Farm

Sunday 4
1 24 Alexander Avenue
21 Harrells Hardy Plants Nursery Garden
46 Round Lodge

Thursday 8
43 Red House Farm

Saturday 10
30 Marlbrook Gardens (Evening)

Wednesday 14
14 The Cottage

Thursday 15
43 Red House Farm

Saturday 17
48 Shuttifield Cottage

Sunday 18
21 Harrells Hardy Plants Nursery Garden

Thursday 22
43 Red House Farm

Sunday 25
18 Frogs Nest

Thursday 29
43 Red House Farm

October

Thursday 6
43 Red House Farm

Friday 7
15 Croome Park

Gardens open to the public

15 Croome Park
19 The Greyfriars
20 Hanbury Hall
21 Harrells Hardy Plants Nursery Garden
22 Harvington Hall
28 Little Malvern Court
43 Red House Farm
44 Riverside Gardens at Webbs of Wychbold
49 Spetchley Park Gardens
50 Stone House Cottage Gardens
58 Whitlenge Gardens

By appointment only

4 Barnard's Green House
13 Conderton Manor
31 Meadow Farm
35 New House Farm, Elmbridge
37 Orleton House
38 Overbury Court
53 Tythe Barn House

Also open by Appointment ☎

1 24 Alexander Avenue
3 Astley Towne House
14 The Cottage
17 The Croft, Eckington Gardens
16 Dial Park
23 High Bank
24 High View
25 Hiraeth
26 Hunters End
27 22 Layton Avenue, Layton Avenue Gardens
32 74 Meadow Road
34 New House Farm, Cutnall Green
30 Oak Tree House, Marlbrook Gardens
40 4 Poden Cottages
41 Pump Cottage
30 Round Hill Garden, Marlbrook Gardens
30 Saranacris, Marlbrook Gardens
47 Seechem Manor
48 Shuttifield Cottage
51 Toll House Cottage
52 The Tynings
55 Westacres
56 Whitcombe House
57 White Cottage
60 68 Windsor Avenue
62 21 Woodfarm Road

A wonderful range of five country gardens of great variety, in picturesque, peaceful and colourful settings . . .

The Gardens

■1 24 ALEXANDER AVENUE

Droitwich Spa WR9 8NH. Malley & David Terry, 01905 774907, terrydroit@aol.com. *1m S of Droitwich. Droitwich Spa towards Worcester A38.Or from M5 J6 to Droitwich Town centre.* **Adm £3, chd free. Suns 24 Apr; 3 July; 4 Sept (2-6).** Visitors also welcome by appt.

Beautifully designed giving feeling of space and tranquillity. 100+ clematis varieties interlacing high hedges. Borders with rare plants and shrubs. Sweeping curves of lawns and paths to woodland area with shade-loving plants. Drought-tolerant plants in S-facing gravel front garden. Alpine filled troughs. April spring bulbs, June clematis. Featured in GGG.

 ⚙ ☎

GROUP OPENING

■2 ASTLEY COUNTRY GARDENS

Astley, nr Stourport-on-Severn DY13 0SG, 01299 823769. *3m SW of Stourport-on-Severn. Take A451 out of Stourport, turn L onto B4196 for Worcester. Start at Astley Village Hall where map and descriptions of gardens are available. Car parking available at each location as distances between most gardens too great to walk.* Home-made teas at various gardens. **Combined adm £5, chd free. Sun 19 June (1-6).**

ASTLEY TOWNE HOUSE
Astley. Tim & Lesley Smith

HALL BARN
Dunley. Susan Chandler & Richard Davenhill

LONGMORE HILL FARMHOUSE
Larford Lane, Astley. Roger & Christine Russell

THE WHITE HOUSE
Dunley. Tony & Linda Tidmarsh

NEW THE WHITE HOUSE - ASTLEY BURF
John & Joanna Daniels

A wonderful range of 5 country gardens of great variety, in picturesque, peaceful and colourful settings. These incl the garden of a Grade II listed half timbered house with sub tropical planting, stumpery with tree ferns and woodland temple, underground grotto and water features; beautiful walled garden of Grade II listed C18 barn conversion; classical style garden with a variety of features celebrating events in the owner's family; ½ - acre garden with mixed borders, 'wheel' herbery and large paddock with specimen trees overlooking the Severn Valley; a Grade II listed C16 farmhouse garden with mixed borders, small feature courtyard leading to a part-walled terrace and lily pond. Astley Towne House, featured in Gardeners World.

🐦 ⚙ ☕

■3 ASTLEY TOWNE HOUSE

Astley DY13 0RH. Tim & Lesley Smith, 01299 822299, tim@tmsmithbuilders.co.uk. *3m W of Stourport-on-Severn. On B4196 Worcester to Bewdley Road.* Home-made teas. **Adm £4, chd free. Suns 29 May; 31 July; 28 Aug (1-5). Also open with Astley Country Gardens Sun 19 June.** Visitors also welcome by appt.

2½ acres incl sub-tropical planting. Winding paths of jungle garden incorporating bananas, palms and other rare and exotic plants. Features incl stumpery garden, woodland temple, tree top high safari lodge, revolving neo-classical summerhouse, columns with statuary and grotto based on Greek mythology with water features and shell mosaics. Featured in The English Garden & on Gardeners World.

🐦 ⚙ ☕ ☎

■4 BARNARD'S GREEN HOUSE

Hastings Pool, Poolbrook Road, Malvern WR14 3NQ. Mrs Sue Nicholls, 01684 574446. *1m E of Malvern. At junction of B4211 & B4208.* **Adm £3, chd free.** Visitors welcome by appt any day, spring, summer into Sept, coaches permitted, any size group.

2-acre garden with a magnificent cedar has been completely redesigned and replanted. The newly made-over woodland which incls gravel garden and stumpery is covered in spring by euphorbia robbiae, hellebore, leucojum, fritillaria and anemones followed by azaleas and rhododendrons. From June-Sept the herbaceous borders have a wide variety of plants and flowering shrubs. Large vegetable garden and 2 rockeries.

♿ ☎

Birtsmorton Court

5 THE BARTON
Berrow Green. WR6 6PL. David & Vanessa Piggott. *1m S of Martley. On B4197 between Martley & A44 at Knightwick, corner of lane to Broadheath. Parking & lunches (12.30-2.30) at Admiral Rodney PH opp.* Home-made teas. **Adm £3, chd free. Sat 4, Sun 5 June (1-5).**
Started in 2003 this ½ -acre colourful cottage-style garden contains unusual trees, shrubs and herbaceous planting. Large pond with herbaceous terracing, wildlife pond, colour-themed gardens, gravel and grass beds. Roses, clematis and uncommon climbers decorate pergola, arbour and trellises. Vegetable garden. Tender and exotic planting in 'Hot Spot'. Exhibition of Batiks.

To paraphrase the lovely Eric Morecambe 'They're all the right plants, just not necessarily in the right order' . . .

GROUP OPENING

6 BECKETT DRIVE GARDENS
Northwick WR3 7BZ, 01905 451108. *1½ m N of Worcester city centre. Cul-de-sac off A449 Ombersley Rd directly opp Granthams garage, 1m S of Claines r'about on A449.* Home-made teas. **Combined adm £3, chd free. Wed 4 May (7-9) Evening Opening £4, wine & soft drinks; Sun 10 July (10-4.30).**

5 BECKETT DRIVE
Jacki & Pete Ager

6 BECKETT DRIVE
Guy Lymer

Two individual but contrasting gardens both with an abundance of plants and interesting design ideas.

Compost advisers in attendance. A range of quality and good value plants on sale at summer opening. 5 Beckett Drive is a plantsman's garden with a wide variety of colourful planting in distinctly different settings. Hot borders give way to a raised alpine area and a sun-loving bed before moving into a shade garden with hostas and ferns. A walk through this long, narrow garden reveals a number of surprising features that have inspired previous visitors. 6 Beckett Drive exploits even the smallest spaces with an eclectic mix of planting, modern sculpture, water and lighting. Year round foliage colour is complemented by exotic plants and natural arbour. A tranquil atmosphere is created by the rear garden's centrepiece; a contemporary water-feature within a wildlife pool.

7 BIRTSMORTON COURT
nr Malvern WR13 6JS. Mr & Mrs N G K Dawes. *7m E of Ledbury. On A438.* Home-made teas. **Adm £4.50, chd free. Sun 12 June (2-5.30).**
Fortified manor house (not open) dating from C12; moat; Westminster pool laid down in Henry VII's reign at time of consecration of Westminster Abbey. Large tree under which Cardinal Wolsey reputedly slept in shadow of ragged stone. White garden, potager; topiary.

8 NEW BLACKMORE GRANGE
Blackmore End, Hanley Swan, Worcester WR8 0EE. Mr & Mrs D Robertson. *4m E of Malvern, 4½ m NW of Upton on Severn. From town centre of Hanley Swan on B4209 take Worcester rd past Butcher's shop on R, RC church on L for ¾ m. Parking in field just before rd bends to R.* Home-made teas. **Adm £3.50, chd free. Tue 5 July (10.30-4.30).**
All-yr round 2-acre rural garden surrounds the family home. Packed with a large variety of plants, shrubs and trees. The swimming pool has been transformed into the stable garden, an outstanding area of traditional cottage-style planting. Also a mixed orchard, woodland walk, mixed planting beds and kitchen garden. Described by Chris Beardshaw as 'A natural garden full of interest and variety'.

9 NEW BOWCASTLE FARM
Tanners Hill, Bewdley DY12 2LN. Thelma & Cedric Quayle. *1m W of Bewdley town centre. Off B4190 signed Tenbury. Turn off B4190 at Hop Pole Inn, bear L in 100yds down Tanners Hill. Follow single track rd approx 500yds. Parking in field.* Home-made teas. **Adm £3, chd free. Sat 21 May (11-5).**
½ -acre garden, looked after for over 40yrs by same owners, who seem to be getting the hang of it at last! Set among C18 farm buildings and old cherry, pear and apple orchards (SSSI), with fine long views. Informal planting of interesting trees, shrubs and herbaceous, around a lawn, old cider press and stone troughs, pond and seating. An ever-growing collection of clematis. Why not stroll through nearby ancient Wyre Forest after your tea?. Some narrow paths of bark and grass.

BROAD MARSTON & PEBWORTH GARDENS
See Warwickshire.

10 NEW BROOK FARM
Berrington, nr Tenbury Wells WR15 8TJ. Sarah & William Wint. *2m W of Tenbury Wells. From Tenbury take A4112 towards Leominster. After 3m turn R, follow to end/parking signs.* Home-made teas. **Adm £3, chd free. Fri 24 June (12-5).**
A relaxed country garden. It's been described as a cottage garden, wildlife garden and chaotic garden. To paraphrase the lovely Eric Morecambe 'They're all the right plants, just not necessarily in the right order'. 1½ -acre garden, 7 acres woodland and wilderness. His and her guides, teas, some weeds.

11 NEW BYLANE
Worcester Road, Earls Croome WR8 9DA. Shirley & Fred Bloxsome. *1m N of Upton on Severn turning. On main A38 directly past Earls Croome Garden Centre, signed Bridle Way.* Home-made teas. **Adm £3, chd free. Weds 6 Apr; 1 June (11-4).**
Herbaceous garden, paddock with pond (wildlife), small vegetable garden, chickens, wood with mature trees and bluebells. Sensible shoes needed.

CAVES FOLLY NURSERY
See Herefordshire.

12 1 CHURCH COTTAGE
Defford WR8 9BJ. John Taylor. *3m SW of Pershore. A4104 Pershore to Upton rd, turn into Defford, black & . white cottage at side of church. Parking in village hall car park.* Light refreshments & home-made teas. Adm £2.50, chd free. **Sats, Suns 30 Apr, 1 May; 28, 29 May (11-5).** True countryman's ¹/₃ -acre garden. Interesting layout, with new Japanese -style feature. Specimen trees; water features; vegetable garden; aviary, poultry and cider making.

13 CONDERTON MANOR
nr Tewkesbury GL20 7PR. Mr & Mrs W Carr, 01386 725389, carrs@conderton.wanadoo.co.uk. *5¹/₂ m NE of Tewkesbury. On Bredon - Beckford rd or from A46 take Overbury sign at Beckford turn.* **Adm £4. Visitors welcome by appt.**
7-acre garden, recently replanted in a contemporary style with magnificent views of Cotswolds. Flowering cherries and bulbs in spring. Formal terrace with clipped box parterre; huge rose and clematis arches, mixed borders of roses and herbaceous plants, bog bank and quarry garden. Many unusual trees and shrubs make this a garden to visit at all seasons. Featured in Worcestershire Life & Cotswold Life. Mainly grass paths, steep slopes.

14 THE COTTAGE
Broughton Green, Droitwich WR9 7EF. Terry Dagley, 01905 391670. *5m E of Droitwich. B4090 4m towards Feckenham. Turn R at sign Broughton Green & Earls Common. 1m (just before T junction) Cottage up track on R, 300yds.* Teas. Adm £3, chd free. **Weds 9, 30 Mar; 11 May; 22 June; 13 July; 24 Aug; 14 Sept (2-5). Visitors also welcome by appt.**
Plantsmans ¹/₂ -acre garden, structured by formal hedges, topiary and mature fruit trees. Year round colour and interest provided by unusual plants and shrubs. Special 9 month coloured grass area Sept to May by bulbs and tubers, plus snowdrops and crocus lawns in spring. Exhibition of paintings and prints by owner.

15 ◆ CROOME PARK
nr High Green WR8 9DW. National Trust, 01905 371006, www.nationaltrust.org.uk/croomepark. *4m W of Pershore. Signed from A38 & B4084.* **Adm £6.50, chd £3.25. For NGS: Fri 7 Oct (10-5).** For other opening times and information, please phone or see garden website.
700 acre landscape park designed by Capability Brown in mid 18th. Restored shrubberies and flowering studs, ornamental lake and restored parkland. Featured on BBC The One Show, A place in the Country - Midlands Today and in local press.

16 DIAL PARK
Chaddesley Corbett DY10 4QB. David & Olive Mason, 01562 777451, olivemason75@btinternet.com. *4¹/₂ m from Kidderminster, 4¹/₂ m from Bromsgrove. On A448 midway between Kidderminster & Bromsgrove. Limited parking at garden, or park in village or at village hall.* Adm £3, chd free. **Wed 23 Feb (11-4). Visitors also welcome by appt all yr-round for groups & individuals, coaches permitted.**
A garden for all seasons with a wide variety of plants, many rare. Approx ³/₄ -acre in rural setting. Specialities incl large collection of snowdrops, old varieties of daffodils, primroses and hardy ferns. Small collection of country tools and bygones. Featured in Gardens Monthly.

DORSINGTON GARDENS
See Warwickshire.

GROUP OPENING

17 ECKINGTON GARDENS
WR10 3BH, 01386 751924. *A4104 (from B4084 through Pershore) to Upton & Defford, L turn B4080 to Tewkesbury/Eckington, R Drakes Bridge Rd, L Manor Rd round s bend - 2nd entrance on R, stonewall entrance.* Light refreshments & home-made teas at Brook House; wine at The Croft. **Combined adm £4, chd free. Sat 28, Sun 29 May (11-5).**

BROOK HOUSE
Manor Road. George & Lynn Glaze

THE CROFT
Upper End. Mr & Mrs M J Tupper.
Garden has electric gates, admission requires pressing a button on a VDU screen to obtain entrance
Visitors also welcome by appt. 01386 750819

NAFFORD HOUSE
Nafford Road. Janet & John Wheatley.
From the Xrds in centre of Eckington (by war memorial) Take rd, signed The Combertons (L if coming from Worcester), follow for 3m. On L at top of hill

3 diverse cottage and formal gardens with topiary, ponds and wildlife. Set in lovely village of Eckington with riverside parking, picnic site. Brook House: 1-acre cottage garden with perennial planting, large pond with koi, surrounded by alpine rockery. The Croft; a formal garden with fish pond, topiary, dew pond with ducks and geese. Hedges & stone paths, gazebo overlooking garden. Nafford House is a 2 acre mature natural garden with slopes to R Avon. Formal gardens around house and magnificent wisteria. Gravel paths.

> A formal garden
> with fish pond,
> topiary, dew pond
> with ducks and
> geese . . .

18 FROGS NEST
8 Stratford Road, Honeybourne, Evesham WR11 7PP. Nina & Steve Bullen. *6m E of Evesham. 5m N of Broadway, 5m S of Bidford. Parking at the Gate Inn.* Light refreshments. Adm £3, chd free. **Suns 15 May; 3 July; 25 Sept (11-5).**
Small garden is worth the journey! 2 quite different gardens make it a special visit. Front garden is quite formal with herbaceous borders and tongue-in-cheek woodland walk complete with boathouse. Back garden has ponds and all-yr colour interest.

Brook Farm

1-acre site consists of beds and borders accessed by bark paths, with several seating areas giving views over the garden. Featured in The English Garden, Worcs Evening News, Gloucester Echo, BBC Hereford & on Worcester Radio.
❀ ☕

22 ◆ **HARVINGTON HALL**
Harvington DY10 4LR. The Roman Catholic Archdiocese of Birmingham, 01562 777846, www.harvingtonhall.com. *3m SE of Kidderminster. ½ m E of A450 Birmingham to Worcester Rd & about ½ m N of A448 from Kidderminster to Bromsgrove.* **Adm £3, chd £1, concessions £2. For NGS: Sat 2, Sun 3 July (11.30-4).** For other opening times and information, please phone or see garden website.
Romantic Elizabethan moated manor house with island gardens, small Elizabethan-style herb garden, all tended by volunteers. Tours of the Hall, which contains secret hiding places and rare wall paintings, are also available.
♿ ❀ ☕

23 **HIGH BANK**
Cleobury Road, Bewdley DY12 2PG. Stuart & Ann McKie, 01299 401342, stuartmckie135@hotmail.com. *3½ m W of Kidderminster. A456. ½ m W of Bewdley town centre on B4190 (signed Tenbury). Parking available opp garden entrance.* Home-made teas. **Adm £3, chd free. Suns 26 June; 7 Aug (11-5). Visitors also welcome by appt June to mid July.**
Award winning mature garden approx ⅓ acre surrounded by many old and protected trees. Restored in keeping with Edwardian house (not open). Large collection of roses, hemerocallis, herbaceous borders, courtyard garden, pergola walk, secret children's garden with gazebo, new woodland garden in development. Winner of 1st prize in Large Garden - Bewdley in Bloom 2010.
🏮 ❀ ☕ ☎

24 **HIGH VIEW**
Martley WR6 6PW. Mike & Carole Dunnett, 01886 821559, mike.dunnett@virgin.net. *1m S of Martley. On B4197 between Martley & A44 at Knightwick.* Home-made teas. **Adm £4, chd free.**

19 ◆ **THE GREYFRIARS**
Friar Street, Worcester WR1 2LZ. National Trust, 01905 23571, www.nationaltrust.org.uk. *In Friar Street within the centre of Worcester. Please use city car parks.* **Adm £2 (incl NT members), chd free. For NGS: Mon 9 May (11-4.30).** For other opening times and information, please phone or see garden website.
Delightful city garden created from the clearance of back to back housing. An archway leads through to the walled garden containing an eclectic mix of styles and plants.
❀

20 ◆ **HANBURY HALL**
School Road, Droitwich, Hanbury WR9 7EA. National Trust, 01527 821214, hanburyhall@nationaltrust.org.uk. *3m NE of Droitwich. 6m S of Bromsgrove. Signed off B4090 and B4091.* **Garden adm £6, chd £3. For NGS: Sat 16 July (11-5).** For other opening times and information, please phone or see email.
Re-creation of C18 formal garden by

George London. Parterre, fruit garden and wilderness. Mushroom house, orangery and ice house, William and Mary style house dating from 1701. Opportunity to meet the gardeners and to see behind the scenes in the Walled Garden.
♿ ❀ ☕

21 ◆ **HARRELLS HARDY PLANTS NURSERY GARDEN**
Rudge Road, Evesham WR11 4JR. Liz Nicklin & Kate Phillips, 01386 443077, www.harrellshardyplants.co.uk. *¼ m from centre of Evesham. From High St turn into Queens Rd opp Catholic church. Turn R at end of Queens Rd, then L into Rudge Rd. Approx 150yds on R is a small lane to nursery gardens.* **Adm £2.50, chd free. For NGS: Suns 5, 26 June; 10, 24 July; 4, 18 Sept; Thurs 16 June, 14 July (2-5).** For other opening times and information, please phone or see garden website.
This garden is naturalistic in style and informally planted with a glorious array of hardy perennials, grasses and a large range of hemerocallis. The

Sun 7 Aug (11-5). Visitors also welcome by appt.
Intriguing and mature 2½ acre garden developed over 35yrs. Visitors have described the garden as magical, inspirational and one of the best kept horticultural secrets of Worcestershire! With its superb views over the Teme valley, vast range of plants and many interesting features, it is a garden not to be missed. Diisplay of garden sculptures. Access to garden via steep slopes and steps.

HIRAETH
30 Showell Road, Droitwich WR9 8UY. Sue & John Fletcher, 07752 717243 / 01905 778390, jfletcher@inductotherm.co.uk. *1m S of Droitwich. On The Ridings estate. Turn off A38 r'about into Addyes Way, 2nd R into Showell Rd, 500yds on R. Follow the yellow signs!* Home-made teas. **Adm £3, chd free. Weds 11 May; 29 June; 10 Aug (12-5) ; Suns 12 June; 17 July (2-6).** Visitors also welcome by appt.
'A haven on the way to heaven' - description in Visitors Book. Front, rear gardens contain unusual plants, traditional cottage garden, herbaceous, hostas, ferns, arches, pool, waterfall, 200yr-old stile, oak sculptures, metal animals, birds etc including, giraffes, elephant. An oasis of colours in a garden not to be missed.

HUNTERS END
Button Bridge Lane, Button Bridge. Kinlet, Bewdley DY12 3DW. Norma & Colin Page, 01299 841055, norma_and_colin@hotmail.co.uk. *6m NW of Bewdley. A4194 from Bewdley at Button Bridge, turn R down Button Bridge Lane, garden ¾ m on L (look for horses heads).* Home-made teas. **Adm £3, chd free. Suns 22 May; 19 June (11.30-5).** Visitors also welcome by appt May - Aug, mini coaches accepted.
This ¾ -acre garden with plants and decorative features will create a smile and a laugh from beginning to end of your tour. Quirky displays enhance the humour. Soak up the atmosphere and tranquillity of the garden. Relax in one of the many seating areas and enjoy your tea and cake. Jams, curd, marmalade, chutney & sauces for sale. Featured in Amateur Gardening. Some gravel. Partly sloping.

GROUP OPENING

LAYTON AVENUE GARDENS
Malvern WR14 2ND. *7m S of Worcester, 5m NW of Upton on Severn. From Worcester approach Malvern on A449. Turn L at r'about into Townsend Way (signed A4208 Welland). After 3 r'abouts take 2nd R (Charles Way), then 2nd L into Layton Ave. From Upton approach Malvern on A4211. Take 3rd exit at Barnards Green r'about (Pickersleigh Rd). After 1m turn R at T-lights (signed A4208) Worcester) take 2nd L, then 2nd L again.* Home-made teas at all venues. **Combined adm £3.50, chd free (share to Acorns Hospice, Worcester). Sat 11, Sun 12 June (11-4).**

10 LAYTON AVENUE
David Ranford

22 LAYTON AVENUE
Brian & Jenny Bradford
Visitors also welcome by appt July/Aug only. Groups of 10 - 15. 01684 565 994

159 PICKERSLEIGH ROAD
Phil & Karen Hopkinson.
Round the corner from 10 Layton Ave

This group comprises three quite different gardens. At No. 10 Layton Avenue the garden surrounds the house. To the front and side are lawns and borders stocked with shrubs and perennial flowers. To the rear a secluded courtyard garden with raised pond, containing Koi carp and an unusual fountain.At 22 Layton Avenue the garden is in three parts. To the front are raised shrubbery beds. To the rear is a lawn area with well stocked borders, gazebos, pond and streamside garden reached via steps and bridge. There will be an exhibition of Jenny Bradford's paintings and carvings. 159 Pickersleigh Road features lawns, surrounded with mixed borders and bisected by a pond fed by its own stream with waterfalls. There are also greenwood structures created by Phil Hopkinson and a large fruit and vegetable area. Dogs welcome at 159 Pickersleigh Road only. Plant sales at 22 Layton Ave & 159 Pickersleigh Rd. Featured in Malvern Gazette & Worcester Evening News. Disabled access at 10 Layton Avenue.

LITTLE MALVERN COURT
Little Malvern WR14 4JN. Mrs T M Berington, 01684 892988, littlemalverncourt@hotmail.com. *3m S of Malvern. On A4104 S of junction with A449.* Tea & cakes. **Adm £5, chd 50p. For NGS: Sun 20 Mar (2-5).** For other opening times and information, please phone or email.
10 acres attached to former Benedictine Priory, magnificent views over Severn valley. Intriguing layout of garden rooms and terrace round house designed and planted in early 1980s; water garden below feeding into chain of lakes; wide variety of spring bulbs, flowering trees and shrubs. Notable collection of old-fashioned roses. Topiary hedge and fine trees.

LONGACRE
See Herefordshire.

'A haven on the way to heaven' – description in Visitors Book . . .

LUGGERS HALL
Springfield Lane, Broadway WR12 7BT. Kay & Red Haslam. *5m S of Evesham. Turn off Broadway High St by Swan Hotel, bear L into Springfield Lane. Luggers Hall is on the L approx 300yds along. Some parking but limited - if possible use car parks which are close by.* Home-made teas. **Adm £3, chd free. Suns 29 May; 19 June (2-6).**
2½ -acre formal garden originally designed by the famous Victorian garden artist Alfred Parsons. Features incl rose garden; parterre; walled garden; potager; white garden; koi pool and herbaceous borders, all connected by gravel paths with seating areas. An abundance of clipped box and yew hedging; plus Victorian hazel walk. Children with caution due to deep water feature. Featured in Worcestershire Life. Gravel paths.

GROUP OPENING

30 MARLBROOK GARDENS
Bromsgrove B60 1DY,
www.marlbrookgardens.com. *2m N of Bromsgrove. 1m N of M42 J1, follow B4096 signed Rednal, turn L at Xrds into Braces Lane. 1m S of M5 J4, follow A38 signed Bromsgove, turn L at T-lights into Braces Lane. Parking available.* **Combined adm £5, chd free. Suns 29 May; 10 July; 14 Aug (1.30-5.30). Evening Opening £6, wine, Sat 10 Sept (6.30-10).** Visitors also welcome by appt (groups of 10+ preferred) to all, two or individual gardens from mid May to end Sept. Coaches welcome, lunches by prior arrangement for larger groups.

OAK TREE HOUSE
504 Birmingham Road. Di & Dave Morgan
Visitors also welcome by appt.
0121 445 3595
meandi@btinternet.com

ROUND HILL GARDEN
24 Braces Lane. Lynn & Alan Nokes
Visitors also welcome by appt.
0121 445 5520
alyn.nokes@btinternet.com

SARANACRIS
28A Braces Lane. John & Janet Morgan
Visitors also welcome by appt.
0121 445 5823
saranacris@btinternet.com

Can you afford to miss this opportunity to experience a trio of unique gardens, rated by one national paper in the top small gardens open to the public? Each an individually stunning garden, together they offer breathtaking experience of contrasting styles and topography from gentle slopes to the steep terraces of a former sand quarry. Gardens styles incl jungle, traditional and cottage garden, all overflowing with an abundance of plants for sun and shade, incl rare exotics and vegetables areas. Streams, ponds, patios, artefacts, sculptures, glass houses and special collections add to the individuality of the gardens. Recognised for excellence, the gardens are continually evolving and our many repeat visitors enjoy sharing with us their new discoveries. Visit us during the year and then come along to our party celebration in September, journey through a myriad of lights sparkling throughout all the gardens,
with a glass of wine in hand. Sept only - All gardens illuminated from dusk.

🌼 ☕ ☎

31 MEADOW FARM
33 Droitwich Road, Feckenham B96 6RU. Robert & Diane Cole, 01527 821156, meadowfarm33@aol.com. *½ m W of Feckenham. On B4090, Droitwich Rd.* Home-made teas. **Adm £4 incl tea, chd free. Visitors welcome by appt** for groups 20+, coach welcome.
1-acre garden created since 1999 by enthusiastic husband and wife team, and intensively planted with herbaceous perennials. Particularly colourful between June and Sept, but planted for all season interest. 1¼ acre wild flower meadow, and ¾ acre nursery not normally open to the public. Worcestershire's best kept secret. Featured in The English Garden.

🌼 ☕ ☎

32 NEW 74 MEADOW ROAD
74 Meadow Road, Wythall B47 6EQ. Joe Manchester, 01564 829589. *4m E of Alvechurch. 2m from J3 M42 take A435 to Wythall.* Home-made teas. **Adm £2.50, chd free. Sat 28, Sun 29 May (2-5).** Visitors also welcome by appt.
An urban garden dedicated to woodland, shade-loving plants. 'Expect the unexpected' in a few tropical and foreign species. Meander through the garden under the majestic pine, eucalyptus and silver birch. Sit and enjoy the peaceful surroundings and see how many different ferns and hostas you can find.

🌼 ☕ ☎

33 MODEL FARM
Montpelier Road, West Malvern WR14 4BP. Deirdre & Phil Drake. *W side of Malvern Hills. West Malvern Rd, B4232 at Elim Pentecostal H.Q (stately stone building). Turn immed down Croft Bank then 200yds turn L into Montpelier Road. Narrow private no-through rd with limited turning space. Visitors are requested to park on Croft Bank & walk down Montpelier Road (250 yards) to Model Farm.* Home-made teas. **Adm £4, chd free. Suns 8, 22 May; 5 June (2-5.30).**
Stunning 2-acre tranquil garden in the Malvern Hills. Victorian tudor-style
house (not open) surrounded by well-stocked borders, patio and courtyard. Picturesque contours of garden complemented by natural stream, ponds, mixed borders, orchard, bog garden, meadow. Ancient oaks, specimen trees, acers, panoramic views to Hay Bluff. Steep in some areas. Wonderful spring bulbs, wisteria and clematis. Three wildlife ponds with common, palmate and great-crested newts. Featured in BBC Hereford & Worcester Gardening Show.

🌼 ☕

MOSELEY GARDENS SOUTH
See Staffordshire Birmingham & part of West Midlands.

34 NEW NEW HOUSE FARM, CUTNALL GREEN
Droitwich Spa WR9 0PW. Mrs Rachel Barnes, 01299 851013, barnes.p7@sky.com. *A442 Droitwich to Kidd rd. Enter village of Cutnall Green after sign on L. New House Farm is located.* Home-made teas in tea room. **Adm £3.50, chd free. Sats, Suns 25, 26 June; 30, 31 July (10-5).** Visitors also welcome by appt June & July only.
1 acre of country garden surrounding Victorian farmhouse (not open), offering many old features, with new planting schemes and views over open countryside giveing this garden a wealth of interest. The creativity is abundant due to resident designer who runs an interior design/craft shop and tea room. Hatfield Interiors in garden grounds offers tea room, interior design gifts for the home and garden, craft workshops, a hub of ideas for both home and garden. Gravel paths in vegetable garden and some areas of parking.

♿ 🐕 🌼 ☎

35 NEW HOUSE FARM, ELMBRIDGE
Elmbridge Lane, Elmbridge WR9 0DA. Charles & Carlo Caddick, 01299 851249. *2½ m N of Droitwich Spa. From Droitwich take A442 to Cutnall Green. Take lane opp The Chequers PH and proceed 1m to T-junction, turning L towards Elmbridge Green & Elmbridge. Continue along lane passing church and church hall. At T-junction turn into Elmbridge Lane, garden on L.* Home-made teas. **Adm £4, chd free. Visitors welcome by appt** May to July & Sept, 10 to 55 visitors, coaches permitted.

This charming garden surrounding an early C19 red brick house, has a wealth of rare trees and shrubs under planted with unusual bulbs and herbaceous plants. Special features are the 'perry wheel', ornamental vegetable gardens. Water garden, dry garden, rose garden, mews, the retreat, potager and greenhouse. Topiary and tropical plants complete the effect.

Rose Villa

36 NEW OLD CASTLE FARM
Evendine Lane, Colwell, Malvern WR13 6YS. June & Clive Greig-Bartram. *From Ledbury take A449 Worcester Road, after approx 3m turn L B4218 signed Colwell. From Great Malvern take A449 towards Ledbury after approx 1/2 m turn R B4218 signed Colwall. Drive through Colwell Village to T-lights on Bridge.* Light refreshments & teas. **Adm £4, chd free. Sun 18 Sept (11-4).**
Shakespeare's Falstaff was St John Old Castle a Yeoman and Old Castle Farm was owned by him. He was tried for treason for being a Lollardy, political religious movement. Why not tread his garden which consists of large informal gardens in progress and walk The Fish Ponds. A poem was written about the ponds centuries ago which was a square moat in his time. Stream, pergola planted with roses, trees and wisteria, a secluded rose garden with lots of lovely walks, constant planting schemes, best views in the area. I hope we have whetted your appetite. Come and see this new garden develop from the early stages 'A new garden in progress'. No coaches.

THE ORCHARDS
See Herefordshire.

37 ORLETON HOUSE
Orleton, Stanford Bridge WR6 6SU. Jenny & John Hughes, 01584 381253, jenny@orleton.co.uk, www.orletonhouse.co.uk. *6m E of Tenbury Wells. 15m NW of Worcester. A443 from Worcester for 10m then B4203 towards Bromyard. Cross R Teme at Stanford Bridge then next R turn. 1m down this lane.* **Visitors welcome by appt** May to July, groups welcome with lunch, high tea or supper min 20, max 50. Individuals may visit with pre-purchased tickets only, please see website.
Approx 3 acres surrounding C19

Grade II listed building (not open) in the heart of the beautiful Teme Valley. Borders with rare and unusual plants alongside familiar cottage garden favourites. Magnificent mature trees, hidden tree house, magical shaded walks, natural stream, gravelled terrace with sun-loving flowers in abundance. Croquet lawn, small orchard, wooded areas and paddocks complete an idyllic setting.

38 OVERBURY COURT
nr Tewkesbury GL20 7NP. Mr & Mrs Bruce Bossom, 01386 725111, garden@overbury.org. *5m NE of Tewkesbury. Village signed off A46.* **Adm £3.50 pp, min charge £15. Visitors welcome by appt.**
Georgian house 1740 (not open); landscape garden of same date with stream and pools; daffodil bank and grotto. Plane trees, yew hedges; shrubs; cut flowers; coloured foliage; gold and silver, shrub rose borders. Norman church adjoins garden. Some slopes, while all the garden can be viewed, parts are not accessible to wheelchairs.

39 PERSHORE GARDENS
Pershore WR10 1BG, 01386 553197, www.visitpershore.co.uk. *On the B4004 between Worcester and Evesham. Tickets and maps can be obtained from Number 8 Community Arts Centre opp Angel Hotel or any garden.* Light refreshments & teas at No. 8 Arts Centre, The Abbey Tea Rooms, The

Holy Redeemer School. **Combined adm £6, chd free. Sun 12 June (1-6).**
Explore a variety approx 18 - 20 of large and small gardens in the market town of Pershore. These include gardens tucked away behind Georgian town houses, gardens which sweep down to R Avon, tiny courtyards and walled gardens, gardens with beautiful views and a Primary School garden. The Angel Hotel, The Star and Brandy Cask will be serving lunches and all have riverside gardens. Teas will be served at various locations.

THE PICTON GARDEN
See Herefordshire.

40 4 PODEN COTTAGES
Honeybourne WR11 7PS. Patrick & Dorothy Bellew, 01386 438996, pots@poden.freeserve.co.uk. *6m E of Evesham. At the Gate Inn take the Pebworth, Long Marston rd, turn R at end of the Village for Mickleton. 1m on Mickleton Rd.* Home-made teas. **Adm £3, chd free. Sun 24, Mon 25 Apr (11-5); Sun 19 June (2-6). Visitors welcome by appt.**
1/3 -acre cottage garden which has been planted by the owners. Paths wind through mixed herbaceous borders. Roses old and modern, shrubs, small terrace and pond. Fine views over the Cotswold Hills. All-yr colour. Small vegetable garden. Gravel drive.

41▶ PUMP COTTAGE
Hill Lane, Weatheroak B48 7EQ.
Barry Knee & Sue Hunstone,
01564 826250,
barryknee.1947@btinternet.com.
*3m E of Alvechurch. 1¹/₂ m from J3
M42 off N-bound c'way of A435
(signed Alvechurch). Parking in
adjacent field.* Home-made teas.
Adm £3, chd free. **Sat 18, Sun 19,
Mon 20 June (11-5).** Visitors also
welcome by appt Apr-Oct, groups
welcome.
C19 cottage in rural setting.
Enchanting, romantic 1-acre
'plantaholic's garden. Extensively
planted, colourful borders, roses,
rockery, water features, bog garden,
large natural pool, water lilies and
wildlife area. Victorian style
greenhouse, brick features, folly,
numerous artefacts and ornaments.
New fernery. Continually developing,
especially unusual woodland plants
and bulbs for springtime. Featured on
BBC's Open Gardens. Restricted
wheelchair access.
&⬤ ☕ ☎

RAGLEY HALL GARDENS
See Warwickshire.

42▶ RECTORY COTTAGE
Old Rectory Lane, Alvechurch B48
7SU. Celia Hitch. *From A441 at
Alvechurch, turn into Old Rectory
Lane, continue along, after sharp R
bend, next house on L.* Home-made
teas. Adm £3, chd Free. **Sun 5 June
(1-6).**
Courtyard garden with pergolas and
many plants including roses and
hostas. Aviary with budgerigars.
Wonderful long, riverside gardens -

secret garden, waterside borders,
patios, 'dragon's den', bridge, ponds,
waterfall.
🛏 ☕

43▶ ♦ RED HOUSE FARM
Flying Horse Lane, Bradley Green
B96 6QT. Mrs M M Weaver,
01527 821269,
www.redhousefarmgardenand
nursery.co.uk. *7m W of Redditch. On
B4090 Alcester to Droitwich Spa.
Ignore sign to Bradley Green. Turn
opp The Red Lion PH.* Adm £2, chd
free. **For NGS: Every Thurs 3 Mar
to 6 Oct (11-5). For other opening
times and information, please
phone or see garden website.**
Created as a peaceful haven from its
working farm environment, this
mature country garden offers yr-round
interest. In densely planted borders a
wide range of traditional favourites rub
shoulders with the newest of
introductions and make each visit a
pleasurable and rewarding
experience. Adjacent nursery open
daily 10-5. Featured in Redditch
Advertiser, Bromsgrove Advertiser &
Worcester Evening News.
⬤

**44▶ ♦ RIVERSIDE GARDENS AT
WEBBS OF WYCHBOLD**
Wychbold, nr Droitwich WR9 0DG.
Webbs of Wychbold, 01527
860000, www.webbsdirect.co.uk.
*2m N of Droitwich Spa. 1m N of M5
J5 on A38. Follow tourism signs from
motorway.* **Adm free for NGS to
gardens all yr. For opening times
and information, please phone or
see garden website.**
2¹/₂ acres. Themed gardens incl

National Collection of Shrubby
Potentilla. Colour spectrum, tropical
and dry garden, David Austin Rose
collection, grassery and
bamboozelum. New Wave gardens
opened in 2004, designer Noel
Kingsberry, to create natural seasonal
interest with grasses and perennials.
The patio gardens are 6 themed
gardens which showcase what to do
with a small space.
& ⬤ **NCCPG**

45▶ ROSE VILLA
Main Street, Beckford GL20 7AD.
*5m NE of Tewkesbury. Off A46
between Tewkesbury & Evesham.
Approx 5m from J9 M5. Centre of
village opp church.* Home-made teas.
Adm £3.50, chd free. **Sun 19 June
(2-6).**
Created in 2000 in a wilderness
behind an early C19th house (not
open). The designer Charles
Rutherfoord met the owner's request
for a brick built garden room and
water feature (canal), these are the
centrepiece of the garden which
combines a small wild flower
meadow, neat lawns and traditional
elements with luxurious planting to
give a contemporary feeling. Gravel in
front garden (point of entry, approx
50yds).
& 🌿 ☕

46▶ ROUND LODGE
5 Court Mews, Jennett Tree Lane,
Callow End WR2 4UA. Cathy
Snelgar. *4m S of Worcester. From
Worcester take A449 Malvern Rd to
Powick, L onto B4429 signed Upton,
to Callow End, turn R in Jennett Tree
Lane, Stanbrook Abbey on corner.
Court Mews is ¹/₂ m on L. Disabled
parking only next to house, park in
lane.* Home-made teas. Adm £3, chd
free. **Sun 4 Sept (11-5).**
¹/₄ -acre country garden within part of
early Victorian walled garden. 2
distinct areas divided by original
kitchen garden wall. Colour themed
borders, original pond, island bed,
lawns and terrace. Through wall to
small shade garden, orchard and
kitchen garden. Delightful evocative
garden with many old features. Some
gravel paths.
& ⬤ ☕

47▶ SEECHEM MANOR
Rowney Green Lane, Alvechurch
B48 7EL. B & Nicky Sethia,
0121 445 2240,
nicolasethia@hotmail.co.uk. *1¹/₂ m
SE of Alvechurch. 3¹/₂ m from J2 M42*

Little Malvern Court

take A441 Birmingham, follow signs to Alvechurch. From village turn L into Radford Rd, proceed 1m turn R into Rowney Green Lane. Light refreshments & home-teas. **Adm £3.50, chd free. Sat 11 June, Suns 12 June; 10 July (11-5). Visitors also welcome by appt June & Aug only. Groups of 10+, coaches permitted, refreshments available.** Oak tree lined drive with wildlife pond and meadow. 3-acre garden surrounding the medieval grade 2* manor house (not open). Climbing roses, clematis and wisterias adorn the property. Herbaceous borders, rose walk, ponds with water feature and abundant wildlife create a peaceful rural haven. The orchard vegetable garden and mixed poultry provide yr round produce. Arts and crafts exhibition.

48 SHUTTIFIELD COTTAGE
Birchwood, Storridge WR13 5HA. Mr & Mrs David Judge, 01886 884243, judge.shutti@btinternet.com. *8m W of Worcester. Turn R off A4103 opp Storridge Church to Birchwood. After 1¼ m L down steep tarmac drive. Please park on roadside but drive down if walking is difficult.* Home-made teas under thatch. **Adm £3.50, chd free. Sats 30 Apr; 14 May; 4, 25 June; 16 July; 20 Aug; 17 Sept (1.30-5). Visitors also welcome by appt, no coaches.** Superb position and views. Unexpected 3-acre plantsman's garden, extensive herbaceous borders, primula and stump bed, many unusual trees, shrubs, perennials, colour-themed for all-yr interest. Walks in 20-acre wood with ponds, natural wild areas, anemones, bluebells, rhododendrons, azaleas are a particular spring feature. Large old rose garden with many spectacular mature climbers. Good garden colour throughout the yr. Small deer park, vegetable garden.

49 ◆ SPETCHLEY PARK GARDENS
Spetchley WR5 1RS. Mr John Berkeley, 01453 810303, www.spetchleygardens.co.uk. *2m E of Worcester. On A44, follow brown signs.* Adm £6, chd free, concessions £5.50. **For NGS: Fri 22 Apr; Sun 3 July (11-6). For other opening times and information, please phone or see**

garden website.
Surrounded by glorious countryside and deer park, virtually hidden from the road, this 30-acre Victorian paradise, belonging to the Berkeley family has been lovingly created by successive generations and boasts an enviable collection of plant treasures from every corner of the globe. Partial wheelchair access.

STANTON GARDENS
See Gloucestershire North & Central.

50 ◆ STONE HOUSE COTTAGE GARDENS
Stone DY10 4BG. James & Louisa Arbuthnott, 01562 69902, www.shcn.co.uk. *2m SE of Kidderminster. Via A448 towards Bromsgrove, next to church, turn up drive.* Adm £3, chd free. **For times and information, please phone or see garden website.**
A beautiful and romantic walled garden adorned with unusual brick follies. This acclaimed garden is exuberantly planted and holds one of the largest collections of rare plants in the country. It acts as a shop window for the adjoining nursery. Partial wheelchair access.

51 TOLL HOUSE COTTAGE
Stourport Road, Bewdley DY12 1PU. Joan & Rob Roberts, 01299 402331. *1m S of Bewdley. 2m N of Stourport, 3m W of Kidderminster. On A456 between Bewdley & Stourport, Opp Blackstone car park & picnic site (free parking). Disabled parking on drive.* Home-made teas. **Adm £3, chd free. Sun 15 May (11-5); 17 July (11.30). Visitors also welcome by appt.** Developing 0.4 acre garden started in 2008 in 2 sections. An informal collection of herbaceous and shrubs around a lawn. Developing mini arboretum and grass walks, vegetable patch and natural pond with beach for wildlife. A painter's garden. Painting and woodturning studio open for viewing.

Lovely view of
the church and
surrounding
countryside . . .

52 THE TYNINGS
Church Lane, Stoulton, nr Worcester WR7 4RE. John & Leslie Bryant, 01905 840189, john.bryant@onetel.com. *5m S of Worcester; 3m N of Pershore. On the B4084 (formerly A44) between M5 J7 & Pershore. The Tynings lies beyond the church at the extreme end of Church Lane. Ample parking.* Home-made teas (Sun). Light refreshments (Fri). **Adm £3, chd free. Sun 31 July (2-5). Evening Opening Sat 6 Aug (6-8). Visitors also welcome by appt late May to Aug, coaches permitted.** Acclaimed plantsman's ½ -acre garden, generously planted with a large selection of rare trees and shrubs. Features incl specialist collection of lilies, many unusual climbers and rare ferns. The colour continues into late summer with dahlia, berberis, euonymus and tree colour. Surprises around every corner. You will not be disappointed. Highly praised by Roy Lancaster.

53 TYTHE BARN HOUSE
Chaddesley Corbett DY10 4QB. Judy & John Berrow, 01562 777014, jdberrow@btinternet.com. *4½ m from Bromsgrove; 4½ m from Kidderminster. On A448. 150yds towards Kidderminster from the turn into Chaddesley Corbett village Parking in village (The Talbot) or at village hall (200 yds). Walking difficulties park in private lane.* Adm £3, chd free. **Visitors welcome by appt groups of 10+, coaches must be notified. Refreshments on request.** Approx ¾ -acre romantic garden created in old farm rickyard, within old farm building complex in conservation area surrounded by sheep. Incl old and modern roses; herbs and herbaceous borders. Small terrace garden. Shrubs and trees together with vegetable plot and greenhouse. Lovely view of the church and surrounding countryside. Featured in Limited Edition, Garden News.

54 THE WALLED GARDEN
6 Rose Terrace, off Fort Royal Hill, Worcester WR5 1BU. Julia & William Scott. *½ m from cathedral. Via Fort Royal Hill, off London Rd (A44). Park on first section of Rose Terrace & walk the last 20yds down track.* Adm £3, chd free. **Sats 16 Apr; 25 June; 6 Aug (1-5).** History, symmetry and historic tributes

are the foundation of this peaceful oasis in a C19 walled kitchen garden. A tapestry of culinary and medicinal herbs, vegetables, flowers and fruit grow organically in herb and flower beds and potager. Whilst preserving its history, the garden continues to change and flourish.

55 WESTACRES
Wolverhampton Road, Prestwood DY7 5AN. Mrs Joyce Williams, 01384 877496. *3m W of Stourbridge. A449 in between Wall Heath (2m) & Kidderminster (6m). Ample parking Prestwood Nurseries (next door).* Home-made teas. **Adm £3, chd free. Sat 23, Sun 24 July (11-4).** Visitors also welcome by appt.
³/₄ -acre plant collector's garden, many different varieties of acers, hostas, shrubs. Woodland walk, large koi pool, covered tea area with home-made cakes. Come and see for yourselves, you won't be disappointed. Ample parking. Plant sales. Featured in local press & radio.

56 WHITCOMBE HOUSE
Overbury, nr Tewkesbury GL20 7NZ. Faith & Anthony Hallett, 01386 725206, faith@whitcombeassocs.co.uk. *9m S of Evesham. From M5 J9, A46 towards Evesham to r'about junction with A435 & B4077, 1st exit down small lane. From Cheltenham, A435 to A46/B4077 r'about above (2nd exit). From Evesham, R off A46 at Beckford Inn. From Tewkesbury, B4080 through Bredon, then straight on via Kemerton to Overbury.* Light refreshments & teas in village hall (May). Home-made teas (June & July). **Adm £2, chd free (May). Adm £3, chd free (June & July). Sat 14, Sun 15 May; (10-4); Suns 12 June; 3 July (2-5).** Visitors also welcome by appt even at very short notice, especially between daffodil flowering & Sept, groups 10+ preferred but not essential, coaches welcome.
1 acre walled garden planted for every season in a beautiful Cotswold village. After spring bulbs, a cool blue and white border and allium varieties take over before passing the baton the roses, summer pastels and fiery oranges, reds and yellows. The stream flows through self seeded primula, poppy and foxgloves, rose cascade and flowering shrubs abound. In late summer, asters and cosmos produce a blousy final flourish

and the roses keep on flowering. Lots of seats for contemplation and relaxation. Exhibition of quilting & stitch in adjoining village hall 14 & 15 May, proceeds of the day Share to Help for Heroes. Featured in Gloucester Echo & Worcestershire Life. For wheelchair access please contact us in advance for details.

57 WHITE COTTAGE
Earls Common Road, Stock Green, nr Inkberrow B96 6SZ. Mr & Mrs S M Bates, 01386 792414, cranesbilluk@aol.com. *2m W of Inkberrow, 2m E of Upton Snodsbury. A422 Worcester to Alcester, turn at sign for Stock Green by Red Hart PH, 1¹/₂ m to T- junction, turn L.* **Adm £2.50, chd free. Suns 22 May; 12 June (10-5).** Visitors also welcome by appt.
2 acres, herbaceous and shrub beds, stream and spring wild flower area, rose garden, raised woodland bed, large specialist collection of hardy geraniums and echinacea. Featured in Country Living.

58 ♦ WHITLENGE GARDENS
Whitlenge Lane, Hartlebury DY10 4HD. Mr & Mrs K J Southall, 01299 250720, keith.southall@ creativelandscapes.co.uk, www.creativelandscapes.co.uk. *5m S of Kidderminster, on A442. Take A449 from Kidderminster towards Worcester, then A442 (signed Droitwich) over small island, ¹/₄ m, 1st R into Whitlenge Lane. Follow signs.* **Adm £3, chd free. For NGS: Suns, Mons 24, 25 Apr; 1 2, 29, 30 May; 28, 29 Aug (9-5). For other opening times and information, please phone or see garden website.**
3 acre show garden of professional designer with over 800 varieties of trees, shrubs etc. Twisted pillar pergola, camomile lawn, waterfalls and pools. Mystic features of the Green Man, 'Sword in the Stone' and cave fernery. Walk the labyrinth and take refreshments in The Garden 'Design Studio' tearoom.

GROUP OPENING

59 WICK VILLAGE
WR10 3NU, 01386 550007. *1m E of Pershore on B4084, signed Post to Wick, almost opp Pershore*

Horticultural College. Home-made teas. **Combined adm £6, chd free. Sun 26 June (1-6).**

AALSMEER
Main Street. Peter Edmunds

NEW **THE BARN**
Main Street. Alison Scott

CONFETTI FIELD
Yock Lane. Charles Hudson
www.confettidirect.co.uk

NEW **LAMBOURNE HOUSE**
Main Street. Mr & Mrs G Power

THE OLD FORGE
Main Street. Sean & Elaine Young

NEW **RYECOT**
Owletts Lane. Margaret & Michael Williams

NEW **SHIELINGS**
Owletts Lane. Tony & Val Taylor

TUDOR HALL
Main Street. Mr & Mrs A Smart

VENEDIGER
Wick House Close. Alan & Barbara de Ville

5 WICK HOUSE CLOSE
Jill & Martin Willams

WILLOW CORNER
Wick House Close. Marjorie Donaldson

WOODWARDS HOUSE
Cooks Hill. Garth & Lynne Raymer

WYKE MANOR
Main Street. Charles Hudson

Once again Wick offers you the opportunity to see the spectacle of acres of farmland in colourful bloom before the harvest of flower petals for confetti. This year we have a group of very varied gardens ranging from the romantic Wyke Manor garden that has evolved over several hundred years, to those that have been designed only recently. With some gardens opening for the first time your tour will incl gardens with secluded spaces, courtyards with ornamental features, not to mention a garden with two giant Sequoiadendron giganteum (Wellingtonia). We also have gardens with fruit orchards, vegetable plots, and that have been created to become wildlife havens. Wick is the home of The Real Flower Petal Company featured on Countryfile & in many magazine articles.

60▶ 68 WINDSOR AVENUE
St Johns WR2 5NB. Roger &
Barbara Parker, 01905 428723,
robarpark@googlemail.com. *W area
of Worcester. Off the A44 to
Bromyard into Comer Road, 3rd L
into Laugherne Rd, 3rd L into
Windsor Ave.* Teas with cakes &
biscuits. **Adm £3, chd free. Sun 5
June (11-4).** Visitors also welcome
by appt max 25 visitors, no
coaches.
In a cul-de-sac, behind a 1930s semi-
detached house is almost 1 acre of
garden with 4 ponds in very different
styles. Split into 3 areas, the garden
has flower beds, bog gardens, an
'oriental' area and vegetable patch.
Plus 4 greenhouses and chickens.

GROUP OPENING

61▶ WITHYBED GREEN
B48 7PP, 0121 445 1321. *3m N of
Redditch. W of Alvechurch, 11m SW
of Birmingham. 6mins from J2 M42
signed N to Birmingham at 1st
r'about turn L signed Alvechurch.
From Redditch A441 to Bordesley
r'about. Take 1st exit on B4120 to
Alvechurch, via Tanyard Lane or Bear
Hill. Follow NGS signs along Snake
Lane & Withybed Lane. By rail
Alvechurch, with a pleasant 15min
stroll along towpath.* Home-made
teas. **Combined adm £5, chd free.
Sun 26 June (2-6).**

FAIRVIEW
Birches Lane. Bryan & Angela
Haycocks

6 FRONT COTTAGES
Withybed Green. Malcolm &
Juliet Horne

2 FRONT COTTAGES
Withybed Green. Ann & Clive
Southern

THE MOUSEHOLE
4 Forward Cottages. David &
Lucy Hastie

6 REAR COTTAGES
Withybed Green. John Adams &
Amelda Brown

SELVAS COTTAGE
Birches Lane. Mr & Mrs J L
Plewes

Withybed Green is a secret hamlet to
the W of Alvechurch set between
semi-wooded hillsides and the
Birmingham Worcester Canal. The
gardens provide a range of sizes and
styles to give interest for all - incl a
rose garden, ancient woodland,
allotments, small cottage gardens and
a stream-side walk. The site is
compact and in a charming
environment and you can easily walk
round all six. The houses and
cottages mostly date from C19, built
for farm workers, nail makers, canal
and railway builders. Withybed has its
own canal-side pub, The Crown.

**62▶ NEW▶ 21 WOODFARM
ROAD**
Malvern Wells WR14 4PL. Jill &
David Briggs, 01684 563446,
david@briggs34.wanadoo.co.uk.
*2m S of Great Malvern. Off B4209
(Hanley rd) close to Junction with
A449, signed Worcs Golf Club. Park
on rd immed on entering Woodfarm
Road.* Home-made teas. **Adm £2.50,
chd free. Sat 16, Sun 17 July (2-5).**
Visitors also welcome by appt
May-Oct, individuals and small
groups, daytime preferred.
Plantswoman's small garden featuring
a wide range of hardy herbaceous

perennials and shrubs, many with
coloured foliage. Sunny borders,
shady damp areas, stumpery with
ferns, raised blue and yellow bed,
packed with colour from May to Oct.
A visual feast. Steps and grassy
slope, so flat shoes advisable.

63▶ NEW▶ THE WOODLANDS
Dunclent, Stone, Kidderminster
DY10 4AY. Pat & Phil Gaskin. *2m SE
of Kidderminster. A448 Bromsgrove
rd. Turn into Dunclent Lane, follow
signs down narrow lane onto
unadopted rd, short distance.* Home-
made teas. **Adm £3, chd free. Suns
26 June; 24 July (11.30-4.30).**
Intriguing approx ³/₄ -acre garden in
rural woodland, open fields haven.
Developed last 7yrs, designed on
various levels, with secret winding
paths, steps to coloured themed
herbaceous/shrub borders, large
vegetable garden, tomato
greenhouses, all grown from seed.
Courtyard, waterfall, pergola walk,
pond, swimming pool garden,
hanging baskets and tubs.

64▶ WOODMANCOTE
Mill Lane, Wadborough WR8 9HB.
Ila Walmsley. *4m NW of Pershore.
Between Worcester & Pershore. Off
4084 Please park considerately at the
Masons Arms (400yds), bar meals
available.* Cream teas. **Adm £2.50,
chd free. Suns 22, 29, Mon 30 May
(11-5).**
³/₄ -acre, early summer garden. Wide
lawns, island beds with a relaxed style
of planting. Old and modern roses,
clematis. A riot of colour. 2 ponds.

WOODPECKERS
See Warwickshire.

Worcestershire County Volunteers

County Organiser
Judy Berrow, Tythe Barn House, Chaddesley Corbett DY10 4QB, 01562 777014, jdberrow@btinternet.com

County Treasurer
Cliff Woodward, 11 Trehernes Drive, Pedmore, Stourbridge DY9 0YX, 01562 886349

Publicity
David Morgan, Oak Tree House, 504 Birmingham Road, Marlbrook B61 0HS, 0121 445 3595, meandi@btinternet.com

Advertising & Leaflet Coordinator
Alan Nokes, 24 Braces Lane, Marlbrook, Bromsgrove B60 1DY, 0121 445 5520, alyn.nokes@btinternet.com

Assistant County Organisers
Richard Armitage, 11 Myatts Field, Harvington, Evesham WR11 8NG, 01386 871211
Valerie Austin, Primrose Cottage, 6 Wyre Hill, Bewdley DY12 2UE, Tel 01299 409441
Mike George, 55 Hawkwood Crescent, Worcester WR2 6BP, 01905 427567
Marie Paginton, Hillrise, Richmond Pitch, Kings Road, Malvern DY12 2UE, 01684 567039, mariepaginton@aol.com

Visit the website for latest information

YORKSHIRE

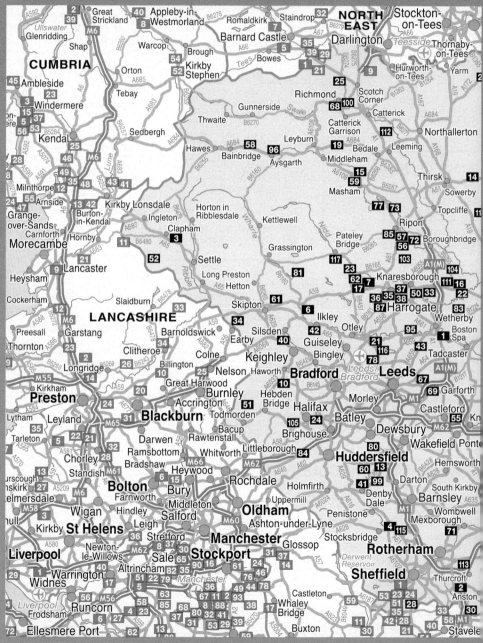

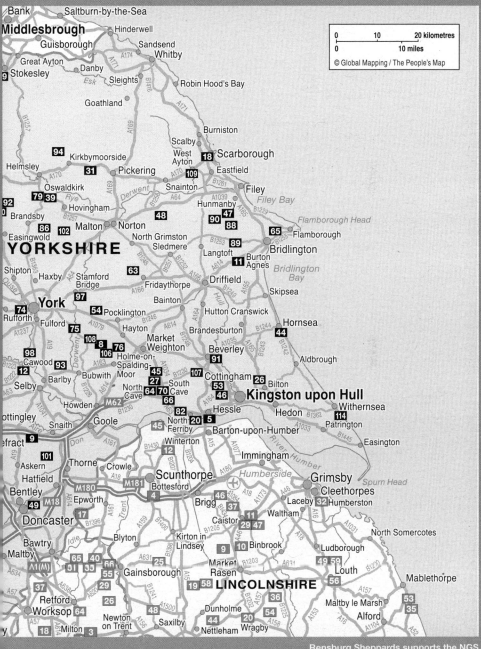

Opening Dates

March

Sunday 20
- **27** Fawley House

Sunday 27
- **33** Goldsborough Hall

April

Sunday 10
- **1** Acorn Cottage
- **13** The Circles Garden

Sunday 17
- **15** Clifton Castle
- **31** Friars Hill
- **83** 130 Prince Rupert Drive

Sunday 24
- **41** Highfields
- **106** Weathervane House

Friday 29
- **92** Shandy Hall Gardens (Evening)

May

Sunday 1
- **22** Croft Cottage
- **29** Fir Trees Cottage

Monday 2
- **29** Fir Trees Cottage

Wednesday 4
- **6** Beacon Hill House

Sunday 8
- **30** Firvale Allotment Garden
- **86** Rewela Cottage

Sunday 15
- **20** The Court
- **43** Hillbark
- **98** Stillingfleet Lodge
- **105** Warley House Garden

Wednesday 18
- **85** 24 Red Bank Road

Saturday 21
- **53** Linden House

Sunday 22
- **5** Beacon Garth
- **41** Highfields
- **48** Jacksons Wold
- **53** Linden House
- **85** 24 Red Bank Road
- **88** The Ridings

Wednesday 25
- **82** Park House

Saturday 28
- **94** Sleightholmedale Lodge

Sunday 29
- **21** Creskeld Hall
- **94** Sleightholmedale Lodge

Monday 30
- **16** Cobble Cottage
- **104** Tinkers Hollow

June

Wednesday 1
- **42** 5 Hill Top

Saturday 4
- **47** Hunmanby Grange
- **77** Old Sleningford Hall

Sunday 5
- **25** Easingtown
- **42** 5 Hill Top
- **44** Hornsea Gardens
- **46** 56 Hull Road
- **47** Hunmanby Grange
- **49** Jasmine House
- **68** Millgate House
- **77** Old Sleningford Hall
- **82** Park House
- **100** Swale Cottage

Wednesday 8
- **107** 26 West End

Thursday 9
- **82** Park House (Evening)

Saturday 11
- **11** Burton Agnes Hall
- **79** Oswaldkirk Hall

Sunday 12
- **11** Burton Agnes Hall
- **15** Clifton Castle
- **73** Norton Conyers
- **75** The Old Coach House
- **78** The Orchard
- **79** Oswaldkirk Hall
- **107** 26 West End
- **111** Whixley Gardens

Wednesday 15
- **58** Lodge Yard
- **81** Parcevall Hall Gardens
- **93** Skipwith Hall

Friday 17
- **54** Linden Lodge (Evening)

Saturday 18
- **54** Linden Lodge

Sunday 19
- **4** Avenue Cottage
- **7** Birstwith Hall
- **39** Havoc Hall
- **48** Jacksons Wold
- **54** Linden Lodge
- **98** Stillingfleet Lodge
- **101** Sykehouse Gardens
- **115** Wortley Hall

Look out for the gardens with the ☎ – enjoy a private visit . . .

Wednesday 22
- **2** Aston Gardens
- **111** Whixley Gardens

Friday 24
- **92** Shandy Hall Gardens (Evening)

Saturday 25
- **28** Fernleigh
- **102** Terrington House

Sunday 26
- **10** Brookfield
- **28** Fernleigh
- **43** Hillbark
- **55** Little Eden
- **69** Millrace Nursery
- **102** Terrington House
- **113** Winthrop Park Gardens
- **117** Yorke House

Wednesday 29
- **10** Brookfield

July

Saturday 2
- **112** The Willows

Sunday 3
- **8** Boundary Cottage
- **23** Dacre Banks & Summerbridge Gardens
- **26** Evergreens
- **60** Lower Crawshaw
- **88** The Ridings
- **112** The Willows

Tuesday 5
- **14** Cleaves House (Evening)

Wednesday 6
- **14** Cleaves House

Thursday 7
- **80** Overthorpe J I & N School (Evening)

Saturday 9
- **12** Cawood Gardens

Sunday 10
- **5** Beacon Garth
- **12** Cawood Gardens
- **43** Hillbark
- **52** Lawkland Hall
- **71** Mon Abri
- **84** 2 Prospect Place
- **101** Sykehouse Gardens
- **109** Whispadales

Wednesday 13
- **17** Cold Cotes (Evening)
- **63** Manor Farm

Friday 15
- **91** St John's RC Primary School

Saturday 16
- **94** Sleightholmedale Lodge

Sunday 17
- **9** Bridge Farm House
- **40** High Hall
- **59** Low Sutton
- **74** The Nursery
- **89** Rudston House

Enjoy a day out – look out for a Group Opening

91 St John's RC Primary School
94 Sleightholmedale Lodge

Wednesday 20
18 Combe Hay
34 The Grange

Friday 22
74 The Nursery (Evening)

Sunday 24
28 Fernleigh
33 Goldsborough Hall
66 39 Market Place
86 Rewela Cottage
97 Stamford Bridge Gardens
73 Westfield Farm

Sunday 31
39 Havoc Hall
103 Thorpe Lodge
114 Withernsea Gardens

August

Wednesday 3
34 The Grange

Friday 5
99 Sue Proctor Plants Nursery
Garden (Evening)

Saturday 6
65 Mansion Cottage

Sunday 7
8 Boundary Cottage
24 Dove Cottage Nursery Garden
65 Mansion Cottage
67 Mere'stead

Sunday 14
3 Austwick Hall
34 The Grange
55 Little Eden
56 Littlethorpe Gardens
69 Millrace Nursery

Sunday 21
28 Fernleigh
39 Havoc Hall

Sunday 28
17 Cold Cotes
99 Sue Proctor Plants Nursery
Garden

September

Sunday 4
90 Rustic Cottage

Sunday 11
8 Boundary Cottage
98 Stillingfleet Lodge

Sunday 18
27 Fawley House
70 Millview Cottage
83 130 Prince Rupert Drive

October

Saturday 1
14 Cleaves House

Sunday 2
14 Cleaves House

Saturday 8
14 Cleaves House

Sunday 9
14 Cleaves House

February 2012

Wednesday 22
3 Austwick Hall

Gardens open to the public

11 Burton Agnes Hall
19 Constable Burton Hall Gardens
48 Jacksons Wold
51 Land Farm
72 Newby Hall & Gardens
73 Norton Conyers
81 Parcevall Hall Gardens
87 RHS Garden Harlow Carr
92 Shandy Hall Gardens
98 Stillingfleet Lodge
116 York Gate

By appointment only

35 Harrogate Gardens
36 Lavender Garden
37 The Mews Cottage
38 Stonehaven
45 Hotham Hall
50 Kelberdale
57 Littlethorpe Manor
61 Lower Heugh Cottage Garden
62 Lowfold
64 Manor House
76 The Old Priory
95 Spring Close Farm
96 Stainsacre
110 The White House

Also open by Appointment ☎

1 Acorn Cottage
12 9 Anson Grove, Cawood
Gardens
3 Austwick Hall
6 Beacon Hill House
7 Birstwith Hall
101 B J Nurseries, Sykehouse
Gardens
9 Bridge Farm House
10 Brookfield
14 Cleaves House
16 Cobble Cottage
17 Cold Cotes
20 The Court
22 Croft Cottage
26 Evergreens
28 Fernleigh
30 Firvale Allotment Garden

31 Friars Hill
33 Goldsborough Hall
34 The Grange
12 21 Great Close, Cawood
Gardens
39 Havoc Hall
41 Highfields
46 56 Hull Road
49 Jasmine House
53 Linden House
54 Linden Lodge
55 Little Eden
65 Mansion Cottage
66 39 Market Place
68 Millgate House
69 Millrace Nursery
74 The Nursery
44 Nutkins, Hornsea Gardens
78 The Orchard
82 Park House
83 130 Prince Rupert Drive
86 Rewela Cottage
88 The Ridings
89 Rudston House
90 Rustic Cottage
94 Sleightholmedale Lodge
97 Stamford Bridge Gardens
99 Sue Proctor Plants Nursery
Garden
102 Terrington House
106 Weathervane House
107 26 West End
109 Whispadales
113 Winthrop Park Gardens
23 Woodlands Cottage, Dacre
Banks & Summerbridge Gardens
115 Wortley Hall
117 Yorke House
23 Yorke House, Dacre Banks &
Summerbridge Gardens

The Gardens

1 **ACORN COTTAGE**
50 Church Street, Boston Spa
LS23 6DN. Mrs C M Froggatt,
01937 842519. *1m SE of Wetherby.
Off A1 on A659 Church St opp
Central Garage.* Light refreshments &
home-made teas. **Adm £3, chd free.**
Sun 10 Apr (11-5). Visitors also
welcome by appt mid March to mid
April.
You are invited to come and spend
peaceful time in this small, well-
established alpine garden full of spring
delights. Three generations of the
family have collected the plants and
bulbs, and these have recently been
rearranged and the garden
significantly altered for ease of
maintenance and access without
losing the character and uniqueness
of this fine collection.
☕ ☎

Be tempted by a plant from a plant stall ⊛

12 ANSELL ROAD
See Derbyshire.

GROUP OPENING

2 ASTON GARDENS
Aston S26 2BD. *11m SW of
Sheffield. M1 J31 A57 Sheffield
(Aston Way) Turn R immed signed
'Sheffield Central' (Worksop Rd). 2nd
L after 500yds (Green Lane). Please
park at Yellow Lion PH on Worksop
Rd (Lower Car Park), approx 50yds to
Aston Gardens. No parking in Green
Lane.* Home-made teas. **Combined
adm £3, chd free.** Wed 22 June
(12-5).

JASMINE COTTAGE
Green Lane. Mr & Mrs M C Soul

RIVELIN COTTAGE
1 Green Lane. Mr & Mrs S
Pashley

Aston is a small village 2m from
Rother Valley County Park. The
nearby Church of All Saints features in
the Domesday Book and dates back
to the C12. Situated in conservation
area in the old part of Aston. Planted
and furnished with vintage finds by
two enthusiastic female gardeners.
Jasmine Cottage is a pretty cottage
and garden with overflowing
herbaceous borders enclosed by box
hedging. Lawned area. Featuring old
and modern roses both climbing and
shrub. Shrubbery. Water feature.
Steps to enclosed seating area with
limited colour pallet of pink and white.
Rivelin Cottage has sweeping
herbaceous borders with backbone of
trees and shrubs. Thoughtfully
planted as to interest and form, with
the emphasis on colour co-ordination.
Pergolas covered in roses and
clematis. Water feature. Ornamental
vegetable garden. Wide variety of
plants and interest. For the cottage
garden lover...

🌐 ☕

---

3 AUSTWICK HALL
Town Head Lane, Austwick, nr
Settle LA2 8BS. Eric Culley &
Michael Pearson, 015242 51794,
austwickhall@austwick.org,
www.austwickhall.co.uk. *5m W of
Settle. From A65 to Austwick Village.
Pass Game Cock Inn on L. After
Primary School turn L up Town Head
Lane. No parking adjacent to hall,
please park in village.* Home-made
teas. **Adm £3.50, chd free.**

Sun 14 Aug (12-5); 2012 Wed 22
Feb. **Visitors also welcome by appt
all yr,**
Set in the dramatic limestone scenery
of the Dales the garden nestles into a
steeply wooded hillside. Features incl
herbaceous borders, juniper walk,
fern border leading to a moongate.
Thatched gazebo overlooking a pond
in the jungle garden, and shrubbery.
New developments incl a woodland
sculpture trail, walled kitchen garden
and winter snowdrop walk. Plant
sales.

🌐 ⌷ ☕ ☎

---

900 feet up the
southern slope of
Beamsley Beacon,
the garden is
sheltered by
woodland on the
north and a
Victorian windbreak
to the west . . .

---

4 AVENUE COTTAGE
Wortley Village S35 7DB. Vega
Shepley & Roger England. *9m NW
of Sheffield, 5m SW of Barnsley. On
A629 Huddersfield - Sheffield Rd in
Wortley Village, signed Wortley Hall &
Gardens.* **Adm £4.50, chd free.** Sun
19 June (12-4). **Also open Wortley
Hall.**
Within the walled kitchen garden of
Wortley Hall and attached to original
gardener's cottage the garden
overlooks the tree line of Wortley Hall
Gardens. Gravelled island beds with
Mediterranean style plantings are set
in lawn. Areas for wildlife, large mixed
shrubbery, and vegetable garden on
raised beds. Garden is totally organic.

🌐 ☕

---

5 NEW BEACON GARTH
Redcliff Road, Hessle, Hull
HU13 0HA. Ivor & June Innes.
*4½ m W of Hull. Humber Bridge
r'about. Toward Hessle. R (S) at T-
lights. Travel toward river along Heads
Lane, over Xrds into Woodfield Lane,
approx
½ m sharp bend L. House on RH-*

---

*side at junction of Cliff Rd & Redcliffe
Rd.* Home-made teas. **Adm £3.50,
chd free.** Suns 22 May; 10 July
(10-5).
Edwardian, Arts & Crafts House (not
open) and S-facing garden set in
3½ acres, in an elevated position
overlooking the Humber. Stunning
sunken rock garden with bulbs and
specimen trees, hostas and ferns.
Mature trees, large lawns and
herbaceous borders. Gravel paths,
box hedges and topiary. Child friendly.
Limited wheelchair access.

♿ ☕

---

6 BEACON HILL HOUSE
Langbar, nr Ilkley LS29 0EU.
Mr & Mrs D H Boyle, 01943 607544.
*4m NW of Ilkley. 1¼ m SE of A59 at
Bolton Bridge.* Home-made teas.
Adm £3.50, chd free (share to
Riding for the Disabled). Wed
4 May (1.30-5). **Visitors also
welcome by appt, written
application preferred.**
900ft up the southern slope of
Beamsley Beacon, the garden is
sheltered by woodland on the north
and a Victorian windbreak to the
west. Rhododendrons, magnolias and
other early flowering shrubs and trees
benefit from this. Later, large
scrambling roses and borders with
unusual plants provide interest.

🌐 ☕ ☎

---

7 BIRSTWITH HALL
High Birstwith, nr Harrogate
HG3 2JW. Sir James & Lady
Aykroyd, 01423 770250. *5m NW of
Harrogate. Between Hampsthwaite &
Birstwith villages, close to A59
Harrogate/Skipton rd.* Home-made
teas. **Adm £3.50, chd free.** Sun 19
June (2-5). **Visitors also welcome
by appt, coaches permitted.**
Large 8-acre garden nestling in
secluded Yorkshire dale with formal
garden and ornamental orchard,
extensive lawns, picturesque stream,
large pond and Victorian greenhouse.

♿ 🐾 🌐 ☕ ☎

BOTTESFORD GARDENS
See Lincolnshire.

---

8 BOUNDARY COTTAGE
Seaton Ross, York YO42 4NF.
Roger Brook. *5m SW of Pocklington.
From A64 York, take Hull exit &
immed B1228, approx 9m, then
follow signs Seaton Ross. From M62
Howden N on B1228 approx 11m, R
turn to Seaton Ross. Garden 1m
before Seaton Ross. From Hull turn R*

100yds before Seaton Ross. **Adm £3.50, chd free.** Suns 3 July; 7 Aug; 11 Sept (11-4). Boundary Cottage, plantsman's no dig garden without boundaries and borrowed landscape! Ponds and lined streams in bog gardens, extensive yet intimate mixed plantings, giant island herbaceous borders, National dicentra collection. Acre garden has 50 maturing specimen trees, gravel gardens, outdoor cacti, rock gardens, roof-less roof garden, alpine troughs and seasonal displays. Unorthodox fruit and veg. Also see village plot in Seaton Ross! Friendly teas next door. Artist in garden.

᚛ 🌳 ❀ **NCCPG** ☕

9 BRIDGE FARM HOUSE

Long Lane, Great Heck, Nr Selby DN14 0BE. Barbara & Richard Ferrari, 01977 661277, barbaraferrari@mypostoffice.co.uk. *6m S of Selby. 3m E of M62 (J34) A19 turn E at r'about to Snaith onto A645, straight on at T-lights then 1st R to Great Heck. House 1st on L, park in adjacent field.* Teas in church opposite. **Adm £3, chd free.** Sun 17 July (12-4). **Visitors also welcome by appt** in June, min 10+, £5 per visitor incl refreshments.

2-acre garden, divided into rooms by ½ m of hedges, to house a varied collection of plants, many unusual, rarely seen and of yr round interest. Garden developed by owners from 2002, incl bog gravel, ponds and 130ft long double mixed borders. Happy hens, extensive compost heaps and wildlife.

᚛ ❀ ☕ ☎

10 BROOKFIELD

Jew Lane, Oxenhope BD22 9HS. Mrs R L Belsey, 01535 643070. *5m SW of Keighley. Take A629 towards Halifax. Fork R onto A6033 towards Haworth. Follow signs to Oxenhope. Turn L at Xrds in village. 200yds after PO fork R, Jew Lane.* Home-made teas. **Adm £3, chd free.** Sun 26, Wed 29 June (1.30-5). **Visitors also welcome by appt** May to July & early Aug.

1-acre, intimate garden, incl large pond with island and mallards. Many varieties of candelabra primulas and florindaes, azaleas, rhododendrons. Unusual trees and shrubs, osrose, greenhouses and conservatory. Series of island beds. Children's quiz. Limited wheelchair access, steps and slope.

🌳 ❀ ☕ ☎

Linden Lodge

11 ◆ BURTON AGNES HALL

Driffield YO25 4ND. Mrs S Cunliffe-Lister, 01262 490324, www.burtonagnes.com. *Between Driffield & Bridlington. Burton Agnes is on A614.* **Adm £4.50, chd £2.50, concessions £4 for Gardener's Fair (donation to NGS). For NGS:** Sat 11, Sun 12 June (11-5). **For other opening times and information, please phone or see garden website.**

Beautiful award-winning gardens of Burton Agnes Hall are home to 4,000 different plant species, herbaceous borders, a jungle garden, potager, coloured gardens, giant games, a maze and National Collection of campanulas. Surrounded by lawns, clipped yews, fountains and a woodland walk. Collections of hardy geraniums, clematis, penstemons and unusual perennials. Gardener's Fair - 50+ stalls selling plants and garden accessories.

᚛ 🌳 ❀ **NCCPG** ☕

GROUP OPENING

12 CAWOOD GARDENS

YO8 3UG. *5m N of Selby. On B1222 5m NW of Selby & 7m SE of Tadcaster. Between York & A1 on B1222.* Village maps given at all gardens. Home-made teas. **Combined adm £5, chd free.** Sat 9, Sun 10 July (12-5).

9 ANSON GROVE
Tony & Brenda Finnigan
Visitors also welcome by appt.
01757 268888

ASH LEA
Michael & Josephine Welbourn

21 GREAT CLOSE
David & Judy Jones
Visitors also welcome by appt.
01757 268571

An attractive, historic, riverside village. C11 church also open. 9 Anson Grove is a small garden with tranquil pools and secluded sitting places. Narrow winding paths and raised areas give views over oriental styled pagoda, bridge and Zen garden. Ash Lea has shrubs and fernery which lead to colourful formal borders, in contrast to a relaxed atmosphere by a clear pool, leading to dining area and traditional vegetable garden edged in clipped box. 21 Great Close has all-yr interest, with mixed planting in ever-changing borders, incl vegetables, herbs, grasses and many unusual and some exotic perennials. Ponds, stream and rose walk make a colourful garden with small summerhouse. Plenty of places to sit and enjoy the views. Crafts and paintings on sale at 9 Anson Grove.

❀ ☕ ☎

---

13 THE CIRCLES GARDEN

8 Stocksmoor Road, Midgley, nr Wakefield WF4 4JQ. Joan Gaunt. *Equidistant between Huddersfield, Wakefield & Barnsley, W of M1. Turn off A637 in Midgley at the Black Bull PH (sharp bend) onto B6117 (Stocksmoor Rd). Please park on L adjacent to houses.* Home-made teas. **Adm £3, chd free. Sun 10 Apr (1.30-5).**

First spring opening for this ¹/₂ -acre plantswoman's garden on gently sloping site overlooking fields and woods. Designed and maintained by owner. Interesting herbaceous and shrub plantings linked by grass and gravel paths, incl varieties of S African plants, half-hardy and tender plants, perennials, holly, fruit trees and ferns. Terrace with pots, greenhouse, circular gravel garden and woodland beds.

14 CLEAVES HOUSE

Thirlby YO7 2DQ. Margaret & Tony May, 01845 597606. *3m E of Thirsk. From A170 in Sutton under Whitestone Cliff take turning signed Felixkirk. Almost immed take rd R signed Thirlby.* Home-made teas. **Adm £3.50, chd free.** Evening Opening wine, Tue 5 July (6-9); Wed 6 July; Sats, Suns 1, 2, 8, 9 Oct (11-5). Visitors also welcome by appt from mid Sept. No coaches.

Informal 2-acre garden set against backdrop of a cliff with wonderful far reaching views. Bold interesting planting with emphasis on contrasting trees, shrubs, roses and plants chosen for autumn interest. Pond and bog areas. Newly developing shade garden. Partial wheelchair access.

15 CLIFTON CASTLE

Ripon HG4 4AB. Lord & Lady Downshire. *2m N of Masham. On road to Newton-le-Willows & Richmond. Gates on L next to red telephone box.* Home-made teas. **Adm £4, chd free.** Sun 17 Apr; Sun 12 June (2-5).

Fine views, river walks, wooded pleasure grounds with bridges and follies. Cascades, wild flower meadow and 19C walled kitchen garden. Featured in As featured in Valentine Warner's 'What to eat now - summer' on BBC in 2010. Gravel paths and steep slopes down to the river.

16 COBBLE COTTAGE

Rudgate, Whixley, Nr York YO26 8AL. John Hawkridge & Barry Atkinson, 01423 331419. *6m E of Knaresborough. 8m W of York. 3m E of A1 off A59 York - Harrogate.* Home-made teas at The Old Vicarage (June). **Combined with Tinkers Hollow adm £3.50, chd free. Whixley Gardens adm £5, chd free, 12, 22 June 1-5.** Mon 30 May (11-5). Visitors also welcome by appt June & July, min 12+.

Imaginatively designed, constantly changing, small cottage garden full of decorative architectural plants and old family favourites. Interesting water garden, containers and use of natural materials. Black and white courtyard garden and Japanese style garden with growing willow screen.

COBWEBS NURSERY & GARDEN
See Lincolnshire.

17 COLD COTES

Cold Cotes Road, nr Kettlesing, Harrogate HG3 2LW. Penny Jones, Ed Loft, Doreen & Joanna Russell, 01423 770937, info@coldcotes.com, www.coldcotes.com. *7m W of Harrogate. Off A59. After Black Bull PH turn R to Menwith Hill/Darley.* Home-made teas & Light Refreshments. **Adm £3.50, chd free.** Evening Opening wine, Wed 13 July (3-9); Sun 28 Aug (11-5). Visitors also welcome by appt.

Large peaceful garden with expansive views is at ease in its rural setting. Series of discrete gardens with year-round interest incl formal areas around house, streamside walk and sweeping herbaceous borders inspired by the designer Piet Oudolf which are at their height in late summer, lead to a newly developed woodland garden with wonderful autumn colour. Art & Craft activities. Garden & nursery open from March to Nov (closed Mon & Tues except BH).

Plantswoman's garden on gently sloping site overlooking fields and woods . . .

18 NEW COMBE HAY

Stepney Road, Scarborough YO12 5DJ. The George Edward Smart Homes, www.combe-hay.co.uk. *1m W of Scarborough town centre. From Whitby take A171 after Scarborough Hospital follow sign for A170 onto Stepney Drive. From Thirsk follow A170 to sixth form college L at r'about 150 metres on R, A64 into Scarborough L onto A171 follow signs for Thirsk A170. At r'about L Stepney Drive.* Home-made teas. **Adm £4, chd free.** Wed 20 July (10-4).

Situated in attractive and tranquil landscape grounds of approx 4¹/₂ acres. The award winning garden is designed for relaxation, with summerhouses and seating areas to admire the large variety of trees and shrubs/colourful herbaceous/annual borders. Other features of interest incl orchard, vegetable garden and pond. Silver Award Yorkshire in Bloom, Gold Award Scarborough in Bloom.

19 ◆ CONSTABLE BURTON HALL GARDENS

nr Leyburn DL8 5LJ. Mr Charles Wyvill, 01677 450361, www.constableburtongardens.co.uk. *3m E of Leyburn. Constable Burton Village. On A684, 6m W of A1.* **Adm £4, chd 5 - 16 50p, Concessions £3.** For opening times and information, please phone or see garden website.

Large romantic garden with terraced woodland walks. Garden trails, shrubs, roses and water garden. Display of daffodils and over 5000 tulips planted annually amongst extensive borders. Fine John Carr house (not open) set in splendour of Wensleydale countryside. Featured on Gardeners World (Tulips).

20 THE COURT

Humber Road, North Ferriby HU14 3DW. Guy & Liz Slater, 01482 633609, guyslater@guyslater.karoo.co.uk. *7m W of Hull. Travelling E on A63 towards Hull, follow sign for N Ferriby. Through village to Xrds with war memorial, turn R & follow rd to T-junction with Humber Rd. Turn L & immed R into cul-de-sac, last house on LH-side.* Light refreshments & home-made teas. **Adm £3, chd free.** Sun 15 May (1-5). Visitors also welcome by appt.

Romantic and restful with hidden

seating areas offering different vistas. Roses and clematis scrambling up walls and trees. 2 summerhouses, small pond and waterfall with secluded arbours and historical items. A long tunnel of wisteria, clematis and laburnum leads to a little path with betula jacquemontii, small stumpery, and grown up swing. Artist in the garden.

21 CRESKELD HALL
Arthington, nr Leeds LS21 1NT. J & C Stoddart-Scott. *5m E of Otley. On A659 between Pool & Harewood.* Home-made teas. **Adm £4, chd free.** Sun 29 May (12-5). Historic picturesque 3¹/₂ -acre Wharfedale garden with beech avenue, mature rhododendrons and azaleas. Gravel path from terrace leads to attractive water garden with canals set amongst woodland plantings. Walled kitchen garden and flower garden. Specialist nurseries.

22 CROFT COTTAGE
Boroughbridge Road, Green Hammerton, Nr York YO26 8AE. Alistair & Angela Taylor, 01423 330330, angie-48@hotmail.co.uk. *6m E of Knaresborough. 3m E of A1M adjacent to A59. Entrance on Boroughbridge Rd between Social Club and hairdresser.* Home-made teas. **Adm £3.50, chd free.** Sun 1 May (12-5). Visitors also welcome by appt. Secluded ¹/₂ -acre cottage garden divided into a number of garden rooms. Conservatory, clipped yew, old brick, cobbles and pavers used for formal areas leading to water feature, mixed borders and orchard with wild flowers. Edwardian children's playhouse open for games.

GROUP OPENING

23 DACRE BANKS & SUMMERBRIDGE GARDENS
nr Summerbridge, Nidderdale HG3 4EW. *4m SE of Pateley Bridge, 10m NW of Harrogate. 4m SE of Pateley Bridge 10m NW of Harrogate on B6451 & B6165. Parking at Yorke House.* Low Hall & Woodlands Cottage. *Footpath access to Riverside House from Woodlands Cottage. Maps will be available to*

show locations. Home-made teas at Yorke House & Low Hall. **Combined adm £6, chd free.** Sun 3 July (11-5).

LOW HALL
Mrs P A Holliday

NEW RIVERSIDE HOUSE
Joy Stanton. *On B6165*

WOODLANDS COTTAGE
Summerbridge. Mr & Mrs Stark. *On the B6165* Visitors also welcome by appt. 01423 780765

YORKE HOUSE
Anthony & Pat Hutchinson Visitors also welcome by appt. 01423 780456 pat@yorkehouse.co.uk www.yorkehouse.co.uk

Dacre Banks and Summerbridge Gardens are situated in the beautiful countryside of Nidderdale and designed to take advantage of the scenic views of the Dales landscape. The gardens are linked by an attractive walk along the valley. All the owners are passionate about the conservation of local flora and fauna and together the gardens contribute to the 'wildlife corridor' of the Dale. Gardens may be accessed individually by car, except Riverside House. Low Hall has a romantic walled garden set on different levels around the historic C17 family home (not open) with extensive herbaceous borders, shrubs, climbing roses and tranquil water garden. New asymmetric pergola, covered with roses and clematis links the orchard to the front garden. Riverside House is a mysterious waterside garden on many levels. The N-facing site supports many shade-loving plants and incorporates Victorian folly, fernery, courtyard and naturalistic riverside plantings. Woodlands Cottage is a 1 acre plantswoman's garden, designed to harmonise with the adjacent natural rock outcrops. It has several different areas of planting with many unusual plants, wild flower meadow, knot garden and productive kitchen garden. Yorke House (see separate entry) for colour themed borders and secluded millennium garden full of fragrant plants and rambling roses. Visitors are welcome to use the picnic area in the orchard of Yorke House.

DEMETER HOUSE
See Lincolnshire.

124 DOBCROFT ROAD
See Derbyshire.

122 DOBCROFT ROAD
See Derbyshire.

Edwardian children's playhouse open for games . . .

24 DOVE COTTAGE NURSERY GARDEN
Shibden Hall Road, nr Halifax HX3 9XA. Kim & Stephen Rogers, www.dovecottagenursery.co.uk. *1m W of Hipperholme. 2m E of Halifax. J26 M62 take A58 Halifax. Turn 2nd L after Hipperholme T-lights (4m from J26). From Halifax turn L off A58 at yellow sign. Signed Claremount, Horley Green. Follow yellow signs for 1m. Car park for disabled & elderly otherwise please park on Shibden Hall Rd.* Light lunches & home-made teas. **Adm £3, chd free.** Sun 7 Aug (10-5). Hedges and green oak gates enclose ¹/₃ acre sloping garden, generously planted by nursery owners over 14yrs. A beautiful mix of late summer perennials and ornamental grasses. Winding paths and plenty of seats incl a romantic oak tulip arbour. Tea, cakes and sandwiches served on the garden terrace with a view down the garden. Plants for sale in the nursery. Featured in Readers Digest - The Most Amazing Gardens In Britain and Ireland.

25 EASINGTOWN
Hartforth, nr Richmond DL10 5JR. John & Kate Stephenson. *1m from Gilling West. From Richmond follow signs to Gilling West B6274, follow signs for Hartforth (1m).* **Adm £3, chd free.** Sun 5 June (11-5). Also open Millgate House & Swale Cottage. Traditional box-edged potager with apple step-overs and rose arches. Derelict fernery with lichen-covered cobbled floor and ivy-clad walls.

Visit the website for latest information

The Old Vicarage

Exuberantly planted cottage garden. Old English rose garden, sunken garden with reclaimed timber laburnam tunnel, shady streamside planting, deep carp-filled pool, graded colour planting, acers and summer house.

  ♿ 🐕 ❀ ☕

26 ▶ EVERGREENS
119 Main Road, Bilton, Hull HU11 4AB. Phil & Brenda Brock, 01482 811365. *4m NE of Hull. Leave city by A165. Exit B1238. Bungalow ¹/₂ m on L opp Asda car park entrance.* Light refreshments, tea, coffee, cakes & trifle. **Adm £2.50 incl tea, chd free.** Sun 3 July (1-5). **Visitors also welcome by appt.** 1 acre with mosaics, sundials, African carvings, tower, rockeries and landscaped pond, Japanese and seaside gardens, summerhouse and children's play area with children's

oriental play house. The garden features mainly conifers and 'fun' items. Photographs showing development of the area. Front garden redesigned 2005.

  ♿ 🐕 ☕ ☎

FANSHAWE GATE HALL
See Derbyshire.

27 ▶ NEW FAWLEY HOUSE
7 Nordham, North Cave HU15 2LT. Mr & Mrs T Martin. *15m W of Hull. M62 E, J38 turn L to N. Cave. On B1230 E of village, turn L before church. Over bridge (car park ahead) House is 3rd on L after L hand bend.* Home-made teas. **Adm £3.50, chd free.** Suns 20 Mar; 18 Sept (12-4). **Also open Millview Cottage 18 Sept.**
Tiered, 2¹/₂ -acre garden with mature trees, formal hedging and gravel pathways. Mixed shrub/herbaceous

borders. Fruit, vegetable and herb gardens. Terrace with vines, peach and fig, overlooking white planting. Woodland with bulbs and ferns. Naturalistic planting to stream/spring area. Quaker Well. In March 2010, a hot garden was developed. Artist in the garden. Plants for sale (March only). Wheelchairs welcome to view garden from top and for teas, access to garden not possible.

  ❀ ☕ 🛏

28 ▶ FERNLEIGH
9 Meadowhead Avenue, Sheffield S8 7RT. Mr & Mrs C Littlewood, 01142 747234. *4m S of Sheffield city centre. A61, A6102, B6054 r'about, exit B6054 towards Holmesfield. 1st R Greenhill Ave, then 2nd R Meadowhead Ave.* Home-made teas. **Adm £2.50, chd free.** Sat 25, Sun 26 June; (1-5); Suns 24 July; 21 Aug (11-5). **Visitors also welcome by appt June to Aug, groups of 10 to 20.**
Plantswoman's ¹/₃ -acre cottage style garden with large variety of unusual plants set in differently planted sections to provide all-yr interest. Auricula theatre and paved area for drought resistant plants in pots. Seating areas to view different aspects of garden. Patio with gazebo and greenhouse. Miniature log cabin with living roof. Sempervivum, alpine displays and 'Wildlife 'Hotel'.

  ❀ ☕ ☎

FIELD HOUSE FARM
See Lincolnshire.

29 ▶ FIR TREES COTTAGE
Stokesley TS9 5LD. Helen & Mark Bainbridge, 01642 713066, www.firtreespelargoniums.co.uk. *1m S of Stokesley. On A172 garden will be signed Pelargonium Exhibition.* Home-made teas. **Adm £3, chd free.** Sun 1, Mon 2 May (2-5).
1 acre mixed shrubaceous borders, large rockeries, spring bulbs, species tulips, mature conifers, fritillaries, erythroniums and secluded ornamental pond. Hosta collection and garden sculpture. Tranquil garden surrounded by farmland with views to Cleveland Hills and Roseberry Topping. Designed and maintained by owners since 1992 with low maintenance in mind. Pelargonium Exhibition - The nursery has won 71 RHS GOLD Medals and 7 Chelsea gold medals for its displays of pelargoniums.

  ♿ 🐕 ❀ ☕

ALLOTMENT

 FIRVALE ALLOTMENT GARDEN
Winney Hill, Harthill S26 7YN. Don & Dot Witton, 01909 771366, www.euphorbias.co.uk. *12m SE of Sheffield, 6m W of Worksop. M1 Jct 31 A57 to Worksop. Turn R to Harthill. Allotments at S end of village, 26 Casson Drive at N end on Northlands estate.* Light refreshments & teas at 26 Casson Drive. **Adm £2, chd free.** Sun 8 May (1-4). **Visitors also welcome by appt April-July.** Large allotment containing 13 island beds displaying 500+ herbaceous perennials. Organic vegetable garden. Refreshments, WC, plant sales at 26 Casson Drive - small garden with mixed borders, shade and seaside garden. National Collection of Hardy Euphorbia will be at its peak with over 100 varieties in flower. Featured in the 2010/11 'Good Gardens Guide'.

 FRIARS HILL
Sinnington YO62 6SL. Mr & Mrs C J Baldwin, 01751 432179, Friars.Hill@abelgratis.co.uk. *4m W of Pickering. On A170.* **Adm £3, chd free.** Sun 17 Apr (1-5). **Visitors also welcome by appt.**
1³/₄ -acre plantswoman's garden containing over 2500 varieties of perennials and bulbs, with yr-round colour. Early interest with hellebores, bulbs and woodland plants. Herbaceous beds. Hostas, delphiniums, old roses and stone troughs.

THE GARDEN HOUSE
See Lincolnshire.

GOLDSBOROUGH HALL
Church Street, Goldsborough HG5 8NR. Mr & Mrs M Oglesby, 01423 867321, info@goldsboroughhall.com, www.goldsboroughhall.com. *2m SE of Knaresborough. 3m W of A1M. Off A59 (York-Harrogate) car-park 300yds past PH on R.* Light refreshments, cream teas & wine. **Adm £5, chd free.** Sun 27 Mar 12-4) by telephoned prebooking due to car parking restrictions; Sun 24 July (12-5) (no prebooking requied). **Visitors also welcome by appt min 15+ all-yr.**
Opened last year for NGS for the 1st time since 1930 and beautifully restored by present owners. 11-acre garden and formal landscaped grounds in parkland setting and Grade 2*, C17 house, former residence of the late HRH Princess Mary, daughter of George V and Queen Mary, Gertrude Jekyll inspired replanted 120ft double herbaceous borders and rose garden. ¹/₄ m lime tree walk planted by Royalty circa 1920 underplanted with 50,000 naturalised daffodils. Woodland walk and specimen trees. Adjacent village church St Mary's open. Featured widely in national press and on local TV. Gravel paths and some steep slopes.

Frequent pauses are encouraged by quirky ornaments, small water features and scattered seating . . .

THE GRANGE
Carla Beck Lane, Carleton, Skipton BD23 3BU. Mr & Mrs R N Wooler, 07740 639135, margaret.wooler@hotmail.com. *1¹/₂ m SW of Skipton. Turn off A56 (Skipton-Clitheroe) into Carleton. Keep L at Swan PH, continue through to end of village & turn R into Carla Beck Lane. From Skipton town centre follow A6131. Turn R to Carleton.* Cream teas (Weds), home-made teas (Sun). **Adm £4, chd free (share to Sue Ryder Manorlands Hospice).** Weds 20 July; 3 Aug, Sun 14 Aug (1 5). Visitors also welcome by appt for groups 15+ in Aug.
Now reaching maturity, a plantsman's garden of over 4 acres of different features restored by the owners during the last 15yrs. Large herbaceous border with ha-ha, walled garden, rose and clematis walk, ornamental grass beds, water features and vegetable beds, some unusual mature tree specimens. Formal parterre garden. Gravel paths and steps.

THE GREEN
See Derbyshire.

GRINGLEY GARDENS
See Nottinghamshire.

16 THE GROVE
See Derbyshire.

GROUP OPENING

NEW HARROGATE GARDENS
Harrogate HG1 2PZ. Visitors welcome by appt by all three gardens, Lavender Garden, The Mews Cottage & Stonehaven, please see below for details. Harrogate is an attractive Victorian Spa town renowned for its floral displays, Valley Gardens, the Stray, Bettys Tea Rooms and RHS Harlow Carr. The Mews Cottage and Lavender Garden are close to the Valley Gardens and Spa, Stonehaven is on the South side across the Stray, a 20min walk from the town centre down Stray Rein or a short car, taxi or bus ride.

NEW LAVENDER GARDEN
11 Rutland Road, Harrogate HG1 2PY. Mike & Dawn Fletcher, 01423 526118, mikefletcher@waitrose.com. *From Cornwall Rd, N-side of Valley Gardens, 1st R (Clarence Dr), 1st L (York Rd), 2nd L (Rutland Rd).* Wine. **Adm £2.50. Visitors welcome by appt May to Sept, max 12 visitors.** An award-winning tiny, hidden S-facing courtyard garden with winding, interlocking paths leading among small trees, shrubs and plants selected for year-round shape, texture and colour of foliage. Also incl a collection of acers and unusual ferns (incl tree ferns). Frequent pauses are encouraged by quirky ornaments, small water features and scattered seating. 1st prize Small Garden Category, Ackrill Media Group Glorious Gardens.

37 THE MEWS COTTAGE
1 Brunswick Drive, Harrogate HG1 2PZ. Mrs Pat Clarke, 01423 566292, patriciaclarke19@googlemail.com. *W of Harrogate town centre. From Cornwall Rd, N side of Valley Gardens, 1st R (Clarence Dr), 1st L (York Rd), 1st L (Brunswick Dr).* Home-made teas. **Adm £2.50.** Visitors welcome by appt May to Sept, individual & groups max 30 visitors, coaches welcome.
Small tranquil garden on sloping site featuring a terracotta tiled courtyard with trompe-l'oeil. A garden of special interest to hardy planters over a long season; recommended for an August visit when a large collection of phlox paniculata is in flower.

38 NEW STONEHAVEN
Belgrave Crescent, Harrogate HG2 8HZ. Denise & Paul Dyson, 01423 538141, paul-dyson@sky.com. *From Harrogate town centre take A61 towards Leeds. Turn 1st L at 2nd r'about down South Dr over Xrds and railway bridge. Turn 2nd R into Belgrave Crescent.* Home-made teas. **Adm £2.50.** Visitors welcome by appt May to Sept, max 12 visitors.
A gem of a small, enclosed garden re-created from 2007. Partly raised and traditionally planted with an interesting selection of herbaceous perennials suitable for both sun and shade. Generously planted pergolas support roses and clematis, underplanted with hardy cyclamen, unusual primulas, violas, hardy geraniums and much more.

39 NEW HAVOC HALL
York Rd, Oswaldkirk, York YO62 5XY. David and Maggie Lis, 01439 788846, maggielis@hotmail.com. *21 m N of York. First house on the R as you enter Oswaldkirk on the B1363 from the S and the last house on the L as you leave the village from the north.* Home-made teas. **Adm £3, chd free.** Suns 19 June; 31 July; 21 Aug (1-5.30). Visitors also welcome by appt Mons pm, June, July, August.
Started in 2009, comprising 6 areas; knot, herbaceous, mixed shrub and flower gardens, a courtyard, vegetable area and orchard, woodland walk and a large lawned area with hornbeam trees and hedging and avenues of amelanchiers. To the south is a 2 acre wildflower meadow and small lake. Plants for sale. Most areas accessible but some steps and gravel drive.

40 NEW HIGH HALL
St Stephen's Road, Keighley BD20 6SB. Roger & Christine Lambert. *3m W of Keighley. Enter Steeton village from A629. Turn R at T-lights, then R after 100yds down St Stephens Rd. Entrance on L immed after church. No parking available adjacent to garden, please follow signs for car parking in the village.* Light refreshments & home-made teas. **Adm £3, chd free.** Sun 17 July (11-5).
2 acre surprising suburban Arts & Crafts garden and historic house (not open) adjacent to St Stephens Church. Formal walled garden with tanks, pond, belvedere, pergola, dovecote, summerhouse and ancient yew, riotous herbaceous planting in formal beds connected by gravel paths. Walled kitchen garden with vegetable beds and fruit trees. Natural woodland area and small croquet lawn. Historical notes available.

Generously planted pergolas support roses and clematis, underplanted with hardy cyclamen, unusual primulas, violas, hardy geraniums and much more . . .

41 HIGHFIELDS
Manorstead, Skelmanthorpe, Huddersfield HD8 9DW. Julie & Tony Peckham, 01484 864336, julie-tony@tiscali.co.uk. *8m SE of Huddersfield. M1 (J39) A636 towards Denby Dale. Turn R in Scissett village (B6116) to Skelmanthorpe. After 2nd Police Speed Check sign turn L (Barrowstead), continue to top of hill.*
Adm £2, chd free. Suns 24 Apr; 22 May (2-5). Visitors also welcome by appt, between 25 April & 18 June.
Small garden which shows creativity within metres rather than acres! 2 ponds, gravel bed, box parterre with obelisk water feature, arbours, arches and vertical structures. Incl collection of 30+ hebes in raised beds, a collection of muscari and rock garden with a growing collection of alpines. Spring/early summer garden with bulbs, woodland plants and alpines. Featured in Garden News 'Readers Gardens' as a regular contributor.

42 5 HILL TOP
Westwood Drive, Ilkley LS29 9RS. Lyn & Phil Short. *½ m S of Ilkley town centre. Turn S at town centre T-lights up Brook St, cross The Grove taking Wells Rd up to the Moors.* Home-made teas. **Adm £2.50, chd free.** Wed 1, Sun 5 June (11-4.30).
Delightful ²/₃ -acre steep garden on edge of Ilkley Moor. Sheltered woodland underplanted with naturalistic, flowing tapestry of foliage, shade loving flowers, shrubs and ferns amongst large moss covered boulders. Natural stream, bridges, meandering gravel paths and steep steps lend magic to 'Dingley Dell'. Lawns, large rockery and summerhouse with stunning views. Steep slopes and gravel paths.

43 HILLBARK
Church Lane, Bardsey, Nr Leeds LS17 9DH. Tim Gittins & Malcolm Simm, www.hillbark.co.uk. *4m SW of Wetherby. Turn W off A58 into Church Lane, garden on L before church.* Home-made teas. **Adm £3.50, chd free.** Suns 15 May; 26 June; 10 July (11-5).
Award winning 1-acre country garden. 3 S-facing levels, hidden corners; surprise views. Formal topiary: relaxed perennial planting. Dramatic specimen yew. Ornamental ponds, summerhouse overlooking gravel, rock and stream gardens, large natural pond with ducks. Marginal planting incl bamboo. Woodland area. Large rambling roses. Unusual ceramics. Featured in RHS The Garden. Dream Gardens of England-100 inspirational gardens Barbara Baker & Jerry & Marcus Harpur.

GROUP OPENING

44 NEW HORNSEA GARDENS
Hornsea HU18 1UR. *12 NE of Beverley. On B1242 S-side of Hornsea between Freeport& golf course.* Tea at Nutkins. **Combined adm £4.50, chd free. Sun 5 June (11-4).**

NEW NEW HOUSE
Belvedere Park HU18 1JJ. Mrs Kate Willans
N end of Cliffe Rd, opp bus arage. Garden halfway down L hand fork.

NUTKINS
72 Rolston Road, Hornsea HU18 1UR. Alan & Janet Stirling **Visitors also welcome by appt adm £3.** 01964 533721 ashornsea@aol.com

Two gardens set in the popular seaside town. The first, larger with many different areas and fun for children. The second, smaller, but a real gem with plants for the enthusiast. Hornsea has seaside attractions, as well as the Mere, Museum, Freeport and Honeysuckle farm nearby. Nutkins covers over $^3/_4$ -acre with herbaceous borders, bog garden, streamside walk and woodland garden with features for children of all ages. Pergolas, gazebo and plenty of seating to linger and enjoy different views of the garden, and see light play on many pieces of stained glass. New House has a small garden, very close to the sea, packed with both hardy and tender herbaceous planting in borders and island beds; a wildlife pond and succulent collection, with paved areas for seating. Plant sale at New House. Wheelchair access at Nutkins. Hornsea Garden Fair Sun 8 May 10-4 at the Floral Hall.

♿ ❀ ☕

Pergolas, gazebo and plenty of seating to linger and enjoy different views of the garden, and see light play on many pieces of stained glass . . .

45 HOTHAM HALL
Hotham YO43 4UA. Stephen & Carolyn Martin, 01430 422054, carolynandstephenmartin@ btinternet.com. *15m W of Hull. Nr North Cave, J38 of M62 turn towards North Cave, follow signs for Hotham.* **Visitors welcome by appt.**
C18 Grade II house (not open), stable block and clock tower in mature parkland setting with established gardens. Lake with bridge over to newly planted island (arboretum). Garden with Victorian pond and mixed borders. Selection of spring flowering bulbs. Gravel paths.

♿ ❀ ☎

46 56 HULL ROAD
Cottingham HU16 4PU. Keith & Mary Gregersen, 01482 849488, keith.gregersen@hotmail.co.uk. *NW edge of Hull. From Hull, Cottingham Rd & Hull Rd (continuation), L after West Bulls PH. From Cottingham $^1/_4$ m from r'about.* Home-made teas. **Adm £3, chd free. Sun 5 June (1-5). Visitors also welcome by appt.**
This varied and interesting $^1/_3$ -acre suburban garden leads visitors through several distinct areas featuring mature trees and shrubs, mixed borders, patio and pergola with old wisteria, formal pond, yew hedges, fernery, gravel garden, antique summer house and lots of seating areas to rest and enjoy the views.

♿ ❀ ☕ ☎

47 HUNMANBY GRANGE
Wold Newton YO25 3HS. Tom & Gill Mellor. *12$^1/_2$ m SE of Scarborough. Hunmanby Grange is a farm between Wold Newton & Hunmanby on the rd from Burton Fleming to Fordon.* Tea. **Adm £3, chd free. Sat 4, Sun 5 June (11-5).**
3-acre garden created from exposed open field, on top of Yorkshire Wolds nr coast. Hedges and fences now provide shelter from wind, making series of gardens with yr-round interest and seasonal highlights. The Wold Top Brewery open to visit with the garden.

♿ ❀ ☕

48 ◆ JACKSONS WOLD
Sherburn. Mr & Mrs Richard Cundall, 07966 531995, www.jacksonswoldgarden.com. *11m E of Malton, 10m SW of Scarborough. A64 in Sherburn. T-lights take Weaverthorpe Rd. R fork*

to Helperthorpe. E & W Lutton. **Adm £3, chd free. For NGS: Suns 22 May; 19 June (1-5). For other opening times and information, please phone or see garden website.**
2-acre garden with stunning views of the Vale of Pickering. Walled garden with mixed borders, numerous old shrub roses underplanted with unusual perennials. Woodland paths lead to further shrub and perennial borders. Lime avenue with wild flower meadow. Traditional vegetable garden with roses, flowers and box edging framed by Victorian greenhouse. Adjoining nursery. Featured in The GGG.

♿ ❀ ☕

49 JASMINE HOUSE
145 The Grove, Wheatley Hills, Doncaster DN2 5SN. Ray & Anne Breame, 01302 361470. *2m E of Doncaster. 1m E of Doncaster Royal Infirmary off A18. Turn R into Chestnut Ave (Motor Save on corner).* Home-made teas. **Adm £2, chd free. Sun 5 June (1-5). Visitors also welcome by appt.**
Colourful tropical to traditional, plant packed haven. A real surprise awaits you on entering this town 'garden for all seasons'. Climbers festoon archways that lead to enclosed gardens displaying the gardener's love of rare and unusual plants, from ferns and alpines to bonsai and tender perennials. Featured in Dalesman, Yorkshire Today and Yorkshire Post.

❀ ☕ ☎

50 KELBERDALE
Wetherby Road, Knaresborough HG5 8LN. Stan & Chris Abbott, 01423 862140, chrisatkelberdale@btinternet.com. *1m S of Knaresborough. On B6164 Wetherby Rd. House on L immed after ring rd (A658) r'about.* **Visitors welcome by appt May to July, groups of 15+, coaches welcome.**
Winner of 3 national awards, this owner-made and maintained plantsman's garden overlooking the R Nidd has a bit of everything. Full of yr round interest with large traditional herbaceous border, colour themed beds, pond and bog garden, alpine house and troughs and vegetable garden. The wild garden with large pond and meadow is a haven for wildlife.

♿ ❀ ☎

51 ♦ **LAND FARM**
Colden, Hebden Bridge HX7 7PJ.
Mr J Williams, 01422 842260,
www.landfarmgardens.co.uk. *8m W of Halifax. From Halifax at Hebden Bridge go through 2 sets T-lights. Take turning circle to Heptonstall. Follow signs to Colden. After 2³/₄ m turn R at Edge Lane 'no through' rd, follow signs from bus stop at Colden.* Adm £4, chd free. For NGS: weekends & BH May to end of Aug (10-5). For opening times and information, please phone or see garden website.
6 acres incl alpine, herbaceous, formal and newly developing woodland garden, meconopsis varieties in June, cardiocrinum *giganteum* in July. Elevation 1000ft N-facing. C17 house (not open). Art Gallery and garden sculpture. The garden is listed on LAPMAG for garden visitors as being one of the best 80 gardens of England and Wales. Limited wheelchair access.

&♿ ⚘ ☕

52 ▶ **LAWKLAND HALL**
Austwick LA2 8AT. Mr & Mrs G Bowring. *3m N of Settle. Turn S off A65 at Austwick/Lawkland Xrds or Giggleswick/Lawkland Xrds signed Lawkland/Eldroth. Follow signs to Lawkland.* Home-made teas. Adm £4, chd free. Sun 10 July (11.30-5).
C17 Grade 1 listed hall (not open) set in 2 acre garden with lake. Developed over the last 10yrs by horticulturist owner, doors in high stone walls, gates and openings in hedges lead into series of outdoor rooms. Black thatch and green oak rustic gazebo in rose garden with mixed planting surrounded by low box hedges. Old stone potting shed in pink garden. Cone shaped yews form vista to woodland beyond lake. Borders backed by house walls and yew hedges combine herbaceous perennials, shrubs and roses. Kitchen garden with summerhouse. Plant sales.

⚘ ⌂ ☕

THE LEYLANDS
See Derbyshire.

53 ▶ **LINDEN HOUSE**
16 Northgate, Cottingham HU16 4HH. Eric Nicklas, 01482 847788,
mrnick@mrnick.karoo.co.uk. *4m NW of Hull. On A164 turn onto B1233 signed Cottingham, garden on L 50yds before railway Xing. From*

A1079, turn onto B1233, straight on at bowling club, over Xing then 50yds on R. Light refreshments and teas. Adm £2.50, chd free (share to Hospice in Hull). Sat 21, Sun 22 May (11-5). Visitors also welcome by appt.
This interesting small garden with a thoughtfully curved lawn, numerous shrubs, pond and aviary which blend well together. (A garden well worth seeing.) Craft demonstration.

&♿ ⚘ ☕ ☎

Doors in high stone walls, gates and openings in hedges lead into series of outdoor rooms . . . .

54 ▶ **LINDEN LODGE**
Newbridge Lane, nr Wilberfoss, York YO41 5RB. Robert Scott & Jarrod Marsden, 07900 003538,
rdsjsm@gmail.com. *10m E of York. A1079 Hull/York rd, E of Wilberfoss and NW of Barmby Moor. Take turn signed Bolton, onto Bolton Lane. At Xrds turn L, garden after Bolton Hall on R.* Cream Teas at Refreshments served in the marquee. Fri 17 June: Preview evening includes wine/juice & nibbles, Sat 18 - Sun 19 June: cream teas. Adm £4, chd free. Sat 18, Sun 19 June (11-5) Evening Opening £6, wine, Fri 17 June (6-8.30).
Visitors also welcome by appt Minimum of 15.
1-acre garden, owner-designed and constructed since 2000, with many choice and unusual plants and trees. Gravel paths edged with box and lavender lead to herbaceous/mixed borders, wildlife pond and summerhouse. Kitchen garden, glasshouse, orchard and woodland area and formal garden with pond and water feature. 5 acres of developing meadow. Open Garden Weekend: Craft stalls, plant sales. Refreshments served in the marquee. Featured in The 100 Inspirational Gardens of England, published by Merrell.The Yorkshire Post.The Journal, East Riding of Yorkshire.The East Riding Mail. Some gravel paths.

&♿ ⚘ ☕ ☎

55 ▶ **LITTLE EDEN**
Lancaster Street, Castleford WF10 2NP. Melvyn & Linda Moran, 01977 514275,
melvynmoran609@btinternet.com. *2¹/₂ m NW of M62 J32. A639 (Castleford). 1st r'about 2nd exit B6136 (Ferrybridge). At top of hill turn L at T-lights (Fryston Rd), straight over next r'about, 3rd R (Elizabeth Drive) 2nd L (Dunderdale Crescent), 3rd L (Lancaster St).* Home-made teas. Adm £3, chd free. Suns 26 June; 14 Aug (10-4). Also open Millrace Nursery. Visitors also welcome by appt.
Plant lovers' small hidden oasis of unusual, tender, exotic and tropical plants in the midst of large housing estate. Trellis and archway festooned with climbers, colourful pots and hanging baskets. Herbaceous perennials, succulents, tree ferns, palms, bananas, pond and decorative summerhouse.

&♿ ⚘ ☕ ☎

GROUP OPENING

56 ▶ **LITTLETHORPE GARDENS**
nr Ripon HG4 3LG. *1¹/₂ m SE of Ripon. Off A61 Ripon bypass, follow sign to Littlethorpe. Parking at Field Cottage, at Greencroft & Village Hall for Kirkella. Field Cottage & Greencroft are 1m apart. No footpaths.* Home-made teas at village hall, excellent facilities. Combined adm £6, chd free. Sun 14 Aug (12-5).

FIELD COTTAGE
Littlethorpe Road. Richard & Liz Tite

GREENCROFT
Pottery Lane. David & Sally Walden

KIRKELLA
Pottery Lane. Jacky Barber

Littlethorpe is a small village on the southern edge of Ripon characterised by houses interspersed with fields. St Michael's church consecrated in 1878, is a 'Chapel of Ease'. Established in 1831 Littlethorpe Pottery is still using its own clay. Field Cottage is a 1 acre plantsman's garden on a dry, freely draining soil with a formal walled garden, vegetable and cut flower plot, 18' Victorian style greenhouse with a pelargonium collection, extensive range of unusual and tender plants in containers, mixed island beds incl brilliant clashing coloured autumn border of late flowering perennials, mainly dahlias, heleniums, asters and grasses. Greencroft a ¹/₂ acre informal garden made by the owners who are local builders. Special ornamental features incl gazebo, temple pavilions, stone-wall with mullions, pergola and formal pool. Long herbaceous borders planted with late flowering perennials, annuals and exotics. A circular garden with views through stone wall mullions to log cabin with shingle roof and large wildlife pond. Kirkella a small bungalow garden in the heart of the village, recently created by a plantswoman and flower arranger to give constant interest. The front gravel garden has a Mediterranean feel; the paved rear garden with a decorative summerhouse is densely planted with unusual and half-hardy perennials, incl many salvias, collections in pots, small water feature and living willow hedge concealing a small productive vegetable pot. Limited wheelchair access.

57 LITTLETHORPE MANOR

Ripon HG4 3LG. Mr & Mrs J P Thackray,
thackray@littlethorpemanor.com.
Outskirts of Ripon by racecourse. Ripon bypass A61. Follow Littlethorpe Rd from Dallamires Lane r'about to stable block with clock tower. Map supplied on application. Light refreshments & teas served in marquee. **Adm £6, chd free. Visitors welcome by appt** from end May to start Sept, groups of 20+.
11 acres. Walled garden based on cycle of seasons with box, herbaceous, roses, gazebo. Sunken garden with white rose parterre and herbs. Brick pergola with white wisteria, blue and yellow borders. Terraces with ornamental pots. Formal lawns with fountain pool, hornbeam towers and yew hedging. Box headed hornbeam drive with Aqualens water feature. Parkland with lake, late summer planting and classical pavilion. Cut flower garden. Spring bulbs. Winter garden.

58 LODGE YARD

Main Street, Askrigg, nr Leyburn DL8 3HQ. Holiday Property Bond.
On the main st of Askrigg, opp The White Rose Hotel, through the arch. Parking in public car park or nr

Rivelin Cottage

church. Limited disabled parking at Lodge Yard.* **Adm £3.50, chd free. Wed 15 June (11-4).**
A garden with stunning views of the Yorkshire Dales, sheltered by stone walls softened with climbers incl many roses and clematis. Large terraced garden at rear created by sleepers topped by box hedging and abundant mixed planting. Wild flower area, with fruit trees. Slowworm Havens. Courtyard gardens.

59 NEW LOW SUTTON

Sutton Lane, Masham HG4 4PB.
Steve & Judi Smith. *1¹/₂ m W of Masham. 1¹/₂ m from Masham towards Leyburn A6108. L turn into Sutton Lane which is a single track tarmac road. Low Sutton is ¹/₄ m on L.* Light refreshments and teas. **Adm £2.50, chd free. Sun 17 July (11.30-5).**
Developing since 2007 a fresh approach to Cottage Gardening. Concentric circular floral colour wheel surrounded by scented Roses and Clematis. Abundant variety of fruit and vegetables decoratively grown in raised beds, fruit cage, greenhouse and coldframe. Perrenial border, grasses, fernery and courtyard

surround the house, all set within six acre smallholding. Plants for sale.

60 LOWER CRAWSHAW

Off Stringer House Lane, Emley, nr Huddersfield HD8 9SU. Mr & Mrs Neil Hudson. *8m E of Huddersfield. From Huddersfield turn R to Emley off A642 (Paul Lane). M1 J39 (A636) direction Denby Dale, 1m after Bretton r'about turn R to Emley, ¹/₂ m beyond Emley village turn R (Stringer House Lane) continue for 1/2mile. Blind corner on approach to field carpark, please take care of oncoming cars on approach to carpark.* Home-made & cream teas. **Adm £4, chd free. Sun 3 July (12-5).**
Large country garden with extensive views and incorporating the borrowed landscape. Surrounds 1690s farmhouse (not open) with extensive range of old farm buildings. A natural stream runs through the garden, dammed on several levels and opening into 2 large ponds. Walled vegetable garden, enclosed rose garden, orchard, and courtyard. Naturalistic planting of shrubs, trees and perennials.

61 LOWER HEUGH COTTAGE GARDEN

Kirk Lane, Eastby, Skipton BD23 6SH. Trevor & Marian Nash, 01756 793702, nash862@btinternet.com. *2¹/₂ m NE of Skipton. Follow the A59/65 N ring rd around Skipton, turn at signs for Embsay (railway) & Eastby. In Embsay follow signs for Eastby & Barden onto Kirk Lane. 6th house on R.* Adm £5, chd free (incls conducted tour & home-made refreshments). Visitors welcome by appt any time, max 30.
A chattering waterfall invites visitors into this 1 acre S-facing kaiyushiki (Japanese Stroll Garden) and the meikakuri design conveys a sense of peace and calm. The many questions posed by this unique garden high in the Yorkshire Dales are answered during the 60+ minute owner led tour through the Karensansui area and the Roji(tea garden) via the Tori gate; the courtyard corner with Japanese wall and moongate; the ladies garden, woodland area, then to rest in the bamboo pavilion. From here view the Hashi and Chisen areas to hills and crags beyond (Shakkei). Carefully sited Ishitoro (lanterns) amongst mature conifers, acers and oriental plants give colour, shape and texture to this immaculate owner maintained beautiful yr round garden. Yorkshire in Bloom Gold Award.
 🐕 🏨 ☕ ☎

A small enclosed English town garden with an Italian twist lovingly developed and cared for by owners . . .

62 LOWFOLD

Silverdale Close, Darley, nr Harrogate HG3 2PQ. Julian & Pat Brockway, 01423 781248, patbrockway@uwclub.net. *7m NW of Harrogate. A59 (Harrogate-Skipton) turn R after Black Bull PH to Darley & Menwith Hill, straight over at xrds. Turn L at T-junction in Darley village. Silverdale Close is opposite Post Office. Veer left in Close and drive to end of private lane.* Home-made teas. Adm £3, chd free.

Visitors welcome by appt July to mid-Aug, for groups 8+.
Tranquil plantsman's garden, brimming with plants, in a lovely dales setting with beautiful views. Grass paths lead and entice giving different aspects at every turn. Perennials border, flowering shrubs, mature rock garden, exuberant bog garden, foliage plants, ornamental grasses, roses and clematis.
 ♿ ☕ ☎

63 MANOR FARM

Thixendale, Malton YO17 9TG. Charles & Gilda Brader, www.manorfarmthixendale.co.uk. *10m SE of Malton. Unclassified rd through Birdsall, ¹/₂ m up hill, turn L at Xrds for Thixendale - 3m, 1st farm on R. 17m E of York, turn off A166 rd at the top of Garrowby Hill, follow signs for Thixendale, 4m turn into village, drive through to end, farm on L.* Home-made teas. Adm £3, chd free. Wed 13 July (2-6).
Created since 1987. 1 acre divided up into many areas of interest. Pergolas, garden room, alpine areas, small knot garden with ruined shed, rocks and water, lawns, herbaceous and shrubs and shaded area, new projects and planting.
 ❀ 🛏 ☕

64 MANOR HOUSE

Church Street, North Cave, Brough HU15 2LW. Mr & Mrs Christian Carver, 01430 421418, christiancarver@btinternet.com. *1¹/₂ m from M62, J38. B1230 E of North Cave, leaving village next to church.* Home-made teas. Adm £3.50. Visitors welcome by appt, between mid May & end of June.
Next generation of family in situ. 2-acre garden surrounding C18 farmhouse with octagonal dovecote, stream and lake. Parterre for late-summer interest; herbaceous border, glasshouse with productive garden and small orchard. Naturalistic planting at rear running into 20yr-old arboretum with spring bulbs and wild flowers and woodland walk by lakeside.
 ❀ ☕ ☎

65 MANSION COTTAGE

8 Gillus Lane, Bempton, Bridlington YO15 1HW. Polly & Chris Myers, 01262 851404, chrismyers@tinyworld.co.uk. *2m NE of Bridlington. From Bridlington take B1255 to Flamborough. 1st L at T-lights, go up Bempton Lane, turn*

1st R into Short Lane then L at T-junction. Cross railway into Bempton, Gillus Lane is L fork at church. Adm £3, chd free. Sat 6, Sun 7 Aug (10-4). Visitors also welcome by appt during Aug, groups of 10+.
Exuberant, lush, vibrant perennial planting highlighted with grasses in this hidden, peaceful and surprising garden offering many views and features. Visitors book comments 'Wonderful garden, a real treat full of colour and creativity' 'Shangri-la heaven, awesome lunch', 'It is bliss here'. New for 2011 - apothecary garden. Delicious home-made lunches, teas and produce. Local photographic exhibition.
 🐕 ❀ ☕ ☎

66 39 MARKET PLACE

South Cave HU15 2BS. Lin & Paul Holland, 01430 421874, paulandlin@btinternet.com. *12m W of Hull. From A63 turn N to South Cave on A1034. House on LH-side opp PO, before Xrds.* Home-made teas. Adm £3, chd free. Sun 24 July (2-5). Visitors also welcome by appt.
Small walled garden with eclectic planting. Established trees, cottage garden plants and evergreen shrubs. Rockeries, gravel fernery with grasses and water feature. Interesting stonework and lots of nooks and crannies. A few shallow steps and gravel paths.
 🐕 ❀ ☕ ☎

67 NEW MERE'STEAD

28 Kelmscott Garth, Manston Crossgates, Leeds LS15 8LB. Mr & Mrs Renzi. *6m E of Leeds. 1m from M1 J46 follow A63 towards Leeds. Take ring-road (A6120) then follow signs to Barwick-in-Elmet. At 2nd T- light turn R (Penda's Way), then 1st L.* Home-made teas. Adm £2.50, chd free. Sun 7 Aug (12-5).
A small enclosed English town garden with an Italian twist lovingly developed and cared for by owners. Mature trees, magnolia and cedar deodara, underplanted with interesting perennials and bulbs giving colour and foliage interest throughout the year. Arches festooned with climbers, small wildlife pond, pots with succulents, colourful summer bulbs and alpine troughs. Winner of Leeds in Bloom for the last 4yrs.
 ❀ ☕

MILL FARM
See Lincolnshire.

68 MILLGATE HOUSE
Millgate, Richmond DL10 4JN.
Tim Culkin & Austin Lynch,
01748 823571,
www.millgatehouse.com. *Centre of Richmond. House is located at bottom of Market Place opp Barclays Bank. Next to Halifax Building Soc.* **Adm £2.50, chd £1.50. Sun 5 June (8-9). Also open Easingtown & Swale Cottage. Visitors also welcome by appt.**
SE walled town garden overlooking R Swale. Although small, the garden is full of character, enchantingly secluded with plants and shrubs. Foliage plants incl ferns and hostas. Old roses, interesting selection of clematis, small trees and shrubs. RHS associate garden. Immensely stylish, national award-winning garden. Collections of ferns, hostas, old roses and snowdrops.

69 MILLRACE NURSERY
84 Selby Road, Garforth, Leeds LS25 1LP. Mr & Mrs Carthy, 0113 2869233, carol@millrace-plants.co.uk, www.millrace-plants.co.uk. *5m E of Leeds. On A63 in Garforth. 1m from M1 J46, 3m from A1.* Home-made teas. **Adm £3, chd free. Suns 26 June; 14 Aug (1-5). Also open Little Eden. Visitors also welcome by appt Groups of 10+.**
Overlooking a secluded valley, garden incl large herbaceous borders containing over 3000 varieties of perennials, shrubs and trees, many of which are unusual and drought tolerant. Garden includes an ornamental pond, vegetable garden and walled terraces leading to wildflower meadow, small woodland, bog garden and wildlife lakes. 14 Aug seed collecting opportunity. Specialist nursery.

70 NEW MILLVIEW COTTAGE
21 Church Street, North Cave, Brough HU15 2LJ. Emma Jackson. *15m W of Hull. M62E, J38 turn L to N.Cave B1230 E of village on R of Church St. For car park, follow directions to Fawley House.* Teas at Fawley House. **Adm £2.50, chd free. Sun 18 Sept (12-4). Also open Fawley House.**
An inspirational cottage garden, long and narrow, split into different styled sections. A rear extension, of Scandinavian influence links the house to a contemporary outdoor

room with terrace, raised beds, wooden walkway, water feature and exotic planting. A more traditional area leads to a family garden, with vegetables, and greenhouse. Featured in East Riding Journal and House Beautiful.

71 MON ABRI
Golden Smithies Lane, Swinton S64 8DL. Fred & Mona Marklew, Vivien Kerry. *5m E of Rotherham. A653 Rotherham to Wath upon Dearne. Turn R at r'about A6022 (Rockingham Rd) to Swinton. 3rd L at T-lights & PH (Golden Smithies Lane).* Light refreshments & home-made teas. **Adm £2.50, chd free. Sun 10 July (10.30-4).**
An enclosed $^1/_2$-acre garden beneath mature trees maintained by owners with a passion for plants. Island beds have evolved into a series of 'garden rooms' with seating, planted for full sun and deep shade. Collections of camellias, rhododendrons, shrubs and herbaceous perennials give colour and interest all year. Water features, small greenhouse. Featured in Barnsley Chronicle, Rotherham Advertiser & Weekender. Partial wheelchair access.

72 ◆ NEWBY HALL & GARDENS
Ripon HG4 5AE. Mr R C Compton, 01423 322583, www.newbyhall.com. *2m E of Ripon. (HG4 5AJ for Sat Nav). Signed from A1 & Ripon town centre.* **For opening times and information, please phone or see garden website.**
40 acres extensive gardens laid out in 1920s. Full of rare and beautiful plants. Formal seasonal gardens, stunning double herbaceous borders to R Ure and National Collection holder *Cornus*. Miniature railway and adventure gardens for children. Contemporary sculpture park set in a peaceful woodland (June - Sept).

9 NEWFIELD CRESCENT
See Derbyshire.

73 ◆ NORTON CONYERS
Wath, nr Ripon HG4 5EQ. Sir James & Lady Graham, 01765 640333, norton.conyers@btinternet.com. *4 m N of Ripon. Take Melmerby & Wath sign off A61 Ripon-Thirsk. Go*

through both villages to boundary wall. Signed entry 300metres on R. **Adm £5, chd free. For NGS: Sun 12 June (2-5). For other opening times and information, please phone or email.**
Large C18 walled garden of interest to garden historians. Interesting iron entrance gate; herbaceous borders, yew hedges and Orangery (open to the public) with an attractive little pond in front. Small sales area specialising in unusual hardy plants, fruit in season. House, visited by Charlotte Brontë and inspiration for Thornfield Hall in 'Jane Eyre' is closed for major repairs. Access to Orangery via sloping gravel path.

> The garden is full of character, enchantingly secluded with plants and shrubs . . . Immensely stylish . . .

74 THE NURSERY
15 Knapton Lane, Acomb, York YO26 5PX. Tony Chalcraft & Jane Thurlow, 01904 781691. *2½ m W of York. Follow B1224 towards Acomb & York city centre, from A1237 York ring road. Turn L at first mini r'about into Beckfield Lane. Knapton Lane 2nd L after 150 metres.* Home-made teas. **Adm £2.50, chd free. Sun 17 July (1-5). Evening Opening Fri 22 July (6-9). Visitors also welcome by appt, groups 10 +.**
Hidden attractive and productive 1-acre organic garden behind suburban house. Wide range of top and soft fruit (incl 40+ varieties apples and pears). Many different vegetables grown both outside and under cover including a large greenhouse. Productive areas interspersed with informal ornamental plantings providing colour and habitat for wildlife. Produce for sale. Tomato tasting on 22 July.

Jasmine Cottage

and huge beech hedges. An award winning forest garden for those keen about permaculture. Several plant and other garden stalls. We are open from noon so please bring a picnic round the mill pond if it's fine weather.

78 THE ORCHARD
4a Blackwood Rise, Cookridge LS16 7BG. Carol & Michael Abbott, 01132 676764. *5m N of Leeds centre. Off A660 (Leeds-Otley) N of A6120 Ring Rd bear L onto Otley Old Rd. Before radio mast turn L (Tinshill Lane). Please park in Tinshill Lane after passing council flats.* Light refreshments & home-made teas. **Adm £2.50, chd free.** Sun 12 June (12.30-5.30). Visitors also welcome by appt evening visits 29 May to 10 July. Groups 10+.
1/4 -acre hidden suburban oasis of peace and tranquillity. Differing levels made by owners using old stone, found on site, planted for yr round interest. Long rockery, fruit tree arbour and sheltered oriental styled seated area linked by narrow grass lawns and steps. Mixed perennials, bulbs and pots amongst paved and pebbled areas. Silver medal - Leeds in Bloom.

75 THE OLD COACH HOUSE
Church Lane, Elvington YO41 4HD. Simon & Toni Richardson. *8m SE of York. From A1079 immediately after York outer ring road, turn on B1228 for Elvington. Disabled parking only on Church Lane. Please park in village.* Light refreshments & teas at village hall. **Adm £3, chd free.** Sun 12 June (12-5).
Delightful atmospheric owner-made 2-acre garden. Extensive mixed long borders, hosta garden and large natural wildlife pond leading to summerhouse, vegetable garden and long rose pergola. Enclosed flower garden with ornamental pool adjacent to house. Fun for all the family on the village green with Elvington village fete.

76 THE OLD PRIORY
Everingham YO42 4JD. Dr J D & Mrs H J Marsden, 01430 860222, marsd13@aol.com. *15m SE of York, 5 1/2 m from Pocklington. 2m S of the A1079 York-Hull Rd. Everingham has 3 access rds, the Old Priory is to the east of the Village.* Visitors welcome

by appt. Garden best last 2 weeks of May & first 2 weeks of June. Country garden of 2 acres on dry sandy loam and wet peat land. Polytunnels, walled vegetable garden. Mixed herbaceous borders drop down to bog garden where paths bridge the stream into less formal garden which leads to lake. New 1/4 -acre wildlife pond. Interesting wild flora and fauna.

77 OLD SLENINGFORD HALL
Mickley, nr Ripon HG4 3JD. Jane & Tom Ramsden. *5m NW of Ripon. Off A6108. After N Stainley turn L, follow signs to Mickley. Gates on R after 1 1/2 m opp cottage.* Home-made teas & light refreshments. **Adm £5, chd free.** Sat 4, Sun 5 June (12-4.30).
A unique opportunity to see both a large English country garden and developing 'Forest Garden'. Early C19 house (not open) and garden with original layout; wonderful mature trees, woodland walk and Victorian fernery; romantic lake with islands, watermill, walled kitchen garden; beautiful long herbaceous border, yew

79 NEW OSWALDKIRK HALL
Oswaldkirk, York YO62 5XT. David & Sara Craig. *4m E of Helmsley. Take road through Oswaldkirk village signposted Ampleforth. Pass pub and church, house last on left with long stone wall.* Home-made teas. **Adm £3, chd free.** Sat 11, Sun 12 June (1-5).
4 acre garden surrounding C17 listed country house, on a slope. Large kitchen garden, orchard, stumpery, herbaceous borders, white garden, sculpture. Fabulous views across the valley towards Howardian Hills.

80 NEW OVERTHORPE J I & N SCHOOL
Edge Top Road, Thornhill, Dewsbury WF12 0BH. www.overthorpe.kgfl.digitalbrain. com. *1m S of Dewsbury. South leave M1 at J38, signed Yorkshire Sculpture Park, through West Bretton. At large r'bout go over,turn R onto B6117 after Black Bull PH. Through Netherton to Middlestown, L at lights, after 100metres R at GO Outdoors Store, signed Dewsbury. After 2 m, L onto Overthorpe Rd, which becomes*

Edgetop Rd, school is on your R Thornhill Trojans Rugby club. North leave M1 J40, follow A638 to Dewsbury. In town centre, follow ring rd signed to Huddersfield. Turn L onto B6409 at Dewsbury Minster. Keep on 1m. At double mini r'abouts keep left, continue on for 1m before turning R onto Overthorpe Rd (which becomes Edgetop Rd) at the brow of the hill. Light refreshments & home-made teas. **Adm £2.50, chd free.** Evening Opening Thur 7 July (4-7.30).
A rare opportunity to visit the grounds of a primary school that are managed for outdoor learning, play and wildlife. Large kitchen and vegetable garden, orchard, wildlife garden and ponds, meadows, WW2 themed garden. Woodland and natural play areas, all richly planted to create opportunities for play and learning in a natural setting. Drama and music in the grounds. Refreshments provided by children from school grown produce. Plant sale. Gold Award Yorkshire in Bloom, Chairman's Discretionary Young Person's Award.

OWL END
See Derbyshire.

81 ◆ **PARCEVALL HALL GARDENS**
Skyreholme BD23 6DE. Walsingham College, 01756 720311, www.parcevallhallgardens.co.uk. *9m N of Skipton. Signs from B6160 Bolton Abbey-Burnsall rd or off B6265 Grassington-Pateley Bridge.* Tearoom. **Adm £6, chd free, concessions £5.** For NGS: Wed 15 June (10-6). For other opening times and information, please phone or see garden website.
The only garden open daily in the Yorkshire Dales National Park. 24 acres in Wharfedale sheltered by mixed woodland; terrace garden, rose garden, rock garden, fish ponds. Mixed borders, tender shrubs (desfontainea, crinodendron, camellias); autumn colour. Bird watching, old apple orchard for picnics.

82 ▶ **PARK HOUSE**
Creyke Lane, Welton HU15 1NQ. Noel & Jane Thompson, 01482 666935. *9m W of Hull. From A63 E towards Hull, follow signs for Welton. Park in village. Creyke Lane is unmade rd to side of Green Dragon*

PH, rough for approx 50yds. Home-made teas. **Adm £3.50, chd free.** Wed 25 May (1-5); Sun 5 June (11-4.30); Evening Opening £4.50, wine, Thur 9 June (6-9). Visitors also welcome by appt.
Informal 1-acre plot with mature beech trees, the garden is planted for yr-round interest. Featuring naturalistic mixed planting, woodland walk, copper rill, pergolas, ornamental herb garden and raised vegetable bedsNEW! Gravel garden and secret garden. Vintage cars on display - weather permitting.

PINEFIELDS
See Lincolnshire.

PRIMROSE COTTAGE
See Nottinghamshire.

83 ▶ **130 PRINCE RUPERT DRIVE**
Tockwith, York YO26 7PU. Mr & Mrs B Wright, 01423 358791, anneswright@hotmail.com, www.dryad-home.co.uk. *7m E of Wetherby. From B1224 Wetherby/York rd turn N to Cattal, after 1m turn R at Xrds to Tockwith. 1st turning on R in village. Please do not park in the cul-de-sac.* Home-made teas. **Adm £3, chd free.** Suns 17 Apr (1-4); 18 Sept (1-5). Visitors also welcome by appt within 2 weeks of main openings, min 20 visitors.
¹/₂ -acre enthusiast's garden planted for yr-round interest from early hellebores, cyclamen and bulbs to late perennials and grasses mixed with our large fern collection, in beds connected by gravel paths. Many plants grown from seed, incl wild-collected seed. Rock and bog gardens, pond and pergola, glasshouses, shade house, kitchen garden with vegetables and trained fruit, small nursery.

Drama and music in the grounds. Refreshments provided by children from school grown produce . . .

84 ▶ **2 PROSPECT PLACE**
Outlane, Huddersfield HD3 3FL. Carol & Andy Puszkiewicz. *5m N of Huddersfield. 1m N of M62. J24 (W) take A643 to J23 (E) follow A640 to Rochdale. Turn R immed before 40mph sign (Gosport Lane). Parking in adjacent field.* Home-made teas. **Adm £2.50, chd free.** Sun 10 July (12-5).
1-acre long, intimate garden high in the Pennines (900ft). Narrow paths lead from cottage herbaceous borders and pond to shade areas and secret garden with camomile lawn, chocolate and silver borders surrounding circular bed and productive kitchen garden with trained fruit and herbs. Evolving wild area with native trees, large pond with indigenous planting, narrow stream and meadow.

85 ▶ **24 RED BANK ROAD**
off Whitcliffe Lane, Ripon HG4 2LE. Margaret & David Rivers. *From r'about at S end of Ripon bypass (A61), head N for city centre. After approx ¹/₂ m take 7th turning L up Whitcliffe Lane (opp South Lodge PH). Red Bank Rd is 3rd R (750yds).* **Adm £2.50, chd free.** Wed 18, Sun 22 May (2-5).
Plant enthusiasts' small garden constantly developing, now planted for yr-round interest. Raised beds, rockeries and gravel contain wide variety of perennials incl species peonies (some grown from seed), alpines and shrubs chosen to be able to cope with the difficult conditions of dry sun and dry shade.

RENISHAW HALL GARDENS
See Derbyshire.

86 ▶ **REWELA COTTAGE**
Skewsby, York YO61 4SG. John Plant & Daphne Ellis, 01347 888125, plantjohnsgarden@btinternet.com. *4m N of Sheriff Hutton, 15 miles N of York. After Sheriff Hutton, towards Terrington, turn L towards Whenby & Brandsby. Turn R just past Whenby to Skewsby. Turn L into village. 400yds on R.* Light refreshments, home-made & cream & teas. BBQ sausage & onions. **Adm £3.50, chd free.** Suns 8 May; 24 July (10-5). Visitors also welcome by appt May & June only, groups of 10+.
³/₄ -acre ornamental garden, designed by current owner, featuring unusual

Be tempted by a plant from a plant stall ✿

trees, shrubs, and architectural plants. Other features include a pond, pergola, natural stone sunken garden, breeze house, raised vegetable garden. May for Rhododendrons, Azaleas, Magnolias and spring bulbs. July for summer flowering plants, year round interest. All unusual trees and shrubs have labels giving full descriptions, picture, and any cultivation notes incl propagation. Plant sales are specimens from the garden. Featured in York Evening Press, Yorkshire Life, Yorkshire Gardens and Barnsley's Mosaic magazine. Some slopes and gravel.

87 ◆ RHS GARDEN HARLOW CARR
Crag Lane, Harrogate HG3 1QB. Royal Horticultural Society, 01423 565418, www.rhs.org.uk/harlowcarr. *1½ m W of Harrogate town centre. On B6162 (Harrogate - Otley).* **For opening times and information, please phone, or see garden website.**
One of Yorkshire's most relaxing yet inspiring locations! Highlights incl spectacular herbaceous borders, streamside garden, alpines, scented and kitchen gardens. 'Gardens Through Time', woodland and wild flower meadow. Events all yr.

88 THE RIDINGS
Bridlington Road, Burton Fleming, Driffield YO25 3PE. Roy & Ruth Allerston, 01262 470489. *11m NE of Driffield. 11m SW of Scarborough. 7m NW of Bridlington. From Driffield B1249 before Fox Holes turn R to Burton Fleming. From Scarborough A165 turn R to Burton Fleming.* Home-made teas. **Adm £2.50, chd free. Suns 22 May; 3 July (1-5). Visitors also welcome by appt.**
Tranquil cottage garden designed by owners in 2001 on reclaimed site. Brick pergola and arches covered with climbers lead to secret garden with lavender edged beds. Colour-themed mixed borders with old English roses. Paved terrace with water feature and farming bygones, gravel garden and small potager. Art exhibition by local artists.

89 RUDSTON HOUSE
Long Street, Rudston, nr Driffield YO25 4UH. Mr & Mrs Simon Dawson, 01262 420400. *5m W of*

Bridlington. On B1253. S at Bosville Arms for approx 300yds. Light refreshments & teas. **Adm £3.50, chd free. Sun 17 July (11-5). Visitors also welcome by appt Jun-Aug, groups any size, coaches permitted.**
Birthplace of authoress Winifred Holtby. Victorian farmhouse (not open) and 3 acres of exuberant garden with fine old trees, lawns, paths with clipped box hedges, conifers, shrubs, greenhouses, roses, interesting potager with named vegetable varieties, hosta beds with lilies, and short woodland walk, with pond. Plenty of seats and interesting corners and features; children love to explore. Partial wheelchair access, ramp access, gravel paths, negotiable with assistance.

90 ◆ RUSTIC COTTAGE
Front Street, Wold Newton, nr Driffield YO25 3YQ. Jan Joyce, 01262 470710. *13m N of Driffield. From Driffield take B1249 to Foxholes (12m), take R turning signed Wold Newton. Turn L onto Front St, opp village pond, continue up hill garden on L.* Home-made teas. **Adm £2.50, chd free. Sun 4 Sept (11-4). Visitors also welcome by appt.**
Plantswoman's cottage garden of much interest with many choice and unusual plants. Hellebores and bulbs are treats for colder months. Old-fashioned roses, fragrant perennials, herbs and wild flowers, all grown together provide habitat for birds, bees, butterflies and small mammals. It has been described as 'organised chaos'! The owner's 2nd NGS garden.

This school garden illustrates the enthusiasm of the younger generation 'to grow' and learn in an outdoor environment . . .

91 NEW ST JOHN'S RC PRIMARY SCHOOL
Wilberforce Crescent, Beverley HU17 0BU. St John of Beverley RC Primary School. *½ m E of Beverley town centre. From Hull A1174 to Swine Moor Lane L Grovehill Rd. 3rd R Coltman Ave onto Wilberforce Crescent.* Cream teas. **Adm £2.50, chd free. Fri 15, Sun 17 July (1-5).**
Organic vegetable garden, wildlife garden, peace garden with willow sculptures, small orchard and sub-tropical poly-tunnel with 'weird and wonderful' theme. Guided tours by pupils, horticultural demonstrations/ gardening activities, suitable for families. This school garden illustrates the enthusiasm of the younger generation 'to grow' and learn in an outdoor environment. Featured in Hull Daily Mail and Beverley Advertiser. Winner ofYorkshire in Bloom gold medal & best in category. RHS partner school.

92 ◆ SHANDY HALL GARDENS
Coxwold YO61 4AD. The Laurence Sterne Trust, 01347 868465, www.laurencesternetrust.org.uk. *N of York. From A19, 7m from both Easingwold & Thirsk, turn E signed Coxwold.* **Adm £2.50, chd £1. For NGS: Evening Openings Fris 29 Apr; 24 June (6.30-8.30). For other opening times and information, please phone or see garden website.**
Home of C18 author Laurence Sterne. 2 walled gardens, 1 acre of unusual perennials interplanted with tulips and old roses in low walled beds. In old quarry, another acre of trees, shrubs, bulbs, climbers and wild flowers encouraging wildlife, incl over 150 recorded species of moths. Moth trap, identification and release. Access to wild garden by arrangement.

93 SKIPWITH HALL
Skipwith, Selby YO8 5SQ. Mr & Mrs C D Forbes Adam. *9m S of York, 6m N of Selby. From York A19 Selby, L in Escrick, 4m to Skipwith. From Selby A19-York, R onto A163 to Market Weighton, then L after 2m to Skipwith.* Home-made teas. **Adm £4, chd free. Wed 15 June (11-4).**
4-acre walled garden of Queen Anne house (not open) fronted by ancient mulberry. Extensive mixed borders surrounding front and main lawn. Re-created working kitchen with

15' beech hedge, pleached trees, maze and new pear walk. Decorative orchard with espalier and fan-trained fruit, malus and allium. New buddleia walk in woodland. Secret Italian garden (under restoration). Featured in Country Life. Gravel paths.

94 SLEIGHTHOLMEDALE LODGE
Fadmoor YO62 7JG. Dr & Mrs O James, 01751 431942. *6m NE of Helmsley. Parking can be limited in wet weather.* Home-made teas. **Adm £3.50, chd free. Sats, Suns 28, 29 May; 16, 17 July (2-6).** Visitors also welcome by appt weekdays only for groups or individuals.
Hillside garden, walled rose garden and herbaceous borders with delphiniums, roses, verbascums in July. Species tulips and meconopsis in May. Views over peaceful valley in N. Yorks Moors. Featured in Country Life, Gardens Illustrated & The English Garden.

95 SPRING CLOSE FARM
Gill Lane, Kearby LS22 4BS. John & Rosemary Proctor, 01132 886310, jhproctor@bigfastweb.net. *3m W of Wetherby. A661 from Wetherby town centre, turn L at bottom of Spofforth Hill to Sicklinghall. 1m after village turn L at Clap Gate towards Kearby.* Home-made teas. **Adm £5, chd £3. Visitors welcome by appt 18 Apr to July.** Groups 10 - 50, coaches permitted. Plants sales can be arranged on request.
Large mature yet evolving quiet country garden, originally an exposed site, now divided into garden rooms sheltered by clipped yew and beech hedging, with allées and tranquil water garden leading to new orchard with ha-ha and stunning views over Wharfe Valley. Underplanted roses, mulberry trees and herbaceous borders with archways to walled garden with small greenhouse, and enclosed cottage garden.

SQUIRREL LODGE
See Nottinghamshire.

96 STAINSACRE
Carperby DL8 4DD. Colin & Pat Jackson, 01969 663740, stainsacrepat@hotmail.com. *7m W of Leyburn. From A684 1m N of Aysgarth Falls.* Tea. **Adm £3.50, chd**

free. Visitors welcome by appt Groups welcome.
1-acre site on S-sloping hillside created by owners since 1996. Deep mixed borders and island beds with wide variety of hardy and unusual perennials. 2 small wildlife ponds and artificial stream. Open grassed area with native trees and gravel area with specimen hostas. Partial wheelchair access.

Patio planters with summer flowers and hanging baskets displaying a kaleidoscope of colour . . .

GROUP OPENING

97 NEW STAMFORD BRIDGE GARDENS
Stamford Bridge YO41 1PD. 01759 373838 (Mr Tattersall). *Approx 7m E of York on the A166 rd to Bridlington. Please use main car park in the village or station car park on Church Rd.* Cream teas at Daneswell. **Combined adm £5, chd free. Sun 24 July (11-5).** Visitors also welcome by appt July & Aug, groups & coaches welcome to all three gardens.

NEW DANESWELL HOUSE
35 Main Street. YO41 1AD
Pauline Alisha Clayton

NEW GROVE LODGE
2 Butts Close. YO41 1PD
Mr & Mrs G Tattersall

NEW MILL TIMBER
Viking Close, off Viking Road. YO41 1ER Mr & Mrs K Chapman

Three interesting and contrasting gardens situated in the historic village of Stamford Bridge. Grove Lodge is a true plantsman's garden with a large collection of plants grown from seed or propagated from cuttings, by the owner. There are small number of vegetables grown in planters, fruit trees and greenhouse that contains a variety of salad vegetables. Plants for sale. Mill Timber has a vast collection of different types of perennials. The garden is sheltered on one side by

mature trees. Patio planters with summer flowers and hanging baskets displaying a kaleidoscope of colour. Daneswell House is a ³/₄ -acre terraced garden that sweeps down to the R Derwent. Pond and water feature with walk over bridge. Large lawned area with mixed borders and shrubs attracts wildlife.

98 ◆ STILLINGFLEET LODGE
Stewart Lane, Stillingfleet, Nr York YO19 6HP. Mr & Mrs J Cook, www.stillingfleetlodgenurseries.co.uk. *6m S of York. From A19 York-Selby take B1222 towards Sherburn in Elmet.* Light Refreshments. Teas in aid of the local church. **Adm £4, chd free. For NGS: Suns 16 May; 13 June; 5 Sept (1-5).** For other opening times and information please visit garden website .
Plantsman's garden subdivided into smaller gardens, each based on colour theme with emphasis on use of foliage plants. Wild flower meadow and natural pond. 55yd double herbaceous borders. New modern rill garden. Rare breeds of poultry and adjacent plant nursery. Finalist in White Rose Awards for small visitor attraction.

99 NEW SUE PROCTOR PLANTS NURSERY GARDEN
Ings Mill Avenue, Clayton West, Huddersfield HD8 9QG. Sue & Richard Proctor, 01484 866189, sueproctor@talktalk.net. *9m NE of Holmfirth, 10m SW of Wakefield. Off A636 Wakefield & Holmfirth. From M1 J39 in Clayton West Village turn L signed Clayton West, High Hoyland, then R signed Kaye's F & N School. Turn 1st R to Ings Mill Avenue.* Home-made teas. **Adm £2.50, chd free. Evening Opening wine Fri 5 Aug (5-9). Sun 28 Aug (11-5).** Visitors also welcome by appt.
Small, mainly sloping, suburban garden packed full of interest. Summer highlights incl exuberant plantings of flowering perennials with some rare and unusual plants and many varieties of crocosmia. Gravel and rock gardens show off grasses, architectural and foliage plants, ferns and spectacular variety of hostas, especially miniatures, the nursery specialism. The Kirklees Light Railway is closeby. Steam trains and many other attractions for children. Station platforms decorated by garden owners.

SUNNYSIDE COTTAGE
See Nottinghamshire.

100 SWALE COTTAGE
Station Road, Richmond DL10 4LU.
Julie Martin & Dave Dalton.
*Richmond town centre. On foot,
facing bottom of Market Place, turn
L onto Frenchgate, then R onto
Station Rd. House 1st on R.* Cream
Teas. **Adm £2.50, chd free. Sun 5
June (1-5). Also open Easingtown
& Millgate House.**
¹/₂ -acre urban oasis on steep site,
with sweeping views and hidden
corners. Several enclosed garden
rooms on different levels. Mature
herbaceous, rose and shrub garden
with some areas of recent
improvement. Magnificent yew and
cedar. Organic vegetables and soft
fruit and pond. Adjacent orchard and
paddock with sheep and hens.
Featured in 'Amateur Gardening'.
Some gravel paths and inaccessible
areas.

    •

GROUP OPENING

101 NEW SYKEHOUSE GARDENS
Broad Lane, Goole DN14 9AX. *7m
NE of Doncaster. M18 J6, A614
towards Goole, 1st L, follow rd to
junction, approx 3m, turn L, 1st
garden behind arena - 2nd on R.
From A19 towards Doncaster L at
Asken, 4m to Sykehouse.* Home-
made teas at BJ Nurseries.
**Combined adm £5, chd free.
Suns 19 June; 10 July (10-5).**

NEW THE AUCKLANDS
David & Christine Gilson

B J NURSERIES
Broad Lane. Jim & Linda
Bennett
*Visitors also welcome by appt
May to Aug, coaches permitted,
groups 10+. 01405 785277
lindarose59@live.co.uk*

Two very different gardens, one
'supersized' with enormous, stunning
herbaceous borders and the second
(new) with an abundant vegetable
area, and cheerful garden with bright
bedding in addition to more
permanent planting. BJ Nurseries
5- acres of mixed planting,
sympathetic to rural outlook. Over
500 varieties of perennials with mass
planting. Exciting group combination
in island beds and deep borders,

results in a garden flowing with
stunning colour. Approaching the
woodland and lake, natural planting
attracts an array of wildlife. Adjacent
nursery. Picnic area. The Aucklands
has borders containing a colourful mix
of herbaceous and bedding plants.
Hostas, various conifers, hanging
baskets and containers. Seating area
to enjoy the peaceful charm. In
addition there's a well laid out
traditional kitchen garden. Featured in
The Journal (BJ Nurseries).

---

102 TERRINGTON HOUSE
Terrington YO60 6PU. Mr & Mrs
James Fenwick, 01653 648470,
lindatex7@yahoo.com. *15m NE of
York. Last house in village on R if
coming from Sheriff Hutton or 1st on
L coming from A64 & Castle Howard
road.* Light Refreshments. Elderflower
and Cupcakes! **Adm £3.50, chd free.
Sat 25, Sun 26 June (11-4). Visitors
also welcome by appt.**
Formal garden set in 3 acres with
exquisite shell house, herbaceous
and mixed borders incl roses, peonies
and hostas. Impressive trees, herb
garden parterre and vegetable
garden.

Seating area to
enjoy the peaceful
charm. In addition
there's a well laid
out traditional
kitchen garden . . .

THISTLE FARM
See Nottinghamshire.

103 THORPE LODGE
Knaresborough Road, Ripon
HG4 3LU. Mr & Mrs T Jowitt. *1m S
of Ripon. On Ripon-Bishop Monkton-
Knaresborough rd ³/₄ m from Ripon
bypass.* Home-made teas. **Adm £5,
chd free. Sun 31 July (1-6).**

Beautiful, large country garden of
12 acres with extensive colour-
themed flower borders, walled rose
garden, canals and fruit trees.
Pleached hornbeam walk and
allées lead to walks through mature
woodland with vistas and ponds.
Courtyard with exotic shrubs and
tender plants in pots. Area for
picnics.

104 TINKERS HOLLOW
Church Field Lane, Great
Ouseburn, nr York YO26 9SG.
Heather & Eric Sugden. *Between
York & Harrogate off B6265. 4m E of
A1 (M) J47, (A59) towards York.
Before Green Hammerton take B6265
towards Boroughbridge. Follow signs
to Great Ouseburn. Car parking at
Tinkers Hollow.* **Combined with
Cobble Cottage adm £3.50, chd
free. Mon 30 May (11-5).**
Just over 1 acre, with wide range of
features. Ponds connected by
waterfall and small stream help
extend the diverse range of plants
grown. Several pergola walk-ways
provide interesting and varied routes
linking bog, perennial and shrub
borders. By complete contrast the
most distant part of the garden is left
to nature with wild pond and folly to
add intrigue.

105 WARLEY HOUSE GARDEN
Stock Lane, Warley, Halifax
HX2 7RU. Dr & Mrs P J Hinton,
www.warleyhousegardens.com. *2m
W of Halifax. From Halifax take A646
(Burnley). Turn R up Windleroyd Lane
approx 1m after A58, A646 junction
(King Cross). Turn L at T-junction into
Stock Lane. Park on rd before Warley
Village.* Tea & Home-made teas &
Light Refreshments. **Adm £3.50, chd
free. Sun 15 May (1-5).**
Following the demolition of original
early C18 house and years of neglect
the partly walled 2¹/₂ -acre garden is
being renovated by the present
owners. Rocky path and Japanese
style planting leads to lawns and
lovely S-facing views over open
countryside. The alpine ravine is now
planted with ferns, and fine trees give
structure to the developing woodland
area. Drifts of groundcover, shrub and
herbaceous plantings, wild flowers
and heathers maintain constant
seasonal interest. Some paths are not
suitable for wheelchairs.

106 **WEATHERVANE HOUSE**
Mill Lane, Seaton Ross YO42 4NE.
Julie & Peter Williams,
01759 318663,
peteandjuliew@googlemail.com.
*5m S of Pocklington. From A64 York,
take Hull exit & immed B1228 approx
9m, then follow signs to Seaton Ross.
From M62 Howden N on B1228
approx 11m R turn Seaton Ross.
From Hull A1079 turn L at Hayton.
Garden on L soon after entering
village.* Home-made teas. **Adm £3,
chd free. Sun 24 Apr (12-5).**
Visitors also welcome by appt,
April & May, groups from 8 to 30.
Two acre garden with semi-mature
woodland, magnolias,
rhododendrons, azaleas, flowering
trees and shrubs, wide range of
spring bulbs together with mixed
herbaceous borders, lawns and
circular mini-meadow. Fruit garden,
glasshouse and large polytunnel with
specimen acers, camellias and
rhododendrons. Gravel drive and
paths but wheelchair passage
possible.

WEST BARN
See Lincolnshire.

107 **26 WEST END**
Walkington HU17 8SX. Miss
Jennifer Hall, 01482 861705. *2m
SW of Beverley. On the B1230,
100yds beyond Xrds in centre of
village on the R.* Home-made teas.
**Adm £3.50, chd free. Wed 8, Sun
12 June (1.30-5).** Visitors also
welcome by appt June & July, for
groups 6+.
Exceptionally charming and
interesting 1-acre cottage garden
attractive to wildlife, particularly bees.
The garden opens into an old
wooded gravel pit still being
developed by owner. Many rare plants
collected over more than 20yrs.

108 **NEW** **WESTFIELD FARM**
Melbourne, York YO42 4SX. Carol
& Howard Wilson. *10m SE of York.
From York follow B1228 from
Grimston r'about, though Elvington &
Sutton, Derwent to Melbourne.
Garden is ¹/₂ m before village on L.*
Light refreshments & teas. **Adm £3,
chd free. Sun 24 July (1-5).**
A 1¹/₂ -acre garden partly situated in
original farm fold yard. Features incl
herb garden with box hedging,
vegetable garden with raised beds
and greenhouse; fruit trees, shrubs

and numerous borders and beds.
Ornamental fish pond with bridge,
wildlife pond, footbridge over stream
to woodland area and rare breeds.

109 **NEW** **WHISPADALES**
48 Candler Avenue, West Ayton,
Scarborough YO13 9JN. Mr & Mrs
Birch, 01723 864932,
terryhw48@aol.com. *4m W of
Scarborough. From West; turn R off
the A170 into Garthend Rd before the
dual carriageway in West Ayton, 3rd R
into Hewley Drive, 1st L and L again
into Cul de Sac. From East; 1st
turning L after the Forge PH on A170
into Garthend Road. Queuing into the
gardens a possibility. Parking limited
in Candler Ave (please don't block the
driveway).* Home-made teas. **Adm
£3.50, chd free. Sun 10 July (11-5).**
Visitors also welcome by appt
spring to Aug.

A delightful pocket handkerchief of a
garden showing creativity in a small
area with extensive mixed planting of
over 100+ foliage plants. Some
unusual; hostas, ferns, clematis,
trees, shrubs, statues, fish pond,
water features, raised alpine bed,
2 glass houses, with cactus and
succulents, seating areas. A gem,
from spring through to summer.
Wheelchairs: viewing point onlyon
driveway, or path on cul de sac.

110 **THE WHITE HOUSE**
Husthwaite YO61 4QA. Mrs A
Raper, 01347 868688. *5m S of
Thirsk. Turn R off A19 signed
Husthwaite. 1¹/₂ m to centre of village
opp parish church.* Visitors
welcome by appt.
Come and meet the gardener, an
enthusiastic plantswoman. Exchange
ideas and visit a 1-acre country

Field Cottage

garden with walled garden, conservatory and gardens within the garden. Herbaceous - of special interest a fresh lavender and purple palette in late spring and a hot summer border. Many unusual plants and shrubs. Strong collection of clematis, landscaping, planting and a recently extended and restructured bed of English and shrub roses in the old orchard. A garden for all seasons. ♿ ⚘ ☎

> A delightful pocket handkerchief of a garden showing creativity in a small area with extensive mixed planting of 100+ foliage plants . . .

GROUP OPENING

111 WHIXLEY GARDENS
nr York YO26 8AR. *8m W of York, 8m E of Harrogate, 6m N of Wetherby. 3m E of A1(M) off A59 York-Harrogate. Signed Whixley.* Specialist nurseries & home-made teas at The Old Vicarage. **Combined adm £5, chd free. Sun 12, Wed 22 June (1-5).**

ASH TREE HOUSE
High Street. Mr & Mrs E P Moffitt

THE BAY HOUSE
Stonegate. Mr & Mrs Jon Beckett

COBBLE COTTAGE
John Hawkridge & Barry Atkinson
(See separate entry)

THE OLD VICARAGE
Mr & Mrs Roger Marshall

Attractive rural yet accessible village nestling on the edge of the York Plain with beautiful historic church and Queen Anne Hall (not open). The Gardens are spread throughout the village with good footpaths. A plantsman's and flower arranger

garden at Cobble Cottage (see separate entry) has views to the Hambleton Hills. Ash Tree House further towards the village centre is a small well designed garden on a steeply sloping site with extensive rock garden and borders full of established herbaceous plants, shrubs and roses creating a tapestry of soft colour and textures achieving a cottage garden effect and the Bay House has a hidden densely planted small courtyard. In front of the Church of the Ascension stands The Old Vicarage, overlooking the old deer park, with its delightful ³/₄ -acre walled flower garden. The walls, house and various structures within the garden are festooned with climbers. Mixed borders, old roses, hardy and half-hardy perennials, topiary, bulbs and hellebores give interest all yr. Gravel and old brick paths lead to hidden seating areas creating the atmosphere of a romantic English garden. Featured in 100 Dream Gardens of England.
⚘

112 NEW THE WILLOWS
Lumley Lane, Kirkby Fleetham, Northallerton DL7 0SH. Jean Morley and Sheila Minto. *4m N of Leeming, 7m S of Scotch Corner. Kirkby Fleetham is just to the E of the A1. The Willows is next to The Black Horse Inn. Visitors to the garden, please use the Inn car park.* Home-made teas. **Adm £2.50, chd free. Sat 2, Sun 3 July (1-5).**
A small (circa ¹/₄ acre) south-facing, gently sloping, evolving cottage garden created by enthusiastic amateur owners over the last 5 years. Well-stocked mixed herbaceous borders. Raised terrace incorporating insect hibernation house. Pond with range of fish. Patio and pebbled areas displaying a range of container planting. Black Horse Inn (next door) open all day for good food. Wheelchair access to viewing point and to refreshments.
♿ ⚘

113 WINTHROP PARK GARDENS
Second Lane, off Newhall Avenue, Wickersley, Rotherham S66 1EE. David & Carol Bowser, 01709 709335, c.bowser@winthroppark.co.uk, www.winthroppark.co.uk. *4m E of Rotherham. M18 J1, follow A631 to Rotherham. In Wickersley turn L at*

r'about B6060 to Thurcroft, after 6 speed humps turn L (Newhall Ave). Light refreshments & teas, lovely sandwiches, delicious cakes and hot & cold drinks served all day. **Adm £2.50, chd free. Sun 26 June (10-5). Visitors also welcome by appt, to book a group evening visit.** Beautiful award winning gardens and nature therapy park honoured by the Queen in 2009. An opportunity to see something very special. Paths lead to themed areas planted with thousands of colourful and scented plants, shrubs and trees to delight and stimulate the senses as well as creating an oasis of rest, tranquillity and peace. Unusual design features, garden art, sculpture, conservatory, craftwork and gifts, and Chataway's Tea Room. Seating around the gardens. Plant sales area and advice from our head gardener throughout the day. Featured in Garden Answers.
♿ ⚘ ☕ ☎

GROUP OPENING

114 WITHERNSEA GARDENS
HU19 2PJ. *23m E of Hull, 16m S of Hornsea. Enter Withernsea from A1033 onto Hollym Rd. From Hornsea, B1242, through town onto Hollym Rd.* Home-made teas. **Combined adm £5, chd free. Sun 31 July (12-6).**

CRANFORD
35 Hollym Road. Linda & Maurice Beever

54 HOLLYM ROAD
Mr Matthew Pottage

Two interesting, contrasting gardens opp each other in Withernsea. Cranford is transformed from an abandoned plot to a picturesque refuge, with colourful herbaceous borders planted with annuals, perennials, grasses, evergreens, shrubs and trees. There's also a pond feature, vegetable garden and chicken run. In 2010, a secret garden with wishing well was added. 54 Hollym Road is a well stocked garden mixing the interesting with the unusual, demonstrating what can be achieved on clay soil in a coastal garden. See Leylandii hedging in a new light and marvel at the collection of meticulously cared for succulents on display in the garden and greenhouse.
♿ ⚘

115 WORTLEY HALL
Wortley Village S35 7DB, 0114 2882100, info@wortleyhall.com, www.wortleyhall.com. *9m NW of Sheffield & 5m SW of Barnsley. On A629 Huddersfield - Sheffield rd in Wortley village, signed Wortley Hall & Gardens.* Light refreshments & cream teas. **Combined with Avenue Cottage** adm £4.50, chd free. Sun 19 June (12-4). Visitors also welcome by appt Mon - Fri, 8-4, groups min 15 for guided tour. (State NGS party, £2.50 to NGS). 26 acres of elegant Italianate gardens set within landscaped parkland. Formal gardens with sunken garden, arbour and clipped yew balls all framed with seasonal bedding and mixed borders leading to walled organic kitchen garden. Informal walks through pleasure grounds reveal C18/19 plantings incl 500yr old hollow oak, lake and ice house and recently uncovered fernery. Organic kitchen garden open with produce for sale. Garden tour 2pm. Award winner Yorkshire in Bloom & Green Pennant. Partial wheelchair access, steep slopes and steps.

&♿ ⊕ ⛺ ☕ ☎

116 ◆ YORK GATE
Back Church Lane, Adel, Leeds LS16 8DW. Perennial, 0113 2678240, www.yorkgate.org.uk. *5m N of Leeds centre. 2¼ m SE of Bramhope, signed from A660. Park in*

South-facing, gently sloping, evolving cottage garden created by enthusiastic amateur owners over the last five years . . .

Church Lane in lay-by opposite church and take public footpath through churchyard to garden. Light refreshments. **Adm £4, chd free. For opening times and information, please phone or see garden website.**
One-acre masterpiece and outstanding example of C20 garden design. A series of smaller gardens with different themes and in contrasting styles are linked by a

succession of delightful vistas. Striking architectural features play a key role throughout the garden which is also noted for its exquisite detailing. Featured in House & Garden magazine and on BBC Gardeners' World.

⊕ ☕

117 YORKE HOUSE
Dacre Banks, nr Summerbridge, Nidderdale HG3 4EW. Tony & Pat Hutchinson, 01423 780456, pat@yorkehouse.co.uk, www.yorkehouse.co.uk. *4m SE of Pateley Bridge, 10m NW of Harrogate. On B6451. Car park.* Home-made teas. **Adm £3, chd free. Combined with Dacre Banks & Summerbridge Gardens** adm £6 chd free, 3 July. Sun 3 July 11-5. Sun 26 June (11-5). Visitors also welcome by appt June/July, groups of 10+, coaches permitted.
Flower arranger's 2-acre garden with colour-themed borders full of flowering and foliage plants and shrubs. Extensive water feature incl large ornamental ponds and stream. Other features incl nut walk, rose walk, patios, gazebo, Millennium garden and wildlife area. The garden enjoys beautiful views across Nidderdale. Picnic area. Winner - Harrogate Glorious Gardens.

&♿ 🐕 ⊕ ☕ ☎

Firgrove, NE Wales

WALES

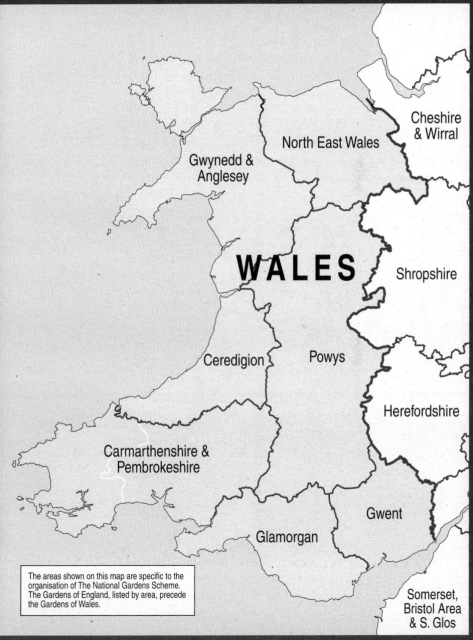

Cheshire & Wirral

North East Wales

Gwynedd & Anglesey

WALES

Shropshire

Ceredigion

Powys

Herefordshire

Carmarthenshire & Pembrokeshire

Glamorgan

Gwent

The areas shown on this map are specific to the organisation of The National Gardens Scheme. The Gardens of England, listed by area, precede the Gardens of Wales.

Somerset, Bristol Area & S. Glos

CARMARTHENSHIRE & PEMBROKESHIRE

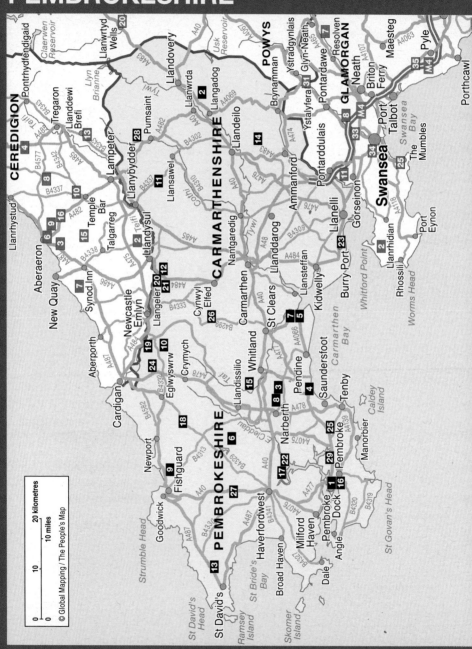

Rensburg Sheppards supports the NGS

Opening Dates

February

Saturday 26
13 Golwg Yr Ynys
Sunday 27
13 Golwg Yr Ynys

March

Every Saturday & Sunday
13 Golwg Yr Ynys

April

Every Saturday & Sunday
13 Golwg Yr Ynys
Sunday 17
29 Upton Castle Gardens

May

Every Saturday & Sunday
13 Golwg Yr Ynys
Daily (not Weds) from 15 May
18 Moorland Cottage Plants
Monday 2
13 Golwg Yr Ynys
Sunday 8
10 Ffynone
Saturday 14
4 Colby Woodland Garden
13 Golwg Yr Ynys
Sunday 15
4 Colby Woodland Garden
Sunday 22
28 Ty'r Maes
Saturday 28
21 Pantyfedwen
Sunday 29
15 Llwyngarreg

June

Every Saturday & Sunday
13 Golwg Yr Ynys
Daily (not Weds)
18 Moorland Cottage Plants
Sunday 5
5 The Cors
26 Tradewinds
Sunday 12
3 Coed-y-Ffynnon
Saturday 18
0 Coed y Ffynnon
Sunday 26
22 Picton Castle & Woodland
Gardens

July

Every Saturday & Sunday
13 Golwg Yr Ynys
Daily (not Weds)
18 Moorland Cottage Plants
Saturday 2
20 The Old Vicarage
Sunday 3
20 The Old Vicarage
Sunday 10
15 Llwyngarreg
24 Rhosygilwen Mansion
Saturday 16
23 Red Roofs
Sunday 17
23 Red Roofs
25 Rosewood
27 Treffgarne Hall
Friday 22
1 Bluebell Lodge
16 Mead Lodge
Saturday 23
1 Bluebell Lodge
16 Mead Lodge
21 Pantyfedwen
Sunday 24
1 Bluebell Lodge
2 Cilgwyn Lodge
16 Mead Lodge
Monday 25
1 Bluebell Lodge
16 Mead Lodge

August

Every Saturday & Sunday
13 Golwg Yr Ynys
Daily (not Weds)
18 Moorland Cottage Plants
Sunday 7
9 Dyffryn Fernant
Sunday 14
28 Ty'r Maes
Sunday 21
26 Tradewinds

September

Every Saturday & Sunday
13 Golwg Yr Ynys
Thursday 1
18 Moorland Cottage Plants
Friday 2
18 Moorland Cottage Plants
Saturday 3
18 Moorland Cottage Plants
Sunday 4
18 Moorland Cottage Plants

October

Every Saturday & Sunday
13 Golwg Yr Ynys

Gardens open to the public

4 Colby Woodland Garden
9 Dyffryn Fernant
22 Picton Castle & Woodland
Gardens
29 Upton Castle Gardens

By appointment only

6 Cwm Pibau
7 Delacorse
11 Gelli Uchaf
12 Glandwr
14 Llwyn Cyll
17 Millinford
19 Nant-yr-Eryd

Also open by Appointment ☎

2 Cilgwyn Lodge
3 Coed-y-Ffynnon
5 The Cors
8 Dyffryn Farm
10 Ffynone
13 Golwg Yr Ynys
15 Llwyngarreg
16 Mead Lodge
18 Moorland Cottage Plants
21 Pantyfedwen
23 Red Roofs
24 Rhosygilwen Mansion
25 Rosewood
27 Treffgarne Hall
28 Ty'r Maes

Wildflower
meadow and
bamboo groves
for children to
explore . . .

The Gardens

1 BLUEBELL LODGE
Imble Lane, Pembroke Dock, Pembrokeshire SA72 6PN. Smith & Mike O'Connor. *From A4139 between Pembroke & Pembroke Dock, take B4322 signed Pennar & Leisure Centre. After ¹/₂ m turn L into Imble Lane. Bluebell Lodge 1st L after cricket club next to farm.* Adm £2.50, chd free. **Fri 22, Sat 23, Sun 24, Mon 25 July (11-5). Also opening Mead Lodge.**
1/3 acre gently sloping, densely planted, lawn-free garden. Unique and quirky. Shade-loving and sun-tolerant. Small dew pond, acers, white birch, cordylines, fern varieties, hostas, tree ferns plus bananas, bamboos, *Shefflera tetrapanax*, grasses, chusan, jujub, tree dahlia and many more. Juxtapositions where leaf shape, size and colour are important. Places to sit and look. Gravel and paved paths, gentle slope.

2 CILGWYN LODGE
Llangadog, Carmarthenshire SA19 9LH. Keith Brown & Moira Thomas, 01550 777452, keith@cilgwynlodge.co.uk, www.cilgwynlodge.co.uk. *3m NE of Llangadog village. 4m SW of Llandovery. Turn off A40 into centre of Llangadog. Bear L in front of village shop then 1st R towards Myddfai. After 2¹/₂ m pass Cilgwyn Manor on L then 1st L. Garden ¹/₄ m on L.* Home-made teas. Adm £3, chd free. **Sun 24 July (1-5). Visitors also welcome by appt. Coaches & parties welcome.**
Fascinating and much-admired 1-acre garden with something for everyone. Wide variety of herbaceous plants displayed in extensive colour-themed borders, large collection of hostas, a growing collection of clematis, hardy, rare or unusual plants. Traditional vegetable and fruit garden and large waterlily pond. A Welsh Wonderland. Featured in Carmarthenshire Life & finalist in Daily Mail, National Garden Competition. Part of garden is wheelchair accessible, the other has slopes and gravel paths.

3 COED-Y-FFYNNON
Lampeter Velfrey, Pembrokeshire SA67 8UJ. Col R H Gilbertson, 01834 831396. *2¹/₂ m SE of Narberth. From Penblewin roundabout on A40 follow signs to Narberth & then to crematorium. Straight on through Llanmill & Lampeter Velfrey. Garden ¹/₂ m on L.* Adm £2.50, chd free. **Sun 12, Sat 18 June (2-6). Visitors also welcome by appt.**
Enthusiast's 1-acre garden with over 140 varieties of old-fashioned roses. Informal planting and very naturalistic garden style with ample provision for wildlife. Roses at their best early June to early July. Relaxed rural setting, lots of rough grass; don't expect manicured lawns.

4 ◆ COLBY WOODLAND GARDEN
Narberth, Amroth, Pembrokeshire SA67 8PP. National Trust, 01834 811885, www.nationaltrust.org.uk. *6m N of Tenby. 5m SE of Narberth. Signed by brown tourist signs on coast rd & A477.* Adm £4.60, chd £2.30. **For NGS: Sat & Sun 14, 15 May (10-5). For other opening times and information, please phone or see garden website.**
8-acre woodland garden in a secluded and tranquil valley with fine collection of rhododendrons and azaleas. Wildflower meadow and bamboo groves for children to explore. Delightfully planted walled garden incl unusual gazebo, designed by Wyn Jones, with internal tromp l'oeil. Artificial rill divides part of this garden. Incl in the *Register of Historic Parks and Gardens: Pembrokeshire.* Short film showing the garden through the seasons. The upper reaches of the woodland garden are difficult to access with wheelchairs.

Exceptional, elegant plantsman's garden with unusual architectural and exotic planting . . .

5 THE CORS
Newbridge Road, Laugharne, Carmarthenshire SA33 4SH. Nick Priestland, 01994 427219, nickpriestland@hotmail.com. *12m SW of Carmarthen. From Carmarthen, turn R in centre of Laugharne at The Mariners PH. At bottom of Newbridge Rd on R. Use public car parks, 5 mins walk.* Home-made teas. Adm £3.50, chd free. **Sun 5 June (2-6). Visitors also welcome by appt, generally any time. Min group size 8, max 30. No parking available for coaches.**
Approx 2¹/₂ acres set in beautiful wooded valley bordering river. Large bog garden with ponds, *Gunnera*, bamboos and tree ferns. Exceptional, elegant plantsman's garden with unusual architectural and exotic planting incl *Tetrapanax papyrifer*, *Blechnum chilensechusan* palms and sculptures.

6 CWM PIBAU
New Moat, Pembrokeshire SA63 4RE. Mrs Duncan Drew, 01437 532454. *10m NE of Haverfordwest. 3m SW of Maenclochog. Off A40, take B4313 to Maenclochog, follow signs to New Moat, pass church, then 2nd concealed drive on L, ¹/₂ m rural drive.* Adm £3, chd free. **Visitors welcome by appt.**
5-acre woodland garden surrounded by old deciduous woodland and streams. Created in 1978, contains many mature, unusual shrubs and trees from Chile, New Zealand and Europe, set on S-facing sloping hill. More conventional planting nearer house.

7 DELACORSE
Laugharne, Carmarthenshire SA33 4QP. Annie Hart, 01994 427728, annie.hart@ymail.com. *13m SW of Carmarthen. On A4066 from St Clears, take the 1st L after Cross Inn at 'no footway' rd sign, continue ¹/₂ m. At bend, carry straight on to farm track for further ¹/₂ m. Alternatively, on foot from Laugharne, 20 mins walk along footpath up-river from Dylan Thomas Boathouse Museum.* Adm £4, chd free. **Visitors welcome by appt May - Sept. Any size group welcome (£3.50 each for 10+) Access limited to size of large minibus.**
3-acre garden beside Tâf Estuary, in peaceful, beautiful landscape with fine

views. Scented walled garden; sheltered courtyard with exotics; fernery; mixed borders for all-yr interest; living willow work; mill pond; lawns; orchard and carefully managed informal areas merging into woodland, reed beds and salt marsh. Extensive organic kitchen garden. Information on living willow work, notes and tips on organic cultivation of fruit and veg incl pest control. Featured in ITV Wales - A Little Piece of Paradise and S4C - Wedi 3. Gravel courtyard, steep slope, steps to mill pond & orchard.

&. 🛈 ☎

Cilgwyn Lodge

8 ▸ DYFFRYN FARM

Lampeter Velfrey, Narberth, Pembrokeshire SA67 8UN. Dr & Mrs M J R Polson, Mr & Mrs D Bradley, 01834 861684, www.pembrokeshireplants.co.uk. *3m E of Narberth. From junction of A40 & A478 follow signs for crematorium, continue down into Llanmill. Then uphill, at brow turn L at Bryn Sion Chapel Xrds (before Lampeter Velfrey). After ¹/₂ m rd turns R under railway bridge. Dyffryn Farm straight ahead, parking under bridge and immed on R.* **Adm £3, chd free (share to Paul Sartori Foundation). Sun 28 Aug (1-5). Visitors also welcome by appt. Only small coaches.**
Large garden, in several areas on different levels, in 'naturalised' manner (not landscaped or contrived) using secluded valley backcloth. Highlights incl 70+ bamboos; grasses, herbaceous plants, unusual shrubs; stream, pond with island and small woodland; all in relaxed style with 'hidden' havens. Supervised children very welcome. Bamboos and other plants for sale.

🛈 ⊛ ☕ ☎

9 ◆ DYFFRYN FERNANT

Llanychaer, Fishguard, Pembrokeshire SA65 9SP. Christina Shand & David Allum, 01348 811282, www.genuslocus.net. *3m E of Fishguard, then ¹/₂ m inland. A487 Fishguard to Cardigan. After approx 3m, at end of long straight hill, turn R signed Llanychaer with blue rd signs 'unsuitable for long vehicles'. After exactly ¹/₂ m is Dyffryn track, on L behind LH bend, with wooden sign.* **Adm £4.50, chd free. For NGS: Sun 7 Aug (2-6).** For other opening times and information, please phone or see garden website.
'I am truly inspired by this place, to see what intelligent and interesting things you can do with plants, how plants can transform a space, is really exciting. Also the way they have planned the routes and the vistas and created a narrative around this space - wonderful' - Landscape Man.

⊛ 🛏 ☎

10 ▸ FFYNONE

Boncath, Pembrokeshire SA37 0HQ. With the kind permission of the Lloyd George Family, 01239 842070. *9m SE of Cardigan. 7m W of Newcastle Emlyn. From Newcastle Emlyn take A484 to Cenarth, turn L on B4332, turn L again at Xrds just before Newchapel.* Home-made teas. **Adm £3, chd free. Sun 8 May (1-5). Visitors also welcome by appt.**
Large woodland garden designated Grade I on Cadw Register of Historic Parks & Gardens in Wales. Lovely views, fine mature specimen trees; formal garden nr house with massive yew topiary; rhododendrons, azaleas, woodland walks and bluebells. House (also Grade I) by John Nash (1793), not open. Later additions and garden terraces by F Inigo Thomas c1904. Limited wheelchair access. Some steep paths & steps.

&. ⊛ ☕ ☎

11 ▸ GELLI UCHAF

Rhydcymerau, Llandeilo, Carmarthenshire SA19 7PY. Julian & Fiona Wormald, 01558 685119, info@thegardenimpressionists.co.uk, www.thegardenimpressionists.co.uk. *5m SE of Llanybydder. 1m NW of Rhydcymerau. In Rhydcymerau on the B4337 turn up Mountain Rd for Llanllwni(by BT phone box). After approx 300 yds turn R up private track continue ¹/₂ m bearing R up steep hill.* Tea & Cream Teas. Picnics welcome. **Adm £2.50, chd free. Visitors welcome by appt. Please ring or email to arrange a visit.** Complementing a listed C18th longhouse and smallholding, a fascinating 1-acre garden with stunning views and a mainly naturalistic planting style. Much to see from early Spring to late Autumn. Many native flowers for maximum biodiversity. A unique fruit and vegetable garden with over 50 apple and pear varieties. Exhibition of images of garden moths and butterflies. Plant and seed sales. Cards, prints, mugs and silk scarves - designs created from photos of flora & fauna in the garden. Featured in the NGS Spring Newsletter; and S4C.

❀ ☕ ☎

12 GLANDWR
Pentrecwrt, Llandysul, Carmarthenshire SA44 5DA. Mrs Jo Hicks, 01559 363729, leehicks@btinternet.com. *15m N of Carmarthen, 2m S of Llandysul, 7m E of Newcastle Emlyn. On A486. At Pentrecwrt village, take minor rd opp Black Horse PH. After bridge keep L for ¹/₄ m. Glandwr is on R.* **Adm £2.50, chd free. Visitors welcome by appt.**
Delightful 1-acre cottage garden, bordered by a natural stream with country views. Some single coloured beds and borders, a rockery and many shrubs and climbers. Walk in the mature woodland transformed into an adventurous intriguing place, with shade loving shrubs and plants, ground covers and many surprises.

13 GOLWG YR YNYS
Carnhedryn, St Davids, Pembrokeshire SA62 6XT. Paul & Sue Clark, 01437 721082, susanpaulc@googlemail.com, www.golwgyrynys.com. *4m E of St Davids, 11m SW of Fishguard, 2m N of Solva. Village of Carnhedryn, off A487 between Fishguard and St Davids.* **Adm £2.50, chd free. Sats, Suns, 26 Feb to 30 Oct; (1-5); Fri 22, Mons 25 Apr; 2, 30 May; 29 Aug (1-5). Visitors also welcome by appt.**
A garden for plantaholics with yr-round floral colour and foliage interest. Intriguing layout of sheltered 'rooms'

full of surprises. Unfolds to reveal ¹/₃ acre of borders, colour themed beds packed with unusual shrubs and garden favourites. Specialities are Hebes (30 varieties) and Hydrangeas (15 varieties). Spacious grassland walk beyond. Featured in Amateur Gardening.

❀ ☎

14 LLWYN CYLL
Trap, Carmarthenshire SA19 6TR. Liz & John Smith, 01558 822398. *3m SE of Llandeilo. In Trap turn towards Glanaman & Llandybie (at The Cennen Arms). Llwyn Cyll is ¹/₂ m on L adjoining Llwyn Onn. Parking limited.* Home-made teas. **Adm £2.50, chd free. Visitors welcome by appt April, May & June.**
3¹/₂ -acre country garden of yr-round interest. Abundant, colourful terraced and walled borders, orchard, vegetable garden. Sun and shade areas with sympathetic planting. A plantsman's garden with many rarities and specimen trees. Up to 40 different magnolias in the arboretum, many in flower late Apr to early June. Scenic view of Castle Carreg Cennen.

❀ ☕ ☎

Walk in the mature woodland transformed into an adventurous intriguing place . . .

15 LLWYNGARREG
Llanfallteg, Whitland, Carmarthenshire SA34 0XH. Paul & Liz O'Neill, 01994 240717, lizpaulfarm@yahoo.co.uk. *19m W of Carmarthen. A40 W from Carmarthen, turn R at Llandewi Velfrey,2¹/₂ miles to Llanfallteg. Go through village, garden ¹/₂ m further on: 2nd farm on R.* Home-made teas. **Adm £3.50, chd free. Suns 29 May; 10 July (2-6). Visitors also welcome by appt. Parking for 1 coach available in layby.**

3-acre plantsman's garden with many rare trees. Bog garden, woodland garden, deep borders, gravel gardens, vegetable plot, rhododendrons, bamboos, willow structures, magnolias, *Meconopsis*, acers, primulas and massed grasses planted to give yr-round interest. Beautiful even in rain! Several deep ponds - young children need close supervision. Limited wheelchair access.

♿ ❀ ☕ ☎

16 MEAD LODGE
Imble Lane, Pembroke Dock, Pembrokeshire SA72 6PN. John & Eileen Seal, 01646 682504, eileenseal@aol.com. *From A4139 between Pembroke and Pembroke Dock take B4322 signed Pennar and Leisure Centre. After ¹/₂ m turn L into Imble Lane. Mead Lodge at end.* Home-made teas. **Adm £3, chd free. Fri - Mon 22, 23, 24, 25 July (11-5). Also open Bluebell Lodge. Visitors also welcome by appt June to September.**
Unexpected, secluded country garden, a relaxing oasis on S-facing slope overlooking the Pembroke River estuary. Varied ³/₄ -acre garden reflects the owners' keen interest in ferns, grasses and herbs. Incl terraces with Chinese and Mediterranean influences, colour-themed beds, small arboretum, fernery and vegetable garden. Pond and bog garden now established. Featured in Western Mail and Pembrokeshire Life.

❀ ☕ ☎

17 MILLINFORD
The Rhos, Pembrokeshire SA62 4AL. Drs B & A Barton, 01437 762394. *3m E of Haverfordwest. From Haverfordwest on A40 to Carmarthen, turn R signed The Rhos, take turning to Millin. Turn R at Millin Chapel then immed L over river bridge.* **Adm £3, chd free. Visitors welcome by appt all yr. No limitations on group size. Please call for appointment.**
Spacious, undulating and peaceful garden of 4 acres on bank of Millin Creek. Varied collection of over 125 different trees, many unusual, plus shrubs, herbaceous plants and bulbs in beautiful riverside setting. Impressive terracing and water features. Visit in spring, summer and early autumn.
☎

18 MOORLAND COTTAGE PLANTS
Rhyd-y-Groes, Brynberian, Pembrokeshire SA41 3TT. Jennifer & Kevin Matthews, 01239 891363, www.moorlandcottageplants.co.uk. *12m SW of Cardigan. 16m NE of Haverfordwest, on B4329, 3/4 m downhill from cattlegrid (from Haverfordwest) and 1m uphill from signpost to Brynberian (from Cardigan).* **Adm £3, chd 50p (share to Paul Sartori Foundation). Daily (not Weds) 14 May to 4 Sept; (10.30-5). Visitors also welcome by appt.**
1½ -acre garden at 700ft on wild NE hillside. Abundantly planted, wide range of plants providing propagating material for the adjacent nursery. Secretive, enclosed areas where carpets of spring flowers give way to jungly perennials, grasses and bamboos contrast with deep, parallel herbaceous borders and new, informal shrubberies providing stunning mountain and moorland vistas. Gardening without insecticides/fungicides encourages abundant wildlife. Diverse mollusc-proof plantings demonstrate what can be achieved without using any slug and snail controls. Featured in 'RHS Garden Finder'.
⚛ ☎

19 NANT-YR-ERYD
Abercych, Boncath, Pembrokeshire SA37 0EU. Alan & Diana Hall, 01239 682489, diana.hall4@btinternet.com. *5m SE of Cardigan, 5m W of Newcastle Emlyn. Off B4332 Cenarth to Abercych, Boncath Rd. Turn N to Abercych, through village and take L fork.* Home-made teas. **Adm £2.50, chd free. Visitors welcome by appt March, April, May & June.**
Charming well-maintained cottage garden of 1-acre. 60 varieties of daffodils in spring. Mature and new topiary gardens. Exotic fernery and other displays in original outbuildings. Well worth visiting in summer. Beautiful roses including Rosa Mundi, and William Lobb, Abraham Darby, Dortmund, and Abbotswood. Also wild flower meadow.
☕ ☎

20 THE OLD VICARAGE
Llangeler, Carmarthenshire SA44 5EU. Mr & Mrs J C Harcourt. *4m E of Newcastle Emlyn. 15m N of Carmarthen on A484. From N Emlyn turn down lane on L in Llangeler before church.* Home-made teas. **Adm £2.50, chd free. Sat & Sun 2, 3 July (11-6).**
A garden gem created since 1993. Less than 1 acre divided into 3 areas of roses, shrubs and a semi-formal pool with an interesting selection of unusual herbaceous plants. Ever changing scene. Garden images by Charles Hawes on display. Gravel access.
♿ ⚛ 🛍 ☕

Secretive, enclosed areas where carpets of spring flowers give way to jungly perennials, grasses and bamboos . . .

21 NEW PANTYFEDWEN
Drefelin, Drefach Felindre, Llandysul SA44 5XB. Steven & Viki Harwood, 01559 371807, steven@harwoodsartsandcrafts.co.uk. *Drefach Felindre is signed from A484 approx 16m from Carmarthen & Cardigan, 5m from Newcastle Emlyn.* Home-made teas. **Adm £2.50, chd free. Sats 28 May; 23 July (11-6). Visitors also welcome by appt May - Sept. Small groups only.**
Small front water garden with stream, surrounded by lush architectural plantings. Hillside garden behind house, informally managed, with unusual plants and seating areas giving views over the valley. Quirky garden of about 1/3 acre, on 5 levels, culminating in a tranquil woodland garden. For the sure-footed only. Arts & Crafts for sale incl wood turning.
⚛ 🛍 ☕ ☎

22 ◆ PICTON CASTLE & WOODLAND GARDENS
The Rhos, Pembrokeshire SA62 4AS. Picton Castle Trust, 01437 751326, www.pictoncastle.co.uk. *3m E of Haverfordwest. On A40 to Carmarthen, signed off main rd.* **Adm £5, chd £2.50. For NGS: Sun 26 June (10-5). For other opening times and information, please**
phone or see garden website.
Mature 40-acre woodland garden with unique collection of rhododendrons and azaleas, many bred over 41yrs, producing hybrids of great merit and beauty; rare and tender shrubs and trees incl *Magnolia*, myrtle, *Embothrium* and *Eucryphia*. Wild flowers abound. Walled garden with roses; fernery; herbaceous and climbing plants and large clearly-labelled collection of herbs.
♿ ⚛ ⚛ ☕ ☎

23 RED ROOFS
129 Elkington Road, Burry Port, Carmarthenshire SA16 0AB. Elaine Morgan, 01554 832418, eddiemorgan44@hotmail.com. *4m W of Llanelli. A484. L at pelican crossing. Bear R. Garden 100 yds on R.* Home-made teas. **Adm £2, chd free. Sat & Sun 16, 17 July (2-6). Visitors also welcome by appt during July.**
A town garden of approx 1/3 -acre in a coastal location. Colourful perennial borders surrounding lawns with a mix of unusual plants such as *Hedychium*, Oleander, *Acacia dealbata* and *Roscoea*. Small water feature with Koi pond, container grown plants incl bonsai and fuchsias. Seating in shaded areas. Additional parking in Jerusalem Chapel car park on A484 150yds Unusual plants for sale.
♿ ⚛ ⚛ ☕ ☎

24 RHOSYGILWEN MANSION
Cilgerran, Cardigan, Pembrokeshire SA43 2TW. Glen Peters & Brenda Squires, 01239 841387, enquiries@retreat.co.uk, www.rhosygilwen.co.uk. *5m S of Cardigan. From Cardigan follow A478 signed Tenby. After 6m turn L at Rhoshill towards Cilgerran. After 1/4 m turn R signed Rhosygilwen. Mansion gates 1/2 m.* Light refreshments & teas. **Adm £3, chd free. Sun 10 July (11-4). Visitors also welcome by appt.**
20 acres of garden in 55 acre estate. Pretty 1/2 m drive through woodland planting. Spacious lightly wooded grounds for leisurely rambling, superb 1-acre walled garden fully productive of fruit, vegetables and flowers; authentically restored Edwardian greenhouses, many old and new trees, small formal garden. Children must be supervised. Gravel paths & slopes in some areas.
♿ ☕ ☎

Red Roofs

25 ROSEWOOD
Redberth, nr Tenby, Pembrokeshire SA70 8SA. Jan & Keith Treadaway, 01646 651405. *3m SW of Kilgetty. Coming from W, turn for Sageston and almost immed R towards Redberth. 1st cottage after village boundary sign. From E, turn for Redberth and continue along old A447, 2nd cottage after village turn. Ample parking on roadside, and in field if dry.* Home-made teas. **Adm £3, chd free (share to Paul Sartori Foundation). Sun 17 July (1-5). Visitors also welcome by appt.**
Intimate and well-maintained $\frac{1}{4}$ -acre garden, cleverly designed in different areas, with abundant, colourful mixed plantings incl scattered exotic species and a National Collection of clematis (subgenus *viorna*) plus many other clematis in bloom all yr, but especially in summer. Fruit and vegetable area in field opposite being redeveloped. Featured in Local press and Pembrokeshire Life.

Exuberantly informal planting, full of cottage garden favourites . . .

26 TRADEWINDS
Ffynnonwen, nr Trelech, Penybont, Carmarthenshire SA33 6PX. Stuart & Eve Kemp-Gee. *10m NW of Carmarthen. A40 W from Carmarthen approx 4m, then turn R onto B4298 to Meidrim. In Meidrim R onto B4299 to Trelech. After approx 5$\frac{1}{2}$ m turn R at Tradewinds sign, then approx $\frac{1}{2}$ m, next to 2nd farm.* **Adm £3, chd free.**

Suns 5 June; 21 Aug (1-5).
2$\frac{1}{2}$ -acre plantsman's garden with abundance of herbaceous perennials, shrubs and trees giving yr-round interest. Mixed borders, natural streams and natural pond. Picturesque garden in tranquil setting. 100ft grass, 100ft herbaceous and 80ft conifer borders. The arboretum incl *Quercus cerris* Argenteovariegata, *Aralia elata* 'Variegata', *Salix fargesii* plus numerous rhododendrons and azaleas. Stream banks planted with many moisture loving plants. Disability buggy available.

27 TREFFGARNE HALL
Treffgarne, Haverfordwest, Pembrokeshire SA62 5PJ. Mr & Mrs Batty, 01437 741115. *7m N of Haverfordwest, signed off A40. Proceed up through village and follow rd round sharply to L, Hall $\frac{1}{4}$ m further on L.* Home-made teas. **Adm £3, chd free. Suns 1 May; 17 July (1-5). Visitors also welcome by appt.**
4-acre garden under development since 2003 situated atop a s-facing ridge with panoramic views. The $\frac{1}{2}$ -acre walled garden with double rill contains a substantial collection of plants from Australia, S. Africa and S. America. Other features incl a broadwalk border, rockery, heather bed and stumpery as well as various statuary.

28 TY'R MAES
Ffarmers, Llanwrda, Carmarthenshire SA19 8JP. John & Helen Brooks, 01558 650541, johnhelen@greystones140. freeserve.co.uk. *7m SE of Lampeter. 8m NW of Llanwrda. 1$\frac{1}{2}$ m N of Pumsaint on A482, opposite turn to Ffarmers.* Home-made teas. **Adm £3, chd free. Suns 22 May; 14 Aug (2-6). Visitors also welcome by**

appt, coaches & parties.
Recently developed 3-acre garden with splendid views. Herbaceous and shrub beds - formal design, exuberantly informal planting, full of cottage garden favourites and many unusual plants. Burgeoning arboretum (200+ types of tree); formal and wildlife ponds, pergola, gazebos, post and rope arcade covered in climbers. Gloriously colourful; spring (rhododendrons, azaleas, primula, 1000's bulbs); late summer (tapestry of annuals/perennials). Craft Stalls. Partial wheelchair access. Some gravel paths.

29 ♦ UPTON CASTLE GARDENS
Cosheston, Pembroke Dock, Pembrokeshire SA72 4SE. Prue & Stephen Barlow, 01646 689996, info@uptoncastle.com. *4m E of Pembroke Dock. 2m N of A477 between Carew and Pembroke Dock. Follow brown signs to Upton Castle Gardens through Cosheston.* Light Refreshments. **Adm £3, chd free. For NGS: Sun 17 Apr (10-5). For other opening times and information, please phone or see garden website.**
35 acres of mature gardens and arboretum with many unusual camellias, magnolias, rhododendrons and other rare trees and shrubs incl a 50yr-old *Davidia involucrata* (handkerchief tree). *Vagus sylvatica* var *heterophylla*, *Drimys winteri*, formal rose gardens, herbaceous borders, Victorian kitchen garden (now being restored), wild flower meadow, woodland walk to the estuary and C13 chapel. Included in the *Register of Historic Parks & Gardens - Pembrokeshire*. Limited wheelchair access, disabled may alight near house.

Carmarthenshire & Pembrokeshire County Volunteers

County Organiser
Mrs Jane Stokes, Llyshendy, Llandeilo SA19 6YA, 01558 823233, jane.h.stokes@btinternet.com

County Treasurer
Mrs Christine Blower, Glangwilli Lodge, Llanllawddog, Carmarthen SA32 7JE, 01267 253334, cheahnwood@toucansurf.com

Publicity
Pembs   Position vacant. Expressions of interest to County Organiser please
Carms   Mrs Jane Stokes, Llyshendy, Llandeilo SA19 6YA, 01558 823233, jane.h.stokes@btinternet.com

Assistant County Organisers
Mrs Jackie Batty, Treffgarne Hall, Treffgarne, Haverfordwest, Pembs SA62 5PJ, 01437 741115, bathole2000@aol.com
Mr Ivor Stokes, Llyshendy, Llandeilo SA19 6YA, 01558 823233, ivor.t.stokes@btopenworld.com

Follow us on Facebook and Twitter

Ceredigion

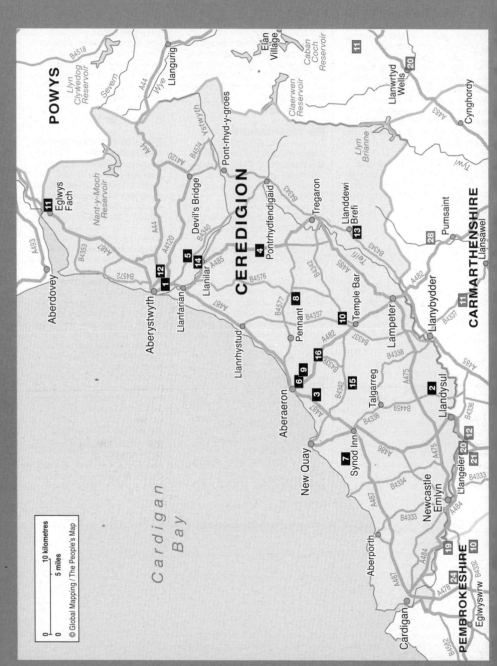

Opening Dates

April

Sunday 17
15 Perth Yr Eglwys

May

Sunday 8
11 Llwyncelyn

Sunday 15
3 Arnant House

Sunday 22
5 Bwlch y Geuffordd
7 Heddfan (Evening)

Sunday 29
2 Alltyrodyn Mansion
12 Mentro Lluest

June

Sunday 5
7 Heddfan
14 Penbanc

Sunday 12
13 Pantyfod
15 Perth Yr Eglwys

Saturday 18
6 Gerallt

Sunday 19
10 Llanllyr

Sunday 26
1 Aberystwyth Allotments

July

Saturday 2
8 Isfryn

Sunday 3
8 Isfryn

Thursday 7
9 Llanerchaeron (Evening)

Sunday 17
13 Pantyfod

Sunday 31
16 Ty Glyn Walled Garden

Gardens open to the public

9 Llanerchaeron
16 Ty Glyn Walled Garden

Also open by Appointment 🕿

2 Alltyrodyn Mansion
3 Arnant House
4 Bwlch y Geuffordd
8 Isfryn
10 Llanllyr
11 Llwyncelyn

The Gardens

1 NEW **ABERYSTWYTH ALLOTMENTS**
Caeffynnon, Penparcau, Aberystwyth SY23 1RE. Ceredigion County Council, Call Pat Causton 01974 272619. *On S side of R. Rheidol on Aberystwyth by-pass. From N or E, take the A4120 between Llanbadarn and Penparcau. Cross bridge then take 1st R into Minyddol. Allotments ¼ m on R. Home-made teas.* **Adm £3, chd free. Sun 26 June (2-5).**
Group of 27 plots in lovely setting alongside R Rheidol close to Aberystwyth. Wide variety of produce grown, vegetables, soft fruit, top fruit, flowers. Sample tastings from allotment produce. Limited wheelchair access.
♿ ☕

Unique garden
sculptures
including a cave,
gazebo and jungle
hut . . .

2 **ALLTYRODYN MANSION**
Capel Dewi SA44 4PS. Mr & Mrs Donald Usher, 01545 590206. *8m W of Lampeter, off A475. Take B4459 at Rhydowen to Capel Dewi. Entrance on R by South Lodge. Home-made teas.* **Adm £3, chd free (share to Capel Dewi Church). Sun 29 May (11-5). Visitors also welcome by appt.**
Early C19 garden. Approx 8 acres, mostly mature woodland with many fine trees. Rare stone-built gothic cold bathhouse. Early C20 lake, Dutch garden and rhododendron plantings. Garden is best in spring when rhododendrons and azaleas are in bloom. Steep slopes.
♿ 🐕 ❀ ☕ 🕿

3 **ARNANT HOUSE**
Llwyncelyn, Aberaeron SA46 0HF. Pam & Ron Maddox, 01545 580083. *On A487, 2m S of Aberaeron. Next to Llwyncelyn Village Hall. Parking in lay-by opp house.*

Home-made teas. **Adm £2.50, chd free. Sun 15 May (12-5). Visitors also welcome by appt.**
Garden created in 9yrs from derelict ground. 1 acre, in Victorian style and divided into rooms and themes. Laburnum arch, wildlife ponds, rotunda and tea house. Wide, long borders full of perennial planting with a good variety of species, numerous statues and oddities to be discovered. Several different magnolias, rhododendrons in May, plus about 50 different types of Clematis. Also a good selection of hellebores in many colours.
🐕 ❀ ☕ 🕿

4 **BWLCH Y GEUFFORDD**
Bronant, Aberystwyth SY23 4JD. Mr & Mrs J Acres, 01974 251559, gayacres@aol.com. *6m NW of Tregaron. 12m SE of Aberystwyth off A485. Take turning opp Bronant school for 1½ m then turn L up a ½ m track.* **Adm £3.50, chd 50p. Visitors also welcome by appt any time, but it is advisable to phone beforehand to check that we are available.**
1000ft high, 3-acre, constantly evolving wildlife garden featuring a lake and several pools. There are a number of theme gardens, incl Mediterranean, cottage garden, woodland, oriental, memorial and jungle. Plenty of seating. Unique garden sculptures and buildings, incl a cave, gazebo and jungle hut. Developing as a healing garden for cancer sufferers and their carers. Featured in Holy Wells of Wales by Phil Cope and Byw yn yr Ardd on S4C 2011.
🐕 🕿

5 NEW **BWLCH Y GEUFFORDD**
New Cross, Aberystwyth SY23 4LY. Manuel & Elaine Grande, 01974 261196. *5m SE of Aberystwyth. On B4340 Trawsgoed Road. Parking in lay-bys opp house. Home-made teas.* **Adm £3, chd free. Sun 22 May (11-5).**
Recently developed 1-acre hillside garden with views of the surrounding countryside. Plenty of places to sit and look. Casual cottage garden with herbaceous borders, shrubs, trees, fish pond and waterfall. Azaleas, rhododendrons and spring bulbs. Some areas are still under development.
🐕 ☕

Llanerchaeron

plantation, a large number of young trees and shrubs, newly constructed maze, ducks, lake and wildlife areas. Children must be supervised. Eggs, produce and plants available. Limited wheelchair access.

9 ◆ LLANERCHAERON

Ciliau Aeron, Lampeter SA48 8DG. National Trust, Call Kevin O'Donnell 01545 570200, www.nationaltrust.org.uk. 2¹/₂ m E of Aberaeron. On the A482 Lampeter to Aberaeron. Adm £3.50, chd free. For NGS: Evening Opening wine, music & refreshments, Thur 7 July (6-9). For other opening times and information please visit website or telephone.
Llanerchaeron is a small C18 Welsh gentry estate set in the beautiful Dyffryn Aeron. The estate survived virtually unaltered into the C20. 2 extensive restored walled gardens produce home-grown vegetables, fruit and herbs for sale. The kitchen garden sits at the core of the estate with a John Nash villa built in 1795 and home farm, all virtually unaltered since its construction. Music.

6 GERALLT

Bro Allt y Graig, Aberaeron SA46 0DU. Huw & Dilys Lewis, 01545 570591. Off A482 Aberaeron - Lampeter rd. Turn at D & L Davies Garage. Entry at first bend where road divides. Please park at Memorial Hall on A482 in Aberaeron. Home-made teas. Adm £3, chd free. Sat 18 June (11-5).
Mature 1920s bungalow garden containing a large variety of shrubs, lavenders and roses such as Chapeau de Napoleon. Sections incl a pond-side area with gunnera and bamboo, a slate bed, woodland glade and a herb plot with a wide variety of herbs both culinary and medicinal. Some slopes & steps.

7 HEDDFAN

Pendderw, Llwyndafydd, Llandysul SA44 6BZ. Mrs S Makepeace. 5m S of New Quay, 12m N of Cardigan. Off A487, at Plwmp PO, take Llwyndafydd rd. Turn L at T-junction. 2nd L (on bend). At next T-junction turn L. After 20yds take 'No Through Rd' on R. Garden 1m on R. Home-made teas & light refreshments. Adm £3.50, chd free. Suns 5 June (10.30-5.30) Evening Opening wine, 22 May (4-8.30).
Beautiful garden of keen

plantswoman, which forms the backdrop to an artisan designed house, lying in the remnants of an old estate surrounded by mature trees. Water features incl large pond with water lilies, a beautifully designed bridge. Small stream, shade area, rose bed, large borders, courtyard garden, Mediterranean area, sculptures, summer house, lots of interest. Ever developing. Plants for sale. Garden partially lit for evening opening 22 May, a mass of floating candles will delight.

8 ISFRYN

Bethania, nr Llanon SY23 5NP. Mrs Julie Langford, 01974 272257, backyardacres@googlemail.com, 15m SW Aberystwyth. B4337 from Llanrhystud or B4577 from Aberarth to Cross Inn. Turn L or continue along B4577 for 2m. At Xrds turn R. 3rd house on L. Home-made & cream teas. Adm £3, chd free. Sat 2, Sun 3 July (11-5). Visitors also welcome by appt Large groups. Coach parties catered for - 2 weeks notice required.
5-acre garden, ever evolving shrub and herbaceous borders, kitchen garden, poultry runs, fruit areas, vegetable beds and polytunnels. 1-acre woodland with paths, field with lawns and paths, strawberry

10 LLANLLYR

Talsarn, Lampeter SA48 8QB. Mr & Mrs Robert Gee, 01570 470900, lgllanllyr@aol.com. 6m NW of Lampeter. On B4337 to Llanrhystud. Home-made teas. Adm £4, chd under 12 free. Sun 19 June (2-6). Visitors also welcome by appt.
Large early C19 garden on site of medieval nunnery, renovated & replanted since 1989. Large pool, bog garden, formal water garden, rose & shrub borders, gravel gardens, laburnum arbour, allegorical labyrinth and mount, all exhibiting fine plantsmanship. Yr-round appeal, interesting & unusual plants. Specialist plant fair by Ceredigion Growers Association.

11 LLWYNCELYN

Glandyfi, Machynlleth SY20 8SS. Mr & Mrs Stewart Neal, 01654 781203, joyneal@btinternet.com. 12m N of Aberystwyth. On A487 Machynlleth (5¹/₂ m). From Aberystwyth, turn R just before Glandyfi sign. Home-made teas. Adm £3.50, chd free. Sun 8 May (12-5). Visitors also welcome by appt throughout the year but please ring beforehand.

13-acre woodland hillside garden and arboretum alongside Dyfi tributary with scenic waterfalls. Collections of hybrid and species rhododendrons flowering from Christmas until Aug. Mollis azaleas in many shades, bluebells in ancient oak wood. Collection of species and hybrid hydrangeas. Large fernery, many overseas taxa added to natives. Formal garden contains terrace, parterre, potager and prairie grasses. Large plant sale. The area around the house is flat but gravelled, other parts on slopes.

Stunning,
panoramic views
of the Teifi Valley
and mountains . . .

12 **NEW** **MENTRO LLUEST**
Llanbadarn Fawr, Aberystwyth SY23 3AU. Chris Glover, 01970 612114, chris@mentrolluest.org, www.mentrolluest.org. *1.5m E of Aberystwyth. From Aberystwyth take A487 north, turn right at top of Penglais hill to Waunfawr. Follow the road to T-junction, turn left and entrance is 20 yards on right.* Home-made teas. Catering provided on NGS open days. **Adm £3, chd free.** Sun 29 May (11-5).
Community garden run by small charity, worked by volunteers. Working garden, used by many local support agencies, produces organic fruit and vegetables as end result of horticultural therapy. Sub-divided into areas separated by hedges and wildlife corridors. Managed on holistic principles, abundant bird, insect and amphibious life. Plenty of seating.

Perennial plants and organic produce for sale. Sensory garden, maritime garden, willow structures, conservation area, polytunnels. Wheelchair access to many parts but not all.

13 **NEW** **PANTYFOD**
Llanddewi Brefi, Tregaron SY25 6PE. David & Susan Rowe, 01570 493505, www.pantyfodgarden.co.uk. *From Llanddewi Brefi village square, take right fork past Community Centre, continue up hill past turning to Ffarmers, over bridge in a dip, up hill to top. Pantyfod is on right, about .75 miles from village.* Home-made teas. **Adm £3, chd free.** Sun 12 June; Sun 17 July (11-5).
Tranquil, intriguing, largely established 3$\frac{1}{2}$ -acre garden with wide variety of perennials, trees and shrubs, many unusual. Varying habitats including terraces, woodland, mature trees, natural ponds. Hardy geraniums, Iris sibirica, grasses and rugosa roses. Wildlife friendly. Stunning, panoramic views of the Teifi Valley and mountains beyond. Plants for sale. Limited wheelchair access. Gravel paths,steps and steep slopes.

14 **PENBANC**
Llanilar, Aberystwyth SY23 4NY. Enfys & David Rennie, 01974 241754. *Off A487, 6m SE of Aberystwyth. From Llanfarian take A485 signed Tregaron for 2$\frac{1}{2}$ m. Turn L into lane immed after Cwmaur Estate. Penbanc in $\frac{1}{2}$ m, overlooking river bridge. Park in field next to river.* Home-made teas. **Adm £3, chd free.** Sun 5 June (2-6).
$\frac{1}{2}$-acre, S-facing sloping cottage garden alongside R Ystwyth with views over valley. Established orchards, large vegetable garden and densely planted herbaceous borders

created in 2005, with masses of roses, clematis, campanula lactiflora, hardy geraniums, grasses and shrubs. Riverside wildlife walk.

15 **PERTH YR EGLWYS**
Mydroilyn, Lampeter SA48 7QX. Elizabeth Gould & Christopher May, 01545 580066. *Off A 487, 4m S of Aberaeron. Turn L at Llanarth, signed Mydroilyn. Through village to chapel, R to school, R again at school, 300yds.* Home-made teas. **Adm £3, chd free.** Suns 17 Apr (2-5); 12 June (11-5).
3-acre established garden and mature arboretum with flowering trees incl cherries and a variety of magnolias. Many unusual shrubs incl camellias, rhododendrons and hellebores. Large areas of spring bulbs with erythroniums, coum cyclamen, species of daffodils and fritillaria. Stream-side and woodland walks.

16 ♦ **TY GLYN WALLED GARDEN**
Ciliau Aeron, Lampeter SA48 8DE. Ty Glyn Davis Trust, 01970 832268, ros.laidlaw@hotmail.co.uk. *3m SW of Aberaeron. Turn off A482 Aberaeron to Lampeter at Ciliau Aeron signed to Pennant. Entrance 700metres on L.* **Adm £3, chd free.** For NGS: Sun 31 July (11-5). **For opening times and information please visit website or telephone.**
Secluded walled garden in beautiful woodland setting alongside R Aeron, developed specifically for special needs children. Terraced kitchen garden overlooks herbaceous borders, orchard and ponds with child orientated features and surprises amidst unusual shrubs and perennials. Newly planted fruit trees selected from former gardener's notebook of C19.

Ceredigion County Volunteers

County Organiser
Pat Causton, Plas Treflys, Llangwyryfon, Aberystwyth SY23 4HD, 01974 272619, dandpcauston@btinternet.com

County Treasurer
Dr. David Shepherd, Bron-y-Craig, 4 Bont Estate, Llanon, Aberystwyth SY23 5LT, 01974 202897, lymphocdomamidwales@btinternet.com

Publicity
Joy Neal, Llyncelyn, Glandyfi, Machynlleth SY20 8SS, 01654 781203, joyneal@btinternet.com

Assistant County Organiser
Lisa Raw-Rees, The Old Mill, Water Street, Aberaeron SA46 0DG, 01545 570107, hywelrawrees@hotmail.com
Daphne Watson, Bwthyn Rhosyn Gwyllt, Bontgoch, Aberystwyth SY23 5DP, 01970 832188, daphnewatson77@btinternet.com

Sign up to our eNewsletter for news and updates

GLAMORGAN

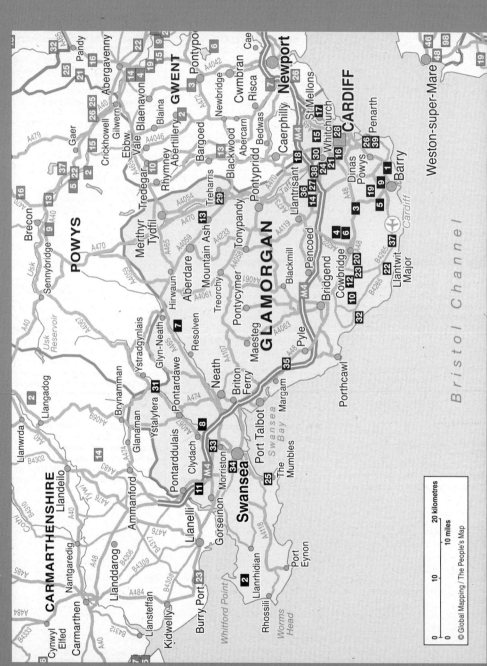

Opening Dates

April

Saturday 16
32 Slade
Sunday 17
32 Slade

May

Sunday 1
9 Cae Gwyn
Saturday 7
21 Llandaff Gardens
Sunday 8
24 Monkstone
34 Tony Ridlers Garden
Sunday 15
15 Cyncoed Gardens
30 Rhiwbina Open Gardens
Sunday 22
33 Springfield
Sunday 29
20 Llanblethian Gardens
28 Penylan Gardens
29 Pontygwaith Farm
Monday 30
29 Pontygwaith Farm

June

Saturday 4
31 Rhos y Bedw
Sunday 5
17 Greenfields
22 Llantwit Major & Llanmaes Gardens
23 Llysworney Gardens
31 Rhos y Bedw
34 Tony Ridlers Garden
Sunday 12
3 Bonvilston Village Gardens
4 Bordervale Plants
9 Cae Gwyn
12 Colwinston Village Gardens
27 Pentyrch Gardens in June
Wednesday 15
36 Ty Deri
Saturday 18
18 Hafod y Milgi
26 Penarth Gardens
29 Pontygwaith Farm
Sunday 19
2 Big House Farm
7 Brynheulog
10 Castle Upon Alun House
16 Dyffryn
18 Hafod y Milgi
29 Pontygwaith Farm
Saturday 25
11 3 Clos Brynlliw

July

Sunday 26
11 3 Clos Brynlliw
19 Hen Felin & Swallow Barns
35 Twyn yr Hydd
37 Wilcot

Sunday 3
5 Broadclose Farm
8 Brynyrenfys
25 Mumbles Gardens
30 Rhiwbina Open Gardens
Sunday 17
38 6 Windsor Avenue
Sunday 24
14 Creigiau Village Gardens
15 Cyncoed Gardens
28 Penylan Gardens
Saturday 30
1 Barry Gardens
6 Bryn-y-Ddafad
Sunday 31
6 Bryn-y-Ddafad

August

Saturday 27
36 Ty Deri
Sunday 28
36 Ty Deri
Monday 29
4 Bordervale Plants

September

Saturday 17
26 Penarth Gardens
39 Witsend

Gardens open to the public

4 Bordervale Plants
35 Twyn yr Hydd

By appointment only

13 The Cottage

Also open by Appointment ☎

28 6 Alma Road, Penylan Gardens
6 Bryn-y-Ddafad
8 Brynyrenfys
9 Cae Gwyn
19 Hen Felin & Swallow Barns
1 1 North Walk, Barry Gardens
14 50 Parc-y-Bryn, Creigiau Village Gardens
1 104 Pontypridd Road, Barry Gardens
29 Pontygwaith Farm

31 Rhos y Bedw
32 Slade
33 Springfield
34 Tony Ridlers Garden
37 Wilcot

The Gardens

GROUP OPENING

1 **BARRY GARDENS**
Barry CF63 2AS. *6m SW of Cardiff.* Home-made teas at 11 Arno Road. **Adm £5, chd free. Sat 30 July (2-6).**

47 ANEURIN ROAD
Dave Bryant

11 ARNO ROAD
Debbie Palmer

1 NORTH WALK
Sue Hyett
Visitors also welcome by appt.
01446 722805

NEW **104 PONTYPRIDD ROAD**
Barry & Susan Neilson
Visitors welcome by appt.
01446 419428
sueneilson42@hotmail.co.uk

Barry enjoys panoramic views of the Bristol Channel and is close to the rural vale. It is close enough to Cardiff to enjoy the city. Four lovely gardens situated in picturesque surroundings. Small plant lovers garden with ponds, rock gardens, alpine sinks and winter flowering shrubs, snowdrops and hellebores. New for this year, enjoy Pets Corner a lovely arrangement of plants named after animals in this ever changing garden with over 600 containers. The third garden has a more formal front garden with herbaceous perennials and cottage-style rear garden incl wildlife pond and quirky touches throughout. The fourth garden at 104 Pontypridd is a new and a very welcome addition. Dyffryn Gardens are close by and the National Botanic Garden of Wales is only 1 hour away.
❁ ☕

2 **BIG HOUSE FARM**
Llanmadoc SA3 1DE. Mark & Sheryl Mead, 07831 725753. *15m W of Swansea. M4 J47. Take A483 signed Swansea. Next r'about R A484 signed Llanelli. 2nd r'about L B4296 signed Gowerton. R at 1st T-lights onto B4295. 10m after Bury*

Green, R to Llanmadoc. Pass Britannia Inn, L at T-junction uphill past red tel box. 100 yds turn R. Honesty car park on R. Home-made teas. **Adm £3, chd free. Sun 19 June (1-6).**
Award winning inspirational garden of just under an acre combines colour form and texture in this beautiful much loved Gower village, described by one visitor as, the best I've seen this season. Large variety of interesting plants and shrubs, with ambient cottage garden feel, Mediterranean garden, Kitchen garden, beautiful views. Winner - Swansea in Bloom.

♿ 👁 ☕ ☎

GROUP OPENING

3 BONVILSTON VILLAGE GARDENS
Bonvilston CF5 6TY. *On A48, 3m W of Culverhouse Cross. Limited car parking at Reading Room on A48 in village.* Home-made teas at The Old Barn. **Adm £3, chd free. Sun 12 June (12-5).**

> **NEW** MAPLES
> Colin Jones

> **THE OLD BARN**
> Jan, Jim & Viv Hayes

> **NEW** PLAS Y COED
> Hugh & Gwenda Child

> **PLASNEWYDD**
> Mr & Mrs Ian Lane

> **TY NEWYDD**
> Mr & Mrs Anthony Provis

> **3 VILLAGE FARM**
> Geoff & Fran Mitchell

Only 7m from the centre of Cardiff on the busy A48, Bonvilston is a pleasant rural village with a mix of interesting old houses and more recent small developments. Gardens incl a colourful, productive garden on a modest plot, offering yr-round colour and interest, productive kitchen garden and patio area.1 acre garden surrounding a C17 barn conversion comprising herbaceous and shrub borders, vegetable garden, chickens, ducks and much more. Courtyard garden with wonderful views across the Vale of Glamorgan, a Japanese style garden, and last but certainly not least, a garden lovingly created by the owners, based on a design by Philip Norman with ironwork by Angharad Jones. A garden of vistas. Lovely

views across the rural vale towards the coast. Flower Festival at C13 Church. Cosy PH & village shop. Featured in Cowbridge Gem local newspaper.

♿ 👁 ☕

4 ♦ BORDERVALE PLANTS
Sandy Lane, Ystradowen, Cowbridge CF71 7SX. Mrs Claire Jenkins, 01446 774036, www.bordervale.co.uk. *8m W of Cardiff. 10 mins from M4. Take A4222 from Cowbridge. Turn R at Ystradowen postbox, then 3rd L & proceed $^1/_2$ m, following brown signs. Garden on R. Parking in rd past corner.* **Adm £2.50, chd free. For NGS: Sun 12 June; Mon 29 Aug (10-5). For further information see website.**
Within mature woodland valley (semi-tamed), with stream and bog garden, extensive mixed borders; wild flower meadow, providing diverse wildlife habitats. Children must be supervised. The nursery specialises in unusual perennials and cottage garden plants. Open Fri - Sun, Mar - Sept (10-5) NOT FOR NGS.

👁 ☎

5 **NEW** BROADCLOSE FARM
Broadclose Lane, Moulton, Vale of Glamorgan CF62 3AB. Anthea Gutherie. *2m North of Barry. From Barry, A4226 2m, turn L into Moulton (signed Moulton), into village and fork right at Three Horseshoes PH, Broadclose Farm is 2nd on the R about 200 yards. From Cowbridge A48 to Cardiff, turn R on to A4226, after 3m turn R into Moulton (signed Moulton), into village and fork R at the Three Horseshoes PH, Broadcose Farm is second on the right about 200 yards.* Home-made teas & crepes available. **Adm £3, chd free. Sun 3 July (12-6).**
Garden planted from scratch 13 yrs ago, orchard with many unusual varieties e.g. apricots, mulberries, perry pear. Roses in borders and over arches. Chickens and quails. Many left overs from show gardens - statues, woven willow sheep as seen at Hampton Court last yr. Box edged herbaceous borders. Herbs and soft fruit. Gold medal Hampton Court RHS, As you Like It Show Garden. Mainly flat mown paths. Some gradual slopes.

♿ 👁 ☕

6 **NEW** BRYN-Y-DDAFAD
Welsh St Donats, Cowbridge CF71 7ST. Glyn & June Jenkins, 01446 774451, junejenkins@bydd.co.uk. *10m W of Cardiff. 3m E of Cowbridge. From A48 follow signs to Welsh St Dowats. Follow brown tourist signs from Xrds.* Home-made teas. **Adm £3.50, chd free. Sat & Sun 30, 31 July (10-6). Visitors also welcome by appt May to end Sept.**
From an overgrown wilderness purchased 30yrs ago to a small formal front garden and terraced rear garden. Beds of colourful perennials and mature shrubs and trees. Lily pond and pergola of roses crossing the natural stream leading to a wild flower area and bank of rhododendrons and azaleas. Do come and share our passion with us.

♿ 👁 🛌 ☕ ☎

Orchard with apricots, mulberries, perry pear. Roses in borders and over arches. Chickens and quails . . .

7 BRYNHEULOG
45 Heol y Graig, Cwmgwrach, Neath SA11 5TW. Lorraine Rudd. *8m W of Neath. From M4 J43 take A465 to Glyneath, then rd signed Cwmgwrach. Entering village pass Dunraven PH, turn L at school sign, approx 100yds fork L into Glannant Place. Up hill, bear sharp R, approx 200yds turn L up steep track. 2nd house on L.* Home-made teas. **Adm £3.50, chd free. Sun 19 June (10-5).**
This keen plantswoman's hillside garden perfectly reflects the dramatic setting and surrounding natural beauty. $^3/_4$ -acre plot with many levels with cottage style planting, tropical greenhouse, wildflower areas, large rockery and ponds. Polytunnel houses all yr-round vegetables. Lots of scent and colour with roses and lilies. Wildflower area & wildlife garden. Featured in A Little Piece of Paradise on ITV Wales.

👁 ☕ ☎

8 BRYNYRENFYS
30 Cefn Road, Glais, Swansea
SA7 9EZ. Edith & Roy Morgan,
01792 842777. *8m N of Swansea.
M4 J45, take A4067 R at 2nd r'about,
then 1st R and follow yellow signs.*
Home-made teas. **Adm £3.50, chd
free. Sun 3 July (12-6)** Also open
**Broadclose Farm & Mumbles
Gardens. Visitors also welcome by
appt April - Aug, coaches /parties
welcome.**
If you love plants you'll be at home
here. A small surprising garden full of
interest. Unusual trees, shrubs and
perennials vie for attention with the
panoramic view. Wildlife and weed
friendly with no bedding! Seating on
different levels, so stay a while,
unwind and be welcome. Croeso i
bawb! Rare and unusual plants for
sale.

9 NEW CAE GWYN
24 Port Road East, Barry CF62 9PT.
Kay & Crandon Villis, 01446
722450. *6m SW of Cardiff. A4050
Cardiff to Barry. Go through 5
r'abouts, turn R into lay-by. 1st
bungalow next to Brynhill Golf Club.*
Light refreshments & teas. **Adm
£3.50, chd free. Suns 1 May;
12 June (12-5).** Also open Sun
**12 June Bonvilston Gardens,
Bordervale Plants & Pentyrch
Gardens Please see separate
entries for opening times. Visitors
also welcome by appt in May, June
& July.**
Large secret garden surrounded by
woodland with many attractive
features incl gravel gardens, pergolas,
sweeping lawns, vegetables and a
large pond. Although we are still
developing there is still plenty to see
with colourful planting and hardy
exotics. Plenty of seating areas
throughout, although we never have
time to use them.

**10 NEW CASTLE UPON ALUN
HOUSE**
St Brides Major, Bridgend
CF32 0TN. Lady Inkin. *7m W of
Cowbridge. Take B4265 to St. Brides
Major. Opposite pond & next to
Farmers Arms, take rd to Castle Upon
Alun, then follow NGS signs.* Home-
made teas. **Adm £4.50, chd free.
Sun 19 June (1-6).**
Grade II listed enclave incl 2-acre
walled garden which was redesigned
and replanted from 1998. Rose
walks, pleached lime walk,

herbaceous borders, extensive lawns
and an ornamental pond garden.
Good trees. Roses a speciality.

11 3 CLOS BRYNLLIW
Grovesend SA4 8DF. Val & Tony
Hopkins. *8m W of Swansea. M4 J47
3rd exit on r'about to Gorsenion.
Straight ahead at 4 r'abouts. T-lights
in centre Gorsenion turn R onto
B4296. 1¹/₂ m to Grovesend. Garden
on R as you leave village. Parking in
surrounding area.* Home-made teas.
**Adm £2, chd free. Sat 25, Sun 26
June (11-6).**
Explore the cottage garden with
greenhouses, fruit and vegatables
mingled with flowering perennials and
hostas, wander through the bamboo
and eucalyptus jungle, sit awhile in
the arbour overlooking the English
rose garden, before reaching the
urban courtyard garden with lilies,
roses and grapevines in raised beds
and pond with mirrored steel
cascade.

GROUP OPENING

**12 NEW COLWINSTON
VILLAGE GARDENS**
Colwinston, Cowbridge CF71 7NE.
*Off A48 3m W of Cowbridge. 1st
turning L after Pentre Meurig. 3m E of
Bridgend from Waterton r'about, turn
R on Crack Hill.* Home-made teas at
Village Hall. **Combined adm £5, chd
free (share to St Michael & All
Angels Church Fund). Sun 12 June
(12-5).**

> **NEW CORNERWAYS**
> Richard & Cynthia Gibb
>
> **NEW CYNMA HOUSE**
> Malcolm & Cynthia Jones
>
> **NEW 3 MAES Y BRYN**
> Evan Thomas
>
> **NEW 8 MAES Y BRYN**
> Clive & Sheila Hawkins
>
> **NEW OLD SCHOOL HOUSE**
> Pamela Haines
>
> **NEW ROSEWOOD LODGE**
> Colin & Hilary Jones
>
> **NEW VILLAGE FARMHOUSE**
> Andrew & Heather Maclehose

Colwinston is a rural village of mixed
developments with its beautiful C12
church at its centre. Visit around 8
contrasting village gardens from

formal to cottage gardens and
productive vegetable gardens.
Several of the gardens have delightful
S-facing views over the surrounding
countryside. **Cornerways** mature
garden, contrasting shrubs, borders,
vegetable plot, greenhouse and pond.
Well laid out. **Cynma House** Large
S-facing garden with mature shrubs,
borders, vegetable plot and paddock
leading to C19 Baptism pool. **3 Maes
y Bryn** is an old fashioned vegetable
garden which is highly productive.
Nurtured for many yrs by 91yr old
owner! **8 Maes y Bryn** is a cottage
garden with a variety of flowerbeds,
perennials, small vegetable plot and
greenhouse. **Old School House**
Cottage style garden with mature
shrubs in a country setting.
Rosewood Lodge is a well laid out
garden on different levels, thickly
planted with a variety of shrubs and
trees and offering extensive views.
Village Farmhouse Well laid out
cottage style garden with vegetable
plot, pond and bowls area. Lunches
available at local PH.

> Wander through the
> bamboo and
> eucalyptus jungle,
> sit awhile in the
> arbour overlooking
> the English rose
> garden . . .

13 THE COTTAGE
Cwmpennar, Mountain Ash
CF45 4DB. Helen & Hugh Jones,
01443 472784,
hhjones1966@yahoo.com. *18m N of
Cardiff. A470 from N or S. Then
follow B4059 to Mountain Ash. Follow
signs for Cefnpennar then
Cwmpennar.* Tea. **Adm £3, chd free.
Visitors welcome by appt** May to
Aug Maximum 12 visitors in group.
4 acres and 30 years of amateur
muddling have produced this
enchanting garden incl bluebell wood,
rhododendron and camellia shubbery,
herbaceous borders, rose garden,
small arboretum, many uncommon
trees and shrubs. Garden slopes
NE-SW.

GROUP OPENING

14 CREIGIAU VILLAGE GARDENS
Creigiau CF15 9SE. *M4 exit 34 A4119 (for Rhondda) turn R at T-lights (filter) through Groesfaen, turn L after PH & church. Turn L at T-junction then 1st R into Creigiau. From Cardiff A4119 pass BBC studios over M4 2nd R signed Creigiau. From N (A470) take rd to Pentyrch-Creigiau to ctre of village (Creigiau Inn) Easy roadside parking. Maps given to all visitors with ticket.* Home-made teas. **Adm £5, chd free. Sun 24 July (2-6).**

BRYNTEG
Alison Knight

31 MAES Y NANT
Frances Bowyer

28 MAES Y NANT
Mike & Lesley Sherwood.
Please park on Fford Dinefwr - parking not always available in Maes y Nant (cul de sac)

50 PARC-Y-BRYN
Bryan & Jan Thomas
Visitors also welcome by appt Month of June.
2920890430
bryanjan.thomas@tesco.net

Four varied gardens in large friendly village. Some mature, some more recently created. Mixed styles incl mixed herbaceous borders and vegetable gardens, ponds, formal pool, large cacti collection. Local PH central to all gardens.

We love our garden and have enjoyed finding plants that survive in this elevated and sometimes windy position . . .

GROUP OPENING

15 NEW CYNCOED GARDENS
Cyncoed, Cardiff CF23 6NA. *Leave A48 at Pentwyn, 2nd exit onto Bryn Celyn Rd, L to Pentwyn drive, R to Glyn Coed Rd. At r'about L up Hollybush Rd. Follow NGS signs to Cyncoed Crescent and Danycoed Rd. Alternatively, from Cyncoed Road or Rhydypenau Rd follow NGS signs.* Tea & cake available. **Adm £3, chd free. Sun 15 May; Sun 24 July (2-6).**

NEW 8 CYNCOED CRESCENT
Alistair and Teresa Pattillo

NEW 22 DAN Y COED
Alan and Miranda Workman

These suburban gardens were carved out of woodland in the 1930s when the houses were built and they are surrounded by trees. They have a multitude of shrubs, climbing roses, clematis, hostas and ferns and many unusual plants. The owners include sculptures and whimsical features in their gardens and spend time on landscaping. Cyncoed Crescent is the larger of the two and has large, recently planted new beds. There are plans for a pond and bog garden and new planting for the lower paved area over the winter of 2010-11. Dan Y Coed Road has established beds and a wildlife pond; and also a summerhouse and greenhouse. All of this is enhanced by the backdrop of the Nant Fawr woodland. Even though they are close to the centre of Cardiff, in both of these gardens the city seems far away.

16 NEW DYFFRYN
3 Ely Road, Llandaff, Cardiff CF5 2JE. Carolyn & Wynne Jones. *1m N of Cardiff. Follow signs for Llandaff (A48) in Llandaff village turn down Ely Rd at Malsters PH, then follow NGS signs.* Home-made teas. **Adm £3, chd free. Sun 19 June (2-6).**
The children having flown the coop, the slides and swings having all gone, Carolyn has had the chance to transform this old Victorian garden into a haven, with approx 150 roses, shrubs and trees in this still evolving garden. Limited wheelchair access.

17 GREENFIELDS
Newport Road, St Mellons CF3 5TW. Roger & Kate Verrier Jones. *3m E of Cardiff. S-side Newport Rd (B4487) on top of hill 1/4 m W of St Mellons village, 200yds E of St Llltyd's sch. Park at Fox & Hounds, Old Hill or Quarry Hall nursing home.* Home-made teas. **Adm £2.50, chd free. Sun 5 June (12-6).**
3/4-acre garden incl a cottage style front garden with herbaceous and wild areas. Pergola, vista to formal pond and beyond, knot garden and water feature. Rear garden open and terraced with topiary, shady areas and views of Bristol Channel leading to newly developed parterre style kitchen garden and fruit cage. Sale of cards, handicrafts, home-made food & plants.

18 HAFOD Y MILGI
Heol y Wenallt, Thornhill CF83 1ND. Eric & Angharad Roberts. *4m from Cardiff centre. From Cardiff take A469 to Caerffili, past Thornhill crematorium. House at junction with Wenallt Rd opp Travellers Rest PH. From Caerffili A470 signed.* Home-made teas. **Adm £2.50, chd free. Sat & Sun 18, 19 June (2-6).**
We love our garden and have enjoyed finding plants that survive in this elevated and sometimes windy position. The aim has been to create sheltered places to sit and enjoy the pond, flowers and views of Nofydd Valley and Garth Mountain. Come and enjoy it with us. Short ramp, some sloping paths in addition to flat patio.

GROUP OPENING

19 HEN FELIN & SWALLOW BARNS
Vale of Glamorgan, Dyffryn, Dyffryn CF5 6SU, 02920 593082, rozanne.lord@blueyonder.co.uk. *3m from Culverhouse Cross r'about. M4 J33, A4232 to Penarth, 1st exit to Culverhouse Cross r'about. A48, follow signs to Cowbridge. At St Nicholas turn L at T-lights down Dyffryn Lane, past Dyffryn House. R at T-junction, both houses on L. Follow signs. Parking in paddock at rear of Hen Felin.* Cream Teas & light refreshments. Barbecue from (12- 2) at Hen Felin. **Adm £5, chd free.**

Sun 26 June (12-7). Visitors also welcome by appt.

THE BARNS
Mrs Janet Evans

HEN FELIN ⊫
Rozanne Lord
Visitors also welcome by appt
June 15th to end of July.
02920 593082
rozanne.lord@blueyonder.co.uk
Artsattheoldmill.co.uk

Dyffryn hamlet is a hidden gem in the Vale of Glamorgan; despite the lack of a PH there is a fantastic community spirit. Wheelchair access possible to most of the two gardens.
Unprotected river access, children must be supervised in both gardens. Yr Hen Felin: Beautiful cottage garden with stunning borders, breathtaking wildflower meadows, oak tree with surrounding bench, 200yr old pig sty, wishing well, secret garden with steps to river, lovingly tended vegetable garden and chickens. Mill stream running through garden with adjacent wild flowers. Swallow Barns: Cross the bridge over the river and pass under the weeping ash to enter Swallow Barns garden, a 15yr old garden with packed herbaceous borders - formal and informal, orchard, hens, herb garden, lavender patio, willow arches leading to woodland walk and deep secluded pond. We welcome all visitors - old and new. Home-made jams, Pimm's at the pond, cheese and wine, artists' stall, face painting, white elephant stall, jewelery stall and plant stall. Featured in BBC 3 program; Don't tell the Bride.
&♿ 🐕 ⊗ ⊫ ☕

Greenfields

GROUP OPENING

20 ▶ LLANBLETHIAN GARDENS
Llanblethian CF71 7JU. *7m E of Bridgend. From Cardiff A48 W through Cowbridge, L up hill towards Llantwit Major. L at Cross Inn PH.* Home-made teas at Llanbleddian village hall. Adm £3.50, chd free (share to West Wales Prostate Cancer Support Group). Sun 29 May (2-6).

MALTSTERS COTTAGE
Mr & Dr Lipp

STALLCOURT MEWS
Dick & Beverly Tonkin

Picturesque hillside country village, quiet and unspoilt. Adjacent to popular market town of Cowbridge. Malsters Cottage courtyard leads through to a pretty cottage garden which invites you to meander through and sit to enjoy the variety of colour and peaceful aspect. Stallcourt Mews is a front terraced courtyard garden. Side and rear sloping garden with 60m stream (unfenced) and ponds. Largely impulse planting so quite varied; vegetable garden and short woodland walk.
&♿ 🐕 ⊗ ☕

GROUP OPENING

21 ▶ LLANDAFF GARDENS
Llandaff, Cardiff CF5 2QH. *1m N of Cardiff. From Llandaff city and Cathedral along Cardiff Rd, A4119. Take 2nd exit onto A4054, Bridge Rd. Turn L at bus stop into Radyr Court Rd. Park next to railings.* Home-made teas & light refreshments. Adm £3, chd free. Sat 7 May (11-4).

GAYNORS GARDEN
Gaynor Witchard

ROSEMARY'S GARDEN
Rosemary Edwards

Set in beautiful location along the River Taff and a short distance from the picturesque Llandaff Cathedral. The owners are enthusiastic gardeners who have many years of experience in horticulture and are more than happy to share their knowledge. Gaynor's Garden is a sheltered sloping garden full of spring bulbs and cottage garden plants. An arbour, octagonal greenhouse & small pond complete the scene. Under a pergola covered in a mature grapevine and clematis, a deck path leads to a quiet area at the top of the garden. Rosemary's Garden - walk through a small woodland garden with specimen Hydrangea and Rhododendron, spring bulbs, stunningly white silver birch. Raised herb bed beside a decked path leading to seasonal containers and a pergola covered in Wedding Day climbing rose. Follow a newly installed stream around a well stocked raised planting area. Plants, hand painted pots and garden ephemera for sale at Gaynor's garden.
⊗ ☕

GROUP OPENING

LLANTWIT MAJOR & LLANMAES GARDENS
Llantwit Major CF61 1SD. *5m S of Cowbridge. From Barry on B4265 at 2nd set of T-lights on outskirts of Llantwit Major take L turn to town centre or R turn to Llanmaes. From Bridgend take B4265 to outskirts of Llantwit Major at 1st T-lights, R turn to town centre or L to Llanmaes & follow yellow signs.* Tea & cake at Old Froglands, Mehefin light lunch, Flanders Barn light refreshments. Adm £3, chd free. **Sun 5 June (11-5).**

FLANDERS BARN ╠═╡
Ann John

IVY COTTAGE
Mrs Lesley Hunt

MEHEFIN ╠═╡
Mrs Alison Morgan

OLD FROGLANDS
Dorne & David Harris

SWINEBRIDGE FARM
Anton Jones

Llantwit Major is only a 30 minute drive from Cardiff in the beautiful Vale of Glamorgan. Llanmaes, a mile or so from Llantwit Major, is a pretty village with attractive village green and stream running through. Front and back gardens are an eclectic mix of large and smaller gardens attached to historic houses, farmhouses, modern houses and cottages. Plantings are varied from cottage garden style to formal with clipped yew and box hedging. There are vegetable plots, water features, ponds, streams and woodland settings, container gardens, ducks and chickens. Come and share the scents, sounds, sights and taste with us.

❀ ☕

GROUP OPENING

LLYSWORNEY GARDENS
Cowbridge CF71 7NQ. *2m SW of Cowbridge. W along A48 passing Cowbridge. Turn L at Pentre Meyrick on B4268 signed Llysworney & Llantwit Major.* Home-made teas. **Sun 5 June (2-6).**

BLACK BARN HOUSE
Linda & Bryn Miles

BROCTON HOUSE
Peter & Colette Evans

`NEW` THE CHASE
Mr & Mrs David Gibson

`NEW` SPRINGFIELD HOUSE
Sue & Francis Hayes

WOLF HOUSE
Martyn & Melanie Hurst

Llysworney is a charming small rural village with PH, church, duck pond and friendly people! Five gardens will be open together with St Tydfil's Church which dates back to C13 to incl **Black Barn House** a garden designed on circular linking themes which are divided by using trellis, archways and trees. Established in 2007 with a good variety of plants with the emphasis on cottage style. **Brocton House** offers a recently extended and renovated garden arranged in terraces overlooking open farmland and countryside. Also fruit and vegetable gardens. **The Chase** is an informal garden backing on to farmland with an interesting mix of perennials, shrubs and roses. **Springfield House** is a terraced garden offering beautiful views from the front. There is also a pond, rhododendrons, herbaceous borders and an abundance of wildlife in a quiet little lane. **Wolf House** is an old established walled cottage offering mainly perennials and roses. After your visit why not join us by the pond for tea and cakes accompanied by music. Plant sale at Wolf House.

❀ ☕

11 Arno Road

See more garden images at www.ngs.org.uk

24 ▶ NEW ▶ MONKSTONE
21 Windsor Road, Radyr, Cardiff
CF15 8BQ. **Mrs Antonia Wigley.** *4m
NW of Cardiff. From Cardiff take
A4119, Llantrissant Rd, past BBC
building Llandaff. At 3rd r'about turn
R into Radyr on B4261. Immed after
pelican crossing turn L into Windsor
Rd. Garden up hill on LHS of bend.
Radyr is close to J32 of M4. Take
A470 towards Merthyr (be ready to
take 1st exit & follow signs into
Radyr), opp Spar shop turn R into
Windsor Rd immed before pelican
crossing.* Home-made teas. **Adm
£2.50, chd free (share to Radyr &
District Good Neigbour Scheme).
Sun 8 May (12-6).**
Our family garden of approx ⅓ acre
was originally laid out in the 1920s.
The mature planting incl acers,
magnolias, azaleas and a wisteria.
There are mixed beds, an alpine area,
kitchen garden, lawn and sitting
areas. Care is needed to negotiate
some of the stone steps and paths.
❀ ☕

GROUP OPENING

25 ▶ NEW ▶ MUMBLES GARDENS
SA3 5EY. *5m SW of Swansea. At
r'about on Mumbles Rd A4067 take
2nd exit (Fairwood Rd) then 1st L
onto Westcross Lane & follow yellow
signs.* Home-made teas. **Combined
adm £3, chd free. Sun 3 July (2-6).**

NEW ▶ 5 MOORSIDE ROAD
Ceri Macafarlane & Mike
Gravenor

NEW ▶ 3 RIVERSIDE ROAD
Catherine & Graeme Harris

Two urban gardens recently planted
on a budget by enthusiastic,
passionate yet interrupted gardeners.
Close to the picturesque seaside
village of Mumbles. 5 Moorside Road
is a long narrow garden on many
levels, where a wide variety of densely
planted herbaceous perennials,
grasses and shrubs jostle with the
trappings of family life. The garden is
constantly evolving through the
owners' experimentation with
balance, colour and form. 3
Riversdale Road has an eclectic mix
of shrubs, trees, cottage plants and
quirky elements that make this garden
a humorous yet tranquil family oasis
filled with colour. A garden grown
from scratch, after building works
3yrs ago. Ornamentals and perennials
compete with the doll's tea parties

and footballs. Steps & narrow paths
make access difficult for less mobile
visitors.
❀ ☕

Full of seasonal colour and the fragrance of honeysuckle, roses and sweet peas . . .

GROUP OPENING

26 ▶ PENARTH GARDENS
Penarth, Penarth CF64 2SR. *3m
SW of Cardiff. Leave M4 at J33 take
A4232 for Cardiff Bay, then B4160
(B4055) for Penarth & Barry to
t'lights, Merry Harrier PH on R. L into
Redlands Rd (B4267). For Witsend
(77) 4th L into Cornerswell Rd then
1st L Coleridge Av. No.77 on LHS.
For Honeysuckle Cott (118a) continue
Redlands Rd to Lavernock Rd, No.
118a on LHS.* Home-made teas.
Honeysuckle Cottage, 18th June only.
**Combined adm £3, (June), £2
(Sept) chd free. Sats 18 June;
17 Sept (11-5).**

HONEYSUCKLE COTTAGE
Louise Sawyer
Not open 17th Sept.

WITSEND
Diana Mead,
www.dianamead.net

Set in the charming Victorian seaside
town of Penarth, 2 small pretty
gardens with lots of big ideas for
making the most of limited space.
Honeysuckle Cottage - tranquil,
sunny cottage-style garden full of
seasonal colour and the fragrance of
honeysuckle, roses and sweet peas.
Several secluded seating areas,
greenhouse and intriguing trompe
l'oeil door at the end of the drive.
Witsend - comprises three small,
awkwardly shaped plots each planted
to create an individual small garden.
Cottage-style front has alpine-planted
gravel path, bird's drinking ponds and

shade area. Side garden is the
vegetable plot with apple trees and
herbs. Sheltered rear garden has
pears, vine, roses, frog pond and
tender plants. Art exhibition at
Witsend on both open days and
produce stall at the September
opening. Plants for sale at both
gardens at June opening. Witsend
only in September.
❀ ☕

GROUP OPENING

**27 ▶ PENTYRCH GARDENS IN
JUNE**
Pentyrch, Cardiff CF15 9QD. *2m N
of Cardiff. M4 J32 - A470 to Merthyr.
After ½ m exit signed Taffs Well &
Radyr. 1st exit at r'about onto B4262
signed Radyr, Gwaelod & Pentyrch.
Next r'about R. L at T-junction. 1st
house on L.* Home-made teas. **Adm
£5, chd free. Sun 12 June
(11-5.30).**

5 DAN Y RODYN
Stephen Evans

9 HEOL Y PENTRE
Chris & Ken Rogers

MAES-Y-GOF
Jeanette & Chris Troughton

SUNNY BANK
Chris & Dave Bilham

TY DERI
Hanni & Lyn Davies
(See separate entry)

Group of 5 gardens offering
something to suit all interests. Maes-
y-Gof a medium sized cottage garden
with exuberantly planted herbaceous
borders, roses, clematis, ferns and
palms. 5 Dan y Rodyn uses much
ingenious recycling, and is a haven for
wildlife - but this garden is beautifully
groomed and neat as well. 9 Heol-y-
Pentre is a corner plot with perennial
borders, acers, climbers and small
gravel garden. Ty Deri is an award
winning front garden with water
feature surrounded by seasonal
herbaceous borders. Rear garden has
raised vegetable beds, fruit cage,
greenhouse and herbaceous borders.
Sunny Bank is a 200yr-old cottage
with a wisteria-covered veranda,
formal terrace and informal garden
Pond with bridge leading to a
summerhouse. Tries to be as organic
as possible.
☕

GROUP OPENING

28 PENYLAN GARDENS
Penylan, Cardiff CF23 5BD. 1½ m NE of Cardiff city centre. M4 J29, Cardiff E A48, then Llanedeyrn/Dock exit, towards Cyncoed and L down Penylan Hill. Marlborough Rd is L at T-lights at bottom of hill. Look out for NGS signs. Tea. **Adm £4, chd free. Sun 29 May (2-6); Sun 24 July (1-6).**

6 ALMA ROAD
Melvyn Rees
Visitors also welcome by appt.
02920 482200
melvyn.tymel@gmail.com

7 CRESSY ROAD
Victoria Thornton

102 MARLBOROUGH ROAD
Mrs Judith Griffiths

128 PENYLAN ROAD
John & Judi Wilkins

NEW 5 SOUTHCOURT ROAD
Pat & Mel Griffiths

5 gardens in this Victorian suburb of mostly terraced houses with small gardens and many parks.The gardens open, show a variety of ways of adding interest and individuality to a small space incl mediterranean-style sunny patio areas, informal mix of cottage plants, slate used as paving material, a riot of exotic foliage, stone walled SE facing cottage garden offering colour and peace away from the busy main rd and a bijou terrace garden profusely planted with an abundance of unusual and exotic plants.

29 PONTYGWAITH FARM
Edwardsville, nr Treharris CF46 5PD. Mrs D Cann, 07527 564116. 2m NW of Treharris. N from Cardiff on A470. At r'about take A4054 (old Ponytpridd to Merthyr rd), travel N towards Aberfan for approx 3m through Quakers Yard and Edwardsville. 1m after Edwardsville turn very sharp L by old black bus shelter, garden at bottom of hill. Light refreshments & teas. **Adm £3, chd free. Sun, Mon 29, 30 May; Sat, Sun 18, 19 June (10-5).** Visitors also welcome by appt Apr to Aug. Drop in visitors also welcome via Trevithick's Tramway.
Large garden surrounding C17 farmhouse adjacent to Trevithick's Tramway. Situated in picturesque wooded valley. Fish pond, lawns, perennial borders, lakeside walk and rose garden. Grade II listed humpback packhorse bridge in garden, spanning R Taff. A lovely day out for all the family. Featured in film; Caught in the Act. Steep slope to river.

A lovely day out for all the family . . .

GROUP OPENING

30 RHIWBINA OPEN GARDENS
Rhiwbina CF14 6EL. M4 J32. 1st L to mini r'about, turn R into village at T-lights, turn R to Pen Y Dre. Home-made teas & light refreshments at most gardens. **Adm £5, chd free. Sun 15 May; Sun 3 July (11-6).**

89 PEN-Y-DRE
Lorraine & Emil Nelz

BARCIES GARDEN
Ms Amerjit Barrett

JAPANESE GARDEN
Mr B A Harding
Not open May 15th.

NEW 7 PEN Y DRE
Christine Lewis
Not open May 15.

Four lovely gardens incl Emil & Lorraine's garden at 89 Pen-y-Dre, small but very interesting containing palms, tree ferns perennials and a conservatory with several cacti, also a fish pond with some very large Koi. Christine Lewis at 7 Pen-y-Dre, a suburban garden approached by a narrow wooden bridge over a babbling brook. Front garden is lawned with a mixture of flowering shrubs, rear cottage garden landscaped with a profusion of perennials and small trees. The Japanese Garden at 42 Lon-Isa was recently featured on ITV's 'A Little Piece of Paradise, and incl a pond with Koi and a Japanese Tea Room. Barcies Garden at 14 Lon Ysgubor is a terraced garden with shrubs, perennials and fern and hosta collections. Lon Ysgubor is not recommended for those with walking difficulties. Featured in The Japanese Garden, ITV; A Little Piece of Paradise. 89 Pen-y-Dre has won several prizes with Cardiff in Bloom.

31 RHOS Y BEDW
4 Pen y Wern Rd, Ystalyfera, Swansea SA9 2NH. Robert Davies & Helen Dyer, 01639 843306. 13m N of Swansea. M4 J45 take A4067. Follow signs for Dan yr Ogof caves across 5 r'abouts. After T-lights follow NGS signs. Parking above house on rd off to R. Cream teas & gluten free cakes available. **Adm £2, chd free. Sat & Sun 4, 5 June (12-6).** Visitors also welcome by appt June to Sept.
Compact offset plot on side of hill with panoramic views of the upper Swansea valley. This newly created garden incl shrubs and perennials with a large selection of heucheras. The garden also has bog, shade, bank, vegetable, herb and alpine areas. Seating throughout, relax and enjoy.

32 SLADE
Southerndown CF32 0RP. Rosamund & Peter Davies, 01656 880048, ros@sladewoodgarden.plus.com, www.sladefarmorganics.com. 5m S of Bridgend. M4 J35. Follow A473 to Bridgend. Take B4265 to St Brides Major. Turn R in St Brides Major for Southerndown. At Southerndown tur L opp 3 Golden Cups PH onto Beach Rd. Follow rd into Dunraven Park. Turn 1st L over cattle grid on to Slade drive. Home-made teas. **Adm £3, chd free. Sat & Sun 16, 17 Apr (11-5).** Visitors also welcome by appt.
Set in 6 acres, Slade garden is an unexpected gem with masses of spring flowers. The terraced lawns, mature specimen trees, living willow arbours, rose and clematis pergola, orchard and herbaceous borders, create a very natural garden that also has extensive views over the Bristol Channel. Heritage Coast wardens will give guided tours of adjacent Dunraven Gardens with slide shows every hour from 2pm. Featured in South Wales Echo on gardening page.

SPRINGFIELD
176 Clasemont Road, Morriston
SA6 6AJ. Carole & Stuart Jones,
01792 773827,
springfield@virgin.net. *4m N of
Swansea. From M4 J46 follow A48
E for 1m. From Morriston Cross take
A48 W for 1m, garden on A48 50yds
from entrance to Morriston Golf Club.*
Home-made teas. **Adm £2.50, chd
free.** Sun 22 May (12-6). **Visitors
also welcome by appt for small
groups, max 20, May to Aug.**
Small informal suburban garden with
interesting mix of trees, shrubs, bulbs
and perennials to give yr-round
interest. Incl small pond and pebble
pond and many containerised plants.
Several seating areas give the garden
a relaxed feel. A real plantaholics
garden.
🌼 ☕ ☎

**34 NEW TONY RIDLERS
GARDEN**
7 St Peter's Terrace, Cockett
SA2 0FW. Tony & Caroline Ridler,
01792 588217,
tony@ridlerwebster.co.uk. *From M4
J47 take A483 towards Swansea at
Fforestfach Cross T-lights turn R on
Station Rd A4216 at next T-lights turn
L on St Peters Terrace.* **Adm £3.**
Suns 8 May; 5 June (2-5). **Visitors
also welcome by appt.**
Graphic designer's ¹/₃ acre garden
behind a modest terrace house. the
garden is divided into a series of
formal spaces and vistas largely
defined by narrow stepped pathways,
sculptures, yew hedges and box
topiary. Regret, no children. Featured
in Discovering Welsh Gardens by
Stephen Anderton.
☕ ☎

TREDEGAR HOUSE & PARK
See Gwent.

35 ◆ TWYN YR HYDD
Margam Country Park, Margam
SA13 2TJ. Neath Port Talbot
College, 01639 648261,
www.trainingwales.com. *2m W of*

Pyle. M4 J38, take A48 signed
Margam Park. Pass entrance to Park,
after ¹/₂ m turn L into garden.* Light
Refreshments. Barbecue (weather
permitting) and home made cakes
and produce. **Adm £3.50, chd free.**
For NGS: Sun 26 June (11-3). **For
opening times and information
please visit website or telephone.**
Spread out over 11-acre site and
containing gardens designed and
constructed by horticulture students.
Incl herb, prairie, woodland and a
vegetable garden. Grounds also
contain walled garden designed by
Arts and Crafts designer Ralph
Hancock. Gardens will house the
largest collection of hebes in Wales.
Plants grown by students, always
available for sale. Featured in BBC
Gardeners World.
♿ 🌼 🌼 ☕ ☎

Front garden is a blaze of colour with flower beds, hanging baskets and tubs . . .

36 TY DERI
Pentyrch CF15 9NP. Hanni & Lyn
Davies. **Adm £3, chd free.** Wed 15
June; Sat & Sun 27, 28 Aug (11-6).
Award winning garden with specimen
trees, water feature surrounded by
seasonal herbaceous borders. Rear
garden incl unusual plants, raised
vegetable beds, large fruit cage and
greenhouse. 1st prize Cardiff &
Bloom; 3rd prize Super Gardener,
Cardiff & District & 1st prize Election
Area.
♿ 🌼

37 WILCOT
Higher End, St Athans, Nr Barry
CF62 4LW. Jan & Tony Simmonite,
01446 753609. *6m S of Cowbridge
off A48. Take B270 from Cowbridge*

or B4265 from Barry. Follow signs to
St Athans then NGS arrows.* Home-
made teas. **Adm £3, chd free.**
Sun 26 June (11-5). **Visitors also
welcome by appt.**
A very special garden with
architectural features that lead you to
meander around fishponds where
waterfalls add interest to the habitat
of many fish. Abundance of flowers,
shrubs and trees ensures yr-round
colour and interest. Fruit and
vegetables. Seating invites you to
stop and enjoy this labour of love.
🐱 ☕ ☎

38 NEW 6 WINDSOR AVENUE
Windsor Avenue, Radyr CF15 8BW.
Norman Clewer. *N of Cardiff. M4 J32
-A470 to Merthyr. After ¹/₂ m exit &
follow signs to Radyr. Turn off main rd
through Radyr by Methodist Church,
take Windsor Rd which leads into
Windsor Av. Look for NGS signs.*
Home-made teas. **Adm £3, chd free.**
Sun 17 July (2-6).
Front garden is a blaze of colour with
flower beds, hanging baskets and
tubs surrounding 2 small lawns. It has
won many prizes in the Cardiff in
Bloom competition. Rear garden,
though not large, is terraced with
lawns, herbaceous borders, ponds
and vegetable plot with greenhouse.
☕

39 WITSEND
77 Coleridge Avenue, Penarth
CF64 2SR. Ms Diana Mead,
www.dianamead.net. **Adm £2.50,
chd free.** Sat 17 Sept (11-5).
Artist-gardener's small awkward plot
designed to give all yr colour and
interest. Three linked areas; cottage
style front with serpentine gravel path
planted to create river-bed effect.
Shrubs, perennials, shade area. Side
vegetable plot with apples and herbs.
Sheltered tiny rear garden with vine,
tender plants, pear trees and frog
pond. September opening for Autumn
colour and fruit harvest.
🌼

GWENT

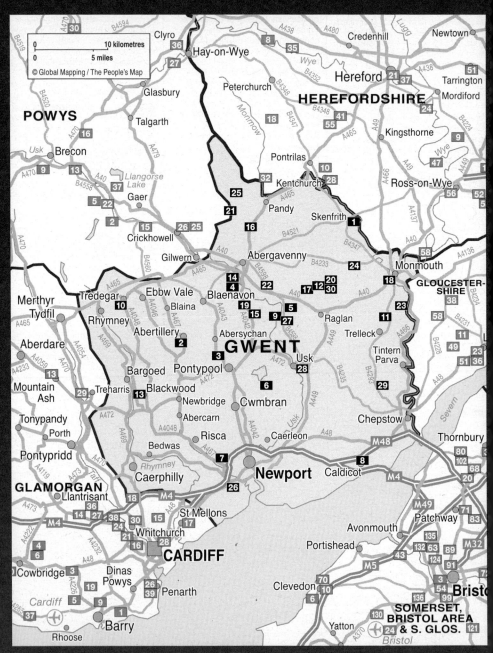

Opening Dates

March
Sunday 27
15 Llanover

April
Sunday 17
8 Dewstow Gardens & Grottoes

May
Sunday 1
27 Trostrey Lodge
Monday 2
27 Trostrey Lodge
Sunday 8
11 High Glanau Manor
Sunday 15
12 High House
30 Woodlands Farm
Sunday 22
6 Coed-y-Paen Village Gardens
Saturday 28
13 Hillcrest
22 Penpergwm Lodge
Sunday 29
13 Hillcrest
22 Penpergwm Lodge
Monday 30
13 Hillcrest

June
Sunday 5
4 Castell Cwrt
20 The Old Vicarage, Penrhos
Saturday 11
21 The Pant
Sunday 12
14 Llanfoist Village Gardens
21 The Pant
Saturday 18
23 Pentwyn Farm & Wyeswood Common
Sunday 19
16 Llanthony and District Gardens
19 Ochran Mill
Saturday 25
28 Usk Open Gardens
Sunday 26
28 Usk Open Gardens
Wednesday 29
29 Veddw House (Evening)

July
Saturday 2
9 Glebe House

Sunday 3
9 Glebe House
Sunday 10
19 Ochran Mill
26 Tredegar House & Park
Saturday 16
18 Monmouth Allotments and Two Rivers Meadow Community Orchard
30 Woodlands Farm
Sunday 17
18 Monmouth Allotments and Two Rivers Meadow Community Orchard
30 Woodlands Farm
Saturday 23
2 Bishop Street Allotments and Leisure Gardens
10 80 Gwent Way
Sunday 24
10 80 Gwent Way
MSaturday 30
3 Bramble Cottage
25 Tair-Ffynnon, 'The Garden in the Clouds'.
Sunday 31
25 Tair-Ffynnon, 'The Garden in the Clouds'.

August
Saturday 6
13 Hillcrest
Sunday 7
13 Hillcrest
Sunday 28
7 Croesllanfro Farm

September
Sunday 18
8 Dewstow Gardens & Grottoes
17 Longhouse Farm

Woodland and haymeadow walk, livestock in fields and family pets. Children very welcome, animals to see and space to let off steam . . .

Sunday 25
24 Sunnyside

Gardens open to the public
1 The Bell at Skenfrith
8 Dewstow Gardens & Grottoes
26 Tredegar House & Park
29 Veddw House

By appointment only
5 Clytha Park

Also open by Appointment ☎
6 April House, Coed-y-Paen Village Gardens
3 Bramble Cottage
7 Croesllanfro Farm
9 Glebe House
10 80 Gwent Way
11 High Glanau Manor
13 Hillcrest
15 Llanover
20 The Old Vicarage, Penrhos
22 Penpergwm Lodge
24 Sunnyside

The Gardens

1 ◆ **THE BELL AT SKENFRITH**
Skenfrith NP7 8UH. William & Janet Hutchings, 01600 750235, www.skenfrith.co.uk. *In the village of Skenfrith on B4521, opp the Norman castle. Parking is in field adjacent to garden as indicated.* Light refreshments & teas. **Visitors welcome anytime between 22 Apr & 22 Oct (11-5). Adm £3.50, chd free. Donation to the NGS.** Productive organic kitchen garden with formal area of raised beds edged with edible delights. Less formal area where more space consuming plants are grown. Produce grown incl herbs, salads, vegetables, flowers (edible and cutting), soft and hard fruits. All produce grown used in the restaurant at The Bell. Vegetables, herbs, flowers and plants for sale, depending on season. Featured in ITV Wales, A Little Piece of Paradise. Some slopes, so care required for wheelchair users.
&. ⊛ ⇌ ☕ ☎

2 BISHOP STREET ALLOTMENTS AND LEISURE GARDENS

Bishop Street, Abertillery NP13 1ET. Judith Williams. *On E side of Abertillery. At T-lights on A467 turn into Abertillery. 1st L, up Station Hill, over Foundry Bridge, 1st L Tillery Street, 1st R Newall Street. Allotments at top. Parking in streets beside allotments.* Home-made teas. **Adm £3, chd free. Sat 23 July (11-4).**

Situated on the mountainside above Abertillery, the allotments were started in the 1880s so that miners could feed their families. They are kept to a very high standard, regularly winning prizes. 36 people garden on the site which will be at its productive best, full of colourful vegetables and flowers. Some of the allotments are organically gardened. Areas to encourage wildlife. Green Pennant holders, Winners Blaenau Gwent in Bloom.

3 NEW BRAMBLE COTTAGE

1 Lower Leigh Road, Pontnewynydd NP4 8LQ. Don Kerr & Serge Demade, 01495 740774, kerr-demade@hotmail.co.uk. *Approx 1m from Pontypool town centre. From Pontypool take A4043 to Blaenafon, at 2nd r'about after Tesco turn R before Texaco garage. Follow NGS signage to T-junction, turn L to Lower Leigh Rd.* Home-made teas. **Adm £3, chd free (share to Alzheimers & MIND). Sat 30 July (10-4.30).** Visitors also welcome by appt 1 May - 30 Sept. Small groups welcome.

$1/4$ -acre of steep S-facing terraced garden, many steps and narrow paths. Not for the faint hearted but well adapted to a tricky site. Dry stone walls, good selection of plants, shrubs and loquat from Corfu create a Mediterranean feel. Lots of areas to sit and enjoy the views.

4 CASTELL CWRT

Llanelen, Abergavenny NP7 9LE. Lorna & John McGlynn. *1m S of Abergavenny. From Abergavenny/ Llanfoist take B4269 signed Llanelen. After passing Grove Farm turn R up single track rd. Rd climbs up steeply over canal. Approx 500yds entrance to Castell Cwrt 2nd on L. Separate disabled parking available.* Home-made teas. **Adm £2.50, chd free. Sun 5 June (12-5).**

Large informal family garden in 10-acre small holding with fine views overlooking Abergavenny. Lawns with established trees and shrubs borders. Organic soft fruit and vegetable gardens. Woodland and haymeadow walk, livestock in fields and family pets. Children very welcome, animals to see and space to let off steam. gravel & grass paths.

5 CLYTHA PARK

Abergavenny NP7 9BW. Sir Richard & Lady Hanbury-Tenison, 01873 840300, etenison673@btinternet.com. *Half-way between Abergavenny (4m) and Raglan (4m). On old rd signed Clytha at r'abouts at either end.* **Adm £3.50, chd free. Visitors welcome by appt Easter to end October. Please call and leave details.**

Large C18 garden around $1\frac{1}{2}$ -acre lake with wide lawns and good trees. Visit the 1790 walled garden or walk around the lake on a serpentine path laid out over 250 yrs ago. Ravens always around and possibly the largest Tulip tree in Wales.

GROUP OPENING

6 COED-Y-PAEN VILLAGE GARDENS

Coed-Y-Paen NP4 0TH, www.coedypaenopengardens.org. *3m SW of Usk. From Usk take rd to Caerleon, 1st R to Coed-y-paen. 1m R, 2m to village. From Cwmbran A4042 towards Newport at Croesyceiliog/Crematorium r'about take 1st exit to Llangybi, 1st L after $1/2$ m to village. Map provided. Mini bus available to outlying gardens.* **Combined adm £5, chd free. Sun 22 May (11-5).**

APRIL HOUSE
Dr C Fleming
Visitors also welcome by appt.
07917 319533
charlotte.fleming00@gmail.com

HILLCREST
Sheila & Chris Gifford

HONEYWELL COTTAGE
Maggie & Patrick Harkness

THE OLD SCHOOL
Carol Orchard

THE ORCHARD
Mrs Chrissie Hayes

SPINDLE TREE COTTAGE
J Hargreaves

TY-PERROTT COTTAGE
Ms A Broben

WINDRUSH
Mrs E J Stickland

Coed-y-Paen is in a beautiful, undiscovered part of Monmouthshire with wonderful views and terrific PH. 8 plus gardens from formal to quirky, humble to ambitious, newly established to mature, hilltop to forest clearing with inspiration for all. A very warm welcome awaits.

7 CROESLLANFRO FARM

Groes Road, Rogerstone NP10 9GP. Barry & Liz Davies, 01633 894057, lizplants@gmail.com. *3m W of Newport. From M4 J27 take B4591 to Risca. Take 3rd R, Cefn Walk (also signed 14 Locks Canal Centre). Proceed over canal bridge, continue approx $1/2$ m to island in middle of lane. White farm gate opp. Limited parking.* Home-made teas. **Adm £4.50, chd free. Sun 28 Aug (2-5). Visitors also welcome by appt May - end Sept.**

An ever evolving 2-acre garden of contrasts. New formal courtyard on 6 levels leads to a tythe barn (open). Large sweeping borders of mass planted perennials and grasses invite the visitor to explore the paths, terracing and folly. A garden for all moods. Quiz for children. Gravel paths and some steps.

Large sweeping borders of mass planted perennials and grasses invite the visitor to explore the paths, terracing and folly . . .

High Glanau Manor

8 ◆ DEWSTOW GARDENS & GROTTOES

Caerwent, Caldicot NP26 5AH. John Harris, 01291 430444, www.dewstow.co.uk. *5m W of Chepstow. From A48 Newport to Chepstow rd, R to Caerwent & Dewstow golf club. Garden next to golf club. Coaches permitted.* **Adm £5, chd free. For NGS: Suns 17 Apr; 18 Sept (10.30-4). For other opening times and information, please phone or see garden website.**

5-acre Grade 1 listed unique garden which was buried and forgotten after World War 11 and rediscovered in 2000. Created around 1895 by James Pulham & Sons, the garden contains underground grottoes, tunnels and ferneries and above ground stunning water features. You will not be disappointed. Wheelchair access very limited.

9 GLEBE HOUSE

Llanvair Kilgeddin NP7 9BE. Mr & Mrs Murray Kerr, 01873 840422, joanna@amknet.com. *Midway between Abergavenny (5m) and Usk (5m). On B4598.* Home-made teas. **Adm £3.50, chd free. Sat & Sun 2, 3 July (2-6). Visitors also welcome by appt April - end July.**

1¹/₂ acres with herbaceous borders overflowing with colourful perennials, annuals and shrubs. S-facing terrace with climbers, ornamental vegetable garden and orchard - all surrounded by picturesque Usk Valley. Old rectory of St Mary's, Llanvair Kilgeddin with famous Victorian scraffito murals which will also be open.

GLIFFAES COUNTRY HOUSE HOTEL
See Powys.

THE GRIGGS
See Herefordshire.

10 80 GWENT WAY

Tredegar NP22 3HT. Mr Robert Edward, 01495 711413 or 07774 440707, robert-je@hotmail.com. *2m W of Ebbw Vale. From A465 take the A4048 to Tredegar and follow signs to Ashvale Industrial Park. Park on the service road to the industrial estate at the bottom of Gwent Way.* Home-made & cream teas. **Adm £3, chd free. Sat 23, Sun 24 July (2-5). Visitors also welcome by appt.**

Small town garden crammed with interest front and back. Terraced front with small shrubbery, alpines, hanging baskets and pots. Sculpted metal pergola across width of back garden, two ponds and a rill, climbers on all walls and fences with numerous pots and hanging baskets. Featured in Gwent Gazette as Winner of Gwent in Bloom 2010.

Take a seat, soak in the garden's ambience, enjoy the views with a sublime cream tea . . .

11 HIGH GLANAU MANOR

Lydart, Monmouth NP25 4AD. Mr & Mrs Hilary Gerrish, 01600 860005, helenagerrish@hotmail.co.uk. *4m SW of Monmouth. Situated on B4293 between Monmouth & Chepstow. Turn into Private Road opp Five Trees Carp Fishery.* Home-made teas. **Adm £4, chd free. Sun 8 May (2-6). Visitors also welcome by appt.**

Listed Arts and Crafts garden laid out by H Avray Tipping in 1922. Original features incl impressive stone terraces with far-reaching views over the vale of Usk to Blorenge, Skirrid, Sugar Loaf and Brecon Beacons. Pergola, herbaceous borders, Edwardian glasshouse, rhododendrons, azaleas, tulips, orchard with wild flowers and woodland walks.

12 HIGH HOUSE

Penrhos NP15 2DJ. Mr & Mrs R Cleeve. *4m N of Raglan. From r'about on A40 at Raglan take exit to Clytha. After 50 yds turn R to Llantilio Crossenny and follow garden open signs to High House - 10mins through lanes.* Home-made teas. **Combined adm with Woodlands Farm £6, chd free. Sun 15 May (2-6).**

3-acres of spacious lawns and trees surrounding C16 house (not open) in a beautiful, hidden part of Monmouthshire. Large extended pond, orchard with chickens and ducks. S-facing terrace and extensive bed of old roses. Areas of grass with tulips, camassias, wild flowers and far reaching views.

13 HILLCREST

Waunborfa Road, Cefn Fforest, Blackwood NP12 3LB. Mr M O'Leary & Mr B Price, 01443 837029, www.hillcrestgarden.co.uk. *3m W of Newbridge. Follow A4048 to Blackwood town centre or A469 to Pengam T-lights, then NGS signs.* Cream teas & light refreshments. **Adm £3.50, chd free. Sat 28, Sun 29, Mon 30 May; Sat 6, Sun 7 Aug (12-6). Visitors also welcome by appt. April to September, groups of any size.**

Popular 1.33 acre garden, regarded by many visitors as their personal 'secret' haven of horticultural treasure and tranquillity. Experience the warmest welcome. Explore secluded gardens each cascading into the next and revealing hidden delights around every corner. Take a seat, soak in the garden's ambience, enjoy the views with a sublime cream tea.

14 LLANFOIST VILLAGE GARDENS

NP7 9NF. Jayne Smith. *1m SW of Abergavenny on B4246. Map provided with ticket. Most gardens within easy walking distance of the village centre. Free minibus to others. Limited wheelchair access to some gardens.* Light refreshments, teas and lunch served in village hall. **Combined adm £5 (donation to NGS), chd free. Sun 12 June (10.30-5.30).**

Make this a great day out. Visit around 15 exciting and contrasting village gardens, both large and small, set just below the Blorenge Mountain on the edge of the Black Mountains. This is our 9th annual event. A number of new gardens opening along with many regulars. Canal boat trips and fantastic food not to be missed.

15 LLANOVER

nr Abergavenny NP7 9EF. Mr & Mrs M R Murray, 07753 423635, elizabeth@llanover.com, www.llanovergarden.co.uk. *4m S of Abergavenny, 15m N of Newport. On A4042 Abergavenny - Pontypool.* Home-made teas available & by prior arrangment only on private visit days. **Adm £4.50, chd free. Sun 27 Mar (2-5). Visitors also welcome by appt. Minimum group 15. Sept to end May.**

15-acre listed garden and arboretum with lakes, streams, cascades and a dovecote set in an unusual circular walled garden. Champion trees present. The woodland garden has numerous spring bulbs, Camellias and Magnolias which give plenty of colour and interest. Home of Llanover Garden School. Traditional Welsh dancing and music. Plants for sale. Park walk. Wheelchair access to all of the garden via grass and gravel paths, lawns and a tarmac drive.

GROUP OPENING

16 LLANTHONY AND DISTRICT GARDENS
Llanthony NP7 7LB. *5m N of Abergavenny. From Abergavenny roundabout take A465 N towards Hereford. 4.8m turn L onto Old Hereford Rd signed Pantygelli 2m. Mione is ¹/₂ m on L. Directions to the other gardens provided.* Home-made teas & light refreshments. **Adm £5, chd free. Sun 19 June (10.30-4.30).**

GROVE FARM
Walterstone. David & Christine Hunt

MIONE
Llanvihangel Crucorney. Yvonne & John O'Neil

PERTHI CRWN
Cwmyoy. Jim Keates

NEW TRWYN TAL
Capel-y-ffin. Mr & Mrs Hart

Located in an area of outstanding beauty within the Black Mountains rural communities of Walterstone, Cwmyoy, Capel-y-ffin and the village of Llanvihangel Crucorney. The garden settings reflect the diversity of the local landscape with views across valleys, mountains and forests. They include, a remote and atmospheric mountainside garden, a farmyard transformed into a tranquil courtyard, a cottage garden with pergolas covered in clematis and roses and a walled garden in a stunning setting.

17 LONGHOUSE FARM
Penrhos, Raglan NP15 2DE. Mr & Mrs M H C Anderson. *Midway between Monmouth & Abergavenny. 4m from Raglan. Old Raglan/ Abergavenny rd signed Clytha. At Bryngwyn/Great Oak Xrds take turn to Great Oak. In Great Oak follow NGS signs from red telephone box down narrow lane.* Home-made teas. **Adm £3.50, chd free. Sun 18 Sept (2-6).**

15 years, and on going, of developing this hidden 2 acre garden with a south facing terrace, millrace wall, pond, spacious lawns, colourful and unusual plants varying from blossom, irises, summer bulbs, roses, vegetables to asters, grasses and a malus avenue of autumn colour. Unspoilt vistas of Monmouthshire.

18 MONMOUTH ALLOTMENTS AND TWO RIVERS MEADOW COMMUNITY ORCHARD
Monmouth Town NP25 3EG. Mrs Sue Carter. *Western Edge of Monmouth. At bottom of Monnow St turn L, opp Gatehouse PH, at public WC's and follow track beside river to car park at allotments.* Home-made teas. **Adm £3.50, chd free. Sat 16, Sun 17 July (12-5).**
Approx 60 allotments full of flowers and vegetables and newly planted community orchard of mixed fruit with biodiverse meadow. Footpath to conjuction of R Wye and Monnow in beautiful Wye Valley.

An abundance of colour and lush growth packed with many varieties of herbaceous perennials and colourful shrubs . . .

MOOR PARK
See Powys.

THE NEUADD
See Powys.

19 OCHRAN MILL
Llanover NP7 9HU. Elaine & David Rolfe, www.ochranmill.co.uk. *3m S of Abergavenny. On A4042 midway between Llanover & Llanelen.* Home-made teas. **Adm £3, chd free. Suns 19 June; 10 July (1-6).**
Grade II listed water mill (not working) in approx 2-acres. An abundance of colour and lush growth packed with many varieties of herbaceous perennials and colourful shrubs. Interest from early spring to late autumn, hellebores, roses, asters and

many more. Field for picnics. Pinball and arcade collection (very popular with non-gardeners and children). Some gravel paths & gentle slopes.

20 THE OLD VICARAGE, PENRHOS
Raglan NP15 2LE. Professor & Mrs Luke Herrmann, 01600 780524, georginaherrmann@btopenworld.com. *3m N of Raglan. At Raglan turn off A40 for Mitcheltroy. Almost immediately turn L for Tregaer. Follow signs for Tregaer, then Penrhos.* Home-made teas. **Adm £3.50, chd free. Sun 5 June (2-6). Visitors also welcome by appt on Suns 27 Mar; 10 Apr only, for Hellebores. Please call or email for more details.**
Traditional garden surrounding beautifully sited Victorian Gothic house (not open) with spendid views over Monmouthshire countryside. Hellebores and early spring flowers, rhododendrons, azaleas and magnolias, early summer roses. Also gazebo, gravel and formal kitchen gardens and ponds. Plant stall.

21 NEW THE PANT
Forest Coal Pit, Abergaveny NP7 7LT. Dr & Mrs Jeremy Swift & Mr & Mrs Andrew Bruce. *5m N of Abergaveny. From Abergaveny take Hereford rd A465 to Llanvihangel Crucorney. Follow signs to Llanthony Abbey. After 1¹/₂ m turn L to Forest Coal Pit. After further 1¹/₂ m at fiveways X-roads, turn sharp R uphill & follow signs.* Home-made teas. **Adm £4, chd free (share to Maggie's Centre). Sat & Sun 11, 12 June (2-6).**
Two adjoining gardens set in secluded, spectacular Black Mountains scenery with 25-acres of landscaped woods, orchard, knot garden, walled garden, Islamic garden and green threatre with string quartet. Large dry stone turtle, ruined village, curious whale shaped lake, all with wonderful views. Demonstrations of coppicing, yurt building, charcoal making, dry stone walling, turtling.

22 PENPERGWM LODGE
nr Abergavenny NP7 9AS. Mr & Mrs Simon Boyle, 01873 840208, boyle@penpergwm.co.uk. *3m SE of Abergavenny, 5m W of Raglan. On B4598. Turn opp King of Prussia Inn. Entrance 150-yds on L.* **Adm £4, chd free. Sat & Sun 28, 29 May (2-6).**

Visitors also welcome by appt. 3-acre garden with Jubilee tower overlooking terraced ornamental garden containing canal, cascading water and new loggia at head of canal. S-facing terraces planted with rich profusion and vibrant colours all surrounded by spacious lawns and mature trees. New brick waisted tower. Some gravel paths.

🔥 🏠 ❀ 🛏 ☕ ☎

23 NEW PENTWYN FARM & WYESWOOD COMMON

Penallt, Abergavenny NP25 4SE. Gwent Wildlife Trust. *3m SW of Monmouth. S of Monmouth on B4293 to Mitchell Troy & Trelleck. Approx 1m from Monmouth turn L for Penallt & Trelleck, after 2m turn L to Penallt. On entering village turn L at X-roads and R at war memorial. Reserve is adjacent to the Bush Inn PH.* Home-made teas. **Adm £3, chd free (share to Gwent Wildlife Fund). Sat 18 June (10-4).**
A wild garden in meadows as beautiful as anything under cultivation. Gwent Wildlife Trust would like to invite you to view the wildflowers of Pentwyn Farm, famous for its orchids, teeming with butterflies and with spectacular views over the Usk Valley. Guided walks at 11am & 1pm, 3pm covering Pentwyn Farm and Wyeswood Common with its flock of Hebridean sheep & lambs. Visitors have the rare chance to picnic on the reserve. Featured in Wye Valley Life, S Wales Argus.

🏠 ❀ ☕

24 SUNNYSIDE

The Hendre NP25 5HQ. Helen & Ralph Fergusson-Kelly, 01600 714928, helen_fk@hotmail.com. *4m W of Monmouth. On B4233 Monmouth to Abergavenny rd. Parking in field 50metres from garden.* Home-made teas. **Adm £3, chd free. Sun 25 Sept (12-5). Visitors also welcome by appt May to Oct, eves & w/ends for small groups.**
Late summer colour: the last soft blooms of summer perennials and shrubs give way to the biscuit and russet tones of grasses and then bold injections of scarlet, cerise, violet and gold from bulbs, perennials and trees. All this in a sloping 1/3 acre garden on the old Rolls estate. Seating areas to enjoy views of the Monmouthshire countryside. Some gravel paths.

❀ ☕ ☎

25 TAIR-FFYNNON, 'THE GARDEN IN THE CLOUDS'.

nr Llanvihangel Crucorney,, Abergavenny NP7 7NR. Antony & Verity Woodward, www.gardenintheclouds.com. *8m N of Abergavenny. Off A465 Abergavenny-Hereford rd. At Llanvihangel Crucorney turn downhill at Skirrid PH and 1st R over hump-back bridge, then follow yellow signs. Challenging, very steep and narrow single-track lanes. Reversing may be necessary for last 1 1/2 m. If wet, parking may be a 15-minute walk away.* Home-made teas & light refreshments. **Adm £4, chd free. Sat 30, Sun 31 July (12-6).**
Tair-Ffynnon is the inspiration behind the recent book The Garden in the Clouds. 6-acre smallholding in National Park reaching nearly 1600ft to Offa's Dyke footpath. For anyone fit and intrepid who sees beauty in wild places - in upland wild flower meadows, dry stone walls and mountain springs, forgotten farm machinery in field corners and gateways framing 70-mile views. Drifts of wild grasses and cloud strewn vistas found only in Wales. Featured in The Sunday Times 'the pinnacle of beauty'; Reader's Digest 'untamed but stunningly beautiful'; Guardian 'magical views to nine counties' Appreciate all this with a free cup of tea. Signed books for sale.

🏠 ☕ ☎

Wonderful day out for all the family with lots of places to eat and drink with picnic places down by the River Usk. Unmissable . . . !

26 ◆ TREDEGAR HOUSE & PARK

Newport NP10 8YW. Newport City Council, 01633 815880, www.newport.gov.uk/tredegarhous e. *2m SW of Newport town centre. Signed from A48 (Cardiff rd) & M4 J28.* **Adm £3.50, chd free, concessions £3. For NGS: Sun 10 July (11-5). For other opening times and information, please**

phone or see garden website. Three walled gardens; the Cedar Garden with herbaceous borders containing an obelisk erected in the memory of the horse 'Sir Briggs' who carried Viscount Tredegar at the Charge of the Light Brigade, the orangery which is fronted by a parterre garden of lawns, sand and sea shells and the secret cottage garden maintained by 'Growing Space' a mental health charity. Garden paths gravelled and level. Dedicated disabled parking approx 260m from house.

🔥 ❀ ☕ ☎

27 TROSTREY LODGE

Bettws Newydd, Usk NP15 1JT. Roger & Frances Pemberton. *4m W of Raglan. 7m E of Abergavenny. Off the old A40 (unnumbered) Abergavenny - Raglan. 1m S of Clytha Gates and 1 1/2 m N of Bettws Newydd.* Home-made teas. **Adm £3.50, chd free. Sun & Mon 1, 2 May (12-6).**
A peaceful garden within old stone walls and buttresses. Approach the Regency house (not open) over a ha-ha, past a spectacular tulip tree and on to a colourful planting of spring flowers with fine carelessness in a structured pattern. Greenfields, old oak trees and R Usk surround. Good range of plants for sale.

🏠 ❀ ☕

28 USK OPEN GARDENS

Monmouthshire, Usk, Usk Town NP15 1HN, www.uskopengardens.com. *From M4 J24 take A449, proceed 8m to Usk exit. Good free parking in town. Map of gardens provided with ticket.* Home-made teas at various locations. **Adm £6, chd free. Sat 25, Sun 26 June (10-5).**
Proud winner of Wales in Bloom for many years, with colourful hanging baskets and boxes - a sight not to be missed! The town is a wonderful backdrop to the 25+ gardens from small cottages packed with colourful and unusual plants to large gardens with brimming herbaceous borders. Wonderful romantic garden around the ramparts of Usk Castle. Gardeners' Market with wide selection of interesting plants. Wonderful day out for all the family with lots of places to eat and drink incl picnic places down by the R Usk. Unmissable!

🔥 ❀ 🛏 ☕

29 ◆ **VEDDW HOUSE**
The Fedw, Devauden NP16 6PH.
Anne Wareham & Charles Hawes,
01291 650836, www.veddw.co.uk.
*5m NW of Chepstow. Off B4293.
Signed from PH on the green at
Devauden.* Adm £6.50, chd £1.50.
**For NGS: Evening Opening wine,
Wed 29 June (5-7.30). For other
opening times and information,
please phone or see garden
website.**
Two acres of ornamental garden and
two of woodland. 'The most
controversial garden in Wales', Helena
Attlee. 'One of the most influential and
important gardens of the last 10
years', Tim Richardson, Garden
Design Journal. Anne Wareham is the
author of: The Bad Tempered
Gardener. Reflecting pool, grasses
parterre, meadows, unusual planting
and hedges. Featured in various
publications. Wheelchair access to
some parts of garden.

Continually evolving garden . . . the new 'ruin' adds structure and whimsy . . .

30 ▶ **WOODLANDS FARM**
Penrhos NP15 2LE. Craig Loane
and Charles Horsfield. *3m N of
Raglan. At Raglan, turn off A40
towards Mitchel Troy. Almost
immediately turn L for Tregaer, then
Penrhos and follow NGS signs.*
Home-made teas. **Combined adm
with High House £6 Sun 15 May;
£3.50 Sat & Sun 16, 17 July, chd
free (2-6)**
Continually evolving garden where the
new 'ruin' adds structure and whimsy.
Surprising and stimulating as
conventional it is not. See the
changes or enjoy its eccentricity for
the first time, not only a visual treat
but also produce (on sale) forms an
intergral part of this working garden.

Dewstow Gardens & Grottoes

Gwent County Volunteers

County Organiser
Joanna Kerr, Glebe House, Llanvair Kilgeddin, Abergavenny NP7 9BE, 01873 840422, joanna@amknet.com

County Treasurer
Helen Fergusson-Kelly, Sunnyside, The Hendre, Monmouth NP25 5HQ, 01600 714928, helen_fk@hotmail.com

Assistant County Organiser
Sue Carter, St Pega's, 47 Hereford Road, Monmouth NP25 3HQ, 01600 772074, stpegas47@hotmail.co.uk

Sign up to our eNewsletter for news and updates

GWYNEDD, ANGLESEY & CONWY

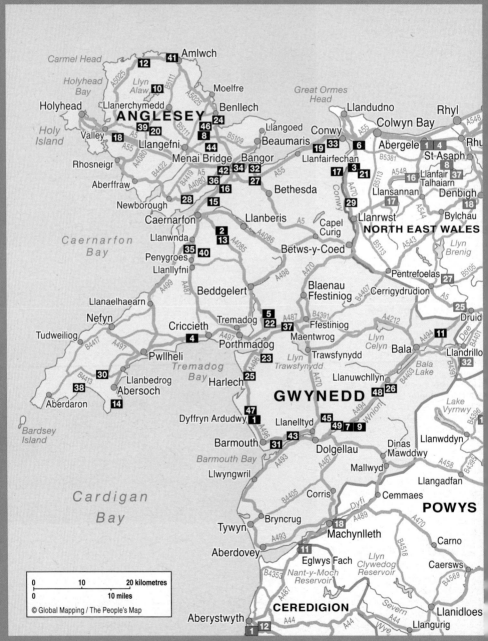

Carmel Head

Holyhead Bay

Amlwch

12 **41**

Llyn Alaw **10**

Moelfre

Great Ormes Head

Llandudno

Rhyl

Holyhead

Llanerchymedd

Benllech

Colwyn Bay

A548

Holy Island

Valley **18**

ANGLESEY

39 **20**

46 **24**

8

Llangoed

Conwy

Abergele **1** **4**

Rhu

Rhosneigr

Llangefni

44

Beaumaris

19 **33**

6

St Asaph

8

B5381

Aberffraw

Menai Bridge

Bangor

Llanfairfechan

Llanfair Talhaiarn **37**

Newborough

42 **34** **32**

36 **16** **27**

28 **15**

Bethesda

17 **3**

21

A548 **16**

Llansannan

Denbigh

Caernarfon

Llanberis

29

Llanrwst

17

Bylchau

18

Llanwnda

2

13

Capel Curig

NORTH EAST WALES

Caernarfon Bay

Penygroes

35 **40**

Betws-y-Coed

Llyn Brenig

Llanllyfni

Beddgelert

Blaenau Ffestiniog

Pentrefoelas

Cerrigydrudion

27

Llanaelhaearn

Nefyn

Tremadog **5**

22

Ffestiniog

25

Druid

Tudweiliog

Criccieth **4**

37

Maentwrog

Bala

11

Llandrillo

Pwllheli

Porthmadog

23

Trawsfynydd

Llanuwchllyn

32

Llanbedrog

30

Abersoch **14**

Harlech **25**

GWYNEDD

48 **26**

Lake Vyrnwy

Aberdaron **38**

Bardsey Island

Dyffryn Ardudwy **47** **1**

Llanelltyd

45

49 **7** **9**

Llanwddyn

Barmouth

31

43

Dolgellau

Dinas Mawddwy

Llangadfan

Barmouth Bay

Llwyngwril

Mallwyd

POWYS

Cardigan Bay

Corris

Cemmaes

Tywyn

Bryncrug

Dyfi

Carno

Aberdovey

18

Machynlleth

Caersws

Eglwys Fach

Llyn Clywedog Reservoir

Nant-y-Moch Reservoir

CEREDIGION

Llanidloes

Aberystwyth **1** **12**

Llangurig

0 10 20 kilometres
0 10 miles
© Global Mapping / The People's Map

Opening Dates

February

Saturday 19
32 Penrhyn Castle

April

Sunday 3
25 Llyn Rhaeadr

Monday 4
25 Llyn Rhaeadr

Friday 22
36 Plas Newydd Country House & Gardens

Saturday 23
25 Llyn Rhaeadr

Sunday 24
4 Bont Fechan Farm
25 Llyn Rhaeadr

Monday 25
4 Bont Fechan Farm
25 Llyn Rhaeadr

Wednesday 27
34 Plas Cadnant

May

Sunday 1
25 Llyn Rhaeadr
31 Pen y Bryn
43 Tanybryn

Monday 2
25 Llyn Rhaeadr

Sunday 8
17 Gilfach

Wednesday 11
16 Foxbrush

Sunday 15
4 Bont Fechan Farm
7 Bryn Gwern

Monday 16
38 Plas Yn Rhiw (Evening)

Saturday 21
18 Gwaelod Mawr

Sunday 22
18 Gwaelod Mawr
27 Llys-y-Gwynt
29 Maenan Hall
35 Plas Mawr
41 Sunningdale

Saturday 28
5 Brondanw Gardens
22 Hen Ysgoldy

Sunday 29
5 Brondanw Gardens
6 Bryn Eisteddfod
22 Hen Ysgoldy
25 Llyn Rhaeadr
35 Plas Mawr

Monday 30
25 Llyn Rhaeadr

Tuesday 31
25 Llyn Rhaeadr

June

Saturday 4
15 Crug Farm

Sunday 5
48 Tyn y Cefn

Saturday 11
10 Cae Newydd

Sunday 12
9 Brynifor Woodland Garden
10 Cae Newydd
11 Caerau Uchaf
14 Crowrach Isaf
17 Gilfach
19 Gwel Yr Ynys
33 Pensychnant
44 Treffos School

Saturday 18
2 Antur Waunfawr
23 Hotel Maes-y-Neuadd
28 Maen Hir

Sunday 19
28 Maen Hir
46 Ty Gwyn

Wednesday 22
16 Foxbrush

Saturday 25
8 Bryn Seiri
24 Llanidan Hall

Sunday 26
8 Bryn Seiri
10 Cae Newydd

Monday 27
8 Bryn Seiri (Evening)

July

Saturday 2
12 Cemaes Bay

Sunday 3
12 Cemaes Bay
27 Llys-y-Gwynt

Wednesday 6
13 Cilfechydd
20 Gwyndy Bach

Saturday 9
24 Llanidan Hall

Sunday 10
33 Pensychnant

Saturday 16
3 Bodnant Garden

Monday 25
40 St John the Baptist & St George

Sunday 31
25 Llyn Rhaeadr

August

Monday 1
25 Llyn Rhaeadr

Tuesday 2
25 Llyn Rhaeadr

Wednesday 3
25 Llyn Rhaeadr

Thursday 4
25 Llyn Rhaeadr

Friday 5
25 Llyn Rhaeadr

Sunday 7
21 Gyffylog
49 Tyn-Twll

Sunday 14
7 Bryn Gwern
17 Gilfach
29 Maenan Hall

Sunday 28
25 Llyn Rhaeadr

Monday 29
23 Hotel Maes-y-Neuadd
25 Llyn Rhaeadr
37 Plas Tan Y Bwlch

September

Sunday 4
1 An Artist's Garden
48 Tyn y Cefn

February 2012

Saturday 11
32 Penrhyn Castle

Gardens open to the public

2 Antur Waunfawr
3 Bodnant Garden
5 Brondanw Gardens
15 Crug Farm
23 Hotel Maes-y-Neuadd
32 Penrhyn Castle
33 Pensychnant
36 Plas Newydd Country House & Gardens
37 Plas Tan Y Bwlch
38 Plas Yn Rhiw

Look out for the gardens with the ☎ – enjoy a private visit . . .

By appointment only

- **26** Llys Arthur
- **30** Nanhoron
- **39** Rhyd
- **42** Tan Dinas
- **45** Ty Capel Ffrwd
- **47** Ty Newydd

Also open by Appointment

- **4** Bont Fechan Farm
- **7** Bryn Gwern
- **10** Cae Newydd
- **11** Caerau Uchaf
- **13** Cilfechydd
- **16** Foxbrush
- **17** Gilfach
- **18** Gwaelod Mawr
- **19** Gwel Yr Ynys
- **20** Gwyndy Bach
- **21** Gyffylog
- **24** Llanidan Hall
- **25** Llyn Rhaeadr
- **27** Llys-y-Gwynt
- **29** Maenan Hall
- **34** Plas Cadnant
- **35** Plas Mawr
- **48** Tyn y Cefn
- **49** Tyn-Twll

The Gardens

1 NEW AN ARTIST'S GARDEN

Ty Llwyd, Dyffryn Ardudwy LL44 2EP. Karen Hall. *5m N of Barmouth on A496.* Home-made teas. **Adm £3, chd free. Sun 4 Sept (11-5).**
An Artist's Garden is a 140ft garden, with slate paths leading to ponds, vegetable plots, cutting borders and colourful late summer perennial planting. At the bottom of the garden is a textile studio which will open to visitors. The garden is a work in progress and is located in a busy village.

2 ◆ ANTUR WAUNFAWR

Bryn Pistyll, Waunfawr, Caernarfon LL55 4BJ. Menna Jones, 01286 650721, www.anturwaunfawr.org. *4½ m SE of Caernarfon. On A4085. Waunfawr village, turn L following signs, bear L for approx ½ m.* **Adm £3, chd free. For NGS: Sat 18 June (11-3). For other opening times and information, please phone or see garden website.**
Gardens and 7-acre Nature Park developed by Antur Waunfawr, a community venture providing employment opportunities for people with learning disabilities. Meadows, woodland walks, wildlife and ornamental ponds, soft fruit garden, herbaceous perennial beds and greenhouses. Wheelchair assisted access as site can be uneven.

ARFRYN
See North East Wales.

3 ◆ BODNANT GARDEN

Tal-y-Cafn, nr Colwyn Bay LL28 5RE. National Trust, 01492 650460, www.bodnant-garden.co.uk. *8m S of Llandudno. From A55 exit at J19. Follow brown signs to garden. Just off A470 on B rd to Eglwysbach.* **Adm £8.50, chd £4.25. For NGS: Sat 16 July (10-5). For other opening times and information, please phone or see garden website.**
Among the finest gardens in the country with rhododendrons, magnolias, camellias and the famous laburnum arch. Summer colours incl roses, water lilies, herbaceous borders and hydrangeas. Superb autumn colours in October. Formal Italianate-style terraces contrast with steeply sided shrub borders and the dell. Gravel paths & steep slopes. Route marked for wheelchairs to avoid steps.

4 ◆ BONT FECHAN FARM

Llanystumdwy LL52 0LS. Mr & Mrs J D Bean, 01766 522604. *2m W of Criccieth. On the A497 to Pwllheli on L of main rd.* Home-made teas. **Adm £2.50, chd free. Sun & Mon 24, 25 Apr; Sun 15 May (11-5). Visitors also welcome by appt.**
Cottage garden with rockery, fish pond, herbaceous border, steps to river. Large variety of plants. Nicely planted tubs; good vegetable garden and poultry. Rhododendron and azaleas.

5 ◆ BRONDANW GARDENS

LL48 6SW. Brondanw Estates, 01766 770853, www.brondanw.org.uk. *5m E of Porthmadog on A4085. Off A498 Caernarfon, Beddgelert Rd, R on the B4410 following Osprey signs until Garreg on A4085. L then R at Gate House.* Car Park on L. Light refreshments. **Adm £3.50, chd free. For NGS: Sat & Sun 28, 29 May (open from 9am). For other opening times and information, please phone or see garden website.**
Plas Brondanw is amongst Clough Williams Ellis' best example of his talent for creative landscape design. The main features were laid down during the early part of the C20 before he began Portmeirion. Over seventy years Sir Clough created a unique and characteristic, romantic landscape. One of the truly great Welsh gardens. Slate paths, slopes on some lawns.

> Williams Ellis' best example of his talent for creative landscape design. The main features were laid down during the early part of the C20 . . .

6 ◆ BRYN EISTEDDFOD

Glan Conwy LL28 5LF. Dr Michael Senior. *3½ m SE of Llandudno. 3m W Colwyn Bay. Up hill (Bryn-y-Maen direction) from Glan Conwy Corner where A470 joins A55.* Home-made teas. **Adm £3, chd 50p. Sun 29 May (2-5).**
8 acres of landscaped grounds incl mature shrubbery, arboretum, old walled 'Dutch' garden, large lawn with ha-ha. Extensive views over Conwy Valley, Snowdonia National Park, Conwy Castle, town and estuary.

7 BRYN GWERN

Llanfachreth LL40 2DH. H O & P D Nurse, 01341 450255, antique_pete@btinternet.com. *5m NE of Dolgellau. Do not go to village of Llanfachreth, stay on A494 Bala-Dolgellau rd: 13m from Bala. Take 1st Llanfachreth turn R. From Dolgellau 4th Llanfachreth turn L, follow signs. No coach parking.* Cream teas. **Adm**

£3, chd free. Suns 15 May; 14 Aug (10-5). Visitors also welcome by appt.
Unusual natural garden in 2-acres, planted with paulona tormentosa, clerodendron, pieris, arbutus, magnolias, azaleas, rhododendrons and many other trees and shrubs, bulbs, herbaceous, water and bog plants, clematis, honeysuckle, akebia quinlata. Where ducks, guinea fowl and chickens roam free. Enjoy your cream tea to the fantastic views Cader Idris. Quilting expert - buy or ask advice. Featured on S4C (TV).

Rhyd

8 ▶ BRYN SEIRI
Talwrn, Llangefni LL77 8JD. Mr & Mrs Phillip Tolman. *3m N of Llangefni. From Llangefni take B5110 signed Benllech. 2m R to Talwrn. 1st L. (F)3/4(/F)m very sharp L hand bend. Do not go round bend. Bryn Seiri drive on R. Limited parking. May need to park in lane.* Home-made teas. Adm £3.50, chd free. Sat & Sun 25, 26 June (2-6) Evening Opening Mon 27 June (5.30-8.30).
A relaxed, colourful 2-acre cottage garden. Incl's generous herbaceous borders, developing sloped woodland garden, pergola, pond (unfenced), gravel garden, sloping lawns, dry stone walls and paths. Many roses and unusual shrubs. Views to Red Wharf Bay, the hills and Snowdonia. Gravel paths, steps & slopes.

9 ▶ NEW ▶ BRYNIFOR WOODLAND GARDEN
Bryncoedifor, Dolgellau LL40 2AN. Malcolm & Jacqueline Quick. *4m W of Dolgellau. A494 from Bala (15-20 mins drive). Signage to turn L for Bryncoedifor. A494 from Dolgellau - 4m signage to turn L for Bryncoedifor. Having turned, 200yds up lane, pass chapel, driveway opp small cottage.* Cream teas. Adm £3, chd free. Sun 12 June (10.30-5).
9-acre woodland garden set in the Einion Valley with lawns, garden pathways and panoramic views. Garden originally set 100yrs ago with a profusion of rhododendrons, azaleas, gunnera and quince which culminates in a blaze of colour come May and June. Also featuring ¹/₂ -acre pond, weir, streams, waterfall and secret steps leading to who knows where! You will just have to come and see for yourself. Wheelchair access available to main area only.

10 ▶ CAE NEWYDD
Rhosgoch, Anglesey LL66 0BG. Hazel & Nigel Bond, 01407 831354, nigel@cae-newydd.co.uk. *3m SW of Amlwch. Turn L immediately after Amlwch Town sign on A5025 from Benllech, follow signs for leisure centre & Lastra Farm. After L turn for Lastra Farm, follow rd for approx 3m, pass through Rhosgoch, keep to main rd, follow signs for Llyn Alaw, ¹/₄ m. Garden/car park on L.* Light refreshments & teas. Adm £3, chd free. Sat 11, Suns 12, 26 June (11-5). Visitors also welcome by appt.
A fairly new garden which blends seamlessly into the open landscape with stunning views of Snowdonia and Llyn Alaw. Good variety of shrubs and trees, large wildlife pond, meadow areas, polytunnel, vegetable garden and chicken run. Adjacent sheltered paddock garden. Formal pond and patio area, raised beds. All yr-round interest, Apr for spring bulbs, May and June for aquilegias, roses etc. Hay meadow best seen in June. New this yr, rose garden for perfume and colour.

11 ▶ CAERAU UCHAF
Sarnau, Bala LL23 7LG. Mr & Mrs Toby Hickish, 01678 530493, info@summersgardens.co.uk. *3m NE of Bala. From A5 N of Corwen turn L A494 to Bala. Approx 5m turn R into Sarnau, keep R up hill approx 1m. From Bala take A494 NE. After approx 3m turn L into Sarnau, keep R up hill approx 1m. Coaches strictly by appt.* Lunches and home-made teas. Adm £3.50, chd free. Sun 12 June (2 til late). Visitors also welcome by appt, coaches by prior notice only.
3-acres of gardens with potager vegetable garden, wildlife garden, herbaceous borders, woodland walks and much more. Added to each yr by RHS show garden designers Toby and Stephanie Hickish. Stunning views at over 1000ft. Plant sales. Adventure playground & sunken trampoline. Open from Easter to the end of Oct. Gravel paths, steep slopes but main gardens accessible.

GROUP OPENING

12 ▶ NEW ▶ CEMAES BAY
LL67 0LJ. *12m E of Valley. 5m W of Amlwch. On A5025 from r'about take exit to High St. 1st L to car park. Follow signs for the short walk to Tyddyn Bach. Disabled parking only at garden.* Home-made teas at 5a Tyhhyn Bach. Combined adm £3, chd free. Sat & Sun 2, 3 July (11-4).

NEW ▶ FRENSHAM
Peter & Barbara Rowe

NEW ▶ PAULINE'S GARDEN
Mrs Pauline Johnston

Cemaes, the most northerly village in Wales is set in an AONB. The village incl a sheltered natural harbour and the main beach is particularly safe with gentle sloping sand and rock pools. A dedicated team of volunteer gardeners, led by Community Gardener Pauline Roberts, look after the many floral displays and flower beds in and around the village which has resulted in Cemaes winning the Village category in the Wales in Bloom competition several times. A varied list of interesting events take place in the village during the spring and summer months incl RNLI Lifeboat Days, Fishing Competitions, Dog Show and Flower Show. Two pretty cottage style garden set in a tranquil cul-de-sac. Both have won awards in the annual Cemaes in Bloom competition. Limited wheelchair access at both gardens.

    ✿ ☕

13 NEW CILFECHYDD
Waunfawr. Caernarfon LL54 7AJ. Mr & Mrs Newsham, 01286 650020, newsham.stuart@googlemail.com. *4¹/₂ m SE of Caernarfon. On A4085 past Snowdonia Parc Tavern, on R after 150yrds next to Dudley Park Nature Reserve. Postcode not suitable for SatNav. Parking at PH & Nature Reserve. Disabled parking only at house.* Home-made teas. **Adm £3.50 (share to Llanberis Mountain Resue Team). Wed 6 July (11-5). Visitors also welcome by appt.**
Award winning nature garden with stream fed pond full of natural plants. Various interesting garden areas with many roses, both cultivars and species. Polytunnel, fruit gardens incl newly planted 50 tree orchard. Large vegetable plot with pottager. Garden alongside own small holding with free range poultry and pigs etc. Gold Award, Wildlife Gardening North Wales. Limited wheelchair access.

    ✿ ☕ ☎

14 CROWRACH ISAF
Bwlchtocyn LL53 7BY. Margaret & Graham Cook. *1¹/₂ m SW of Abersoch. Follow rd through Abersoch & Sarn Bach, L at sign for Bwlchtocyn for ¹/₂ m until junction and no-through rd - Cim Farm. Turn R, parking 50metres on R.* Cream teas. **Adm £3, chd free. Sun 12 June (11-4).**
2-acre plot incl 1 acre fenced against rabbits, developed from 2000. incl island beds, windbreak hedges and

wide range of geraniums, shrubs and herbaceous perennials. Views over Cardigan Bay and Snowdonia. Grass and gravel paths, some gentle slopes.

    ✿ ☕

15 ◆ CRUG FARM
Caernarfon LL55 1TU. Mr & Mrs B Wynn-Jones, 01248 670232, www.crug-farm.co.uk. *2m NE of Caernarfon. ¹/₄ m off main A487 Caernarfon to Bangor rd. Follow signs from r'about.* **Adm £3, chd free. For NGS: Sat 4 June (10-5). For other opening times and information, please phone or see garden website.**
3 acres; grounds to old country house (not open). Gardens filled with choice, unusual collections of plants. Collected by the Wynn Jones, winners of the Sir Bryner Jones Memorial Award for their contribution to horticulture. National Collection of Paris. Gold Medal RHS Vincent Square, Silver Gilt Gardening Scotland; top prize at Lucca, Italy. Limited wheelchair access.

    ✿ NCCPG ☎

Spanish style patio and laburnum arch lead to sunken garden and wooden bridge over lily pond with fountain and waterfall . . .

CYFIE FARM
See Powys.

16 FOXBRUSH
Felinheli LL56 4JZ. Mr & Mrs B S Osborne, 01248 670463. *3m SW of Bangor. On Bangor to Caernarfon rd, entering village opp Felinheli signpost.* Cream teas. **Adm £2.50, chd free. Weds 11 May; 22 June (2-7). Visitors also welcome by appt March to end June.**
Fascinating country garden created over 40 years around winding river. Rare and interesting plant collections incl rhododendrons, ferns, Hydrangea, clematis and roses cover

a 45ft long pergola. Fan-shaped knot garden, 3 bridges and new plantings have replaced those lost in the horrendous devastation caused by floods of 2004. New feature this yr, Mill Pond.

    🏠 ✿ ☕ ☎

17 GILFACH
Rowen LL32 8TS. James & Isoline Greenhalgh, 01492 650216. *4m S of Conwy. At Xrds 100yds E of Rowen S towards Llanrwst, past Rowen School on L; turn up 2nd drive on L.* Home-made teas. **Adm £3, chd free. Suns 8 May; 12 June; 14 Aug (2-5.30). Visitors also welcome by appt.**
1-acre country garden on S-facing slope with magnificent views of the R Conwy and mountains; set in 35 acres of farm and woodland. Collection of mature shrubs is added to yearly; woodland garden, herbaceous border and small pool.

    ☕ ☎

GRANDMA'S GARDEN
See Powys.

18 GWAELOD MAWR
Caergeiliog, Anglesey LL65 3YL. John & Tricia Coates, 01407 740080. *6m E of Holyhead. ¹/₂ m W of Caergeiliog. From A55 J4. R'about 2nd exit signed Caergeiliog. 300yds, Gwaelod Mawr is first house on L.* Home-made teas. **Adm £3, chd free. Sat & Sun 21, 22 May (11-5). Visitors also welcome by appt May, June, & July only.**
2¹/₂ -acre garden created by owners over 20yrs with lake, large rock outcrops and palm tree area. Spanish style patio and laburnum arch lead to sunken garden and wooden bridge over lily pond with fountain and waterfall. Peaceful Chinese orientated garden offering contemplation. Separate Koi carp pond. Abundant seating throughout. Gravel paths.

    🏠 ✿ ☕ ☎

19 NEW GWEL YR YNYS
Parc Moel Lus, Penmaenmawr LL34 6DN. Mr Dafydd Lloyd-Borland, 07968 243119. *Take J16 off A55 signed Penmaenmawr. Taking R corner to main village along Conwy Rd for appprox ¹/₂ m. Past Mountian View Hotel on L prceed to village pedestrian crossing, turn L at NatWest Bank. Parking in car park on R. Shuttle bus available to garden.* Home-made teas. **Adm £3, chd free. Sun 12 June (11-5). Visitors also welcome by appt.**

New ³/₄-acre garden in an elevated position above village parallel with Mountain Lane offering fantastic views of Anglesey, Puffin Island and Foel Lus behind. Dynamic and exciting garden with many influences apparent with a hillside garden. Much natural planting incl large range of herbaceous plants. Garden structure benefits from stream, freshwater pond, woodland area, bog garden. Chickens.

⚘ ☕ ☎

20 ▶ GWYNDY BACH
Llandrygarn LL65 3AJ. Keith & Rosa Andrew, 01407 720651. *5m W of Llangefni. From Llangefni take B5109 towards Bodedern, cottage exactly 5m out on the L.* Home-made teas. **Adm £3, chd free. Wed 6 July (11-4). Visitors also welcome by appt May, June & July only.**
³/₄-acre artist's garden, set amidst rugged Anglesey landscape. Romantically planted in informal intimate rooms with interesting rare plants and shrubs, box and yew topiary, old roses and Japanese garden with large Koi pond. National Collection of Rhapis miniature Japanese palms. Studio attached. Featured in Amateur Gardening. Gravel entrance to garden.

& NCCPG ☕ ☎

21 ▶ GYFFYLOG
Ffordd Gyffylog, Eglwysbach, Colwyn Bay LL28 5SD. Chris & Carol Potten, 01492 651093, chris.potten@googlemail.com. *2m from Bodnant Gardens. 1 ¹/₂ m from Eglwysbach. From A55 take A470 signed Bodnant Gardens, passing Bodnant Gardens on R towards Eglwysbach. Before village pass cream chapel on L. L at Ffordd Gyffylog for 1m. At green railings turn R, park in field at end of lane.* Home-made teas. **Adm £3, chd free. Sun 7 Aug (11-4.30). Visitors also welcome by appt.**
Set in 26 acres of woodland with stunning views of the Snowdonia foothills. Entrance is a Welsh slate patio with water feature and knot garden. Mature herbaceous flower beds extend around the house. Orchard, vegetable garden and chickens. Footpath to waterfall, walks to Oak wood and to lake. Photographic opportunities, nature walks. Some areas not accessible for wheelchair users.

& 🐸 ⚘ ☕ ☎

22 ▶ NEW ▶ HEN YSGOLDY
Llanfrothen, Penrhyndeudraeth LL48 6LX. Mr K Gurney. *1m SE of Plas Brondanw. At centre of Llanfrothen, take rd behind shop, B4410 towards Rhyd, after approx ¹/₄ m, turn L at Y Wern B&B sign. Hen Ysgoldy is ¹/₄ m up lane on R.* **Adm £3.50, chd free. Sat & Sun 28, 29 May (10.30-5.30). Also open with Plas Brondanw.**
First established 50yrs ago, the lower garden at Hen Ysgoldy is now undergoing gentle restoration work, bordered on 2 sides by tumbling streams, it has a water-side character with mature shelterbelts of magnolia, rhododendrons, acer and oak creating shady and peaceful sloping dell.

⚘ ☕

23 ▶ ◆ HOTEL MAES-Y-NEUADD
Talsarnau, nr Harlech LL47 6YA. Mr & Mrs P Jackson & Mr & Mrs P Payne, 01766 780200, www.neuadd.com. *3m NE of Harlech. Take B4573 old Harlech rd at T-junction with A496. Hotel signed ¹/₄ m on L. Take small lane on L immed after sign, just before small bridge on bend. Hotel entrance & car park ¹/₂ m up hill, through small hamlet (tel box on L). Follow brown signs.* **Adm £3, chd under 12 free. For NGS: Sat 18 June; Mon 29 Aug (10-5). For other opening times and information, please phone or see garden website.**
Gardens and grounds of country house hotel, parts of which C14. Views towards Snowdon, Cardigan Bay and Lleyn Peninsula. 80 acres, meadows, woodland walks, 2 working walled gardens, unusual cultivars, cut flower borders; innovative, intensive, organic gardening methods with aesthetic appeal. Fruit and vegetables for sale. Suitable for assisted wheelchair users only. Slate & gravel paths to all vegetable gardens, gravel drive. External lift available for access to hotel & ramps inside.

& 🐸 ⚘ 🛏 ☕ ☎

24 ▶ LLANIDAN HALL
Brynsiencyn LL61 6HJ. Mr J W Beverley (Head Gardener), 07759 305085, beverley.family@btinternet.com. *5m E of Llanfair Pwll. From Llanfair PG (Anglesey) follow A4080 towards Brynsiencyn for 4m. Turn at Groeslon PH. Continue for 1m, garden entrance on R.* Light refreshments & teas. **Adm £3.50, chd free (share to CAFOD). Sats 25 June; 9 July (10-4). Visitors also welcome by appt.**
Walled garden of 1³/₄ acres. Physic and herb gardens, ornamental vegetable garden, herbaceous borders, water features and many varieties of old roses. Sheep, ponies, rabbits and hens to see. Children must be kept under supervision. Llanidan Church will be open for viewing. Gravel paths, some slight slopes.

& ⚘ ☕ ☎

Stunning views of the Snowdonia foothills . . . footpath to waterfall, walks to Oak wood and to lake . . .

25 ▶ LLYN RHAEADR
Parc Bron-y-Graig, Centre of Harlech LL46 2SR. Mr D R Hewitt & Miss J Sharp, 01766 780224. *From A496 take B4573 into Harlech, take turning to main car parks S of town, L past overspill car park, garden 75yds on R.* **Adm £3, chd free (share to WWF UK). Sun & Mon 3, 4, Sat - Mon 23, 24, 25 Apr; Sun & Mon 1, 2, Sun - Mon 29, 30, 31 May; Sun 31 July; Mon - Fri 2, 3, 4, 5; Sun & Mon 28, 29 Aug (2-5). Visitors also welcome by appt all year (2-5) max group 20.**
Hillside garden blending natural wildlife areas with garden plants, shrubs, vegetables and fruit. Small lake with 20 species of waterfowl with ducklings in spring and summer. Fish pond, waterfalls, woodland, rockeries, lawns, borders, snowdrops, daffodils, heathers, bluebells, ferns, camellias, azaleas, rhododendrons, wild flowers, views of Tremadog Bay, Lleyn Peninsula. Good paths and seating. Car park, toilets and refreshments all within 200yds in Harlech

☎

Gwyndy Bach

26 **LLYS ARTHUR**

Llanuwchllyn, nr Bala LL23 7UG.
Mr & Mrs E Morgan, 01678 540233,
tedanded@hotmail.co.uk. *On A494,
on Dolgellau side of Llanuwchllyn,
opp Penial Chapel, over bridge, 1st
house on L.* Visitors welcome by
appt.
At the foot of the Aran, this 1-acre
garden has been created from
nothing during the last 22yrs. Lots of
interesting plants and features, large
vegetable garden, polytunnel and
battery rescue chickens, fish pond,
wildlife pond and lots of places to sit
and enjoy the beautiful Welsh
countryside.

🏡 ✿ ☕ ☎

27 **LLYS-Y-GWYNT**

Pentir Road, Llandygai LL57 4BG.
Jennifer Rickards & John Evans,
01248 353863. *3m S of Bangor.
300yds from Llandygai roundabout at
J11 of A5 & A55, just off A4244.
From A5 & A55 follow signs for
services (Gwasanaethau) and find 'No
Through Road' sign 50yds beyond.
Turn R then L. (Sat Nav does not find
us due to large postcode area).*
Home-made teas. **Adm £3, chd free.**
Suns 22 May; 3 July (11-4). Visitors
also welcome by appt, coaches
welcome.
Rambling 2-acre garden in harmony
with and incl magnificent views of
Snowdonia. Incorporating large
Bronze Age cairn. Designed to
wander, with paths to provide shelter
and interest. The exposed site
planted for wind tolerance, yr-round
colour and wildlife. Pond, waterfall
and N-facing rockery. Good family
garden.

♿ ✿ ☕ ☎

28 **MAEN HIR**

Dwyran, Anglesey LL61 6UY. Mr &
Mrs K T Evans. *6m SE of
Llanfairpwll. From Llanfair P.G
(Anglesey) follow A4080 through
village Brynsiencyn. Continue on this
rd for approx 2m. Maen Hir on R.*
Home-made teas. **Adm £3, chd free.**
Sat & Sun 18, 19 June (11-5).
Set in 7 acres incl beautiful walled
garden with gazebo, old roses and
mixed herbaceous borders replanted
2007. Courtyard, outer garden,
woodland walks, greenhouse, potting
shed, cutting patch and hay meadow.
Maen Hir enjoys magnificent views of
Snowdonia range. Musical
entertainment on front lawn plus
various attractions in the woods.

♿ 🏡 ✿ ☕

29 **MAENAN HALL**

Maenan, Llanrwst LL26 0UL. The
Hon Mr & Mrs Christopher Mclaren,
0207 602 1983,
cmmclaren@gmail.com. *2m N of
Llanrwst. On E side of A470, ¼ m S
of Maenan Abbey Hotel.* Home-made
teas. **Adm £4, chd £3 (share to St
David's Hospice).** Suns 22 May; 14
Aug (10.30-5.30) last entry 4.30pm.
Visitors also welcome by appt.
Superbly beautiful garden (about
4 hectares) on the slopes of the
Conwy Valley, with dramatic views of

Snowdonia, set amongst mature hardwoods. Both upper part, with sweeping lawns, ornamental ponds and retaining walls, and bluebell carpeted woodland dell contain copious specimen shrubs and trees, many originating at Bodnant. In spring magnolias, rhododendrons, camellias, pieris and cherries amongst many others make a breathtaking display. Upper part of garden accessible but on gentle slope.

  ♿ 🐕 ✿ ☕ ☎

 NEW NANHORON
Pwllheli, Gwynedd LL53 8DL. Mr & Mrs David Harden, 01758 730610, bettina.harden@farming.co.uk. *8m W of Pwllheli. On B4413 between Mynytho & Botwnnog.* **Adm £4.50, chd free.** Visitors welcome by appt April - Oct. No coaches.
Two fine walled gardens, a woodland walk and parkland surround a peaceful Regency house. There is something to see throughout the yr, especially in the spring with sheets of bluebells among fine rhododendrons, azaleas and camellias. June is full of roses and hydrangeas add colour to the late summer. Gravel paths.

  ♿ 🐕 ☎

 PEN Y BRYN
Glandwr, Barmouth LL42 1TG. Phil & Jenny Martin. *2m E of Barmouth. On A496 7m W of Dolgellau, situated on N side of Mawddach Estuary. Park in or nr layby and walk L up narrow lane.* Cream teas. **Adm £3, chd free** (share to Gwynedd Hospice at Home). Sun 1 May (11-5).
A glorious hillside garden with panoramic views of The Mawddoch Estuary. Woodland walks awash with Bluebells in the spring. Lawns on different levels with vibrant rhododendrons and azaleas, arches of clematis, honeysuckle and roses. Heather filled natural rocks, unusual conifer feature, a rock cannon and a pond for wildlife.

  ✿ ☕

32 ◆ PENRHYN CASTLE
Bangor LL57 4HN. National Trust, 01248 353084, www.nationaltrust.org.uk. *3m E of Bangor. On A5122. Buses from Llandudno, Caernarfon, Betws-y-Coed; alight: Grand Lodge Gate.* J11 A55, signed from thereon. **Adm £3, chd £1.** For NGS: Sat 19 Feb (11-3); Sat 11 Feb 2012. For other opening times and information please visit website or telephone.

Large grounds incl Victorian walled garden; fine trees, shrubs, wild garden, good views, snowdrop walks. Gravelled & grassed paths, some steps, exposed tree roots, some surfaces bark & chippings.

  ♿ ☕ ☎

Sweeping lawns, ornamental ponds and retaining walls, and bluebell carpeted woodland dell . . .

33 ◆ PENSYCHNANT
Sychnant Pass, nr Conwy LL32 8BJ. Pensychnant Foundation Wardens Julian Thompson & Anne Mynott, 01492 592595, jpt.pensychnant@btinternet.com. *2¹/₂ m W of Conwy. Top of Sychnant Pass between Conwy & Penmaenmawr. From Conwy turn L into Upper Gate St by Heddlu/Police; after 2¹/₂ m Pensychnant's drive signed on R. From Penmaenmawr, fork R by Mountain View PH; summit of Sychnant Pass after walls, Pensychnant's drive on L.* **Adm £2, chd 50p.** For NGS: Suns 12 June; 10 July (11-5). For other opening times and information, please phone or see garden website.
Diverse herbaceous 'cottage garden' borders surrounded by mature shrubs, banks of rhododendrons, ancient and Victorian woodlands. 12 acre woodland walks with views of Conwy Mountain and Sychnant. Woodland birds. Picnic tables, archaeological trail on mountain. A peaceful little gem. Large Victorian gothic house (open) with art exhibition. Partial wheelchair access, please phone for advice.

  ♿ ✿ ☕ ☎

34 ◆ PLAS CADNANT
Menai Bridge LL59 5NH. Mr A J Tavernor, 01248 717007, garden@plascadnant.co.uk, www.plascadnant.co.uk. *¹/₂ m E of Menai Bridge. Turn off A545 ¹/₂ m E of Menai Bridge, at Cadnant Bridge, follow drive over cattle grids.* Light refreshments. **Adm £6, chd free**

(share to Anglesey Red Squirrel & Air Ambulance). Wed 27 Apr (1-5). Visitors also welcome by appt Apr to Sept, groups of 20+, coaches welcome.
Early C19 Picturesque garden that has been undergoing restoration since 1996. Work still ongoing, but much to see incl valley garden with waterfalls, large walled garden (now an ornamental garden with herbaceous planting) and early pit house. Some steps, gravel paths and steep slopes. Featured in Coutry Living. Rural Wales Award. Limited wheelchair access. Some steps, gravel paths, slopes.

  ♿ ✿ ☕ ☎

35 PLAS MAWR
Groeslon, Caernarfon LL54 7UF. Mrs Pam Marchant & Mrs Tracey Jones, 01286 830628. *Off A487 Caernarfon - Porthmadog road. From Caernarfon take 3rd exit at Groeslon r'about. Property is approached across cattle grid immed to the R.* Home-made teas. **Adm £3, chd free** (share to Hospice at Home). Suns 22, 29 May (1-5). Visitors also welcome by appt May & Jun only. Groups of 10+ only.
2-acre wildlife garden with streams, ponds and woodland walks. Cultivated areas incl herbaceous borders, rockeries, vegetable garden, polytunnel and greenhouse. Plenty to delight children with dens and places to explore. Wellies advisable and adult supervision essential. Garden plant sale. Some wheelchair access. Help available if required.

  ♿ ✿ ☕ ☎

36 ◆ PLAS NEWYDD COUNTRY HOUSE & GARDENS
Anglesey LL61 6DQ. National Trust, 01248 714795, www.nationaltrust.org.uk. *2m S of Llanfairpwll. A55 junctions 7 & 8 on A4080.* **Adm £7.30, chd £3.65.** For NGS: Fri 22 Apr (11.30-5.30). For other opening times and information please visit website or telephone.
Plas Newydd is a beautiful C18 country house with spectacular panoramic views across the Menai Strait to Snowdonia. Set in beautiful gardens, there are tranquil walks, an Australasian arboretum and a pretty Italianate Terrance Garden. The house is the family name of the Marquesses of Anglesey. Some slopes and gravel paths.

  ♿ ☕ ☎

37 ◆ **PLAS TAN Y BWLCH**
Maentwrog LL41 3YU. Snowdonia
National Park, 01766 772617,
www.plastanybwlch.com. 7m SW of
Porthmadog. By Oakley Arms A487
turn L and immediately L again. Drive
up to Plas approx ½ m. Adm £4.50,
chd free. For NGS: Mon 29 Aug
(10-5). For other opening times and
information, please phone or see
garden website.
Picturesque historic garden where
exotic and mature plants sit side by
side. Chance to enjoy a garden using
wildlife friendly practises. Numerous
woodland paths which are well
maintained. Oak trees and old
plantations of rhododendron
arboreum varieties are a feature.
Several new plantings underway.
Guided tour by head gardener, Chris
Marshall, 11am & 2 pm lasting approx
1hr. Restricted wheelchair use due to
steep slopes & stairs. Access allowed
at House & Sensory Garden.
&♿ 🐛 ⊨ 🕿

38 ◆ **PLAS YN RHIW**
LL53 8AB. National Trust,
01758 780219,
www.nationaltrust.org.uk. 4m E of
Aberdaron. 12m from Pwllheli,
signposted from B4413 to Aberdaron.
Adm £3, chd free. For NGS:
Evening Opening Mon 16 May
(6-8). For other opening times and
information, please phone or see
garden website.
Essentially a cottage garden of ¾ acre
laid out around C17 manor house (not
open) overlooking Porth Neigwl.
Flowering shrubs and trees flourish in
compartments framed by formal box
hedges and paths. On summer days,
scented plants infuse the air. A place
of romance and charm.
✿ 🍵 🕿

39 **RHYD**
Trefor, Anglesey LL65 4TA.
Jeff Hubble, 01407 720320,
jeffh43@btinternet.com. 7m W of
Llangefni. Nr Holyhead. From
Bodedern 2¼ m along B5109
towards Llangefni, turn L. From A55
take J5 to Llanerchymedd turn L
Trefor Crossroads, 1st R, house on R.
Adm £3, chd free. Visitors
welcome by appt May to end Aug,
any size group, no coaches.
5 acres of gardens, arboretum,
meadows and nature reserve.
Herbaceous beds, pergolas, ponds,
stream, rockery, garden room,
decking and fernery. Many species of
roses, climbing and standard.

Clematis and rhododendron. Wide
variety of herbaceous plants
especially hosta and primula. Many
places to sit and ponder or watch the
wildlife.
&♿ 🕿

40 **ST JOHN THE BAPTIST &
ST GEORGE**
Lon Batus, Carmel LL54 7AR.
Bishop Abbot Demetrius. 7m SE of
Caernarfon. On A487 Porthmadog
Rd, at Dinas r'about exit 1st L to
Groeslon, turn L at PO for 1½ m. At
village centre turn L & L again at Xrds.
Adm £1, chd free. Mon 25 July
(2-5).
Holy community in the making under
the authority of The Orthodox
Catholic and Holy Synod of Malan.
This is not a garden in the traditional
sense but a spiritual retreat from the
stresses and strains of modern life,
surrounded on all sides by space and
rural tranquillity. We are privileged to
share a glimpse of a more
contemplative life.
☕

41 NEW **SUNNINGDALE**
Bull Bay Road. LL68 9SD. Michael
Cross & Gill Boniface. 1½ m NW of
Amlwch. A55 over Britania Bridge,
2nd turning Amlwch (17m). A5025 to
Amlwch. Keep on A5025 past golf
course. Trecastell Hotel on L, parking
at Hotel. Garden 5 houses further on.
Home-made teas. Adm £3, chd £1.
Sun 22 May (12-6).
Not a large garden, but packed with
plants and ideas. Mini orchard, soft
fruit area, herbaceosu beds, wild area
with bug hotel and many paths and
pots. Very bird and bee freindly.
Cottage garden with modern twist
built on slope which has to withstand
wind and salt. The Headland will be
open. wild beaches and caves.
narrow paths and sheer drops.
Spectacular views. Access via steps.
Children must be strictly supervised.
Amlwch Council Garden Competition.
⊨ ☕

This is not a garden
in the traditional
sense but a spiritual
retreat from the
stresses and strains
of modern life . . .

42 **TAN DINAS**
Llanfairpwll, Anglesey LL61 5YL.
Charles Ellis, 01248 714373,
charles.ellis@tesco.net. 2m W of
Menai Bridge. On A5 between
Britannia Bridge and Llanfairpwll
village. Below Marquess of Anglesey's
Column. Parking for up to 6 cars,
more parking in Column car park
250yds. Adm £3, chd free. Visitors
welcome by appt Feb - Aug.
Individuals & groups, max 20
persons.
Small cottage garden of less than an
acre. Overlooked by the Marquess of
Anglesey's Column. Carefully
designed and planted on 3 levels with
many interesting plants, careful
planting ensures colour throughout
the year, incl snowdrops in Feb.
🕿

43 NEW **TANYBRYN**
Bontddu, Dolgellau LL40 2UD.
Mrs Beryl Jones. From Barmouth to
Dogellau an A496 in the village of
Bontddu. Cream teas. Adm £3, chd
U12 free. Sun 1 May (10-5).
In the village of Bontddu with a view
of Cader Idris across the R
Mawddach. Approx 1 acre of
woodland garden with unusual
shrubs, shade loving plants, azaleas,
rhododendrons and mixed borders.
The Afon Cwmllechen forms the
boundary on 2 sides with a small
stream running through the garden
and small wild-life pond and many
wild birds.
&♿ 🍵

44 **TREFFOS SCHOOL**
Llansadwrn, Anglesey LL59 5SL. Dr
& Mrs Humphreys. 2½ m N of Menai
Bridge. A5025 Amlwch/Benllech exit
from the Britannia Bridge onto
Anglesey. Approx 3m turn R towards
Llansadwrn. Entrance to Treffos
School is 200yds on LH-side. Cream
teas. Adm £3, chd free. Sun 12
June (12-4).
7 acres, child-friendly garden, in rural
location, surrounding C17 house now
run as school. Garden consists of
mature woodland, underplanted with
spring flowering bulbs and
rhododendrons, ancient beech
avenue leading down to rockery,
herbaceous borders and courtyards.
Childrens activities; garden trails, art &
crafts, story telling in the woods.
&♿ ✿ 🍵

45 TY CAPEL FFRWD
Llanfachreth LL40 2NR. Revs Mary & George Bolt, 01341 422006, www.plasgwynfryn.co.uk. *4m NE of Dolgellau, 18m SW of Bala. From A470 nr Dolgellau take A497 towards Bala. Turn L after 200yds signed Dolgellau. 1st R signed Llanfachreth, 4m. Uphill to village, L at T-junction, past war memorial on L, 1/2 m. Park nr chapel, walk 30yds downhill to garden. No parking beside cottage. From S via Trawsfynydd, go through Ganllwyd, 1st L signpost Llanfachreth. Parking in field or beside chapel.* Home-made teas & light refreshments. **Adm £3, chd free. Visitors welcome by appt** only. **For opening details please call.**
True cottage garden in Welsh mountains. Azaleas, rhododendrons, acers; large collection of aquilegia. Many different hostas give added strength to spring bulbs and corms. Stream flowing through the garden, 10ft waterfall and on through a small woodland bluebell carpet. I will let you into the secret of hostas without holes! Vibrant bird life due to the cottage's isolated location & surrounding countryside. Sale of plants sourced from the garden. Featured in Welsh magazine, Golwg. Article in the Cambrian News.

46 TY GWYN
Llanbedrgoch, Anglesey LL76 8NX. Keith & Anna Griffiths. *2m inland W of Red Wharfe Bay. A5025 from Menai Bridge through Pentraeth. Turn L to Llanbedrgoch. L at staggered Xrds in village on road to Talwrn. After 1m turn R up unmade road of concrete strips. Garden 1m on L at bottom of small dip.* Home-made teas. **Adm £3, chd free. Sun 19 June (12-5).**
Wildish 9-acres incl wild flower meadow, limestone pavement and hazel copses together with landscaped formal lawns and gardens separated into a number of 'green rooms' of different interest incl gazebo and fish pond, small walled garden, topiary yews and box hedging. Adjacent to several SSSI's, incl Cors Goch, an International Wetlands Nature Reserve.

47 TY NEWYDD
Dyffryn Ardudwy LL44 2DB. Guy & Margaret Lloyd, 01341 247357, guylloyd@btinternet.com. *5 1/2 m N of Barmouth, 4 1/2 m S of Harlech. A496 Barmouth to Harlech rd, 1/2 m N of Dyffryn Ardudwy, area sometimes referred to as 'Ty Canol'. At bus shelter and phone box turn down lane towards sea, driveway 30yds on L.* **Visitors welcome by appt** yr-round. **May - July garden at best.**
3 1/2 -acre maritime garden diversley planted with trees and shrubs to provide yr-round interest through contrasting foliage colours and forms as well as floral displays. Plants incl a number of more tender subjects such as echium, grevilleá and pittosporum. Areas devoted to fruit and vegetable growing and the so called Diamond apple tree.

48 TYN Y CEFN
Llanuwchllyn LL23 7UH. Trevor and Diane Beech, 01678 540 551. *6m W of Bala. From Bala take A494 towards Dolgellau. Small lane on L approx 2 1/2 m after Llanuwchllyn. From Dolgellau take A494 towards Bala. Small lane on R approx 4m after turn to Drws y Nant.* Home-made teas. **Adm £3, chd free. Suns 5 June; 4 Sept (12-5). Visitors also welcome by appt** June, July and August - regret no coaches.
1 1/2 acre very exposed sloping meadow garden at foot of the Aran with panoramic views. Features sheltered, enclosed garden for tender plants and trees. Wildlife area incl 2 ponds and developing woodland to attract birds. Mature shrub beds and feature trees incl majestic eucalyptus. Display of garden sculptures created by the owners. Featured in weekly Welsh language magazine Golwg. Some steep slopes & unfenced ponds.

I will let you into the
secret of hostas
without holes . . . !

49 TYN-TWLL
Llanfachreth LL40 2DP. Sue & Pete Nicholls, 01341 450673, sue-nicholls@hotmail.com. *1 1/2 m NE of Llanfachreth. From Dolgellau on Bala rd (A494), 1st L to Llanfachreth opp Brithdir sign. Continue up hill, 1st R then 1st L and follow signs to Tyn Twll.* Home-made teas. **Adm £3, chd free. Sun 7 Aug (10-5). Visitors also welcome by appt.**
Created by 2 artists. 2 acres of ancient woodland with imaginative architectural features using local materials. Traditional planting, rockeries, walled fruit and vegetable garden, short woodland walk and pond area in sheltered setting, providing a haven for wildlife. Recent addition sculpture of a 35ft sleeping giant - inspired by Welsh legends. Garden still developing. Planters, bird boxes & feeder for sale plus Wildlife & Nature cards. Featured in Cumbrian News & The Dydd.

Gwynedd County Volunteers

County Organisers
North Grace Meirion-Jones, Parc Newydd, Rhosgadfan, Caernarfon LL54 7LF, 01286 831195
South Hilary Nurse, Bryn Gwern, Llanfachreth, Dolgellau LL40 2DH, 01341 450255

County Treasurers
South Michael Bishton, Bronclydwr, Rhoslefain, Tywyn LL36 9LT, 01654 710882, m.bishton@btopenworld.com
North Nigel Bond, Cae Newydd, Rhosgoch, Amlwch, Anglesey LL66 0BG, 01407 831354, nigel@cae-newydd.co.uk

Assistant County Organisers
North Hazel Bond, Cae Newydd, Rhosgoch, Amlwch, Anglesey LL66 0BG, 01407 831354, nigel@cae-newydd.co.uk
North Janet Jones, Coron, Llanbedrog, Pwllheli LL53 7NN, 01758 740296, coron@hotmail.co.uk
South Sue Nichols, Tyn Tyll, Llanfachreth LL40 2PP, 01341 450673

NORTH EAST WALES

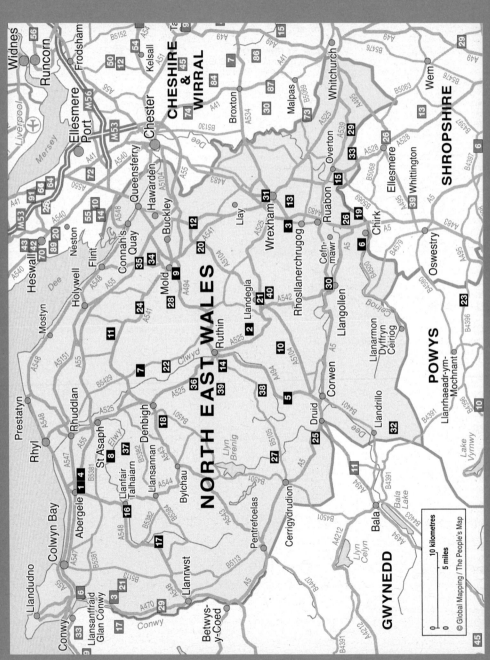

Opening Dates

April

Thursday 7
29 Park Cottage

Sunday 10
27 The Old Rectory, Llanfihangel Glyn Myfyr

Saturday 16
35 90 St Peters Park

Saturday 30
10 Dibleys Nurseries

May

Every Tues & Thurs
14 Firgrove

Sunday 1
10 Dibleys Nurseries

Monday 2
10 Dibleys Nurseries

Thursday 5
29 Park Cottage

Friday 6
13 Erddig Hall

Sunday 22
15 The Garden House
25 Maesmor Hall

Saturday 28
35 90 St Peters Park

Sunday 29
4 33 Bryn Twr & Lynton
20 Leeswood Green Farm

Monday 30
20 Leeswood Green Farm

June

Every Tues & Thurs
14 Firgrove

Thursday 2
14 Firgrove

Sunday 5
29 Park Cottage

Friday 10
38 Ty Uchaf (Evening)

Sunday 12
15 The Garden House
22 Llandyrnog Village
38 Ty Uchaf

Saturday 18
6 Chirk Castle

Sunday 19
8 The Cottage Garden Melin-y-Ddol
18 Gwaenynog
19 Hillside
23 Llangedwyn Hall
26 Meadowside

Sunday 26
1 Abergele Gardens
28 Pantymwyn Village Gardens

July

Every Tues & Thurs
14 Firgrove

Sunday 3
27 The Old Rectory, Llanfihangel Glyn Myfyr

Thursday 7
29 Park Cottage

Sunday 10
9 The Cottage Nursing Home
24 Maes-y-Cyffion
31 Prices Lane Allotments

Sunday 17
34 Soughton House Walled Kitchen Garden

Sunday 24
21 Llandegla Village Gardens

Sunday 31
5 Caereuni
12 Dove Cottage

August

Every Tues & Thurs
14 Firgrove

Thursday 4
29 Park Cottage

Sunday 7
3 Bramley House

Friday 26
13 Erddig Hall

Sunday 28
5 Caereuni
36 Stella Maris

Monday 29
5 Caereuni
36 Stella Maris

September

Every Tues & Thurs
14 Firgrove

Thursday 1
29 Park Cottage

Sunday 4
5 Caereuni
15 The Garden House

Situated on hillside 800ft above sea level. 2-acre garden designed for year-round interest . . .

October

Saturday 8
35 90 St Peters Park

Gardens open to the public

6 Chirk Castle
13 Erddig Hall
15 The Garden House

By appointment only

2 Arfryn
7 Clwydfryn
11 Donadea Lodge
16 Garthewin
17 Glog Ddu
30 Pear Tree Cottage
32 Rhyd Gethin
37 Tal-y-Bryn Farm
39 Tyddyn Bach
40 Y Graig

Also open by Appointment ☎

3 Bramley House
4 33 Bryn Twr & Lynton
12 Dove Cottage
14 Firgrove
21 Glan-yr-Afon, Llandegla Village Gardens
20 Leeswood Green Farm
27 The Old Rectory, Llanfihangel Glyn Myfyr
29 Park Cottage
35 90 St Peters Park

Pantymwyn Village Gardens

Gwaenynog

The Gardens

GROUP OPENING

1 NEW ABERGELE GARDENS
Abergele LL22 8DD. *Zones A & B will be signed on entry to the town centre. Signs will be up from both junctions for Abergele off A55.* Home-made teas at Lynton. **Combined adm £5, chd free (share to St Kentigern Hospice). Sun 26 June (11-5).**

> **NEW BRANAS**
> Mr D Prys Jones

> **NEW 12 BRYN DERWEN**
> Mr & Mrs G Jones

> **NEW 11 BRYN ONNEN**
> Mrs Margaret Flaherty

> **NEW 33 BRYN TWR & LYNTON**
> Mr & Mrs C Knowlson

> **NEW ERDDIG**
> Lis & Eifion Parry

> **NEW 25 KINMEL AVENUE**
> Mr G W Davies

> **NEW 23 KINMEL AVENUE**
> Mr & Mrs D Evans

> **NEW 45 KINMEL AVENUE**
> Mr D J Moore

> **NEW 38 KINMEL AVENUE**
> Mr & Mrs Lees

> **NEW 34 KINMEL AVENUE**
> Mr & Mrs R A Krinks

> **NEW 36 KINMEL AVENUE**
> Mrs D Novak

> **NEW 22 KINMEL AVENUE**
> Mrs Cyndy Hurley

> **NEW MELIDEN**
> Mr & Mrs R Hampshire

12 varied gardens in two zones, owned by enthusiasts who are keen to make the best of the plots they have and share with others. Zone A near Pentre Mawr Park will have the plant sale at 22 Kinmel Avenue and tickets will be available both there and in Zone B at 33 Bryn Twr which also has the teas. Several have vegetable patches, one has hens, there are several ponds of various sizes with fish and nearly all have selection of pots full of colour. Trees, climbers, shrubs and perennials are all well represented. Wheelchair access available to over 50% of gardens.

---

2 ARFRYN
Pentrecelyn, nr Ruthin LL15 2HR. Aaron & Ruth Davies, 01978 790475, arfrynpentrecelyn@btinternet.com. *4m S of Ruthin. On A525 Wrexham/Ruthin rd. 4m out of Ruthin by Llysfasi College take B5429 to Graigfechan. Follow NGS signs.* **Visitors welcome by appt** June & July Only, groups 10+.
Situated on hillside 800ft above sea level. 2-acre garden designed for yr-round interest, overlooking wonderful views. Divided into separate rooms - secret garden filled with old roses and hardy geraniums, cottage garden, wild flower bank and lawned gardens with herbaceous and shrub beds. Latest project - long borders created for late summer colour.

3 BRAMLEY HOUSE
Bronwylfa Road, Legacy, Wrexham LL14 4HY. Susan & John Droog, 01978 846935, john_sue.droog@btinternet.com. *2m W of Wrexham. Leave A483 at the Rhosllanerchrugog exit, then B5605 signed Johnstown. 1st R, after roundabout. L at T-junction on to B5097. After 1m follow signs for field parking.* Home-made teas & light refreshments. **Adm £3, chd free. Sun 7 Aug (12.30-6).** Visitors also welcome by appt July & Aug, groups 10+, coaches permitted.
Set in ¹/₂ acre with open views across farmland to nearby woods. S-facing, formal and gravel gardens to the front moving to mixed borders, shrubs, trees and large lawned area. Water features further complemented by a stream running through the main body of the garden. Tombola.

4 33 BRYN TWR & LYNTON
Bryn Twr, Abergele LL22 8DD. Mr & Mrs Colin Knowlson, 01745 832002, apk@slaters.com. *From A55 heading W, take slip rd to Abergele. Turn L at r'about then over T-lights; 1st L signed Llanfair T H. 3rd rd on L, 33 Bryn Twr is on L.* **Adm £3, chd free. Sun 29 May (11-5).** Visitors also welcome by appt.
Large changes have been made to incorporate 2 gardens into one. Approx ³/₄ acre in total with patio and pond area, mixed herbaceous and shrub borders, some trees plus many unusual plants. New areas maturing well. Wisteria should still be flowering for May opening.

5 CAEREUNI
Ffordd Ty Cerrig, Godre'r Gaer, nr Corwen LL21 9YA. Mr S Williams. *1m N of Corwen. Take A5 to Bala. Turn R at T-lights onto A494 to Chester. 1st R after lay-by; house ¹/₄ m on L.* Home-made teas. **Adm £3, chd free. Sun 31 July; Sun & Mon 28, 29 Aug; Sun 4 Sept (2-5).**
Third of an acre international quirky themed fantasy garden with unique features incl; Japanese smoke water garden, old ruin, Spanish courtyard, Welsh gold mine, Chinese peace garden, woodman's lodge and jungle, Mexican chapel, 1950s petrol garage all forming a dramatic background to a plantsman's collection of rare trees, shrubs and plants. Innovative container planting of tender perennials and topiary.

6 ◆ CHIRK CASTLE
nr Wrexham LL14 5AF. National Trust, 01691 777701, www.nationaltrust.org.uk. *7m S of Wrexham, 2m W of Chirk Village. Follow brown signs from A483 to Chirk Village. 2m W on minor rds.* **Adm £7.20, chd £3.60. For NGS: Sat 18 June (10-6).** For other opening times and information please visit website or telephone.
5¹/₂ -acre hilltop garden with good views over Shropshire and Cheshire. Formal garden with outstanding yew topiary. Rose garden, herbaceous borders, more informal further from the building with rare trees and shrubs, pond, thatched hawk house, ha-ha with terrace and pavilion. Compact gravel paths, some slopes & grass paths.

Third of an acre international quirky themed fantasy garden with unique features . . .

7 CLWYDFRYN
Bodfari LL16 4HU. Keith & Susan Watson, 01745 710232. *5m outside Denbigh. Halfway between Bodfari and Llandyrnog on B5429.* **Adm £3.50, chd free. Visitors welcome by appt** from January to end June. Groups welcome.
³/₄ -acre plantswoman's garden, well worth a visit any time of the yr. Collection of epimediums, hellebores and daffodils in spring. Many unusual spring shade loving plants and perennial borders in summer. Grasses border, orchard and colourful cottage garden potager. Long, fairly steep slope to gain access to most of the garden.

8 THE COTTAGE GARDEN MELIN-Y-DDOL
Marli, Abergele LL22 9EB. Tom & Jenny Pritchard. *1¹/₂ m N of Llannefydd. 3m S of Bodelwyddan. 3m S of A55 between Llannefydd & Glascoed. On R Elwy adj to Pont-y-Ddol. Entrance on S side of bridge.* Home-made teas. **Adm £3, chd free (share to St Mary's Church, Cefn). Sun 19 June (2-5).**
Many cottage garden plants in informal borders. Small bog areas, laburnum arch, wildlife area, fruit and vegetables, cut flower border. Elemental 'white witches' garden. Dyers and aromatherapy plant areas. Old mill stones from the mill are used throughout garden. Living willow structure. Riverside walk. Working cottage garden, sometimes repeat flowering sacrificed for seed production. All in magical setting. Adjacent nursery featuring plants propagated from garden. Wheelchair access to some parts. Narrow approach to garden, gravel paths in some areas.

9 THE COTTAGE NURSING HOME
54 Hendy Road, Mold CH7 1QS. Mr & Mrs A G & L I Lanini. *10m W of Chester. From Mold town centre take A494 towards Ruthin. 2nd R into Hafod Park. Straight on to T-junction. Turn R onto Hendy Rd. Garden at junction of Hendy Rd & Clayton Rd.* Home-made teas. **Adm £2, chd £1 (share to British Heart Foundation, Mold). Sun 10 July (2-5).**
Beautiful garden set in approx 1 acre. Well-established shrubs, herbaceous plants and abundance of colourful window boxes and tubs. Heart-shaped patio, incl water feature and pergola, with natural reclaimed stone walling.

10 DIBLEYS NURSERIES
Cefn Rhydd, Llanelidan LL15 2LG. Mr & Mrs R Dibley. *7m S of Ruthin. Take A525 to Xrds by Llysfasi Agricultural College. Turn onto B5429 towards Llanelidan. After 1¹/₂ m turn L, 1m up lane on L. Brown tourist signs from A525.* Home-made teas. **Adm £3, chd free. Sat, Sun, Mon 30 Apr, 1, 2 May (10-5).**
8-acre arboretum with wide selection of rare and unusual trees. There will be a lovely display of rhododendrons, magnolias, cherries and camellias. Ride through the garden on a

miniature railway. ³/₄ acre of glasshouses are open to show a spectacular display of streptocarpus and other house plants. National Collection of *Streptocarpus*. 21 RHS Gold Medals at Chelsea Flower Show.
⊛ **NCCPG** ☕

11 ▶ DONADEA LODGE
Babell CH8 8QD. Mr P Beaumont, 01352 720204. *7m NE of Denbigh. Turn off A541 Mold to Denbigh at Afonwen, signed Babell; T-junction turn L. A55 Chester to Conwy take B5122 to Caerwys, 3rd turn on L.* Adm £2.50, chd free. Visitors welcome by appt, June & July only (11-5) no minimum size, coaches permitted.
1-acre shady garden showing 25yrs of imaginative planting to enhance the magic of dappled shade, moving through different colour schemes, with each plant complementing its neighbour.
ᕚ ☎

12 ▶ DOVE COTTAGE
Rhos Road, Penyffordd, Nr Chester CH4 0JR. Chris & Denise Wallis, 01244 547539, dovecottage@supanet.com. *6m SW of Chester. From Chester A55 S exit A550 follow signs for Corwen. Turn L immed opp Penyffordd railway stn. From Wrexham A541 for Mold, R at Pontblyddyn for Chester, turn R immed opp Penyffordd railway stn.* Home-made teas. Adm £3, chd free. Sun 31 July (2-5). Visitors also welcome by appt.
Approx 1¹/₂-acre garden, shrubs & herbaceous plants set informally around lawns. Established vegetable area, 2 ponds (1 wildlife), summerhouse,and woodland planted area.
ᕚ ⊛ ⊨ ☕ ☎

13 ▶ ◆ ERDDIG HALL
nr Wrexham LL13 0YT. National Trust, 01978 355314, www.nationaltrust.org.uk. *2m S of Wrexham. Signed from A483/A5125 Oswestry rd; also from A525 Whitchurch rd.* Adm £7, chd £3.50. For NGS: Fris 6 May; 26 Aug (11-4). For other opening times and information please visit website or telephone.
Important, listed Grade 1, historic garden. Formal C18 and later Victorian design elements incl pleached lime tree avenues, trained fruit trees, wall plants and climbers, herbaceous borders, roses, herb

border, annual bedding, restored glasshouse and vine house. National Collection of Hedera. Free garden tours for NGS visitors.
ᕚ ⊛ **NCCPG** ☕ ☎

14 ▶ FIRGROVE
Llanfwrog, Ruthin LL15 2LL. Philip & Anna Meadway, 01824 702677, panda.meadway@btinternet.com. *1¹/₂ m SW of Ruthin. Exit Ruthin on B5105 towards Cerrigydrudion. After church & inn, garden is ¹/₂ m on the R.* Tea & Cream Teas. Adm £2, chd free. Every Tues & Thurs from 3 May until 29 Sept, (12-3.30). Visitors also welcome by appt 3rd May to 29th Sept.
1¹/₂ -acre mature plantsman's garden that is still developing. A garden for all seasons whose microclimate allows tender and unusual shrubs to thrive. Some underplanted with streptocarpus for the summer. A collection of large exotics for summer containers. Many varieties of pittosporum, camellias, magnolias, buddleia colvii and alternifolia. Clematis up the trees. Featured in Winner of Ruthin Show Society Best Town Garden.
ᕚ ⊨ ☕ ☎

15 ▶ ◆ THE GARDEN HOUSE
Erbistock LL13 0DL. Mr & Mrs S Wingett, www.simonwingett.com. *5m S of Wrexham. On A528 Wrexham to Shrewsbury rd. Follow signs at Overton Bridge to Erbistock Church.* Adm £4, chd free. For NGS: Suns 22 May; 12 June; 4 Sept (2-5). For other opening times and information please visit website or telephone.
Shrub and herbaceous plantings in monochromatic, analogous and complementary colour schemes. Rose pergolas, National Collection of hydrangea (over 300 species and cultivars). Sculpture Garden. Large lily pond, Victorian dovecote.
ᕚ ᕚ ⊛ **NCCPG** ⊨ ☕

A garden for all seasons whose microclimate allows tender and unusual shrubs to thrive . . .

16 ▶ GARTHEWIN
Llanfair T.H., LL22 8YR. Mr Michael Grime, 01745 720288. *6m S of Abergele & A55. From Abergele take A548 to Llanfair TH & Llanrwst. Entrance to Garthewin 300yds W of Llanfair TH on A548 to Llanrwst.* Adm £3, chd free. Visitors welcome by appt in April, May & June only. No coaches.
Valley garden with ponds and woodland areas. Much of the 8 acres have been reclaimed and redesigned providing a younger garden with a great variety of azaleas, rhododendrons and young trees, all within a framework of mature shrubs and trees. Small chapel open.
ᕚ ☎

17 ▶ GLOG DDU
Llangernyw, Abergele LL22 8PS. Pamela & Anthony Harris, 01745 860 611, anthony.harris@btinternet.com. *1m S of Llangernyw. Through Llangernyw going S on A548. R into Uwch Afon. L after 1m at grass triangle. Follow rd, past new houses, down narrow lane. Glog Ddu is the house on R at end.* Adm £3, chd free. Visitors welcome by appt Early May to Mid October. Parking for 12 cars. Narrow road unsuitable for coaches.
The result of three generations of gardening enthusiasm, a garden inspired by an Edwardian plantsman with a fascinating history. Approx 2-acres consisting of snowdrops rhododendrons, herbaceous borders, extensive area of rare trees and shrubs, many grown from seed. Planted for yr-round interest with an emphasis on autumn colour.
⊛ ☎

18 ▶ GWAENYNOG
Denbigh LL16 5NU. Major & Mrs Tom Smith. *1m W of Denbigh. On A543, Lodge on L, ¹/₄ m drive.* Cream teas. Adm £3, chd free (share to St James' Church, Nantglyn). Sun 19 June (2-5.30).
2 acres incl the restored kitchen garden where Beatrix Potter wrote and illustrated the 'Tale of the Flopsy Bunnies' in 1909. Small exhibition of some of her work. C16 house (not open) visited by Dr Samuel Johnson during his Tour of Wales. Restoration work is taking place in some flower beds and a new greenhouse is being built. Featured in local press and on TV during Launch of Statue of Beatrix Potter.
ᕚ ⊛ ☕

19 NEW **HILLSIDE**
Pont-y-Blew, Chirk LL14 5BH.
Ferelith & Robert Smith. *2m E of
Chirk. Follow NGS signs to Chirk.
Turn down Colliery Rd, follow signs to
Pont-y-Blew, or follow NGS signs
from Halton r'about (McDonalds).*
Home-made teas at Meadowside.
**Combined adm with Meadowside
£3.50 (share to NSPCC), chd free.**
Sun 19 June (2-5).
Country cottage garden in fabulous
setting, looking across the lower
Ceiriog Valley. C17 half-timbered
cottage (not open) in middle of
³/₄ -acre lawned garden with mixed
borders, woodland stream, roses, fruit
and vegetable gardens. Wild flower
bank. Stream and lower garden
accessible by steep paths.

20 **LEESWOOD GREEN FARM**
Leeswood CH7 4SQ. John Glenn &
Anne Saxon, 01352 771222,
annemsaxon@yahoo.co.uk. *3m SE
of Mold. 9m NW of Wrexham. Off
A541 W. At Pontblyddyn, from
Wrexham, turn L after garage into
Dingle Rd. After ¹/₂ m at T-junction
turn L. Garden after 50yds on R
approached by lane.* Home-made
teas. **Adm £3, chd free.** Sun 29,
Mon 30 May (11-5). **Visitors also
welcome by appt No access for
coaches.**
Plantswoman's garden surrounding
C15 farmhouse in lovely rural location.
Many unusual trees, shrubs and
perennials set around lawns,
ornamental vegetable garden, orchard
and paved areas with some unusual
features. Small meadow, wildflowers
and seating to enjoy the vistas.

Look out for
the gardens with
the ☎ – enjoy
a private visit . . .

GROUP OPENING

21 **LLANDEGLA VILLAGE
GARDENS**
Llandegla LL11 3AP. *10m W of
Wrexham. Off A525 at Llandegla
Memorial Hall. Parking & mini bus
from hall.Please park in centre of
village because parking is difficult for
some gardens.* Tea & Cream Teas at
Llandegla Memorial Hall and some
gardens. **Adm £5, chd free.** Sun
24 July (2-6). **Visitors also welcome
by appt at some gardens.**

> **BRYN EITHIN**
> Mr & Mrs A Fife

> NEW **4 CHURCH
> TERRACE**
> Phil and Brenda Cottrell

> **ERW LLAN**
> Mr & Mrs Keith Jackson

> **GLAN-YR-AFON**
> Mr & Mrs D C Ion
> **Visitors also welcome by
> appt.**
> 01978 790286
> val@dunvalion.co.uk

> **OLD TY HIR FARM**
> Mr & Mrs D M Holder

> **SWN Y GWYNT**
> Phil Clark

> **TY SIONED**
> Mr & Mrs Muia

Selection of 7 varied gardens set in
and around the picturesque village
with many stone cottages. There is
a new addition, 4,Church Terrace.
This compact cottage garden,
situated to the rear of a mid 19th
century typical Welsh cottage is full
of colour, with a wide variety of
interest. Ty Sioned is a terraced
garden with an Italian flavour and
panoramic views of Clwydian Hills.
Bryn Eithin has colourful bedding
plants and orchard while Swn y
Gwynt is a real plantsman's garden
of ¹/₄ -acre. Old Ty Hir Farm has 1-
acre of open plan garden and many
secret areas to explore. There is the
informal country garden of Glan-yr-
Afon, surrounding 200yr old
farmhouse incl stream, ponds and
several ancient trees. Erw Llan is a
¹/₄ acre garden made to attract wild
life. Plants are grown for birds and
butterflies, trees for nesting sites
and there is a pond to encourage
toads, newts, frogs and damsel flies.
St Tegla's Church and ancient Well.
Extensive views over surrounding

areas of natural beauty such as the
Clwydian range, Horseshoe Pass and
Llandegla moor.

GROUP OPENING

22 NEW **LLANDYRNOG
VILLAGE**
LL16 4EY. *5m N E of Denbigh.
Parking available in village hall/school
car park.* Home-made teas.
Combined adm £4, chd free.
Sun 12 June (2-5).

> NEW **CRAIG LEA**
> Mrs Hilary Wilcox

> NEW **GER Y LLAN**
> Olga & Elwyn Evans

> NEW **SPRINGERS**
> Mrs Sue Vine

Take a walk through the thriving
village of Llandyrnog, situated in the
heart of the Vale of Clwyd, in an area
of outstanding natural beauty and
enjoy 4 colourful gardens, some of
which take advantage of the spendid
views of the surrounding countryside.
Craig Lea Cottage garden bursting
with colour throughout the summer.
New feature to incl green architectural
planting. **Ger Y Llan** Informal village
garden with yr-round colour. Excellent
rural views nestling in the heart of the
village. **Springers** Compact cottage
garden, bursting with colour and
offering views of the beautiful Vale of
Clwyd. Whilst here, why not enjoy a
spot of lunch at one of our 3 local PH
and complete your walk/drive to our
excellent local plant nursery.
Wheelchair access at Glan yr Afon &
Ger y Llan only.

23 **LLANGEDWYN HALL**
Llangedwyn SY10 9JW. Mr & Mrs T
M Bell. *8m W of Oswestry. On
B4396 to Llanrhaeadr-ym-Mochnant
about 5m W of Llynclys Xrds.* Home-
made teas. **Adm £3.50, chd free.**
Sun 19 June (12-5).
Approx 4-acre formal terraced
garden on 3 levels, designed and laid
out in late C17 and early C18.
Unusual herbaceous plants, sunken
rose garden, small water garden,
walled kitchen garden and woodland
walk.

25 ▶ MAESMOR HALL

Maerdy, Corwen LL21 0NS. Mr & Mrs G M Jackson. *5m W of Corwen. Take A5 from Corwen, through 2 sets of T-lights. In Maerdy take 1st L after church and opp The Goat PH.* Home-made teas. **Adm £3, chd free (share to St Dunstans (charity for injured soldiers). Sun 22 May (1-5).** Well-established garden with riverside and estate walks featuring a water garden and white plant garden. The rhododendrons are extensive and provide a fitting backdrop to the parkland. Large azalea beds are a mixture of colour. Wooded walks around the hall together with bluebells and bulbs and an arboretum are also an attraction. 100yr old Fig House has been restored and incl exotic plants and flowers incl pomegranates, lemons, bananas etc. Patios and front of hall displays. Enormous stone table has been brought down from the surrounding mountain - could have been King Arthur's. Gravel paths.

  ♿ 🐕 ☕

24 ▶ MAES-Y-CYFFION

Rhes-y-Cae Road, Nannerch CH7 5QW. Mr Cliff Halsall. *5m NW of Mold on A541. Towards Denbigh from Mold (5m) look for X-roads signed Cilcain (L), Rhes-y-Cae (R), turn R, then immed L to drive gate.* Ample off road parking. Home-made teas. **Adm £3, chd free. Sun 10 July (2-6).** Cottage garden of about ½ acre with traditional planting, mostly herbaceous, at varying levels, colourful and rising to limestone rock face. Very productive kitchen garden with soft fruit and orchard trees. Limited wheelchair access on gravel.

  ♿ ❀ ☕

26 ▶ NEW ▶ MEADOWSIDE

Halton, Chirk LL14 5BD. Nick & Ingrid Davies. *10m SW of Wrexham. Follow A483, exit at Halton r'about, at next r'about take 1st exit L into Black Park. House on R at end of village.* Home-made teas. **Adm £3.50, chd free. Sun 19 June (2-5). Combined with Hillside.** Meadowside is an informal ¼ -acre garden set in an idyllic situation with lovely countryside views, close to the proposed site of 'Waking the Dragon' project. Garden planted with wildlife in mind. Borders encourage insects and provide homes for birds, bats and hedgehogs. Mixed shrubs, trees and herbaceous perennials. Some steep slopes and gravel paths.

☕

27 ▶ THE OLD RECTORY, LLANFIHANGEL GLYN MYFYR

Corwen LL21 9UN. Mr & Mrs E T Hughes, 01490 420568, elwynthomashughes@hotmail.com. *2½ m NE of Cerrigydrudion. From Ruthin take B5105 SW for 12m to Llanfihangel Glyn Myfyr. Turn R just after Crown PH (follow signs). Proceed for ⅓ m, garden on L.* Home-made teas. **Adm £3.50, chd free (share to Cancer Research U.K.). Suns 10 Apr; 3 July (2-5). Visitors also welcome by appt.** Garden of approx 1 acre set in beautiful, tranquil, sheltered valley. A garden for all seasons; hellebores; abundance of spring flowers; mixed borders; water, bog, and gravel gardens; walled garden with old roses, pergola, bower and garden of meditation. Also hardy orchids, gentians, daffodils, rhododendrons and acers.

  ♿ ❀ ☕

GROUP OPENING

28 ▶ PANTYMWYN VILLAGE GARDENS

Mold CH7 5EN. *3m W of Mold. From Mold A541 to Denbigh turn L at first mini r'about, signed Pantymwyn approx 3m. From Ruthin A494 to Mold turn L after Flintshire Boundary signed Pantymwyn 1½ m. At end of rd turn L.* Live music, Home-made teas and plant stall at Wych Elm (not open). **Combined adm £4.50, chd free. Sun 26 June (2-6).**

> **BRYN MOR**
> Pam & Andy Worthington
>
> **NEW ▶ CHARLESVILLE**
> Peter & Carol Garrett
>
> **COEDLE**
> Richard & Shirley Hughes
>
> **NEW ▶ CRUD-Y-GWYNT**
> Pete & Sue Dodd
>
> **GREENHEYS**
> Roy & Carol Hambleton
>
> **LONG SHADOWS**
> Dave & Agnes Christmas
>
> **ROWANOKE**
> Ron & Clare Exley
>
> **NEW ▶ WHITE LODGE**
> George & Edwina Hattersley

Visit 8 diverse gardens in this small scenic village close to Loggerheads Country Park in AONB. As you walk the garden route there are wonderful views of the Clwydian range and Moel Famau. **Bryn Mor** features an organic ornamental kitchen garden and live music to accompany scenic views. New this year is **Charlesville**, which is an evolving garden with terraces and pond with a woodland backdrop. **Coedle** is a country cottage style garden on a limestone hillside with herbaceous borders, small pond and woodland area. **Crud y Gwynt** is new this year and has a paved arbour, pond, borders, shrubs, herb/kitchen gardens. **Greenheys** has relaxed style planting of perennials and climbers especially clematis but has occasional formal touches. **Long Shadows** has spectacular views from its sloping garden with rocky outcrops and is full of shrubs, flowers and trees. **Rowanoke** is a limestone hillside garden on different levels with a wildlife pond and natural woodland. **White Lodge** is new this year and has an interesting variety of shrubs and flowers in a terraced garden. En route enjoy home-made teas, a plant stall and Welsh music performances courtesy of Wych Elm (B&B) (not open)

  ❀ ☕

The rhododendrons are extensive and provide a fitting backdrop to the parkland . . . large azalea beds are a mixture of colour . . .

Caereuni

29 PARK COTTAGE

Penley, Wrexham LL13 0LS. Dr S J Sime, 01948 830126, sjsime@hotmail.com. *12m SE of Wrexham. Signed from A539, 3m E of Overton-on-Dee. No parking at house please. Roadside parking in village, 250yd walk from road to garden.* Tea/coffee Thurs. Full tea Suns. **Adm £3, chd £1, (June) £4,chd £1.** Thurs 7 Apr; 5 May; 7 July; 4 Aug; 1 Sept (2-4) Sun 5 June (2-5.30). Also opening with **Shilling Barn Cottage** 5 June. Visitors also welcome by appt, groups 10+.

5-acre garden designed to provide distinct and appropriate habitats for plant collection of over 3000 labelled species and varieties, specialising in flowering shrubs, small trees, grasses and shade-loving plants, featuring shrubby caprifoliaceae, clethra, aronia, eucryphia, herbaceous berberidaceae, woodland aroids and hydrangeaceae.

Look at the mountains and trees, listen to the river and birds, smell the roses and let our garden touch your senses . . .

30 NEW PEAR TREE COTTAGE

Geufron, Llangollen LL20 8DY. Mr & Mrs M Davies, 01978 861704, tolly17@hotmail.co.uk. *½ m N of Llangollen. From Llangollen take A542 towards Ruthin. Turn R immed after Llangollen Pavilion, up Tower Rd, straight at Xrds, up steep hill to Xrd. Turn R down lane to garden. From Horseshoe Pass turn L into Tower Rd just before brown Llangollen Pavilion sign.* **Adm £3, chd free.** Visitors welcome by appt June & Sept only, no coaches.

Steeply sloping s-facing cottage garden full of colourful plants and vegetables many propagated by the owners. Wide steps edged with showy pots, lead down to the pond and terrace where the magnificent views can be admired.

ALLOTMENTS

31 PRICES LANE ALLOTMENTS

Prices Lane, Wrexham LL11 2NB. Wrexham Allotment & Leisure Gardeners Association. *1m from town centre. From A483, take exit for Wrexham Ind Estate and follow A5152 towards the town centre. Allotments signed from there.* **Adm £3, chd free.** Sun 10 July (12-6).

120 plus plots, growing a good variety of flowers, fruit and vegetables. Plots for the disabled and school children. Association shop, selling a wide range of garden requisites and seeds.

32 RHYD GETHIN

Pennant Road, Llandrillo, Corwen LL21 0TE. Tony & Jenny Leeson, 01490 440213. *Between Corwen & Bala. Take B4401 signed Llandrillo. In village turn at shop /PO. 50yds fork L onto Pennant Rd. 2m down single track. Fork R at telephone box.* Home-made teas. **Adm £3, chd free.** Visitors welcome by appt May, June & July - individs & groups welcome. Access unsuitable for coaches.

Look at the mountains and trees, listen to the river and birds, smell the roses and let our garden touch your senses. Oh! to taste the teas and feel the peace of this garden filled with old roses, shrubs and herbaceous plants. Mature woodland area with pond, rock garden.

33 SHILLING BARN COTTAGE

LL13 0NA. Jean & Trevor Thomas. *12 m SE of Wrexham. On A539 approaching Penley from Overton, turn R onto Red Hall Lane (signed Ellesmere).* **Combined with Park Cottage adm £4, chd free.** Sat 5 June (2-5.30).

Just under ½ -acre of mainly herbaceous perennials, incl hardy geraniums. Beginning 6yrs ago it was carved out of heavy clay to produce dry and wet areas. Space has to be created constantly for the results of various 'seed distribution schemes', some of which are rather strange.

34 NEW SOUGHTON HOUSE WALLED KITCHEN GARDEN

Hall Lane, Sychdyn, nr Mold CH7 6AD. Mr & Mrs David McLean. *½ m off Mold-Northop Rd. Leave Mold on the Northop Rd (A5119), go through Sychdyn and take 1st R, follow signs for NGS. From Northop take Mold Rd & turn 1st L then follow signs for NGS.* Light refreshments. **Adm £3, chd free** (share to Nightingale House Hospice). Sun 17 July (2-6).

Beautifully restored and maintained Victorian walled kitchen garden with a selection of thirty five fruit trees and soft fruit. The greenhouse contains figs, peaches, apricots, grapes and other fruit. Low boxwood hedges surround many of the 14 plots. Allotment holders grow a wide selection of vegetables and actively encourage biodiversity. A harpist will play during the afternoon. Featured on BBC Wales TV & radio, in Daily Post & Daily Mail. Brick paving around the garden.

35 90 ST PETERS PARK

Northop CH7 6YU. Mr P Hunt, 01352 840758, philipbhunt@hotmail.co.uk. *3m N of Mold, 3m S of Flint. Leave A55 at Northop exit. Opp cricket ground, turn R. Fifth turning on R. Garden on R.* Tea & Light Refreshments. **Adm £3, chd free** (share to Chester Cathedral; Northop Parish Church; Northop Silver Band). Sats 16 Apr; 28 May; 8 Oct (2-5.30). Visitors also welcome by appt.

Garden planted by professional botanist and horticulturalist. A plantsman's garden with exotic and rare species of trees and ornamental plants. Unique garden cruck house with sedum roof, beamed ceilings, stained glass windows and inglenook fireplace. Other interesting timber framed structures.

36 STELLA MARIS

Mynydd Llech, Llanrhaeadr LL16 4PW. Mrs J E Moore. *3m SE of Denbigh. Take A525 Denbigh to Ruthin rd. After 3m from Denbigh or 4m from Ruthin turn W to Mynydd Llech. Garden ½ m on L.* Cream & Home-made teas. **Adm £3, chd free.** Sun 28, Mon 29 Aug (2-6).

1-acre garden created to enjoy the wonderful, ever changing views over the Vale of Clwyd. Good collection of specimen trees, interesting shrubs, herbaceous borders with yr round interest, gravel garden and ponds. New areas of late flowering shrubs and herbaceous plants, complement the outstanding scenery. Some lawned slopes and gravel drive.

37 **TAL-Y-BRYN FARM**
Llannefydd LL16 5DR. Mr & Mrs Gareth Roberts, 01745 540256, llaeth@villagedairy.co.uk. *3m W of Henllan. From Henllan take rd signed Llannefydd. After 2¹/₂ m turn R signed Bont Newydd. Garden ¹/₂ m on L.* Adm £3, chd free. **Visitors welcome by appt Groups 6+.**
Medium-sized working farmhouse cottage garden. Ancient farm machinery. Incorporating ancient privy festooned with honeysuckle, clematis and roses. Terraced arches, sunken garden pool and bog garden, fountains and old water pumps. Herb wheels, shrubs and other interesting features. Lovely views of the Clwydian range. Water feature. Featured in Denbighshire Free Press.

38 **NEW** **TY UCHAF**
Clawddnewydd LL15 2NL. Tom & Sarah Roberts. *4.6m S of Ruthin. Exit Ruthin on B5105 towards Cerrigydrudion. At Clawddnewydd pass pond & PH on L. After 200m take L fork past community centre & shop signed Derwen. Follow yellow signs.* Home-made teas. **Adm £3, chd free. Sun 12 June (2-6)**

Evening Opening Fri 10 June (6-9).
Approximately 1-acre garden set on hillside with panoramic views of Clwydian Range, Berwyn Mountains and Snowdonia, comprising established vegetable, fruit and herb garden, large selection of shrubs, mixed herbaceous borders and terraced cottage and rose gardens. Cake stall. Gravel path to large terrace, grassy slopes.

1-acre garden set on hillside with panoramic views of Clwydian Range, Berwyn Mountains and Snowdonia . . .

39 **TYDDYN BACH**
Bontuchel, Ruthin LL15 2DG. Mr & Mrs L G Starling, 01824 710248. *4m W of Ruthin. B5105 from Ruthin, turn R at Cross Keys PH, on road to Bontuchel/Cyffylliog. Go through Bontuchel, without turning, heading towards Cyffylliog. 400yrds (river on*

R) turn L up narrow rd, steep hill just before next bridge at chevron signs. House 1st on L. Ignore final Sat Nav instructions. Adm £3, chd free. **Visitors welcome by appt July & August, individuals & groups welcome. Limited parking, not suitable for coaches.**
Mainly organic, very pretty cottage garden with prolific vegetable garden. Wildlife friendly with hedges and wood pile. Greenhouse packed with plants for both pots and the garden. Small wildlife pond completed in May 2010.

40 **Y GRAIG**
Llandegla, Wrexham LL11 3BG. Janet Strivens & Phillip Tidey, 01978 790657, ygraig@btopenworld.com. *8m SE of Ruthin. From Wrexham take A525 towards Ruthin. After approx 7m turn L immed before The Plough PH on L, garden is 1m up the narrow winding rd.* Light refreshments & teas, if required. Adm £3, chd free. **Visitors welcome by appt May to Aug, individuals and groups, (max 20) No coaches.**
¹/₂ acre of enchanting informal hillside garden at over 1000ft beneath a limestone outcrop. Herbaceous beds full of colour, rockeries, many clematis and old roses, small ponds and water lilies. 3 acres of field with recently established woodland incl specimen trees. Vegetable garden and wonderful views over the Clwydians. Some paths difficult to access, gravel surfaces, steps and steep slopes.

North East Wales

County Organiser
Jane Moore, Stella Maris, Mynydd Llech, Llanrhaedr, Denbigh LL16 4PW, 01745 890475, jemoore01@live.com

Booklet Coordinator
Roy Hambleton, Greenheys, Cefn Bychan Road, Pantymwyn, Mold GH7 5EN, 01352 740206, royhambleton@btinternet.com

County Treasurers
Elizabeth Sasse, Ty'r Ardd, High Street, Caerwys, Mold CH7 5BB, 01352 720220, Elizabeth.sasse246@btinternet.com
Wendy Sime, Park Cottage, Penley, Wrexham LL13 0LS, 01948 830126, sjsime@hotmail.com

Press & Publicity Officer
Ann Rathbone, Woodfirld House, Station Lane, Hawarden CH5 3EG, 01244 532948, rathbone.ann@talktalk.net

Assistant County Organisers
Fiona Bell, Plas Ashpool, Llandyrnog, Denbigh LL16 4HP, 01824 790612, bell_fab@hotmail.com
Ruth Davies, Arfryn, Pentrecelyn, nr Ruthin LL15 2HR, 01978 790475, arfrynpentrecelyn@btinternet.com
Bill & Dawn Jones, Tan y Coed, Llanasa, nr Holywell CH8 9NE, 01745 889919, w.jones844@btinternet.com
Mrs Ann Knowlson, Lynton, Highfield Park, Abergele LL22 7AU, 01745 828201, apk@slaters.com
Ann Rathbone, Woodfield House, Station Lane Hawarden CH5 3EG, 01244 532948, rathbone.ann@talktalk.net
Anne Saxon, Leeswood Green Farm, Leeswood, Mold CH7 4SQ, 01352 771222, annemsaxon@yahoo.com
Susan Watson, Clwydfryn, Bodfari, Denbigh LL16 4HU, 01745 710232, clwydfryn@btinternet.com

Enjoy a day out – look out for a Group Opening

POWYS

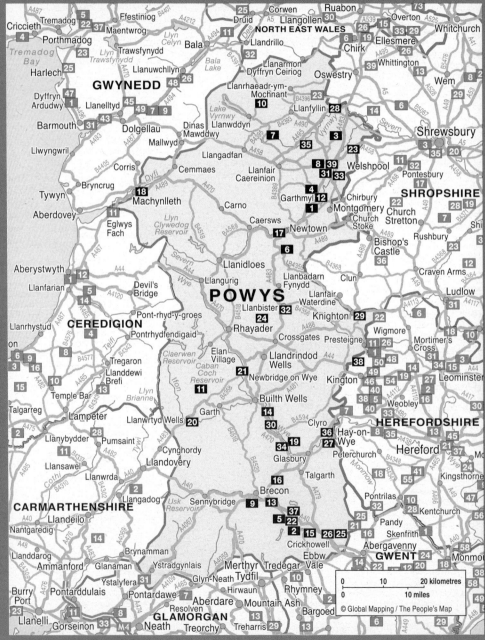

Opening Dates

April

Sunday 3
23 Maesfron Hall and Gardens

Tuesday 5
2 Ashford House

Sunday 10
38 The Walled Garden

Tuesday 12
2 Ashford House

Sunday 17
3 Cartref

Tuesday 19
2 Ashford House

Sunday 24
1 Abernant
39 Welshpool's Secret Gardens

Monday 25
39 Welshpool's Secret Gardens

Tuesday 26
2 Ashford House

May

Sunday 1
25 Moor Park

Monday 2
24 Mill Cottage

Tuesday 3
2 Ashford House

Saturday 7
35 Tan-y-Llyn

Sunday 8
35 Tan-y-Llyn

Tuesday 10
2 Ashford House

Friday 13
12 Glansevern Hall Gardens

Saturday 14
8 Dingle Nurseries & Garden

Sunday 15
8 Dingle Nurseries & Garden
14 Glanwye

Tuesday 17
2 Ashford House

Saturday 21
30 Pontsioni House

Sunday 22
3 Cartref
6 Cwm-Weeg
15 Gliffaes Country House Hotel
21 Llysdinam

Tuesday 24
2 Ashford House

Sunday 29
6 Cwm-Weeg
7 Cyfie Farm
10 Foel Ortho

34 Stockley Cottage

Monday 30
19 Llanstephan House

Tuesday 31
2 Ashford House

June

Saturday 4
35 Tan-y-Llyn
39 Welshpool's Secret Gardens

Sunday 5
6 Cwm-Weeg
9 Ffrwdgrech House
20 Llanwrtyd Gardens
26 The Neuadd
32 The Rock House
35 Tan-y-Llyn
39 Welshpool's Secret Gardens

Tuesday 7
2 Ashford House

Wednesday 8
31 Powis Castle Garden

Sunday 12
6 Cwm-Weeg
38 The Walled Garden

Tuesday 14
2 Ashford House

Saturday 18
4 Cil y Wennol

Sunday 19
3 Cartref
6 Cwm-Weeg
13 Glanusk

Tuesday 21
2 Ashford House

Sunday 26
6 Cwm-Weeg
11 Gilwern
16 Glyn Celyn House
29 Pont Faen House

Tuesday 28
2 Ashford House

July

Saturday 2
35 Tan-y-Llyn

Sunday 3
6 Cwm-Weeg
27 Pen-y-Maes
35 Tan-y-Llyn
37 Treberfydd

Tuesday 5
2 Ashford House

Thursday 7
10 Glansevern Hall Gardens

Friday 8
28 Pen-y-Maes (Evening)

Sunday 10
6 Cwm-Weeg
22 Lonicera

Tuesday 12
2 Ashford House

Sunday 17
6 Cwm-Weeg

Tuesday 19
2 Ashford House

Sunday 24
6 Cwm-Weeg

Tuesday 26
2 Ashford House

Sunday 31
6 Cwm-Weeg

August

Tuesday 2
2 Ashford House

Sunday 7
6 Cwm-Weeg
21 Llysdinam

Tuesday 9
2 Ashford House

Sunday 14
6 Cwm-Weeg

Tuesday 16
2 Ashford House

Sunday 21
6 Cwm-Weeg

Tuesday 23
2 Ashford House

Wednesday 24
18 Grandma's Garden

Sunday 28
6 Cwm-Weeg

Tuesday 30
2 Ashford House

September

Sunday 4
23 Maesfron Hall and Gardens

Tuesday 6
2 Ashford House

Sunday 11
16 Glyn Celyn House

Tuesday 13
2 Ashford House

Friday 16
12 Glansevern Hall Gardens

Tuesday 20
2 Ashford House

Tuesday 27
2 Ashford House

October

Saturday 15
8 Dingle Nurseries & Garden

Sunday 16
8 Dingle Nurseries & Garden

You are always welcome at an NGS garden

Gardens open to the public

2 Ashford House
8 Dingle Nurseries & Garden
12 Glansevern Hall Gardens
18 Grandma's Garden
31 Powis Castle Garden

By appointment only

5 Coity Mawr
17 Glynderyn
33 Rowan
36 Tawryn

Also open by Appointment ☎

1 Abernant
7 Cyfie Farm
39 Glandwr. Welshpool's Secret Gardens
21 Llysdinam
24 Mill Cottage
39 Oak Cottage, Welshpool's Secret Gardens
29 Pont Faen House
34 Stockley Cottage
35 Tan-y-Llyn
38 The Walled Garden

Meandering paths join different areas and give unexpected views within the garden . . . .

The Gardens

1 ABERNANT
Garthmyl SY15 6RZ. J A & B M Gleave, 01686 640494. *On the A483 Mid-way between Welshpool (9m) & Newtown (9m). 1¹/₂ m S of Garthmyl. Approached over steep humpback bridge, then straight ahead through gate. No parking for coaches.* Home-made teas. **Adm £3.50, chd free. Sun 24 Apr (11-5). Visitors also welcome by appt mid Apr to end July.**
Approx 3 acres incl cherry orchard, roses, knot garden, lavender, box hedging, rockery, pond, shrubs, ornamental trees, potager, raised specimen fern beds in natural setting. Examples of archaic sundials,

fossilised wood and stone heads. Additional woodland of 9-acres, pond and stream with borrowed views of the Severn Valley.

☕ ☎

2 ◆ ASHFORD HOUSE
Talybont-on-Usk LD3 7YR. Mrs E Anderson, 01874 676271. *6¹/₂ m SE of Brecon. Off A40 on B4558. 1m SE of Talybont-on-Usk.* **Adm £3, chd free. For other opening times and information, please phone.**
For NGS: Every Tues, April to Sept (2-6).
1-acre walled garden surrounded by woodland and wild garden approx 4 acres altogether. Mixed shrub and herbaceous borders; meadow garden and pond; alpine house and beds; vegetables. A relaxed plantsman's garden. Weekly openings mean visitors may enjoy a peaceful garden in its everyday state.

♿ 🏵 ⚘ ☎

BRYAN'S GROUND
See Herefordshire.

3 NEW CARTREF
Sarnau, Llanymynech SY22 6QL. Neil & Stella Townsend. *8m N of Welshpool. Take A483 from Welshpool towards Oswestry. Turn L after 6m at Ardleen, bear R then turn R towards Sarnau. Turn R after 1m. Continue for approx ¹/₂ m. Cartref is on L.* Home-made teas. **Adm £3, chd free. Suns 17 Apr; 22 May; 19 June (1-5).**
A modern cottage garden matured over three decades. Woodland, ponds, perennial borders, mobile topiary and a kitchen garden give yr-round interest and attract wildlife. Spring bulbs and tadpoles feature in April, pond side irises and dragon flies in June. Meandering paths join different areas and give unexpected views within the garden.

🏵 ⚘ ☕

4 CIL Y WENNOL
Berriew, Welshpool SY21 8AZ. Willie & Sue Jack. *5m SW of Welshpool. Berriew is off the A483 Welshpool to Newtown rd. By Berriew School take B4385 towards Castle Caereinion. Cil y Wennol is ³/₄ m along the B4385.* Home-made teas. **Adm £3, chd free. Sat 18 June (2.30-5).**
3¹/₂ -acre established garden set around Tudor cottage (not open). Long curving drive, through terraced landforms leads to front garden of traditional formal cottage design with

more recent influences. Rear gardens: sweeping array of new-style prairie planting, spectacular views, enclosed vegetable garden, croquet lawn. Crescent-shaped hedges, slate walls, amphitheatre steps and congruent sculptures. Some steep steps.

🏵 ☕ ☎

5 COITY MAWR
Talybont-on-Usk LD3 7YN. Mr & Mrs William Forwood, 01874 676664. *6m SE of Brecon. Leave Talybont village on B4558 towards Brecon. Approx ¹/₂ m at pink cottages take L signed Talybont reservoir, then 1st R up to rd junction; turn L to Coity Mawr at top on R.* **Adm £3, chd free. Visitors welcome by appt Spring to Autumn, groups also welcome, please telephone first.**
4¹/₂ acres at 850ft created over 17yrs; work still in progress incl Cornus Wood. Terraced with spectacular view of Black Mountains across Usk valley. Mature trees, unusual plants and shrubs; rose and water gardens; parterre; willow arbour.

♿ 🏵 ☎

6 CWM-WEEG
Dolfor, Newtown SY16 4AT. Dr W Schaefer & Mr K D George. *4¹/₂ m SE of Newtown. Take A489 E from Newtown for 1¹/₂ m, turn R towards Dolfor. After 2m turn L down farm track, signposted at entrance.* Light Refreshments. **Adm £3.50, chd free. Suns, 22 May to 28 Aug; (2-5).**
2¹/₂ -acre garden set within 22 acres of wild flower meadows and bluebell woodland with stream centred around C15 farmhouse (open by prior arrangement). Formal garden in English landscape tradition with vistas, grottos, lawns and extensive borders terraced with stone walls, translates older garden vocabulary into an innovative C21 concept.

☕

7 CYFIE FARM
Llanfihangel, Llanfyllin SY22 5JE. Group Captain Neil & Mrs Claire Bale, 01691 648451, info@cyfiefarm.co.uk. *6m SE of Lake Vyrnwy. B490 N from Llanfyllin, turn L B4393 after ¹/₂ m towards Lake Vyrnwy. After approx 4m, L B4382 signed Llanfihangal/Dolanog. Through Lllanfihangal ¹/₂ m towards Dolanog, 1st L, 3rd on L.* Light Refreshments. **Adm £3.50, chd free. Sun 29 May (5.30-8.30). Visitors also welcome by appt Mar - Sept 1st.**

Enjoy an evening with wine and music in our beautiful 1-acre hillside garden with spectacular views of Vyrnwy valley and Welsh hills. Live sculpture event. Linger over the roses or wander through the woodland garden with rhododendrons and bluebell banks. Many places to sit and contemplate the stunning views to the sound of peaceful Welsh Music. Sculptures by local artist as garden exhibits. Live sculpture event. Plant Sale. Spectacular views. Featured in Llanfyllin Chronicle. Live feed into visitmidwales.co.uk activities website.

🛏️ ⊛ 🛏️ ☕ ☎

8 ◆ DINGLE NURSERIES & GARDEN
Welshpool SY21 9JD. Mr & Mrs D Hamer, 01938 555145, www.dinglenurseries.co.uk. *2m NW of Welshpool. Take A490 towards Llanfyllin and Guilsfield. After 1m turn L at sign for Dingle Nurseries & Garden.* **Adm £3.50, chd free.**
For NGS: Sats & Suns 14, 15 May; 15, 16 Oct (9-5). For other opening times and information, please phone or see garden website.
RHS recomended 4.5 acre garden on S-facing site, sloping down to lakes surrounded by year round interest. Beds mostly colour themed with a huge variety of rare and unusual trees, ornamental shrubs and herbaceous plants. Set in hills of mid Wales this beautiful and well known garden attracts visitors from Britain and abroad. Featured in Discovering Welsh Gardens by Stephen Anderton, local & national press. Open all year (9-5) except 24 Dec to 2 Jan. Featured in Shropsire Life, RHS Garden Magazine.

🛏️ ⊛ ☕ ☎

9 FFRWDGRECH HOUSE
Brecon LD3 8LB. Mr & Mrs Michael Evans. *¹/₂ m W of Brecon. Enter Brecon from A40 bypass. Take 3rd turning on R, Ffrewdgrech Road. In ³/₄ m at oak gate, Lodge on L.* Home-made teas. **Adm £3, chd free. Sun 5 June (2-5).**
7-acre Victorian pleasure garden, lake, specimen trees incl fine examples of ginkgo, swamp cyprus, davidia involucrata, subtropical shrubs, rhododendrons and azaleas. Beautiful stream and waterfall, woodland walks. Views of Brecon Beacons.

♿ 🛏️ ☕

The Rock House

10 NEW FOEL ORTHO
Penybontfawr SY10 0HU. Eddie Matthews & Jenny Miller, www.farmhouseinwales.com or www.bunkhouseheaven.com. *16m W of Oswestry. 2m S of Penybontfawr. From Penybontfawr take rd towards Lake Vyrnwy. After ¹/₄ m bear L up steep hill then along side of valley for 1m. Sign on LHS follow rough farm track.* Home-made teas. **Adm £3.50, chd free. Sun 29 May (2-5).**
Exciting, eccentric, steeply terraced hillside garden. Paths through lovely planting wind upwards past water, through turrets, boules arena to 'pueblo' all set in remote idyllic landscape. Live Music. Featured in local press. Due to steep steps children must be supervised by an adult at all times.

☕

11 NEW GILWERN
Beulah LD5 4YG. Mrs Penelope Bourdillon. *2m N of Beulah. From Builth Wells take A483 towards Llandovery. After 9m at Beulah take 2nd R to Newbridge-on-Wye B3458 (by Trout Inn) then take 3rd turn on L (marked no through rd) at give way sign with painted blue pole. Follow rd up hill to R & after 1m turn L at T-junction. After 600yds drive forks down to L.* Cream teas. **Adm £3, chd free. Sun 26 June (2-5).**
Terraced 2-acre garden in the making, on very challenging site situated on steep rocky hillside in the beautiful and secluded Cammarch Valley. Roses, herbaceous and shrub borders. Fine walling and gate posts making use of stone found in the garden. Box house. Woodland area (with adventure playground).

♿ 🛏️ ☕

12 ◆ GLANSEVERN HALL GARDENS
Berriew, Welshpool SY21 8AH. Thomas Family, 01686 640644, www.glansevern.co.uk. *5m SW of Welshpool. On A483 at Berriew. Signposted.* Light Refreshments. **Adm £6, chd free. For NGS: Fri 13 May; Thur 7 July; Fri 16 Sept (12-5).**
Over 25 acres of glorious gardens surrounding a Greek revival house (not open). Lakeside walks, large walled garden divided into rooms. Ornamental fountains, huge rock garden, orangery, follies and sculptures. Many unusual trees, bird hide on banks of R Severn and ornamental shelters. Herbaceous borders, pergola and orangery. Colour throughout yr. Garden open Thursday, Friday and Saturday and Bank Holiday Mondays from May to end of Sept.

♿ 🛏️ ☕ ☎

13 GLANUSK
Llanfrynach, Brecon LD3 7UY. Mike & Lorraine Lewis. *1¹/₂ m SE of Brecon. Leave A40 signed Llanfrynach, Pencelli. Cross narrow bridge (R Usk), 40 metres on R.* Home-made teas. **Adm £4, chd free. Sun 19 June (2-5).**
1¹/₂ -acre garden on the Usk. The steep N-facing river bank has prairie and perennial planting criss-crossed with paths.The remains of an orchard and a small wood contain some specimen trees. The reorganised shrubbery and formal garden incl borders, box balls, a rose pergola, garden and walk.

14 GLANWYE
Builth Wells LD2 3YP. Mr & Mrs H Kidston. *2m SE Builth Wells. From Builth Wells on A470, after 2m R at Lodge Gate. From Llyswen on A470, after 6m L at Lodge Gate.* Home-made teas. **Adm £3, chd free. Sun 15 May (2-5).**
Large Edwardian garden, spectacular rhododendrons, azaleas. Herbaceous borders, extensive yew hedges, lawns, long woodland walk with bluebells and other woodland flowers. Magnificent views of upper Wye Valley.

15 GLIFFAES COUNTRY HOUSE HOTEL
Gliffaes Rd, Crickhowell NP8 1RH. Mr & Mrs N Brabner & Mr & Mrs J C Suter, www.gliffaes.com. *2¹/₂ m NW of Crickhowell. 1m off A40.* Cream Teas. Afternoon tea at hotel. **Adm £3, chd free. Sun 22 May (2-5).**
Large garden; spring bulbs, azaleas and rhododendrons; ornamental pond; heathers, shrubs and ornamental trees; fine maples; superb position high above R Usk.

16 GLYN CELYN HOUSE
Felinfach, nr Brecon LD3 0TY. Mr & Mrs N Paravicini. *4m NE of Brecon. On A470 east of Brecon on hill above Felinfach.* Home-made teas. **Adm £4, chd free. Suns 26 June; 11 Sept (2-5).**
7-acre sloping garden still in the making after 14yrs. 2 streams supply water to fountains and lake. Mixed planting within yew and hornbeam hedges. Woodland walks lead to lake and unusual grotto. Well-established and newly planted trees. Pretty

kitchen garden with raised beds and rose and sweet pea covered arches. Glorious views over the Black Mountains.

17 GLYNDERYN
Milford Road, Newtown SY16 3HD. Janet & Frank Podmore, 01686 626745. *¹/₂ m W of Newtown. B4568 Newtown - Aberhafesp Rd. 1st gate past Dolerw Park Drive on L.* Home-made teas. **Adm £4.50 (incl home-made tea), chd free. Visitors welcome by appt** for small groups (max 20), March to end Sept.
Much loved secluded garden in decline, being lovingly restored by plant enthusiast. ¹/₄ -acre garden with long curved pergola for wisteria and clematis, raised alpine, herbaceous and rose beds. Small pond, trees, shrubs, camellias, azaleas, rhododendrons and bulbs begin colourful yr-round interest garden. Small fruit and vegetable area.

Inspiration for the senses, unique, fascinating, educational and fun . . .

18 ◆ GRANDMA'S GARDEN
Solstar, Plas Dolguog Estates, Machynlleth SY20 8UJ. Diana & Richard Rhodes, 01654 703338, diana.grandmasgarden@tiscali.co. uk. *1¹/₂ m E of Machynlleth. Turn L off A489 Machynlleth to Newtown rd. Follow brown tourist signs to Plas Dolguog Hotel.* **Adm £4, chd £1.50. For NGS: Wed 24 Aug (10-5.30).**
Inspiration for the senses, unique, fascinating, educational and fun. Strategic seating, continuous new attractions, wildlife abundant, 9 acres of peace. Sculptures, poetry arboretum. Seven sensory gardens, wildlife pond, riverside boardwalk, stone circle, labyrinth. Azaleas and bluebells in May. Children welcome,. Open all yr Sundays & Wednesdays. Featured on ITV Wales, A Little Piece of Paradise. David Bellamy Gold & Special Awards for conservation. Access statement available. Owner wheelchair user with assistance dog.

THE GRIGGS
See Herefordshire.

HILL HOUSE FARM
Knighton. See Herefordshire.

IVY COTTAGE
See Herefordshire.

LLANGEDWYN HALL
See North East Wales.

19 LLANSTEPHAN HOUSE
nr Llyswen, Powys LD3 0YR. Lord & Lady Milford. *10m SW of Builth Wells. Leave A470 at Llyswen onto B4350. 1st L after crossing river in Boughrood. Follow yellow signs. From Builth Wells leave A470 at Erwood Bridge. 1st L then follow signs.* Home-made teas. **Adm £3, chd free. Mon 30 May (2-5).**
Large garden with rhododendrons, azaleas, shrubs, water garden, shrub roses, walled kitchen garden, greenhouses and very fine specimen trees. Beautiful views of Wye Valley and Black Mountains.

LLANTHONY AND DISTRICT GARDENS
See Gwent.

GROUP OPENING

20 LLANWRTYD GARDENS
Llanwrtyd Wells LD5 4RG. John & Rosemary Rowlands. *13m SW of Builth Wells. 11m NE of Llandovery on A483.* Home-made teas. **Combined adm £5, chd free. Sun 5 June (2-5).**

BRYNTEG
Verity & Arthur Price

LLYS-Y-COED
Kathy & Paul Biggs

MEADOW WAY
John & Rosemary Rowlands

Lovely diverse group of gardens in the smallest town in Britain! **Brynteg**: a small terraced garden with big impact. Great use of interesting plants and eye level alpine area. Clever use of the natural slope. **Llys-y-Coed**: Fascinating, well designed garden of many areas. Secret garden, children's play area. Seating spots to admire well planted borders, ducks, fabulous vegetable patch. Polytunnel. Newly planted orchard. Great use of materials, incl railway platform edging, brick, stone, wood and gravel. Work in progress. **Meadow Way**: Wildlife friendly 1¹/₃ -acre garden with paths through meadow areas. Lawns, shrubs, perennials, mature trees, an old apple orchard and hazel tunnel. Work in progress to create herb garden. Spectacular views.

  🚻 🐕 ✿ ☕

LLWYNCELYN
See Ceredigion/Cardiganshire.

21▶ LLYSDINAM
Newbridge-on-Wye LD1 6NB. Sir John & Lady Venables-Llewelyn & Llysdinam Charitable Trust, 01597 860190, elster@f25.com. *5m SW of Llandrindod Wells. Turn W off A470 at Newbridge-on-Wye; turn R immed after crossing R Wye; entrance up hill.* Cream teas. **Adm £3, chd free. Suns 22 May; 7 Aug (2-6).** Visitors also welcome by appt April to Sept, groups also welcome. Please ring first.
Large garden. Azaleas, rhododendrons, water garden and herbaceous borders, shrubs, woodland garden, Victorian kitchen garden and greenhouses. Fine view of Wye Valley. Some gravel paths and slopes.

  🚻 🐕 ✿ ☕ 📞

22▶ LONICERA
Station Road, Talybont-on-Usk LD3 7JE. Gareth & Eirona Davies. *5¹/₂ m S of Brecon. Off A40 signed to Talybont-on-Usk. 1st house on L after crossing R Usk.* Teas at Usk Hotel. **Adm £3, chd free (share to Arthritis Research Campaign). Sun 10 July (2-5).**
¹/₂ -acre garden of varied interest incorporating several small feature gardens. Rose garden; heather garden with conifers; herbaceous and woody perennials; colourful summer bedding displays; window boxes, hanging baskets and patio tubs forming extensive frontage display; greenhouses.

  🚻 ✿ ☕

23▶ MAESFRON HALL AND GARDENS
Trewern, Welshpool SY21 8EA. Dr & Mrs TD Owen. *4m E of Welshpool. On A458 Shrewsbury to Welshpool road.* Home-made teas. **Adm £4, chd free. Suns 3 Apr; 4 Sept (2-5).**
Georgian house (not open) built in Italian villa style set in 4 acres of S-facing gardens on lower slopes of Moel-y-Golfa with panoramic views of The Long Mountain. Terraces, walled kitchen garden, tropical garden, restored Victorian conservatories,

tower and shell grotto. Woodland and parkland walks with wide variety of trees. Some gravel paths.

  🚻 🐕 ☕

24▶ MILL COTTAGE
Abbeycwmhir LD1 6PH. Mr & Mrs B D Parfitt, 01597 851935. *8m N of Llandrindod Wells. Turn L off A483 1m N of Crossgates roundabout, then 3¹/₂ m on L, signed Abbeycwmhir.* Limited parking. **Adm £3, chd free. Mon 2 May (12-6).** Visitors also welcome by appt Apr - Sept. Please ring first.
¹/₃ -acre streamside garden in spectacular valley setting on the Glyndwr Way, consisting mainly of mature, rare and unusual trees and shrubs, particularly interesting to the plantsman. Rockery with numerous ericaceous plants and interesting water feature. Beautiful church and Abbey ruins nearby.

  ✿ 🛏 ☕ 📞

25▶ MOOR PARK
Llanbedr NP8 1SS. Leolin Price. *2m NE of Crickhowell. Turn off A40 at fire stn in Crickhowell; continue 2m, signed Llanbedr.* Home-made teas. **Adm £3, chd free. Sun 1 May (2-5).**
5-acre organic kitchen garden with trained figs, apricots, pears and apples. Spring bulbs, lawns, borders, roses. Lake with swans, water garden, tree house and island theatre. Great trees and woodland walk.

  🚻 🐕 ☕

26▶ THE NEUADD
Llanbedr, nr Crickhowell NP8 1SP. Robin & Philippa Herbert. *1m NE of Crickhowell. Leave Crickhowell by Llanbedr Rd. At junction with Great Oak Rd bear L and continue up hill for 0.9m, garden on L. Ample parking.* Home-made teas. **Adm £3, chd free. Sun 5 June (2-5).**
Robin and Philippa Herbert have worked on the restoration of the garden at the Neuadd since 1999 and have planted a wide range of unusual trees and shrubs in the dramatic setting of the Brecon Beacons National Park. One of the major features is the walled garden, which has both traditional and decorative planting of fruit, vegetables and flowers. There is also a woodland walk with ponds, streams and a formal garden with flowering terraces. Philippa uses wheelchair and nearly all garden accessible, however some paths are quite steep.

  🚻 🐕 ☕

THE PANT
See Gwent.

27▶ PEN-Y-MAES
Hay-on-Wye HR3 5PP. Sh,n Egerton. *1m SW of Hay-on-Wye. On B4350 towards Brecon.* Home-made teas. **Adm £4, chd free. Sun 3 July (2-5).**
2-acre garden incl mixed herbaceous borders; young topiary; walled formal kitchen garden; shrub, modern and climbing roses, peony borders, espaliered pears. Fine mulberry. Beautiful dry stone walling and mature trees. Great double view of Black Mountains and the Brecon Beacons. Emphasis on foliage shape and colour.

  🚻 🐕 ✿ ☕

28▶ NEW PEN-Y-MAES
Llansantffraid SY22 6TL. Mrs Heike O'Hanlon. *From Llansantffraid towards Oswestry on A495 after delimit 3rd turn L.* Light refreshments. **Adm £3, chd free. Evening Opening Fri 8 July (6-8).**
Landscape garden with borrowed views incl Rodney's Pillar, Offa's Dyke, Wellingtonia and lebanon cedar, other specimen trees. Roses. Semi walled vegetable garden. Pool which can be used by children accompanied by adult. Cobbled yard.

  🚻 🐕 ☕

> Floriferous arches and gazebos lead from shady, ferny corners to deep borders . . .

29▶ NEW PONT FAEN HOUSE
LD7 1LA. Mr John & Mrs Brenda Morgan, 01547 520847. *S of Knighton off Ludlow Rd. W from Ludlow on A4113 into Knighton. 1st L after 20mph sign before school.* Home-made teas. **Adm £3, chd free. Sun 26 June (2-5).** Visitors also welcome by appt April to Sept.
Colourful ¹/₂ -acre garden, full of flowers surrounds house on edge of town. Paths through floriferous arches and gazebos lead from shady, ferny corners to deep borders around lawns. Trees incl specimen beech, shrubs, perennials and annuals, fish pond and small vegetable plot. Seats with vistas through garden to hills beyond.

  🚻 🐕 ✿ ☕ 📞

Tan-y-Llyn

30 NEW PONTSIONI HOUSE
Aberedw, Builth Wells LD2 3SQ.
Mrs Jonathan reeves. *3m SE of Builth Wells. On B4567 between Erwood Bridge & Aberedw on Radnorshire side of R Wye.* Home-made teas. **Adm £3, chd free.**
Sat 21 May (2-6).
Approx 1-acre mainly created over the last 8yrs, with wide views of the Wye Valley and has rocky woods rising above it. Lawns, ha-ha, shrubs and herbaceous borders, terrace, natural rockery and young rhododendron walk. Also walks along the old railway line and up to the adjoining Aberedw rocks (common land).

31 ◆ POWIS CASTLE GARDEN
Welshpool SY21 8RF. National Trust, 01938 551929, www.nationaltrust.org.uk. *1m S of Welshpool. Turn off A483 ³/₄ m out of Welshpool, up Red Lane for ¹/₄ m.* **Adm £8.20, chd £4.10.**
For NGS: Wed 8 June (11-5.30).
For other opening times and information, please phone or see garden website.
Laid out in early C18 with finest remaining examples of Italian terraces in Britain. Richly planted herbaceous borders; enormous yew hedges; lead statuary, large wild flower areas. One of the National Trust's finest gardens. National Collection of *Laburnum*. Short tours 'behind the scenes'

throughout day by careership gardeners. Motorised wheelchairs only permitted on top terrace due to steep gradient of paths.

32 THE ROCK HOUSE
Llanbister LD1 6TN. Jude Boutle & Sue Cox. *10m N of Llandrindod Wells. From Llandrindod Wells, turn R off A483 at Llanbister onto B4356. Go through village, past school & war memorial on L, up short hill, over cattle grid and turn immed R up track (take care). Park on track.* Home-made teas. **Adm £3.50, chd free.**
Sun 5 June (2-5).
An acre of informal hillside garden at 1000ft, with sweeping views over Radnorshire Hills, managed using organic principles. Created over 13yrs from a rocky clay-covered field with plantings of hebes bamboos and hardy perennials. Raised beds, bog gardens with raised walkway, dry shady borders, gravel garden, pond and grazed bluebell meadow and laburnum arch.

33 ROWAN
Welshpool SY21 8HJ. Tinty Griffith, 01938 552197. *2m E of Welshpool. From Welshpool take B4388 (Buttington to Montgomery). At Leighton turn L after school then at church straight ahead between stone pillars. 1st on R, parking in churchyard.* Tea & cake. **Adm £3,**

chd free. Visitors welcome by appt April to mid July (2-5).
1 acre of traditional plantsman's country garden with village church as backdrop. Discrete paths meander around island beds and mixed borders with irises, roses, unusual and rare plants, trees dripping with climbers and a series of planted pools and marshy areas. Lovely views over Montgomeryshire countryside and the borrowed landscape. Gravelled entrance, level grassed areas, some slopes.

STAUNTON PARK
See Herefordshire.

34 STOCKLEY COTTAGE
Erwood, Nr Builth Wells LD2 3TQ.
Mr & Mrs Brian Hepton, 01982 560367, brianhepton@btinternet.com. *7m SE of Builth Wells. 2m from Llyswen on A470. On L ¹/₂ m from Llangoed Hall.* Home-made teas at local school.
Adm £4, chd Free. Sun 29 May (2-5). Visitors also welcome by appt.
Surrounding old Welsh stone built drinking house; 2-acre garden in woodland setting, opening for the late spring bulbs and naturalised bluebells. Incl many specimen trees, Japanese maples, cornus and magnolias. Landscaped with shrubs and perennials selected for their variegation of coloured leaf combinations. Wildlife pond, collections of hostas, ferns auriculars and succulents. Rare breed bantams running around make a picture perfect, fascinating Wye Valley garden. Willowcraft demonstration. Plants for sale.

35 TAN-Y-LLYN
Meifod SY22 6YB. Callum Johnston & Brenda Moor, www.tanyllyn-nursery.co.uk. *1m SE of Meifod. From Oswestry on A495 turn L in village, cross R Vyrnwy & climb hill for ¹/₂ m. From Welshpool on A490 look for Meifod sign on L just past Groesllwyd.* Home-made teas.
Adm £3, chd free (share to Montgomrtyshire M.S). Sats & Suns 7, 8 May; 4, 5 June; 2, 3 July (2-5). Visitors also welcome by appt.
Set in a quiet valley above Meifod in the old county of Montgomeryshire, Tan-y-llyn sits on a steep hillside surrounded by conifers, broadleaves

Be tempted by a plant from a plant stall

and pastureland. This natural garden grows into the landscape: wild at the edges, but tamer near the house with gravel, terracotta and a raised herb garden. Landscape, flora and abstract painting exhibitions by Louise Edwards (May), Joy Hopson (June) and Joan Baker (July). Acappella music from Nostalgia (July).

36 TAWRYN
6 Baskerville Court, Clyro HR3 5SS. Chris & Clive Young, 01497 821939. *1m NW of Hay-on-Wye. Leave A438 Hereford to Brecon rd at Clyro. Baskerville Court is behind church and Baskerville Arms Hotel. Please park in village.* Teas in the garden. Adm £2.50, chd free. Visitors welcome by appt.
1-acre steeply-terraced garden on an oriental theme. Come and see the Ghost Dragon and the River of Slate. Lots of new crooked paths and planting. Stunning views of the Black Mountains and Kilvert's Church. Colour all yr. Talks by Chris on NGS and its history to garden groups, WI etc. Please call to book appointment.

37 TREBERFYDD
Bwlch, nr Brecon LD3 7PX. David Raikes, www.treberfydd.com. *6¹/₂ m E of Brecon. From Crickhowell leave A40 at Bwlch and take B4560 then L for Penorth. From Brecon leave A40 at Llanhamlach. 2¹/₂ m sign for Llangasty Church, entrance over cattle grid. Tel 01874 730205/07796 897540 or email david.raikes@btinternet.com for further directions.* Home-made teas. Adm £3, chd free. Sun 3 July (1-5).
10 acres of lawns, peaceful woodland walks, rose beds and herbaceous borders designed in 1852 by W A Nesfield for imposing Victorian Gothic house. Cedar of Lebanon 155 yrs old.

Yews, holly oaks, copper beech, orchards and rockery. Wonderful position nr Llangorse Lake. Beacons nursery within walled garden. Tours of the house.

UPPER TAN HOUSE
See Herefordshire.

Come and see the Ghost Dragon and the River of Slate . . .

38 THE WALLED GARDEN
Knill, nr Presteigne LD8 2PR. Dame Margaret Anstee, 01544 267411. *3m SW of Presteigne. On B4362 Walton-Presteigne rd. In Knill village turn R over cattle grid, keep R down drive.* Adm £3, chd free. Suns 10 Apr; 12 June (2-5). Visitors also welcome by appt, please ring first.
4 acres: walled garden; river, bog garden and small grotto; primulas; over 100 varieties of roses, shrub, modern and climbing; peonies; mixed and herbaceous borders; many varieties of shrubs and mature trees; lovely spring garden. Nr C13 church in beautiful valley. Some narrow paths and uneven ground.

GROUP OPENING

39 WELSHPOOL'S SECRET GARDENS
Welshpool SY21 7JP. *Off A458 in Welshpool. Oak Cottage is off the High St, Church Bank leads on to Salop Rd and Glandwr is on Salop Rd opp Peates the undertaker. Follow signs all locations.* Home-made teas

at 1 Church Bank. Adm £4, chd free. Sun & Mon 24, 25 Apr; Sat & Sun 4, 5 June (2-5).

NEW 1 CHURCH BANK
Mel and Heather Parkes

GLANDWR
Janet & Peter Milner
Visitors also welcome by appt.
01938 556720
peter.ribenco@btinternet.com

OAK COTTAGE
Tony & Margaret Harvey
Visitors also welcome by appt
Months of April, May and June (1-5). 01938 559087
tony@montgomeryshire.eu

Three very different hidden gardens offering seclusion, plantsmanship and lovely surprises at every turn! Glandwr is a hidden town garden with beautiful planting. Figs and grapes share a sunny courtyard with a pond. Circle of specimen trees shelters a private glade while a circular woodland path discloses borrowed views of Long Mountain. Georgian wharf on the Montgomery Canal is another feature of this unusual and surprising garden. Oak Cottage is a plantsman's small garden providing an oasis of green in the town centre. Gravel paths and stepping stones meander through a wide variety of plants, including unusual species. Alpines are a favourite (more enthusiasm than knowledge!) 1 Church Bank is a jewel in the town. Gothic arch over a zig zag path leads to exotic arbours in the intimate rear garden of an old town house. The sound of water fills the air and unusual plants fill the space. Selection of plants for sale.

WESTONBURY MILL WATER GARDEN
Pembridge. See Herefordshire.

Powys County Volunteers

County Organisers
South Sarah Lee, Tredwern, Llandefalle, Brecon LD3 5PP, 01874 754627, sarahlee@berringtons.com
North Christine Scott, Bryn-y-Llidiart, Cefn Coch, Llanrhaeadr ym Mochnant, Oswestry SY10 0BP, 01691 780080, christinemargaretscott@yahoo.com

County Treasurer
Gwyneth Jackson-Jones, Bryn yr Aur, Delwyn Lane, Llanfyllin SY22 5LB, 01691 648578, g.jackson-jones@tiscali.co.uk

Publicity
North Group Captain Neil Bale, Cyffie Farm, Llanfihangle, Llanfyllin SY22 5JE, 01691 648451, info@cyfiefarm.co.uk

Assistant County Organisers
North Penny Davies, Plas Derwen, Llansantffraid, Powys SY22 6SX, 01691 828373, digbydavies@aol.com
South Shan Egerton, Pen-y-Maes, Hay-on-Wye HR3 5PP, 01497 820423, sre@waitrose.com

Visit the website for latest information

Early Openings 2012
Don't forget early planning for 2012

Gardens across the country open from early January onwards – before the new Yellow Book is published – with glorious displays of colour including hellebores, aconites, snowdrops and carpets of spring bulbs.

Bedfordshire

Sun 29 January
King's Arms Garden

Buckinghamshire

Sun 19 February
Higher Denham Gardens

Sun 26 February
Magnolia House (see Grange Drive Wooburn)
Quainton Gardens

Cornwall

Sat 11, Suns 19, 26 February
Coombegate Cottage

Cumbria

Sun 19 February
Summerdale House

Devon

Suns 1, 8, 15, 22, 29 January & 5, 12, 19, 26 February
Sherwood

Suns 5, 12, 19 February
Little Cumbre

Sun 5, Thur 16 February
Cherubeer Gardens

Sats, Suns 18, 19, 25, 26 February
Pikes Cottage

Dorset

Sat 25, Sun 26 February
Snape Cottage Plantsman's Garden

Gloucestershire North & Central

Sun 12, Sat 18, Suns 19, 26 February
Kempsford Manor

Suns 12, 19 February
Trench Hill

Gwynedd

Sat 11 February
Penrhyn Castle

Hampshire

Sun 19 February
Bramdean House

Thur, Fri, Sun 23, 24, 26 February
Little Court

Kent

Sun 19 February
Mere House

Sat 25, Sun 26, Wed 29 February
Yew Tree Cottage

Lancashire

Suns 12, 19, 26 February
Weeping Ash

Lincolnshire

Sat 25, Sun 26 February
21 Chapel Street

Northamptonshire

Sun 26 February
Jericho

Nottinghamshire

Sun 22 January
The Beeches

Somerset & Bristol

Sun 5 February
East Lambrook Manor Gardens

Suns 5, 12 February
Rock House

Surrey

Sun 12 February
Gatton Park

Sussex

Tues, Weds, Thurs 14, 15, 16, 21, 22, 23 February
Pembury House

Warwickshire

Sun 19 February
Ragley Hall Gardens

Wiltshire

Sats, Suns 11, 12, 18, 19 February
Lacock Abbey Gardens

Sun 19 February
Avon Cottage

Sun, Mon 19, 20 February
Boscombe Village Gardens

Yorkshire

Wed 22 February
Austwick Hall

You are always welcome at an NGS garden

Garden Visiting Around the World

Heading off on holiday? Whether you're planning to travel a short distance or much further afield you may be going to a country where some truly fantastic gardens can be visited for the benefit of charity.

America

GARDEN CONSERVANCY
Publication Open Days Directory
W www.gardenconservancy.org
Visit America's very best rarely seen private gardens. Open Days is a national program of The Garden Conservancy, a non-profit organisation dedicated to preserving America's gardening heritage.

VIRGINIA'S HISTORIC GARDEN WEEK
16 – 23 April 2011
W www.vagardenweek.org
Every year Virginia plays host to Historic Garden Week and 2011 represents the 78th anniversary. Visitors will be able to step through the gates of more than 250 of Virginia's most beautiful gardens, homes and historic landmarks during 'America's Largest Open House'. Historic Garden Week is the oldest and largest statewide house and garden tour event in the USA.

Australia

AUSTRALIA'S OPEN GARDEN SCHEME
Contact Richard Barley
E national@opengarden.org.au
W www.opengarden.org.au
Around 600 inspiring gardens drawn from every Australian state and territory including tropical gardens, arid-zone gardens and gardens featuring Australia's unique flora.

Belgium

JARDINS OUVERTS DE BELGIQUE – OPEN TUINEN VAN BELGIË
Publication Catalogue of private Belgian Open Gardens, published annually in March
Contact Dominique Petit-Heymans
E info@jardinsouverts.be
W www.jardinsouverts.be
A non-profit organization founded in 1994.

Over 200 remarkable private gardens throughout Belgium open to members.
Membership of €20 entitles you to the full-colour yearly agenda, comprising photograph, description, opening dates and access plan of the gardens.
Most of the proceeds from entry fees support charities chosen by garden owners.

France

JARDINS ET SANTE
E jardinsetsante@wanadoo.fr
W www.jardins-sante.org
Founded in 2004, Jardins et Santé is a charitable voluntary association with humanitarian aims.
Increasing numbers of gardens open each year across many regions of France.
Entry often includes guided tours, exhibitions and concerts. Funds raised from visitor entry fees help finance scientific research in the field of mental illness and also contribute to developing the therapeutic role of the garden, particularly in hospitals and care centres.
Thanks to the generosity of the many visitors and garden owners in 2009, Jardins et Santé is proud to contribute to no less than 11 therapeutic garden projects in hospitals, clinics, mental health centres and retirement homes right across France. The 2010 grant will be awarded for clinical research into childhood migraine.

Japan

THE N.G.S. JAPAN
Contact Tamie Taniguchi
E tamieta@syd.odn.ne.jp
W www.ngs-jp.org
The N.G.S. Japan was founded in 2001. Most of the proceeds from the entry fees support children's and welfare charities as nominated by owners and Japanese garden conservation. It has run a series of lectures entitled 'lifestyle & gardening with charity' since 2004.

Netherlands

NETHERLANDSE TUINENSTICHTING (DUTCH GARDEN SOCIETY, NTS)
Publication Open Tuinengids, published annually in March.
E info@tuinenstichting.nl
W www.tuinenstichting.nl
250 private gardens from all over Holland open on behalf of the Dutch Garden Trust. This is a not-for-profit organisation which was founded in 1980 to protect and restore Dutch gardening heritage consisting of gardens, public parks and cemeteries.

New Zealand

PRIVATE GARDENS OF NEW ZEALAND/GARDENS TO VISIT
W www.gardenstovisit.co.nz
The New Zealand website showcases private gardens of New Zealand which also operate B&Bs and farm stays. In addition some properties can also provide venues for private and corporate hospitality and weddings. Properties may also feature plant, art and sculpture sales, picnics, fishing. Please also check the website for details of guided, multi-day garden tours.

Scotland

GARDENS OF SCOTLAND
Contact Paddy Scott
T 0131 226 3714
E info@sgsgardens.co.uk
W www.gardensofscotland.org
Founded in 1931, Scotland's Gardens Scheme facilitates the opening of Scotland's finest gardens to the public. 40% of funds raised goes to charities nominated by each garden owner whilst 60% net goes to the SGS beneficiaries: The Queen's Nursing Institute Scotland, Maggie's Cancer Caring Centres, The Gardens Fund for the National Trust for Scotland, Perennial and The Royal Fund for Gardeners' Children.

Acknowledgements

Each year the NGS receives fantastic support from the community of garden photographers who donate and make available images of gardens for use in The Yellow Book and NGS publicity material. The NGS would like to thank them for their generous donations.

Images appearing in the listing section this year have been contributed by:

Mandy Bradshaw, David Burton, Brian & Nina Chapple, Leigh Clapp, Val Corbett, Ann Curtis, David Dixon, Carole Drake, Heather Edwards, Suzie Gibbons, Anne Green-Armytage, Linda Greening, Judy Goldhill, Gerry Harpur (Harpur Garden Library), Marcus Harpur (Harpur Garden Library), Helen Harrison, John Hinde, Jacqui Hurst, Rowan Isaac, Lu Jeffery, Louise Jolley, Andrea Jones, Andrew Lawson, Fiona Lea, Sarah Lee, Marianne Majerus, Fiona McLeod, Clive Nicholls, Abigail Rex, Rosalind Simon, Julia Stanley, Nicola Stocken Tomkins, Mike Vardy, Rachel Warne, Susie White.

We also thank the Garden Owners who have kindly submitted images of their gardens.

A catalogue record of this book is available from the British Library.

Typeset in Helvetica Neue font family by Chat Noir Design, France.

The papers used by the NGS are natural recyclable products made from wood grown in sustainable forests.

ISBN 978-1-905942-14-5
ISSN 1365-0572
EAN 9 781905 942008

© The National Gardens Scheme 2011
First published February 2011

If you require this information in alternative formats, please telephone 01483 211535 or email ngs@ngs.org.uk

National Plant Collections®
in the NGS

NCCPG

Approximately 100 of the gardens that open for The National Gardens Scheme are custodians of a National Plant Collection, although this may not always be noted in the garden descriptions. The county that appears after the garden name indicates the section of The Yellow Book where the entry can be found.

Plant Heritage (formerly known as NCCPG) is located at 12 Home Farm, Loseley Park, Guildford, Surrey GU3 1HS. Tel: 01483 447540 Website: www.plantheritage.com

AESCULUS, LIRIODENDRON
West Dean Gardens
Sussex

ANEMONE NEMOROSA CVS.
Kingston Lacy
Dorset

ANEMONE (JAPANESE) & HELLEBORUS
Broadview Gardens
Kent

ARBUTUS
Barton House
Warwickshire

ARUNCUS, FILIPENDULA
Windy Hall
Cumbria

ASPLENIUM SCOLOPENDRIUM, CYSTOPTERIS, DRYOPTERIS, OSMUNDA
Sizergh Castle
Cumbria

ASTER (AUTUMN FLOWERING)
The Picton Garden
Herefordshire

ASTER AMELLUS, A. CORDIFOLIUS, A. ERICOIDES
Upton House & Gardens
Warwickshire

ASTILBE, HYDRANGEA AND POLYSTICHUM (FERNS)
Holehird Gardens
Cumbria

ASTILBE, IRIS ENSATA, TULBAGHIA
Marwood Hill
Devon

BRUGMANSIA
Valducci Flower & Vegetable Gardens
Shropshire

BRUNNERA & OMPHALODES
Hearns House
Oxfordshire

BUDDLEJA, CLEMATIS VITICELLA
Longstock Park Water Garden
Hampshire

BUXUS
Ickworth House Park & Gardens
Suffolk

CAMELLIAS & RHODODENDRONS INTRODUCED TO HELIGAN PRE-1920
The Lost Gardens of Heligan
Cornwall

CAMPANULA
Burton Agnes Hall
Yorkshire

CAMPANULA - ALPINES
Langham Hall Gardens
Suffolk

CARPINUS, CORNUS, CORYLUS, COTONEASTER, HAMAMELIS
Hillier Gardens
Hampshire

CEANOTHUS
Eccleston Square, SW1
London

CENTAUREA
Bide-a-Wee Cottage
North East

CLEMATIS (SUBGENUS VIORNA)
Rosewood
Carmarthenshire & Pembrokeshire

CLEMATIS VITICELLA CVS., LAPAGERIA ROSEA (AND NAMED CULTIVARS)
Roseland House
Cornwall

CORNUS (EXCL C FLORIDA CVS.)
Newby Hall & Gardens
Yorkshire

CORYDALIS
164 Point Clear Road
Essex

CROCOSMIA
The Crocosmia Gardens
Lincolnshire

CYCLAMEN (EXCL PERSICUM CVS.)
Higher Cherubeer, Cherubeer Gardens
Devon

CYDONIA OBLONGA
Norton Priory Museum & Gardens
Cheshire

DAPHNE, GALANTHUS
Brandy Mount House
Hampshire

DICENTRA
Boundary Cottage
Yorkshire

EMBOTHRIUM, EUCRYPHIA, MAGNOLIA SPP. AND RHODODENDRON FORRESTII
Bodnant Garden
Gwynedd

EUCALYPTUS, PODOCARPACEAE & ARALIACEAE
Meon Orchard
Hampshire

EUONYMUS (DECIDUOUS)
East Bergholt Place – The Place for Plants
Suffolk

EUPHORBIAS
Firvale Allotment Garden
Yorkshire

FRAXINUS
The Quinta Arboretum Tatton Garden Society)
Cheshire

GEUMS (PROVISIONAL STATUS)
1 Brickwall Cottages
Kent

GUNNERA
The Mowle
Norfolk

HAMAMELIS
Swallow Hayes
Shropshire

HEDERA
Erddig Hall
NE Wales

HELENIUM
Yew Tree House Garden & Special Perennials Nursery
Cheshire

HELIOTROPIUM
Hampton Court Palace
London

HELIOTROPIUM ARBORESCENS CVS.
The Homestead
Leicestershire

HOSTA (MODERN HYBRIDS)
Cleave House
Devon

HYDRANGEA
The Garden House
NE Wales

JOVIBARBA (BRED BY CORNELIUS VERSTEEG)
Eggleston Village Gardens
North East

JUGLANS
Upton Wold
Gloucestershire North & Central

JUGLANS (INCL REGIA CVS.)
Wimpole Hall
Cambridgeshire

LABURNUM
Powis Castle Garden
Powys

LAMIUM
12 Darges Lane
Staffordshire

LEUCANTHEMUM SUPERBUM (CHRYSANTHEMUM MAXIMUM)
Shapcott Barton Estate
Devon

MALUS (ORNAMENTAL)
Barnards Farm
Gloucestershire North & Central

MUSCARI
16 Witton Lane
Norfolk

NYSSA, OXYDENDRUM
Exbury Gardens & Steam Railway
Hampshire

OENOTHERA (SPP.)
The Old Vicarage, Edington Gardens
Wiltshire

PAEONIA (PRE-1900 AND EARLY POST 1900 LACTIFLORA CVS.)
Green Cottage
Gloucestershire North & Central

PARIS
Crug Farm
Gwynedd

PATRINIA
The Hyde
Hampshire

PELARGONIUM, HEDERA
Ivybank, Broad Marston & Pebworth Gardens
Warwickshire

PENNISETUM, CEANOTHUS (DECIDUOUS CVS.) AND PHYGELIUS
Knoll Gardens
Dorset

PENSTEMON
Mews Cottage
Dorset

Froggery Cottage
Northamptonshire

PENSTEMON CVS. AND SALVIA (TENDER)
Kingston Maurward Gardens
Dorset

PLANTS SELECTED BY SIR FREDERICK STERN
Highdown Gardens
Sussex

POTENTILLA FRUTICOSA CVS.
Riverside Gardens at Webbs of Wychbold
Worcestershire

QUERCUS
Chevithorne Barton
Devon

RHAPIS (SPP. & CVS.)
Gwyndy Bach
Gwynedd

RHODODENDRON (GHENT AZALEAS)
Sheffield Park and Garden
Sussex

ROSA (PRE-1900)
Broomfield Hall
Derbyshire

ROSA (RAMBLING)
Moor Wood
Gloucestershire North & Central

SALVIA SPP.
2 Hillside Cottages
Hampshire

SAXIFRAGA (SUBSECTS. KABSCHIA & ENGLERIA)
Waterperry Gardens
Oxfordshire

SIBERIAN IRIS CVS.
Aulden Farm
Herefordshire

SORBUS
Ness Botanic Gardens
Cheshire

STEWARTIA
High Beeches
Sussex

STREPTOCARPUS
Dibleys Nurseries
NE Wales

STYRACACEAE (INCL HALESIA, PTEROSTYRAX, STYRAX, SINOJACKIA)
Holker Hall Gardens
Cumbria

YUCCA
Renishaw Hall Gardens
Derbyshire

Accommodation available at NGS Gardens

We feature here a list of NGS garden owners or county volunteers who offer accommodation. We have listed them by Yellow Book county and indicated whether they offer Bed & Breakfast (**B&B**), Self-Catering (**SC**), or Hotel (**H**) accommodation. You will also find a reference to accommodation in the main directory with their garden entry, unless the property owner is a member of the county team and does not open their garden.

Bedfordshire

LUTON HOO HOTEL, GOLF AND SPA
Luton Hoo, Luton LU1 3TQ
Elite Hotels (Rotherwick) Limited
T: 01582 734437
E: enquiries@lutonhoo.co.uk
W: www.lutonhoo.com
Accommodation: A luxury 5* hotel with 228 rooms, 18 hole golf course, magnificent spa with swimming pool and 1,065 acres of parkland and gardens created by the famous landscape designer Capability Brown.
H

Berkshire

LITTLECOTE HOUSE HOTEL
Hungerford RG17 0SU
Warner Leisure Hotels
T: 01488 682509
E: functions.littlecote@bourne-leisure.co.uk
W: www.littlecotehouse.co.uk
Accommodation: Commanding an excellent location in the heart of the Berkshire countryside, the hotel has 198 bedrooms including beautifully refurbished 'Historic' rooms and suites in the Old House, luxurious contemporary 'Signature' rooms and comfortable 'Ambassador' rooms in the new wing.
H

21 SIMONS LANE
Wokingham RG41 3HG
Jill Wheatley
T: 0118 377 4040
E: jill.wheatley@btinternet.com
Accommodation: This is a pretty bungalow with a comfortable double bedroom overlooking the front garden. Own bathroom and use of the sitting room and dining room. Meals may be taken in the garden. Further seating in the summer house. This quiet, tree lined road is about a mile Wokingham Town centre and there is a lovely country park with lakes nearby. There is easy access to the M4 motorway system. Parking is on the drive and a dog is allowed. (A small charge will be made. Please phone to discuss pet requirements.)
B&B

SUNNINGDALE PARK
Larch Avenue, Ascot SL5 0QE
De Vere - National School of Government
T: 0844 980 2318
E: sunningdale@deverevenues.co.uk

W: www.devere.co.uk
Accommodation: Set in 65 acres of landscaped gardens, Sunningdale Park is in the heart of Berkshire. 272 tastefully decorated bedrooms, all ensuite, are situated in buildings across the estate. Enjoy our outdoor pool, tennis and superb restaurant.
H

WHITEHOUSE FARM COTTAGE
Murrell Hill Lane, Binfield RG42 4BY
Louise Lusby
T: 01344 423688
E: garden.cottages@ntlworld.com
Accommodation: Whitehouse Farm Cottage is a listed timber-framed house with 2 self-contained buildings in the garden. Garden cottage is a small barn conversion with full height sitting room, dining and kitchen area below the mezzanine floor containing the double bedroom, off the main room is an en-suite shower room, cost per night £90 - £110 incl breakfast. Can also be used for self-catering if desired. The Forge is a delightful self-contained double room with en-suite facilities with a small inglenook fire place with period details showing its former use as a forge. The single room is in the main house with en-suite facilities, cost £65 - £75 incl breakfast
B&B, SC

Buckinghamshire

LAPLANDS FARM
Ludgershall Road, Brill, Aylesbury HP18 9TZ
Roger & Hilary Cope
T: 01844 237888
E: enquiries@intents-marquees.co.uk
W: www.laplands.clara.net
Accommodation: Laplands is set in a quiet rural location. A C16 heavily

beamed house, tastefully refurbished. All bedrooms ensuite. Pretty gardens with ponds and streams. Visitors are welcome to wander and enjoy all the rare breeds.
B&B

MAGNOLIA HOUSE
Grange Drive, Wooburn Green, High Wycombe HP10 0QD
Alan Ford
T: 01628 525818
E: sales@lanford.co.uk
W: www.cottageguide.co.uk
Accommodation: Flat over the garage with either 1 double bedroom or 1 double and one twin bedroom (with en suite), with bathroom, lounge, kitchen. Own entrance. On first floor overlooking garden. See Grange Drive Wooburn for details of garden
SC

Cambridgeshire

CHEQUER COTTAGE
43 Streetly End, West Wickham CB21 4RP
Mr & Mrs D Sills
T: 01223 891522
E: stay@chequercottage.com
W: www.chequercottage.com
Accommodation: Charming C15 cottage in Streetly End, a picturesque conservation hamlet of thatched properties. Spacious annexed accommodation with king size bed, fabulous shower room and loads of luxury. Overlooking the surrounding countryside and our cottage garden where you can relax and take tea beneath the walnut tree. Close to Newmarket races, country houses and gardens, Cambridge and much more. Also near by is Beeches renown nursery in Ashdon. Four Star with Silver award. Room rate £75 pn inclusive. See Streetly End Gardens for details of garden.
B&B

KENILWORTH SMALLHOLDING
West Drove North, Walton Highway, Wisbech PE14 7DP
Marilyn Clarke
T: 01945 881332
E: bookings@kenilworthhouse.co.uk
W: www.kenilworthhouse.co.uk
Accommodation: Self contained double rooms each with ensuite shower and each opening into the garden. Each unit contains a small fridge stocked for self catering breakfast, kettle, toaster, microwave

and hairdryer. Kenilworth is a working smallholding with sheep and goats. It provides a relaxing and tranquil environment. Parking spaces provided.
B&B, SC

MADINGLEY HALL
Madingley CB23 8AQ
University of Cambridge
T: 01223 746222
E: enquiry@madingleyhall.co.uk
W: www.madingleyhall.co.uk
Accommodation: Madingley Hall is a University owned estate set in 7 acres of delightful landscaped gardens, 3 miles west of Cambridge. The Hall has easy access from the M11, the A14 from the North and East, and the A428 from the West, with good links to the three London Airports and ample free car parking on site. The Hall is regularly used for educational and training events and has 61 ensuite bedrooms (13 twin and 48 single) which are welcoming, comfortably furnished and have garden views. Each room has a digital television, free broadband internet, direct dial phone, tea and coffee making facilities and a personal safe.
B&B

Carmarthenshire and Pembrokeshire

THE CORS
Newbridge Rd, Laugharne Carmarthenshire SA33 4SH
Nick Priestland
T: 01994 427219
E: nickpriestland@hotmail.com
W: www.the-cors.co.uk
Accommodation: Hidden from the main street in Laugharne, behind its exotically landscaped grounds, is The Cors, a very special and intimate restaurant and rooms. Converted from an exquisite Victorian house, chef-proprietor Nick Priestland has brought this building to life and created a charming blend of period pieces and modernist artworks both in his restaurant and the two en-suite guest rooms available.
B&B

HAYSTON FARMHOUSE
Merrion, Pembrokeshire, SA71 5EA
Nicky & Johnny Rogers
T: 01646 661462
E: haystonhouse@btinternet.com
W: www.haystonfarmhouse. co.uk
Accommodation: Spacious period

farmhouse with 2 acre garden within National Park. 1 Double bedroom with private bathroom and sitting room. Coach House with double bedroom, ensuite bathroom, kitchen/sitting room. Sumptuous beds and linen.
B&B, SC

THE OLD VICARAGE
Llangeler, Carmarthenshire SA44 5EU
Mr & Mrs J C Harcourt
T: 01559 371168
Accommodation: Cottage attached to main house. 1 double bedroom + cot for child or single bed. Large lounge with dining facilities, large wood burner, logs free. Ensuite shower WC etc. Fully fitted kitchen.
SC

PANTYFEDWEN
Drefelin, Drefach Felindre, Llandysul Carmarthenshire SA44 5XB
Steven & Viki Harwood
T: 01559 371807
E: steven@harwoodsartsandcrafts. co.uk
W: harwoodsartsandcrafts. co.uk
Accommodation: This very informal garden combines a small water garden and a larger terraced hill garden, with clearly defined areas for sitting and enjoying the beautiful views. For the sure footed visitor.
B&B

Y BWTHYN BACH AT DYFFRYN FERNANT
Llanychaer, Fishguard, Pembrokeshire SA65 9SP
Christina Shand
T: 01348 811282
E: christina.shand@virgin.net
W: www.genuslocus.net
Accommodation: Cosy one roomed converted barn in the heart of the garden with wood burning stove. Sleeps 4. Secluded, romantic and peaceful.
SC

Cheshire

HILLTOP
Flash Lane, Prestbury SK10 4ED
Martin & Clare Gardner
T: 01625 829940
E: enquiries@hilltopcountryhouse. co.uk
W: www.hilltopcountryhouse. co.uk
Accommodation: Beautiful 17th century house with 5 acres of gardens to explore. Woodland walk,

Herbaceous borders, Ponds and far reaching views of Pennines. 4 elegant en-suite rooms (two on ground floor) with TV, Tea / Coffee, and wi-fi. AA 4Star highly commended. Ideal base for Cheshire / Peak District visit. Home or local produce, and a warm welcome. Visitors book full of superlatives.
B&B

ONE HOUSE LODGE
Buxton New Road, Rainow
SK11 0AD
Louise Baylis
T: 01625 427087
E: louisebaylis@tiscali.co.uk
W: www.onehouselodgebandb. co.uk
Accommodation: Luxury bungalow set in gardens with stunning views. See website for details.
B&B

Cornwall

THE BARN HOUSE
Higher Penhalt, Poundstock
EX23 0DG
TJ & S Dingle
T: 01288 361365
E: tdingle@toucansurf.com
Accommodation: A comfortable and spacious apartment for two close to the coast path and beaches. A cot or bed are available for small children. Access to the garden and flower rich meadow. Plenty of walking opportunities See Poundstock Gardens for details of garden
SC

BOCONNOC HOLIDAYS
The Estate Office, Boconnoc, Lostwithiel PL22 0RG
Mrs Anthony Fortescue
T: 01208 872507
E: adgfortescue@btinternet.com
W: www.boconnocenterprises. co.uk
Accommodation: The marvel of the Boconnoc Estate today is that it is a world apart, a hidden gem in east Cornwall but only 20 minutes away from many holiday attractions and beaches. There are two self catering cottages situated in the Stable Yard. The Head Grooms sleeps 4/6 with one double room and adjoining shower room and one twin bedded en suite. Large sitting/dining room downstairs, log burner and separate kitchen. Grooms sleeps 6/8 with three twin bedded rooms en suite, one upstairs along with

sitting/dining/kitchen with views of the Church and park. Double sofa beds are available, if required. Dogs welcome on leads. Ample parking.
SC

BONYTHON MANOR
Cury Cross Lanes TR12 7BA
Richard & Sue Nathan
T: 01326 240234
E: sue@bonythonmanor.co.uk
W: www.bonythonmanor.co.uk
Accommodation: 4 properties sleeping 10, 6, 4 and 2. All 5* accommodation with ensuite facilities and private gardens. Bookings through 'Rural Retreats' - 01386 701177. www.ruralretreats.co.uk. Cottage refs: Bonython Farmhouse – CW042, Mews Cottage – CW047, St Corantyn Cottage – CW048, Spring Water Barn – CW058.
SC

CARWINION HOUSE AND GARDEN
Carwinion Road, Mawnan Smith
TR11 5JA
Jane Rogers
T: 01326 250258
E: jane@carwinion.co.uk
W: www.carwinion.co.uk
Accommodation: Carwinion House is a beautiful 18th Century stone manor house tucked away in its own private estate in the lush North Helford area of Cornwall, only a stone's throw from Falmouth. Nature lovers from around the world visit Carwinion to admire its renowned collection of bamboo and to relax among the beautiful and rare plants in these 14 unmanicured acres of tranquil garden. Some stay as bed-and-breakfast guests in the manor house where they are looked after by the lady of the manor herself, Jane Rogers. Some stay as self-catering guests in one of Carwinion's attractive period cottages.
B&B, SC

CREED HOUSE
Creed, Grampound TR2 4SL
Mr & Mrs Jonathan Croggon
T: 01872 530372
E: jrcroggon@btinternet.com
Accommodation: Georgian Rectory - guest wing with one twin, one double - both with ensuite, sitting room, continental breakfast. Prices £90 per night.
B&B

HIDDEN VALLEY GARDENS
Treesmill, Nr Par PL24 2TU
Patricia Howard
T: 01208 873225
E: hiddenvalleygardens@yahoo.co.uk
W: www.hiddenvalleygardens. co.uk
Accommodation: New, fully equipped, "4 star" SC accommodation for 2 or 4 guests in "Garden Studio" & "West Wing" stone barn conversions set in 'hidden' valley with a delightful, award winning, colourful 4 acre display garden. Inside and outside dining. Ideal for a couple, particularly garden lovers, seeking a cosy/romantic getaway holiday. (The West Wing is larger and is suitable for 2 couples holidaying together when booked with the Fountain Suite) See www.hiddenvalleygardens.co.uk for more details and photos.
SC

MAZEY COTTAGE
Tangies, Gunwalloe, TR12 7PU
Peter & Marion Stanley
T: 01326 565868
E: stanley.m2@sky.com
W: www.mazeycottage.co.uk/
Accommodation: Charming C18 cottage _ mile from Loe Pool and sea surrounded by National Trust land. Valley garden and ancient oak woodland with stream and large pond. One luxury double bedroom with private bathroom & shower. Garden open.
B&B

TREVOOLE FARM
Trevoole, Praze-an-Beeble, Camborne TR14 0RN
Mr & Mrs T Stevens
T: 01209 831243
E: beth@trevoolefarm.co.uk
W: www.trevoolefarm.co.uk
Accommodation: Traditional Cornish stone cottage. Ensuite bedrooms, farmhouse kitchen with Rayburn. Sitting room with wood burner. Enclosed courtyard garden. Linen, towels, fresh eggs and vegetables from the kitchen garden included. From £290 per week.
SC

Cumbria

BRACKENRIGG LODGE
Bowness-on-Windermere LA23 3HY
Lynne Bush
T: 015394 47770
E: lynne@brackenriggs.co.uk
W: www.brackenriggs.co.uk
Accommodation: Ideally located, tranquil, rural 3 acre setting. Close to the village and lake. Resident owner guarantees comfortable, clean accommodation. A real home from home. (SC - 1 apartment & 1 cottage).
SC

LAKESIDE HOTEL
Lake Windermere, Newby Bridge, LA12 8AT
Mr N R Talbot
T: 015395 30001
E: sales@LakesideHotel.co.uk
W: www.LakesideHotel.co.uk
Accommodation: The best 4* hotel and spa on the shores of Lake Windermere - a spectacular location. Guests enjoy exclusive use of luxury Health and Leisure Spa. Bedrooms with private gardens available. (75 rooms).
H

LANGHOLME MILL
Woodgate, Lowick Green, Ulverston LA12 8ES
Mr & Mrs G Sanderson
T: 01229 885215
E: info@langholmemill.co.uk
Accommodation: Ten minutes from Lake Coniston with stunning views, this C17 corn mill comprises 4 double bedrooms & large garden designed around the mill race featuring rhododendrons, hostas & acers. Ideal for walkers & families.
SC

LINDETH FELL COUNTRY HOUSE HOTEL
Lyth Valley Road, Bowness-on-Windermere La23 3JP
T: 015394 43286
E: kennedy@lindethfell.co.uk
W: www.lindethfell.co.uk
Accommodation: One of the most beautifully situated hotels in Lakeland, in magnificent gardens above Lake Windermere. Brilliant views and stylish surroundings. Restaurant offers superb modern English cooking with wines to match all at competitive prices. 14 bedrooms. Prices from £65 B&B. Visit Britain three star Gold, Good Hotel guide " English Country Hotel of the Year " 2009.
H

RYDAL HALL
Rydal, Ambleside LA22 9LX
Diocese of Carlisle
T: 015394 32050
E: mail@rydalhall.org
W: www.rydalhall.org
Accommodation: Rydal Hall is a Grade 2 listed house situated in the heart of the English Lake District with recently restored Thomas Mawson Gardens. A number of the ensuite rooms have a wonderful view down the Rothay Valley.
B&B, SC

SWARTHMOOR HALL
Swarthmoor, Ulverston LA12 0JQ
Religious Society of Friends (Quakers)
T: 01229 583204
E: info@swarthmoorhall.co.uk
Accommodation: 3 fully equipped self-catering units sleeping 5,5,4 people, or B&B available.
B&B, SC

Derbyshire

BRICK KILN FARM
Hulland Ward, Ashbourne DE6 3EJ
Mrs Jan Hutchinson
T: 01335 370440
E: robert.hutchinson@btinternet.com
Accommodation: The property is a small holding in a rural setting. Dogs, horses and hens are kept. Available are two bedrooms, one twin and one double, bathroom with bath, shower.
B&B

THE CASCADES
Clatterway, Bonsall DE4 2AH
Mr & Mrs A Clements
T: 01629 822464
E: info@cascadesgardens.com
W: www.derbyshiregarden.com
Accommodation: Set in a beautiful 4 acre garden within The Peak District National Park and close to Chatsworth. Cascades offers a range of luxury 5* accommodation. Ideal for a relaxing short break or holiday.
B&B

SHATTON HALL FARM COTTAGES
Bamford S33 0BG
Angela Kellie
T: 01433 620635
E: ahk@peakfarmholidays.co.uk
W: www.peakfarmholidayo. oo.uk
Accommodation: Three comfortable stone cottages, each with two double bedrooms, open plan living area. 4* accommodation, around listed Elizabethan farmhouse. Secluded location with good access

and within easy reach of Chatsworth House and Haddon Hall. Extensive gardens are to be enjoyed and are open in July.
SC

Devon

DARTINGTON HALL
Dartington TQ9 6JE
Dartington Hall Trust
T: 01803 847147
E: bookings@dartingtonhall.com
W: www.dartingtonhall.com
Accommodation: There are 51 characterful bedrooms within the medieval courtyard. From beamed ceilings to an etching of a C15 Spanish galleon carved onto a wall, history can be discovered all over the courtyard and gardens. Enjoy refreshments at The Grade 1 listed White Hart, where regional produce is creatively delivered by the kitchen team.
H

THE DOWNES
Monkleigh, Bideford EX39 5LB
Richard Stanley-Baker
T: 01806 622244
E: downes.gardens@gmail.com
W: downes-gardens.co.uk
Accommodation: Enjoy the best of Georgian splendor and style in a listed Georgian house on small country estate. Downes Gardens offers luxury self catering accommodation for eight in a secluded rural retreat in North Devon. Conveniently located for surfing, fishing, cycling, golfing, sailing, and coastal walks, the Downes is a great base from which to visit stately homes and historic houses run by the National Trust, and enjoy the many Gardens open to the public nearby such as Rosemoor.
B&B, SC

HEATHER COTTAGE
Yeo Cross, Chagford TQ13 8EX
Nicola Chatterjee
T: 07734 915626
E: nicolachatterjee@hotmail.co.uk
W: www.thegreatdevonescape. co.uk
Accommodation: Heather Cottage is one of Dartmoor's best kept secrets. The enviable location and sumptuous accommodation make it a stopover not to be missed! Alternatively Postbox Cottage is our luxury self-catering cottage for 2. The perfect rural retreat!
B&B, SC

KINGSTON HOUSE
Staverton TQ9 6AR
Michael & Elizabeth Corfield
T: 01803 762235
E: info@kingston-estate.co.uk
W: www.kingston-estate.co.uk
Accommodation: Kingston House,
5 Star - Gold award, has 3 beautiful
suites and nine 5 Star cottages. The
house is set in the gardens, offering
delicious food using garden produce
whenever possible, excellent wine
list. Price on application.
B&B, SC

THE OLD RECTORY
Ashford, Barnstaple EX31 4BY
Ann Burnham
T: 01271 377408
E: annburnham@btinternet.com
Accommodation: You will enjoy
your stay at the recently renovated
Old Rectory. Attractive bedrooms
with full ensuite. Delicious breakfasts;
dinner or supper on request. The
view is superb. Log fires in winter.
B&B

**THE PARK & GARDEN WINGS,
FURSDON HOUSE**
Cadbury, nr Thorverton, Exeter
EX5 5JS
Mrs Catriona Fursdon
T: 01392 860860
E: admin@fursdon.co.uk
W: www.fursdon.co.uk
Accommodation: Park and Garden
Wings, 4* Gold Award, are beautiful
private apartments in historic
Fursdon House overlooking gardens
with far reaching views. Elegant and
spacious, sleeping 6 & 3 respectively,
they are a perfect rural retreat. See
Fursdon for details of garden.
SC

REGENCY HOUSE
Hemyock EX15 3RQ
Mrs Jenny Parsons
T: 01823 680238
E: jenny.parsons@btinternet.com
Accommodation: Regency House
is the most beautiful, spacious,
Georgian rectory. **Accommodation:**
double room, ensuite, 1 twin with
private bathroom. Price £45 per
person
B&B

THE STANNARY
Mary Tavy, Tavistock PL19 9QB
Michael Cook & Ali Fife
T: 01822 810897
E: garden@alifife.co.uk
W: www.alifife.co.uk/garden
Accommodation: The Stannary is a
C16 & Victorian house on the edge
of Dartmoor. Two ensuite guest

bedrooms. Vegetarian breakfast (the
owners previously ran the most
highly-rated vegetarian restaurant in
the country!).
B&B

WHITSTONE FARM
Whitstone Lane, Bovey Tracey
TQ13 9NA
Katie & Alan Bunn
T: 01626 832258
E: katie@whitstonefarm.co.uk
W: www.whitstonefarm.co.uk
Accommodation: Country house
with stunning views over Dartmoor. 1
super kingsized (or twin) room, 1
kingsized room, 1 double sized room
- all ensuite. Prices from £41.50pppn
B&B

Dorset

DOMINEYS COTTAGES
Buckland Newton, nr Dorchester
DT2 7BS
Mr & Mrs W Gueterbock
T: 01300 345295
E: cottages@domineys.com
W: www.domineys.com
Accommodation: 3 delightful highly
commended 2 bdrm self-catering
cottages. Maintained to exceptional
standards - TB4*. Enchanting
gardens peacefully located in
Dorset's beautiful heartland. Flower
decked patios and heated summer
pool. Babies & children over 5 years
welcome. Regret no pets.
SC

HIGHER MELCOMBE MANOR
Melcombe Bingham DT2 7PB
Michael Woodhouse & Lorel Morton
T: 01258 880251
E: lorel@lorelmorton.com
Accommodation: 3 double
bedrooms, 2 with ensuite bathrooms
and 1 with bathroom along the
corridor. All recently refurbished.
Historic C16 manor house with two
acres of garden in a glorious setting.
Near to the Dorset Gap with its
wonderful walks and breathtaking
views.
B&B

KNOWLE FARM
Uploders, nr Bridport DT6 4NS
Alison & John Halliday
T: 01308 485492
E: info@knowlefarmbandb.com
W: www.knowlefarmbandb. com
Accommodation: In an AONB close
to the Jurassic Coast enjoy the
delights of West Dorset and beyond
from this C18 longhouse. We offer a
welcoming, relaxing village base in top

quality accommodation. Double
bedded room, ensuite.Twin room
private bath. Use of large lounge and
garden. Wide, varied breakfast menu.
Great attention to detail will make your
stay memorable. See what guests say
about us by visiting our website and
that of Alistair Sawday 'Special Places
to stay in Britain'. Regret no children
under 12 or visitor's pets.
B&B

Glamorgan

ARTS AT THE OLD MILL
The Old Mill, Dyffryn CF5 6SU
Rozanne Lord
T: 02920 593082 / 07775598636
E: rozanne.lord@blueyonder.co.uk
W: www.artsattheoldmill.co.uk
Accommodation: Arts at the Old
Mill offers a wide spectrum of art
courses, both residential and non
residential. We also cater for away
days, functions and weddings.
B&B

BRYN-Y-DDAFAD
Welsh St Donats, Cowbridge
CF71 7ST
Glyn & June Jenkins
T: +44 (0) 1446 774 451
E: enquiries@bydd.co.uk
W: www.bydd.co.uk
Accommodation: Visit Wales 4 Star
Guest House & Ground floor annex in
a peaceful rural location with easy
access to Cardiff. All rooms en suite,
guest lounge, safe off road parking
and free WiFi. Up to 11 guests may
be accommodated with self catering
option for a maximum of 4. Sorry no
children or pets. Close to Grade 1
listed Dyffryn Gardens and the
historic town of Cowbridge and
Physic Garden. Approximately 1
hour's drive from the National
Botanic Garden of Wales and
Aberglasny. Visit our website for
availabilty and special offers.
B&B, SC

FLANDERS BARN
Flanders Road CF61 1RL
Ann John
T: 01446 794711
E: davidp.john@hotmail.co.uk
W: www.flandersbarn.co.uk
Accommodation: Cottage annexe
of grade 2 listed barn. Lounge with
log fire, fridge and TV. Double
bedroom, ensuite shower room.
Sleeps 2-4. Price from £70 per night,
including breakfast. Visit Wales 4 star
rated. See Llantwit Major & Llanmaes
Gardens for details of garden
B&B

MEHEFIN
Sigginston Lane, Llanmaes
CF61 2XR
Bryn & Alison Morgan
T: 01446 793427
E: bb@mehefin.com
W: www.mehefin.com
Accommodation: Privately owned
B&B in attractive, award winning
village. Two double ensuite
bedrooms. 18 miles from Cardiff.
Close to Dyffryn Gardens and approx
1 hour's drive to National Botanic
Garden of Wales. See Llantwit Major
& Llanmaes Gardens for details of
garden
B&B

Gloucestershire North and Central

BARNSLEY HOUSE
Barnsley House Hotel, Barnsley,
Cirencester GL7 5EE
Calcot Health & Leisure
T: 01285 740000
E: info@barnsleyhouse.com
W: www.barnsleyhouse.com
Accommodation: Relax and indulge
yourself with a stay at Barnsley
House and enjoy the contemporary
rooms and luxury bathrooms and
The Garden Spa. Rooms from £275.
Alternative accommodation available
at The Village Pub, our Cotswold
country pub with 6 letting rooms.
Pub Rooms from £125.
H

BERRYS PLACE FARM
Bulley Lane, Churcham GL2 8AS
Mr G & Mrs A Thomas
T: 01452 750298 / 07950 808022
E: g.j.thomas@btconnect.com
Accommodation: Traditional
farmhouse B&B with fishing lake. 6
miles west of historic Gloucester,
approx 9 miles to Cheltenham Spa
and race course and within easy
reach of the Cotswolds, Forest of
Dean and Wye Valley.
B&B

BYAMS HOUSE
Willesley, Tetbury GL8 8QU
Kena & Sean Magee
T: 01666 880009
E: spbmagee@gmail.com
Accommodation: Two bedroomed
cottage which sleeps 4 in a peaceful,
rural setting near Westonbirt
Arboretum. Convenient for Bath and
Cheltenham. £40 single, £75 double
occupancy. Full English breakfast.
B&B

COOPERS COTTAGE
Wells Cottage, Wells Road, Bisley
GL6 7AG
Mr & Mrs Michael Flint
T: 01452 770289
E: flint_bisley@talktalk.net
Accommodation: Attractive old
beamed cottage, non-smoking,
sleeps 2-4. Stands apart in owners'
large, beautiful garden with lovely
views. Furnished & equipped to high
standard. Very quiet, good walking.
Village shop & 2 pubs nearby. See
Wells Cottage for details of garden.
SC

KEMPSFORD MANOR
High Street, Kempsford GL7 4EQ
Mrs Z Williamson
T: 01285 810131
E: info@kempsfordmanor.com
W: www.kempsfordmanor.com
Accommodation: C17-18 manor
house set in peaceful gardens. Fine
reception rooms. 3-4 double
bedrooms. Price from £40 single
occ. Ideal retreat. Home grown
organic vegetables. Suitable for small
conferences and marquee receptions.
1 mile from Wiltshire border.
B&B

KINGSCOTE PARK HOUSE
Kingscote GL8 8YA
Geoffrey Higgins
T: 01453 861050
E: rebecca@matara.co.uk
W: www.kingscotepark.co.uk
Accommodation: Relax in our
beautiful Regency family home, with
close family and friends
B&B, SC

ORCHARD COTTAGE
Lynch Road, France Lynch GL6 8LP
Tricia Willey
T: 01453 883736
E: willey800@talktalk.net
W: www.cotswolds.info/
webpage/orchard-cottage.htm
Accommodation: Cotswold stone
cottage dating from18th century, with
a large garden in a peaceful hillside
village setting, 20 minutes drive to
Cheltenham or Cirencester. See
France Lynch Gardens for details of
garden
B&B

Gwent

APRIL HOUSE
Coed-Y-Paen NP151PT
Dr C Fleming
T: 01291 673775 or 07971319533
E: charlotte.fleming00@gmail.com
Accommodation: Welcome to our
cottage in a little patch of heaven.
Pretty double room with own
bathroom. Spotless. Lovely views
over the garden and valley beyond.
See Coed-Y-Paen Village Gardens for
details of garden.
B&B

THE BELL AT SKENFRITH
Skenfrith NP7 8UH
William & Janet Hutchings
T: 01600 750235
E: enquiries@skenfrith.co.uk
W: www.skenfrith.co.uk
Accommodation: A C17 coaching
inn on the banks of the River
Monnow with 11 fabulous ensuite
bedrooms, fine dining restaurant and
bar with sumptuous sofas and sunny
terrace overlooking the garden and
organic kitchen garden.
H

PENPERGWM LODGE
nr Abergavenny NP7 9AS
Mr & Mrs S Boyle
T: 01873 840208
E: boyle@penpergwm.co.uk
W: www.penplants.com
Accommodation: A large rambling
Edwardian house in the lovely Usk
valley. Pretty bedrooms have garden
views, bathrooms share a corridor,
breakfast and relax in the spacious
and comfortable sitting room. Great
walking in nearby Brecon Beacons
National Park.
B&B

Gwynedd

HOTEL MAES-Y-NEUADD
Talsarnau, nr Harlech LL47 6YA
Peter & Lynn Jackson & Peter Payne
T: 01766 780200
E: maes@neuadd.com
W: www.neuadd.com
Accommodation: 15 individually
designed ensuite double/twin rooms.
C14 manor house with bar, terrace,
lounge, conservatory and highly
acclaimed restaurant serving fresh,
local produce and home grown fruit
& vegetables. B&B from £49.50
H

PLAS TAN Y BWLCH
PlasTan y Bwlch, Maentwrog
LL41 3YU
Snowdonia National Park Authority
T: 01766 772600
E: plas@eryri-npa.gov.uk
W: www.plastanybwlch.com
Accommodation: Accommodation
for individuals or groups is available
in Plas Tan y Bwlch, the Snowdonia
National Park Authority Study Centre,
an C18 manor house overlooking the
Vale of Ffestiniog. Please call for
availability and prices.
B&B

Hampshire

APPLE COURT
Hordle Lane, Hordle, Lymington
SO41 0HU
Charles & Angela Meads
T: 01590 642130
E: applecourt@btinternet.com
W: www.applecourt.com
Accommodation: Cottage annexe
next to Apple Court. 2 bedrooms,
sleeps 4. Kitchen, dining room,
conservatory/lounge. Non-smoking.
Regret no dogs. Beautiful location
near New Forest, Lymington. From
£450 - £700 per week
SC

12 CHRISTCHURCH ROAD
Winchester SO23 9SR
Mrs P Patton
T: 01962 854272
E: pjspatton@yahoo.co.uk
W: www.visitwinchester.co.uk/
site/where-to-stay
Accommodation: An elegant
Victorian house on the south side of
city. Garden featured in The English
Garden Sept. 2010 Easy walk to city
centre, cathedral, museums,
restaurants etc. Close to long
distance footpaths. Home made
bread, preserves and local produce.
Well behaved dogs welcome.
Luggage can be transported for
walkers.
B&B

DURMAST HOUSE
Burley BH24 4AT
Philip and Margaret Daubeney
T: 01425 402132
E: philip@daubeney.co.uk
W: www.durmasthouse.com
Accommodation: Period house
with garden designed by Gertrude
Jekyll. Separate flat with one
bedroom, sitting room, beautiful
bathroom and fitted kitchen. Walking

in the New Forest, golf, riding and
beaches five miles away. From £300
p/w
SC

THE ELVETHAM HOTEL
Elvetham, Hartley Wintney, Hook
RG27 8AR
T: 01252 844871
E: enq@elvethamhotel.co.uk
W: www.elvethamhotel.co.uk
Accommodation: Set in 35 acres of
formal gardens and grounds, this
magnificent 19th century Victorian
mansion has 70 traditionally styled
bedrooms, including superior rooms
and suites. The gardens include a
tree which was planted by Queen
Elizabeth.
H

TYLNEY HALL HOTEL
Ridge Lane, Rotherwick RG27 9AZ
T: 01256 764881
E: sales@tylneyhall.com
W: www.tylneyhall.com
Accommodation: Set in 66 acres of
glorious Hampshire Countryside,
Tylney Hall Hotel, an elegant Grade II
listed Victorian mansion provides the
perfect location for every occasion.
112 bedrooms are complemented by
award winning dining in the Oak
Room Restaurant. Traditional
afternoon tea is served daily in our
lounges, and leisure facilities include
five beauty treatment rooms, which
offer a wide range of treatments,
along with indoor and outdoor
swimming pools, tennis courts,
jogging trails and croquet.
H

Herefordshire

BROBURY HOUSE
Brobury, Hereford HR3 6BS
Keith & Pru Cartwright
T: 01981 500229
E: enquiries@broburyhouse.co.uk
W: www.broburyhouse.co.uk
Accommodation: House - B&B:
Large double room, ensuite. 1
double & 1 twin large rooms each
with private shower room, all with
beautiful garden views. Prices from
£35 pppn - Cottages - 2 spacious,
recently refurbished, self catering
cottages. Peak period price £440 per
week.
B&B, SC

CAVES FOLLY NURSERY
Evendine Lane, Colwall WR13 6DX
Bridget Evans

T: 01684 540631
E: bridget@cavesfolly.com
W: www.cavesfolly.com
Accommodation: SC cottage on
organic nursery. Idyllic setting in
Malvern Hills AONB. Available to let
nightly or weekly. Sleeps 6. Also self-
catering B&B - choose your organic
breakfast from our shop.
B&B, SC

THE GREAT HOUSE
Dilwyn HR4 8HX
Tom & Jane Hawksley
T: 01544 318007
E: greathousedilwyn@gmail.com
W: www.thegreathousedilwyn. co.uk
Accommodation: 3 double/twin,
ensuite bathrooms. Private sunny
sitting room with door to garden.
Beams, panelling, flag stone floors
and enormous log fires. Price from
£48 pppn, single suppl. £10. Dinner
by arrangement from £20, Licensed
Wolsey Lodge.

HOLME LACY HOUSE HOTEL
Holme Lacy, nr Hereford HR2 6LP
Warner Leisure Hotels
T: 01432 870870
E: sales.holmelacy@bourne-
leisure.co.uk
W: www.holmelacyhouse.co.uk
Accommodation: Set in the idyllic
Wye Valley, this a magical Grade I
listed mansion with 179 bedrooms.
The Historic Rooms and Suites are in
the Old House, whilst the
contemporary 'Signature' rooms and
comfortable 'Ambassador' rooms are
in the new wing.
H

HOPE END HOUSE
Hope End, Wellington Heath HR8 1JQ
Mr & Mrs PJ Maiden
T: 01531 635890
E: sharonmaiden@btinternet.com
W: www.hopeendhouse.com
Accommodation: Hope End House,
surrounded by 100 acres of historic
parkland. This romantic house has
peace at its heart. Our accommoda-
tion has been awarded 5* Gold Award.
Our gardens tranquil and peaceful.
B&B

KENTCHURCH COURT
Kentchurch, Pontrilas, HR2 0DB
Mr & Mrs John Lucas-Scudamore
T: 01981 240228
E: jan@kentchurchcourt.co.uk
W: www.kentchurchcourt.co.uk
Accommodation: Kentchurch Court
is a family home dating back to the
11th Century. John Nash renovated

the house in 1795. The Deer Park was bought from the Knights Hospitalers of Dinmore in 1527. Kentchurch is an ideal base for visiting South Herefordshire and the gardens in the locality. There are a number of churches, notably Kilpeck, built in the the tradition of the Hereford Romanesque School of Stonemasons, Shobden and Dore Abbey. Hay on Wye is also very popular.
B&B

SHIELDBROOK
Kings Caple HR1 4UB
Susan & Oliver Sharp
T: 01432 840670
E: susansharp95@btinternet.com
W: www.shieldbrooksculpture garden.com
Accommodation: Comfortable double room with double bed and ensuite shower in a traditional 300 year old house. Well situated for garden visits. £50 pppn.
B&B

WOLFERLOW HOUSE
Wolferlow, nr Upper Sapey HR7 4QA
Stuart and Jill Smith
T: 01886 853311
E: hillheadfm@aol.com
W: www.ngs.org.uk/gardens/ gardenfinder/garden.aspx?id=21624
Accommodation: Wolferlow House is a large former Victorian rectory set in beautiful countryside on the Herefordshire / Worcestershire border close to interesting centres such as Ludlow, Worcester and Hereford. The fully modernised accommodation comprises two double bedrooms both with en-suite shower room. Delicious home-cooked breakfast included; evening meal available by prior arrangement. £70 per room per night.
B&B

Hertfordshire

106 ORCHARD ROAD
Tewin AL6 0LZ
Linda Adams
T: 01438 798147
E: alannio@btinternet.com
W: www.tewinvillage.co.uk
Accommodation: 1 large double and 1 large twin room with private facilities, in listed C20 house, with many original features. 1 acre garden with year round interest. Peaceful country setting. Parking. Prices from £35 pppn.
B&B

Isle of Wight

NORTHCOURT
Northcourt Gardens, Shorwell
PO30 3JG
Mr & Mrs J Harrison
T: 01983 740415
E: christine@northcourt.info
W: www.northcourt.info
Accommodation: B&B in large C17 manor house in 15 acres of exotic gardens, on edge of the downs. 6 double/twin rooms, all ensuite. Price from £65 per room. Also wing of house for up to 14 self-catering, or 2 wings for up to 25.
B&B, SC

Kent

CANTERBURY CATHEDRAL LODGE
11 The Precincts, Canterbury
CT1 2EH
Dean & Chapter of Canterbury
T: 01227 865350
E: stay@canterbury-cathedral.org
W: www.canterburycathedral lodge.org
Accommodation: The best located accommodation in the City! Canterbury Cathedral Lodge is a unique and contemporary hotel, situated within the private grounds of Canterbury Cathedral. In a peaceful environment but only a couple of minutes walk to Canterbury's many attractions, the Lodge offers stylishly refurbished en-suite bedrooms overlooking the Cathedral and gardens. All rooms in the Lodge benefit from luxury furnishings, LCD screen TVs with free-view and there is complimentary WI-FI throughout. Guests also enjoy free entrance to the Cathedral, worth £8 per person.
B&B, H

3 CHAINHURST COTTAGES
Dairy Lane, Chainhurst TN12 9SU
Heather Scott
T: 01622 820483 / 07729 378489
E: heatherscott@waitrose.com
W: www.chainhurstcottages. co.uk
Accommodation: Comfortable, modern accommodation with private entrance and ensuite bathroom in quiet rural location with good local pubs. Ideal touring base for historic properties and gardens including Leeds Castle & Sissinghurst Garden. Visit Britain 4* Silver award. See Chainhurst Cottage Gardens for details of garden
B&B

COTTAGE FARM
Cacketts Lane, Cudham TN14 7QG
Phil Baxter
T: 01959 534048/532506
E: cottagefarmturkeys@googlemail. com
Accommodation: Delightful country cottage: 1 double and 1 twin room, living room, kitchen and bathroom. Full central heating. From £350 per week self catering. B&B £35 pppn based on 2 sharing double/twin room. £45 single occ. Visit Britain 4*.
B&B, SC

OLD STABLES COTTAGE
Shipbourne TN11 9RX
Mr & Mrs M Cohen
T: 01732 810739
E: oldstablescottage@btinternet.com
Accommodation: The Old Stables self-catering cottage is converted to a high standard with a fully fitted kitchen and large, light open-plan living room opening onto a courtyard garden. It is fully equipped with all the home comforts and off road parking. There is a shower room and one double bedroom on the ground floor, two single beds in the attic bedroom. Please visit www.kent-lets.co.uk to find out more. Shipbourne Gardens
SC

THE SALUTATION
Knightrider Street, Sandwich
CT13 9EW
Mr & Mrs D Parker
T: 01304 619919
E: dominic@the-salutation.com
W: www.the-salutation.com
Accommodation: 9 bedrooms available within 3 cottages within the estate, offering exclusive and private bed and breakfast.
B&B

SISSINGHURST CASTLE FARMHOUSE BED AND BREAKFAST
Cranbrook TN17 2AB
Sue & Frazer Thompson
T: 01580 720992
E: sue@sissinghurstcastlefarmhouse. com
W: www.sissinghurstcastlefarm house.com
Accommodation: Situated next to Sissinghurst Castle Gardens - the magnificent creation of Vita Sackville-West and husband Harold Nicholson, Sissinghurst Castle Farmhouse is a five star bed and breakfast with seven luxury double bedrooms, all with en-suite bathrooms or shower rooms. All of our bedrooms can be

accessed without the use of stairs as we have a lift. The bedrooms are all individual and have spectacular views across the Sissinghurst Estate and many have a view of the Elizabethan Tower. They also have all the luxuries and facilities you would expect in such a special location including digital TV, radio, i-pod docking and broadband connection.
B&B

WICKHAM LODGE
The Quay, 73 High Street, Aylesford ME20 7AY
Cherith & Richard Bourne
T: 01622 717267
E: wickhamlodge@aol.com
W: www.wickhamlodge.co.uk
Accommodation: Beautifully restored house offering every modern comfort situated on the river bank in Aylesford, one of the oldest and most picturesque villages in Kent. Cherith & Richard provide a warm and hospitable welcome for their guests. Winner Kent Life, amateur garden of the year 2010.
B&B, SC

Lancashire Merseyside and Greater Manchester

LITTLE STUBBINS
Stubbins Lane, Claughton-on-Brock, Preston PR3 0PL
Margaret Richardson
T: 01995 640376
E: littlestubbins@aol.com
W: www.littlestubbins.co.uk
Accommodation: Charming B&B with 2 double and 1 twin rooms, all ensuite, 4 star Gold award. Set in rural surroundings, handy for both Junction 32 & 33 of the M6. Conveniently situated 2 miles south of the old market town of Garstang. Guests are welcome to use the lounge and wander /relax in the large garden. Prices from £35 p.p. including breakfast.
B&B

MILL BARN
Goose Foot Close, Samlesbury Bottoms PR5 0SS
Chris Mortimer
T: 01215 853300
E: chris@millbarn.net
Accommodation: Mill Barn is a converted barn. 1 double & 1 twin room, neither ensuite. Guests are accommodated as house guests &

have full access to all shared rooms - lounge, conservatory, studio etc. as well as the garden.
B&B

THE RIDGES
Weavers Brow, Cowling Road Limbrick Heath Charnock, Chorley PR6 9EB
John & Barbara Barlow
T: 01257 279981
E: barbara@barlowridges.co.uk
W: www.bedbreakfast-gardenvisits.com
Accommodation: 4 bedrooms, 2 double ensuite, 1 twin & 1 single sharing a private bathroom. Breakfast room. Prices from £40 single, £70 double.
B&B

SEFTON VILLA
14 Sefton Drive, Sefton Park, Liverpool L8 3SD
Mrs Patricia Williams
T: 0151 281 3687
E: seftonvilla@live.co.uk
W: www.seftonvilla.co.uk
Accommodation: Victorian house. 1 double room decorated in period style with kingsize bed and ensuite with shower. Tea & coffee facilities, TV, hairdryer. See Sefton Park Gardens for details of garden
B&B

Leicestershire and Rutland

BENTS FARMHOUSE
Church Drive, Gilmorton LE17 5PF
Mrs Jill Mackenzie
T: 01455 558566 or 07736 018111
E: fourseasons@harborough.uk.com
W: www.fourseasonsgarden design.com
Accommodation: Georgian Farmhouse with delightful country garden. Double room with balcony, period features, private bathroom roll top bath and shower. Comfortable guest lounge/dining room with French windows to garden and log fires. Self-contained annexe also available SC or B & B. See Gilmorton Gardens for details of garden
B&B, SC

THE GRANGE, KIMCOTE
Kimcote, Lutterworth LE17 5RU
Shaun & Mary Mackaness
T: 01455 203155
E: shaunandmarymac@hotmail.com
W: www.thegrangekimcote. co.uk
Accommodation: An attractive,

Grade II listed, Queen Anne house located on the edge of a small village set in one acre of garden with views over open countryside. Only 4 miles from J.20 of M1 with easy access to M6 and A14. East Midlands, Birmingham and Coventry airports are all close by.
B&B

Lincolnshire

BRUNESWOLD COACH HOUSE
1A Hereward Street, Lincoln LN1 3EW
Jo & Ken Slone
T: 01522 568484
E: kenjo@bruneswoldcoachhouse.co.uk
W: www.bruneswoldcoach house.co.uk
Accommodation: Ground level self catering accommodation within the garden of a Victorian town house in uphill Lincoln, brimming with plants and sculpture. 5 minutes walk away from the historic quarter of Lincoln. Off-road parking. See The Coach House for details of garden.
SC

GOLTHO HOUSE
Lincoln Road, Goltho LN8 5NF
Mrs D Hollingworth
T: 01673 857768
E: s.hollingworth@homecall.co.uk
W: www.golthogardens.com
Accommodation: Fancy a day at the races, or at a championship golf course, maybe walking in the Lincolnshire Wolds or exploring Historic Lincoln. All of these are easily accessible if you stay with us in our comfortable, traditional farmhouse accommodation which includes 1 double room with a four poster bed or 1 double room with a half tester bed both sharing a private bathroom. Guests are also welcome to walk around our delightful 4 acre garden at will.
B&B

London

BALHAM B&B
28 Old Devonshire Road, Balham, London SW12 9RB
Georgina Ivoi
T: 020 8673 7179
E: georgina@balhambandb.co.uk
W: www.balhambandb.co.uk
Accommodation: Spacious double room with private bathroom in

elegant mid Victorian house. Chosen for inclusion in Alistair Sawday's 'Special Places to Stay' and featured in The Weekend Guardian's selection of Gorgeous B&Bs in Central London (September 18th 2010). 'Fantastic stay in lovely surroundings - an oasis in the urban sprawl !' Sal & Adrian. North Yorkshire. July 2010
B&B

THE GARDEN BED AND BREAKFAST
London SW2 4NT
Winkle Haworth
T: 020 8671 4196
E: winklehaworth@hotmail.com
W: www.thegardenbedand breakfast.com
Accommodation: Luxurious and stylish accommodation, with a garden of international repute, listed in the Good Gardens Guide. House and garden have featured in magazines worldwide and been the subject of television programmes both in England and overseas. The garden has won first prize in the English Garden magazine 'Best Town Garden' Competition. Garden owner with a Certificate in Horticulture and Diploma in Garden History. Twin rooms from £95; single rooms from £65
B&B

WEST LODGE PARK
Cockfosters Road, Hadley Wood EN4 0PY
Beales Hotels
T: 0208 216 3900
E: westlodgepark@bealeshotels. co.uk
W: www.bealeshotels.co.uk
Accommodation: 59 bedrooms including Superior, Executive rooms with views over our arboretum. If you are looking for something more modern, try our Chestnut Lodge rooms which can be found in a separate lodge in our gardens.
H

29 WOODBERRY CRESCENT
Muswell Hill, London N10 1PJ
Edwina Roberts
T: 020 8365 3639
E: edwinakellerman@btinternet.com
Accommodation: Large, bright white painted double room with ensuite shower room, comfy bed, books, and television. Downstairs, a sitting room for guest use with French window out to the garden terrace where breakfast is served on sunny days.
B&B

Norfolk

BAGTHORPE HALL
Bagthorpe PE31 6QY
Mrs Gina Morton
T: 01485 578528
E: enquiries@bagthorpehall.co.uk
W: www.bagthorpehall.co.uk
Accommodation: 2-3 large double bedrooms ensuite, big comfortable beds, organic and homemade breakfast. £80 for a double incl breakfast. £50 for single.
B&B

BAY COTTAGE
Colby Corner, nr Aylsham NR11 7EB
Stuart Clarke
T: 01263 734574
E: enchanting@btinternet.com
W: www.enchantingcottages. co.uk
Accommodation: 4* ETB graded country cottage with large garden. Sleeps 7 in 3 bedrooms, plus a self contained garden, oak framed annexe with wheelchair access, which sleeps 2. See The Old Cottage for details of garden.
SC

CHAUCER BARN
Holt Road, Gresham NR11 8RL
James Mermagen
T: 01263 577733
E: info@chaucerbarn.com
W: www.chaucerbarn.com
Accommodation: Award winning Chaucer Barn offers luxury self catering accommodation for up to 18. Set in 5 acres of landscaped gardens. 9 bedrooms, 7 bathrooms, 4 reception rooms, games room, 18 seated dining table. Breathtaking gardens are a mix of contemporary topiary and romantic informal including wild flower meadow, herb garden, pergola with bbq and eating area, lawns, young arboretum, children's play area and woods.
SC

THE LODGE COTTAGE
Main Road, Narborough PE32 1TE
J Merrison
T: 01760 339923 / 01760 338827
E: narboroughgardeners@googlemail.com
W: www.narboroughhall gardens.com
Accommodation: Picture book Victorian Lodge Cottage with own garden. Pretty vintage decoration. Two bedrooms (double), dining room, kitchen, sitting room with open fire, bathroom. Use of Narborough Hall grounds. Swimming pool and tennis in summer.
SC

MANOR HOUSE FARM
Wellingham, nr Fakenham PE32 2TH
Robin & Elisabeth Ellis
T: 01328 838227
E: libby.ellis@btconnect.com
W: www.manor-house-farm.co.uk
Accommodation: Award winning conversion in garden. 2 large airy double bedrooms, ensuite. Comfortable, sitting room with wood burning stove, TV and books etc plus small kitchen. Breakfast in dining room of main house. Also beautiful barn with SC for 2.
H

THE OLD RECTORY
Ridlington, nr North Walsham NR28 9NZ
Peter & Fiona Black
T: 01692 650247
E: blacks7@email.com
W: www.oldrectory.north norfolk.co.uk
Accommodation: Just a minute's drive from the wonderful gardens at East Ruston Old Vicarage we offer both bed and breakfast and self-catering accommodation. 2 double rooms one with ensuite bathroom and one with private bath. Delicious homemade breakfast. Close to lots of other gardens and beaches. The Garden Room is a self-catering studio. One large room with kingsize bed, separate kitchen and bathroom, woodburner, Prices from £60 per night for two.
B&B, SC

SALLOWFIELD COTTAGE
Wattlefield, Wymondham NR18 9NX
Caroline Musker
T: 01952 605086
E: caroline.musker@tesco.net
W: www.sallowfieldcottage. co.uk
Accommodation: One double with private bathroom on the first floor and one double and one twin room, both with ensuite showers, on the ground floor. The cottage is in a quiet location well away from the road surrounded by its own garden with a large pond.
B&B

THE SMALL BARN
Holt Road, Wood Norton, Dereham
NR20 5BL
Jane Lister
T: 01362 684206
E: hoecroft@hotmail.co.uk
W: www.hoecroft.co.uk
Accommodation: Cosy barn
conversion situated 8 miles south of
Holt, comprising of well fitted kitchen
diner, comfortably furnished living
room with French windows opening
onto private terrace and garden.
Sleeps 4 (1 double,1 twin). Access to
Severals Grange garden at all times.
See Severals Grange for details of
garden.
SC

North East

BROACHES FARM
Dalton, Richmond DL11 7HW
Mrs Judith Hutchinson
T: 01833 621369
E: jude1@farmersweekly.net
Accommodation: A warm welcome
awaits you at Broaches Farm. Set in
an idyllic location overlooking open
fields. We offer comfortable,
spacious, ensuite accommodation.
Hearty breakfasts are served in the
sunny conservatory using our own
free range eggs and home-made
preserves.
B&B

CHESWICK HOUSE
Cheswick TD15 2RL
Jean & Peter Bennett
T: 01289 387387
E: info@cheswickhouse.co.uk
W: www.cheswickhouse.co.uk
Accommodation: Detached
picturesque lodge. Cosy lounge with
wood burner. Four-poster bedroom.
Garden Wing - 3 Bedroom apartment
sleeps 5. Large lounge, master
ensuite with four poster. Both one
mile from heritage coast within
secluded private estate. Tennis court.
SC

LOUGHBROW HOUSE
1 mile from Hexham centre
NE46 1RS
Mrs P A Clark
T: 01434 603351
E: patriciaclark351@btinternet.com
W: www.loughbrowhouse
bandb.co.uk
Accommodation: First built in 1780
and overlooking the Tyne Valley,
Loughbrow is a large country house
in 9 acres of garden. Furnished with
family portraits & antiques. 1 double,

2 twin & 2 single bedrooms. from
£40 per person per night.
B&B

THORNLEY HOUSE
Thornley Gate, Allendale NE47 9NH
Eileen Finn
T: 01434 683255
E: enquiries@thornleyhouse.co.uk
W: www.thornleyhouse.co.uk
Accommodation: A B&B for lovers of
fine cats and fine gardens. Beautiful
country house, 1 mile west of
Allendale, near Hadrian's Wall. 3
bedrooms with facilities, TV & tea
makers. 2 lounges with Steinway grand
piano and plasma TV. Resident Maine
Coon cats. B&B from £30 per person.
French Spanish and Russian spoken.
B&B

North East Wales

BODYSGALLEN HALL
Llandudno LL30 1RS
Historic House Hotels Ltd.
T: 01492 584466
E: info@bodysgallen.com
W: www.bodysgallen.com
Accommodation: Standing in over
200 acres of gardens and parkland,
Bodysgallen Hall is acclaimed as
Wales' highest rated country house
hotel and is part of the National Trust.
31 bedrooms, located in the main
hall and cottages in the grounds, an
award-winning restaurant and a
bistro, as well as a health and fitness
spa, make a perfect all-round
experience.
H

BRYN DWR B&B AND PODS
Llandegla LL11 3AW
T: 01978 790612 / 0798 461 3534
E: julietudor@tiscali.co.uk
W: www.bryndwrpodsbandb. co.uk
Accommodation: Bryn Dwr is set in
the heart of Wales 50 yards from the
Offa's Dyke path on the banks of the
River Alyn. We have two twin bedded
rooms with tea and coffee making
facilities. We have a shared
bathroom. Bed and breakfast is
£32.00 per person per night which
includes a full traditional breakfast.
Also available are two camping pods
which sleeps two adults and two
children £40.00 per pod per night.
B&B

33 BRYN TWR & LYNTON
Highfield Park, Abergele LL22 7AU
Colin & Ann Knowlson
T: 01745 832002 or 07712623836
E: apk@slaters.com

Accommodation: Double ensuite
room with separate entrance. Garden
room/lounge. Tea/coffee facilities.
Convenient for Bodnant Gardens,
Conwy & Snowdonia. Some good
walks adjacent.
B&B

DOVE COTTAGE
Rhos Road, Penyffordd, nr Chester
CH4 0JR
Mr & Mrs C Wallis
T: 01244 547539
E: dovecottage@supanet.com
W: www.visitwales.com
Accommodation: Delightful C17
farmhouse. Luxurious
accommodation. 2 double rooms,
ensuite. Single occ. £35-£40, double
£60 per night. Convenient for
Chester & N Wales.
B&B

FIRGROVE
Llanfwrog, Ruthin LL15 2LL
Anna & Philip Meadway
T: 01824 702677
E: panda.meadway@btinternet.com
W: www.firgrovecountryhouse. co.uk
Accommodation: A small Georgian
country house offering 5* B&B
accommodation in a peaceful, rural
setting. Three double bedrooms
equipped with every need of the
modern day visitor. Evening meals
are available with prior notice.
B&B

THE GARDEN HOUSE
Erbistock LL13 0DL
Mr & Mrs S Wingett
T: 01978 781149
E: art@simonwingett.com
W: www.simonwingett.com
Accommodation: 2 double
bedrooms en suite at the Garden
House and Wolsey Lodges
www.wolseylodges.com/lodges/
6980
B&B

RHYD GETHIN
Pennant Road, Llandrillo, Corwen
LL21 0TE
Tony & Jenny Leeson
T: 01490 440213
E: anthony.leeson@tesco.net
Accommodation: Former C16
stone farmhouse in a riverside setting
in a secluded wooded valley. One
bedroom with kingsize four poster
bed and ensuite shower room. One
bedroom with kingsize bed and
private bathroom. Outstanding rural
views. £37.50 pppn.
B&B

RUTHIN CASTLE HOTEL
Castle Street LL15 2NU
Ruthin Castle Ltd
T: 01824 702664
E: reservations@ruthincastle.co.uk
W: www.ruthincastle.co.uk
Accommodation: A magical 62
bedroom hotel in a parkland setting,
rich in history and character, 23 miles
from Chester. The mediaeval castle,
built by Edward 1, & owned by the
monarchy for extended periods, was
re-built in 1826. set in extensive
parkland with rooms from £49 See
Ruthin Town Gardens for details of
garden
H

SIR JOHN TREVOR HOUSE
Castle Street, Ruthin LL15 1DP
Jackie Jones
T: 01824 703176
E: jackie@sirjohntrevorhouse.co.uk
W: www.sirjohntrevorhouse. co.uk
Accommodation: A unique
opportunity to stay in a beautiful
Elizabethan town house, 3 tastefully
furnished, ensuite bedrooms
providing all facilities. Set in a lovely
part of North Wales - access to the
countryside, seaside and cities. An
hour to the nearest airport. See
Ruthin Town Gardens for details of
garden
B&B

STELLA MARIS
Mynydd Llech, Llanrhaeadr
LL16 4PW
Mrs Jane Moore
T: 01745 890475
E: jemoore01@live.com
Accommodation: Suite of bright
comfy rooms. Lounge with
kitchenette, spacious bedroom with
kingsize bed, sofa bed & ensuite
shower room. Peaceful location with
wonderful views over the Vale of
Clwyd. Bodnant, Erddig, Chirk and
Ness are within 45 minutes drive and
many local NGS gardens are open by
appointment. A number of good
restaurants and a health spa are
nearby. Member of County Team.
B&B, SC

**TAL-Y-BRYN FARM GUEST
HOUSE**
Llannefydd LL16 5DR
Gareth & Falmai Roberts
T: 01745 540208
E: llaeth@villagedairy.co.uk
W: www.villagedairy.com
Accommodation: C16 farmhouse,
lovely views and garden with lovely
historical walks. 4 double guest

rooms with ensuite facilities. TV and
internet connections. Tea & coffee
facilities. Dogs by arrangement.
B&B

WYCH ELM
Cefn Bychan Road, Pantymwyn,
Mold CH7 5EL
Martin & Gillian Fraser
T: 01352 740241
E: gandmfraser@btinternet.com
W: www.wychelmbandb.co.uk
Accommodation: Set in woodland
with views of the Clwydian Hills,
Wych Elm is an ideal place to
explore this undiscovered and
unspoilt area of North Wales.
Although not a garden of merit itself,
it is situated mid way between Ness
and Bodnant Gardens. Viewing of
private gardens in the area by
arrangement.
B&B

Northamptonshire

DALE HOUSE
Yew Tree Lane, Spratton,
Northampton NN6 8HL
Fiona Cox
T: 01604 846458
E: cjcatdalehouse@aol.com
Accommodation: Double room with
kingsize bed and own bathroom in
annexe. SC or B&B. Parking in private
drive. Quiet views overlooking garden
and open countryside. See Spratton
Gardens for details of garden
B&B, SC

THE OLD VICARAGE
Broad Lane, Evenley, Brackley
NN13 5SF
Philippa Heumann
T: 07774 415 332
E: philippaheumann@andreas-
heumann.com
Accommodation: Elegant Regency
vicarage set in large attractive garden
in the picturesque village of Evenley.
Two twin bedrooms, two bathrooms.
Ideally situated for visiting gardens in
Central England - approx 5 miles J10
M40. B&B - single £40, double £80
pn.
B&B

Nottinghamshire

GRINGLEY HALL
Gringley on the Hill, Doncaster
DN10 4QT
Dulce & Ian Threlfall
T: 01777 817262

E: dulce@gringleyhall.fsnet.co.uk
W: www.gringleyhall.co.uk
Accommodation: Regency house
located on the borders of
Nottinghamshire, Lincolnshire and
South Yorkshire. The setting for the
true story See Gringley Gardens for
details of garden
B&B

THE SUMMER HOUSE
High Street, Gringley on the Hill,
Doncaster DN10 4RF
Mrs Helena Bishop
T: 01777817248
E: jbt@waitrose.com
Accommodation: A warm friendly
home in an unspoilt village. 1 double
room and 1 twin room @ £40 per
person, with dinner on request. A
member of Wolsey Lodge for over
twenty years.
B&B

**THORESBY HALL HOTEL
& SPA**
Thoresby Park, nr Ollerton, Newark
NG22 9WH
Warner Leisure Hotels
T: 01623 821000
E: thoresbyhall.reception@bourne-
leisure.co.uk
W: www.thoresbyhall.co.uk
Accommodation: Perched on the
edge of Sherwood Forest in
Nottinghamshire, the house,
gardens and parklands of Thoresby
Hall & Spa are as grand an invocation
of the 18th and 19th-Centuries as
you'll find. Balconies and cupolas on
the outside, galleries and tapestries
within and all bound in unforgettable
period elegance; Thoresby Hall has it
all.
H

Oxfordshire

BROUGHTON GROUNDS FARM
North Newington, Banbury
OX15 6AW
Andrew and Margaret Taylor
T: 01295 730315
E: info@broughtongrounds.co.uk
W: www.broughtongrounds. co.uk
Accommodation: One double, one
twin and one single room in C17
farmhouse, on working mixed farm,
located on the Broughton Castle
Estate. Beautiful views and peaceful
location. Prices: £30 pppn.
B&B

BUTTSLADE HOUSE
Temple Mill Road, Sibford Gower,
Banbury OX15 5RX
Mrs Diana Thompson
T: 01295 788818
E: janthompson50@hotmail.com
W: www.buttsladehouse.co.uk
Accommodation: Sympathetically
restored stables of C17 farmhouse in
tranquil English country garden. 1
double and 1 twin bedded room with
private sitting rooms and own
bathrooms. Own bread & cakes
baked daily, seasonal fruit from
garden. SC available, please enquire.
See Sibford Gower Gardens for
details of garden
B&B, SC

CHAPMANS BARN
Nottingham Fee, Blewbury
OX11 9PG
Jenny Craig
T: 01235 851055
E: bnb@chapmansbarn.com
W: www.chapmansbarn.com
Accommodation: A private annexe
to a C17 thatched cottage with 1
bedroom (single, double, twin)
ensuite bathroom, sitting room,
nestled at the foot of the Berkshire
downs. Sun - Thurs £60 Fri - Sat £80
See Blewbury Gardens for details of
garden
B&B

GOWERS CLOSE
Sibford Gower, Banbury OX15 5RW
Judith Hitching and John Marshall
T: 01295 780348
E: j.hitching@virgin.net
Accommodation: C17 thatched
cottage has 1 double and 1 twin,
both ensuite, with low beams and log
fires, enchanting garden for
pampered guests to enjoy. Close to
Hidcote, Kiftsgate and many
Cotswold gardens. Price from £40
pppn. See Sibford Gower Gardens
for details of Garden
B&B

Powys

CYFIE FARM
Llanfihangel, Llanfyllin SY22 5JE
Neil & Claire Bale
T: 01691 648451
E: info@cyfiefarm.co.uk
W: www.cyfiefarm.co.uk
Accommodation: Minutes from
fairytale Lake Vyrnwy, this beautiful,
remote, 5* (Gold), 17th Century
Welsh Longhouse boasts a
magnificent peaceful setting with
stunning views over the magnificent
Vyrnwy Valley. Relax all day in your
own luxurious suite of rooms or in
our lovely gardens nestling into the
hillside. Enjoy the tranquillity from our
hot tub & sauna spa complex with
views across the width of Wales .
Cordon Bleu cuisine. Two beautiful
self-catering cottages available all
year round.
B&B, SC

MILL COTTAGE
Abbeycwmhir, Powys, Llandrindod
Wells LD1 6PH
Mr & Mrs B D Parfitt
T: 01597 851935
E: nkmillcottage@yahoo.co.uk
W: www.Abbeycwmhir.co.uk
Accommodation: C18 cottage in a
peaceful village in the beautiful
Cambrian mountains. 1 double/twin
with private bathroom. 2 singles (one
with dressing room and basin).
Private bathroom. Evening meals by
arrangement. Ideal for walkers and
cyclists.
B&B

PLAS DOLGUOG HOTEL
Felingerrig, Dolguog Estates,
Machynlleth SY20 8UJ
Anthony & Tina Rhodes
T: 01654 702244
E: info@plasdolguog.co.uk
W: www.plasdolguog.co.uk
Accommodation: Family run hotel,
David Bellamy Conservation Award,
9 acres including Grandma's Garden.
Family & ground floor rooms - all
individual with ensuite facilities. Cu
Og's restaurant offers panoramic
views over the Dyfi Valley &
Snowdonia National Park. See
Grandma's Garden for details of
garden.
B&B, H

Shropshire

BROWNHILL HOUSE
Ruyton XI Towns SY4 1LR
Yoland & Roger Brown
T: 01939 261121
E: brownhill@eleventowns.co.uk
W: www.eleventowns.co.uk
Accommodation: Old world
standards, modern facilities & relaxed
atmosphere. Unique 2 acre hillside
garden - must be seen to be
believed. In the garden rich corner
where England meets Wales. Easy
access - Chester to Ludlow,
Snowdonia to Ironbridge. Find out all
about us and our garden on our
website.
B&B

THE CITADEL
Weston under Redcastle SY4 5JY
Beverley and Sylvia Griffiths
T: 01630 685 204
E: griffiths@thecitadelweston.co.uk
W: www.thecitadelweston. co.uk
Accommodation: An unusual red
sandstone mansion overlooking a
Grade 1 listed landscape. Three
double suites are elegant,
comfortable and have beautiful
bathrooms. A very cosseted
experience awaits you.
B&B

EDGE VILLA
Edge, nr Yockleton SY5 9PY
Chris & Bill Neil
T: 01743 821651
E: bill@billneil.fsnet.co.uk
Accommodation: Stable Cottage
annex, double bedroom, bathroom,
sitting room and kitchen. Use of
tennis court. Stunning views over
South Shropshire hills. Walking &
Cycling country. Non Smokers
SC

MAREHAY FARM
Gatten, Pontesbury SY5 0SJ
Carol & Stuart Buxton
T: 01588 650289
Accommodation: 2 ensuite rooms,
one twin, one double in one of the
last idyllic areas of England. Far from
the madding crowd and noble strife!"
B&B from £27.50 per person."
B&B

THE STUDIO APARTMENT
Lightwood, Upton Cressett
WV16 6UL
Margaret & Tony Bill
T: 01746 789645
E: margaret_bill@btinternet.com
W: www.shropshiretourism. co.uk/
accommodationdetails.php?estid=
6865
Accommodation: The Studio is
reached by an external staircase.
Sleeps 2 in open plan area. Kitchen
and shower room. Bridgnorth 4
miles, Ditton Priors 3, in AONB. All
linen provided. Set in 1 acre garden
in open countryside. See
www.shropshiretourism.co.uk/
accommodationdetails.php?estid=
6865 for details. See Heath House
for details of garden.
SC

Somerset and Bristol

BEANACRE BARN
Turners Court Lane, Binegar,
Radstock BA3 4UA
Susan & Tony Griffin
T: 01749 841628
E: smgriffin@beanacrebarn.co.uk
W: www.beanacrebarn.co.uk
Accommodation: Self catering
cottage in the Mendip Hills 4m north
of Wells. 4 Star (English Tourist Bd).
Imaginatively converted beamed
barn, beautifully furnished, equipped
and particularly spacious. All modern
facilities and comfort in a traditional
setting. Sleeps 2. Bath / Bristol 13
miles. Many NT properties and NGS
gardens within easy reach. Own
south-facing walled garden and
patio. See Church Farm House for
details of garden.
SC

BEECH HOUSE B & B
Iron Acton BS37 9XX
John & Hazel Williams
T: 01454 313679
E: bandb@beech-house.biz
W: www.beech-house.biz
Accommodation: Farmhouse
accommodation serving home
grown/local produce for breakfast.
Approved by tourist board. All rooms
en-suite with hospitality tray, TV and
internet. Some with far reaching rural
views. Gardens open to residents all
year round. Sorry no pets or children.
B&B

BINHAM GRANGE
Old Cleeve, Minehead TA24 6HX
Marie Thomas
T: 01984 640056
E: mariethomas@btconnect.com
W: www.binhamgrange.co.uk
Accommodation: A warm welcome
awaits you at Binham Grange,
mentioned in the 13th Century in
association with Cleeve Abbey.
Rooms are individually decorated
with antiques, books and flowers.
Local produce, herbs and vegetables
from own garden simply prepared.
B&B

CADWELL HILL BARN
West Littleton, Chippenham
SN14 8JE
Mrs Elizabeth Edwards
T: 01225 891122 or 07787305500
E: maesdewi1@gmail.com
W: www.cadwellhillbarn.co.uk
Accommodation: A unique barn
with high quality accommodation

having double bedroom with ensuite
shower room and own sitting room.
Two other double bedrooms with
bathrooms and one single bedroom.
Also two lounges with TV.
B&B

CHERRY BOLBERRY FARM
Furge Lane, Henstridge,
Templecombe BA8 0RN
Mrs Jennifer Raymond
T: 01963 362177
E: cherrybolberryfarm@tiscali.co.uk
Accommodation: Farmhouse B&B
on working organic dairy farm with
Jersey dairy cattle & Oxford sheep.
1 double and 1 twin, £30.00 pppn.
Very peaceful setting in no through
lane with far reaching views. T.V, tea
and coffee facilities. Full English
breakfast, mainly with home
produced produce, served in
conservatory overlooking the one
acre garden. Use of heated
swimming pool.
B&B

CRICKET ST THOMAS HOTEL
nr Chard TA20 4DD
Warner Leisure Hotels
T: 01460 30111
E: cricketstthomas.reception@
bourne-leisure.co.uk
W: www.cricketstthomas.co.uk
Accommodation: Cricket St
Thomas Hotel, part of Warner Leisure
Hotels, is an elegant mansion c1820,
set in the heart of Somerset's cider
country.The hotel has 239 bedrooms
including the beautiful 'Historic'
rooms in the Old House. Cricket St
Thomas is noted for the glorious
mature trees and shrubs in its 46
acres of Grade II listed Lakes and
Gardens, the 12th Century parish
church of St Thomas - and centuries
of noble ownership both famous and
diverse. This stunning country hotel
will welcome you as 'to the manor
born' and yes, this was the location
for the famous TV series.
H

FARNDON THATCH
Puckington, Ilminster TA19 9JA
Bob & Jane St John Wright
T: 01460 259845
E: bobstjw@yahoo.co.uk
W: www.bandbinsomerset.com
Accommodation: Beautiful C16
thatched cottage with superb
panoramic views and an acre of
garden - cottage garden style, fine
trees, lawns & sculptures.
Accommodation 2 doubles (1 ensuite
1 private bathroom) both very

comfortably furnished with views
over garden, TV, beverages, filtered
water, hairdryer. Guest sitting room,
full English breakfast with local
produce & own jams. WiFi and
plenty of private parking. Please see
website.
B&B

HANGERIDGE FARMHOUSE
Wrangway, Wellington TA21 9QT
Mrs J M Chave
T: 01823 662339
E: hangeridge@hotmail.co.uk
W: www.hangeridge.co.uk
Accommodation: A family run B&B.
Located in Wrangway near
Wellington on the Somerset/Devon
border. Very peaceful setting down a
country lane, on the edge of the
Blackdown Hills. One double room
with private bathroom and a twin
bedded room.
B&B

HARPTREE COURT
East Harptree BS40 6AA
Mr & Mrs Charles Hill
T: 01761 221729
E: location.harptree@tiscali.co.uk
W: www.harptreecourt.co.uk
Accommodation: 3 large double
en suite rooms in elegant period
house surrounded by beautiful
landscaped grounds including
ponds, waterfall, underground
passage, ice house, lily pond and a
2 acre walled garden. Good local
pub only 300 yards away. You are
encouraged to walk around the 17
acres of woodland and garden. £120
B&B pn incl afternoon tea on arrival
(£75 single occ.)
B&B

HOMEWOOD PARK HOTEL
Abbey Lane, Hinton Charterhouse,
Bath BA2 7TB
von Essen Hotels
T: 01225 723731
E: info@homewoodpark.co.uk
W: www.homewoodpark.co.uk
Accommodation: Beautifully
refurbished, this country house hotel
near Bath is one of the loveliest in the
West Country. A beautiful brand new
luxorious spa, 21 individually designed
contemporary bedrooms, individually
furnished to a high standard. B&B
prices from £70 per person.
H

LOWER SEVERALLS FARMHOUSE

Lower Severalls, Crewkerne
TA18 7NX
Mary Cooper & Mike Wycherley
T: 01460 73234
E: mary@lowerseveralls.co.uk
W: www.lowerseveralls.co.uk
Accommodation: Converted stable and loft next to 17th Century farmhouse located on Somerset Dorset border, perfect for visiting the Classic Gardens of Somerset, the Jurassic Coast and for walking or cycling. 3 acre garden & nursery featured in Gardens Illustrated. Ham stone country. £35 pppn incl. farmhouse or healthy breakfast options. Cards accepted.
B&B, SC

SELF REALIZATION MEDITATION HEALING CENTRE

Laurel Lane, Queen Camel
BA22 7NU
Charitable Trust - SRMHC
T: 01935 850266
E: info@selfrealizationcentres.org
W: www.selfrealizationcentres. org
Accommodation: The accommodation is comfortable, simple, home style and non-smoking with beautiful vegetarian meals available. The spacious grounds include meditation rooms, a heated indoor therapy pool and a lovely sitting room with a log fire. Retreat chalets available.
B&B, SC

SPINDLE COTTAGE

Binegar Green, Binegar, nr Bath
BA3 4UE
Angela Bunting
T: 01749 840497
E: angela@spindlecottage.co.uk
W: www.spindlecottage.co.uk
Accommodation: Fairytale picturesque C17 cottage Sleeps 5, 3 bedrooms. Set in peaceful garden with summer-house, gazebo, conservatory and three magical playhouses. Within the cottage, carvings of mushrooms, spiders' webs, birds and mice. Quite magical.
SC

STOBERRY HOUSE

Stoberry Park, Wells BA5 3LD
Frances Young
T: 01749 672906
E: stay@stoberry-park.co.uk
W: www.stoberry-park.co.uk
Accommodation: Stoberry House is set within 26 acres of parkland with outstanding views over the City of Wells and the Vale of Avalon and within easy walking distance of Wells. The ancient City with its Cathedral has many interesting historical sights. The garden has seats strategically placed to take advantage of our outstanding views and as darkness falls we light the one and a half acre walled garden so our guests can enjoy the visual difference and contrast of light and shadow on the plants and sculptures: it is like painting with light.
B&B

STON EASTON PARK

Ston Easton, Radstock BA3 4DF
von Essen Hotels
T: 01761 241631
E: info@stoneaston.co.uk
W: www.stoneaston.co.uk
Accommodation: A superb Palladian mansion set in one of the West Country's most romantic estates, Ston Easton Park exudes elegance, warmth and comfort. Log fires burn, comfortable antique furniture and exquisite paintings beckon, evoking memories of a more leisured age and providing a welcome you might associate with a magnificent private country house. There is little that can compare with the well preserved classicism of Ston Easton Park.
H

WESTBROOK HOUSE

West Bradley BA6 8LS
Keith Anderson & David Mendel
T: 01458 850604
E: westbrookbandb@aol.com
W: www.westbrook-bed-breakfast.co.uk
Accommodation: Charming B & B in quiet rural village, surrounded by 4 acres of gardens and orchards. 4 miles from Glastonbury and 6 miles from Castle Cary. Dinner available with prior notice.
B&B

WOOLLEY GRANGE HOTEL

Woolley Street, Bradford-on-Avon
BA15 1TX
T: 01225 864705
E: info@woolleygrangehotel.co.uk
W: www.woolleygrangehotel. co.uk
Accommodation: A beautiful Jacobean Manor House standing in 14 acres of grounds on the outskirts of the medieval wool town of Bradford-on-Avon in Wiltshire. Woolley Grange was a family home for 400 years before becoming the first Luxury Family Hotel in 1989. Woolley Grange still retains the atmosphere of home, arriving tired from your journey, formality is replaced with a warm welcome and an understanding that our youngest guests need to let off steam whilst you need some welcome refreshments. No request is too great, Woolley is your home whilst you are with us; relax, unwind and let us take care of you!
B&B, H

Staffordshire Birmingham and part of West Midlands

THE OLD RECTORY

Mavesyn Ridware, nr Rugeley
WS15 3QE
Sandra & Riach Ryder
T: 01543 490792 / 07816 296975
E: sandra@oldrectory-mavesyn.co.uk
Accommodation: Grade II listed building, former 18th Century Rectory steeped in history situated within a peaceful medieval hamlet. Surrounded by beautiful countryside and easy access for walking along the River Trent and canal. Now serving as a comfortable, relaxing retreat for the discerning visitor. The house sits in magnificent gardens. Easy access to main routes.
B&B

WINDY ARBOUR

Hollis Lane, Denstone ST14 5HP
Dave & Gill Brown
T: 01889 591013
E: stay@windyarbour.co.uk
W: www.windyarbour.co.uk
Accommodation: A hilltop farmhouse providing accommodation in either the house or annexes. A peaceful retreat with panoramic views over the surrounding countryside and a relaxing place to stay as a base for exploring Staffordshire, or visiting Alton Towers and the Peak District.
B&B, SC

Suffolk

BAYS FARM BED & BREAKFAST
Forward Green, Earl Stonham
IP14 5HU
Richard & Stephanie Challinor
T: 01449 711286
E: info@baysfarmsuffolk.co.uk
W: www.baysfarmsuffolk.co.uk
Accommodation: Bays Farm is 5
Star accommodation where we offer
luxurious bedrooms, stylishly modern
en-suite facilities, gardens to delight
and a delicious breakfast to ensure
our guests feel completely at home
and totally spoiled. Double / twin
rooms from £75 per room per night
including breakfast.
B&B

FEN HOUSE
Fen Road, Pakenham IP31 2LP
Lynn Patterson & Glynn Evans
T: 01359 234968
E: fen.house@hotmail.co.uk
W: www.fenhouse.net
Accommodation: 4* Silver Award
winning bed & breakfast in
Pakenham (village has a working
windmill and watermill) close to Bury
St Edmunds. 3 double rooms with
en-suites and 1 family suite
comprising 1 room with king bed,
1 room with double bed and
adjoining family bathroom with bath
and large shower. Beds have
memory mattresses, all rooms have
TV/DVD/Freeview/Free Wifi, welcome
trays, hairdryers. All rooms are non-
smoking and we regret we are
unable to accept pets.
B&B

PAVILION HOUSE
133 Station Road, Dullingham,
Suffolk, CB8 9UT
Mrs Gretta Bredin
T: 01638 508005
Mobile: 07776 197709
E: gretta@thereliablesauce.co.uk
W: www.pavilionhousebandb. co.uk
Accommodation: David and Gretta
welcome you to Pavilion House, and
glorious 1 acre garden with stunning
rural views. We are a short walk from
the train station with local
connections to Newmarket (3 miles)
and Cambridge (10 miles).
Dullingham has a great 'local' pub
and also a good restaurant. Our
accommodation consists of one
double, one twin and one single
room, all with private bath or shower
rooms. Prices: £70 for twin or
double, £40 for single or single
occupancy, inclusive of breakfast.
Gretta will give you a great breakfast,
eggs and other home produce.. Well

behaved dogs by arrangement.
Three course dinner by arrangement
from £25
B&B

ROSEMARY
Rectory Hill, East Bergholt CO7 6TH
Mrs Natalie Finch
T: 01206 298241
Accommodation: Situated in the
heart of Constable country within
easy reach of Harwich and Flatford.
Garden featured on Gardeners'
World. 3 twin rooms - with hand
basins, 1 single room. Shared
bathroom. Price £32 per person per
night
B&B

THE WALLOW
Mount Road, Bury St Edmunds
IP31 2QU
Linda Draper
T: 01284 788055
E: info@thewallow.co.uk
W: www.thewallow.co.uk
Accommodation: Two large suites
in Ranch style bungalow, set in 2
acre garden haven, surrounded by
countryside yet close to Bury St
Edmunds town centre.
B&B

Surrey

COVERWOOD FARM
Coverwood Farm, Peaslake Road,
Ewhurst GU6 7NT
Ann Metson
T: 01306 731101
E: coverwoodfarm@coverwoodlakes.
co.uk
W: www.coverwoodlakes.co.uk
Accommodation: C14 farmhouse
on a working farm in the Surrey Hills.
14 acres of lakes and gardens.
Amazing walking, riding and cycling.
1 twin bedded and 1 single room.
Private bathroom, stable and grazing.
B&B

GREAT FOSTERS
Stroude Road, Egham TW20 9UR
The Sutcliffe Family
T: 01784 433822
E: reservations@greatfosters.co.uk
W: www.greatfosters.co.uk
Accommodation: More than
4 centuries of celebrated history have
enriched Great Fosters with
remarkable heritage. Countless
original features remain within this
Grade One listed Historic monument.
The Oak Room restaurant has been
awarded 3 rosettes by the AA.
Bedrooms range from historic

grandeur to more contemporary in
style. Double/twin rooms start from
£175 per night.
H

WALTON POOR HOUSE
Ranmore RH5 6SX
Prue Calvert
T: 01483 282273
E: wnscalvert@btinternet.com
Accommodation: Walton Poor
House was built in 1924/1925. The
Self catering accommodation
comprises a self contained annexe,
kitchen/bathroom, bedroom.
Entrance to garden. The House is
close to RHS garden Wisley,
Polesden Lacey, Clandon Park.
Good walking and cycling area. £50
per night. My husband and I moved
here in 1971 and have developed the
main garden; at the same time Prue
Calvert built up the herb nursery, by
the cottage, specialising in aromatic
and scented plants and a number of
the mature trees were planted at the
same time.
SC

WOTTON HOUSE
Guildford Road, Dorking RH5 6HS
Principal Hayley & Conference
Centres
T: 01306 730000
E: wotton.reservation@principal-
hayley.com
W: www.principal-
hayley.com/venues-and-
hotels/wotton-house
Accommodation: Wotton House
has 111 ensuite facilities. 91 double
rooms, 20 twins and 1 adapted for
disabled use. Each room has: Wi-Fi,
TV, safe, tea & coffee making
facilities, hairdryers, trouser press &
iron. Dry cleaning service.
H

Sussex

BUTLERS FARMHOUSE
Butlers Lane, Flowers Green,
Herstmonceux BN27 1QH
Irene Eltringham-Willson
T: 01323 833770
E: irene.willson@btinternet.com
W: www.irenethegardener.
zoomshare.com
Accommodation: A charming C16
farmhouse in 5 acres of idyllic, quiet
countryside. Enjoy breakfast
overlooking fantastic views of the
South Downs. 3 double rooms. Laze
around outdoor swimming pool.
Herstmonceux and Pevensey Castles

nearby. From £75. As featured in Channel 4 TV's Four in a Bed.
B&B

COPYHOLD HOLLOW
Copyhold Lane, Lindfield, Haywards Heath RH16 1XU
Frances B G Druce
T: 01444 413265
E: yb@copyholdhollow.co.uk
W: www.copyholdhollow.co.uk
Accommodation: Guests' sitting room with inglenook fireplace, oak beams, cotton sheets, ensuite bedrooms, C16 home surrounded by countryside. Double/twin £45/£50 pppn, single £50/£55 pn.4*(Gold Award)
B&B

THE GRANARY
Southerham Lane, Southerham BN8 6JN
Steve & Alison Grint
T: 01273 480728
E: ali899@hotmail.co.uk
Accommodation: Very comfortable, tastefully furnished rooms with ensuite in charming converted granary at the foot of the South Downs. Tea and coffee facilities, TV, hairdryer. Beautiful walks straight on to the Downs. Walk also to historic market town of Lewes - castle, museums, art galleries, flea markets, restaurants. Easy access to Glyndebourne, Brighton, London (1 hour by train). Delicious breakfast served outside if weather permits. See Southerham Gardens for garden details.
B&B

HAILSHAM GRANGE
Hailsham BN27 1BL
Noel Thompson
T: 01323 844248
E: noel@hgrange.co.uk
W: www.hailshamgrange.co.uk
Accommodation: Hailsham Grange is an early 18th century former vicarage located at the heart of the market town of Hailsham. Built in the Mary-Anne style the house with its acre of garden provides a welcome oasis for those who wish to pamper themselves with traditional hospitality and comfort. The house exemplifies classical English decoration while the garden provides on–going interest through the changing seasons, Hailsham Grange provides an ideal location for those wishing to visit the diverse range of gardens to be found in the East Sussex and West Kent area.
B&B

HAM COTTAGE
Highbrook, Ardingly RH17 6SR
Mr & Mrs P Browne
T: 01444 892746
E: aegbrowne@btinternet.com
Accommodation: C18 cottage set in 8 acres of landscaped gardens within the heart of Sussex, providing 2 double & 1 twin room each with its own bathroom.
B&B

KING JOHN'S LODGE
Sheepstreet Lane, Etchingham TN19 7AZ
Jill Cunningham
T: 01580 819232
E: kingjohnslodge@aol.com
W: www.kingjohnsnursery.co.uk
Accommodation: B&B in this historic listed house surrounded by 8 acres of gardens, meadows and plant nursery. All rooms ensuite.
B&B

LORDINGTON HOUSE
Lordington PO18 9DX
Mr & Mrs John Hamilton
T: 01243 375862
E: hamiltonjanda@btinternet.com
Accommodation: Comfortable accommodation offered in double, twin and single rooms with own bath/shower. All rooms have fine views over National Park. Breakfast times flexible. Packed lunches and supper by arrangement. Price from £47.50 pppn
B&B

MOOR FARM
Horsham Road, Petworth GU28 0HD
Richard Chandler
T: 01798 342161
E: richardandflo1@btinternet.com
Accommodation: B&B accommodation on large working arable farm, well off the road, lakeside setting, within sight of Petworth Park. Bring your own horse and explore the local bridleways. Coarse fishing on site. Good parking.
B&B

MORLANDS FARM
Wheatsheaf Road, Henfield BN5 9AT
Pauline McBride
T: 01273 495902
E: morlandsfarm@btinternet.com
W: www.sussexprairies.co.uk
Accommodation: Set within the beautiful Sussex Prairie landscape, our farmhouse offers the highest standard of comfort. Two double & one twin bedrooms all with ensuite facilities. Beautifully and individually decorated with free wifi access and tea and coffee making facilties.

Unlimited access to the Prairie Garden at all times. Delicious breakfast sourced from our farm and garden and quality local suppliers. See Sussex Prairies for details of garden.
B&B

NETHERBY
Bolney Road, Ansty RH17 5AW
Mr & Mrs Russell Gilbert
T: 01444 455888
E: susan@gilbert58.freeserve.co.uk
Accommodation: A warm welcome awaits you in this cosy Victorian cottage. See Ansty Gardens for details of garden
B&B

NETHERWOOD LODGE
Chiddingly, Muddles Green BN8 6HS
Margaret Clarke
T: 01825 872512
E: netherwoodlodge@hotmail.com
W: www.netherwoodlodge. co.uk
Accommodation: A former coach house amidst glorious, quiet countryside. Twin room with ensuite and double room with private bathroom over looking garden. Egyptian cotton linen and luxury toiletries. Home-made bread, preserves and yoghurt. See Laughton Gardens for details of garden
B&B

OCKLYNGE MANOR
Mill Road, Eastbourne BN21 2PG
Wendy & David Dugdill
T: 01323 734121
E: ocklyngemanor@hotmail.com
W: www.ocklyngemanor.co.uk
Accommodation: Grade II listed Georgian house in walled garden. Awarded 3rd in The Independent Newspaper's 50 Best British B&Bs. Free private parking. Once home to Peter Pan illustrator Mavel Lucy Attwell. 5* Gold award Mabel Lucy Attwell. 5* Gold award."
B&B

PINDARS
Lyminster Road, Lyminster, nr Arundel BN17 7QF
Jocelyne & Clive Newman
T: 01903 882628
E: pindars@tiscali.co.uk
W: www.pindars.co.uk
Accommodation: Comfortable, friendly country house with special emphasis on hospitality and good food. Delicious and varied breakfasts, imaginatively cooked. Evening meals on request, with vegetables from the prolific garden!
B&B

SOUTH GRANGE
Quickbourne Lane, Northiam, Rye
TN31 6QY
Mr & Mrs Belton
T: 01797 252984
E: belton.northiam@virgin.net
W: www.southgrange-
northiam.co.uk
Accommodation: Accommodation
consists of one double, one twin-
bedded and one single room with
use of a large private bathroom in a
modern detached house situated on
a quiet country lane on the edge of
the village.
B&B

STANE HOUSE
Bignor RH20 1PQ
Angie Symes
T: 01798 869454
E: angie@stanehouse.co.uk
W: www.stanehouse.co.uk
Accommodation: Beautiful country
location under South Downs with
tremendous views. Luxury well-
appointed ensuite accommodation,
friendly hosts and scrumptious
breakfasts. Set in an acre of classic
English style gardens in a tiny pretty
village. Close to many well known
gardens.
B&B

Warwickshire

SPRINGFIELD HOUSE
School Lane, Warmington OX17 1DD
Roger & Jenny Handscombe
T: 01295 690286
E: jenny.handscombe@virgin.net
W: www.stayatspringfield.co.uk
Accommodation: A warm welcome,
a comfy bed and a wonderful
breakfast - all in superb period
surroundings. Twin, king or super-king
all with private bathroom. Handy for
Cotswolds. Compton Verney and
Shakespeare. No Smoking. £27.50
pppn. See Warmington Village
Gardens for details of garden
B&B

Wiltshire

BECKETTS HOUSE
Tinhead Road, Edington, Westbury
BA13 4PJ
Mrs Susan Bromhead
T: 01380 830100
E: sue@bromhead.org
Accommodation: C16/17/18 listed
house, in lovely village, set in 2½
acres, tennis court, lake, summer
house & superb views. 3 large twin

beds, ensuite/private bathrooms.
Guests' drawing room. Walks on
doorstep. Longleat, Bath, Salisbury
nearby. See Edington Gardens for
details of garden
B&B

BROOMSGROVE LODGE
New Mill, nr Pewsey SN9 5LE
Diana Robertson
T: 01672 810515
E: diana@broomsgrovelodge.co.uk
W: www.sawdays.co.uk
Accommodation: Thatched house
with very comfortable twin and single
accommodation. Own chickens and
large vegetable garden. Close to
Marlborough and the canal, with
wonderful views over Pewsey Vale
and Martinsell Hill.
B&B

89 CHURCH LAWN
Stourhead
National Trust
T: 0844 800 2070
E: cottages@nationaltrust.org.uk
W: www.nationaltrustcottages. co.uk
Accommodation: This charming
stone cottage stands right at the
entrance to Stourhead Garden
overlooking the historic St Peter's
church with the renowned Spread
Eagle Inn just over the road.
Accomodates 7 people.
SC

GOULTERS MILL FARM
The Gibb, nr Castle Combe
SN14 7LL
Alison Harvey
T: 01249 782555
Accommodation: Delightful rooms
in old mill house, all ensuite and
equipped with kingsized beds.
Convenient for Bristol, Bath or
Cotswolds. The house is set in
cottage gardens in a steep sided
valley. See Littleton Drew Gardens for
details of garden
B&B

THE MILL HOUSE
Berwick St James, Salisbury
SP3 4TS
Diana Gifford Mead/Michael Mertens
T: 01722 790331
W: www.millhouse.org.uk
Accommodation: 4 ensuite, 2
single rooms from £60 pp single,
£90, double. High quality
accommodation. Very quiet, beautiful
garden. Highly sourced and organic
food. Part of old farm.
B&B

THE POUND HOUSE
Little Somerford, Chippenham
SN15 5JW
Mrs Michael Baines
T: 01666 823212
E: squeezebaines@yahoo.com
Accommodation: 2 twins, shared
bathroom. 2 doubles, own
bathrooms. Aga breakfast, home-laid
eggs. Old rectory, large well planted
garden, beautiful trees, lots of
animals! Pets by arrangement. 4
miles from J17 M4. Ideal for
Cotswolds and Bath. £35 pppn.
B&B

RIDLEYS CHEER
Mountain Bower, Chippenham
SN14 7AJ
Sue & Antony Young
T: 01225 891204
E: sueyoung@ridleyscheer.co.uk
Accommodation: 1 double with
private bathroom. 1 double and
1 twin bedded room with shared
bathroom. Prices from £90 per night.
Single occ from £55. Dinner £40 per
head.
B&B

WHATLEY MANOR
Easton Grey, Twatley SN16 0RB
Christian Landolt & Alix Landolt
T: 01666 822888
E: reservations@whatleymanor.com
W: www.whatleymanor.com
Accommodation: Privately owned
hotel with 23 individually decorated,
luxury rooms or suites. The hotel's
restaurant, 'The Dining Room', has a
Michelin 2* award. The 'Le Mazot'
brasserie is perfect for informal
dining. Award winning spa. Beautiful
peaceful gardens.
H

Worcestershire

BROOK FARM
Worcestershire, nr Tenbury Wells
WR15 8TJ
Sarah & William Wint
T: 01584 819868
E: sarah@brookfarmberrington.com
W: www.brookfarmberrington. com
Accommodation: Brook Farm
nestles in its own little valley where
we are making a garden on fairly
soggy clay soil. So far, amongst other
things, we've made a cottage
garden, some wild and wiggly beds,
covered a pergola in wisteria and
planted lots of roses. In 2011 we are
planting a new 20 metre Bug Border.
B&B

LUGGERS HALL
Broadway WR12 7BT
Kay & Red Haslam
T: 01386 852040
E: luggershall@hotmail.com
W: www.luggershall.com
Accommodation: 2 king-size
double rooms with beautiful views of
gardens and 1 double room all with
private ensuite bathrooms. Also self-
catering in self contained apartment
plus separate cottage in adjacent
Cotswold village of Broadway. Prices
from £65 per night.
B&B

NAFFORD HOUSE
Eckington, Pershore WR10 3DJ
Mr & Mrs John Wheatley
T: 01386 750233
Accommodation: Nafford House is
situated in 6 acres, 2 acres of mature
gardens sweeping down to the River
Avon, also a copse of specimen
trees. 2 twin rooms with private
bathroom.
B&B

RECTORY COTTAGE
Old Rectory Lane, Alvechurch
B48 7SU
Celia Hitch
T: 0121 445 4824
E: celiaandsteve@reccott.
freeserve.co.uk
W: www.rectorycottage-
alvechurch.co.uk
Accommodation: Rectory Cottage
is a large family home in a lovely
riverside setting offering spacious
and elegant bedrooms, all ensuite
and overlooking the gardens. Family
room, double room, twin bedded
room. Easy access from J2 of M42.
Prices from £35 pppn. Garden opens
for NGS 5 June 2011.
B&B

SEECHEM MANOR
Rowney Green Lane, Alvechurch
B48 7EL
Mrs NJ Sethia
T: 07802494494
E: nicolasethia@hotmail.co.uk
Accommodation: Lovely,
comfortable self-contained one
bedroom annexe with super kingsize
or twin beds. En suite bathroom,
sunny sitting room with sofa bed and
kitchenette. Small private garden with
seating area set within main garden
of 4 acres and grounds of 17 acres.
Good walks and easy access to
pubs and Becketts Farm Shop.
Good base for Worcestershire,
Stratford, Warwick and NEC. £80 per
night. Breakfast by separate
arrangement.
SC

Yorkshire

AUSTWICK HALL
Town Head Lane, Austwick,
Lancaster LA2 8BS
Eric Culley and Michael Pearson
T: 015242 51794
E: austwickhall@austwick.org
W: www.austwickhall.co.uk
Accommodation: Country House
accommodation. An historic Manor
House set in 13 acres. The five
ensuite bedrooms provide spacious
accommodation individually
decorated and furnished with
antiques. Dinner available.
B&B

COLD COTES
Cold Cotes Road, nr. Kettlesing,
Harrogate HG3 2LW
Ed Loft
T: 01423 770937
E: info@coldcotes.com
W: www.coldcotes.com
Accommodation: Cold Cotes'
guests say this is a special place to
stay, tranquil setting, beautiful and
comfortable rooms, excellent
breakfast, an inspiring garden, with
service second to none. We have
6 ensuite guest rooms and facilities
for small events. Prices from £70
double
B&B

DANES WELL HOUSE
Main Street, Stamford Bridge
YO41 1AD
Pauline Clayton
T: 01759 371446
Accommodation: 1930s house has
comfortable bedrooms overlooking
fishpond and sloping garden down to
the River Derwent.
B&B

DOWTHORPE HALL
Skirlaugh, Hull HU11 5AE
Caroline Holtby
T: 01964 562235
E: john.holtby@farming.co.uk
Accommodation: Dowthorpe Hall
provides a twin room, ensuite, a
double room with own bathroom & a
single room, all offering the ultimate
in luxury. Caroline, a cordon bleu
cook, is happy to offer evening meals
with home grown ingredients.
B&B

FAWLEY HOUSE
7 Nordham, North Cave, Brough
HU15 2LT
Mr & Mrs T Martin
T: 01430 422266
E: louisem200@hotmail.co.uk
Accommodation: 2 holiday
cottages1 sleeps 6, and the other
sleeps 2
SC

GOLDSBOROUGH HALL
Church Street, Goldsborough,
Knaresborough HG5 8NR
Mark & Clare Oglesby
T: 01423 867321
E: info@goldsboroughhall.com
W: www.goldsboroughhall.com
Accommodation: Grade II* listed
C17 stately home, former residence
of HRH Princess Mary, the Queen's
aunt. Six luxury suites offering 5*
B&B, highest rated accommodation
in North Yorkshire. 8ft four poster
beds and whirlpool baths. 11 acres
of beautiful landscaped gardens.
B&B

LAWKLAND HALL
Austwick LA2 8AT
Mr & Mrs Giles Bowring
T: 01729 823551
E: diss@austwick.org
Accommodation: Relaxed,
spacious Elizabethan country house.
Choose from 1 double and 3 twin
bedrooms. Large, comfortable
drawing room overlooking the
garden. £45 per person per night.
B&B

LOWER HEUGH COTTAGE
GARDEN
14-16 Kirk Lane, Eastby, Skipton
BD23 6SH
Trevor & Marian Nash
T: 01756 793702
E: nash862@btinternet.com
W: www.cottageguide.co.uk
Accommodation: Immaculate 5*
Gold cottage set in Japanese award
winning garden. Beautiful views of
garden and surrounding fells yet only
3 miles from Skipton. Sleeps 2.
Comprehensively equipped. Open all
year. See website for full details and
charges.
SC

MANOR FARM
Thixendale, Malton YO17 9TG
Charles and Gilda Brader
T: 01377 288315
E: manorfarmthixendale@hotmail.com
W: www.manorfarmthixendale.co.uk
Accommodation: Private spacious
wing of farmhouse. Hot deep baths
and comfy sofas. Situated west end

of isolated village. Substantial breakfasts, fresh fruit, cereals, home-made bread. Buff Orpington eggs. Proper meat cooked in the Aga. Relax in a bygone era.
B&B

MILLGATE HOUSE
Millgate, Richmond DL10 4JN
Tim Culkin & Austin Lynch
T: 01748 823571
E: oztim@millgatehouse.demon. co.uk
W: www.millgatehouse.com
Accommodation: Prepare to be amazed - something very special - exceptional taste, furnishings from all over the world, stunning position, celebrated garden - breakfasts are superb. National Award winning garden selected from 3200 entries. And now named Bed and Breakfast of the Year 2011 by the Good Hotel Guide and the Sunday Times.
B&B, SC

RIVERSIDE FARM
Sinnington, York YO62 6RY
William and Jane Baldwin
T: 01751 431764

E: wnbaldwin@yahoo.co.uk
Accommodation: Situated in stunning, quiet village, Georgian farmhouse offers high class accommodation, private sitting room, wonderful atmosphere. 1 kingsize double ensuite. 1 twin with private bathroom. 1 single room. Price £35 pppn.
B&B

SLEIGHTHOLMEDALE LODGE
Kirbymoorside, York YO62 7JG
Mrs R James
T: 01751 431942
E: info@shdcottages.co.uk
W: www.shdcottages.co.uk
Accommodation: Peaceful, warm cottages round a stone courtyard, adjoining a working farm and garden. Max price - high season - £480 per cottage per week
SC

THORPE LODGE
Knaresborough Road, Ripon HG4 3LU
Tommy & Juliet Jowitt
T: 01765 602088
E: jowitt@btinternet.com

W: www.thorpelodge.co.uk
Accommodation: Listed Georgian house with 2 large double/twin rooms, both ensuite bath & shower, TV and tea/coffee making facilities. Own sitting room and entrance. Dogs kept and welcome.
B&B

WORTLEY HALL
Wortley, Sheffield S35 7DB
Jonathan da Rosa
T: 0114 2882100
E: info@wortleyhall.org.uk
W: www.wortleyhall.org.uk
Accommodation: The Hall itself was originally the ancestral home of the Earls of Wharncliffe and the property can be traced back to 1140 when Sir Thomas Wortley lived in the manor house believed to be Wortley Hall. The Hall fell into decay until the mid 18th Century when Edward Wortley commissioned the rebuilding of the Hall. The Hall has 49 en-suite bedrooms. All bedrooms have a direct telephone line which have a connection point to link a laptop to the Internet.
B&B

Garden Index

This index lists gardens alphabetically and gives the Yellow Book county section in which they are to be found.

Be tempted by a plant from a plant stall ✿

724

Bath/Somerset, Somerton

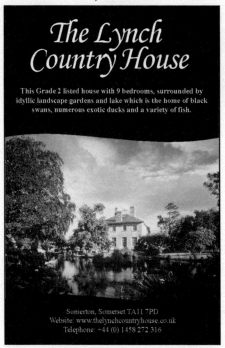

The Lynch Country House

This Grade 2 listed house with 9 bedrooms, surrounded by idyllic landscape gardens and lake which is the home of black swans, numerous exotic ducks and a variety of fish.

Somerton, Somerset TA11 7PD
Website: www.thelynchcountryhouse.co.uk
Telephone: +44 (0) 1458 272 316

Bath/Somerset, Wellington

Hangeridge Farm House

Enjoy a stay at our peaceful, family run B&B situated on the edge of the Blackdown Hills on the Devon/Somerset border. Other meals and packed lunches provided by arrangement

**Wrangway, nr Wellington, Somerset, TA21 9QG
Contact Mrs Chave 01823 662339
www.hangeridge.co.uk**

Bath/Wiltshire, Bath

Glebe House, Chittoe, Wiltshire

Silver award winning country house B & B in the most rural of locations

T: 01380 850864 | M: 07767 608841 | E: gscrope@aol.com
W: www.glebehouse-chittoe.co.uk

Cornwall, Falmouth

Carwinion
Cornwall's Bamboo Garden

- 12 acres of tranquil garden
- Over 200 types of bamboo
- Cream teas
- Dogs welcome

*Mawnan Smith, Nr Falmouth, 01326 250258
www.carwinion.co.uk*

Cornwall, St Agnes

Proprietor run country house three star hotel on the north Cornish coast set in 10 acres. Close to coastal path and 5mins from A30.

Special Offer: From 1st October 2010, stay for 5 nights half board from only **£312.50** per person.

Tel: 01872 552202
www.rose-in-vale-hotel.co.uk

*Offer valid until Easter 2011 and excludes Xmas and New Year

Rose in Vale
THE HOTEL IN THE VALLEY

Dorset, Sturminster Newton

For 30 years this 17th Century Manor House has been run by the Prideaux-Brune family as a restaurant with rooms where guests can enjoy excellent food specialising in local produce. The hotel is open all year round except February and the restaurant is open every night and for Sunday lunch.

PLUMBER MANOR
Sturminster Newton Dorset DT10 2AF
Tel: 01258 472507 • Fax: 01258 473370
www.plumbermanor.com • book@plumbermanor.com

Dorset, Wimborne Minster

Cranborne, Edmondsham, Knoll and
Kingston Lacey Gardens in Dorset

Are close to La Fosse with six comfortable, four-star quality
en-suite accommodations for B&B or B&B, Dinner

Relaxing atmosphere, good food and wine; Local, fresh,
seasonal, traditionally British
with a dash of International menu

Restaurant open for outside guests:
Lunch: Sunday
Dinner: Monday, Friday and Saturday

Private parties we open up any time.

Houseguests and their guests we cook every night, except Sundays

01525 817604
www.la-fosse.com
Restaurant with Rooms, The Square, Cranborne, BH21 5PR, Dorset

East Sussex, Hailsham

HAILSHAM GRANGE
Bed & Breakfast East Sussex

Comfortable accommodation & old fashioned hospitality in gracious early C18 former vicarage and adjoining Coach House.
Close to South Downs and many tourist attractions

For further details contact:
Noel Thompson
T 01323 844248
E noel@hgrange.co.uk
W www.hailshamgrange.co.uk

East Sussex, Newick

NEWICK PARK
HOTEL & COUNTRY ESTATE

RELAX

Come and enjoy the parkland and gardens at Newick Park - including our Royal Ferns - by taking advantage of our special offer:

Dinner, Bed & Breakfast
from £95pp

NEWICK PARK, NEWICK,
EAST SUSSEX BN8 4SB

+44 (0)1825 723633
bookings@newickpark.co.uk

www.newickpark.co.uk

Oxfordshire, Chipping Norton

Oxfordshire

Shropshire, Shrewsbury

Surrey, Dorking

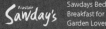

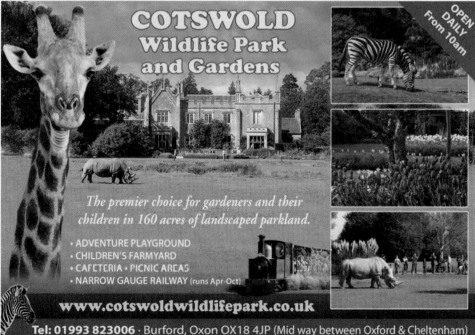

Oxfordshire, Wheatley

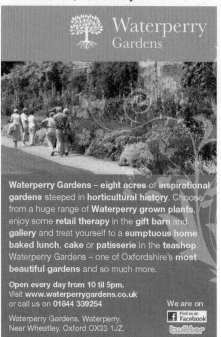

Waterperry Gardens – eight acres of inspirational **gardens** steeped in **horticultural history.** Choose from a huge range of **Waterperry grown plants,** enjoy some **retail therapy** in the **gift barn** and **gallery** and treat yourself to a **sumptuous home** baked lunch, cake or patisserie in the teashop. Waterperry Gardens – one of Oxfordshire's **most beautiful gardens** and so much more.

Open every day from 10 til 5pm.
Visit **www.waterperrygardens.co.uk**
or call us on **01844 339254**

Waterperry Gardens. Waterperry.
Near Wheatley. Oxford OX33 1JZ.

We are on
Find us on Facebook
twitter

Lancashire, Rufford

RUFFORD OLD HALL & GARDEN
Ormskirk, Lancashire, L40 1SG

This fascinating house is surrounded by lawns, herbaceous borders, topiary and an orchard growing old northern varieties of apples. In Spring enjoy the rhododendrons and azaleas, bluebells and the delights of the woodland walk.

Normal admission applies. NT members free.
Open mid March to end Oct, 11-5pm daily except Thurs & Fri. 01704 821254.
www.nationaltrust.org.uk/ruffordoldhall

National Trust
Time well spent   Registered charity No. 205846.

North East, Darlington

B
Raby Castle
Staindrop, Nr Darlington

"Discover One of England's Finest Medieval Castles"

Tel: 01833 660202   www.rabycastle.com

Worcestershire, Droitwich

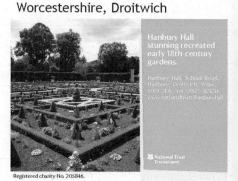

Hanbury Hall – stunning recreated early 18th-century gardens.

Hanbury Hall, School Road, Hanbury, Droitwich, Worc. WR9 7EA. Tel 01527 821214. www.nationaltrust/hanburyhall

National Trust
Time well spent

Registered charity No. 205846.

your time

We'd like to thank the National Gardens Scheme for their on-going support of *Careership*, our training scheme for gardeners. Thanks to this funding, we are able to develop the skills needed to keep over 200 gardens looking their very best. So people, like you, can enjoy a day out in beautiful surroundings.

If you would like to support the work of the National Trust, simply visit **nationaltrust.org.uk/donations**

An independent charity looking after special places for ever for everyone.

Hidcote Manor Garden, Gloucestershire.
Registered charity number 205846.

National Trust
Time well spent

Warwickshire

ngs gardens open for charity

Private Gardens of Somerset

Kilver Court

Departs

26 June 2011
4 days from £375pp

Departure points
London, Reading, Swindon, Bristol

Supplements per person

> Single room £60.00
> Insurance

What's Included

> 3 nights dinner, bed and breakfast at the Webbington Hotel, near Axbridge
> Comfortable coaching throughout. Rail/air connections and overnight accommodation in London or Bristol before or after the tour are available on request
> Visits to the gardens of Badger's Acre, Watcombe, Rose Cottage, Lift the Latch, Wayford Manor, Abbey Farm, Church Farm House, Kilver Court, Somerfoss and Holt Farm Organic Gardens

A 4-day package by air is available from Scotland from £475pp – please ask for details

Over the last few years Brightwater Holidays has been operating a series of exclusive short holidays on behalf of the National Gardens Scheme to scenic regions of England where a contribution per passenger goes to help NGS's sterling fundraising efforts.

One of England's most beautiful counties is of course Somerset, whose lush green pastures, orchards and little villages provide a wonderful backdrop to a most colourful and varied collection of private gardens. By their very nature these gardens are attached to private dwellings and are only opened through the kindness of their owners and we therefore feel very privileged to share them at a time when they will be looking at their absolute best. Over four days we will explore gardens around Axbridge, Blagdon and the Wells area, including a chance to visit the magnificent Wells cathedral. We visit Kilver Court in Shepton Mallet and the south of the county around Crewkerne and Chard, finishing high up on the Mendips with stunning views across The Levels to Glastonbury Tor.

Brightwater Holidays Brochure out now....

01334 657155

brightwater
holidays

Brightwater Holidays Ltd
Eden Park House,
Cupar, Fife KY15 4HS
info@brightwaterholidays.com
www.brightwaterholidays.com

Please go to the NGS Directory online at www.ngs.org.uk/directory

You'll find more information on all these companies and you'll be able to find out more about the NGS.

Gardd Fotaneg Genedlaethol Cymru
National Botanic Garden of Wales

Mae'r Ardd ar agor gydol y flwyddyn ac yn cynnig diwrnod allan arbenning i'r teulu i gyd. Dewch i weld y Tŷ Gwydr un haen mwyaf yn y byd, a nifer o atyniadau eraill gan gynnwys:

Open all year, the Garden offers a great day out for all the family. See the world's largest single span glasshouse and the many varied attractions including:

- Y Tŷ Gwydr Enfawr
- Tŷ Gwydr Trofannol Newydd
- Yr Ardd Siapaneaidd
- Oriel y Stablau
- Canolfan Ymwelwyr a Siop Rhoddion
- Theatr Botanica
- Arddangosfa Planhigion Iechyd
- Lle Chwarae i Blant
- Gwarchodfa Natur Genedlaethol Waun Las

- Great Glasshouse
- Tropical House
- Japanese Garden
- Stables Gallery
- Gift shop & Visitor Centre
- Theatr Botanica
- Plants for Health Exhibition
- Children's Play Area
- Waun Las National Nature Reserve

R'ydym ar agor bob dydd ag eithrio Dydd Nadolig
Haf:10am-6pm/Gaeaf: 10am-4.30pm

Open every day except Christmas Day
Summer: 10am-6pm / Winter: 10am-4.30pm

- **Oedolion £8.50** * Gostyngiadau £7 * Plant (5-16) £4.50
- **Dan 5 AM DDIM** * Tocyn Teulu (2 Oedolyn a 4 o blant) £21

- **Adults £8.50** * Concessions £7 * Children (5-16) £4.50
- **Under 5's FREE** * Family (2 Adults, up to 4 Children) £21

Mae cyfleusterau cynadledd a ac arlwyo ar gael ar gyfer hyd at 400 o bobl.

Addas iawn ar gyfer ymweliadau ysgol.

Conference and catering facilities for up to 400 people available.

School visits highly recommended.

I gael prisiau a rhagor o wybodaeth cysylltwch â: Gardd Fotaneg Genedlaethol Cymru Llanarthne, Sir Gaerfyrddin SA32 8HG

For prices and further information contact: The National Botanic Garden of Wales, Llanarthne, Carmarthenshire SA32 8HG

01558 668 768
www.gardenofwales.org.uk

National Botanic Garden of Wales
Gardd Fotaneg Genedlaethol Cymru

Voted the No1 Garden to visit in Wales by the BBC Gardeners' World Magazine

Great GARDEN DAY TOURS *for 2011*

Visits to raise funds for the NATIONAL GARDENS SCHEME in association with GARDENS ETC.

A TASTE OF SPRING GARDENS THURS 28 APRIL £85
Blossom is on the bough, so seize the moment and visit three gardens, starting at **Eccleston Square**, Belgravia, filled with ceanothus. Then to **Clapham** to see an artist's particularly pretty garden, where nine apple arches should be in blossom. And there's much to enjoy at **Petersham Lodge**, with three acres on the River Thames giving it a country estate feel, as expected for a house built as a royal hunting lodge in 1800 and now home to a prince and princess. There will be bluebells and camassias, and *Rosa banksiae* and wisteria smothering the walls.

NEW WALKING TOUR **SECRET GARDENS OF LONDON** TUES 24 MAY & SAT 9 JULY £50
Walk with us to explore the hidden gardens of the City of London, often unnoticed but redolent with history. On one small piece of pavement alone you will be walking over the bones of four early queens. Some are linked to great figures, like Shakespeare, and many are tucked away beside the old Medieval city walls. But they are not all ancient; we have one or two quite modern surprises, including a lake and water garden, where you may spot London's only pair of nesting peregrines.

SAILING UP THE RIVER WED 25 MAY CHELSEA WEEK £95
We shall explore gardens that bound the river from Blackfriars to Kew during Chelsea Flower Show week. We start at the 'most beautiful of the Temple gardens', **Middle Temple**. Next we embark on our boat, the Kingwood and head west to a palace: **Fulham**, for many centuries home to the Bishops of London. It has a new look thanks to a Lottery grant. After lunch at a riverside restaurant we reach the green oasis of Kew to see four 300ft long gardens in **Kew Green**, behind their elegant 18th century houses with terraces, lawns, rambling roses and woodland walks.

GRANDEUR IN HAMPSTEAD & HIGHGATE THURS 26 MAY £85
The streets are winding, the houses are stylish and we have picked four gardens to surprise you. A prime spot, off Parliament Hill, with two acres and vistas across to Hampstead Heath, **Millfield Place** backs on to the Highgate Ponds. A 17th century merchant's house, **Fenton** is a hidden gem of the National Trust. Head gardener Danny Snapes takes us round the garden and orchard. Few, too, know about the enormous **Hill Garden** created by Lord Leverhulme (the man who sent soap around the world). We won't spoil the surprise, but look out for the pergola. You will never see another like it. Sue Whittington is a dedicated gardener. Her very sloping garden behind the 18th century house, **Southwood Lodge**, is positively packed with unusual, beautiful and amazing plants. *Photo credit: Marianne Majerus*

FINE FARMS & MANORS IN BEDFORDSHIRE FRI 27 MAY £85
Kathy and Simon Brown have carved a magnificent four acre garden over the past 20 years at **The Manor House**, Stevington, with a pergola that is ablaze with laburnum, wisteria and clematis. Since 1980 Geoff Barrett has been stamping his individual character on three acres at **Flaxbourne Farm** to create this 'off the wall' garden, with grottos, temples, ferneries and water everywhere. See it to believe it. Veronica Pilcher's garden at **The Manor House** Barton-le-Clay is a soothing space where gently flowing water is threaded through the garden, fed by a natural spring. All here is wonderful planting and a feeling of peace and antiquity.

NEW WALKING TOUR **SMALL BUT SMART: TRENDY DALSTON GARDENS** WED 6 JULY £65
Dalston is definitely the place to be. Check out some uber-chic spots here, for London's up and coming N by NE crowd is making E8 the postcode to have for the trendsetters; and, well, N1 has been fiercely fashionable for some time now. These urban gardens are small, but all fascinating for their differing styles and planting. All are within easy walking distance of each other, so we will do three in **De Beauvoir** in the morning; stop for a bite to eat and take in four in **London Fields** in the afternoon!

FROM PLOT TO PLATE: EDIBLE SURREY GARDENS FRI 8 JULY £85
Everyone is growing to eat, so we visit **Horsell Allotments**, one of the prettiest and the first allotment to open for the NGS. With 100 gardeners of many nationalities, there's much to admire. At **Vale End**, some steps must be tackled to reach Daphne Foulsham's hillside edible garden, jampacked with fruit and veg, but the bonus is the splendid view. Next stop will be lunch at **Loseley Park**, followed by a tour of the three-acre walled garden, with its vegetable section and a fragrant herb garden. Our last stop, **Stuart Cottage**, is another very tasty morsel: NGS County Organiser Gayle Leader will show us her pretty, productive patch with its apple arches and mini orchard.

Gardens Etc For information/leaflet contact Janine Wookey: 4 Piermont Green, East Dulwich, London SE22 0LP
tel: +44 (0)20 8693 1015 mobile: +44 (0)7711279636 j.wookey@btinternet.com www.gardentoursetc.co.uk

ngs gardens open for charity

740

Scotland

PEND MEMORABLE DAYS VISITING SCOTLAND'S MOST REMARKABLE
AND BEAUTIFUL GARDENS WHICH OPEN TO THE PUBLIC FOR
SCOTLAND'S GARDENS SCHEME AND SUPPORT A VARIETY OF TRULY WORTHY CHARITIES.

For more information refer to our website: www.gardensofscotland.org

Scotland's Gardens Scheme
Gardens open for charity

© Andrea Jones

Charity No. SC011337

Wales

Gregynog

Grade 1 listed formal gardens.

Magnificent yew hedge, rhododendrons, water and rose gardens with ancient oaks forming a SSSI. Colour coded woodland walks through 750 acres of beautiful and varied landscapes.

According to CADW, 'one of the most important parks and gardens in Powys, dating from at least the 1500's'.

Courtyard café and shop with special events throughout the year.

Tel 01686 650224
gregynog@wales.ac.uk
www.gregynog.wales.ac.uk
Located near Newtown,
Powys SY16 3PW

Garden admission £2 per person.
Estate admission administered via a £2.50
car parking charge also applies.

Neuadd Gregynog
Gregynog Hall

Prifysgol Cymru
University of Wales

742

744

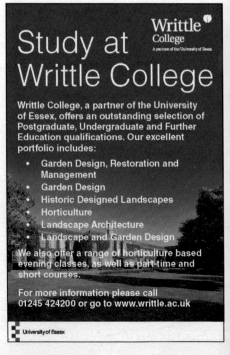